MW01076544

The Kolbrin Bible

21st Century Master Edition with Kolbrin.com Quick Study Reports

The Kolbrin Bible

21st Century Master Edition with Kolbrin.com Quick Study Reports

Janice Manning, Editor

Marshall Masters, Contributor

Your Own World Books
thekolbrinbible.com
yowbooks.com
kolbrin.com

COPYRIGHT

No part of this book may be reproduced or transmitted in any form or by any means, graphic, electronic, or mechanical, including photocopying, recording, taping, or by any information storage retrieval system, without the written permission of the publisher.

The Kolbrin Bible: 21st Century Master Edition
Anonymous Original Authors: 2nd Century B.C.E to 1st Century C.E.
Public Domain Manuscript — Final Compilation: 19th Century C.E., UK
Kolbrin Citation System: Marshall Masters, 2005-2008 USA

First Edition Copyright ©2005 Your Own World, Inc.
USA Copyright Registration Number: TXu-1-262-967

Second Edition Copyright ©2006 Your Own World, Inc.
For Additional Front Matter, Editing and Index
All rights reserved.

Your Own World Books
First Edition – April 2005
Second Edition – May 2006

21st Century Master Edition with Kolbrin.com
Quick Study Reports – February 2008

Trade Paperback
ISBN-10: 1-59772-069-0
ISBN-13: 978-1-59772-069-4

thekolbrinbible.com
kolbrin.com

YOUR OWN WORLD BOOKS
an imprint of Your Own World, Inc.
Silver Springs, NV USA
SAN: 256-1646
yowbooks.com

This edition is dedicated to the memory of those unknown ancients, who labored in the face of future uncertainty, to share their timeless wisdom with generations yet unborn.

— and to —

Those future caretakers who choose to follow in the loving footsteps of generations past.

Table of Contents

Kolbrin.com Quick Study Reports

INTRODUCTION

The Kolbrin Bible: 21st Century Master Edition contains faithful copies of all 11 books of the historical and prophetic anthology formerly known as *The Kolbrin.*

The Kolbrin Bible is an ancient secular academic work; it offers alternate accounts of several stories from the *Holy Bible* and other wisdom texts. Previously named *The Kolbrin*, the work is now titled *The Kolbrin Bible* by the publisher. This is because the term *"Bible"* accurately defines the work and also has its roots in a civilization that played a critical role in its dissemination.

In the classic sense, the term "*Bible*" comes from the Greek "*Biblia*," meaning books, which stems from "*Byblos.*" Byblos was an ancient Phoenician port located in what is now the central coast of Lebanon.

In their day, Phoenician traders operated the most advanced fleets of ocean-going vessels in all the world. Before their fall to the Roman Empire, their principal trade routes stretched throughout the Mediterranean area, out along the shores of Western Europe and up as far North as Britain.

Of note to this body of work is that the Phoenicians imported papyrus from Egypt and sold it abroad along with ancient wisdom texts. In doing so, they distributed the earliest known variant of *The Kolbrin Bible,* called *The Great Book,* to their various ports of call.

The Great Book was originally penned in Hieratic by Egyptian academicians after the Exodus of the Jews (ca 1500 BCE). Its original 21 volumes were later translated using the 22-letter Phoenician alphabet (which later spawned the Greek, Roman and English alphabets of today).

The only known copy of *The Great Book* to survive the millennia was the one exported to Britain by the Phoenicians in the 1st century BCE. Regrettably, much of it was destroyed when the Glastonbury Abbey was set ablaze in 1184 CE. The attack on the Abbey was ordered by English King Henry II, after he accused the Abbey priests of being mystical heretics.

Fearing for their lives, the Celtic priests of the Abbey fled into hiding with what remained of *The Great Book.* There, they transcribed the surviving Phoenician translations to bronze sheets and stored them in copper-clad wooden boxes. This effort became known as *The Bronzebook.*

In the 18th century CE, *The Bronzebook* was merged with a Celtic wisdom text called the *Coelbook* to become *The Kolbrin Bible.*

For more information visit www.kolbrin.com.

Your Own World Books Editions of *The Kolbrin Bible*

Your Own World Books first published several print and electronic editions of *The Kolbrin Bible* in April 2005. Each edition is a faithful copy of the 20th Century Major Edition and uses the Kolbrin Citation System developed by Marshall Masters.

In May 2006, Your Own World Books published second editions of *The Kolbrin Bible.* Updated with over 1,600 typographical corrections based on the *Chicago Manual of Style,* the verbiage remains exactly the same. An index was also added to the print and Adobe eBook editions.

<table>
<tr><th>The Kolbrin Bible</th><th>Books</th><th>Comments</th><th>Paperback Edition</th><th>eBook Formats</th></tr>
<tr><td>21st Century Master Edition</td><td>ALL 1-11</td><td>Published for scholars, this edition is available in an A4 letter-sized paperback with ample margins for notes. The typesetting is easy on old eyes.</td><td>8.268" x 11.693"
Easy on Old Eyes
Wide Margins for Notes</td><td rowspan="3">Adobe
Microsoft
Mobipocket
Palm</td></tr>
<tr><td>Egyptian Texts of the Bronzebook</td><td>1-6 Only</td><td>Recommended for those with an interest in 2012 Mayan prophecies, Planet X (Nibiru) and factual alternate accounts of Noah's Flood and Exodus.</td><td>7.44" x 9.69"
Affordable
Ideal for Home</td></tr>
<tr><td>Celtic Texts of the Coelbook</td><td>7-11 Only</td><td>Recommended for those with an interest in Druid/Celtic philosophy and prophecies. Also contains newly detailed biographical accounts of Jesus Christ with several first-person quotes.</td><td>7.44" x 9.69"
Affordable
Ideal for Home</td></tr>
</table>

Table 1: Your Own World Books Publications, May 2006

For more information about the abridged and unabridged editions of *The Kolbrin Bible: 21st Century Master Edition,* visit www.kolbrin.com.

Languages of *the Kolbrin Bible*

One of the most commonly asked questions is "what was the original language of *The Kolbrin Bible,* and who wrote it." The answer is in multiple parts.

<table>
<tr><th rowspan="4">Book</th><th rowspan="3">The Kolbrin Bible
21st Century
Master Edition</th><th colspan="2">BCE</th><th colspan="3">CE</th></tr>
<tr><th>15th Century</th><th>1st Century</th><th>1st Century</th><th>18th Century</th><th>20th Century</th></tr>
<tr><th>Original</th><th>Translation</th><th>Original</th><th>Translation</th><th>Translation</th></tr>
<tr><th>Book Title</th><th>Egyptian Hieratic</th><th>Phoenician Script</th><th>Old Celtic</th><th>Old English</th><th>Continental English</th></tr>
<tr><td colspan="7">Egyptian Texts of the Bronzebook</td></tr>
<tr><td>1</td><td>Creation</td><td>u</td><td>u</td><td></td><td>u</td><td>u</td></tr>
<tr><td>2</td><td>Gleanings</td><td>u</td><td>u</td><td></td><td>u</td><td>u</td></tr>
<tr><td>3</td><td>Scrolls</td><td>u</td><td>u</td><td></td><td>u</td><td>u</td></tr>
<tr><td>4</td><td>Sons of Fire</td><td>u</td><td>u</td><td></td><td>u</td><td>u</td></tr>
<tr><td>5</td><td>Manuscripts</td><td>u</td><td>u</td><td></td><td>u</td><td>u</td></tr>
<tr><td>6</td><td>Morals and Precepts</td><td>u</td><td>u</td><td></td><td>u</td><td>u</td></tr>
<tr><td colspan="7">Celtic Texts of the Coelbook</td></tr>
<tr><td>7</td><td>Origins</td><td></td><td></td><td>u</td><td>u</td><td>u</td></tr>
<tr><td>8</td><td>The Silver Bough</td><td></td><td></td><td>u</td><td>u</td><td>u</td></tr>
<tr><td>9</td><td>Lucius</td><td></td><td></td><td>u</td><td>u</td><td>u</td></tr>
<tr><td>10</td><td>Wisdom</td><td></td><td></td><td>u</td><td>u</td><td>u</td></tr>
<tr><td>11</td><td>Britain</td><td></td><td></td><td>u</td><td>u</td><td>u</td></tr>
</table>

Table 2: Languages of The Kolbrin Bible

Languages Used Before the Common Era

The *Egyptian Texts of the Bronzebook* (the first six books of *The Kolbrin Bible*) were originally penned in Hieratic as *The Great Book* by Egyptian academicians, following the Exodus of the Jews (ca 1500 BCE).

One of several copies of this work was translated into Phoenician and eventually made its way to Britain. This is because Egypt and Phoenicia were both very powerful nations at the time, and their languages were widely used.

Languages Used During the Common Era

The *Celtic Texts of the Coelbook* (the last five books of *The Kolbrin Bible)* were originally penned in ancient Celtic. Work began on the earliest parts of *The Coelbook* in approximately 20 CE and finished in approximately 500 CE.

Inspired by the scope of the Egyptian texts, the Celts wrote their own historical and philosophical anthology in a similar manner, but in their own language. Viewed as a religious work by many, the Celtic texts offer a timeless insight into Druid folklore, mysticism and philosophy.

According to some historians, *The Coelbook* was also inspired in part by a visit by Jesus Christ to Britain. At the time, Jesus was either in his late teens or middle twenties and traveled via a high-speed Phoenician trading ship to Britain with his great uncle Joseph of Arimathea, who undertook the journey to inspect a tin mine he owned.

These historians further maintain that Jesus studied the Egyptian texts in Britain. This is because the Celtic texts penned following his possible visit contain a never-before published biography of Jesus.

Given the detailed and highly revealing nature of this biography, the case can be made that the biographer personally met Jesus, or interviewed someone who had. Additional corroboration comes from reliable historical accounts that indicate Joseph of Arimathea founded the Glastonbury Abbey in or about 36 CE, and that it eventually became the repository for these texts during the 1st millennium.

Stored together in the Glastonbury Abbey under the watchful eyes of Celtic priests, the texts remained safe and were actively studied until the 12th Century, when the Abbey was attacked and set ablaze by minions of King Henry II.

After the attack, the priests fled with what remained of these ancient works to a secret location in Scotland, where the Egyptian texts were transcribed to bronze sheets. At that time, the two books were still not joined, and the languages of both remained as-is; Phoenician (translated from Egyptian Hieratic) and ancient Celtic, respectively.

In the 18th century, the two books were combined and translated to Old English to form the first identifiable edition of *The Kolbrin Bible*. In the 20th century, the manuscripts were transferred to London and updated to Continental English.

The latest edition of *The Kolbrin Bible* still uses the Continental English update, but has been edited according to modern rules of grammar and punctuation based on the *Chicago Manual of Style*.

The Seven Major Editions of *The Kolbrin Bible*

Born of great wisdom and love, the overall creation span of *The Kolbrin Bible* is greater than that of the *Holy Bible*.

To facilitate a historical study of the work, the publisher has divided the creation span of *The Kolbrin Bible* into seven "master editions" using the criteria of publication era and country.

Master Edition	Publication Era/Country	Description
1st	15th Century BCE *Egypt*	First penned in Hieratic after the Exodus of the Jews from Egypt (ca 1500 BCE). Published as *The Great Book*, a 21-volume work. The surviving volumes are now published as the *Egyptian Texts of the Bronzebook.* The genesis of this secular work was a new Egyptian interest in finding the one true G-d of Abraham as a consequence of their defeat at the hands of Moses. The work contains many historical accounts that parallel those of the *Torah* (Old Testament) and warns of a massive object called the "Destroyer" that is prophesied to return in this time with catastrophic results for the Earth.
2nd	1st Century BCE *Phoenicia (Lebanon)*	The 1st Master Edition is translated into the Phoenician language. The simple 22-letter alphabet of the Phoenicians eventually becomes the root alphabet of the Greek, Roman and English alphabets. Before falling to the Roman Empire, they distribute the work throughout the Mediterranean area, Western Europe and Britain.
3rd	1st Century CE *Britain*	From approximately 20 CE to 500 CE, the last five books of what would eventually become *The Kolbrin Bible* are written. Now published as the *Celtic Texts of the Coelbook,* this part of the work was first penned in ancient Celtic. During this time, the Egyptian texts of the 2nd Major Edition were studied by Celts as well as the children of wealthy and powerful Romans. Copies of the work eventually found their way to the Glastonbury Abbey.
4th	12th Century CE *Scotland*	In 1184, English King Henry II ordered an attack on the Glastonbury Abbey, claiming it's Celtic priests to be heretics. Those who survived the arson and murder fled with the surviving Egyptian texts of the 2nd Master Edition and later engraved them on bronze sheets. Stored for centuries in a secret location in Scotland, this edition is also known as *The Bronzebook*..
5th	18th Century CE *Scotland*	*The Bronzebook* was merged with *The Coelbook,* and then both were translated into Old English. The new anthology was collectively titled *The Kolbrin* by its caretakers, the Hope Trust of Edinburgh, Scotland.
6th	20th Century CE *England New Zealand America*	In the years following WWI, the 5th Major Edition was relocated to London, England, where it was updated to Continental English. This master edition remained unpublished until 1992, when a senior member of the Hope Trust distributed several copies of the work. One distributed copy was printed in 1994 in New Zealand by a small religious order and another in 2005 in America by Your Own World Books. The only differences between the New Zealand (1994) and American (2005) editions appear in the front matter, and the American edition added a new citation system and was published in both print and electronic variants.
7th	21st Century CE *America*	Your Own World Books updates the 6th Major Edition with 2 significant changes. While the Continental English language and spellings remain unchanged, the text is updated to comply with the *Chicago Manual of Style.* Over 1,600 typographical corrections are made. Also new to this master edition is a first-ever index with over 2,700 unique entries. This master edition is also published in 2 abridged editions; the *Egyptian Texts of the Bronzebook* and the *Celtic Texts of the Coelbook.* All editions are published in print and electronic variants.

KOLBRIN CITATION SYSTEM
MARSHALL MASTERS, 2005-2006

All Your Own World Books abridged and unabridged editions of this work use the same Kolbrin Citation System. It is designed to speed collaborative studies between researchers and authors using any of the twenty print or electronic editions published since April 2005.

Book Citation Schema for *The Kolbrin Bible*

There are 2 citation forms: Long and short. The long form uses a whole word to form the book prefix. The short form uses a 3-letter acronym.

Book No.	Master Edition	Egyptian Texts	Celtic Texts	Book Title	Long Form	Short Form
1	u	u		Creation	Creation	CRT
2	u	u		Gleanings	Gleanings	GLN
3	u	u		Scrolls	Scrolls	SCL
4	u	u		Sons of Fire	Sons of Fire	SOF
5	u	u		Manuscripts	Manuscripts	MAN
6	u	u		Morals and Precepts	Morals	MPR
7	u		u	Origins	Origins	OGS
8	u		u	The Silver Bough	Silver Bough	SVB
9	u		u	Lucius	Lucius	LUC
10	u		u	Wisdom	Wisdom	WSD
11	u		u	Britain	Britain	BRT

Each book of *The Kolbrin Bible* contains multiple chapters. Following the book prefix, each citation uses a two-part suffix to denote the chapter and paragraph numbers.

The first chapter in each book is designated as number 1 and each of following chapters are numbered in ascending order.

The same numbering rule applies to paragraphs within each chapter.

Note: this system does NOT reference page numbers.

Kolbrin Short Form Citations

This citation form is used in the text itself and is recommended for use by collaborative research groups.

Short Form Syntax
Short Citation Book Acronym <colon> Chapter No. <colon> Paragraph No.

Examples:

> CRT:3:7 "In this manner, the first Earth was destroyed by calamity descending from out of the skies. The vaults of Heaven had opened to bring forth monsters more fearsome than any that ever haunted the uneasy dreams of men."
>
> Hi Bill:
>
> Just downloaded the 21st Century Master Edition in the Mobi eBook format, and I'm delighted to learn the citation system is the same one used in your 2005 print copy.
>
> Could you give me your thoughts on CRT:3:7 "In this manner, the first Earth was destroyed by calamity descending from out of the skies..."
>
> Many thanks, Bobbi

Kolbrin Long Form Citations

This formal citation form is recommended for use with articles, essays and books that reference this work using footnotes, etc.

Long Form Syntax
Long Citation Book Title <space> Chapter No. <colon> Paragraph No.

Examples:

The Kolbrin Bible: 21st Century Master Edition
Your Own World Books Second Edition
Creation 3:7

> "In this manner, the first Earth was destroyed by calamity descending from out of the skies. The vaults of Heaven had opened to bring forth monsters more fearsome than any that ever haunted the uneasy dreams of men."
>
> "In this manner, the first Earth was destroyed by calamity descending from out of the skies..." — *Creation 3:7*
>
> [4] The Kolbrin Bible: 21st Century Master Edition, "**Creation 3:7**", Your Own World Books (Silver City, NV)

Regardless of how you format the typeface style of your short and long citations, always use the proper syntax to ensure clarity.

Marshall's Motto

Destiny finds those who listen,
and fate finds the rest.

So learn what you can learn,
do what you can do,
and never give up hope!

—Marshall Masters

Book of
Creation

CRT:1:4 The name which is uttered cannot be that of this Great Being who, remaining nameless, is the beginning and the end, beyond time, beyond the reach of mortals, and we in our simplicity call it God.

Table of Chapters

Book of Creation

Chapter One – Creation

CRT:1:1 Mortal knowledge is circumscribed by mortal ignorance, and mortal comprehension is circumscribed by spiritual reality. It is unwise for mortal man to attempt the understanding of that, which is beyond his conception, for there lies the road to disbelief and madness. Yet, man is man and ever fated to reach out beyond himself, striving to attain things which always just elude his grasp. So in his frustration, he replaces the dimly seen incomprehensible with things within his understanding. If these things but poorly reflect reality, then is not the reflection of reality, distorted though it maybe, of greater value than no reflection at all?

CRT:1:2 There are no true beginnings on Earth; for here, all is effect, the ultimate cause being elsewhere. For who among men can say which came first, the seed or the plant? Yet in truth, it is neither, for something neither seed nor plant preceded both, and that thing was also preceded by something else. Always there are ancestors back to the beginning, and back beyond that, there is only God. This, then, is how these things were told in The Great Book of The Sons of Fire.

CRT:1:3 Before the beginning, there was only one consciousness, that of The Eternal One whose nature cannot be expressed in words. It was The One Sole Spirit, The Self Generator, which cannot diminish, The Unknown, Unknowable One brooding solitary in profound pregnant silence.

CRT:1:4 The name which is uttered cannot be that of this Great Being who, remaining nameless, is the beginning and the end, beyond time, beyond the reach of mortals, and we in our simplicity call it God.

CRT:1:5 He who preceded all existed alone in His strange abode of uncreated light, which remains ever unextinguishable, and no understandable eye can ever behold it. The pulsating draughts of the eternal life light in His keeping were not yet loosed. He knew Himself alone; He was uncontrasted, unable to manifest in nothingness, for all within His Being was unexpressed potential.

CRT:1:6 The Great Circles of Eternity were yet to be spun out, to be thrown forth as the endless ages of existence in substance. They were to begin with God and return to Him completed in infinite variety and expression.

CRT:1:7 Earth was not yet in existence; there were no winds with the sky above them; high mountains were not raised, nor was the great river in its place. All was formless, without movement, calm, silent, void and dark. No name had been named, and no destinies fore-shadowed.

CRT:1:8 Eternal rest is intolerable, and unmanifested potential is frustration. Into the solitude of timelessness came Divine Loneliness, and from this arose the desire to create, that He might know and express Himself, and this generated the Love of God. He took thought and brought into being within Himself the Universal Womb of Creation containing the everlasting essence of slumbering spirit.

CRT:1:9 The essence was quickened by a ripple from the mind of God, and a creative thought was projected. This generated power, which produced light, and this formed a substance like unto a mist of invisible dust. It divided into two forms of energy through being impregnated with The Spirit of God and, quickening the chaos of the void within the Universal Womb, became spun out into whirlpools of substance. From this activity, as sparks from a fire, came an infinite variety of spirit minds, each having creative powers within itself.

CRT:1:10 The activating word was spoken; its echoes vibrate still, and there was a stirring movement, which caused instability. A command was given, and this became the Everlasting Law. Henceforth, activity was controlled in harmonious rhythm, and the initial inertia was overcome. The Law divided the materialising chaos from God and then established the boundaries of the Eternal Spheres.

CRT:1:11 Time no longer slept on the bosom of God, for now there was change, where before all had been unchanging, and change is time. Now within the Universal Womb was heat, substance and life, and encompassing it was the Word, which is the Law.

CRT:1:12 The command was given, "Let the smallest of things form the greatest and that which lives but a flash form everlastingness." Thus the universe came into being as a condensation of God's thought, and as it did so, it obscured Him from all enclosed within His solidifying creation. Henceforth, God was hidden, for He has always remained dimly reflected in His creation. He became veiled from all that came forth from Him. Creation does not explain itself; under the Law, it cannot do so; its secrets have to be unravelled by the created.

CRT:1:13 All things are by nature finite; they have a beginning, a middle and an end. An unaccomplishable purpose would be eternal frustration, and therefore, the universe being created purposefully it must have an objective. If it ended without anything else following, then the God existing must slumber indifferent to its activities. But He has made it a living work of greatness operating under the changeless Law.

CRT:1:14 The creating word had been spoken; now, there was another command and the power going forth smote the sun so its face was lit, and it shone with a great radiance pouring warmth and light upon its sister Earth. Henceforth, she would live within the protection of her brother's household, rejoicing in his benevolence and strength.

CRT:1:15 The waters upon the bosom of Earth were gathered together, and dry land appeared. When the covering of water was rolled back, the body of Earth was unstable, damp and yielding. The face of the sun shone down kindly upon his sister, and the dry land of her body became very hard; humidity and dampness were taken away. He gave her a garment of fleece and a veil of fine linen, that she might clothe her body with modesty.

CRT:1:16 From the Great Womb had sprung the Spirit of Life, and it was rampant in the Heavens. It gazed upon Earth and saw her fairness, was filled with desire, and came out of the heavenly spaces to possess her. It came not peacefully as a lover, but tempestuously as a ravager. Its breath howled along her corridors and raged among her mountain tops, but it did not discover the dwelling place of her Spirit. She had withdrawn, as a woman withdraws before force, for modesty must not be outraged in submission. Yet, she desired its embrace, for among all the Radiant Company, she was honoured.

CRT:1:17 The sun saw her perplexity, and he wrestled with the Spirit of Life and overcame it. When it was subdued and the primal struggle had ceased, it was delivered by the sun to his sister. It was chastened and quietened and in silence brooded over Earth's waters; she was stirred in response. Mud eggs of life potential were formed in swamps, at the meeting places of land and two waters. The sun gave quickening heat, and life crawled forth upon the bosom of the Earth.

CRT:1:18 The land dust brought forth the male and the dark water mist the female, and they united and multiplied. The first brought forth the second, and the two produced the third. Earth was no longer virgin, and the Spirit of Life grew old and departed. Earth was left garbed in the matron's mantle of green; herbage covered the face of the land.

CRT:1:19 The waters brought forth fishes and creatures, which move about and twist themselves and wriggle in the waters, the serpents and the beasts of terrible aspect, which were of yore, and reptiles which creep and crawl. There were tall walking things and dragons in hideous form clothed with terror, whose great bones may still be seen.

CRT:1:20 Then came forth from the Womb of the Earth all the beasts of the field and forest. All the creatures of creation having blood in their bodies, and it was complete. Beasts roamed the dry land, and fishes swam in the seas. There were birds in the skies and worms within the soil.

CRT:1:21 There were great land masses and high mountains, wide, barren places and heaving waters. Fertile greenness covered the land, and abundant life swarmed in the seas, for now Earth throbbed with the energy of life.

CRT:1:22 Metals lay hidden in her rocks and precious stones within the soil. Gold and silver were scattered and secreted. There was copper for tools and forests of timber. There were swamps of reeds and stones for every purpose.

CRT:1:23 Everything was prepared, everything was ready, and now Earth awaited the coming of man.

Chapter Two – The Birth of Man

CRT:2:1 The love of God penetrated the third veil and became the Seed of Souls within the Soul Sea. The body of man, God made of water and things of the Earth, breathing into him the Spirit of Life, that he might live. But man, when young, lived only to eat and drink and to fornicate, for, being conscious only of the Earth, he knew only earthly things and earthly ways.

CRT:2:2 Now the Spirit of God moved over the face of the Earth, but was not of the Earth. It held all things and was in all things, but on Earth could not be apart from anything. Without substance, it was awake, but entering substance, it slept.

CRT:2:3 Consider that, which was told by the servants of Eban, of Heavenman, who once wandered the Earth. He had no earthly substance and could not grasp its fruits, for he had no hands. He could not drink its waters, for he had no mouth, nor could he feel the cool winds upon his skin. They tell how the ape tribe Selok, led by Heavenman, perished by flames before the Valley of Lod, only one she-ape reaching the cave heights above.

CRT:2:4 When Heavenman was reborn of the she-ape in the cavern of Woe, could he taste the fruits of the Earth and drink of her waters, and feel the coolness of her winds? Did he not find life good? It is not all a tale of the courtyard!

CRT:2:5 Man, created from earthly substance alone, could not know things not of Earth, nor could Spirit alone subdue him. Had man not been created, who would have known God's wisdom and power? As the Spirit fills the body of man, so does God fill His creation.

CRT:2:6 Therefore, it was that God saw something had to be which joined Earth and Spirit and was both. In His wisdom and by the creative impulse which governs the Earth, He prepared a body for man, for the body of man is wholly of Earth.

CRT:2:7 Behold, the great day came when the Spirit, which is God, was joined with the beast, which is Earth. Then, Earth writhed in the labour of travail. Her mountains rocked back and forth, and her seas heaved up and down. Earth groaned in her lands and shrieked in her winds. She cried in the rivers and wept in her storms.

CRT:2:8 So man was born, born of upheaval and strife. He came wretchedly and tumultuously, the offspring of a distraught Earth. All was in discord, snow fell in the hot wastelands, ice covered the fertile plains, the forests became seas. Where once it was hot, now it was cold and where no rain had ever fallen, now there were floods. So man came forth, man the child of calamity, man the inheritor of a creative struggle, man the battleground of extremes.

CRT:2:9 Earth nurtured man with cautious affection, weaning him in the recesses of her body. Then, when he was grown sufficiently to be lifted so he walked in the uprightness of God, she took him and raised him above all other creatures. She led him even into the presence of God, and she laid him on His Great Altar.

CRT:2:10 A man imperfect, of earthly limitations, a thing unfinished, ungainly and unlearned, but proudly was He presented to Earth's Creator. Not her first-born was man, the son of Earth, the grandchild of God; man the heir of tribulation and the pupil of affliction.

CRT:2:11 God saw man, the offering of Earth to her Lord, unconscious on the High Altar, a sacrifice to Him and a dedication to the Spirit of Fate. Then from out of the unfathomable heights and from behind the impenetrable veil, God came down above the Altar, and He breathed into man the breath of Eternal Life. Into his sleeping body, God implanted a fragment of Himself, the Seed of a Soul and the Spark of Divinity, and man the mortal became man the heir of God and the inheritor of immortality. Henceforth he would have dominion over God's earthly estate, but he also had to unravel the Circles of Eternity, and his destiny was to be an everlasting seeking and striving.

CRT:2:12 Man slept, but God opened the Great Eye within him, and man saw a vision of unsurpassed glory. He heard the voice of God saying, "O man, in your hand is now placed the tablet of your inheritance, and My seal is upon it. Know that all you desire within your heart may be yours, but first it is necessary that you be taught its value. Behold, the Earth is filled with things of usefulness; they are prepared to your hand for a purpose, but the task is upon you to seek them out and learn their use. This is the tuition for the management of your inheritance."

CRT:2:13 "What you know to be good, seek for and it shall be found. You may plumb the seas and pluck the stars. You may live in everlasting glory and savour eternal delights. Above and below and all about, there is nothing beyond your reach; all, with one exception, is yours to attain." Then God laid His hand upon man, saying, "Now, you are even as I, except you sleep there enclosed in matter in the Kingdom of Illusion, while I dwell here in the freedom of Reality and Truth. It is not for Me to come down to you, but for you to reach out to Me."

CRT:2:14 Our Unborn Friends, whatever your circumstances of life, you are the children of the past and heirs of those who have lived and died. We trust you have no cause to reproach those who once held stewardship over your estate. But whatever you think of the heritage, you cannot put it aside, any more than you can refuse that Man then saw a vision of glory encompassing even the Spheres of Splendour. Unbounded wisdom filled his heart, and he beheld beauty in perfection. The ultimates of Truth and Justice were unveiled before him. He became one with the profound peace of eternity and knew the joys of unceasing gladness.

CRT:2:15 The eternal ages of time unrolled as a scroll before his eyes, and he saw written thereon all that was to become and occur. The great vaults of Heaven were opened up unto him, and he saw the everlasting fires and unconsumable powers that strove therein. He felt within himself the stirring of inexpressible love, and unlimited designs of grandeur filled his thoughts. His spirit ranged unhampered through all the spheres of existence. He was then even as God Himself, and he knew the secret of the Seven Spheres within Three Spheres.

CRT:2:16 Then, God lifted His hand from man, and man was alone. The great vision departed and he awoke; only a dim and elusive recollection, no more than the shadow of a dream remained. But deep within the sleeping Soul, there was a spark of remembrance, and it generated within man a restless longing for he knew not what. Henceforth, man was destined to wander discontented, seeking something he felt he knew, but could not see, something which continually eluded him, perpetually goaded him and forever tantalised him. Deep within himself, man knew something greater than himself was always with him and part of him, spurring him on to greater deeds, greater thoughts, greater aspirations. It was something out beyond himself, scarcely realised and never found; something, which told him that the radiance seen on the horizon but dimly reflected the hidden glory beyond it.

CRT:2:17 Man awoke, the revelation and vision gone; only the grim reality of Earth's untamed vastness surrounded him. But when he arose and stepped down onto the bosom of his Mother Earth, he was undaunted by the great powers that beset him or by the magnitude of the task ahead. Within his heart, he knew destiny lay beyond the squalor of his environment, he stepped out nobly, gladly accepting the challenge.

CRT:2:18 He was now a new man; he was different. He looked above and saw glory in the Heavens. He saw beauty about him and he knew goodness and things not of the Earth. The vision of eternal values arose before his inner eye. His Spirit was responding to its environment; man was now man, truly man.

CRT:2:19 The nature of man on Earth was formed after the nature of things in Heaven, and man had all things contained as potential within himself, except divine life. But he was as yet an untrained, undisciplined child, still nurtured simply upon the comforting bosom of Earth.

CRT:2:20 Man grew in stature, but Earth was not indulgent, for she disciplined him firmly. She was ever strict and unyielding, chastening him often with blasts of displeasure. It was indeed the upbringing of one destined for greatness; he was made to suffer cold, that he might learn to clothe himself; sent into the barren places, that his limbs should be strengthened, and into forests, that his eye should become keen and his heart strong. He was perplexed with difficult problems and set the task of unravelling the illusions of Nature. He was beset with hardships of every description. He was tested with frustrations and tempted with allurements; never did Earth relax the vigilance of her supervision.

CRT:2:21 The child was raised sternly, for he needed the fortitude, courage and cunning of a man to fit him for the task ahead. He grew wily and wiry in the hunt; he became adaptable, able to cope with any untoward happening. Overcoming the bewilderments of early days, he found explanations for the perplexities of his surroundings. Yet, the struggle for knowledge, the need for adaptation and the effort to survive were never relaxed. The Earthchild was well trained and disciplined; he was never unduly mollycoddled. He cried for bread and went hungry; he shivered and was cast out; he was sick and driven into the forest. Weary, he was lashed with storms; thirsty, he found the waters dried. When weak, his burden was increased, and in the midst of rejoicing, he was struck down with sorrow. In moments of weakness he cried, "Enough!" and doubted his destiny; but always something fortified and encouraged him; the Earthling never forfeited his godlikeness.

CRT:2:22 For man was man; he was not cowed, nor his Spirit broken; a wise God knew his limitations. As it is written in the wisdom of men, 'over chastisement is as bad as no chastisement at all'. But man was rarely chastised, he was tried, tested and challenged; he was led, prodded and urged; yet nothing was done unnecessarily. The seeming imperfections of Earth, the hazards and inequalities of life, the cruelty, harshness and apparent indifference to suffering and affliction are not what they seem; as it is, Earth is perfect for its purpose. It is ignorance of that purpose, which makes it appear imperfect.

CRT:2:23 Where is there a wiser father than the Spirit of God, or a better mother than Earth? What man is now he owes to these; may he learn to be duly grateful. Above all, let him never forget the lessons learned in his upbringing.

Chapter Three – Destruction and Re-Creation

CRT:3:1 It is known, and the story comes down from ancient times, that there was not one creation but two, a creation and a re-creation. It is a fact known to the wise that the Earth was utterly destroyed once, then reborn on a second wheel of creation.

CRT:3:2 At the time of the great destruction of Earth, God caused a dragon from out of Heaven to come and encompass her about. The dragon was frightful to behold; it lashed its tail, it breathed out fire and hot coals, and a great catastrophe was inflicted upon mankind, The body of the dragon was wreathed in a cold bright light and beneath, on the belly, was a ruddy hued glow, while behind it trailed a flowing tail of smoke. It spewed out cinders and hot stones, and its breath was foul and stenchful, poisoning the nostrils of men. Its passage caused great thunderings and lightnings to rend the thick darkened sky, all Heaven and Earth being made hot. The seas were loosened from their cradles and rose up, pouring across the land. There was an awful, shrilling trumpeting, which outpowered even the howling of the unleashed winds.

CRT:3:3 Men, stricken with terror, went mad at the awful sight in the Heavens. They were loosed from their senses and dashed about, crazed, not knowing what they did. The breath was sucked from their bodies, and they were burnt with a strange ash.

CRT:3:4 Then it passed, leaving Earth enwrapped within a dark and glowering mantle, which was ruddily lit up inside. The bowels of the Earth were torn open in great, writhing upheavals, and a howling whirlwind rent the mountains apart. The wrath of the sky-monster was loosed in the Heavens. It lashed about in flaming fury, roaring like a thousand thunders; it poured down fiery destruction amid a welter of thick black blood. So awesome was the fearfully aspected thing that the memory mercifully departed from man; his thoughts were smothered under a cloud of forgetfulness.

CRT:3:5 The Earth vomited forth great gusts of foul breath from awful mouths opening up in the midst of the land. The evil breath bit at the throat before it drove men mad and killed them. Those who did not die in this manner were smothered under a cloud of red dust and ashes, or were swallowed by the yawning mouths of Earth or crushed beneath crashing rocks.

CRT:3:6 The first sky-monster was joined by another, which swallowed the tail of the one going before, but the two could not be seen at once. The sky-monsters reigned and raged above the Earth, doing battle to possess it, but the many-bladed sword of God cut them in pieces, and their falling bodies enlarged the land and the sea.

CRT:3:7 In this manner, the first Earth was destroyed by calamity descending from out of the skies. The vaults of Heaven had opened to bring forth monsters more fearsome than any that ever haunted the uneasy dreams of men.

CRT:3:8 Men and their dwelling places were gone; only sky-boulders and red earth remained where once they were, but amidst all the desolation, a few survived, for man is not easily destroyed. They crept out from caves and came down from the mountainsides. Their eyes were wild, and their limbs trembled; their bodies shook, and their tongues lacked control. Their faces were twisted, and the skin hung loose on their bones. They were as maddened wild beasts driven into an enclosure before flames; they knew no law, being deprived of all the wisdom they once had, and those who had guided them were gone.

CRT:3:9 The Earth, only true Altar of God, had offered up a sacrifice of life and sorrow to atone for the sins of mankind. Man had not sinned in deed, but in the things he had failed to do. Man suffers not only for what he does, but for what he fails to do. He is not chastised for making mistakes, but for failing to recognise and rectify them.

CRT:3:10 Then the great canopy of dust and cloud, which encompassed the Earth, enshrouding it in heavy darkness, was pierced by ruddy light, and the canopy swept down in great cloudbursts and raging stormwaters. Cool moontears were shed for the distress of Earth and the woes of men.

CRT:3:11 When the light of the sun pierced the Earth's shroud, bathing the land in its revitalising glory, the Earth again knew night and day, for there were now times of light and times of darkness. The smothering canopy rolled away, and the vaults of Heaven became visible to man. The foul air was purified, and new air clothed the reborn Earth, shielding her from the dark hostile void of Heaven.

CRT:3:12 The rainstorms ceased to beat upon the faces of the land, and the waters stilled their turmoil. Earthquakes no longer tore the Earth open, nor was it burned and buried by hot rocks. The land masses were re-established in stability and solidity, standing firm in the midst of the surrounding waters. The oceans fell back to their assigned places, and the land stood steady upon its foundations. The sun shone upon land and sea, and life was renewed upon the face of the Earth. Rain fell gently once more, and clouds of fleece floated across dayskies.

CRT:3:13 The waters were purified, the sediment sank and life increased in abundance. Life was renewed, but it was different. Man survived, but he was not the same. The sun was not as it had been, and a moon had been taken away. Man stood in the midst of renewal and regeneration. He looked up into the Heavens above in fear for the awful powers of destruction lurking there. Henceforth, the placid skies would hold a terrifying secret.

CRT:3:14 Man found the new Earth firm and the Heavens fixed. He rejoiced, but also feared, for he lived in dread that the Heavens would again bring forth monsters and crash about him.

CRT:3:15 When men came forth from their hiding places and refuges, the world their fathers had known was gone forever. The face of the land was changed, and Earth was littered with rocks and stones, which had fallen when the structure of Heaven collapsed. One generation groped in the desolation and gloom, and as the thick darkness was dispelled, its children believed they were witnessing a new creation. Time passed, memory dimmed and the record of events was no longer clear. Generation followed generation, and as the ages unfolded, new tongues and new tales replaced the old.

Chapter Four – Affliction of God

CRT:4:1 This comes from the scroll of Kerobal Pakthermin, who wrote, "The forbears of all the nations of man were once one people, and they were the elect of God who delivered all the Earth over to them, all the people, the beasts of the field, the creatures of the wasteland and the things that grow."

CRT:4:2 They dwelt through long ages in lands of peace and plenty."

CRT:4:3 "There were some who struggled harder, were more disciplined; because their forefathers had crossed the great dark void; their desires were turned Godward, and they were called The Children of God."

CRT:4:4 "Their country was undulating and forested. It was fertile, having many rivers and marshes. There were great mountains to the East and to the West, and in the North was a vast stony plain."

CRT:4:5 "Then came the day when all things became still and apprehensive, for God caused a sign to appear in the Heavens, so that men should know the Earth would be afflicted, and the sign was a strange star."

CRT:4:6 "The star grew and waxed to a great brightness and was awesome to behold. It put forth horns and sang, being unlike any other ever seen. So men, seeing it, said among themselves, 'Surely, this is God appearing in the Heavens above us.' The star was not God, though it was directed by His design, but the people had not the wisdom to understand."

CRT:4:7 "Then, God manifested Himself in the Heavens, His voice was as the roll of thunders and He was clothed with smoke and fire. He carried lightnings in His hand, and His breath, falling upon the Earth, brought forth brimstone and embers. His eye was a black void and His mouth an abyss containing the winds of Destruction. He encircled the whole of the Heavens, bearing upon His back a black robe adorned with stars."

CRT:4:8 "Such was the likeness and manifestation of God in those days. Awesome was His countenance; terrible His voice of wrath; the sun and moon hid themselves in fear and there was a heavy darkness over the face of the Earth."

CRT:4:9 "God passed through the spaces of the Heavens above with a mighty roar and a loud trumpeting. Then came the grim dead silence and black red lit twilight of doom. Great fires and smoke rose up from the ground and men gasped for air. The land was rent asunder and swept clean by a mighty deluge of waters. A hole opened up in the middle of the land; the waters entered, and it sank beneath the seas."

CRT:4:10 "The mountains of the East and West were split apart and stood up in the midst of the waters, which raged about. The Northland tilted and turned over on its side."

CRT:4:11 "Then again, the tumult and clamour ceased, and all was silent. In the quiet stillness, madness broke out among men, frenzy and shouting filled the air. They fell upon one another in senseless, wanton bloodshed; neither did they spare woman or child, for they knew not what they did. They ran unseeing, dashing themselves to destruction. They fled to caves, and were buried and, taking refuge in trees, they were hung. There was rape, murder and violence of every kind."

CRT:4:12 "The deluge of waters swept back, and the land was purged clean. Rain beat down unceasingly, and there were great winds. The surging waters overwhelmed the land, and man, his flocks and his gardens and all his works ceased to exist."

CRT:4:13 "Some of the people were saved upon the mountainsides and upon the flotsam, but they were scattered far apart over the face of the Earth. They fought for survival in the lands of uncouth people. Amid coldness, they survived in caves and sheltered places."

CRT:4:14 "The Land of the Little People and the Land of Giants, the Land of the Neckless Ones and the Land of Marshes and Mists, the Lands of the East and West were all inundated. The Mountain Land and the Lands of the South, where there is gold and great beasts, were not covered by the waters."

CRT:4:15 "Men were distracted and in despair. They rejected the Unseen God behind all things for something, which they had seen and known by its manifestation. They were less than children in those days and could not know that God had afflicted the Earth in understanding and not wilfully, for the sake of man and the correction of his ways."

CRT:4:16 "The Earth is not for the pleasure of man, but is a place of instruction for his Soul. A man more readily feels the stirrings of his Spirit in the face of disaster than in the lap of luxury. The tuition of the Soul is a long and arduous course of instruction and training."

CRT:4:17 "God is good, and from good, evil cannot come. He is perfect, and perfection cannot produce imperfection. Only the limited understanding of man sees imperfection in that, which is perfect for its purpose."

CRT:4:18 "This grievous affliction of man was another of his great tests. He failed and in so doing followed the paths of unnatural gods of his making. Man makes gods by naming them, but where in this is the benefit to him?"

CRT:4:19 "Evil comes into the midst of mankind spawned by the fears and ignorance of men. An evil man becomes an evil spirit, and whatever evil there is on Earth comes either from the evil of spirits or the evil of men."

Chapter Five – In the Beginning

CRT:5:1 Now, the Children of God were moulded by the Hand of God, which is called Awen, and it manifested according to their desires. For all things that have life are moulded by Awen. The fox, shivering in the coldlands, longs for warmth and so its cubs have coats. The owl, clumsy in the dark, longs to see its prey more clearly, and in generations of longing, the desire is granted. Awen makes everything what it is, for all things change under its law.

CRT:5:2 Men, too, are moulded by their desires, but unlike the beasts and birds, their yearnings are circumscribed by the laws of fate and destiny and the law of sowing and reaping. These, the desires, modified by the laws, are called Enidvadew. Unlike the beasts and birds, this, in man, is something relating to him rather than to his offspring, though they are not untouched by it.

CRT:5:3 Destiny may be likened to a man who must travel to a distant city, whether or not he wishes to make the journey, the destination being his destiny. He may choose whether to go by way of a river or by way of a plain; whether across mountains or through forests, on foot or horseback, slow or fast, and whatever befalls because of this decision is fate. If a tree falls on him because he chose the forest path, it was fated, for luck is an element of fate. Destiny leaves no choice; fate gives limited choice which may be good or bad, but it cannot be averted. What is fated must be, for at no point can there be any turning back.

CRT:5:4 The circumstances, Enidvadew, of the traveller conform to the law of sowing and reaping; he may travel in comfort or pain, happily or sorrowfully, with strength or weakness, heavily burdened or lightly burdened, well prepared or ill prepared. When the destination is set according to the degrees of a former life, then the circumstances of the journey should conform with the desire. For what use is it desiring a great destination when the law of sowing and reaping decrees that an intolerable burden must be carried on the way? Far better to have lesser aspirations. The decrees of fate are many; the decrees of destiny are few.

CRT:5:5 When the Earth was young and the race of man still as children, there were fertile, green pastures in the lands where all is now sand and barren wasteland. In the midst of it was a gardenland, which lay against the edge of the Earth, eastward towards the sunrising, and it was called Meruah, meaning The Place of The Garden on the Plain. It lay at the foot of a mountain, which was cleft at its rising, and out of it flowed the river of Tardana, which watered the plain. From the mountain, on the other side, ran the river Kal, which watered the plain through the land of Kaledan. The river Nara flowed westward and then turned back to flow around the gardenland.

CRT:5:6 It was a fertile place, for out of the ground grew every kind of tree that was good for food and every tree that was pleasant to the sight. Every herb that could be eaten and every herb that flowered was there. The Tree of Life, which was called Glasir, having leaves of gold and copper, was within the Sacred Enclosure. There, too, was the Great Tree of Wisdom bearing the fruits of knowledge granting the choice and ability to know the true from the false. It is the same tree, which can be read as men read a book. There also was the Tree of Trespass, beneath which grew the Lotus of Rapture, and in the centre was The Place of Power, where God made His presence known.

CRT:5:7 Time passed, and The Children of God were grown strong and upright under the tempering hammer of God, and Earth, The Anvil of God, became more kindly. All was pleasant and food plentiful, but life palls in such places, for it is against the nature of man to flourish in these circumstances. Earth is not for pleasurable dallying, it is a place of teaching, trial and testing.

CRT:5:8 The Children of God were not yet the heirs of God, nor inheritors of godhood, but there was one among them who had almost completed the Pilgrimage of Enidvadew. He had unravelled the tangled skeins of fate and traversed the tumultuous seas of life to the many ports of destiny, and having paid the debts of sowing and reaping, was one triumphant over Enidvadew.

CRT:5:9 He was Fanvar, son of Auma and Atem. He was wise and knew all things; he beheld mysteries and the secret things hidden from the eyes of other men. He saw sunrise and the sunsetting in their splendour, but longed for things not realisable in the place where he lived. So because he walked with God, he was culled out from his kind and brought to Meruah, The Gardenplace.

CRT:5:10 He came to it across the mountains and wastelands, arriving after many days' journeying. Weary and close to death because of the privations he suffered, he could just reach the refreshing waters, from which he drank deeply, and filled with exhaustion, he slept. In his sleep, he dreamed, and this was the manner of his dreaming: he saw before him a being of indescribable glory and majesty, who said, "I am the God above all, even above the God of your people, I am that which fulfils the aspirations of men, and I am that in which they are fulfilled. You, having traversed all the Circles of Enidvadew and established your worthiness, are now made my governor on Earth, and you shall rule all things here, guiding them in my ways, leading them ever upwards into glory. This will be your labour and, behold, here is your reward."

CRT:5:11 A cloud mist seemed to gather about The Glorious Being, enfolding Him so He was no longer visible. Then, the mist gradually cleared, and the man saw another form emerging. It was that of a woman, but one such as Fanvar had never seen before, beautiful beyond his conception of beauty, with such perfection of form and grace that he was dumbfounded. Yet, the vision was not substantial; she was a wraith, an ethereal being.

CRT:5:12 The man awoke and sought food from the fruits about him and, having refreshed himself, wandered about the garden. Wherever he went he saw the wraith, but was unafraid because she smiled encouragingly, bringing comfort to his heart. He built himself a shelter and grew strong again, but always, wherever he went, the wraith was not far distant.

CRT:5:13 One day, near the edge of the garden, he fell asleep in the heat of the day and awoke to find himself surrounded by the Sons of Bothas, not true men but Yoslings, kinsfolk to the beasts of the forest. Before they could take his strength and wisdom, he loosed himself among them, slaying some in his rage and might before the rest ran away. When it was done, he sat himself down beneath a great tree, for he was wounded and blood gushed out from his side and gathered thickly beside him. He became faint, falling into a deep sleep, and while he slept, a wondrous thing happened. The wraith came and lay beside him, taking blood from his wound upon herself so it congealed about her. Thus, the Spiritbeing became clothed with flesh, born of congealing blood, and being sundered from his side, she rose a mortal woman.

CRT:5:14 In his heart, Fanvar was not at rest, because of her likeness, but she was gentle, ministering to him with solicitude and, being skilful in the ways of healing, she made him whole. Therefore, when he had grown strong again, he made her Queen of The Gardenland, and she was so called even by our fathers, who named her Gulah, but Fanvar called her Aruah, meaning helpmate. In our tongue, she is called The Lady of Lanevid.

CRT:5:15 Now, God enlightened Fanvar concerning the woman, saying, "This woman was drawn from her compatible abode in a realm of beauty through the yearning aspirations of men. Her coming accomplishes something, which would otherwise have taken countless generations, for Earth is more fitting for men to learn manly things than for women to learn womanly ones. This woman is not as other women, being in no way like yourself; every hair of her head is unlike that of a man, every drop of blood and every particle of flesh is that of a woman and quite unlike that of a man. Her thoughts and desires are different; she is neither coarse nor uncouth, being altogether of another, more refined realm. Her daughters will walk proudly, endowed with every womanly perfection and grace. Delicacy, modesty and charm will be the lovely jewels enhancing their womanliness. Henceforth, man will be truly man, and woman will be truly woman, men being girded with manliness and women clothed with womanliness. Yet, they shall walk together, hand in hand, towards the ascending glory before them, each the helpmate and inspiration of the other." So Fanvar and Aruah lived in contentment amid bounty and fruitfulness, with freedom from afflictions and sickness. They delighted in each other and, because of their differences, were drawn closer together.

CRT:5:16 Aruah brought but one thing with her when she crossed the misty frontier, the treasure of Lanevid, the jewel contained in the moonchalice, the stone of inspiration fashioned by the desires of men. Never owned by any but the daughters of Aruah, this, the Lengil, Aruah gave to Fanvar as her dowry and her pledge of purity and exclusiveness. She followed the ways of the cradleland, not the ways of Earth.

CRT:5:17 Within the Gardenland was the Sacred Enclosure, the domain of Fanvar and Aruah, forbidden to those of The Children of God who had now come to this place. It contained the Chalice of Fulfilment, granting any who drank from it the realisation of all things to which they aspired. None might drink from this, save Fanvar and Aruah. Also, there was the Cauldron of Immortality, containing an essence distilled from the fruits growing in the garden, and this guarded against mortal ills.

CRT:5:18 Aruah brought forth a son by Fanvar, and he was called Rautoki, and a daughter who was called Armena. Each knew the mysteries of magic and the ways of the stars. In the fullness of time, Rautoki married among the daughters of the Sons of God and had two sons, Enanari and Nenduka. It was Enanari who first taught the weaving of cloth from plants, and Nenduka was a mighty hunter. Armena also married among the Sons of God and brought forth a son who was called Belenki and daughters called Ananua and Mameta. Ananua knew the making of pots and things of clay, and Mameta the taming of beasts and birds.

CRT:5:19 Nenduka had two sons, Namtara and Kainan. Namtara had two sons also, Nenduka and Dadam, before dying in the fullness of manhood. Belenki married Enidva and had a son called Enkidua and a daughter called Estartha, meaning Maid of the Morning, and she became a great teacher among The Children of God. This was the Estartha who became the first Moonmaiden, being later called Lady of The Morning Star. Enkidua had a daughter, and her name was Maeva.

CRT:5:20 Outside the Sacred Enclosure, known as Gisar, but forming a gateway into it was a circular structure of stones called Gilgal, and within this was a shrine, wherein was kept a sacred vessel called Gwinduiva. This was like a goblet and was made of rainbow-hued crystal set in gold with pearls. Above the cup appeared a shimmering moon-coloured mist like a thin, cold flame. At certain times, when the Heavens were in a proper position, the Gwinduiva was filled with moondew and potions from the cauldron within the Sacred Enclosure, making a pale honey-coloured liquor, and this the people drank from the goblet. However, there were different proportions in the vessel for those of the blood of Fanvar and Aruah and those who were Children of God, but not of their blood. It was the potion from the Gwinduiva which kept sickness and disease away from those who drank it.

CRT:5:21 Dadam the Firstfather married Leitha, and they had a son called Herthew. Dadam then married Maeva who had a daughter, not by him, and this was Gwineva, the cuckoochild fathered by Abrimenid of Gwarthon, son of Namtenigal, whom we call Lewid the Darkfather.

CRT:5:22 About the land of The Children of God was the wasteland where Yoslings, called The Children of Zumat, which means They Who Inherit Death, dwelt. Amongst these, Namtenigal, the wily hunter, was the most wise and cunning; he alone was unafraid of The Children of God, and he alone dared enter the Gardenland.

CRT:5:23 In the days when Estartha was teaching, Namtenigal often came to hear her words, and The Children of God were not displeased, for teaching the wild men about them was a duty with which they had been charged. Namtenigal, therefore, participated in their rites but could not partake of the elixir from the Gwinduiva, because this was forbidden. While it gave health and strength to The Children of God, safeguarding them from the sicknesses of the Yoslings, if given to others, it caused a wasting away. It was also altogether forbidden for any of The Children of God to mate with the Yoslings, for this was deemed to be the most unforgivable of sins.

CRT:5:24 Now, the wily one learned much from Estartha and, in the fullness of time, brought his own son to her and he became as her son, living in her house and forsaking the ways of his people. Estartha called him Lewid the Lightbringer, for it was her intention that he should be taught the ways of those who walked in light, that he might in time enlighten his own people.

CRT:5:25 Lewid grew up tall and handsome; he was quick to learn and became wise. He was also a man of the chase, strong and enduring, a hunter of renown. But there were times when the call of his people was strong; then, he would go out furtively into the night to indulge in their dark rituals. Thus, he became knowledgeable in the ways of the flesh and in the carnal indulgences of the body.

CRT:5:26 Dadam became a servant of the Sacred Enclosure, where the misty veil between the realms could be penetrated, for all those having the blood of Aruah had twinsight, an ability to see wraiths and sithfolk, ansis and spiritbeings, all the things of the Otherworld, not clearly, but as through a veil.

CRT:5:27 Beside the place called Gisar was a pleasant parkland with trees of every kind and a stream, also thickets of flowering bushes and all manner of plants growing lushly. It was the custom of Maeva to wander there in the sunshine, and Lewid also went there; so it came about that they met among the trees. Maeva knew the man but had shunned him in the past; now, she saw he was handsome, possessed of many attractions, so her foot was stayed, and she did not run away.

CRT:5:28 As the days passed they dallied longer together, and Lewid talked of things Maeva had not heard before. She felt a stirring in her blood, but did not respond or heed his temptations, because of the things that were forbidden. So Lewid went to the Moonmother, wise woman of the Yoslings, and telling of his desires, beseeched her to help him. The Moonmother gave him two apples containing a vile substance, which they had drawn through their stalks; this Lewid gave to Maeva who then became helpless in his hands.

CRT:5:29 They met again after this, for Maeva became enamoured towards Lewid, but it happened that she became ill with a strange sickness and was afraid. Then Dadam became ill, and Lewid also, and Lewid said to the woman, "You must obtain the pure essences from within the Sacred Enclosure, and Setina, the Moonmother, will prepare an elixir which will cure us." This he said because none of his kind had ever been able to obtain the Sacred Substances, though they had always coveted what had been denied them. Now, because of her frailty, the woman was pliable in his hands, and Lewid seized the opportunity.

CRT:5:30 To achieve his ends, Lewid gave Maeva a potion which had been prepared by the Moonmother, and she administered this to Dadam and those with him, by guile and deceit, so that they fell asleep. While they slept, Maeva stole from the Sacred Substances and took them to Lewid, who gave them to the Moonmother, and she made a brew.

CRT:5:31 Part of this was given to Maeva, and the rest was drunk by the Yoslings, from their awful ankital during their night rites. When the morning came, they were all smitten with grievous pains, and before the sun set that day, all the Yoslings were stricken with a sickness, such as they had not known before.

CRT:5:32 Maeva took what had been given to her and, finding Dadam, laid low in his bed gave him a draught from her vessel, though she had to use womanly wiles to get him to drink it. She drank the remainder, and they both slept. But when they awoke in the morning, both were suffering pains, and this was something they had not known before. Dadam said to the woman, "What have you done, for what has happened to us cannot be unless the things which are forbidden have been done." The woman replied, "Lord, I was tempted, and I fell, I have done that which is forbidden and unforgivable."

CRT:5:33 Dadam said, "I am bound by duty to do certain things, but first let us go into the Gisar to the place called Bethkelcris, where I will seek enlightenment." So they went there together and stood before the shrine beneath the Tree of Wisdom. There, they were filled with an inflowing vision, seeing themselves as they were and as they should have been, and they were ashamed. He, because he had not followed the proper path of a man and she, because of her falsity. There, in the reflecting mist, the contamination of the woman was revealed, and the man's heart shrivelled within him like a flower licked by flame.

CRT:5:34 Then, they saw a great Spiritbeing materialising in the reflecting mist, and he said to them, "Woe to you and your house, for the greatest of evils has befallen the race of The Children of God, and it is defiled. The heritage of Kadamhapa is lost. The fetid flow defiling the woman results from the incompatible intermingling, but it is not all, for sicknesses and diseases are also generating from the ferments of the impure implantation."

CRT:5:35 Dadam said, "The fault is with the woman; wherefore should I suffer?" The Spiritbeing replied, "Because you two are now as one, the cankerworms of disease and sickness strike both equally, but you shall not again defile this place. Henceforth, the misty veil becomes an impenetrable barrier severing our two realms from each other, so they can no longer be easily spanned. Between us, there will now be no means of communication. Henceforth, man and woman, fated to unite in love divine, shall be divided and set apart, though ever yearning reunion. They may cleave one to the other, seeking the unity, which will rekindle the flame, but unless their efforts transcend the limitations of earthly things, they will be in vain. The spirit of man is now severed from the whole and cast again into unconsciousness, and it too shall long for reunion with the whole. The spark shall seek to return to the fire; for otherwise, it becomes nothing. The web of fate is rewoven and the paths of destiny remade; the design of life is redrawn; again, the progression begins in ignorance, birth and death, pain and pleasure, joy and sorrow, success and failure, love and hate, peace and war, all the light and shade, the many hues making the splendidly intricate pattern of life on Earth. This is a new beginning, but a beginning not in purity and unencumbered, but one already weighted with debts and burdens."

CRT:5:36 The Spiritbeing continued, "Enough wickedness has been wrought by your wilfulness and disobedience, for the decrees forbidding certain things were for your own benefit. Immortality was nearly within your reach, but had you achieved this, you would have brought an even more grievous evil upon yourselves and your inheritors, for freed from servitude to change, you and they would have been unable to progress."

CRT:5:37 The Children of God were driven out of the gardenland by Spiritbeings, and then guardians were set at its gates so none could re-enter. Then, it was withdrawn beyond the misty veil; the waters ceased to flow, and the fertility departed; only a wilderness remained. The Children of God went to dwell in the land of Amanigel, which is beyond the mountains of Mashur by the sea of Dalemuna.

CRT:5:38 From this time onward, man fashioned his own spiritlikeness. Some, who were loathsome in aspect even unto themselves, went apart and were mercifully veiled in dark depths, and they said among themselves, "Let us dwell here in the darkness and prepare a place for others like ourselves, so that when they follow, they abide here and join us." Thus, were the Dark Regions formed and inhabited by demons who are nought but the hideously fashioned spirits of evil men.

CRT:5:39 These things have been written into the record. In Siboit, they used to say this was the manner of man's making, "God sent His creating Craftsman Spirit down to Earth, and the reflection of The One was drawn into a spiritless body, and this became the heart of man."

CRT:5:40 These are the words written by Thonis of Myra in Ludicia in his day:

CRT:5:41 "You ask me what is man, and I answer: He is life becoming aware of itself. He is the intangible knowing the tangible, Spirit in matter, fire in water. When this first happened, none remembers, and only the old folktales remain. There was the beginning and then the garden, and it was in this garden man found himself; before this he was not free, being one with everything about him. As he could not disobey, good and evil could not be; they were non-existent."

CRT:5:42 "Man became free through awareness of himself, and with this knowledge, denied any kinship with the beast. As he was no longer in harmonious relationship with things of the Earth, he became discontented, dissatisfied and restless, he wanted to belong, but felt his place of belonging was not there. He had been reborn as a mangod, and therefore, it is truly said that man was born of Earth and Spirit, under a tree, the symbol of life, and in a garden."

CRT:5:43 "There the eyes of the man and woman were opened and, being above the beasts, they knew they were different and set apart from all else that breathed. They separated themselves, being now ashamed of their state and strangers to each other. The carnal satisfaction of lesser creatures now no longer sufficed; they had lost contact with the Source of Love, but, though knowing something was lacking, knew not what. They had fallen into carnal knowledge which only man can know, for only he feels the reproach of divinity. They were removed from The Garden of Content by an inhalation of the Divine Substance and could not return because of the barrier between man and non-man.

CRT:5:44 Kamelik has written: "The entwined were cut apart and since that day have never known content. They wander restlessly, ever seeking to unite again and together find the jewel, which is lost to Earth forever."

CRT:5:45 Lupisis has written: "This first woman, who came from the void, is the eternally glorified goddess, the inspirer of hearts, the ideal of womanhood honoured by all men, the priestess at the shrines of delicacy and tenderness. She was the ideal woman who, because of man's nature, is always tempted by his twinshade, the beast in his form. If the beast triumphs and she falls, the ideal becomes enshrouded in winding cloths of disillusionment, and something is lost to the heart of a man.

CRT:5:46 These words are also there: "They did not partake of wisdom, and fruit from the tree of knowledge is bitter. Men are denied their true birthright. The fall of man was a fall from loving contact with God into material carnality. The Soul that had shared the consciousness of God fell into unconsciousness by becoming ensnared in matter. The fall severed man from the source of his spiritual sustenance; thereafter, his efforts were to struggle back. In his blind groping for God, after the fall, he discovered demons and found it easier to worship them than to continue the search."

CRT:5:47 "God is always waiting; man has only to look up, but it is easier to go down the hill than to climb it. It is easier for man's spiritual beliefs to degenerate than to evolve. Who among men knows the truth and can write with certain knowledge? Would not this certainty be against the Law? No man was there at the beginning to see and write, but of one thing alone we can be sure; The Creating God knows how and why, and could the acts of One so great be without purpose?

Chapter Six – Dadam And Lewid

CRT:6:1 Maeva fled for her life, and many kinfolk went with her. But Dadam was unable to follow, being laid low with the sickness. This loosened his tongue so it became uncontrollable, making him babble like a child, and the sickness covered his body with red sores, from which came an issue. Lewid also departed for a place far out in the wilderness.

CRT:6:2 Those with Dadam, who looked back towards the place of the garden, saw bright tongues of light licking the sky above it, the whole being interwoven with flickering flames in many hues. Those who sought to return were repulsed with a tingling ache over their bodies, which increased into severe pain as they approached; so, they were driven away.

CRT:6:3 When Dadam recovered so he could stand, only a few remained with him, and they all moved further into the wilderness to a place where there was water and pasture. There, Dadam left Herthew, his son, and the boy's mother, with Habaris the Learned and set out to find Lewid.

CRT:6:4 After many days, Dadam and those with him came upon Lewid and his Yoslings, who were full of sickness, and slew many, but Lewid was not slain, though mortally wounded, and he lay against a great rock. When Dadam came near, Lewid raised an arm heavily and said, "Hail to the victor and benefactor, who has come to terminate our wretchedness." While Dadam stood sternly contemplating him, Lewid said, "To kill me now is your prerogative, for even we lesser beings, who are far removed from godmen have the law of husbandly pride. What I did has been done before and will be done again, but I erred by crossing an unknown barrier which could not be discerned, for we, within ourselves, are no more contagious to each other than are your people. If I then must die, let it be for my part in spawning the cankerworms of disease which have stricken both our peoples."

CRT:6:5 "Back in the dreamingtime, when the Great Gods strove among themselves for dominion of the skyspaces, and the wide expanse of Earth was rent apart by unearthly wildfire, Bemotha was cut apart by the bright arrows of Shemas. Then, this land was given to my people as their dominion, while yours was in another unearthly place far distant. Our domain was a pleasant place and though you teach that because of this, we remained as we are; yet we were content. We know of no great design, nor of any barely attainable objectives, to which men must aspire. Such striving, as you know, is to us no more than purposeless vexation."

CRT:6:6 "I have my God, and you have yours, and as they strove one against the other beforetimes, so will it always be; but now, there is a new battleground with new battlechiefs. I will go to my appointed place, and you will go to yours, and from thence, as leaders of the fray, we shall wage a never ceasing war. Such is fated and must be, but who will win the fair prize of Earth for their king? We shall not strive with clubs and lances, the hurling stone and flying dart, but with more subtle weaponry. This thing is not our choice; we are but playthings of fate. That you and I should head the fray is not because of our qualities, but because we were where we were, when we were. Now we are but two precarious points of life in a hostile wilderness, but what might we be in a hundred generations?"

CRT:6:7 Dadam said, "These things I know too, for my eyes have always been opened. I too have looked out into an endless plain without any horizon, but I shall lead those who have grown strong through seeking and striving, while those in your ranks will be weakened through indulgence in the fleshpots and pleasure places of Earth. We are the disinherited, but not the disowned; we have the seeds of victory within us. You and yours were never more than you are, sons of the easy path, followers of the downhill road."

CRT:6:8 Then, when these things had been spoken, Lewid died, and Dadam and those with him burnt his body. Dadam and those with him wandered the wasteland for many days, then turned southward towards the mountain. Then it happened that one day, Dadam was seated apart, in solitude among rocks, with chin on chest, and a hunter of the Ubalites came upon him from behind. The hunter slung a smooth stone as the man turned, and it struck out his eye. Then, the Ubalite slew him by smashing in his head with a stone.

CRT:6:9 This hunter was the son of Ankadur, son of Enanari, king of the Ubalites, by Urkelah, daughter of the Chaisites. This is known because those who were with Dadam came out of the barren places and learned the ways of builders, becoming great among the Ubalites and raising cities along the rivers. Among them was Enkilgal who built Keridor, which stands between the two great rivers, and Netar and Baletsheramam, who taught men the ways of writing, setting the letters upon a pillar in Herak.

Chapter Seven – Herthew, Son of the Firstfather

CRT:7:1 The Book of Beginnings tells us all things began with Varkelfa, therein called Awenkelifa, from whom flows gwinin, the energiser which stabilises all things so they maintain their proper form and awen, which responds to the moulding desires. This is well enough, but men concern themselves more with the beginnings of their race, and ours is rooted in Herthew the Sunfaced, son of the Firstfather.

CRT:7:2 While Herthew was still young, he was expelled from the lushlands where he was born, and he journeyed across the harshlands in the company and keeping of wise Habaris. After many days, they came to Krowkasis, cradleland of our race, land of mountains and rivers, which is beside Ardis, and they encamped there in a valley. With them were retainers and flocks.

CRT:7:3 Herthew grew to manhood there, and always Habaris was at his side, instructing him in all the things he should know. He taught Herthew the nine essential disciplines of Imain and the secrets of the three sacred vessels. Herthew learned that there was a place of gloom, where the air was foul, and malodorous breezes carried pestilence and poisonous particles. This was the source of all maladies and ailments and of the things which cause putrefaction and decay. This place had been closed off from Earth, for it existed in another realm beyond the ken of mortals; but it had been brought into attunement with Earth when a forbidden act was accomplished. Thus, the bodies of mortals became susceptible to influences from the baleful place.

CRT:7:4 To this and similar parts of the Otherworld, the wicked would be drawn when they passed through the grim gates of death. But Habaris taught a different conception of wickedness, one where lack of effort, indolence and indifference to duty and obligations, the taking of the easy path, were just as wrong as actual deeds of wickedness. He taught that men reach the true goal of life by transmuting lustlove into truelove. That true victory is gained only over the defeated bodies of their vanquished passions and baser selves.

CRT:7:5 These and many other things were taught by Habaris, but many of his teachings displeased the people of Krowkasis who were then as they were before Herthew's forefather was led away. So Habaris concealed many things from them and taught, by simple tales, things within their understanding. He taught them the mysteries concerning the wheel of the year and divided the year into a Summer half and a Winter half, with a great year circle of fifty-two years, a hundred and four of which was the circle of The Destroyer. He gave them the Laws of Weal and Woe and established the folkfeasts of harvest-tide and seeding-tide. He taught them the ritual of Ulisidui.

CRT:7:6 But Habaris instructed Herthew in the ways of the Otherworld. He taught him concerning the three rays from the central invisible sun, which manifest all things, upholding them in stability of form. Also concerning the Oversoul, which filled everything in creation, as the Soulself filled the mortal body. This Soulself, he declared, would develop from mortal sensitivity and feeling transmuted into divine sensitivity and feeling, through suppression of the baser instincts within mortals. It was strengthened by development of feelings of love between man and woman and between these and their kindred by the appreciation of beauty and devotion to duty, by the development of all qualities that pertain to humans and not to animals.

CRT:7:7 Herthew learned that the Soulself is quickened by soul substances outflowing from The Godhead. That the strong soul is transformed and moulded to the soul's desire, but the weak soul is not its own master; it is flabby, unstable and is pulled into a state of distortion by its own vices. In the afterlife, there is unbounded joy for the entry of a noble soul; it will glow with splendour and stand out proudly. The mean soul of the wicked is dull-hued, twisted and drab, and, being drawn towards its own compatible state, it shrinks into the dark places.

CRT:7:8 When Herthew had barely crossed the threshold of manhood, black-bearded spearmen began to ravish the borders of Krowkasis, and Idalvar, king of that country, called his fighting men together and when word came to Herthew, he prepared to depart. But Habaris bid him stay awhile, for he was unprepared for battle. Then, Habaris prepared a strange fire with stones, unlike any fire seen before, and when it burnt low he plucked out that which is called 'child of the green flame' and he beat it out so it became a blade. This he fitted to a horned handgrip and, when it was edged and blooded, gave it to Herthew, saying, "Behold, Dislana the Bitterbiter, faithful servant of he who strikes hard and true." Then, he made a shield of wicker covered with ox-hide and a cap of hide which came down over the face and neck. So equipped, Herthew went to the encampment of Idalvar, taking eight fighting men with him.

CRT:7:9 In those days, men fought with hand-thrown spears and clubs, with flung stones and sticks sharpened by fire and weighted, but they did not close in the battle clash. So when Idalvar saw the battleblade of Herthew, he wondered and it passed his understanding; but when he saw Herthew close on the battleline and the foeman fall before him, he was amazed.

CRT:7:10 No man about the king could understand the making of such weapons, offspring of fire and stone, but Habaris made others, and Herthew became the king's right hand man and the first hero of the Noble Race. The king offered Herthew his daughter's hand in marriage, but Herthew declined, saying, "The days of my manhood are not yet fulfilled."

CRT:7:11 When the war-filled days had passed, Herthew withdrew to the place where Habaris made the bright battleblade, and already he had taught the mysteries of their making to others, sealing their mouths with magic. But Herthew was less concerned with the weaponry of war than with the mysteries of life and the battles of the Spirit beset by mortality. So, while his workmen drew bright blades from the thunderstones, Habaris taught Herthew and his battlebrothers, and these were the things they learned from his mouth.

CRT:7:12 "Beyond God, there is an Absolute, which no man should try to understand, for it exists and has always existed in a state beyond man's finite comprehension. It is from this Absolute that God, The Ultimate in all Perfections, was engendered."

CRT:7:13 "To create, God first visualised in thought, then He produced an outflowing wave of power, which, in a manner of speaking, solidified what might be called building stones. The outflowing power also produced the Celestial Hymn, which brought the building stones together in harmonious forms. So it is truly said that all creation is the harp of God, and it responds to His song and manipulations. It is an everlasting unfoldment. The voice of God can also be heard in the voice of His beautiful daughter who endows all growing things with life and beauty."

CRT:7:14 "There is a divine purpose in creation, which may be known only to the few; this knowledge is the key to all unanswered questions. Acquiring it is like the drawing back of heavy curtains, which have kept a room in gloomy half light, so all things suddenly become clear and distinct. He who gains this knowledge knows the Grand Secret, the answer to the riddle of the ages and knows beyond a shadow of a doubt. This divine purpose, and the divine secret concerning it, is called Gwenkelva."

CRT:7:15 "Apart from Gwenkelva, God gains nothing from His creation, except that as a Being possessing infinite love and goodness, He must have something to receive the gift of love and respond to it. Even among mortal beings, who is there that could find satisfactory fulfilment in self-love? Also, He needed something wherewith He could contrast Himself, some medium wherein He could perform, and this is creation."

CRT:7:16 "Creation is also, for mortals, the school of life. The training ground for godhood. There are Three Circles of Reality, three realms, three stages of existence. They are: Heaven, where perfection visualised on Earth may be realised and desires and ideals materialised; where hard-striven-for aspirations are attained; it is the place where all the properly developed spiritual potential latent in man reaches maturity and fulfilment. Earth, the place of training, development and preparation, the testing ground, the battlefield where men discover their true natures when confronted by life's challenges, contests and contentions; where competition and controversy are the rule. It is here that aims and objectives are conceived and thought-out for realisation later in the proper place. It is a starting point, the beginning of the journey; it is here that the proper road must be wisely chosen. Then, there is the Realm of the Misty Horizon, the intermediate place, the place of spirits, where those above can commune with those below and where free spirits wander within their limitations."

CRT:7:17 These things, which Habaris taught in those far off days, have been rewritten in transmission to accord with our understanding, but it is unwise to voice them in these troublesome days, when words become snares to entrap the unwary.

CRT:7:18 Now, Idalvar desired to learn the secret of the bright blade engendering thunderstones, but no man who came with Habaris or laboured for him would disclose any part of it, and the king was afraid to put them to the test. So, having thought the matter out, the king sent for his daughters and told them what he expected them to do, for he had devised a plan to learn the secret. Then, he sent an invitation to Herthew and Habaris. When they arrived at the king's encampment, they found a great gathering in their honour, and the king's daughters favourably inclined towards them, one smiling upon Herthew and the other upon Habaris who was at the age of hoaryheadedness. Though at first, Habaris was indifferent and wearied her, the king's daughter pandered to him, encouraging even his follies, setting out to charm him with her wit and beauty.

CRT:7:19 It was no great length of time before her womanly wiles ensnared the heart of Habaris, and though he was almost ripe for the surrender of secrets, the damsel's efforts had taxed her, and the game became tiresome, so there came an evening when she could not endure his company. In the midst of the merrymaking, when the alebowls had made many rounds and the sound of song and story was at its height, she slipped away with a young battleman, who attended upon her father. Many who sat among the benches saw this and whispered to one another, nodding knowingly in the direction of Habaris who was not unaware, though he appeared to have drunk to his capacity.

CRT:7:20 Habaris had learned to love the young woman; so he was sorely heartsmitten, but within himself, he knew the tree of Winter love bears only Winter's fruits. Yet he made excuses to himself for her, thinking perhaps it was just some girlishness with no more weight than a floating feather, nothing of serious import, for it was true the merrymaking was better suited to the natures of men than the natures of women. Maybe, he thought, it is just an innocent indiscretion.

CRT:7:21 So when the day came to its fullness and those who had made merry went heavily about their tasks, Habaris approached the king and asked for his daughter's hand in marriage. He said, "Your daughter Klara has delighted me with her winsome ways; she has charmed me with her gaiety and beauty; she has displayed much pleasure in my company; surely I have not misread the signs." The king was not overpleased, for though he greatly desired to know the secret of the bright blade he had not intended giving his daughter's hand to Habaris, but neither did he wish to offend him. Therefore, he was wary in his reply, saying, "It is the custom for any suitor for a highborn woman's hand to be himself highborn and worthily battleblooded. Yet, such is my affection for you that I would not let even the custom become a bar to this marriage, and you may be a battleblooded man among your own people. But let us not enter lightly into this thing, for the girl is still young and it would be well if you established yourself favourably with her. She will be a worthy wife indeed, for she is one who is ever ready to learn, one with an enquiring mind. Nothing gives her greater pleasure than the acquisition of knowledge." So the matter was left.

CRT:7:22 Now, some days later Idalvar and his retinue, accompanied by Herthew and Habaris, went to the gathering place for folkfeasts, some five days journey away. People were accustomed to meeting here every thirteen moons to celebrate the season of fruitfulness, many coming a great distance. Beside the gathering place was the compound of a far-framed seer and warlock called Gwidon, who, in the fullness of the moon on the third night, would prophesy events for the forthcoming year.

CRT:7:23 Idalvar and those with him presented their gifts and took their places before the compound. Presently, Gwidon came out cloaked in the skins of wild dogs, with a horned crown and skull-headed staff. He seated himself before a small fire, into which he threw prescriptions, making a cloud of smoke, which completely enveloped him. When this had drifted away, he seemed to be asleep, but after a while, he lifted his head; then raising himself up, he started to prophesy.

CRT:7:24 He talked awhile of small matters, then told of dangers to the people through enemies who would bear down from the Northlands. He prophesied a great bloodletting, telling people they would be saved by a great war leader, a king knowing the secret of the bright blade, himself a war-wielder of one. He exhorted the people to bestir themselves and prepare, wasting no time in finding their leader.

CRT:7:25 No man among the people knew the mysteries of the bright blade except Habaris, but he was not a man of battle and Herthew was not high born among them. So, though they talked long, they talked in tangles, failing to resolve the issue. It was then decided each should go his own way, but they should meet at the same place again at the next full moon, when Gwidon would be able to help with their decision.

CRT:7:26 When Idalvar returned to his encampment, he was no longer hesitant about the marriage of his daughter, ordering that it should take place forthwith. But he stipulated that Habaris must initiate him and his sons into the mysteries of the bright blade immediately. This being agreed, arrangements for the marriage were put in hand.

CRT:7:27 Habaris and Klara were married, and Idalvar and his sons partially initiated into the mysteries of the bright blade, for the king was told it would take some time for the initiation to be completed. So when they next went to the meeting place, Idalvar was proclaimed the war leader, with his sons to follow according to their ages, should he fall in battle. But Habaris had spoken to Gwidon in secret, and matters were so arranged that should the sons of Idalvar fall, then Herthew would become the battle chief.

CRT:7:28 The king and those with him returned to their home compound where they were to prepare battlemen, but Herthew was to go back to the gathering place and there train fighting men in the battle tactics which brought them clashing into the foe.

CRT:7:29 Now, on their wedding night, when they had retired to their bower, Klara burst into tears and fell weeping with her head on the knees of Habaris, confessing she was not a virgin and had deceived him, begging his forgiveness. Habaris raised her up and said, "Even the wisest of men becomes a fool when his heart blinds him to reason. The older the fool, the bigger the fool. He did not question her regarding love, for he knew she could not love and deceive him; she had given her heart, and with it, her virginity to another. Yet, he made an excuse for her to himself, thinking that she had not wilfully deceived him but had acted out of duty to her father. Also, truly loving someone and wishing to demonstrate that love, she necessarily had to sacrifice the happiness and content, the self-respect of her husband-to-be, the choice had been hers to make. It is ever so. Habaris asked if her father had known how things were and she said, "He suspected, for am I not his daughter?" Thus, Habaris found himself tied to an unloving wife, for he chose to disregard the custom of the people. He wondered, was she also to be an undutiful and unfaithful one?

CRT:7:30 A woman reserves herself for her husband, or she does not, according to her marriage criterion. A woman reserved for marriage is one unlikely to be unfaithful; a woman easily come by before marriage is no less attainable afterwards, for if she says love is the criterion, then she measures by something unstandardised, which may figuratively vary from one inch to a mile. A man declaring his love may have seduction in mind or a lifetime of protective devotion; the marriage proposal determines the difference and establishes the intent.

CRT:7:31 After the marriage, the king showed little concern for Habaris, for he kept Klara's young battleman in his retinue when he should have despatched him elsewhere. Nor did Klara maintain the restraint and decorum, which dignifies wifehood, except in their outward manifestations, which is no more than a deceptive crust disguising the polluted love beneath. Thus, Habaris bore the shame of belittlement in the eyes of men, for Klara was furtively unfaithful.

CRT:7:32 Habaris visited Herthew and, on his return, told the king that he and his sons would now receive their final initiation.

CRT:7:33 So, having made preparation, they set off, accompanied by Klara, to the place of the thunderstones, this being a deeply cleft mountain wherein there was a large cavern, from which flowed a river. Entering the cave, Habaris told those with him to bide where they were, for only Idalvar, his sons and Klara were to accompany him into the place of initiation, a small cave entered through a long narrow passage closed off by a heavy door and lit by a fire already prepared, a fire which burnt tardily with a blue flame.

CRT:7:34 When a length of time had passed, those who waited without grew uneasy, but it was long before they approached the door, and when they did, their throats were seized, so they were affrighted and fled, and one among them died. Then, those who knew the mysteries of the thunderstones came and cleared the way, and all within the cave were found dead. Habaris did what had to be done, for though it is well for men to conform to the laws of men, there is a superlaw, by which men who are men should live, and which sometimes decrees that they must die.

CRT:7:35 Herthew married the daughter of Idalvar, and they had a son who died in his seventh year. Idalvar's daughter died in childbirth. The invaders came and were defeated with a great slaughtering, and Herthew became the first king over all the people of Krowkasis.

Chapter Eight – Gwineva

CRT:8:1 Maeva, one time wife of Dadam, found refuge among people of Ardis, where she gave birth to Gwineva the Cuckoochild, but as the child grew, it was seen that she had red hair. Though all knew there were fair-haired and dark-haired people, none had ever seen anyone with red hair. Also, strange maladies had manifested in Ardis, for which the strangers were blamed; therefore, because of these things, Maeva and her child were driven out.

CRT:8:2 They came to a pool near the border of Krowkasis and built a habitation of reeds, living there for many years. However, Maeva was killed by a wild beast, and Gwineva was left alone, but she learned much from familiars who came to her, and so she became a sorceress.

CRT:8:3 Time went by and the half-folk called Yoslings began to gather around her habitation, and they thought she was a goddess and worshipped her. As her fame spread, word came to Herthew concerning the strange woman, so he sent men to find out about her and report. Gwineva knew about Herthew, but he did not know who she was or that any child of Maeva lived. When Herthew heard the report, he was intrigued and sent men to escort her to him, and she came at his request. They brought her into his presence wearing a cloak of feathers and a garment of doeskin, her hair unbraided like that of other women, falling outside the cloak almost to her knees. He was amazed at the cascade of red hair, and his heart was stirred by her beauty.

CRT:8:4 Herthew gave Gwineva a bower and attendants, but she preferred to be attended by Yoslings, whom the people about Herthew despised. They gossiped about the strange woman, for it was seen that Yosling men freely entered her bower; yet, her bearing was modest and maidenly; the Yoslings showing her every form of respect.

CRT:8:5 It was the season of fruitfulness, and when Herthew went to the gathering place, he took Gwineva with him, but the Yoslings could not be taken there. So they remained behind, but the people removed them. When they arrived at the gathering place and Gwidon saw Gwineva, he was startled, for he had seen such a woman in the darkened waters; but he welcomed her and was surprised at her wisdom and skill at sorcery. When the time came for Gwidon to prophesy and all who came to hear him were gathered about, they became apprehensive, for his coming forth was delayed, and the moon began to disappear, eaten away by the blackness of the night. Then, when they started to jostle and flee, there was a great shout, and Gwidon appeared; as he did, a great fire sprang up on either side of him. The people remained, for each was rooted to the place where he stood.

CRT:8:6 Gwidon spoke at length, telling them that the nightsky sign heralded a new era. That as the moon grew again in brightness, so should their race wax strong and virile, spreading wide across the face of the Earth, driving lesser races before them. That a son of Herthew would lead their sons out of Krowkasis, and his sons and their Sons would continue westwardly, towards Hesperis, meaning Land of Spirits. That there they would meet their final destiny. He told them that there would be a great bloodletting, when brother would fight with brother and father with son, but that this would be the planting of the centrepole, around which the framework for the structure of their race would be woven. He said, "I shall go before the vanguard in spirit."

CRT:8:7 Later, Herthew asked Gwidon to cast the omensticks and read the ashes, as he wished to know things concerning Gwineva. This Gwidon did, telling him that she was his fatemate, one destined to be his wife; that she was indeed a true maiden, and he would not be foreridden. He said, "She acts as she does through innocence and not through brashness." But what Gwidon told Herthew was no more than a grain in the grainsack among all that, which he knew and saw.

CRT:8:8 When Herthew returned to his homesite, he paid court to Gwineva and asked her to marry him, and this she consented to do after one year. The people, hearing what was intended, were displeased and murmured against the marriage, saying it was unseemingly for their king to marry a sorceress and one strange in so many ways. Also, there was a custom forbidding the intermingling of blood, but there was no doubt as to what she was, some thinking she was one who could be acceptable.

CRT:8:9 Gwineva was not the bloodkin of Herthew, so as the marriage would not be incestuous, Gwineva decided she would say nothing of their relationship, for she was in love with him, and love is ever ready to make excuses. Yet, despite her knowledge and wisdom, her heart was full of fears because of her background, but she displayed none of her anxieties. She did not feel at ease among the people, but never asked that the Yoslings be allowed back. She tried to become acceptable by ministering to the sick with simples and remedies, but the more she cured and healed, the more people feared her, and fearing they shunned her, except they were in dire need of her help.

CRT:8:10 However, Herthew remained firm in his resolve to marry, though many advised that if he simply took Gwineva as a concubine or as something less than a wife, it would be more acceptable. They said, "None would object if she were treated as a woman with no standing; mate, but do not marry, for marriage would grant her undue status, and is marriage so necessary? Does a wise man buy the pie, whereof he can freely eat at any time?"

CRT:8:11 Such sayings enraged Herthew, for he knew Gwineva to be a woman reserved for marriage, and this he tried to tell the people, but they laughed, saying, "She has bewitched you; put her to the test." But he replied, "This is unworthy, for it displays doubt and distrust; a virgin is a virgin, whether named so by horn or wand and remains so whatever the conjectures of carnal-minded men who are more familiar with women of lesser repute." Yet, whether the marriage bar applied was still a thing of doubt in the minds of many, for none knew the lineage of Gwineva, nor did she enlighten anyone, though it was customary to recite this at the betrothal. But Herthew and Gwineva remained unbetrothed, though the forthcoming marriage was made known.

CRT:8:12 Now, the nephews and kin of Idalvar nurtured seeds of discord among the people, and because it was a time of peace, when the skills of a warchief were not needed, many heeded their words. So it developed that there were those for Herthew and those against him. Then, Herthew said to the people, "Let this not be something to cut people apart, but something, which can be decided at the next folkfeast."

CRT:8:13 The seedsowing time had passed, but it was not yet harvest-tide, and the young men held spear-throwing contests and tested each other in many manly skills. At such times, seated on a platform against the palisade, Herthew gave judgement and awarded merits. Inside the palisade was a walkway and places, from which great stones could be hurled, and from one such place came a murderous weapon which cut down through Herthew's head to pierce the shoulder of his shield arm, striking him to the ground. Immediately, there was a great tumult and confusion; fighting broke out and men died, but Herthew was carried to safety in the bower of Gwineva. There he was protected by his retainers, but within the palisade, all was taken over by those hostile to Herthew.

CRT:8:14 Before the cowardly blow, those for Herthew had been more numerous and powerful, but after he was so sorely wounded, they were less, and of these, many were inclined to waver, for such is the nature of man. But to contrast with the frail reeds who wavered, those who remained loyal were resolute, for this too is the nature of man.

CRT:8:15 Now, when Gwineva and the wise men attended to Herthew, they saw that while the shield arm had been injured it was not unfeeling, for it grasped the hand of Gwineva, but this the sword arm could not do, though it was uninjured. Therefore, they knew the slaughter-bent weapon had been charmed, and no woman could remove such enchantment, nor could the wise men, for they were unblooded. In the days that followed, the enchantment caused demons to enter through the wound and take up their abode, so Herthew was tormented, and his body wracked before subsiding into the quietness, which precedes death. The demons had abused Gwineva, called her foul names and cried out in loud voices against people, so that they should abandon their king.

CRT:8:16 The place where Herthew lay was near the lakeside and in the lake was an island called Inskris, meaning Isle of the Dead, where those about to die were taken, as well as the dead, before being consigned to the waters. For the people believed that those given into the lake went straight into awareness in the Otherworld, while anyone buried on land was only half aware upon arrival and remained half awake and half asleep for many years. So, those loyal to Herthew carried him down to the boats and accompanied him and Gwineva to the Isle, and they were not molested, for none interfered with those mourning the dead. On the isle were priests and nine holy maidens, who attended to the rites while other women ministered to the newly dead, but Herthew was not dead, though halfway across the threshold.

CRT:8:17 When Herthew arrived, he was placed in the hospice house, where Gwineva attended to him. Gwidon opened Herthew's skull where it had been cleft and let out the demon which had taken up habitation there, and he brewed powerful potions which removed the enchantment. When, after many days, he departed, Herthew was no longer at the door of death, though weak and in many ways like a baby.

CRT:8:18 While Herthew lay so sorely stricken, the kinsfolk of Idalvar were disputing among themselves, and this led to fighting and battles. But none came near the isle to harm Herthew, because it was a sacred place and gave him sanctuary. When it came to the time of the folkfeast, there was a great battle at the gathering place, and Gwidon was slain. There came a day when Herthew, though still not whole, could move about, and then, he and Gwineva departed with those who remained with them. They were married before leaving their isle of sanctuary.

CRT:8:19 They fled to a place afar off where, as the years went by, Herthew became whole again and Gwineva gave birth to sons and daughters. It was a good place, fertile and well watered, and so they prospered. But there came a time of drought, when the waters dried up and their flocks died. So Herthew sent men to Krowkasis, and these came back saying that there, too, the land was stricken and the people distressed. He also sent others to the West, and they returned, saying that there, the land was not stricken, but the people would not accept them except with spears.

CRT:8:20 Herthew then sent men back to Krowkasis to tell the people there of the plenty, which lay to the West, and they came back with a warband led by Ithilis, and many people followed. Herthew could no longer bear weapons, and his sons were as yet young and unblooded. Therefore, he gave his two sons, who were of sufficient age, into the keeping of Ithilis, so they might learn the art of war, and they followed him loyally, becoming men of valour in the conflict, which ensued. Many people left Krowkasis and settled in the land lying to the West, and Herthew and Gwineva also settled there.

CRT:8:21 Time passed, and Herthew became renowned for his wisdom, and Ithilis king of Arania honoured him with lands and servants. Herthew's two sons, who had followed the king and were twins, married the king's two eldest daughters who were also twins. This caused problems, for the king, though having three wives, was sonless; therefore, the twin sons of Herthew became his heirs. The king was perplexed, for the two men could not rule together, and both were of equal standing in his eyes. Yet, it was the king's duty to nominate his heir and proclaim him to the people so there should be no division after his death. Therefore, Ithilis consulted Herthew as to how the judgement should be made, and Herthew said, "Let fate decree who shall be king."

CRT:8:22 In Arania, the people gathered four times a year for the folkfeasts. At such times, it was customary for new laws to be proclaimed, judgements given and all contentious issues settled. So before the next folkfeast, Herthew prepared a manmade stone from sand, clay and other things, and while it was still soft he set the hilt of his great sword, Dislana the Bitterbiter, into it, and when the stone was hardened Dislana was fast. The sword-implanted stone was then set down near the place where the king gave judgement. Around it was drawn a wide circle bisected across.

CRT:8:23 On the day when the people were first assembled to hear his words, Ithilis told them of his perplexity over the problem concerning the twin sons of Herthew and his daughters, he said, "So the people are not divided and the kingdom rent by strife, it is well this matter be settled now. Therefore, I am setting a fair test involving no men other than these two, whom I hold equally dear. Whichsoever of them shall remove their father's great weapon from this stone, so he frees it and grasps the hilt, shall become my lawful heir, with the other being to him as a younger brother. They will each try in turn during the duration of the fall of a feather, the first trier being he who casts his bracelet over the blade. Then, each of Herthew's sons was placed in a spot where the bisecting line joined the circle, so they stood opposite each other, and each had three bracelets. They threw until one encircled the blade with his bracelet.

CRT:8:24 Then, this one tried to withdraw the weapon with his hand, but could not, because of the sharpness. The other tried by placing his two palms on each side of the blade, then pressing them together while lifting, but he could not move it either. The first one tried again, copying what had just been done more powerfully, so the stone almost lifted off the ground, but the sword did not leave the stone. Then, the other approached the stone, but this time he put his hands under the edges of the stone, so he could lift it in his arms, and he dashed it down over a rock which was nearby, so it broke asunder. He then picked Dislana up by the hilt and brandished it over his head. The people acclaimed him while his brother grasped his arms in congratulations. Thus, by wisdom was the problem overcome.

Book of
Gleanings

GLN:1:5 Men struggle daily with the beast and wrest their living from the soil; their day being encompassed with strife and toil. So women bring forth children with suffering, and because they are frail, their husbands rule over them. Man is conceived in the womb of woman, and she brings him forth to life. Therefore, when God raised man up from among the beasts, choosing him as His heir and endowing him with an immortal spirit, He placed a veil over the portals of life. This, that woman should not forget she is unlike all other living creatures and the trustee of a divine mission. For a woman not only gives life to a mortal being; she also bears a spark of divinity to Earth, and there can be no greater responsibility.

Table of Chapters

Book of Gleanings
Table of Chapters (Continued)

Book of Gleanings

Chapter One – Maya and Lila

GLN:1:1 This was formerly called The Book of Conception and said to be The First Book of the Bronzebook. It concerns man's conception of The True God in olden days, during the struggle back towards the light.

GLN:1:2 Once, all men were dark and hairy, and in those days, woman was tempted by the strength and wildness of the beast, which dwelt in the forest, and the race of man was defiled again.

GLN:1:3 Therefore, the Spirit of God was wrathful against woman, for hers was the responsibility to reject the beast within and without, that she might bring forth children of the light to walk in the light; for in man, there is beast and god, and the god walks in light, and the beast walks in darkness.

GLN:1:4 Now, because of the wickedness that was done, there are among men those who are the Children of the Beast, and they are a different people. The race of man alone was punished, for the beast acted according to its nature. In man, the beast and god strive to decide whether he shall take his place among the gods that live or the beasts that die, and woman, in her weakness, betrayed him to the beast.

GLN:1:5 Men struggle daily with the beast and wrest their living from the soil; their day being encompassed with strife and toil. So women bring forth children with suffering, and because they are frail, their husbands rule over them. Man is conceived in the womb of woman, and she brings him forth to life. Therefore, when God raised man up from among the beasts, choosing him as His heir and endowing him with an immortal spirit, He placed a veil over the portals of life. This, that woman should not forget she is unlike all other living creatures and the trustee of a divine mission. For a woman not only gives life to a mortal being; she also bears a spark of divinity to Earth, and there can be no greater responsibility.

GLN:1:6 The eye that sees earthly things is deceitful, but the eye that sees spiritual things is true. Then, because of the things that happened, the Great Eye that saw Truth was closed, and henceforth, man walked in falsity. Unable to perceive Truth. he saw only that which deceived him, and so it shall be until his awakening.

GLN:1:7 Not knowing God, man worshipped Earth who mothered him and supplied his needs. God was not displeased, for such is the nature of children; but when no longer children, they must put aside childish things. Nor, having blinded them, was He wrathful that they could not see, for God is, above all else, understanding. The face of a good father is stern, and his ways are hard, for fatherly duty is no light burden, but his heart is ruled by compassion. His children walk in Truth and uprightness; their feet do not wander, nor are they wilful and wayward.

GLN:1:8 Man is born of mud, sun and Spirit. In the days of conception, the Spirit of God impregnated the receptive Earth, and she brought forth her children. Then came man who walked like a little child, but God took him in hand and taught him to walk in the uprightness of God.

GLN:1:9 A race of men came out of the cold northlands. They were under a wise father, and above them was The Grand Company, which later withdrew in disgust. This race was The Children of God; they knew Truth and lived in the midst of peace and plenty. The Children of Men about them were wild and savage; clothed in the skins of beasts; they lived like beasts. Even more wild were the Men of Zumat who lived beyond them. Among the Children of God, woman had equality with man, for her counsels were known to be wise. She heard with understanding, and her speech was considered; in those days, her words were weighed, for then her tongue did not rattle in her head like seed in a dried pod.

GLN:1:10 Woman knew that, though man could subdue her with his strength, he was weak in his desire for her. In his weakness lay her power, and in those days it was used wisely; it was the foundation of the people. The race was good, but because of its goodness, it was destined to be smitten, for only the good vessel is worthy of the fire. It is burnt, that its shape may be set and its design endure. The path of peace is not the path of progress.

GLN:1:11 The people were not governed by princes or by statutes, but wise men sat in council. They had only a code of conduct and a moral tradition binding each one to the others in a symmetrical web of life. Those who transgressed the code and tradition were deemed to be unworthy of life among the people and were banished into exile.

GLN:1:12 Among The Children of Men, woman was a chattel. She was subject to man, an object for the satisfaction of his lust and the servant to supply his needs. He subdued her and kept her in servitude, for her betrayal of man was known even among them, and it was never forgotten, nor could it be forgiven.

GLN:1:13 The Children of God valued woman highly and protected her from crudeness and cruelty, and her standing was such that she was awarded only to the most worthy of men. They held her in respect, for to them, she was the fountain of life within their race, the designer of its future. Yet even so, they had to restrict her, for she was inclined to be wilful and unheeding of her responsibility.

GLN:1:14 The people flourished and, from generation to generation, grew in stature and comeliness. They were the rising tidewaters of mankind surging towards its destiny. The right of a man to a mate was decided according to his standard of thought, his uprightness, the manner in which he upheld the code and tradition and his dealings with man and woman. The fittest men could choose a mate among all women, but lesser men could seek only among the less desirable, according to a known standard. To some, having only the outward appearance of men, no mate was given, while the noblest men could take additional ones from among the ranks of lesser women. Thus, the race ever tended to improve, to accord with its design.

GLN:1:15 The council of the people knew well the strength of man's desire for woman. The force of the urge was not wasted, for their forbears had harnessed it to the vehicle which carried their race to greatness above others. The race, which could properly channel the forces contained within itself, was ready to control the forces beyond itself. The greatest forces man can harness to his benefit are those lying within himself, but the underlying strength of the people lay in the morality of its women, for this was the strength that governed, because it was the safeguard for something of value. Men strive for gold, and value it because it is something not easily attained. If gold could be gathered by the handful, men would scorn it; its power is in its scarcity.

GLN:1:16 Then it happened that one man became arrogant in the strength of his manhood and pride of place, his thoughts inclined towards himself rather than towards the welfare of the people. He scorned the old ways, declaring the code and tradition an unnecessary burden laid on the backs of men. He said, "Why should we carry the burden of things, which have come down to us from our fathers? How do we know they walked with wisdom? How can we say that what was good for them is good for us?" Because of his unruly speech and wayward ways, the council banished him for a time, and had he remained apart, his heart would have been humbled in wisdom. But among The Children of God, there was a woman, one of the most desirable and fair, who interceded for him so he might return to dwell among them, it being in their code that the wayward could always regain their place.

GLN:1:17 The woman sought him out in the wilderness and, coming upon him, said, "Though, because of my heart, you appear to me as the finest of men, in the eyes of the elders you are unworthy to claim me. Therefore, I have spoken for you; now, come; go before them yourself, and say the wilderness has changed your ways. By so doing, you will find favour with the council and, perchance, I may become your mate. The strength and courage I admire place you high in the regard of men and in favour with the elders, but your wayward and inconsiderate spirit is unworthy of your body. Though you find favour in the eyes of the young and foolish women, who see only the outwardness of your body and thereby become more foolish, the eyes of the wise women see your naked spirit and are not deceived. Therefore, disregard the glances of foolish maidens and carry yourself well. Act in such manner that you find favour in the sight of the wise women." And, said she, "Am I not Maya, the most desirable of women, one whom all men seek? Yet will I remain reserved only for you; therefore, be not unworthy of me."

GLN:1:18 The man came out of the wilderness and wastelands. He went before the council of wise women and said, "What must I do that I may have this woman for a mate? For I desire her above all things, even above my own life, For her, I will become the most worthy of men among the people; her standard being high, I may not possess her otherwise." The wise women answered him, saying, "For so long shall you conduct yourself in this manner," and they set him a time and a task. That it should be well, the task was to be done with heart as well as deed, but the man accepted it gladly, his heart not in that day but in the days to come. The council and the elders said, "what the wise women have done is good; it will be well and to the people's benefit."

GLN:1:19 The man rose manfully to the task and was magnificent in his manhood; his new ways gladdening the hearts of all the maidens, many of whom were disturbed by strange stirrings within their breasts. Among these was one less comely and desirable, whose heart burned hotly for him, her thoughts resting upon him continually; but she knew that in his sights she was of little account. Her name was Lila.

GLN:1:20 It happened that, arising early one day, she saw the man depart into the forest by the swampland, going about his task, and she took counsel with herself and followed him. She came upon the man while he rested in a place of solitude and, approaching, spoke softly, saying, "It is your servant, Lila. O my Lord, are you not weary with the task burdening your days, also that you lack companionable gladness to lighten it? Where is she who set the load upon your strong back? Where is my kinswoman who, without doubt, is more comely and very much more desirable than I and, therefore, a very fitting reward for your heavy labours? Does she rest in the shade, or is she gathering fruit back in the gardens? Without doubt, her thoughts are with you, but is she not unduly hardhearted in that she fails to comfort you, for is it not in the nature of woman to come to man and lighten his burden with her softness? Is it not in the nature of woman to be yielding and submissive, that man may rejoice in his strength? Is it, perhaps that, despite her loveliness, the heart of this woman of your desire is not the heart of a woman? Is it like the mock orange, sweet to look at, but bitter to bite?

GLN:1:21 "Or is her heart in the keeping of the elders, that she prefers the ways of the old to the ways of the young? What has she done to you; has she not humiliated your manliness by harnessing it like an ox to the customs of the people? an it be right that the decrees of old men long dead should come between living man and woman? Is it not more fitting that the customs of men submit to the law of Her who gave us our natures? This desirable woman is yours, providing you toil and wait. She is yours, but not without conditions. She does not come without reservations as a woman should, but like a man who comes to an ass, bridle in hand. Alas, that I lack the loveliness, which places the yoke upon you, but beneath, I lack nothing and am as much a woman as any. My heart burns for you with a flame that comes nigh to consuming my body. Take me; accept my humble offering. I give all freely, I will be yours without any conditions. O my Lord, which of us women truly offers the most? She who concedes nothing, or I who will even be accursed by God and men for your sake? I, who am nothing in your sight, require no sacrifice from you on my behalf. I ask nothing, and I offer all a woman can." Then, Lila knelt at the feet of the man and placed her head on his knee.

GLN:1:22 The man was sorely troubled in his body, and he wrestled with it, but his spirit brought before his eyes the vision of the more desirable maiden, and he was strengthened. He arose and said, "Begone, and tempt me no more!"

GLN:1:23 Then, Lila departed and went her way, but within herself, she brooded, and in the course of days, her thoughts hatched a dark scheme. She mixed a forbidden potion from herbs and, putting it into a pitcher of water with honey, took it to the man as he toiled in the heat of the declining day. Seeing her, the man said, "Wherefore have you come again?" And she answered him, saying "My Lord, your servant brings a much lesser offering, one you need not fear as you did the greater one, a humble gift of refreshment." The day being hot and the toil arduous, the gift was not unwelcome. The man drank heavily from the pitcher and, because of the potion, his spirit slept while the beast entered his body in strength.

GLN:1:24 When the fire of his passion was quenched by the waters of lust, his spirit returned, and he reviled the woman, saying, "What have you wrought?" Would you destroy me in this manner?" The woman replied, "The deed is yours, my Lord, for you are a man and I am a woman." Then the man became afraid, for he knew the code and custom. He became angry after the manner of frightened men and shouted, "Begone from my sight, you viper, lest I crush you!" Lila answered quietly, "My Lord, why be wrathful or afraid without cause? For this thing shall be a secret between us, none will ever know of it. Behold, my Lord, are you not free again and the yoke removed from your neck? Now, you may know the joys a woman can give without submitting to the task; therefore, take your ease, for life is good to you."

GLN:1:25 The words of the woman were not sweet to the ears of the man, for he was filled with remorse for what had been done. He said, "you are not the maiden of my tender desires, in whom my heart delighted and for whom I gladly undertook the task. What now of her, whose beauty compares with the glory of the sun, whose gentleness caresses as the sunbeam, beside whose brightness you are no more than a gloomy shadow?" Lila replied, "She is indeed as the sun; you may worship from afar, but never touch, lest you be burnt and destroyed."

GLN:1:26 "I am the woman of your body whom your flesh has chosen. What has this other woman done for you? Did she not sharpen the sword on which you cut yourself? If one lights a fire among reeds, knowing a man sleeps there, who is to blame for his burning? The fire, he who lit it or the reeds? It is beneath your manliness to turn on me thus; am I not shamed for your sake? And who among women would invite the wrath of gods and men, as I have done? Be content with the wrong your lust has already wrought. This is an evil deed you have committed, but because we are now united in the flesh, no harm shall befall you through me."

GLN:1:27 Thenceforth, among the people they went their separate ways, but flesh called to flesh, bringing them furtively together in secret places. Each dwelt with the reproachful whispers of their spirit, and each walked in the shadow of fear because of the code and tradition.

GLN:1:28 Now, the elders were not without shrewdness, and they saw that the man was no longer diligent in the task and had returned to his former ways. Also, he avoided the eyes of Maya and was no longer reserved with women; having sampled forbidden fruit, he now sought other varieties. He was not a man with an end in view, towards which he strove; his bearing was not that of a free man. The glances between the man and the woman, and their uneasiness, were not difficult to interpret.

GLN:1:29 The elders and wise women said among themselves, "Such is the manner of those carrying a burden in their hearts, whose shadowy love is a feeble, furtive thing blooming shamefully in dark and hidden places." Therefore, they set a watch on the pair. The watch came upon them as they lay together in nakedness upon their skins and mocked them with ribaldry, for their passion was profane and a thing for jest. It was a fungus upon the tree of love.

GLN:1:30 They were brought before the high council, which was the council of elders, and the council of wise women, which questioned them, saying, "Wherefore have you done evil unto us?" The man answered. "The woman put my spirit to sleep with an evil brew, and my body became weak because of my manhood." They replied, "Truly, you have little manhood now and are a lesser man because of this woman."

GLN:1:31 The woman stood up before the high council and answered them boldly, "Am I then the stronger of the two? an I lift the biggest stone or run the fastest race? Do not the strong always prevail against the weak, and is not this man the strongest among men? Is this even a matter for your concern? For in what way have we caused harm to any but ourselves? Shall we be punished for that which concerns us two alone and wrongs no other?"

GLN:1:32 The high council replied, "The deeds of any person affecting the lives of others are the concern of others. Though it were done in secret between yourselves, were not the effects displayed in your eyes for all to see? Does the man serve the people better because of this thing, or does he serve them less well? Has something been added to the people, or has something been taken away? Have not the people lost?"

GLN:1:33 "Therefore, is not that which you did the concern of the people and not of yourselves alone? The deed, of itself, was not wrong, except in the manner of its accomplishment. A woman who places no value on herself steals something from all women, for they are then less valued in the eyes of men. Would men value gold were it gathered by the wayside? Above all this, what of God-given love?" Have you elevated or degraded its means of expression among men and women? Among people who value gold above all else, he who debases or adulterates it commits a wrong against them. Here, where love is valued above all else and woman honoured as its custodian, those who debase it are regarded likewise."

GLN:1:34 "We dwell in a pleasant place, amid peace and plenty, an inheritance from our fathers. The Children of Men have inherited the wastelands. Are our fathers less wise than theirs, that the customs of our fathers should be spurned? What you have done relates to your two selves, and by your two selves shall your punishment be carried out. This is not a punishment for any wrong done to us, for we are old, and it affects us little. We punish, because we have a duty to the young, to the unborn of our race. We have an even greater duty to the hallowed things, which inspire mankind and enthrone man above the beasts."

GLN:1:35 "Your wrongdoing affects no one man or woman; yet, it affects all men and women and, if left unheeded, would not be without effect on children yet unborn. The code and tradition is the pillar of our people, and the pillar may not be struck with impunity. Though it be strong, and one blow will not damage it, many blows will bring down even the stoutest pillar. A blow left unheeded encourages another. A deed disregarded is a deed encouraged'.

GLN:1:36 "A people can be judged by the things it punishes and the things it permits. The swine revels in filth and, therefore, attacks anyone who enters his pen. Were we wholly of the Earth, we need only protect earthly things."

GLN:1:37 "Thus, we banish you for ever from among us, unless in your old age you are permitted, in mercy, to return."

GLN:1:38 In this manner were the man and woman banished from the tilled land to wander the wilderness beyond. They dwelt in a cavern in the wasteland, against the outer border of the tilled land, and they ate weeds and wild creatures. There, they were in a place defended from hostile men and made safe from ambushes. In the first days of their banishment, the man was wrathful against the woman and spoke to her spitefully, saying, "Like a lamp that gives no light, you are a woman without womanly virtue, no longer deserving of the honoured treatment accorded women of our race. You spoke truly when you said that I am strong and you are weak. So be it; henceforth, your weakness shall be my strength; no longer will the weakness of man be the strength of woman and the backbone of a people clinging to things without substance. Henceforth, I am obligated to no one and owe a duty to none but myself. Man is weak only in his desire for woman, but the weakness of woman shall henceforth assure satisfaction of the desire."

GLN:1:39 So the man subdued the woman after the fashion of The Children of Men; she was the wife who ministered unto him, saying, "My Lord, I am but a woman and your handmaiden."

GLN:1:40 The beasts of the wastelands were the keepers of the woman and she was in bondage to the barrenland, for the wilderness was beyond reach of the waters, a place of desolation yielding only weeds and thorns. The man hunted afield for wild creatures, while the woman delved for roots, seeking sustenance among the weeds.

GLN:1:41 Thus, it happened that one day, being overcome with hunger, the woman went among the reeds growing on the edge of the tilled land, for flowering plants grew there, the roots of which could be eaten. While engaged in gathering, she was seen by a husbandman tilling the fields, who, coming upon her stealthily, said, "Woman, I see you; are you not the one who was banished? If so, the custom decrees you will have to die, for it is forbidden to re-enter the fertile land, having been cast out."

GLN:1:42 Then the woman, being still in the water, loosened her girdle and, letting down her hair, said, "Honoured I may no longer be, perhaps die I must, but am I not still a woman while I live? If you see me otherwise than as a woman who can please a man by the ways of women, then I say you cannot be a man. Yes, I am the woman your brother seduced, the frail victim of his lust. Perhaps it is better that I die quickly by your hand than starve slowly in the wasteland. Death can hurt me no more than life, which has revealed me to the evil of men. Let me die now for the wrongdoing of your brother." So saying, she came out of the water.

GLN:1:43 The husbandman did not slay, but instead he dallied with her until the evening. The woman said, ere he departed, "This shall be a secret between us, for there is none other nearby to see us here. Give me food, that my flesh may be firm and my heart gladdened, that I may come often to this place."

GLN:1:44 Thus, in the days that followed, the woman went many times to the waters and in other places where there were other men. Therefore, she no longer had to delve for roots, nor did she toil in the wilderness.

GLN:1:45 Then, The Children of God banished other men into the wastelands because of the woman, and the man, seeing how this came about, said, "Is my affliction because of you never to end?" The woman answered, "My Lord, this thing I did for your sake; see these others; are they not outcasts in the wilderness, men without a chief to rule over them or a hand to guide? Gather them together, that they may hunt for you and serve you; rule over them, and become powerful. What I have done, I have done for you alone. To your strength will be added their strength, and the loss of the people in fertile lands will thus become your gain. What is there that strength cannot obtain? If your desire is for other women, will not strength obtain them? Therefore, revile me not, because I have now placed in your hands the means to that which you desire."

GLN:1:46 "Now I say to you, and speak truly of things only a woman can know, that you are a better man than those who live bound to the tilled lands, whose women secretly despise them for their servility to the code and tradition."

GLN:1:47 The man was stirred up by these words and went out and about to the others, approaching them, saying, "Behold, we have been cast out because we have followed the ways of men according to the nature of men. Our manhood is good within us, let it therefore assert itself so our strength may be greater."

GLN:1:48 So it came about that the men who were outcasts entered the fertile, tilled land stealthily at night time, burning the houses and overthrowing the water towers, saying, "Let this land rejoin the wilderness."

GLN:1:49 They slew menfolk and carried the women and children away. They stole sheep, goats and cattle. Then, they withdrew to the fastnesses of the wastelands. There, they built an encampment and fortified it about with walls and ditches, and they made war upon The Children of Men and prevailed against them. They ruled their women sternly and made them chattels, buying and selling them like cattle. When man said "Come," the woman came, and when he said "Go," she went. On her yielding back and on her submissive head he dissipated his wrath, on her servile body he satisfied his lust.

GLN:1:50 Lila was a true daughter of the woman who betrayed the first race of men. It is written of her that when her sons grew to manhood, she caused then to kill and eat their father, so they might gain lifelong strength and wisdom.

GLN:1:51 Man kept woman in bondage, for he knew from his own knowledge of her ways that she was not to be trusted. Henceforth, she could not walk freely among men, for they knew that, though woman was weak and man strong, by womanly guile, she could exploit his weakness. Among the outcast people and The Children of Men, woman was subject to man, and he imposed his will upon her and dominated her.

GLN:1:52 In this manner, woman wrought her own downfall and the destruction of those who held her in high regard. Her charms she cast at the feet of those who trampled them underfoot. Woman was not yet fitted to be the free guardian of the portals of life. She was never wise enough to choose the fathers of the race, for she was ruled by womanly waywardness, not by wisdom.

Chapter Two – Eloma

GLN:2:1 It came about that the sons of The Children of God mated with the daughters of The Children of Men, who knew well the ways of men and were not reserved. The covenant had been broken and strange women were taken into the households, some even as wives; but though the daughters were lesser women, the sons were wonderfully big and mighty fighting men.

GLN:2:2 These new people came out of the wastelands and crossed to Kithermis. which they divided in three parts between them, and there were rivers on the boundaries. This was when the years of man's life were lessened because he became fully Earth-sustained, but he remained full of vigour though filled with hostility, particularly towards those who loved.

GLN:2:3 To the East was the land of Ubal which was mountainous and the Ubalites were herdsmen. Westward was the land of Chaisen and it joined Ubak on the North. Southward were the land of Utoh and the land of Kayman, whose peoples dwelt on the plains and tilled the soil. Some from the households of The Children of God went into the land of Chaisen and gave the people laws and taught them to build with brick. Netar and Baletsheramam, the sons of Enanari, taught them writing and set their letters on a pillar in Herak. Enkilgal, son of Nenduka, built Keridor, which stands between two rivers.

GLN:2:4 Then came the lengthening of the years, when the time of sowing was confused and seed died in the ground. In those days, Enos came up out of Chaisen and spoke for the god of The Children of Men. in those days, there were many having the blood of The Children of God who inclined their ears towards his words, for they thought the Great God of their fathers had abandoned them. Therefore, the enlightening word of God came to Eloma.

GLN:2:5 Eloma, daughter of Kahema, heard the voice of God and was carried into the wilderness unto a place where there was a cave and clear running waters, and she dwelt there for seven years. Eloma had three sons, and they all heard the voice of God and walked with Him. Her firstborn son was Haryanah and he carried the word of God to the Children of God who dwelt in the Northlands, for they had forgotten His Ways. He married Didi, daughter of a great king and became an even greater king; he had many sons who all became kings among men of renown. Yahama, her secondborn son, carried the word of God to those who dwelt towards the sunrising, and Manum, her thirdborn son, carried it to those towards the sunsetting.

GLN:2:6 When the ear of the Spirit was opened in Eloma, she returned to her people and became The Interpreter of God. In the days when some men left to dwell among The Children of Men, others came to Eloma and said, "Behold, men leave and we become weak, while The Children of Men become strong. an this be the will of our Father?" Then, Eloma called upon God, and He heard her cry and said unto her, "Let your spirit be at peace, for things happen as they will; it is the grain being winnowed from the chaff. It is always easier for men to follow the ways of the flesh than the ways of the spirit; yet, the deeper man descends into the vale of earthly things, the harder the climb out to the heights of glory. A generation to go down, ten generations to rise again. Man must struggle or degenerate, but the path of pleasure is pleasant, while the path of progress is beset with pain and strife."

GLN:2:7 God said to Eloma, His servant, "Behold, I have been good to My children; they have been given everything that is pleasant; everything has come easily to their hand. The lot of The Children of Men is more harsh, and yet they prosper. Childish things are expected from a child, but when it grows up, more is anticipated; yet, still My children come to me as children."

GLN:2:8 God then said, "Go, return to the place from whence you came and remain there for seven years" and she did so. The seven years passed; Eloma returned to the people and, behold, the fertile fields were unsown, the water channels were dry and there was desolation in the midst of the waters. Eloma sought among the fields and when she came upon the habitations, her heart was rent apart. For she saw the daughters of The Children of God consorted with the sons of The Children of Men and were become unlike true women. Then Eloma said to them, "Wherefore has this thing come about?" And they answered, "Behold, men came from out of the wilderness, and our men were like sheep before wolves; see, even now they labour within a pen of servitude." Eloma then went unto the men and said, "Wherefore has this thing come about?" They answered her, "Behold, the god of The Children of Men is, unlike ours, a god of battles, and we were delivered into their hands."

GLN:2:9 Then Eloma was heavy of heart and called upon God, saying, "Behold the plight of your children" and God heard her and answered, "I am not indifferent, for their sufferings are My sufferings. They are not under the whips of men but under the flail of God; the grain is being separated from the chaff. They toil not under the blows of men but under the hammer of God; they are not imprisoned, but are upon an anvil. I am not the God of battles, not the God of nations, not even the God of men. I am the God of Souls, The Keeper of the Treasures of Eternity. I have not turned away from My children; My children have turned away from Me, disobeying my laws. This cry will echo down through the generations of man: "My God, why have You deserted me?" And it will come from those who have deserted their God."

GLN:2:10 "Arise; go seek among the people, and you will find a maiden who is pure at heart, but she is mocked and degraded by being made a swine attendant. Take her with you and go to Shinara; guard her well, for she is the daughter of a new dawning." Eloma sought among the people and found Nanua, Maid of the Morning, and they went into Shinara.

GLN:2:11 The Voice of God came to Eloma in Shinara, saying, "This is the way things shall be with those who aspire to godhood. They must follow only the paths which I have shown through the words of My interpreters. The unfolding spirit residing in those who have the blood of The Children of God, and the greatness that dwells in men shall be magnified in the blood of their children. Their wisdom shall be greatly multiplied, if the tie of blood be strong. As good wine becomes bad if diluted overmuch, so is greatness in the blood of man. There is a virtue in the blood of those whose forbears were The Children of God, and if two people having this blood marry, then this virtue is increased in their children, so it is greater than either parent. There is a law of inheritance from which no man is exempt, for man is governed by the laws of earthly creatures as well as by greater laws. Is not the best ram chosen to sire the new flock? So, let women choose the best among men that they can and let men choose the best among women, and they who heed My words will know which is the best. Let the truly great ones rule."

GLN:2:12 God said, "The creative words remain on this side of the veil, but their echoes resound on your side. The real remains here, but its reflection is there; creation is My mirror, though it is not without distortions. I have created in spirit and in matter, My thoughts have ranged from the unseeable smallest to the incomprehensible largest. My greatest thoughts formed substance for the spirits of the sons and daughters of Earth."

GLN:2:13 "Truth and justice, perfection of beauty and goodness remain with Me, and these you can know on Earth only by their reflection. In the universe of Truth. all things are free from illusion and are seen in reality, but on Earth, even the reflection is distorted. I have created light and called it substance; it is illuminated within by the light of an ever present love potential."

GLN:2:14 "Men call on many gods, though above all there is but One; yet whatever they call Me, I will hear them, for I am The God Above Names, The God Embracing All Names. Whatever men believe, if it serves Good, it serves God. But gold necklaces are not for sheep and outward forms of worship must suffice for the spiritually undeveloped. The rituals of men may often be empty ceremonials, but they may also guard the Great Mysteries behind them."

GLN:2:15 "If a man seeks to enter My presence by prayer and says, "God grant me this or give me that," the thing will be neither granted nor given, unless it be for his spiritual good or benefit another. I am no huxter bargaining blessings in exchange for worship, nothing man can give can add to what I have. Also men do Me little honour when they fail to recognise that I am above concern for mere bodies, which decay and fall apart when the enlivening spirit leaves them. Yet, man is but man, know that I am a God of understanding and compassion. If man cries out to Me, in genuine stress and suffering, he will not go unrelieved and uncomforted. Yet, understand that suffering and sorrow are the lot of man, that he may become Man-god. There is also the Great Law, to which man must conform; there are the intricacies of Enidvadew to be unwoven and the challenging paths of destiny and fate to be followed. Too often, the price to be paid for things done or not done is pain and suffering, sorrow and distress, but where would be the benefit to the debtor were I to wipe out such debts? Yet will I see that never, by even a single grain, will they exceed that which is absolutely necessary and just.

GLN:2:16 On Earth, joy and gladness will always outweigh pain and sorrow."

GLN:2:17 "Earth is Earth; take it as you find it; do not expect to find heavenly things there. It is a place of tuition and the purpose of life is learning. All things of Earth are limited and mortal; immortality will not be found there. When the things of Earth have fulfilled their hidden purposes, each passes away, returning to the dust, from whence it came."

GLN:2:18 "Behold, in the days to come Truth shall be unfolded to all peoples, revealed in a degree and manner, which will accord with their needs and capabilities. It will be passed on from generation to generation and from man to man. The purity of its flame will accord with the quality of the oil of spirituality, with which it is fed and replenished; hence there will be many differing degrees of purity and revelation. The food, which one man enjoys, may sit heavily on the stomach of another, yet, it would be foolish to say that the food enjoyed by one should become the food of all. So it is with the spiritual things which men believe."

GLN:2:19 "I will not send prophets, nor will I appoint spokesmen, but such will arise through their own efforts and enter into conscious union with Me. They will point the way, which will be followed by the spiritually sturdy, but others less strong in spirit must take a slower path, and many will advance only by faith and service, by justice and kindliness towards others."

GLN:2:20 "The spark of divinity in man generates inspiring dreams, which will ever lure him onward and upward; yet, the road is long, the journey wearying and often unpleasant. Man has unnecessarily encumbered himself; he has enshrouded his spirit under a winding sheet of earthly passions. With his Great Eye blinded by indulgence in vice and his spirit corroded by corruption, his fallible senses only are left to him, and these deceive him into believing the mortal vehicle is his total being. Affliction and decay are now the lot of man, and he has passed into a long, dark night of ignorance. Now, only by journeying the long and painful road of earthly experience, can his soul be cleansed and awakened to the realisation of the glory within him."

GLN:2:21 "Man may conceive Me as he will and it will be well. I am not a God of pettishness. As I brought forth the creation, so shall he bring forth the revelation of his God. Unto you, Eloma, My child, I grant the keys of Communion and Union."

GLN:2:22 Then Eloma went out among the people and taught them about their Creator in this manner, "I bring you the soul-whispered words of God, The Eternal Tower of Strength, The Fathomless Ocean of Compassion. He has hung the Earth in the void, surrounding it with nothingness; yet, by his power, it remains in its appointed place. He veils His glory behind the shield of illusion, lest it overpower the spirits of men. He is obscured by the dark cloud of mortal ignorance. He is the inspirational spirit ever entering the hearts of man, striving to arouse them to reach out towards greatness and achievement."

GLN:2:23 "He has moulded the sky above us and bedecked it with splendour and awesome beauty. He taught the stars their song of joy and the winds their wondrous music. All the widespread Earth proclaims His creativity, while the high vaults reveal His skill and handiwork. His messages go out to men, not in the speech of men but in wordless whispers to their hearts. His finger prescribes a course for the fertilising waters which nourish the desolate sands, making tender buds burst forth from the dead soil. The soft waters caress the ground, and pastures arise to become the habitations of great flocks and herds."

GLN:2:24 "The rose unfolds its beauty to honour Him, and the woodbine delights Him with perfume delivered upon the wind. The cornfields bow in humility; then, the wheatstalks raise upwards in praise. The trees spread wide their worshipping branches, and the barleyheads whisper together of His sungiven bounty. He is the Fountainhead of All Life, the Overseer of the Fertilising Waters and the Captain of the Stars."

GLN:2:25 "Men stand beneath the great dome of the nightskies and are overawed by the work of their architect and by the bright mysteries displayed in such a pattern of beauty. They become dismayed at their own smallness, but are reassured by His words, which have come down to them from ancient times."

GLN:2:26 "God has crowned man with life and set the sceptre of intellect in his hand. He has given him the flail of mastery over all other living creatures and set him on the throne of creation. He disciplines us when young and stretches out a welcoming hand when we near the end of life's journey. He accompanies men on their pilgrimage along the road of life, mitigating their misfortunes and rejoicing with them in its pleasant surprises. He balances the lives of all men, so they continually encounter conditions and situations meet for them."

GLN:2:27 "The widespread, mysterious Heavens are His throne and bountiful Earth His footstool; no structure man could build would contain Him. Did He need a residence, no place built by the hands of man could compare with that, which His hands could erect. There is nothing on Earth that man can give God, which could add to God's glory or increase what He has. The only acceptable sacrifice man can offer is service to the will of God, and God's will is that man should spiritualise himself and improve the Earth. To offer goods or money as a sacrifice is an insult to God; it is shirking the needful effort, evading the necessary duty and obligation; it is the easy way and not acceptable."

GLN:2:28 "God is the refuge of the poor and the comforter of the needy. His compassion encompasses men when troubles weigh heavily upon them. Yet, tribulation and adversity, sorrow and suffering are not to be thought of as needless burdens imposed upon the difficulties inseparable from earthly life. They are things of value, which open the eyes to Truth. tempering the spirit, as iron is tempered in the flame."

GLN:2:29 Eloma taught many things, and she forbade any man to fornicate with unwedded matrons whose silver tongue beguiled and whose winsome ways led men astray. She also decreed that men should not fornicate with any maid or another's wife, for none so doing could call himself an honourable man, and such deeds canker the spirit.

GLN:2:30 It was Eloma who taught men the wisdom of the stars, which journeyed according to their destinies. She taught them to interpret the pattern of each man's life, which is woven from the threads of fate and destiny and interwoven with the many coloured strands of Enidvadew. These things were learned and written down by Ishkiga.

Chapter Three – Flood of Atuma

GLN:3:1 Behold, was this not written in the days of our fathers' fathers and of their fathers before them, and given unto us that we should pass it in to you, the children of days yet unborn? That, if the ability of the scribe remains with you it could be read in your generation.

GLN:3:2 Read, O children of the unborn years, and absorb the wisdom of the past, which is your heritage. The enlightening words from a past, which is to you, in days so far away and yet, in Truth so near.

GLN:3:3 We are taught that we live forever, and this is true, but it is equally true that no moment of life must be wasted; for each hour and day on Earth is a shaping for the future. We are the inheritors of a portion of time; we can dissipate it on futile things or utilise it to our everlasting benefit. In the days of our fathers, before barren teachings clogged the thoughts of men, and vain, formal ritual built a wall which obscured understanding, men walked in the light of Truth. Then, they knew there was One God alone, but because they allowed their higher abilities to fall to disuse, they saw less clearly. Because He appeared in different aspects, they thought He was many.

GLN:3:4 Now, in our days, God has many varied forms in the eyes of men, and each declares he alone knows the true name and likeness of God. Here, all men fall into error, though all have spoken truly according to their understanding. But Truth can never bow to the limited understanding of man; the comprehension of man must expand to grasp it.

GLN:3:5 In olden times, there were spawned great monsters and beasts in fearful form, with frightful gnashing teeth and long ripping claws; an elephant was but a rat in comparison with them. Then, because of heavenly rebellion and turmoil, and the terror overwhelming the hearts of men, The Great One hardened the face of the land, which had become unstable, and the beasts were changed to stone. This was beforetimes, when the Destroyer still slumbered in the upper vaults of Heaven.

GLN:3:6 Thus it is written in the record of Beltshera: In those days the people were wicked and though the wise men among them gave many warnings of the wrath to come, they would not listen; such is the way of the wicked. So it came about that the hastening Spirit became stirred up against them because of the odour of wickedness arising from the Earth, for her nostrils abhor the smell of evil. This is a smell no man can know, for as the hounds know the smell of fear, which no man can detect, so can other beings know the smell of wickedness.

GLN:3:7 The great floodgates, which are above Earth, were all opened. Thus, the floodwaters rose up to cover the land, and great rainstorms lashed down. The winds could no longer discover their destinations.

GLN:3:8 The people left the plain of Shinara and fled up into a great mountain rising above the flatlands below, and here, near the summit, they camped. Feeling themselves secured, the wicked mocked, saying, "No water can ever reach up here, for there is not enough of it in Heaven or Earth." Still, the waters rose ever higher and the mouths of the wicked were silenced. The priests of the people danced and chanted in vain, and many rituals were performed to appease the wrath above.

GLN:3:9 There came a period of quietness; then, the people built a gateway to Heaven wherein the Chief of Interpreters might commune with the Other Realm. He entered into the silence and cast his spirit, and when he had done so it contacted the hastening Spirit, which men call by other names. Her voice was heard within his heart and it said, "I am that which has been called forth by the odour of wickedness arising from the bodies of men, which no incense can disguise. For, as the smell of putrefaction assails the nostrils of men, so does wickedness give forth something which assails us in this realm. Wickedness is, therefore, an offence against us. If a man threw filth over the wall into your courtyard, would you not consider this an act of hostility? Could any among you live in harmony with those who were insensitive to your own sensitivity? Thus, I am awakened to happenings in the world of men and am now clothed in a performing substance."

GLN:3:10 The Spiritbeing said, "I have no desire to unduly punish men. Go out to the people, and tell them that if they will but mend their ways and walk no more in the path of wickedness, I shall depart." But when the Chief of Interpreters returned to the people, he found them fearful and distraught, clay in the hands of false priests, devotees of the baleful gods. The false priests were crying out for a sacrifice to their gods and had seized Anis, a young man more handsome than any other, a messenger and runner between cities. Then, though they whispered fearfully among themselves concerning the deed, the people had seized Nanua, handmaiden of Eloma, the Enlightened One, whose life was dedicated to Illana, for she had cried out curses upon their heads when the young man was taken.

GLN:3:11 Nanua and Anis were held by the false priests, and about them surged the great mass of the people, and, though the Chief of Interpreters raised his voice it went unheeded. Then the mass of the people moved down to the water's edge and there they stopped while the priests shouted prayers to the gods raging above. All the Heavens were darkened with great rolling clouds and there were high winds and lightning about the mountain top. The people rent their garments, the women wailed and men struck their forearms. Anis was beaten with a club and delivered to the waters.

GLN:3:12 Then, as he who wielded the club turned towards Nanua, she said to those about her, "Let be, I will deliver myself to the waters, for if I must be sacrificed, I would be a better sacrifice so given." Then she went down to the waters, but as her feet entered she drew back from the cold, dark, watery depths before her. But as the one who wielded the club moved forward, a young man, Sheluat the Scribe, a man of quiet ways, neither handsome nor strong in body, pushed forward and, taking her by the hand, went down into the waters with her.

GLN:3:13 The waters had risen high, and men shared the place where they stood with wild beasts and with sheep and cattle, but now the tumult quietened and the waters drew back. Seeing this, the people shouted praises to the baleful gods and cried out, "Great are the mighty gods and great their holy priests!"

GLN:3:14 The Chief of Interpreters went sorrowfully apart, hiding himself; for now, he was fearful for his life. When the waters had subsided, he cast his spirit and entered into communion with the hastening Spirit, and he said, "Shall I also enter the falling waters as a sacrifice? For life is now futile, as I am without God or honour." The Great One answered, "Men see in events the things they wish to see, they can interpret only according to their understanding. The waters rose to their limitation and did not fall because of the needless sacrifices. The Powers above may ordain events to chasten men, but more often, such events are challenges and tests. However, divine intervention is rare, indeed."

GLN:3:15 "These priests follow another, a longer path, but they too condemn wickedness and they too point the way to Truth. though that way may be indirect and beset with hazards. So, whether they or you reached the ears of the people, the odour of wickedness will be diminished. Divine ends are achieved by diverse means, and the eyes of few men are opened to see either the means or the end."

GLN:3:16 "Life is never futile, but your sacrifice would be. No man can lose his God, for He is always there; but the prestige of a man because of that God such prestige is a worldly thing of little real value. How do you know whether you have lost or gained? Events of the moment cannot be weighed in the moment, but can be assessed only by the judgement of the years. Only eternity knows whether this or that was good or bad, a gain or loss."

GLN:3:17 Then, the Great One opened the eyes of the Chief of Interpreters, so he saw beyond the earthly border into the realm beyond. Behold, he saw Anis who had been strong and handsome on Earth, and now he was something not pleasant to gaze upon. He saw also the true beauty of Nanua, who was now a being of dazzling loveliness, and beside her was Sheluat, who had always loved her secretly, and he was now glowing with youth and handsome as Helith. The Chief of the Interpreters then understood that evil could be transmuted into good, and that men had little knowledge of the true nature of things.

GLN:3:18 Upon the mountain, there is now a grove of trees and a temple built in the form of a circle of white stones, where the people remember the day of their deliverance. But what they recall and what happened are not the same; nor is the cause in their minds the true cause. They say, "We are the children of Atuma who saved us." Many who have gone often to the Temple of Deliverance say they have seen two shades, one radiantly beautiful and one gloriously handsome, wandering hand in hand through the trees or sitting in the sunlit glades. All about is now a place of peace.

GLN:3:19 Men walk under the shadow of dread, and fear of unknown powers fills their hearts. They have fashioned images in the likeness of the things which frighten them in the gloom of their ignorance, and they spurn the real for the unreal. Did they see more clearly, they would know that the things they fear are but gentle and sturdy hands, which can lead them to fields of contentment.

Chapter Four – The Deluge

GLN:4:1 It is written, in The Great Book of The Fire hawks, that Earth was destroyed twice, once altogether by fire and once partially by water. The destruction by water was the lesser destruction and came about in this manner.

GLN:4:2 The people of those times spurned all spiritual things, and men lived only for pleasure, caring little for the good of mankind or the future of the people. Lewdness and lies were upon the tongues of all men, and brother could not deal justly with brother. The princes and governors were corrupt, and proper tribute was not paid; the statutes were held up to scorn. The lives of men were ruled by their desires, and they spent their days in gluttony, drunkedness, fornication, dancing and singing to instruments of music.

GLN:4:3 The land was unattended, for men dissipated their strength in unproductive lusts and pleasures. Women lacked
cast their glances after
among themselves and ev
cause of their lusts for wo
chaste women were not
rejected, for men declined the effort of being worthy of them in the eyes of their fathers. Wives were unhonoured, and only the women of pleasure commanded the attentions of men. Women were unclean and immodest, and men lay with them shamelessly in the presence of one another. Old women were more lustful than the young ones, while virgins were seduced and corrupted in their childhood. Fathers fornicated before their sons and were admired for their prowess. They made no distinction between their sons and other men, or between their wives and other women. Deceit and violence were seen on every hand.

GLN:4:4 To the East and North were high mountains, upon which dwelt a tribe called The Sons of Nezirah, The Men of the Mountains, who were hardy men and mighty hunters, skilful in the chase and valiant in battle. The men were upright; their wives were faithful and their sons noble. In their hearts were no unworthy thoughts, no envy or hate, no malice or deceitfulness. They did not smile before a man's face, uttering smooth words, then when he turned his back, reach out to stab him. In their wives and daughters there was no impure longing, and neither cursing nor lying was heard among them. The womenfolk respected their men and maintained decency and decorum.

GLN:4:5 Yet they were men with men's ways, abhorring all forms of unmanliness and degeneracy. Therefore, the treasures in the cities of the plains and the weakness of the people to whom these belonged did not go unnoticed by The Sons of Nezirah. So they said among themselves, "Let us go down and do a good deed among these people; let us show them the ways of men who are strong, making them slaves and possessing ourselves of their goods." This talk continued among the men in the marketplaces and gatherings, until they were stirred up to deeds, and they gathered together a warband of fighting men. The Mountain Men chose leaders from among themselves, after their custom, and prepared to fall upon the softliving people of the plains and become their masters.

:4:6 When the chiefs of The Mountain Men aw what was happening, they became wroth and ordered their men to return to their flocks and pastures. The chief of chiefs stood up before the gathered warband and said, "It is our decree that this thing shall not be done, you must not go down from these mountains bringing the sword to these people. Leave them alone, as rotted fruit is left on the tree to whither and die. Leave them to follow their own ways a little longer, and in the fullness of time, they will destroy themselves. Make no widows among your own people. If you go down there carrying fire and sword, you may find a trap laid for you among the fleshpots. The attraction of their pleasure and the temptations of their luxury are, to strong men such as you, like the lure the flame has for the moth. Do not lay yourselves open to destruction, even though the manner of its accomplishment be pleasant. If you must destroy this people, then destroy utterly so nothing remains. They are many while we are few, and though by the keen, hardhitting sword we may prevail in battle, yet might we not be lost under a deluge of soft feathers? Will you be wise enough to sup on milk and honey without being drowned in it?"

GLN:4:7 For a time, the fighting men heeded the words of their chiefs, for they were neither wilful nor reckless, but there were some among them who went down to the plains in peace. They returned with tales of treasures and pleasures awaiting below, reporting that the time was ripe for an attack, the warmen hired by the lowlanders having departed. For in those days the gods of Sharapik strove against the gods of Elishdur and Ladek. Then the fighting men disregarded the commands of their chiefs and, choosing war captains from among themselves, went down and fell upon the people of the plain.

GLN:4:8 The people of the plain bowed before the strength of the men of the mountains. They did not fight, for among all their possessions, they regarded their lives as the most valuable thing, precious above all else. They said, "Take whatever we have, our riches and harvests, the treasured things from our dwellings, even our daughters for your amusement, but leave us enough that we may live under your shadow." The sturdy men of the mountains were sickened by these half men who had lived for three generations without fighting, and they despised them.

GLN:4:9 The battlehardened men who had come down from the highlands took whatsoever they desired. The plainsmen demurred, but because their stomachs turned to water before the virility of their conquerors, their protestations were words of wind. The victors clothed themselves in plundered finery and indulged themselves in the wines and delicacies of the food tables. They slept in beds of luxury and dissipation, every want being attended to by the vanquished. They learned the ways of sensuality, which goes with soft-living, and when sated with natural pleasures some lightened their boredom with unnatural ones. The Mountain Men saw that the women of the cities were beautiful, but they were not modest, casting their charms before the masters, unashamed; so it followed they were taken when required and treated as chattels. The women did not complain, though hitherto they had stood equal with their menfolk, but woman's equality with half men is not something of value.

GLN:4:10 With women like this, the men placed no restraint on their lust and went from excess to excess. The women, rejoicing in the strength and vigour of the men, said among themselves, "Here are men indeed, such as we have not known before." Then, in the manner of women, they turned away from their own men and from the households of their husbands and fathers; for now, they despised them. They threw off all womanly restraint and grappled with the victors like ravening beasts, and the strong were vanquished by weakness. Always do women behave thus when their menfolk are defeated in battle; it is for this men fight.

GLN:4:11 None came to do battle with the victors, for they who had fought for the gods had destroyed themselves, and in the fullness of time the victors, too, were destroyed by the fleshpots, by fornication and drunkenness, by ease and luxury. Their fighting strength and valour departed with the passing years; they grew fat and slothful. They who had come down in manly array to fight and win, who could not be challenged in battle by the lesser men of the plains, were eaten up m the mansions of pleasure, in the drinking booths, with music, wine and fine linen.

GLN:4:12 Upon the mountain and in the mountain homes, there was weeping and sadness among the women. Fields were untilled, and cattle strayed away, sheep went unplucked. The best craftsmen were gone, and few remained willing to learn their skill, the teachers of learning taught no more. The gnarled hand that had wielded the sword and terrorised the foe now plucked the strings of psaltery and lyre. The rough jerkins and corselets were cast off, and now garments were of fine linen dyed purple and crimson. Men arrayed their softening bodies in gaudy attire and bathed in scented waters. They rejected their own women for those of the cities whose hands and feet were stained with bright colours and whose faces were marked with blue.

GLN:4:13 One day, from afar off came three men of Ardis, their country having been stricken by a mountain burst. They were worshippers of The One God whose light shines within men, and when they had lived in the two cities for a number of days they were stirred up in heart because of the things they saw. So they called upon their God to see these evil things. Their God sent down a curse upon the men of the cities, and there came a strange light and a smoky mist, which caught at the throats of men. All things became still and apprehensive, there were strange clouds in the skies and the nights were hung with heaviness. Many days passed before a northwind came, and the skies cleared; but then, when women conceived, they bore devils. Monstrosities came forth from their wombs, whose faces were terrible and whose limbs were unproportioned.

GLN:4:14 In those days men knew the art of working clay and making linen in bright colours, and also the use of eye paint. They had knowledge of herbs and magic, of enchantment, and the wisdom of The Book of Heaven; the knowledge of signs and omens, the secrets of the seasons, of the moon and the coming of the waters.

GLN:4:15 The remnants of the Sons of Nezirah remained upon the mountains which are against Ardis, by the land about the encampment of Lamak. In Ardis, there were wise men filled with the inner wisdom, who read The Book of Heaven with understanding and knew the signs. They saw that the deeds of men in all the lands about the mountains had brought them to their hour. Then, the day came when The Lady of the Night changed her garment for one of a different hue, and her form swept more swiftly across the skies. Her tresses streamed out behind in gold and copper, and she rode in a chariot of fire. The people in those days were a great multitude, and a loud cry ascended into Heaven.

GLN:4:16 Then, the wise men went to Sharapik, now called Sarapesh, and said to Sisuda, the King, "Behold, the years are shortened and the hour of trial draws nigh. The shadow of doom approaches this land because of its wickedness; yet, because you have not mingled with the wicked, you are set apart and shall not perish; this, so your seeds may be preserved." Then, the king sent for Hanok, son of Hogaretur, and he came out of Ardis, for there he had heard a voice among the reeds saying, "Abandon your abode and possessions, for the hour of doom is at hand; neither gold nor treasure can buy a reprieve."

GLN:4:17 Then Hanok came into the cities and said to the governors, "Behold, I would go down to the sea and would therefore build a great ship, that I may take my people upon it. With me will go those who trouble you, and they will take the things which cause you concern; therefore, you will be left in peace to your own enjoyment." The governors said, "Go down to the sea, and build your ship there, and it will be well, for you go with our blessing." But Hanok answered, "It has been told to me in a dream that the ship should be built against the mountains, and the sea will come up to me." When he had gone away, they declared him mad. The people mocked him, calling him Commander of the Sea, but they did not hinder him, seeing gain in his undertaking. Therefore, a great ship was laid down under the leadership of Hanok, son of Hogaretur, for Sisuda, king of Sarapesh, from whose treasury came payment for the building of the vessel.

GLN:4:18 It was built on the lake of Namos, close by the river of gold, where it divides. All the household of Hanok was there and the household of his brother who directed the men at the task. Dwyvan, captain of ships, from the land beyond Ardis, was overseer of the craftsmen. The women and children carried and the men built. The length of the great ship was three hundred cubits, and its breadth was fifty cubits, and it was finished off above by one cubit. It had three storeys, which were built without a break.

GLN:4:19 The lowermost was for the beasts and cattle and their provender, and it was laid over with sand from the river. The middle one was for birds and fowls, for plants of every kind that are good for man and beast, and the uppermost one was for the people. Each storey was divided in twain, so that there were six floors below and one above, and they were divided across with seven partitions. In it were cisterns for water and storehouses for food, and it was built with askara wood, which water cannot rot or worms enter. It was pitched within and without, and the cisterns were lined. The planks were edged and the joints made fast with hair and oil. Great stones were hung from ropes of plaited leather, and the ship was without mast or oars. There were no poles and no openings, except for a hatch beneath the eaves above, whereby all things entered. The hatch was secured by great beams.

GLN:4:20 Into the great ship they carried the seed of all living things; grain was laid up in baskets and many cattle and sheep were slain for meat, which was smoked by fire. They also took all kinds of beasts of the field and wild beasts, birds and fowls, all things that crawl. Also gold and silver, metals and stones.

GLN:4:21 The people of the plains came up and camped about to see this wonder; even the Sons of Nezirah were among them, and they daily mocked the builders of the great ship; but these were not dismayed and toiled harder at the task. They said to the mockers, "Have your hour, for ours will surely come."

GLN:4:22 On the appointed day, they who were to go with the great ship departed from their homes and the encampment. They kissed the stones and embraced the trees, and they gathered up handfuls of the Earth, for all this, they would see no more. They loaded the great ship with their possessions, and all their provender went with them. They set a ram's head over the hatch, pouring out blood, milk, honey and beer. Beating upon their breasts, weeping and lamenting, the people entered the great ship and closed the hatch, making it secure within.

GLN:4:23 The king had entered and with him those of his blood; in all fourteen, for it was forbidden that his household go into the ship. of all the people who entered with him, two understood the ways of the sun and moon and the ways of the year and the seasons. One the quarrying of stones, one the making of bricks and one the making of axes and weapons. One the playing of musical instruments, one bread, one the making of pottery, one the care of gardens and one the carving of wood and stone. One the making of roofs, one the working of timbers, one the making of cheese and butter. One the growing of trees and plants, one the making of ploughs, one the weaving of cloth and making of dyes, and one the brewing of beer. One the felling and cutting of trees, one the making of chariots, one dancing, one the mysteries of the scribe, one the building of houses and the working of leather. There was one skilled in the working of cedar and willow wood, and he was a hunter; one who knew the cunning of games and circus, and he was a watchman. There was an inspector of water and walls, a magistrate and a captain of men. There were three servants of God. There was Hanok and his brother and their households, and Dwyvan and six men who were strangers.

GLN:4:24 Then, with the dawning, men saw an awesome sight. There, riding on a great black rolling cloud, came the Destroyer, newly released from the confines of the sky vaults, and she raged about the Heavens, for it was her day of judgement. The beast with her opened its mouth and belched forth fire, hot stones and a vile smoke. It covered the whole sky above and the meeting place of Earth and Heaven could no longer be seen. In the evening, the places of the stars were changed, they rolled across the sky to new stations; then, the floodwaters came.

GLN:4:25 The floodgates of Heaven were opened and the foundations of Earth were broken apart. The surrounding waters poured over the land and broke upon the mountains. The storehouses of the winds burst their bolts asunder, so storms and whirlwinds were loosed to hurl themselves upon the Earth. In the seething waters and howling gales all buildings were destroyed, trees were uprooted and mountains cast down. There was a time of great heat; then came a time of bitter cold. The waves over the waters did not rise and fall, but seethed and swirled; there was an awful sound above.

GLN:4:26 The pillars of Heaven were broken and fell down to Earth. The skyvault was rent and broken; the whole of creation was in chaos. The stars in the Heavens were loosened from their places, so they dashed about in confusion. There was a revolt on high; a new ruler appeared there and swept across the sky in majesty.

GLN:4:27 Those who had not laboured at the building of the great ship and those who had mocked the builders came quickly to the place where it was lying. They climbed upon the ship and beat upon it with their hands; they raged and pleaded, but could not enter inside, nor could they break the wood. As the great ship was borne up by the waters it rolled and they were swept off, for there was no foothold for them. The ship was lifted by the mighty surge of waters and hurled among the debris, but it was not dashed upon the mountainside because of the place where it was built. All the people not saved within the ship were swallowed up in the midst of raging confusion, and their wickedness and corruption was purged away from the face of the Earth.

GLN:4:28 The swelling waters swept up to the mountain tops and filled the valleys. They did not rise like water poured into a bowl, but came in great surging torrents; but when the tumult quietened and the waters became still, they stood no more than three cubits above the Earth. The Destroyer passed away into the fastness of Heaven, and the great flood remained seven days, diminishing day by day as the waters drained away to their places. Then, the waters spread out calmly and the great ship drifted amid a brown scum and debris of all kinds.

GLN:4:29 After many days the great ship came to rest upon Kardo, in the mountains of Ashtar, against Nishim in The Land of God.

Chapter Five – Birth of Hurmanetar

GLN:5:1 Hanok had three brothers by his mother and one by Sadara, two were with him on the great ship, and one was saved in Megin. Hanok ruled all the land of Bokah, and his sons, Labeth and Hatana, were born at Nasirah after the great ship became fast.

GLN:5:2 His brothers divided the water-washed land between them. One went to Tirdana and built a city there, and he ruled the western waters. One ruled the eastern waters and the swamps down to the waters of the sea. The other raised up Eraka in the midst of them, and he was the greatest. The city of Eraka stood for a thousand years, but in the days of King Naderasa, the people made great images with faces of gold and bodies of brass. Children were offered to these demons conceived in wickedness. Then God in His wrath unleashed the winds, and they were swept through the city as a whirlwind. The gold-faced images were thrown one against another and were broken; they fell and were buried under their temples. Eraka was then removed from the eyes of men.

GLN:5:3 All the cities were rebuilt, and the kings were dead; the people had multiplied greatly when Lugadur, he who taught the working of metals, was born. He was the mightiest of kings and his deeds are known to all men and written in his books.

GLN:5:4 Wisdom came to the land by the hand of our father Hurmanetar, who was called Hankadah, born at Egelmek in the land of Khalib under Eraka, of Nintursu, Maiden of the Temple, by Gelamishoar, Builder of Walls, son of Lugadur the Metalworker, son of Dumath the Shepherd, son of Gigitan, the Tiller of the Soil.

GLN:5:5 In the days when the mother of Hurmanetar carried him under her heart with pain, the king, his father, had a dream. He saw a woman and knew he had just lain with her, but could not see her face clearly, for whenever he almost recognised it, the likeness changed to that of another. The woman was purifying herself over a bowl of incense, and while so doing she made water. Then, a great cloud of smoke arose up from out of the bowl and filled all the room, and it went out through the doors and filled all the city and all the temples of the city.

GLN:5:6 The following night the king was disturbed by the same dream Therefore, knowing he had received an omen, upon his arising he hastened to send a messenger to the Temple of the Stargazers. Two wise men came and he told them concerning his dream, requesting that they read its meaning. Having heard the words of the king, they thereupon left, going away to consult The Book of Heaven to discover what was written in the future concerning such a matter. In two days they returned, coming in unto the king as he sat within the hall of judgement, and they bowed before him saying, "Woe unto us your servants for what we have to say, for thus it is written. One is to be born of a woman, whom you have ravished, and he will be a slayer of kings, a destroyer of temples and a contender with the gods. He is one born to be great among men, and his hand will be against you."

GLN:5:7 Hearing this the king bethought himself of the women he had taken by force, but they were many and scattered. So he sent again for the wise men, requesting their aid, and the wise men received his words.

GLN:5:8 Now, the wise men knew these things were written of a son to be born to Nintursu, but they were perplexed not knowing what to do, for she was a Maiden of the Temple of the Seven Enlightened Ones, which had been built in the days of Sisuda. If the blood of one thus born were shed or its breath stopped within the boundaries of the land, the corn would perish within the furrow, and the blossom would fall from the trees, so that they yielded no fruit. yet the wise men were not loath to bring down the wrath of the king upon this temple, for it was one whose god had but small estate, yet it paid no tribute to the god of the land. Nor did they desire to deceive the king in this matter, for if by perchance the deceit were uncovered, they lost their protection.

GLN:5:9 The wise men, therefore, went before the king and spoke thus, "O king, light of our lives, we your servants have discovered this child, though it is yet unborn. It is to be born of a maiden bound to the Temple of the Seven Enlightened Ones; therefore, its blood may not be shed on land worked by the hand of man, nor may its breath be stopped. So now we say unto you, send those who are your most trusted servants; let them take this maiden and carry her away to a place afar off. If it be beyond the boundaries of this land, the child when born can be slain there and no evil will befall the lands of our god." Hearing these words, the king remembered the maiden he had taken for his pleasure, for while hunting he had come upon her as she bathed. Neither the temple nor its god was known to him and he had no fear of its priests.

GLN:5:10 The king called his chamberlain to his side, a man most trusted, and charged him, saying, "Go, take this Nintursu, this temple maiden, and carry her into the land of Kithis, entering by stealth. She is with child, and when it is born, slay it, letting its blood fall upon the soil in the land of Kithis."

GLN:5:11 The chamberlain prepared and departed, taking with him men of blood and their captain. They travelled so they came upon the temple at first light in the morning. Nintursu was taken and they left ornaments of gold and silver.

GLN:5:12 Now, Nintursu was not delivered of the child when they came to the boundary of the land, so they camped there, and in the days that followed, men went out to spy. The captain was a man skilled in war and courageous; a man of many battles, and Nintursu spoke often with him. But between her and the chamberlain few words were spoken.

GLN:5:13 It happened that when Nintursu's time was upon her and the child to be delivered, it was the days of full moon; therefore, the child could not be slain, so they bided until the dark of the moon. Then, when the order of things was right, the chamberlain called the captain and said, "This is a task for a man of blood and I am not such a one, therefore, you take the child and slay it over the border. Seven men will go with you, that all these may bear witness to the deed and swear to it."

GLN:5:14 Now, the men of blood were grim men of battles, strangers to soft beds and the gentle ways of women, but some among them were the companions of Nintursu during the first days of her motherhood. Also, there was one whose father had been a worshipper at the Temple of the Seven Enlightened Ones before it was abandoned by all who followed the king. There were those who murmured, saying, "This is a task for those in high places, who speak with honeyed tongues and carry concealed knives that stab in the back, this is not for fighting men."

GLN:5:15 It was true. This was no task for men of clashing metal, it was a deed more suited to squeamish-stomached courtiers; but, lacking backbone, these have ever needed others to do their dirty work spawned through intrigue and conspiracy. Lord, hasten the day when real men are no longer manipulated by half men!

GLN:5:16 The captain put the child into a basket prepared by Nintursu. It was placed upon an ass. Then, he and his men went over the boundary to a place, where neither tree nor grass grew; but about ten bowshots distant, a stream ran through it to water fields and pastures in the valley below. When they stopped, the captain took down the basket and opened it, but when he gazed upon the face of the child, his heart held his hand. He was a man of battles who slew in war, a slayer of men in combat, not a weak-kneed man of intrigue and slayer of children. He closed the basket and said to those who had come with him, "We will bide our time here until nightfall. If we loose the blood of the child here it will be absorbed into dead soil and do no harm, but if we carry it further, down into the valley, it will fall on living soil." None with him answered, for they were but simple fighting men knowing not that the blood could have been let into the waters. Or maybe they understood the heart of their captain.

GLN:5:17 The captain said, "It is hot, we have time enough before those who dwell below are asleep; therefore, let us drink wine and rest awhile." So they drank wine which had been brought and rested; becoming drowsy they eventually fell asleep. Darkness fell.

GLN:5:18 Now, the ass had not eaten since the morning; nor had it drunk at the stream, and the captain of men bided his time, for he had a plan and this was a place known to him. In the gathering darkness he put the basket, with the child inside, back on the ass. It was a good place of concealment, under an overhanging rock, with thickets of thorn all around, while below, the ground fell away steeply, being covered with rocks and loose stones. Only the captain knew how, in the darkness, a large stone was loosed from above, bringing down many others with it, so that stones fell all about the place where the men lay under the overhang. They were heavy with wine, they shouted, they stumbled and fell; one was struck by a dart, another by a spear; there was a clash in the darkness though none was killed. The ass, loosed from its halter, fled, and none could stop it.

GLN:5:19 Wrathfully the captain shouted, "What kind of men have I been given, why have you not brought trumpets to announce our coming? Who can see the ass among the bushes or hear it among the stones? Then, as lights appeared below and the voices of men were heard in the night, they withdrew.

GLN:5:20 Coming to a place of safety, the men took counsel among themselves, for the captain of the men said, 'If you would go unpunished for this night, then you must slay me now; even then, can you return without me? Also, who knows where the blood will flow? Therefore, shall we not all say, with mine own eyes I beheld the blood of this child and know it is dead? Are we men of wisdom who live, or are we foolish ones who die? Thus, borne on the back of an ass, Hurmanetar came to the land of Kithis.

Chapter Six – Companionship of Yadol

GLN:6:1 Concerning our father Hurmanetar, these things were written in the scroll of Pakhamin, scribe of the Firehawks. Generation had grown out of generation, and the Lord of Light and Life had hidden himself, for He knew the nature of man, and none could find Him. Time passed, and they sought Him no more.

GLN:6:2 Then high riding, ass-borne, came one who was to reveal the Light to men. Praises to the Lord of light and Life for Hurmanetar the Lightbringer! He wandered the hillsides among shepherds who tended their flocks with care, and he learned their ways. This was the wisest of men, and his body was filled to overflowing with manly powers; wide-striding, he measured the mountains' broad pastures. In anger, his face burned like the sun at noontide, while in benevolence, it shed the calm glow of the moon in the night quietness. In courage and skill, none could match him. He was a child like no other; before others crawled he stood upright; he learned his letters at three years; he could read and write at five; he taught those who attended the temple with him when he was seven. He was ten when his foster-father joined his fathers, and the estate was divided through the women. At twelve, he changed the course of the river falling down from the mountains to lead it through new pastures, and thus, his mother became rich. At thirteen, he was sent to the Shepherd of the City and trained with spear and shield. At seventeen, he slew the king's right hand man and fled to the mountains of Akimah.

GLN:6:3 Like a beast of prey, he wandered at will; he was the mountain-dweller, firm of limb and swift-footed, taking according to his whim from those who passed his way. Mighty was his bow of anshan wood; sinew-strung, it sped swiftly his straight-shot arrows.

GLN:6:4 High on the mountains wandered another, Yadol his name, one who lived on herbs and wild honey, tall and long-haired, for no knife had ever touched it. His hand tamed a wild wolf cub, and it was his companion; wherever he went, it followed. The wild beasts did not molest him, and he walked freely among them.

GLN:6:5 Hurmanetar was a trapper of wild beasts; he dug a pit at the place where they came down to water, and other traps were set. Yadol passed that way; the pit was filled in and the traps broken; the ensnared deer was set free. When Hurmanetar returned and found the pit filled in and the traps broken, his heart was seized by a whirlwind; he raged against the skies, he swore against the trees. He sought, for days he sought but could not come upon Yadol, the evasive one, the cunning one. His traps were useless, his pits a vain labour. He hungered, and because he hungered, he became less cautious. When he lay in wait among the bushes to waylay men who passed, he was not held back by thought of their number, but loosed his arrows and leapt among them. Hurmanetar attacked stormy-hearted; like a whirlwind, he attacked, but when they saw he was one alone, they stood fast. Hurmanetar turned back into the bushes, but arrows sent after him found their mark.

GLN:6:6 For three days, he lay in his place upon the mountain; his leg swelled up and he thirsted, for he could not get water. He lay in a body of pain, and his spirit prepared to depart from him. A wolf came, and his hand sought a stone, but weakness held his arm, so it could not be cast. Then lo, the wolf licked his hand and departed. Then, Yadol came; in his hand was a skin filled with fresh water, and he knelt beside Hurmanetar and gave him a drink. Yadol dressed the wounds and brought herbs to eat, and so it came to pass that Hurmanetar grew strong again.

GLN:6:7 Thereafter, Hurmanetar and Yadol dwelt together within a cave among the mountains, but Yadol would neither slay for meat nor eat of it. Yet they roamed the wide mountains together in joyous companionship, and their days sped swiftly by. But Hurmanetar longed for other things and therefore was tempted to attack men who passed, for he desired fine meats and garments and ornaments for his body.

GLN:6:8 These things were brought to the ears of the king, and those about the king said, "Let us take men up into the mountain and slay this wild hill wanderer, this manslayer and robber." But the king bade them hold their hands, for he desired to see the man for himself; he wanted him taken alive, and he said, "Should any man slay him, that man is mine." The king, therefore, took counsel of the wisemen, saying, "How shall we take this man, if man he be and not a spirit of the mountains? I would look upon him with my own eyes, for I know of none such as he. One such, there once was, but he is no more." Then, one among the wise men said, "This man of the mountains, if man he be, will follow the ways of men; therefore, let us procure a harlot from the temple, a woman of pleasure, and let her go and take him; ensnare the hunter in the well baited trap." The king said, "This is no new thing, and perchance, it can bring the wild man of the mountains down to me in chains of silk, even into the city; therefore, go and put your words into deeds." Then, a man was sent to the temple, and he brought back Hesurta, a woman of pleasure, in exchange for gold, and she was taken to the hunters who knew the ways of the mountains.

GLN:6:9 They set off, journeying for some days, the hunters, the harlot and those with her, until they came to a place where there was a waterhole, close by the way of Elamki. They passed beyond the waterhole to the spring above, sending men into the surrounding forest. The day came when one returned saying, "The wild man comes." Then, the chief of the hunters said to the woman, "O woman, bare your breasts and sit beside the waters; use the wiles of your calling, have no shame but welcome him boldly. When he comes up close reveal your secrets, drawing him to you; teach him the arts of the harlot that ensnares men."

GLN:6:10 The woman was not loath to take him, responding well to the task, sitting by the waters, singing. However, Hurmanetar circled warily about the place, but discovered nothing, and no harm came to him. He drew closer, and when he did, the harlot revealed her secret charms and was well pleased by the eagerness he displayed. She instructed him in the harlot's art and they dallied there for several days; but the hunters did not come to take him, for they found no way to come upon him furtively. Then, after seven days, Hurmanetar departed, passing up the incline of the mountainside without looking back. The harlot was afraid, because the hunters murmured against her, but it was not her fault, and the chief of hunters said, "Wait and see, let us bide a while yet."

GLN:6:11 Hurmanetar returned to the place where the wild deer grazed, but Yadol was not there, and when he crossed the wind of the deer, they fled away.

GLN:6:12 He went to the cave, where they shared their rest, but Yadol was not there. The wolf alone lay close by and Hurmanetar called out to it, but the wolf stayed afar off, it would not come near, because Hurmanetar was not purified from contact with the harlot.

GLN:6:13 For a day and a night, Hurmanetar stalked the mountainside, wide-striding along its paths, but he did not find Yadol; therefore, he returned to the place where he had left the woman. She greeted him warmly, making him welcome with cooked meats, rejoicing in her heart. They remained there for three days, and she tamed him to the need for a woman. Then, the day came when she said, "You are wise; You are strong even as a bull, why run wild upon the mountainsides with one who deserts you at will? Come with me unto the king, for he has heard tales of your might and would close his eyes to your deeds. He will give you a house and gold, and I, Hesurta, will become your servant. The temple of love will be opened for you, and I will show you the delights within. Come and dwell under the shadow of the king, for he is mighty, he is the wild bull, which roars over men."

GLN:6:14 Hurmanetar thought and said, "No, I will not go before the king, for he does no good in my sight. Do not the people murmur against him, saying, "Woe for these days. The hand of the king rests heavily upon us, his pride knows no bounds and no maiden is left virgin for her husband. Neither the daughter of a man of blood nor the wife of a prince walks freely in the city. Are not all its doors shut like the doors of prisons?"

GLN:6:15 The woman thought awhile, then said, "Who tells these things of the king? Are their words established? He is the great king; a mountain licked by ten thousand tongues, the king whose whisper fills the judgement hall, whose voice echoes a thousand leagues away. He is the glorious king, a man perfect in strength and proportion; his body is one to delight the eyes of any woman. None other has his wisdom and knowledge. Therefore, men talk against him, for it is the nature of men to be jealous of those who so much excel.

GLN:6:16 "Let us go; let the king see you face to face and rejoice, for you are alike. O come with me to where each day brings new delights, where the young women are gaily robed and the young men wonderful to look upon. Come to where breezes are filled with sweet smells, where beds are soft and rooms perfumed. Come to the place where life is enjoyed. Come, serve the king; as you are now, so was he in his youth, but youth departs, albeit slowly. He is the never resting one, the son of The Lady of Battles. Come and do not fear; all will be made ready for you; even now the wise men tell of your coming, and men wait to escort you in peace."

GLN:6:17 Hurmanetar was swayed by her words and said, "So let it be; where you go, there go I." Then Hesurta gave him a necklace she had brought and led him to the tents of the hunters. But when they saw him face to face, they were afraid; such was the light held in the eyes of the stalwart, wide striding one. Yet they recognised him as a man like themselves, and their fear passed. So it was that Hurmanetar went with them and with the woman, came to the city and went before the king, and the king looked upon him with favour. He gave Hurmanetar wine, and he was drunk; and oil for his body, and he was anointed. He was arrayed in three robes, he became a man of rank; he was given a house and servants and he was given a watchman. He became captain of the guards, and none was like him.

GLN:6:18 To the woman of pleasure, the harlot, the king gave bracelets of gold and sent her away, saying, "Go to your proper place, for you have completed the thing required of you. There, you will be great among women, while here, you will be degraded among them." Hesurta departed in sorrow, for even a harlot can feel faint stirrings of affection through the oft soiled, winding cloth which enwraps her sordid spirit.

GLN:6:19 Hurmanetar learned the ways of the palace and walked as he willed, but soon he became restless, for his thoughts turned towards Hesurta. He missed her ways. Yet, many women cast their glances towards him, but behind these was the threat of the sword. He was not a man of smooth and subtle ways, being unskilled in the deceit which flourishes under the shadow of kings. Though favoured by the king and safe under his mantle, he was a man alone in the palace and courtyards. He set out to find Hesurta, seeking her at the temple of pleasure within the temple gate, where she had served as a harlot, but the priest said, "The woman is no longer here, for a harlot, given gold, thinks herself a queen, and the women have driven her out." Hurmanetar sought her throughout the city, but she was nowhere to be found. Persisting, he eventually found her at a harlot's post beside the river, among wineskins and men of the waters. There was one who sat with her, and he was a man of blood; therefore, armed. So when Hurmanetar came up to them seeking to talk with the woman, he drew his sword. When the man of blood saw that Hurmanetar was undismayed by this and prepared to settle the issue, he mocked him, saying, "Why should men fight when women are plentiful and we have half a measure of corn?"

GLN:6:20 Hurmanetar bought the woman from those who grow rich on the defiled bodies of women and established her in his house. The men about the king murmured against him, speaking poisoned words in the ear of the king. The women of the palace also turned from him. Meeting Hesurta on the street, they caught her and tore her veil off her face, while men of subtle ways who served the king mocked behind their hands. The men of blood serving the king set their faces against Hurmanetar, while in the city, men said, as he passed, "There goes the great one who bathes in dirty water." Therefore, Hurmanetar departed from the city, going to dwell without its walls among men who tilled the soil.

GLN:6:21 It was not long before the day came when the woman saw that Hurmanetar was downcast, and so she said to him, "O man of might, when my eyes rest upon you I am raised above all women, and now my heart is cleansed of all that polluted it, my body rejoices in freedom and my life is a song of gladness. Yet, I am saddened because my heart tells me you are sorrowful and not at ease within yourself, that half your heart remains in the mountains. Therefore, hear what I say, go there once more while I remain here to await your return, perhaps this time you will find Yadol." Her words made Hurmanetar sad and he said, "How can I go away and leave you here? Who will protect you? What man can I place over you who will not know you? Yet go to the mountain, I must, therefore you shall come with me."

GLN:6:22 They departed, crossing by way of Hamrama, and came to the mountains high standing and steep-sided. They searched many days, but Yadol could not be found, neither would any bird or beast approach them. They wandered the mountains, they searched the valleys and they grew weary in the search. They returned to the foot of the mountains, below the place where shepherds dwelt and into the tillage, where there was a city. It was the time of Akitoa, and Sharah, chief of the city dwellers, was to be married. Being invited to remain in the city as guests, they stayed there. When the days of feasting commenced, men came in from the mountains and tillage, and there was much dancing and singing. Hurmanetar and Hesurta were made welcome, taking their places among the guests and storytellers, eating and drinking their fill. There was strong drink brewed from corn and wine from the palm, and Hurmanetar became overfilled with these and, drunk, he fell asleep. While he slept, a man came upon Hesurta and seized her, saying, "Come, let us be together, so I may have pleasure, and you may have silver. I know you are a woman of many pleasures, a servant to the vices of men." When she denied him his desire, he sought to take her by force, but she drew a knife and slew him, for a woman cannot be taken by man, except she surrender herself to his needs.

GLN:6:23 Hearing the clamour, men came and, seeing what had happened, they seized the woman. Others took Hurmanetar and both were brought before the headman, who delivered them to a place of confinement. When the feasting was over they were brought before Pitosi, one who sat in judgement. Pitosi said to Hurmanetar, "You have come among us as a guest and a man of good standing; therefore we know not whether you have been wronged or whether a man of this city has been slain unjustly. If you have been wronged, then also establish the standing of this woman. It is said that she is a harlot without standing, this being so, then you shall pay the price of he who is slain to his kindred and no more will be required of you."

GLN:6:24 Hurmanetar answered Pitosi thus, "You are one filled with the essence of wisdom, who justly occupies the seat of judgement. I ask with due humility that you give ear to my plea for this woman, who may not speak for herself. Denounce her I cannot; instead, I will claim her as wife under the law of Hudashum, for she has dwelt with me for twenty months and in that time has not known another man, nor have I cause for complaint."

GLN:6:25 Hearing this, and because Hurmanetar made claim to the law of Hudashum, Pitosi sent for Enilerich, priest of the Great Temple, that he should say whether or not Hesurta stood before him as the wife of Hurmanetar. When the priest came he enquired of the woman whether she were a virgin when Hurmanetar took her. Had she said "yes", then the passage of three months would have given her the standing of a wife; but she answered "no." The priest asked her if she were a widow when Hurmanetar took her. had she answered "yes", then the passage of twenty months would have given her the standing of a wife; but she answered "no." Then the priest asked if she were a harlot when Hurmanetar took her and she answered "yes." Therefore, as seven years had not yet passed since Hurmanetar first took her, she could not have the standing of a wife. Nor could she claim to be a harlot of the temple, for she had left its protection.

GLN:6:26 Now the mark of a harlot was upon her and Hurmanetar had forfeited his standing in the place of judgement. So, Pitosi gave judgement upon them and it was decreed that when Gaila came they would be led to the enclosure of death and there tied back to back. The woman would be strangled with cords, after the manner of harlots, while Hurmanetar would be left to carry her as a burden within the enclosure for seven days. Then, if the gods willed that he lived, he would be let out to wander as he willed, all he might take with him being three handfuls of corn and a gourd of water, The judgement was fulfilled. Hurmanetar lived. He departed and went his way, and the kindred of the slain men failed to catch him.

GLN:6:27 Hurmanetar passed across the land, coming at last to the temple of the Seven Illuminated Ones, and his mother was there. She dwelt alone with only an old serving woman, for now the temple was desolate and without walls, For two years, Hurmanetar dwelt with his mother, but then his heart went out again to the companion he had left upon the mountainside. He said to his mother, "I must depart, for my heart cries out for one who saved my life and whose ways are mine. Great is the love of man for woman, but greater the love of man for man."

GLN:6:28 So Hurmanetar came again to the mountains, and lo, he had entered the forest but half a day when he came upon Yadol. How warm was the greeting, how strong the embrace! Hurmanetar said, "Long have I sought you and found you not; yet I come again, and you are here." Yadol answered, "It was because of the harlot, I was here, but you saw me not, nor could I make myself known to you."

GLN:6:29 Hurmanetar returned with Yadol to the place where his mother dwelt, and they remained there, none knowing what they were, for they were garbed as priests. They tilled the ground about the place, enjoying its fruitfulness, and both were nourished by the wisdom of Hurmanetar's mother.

GLN:6:30 Nintursu was the last of the line of Sisuda. Ten thousand generations had passed since the beginning and a thousand generations since the recreation. The Children of God and The Children of Men had passed into dust, and only men remained. One hundred generations had passed since the overwhelming deluge and ten generations since The Destroyer last appeared. Once man lived for less than two score years, now his years were three score and ten. Once, God had walked with men, and men knew only God. Now, He was hidden behind many veils, and few saw Him, and then but dimly and with great distortion. Where once there was one God, now gods were as numbered as the stars. Yet the Great Key remained in the midst of men, and it was here, at the Temple of the Seven illuminated Ones, the Key of Life, the Key which was given into the keeping of our father, Hurmanetar. It is a secret thing, something exceedingly great. It is not lost but has come down to us and is known in our times.

GLN:6:31 Now, one day, as Hurmanetar sat beneath a tree, enjoying its shade at the height of noon, he saw a stranger approaching. The man was weary and staggered, so Hurmanetar sent his servant to bring him into the shade. The servant hastened out and brought him in. He was given refreshment and his feet washed, and when this had been done Hurmanetar asked him where he was bound, and the stranger replied, "I go to Tagel, for in that place, there is a mighty man and a just one who will give ear to my plea, for untoward things are happening in the great city, things which should not be, The people cry out in the place of assembly, but they cry to the wind. Gilnamnur has seized the heart of the king and now rules. In twelve days I am pledged to marry, but there is no lightness of a bridegroom in my heart, for the king elects to be first with the bride. This is the custom come down to us from the gods of old, but my heart is wrung like a grape. I cannot find it within me to give her into his keeping on the wedding night. Therefore, I go to find one who can challenge him at the door of the bridal chamber, as the custom permits, for this is no low born woman. But this is a thing none has heard of as having been done before in our times, for men fear the gods. I know of none other who may stand before the king as one sanctified."

GLN:6:32 Hurmanetar heard him and replied, "Be of good heart, and go no further, for I am that man." Hearing this, the stranger, filled with gratitude, fell upon his knees before Hurmanetar and said, "How can I thank you, how can I repay you, what can I give?" But Hurmanetar answered, "When a man does what has to be done, then payment and reward sully the deed." Then he called Yadol and said, "Prepare, for we go into the city of the king, and because he was sanctified, Hurmanetar claimed the protection of Erakir. Then, they offered prayers in the antechamber between Heaven and Earth.

GLN:6:33 They dwelt with the brother of the bridegroom until the day of the wedding feast came, for the bridegroom was not of this city. When the feast was over, and before the guests departed, the bridal chamber was made ready with the bride within, and the young messenger of the temple went about making his call. Then the king came to the antechamber, passing by the husband who was to wait without. But there, standing before the door, was Hurmanetar, his right hand on the pillar, for none might otherwise challenge the king, and in his left hand were the reeds.

GLN:6:34 Those who were gathered there, the men and the women, drew back and men of the king's guard came forward, each claiming the right to enter the combat on behalf of the king; for one man could precede the king, but no more. Such was the custom. The choice of whom to fight from among those who came forward lay with Hurmanetar, and because he chose the captain of the guard, a man skilled in war, the people were amazed. But Hurmanetar knew the man's weakness. No more than five blows were struck when Hurmanetar, leaping to the left hand side of the captain of the guard, drove up under his armpit, so that he fell to the ground and died.

GLN:6:35 Then Hurmanetar and the king girded themselves and fought in the high courtyard, and it was a fight such as men had not seen before. The young and the old, agility against experience, stamina against cunning, they were both equal in the fight. They slashed at each other until their weapons broke and their shields split. They grappled, they stamped, they rolled in the dust, they lashed out at each other, and the combat went on until the water ran out, and still they both stood. Then, they could not fight with weapons but stood disarmed, and this time, neither might cause the death of the other. They circled each other warily, keeping away from the balustrade. Then Hurmanetar jumped aside and with a swift movement caught the king to him, twisting him so they both fell down into the courtyard below the ground, and the king fell over his shoulder, so that his breastbone broke, and he remained on the ground. Then the king's guard gathered about him, and a man skilled with medicines came forward; though grievously hurt the king would not die. Hurmanetar gave his seal and right to the husband and, with Yadol, parted the men who stood about in silence, for they could not harm them. So Hurmanetar and Yadol departed from the land, for it became closed to them and, mounted on mountain asses, they set out on the way of Anhu.

GLN:6:36 Hurmanetar crossed the wide plains with Yadol until they came safely to the stream of bitter waters, brought there by Mamanatum, and so they came up to Machur close by the forest of cedars and dwelt there. This is the place where there was a temple to Humbanwara, the Guardian.

Chapter Seven – Death of Yadol

GLN:7:1 Hurmanetar married Astmeth, daughter of Anukis, governor of all the Western parts of Hamanas, and the mother of Astmeth was Neforobtama, daughter of Hahuda, prince of Kerami. In those days, Daydee, daughter of Samshu, king of all the lands to the North, even to the land of everlasting night, ruled all the Eastern parts of Hamanas, and of all women, she was the most beautiful.

GLN:7:2 Now, as time passed Hurmanetar grew rich; he built himself a great house of cedar wood and had many servants and concubines. In these, the days of his greatness, he forgot the teachings of Nintursu, and the Great Key lay hidden, for the hours of his days were filled with worldly matters.

GLN:7:3 The overseer of Hurmanetar's cornfields was Noaman, a man of Loza, a man whose word was not worth an obal of sand, for he falsified the measure. Therefore, fingers were removed from him, and he was driven forth out of the lands of Hurmanetar, and he became the servant of one Sabitur. This Sabitur dwelt on the road to Milikum, outside the city of Kithim where Daydee ruled, and Daydee was a great queen.

GLN:7:4 In the days when men came to Kithim and Lodar to buy and sell, before the feast when new-milled corn was offered to the Bull of Yahana, Hurmanetar went up into the city of Kithim to pay his tribute.

GLN:7:5 Now, Gilamishoar, the king, had died because of the thing hidden in an earthenware box, and the new king, wishing to know where he stood with the gods, sent for wise men who threw bundles of cedar wood before him. They saw he was destined to reign in greatness and prosperity, providing that he never quarrelled with a queen or killed a child. Therefore, the king deemed it wise to strengthen his peace with Daydee and sent his son to her with many gifts.

GLN:7:6 The prince journeyed some days; then, stopped at an inn a day's journey from Kithim, and supped there; and while he ate, word was brought to him that someone wished to speak with him. It was Noaman, and he spoke poisoned words regarding Hurmanetar, so these should be brought to the ear of the queen. Thus, when Hurmanetar entered the city of Kithim, he was seized and brought before the queen. But when she saw him and spoke with him, Daydee found no fault with him and looked upon him with favour. Therefore, though the prince departed, Hurmanetar dallied at the court of queen Daydee.

GLN:7:7 Time passed, and Hurmanetar came frequently to the court and he was well-favoured, but it came about that strife arose in the lands about, for the Mother of the Gods strove with the Father of the Gods. It was a time of turmoil, when the hand of brother was against brother, and all the while Hurmanetar rose in the esteem of the queen. So it came about that a son was born to Hurmanetar and Daydee. While the lands about had been ravaged by war, there was peace in Kithim, but when the son of Hurmanetar and Daydee was scarce one year old, men came bearing tidings of war; the hosts of the king had gathered and voices were crying in the market place. "Prepare to die, for those who are mightier than the Humbala are upon us. None shall be spared from the fire of the pit, neither old men, nor women and children." For those who came were The Children of Githesad the Serpent, the Cunning One, whose mother was one of those who brought defilement into the race of men. These people knew neither justice nor mercy.

GLN:7:8 The priests and the people went up into the mountain to gather before the cave of Yahana. They cried out to be delivered; they were overpowered with weakness and their teeth shook, their knees became weak. But Daydee remained in the city, and she appointed Hurmanetar captain of her war hosts, and he gave the orders. The armsmakers bent to the task, making spears of willow wood and casting axes. Hurmanetar freed Turten, because he had renounced his father, had become a slave, and gave him command of the bowmen. For Turten was a man of might and a bowman of renown.

GLN:7:9 In the days when men feared because of the bull of Heaven, the war hosts of The Children of Githesad gathered on the plain, and the fires of their encampment were, at night, numbered like stars. The men of Hurmanetar encamped against them, and when he led the war hosts of queen Daydee out in the morning light the men of blood faced one another. Turten, the bowman, had been made a war captain and he went out before the host of Daydee to see how those who stood against them were arrayed. When he returned, he spoke thus to Hurmanetar, "Behold my Lord, great is the host of The Children of Githesad and well set in their order of battle. Behold the long-limbed spearman, Kami the Mighty, far famed among men, leads them. See the powerful bowmen, whose wide ranging arrows speed from behind tall shields, which stand before them. What has Hoames failed to teach these people? Behold the hosts of the Husigen who are with them, led by Aknim of the firm standard. See to their left the spearmen of ever mighty Marduka; they stand firm in line; they are like the point of a nail, ready to thrust inward. See, already the horns of the bull spread out for the encircling clash. Slingers already harass our foreguard, while bowmen sting us on either side."

GLN:7:10 "Still let us take heart. Have we not, ourselves, many mighty men ready to give their life's blood for you? Are they not all armed with every kind of weapon and masters of war? There are far throwing slingers and keen-eyed bowmen, there is tall Lugal with the flashing weapons of fire. Yet, we can number our host, while the numbers of those who stand against us seem countless as the sands.

GLN:7:11 Then Hurmanetar raised his voice, calling upon his men to stand firm-footed in line to await the clash and bear up before it. He said, "Think of your duty, and do not waver before the thrusts. To step back in battle is to step back from manhood. To take flight would cause men to tell of your dishonour now and in the days to come, and to an honourable man the disgrace of dishonour is worse than death itself. If any of you run, the staunch ones who stood firm will say you have fled the battle through fear, and your comrades who expected your support will treat your name with scorn. Those who stand against us on the field of blood will speak of you with contempt and derision. They will mock your courage, and for a true man there can be no more shameful fate."

GLN:7:12 Then, to encourage those who were faint-hearted, Hurmanetar sounded the loud, thunderous war cry. It resounded like the roar of ten bulls. Then he caused his companion of the shield to blow the far-sounding war horn. After this came a rolling boom of war drums, the ringing sound of clashing cymbals, the loud shrilling of trumpets, and even louder trumpets filled the sky above with thunder.

GLN:7:13 Turten, of the powerful bow, and Lugal, of the bright weapons, prepared their men to meet the clash. The war hosts drew closer, and the flight of arrows and slingstones began, followed by the hurling of flight spears. Heaven and Earth trembled under the fearful sound of war cries and the clamour of war horns; even the hearts of stout fighting men shook before they commanded themselves. Yet, those with Hurmanetar stood firm, eager for the clash and saying, "Let us smite those who come full of fight and fury to do the evil will of their dark king."

GLN:7:14 Now I, Ancheti, stood behind the slingers' wall; my limbs trembled and my mouth was dry, my tongue craved for water. My scalp moved in fear and my hands loosened their grip through moisture. My heart thumped in confusion and I saw a mist of redness before my eyes, for this was my first battle, and I was but a youth. Beside me stood Yadol, the wild tender man, and he said, "I see no gladness in victory, if victory be granted. I crave no kingdom that I may rule over other men. What would be its pleasures to one such as I? For what do men slay one another? Which man seeks spoil and its pleasure and which man the joys of life? Against us stand men of living flesh and blood, men who have mothers and wives, men who have children, men who are good, even if those who lead them are evil. These good men, I have no wish to slay, better would it be, were I to be slain myself. Not a man will I slay with these hands, not even for the kingdom of the three spheres would I do it, much less an earthly kingdom. Were those who stand against us all men of evil, it would perhaps be a good deed to slay them; but in the clash of war, the good slay the good and the evil ones live safely behind the shields."

GLN:7:15 "an we slay men made in our own likeness, brother beings? What peace shall we henceforth enjoy in our hearts? Will not the memory make our hearts heavy, so that life becomes an unbearable burden? Even if there are others among these great war hosts who are so overcome with greed for spoil that they see no evil in the slaying of men, shall we not withhold our blows from this awful deed of blood?"

GLN:7:16 "O doom of darkness, O day of sorrows, what evil has moved the hearts of rulers that men be slain in thousands for the gain of treasure and the rule of an earthly kingdom? What do we here on this field of blood, we who are men of peace and goodwill? Better by far that I stood unarmed, my breast bared, unresisting, and let them slay me, that I might lay in my own innocent blood!. Thus spoke Yadol as the clash drew nigh, but only I, Ancheti, heard him.

GLN:7:17 Then the lunge and thrust was upon us, and I heard another voice beside me, that of my uncle, Hurmanetar, who was there, red sword in hand. The press of the foe drew back, and in the lull, Hurmanetar stood beside Yadol, the companion of his wanderings, and placed a hand on his shoulder in compassion, for Yadol was a man without fear, a man of more courage than Ancheti. On the field of blood, the craven-hearted are truly separated from the men of peace and goodwill.

GLN:7:18 The foe swept upon the thinning ranks again; they came like waves breaking upon a beach. They swept in, then sullenly, tardily, they rolled back, only to reform and crash again. As they came, I heard Hurmanetar open his mouth and cry out, "They come yet again, they are upon us, arise and greet them; arise above this field of blood like men, for this is the day of heroes. This is the final test, this is the last trial of strength, the last effort to cast back. Why this lifeless rejection of all that is manly? Strong men cannot despair in their hearts when facing conflict and death; this gains neither victory on Earth, nor peace in Heaven. Stand as you have done, firm-footed, rising to the battle clash like the whirlwind that carries all before it. We are but men who know nothing of the causes of gods and their ways. I fight for the cause of loyalty and honour, I know not whether their victory or ours be best for the true cause of God, but I fight. Come, rise to the clash."

GLN:7:19 Then, the remnants of the war hosts came together in the clash of arms. The cruel weapons struck one against the other, blow and counter blow. There were dull cries of death, the shrieks of pain and the shrill shout of victory, the last efforts of weary bodies, the last cries of dry-throated voices. The men of Hurmanetar stood firm in the line, and the war hosts of those who sought to overwhelm them broke like a wave upon the seashore; they came no more. Hurmanetar stood blooded and proud in the exultation of victory, but it passed in a moment when he saw Yadol lying among the dead and dying; wounded to death, but not yet dead. He had taken upon himself the spear thrust meant for Ancheti.

GLN:7:20 Hurmanetar lifted him up, his knee under his head, and Yadol opened his mouth and said, "The Great One has given you the victory, and for you, behind and beyond the victory, I see a great destiny, and therefore a difficult one. Be not heavy-hearted, nor let your spirit grieve, heavy-laden with sorrow because of me. Weep not, for this I know; he who thinks he can slay another or be slain by him is devoid of enlightening truth. The spirit of man cannot perish by the sword or be overwhelmed by death."

GLN:7:21 "The sharp weapons of war cannot harm the spirit, nor can fire burn it. Waters cannot drown it and soil cannot bury it. My spirit departs to its abode beyond the power of sharp sword, beyond the reach of thrusting spear, beyond the range of swift arrow. Now, face to face with what must be and cannot be altered, face to face with the ultimatum of destiny, cease from sorrow."

GLN:7:22 "What is this passing thing called life? This fragile flower so tenderly cherished, seen in its true frailty here on the field of blood. Does it have any real meaning? Here on the field of blood the dead sleep to awake to glory. To the victorious ones remaining alive there is glory on Earth. So, do not dally here with the dying. Arise, go to your proper reward and lay me down to mine. Fear not for me, already I see the welcoming light beyond the veil. We shall meet again."

GLN:7:23 Thus, Yadol departed from Earth, and he was laid to rest in glory. He sleeps among the hills and trees, among the wild birds and beasts, which were his friends. These words are cut on his tomb, 'He was a man of peace and died because other men were not as he'.

Chapter Eight – Hurmanetar Journeys to the Nether World

GLN:8:1 Perhaps no man of his day properly honoured Yadol, for he was beyond their understanding, but Hurmanetar loved him and Ancheti never forgot him. Long days, the thoughts of Hurmanetar rested upon Yadol, his friend, the companion in the joyous hunting on the mountains. Long he thought, "What manner of sleep is this, if sleep it be, that fell upon Yadol? Has he decayed into dust to become nothing, as my eyes declare? Or does he live in some strange way? Did not the worm fasten onto his body before it was laid to rest? Yet he knew it not." Long hours had Hurmanetar sat at the feet of Nintursu the wise, yet faced with the blank stare and deaf ears of his companion he had begun to fear the certainty of death. Like many before him he sought to penetrate the veil.

GLN:8:2 Therefore, having claimed audience, Hurmanetar came before the queen to state his intention. Daydee, having been victorious, was exalted in her own eyes and cared little that the battle had been won for her by Hurmanetar and others. Now that the danger was past, she dallied with new favourites, not knowing the day of retribution would come, as come it surely did, for she was carried off captive in chains, to become the plaything of a cruel king.

GLN:8:3 Having come before the queen, Hurmanetar spoke thus, "O great queen, exalted above all others, great lady of battles, though dwelling here under your great shadow, I am as a cat among pigeons, as a wild boar among a docile herd. Therefore, I would spread my wings, going to a distant place to communicate with my God. I would seek entry into the Place of the Dead. My heart is consumed with sorrow because of the uncertainty that grasps my heart; my spirit is restless. I shall seek to discover if my friend and companion yet lives in the Land of Shadows, or whether he is no more than mere dust, the plaything of the winds."

GLN:8:4 Queen Daydee answered, "Wherefore must you go to some distant place to communicate with your God? Is He some little god to be found only in one place? Hurmanetar replied, "O great queen, no little god is this, but the Greatest God of All. It is not because of His littleness that I seek Him out but because of His Greatness. The handmaiden goes to the dressmaker, but the dressmaker comes to the queen." Then, Daydee enquired from Hurmanetar as to the nature of this God, for she was curious, he not having previously discussed such things with her. She asked him for which God he fought, but Hurmanetar said he had fought only for her.

GLN:8:5 Hurmanetar said, "We have a god, you and I, and you have a god and I have a god. The people have their gods and the strangers within your gates have their gods; but hidden behind all these is another God. These lesser gods are no more than His members. It is this God, whom I seek. How can I, a mere mortal, describe Him? Only this do I know, as I learned it in a remote temple. This God came into existence before all else. He ever was, so none could know Him in the beginning, and none knows His mysterious nature. No god came into existence before Him. How can I even name One who had no mother after whom His name might have been made? He had no father who could have named Him and said, "This is I, your father." None can display His likeness in writing, nor can it be cut with knife in wood or stone. He is too great, that men should even enquire about Him. With what words could He be described to their understanding? No other god knows how to call Him by name, even the greatest of them being less than a servant before Him. Yet this I have been told, that the spirit of man can know this Great God and can even know His nature; therefore, perchance the spirit of man is greater than any of the gods."

GLN:8:6 At this those who stood about queen Daydee murmured against Hurmanetar, but she gave no heed to them, gazing long upon him. Then she spoke, "Perchance, too, this Great God does not exist. Who besides you knows of Him? If He be so great, is it not more likely that He would be worshipped by gods rather than by men? Is it not more likely that lesser gods stand intermediate between Him and men'? If a shepherd or husbandman comes to the palace seeking justice or grace, does he see me or an official under me? You say your God is approachable by anyone. Does this enhance His stature? Which is greater, the ruler who judges disputes between swineherds and listens to their complaints, or the ruler who appoints effective officials to deal with swineherds? Surely the former rules amid chaos while the latter rules with efficiency. Do not both of us believe, as all men believe, that there is One Great God above all gods, but we believe that being so great, this Being is beyond approach by mere mortals. Only in this do we differ, you and I."

GLN:8:7 Hurmanetar answered her, saying, "I know him not as He is; all I know is that He exists. Look about you, you who are enthroned so mightily high that your eyes are bedazzled by your surroundings, so you cannot see the Truth lesser beings discover for themselves. Why, even the lowly worm crawling beneath your palace proclaims that nothing less than an almighty God could have created it!"

GLN:8:8 "Wise were our fathers in olden times, and wiser our fathers' fathers. Whence came their wisdom? Did it not come from the Great God, who holds the key to the meeting place of the two kingdoms, which now stand apart? Who lifted the lofty vaults of Heaven and spread Earth out in wide expanse?"

GLN:8:9 Daydee said, "Does it matter, whether it was this God or that? Your God or mine? Suffice it was some god, named or unnamed. These are labyrinthine arguments unsuited to those to whom time is precious."

GLN:8:10 Then, those who stood about the queen set a snare for Hurmanetar, asking him whether the Great Being of whom he spoke was The Mother of All or The Father of All. But Hurmanetar answered, "Let he who has examined the Great Being answer, for I am but a mere mortal man, one not even claiming to be wise. Let the wise among you answer for me."

GLN:8:11 Then Hurmanetar departed from the presence of queen Daydee. In a few days, he left her land, driven by the God-given restlessness that marks the true seeker after light. With him went the youth, Ancheti. Tame goats guided them to the border of the land, and from thence they followed the Way of the Chariot until they came to the land of Mekan, where they rested. In this place dwelt Formana, the strong-limbed, who gave them shelter.

GLN:8:12 Formana asked Hurmanetar whither he went, and Hurmanetar replied, "I go to seek the abode of Hamerit, which is set atop a mountain in the midst of this great forest, just beyond the river. There is a door therein, which I would open, to which I hold a key." Formana said, "This is an enterprise doomed for failure, for none may pass that way and return. I, who have dwelt here for many long years, know the truth of this; nor do I understand this talk of a key; this is a thing new to my ears." So Hurmanetar drew forth the Great Key, shaped like a sword, but like no other sword, for it could not be gazed upon for more than a moment without blindness striking the beholder. Yet within its strange scabbard, it harmed none.

GLN:8:13 Formana said, "This many-hued weapon is a strange thing, indeed, and I have no knowledge of its like or its power. But this I do know;, it is an unequal struggle when men alone, however weaponed, have to face dread Akamen, the Terrible One. This is not all, for first they must pass the fearsome watchman at the gate, and he never sleeps." Hurmanetar said, "I have set my heart on this enterprise because of my friend; also, if there is an evil thing lurking within the forest it must be destroyed. I am one whose destiny is already written; I must die that men might live. What a man cannot escape he must face manfully."

GLN:8:14 Then Hurmanetar left Formana to go apart into a place of solitude where he prayed, "O Father of the Gods, hear me. Hear me, O Father of the Gods, for there is evil abroad in the land and men die of despair. Even the tallest of men cannot reach the Heights of Heaven, or the swiftest of them encompass the Earth. Yet, men must struggle against things beyond their reach and overcome evils, which overshadow the whole land contained within the bitter waters. My destiny is decreed; I alone will enter the gate at the abode of Akamen. O Father of the Gods, when I return I will set up Your Name where now the name of other gods are written, little gods of no standing before you. I will raise a great straight monument to Your sacred Name, if I could but know it."

GLN:8:15 "Why did You move me, Father of the Gods, to embark on this enterprise unless I were destined to accomplish it? Why fill me with the restless desire to perform it? How can I, a mere mortal, succeed without aid? I sought no more than to know the lot of my friend; yet, a greater burden has been allotted to me. If I die, it may be without fear, but if I return may that return be glorified by the knowledge of Truth. O Father of the Gods, stand by my side, help me overcome the lurking thing and show it the strength of a son of Sisuda."

GLN:8:16 When Hurmanetar returned he felt strengthened, but Formana tried to turn him away from his intention, saying, "Desist from this thing; put this enterprise from your thoughts. You have courage, and it carries you far, but does it not also sweep you along, as one caught in the swift river current is swept to destruction? You cannot know what this means; the Guardian at the Gate alone is like nothing on Earth; his weapons are like no others, for they are invisible and strike down from afar. Why strive to do this thing? It is no equal struggle." Hurmanetar replied, "My heart is set on this matter. Though I must journey along an unknown road, perhaps a road of no return, and fight a strange battle, go, I will. I fear not the Terror at the Gate, nor that, which dwells within the abode of Akamen."

GLN:8:17 Formana said, "If go you must, then I who have seen many pass this way will go with you to the gate. Even through the forest, I will accompany you, for am I not one who has been purified before the Sacred Flame? But is it wise that any other should go with such as we? Surely, this youth, your attendant, this young man of few years, inexperienced in things such as we must face, should not accompany us. Is it not more fitting that he remain here to protect my daughters? Is it not better to exchange his inexperience for my experience, his youthful strength for my wisdom and cunning, his endurance for my steadfastness?"

GLN:8:18 Though Ancheti protested, it was agreed that he should remain behind at the dwelling place of Formana.

GLN:8:19 So, making things ready, Hurmanetar and Formana departed in the morning light, while Ancheti remained behind, a guardian of young women, and his heart was sore. He raised his voice to Heaven, saying, "O Father of the Gods, whom Hurmanetar knows, why did You give him this restless heart? Why did You bestow it upon him? You have stirred his spirit, so now he goes into unimaginable danger. O Father of the Gods, of whom I am ignorant, overlook my shortcomings and hear my voice; from this day until he overcomes the Evil Thing and returns, let him ever rest in Your thoughts. Stand by him when he faces the Watchman at the Gate. Strengthen his arm when he strikes at the things that lurk to devour. What these might be or their nature is beyond my imagination. I know them only from the talk of men, each of whom sees them from a different stance. Yet, have any truly seen and lived to return? I know not, but I pray sincerely for him, whom I serve."

GLN:8:20 When Hurmanetar and Formana came to the edge of the forest, they were attacked by lions, but they slew the beasts. Then they entered the forest and saw great trees, such as they had not seen before. They went sleepless, for dread things lurked in the murky light of the forest. They pressed on, coming to the foot of the mountain where they camped and slept, for it was an open place.

GLN:8:21 Then, as the sun rose next day, they climbed the mountain until they came to a cleared place before the cave known as the Portal of the Dead. Here Hurmanetar took leave of Formana, who remained in a hut just beyond the cleared place.

GLN:8:22 Now, Hurmanetar looked about, seeking the Guardian, for he knew what had to be done before he could enter the cave. Then he saw, to his right and beside the cave, a stone hut, and seated before it was a very old woman. Going up to the woman he greeted her and said, "I am one who would enter the dread place, the Abode of Death, the Threshold of the Otherworld, the Door Replacing the Misty Veil. I am one sanctified, one knowing the Lesser Mysteries, I am an Enlightened One."

GLN:8:23 The woman replied by asking the three questions, which all who would span the spheres must answer, and when this was done correctly, she invited Hurmanetar into the hut. Inside, she indicated a stool, and when he was seated she spread a cord around him in a circle. Then she placed a firepot before him, onto which she poured the contents of a small leather bag. She also gave him a pot of green water, which he drank.

GLN:8:24 Some time later, after he had slept awhile, Hurmanetar was conducted to the cave and left there at a spot known as the Devil's Mouth, for there, an evil breath came from an opening in the ground. He remained there for awhile, and again he slept. Awaking, he moved forward into a dark passage, but his movement was strange and he saw as through a narrow tunnel, while his body appeared light and airy.

GLN:8:25 He came to the place where the Watchman kept guard at the gate and beside him the Terror squatted. Hurmanetar drew his sword and faced the awful pair; he advanced cautiously towards them. Then, when they met, the air was filled with a loud clamour, great hissing noises beat at the ears; shouts and screams tore overhead. There was a howling such as no mortal has heard outside of that awful place. Hurmanetar drew back a pace, then advanced again and, behold, both the Watchman and the Terror suddenly vanished, and the hideous clamour was stilled.

GLN:8:26 Hurmanetar passed through the portal and came to a wider, more open place wherein there was a pool of water. It was deep, dark and still. He gazed into the water, and surely no mortal has ever seen such sights as he saw pictured in its stillness. He passed it by. Terrifying shadows leaped and quivered over the walls as he entered a narrowing passage, cast by some hidden ruddy light which seemed to dance as though alive. Then he saw daylight ahead.

GLN:8:27 He came out into the daylight; on one hand, the mountainside reared up; on the other was a vast chasm, between the two ran a narrow path and up this he went. Great birds attacked him, eagles and birds with strange heads. He fought them off and continued upward until he came within sight of the abode of Akamen. He came to it after the long journey upward and stood before the great brazen doors, the seven-bolted doors.

GLN:8:28 Hurmanetar saw no Guardian before the doors, but he heard its voice as it asked the seven questions. He who had sat at the feet of Nintursu remembered well the replies to make, and as each was answered, a bolt slid back. Seven questions were asked, and seven answers rightly given. The great doors swung apart and Hurmanetar passed through, entering the courtyard of Akamen.

GLN:8:29 Within the courtyard, Hurmanetar fought and overcame the four great beast Beings, which feast on the bodies of men, but the sword of Hurmanetar laid them low. He passed through the Hall of Contest, where good and evil spirits fight an eternal battle for the souls of men, coming into the Chamber of Death. Now weary, he sat himself down on the stone called the Seat of Makilam, for it was then in this place, and he waited.

GLN:8:30 Then, Akamen the Terrible came, and Hurmanetar strove with him for half a day and prevailed, and so, he entered into the place where stood the Door of the Spheres. This, Hurmanetar opened with the Great Key; he passed through and entered the Abode of the Dead. He held fast to the Great Key, for without it there was no return, nor could it be held by his own powers alone, but only through the additional powers of those who might come to his aid.

GLN:8:31 A mist gathered before him, gradually thickening, and as it thickened, it gave off an ever increasing brilliant light, at the same time shaping itself into a glorious form of brightness. When the shaping was complete, a Being stood there, radiant as the sunlight and lovely as the moonbeam. Hurmanetar heard a voice coming out from the Glorious Being, which said, "Who are you that comes hither, wan of cheek and with lowered countenance, heavy-hearted and dejected in spirit, weary from a strange fray? There is lamentation, in your heart and surely none such as you has entered here beforetimes. Brave indeed is the one who seeks entry by force of arms." Hurmanetar answered, "O beautiful vision, indeed my heart is not light, for I have fought an inhuman contest. I have been assailed by hideous things unknown on Earth, things, which haunt the night dreams of men and are spoken of only in whispers. I have come seeking a friend, a companion of the hunt, the loyal one of my wanderings. His death lies heavily upon my heart; therefore, I have dared to come even unto this place."

GLN:8:32 The Form of Beauty said, "He whom you seek lies beyond the Waters of Death, but you who have passed the Guardians are permitted to go thence. One thing, however, you must not do. In the midst of the waters grows the plant of eternity, the forbidden tree, of which you and all men may not eat, a fruit of which was stolen by the serpent of ancient times. Partake of it now and you will suffer everlasting changelessness, the most dreadful of all fates. Go; tarry awhile, then return this way."

GLN:8:33 Hurmanetar passed over the still sullen waters to the Land of Waiting, where all spirits shine redly. He passed through the Great Doorway and came to the Place of Glory, the Land of Eternal living. He saw his friend, his companion of the hunt, the loyal one during his wanderings. Behold, there before his eyes was Yadol. Hurmanetar knew him, though he stood forth in a form more glorious than can be described to the understanding of men. He was here; life was in him, he was here in a bright and flowering place, a place of trees and waters, a place such as no man can describe.

GLN:8:34 Yadol spoke with Hurmanetar, and he spoke of things long forgotten by men and revealed truths unknown since the days when men walked with their Father. They spoke one with the other, they rested in pleasant places, they embraced, and they parted. Before Hurmanetar left, Yadol said, "As you have passed through the Portal of Death while yet uncalled from the embrace of the flesh, for no purpose other than gaining assurance that the dead do not pass into dust, it is decreed by the ordinance of this place that your life shall be shortened. Time enough, you will have; therefore, record the things of which we have spoken, that they may be guiding lights to men. Set them down in two books, one recording the Sacred Secrets, more precious than life itself and for the elect alone, The other recording the Sacred Mysteries for those who sit at the feet of the elect. One will be the Book of Truth Unveiled and the other the Book of Veiled Truth. the Book of Hidden Things."

GLN:8:35 Yadol continued, "Once men could pass easily from one sphere to another, then came the misty veil. Now men must pass a grim portal to span the spheres and, as the generations pass, this, too, will be closed to men. The secret of the substances, which, compounded together, become the horse which can bear men here, will remain with those who know the mysteries, but these will become even harder to reach. As the ages roll by, there will be many false mysteries, and perhaps the path will become closed or the way lost." These things Yadol said, and they talked of other things.

GLN:8:36 Hurmanetar returned. He passed over the Waters of Death, he was upheld by the Guardians of Form, by those who safeguarded the powers of the Great Key. He saluted the Glorious Being; he passed through the manifold chambers, through the courtyard and the manybolted doors, down the winding path lit by strange torches, through the cavern and out through the cave.

GLN:8:37 At the entrance, Formana still waited; he arose from his watch and greeted Hurmanetar warmly, saying, "I saw you as one dead, lying stiff between the twin flames, and I feared for you. Now, behold, you come forth with shining countenance, as one in whom life has been renewed. My heart rejoices for you, but let us not delay, let us depart from this dread place, for I have spent the whole long vigil in fear-enshrouded watchfulness."

GLN:8:38 They departed the mountain; they passed through the forest. They fought with things that lurked in the gloom beneath the tall, overhanging trees. They came through the Gate of Many Cubits and back to the pleasant pastures of Formana.

Chapter Nine – Asarua

GLN:9:1 Ancheti had been left with the daughters of Formana, who, having just reached maidenhood, were wilful and vexed him sorely, so that he sought places of solitude, being an unbearded youth unlearned in such matters. Beyond the place where they dwelt there was a river, and from the hillside, away from the forest, a small stream flowed down to join it. Upward of the stream was a valley, in which lay a small lake fed by an unfailing stream of sweet water. Here, in a house of wattle, dwelt a maiden whose name was Asarua, and she lived with her mother, Mamuah, who was a wise woman and blind.

GLN:9:2 The young woman had barely reached maidenhood and neither hunted for food nor dug in the ground. She dwelt in a garden of trees, her implements of toil being pruning hook and knife. Her days were spent in joyful tasks, and a song was ever on her lips. She worked happily among the trees, loosening the soil about their roots, cutting away the overgrowth and pulling up the weeds. She knew the art of fostering twigs so that fruits grew on trees strange to them. She grew vines, the fruits of which were not used for wine, and these she twined around bowers and over the branches of trees.

GLN:9:3 The women dwelt under the protection of Asarua's father, but the mother of Asarua was not of his household, for he was a strange king, though a mighty one. The place wherein they dwelt was fenced about and guarded by seven fierce hounds, tawny-coated and long of body. The maiden was supple and firm-breasted, she was tall and graceful, red of cheek and light of skin. Her sole garment was plainly woven and unadorned, for she lacked all the things, with which women bedeck themselves. Upon her head she wore a garland of leaves, and her only ornaments were flowers. She was shy and restrained of glance; nevertheless, she was not unobserved, for the eyes of men had fallen upon her from outside the place wherein she dwelt. They did not enter the place, for to them it was sacred ground, upon which men feared to trespass.

GLN:9:4 One day, a hunter passed by and became smitten by her beauty and modesty. He thought also of what she had to offer, fine fruits and green growing herbs, a garden of plenty where, in her embrace, he could find rest from the rigours of the hunt. He came to pay his court, garbed as for the chase with bow on back and spear in hand. He brought with him two wild geese and a young piglet to lay at her feet, but when his steps brought him within the fence, the hounds were loosed upon him. The hunter, seeing that he was unwelcome, took counsel with himself and thought, "Perhaps if I am uncouth in her sight, my brother the shepherd will seem better in her eyes."

GLN:9:5 Therefore, the shepherd came and sat on the grass outside the fence, paying his court with music from the pipes, but she paid no heed to him. Still he remained, until wearying of his piping, she called out, "Go, for what want I with one who sits blowing wind all day? Go learn music from the flowing waters."

GLN:9:6 In the days that followed, others came, among them a merchant, a rich man, a lord of grainfields and vineyards. Word of her beauty had been brought to him, and he was challenged by her inaccessibility. So he thought, "If indeed it is as men say, then I will have this woman for my own. Have I not riches enough to provide all that gladdens the heart of a woman? So he came wearing a mantle of scarlet with brooches of bronze. He wore buckles of silver and ornaments of carnelian and gold. He was a man possessed of a smooth, well oiled tongue, the owner of a storehouse of fine words. He came with attendants who drove off another who sat outside the fence. The merchant came boldly through the gate of the fence, but Asarua met him. When he paid court with bejewelled words, she said, "What have you to offer but gold and treasure? Think you that such unfeeling things can capture my heart? Am I to be bought as a woman bound within her father's household? Am I to be another counted among the many women you have known? An occupant of a cornerplace within your heart, O man of many lovers?" Then he was wrath with her; but she took no heed and the hounds drove him off, even the lordly one, for the ground here was sacred.

GLN:9:7 One day, not much later, the young Ancheti came that way and in passing, he saw the maiden Asarua, but because of his unfamiliarity with women, he hesitated to speak, though he, too, was smitten by her beauty and maidenly bearing.

GLN:9:8 Passing that way again Ancheti stopped by the place and seeing an old woman seated beneath the tree, he said to her, "Mother, may I have some water, for I am thirsty from journeying." The woman replied, "My son, there is water in plenty below on the other side of this place, which young ears should hear, but I am blind and cannot see. I, too, thirst and therefore I beg that you enter and bring me cool water from the pool below the waterfall." So Ancheti entered and drank, and he gave water to the woman. Though Asarua espied him from afar, she did not come near, but neither were the hounds allowed near him.

GLN:9:9 Hurmanetar had returned from his strange journey, but was puzzled when he saw Ancheti was silent and spoke little, that his thoughts were not inside him. So Hurmanetar questioned him, "Wherefore are you sick? What ails you? "Then, when Ancheti spoke to him of the maiden he had seen, Hurmanetar said, "This is a delicate matter and one not for the heavy tactics of men. Does not the fawn take flight at the sight of the hunting hound? While the moonflower that closes its petals at the touch of a man opens them at the touch of a woman. Your heart has guided you rightly when counselling caution, for you are ill equipped to catch this rare bird of beauty when unaided by wisdom. For a woman's errand, let us send a woman, the nightingale sings in the presence of the owl, but hides in silence when the hawk roosts nearby."

GLN:9:10 Then Hurmanetar spoke with the maidservant of she who had mothered the daughters of Formana, and the maidservant agreed to do the things he told her. Thus, on the morrow, she went forth unaccompanied, and coming to the place where Asarua dwelt, sat down outside the gate. When the eyes of the maiden eventually fell upon her Asarua saw the bent, old woman, weary and travel-stained from the journey; and out of kindness, for she was gentle and compassionate by nature, brought the old woman in, that she might sit under the shade of a tree to rest herself and eat some fruit.

GLN:9:11 After the maidservant had rested in the shade and refreshed herself, she spoke to Asarua and said, "How lovely is your garden, how well watered, how bright and refreshing its many fruits. I have heard much of this place, but more of you and your beauty; but no words of men have done justice to what I see with my own eyes." Asarua said, "The words of men often differ from the thoughts of their hearts; while flattering words are bait above a well set trap. Let us not talk of men and their wiles but of more pleasant things. Come, let us walk around the garden."

GLN:9:12 They walked and came to a place where grew a tamarisk tree, and about the tamarisk entwined a vine holding many bunches of grapes. The old maidservant said, "Behold this tree, of what value would it be were it not for the vine? Would it have any value, except as firewood? And what of the tree to which it clings, would it not straggle along the ground, laying in the dust to be crushed underfoot by any passer-by? It would be a helpless thing unable to raise itself up, a barren creeper bearing no fruit. So, see what benefit comes from their union, and learn wisdom. Is not the tree named as a man is named and the vine as a woman is named? We who are old see lessons in such things and, in learning from them, gain wisdom. The young are ever loath to even read to their benefit from the book which is always open before their eyes."

GLN:9:13 Asarua listened, but said little, and as they walked the maidservant spoke of the young daughters of Formana whom she had nursed, and of the ways of man and woman. She spoke as such women speak, her tongue following a winding road. The speech of men comes out like an arrow, but the speech of women comes out like a puff of smoke. Men talk with the naked tongue, but words from the mouth of a woman are veiled and devious. The tongue of a woman is a sword sheathed in silk. Not for nought are women called the twin-tongued. Perchance, these words were added in the days of Thalos, for not all men think thus of women.

GLN:9:14 The maidservant had an inexhaustible supply of words, and Asarua was so taken aback to hear the things of which she spoke that she could find no words to answer. Thus speaking, they came to the small dwelling place, where the mother of Asarua was preparing a meal. She invited the maidservant to eat with them and to sleep there that night, and this the maidservant gladly accepted.

GLN:9:15 After they had eaten, the maidservant spoke with Mamuah, the mother of Asarua, and the talk was of unfortunate women, whose daughters were fair yet refused to be married, daughters who closed their ears even to good advice on marriage, whether such women were true women or unnatural women. The words which mattered were few while the words in which they were buried were many, but the former were not lost on Mamuah, whose ears were not closed to such talk, and they entered her heart. She gave attentive ears when the other spoke of Ancheti who, though but a youth, was wise. Though he had not yet drunk deeply from the waters of wisdom, nevertheless the well from which he drew them was a never failing one. "Be wise," said the maidservant. "Choose this young man, for surely none better will come this way. He does not wander from his place of duty; he is not slothful in manner, nor does he spend his days in futile pleasures. He does not go from woman to woman, and while it is true that this could be because of his age, yet he speaks of women only with respect, which is not the way with budding fornicators. He is manly; he is of the blood of kings, and above all, he is wise, because he has a wise instructor. He is a youth of good promise and one who would not bestow his love lightly."

GLN:9:16 The mother of Asarua heard the words of the maidservant with both ears, and when the maidservant was departing said, "Come again when the moon is new, that we may speak more of these matters." Ancheti visited the place again and when the maidservant returned at the new moon, Mamuah said, "It is well, my daughter will marry the youth, Ancheti. But first he must bide in the place where he now serves for one year; then, he must labour in this place for one year; after this he may marry Asarua with my blessing." This seemed good in the eyes of Ancheti, and so it was that he laboured two years in order to marry Asarua.

Chapter Ten – Death of Hurmanetar

GLN:10:1 In the days when the Elshumban were gathered in war hosts, Hurmanetar departed with his household and the household of Ancheti to dwell in the land between the Great River of Sweet Waters and the Bitter Waters of the West, and they built an encampment there. They were in a land where some men spoke as Hurmanetar spoke, and though there were men of blood with them, the people of the land let Hurmanetar and those with him dwell in peace among them, because in those days men were inflicted with Inahana.

GLN:10:2 When the task set upon him was nigh finished, Hurmanetar knew that his days in the land of the living were not to be many more; therefore, he betook himself into a place of solitude. There he fasted for many days, casting his spirit that it might commune with the Father of the Gods, but the voice of God remained silent. Then, he left that place, going into a cave, where he dwelt in the half light for many days; but again there was no response from the Father of the Gods. So Hurmanetar departed from the cave and returned to his people, where he was heard to say, "Woe, for truly my God has forsaken me and remains dumb against my pleadings. yet, I have done all the things told me beforetimes and written in the great Book, wherefore have I failed?

GLN:10:3 Then he went apart from the people and slept alone, for his heart was heavy. But behold, in the night he had a dream. In it, he saw the Sacred Symbols spread out upon a cloth of white linen, and each was displayed according to its form. As he gazed upon them and numbered them, each by its own number, an ass came and ate up the Sacred Symbols, and lo, the ass became a falcon. Then as he looked, the falcon became a cow, and between its horns was a crown of silver and a crown of gold, and the cow spoke to Hurmanetar, saying, "Drink of my milk, and anoint your eyes with it; thus they will be opened and you will see." Hurmanetar drank the milk and anointed his eyes, and then he awoke. Remembering the dream and being wise, he needed no other to interpret it for him. So then, he straightway did the things which had to be done, about which those with understanding will know, and departed from the people.

GLN:10:4 Hurmanetar went out towards a place of solitude, about one day's journey distant. Having gone about half the way, he became weary under the noonday sun, and so sat down beneath a tree to rest in its shade. Then, as he drowsed, behold, a great flash of light came down from out of Heaven, and it smote the ground before him. He heard a great noise like a mighty whip crack, and he was blinded. Then, he heard a voice saying, "Behold I am here, the God of Gods and the God of Men in the beginning." Hearing this, Hurmanetar fell upon his face and cried, "O Great One, I am Your servant."

GLN:10:5 Then God said, "Wherefore would you open a door unto me? Because the race of man has been defiled, and men are no longer with Me, am I not the withdrawn One, the Hidden One?"

GLN:10:6 Hurmanetar, still on the ground, answered, "O Father of the Gods, I Your servant would know Your will. I have a task nigh finished and seek to know whether it is well in Your sight, or whether it is a thing done without Your blessing."

GLN:10:7 God answered Hurmanetar, saying, "Is this not a Sacred Thing, a heritage saved and handed down from the days when men walked with Me? Therefore, it is a good thing, though care must be taken to ensure it is not disclosed to the eyes of profane men. The concoctions, which, when properly compounded, will enable men to span the spheres can also, used otherwise, give men near unlimited potency and extreme pleasure with woman-kind. Therefore, such things must be carefully safeguarded, for in the hands of lesser men, they will certainly be abused. But let it all be as it is written; do with it as you have been instructed."

GLN:10:8 "You call upon Me as the Father of the Gods, nor do you err in this. Yet I am the Hidden God, the God of Secret Manifestation, the Wronged God, the Betrayed God, the Disappointed God. I am the God who sought to give love Divine to men by making them My heirs, making them partakers of divinity, co-creators with Me. But men spurn their birthright, not through wickedness alone, but through their weakness and love of pleasure. Therefore, the love once offered cannot now be displayed in all its glory; it cannot be revealed in its beauty; it must now be leavened with severity and chastisement. This, so that those who are the inheritors of divinity may return to it with undiminished powers, but purged of their weaknesses and love of unprofitable pleasure. This you should know, that men may know: Divinity of itself is not a created thing and cannot be bestowed as a gift. It comes as the crown of achievement. I, the Almighty God who, by taking thought can create ten thousand worlds, say this."

GLN:10:9 "Men have said, as they will say throughout the ages, 'Why, if God be almighty, can He not create perfection immediately? Why does He not create beings having the knowledge of divine love forthwith? Why have Earth, with all its trials and tribulations?' Know this; what appears to you as ages in time is, to me, but a flash of thought in a moment of eternity. I breathed in, the hosts of earths and the spheres were not. I breathed out and the hosts of earths and spheres were. I breathe in, and they are no more. All things exist within the Eternal One and that which men know as the span of time is the act of creation."

GLN:10:10 "Mark the flight of an arrow from the hands of a bowman. It flies from the bent bow; time passes, then it finds its mark. But to Me, the arrow leaves the bow and strikes the mark together. Distance, time and change are not with Me. Once I, your God, was not apart from man, My offspring. Now I am veiled from his sight, not because I have willed it so, but because man has chosen to bring this about. The barrier between us grows ever more dense, as man wantonly spurns his birthright; henceforth, it may be penetrated only by long and arduous preparations, and even then those who would do so must know the key. I come to you, not because of your preparations but because your God is ever ready to incline towards men. Though there is this barrier between us, it is not impervious to the sincere prayers of a pure heart. This, men should know. As for you, your days are numbered, you are now no more than the basket holding the seeds, which will be strewn and sown by another hand. Many things of which I have spoken are not for the ears of men, for such knowledge, freely bestowed, would not benefit them. Other things are beyond their present understanding; let these, therefore, be recorded unto the generations of men yet unborn. Men are now as children and must learn again as children, being taught childish tales."

GLN:10:11 "Therefore, go hence, go to Ancheti, and tell him of these things. Say also that his God, I Who Am, chooses him as the sower of seeds. Let him know that I Who Am will guide his steps and will open a door in the barrier, that he may hear my voice. Let your eyes now see again and, behold, I Am Who I Am."

GLN:10:12 Then Hurmanetar left the place where he had seen the face of the Father of Gods, returning to the encampment of his people, which had been set up in the midst of pastureland. When he drew nigh he saw cattle lying beside the running waters, and men were moving among them. The cattle were dead and their bellies swollen. Men came up to Hurmanetar and cried, "Behold, the sustenance of our children is taken from their mouths. The cattle have eaten a herb that burns as fire in their bellies so they crave water, drinking until they become overfilled, and their bellies burst from within; therefore they die. Who is this whom you call Father of the Gods? Perchance the gods do have a father, but where is the god who protects men? Where is the god who is the Father of Men? While you leave us to pay homage to the Exalted One, who may concern Himself with the affairs of the gods but has no concern for the welfare of men, our cattle die. Because of your words, we have neglected to build an altar to Shemakin or to pay homage to Yahana; truly we are men who have been deceived and led astray. We are men who have walked with their eyes turned upward and fallen into a quicksand. Tell us then, O wise one, who are the gods of men and of cattle?"

GLN:10:13 This filled the heart of Hurmanetar with ire, and he cried out to the wrathful people, "Wherefore do you cry out to me and seek some god to come to your aid? There is but one God, and these that you call gods are but manifestations of His members. Why do you seek to cast blame on God for your own neglect? Has He not relinquished His hold on all creatures that serve man and given them into your hands? Behold the beasts of the forest and wilderness; do they eat of the herb that poisons? Are they not able to know the herb that is harmful and the herb that nourishes? The herb that heals in sickness and the herb that brings death? Who taught them this wisdom? There are creatures under the care of God, which know not the slothful care of man, therefore they are safe from the deadly herb and pass it by. But you, having taken these poor beasts to benefit from them, are solely responsible for their wellbeing. They are your responsibility."

GLN:10:14 "The Father of the Gods made cattle as He made all creatures, and while He ruled their ways, they were protected from the deadly herbs. Then men took them unto themselves so they might serve them. They yielded milk and cheese to nourish them and firm meat to sustain them, their hides covered them warmly as they slept. These things the cattle gave, not unto God, but unto man. Therefore, who should protect and care for them, he who benefits or He who does not? Do you expect God to herd your cattle? To keep them from the deadly herb while you slumber in the shade? Is this not a just reward for your slothfulness? You know that the herb is deadly, but these cattle, the dumb servants of man, know it not, for they are delivered into your care. Would you take all they give while denying them the diligence of your protection? What kind of men are you who cry, "Woe unto us, whom God has forsaken." Who wring their hands, saying, "What god shall we seek to aid us in our self-wrought calamity? Arise like men, to shoulder the burden of your own slothfulness and lack of diligence. Never fear that God will fail man, for if man does the duties of man, God will do the duties of God, for it is man who falls short. It is man who seeks to take more than he gives. Surely whatever man takes for his benefit, also becomes his responsibility. God decrees that man may take whatever he will for his own use, but in so doing, he must also assume responsibility for its care and rightful use. Is this unjust?" The men said no more.

GLN:10:15 Hurmanetar then made the men draw the cattle up out of the water, and some which had eaten of the deadly herb were saved. He then divided the pastures and sent men to seek out the places of the deadly herb and cut it from the soil.

GLN:10:16 One day, Hurmanetar was going about the encampment, and he came upon a man burying his newly born daughter, and Hurmanetar was wrathful at the man for such a deed. It was an abomination performed by the sand wanderers and the wild men who dwelt in the wilderness. Taking the child, Hurmanetar brought it to the wife of Ancheti, who saved it so it lived. It was named Mahat, meaning pure of heart, but because of the sand which had filled her eyes, she was blind.

GLN:10:17 The strangers about the encampment became enraged against Hurmanetar because of what he had done. Also, because he had struck the father of the child so he bled, they demanded that the blood be requited. They said, "This is an unjust deed, for he who buries a daughter because he lacks sustenance for her does no wrong in our eyes. Is it not better that she be buried in the ground out of sight than kept with disgrace? Is it not for the father to decide whether a daughter should live? Has a woman a soul of her own? Is she not no more than the maker of the body, while the soul is given into her keeping by man?"

GLN:10:18 The strangers about the encampment were not so many, while those with Hurmanetar were many and strong, but he dealt justly with those claiming payment for the blood. They were given a piece of silver and a calf that was ready for the slaughter. Thus, Mahat came into the household of Ancheti.

GLN:10:19 Hurmanetar was sitting with Ancheti and said to him, "I have spoken to you of the happening while I sat beneath a tree in a place of solitude, and of matters which you should know in order to be wise. Into your keeping have been given the treasures I have wrought by my own hands, and you are well instructed in the Sacred Things and the Mysteries. You have a destiny upon you, which may not be fulfilled in this place, while the sustenance obtainable here declines day by day. Therefore, let us depart and go a long journey by way of the bitter waters, for should we go by way of the forest or through the great wilderness, we may not live. Our flocks and herds can be driven before us, for the road is wide and well watered. Let us not delay in this place, for already there is a restlessness among the people here."

GLN:10:20 So they departed from that place, journeying towards the bitter waters and when they came there they turned southward, continuing until they came to Basor. There, they encamped, for the death sickness had come upon Hurmanetar. As he lay upon a couch of sheepskins, he called for Ancheti, but he did not come, for he had gone before them to spy out the land. However, Ancheti did come before Hurmanetar passed from Earth, and Hurmanetar knew he was there and called him to his side. Then Hurmanetar said, "My hour is at hand, but I am without fear, knowing I go not to a place where men eat dust, where all is darkness and gloom. The fears of my youth are but shadows having no substance; they flee before the pure light of Truth."

GLN:10:21 "Upon you there is a great destiny, may you reach out and grasp that, which your heart desires, and having attained it, use it to deliver all men from the darkness of ignorance. Go forth like the sun who throws his rays down like a net over the land to enlighten it. Go to a land where the honest man will be made rich and the dishonest man impoverished, for the balances must be adjusted so that riches cease to be the reward of dishonesty and deceit. Go to a land where those holding places of power and position will stand forth as examples of goodness and honesty; where none but the worthy occupy high positions; where those who have possessions and estate use these to succour the needy and resist the strength of those who oppress the weak and unprotected."

GLN:10:22 Ancheti said, "But where is this land, and how shall I find it?' Hurmanetar answered, "Were there such a place, what good purpose would you serve by going there'? What you will have to do would have been done already by another."

GLN:10:23 Hurmanetar died and was buried deep within the ground ,and none knows his tomb. May he live forever and dwell with the Father of the Gods whom he served!

GLN:10:24 These things concerning Hurmanetar have been rewritten many times, but the copies have always been true. That which follows has been added on, but when made and by whom, it is impossible to discover.

GLN:10:25 Hurmanetar is buried in the land of Philistia. Is this Okichia?

GLN:10:26 The father of Hurmanetar was Nimrod of the Twin Bows. This, I doubt, and it is not stated.

GLN:10:27 The stone of Makilim is at Bethgal even now. The words on the tomb of Yadol are: 'He died because he was not as other men'. I, Frastonis, have seen it.

GLN:10:28 Could this be when eighty generations have passed? Men of this race are unsound witnesses. The Samarites say Yadol was not mortal man.

GLN:10:29 This we know in truth: the deeds of Hurmanetar and Yadol are more fully told in The Tales of the Hithites.

GLN:10:30 The shield of Ancheti was called the Big Shaker, and painted upon it was a likeness of the mudhopping bird. It was this bird that taught men writing, for it left mud marks, which men first read as omens, later forming them into signs, which could be read. They are not as ours, though men among us can read them.

GLN:10:31 Ancheti taught the mystery of metals in Okichia, a land of beer, bread and milk. He was renowned in the Twinlands of Light.

GLN:10:32 Mahat, the blind one who remained virgin, guided Ancheti to this land while yet a child. She was filled with the inner light of wisdom and saw with the spirit. When he knew not which way to go, her father sat her on the ground and held a breast feather before her, upon which she blew. He went whichever way it inclined and was never led astray. Later, she used this method when settling disputes and giving judgements. She was greatly honoured, for in the whole land, there was no wiser woman.

GLN:10:33 We who make these writings indestructible have abandoned the Book of Ancheti, for it has nought of value to those who follow us, and this is a work of much labour. It contains laws for a people living in a land called Okichia, who must have been less than barbarians, for he forbade such things as the eating of children newly born, the mixing and drying of their blood for eating in uniting brothers and the hanging up of women in travail. Also the cutting of a woman's private parts and the deballing of men.

Chapter Eleven – Teachings of Yosira

GLN:11:1 These are the words for the Sons of the True Doctrine, written in the temple of Sacred Mysteries at Yankeb in the Days of Darkness, by the Unnamed Lord of the Secret Belief, who then lived. The true knowledge of the teachings and mysteries of Yosira concerning the spirit within the body, taken from his books and rewritten truly after the custom of writing.

GLN:11:2 Yosira spoke to his Sons in this manner, "I am the Viceregent of the God of Gods. I am the custodian of the Books of Power. I am the Voice of Heaven. I am one sent into Tamerua as a lightbearer, that a call may go thence throughout all lands. Let every man be watchful of his deeds and ways. Whosoever be watchful of himself is a man of wisdom, for he shall be saved from the terror of everlasting darkness."

GLN:11:3 "I am the torchbearer running before the chairlitter of Truth. I come to reveal the greatness of men, to tell them of their immortal selves, of their spirits which have to be ransomed from the doom of devouring darkness."

GLN:11:4 "The God of Gods spoke unto me, saying, "Long have you dwelt under my shadow and listened to my words. Now, arise and go hence to a land where these things, of which we have spoken, can be established. To a place whither I shall lead you, for it is not proper that those who dwell there should remain uninstructed. Behold, I have given you the secret of immortality, but know that, though all men are born into a heritage of immortality, not all enjoy it. The God of Gods, in His infinite mercy, plunges many into the waters of forgetfulness. Yet even from there, they may return to be renewed, not of themselves but through the supplications of others."

GLN:11:5 When Yosira came into Tamerua, he gathered his sons together on the stones beneath the place called Homtree and spoke to them in this manner, "I am the Dawnlighter and a torchbearer for the God of Gods. These are my words, which you will do well to absorb, as the dry sands soaks up water. Though they are words of wisdom, they are useless unless accepted by men who have control over themselves. They have no value to men who are unable to feel compassion for others or who close their ears to Truth."

GLN:11:6 "You are the few chosen ones, my sons, light of my light, who shall hand the light on down through the generations. To you, I give the true conception of God. To you, I give this standard, that it may be a rallying point for those who will accompany us; for we stand on the borders of a land, which has found favour in the eyes of our God."

GLN:11:7 "With us are fighting men, but they are few, while those who stand ready to repel us are many. Therefore, we will not set ourselves against them in battle array, but go among them with guile, to gather many who will fight with us. You shall be the light of the fighting men, even as I am your light and the God of Gods my light."

GLN:11:8 "The light that is with me was kindled at The Supreme Source, which is the God of Gods. Therefore, my light shines with such brilliance that it must be veiled in part, lest it blind you. It is even as the sun be seen through a veil of cloud, it may be gazed upon for as long as desired. Seen thus, it is a thing of beauty and mystery, not something, which burns and consumes the eyes of the beholder."

GLN:11:9 "Therefore, even as I veil my light from you, so shall you veil your lights from the eyes of the uninstructed. Yet, in all matters not pertaining to the light, you shall instruct them in the fullness of Truth. In all matters concerning their bodies, you shall instruct them in Truth. But in all matters concerning the Lord of the Body, you shall instruct them with a light that is veiled."

GLN:11:10 "Behold the nature of man. Within him is a spark from the Divine Source, and this is the Lord of the Body. This alone is everlasting, this alone of man is his true self. This spark is enwrapped within a heavy mantle of matter; it is enclosed in a covering of earthly clay. This spark alone is the seat of life; it alone has understanding and thought. Such things are not with the clay of the flesh, neither are they kin to the stones from which the bones come. The life within man radiates out from the enclosed spark, and through the blood, endows the body with life and heat. Life gives forth heat, and the greater the life, the greater the heat."

GLN:11:11 "As the sun gives light and fire spreads heat, as the flower radiates perfume, so does the Central Light give forth a vaporous unseeable glow, and this our fathers called the Breath of God. This Breath comes forth in two manifestations: there is a heavy form and a light form, and from these, all things are compounded. From The One comes the Sacred Glow in its two aspects, which men call the Breath of God, and from this are made all things, which are in Heaven and Earth."

GLN:11:12 "Above is the God of Gods, and below Him are Heaven and Earth. Heaven is divided in twain; there is a Place of Light and a Place of Darkness. Within the Place of Light dwell the spirits of Good and within the Place of Darkness dwell the spirits of evil. Between them, the boundary is not fixed but flows back and forth according to their fluctuating strengths. But they who abide in the light shall always prevail, for light will ever dispel darkness. Therefore, those who dwell in darkness withdraw before the brilliance of those who dwell in the light. This light and darkness are not such as men can understand, for it is not the light and darkness known on Earth."

GLN:11:13 "Before the Gates of Heaven is the Land of the Horizon, whence go all who depart from their earthly body. From here, there are two great gates, one leads to the Place of Light, and the other to the Place of Darkness, and the Lord of the Body is admitted into its appointed place according to its likeness. He who is filled with the light and is a k cannot go to the Place of Darkness, for it would draw back before him. Neither can he who is a Dark One go into the Place of Light, for there, he would shrivel before the light, as the white worm coming forth from the damp darkness of its hole shrivels in the light of the sun."

GLN:11:14 "Between Heaven and Earth, there is a great gulf across which the dwellers in Heaven may not return, but Earth is not wholly beyond their reach. Man receives, from the Place of Light, that which influences him for good, and from the Place of Darkness, that which affects him for evil. These things may be written, but the secret things concerning them may not be recorded in such manner that they come to the knowledge of the unenlightened men."

GLN:11:15 "That which comes from Heaven, whether influencing for good or evil, comes forth as shades in the likeness of men, which is rare; or much more often as lukim, which are like unto motes. It may also come as waves of air, but not air such as we breathe and feel. It is something altogether different in nature. Things come forth which are not stable, and these are the formless Ones. All things are held in form by the Breath of God, which changes formlessness, but the formless Ones can alter form into instability."

GLN:11:16 'There are three great spheres, and that containing the Earth is held together by the Great Glow outflowing from the God of Gods. That part of the Great Glow, which is light and contains life is called Manah, while that which is heavy and contains the flesh of things of the Earth is called Manyu."

GLN:11:17 "The One Who is the God of Gods is so great that He cannot be defined in the speech of men. Neither can they conceive Him in their thoughts, for He is beyond their understanding. Mortal man has limitations; therefore, let men conceive Him as they will. It is of no importance, providing their conception serves both His purpose and the glorification of man."

GLN:11:18 "Man is not yet great, and until he becomes so it is well that he worship the many Godforms conceived within his thoughts, providing they be such as tend to raise him above himself. Nor do ritual and worship do harm of themselves, unless they, too, thickly overlay the truth so it is buried from sight. Ritual and outward forms of worship can be aids to purification of thought and provide a kind of sustenance for the Lord of the Body. What are the Lesser Gods beloved by unawakened men but thought-conceived friends and guides? Yet, this is a dangerous path men tread, balanced between light and darkness. Therefore, when man wanders towards the abyss of darkness, reveal a little more light, that he may see and so return to the path. Beware, too, lest he follow gods that are false guides and would lure him into the quicksand of carnality, or into the wilderness of ignorance."

GLN:11:19 Before crossing into Tamuera, Yosira chose captains to be over the fighting men, and they sent forth men to spy out the land. He also sent some from among his sons into the land of Tewar, that they might talk with the people there, and these came back bringing hostages from the governors of the land of Tewar. Then, Yosira spoke with the sons of the governors and they gave ear to his words; they were receptive to his speech.

GLN:11:20 Yosira spoke to the people, "These are the words of the God of the Gods. Henceforth, no child shall be sold into bondage by its father or by any man who has ward over it. Such may not yet be the custom of all the people in this land, but if they become mighty, this they may do, for such is the nature of men.

GLN:11:21 "If a man have a woman in bondage, he shall not cause her to become a harlot unto men, for this is a great wickedness and he shall not go unpunished. If she become with child unto her master, then neither she nor the child shall be given in bondage to another. But if she be given to a freeman who takes her in marriage, then it will be well."

GLN:11:22 "The greatest wickedness in the eyes of the God of Gods is all incest of the first degree, which is that between mother and son or father and daughter; or between the mother's mother and the son of the mother, or between the mother's father and the daughter of the mother; or between the father's father and the father's daughter, or between the father's mother and the father's son. This is a wickedness unto the God of Gods, for it calls forth the strongest of the Formless Ones, causing it to enter into an earthly body to become an abomination before the eyes of God and man. Therefore, they who commit such an act shall perish by fire. If it be committed with a child, then, the child shall not perish, but it shall be branded with the mark of incest."

GLN:11:23 "Adultery is a foul and evil thing which you shall abhor, for it permits the lukim to pollute the fountain of life. In a far off land there lived a queen more beautiful than the Dawnflower, who, because she was powerful, disregarded her heritage of womanhood. As powerful kings had many wives, she thought she could do likewise with men. The God of Gods and Creator of Life created men and women intending that each should play a different role. They are in no wise alike, for as men have their function, so do women have theirs. What is meet for one is not meet for the other, and because the Creator made them as they are, each should follow their own path, never seeking to journey along the other's. Now, while the seed of one man was yet with her, this queen took the seed of another, and the seed of one man strove with that of the other so that both perished and became a corrupt pasture. Thus, the way was cleared for lukim to enter into the antechamber of life and the sacred shrine of life was polluted, becoming the breeding place of foulness. So it was that when other men came unto her, the flesh of their bodies was seized upon by the lukim and corrupted, for foul lukim had made their abode within the woman. So the wellspring of life became a fountain of polluting evil. Adultery is an abomination to the Bestower of Life; therefore, let it not go unpunished."

GLN:11:24 "None shall sleep in the bed of another, unless the spell of his presence be first removed. For he who goes into any place or takes up any thing while it is under the spell of another's presence, shall surely suffer. They who are of the same kin living under the one roof will not suffer unless sickness already be there."

GLN:11:25 "None shall eat from the platter of another or drink from his drinking vessel until the spell of his presence has been removed. None among those who know the God of Gods shall walk in anything poured out for a libation unto strange gods, neither shall he touch any part of the libation. If it come upon him he shall go forthwith to the Master of Mysteries and be cleansed."

GLN:11:26 Yosira said unto the people, "These are the words of the God of Gods. None among you shall wash himself in water used by another and contained within anything made by the hand of man. None among those who know God shall touch a woman while the days of her heritage are upon her. No man shall go unto a woman with unwashed hands, and when man and woman have lain together, both shall purify themselves before going about their tasks."

GLN:11:27 "Among the lukim none is more subtle than the nableh, which seek sustenance among the food of men. Therefore, if you have bread within your dwelling, then it shall not be hung up; but if there be meat or fish, then it shall be suspended within the dwelling. If you have bran or meal which has been pounded, then it shall be kept in a capped container with nowrata flowers; thus the lukim will not come upon it. Neither crushed corn nor the crumbs of any repast shall be left within the sight of man or within the boundaries of the dwelling, lest the nableh seize upon them for sustenance. All things that have held life but have not been used for food shall be buried within the ground. All vessels which have held food but hold it no longer shall be made clean with sun and sand."

GLN:11:28 "When the flesh of any beast or of fish or fowl becomes dark in your keeping or has the smell of rottenness upon it, then it is a sign that the nableh have come upon it and it shall be taken out and buried where no beast can come upon it. Thus, the nableh are left without sustenance and will be forced back into their dark abode. But if you permit them to sustain themselves, then they will come in their hosts and, being fattened and strengthened, will afflict you with many terrors during night watches."

GLN:11:29 "If the pouring place or the spout of any pitcher or pot have a blackness upon it, then that pitcher or pot shall be broken, for it has been entered by the fiery lukim. If any who know God eat with strangers, they shall purify themselves at the rising of the sun on the following day. If any among you eat with a hand uncleansed by water or sand, then be prepared for attack by the lukim of the night. He who draws the blood of any beast must cleanse himself of all blood, lest he be attacked by the dark lukim. Neither food nor drink of any kind shall be kept under a bed or against a sleeping place, lest the lukim of the night come and take up their abode therein." These are words of the God of Gods spoken through the mouth of Yosira.

GLN:11:30 Yosira said this also, "All things, which may sustain the lukim are to be buried or burnt. Anything coming forth from the nostrils or mouth of any man or woman is rejected from within and becomes sustenance for the lukim. Still waters that lie upon the ground are their drinking places and forbidden to men. Water shall not be used as drink unless it be drawn from within the ground, or be in a place where it is shaded by trees."

GLN:11:31 "Eat only food known to be wholesome and which gives contentment to the stomach. In taste, it should be soothing and refreshing, never bringing pain and discomfort. Eat not of anything that is too dry or oversalted, or which brings sickness upon you. Any food, of which men eat and has become rotten or mouldy has been seized by the lukim for sustenance; this you can see, for the rottenness and mould upon it is the excreta of lukim."

GLN:11:32 "Anything that has blood in it and is dead, having died of itself, shall not be eaten, for the lukim have made their abode in it. No man shall eat uncooked meat; even that, which the sandfarers carry shall not be eaten."

GLN:11:33 "The slaying of any man or any woman is forbidden, but it is not unlawful to slay in war or in self-defence, or to uphold the purity of the household and home. To kill deceitfully or to strike from behind is murder and shall not go unpunished. If blood be shed, it shall not cry out from the ground in vain, and unto the kinsmen of each one slain shall be the order of revenge."

GLN:11:34 "If you swear an oath one with another, saying, "Great God, bear witness" or before any strange god, to deceive another man, then consider, for only the most foolhardy turn their back on such an oath. For it is sworn on the life of the Lord of the Body, and if it be broken, the Lord of your Body will be everlastingly disfigured with an unremovable scar. Man has many trials to overcome in his life, and not the least of these tests is oathkeeping. Though an oath may diminish and become nothing with the passing years according to the memories of men, it is everlastingly impressed on the Lord of the Body. Wiser far is he who never makes an oath."

GLN:11:35 "If any man say, "The whirlwind and the sandstorm, the floodwaters and the burning fire, these do I fear because these I see, but the lukim, which I see not neither do I fear, that man is a fool, for he knows not the deficiencies of his own eyes. The lukim, he will learn to know by their manifestations, for they will seize upon his body and torment it, sometimes even unto death. It is likewise with the God of Gods; none may see Him, but by His manifestations is He made known unto men."

GLN:11:36 Yosira spoke to the captains of the fighting men and to those who were with them and said, "When we come into this new land, all things that the people who dwell therein hold sacred you will neither defile nor mock. Neither shall you stir up strife with any man, for we come to them as friends, not foes." Therefore, when Yosira and all those with him came up into the land of Tewar and dwelt there, peace was in the land.

GLN:11:37 Then Yosira taught the people of Tewar the weaving of cloth and the working of metals, and showed them how to make tools and weapons of metal cast in a mysterious manner. But the secret of the sharp-edged weapons, he revealed only to his own.

GLN:11:38 The people of Tewar built a habitation for Yosira and a temple of brick bound with reeds. There were skins upon the walls and on the floor, and the doors were of wood. Then Yosira spoke to his sons in this manner, "These are the things in which the people of this place shall be instructed: The dove is the most sacred of birds and shall not be eaten, but if people say, "Forbid it not to us for sacrifice to our gods," then, it shall not be forbidden them."

GLN:11:39 "The milk of all beasts which do not have horns and part the hoof is not for the sustenance of man, but if the people say, "Forbid it not, for it is our custom," then it shall not be forbidden them."

GLN:11:40 "The sacrifice of breast children at the burial of the dead shall be forbidden, for the blood of the young cannot provide life for the old, each man being the fashioner of his own destiny. He that has life shall bear it with him, and none can possess the body and life of a breast child except the God who gave it life. He who buries a living breast child with the dead shall himself die."

GLN:11:41 "All things buried with the departed one, whether they be weapons or dishes, instruments or ornaments, shall have the form released from them before they are placed within the ground."

GLN:11:42 "This shall be the law unto all those who work with metal, whether it be gold, silver or copper: One day in seven shall be a day of rest for the fires herewith the metals are wrought. On this day no fire will be lit and no metal touched or moved from its place. On the even of this day, all things of metal that have been made since the last day of rest shall be placed in a trough of sanctified oil, remaining there until their appointed time. Nothing shall go out from the workplace of a craftsman in metal until it has passed through the oil."

Chapter Twelve – Rule of Yosira

GLN:12:1 Yosira gathered his sons about him and spoke to them thus: "These are the days of the dawnlight, and I am the Dawnlighter from beyond Bashiru. I am the Torchbearer for the God of Gods. These are the laws, which I made for my people in the land of Tewar, the laws of one speaking with the mouth of the God above all gods."

GLN:12:2 "He who places a spear or arrow within a dead body shall be accursed, and his hand and arm will become things of evil. They will swell up and become consumed by fire. Likewise shall be accursed who looses these weapons against another, but if it be a man of Tamuera who looses the weapons, then he shall die by them himself, for he is beyond the reach of the curse."

GLN:12:3 "A tree that reaches up above twice the height of a man shall not be stricken for burning or to take away its land. But if it be dedicated to the adze and is then used by a craftsman in wood, then it may be stricken and cut. Trees are not things to be lightly dealt with, for they move the winds, which cross the face of the Earth and generate these in great forests of the North and South. The slaughter of a tree is no less wrong than the slaughter of an ox or a sheep, for the same breath of life is in each. Therefore, never bring them low wantonly. Are not trees held sacred by the people of this land? Is it not more reasonable to dedicate a mighty tree or a grove of trees to a god than a mute stone or object cut from wood?"

GLN:12:4 Therefore, when Yosira moved among the people he did not forbid them their grave groves, nor did he silence the words of the women, who tended them. But Yosira said, "These things are for women and not for men, let the women bide, but men should follow the callings of men and their place is not among the grave groves."

GLN:12:5 Now, when Yosira came among the people, they dwelt away from the river, fearing the god of moving waters who molested them at night. But Yosira bound the god of moving waters, so he no longer troubled the people. Then Yosira bade them build their dwelling places beside the moving waters, decreeing that none should dwell beside still waters unless the still waters be filled with the life of fishes.

GLN:12:6 In those days men sought to appease the Formless Ones and the Spirits of the Night with offerings and worship.

GLN:12:7 But Yosira forbade them this, and he surrounded the whole land with a protective wall, which no Dark Spirit could penetrate, while all those within were dissolved. Every Dark Spirit being neither male nor female and every Dark Spirit, which clothed itself in the shape of a beast or bird was bound and cast back into the Place of Darkness.

GLN:12:8 All men who were blood kindred with the beasts of the forest or with fowl or with serpent, dwelt together according to their kinship, and were divided thereby. Yosira forbade them not their kinship but did forbid the rule of blood. He spoke to the people in this manner: "Great are the ties of that thing, which binds men together and joins them with their forefathers, but greater still is each man in himself, his destiny lying within himself alone and not within his kindred. Man is not a drop of water in the stream of life, but a fish that swims within the stream. Yet insofar as these things have ever been, the twenty-four great kinships shall remain secured in their establishment."

GLN:12:9 Before the coming of Yosira, a man could not take to wife a woman of his own blood, but Yosira redeemed the land with blood, safeguarding it against barrenness. So henceforth men could take wives from among their own blood kindred, and the land remained fruitful. This, the Spirit of Life, became strong among men, for it was not spread out to become diluted and weakened.

GLN:12:10 Until Yosira came, none in this land knew of hokew, and it filled men with fear and awe, but Yosira revealed all its secrets to his sons, and the secrets are known even in these days. Hokew is that, which sustains the Dawndwellers. It is but thinly spread throughout the Earth, and before the days of Yosira, men could gather it, storing it in stones and in sacred objects. It may be drawn upon by the spirits of men, as women draw water from a well. It is hokew, which bestows fertility, causing flocks to multiply and crops to increase. Its secrets are known by the Twice Born.

GLN:12:11 Though in the days of his distress, Yosira called upon his Father in Kanogmahu, he forbade his sons to call upon Him likewise, for Yosira was their father on Earth and their advocate in the Hall of Admission. Therefore, none can call upon Him with impunity, for if He dealt with them, He would neglect His task among the Dawndwellers. Nor is any man justified in calling upon the spirit of a Departed One, for they are beyond concern for the everyday affairs of men.

GLN:12:12 When the Sons of Yosira had established their rule over the people, the leaders of the people came to Yosira desiring to make him their king, so he would rule over them. But when they came before him, Yosira replied to their wish in this manner, "I am the mouth of the God of Gods and the light of my people. I will be the father of your king and the director of his footsteps, but your king I cannot be, for I am dedicated in service to the God of Gods." Saying this, Yosira then took his son, who was grown to manhood, and led him forth by the hand, giving him to the people to be their king.

GLN:12:13 Later, while the leaders and governors of the people still remained gathered after the anointing of their king, Yosira spoke to them as the mouth of God. He said, "To judge justly between man and man is one of the greatest obligations of a king and those who stand in his place. So from this day hence, judgement shall not be given by those who sit under the trees, listening to the words whispered among the leaves. However, if three men sit far apart and each gives alike judgement, the words from their mouths being the same, then the judgement shall be good. However, if it is a matter where a life can be forfeit or property taken away, a family divided or a man or woman enslaved, then judgement shall be given only by the king or by one who wears his mantle and bears his burden."

GLN:12:14 "Sacred waters are living waters filled with the power of hokew and shall no longer be used for any purpose other than sanctification and purification. No longer shall they be used to decide whether a wife be guilty of adultery; henceforth, she shall be tested by the bitter draught alone."

GLN:12:15 "He who eats the flesh of swine shall be accursed, for to eat the flesh of swine is to eat something dedicated to the fathers of men and an abomination. Flesh of the ass shall not be eaten, for it diminishes the vigour of men."

GLN:12:16 "Henceforth, the bodies of the dead shall not be broken or burnt, for the hokew within them departs with the Lord of the Body. Therefore, nothing can be added unto a Victorious One by rendering up the essence of his earthly mantle through the flames of the fire."

GLN:12:17 "The people shall not be denied their feasts, nor shall they be forbidden the rituals of fruitfulness. Their offerings to any god shall not be taken away. As the gods of the people are today, so shall they remain, for they serve their end. They may depict their gods after their own fashion, for the likeness of such gods is of small consequence. But the likeness of the God of Gods shall not be fashioned by any man, for He is beyond the understanding of men. No man shall seek to find His likeness in water."

GLN:12:18 "The festival to the god who draws up the land is not to be denied the people, but no longer shall they eat the flesh of asses, for now this is forbidden. The days for the feast of the forefathers shall not be diminished, lest the gift of long life be thereby curtailed. With them alone is the distribution of the life forces and in their keeping are the powers granting fertility and good fortune. Unto those who control the sprouting of corn, the increase of herds and the harvests of fishes, the potency of men and the fertility of women, success in hunting and victory in war shall be given all due honour and worship."

GLN:12:19 "He who causes injury or death, sickness or suffering by drawing the likeness of another in sand and piercing it with a fire-hardened stick, or who makes the likeness of another in wax to burn in the fire, or in clay to be pierced by stake or thorn, is henceforth accursed. He will be delivered to the lukim of disease or death."

GLN:12:20 "He shall be accursed who mixes living grain with fat to enslave the earthshade of another man or woman. He shall be accursed who calls up the nightshade of another or the night-frightener. All who are so accursed will be delivered to the lukim of sickness or shall become the prey of Formless Ones."

GLN:12:21 "It is not wrong to make an image of a breast child, that a woman may conceive, but to make the likeness of a man's private organ so that a woman may conceive is wrong and any woman making or lying with such a likeness shall be accursed. She who is so accursed will be delivered to the lukim of sickness and pain."

GLN:12:22 When Yosira came up into Harfanti, he found there people with strange customs, which displeased him, but he forbade them none except those which were evil in the sight of the God of Gods. While there, he laid a great curse upon any who transgressed his laws.

GLN:12:23 These were words spoken through the mouth of Yosira, which he caused to be recorded: "Henceforth, no maiden shall be enclosed in bark and kept in darkness for seven days before marriage, but she may be kept in seclusion among women. If she has to be purified, it must be done with water and not with fire. A woman shall never be mutilated to purge her wickedness."

GLN:12:24 "Henceforth, the private parts of young women shall not be sewn up to preserve their maidenhood. This shall remain in their own keeping and in the keeping of the young women's kindred in good faith and trust. To sew or cut the private parts of any woman is a great wickedness, for this is the portal of life, and woman is not an unworthy guardian. It is best that women remain maidens, until their marriage day, of their own free will and choice; but if, because of the maiden's weakness, this seems doubtful, then the obligation shall be on her kindred."

GLN:12:25 "The custom of the Habshasti, whereby the legs of young women are bound together, after which young men may enter their chamber to lie with them, is a thing of wickedness and no longer permitted. Now, if any man discover the nakedness of a maiden, he shall not go unpunished."

GLN:12:26 "Man shall not see the nakedness of woman in childbirth, even though the woman be his wife. The hut of childbirth and all within its circle is a place forbidden unto men. Henceforth, no woman shall be suspended at childbirth."

GLN:12:27 "If the wife of a hunter lie with another man while her husband is absent so that he be slain or wounded during the hunt, then no wrong is done if her husband or the kindred of her husband slay her. Neither shall it be cause for bloodslaying if the kindred or husband slay he who lay with her."

GLN:12:28 "The foreskin of a man is cut to defy the lukim of impotency. This is not forbidden to the people, but they shall not preserve the foreskin in fat and use it to endow stones with hokew. The binding of foreskins is forbidden."

GLN:12:29 Yosira laid the greatest of all curses upon those who captured and enslaved the Lord of the Body belonging to another. Since that day, none has done so and lived. He also laid a curse upon women who baked their new born children and ate them because of the barrenness of the land. He also cursed the chief of the women's kindred.

GLN:12:30 Beforetimes, that which grew to fullness within the wombs of cattle and sheep was sustenance for men alone, but when the beast cast it forth before its day, it became sustenance appointed for women. Yosira forbade this and cursed all that came forth from the womb of beast before its time.

GLN:12:31 Yosira had these things recorded in Yapu: "No child shall be slain wilfully, saying, 'Our god has denied it proper sustenance.' Above all gods is the God of Gods who is the God of Life and they who proclaim these things proclaim a falsehood against Him. Yet they shall not be accursed until after the day when they have heard the laws of the God of Gods spoken unto them. Before then they have been led astray by those who should guide them, and on the leaders shall be the curse."

GLN:12:32 "Henceforth, the empty body shall not be bound tight against itself, but stretched out, for the earthly body cannot be reborn once its Lord has departed. The people shall not be forbidden the carrying of it, nor shall they be stopped from elevating it, but it shall not be hung over the living waters, lest it call forth a Formless One in the darkness of the night."

GLN:12:33 "If the kindred of a man come up to molest him at night, the nightshade shall be bound by the power of hokew transmitted into a hollow log filled with fire-retaining substances. The log will then be burnt in purifying fire and the ashes buried after the fashion of your fathers, but the hokew shall not be given back. That hokew, which comes from a man whose crops and trees yield abundantly is best."

GLN:12:34 "The spirit of the life of men does not dwell in the moving waters and therefore it cannot enter into a woman from the waters, neither does her own water bear it up from the ground. Even as a tree springs out from a single seed and the barley from a single grain, so is it with the seed of men. That which forms within the womb of woman is not built up from many outpourings of man, once will suffice. If the blood of a woman be not stopped, then she carry no child, for the life within is blood of her blood."

GLN:12:35 "No man shall fashion the likeness of any beast to lay with it so that his flocks and herds be increased, for henceforth he who does so, and all his beasts, shall be accursed so they sicken and perish. Nor shall any man spill his seed into an object of wood or stone and bury it If he does so, then be he accursed, so that he is forever molested by the nightshades of terror."

GLN:12:36 "It is foolishness to resort to the charmers who make likenesses of beast so their kind may be brought to the arrow and spear. Unless he who seeks the wild beasts be empowered with the hokew gathered by the kindred of his habitation, nought can guide his steps or strengthen his arm, neither will his eye see keenly. The success of the hunter is not to be found with the charmers, but lies in the goodness and uprightness of the kindred within his habitation."

GLN:12:37 "If a woman take seed from a young man and deliver it to the charmers so that barrenness be removed from her, then she and the youth, and if she bear any children, they also shall be accursed. The young man will be seized by the lukim which feasts on the hearts of men, and the woman by those which tear open the bowels."

GLN:12:38 "It is an abomination in the sight of the God of Gods for men to deball themselves, and all who do shall be accursed. Those who would deball themselves for the sake of their god may instead make an offering of their foreskin, and this will be acceptable by any god. The prayer of thankfulness that they are not born women shall be made at the time of sacrifice upon the altar."

GLN:12:39 "The excreta of man and woman shall never be left exposed to the eyes of anyone, nor in a place where its smell can come to the nostrils. Nor shall anyone pass water where another can smell it, for they whose nostrils the smell enters thereby gain power over the other. The smell from human waste draws up the formless lambata, which afflict men and women at night and turn their bowels to water."

GLN:12:40 "No offering of meat shall be eaten raw. It shall be roasted before a fire and the bones pounded into flour and eaten with meal. If the offering be consumed within a dwelling place, then the blood which has been spared must be smeared upon the door posts, so that the dark shades of the night haunters and the death bringers be repulsed by the power of life."

GLN:12:41 "It is the duty of a son to provide sustenance for a Departed One who was his mother or his father, and he shall not neglect his brother or his sister or any of his kinsfolk who lack children. If he be neglectful of his duty, he shall not escape molestation by the earthshades of the Departed Ones, which will wander relentlessly until satisfied. if Formless Ones be called forth by neglect so that they reach stability on Earth, they will haunt the dark watches of the night and suck life-filled blood to sustain their awful forms. No man may keep them from his dwelling, for they will slide in stealthily, even as snakes."

GLN:12:42 "It is wrong for charmers to call forth Dark Spirits. Any charmer so doing within the borders of the enlightened land shall be accursed, so he be seized by the nightfiend. if such be done, and the Dark Spirits wander out of control, then one of the Twice Born shall be called upon to return them to their dark abode."

GLN:12:43 "It is not sufficient for men to shun the ways of wickedness, for unless the Lord of the Body be clothed in brightness, they who watch for him in the Land of the Dawning will wait in vain. Those who lack that, which would bring them into the Place of Light will fall prey to the Lords of the Dark Places and be forever lost to those who love them."

GLN:12:44 "All those who are Awakeners of the Dead shall be accursed and delivered to the lukim of madness. If any of my people deal with them, then they too shall be accursed so that they become prey to the terrors of the night. It is futile to consult the Departed Ones, for what can they do but advise on matters of little import? If they have anything of importance to impart they will come unbidden to men of understanding and make it known."

GLN:12:45 When Yosira came with his sons and those with them into the true land of Tamerua, he strove with the people of Kantiyamtu who followed the ways of wickedness and ignorance. He remained among the people of Tamerua during the days of Gabu, dwelling at the place where now stands the Temple of the Skyseer, in an abode of reeds, by the moving waters.

GLN:12:46 In those days, the people of Earth united themselves with those who were in the land of Morning Light by the powers within the body of a womanchild, seeking in this manner to preserve the hokew of their kindred. When Yosira saw the wickedness of the custom he placed a great curse upon all the land and upon those who split the body of a womanchild, so that her flesh cried out from within them. Therefore, the land became stricken with a great plague. Since then never has anyone in the enlightened lands eaten the flesh of man or woman, and no womanchild is violated in the great wickedness of ignorance. The people of Tamerua greatly feared the curse of Yosira.

GLN:12:47 Yosira taught the people that the power of hokew resided not in the flesh of the body but in the bones, and that each bone contained the essence of all the being, man and woman. Then the people began to seek union with the Departed Ones in the land of the Morning Light, by the power of the bones, and Yosira forbade this not, though he knew it was futile. But where there was healing in the bones and they were able to draw it forth, Yosira was not displeased, for all things pertaining to the good of the people were well in his sight. Nevertheless, he forbade to women the burden of the bones of their husbands, and since then no shades have risen to molest them. This was because of the protecting power, which he drew forth to fill all the land; it relieved the women of their burden, raising it from their backs.

GLN:12:48 All the charmers who brought forth shades from the Land of Dawning and all the

Questioners of the Dead and the Awakeners of the Dead were cursed, and this curse hovers over the land even to this day. Yet there are still some who seek to call forth a shade from the swathed body made eternal, but all they raise up is an ill-omened messenger from the Place of Darkness.

GLN:12:49 Yosira did not forbid to the people the rites of homage due to their departed kinsfolk, for in the Place of Morning Light, these were the powers most interested in the welfare of any mortal man. Yosira never forbade anything that was to the benefit of men, taking away nought but the things which were futile or harmful. In those days, there were no rites of written record, but Yosira caused them to be given to the people. Not so that these should renew life in the Departed Ones upon Earth, but so that the Lord of the Body should be sustained and strengthened in the Place of the Morning Light by the link of hokew, sacrificed by those remaining on Earth.

GLN:12:50 Yosira spoke to the people, giving them laws which were recorded in this manner: "These are words of the God of Gods, Who created man and beast upon the sacred island. No beast shall be mated with another not of its kind, and if this happen, then both shall be slain and their bodies burnt. If this be done with the permission of a man, that man will be accursed. Neither shall any beast be yoked together with another not of its own kind. During the first year of its life, no beast shall be made to take up the burden of man."

GLN:12:51 When Yosira came to Kambusis, he found there a man of the Hestabwis bound and prepared for sacrifice, and he cried out against the deed, but none gave ear to his word. So, standing off, Yosira placed a staff of power upright into the ground and danced around it, singing the song for drawing forth the spirit. When they saw this, the people were wroth against him and called upon their charmers to curse him so he departed from the Earth. Their curses were ineffective, and when one charmer approached the dance ring of Yosira, Yosira called forth a tongue of flame, which consumed the charmer. Then the people became afraid and fled. So Yosira released the man who was bound upon the place of sacrifice, but he was not yet whole. Yosira also cursed all those who offered the Hestabwis as a sacrifice to their gods; since that day no man of the Hestabwis was ever slain upon the altars.

GLN:12:52 Yosira did not curse the charmers of that place; instead, he called them to him and gave them dominion over the Dark Spirits which left their abode to wander Earth, molesting men in their habitation. Thus, the charmers became greater in the eyes of the people, and from that day onward, they have cleansed the land of all Dark Spirits. However, Yosira forbade them the calling forth of the Lord of the Body from any man so that he became the servant of another, and he placed a great curse upon any charmer who disobeyed this law. Yet, this is done even now, but those who transgress the laws of Yosira do not escape the awful fate due to them, for his power is yet potent in the lands of his people. When the transgressors stand before him in awful judgement, their deeds will witness against them.

GLN:12:53 Yosira forbade those who sat in judgement the right to judge men by the fat of crocodiles or by the horn or skin. Instead, he revealed to them the manner of making judgement through corn and by the burning sword. He also taught them how to brew drink, which loosened the bonds from the tongues of men, so that Truth was no longer restrained.

GLN:12:54 The people dwelling among the trees, along the banks of the moving waters, lived in fear of tree apes. They held these sacred and would never harm them. They believed that these tree apes snatched the departing Lord of the Body and ate it, that they lurked in wait to catch it in a mighty, unseen net. So Yosira went about cursing the food reserve for the tree apes so that it became fire in their bellies, causing the life within them to come up as foam out of their mouths. Thus the land was freed from fear of the tree apes, and henceforth the Departed Ones have gone in peace, no longer being molested by the tree apes.

Chapter Thirteen – The Way of Yosira

GLN:13:1 Yosira taught that within each man resides a little man who is the Lord of the Body, and this is the life of men. While man sleeps, the little man wanders abroad to journey as it will, at death, departing from him forever.

GLN:13:2 The Lord of the Body cannot be seen by mortal eyes, but it is not hidden from all-seeing eyes of the Twice Born. When departing at death, it comes out from the mortal mouth, waiting awhile until it grows celestial wings. Then it flies away to the Western Kingdom, where the wings are shed.

GLN:13:3 In the place whither it journeys, the Lord of the Body needs no earth-made abode; therefore, burning the earthly habitations of a Departed One is futile. However, if the habitation remains and it is not purified, it becomes the gathering place for shades arising from the Place of Darkness, for the habitation need not be destroyed, but it must be purified by incense and water and refilled with protective hokew.

GLN:13:4 If a man come upon another asleep, the sleeper must be awakened quietly and with gentleness, so the Lord of the Body may re-enter peacefully. For if the sleeper be awakened before it has re-entered, or if it jump back in fright, then the man will become sick. Therefore, when awakening a sleeper, it is well to call gently to the being without.

GLN:13:5 When the mortal body becomes sickened without the heat of the lukim being present, or if the man or woman be seized and tormented by the Dark Spirits of madness, this may be caused by the daysleeping of the Lord of the Body. Thus, if the Lord of the Body be awakened from its daysleeping, or restored from its restlessness, then the man or woman may be cured. These things, Yosira permitted to be done after the fashion of charmers.

GLN:13:6 Yosira taught the curing of many kinds of ills within the mortal body and the use of draughts containing the life of herbs and growing things. He used fire to stop life leaving the mortal body. The manner of effecting these things is written in the Book of Medications.

GLN:13:7 When Yosira came with his sons into the land of Tamuera, the people there dwelt in darkness, and they were ignorant of all knowledge. They were divided among themselves into many kindreds, and strife was frequent. They had no kings, and only the old men ruled. There were many charmers who ruled the people by delusions and also those called the Keepers of Customs and the Teller of Tales.

GLN:13:8 One people dwelt among great trees and thick forests in the midst of swamplands. Their habitations were made of reeds and stood upon high platforms. These people were called the Children of Panheta, for he was their god in the days following those, during which men were first created in the midst of the waters.

GLN:13:9 Another people dwelt beyond reach of the waters and away from the trees, and they were nameless. They dug holes for their habitations or sought abodes in caves within the hillsides. This people had no gods, but worshipped the Dark Spirits and the Kamawam of the forest, which seized men at night. When the men who had been seized returned to their kindred, they were without words, being dumb. They died in the midst of madness, tearing at their bodies. But there was no Kamawam in the forest, this madness being the work of charmers wishing to instil fear into the hearts of men.

GLN:13:10 This is the manner, in which it was brought about: When the charmers seized men at night, they took them to a secret place, where their tongues were pierced well back with thin thorns. Thus the tongue swelled up, so they whose tongues were so pierced lost the power of speech. The charmers also pierced the victims about the waist with slivers of wood, so none could discover where they were inserted. They drove other splinters into them at the bridge between the private parts and the rear channel, and none could discover them there and know the victim was pierced with thorns and splinters.

GLN:13:11 Yosira cursed all the charmers who practised this evil with a great curse, so they were driven to madness by a demon which ate away their bellies. Since then, the Kamawam has been known no more in the land.

GLN:13:12 Yosira taught men to beat metal out of stones and to burn stones, so that they gave up their heat. He taught men to work with clay and he taught them the weaving of cloth and the making of beer.

GLN:13:13 When Yosira came into the land, the people knew nought about the cutting of water channels and the sowing of corn, but Yosira taught them these things. It was he who brought fertility to the land; it was he who died in the midst of the waters to give them life, and his life is in them still. Therefore, it was through the Spirit of the Great One who died in the days of old that the soil became fruitful. Beyond the reach of the living waters which rise and fall like the chest of a breathing man, the land is dead. It remains barren like a woman who has not known a man. It was known even to the men of old that if the land was not refreshed with the living waters, but with other waters, then its increase would diminish from year to year until it became waste. The increase within the soil comes not from water alone but from the life within the water. Life comes forth from life, and that ,which has not life cannot beget life.

GLN:13:14 Therefore, the good land is that, which is married to the threefold god, and land not so married remains barren. The married land is covered with the rising waters, but the land not married is ignored by them.

GLN:13:15 These things were written concerning The Children of Panheta: Yosira spoke with Panheta as man speaks to man; therefore, the laws of the Inta were not changed, remaining to bind alike those of them who dwelt on the soil or dwelt on the sand. If any man went among the Inta, their laws became his laws and if any woman left the people to dwell among the Inta, she became even as they and might not return.

GLN:13:16 Even as the Sunspirit journeys on a road set between the stars, so does the spirit of man journey with the movement of the waters. Therefore, when a man dies, his body shall be buried lengthwise with the great river.

GLN:13:17 Even as the land, upon which things grow belongs to the kindred whose blood is within it, so shall no man own to himself alone anything growing up from it, whether it be grass or herb or tree. But each man and woman may take of every herb and fruit as much as can be gathered in the hands and eaten before sunsetting.

GLN:13:18 Of all things which are a seed and can be eaten, each one may gather for themselves as much as can be stored within a jar or suspended from the foodpole. All things which are a seed and can be eaten, but which are not stored in ajar or suspended from a foodpole, shall be stored in the pit of the kindred. Nothing shall be placed within the pit unless it has been heated by fire and cooled.

GLN:13:19 Even as the Spirit of Life resides in the things, which men eat, so does it reside in the living things, from whence they came. Therefore, any tree or bush bearing the food of men shall not be cut or broken.

GLN:13:20 The blood of beasts cries from the soil even as does the blood of men; therefore, if shed it must be appeased. Slay no beast unless it be needed for food, and bury the head and whatever comes out of its belly. Every other part which is taken shall be eaten or burned, except for the bones and the skin, which are to be used.

GLN:13:21 Fire serves man, but it can also become his master. Consider its nature. Does it spring out of the wood unbidden or of its own volition, or does it require the agency of man? Does it reside in the wood or is there a firespirit? Only the fools among men start something, which they cannot control. Never let a fire grow into a thing of much smoke, keep it bright, using no more wood than is needful for the purpose. Let it not stray from its proper place, which is the place where it serves without menace.

GLN:13:22 When they become of an age to do so, every man and woman should take themselves a mate. Those who fail to do so are not held in the highest esteem.

GLN:13:23 By the things whereby a man commits a wrong, so shall he be punished. Likewise, he shall be dealt with according to the nature of the wrong. The customs from times past are not unhelpful guides.

GLN:13:24 When Yosira came to the place where the Inta dwelt, they made him welcome in this manner, 'When we saw you, our hearts were gladdened. The life was renewed in us and though content as we were, you brought refreshment and joy.' Yosira called these people his unweaned children.

Chapter Fourteen – Tribulations of Yosira

GLN:14:1 These things were written in the Book of the Two Roads: Yosira, who is therein called Yoshira, came from beyond the Realm of Athor and was the first king of Tehamut. He established the festivals of the new moon, the festival of wool drawing and the days of devotion. When first he brightened this land by his presence, the welfare of its people was in the hands of false priests who taught that man was a double-spirited being, in whom the Spirit of Good struggled with the Spirit of Evil for possession of his soul. Each deed and thought was said to strengthen one or other of the opponents. The people were not completely deceived in accepting this; it is perhaps an earthly distortion of reflected Truth. but neither is it wholly true. In the days of old, men saw Truth but dimly, for it could be only partially revealed in accordance with their ability to understand it. Truth is a light growing even brighter in the darkness of man's ignorance, and as the generations pass and go down into dust, men see more clearly. Each lightbearer dispels a little more darkness, and Yosira was a lightbearer, the greatest of them all.

GLN:14:2 Before Yosira came, bearing the lamp of brilliant light, Truth was but dimly perceived in this land. The false priests of those days taught that when the Great God created man, He held back immortality as a special gift for those whom he favoured. This is not the attitude of One Who is Great, and therefore such doctrine cannot be accepted. That these priests were misled themselves was not so great an evil as their misleading of others who trusted them. A true priest should approach as close as possible to the shrine of Truth and interpret whatever he sees there as clearly as his ability and the understanding of his followers permit. In those olden days, no man had yet been reborn to wisdom and enlightenment. Therefore, nothing was known about the Gardens of Light, and men believed in the Dark Abode alone, This Dark Abode was a place where sand and dust were the sustenance of the dead, whose bodies were clothed in long hair and feathers. Men, in those olden days, knew little more than that.

GLN:14:3 They also believed that souls risen to glory really consumed the food and wore the garments and ornaments provided for their use. They did not know, as we do, that as the soul is subtle, itself, so can it use nought but the subtle elements of earthly things. Even now, incense is burned before the statues of those risen to glory, so that they may receive their portion. There are those who believe that the sustenance of the soul, and its continued life, depends upon the monthly communion sacrifice of its kinsmen on Earth.

GLN:14:4 As a man who walks with a lamp at night is attacked by those who lurk in the darkness, so are enlighteners who seek to bring light into the gloom of ignorance attacked by those whom it would reveal in their true likeness. Thus, when Yosira cried out against those who, while not permitting the slaying of men and women in their daily lives, nevertheless allowed a child to be slain as sacrifice, or buried beneath the pillars they raised up, he was condemned as an enemy of the gods.

GLN:14:5 When Yosira was in the land far up the River of Life, one named Azulah who stood close to the right hand of Yosira slew a man who was kindred to the Leopard. This enraged the god of these people, for the slain man's blood cried out to him. Therefore, men of the Leopard came into the land of the East seeking to slay Azulah for his offence against their god, but he had withdrawn to a place of hiding. So when they found their search to be in vain, the men of the Leopard returned to their place, informing their priests of their failure. The priests then held the rituals for calling down the war power, drawing it down in strength. Then, because Yosira was the overlord of Azulah, the men of the Leopard went forth against him, claiming the right of war.

GLN:14:6 But in the night, when the hostile host waited before the camp of Yosira, the war priest defiled himself, and so the war power failed to make faint the hearts of those with Yosira, the war priest having lost control over it. Thus, the war power came into the hands of Yosira, and he cast it back so it fell upon the Men of the Leopard, and their knees were loosened, and their bowels went to water, and they fled from that place.

GLN:14:7 The Men of the Leopard dwelt within the forests, towards the sunsetting side of the moving waters, and Yosira pursued them there. He did not enter the thick forest, but, coming to an island in the midst of the waters, he made camp there. He had a prisoner whom he released, sending him to the priests with this message, "Come in peace, that I may hear your complaint and judge whether it be just." But the priests of the Men of the Leopard came down only to the edge of the waters and would go no further, and they called out across the waters, "What was just heretofore is just no longer, for this is now a matter to be settled between our kindred and those who are with you, for blood still cries out for blood."

GLN:14:8 Hearing this, Yosira answered, "Let us be wise; there are judges above us, so let the God of the Moving Waters decide the matter." To this the priests said, "It is well." Then Yosira took Azulah into a boat, rowing him through the waters against the South wind. Stopping the boat, Yosira commanded Azulah to leap into the waters, so he might be tested by swimming, and this Azulah did. He swam powerfully and the God of the Moving Waters did not take him, for Yosira had covered the waters with his power, so the waters bore up the swimmer, carrying him in safety to the shore.

GLN:14:9 Then Yosira sat down with the chiefs of the Men of the Leopard and made a covenant with them and with other peoples likewise. This was that when a man slays another among his own kindred, none among them shall protect him, and he shall be either slain or cut off from those of his own blood. However, if the slain man be of a kindred different to that of the slayer, then the slayer may be slain by men of either kindred. If the kindred of the slayer would avoid the toll of blood, then they must send a token to the kindred of the slain man, together with an account of the deed. They must also agree that the blood be upon their own heads and revenge in their hands, and account of such revenge shall be sent to the kindred of the slain man together with their forfeiture.

GLN:14:10 Then all the kindred bound themselves with a great oath, declaring that, if blood cried out from the ground in vain, then the night terrors and blood shades would be called upon to fall upon the kindred of the slayer and not upon the kindred of the slain.

GLN:14:11 It was at the time when this covenant was made that Yosira spoke in this manner to his sons, "These are the meats, which are accursed and shall not be eaten. All the meat of any beast which dies of itself. All the meat of any beast, which has been slain as a sacrifice to the small gods. All the meat of any beast, which has been slain by wild beasts and all meat, which has been offered up on the door stones. These are unclean meats."

GLN:14:12 When Yosira had gone throughout the land and purified it, and bound up its wickedness with curses, he taught those who dwelt there the making of waterways. He also instructed them in the meanings of the heavenly signs. He built Piseti in the midst of the reedlands and drained the swamps. Then he raised up the first temple of brick and stone. At this time, he established those who were recorders of the days and seasons.

GLN:14:13 While Yosira was at Piseti, the priests stirred up the people against him, and so he fled to the Land of God with his sons and blood kindred. But his wife and youngest son did not go with him, for they were with her father in the land, from whence the great river flowed. This was the land of Kantoyamtu, where priests taught that death is not the normal lot of man. These priests said that though their forefathers of old were just as mortal as men, their forefathers' fathers were heirs to immortality on Earth. This is an erroneous teaching, one belonging to the childhood of man, but later men were taught that death is just the departure of life, which takes flight with the soul.

GLN:14:14 While Yosira was at Piseti, his true son, Manindu, commanded the Mesiti who were a host of men and workers in brass. They subdued the whole land, returning it to Yosira. Later, it was delivered into the hands of Manindu whose seal is on it even yet.

GLN:14:15 After the time of Manindu, the people forgot the God of Gods, for He appeared distant from them, and they worshipped other gods whom the priests devised. The light was dimmed and only poorly reflected in small, hidden shrines.

Chapter Fifteen – The Voice of God

GLN:15:1 The Voice of God came out of the Heavens unto His servants even before the days of

Wunis, but in these days, it has come to certain of His Devoted Ones who heard it within the cavern of visions. Afterwards, each wrote it down according to his own hearing, and lo, when they came together, it was seen that each had recorded the same words. Thus, the things, which were heard by the three and set down by them in writing, all being agreed alike are things recorded forever.

GLN:15:2 "I am the Voice of God Who is the God of All Men and Ruler of their Hearts. I have many aspects and come differently to all men, I am the God of Many Faces. To you, My servants, I give these words, that they may be carried to all men. Obey My commands, and I will be your God. I will enlighten and instruct you, guiding you along the way. I desire your love and loyalty, and your adherence to My plans, but I do not desire your servility. I am not only your God, but your Commander, as well, and so I expect obedience and discipline, as befits those who prepare for harsh and grim battles such as those, which lie ahead."

GLN:15:3 "My desire is for love rather than futile sacrifices of burnt offerings, but it should not be a passive love but one expressing service in My Cause. A certain knowledge of right and wrong, with free choice of the former, is of greater value in My sight than pointless, ritualistic worship. I derive no pleasure from the wasteful shedding of blood from bulls and lambs. I gain nothing from the fat of sheep and the flesh of goats. I am the Creator of All, so what can men give that would increase My greatness? Men are misled if they believe that their sins can be purged by vain rituals. Only active goodness can obliterate the stain of sin."

GLN:15:4 "Men approach Me in fear; they come to me with servility. They beg forgiveness for their sins and request My help in worldly matters. To sing My praises is their excuse for coming into places made sacred unto Me, but they come wanting something, be it only reassurance. With this attitude towards Me, do you wonder that I remain mute before their pleas? Bring Me no more vain offerings of flesh and blood, for such wastefulness of life is an offence to the God of Life. What benefit do I derive from all your feasts or festivals? Give me dedication and effort; that is all I ask. Above all be true to yourselves, for I abhor the face of hypocrisy, the face now all too familiar when men approach Me."

GLN:15:5 "Men bring Me meat and wine, fine flour and wheaten cakes, thinking I can consume these, or that I have need of such sustenance. I would be far better served were these to be given to the widow and orphan, to the multitudinous poor whom you suffer to exist in your midst. Poverty is man-made, and it is not sufficient for the wealthy to give alms to the poor; those with power and position, with wealth and plenty must strike at the roots of poverty. If they fail to do this, then the alms they give have no merit in My sight."

GLN:15:6 "Your solemn assemblies, your tedious processions, your long faces and melancholy expressions bring no gladness to My heart. Your burdensome ceremonials and futile offerings of life and food benefit Me in no way at all. Men themselves may derive benefit from these, but their hypocrisy when they proclaim they do this in My name is not hidden from Me."

GLN:15:7 "The reek of your incense smoke rises and disappears into the air, but it comes not unto Me, nor do I have need of it. Yet, I will not deny you the pleasure of its fragrance ,which can bring inner harmony and peace by soothing the spirits of men. Nor will I deny you your feasts, if the fetters of wickedness be thereby loosened from your souls, but do not say they are undertaken for My benefit or glorification. Fasting and the denial of bodily appetites may serve useful ends for men, but though you may deceive yourselves regarding their intent, do not try to deceive Me by misstating their purpose. I have no desire to repress the joy and exuberance welling up in the hearts of men; far rather would I prefer that such humanising emotions be cultivated. Therefore, pray if prayer serves its true purpose, which is to harmonise your spirit with Mine so communication becomes possible. Keep your festivals and feasts if they serve their purpose, which is to inspire and refine your spirit. Do all that elevates your spirit and develops your souls; that is the true purpose of life. Do all that is good for you; nothing wholly beneficial is denied you, but do not declare that in so doing you confer benefit upon Me. I am the God Above and Beyond All."

GLN:15:8 "I do not deny you your rituals and ceremonials; worship Me if you will as you will, but bear in mind that this cannot substitute for your obligations. Ritual and worship cannot be an adjustment or payment for the things you have failed to do, or be an apology for your own shortcomings. Neither do they compensate for iniquities against your fellowmen. If you attach importance to ritual and ceremonial, let it be in a proper proportion, and never let them dull your conscience against deeds of wickedness, of usury and injustice. Never let your duty and obligations be neglected because you worship Me diligently, following a formalised ritual and ceremonial. Let this not become an excuse for failing to share your bread with the hungry or for neglecting the needs of the destitute or weak. I am not deceived. A life dedicated to Me is not one preoccupied with worship; that is more the life of a coward trembling before the unknown. He who dedicates his life to Me gives shelter to the homeless and succours those in distress, but even these are not the ultimate in goodness, for they are passively accepted. The ultimate in goodness is to actively combat all the root causes of evil. Those who are my true followers live a life of service and goodness. They live in harmony with their neighbours, harm none and do not shirk the burdens and obligations of earthly existence."

GLN:15:9 "I am better served by obedience to My laws and conformity with My plans than by ritual and offerings. To listen to the words of the Sacred Writings while striving to understand them is better in My sight than offerings of flesh and treasure which benefit the priests more than they do Me. Among the things, which I abhor, few are more detestable than the hypocritical offerings of the evildoer. The offerings and worship of a hypocrite are an abomination to Me. Evil enters the realm beyond Earth as a foul smell, and the worse one of all is the smell of hypocrisy. Those who pander to hypocrites or do not actively oppose them are also creatures of evil."

GLN:15:10 "I know too well the deceit, to which men are prone. The adulterer and fornicator preach chastity for others, while the liar declares the virtues of Truth. The thief preaches honesty and the lewd-minded professes modesty. Men say one thing and mean another, while all too often the half or slanted truth replaces the real thing. Men may deceive themselves and other men, but I am not deceived. Now I say, let men first cleanse their own souls and eradicate hypocrisy before presuming to approach Me. Men may well cry out, "Why does God remain mute; why has He deserted Me?" Do they think their deeds are hidden or that I cannot read the secrets of their hearts?"

GLN:15:11 "Worship by men of iniquity is mere mockery. How rare the sincere and genuine heart! Were men indeed deserted by their God, they would have none to blame but themselves. Do men think their lack of kindness and consideration for others, their insincerity and inconsistency are truly hidden from Me? I am the All Knowing One. I see too little love of goodness in the hearts of men and too much fear for the consequences of their deeds."

GLN:15:12 "Real and sincere worship is to obey My laws and to shoulder the responsibilities of men, to steadfastly conform to My plan and to live in neighbourly harmony. He who devotes his life to Me also devotes it to his own welfare. He who serves Me well likewise serves himself. This is the Law of Laws. For the whole purpose of life is not the service of God, but the development of the soul of man. He who worships Me with empty ritual and vain ceremonial, but neglects the wellbeing of his own soul, does not serve Me well, for he thwarts My purpose. I have endowed the creature made in My likeness with a religious instinct, for this springs from its everlasting spirit, as fire generates heat; therefore, to worship is not unnatural. But blind worship lacks the vitalising element; it defeats its own end, for in true worship, man should reach out beyond himself to discover his own soul. Then, having done so, he should develop it until the soul aspires to godhood itself."

GLN:15:13 "Therefore, dedicate all your labours and the skill of your hands unto Me, and let your heart ever dwell on the borders of the spiritual. Let the life, which you cherish, be the spiritlife. Free yourself from all vain hopes and selfish thoughts; from all worthless encumbrances; from ungainful avarice and unbeneficial lusts; from the domination of the flesh. Life is not easy, nor is it wholly pleasant; it is not meant to be, but bear your burdens with cheerfulness and fortitude. Entrench yourself within an inner fortress of peace."

GLN:15:14 "Whatever you do or give, do or give in My name, and whatsoever sufferings descend upon you, suffer them for Me. Thus, you will avoid the stigma of false pride and all given and suffered will be without any taint of self-interest."

GLN:15:15 "The path of godliness is not an easy one to follow, for it is beset with the pitfalls of perplexity and doubt. Then, too, there is not one path, but several, and few among men know which is the best. There are many false paths leading nowhere, there are paths that lead to a wilderness of disillusion and some, which lead to destruction. Yet among the many beliefs springing up from time to time in various lands, there are always those, which lead to the same Truth. to the one Fountainhead of Light, though some may be devious and some wander through dangerous territory. They are like many roads leading pilgrims to the one shrine. Though all true paths are lit by the guiding light of Truth. not all see it alike; but the fault lies not so much in the light as in the beholder. It is this, which leads to misunderstandings concerning each other's teachings and to disputes between those who prefer one road and those preferring another. Each considers his own way, his own interpretation of the light to be the best, if not the only, way."

GLN:15:16 "There are few, even among truly enlightened men, who are able to conceive My true nature, and these know that I am even above unchangeability in manifestation. I can think of Myself as some other, and forthwith, that other comes into being. There are those among men who declare all life, all My creation to be an illusion of the senses, a dream without sustenance. They are in error, for all that is real and all that exists was ever latent, awaiting the awakening kiss. Because men cannot know reality as it actually is, but only as they can conceive it to be with their deceptive sense, does not make it any less real. If all men were blind, the stars would still exist."

GLN:15:17 "Neither reality nor Truth. nor the God Who is beyond and above both will be inconceivable to the minds of the ultimate man. Only man in his present undeveloped state and in his ignorance cannot conceive such things and therefore, because in his blindness they are beyond his sight, he says they do not exist."

GLN:15:18 "In the beginning, I established the Law, without which the souls of men could not develop and progress. As each soul is itself a divine fragment, with all the powers of divinity latent within itself, it can modify all but the Great Law. Man thinks, but his thoughts alone do not create, for, as yet, he lacks knowledge of the power, which creates in substance. First, I created the firmament, which is the matrix of all; then when I took thought, the creative power flowed outward and, operating upon the medium, brought into being things of substance."

GLN:15:19 "My creation arose before Me as light does before a flame or heat before a fire. It came and still comes into being because I exist, it is because I Am.

GLN:15:20 Creation in no way affects Me any more than a man is affected by his shadow, or light by its reflection. As raindrops, waves, rivers, dew and mist are all forms of water, so is everything existing and knowable by man but various forms of the one substance. This substance has its origin in Me, but it is not Me."

GLN:15:21 "I am the source of all things, supporting but not being supported by them. Even as the mighty winds which sweep across the Earth find their rest in the tranquil vastness above, so all beings and all things have their rest in Me. It is a power outflowing from Me, which holds all things in stability and form."

GLN:15:22 "They who devote their lives to My service must do more than love and worship Me, for such service entails the elevation of mankind, the spreading of good and the combating of evil. They must not only fight against the ungodly, but also overcome the wickedness welling up in their own thoughts. They who love Me desire the wellbeing of all men, and their souls are filled with harmony and peace. Dearer to Me than their love for Me is the labour and tribulations of those who serve Me. I am their end. I am never the God of Inertia but the God of Effort; if you offer no more than deeds done in My service or in conformity with My design, then you serve Me adequately."

GLN:15:23 "However, too rarely do the ways of men conform to My plan and the ranks of those who serve are too thin. Therefore, I shall call forth leaders from among men and send out the clarion cry to service. I shall seek out men who will serve Me diligently and loyally. They will be men of goodwill who are of a friendly nature. They will be kind and compassionate, men who can love deeply and truly, whose steadfastness is the same in pleasure and affliction; whose resolve remains equally unbroken in the sweet embrace of good fortune as under the harsh blows of misfortune. I will send men who are fair and just, proud and resolute, but these qualities mean nothing unless they also have courage and resolution, fortitude and tenacity."

GLN:15:24 "I shall seek the man who is himself ever seeking, who seeks to unravel the riddle of life. One whose determination is strong, who detests wickedness and delights in the good; whose heart and inner vision reach out for enlightenment. His tranquillity will remain unshaken under stress, and within his heart will be a haven of peace beyond the reach of excitement and anger. He will be a lover of wisdom and seeker of truth. He who is wise, he who knows what to do, who remains calm when others lose their self-control; he who is clear-headed under stress, who enjoys the challenge of the task, that man is Mine. He who labours uncomplainingly, who disdains to satisfy deforming lusts, whose spirit remains the same under the temptations of honours or the pressure of disgrace; he who is free from the shackles of unworthy earthly attachments, who retains his balance under praise or blame, who can shoulder his own burdens, whose spirit is calm, silent and strong under all circumstances; he who can bear the responsibilities of life and the obligations of love, that man is Mine. I am the God of Inspiration, I am the God of Love."

GLN:15:25 "I am the Knower, and you are the known. I am the Source of Life. In the vastness of My nature I place the seed of things to be, from which come forth all things that are now or ever will exist."

GLN:15:26 "Men must nourish their spirit and sustain it with spiritual fare. They must also learn that the spirit is not something separate from man, or something within him. Man is spirit; man is soul. There is no need to engage in long-winded, empty discussions about far away things lying beyond the reach and understanding of men. To know the reality of the spirit and to establish the existence of the soul, man has only to delve within his nature, to seek within himself. The spiritual part of man is not a mysterious something outside his being, or a thing difficult to understand. To discover it requires no more than the effort of seeking."

GLN:15:27 "Men with sincere hearts, seeking a path ask for a starting point. However, for most, the key is self-discipline, and this is the reason for many laws and restrictions. But these must never be unnecessarily restrictive; each must have a definite purpose and beneficial end, obscure though these may be. The means for overcoming unwholesome desires and for harmonising with the divine chord lie within the reach of all, but effort must be expended in their cultivation. If the end is great beyond man's conception, it is no less true that the task before man is arduous and difficult in the extreme. To master himself and gain complete self-control is no more than the first step along the path."

GLN:15:28 "Though men may despair because I am veiled from them, though they may seek without finding, I am not indifferent to their needs and desires. Doubt and uncertainty are essential earthly conditions serving a definite end. I have not surrounded men with perplexities and obscurities unnecessarily. The climate of unbelief and materialism, strange though it may seem to men, is best for their spiritual health. I know better than men themselves what is best for them, for I alone can see the broad design spread over the ages, I alone see the end and objective. Though unenlightened men expect it, it is not meet for Me to interfere unduly in the affairs of Earth."

GLN:15:29 "All things are Mine and under My dominion, but man may deal with them as he will. I do not interfere, but finally man is accountable. Though I have all and nothing can add to My grandeur, with all this I still labour. Therefore, man should never disdain to labour, for this is an attribute of the Highest. I do not require of any man that he do something I would not do, or be something I would not be, I am the God of Righteousness. If ever I ceased to labour, the universe would be without order, chaos would prevail and precede its destruction

GLN:15:30 "I am the God of Many Aspects, for men may conceive Me in any form they wish, or even as something without form. I am the God of Men's Hearts. In whichever way and by whatever name men serve Me, abiding by My laws and conforming with the Great Design, is right in My eyes. Any path, which will bring man to his goal is the right road. Truly the paths chosen by men are many and varied; some are even devious, but if they be true paths of enlightenment and development, they are acceptable in My sight. However, those who lust for earthly power, offering sacrifice and worship to earthly gods conceived to accord with their desires, are not acceptable to Me. It is true that earthly success and power may come to those who strive for them, but do they achieve anything more than fleeting satisfaction? What manner of being would now dominate Earth, had all men been without divine enlightenment from the beginning, if earthly ends alone had dominated men's minds? Consider what earthly life would have been like, had it been left to develop predominated by materialism, if it had not been mitigated by injections of the divine."

GLN:15:31 "There are four main types of men who are good and serve Me well. They are those who suffer courageously the afflictions and sorrows, which develop the soul. Those who labour, that Earth and man may benefit. Those who seek after Truth and those with vision and creativity. Yet how rare are those among these who do not besmirch their record with deeds of evil and thoughts of wickedness? All too many may have, by their carnal desires and acts of wickedness, countered their goodness to the detriment of their immortal souls."

GLN:15:32 "If a man follow a false god with goodwill and honesty, serving men well and living in accordance with My laws, I will not repudiate him, and he will not be denied enlightenment on the way. There are many roads along which the soul may travel to bring about its development and awakening to self-consciousness, but is it not advantageous to choose the best one? Only the foolish travel blindly, without seeking guidance and directions. Those who have little wisdom or who are easily misled follow roads which go nowhere. They who follow a barren faith reach a barren destination, they find only an empty place devoid of hope, incapable of fulfilling their dreams and aspirations."

GLN:15:33 "Those who worship gods of their imagination, gods in strange likenesses, which have been brought into being by man's creative conceptions, will go to these gods who have an existence in a dim shadow realm. Those who worship lower spirits will go to them and those who worship the demons of darkness will join them, for what a man desires, he deserves. There is a link between that, which men desire and what becomes established in existence. Provision is made for man to receive the fruits of his own creations."

GLN:15:34 "Whatsoever you do, whatsoever you plan or create, whatsoever you suffer, let it be an offering unto Me, not for My sake but for yours. I am the God of Compassion, the God of Understanding. From those who in their devotion offer Me but a single leaf, a flower or fruit, or even a little water, this I will gladly accept, thus lightening their loving spirit, for it is offered in sincerity of heart. He who comes before any god, whatsoever its image, with pureness of heart and good motives, comes unto Me, for I gaze upon him with compassion and understanding. I am not concerned with the deeds alone of men, but with their motives. Empty gestures are ignored, but that, which is done with good intent and a loving heart never goes unheeded."

GLN:15:35 "I am the Hidden God, hidden to serve an end. Veiled in mystery, I am further obscured by the mists of mortal delusion. Unable to see me, men declare I do not exist, yet I declare to you that man, with his mortal limitations, sees only a minute part of the whole. Man is the slave of illusion and deception. Though man is born to delusion, for it is a needful state, he is further inflicted by deceptions wrought by men. Though man cannot perceive the greatness above him, because of its greatness, neither can he see the smallness beneath him, because of its smallness. From the greatest came the smallest and from the smallest came creation, and within the smallest is greatness and power. For the smallest is far less than the mote, yet it is the upholder of the universe, and it shines like the sun beyond the darkness. It lies out towards the edge of the reach of man's thought. In the beginning, all things arose from the invisible, and into the invisible, all things will disappear in the end, but the end is not the end of the spirit. Out beyond this material creation born of the invisible, there is a higher eternal invisible of greater substance. When all material things have passed away, this will remain. Above all is timelessness, which is eternity, and there is My abode, the supreme goal of man, and those who attain it dwell in eternity. I am the Eternal God."

GLN:15:36 "Few are they who can conceive of Me as I really am, the Unborn and Uncreated, Beginningless and Without End, Lord of All the Spheres. Those few who can conceive Me as I am are awakened spirits freed from mortal delusions. As thick clouds of smoke rise up and spread out from a fire burning in damp wood, so did the material universe come forth from Me. As a lump of salt dropped into a pool of water dissolves and cannot be removed afterwards, yet from whatever part of the water you draw there is salt, so it is with My pervading Spirit. I am the Great Luminary, the everlasting source of light sparks, which, imprisoned in matter, become the slumbering souls of men. These, unconsciously guided, spread out the five senses under the control of unconscious thought. That, which the senses harvest departs with the spirit. It is borne away by the spirit, even as perfume is carried by the wind. I am the Boundless One, The One Beyond Limitations. I remain free and unencumbered by the effort of creation. I Am, and I watch life unfold. I set the course, which nature follows to bring forth all that lives.

GLN:15:37 "The fools on Earth who shut their eyes and complain because they stumble, the ignorant who choose to walk in darkness and the apathetic who choose paths of ease and comfort, have no knowledge of Me. Their hopes are sterile. Their s the choice of darkness; theirs the choice of ignorance, theirs the choice of apathetic inertia. Their learning is futile, their thoughts fruitless and their deeds without purpose. Though man is born in ignorance and darkness, he is also heir to the guiding light which dispels them. The light is his for the taking. Then there are the awakened souls among men, their sustenance is My own nature. They know My Spirit is among men as an everlasting source of strength and refreshment to the weary and disheartened. They are in harmony with My Spirit and therefore know Me."

GLN:15:38 "Men call Me the God of Battles, which I am not, for good men fight each other when kings declare war. Men call Me many things, but this does not make Me become what they think I am. I am the hidden power, which ultimately rights all wrongs, which will eventually redress all injustices. I come to all who are worthy, but it is the lonely, the unwanted, the undesirable whom I seek. To Me, the dispirited, the perplexed, the sorrowful and humiliated soul is an irresistible magnet. I am the welcoming light at the end of the road, the companion who watches in compassionate silence, the understanding friend, the ever ready arm. I am He Who presides over the haven of peace within your heart."

GLN:15:39 "To those who unite their spirit with Mine and to those who are in harmony but not united, I increase that, which they have and provide what they lack. I turn a like countenance to all men. My love for them remains constant, but those who join Me in devotion to My cause are truly in Me and I am in them. This is My everlasting and unchanging promise unto me: He who walks with Me, serving My cause, shall not perish. So join your spirit with Mine, giving me your confidence and trust, and thus united in a harmonious relationship, you will come to know the supreme goal. Men say they cannot know Me through their senses, and this is true, for I am above and beyond the reach of their finite senses. The senses of man are not meant to be the means for experiencing Me, they are for experiencing the material spheres. They are also limiting, shutting out far more than they reveal. Yet men have within them a greater sense, which can know Me, but it lies dormant in the mass of men. I am the God of Men's Hearts, the Consciousness of All Living Things. I am the God of Consciousness, the Listener in the Silences."

GLN:15:40 "I do not manifest to man through his mortal senses, for these are bounded by earthly limitations. I manifest through the great sense which is of the spirit, the sense of the soul. As pure light hides many colours, so am I hidden in the hearts of men. As sparks fly from a bellows-blown fire, so from the Eternal Fire, the life sparks fly out to glow for an instant in matter and then fall back. As the sun radiates heat, a flower perfume and a lamp light, so does the heart of man create his own spiritual state. The eye of man sees a pebble, a star, a sheep or a tree, and these do not appear to him in anyway alike. Yet all are differing forms manifesting in the one outflowing force originating with Me. This outflowing force generated that, which gave birth to substance and endowed it with the matrix for form. The fragments of Divine Spirit interpret that, which the Divine Spirit created, but they cannot know it in its reality, for, enshrouded in matter, they sleep. Because the material sphere is a separate part of the greater whole, the mortal part of man can never hope to know in full its boundless beauty, or experience its limitless bliss. Out beyond the limits of man's thought and conception, beyond reach of even the most vivid imagination, the wonder and glory of it all stretch out into absolute perfection. Even at the outer reaches, where eternity begins, the wonder of the inner glory remains veiled. No words of man can ever hope to describe the true nature of divine things; to the divine alone can the divine be known. The radiant living heart pulsating with love can never be known to man as man, but when man becomes more than man, he may take his first glimpse behind the veil. I am the Inspiration and Goal of Man."

GLN:15:41 "Before creation, I was the One Alone. I thought, and the thought became a command of power, and into the void of the invisible came that, which was the potential of substance, though itself then part of the invisible. Light was born of the power, and My Spirit was in the midst of the light, but it was not that light which lightens the day. A firmament became the foundation of all things, matter gradually forming there, becoming ever denser as it thrust outward from the invisible. It moved from a subtle state to something more solid, from intangibility to substance, from incoherent substance into a state of density and form. I commanded the subtle substance, with light but without form, to mate with the subtle substance of darkness and become dense. It did so and became water. Then I spread water over the darkness below the light, placing a fountain of light about the waters. This brought forth the light of mortal vision, which is not the light of the spirit, nor the light of power. At that time, the universe was made, and then Earth received her form. It slept warmly in the midst of the waters, which were not the waters of Earth, and this was before the beginning of life in earthly substance. I am the God of Creation."

GLN:15:42 "At the foundations of My creations are Truth and Reality, these are with Me and of Me, but they are not My substance, neither are they things comprehensible on Earth. These are truly great things indescribable in the inadequate words of men, which can do no more than form an imperfect, incomplete and distorted picture of them; simple things can be described clearly in a few words to the understanding of man, but greater things become increasingly difficult to deal with through mere words. What words of man can be used to describe the indescribable? How can things beyond the comprehension of mortal men be brought within the limits of their understanding? Before the shadow, there was the reflecting light, a light so bright that, were it not veiled in the darkness, it would consume the shadow. Seeking to explain and describe transcendental things in the limited language of man only leads to obscurity and confusion; the words form incomprehensible sentences, and unthinking men will declare them to be incoherence. Therefore, look behind the sentences strung together with mere words. I am the Unknown God veiled from man by man's mortal limitations."

GLN:15:43 "The universe came into being and exists because I AM. It is My reflection in matter. As a man remains unaffected by the manifestations of his shadow, so do I remain unaffected by the material creation. As heat comes forth from fire and contains its essence and nature, though it is not fire, neither has it the substance of fire, so does My creation relate to Me. I am as an object reflected in water. The water may not know the reflection or find it within itself, but this inability has no effect on the reality of the object, nor on the fact of its reflection. It is as a man looking into clear water on a calm day sees his reflection therein, but if the wind blows the image becomes distorted, and if the sun hides its face, the image disappears. Yet, none of these effects touches upon the image itself, nor upon that which casts the image. When the wind drops, the cloud vanishes and the sun reappears, both distortion and deception end, and the reality is again reflected. Within My creation is My Spirit, which supports it, and this Spirit is the bond between My creation and Myself. No man acknowledges the air because it is still, but when this same air becomes a whirlwind men give it their whole attention. With Me, all is real, while with man all is illusion; but man may abandon his illusions in seeking Me, and he will thereby discover reality. I am the Reality Behind the Reflection; I am the Uncaused Cause."

GLN:15:44 "Those who turn away from the glorious jewel within to seek an outside god, a separate, unresponsive being, are looking for a mere trinket, while disregarding the priceless treasure already in their keeping. Men of light worship the vision of light; men of darkness and ignorance worship ghosts and dark spirits, demons of the night. There are men who, moved by dark beliefs or their carnal lusts and perverted passions, perform awful austerities and self-mutilations never ordained by Me. They delight in tormenting the life and spirit within their bodies. They are truly deluded victims of the darkest form of ignorance. Yet, some derive pleasure from their pains and torments, and so continue them, but these may be truly described as mutilated souls. Some men follow gods who punish wickedness and reward good, and therefore tend towards goodness, but is it not folly to follow non-existent gods? All men choose their own spiritual destiny, whether it be done knowingly or not, for under the Law, their future state must rest in their own hands. I am the God Who ordained the Law, and nothing man can do will change it. My love alone mitigates the consequences of man's unredeemed wickedness. I am the Changeless One. Could a God of Love become a God of Vengeance? Revenge is something alien to Me. Therefore, is it reasonable that men should believe I could be one thing today and then, because they fall into error, become something else tomorrow? My nature is not as that of man. I AM as I AM.

GLN:15:45 "I am not influenced by the mere formal actions of men, or by empty sacrifice. Lighted lamps and candles, days of fasting and self-mortification by man cannot sway Me in his favour. I am not to be bribed, for I am God. He who handles fire carelessly and gets burnt cannot blame the fire; neither can he who goes into swift waters and drowns blame the waters. There are laws, the violation of which brings retribution in its train. They who by their own deeds bring pain and suffering upon themselves cannot blame Me for what ensues. These are the effects of the lesser laws which are easily understood, but above these is the Great Law, which is not so incomprehensible. Under this, the link between the deed and its effect is not so apparent; men bring down calamity and suffering upon their own heads and blame Me, when the fault lies with them and the cause is their own misconduct or misconception. Men reap as they sow and I am the Fertile Field, which takes no part in the sowing or the reaping Man is his own master and the lord of his own destiny. He cannot expect help from any great power, unless he himself expend effort to contact such power or be deserving of help. Everything a man is or becomes is the result of his own striving and efforts, or his lack of them. I made man to be a man, not a mere puppet or nursling. I am the God of the Law. I am the God of the Stalwart."

GLN:15:46 "Man is the heir to divinity, and the road to divinity is spirituality. Man cannot become spiritual except through his own efforts and striving. He cannot achieve it by being led by the hand or through fear of punishment, nor by greed through anticipation of a reward. He who enters into his heritage of divinity will be no weakling; he will have trodden a hard and stony path."

GLN:15:47 "Man has two ways of knowing Me. He can know Me through his own spiritual awakening or through the continued revelation of moral law and divine purpose by My inspired servants. To know Me through a spiritually awakened self is the way of certainty, but few can suffer its austerities and disciplines."

GLN:15:48 "When the spirit of man is unawakened, he cannot know the great self within him, of which he is apart. Not knowing his true nature and unable to see clearly, he is blinded by material delusions. Would not the creatures of the night, which never see the sun, deem the moon to be the most brilliant light in the sky above? So it is with the man walking in the darkness of spiritual unconsciousness. He says, "I am the body, and the body is my whole being," and in the delusion of that belief he becomes ensnared in an existence bound to matter. Like the creatures bound to an existence in the night, which cannot know the glories of things flourishing in the brilliance of daylight, so it is with men bound to the darkness of spiritual ignorance."

GLN:15:49 "As a shadow in the night is mistaken for an intruder, or a mirage is mistaken for a pool of clear water, so does the spiritually immature man mistake the material body for the whole living being. As the shimmering heat haze appears like solid water, so does the outer body appear as the whole being to the spiritually unawakened. As, to a man in a moving boat, another boat lying still on the water will often appear to be moving, while he himself seems to remain still, so the unawakened spirit is deluded by appearances, seeing the mortal body as a whole being. When in fact the clouds are flying overhead, it appears as though the moon itself is speeding across the Heavens, it is only the knowledge and experience we have of the skies above, which tell us this cannot be the truth. Thus it is with the spiritually unawakened man who, in his ignorance, thinks the mortal body is the whole being, and, having no knowledge or experience of the spiritual region, is deceived. In fact all the beliefs of man which hold that the mortal body is the whole being are generated in the darkness of ignorance. A man may be wise in the ways of men, but completely ignorant and unaware of the higher, more glorious things, which are revealed in the light of the spirit."

GLN:15:50 "The man held in bondage to delusion says, "If there be another body, a part of me of which I am unaware, it cannot be real, neither can I know it. My eyes are infallible guides, seeing things just as they are, and any feelings I may experience have their origin within my mortal being. I am the child of my body." This man is deluded, like the creatures of the night, or as the man who sees a mirage. Are the eyes, which see mirages totally reliable? Motes swimming in the sunbeam are unsubstantial things, yet things such as these are the bricks of man's body, the eyes making them appear solid and substantial, the unreal for the real, his mortal body for his whole self. The deluded man ignores the spiritual part of his being and its needs. He cherishes the mortal body, gratifying its desires with earthly pleasures. Like the silkworm, he becomes captive in a cocoon of his own making. The man who lavishes undue care on the mortal body displays his own spiritual ignorance and inadequacy. To be free from existence in the darkness of ignorance, to know the glory of life in the light of spiritual consciousness, a man must first awaken his spirit; in this way alone can he become aware of his true nature."

GLN:15:51 "Ask yourselves, 'What am I? What is real within myself? What comprises the whole man? an it be that I am truly no more than this fleshy thing, the petty, immature, unstable being balanced between futile unearthly ideals and carnal cruelty and lust? Or am I something greater, which is undiscoverable by mortal senses? Am I really akin to something divine and glorious, from which source alone could have come the ideals and virtues which transcend the mundane needs of earthly existence?' Ask yourselves, in the solitudes, and perchance you will not go unanswered. I am the God of Silences."

GLN:15:52 "The words of men are inadequate to express just what man really is, the knowledge of his true nature is beyond the understanding of the unawakened spirit. The inheritance within the grasp of man is without limitation, for it is the totality of all things. Man has not been misled in the hope and belief that the seemingly mortal is in fact immortal. The spirit does not mislead men. They are deceived by their own eyes; they are misled, so they are unable to see things as they are in reality. All that men see and experience throughout earthly existence is veiled in illusion. Man may think his eyes reveal things as they are, but no mortal eye has ever beheld a thing as it actually is. It appears to man through the coloured distorting glass of his own mortality. Spiritually, men as a whole are little different from the madman who builds himself a kingdom from the fabric of his imagination. The flowing life existence about him is seen as a distorted image, a distortion, which his own defects have imparted to it. Yet it was meant to be thus, for man is surrounded by the conditions meet for him. It is for man to discover why this is so, and in discovering, he will find himself. I am the Truth. I am the Reality."

GLN:15:53 "This earthly life, which I have given you, should not be viewed in its minute aspect but in the light of infinitude. All the suffering and disillusionment, the futility, the forlorn hopes and wasted efforts, the oppressions and injustices are not without a purpose. That purpose is beyond anything man can understand and infinitely greater than his conception can grasp. The truly awakened man, alone among men, can have any insight into life's end and goal."

GLN:15:54 "These are divine things, yet they can be set down only in the mere words of men and will thus be reduced to things of mortal frailty.

Mere words will be read, and the pattern formed by them will be far short of Truth and Reality. The taste of a fruit or the fragrance of a flower cannot be known by reading about them. The fruit must be eaten, and the flower smelt. Only in union with Me, spirit communicating with Spirit, can proof of My reality be found. yet, because things are as they are, Truth must ever be veiled from man as man. But who would labour, if labourers were paid whether they worked or not? Were they revealed to him, the ignorant man would not comprehend great things, therefore the light is not for him. The insincere and shallow seeker after diversion and pleasure will find little entertainment in these words. The really illuminated man will already know something of the Truth and will therefore seek it more diligently along a higher path. So these words are given just for those sincere seekers who are aware of their own shortcomings and ignorance. These will be people whose thoughts are not smothered by prejudice, who are not set in their opinions. For who among men is the most confirmed in his opinions? Who states things in the most assertive manner and talks with the loudest voice? Is it not the most ignorant? I will not let the sincere seeker go unguided. I am the Light on the Path."

GLN:15:55 "Well do I know the hearts of men; they ever seek to deceive themselves. They clearly see the errors and follies of others, but are blind to their own. There are those whose idea of righteousness is mumbled words and repetitious prayers. Their souls are warped with selfish desires, and their Heaven is the fulfilment of these. Their prayers are pleas for pleasure or power, for freedom from the things which develop the spirit. The lovers of pleasure and power delight in following the path of their own inclinations, they build a creed of their own desires. They have neither courage nor the will to follow a sterner and true path. Avoid the companionship of such as these, setting your heart upon the task in hand rather than the reward. I am the Knower; I am the Rewarder."

GLN:15:56 "If a man fixes his attention wholly upon one goal or one thing for his own selfish purpose, as if it were an independent, all unrelated to others, thing, then he moves in darkness of ignorance. If he undertakes a task with a confused mind, not considering the outcome or where it will lead him, or the harm it may do to others or himself, then it is an undertaking of evil. There is a wisdom, which knows when to go and when to stay, when to speak and when to remain silent, what is to be done and what is to be left undone. It knows, too, the limitations set by fear and by courage, what constitutes bondage and what freedom. This is the wisdom I have placed at the disposal of man, if he would but seek it, the true wisdom of the spirit. Opposed to this clear-sighted wisdom is the false, man-made wisdom obscured by the darkness arising from delusion. Here, wrong is thought to be right, and error passes as Truth. things are thought to be what they are not. The unenlightened men dwelling in comfortable darkness, unperturbed by the challenge of reality as revealed by the light of Truth. lack any understanding of true values. That which appears to them to be no more than a cup of sorrow is in fact a chalice filled with the wine of immortality. The vain pleasures that come from pandering to the carnal cravings of the senses appear at first to be a cup of sweetness, but in the end it is found to hold the brew of bitterness. He who does right does it not for Me but for himself; he is the one who benefits, not his God. He who does wrong inflicts himself for it, and he is the sufferer. He who does right does it to his own good, and he who works wickedness does it to his own hurt. It could not be possible, in a just creation, that those whose ways are evil should be dealt with as are those who live goodly lives and perform good deeds. The fate of the selfish and that of the unselfish could not be alike. I am the God of Justice, the Maker of the Law."

GLN:15:57 "The spirit of man has the potential for doing all things; it can even rise above earthly limitations. The awakened soul can do whatsoever it wills. Man makes the environment for his own development; as it is now, so countless wills from the past have fashioned it. When the body awakens in the morning, it is like a man entering his habitation, it becomes a place of awareness. The soul becomes active in matter, that with which you hear, taste, smell and feel is the soul. Physically, the ear of a dead man is still in perfect condition for hearing, but the hearer, the interpreter, has gone. The eyes of a corpse are not blinded, but that which operated them is no longer there."

GLN:15:58 "So long as the soul looks outward only, into the deceptive environment of matter and is satisfied with the material pleasures it finds there, and which its baser body finds compatible, it remains cut off from the greater realm of the spirit. It binds itself to matter, failing to find the greater pleasures always there in the silent depths of its being. Confirmed in his attitude by experiences in a deceptive environment, mortal man becomes convinced that all desirable things lie outside himself. He concludes that satisfaction comes from gaining the things which promote material welfare. This is the folly of the unbalanced man. However, balance is the keyword, for it is equally foolish to turn away from material things altogether. Man is made of earthly things, because it is intended that he should live and express himself on Earth. It is also intended that he should discover his nature through earthly conditions and experiences."

GLN:15:59 "However, the Divine Spark must kindle the spirit. It must not be smothered. Balance is the ideal, the whole becoming neither wholly inwardly nor outwardly orientated. Man needs his body and must not repudiate it, and if it requires man's labour to sustain it, then is not man entitled to enjoy its pleasures? Here also it is simply a matter of proper balance. Man lives in a sea of material manifestation where I am only indirectly reflected, as the soul of man is indirectly reflected in his body. If a man sees with nothing but the eyes of the body, then he cannot perceive Me, for I am beyond his vision. I am the God veiled Behind Matter; I am the God of the Spirit."

GLN:15:60 "Yet there is a vision possible to man, which pierces the universal veil, a vision free from all obscurity, a vision uncontaminated by the dark shadows of base desires or fear, by unstable emotions or unworthy motives. It is the vision seen when man develops a new faculty, a new sense. It is an inward vision of splendour. A wave of spiritual light will engulf him; a mysterious power indescribable in mere words sweeps like a shooting star over the expanse of his spirit, giving a sudden illuminating flash which floods his whole inner being, his soul, with a glorious light. In its brilliance he is granted, for a brief moment in time, a glimpse of the vision splendid. He is then united with the living heart of the universe by a bond reaching out to infinity. Nothing known to man, no symbols of his conception can express the joyousness which floods his whole being. It can be experienced in quiet tranquillity of spirit. It can burst all the bounds of restraint, expressing itself in an all-embracing, overwhelming feeling of love. Lost in an unfathomable sea of silent contemplation, the body will shine with radiance from the inner light, and all about will be bathed in a luminous, spiritual glow. Having once been in divine communication, these awakened spirits know a joy supreme, and never again do they walk through the veil of mortal sorrows. The truly awakened soul is beyond carnal lust and mortal grief; his love is alike for all My creation, and thus he shows supreme love for Me. By this love alone he knows Me in Truth. Who and What I am, and knowing Me in Truth he participates in My Whole Being. Those who seek union with Me must first prepare a dwelling place for Me in their hearts; but those who are not pure, those who do not fight for Me, those who have not suffered under the discipline of love and those without wisdom cannot attain union, no matter how much they strive. I am the God of Illumination; I am the God of Enlightenment."

GLN:15:61 "Would you know the ultimate state of man when he has finally reached his goal, when he has entered into his inheritance of divinity? It is a state of glory transcending anything conceivable by him during an earthbound existence. His consciousness expands to embrace everything, all that ever was or will be. He sees all. He knows all. He is in all, and he contains all. These things come to him through infinite powers of perception; yet he is above all such powers. He is beyond all yet within all. He is beyond the realm of matter, freed from all restrictions; yet he is not denied its joys and may, if he so desires, manifest again in matter. His thoughts have the power of creation. He is one with the Light of Lights, the Light transcending vision. He is the partaker of My Substance, My son in eternity, the inheritor of everlasting life. I am your God, the Father of Man."

Chapter Sixteen – The Spirit of God

GLN:16:1 "I am the immortality latent in all things mortal. The light filling all things with radiance, the power holding all things to their form. I am the pure, invulnerable stream untouchable by evil, the supreme fountainhead of thoughts, the unfailing well of consciousness, the light of eternity. I am that to which the soul of man is related. I am its power, its life, its strength. I am that to which it responds."

GLN:16:2 "I am the sweet coolness in refreshing waters and the comforting warmth in the sun. I am the calmness of peace in the radiance of the moon and the delicacy in the moonbeam. I am the sound heard in the stillness, the companionship felt in the solitude and the stirring in the hearts of men. I am the cheerfulness in the laugh of a youth and the gentleness in the sigh of a maiden. I am the joy in the life of all living things and the content in the hearts of awakened souls. I am the beauty in the beautiful and the fragrance in the fragrant. I am the sweetness in honey and the scent in perfume. I am the power in the strong arm and the wistfulness in a smile. I am the urge in good and moderate desires. I am the gaiety in gladness, the restlessness in life, the refreshment in sleep. Yet though I am in all these, I am not contained in them, and they are in me rather than I am in them. How pitiful are the words of men to depict sublime things! With the souls of men asleep, enwrapped in clouds of delusion, how can I be known to them?"

GLN:16:3 "I am of the Supreme, the Eternal, of God and from God, yet not God. As heat to fire, as fragrance to flowers, as light to a lamp, so am I to God. I am the power of God operating in matter. I am the first created of creation, I am the eternal thread, upon which all creation is strung. I am the effective thought of God. I am that brought forth by His creating command, wherein all things share life. I am the Lord of forms holding all things together."

GLN:16:4 "I am the power giving form, I am the comforting companion of the way. I am that which gives substance to the hopes and desires of men. Think of me therefore in any way you will. I am the companionable one, the comforter. I am the waters of inspiration springing from the Eternal Fount. I am the glory of love shining forth from the Central Sun. I am in all things."

GLN:16:5 "I am the root of the tree of life, the words written in the Book of God. I am the guardian of knowledge, the wisdom of the soul. I am the harmoniser of sound, the controller of power, the keeper of matter and the sustainer of shapes. I unroll the scroll of time and record its changes. I am the reader of past and present, the scribe of change, the chooser of chance."

GLN:16:6 "I am victory and the struggle for victory, but I am more, I am that, which defeats defeat, for I am the victory in defeat. I am the goodness of those who are good, but I am more, for I am the success that arises out of failure. I am the achievement remaining when all else has gone."

GLN:16:7 "I am the sublime veiling secret mysteries. I am the guardian who jealously discloses hidden things. I am the knowledge of the knower. I am the seed within the seed, from which all things spring. I am the bricks of which all things are built. I am more; I am the clay and water within the bricks. I am the motion in all things that move, without me there is no movement. I am the stability in all things stable, without me no thing holds to its shape."

GLN:16:8 "I am the craftsman with innumerable shapes, the artist with countless colours. My labours are outside the knowledge of men, my works beyond their sight. My masterpieces will never be seen by mortal eyes."

GLN:16:9 "That which abides in breath and yet is other than breath, which breath itself cannot know or influence, which controls it from within itself, that am I. That which is behind the voice, which voice itself cannot know or influence, which controls it from behind itself, that am I. That which is in the eye, yet is other than the eye, which the eye itself cannot know or influence, which controls it from within, that am I. That which is behind the touch, and yet is other than touch, which touch itself cannot know or influence, which manipulates it from behind itself, that am I. Yet this you must know: I am not you, nor are you me, though I abide in you as you abide in me. Let wisdom disentangle these feeble words set down through the hands of mortal men."

GLN:16:10 "The glory that shines from the Lord of the Day, the gentle gleam radiating from the Mistress of the Night, the comforting glow from the hearth fire; all these are of my substance. I penetrate Earth with love. I raise up the seed. I am the breath within the breath of all living things. I am the sweet scent of flowers and the bitter tang of vinegar. I am the differentiating essence in all things."

Chapter Seventeen – The Song of the Soul

GLN:17:1 "I am the sleeper awakened from slumber. I am the seed of life eternal. I am the everlasting hope of man. I am a shoot of the Spirit Divine. I am the soul."

GLN:17:2 "I have been since the beginning of time and shall be forever. I am the design interwoven in the warp and weft of creation. I am the indestructible essence of life. I am the treasure chest of man's hopes and aspirations, the storehouse of lost loves and fulfilled dreams."

GLN:17:3 "Before time, I was an unconscious spirit potential, united with the Supreme All. Ever since time began, I was in the slumbering sea of spirit, waiting to be drawn forth into separate mortal incarnation. Now, though the mortal body enwrapping me fall apart and decay, I remain everlasting and immortal. Through all the ebb and flow of life, whatever destiny decrees, I remain the everlasting jewel of ages, invisible to mortal eyes and untouchable by mortal hands."

GLN:17:4 "I am the eternal bride of mortal men, ever awaiting the awakening kiss, the whisper of recognition. O being of flesh, deny me not; let me not dwell in forgotten solitude, left alone, unwanted and unheeded. Hold me to you as a lover holds the beloved; reach out beyond earthly things and kiss the lips that are yours eternally. Look out beyond the sphere of earthly opposites, out beyond the pettiness of gains and possessions. Grasp and possess me, your own everlasting and responsive soul."

GLN:17:5 "You will not find me where emotional tempests rage, or while sensual storms bring turmoil and disquiet. First subdue these, for I await beyond, in the quietness of calm waters. I must be sought as a lover seeks the loved one, in solitude, amid quietness and tranquillity, only there will I respond to the awakening kiss of recognition."

GLN:17:6 "Do not neglect me, O my beloved, or tarnish me; for I come to you as an inestimable treasure. I bring beauty and innocence, gaiety and wholesomeness, decency and consideration, a jewel of potential perfection. Do not drag me down with you into the demon-haunted regions of darkness and terror. I am yours, closer to you than any loved one of Earth. If you spurn me, I go down to a terrible doom in darkness, there to be purged and purified from the corruption of your touch. The best I can then hope for is to be bestowed upon another."

GLN:17:7 "I am the sublime vehicle awaiting the command to bear your trueself to its destiny of glory. Could anyone be so foolhardy as not to cherish me? Without moving, I am swifter than thought; on celestial wings I far outstrip the range of mortal senses. I drink at the fountain of life and feed on the fruits of eternal energy."

GLN:17:8 "What are you, my beloved, but a passing thing fashioned of clay? A handful of dust given life by a spark from the everlasting flame. I, myself, am no more than potential. Yet together, we are so great that Earth of itself alone cannot contain us, we transcend it to reach out into the spheres of divinity. Take me, awaken me, acknowledge me, cherish me, and I will carry you to realms of glory unimaginable on Earth."

GLN:17:9 "I am the imprisoned captive longing for return to the freedom of the infinite. Yet, because of my mortal love I feel heartpangs of sorrow for things that pass away. But I know that beyond the pains inseparable from a sojourn in the vale of tears, there shines a glorious rainbow of hope and joy. There is a place of abiding love centred on the infinite; there, if you will but cherish me, we shall not be denied expression."

GLN:17:10 "I am drawn, by the law of spiritual gravitation, towards union with the Universal Soul and can no more escape return there than the mortal elements of man can escape their return to dust. Man sees glory by the reflected light of glory within him, he knows love by the love within himself. The sun is seen by the light of the sun and not by any light within man. Man sees the spirit by the light of the spirit, and not by any light within his mortal self. Only by the light of the spirit can the spirit of man be lit."

GLN:17:11 "I am at peace when awakened to communion with my God. I am joyful when enthroned in consciousness and when endowed with wisdom and vision transcending that of Earth. I delight in communion with the great sphere, with which I am akin. I rejoice in union with the Divine Spirit from whence I came. I am your own trueself, which should be forever cherished. By listening to my whispers, by letting your thoughts dwell on me and by knowing me, the whole glory of the greater spheres is opened unto you."

GLN:17:12 "I am that which reads what the eye sees, understands what the ear hears, knows what the hand feels, tastes whatever enters the mouth and smells whatever is borne on the nose. I am the indwelling consciousness, which knows and enjoys all the good things of Earth. Those who dwell in the darkness of delusion cannot know me, and to them is lost the greatest glory of life. All conceptions of beauty, love and kindness are due to the consciousness residing in me. When I depart from my earthly abode, I will carry with me the knowledge of the senses, as the wind carries perfume from the flower."

GLN:17:13 "I am not born, nor will I ever die. Once awakened to an existence in consciousness, I can never become nothingness. I am the everlasting one who dies not when life departs from the body. O call me forth; awaken me from sleep with the kiss bestowing conscious life. Let me not lie unnoticed, wrapped in the heavy mantle of perpetual slumber, dreamless, unknowing."

GLN:17:14 "I am the indestructible one. Fire cannot burn me, swords cannot maim me or water smother me. When a drum is beaten, the sound it gives forth cannot be grasped or held. As that sound, so am I. When a shell is blown, the note it gives forth cannot be grasped or held. As that note, so am I. When a pipe is played, the music it gives forth cannot be grasped or held. As that music, so am I. I am the immaterial in the material awaiting recognition, but in my own sphere I am the substantial one. There, man-known matter is no more substantial than the dawn mists are here."

GLN:17:15 "I am the fire of life in all things that breathe, and in union with the breath I consume the nourishing substance within the food, which feeds the body. I am the kernel within the seed in the heart of all. I am the guardian of memory and the arbiter of wisdom."

GLN:17:16 "These things are mine and ever with me. They are to me what the bones and muscles are to the mortal body. The waking and sleeping consciousness. The awareness of self. The five powers of feeling and the five of activity. The controlling spirit, which is the sensitive being."

GLN:17:17 "I am the living consciousness within you; I am the knower. The things seen by the eye and the things smelt by the nose are received by me. The things heard and the things felt are registered by me. I am the inner being causing all decisions to be made, though the tongue report back outside the things that I, the soul and the spirit, hold recorded. Everything done and undertaken, such as the working of the hands and movement of the legs, all are done in accordance with my command."

GLN:17:18 "When I depart, the body without me is as useless as a worn-out garment, which is discarded and cast aside. Do we go together, my beloved, hand in hand as lovers? Do I return home radiant in the pride of blooming consciousness, or, spurned and humiliated, return without sensitivity, memory or knowledge? Do I return to be welcomed with joy in the light of glory, or must I shamefully seek refuge in the darkness? I am yours, my beloved, do with me as you will. I am yours everlastingly."

Book of
Scrolls

SCL:1:8 These are the words to be spoken to those who peer from beyond the Dark Portal: His arm was ever ready to help those who did good for others, and he lent his power to those who ordered what was good. He stood for those who could no longer stand and commanded for those who could no longer command. He carried the weary and succoured the helpless. He never oppressed the weak, nor did he permit injustices to go unpunished and unrectified.

Table of Chapters

BOOK OF SCROLLS
Table of Chapters (Continued)

Book of Scrolls

Chapter One –
The Sacred Registers – Part 1

SCL:1:1 Herein are recorded sacred things, which should never be written, but the memory of man is like a storehouse made of straw, or like a storepit dug in sand.

SCL:1:2 Even less enduring is his body, for it is a frail thing of fleeting substance, which passes away like the dew in the morning. And what of the mortal chain, which links the generations in knowledge? Behold, it is a thing prone to distortion, a transmuter of tradition and Truth.

SCL:1:3 Therefore, when the command went forth from the Great One illuminated with wisdom and came to your servant, he saw fit to quell the doubts engendered by fear and undertook to do the thing, which had not been done before, placing his trust fully in the protecting wings which are spread by the words issuing from the Royal Residence.

SCL:1:4 These are the words spoken by the Great interpreter, who, through the powers inherited by him from above and by the powers now in his keeping, all freely bestowed upon him by the grateful hearts of his people below, will lead us into the Fields Of Everlasting Glory.

SCL:1:5 O Exalted One, intermediate between gods and men, what we now do for you do you for us. Let your deeds and your words become our words. Thus it ever was, and thus it will ever be while mortal beings make pilgrimage through this valley of tears.

SCL:1:6 Speak thus in your hour: the High Born One has not blasphemed the Divine Powers, nor has he paid undue homage to earthly desires. He has not been loudmouthed in the Sacred Places, nor laughed when he should have been grave. His tongue is pure, for when fed with the words of men, he absorbs Truth and excretes falsehood. His mouth has never spewed forth words of malice or envy; words of oppression or injustice never passed his lips.

SCL:1:7 Look now at the great dark water mirror and see what is reflected there from the mists swirling along the corridor of time. Seeing your place, make ready, so that when the summons comes from the Dark One, you are not caught unprepared.

SCL:1:8 These are the words to be spoken to those who peer from beyond the Dark Portal: His arm was ever ready to help those who did good for others, and he lent his power to those who ordered what was good. He stood for those who could no longer stand and commanded for those who could no longer command. He carried the weary and succoured the helpless. He never oppressed the weak, nor did he permit injustices to go unpunished and unrectified.

SCL:1:9 He stood by the side of the Great Potter, and because of his plea, the clay was shaped to a more pleasing form. He erased disfiguring faults and smoothed the roughness. He added stiffness to the mixture.

SCL:1:10 He has done no evil; his words have always been true. He stands unashamed and fearless before the twin shrines. Even as it was in the Land of the Great River, so let it be here. Let him not be cut off by distance.

SCL:1:11 Let not his power be cut off, for he stands between the worlds. Let it flow out like living waters unto the living and be as shining rays to the Radiant Ones. For here, we see the power darkly, while beyond the horizon it shines brightly.

SCL:1:12 He is everlastingly faithful in heart, for he has admitted no other who would defile him. He has remained loyal to the sacred words and has diligently perused the great writings. He has navigated the shallows of the winding waters. Now, he draws near.

SCL:1:13 He has left his kingdom of trial, he has overcome the challenges of life, he has done all things written on the tablets of Truth, and he has sojourned in the Chamber of Profound Silence. He has done all things which are proper and been reassured that he has followed the right path. He does not fear judgement.

SCL:1:14 Let him reunite with The Supreme One who sent him forth, so that he will not be separated from the waters of life. Let the Holy Heat enwrap him when he passes through the Place of Coldness. Let his nostrils inhale the breath of nourishment, that he may live and that we may partake of his existence.

SCL:1:15 Do not repudiate him, but make him welcome. Do you not recognise the one you endowed with power? Has he become too radiant? Is his form too glorious? Read what is written in the books of his heart. You set him in darkness, and he saw. You set him in silence, and he heard. You set him in emptiness, and he felt. You established him in nothingness, and he gathered substance. Therefore, he returns with manifold powers. He is well fitted to be presented to those who stand before The Supreme One.

SCL:1:16 When the bright sun shines with splendour in the dayskies above, the gentle morning star hides her face in modesty and becomes unseen. All the great Company of the radiant nightlights withdraw before the majesty of the greater light. Yet, when darkness eats the shining disk we know again the comforting presence of the eternal stars, so let it be with your servant.

SCL:1:17 The Dark Ones who dwell in their compatible gloom cannot claim him as one of their own; he cannot be numbered among their dreadful company. His heart is pure, his deeds were good, no creature spawned in murkiness has gained control of his thoughts. His desires have not been generated by denizens of the darkness.

SCL:1:18 He who was afflicted here is not afflicted forever; he is made whole; he is freed from pain; his sickness has departed. He rejoices in the light; therefore, let him be drawn towards the greater light where you are. Let him not see the place of darkness; let him not behold the Hideous Ones fashioned by wickedness, the Dwellers in the Dark Recesses, who shrink before the light, or the Twisted Ones moulded by lewd desires.

SCL:1:19 He brings with him a lamp lit from the flame of Truth. he bears the rod of righteousness which rewards those who have overcome tribulations. O let him pass to the right side of the dividing flame! He has left us, he is coming to you, he approaches, he throws off the earthly wrappings, he stands free, he stands glorious. Does he not glow with splendour? Behold him, your worthy companion in brightness. Is he not wholly compatible with those of your company? See, he is a Shining One, a Hero of the Horizon. Is he not one destined to abide everlastingly? Take him, lead him to the Realm of Glory, show him his place in the Spheres of Splendour.

SCL:1:20 The eyes that were deceived on Earth now see clearly. O what splendours are revealed! The music unheard by earthly ears now sounds sweet melodious music. O what joyous rapture it brings! The nostrils inhale perfumes too delicate for the earthly nose, O how the heart sings! All drabness, all dullness and all sordidness, which are of the Earth, are left behind. Turn him from the place where these can regather about him.

SCL:1:21 The unmoving, empty body remains here before our eyes; it is nothing, it sees not, it hears not, it speaks not, it smells not, its breath is stilled, it begins to fall apart. There is no life, and the overseer has departed. Nothing remains here with us but this unresponsive thing. The greatness, the feeling, the sensitivity have departed from the body and are now beyond our ken. These are with the real surviving being. O receive him into the life of splendour! We, who are here, stand blinded behind the veil of flesh; we cannot see beyond ourselves; we hope, we believe and we trust. Thus it has ever been with men, for they pass their lives behind a wall of limitations, there is a barrier shutting them in. They are imprisoned within a mortal body. O grant us fulfilment, grant us that which is the ultimate desire and aspiration of men!

SCL:1:22 We speak for this man. He is one who came with us from afar. He is one who has travelled a long weary road. No taint of meanness stained the purity of his spirit, no corruption of deceit discoloured the garments of his soulself. He has gone over shining in radiant splendour, so even the doomed in their darkness can hope when they sight his distant glow. May it shed some small warmth into their grim coldness!

SCL:1:23 O Great Welcomer, who greets the newcomers, help our departed one. He served well in this place of trial and tribulation; let him not go unrewarded. He is the son of hope. Like us, like those who went before, he hoped as men have always hoped, for this is not a place of certainties. If it were, our heritage of glory would be badly earned.

SCL:1:24 He lives because it is ordained that he live; he lives, for all men live everlastingly. They die not, they perish not, they endure through ages. His Kohar awaits him and needs hide no awful aspect in shame. Let his face shine in greeting; welcome home the wanderer.

SCL:1:25 This tombed structure is not a place of finality. The grave is not the goal of earthly life, any more than the soil is the goal of the seed. Does seed die within the ground? Is it planted intending that it be mingled with the soil and lost'?

SCL:1:26 O Great Welcomer, let your face shine with gladness when you greet the homecoming wanderer. Lead him to the Kohar, which is his inheritance, that he may enter into it and enjoy its embrace. Let him find completion and fulfilment by absorption into his Kohar.

SCL:1:27 Our departed one was the whole part which came forth from the whole, and he returns to the whole. Nothing is lost, nothing is gone. He lives over there, lives more fully than he ever lived. He lives in splendour, he lives in beauty, he lives in knowledge and in the waters of life. He is everlasting.

SCL:1:28 O departed one risen to glory, you are now a released spirit united with your spirit whole, the companionable Kohar, the everlasting one. Arise alive in the Land Beyond the Horizon, and journey to the Land of Dawning; the stars accompanying you will sing for joy, while the heavenly signs voice hymns of praise and gladness. You are not far removed from us; it is as if we were in one room divided by a curtain, therefore we are not sorrowful. If we weep it is because we cannot share your joys and because we no longer know your touch.

SCL:1:29 O everlasting Kohar, take this man of goodness into your eternal embrace; let your life become his life and your breath his breath. He is your own; he is the drop returning to the filled pitcher, the leaf returning to the tree; you are the repository of his incarnations. As you grew there, so he grew here; you are everlastingly, whole, and he lives in you. If he is not even as you in face, let him enter; hide his faults, for they are not many. For this you were fashioned; for this you came into being. You are the overbody awaiting the returning spirit, and the spirit now comes. You are that which will clothe the newly arrived spirit in heavenly flesh. You are that in which our departed one will express himself.

SCL:1:30 O Kohar, hear us. Here is your vitalising essence; before you were incomplete; now you are whole. Draw your own, your compatible one, to you and observe the many likenesses.We send fragrances, that they may spread around you. Now take the eye, which will perfect your face; it is the perfecting eye, the eye which sees things as they are. See the fluctuating wraith; is it not beautiful? Does it not come with an aura of fragrance, sweetness filling the air? It has been purged of all impurities; all about it is fragrant. Therefore, grant it your substance, that it may become solid and firm.

SCL:1:31 O Kohar, long have you awaited the day of fulfilment, the day of your destiny. That day is here; it is now; therefore, take the spirit, which is your own and enfold it with your wings. Each to his own and to his own each goes. You and he are bound together with unseverable bonds; each without the other is nothing. Now bear him up, for in that place you are greater than he, for you are the generator. While he rested in the womb, you were active; as he grew, you grew before him. If he has done wrong, and who among men is guiltless, then in you let the wrong be adjusted. You are his hope, you are his shield and you are his refuge.

SCL:1:32 This we say to the Brilliant One, the Guardian of Goodness: The departed one has not walked with ignorance; he has not been slothful in carrying the burden of his duty. He has not been swayed by passions of the body; he has not despoiled the house of another; he has not caused undue sorrow, nor has he maltreated a child for pleasure. He has succoured the poor and weak; he has done all that is good; therefore, let none of Those Who Lurk in Darkness seize him. His radiant light is strong; those who would seize him are repulsed by the light and slink away. He lives; he lives forever.

SCL:1:33 He has lived worthily; he has been purified by the fires of earthly life; he has been refined in the furnace of tribulation, he has overcome all earthly temptations. He has lived the life which enhances goodness; he has prepared himself for life in the light. Receive him, O Brilliant One!

SCL:1:34 O Kohar, absorb into yourself the life-force; it was meant for you; it is yours. It is the enlivening spirit, which spans the two worlds. He, the departed one, was you, and even more so were you he. Come to him as the Beauteous One came to Belusis, a great king, and gathered him in compassion and love. Come, that he may awaken to new life in your arms.

SCL:1:35 This man, the departed one, who in unity with you becomes the Glorious One, was born of a god and is the child of two gods, after the nature of greater men. Now, you are impregnated with the living spirit of he who was prepared by trial on Earth for you. Behold, in unity your twain are now throbbing with life, and your brightness bedazzles the eyes. You are now a Star of Life, a Living Star, and to a star, you shall ascend to rule its life.

SCL:1:36 The departed one is now freed, he is loosed from the bonds of illusion, he is saved from the dark waters of unreality and is one with the Eternal Light. These things we declare, so let them be. Our thoughts mould a new reality beyond the present real, and this becomes the reality of tomorrow.

SCL:1:37 O great, substantial Kohar, protect this departed one, your own, from the accusations of false-fronted beings, remembering the faithful heart ever prevailing before the balances of our forefathers from far away. Put into his mouth those words, which open doors. Let the goodness in him prevail, but you, yourself, stand up and bear witness for him. He suffered from the frailties of men. He was wrathful when provoked and surly when enduring great burdens. His temper flashed quickly when his words were not accepted or his ways followed, and at times, he lacked consideration. However, these are small things inseparable from the frailties of mortal men, and in all greater things, he was good. Let not the false-fronted one disguised in his brother's form possess him; guard him from the beings lurking in the shadows this side of the darkness.

SCL:1:38 I see this, my brothers. Behold, the departed one goes to meet his own image. It is his own self reflected in his image. It is his own self that comes to greet him. It is his Kohar, which embraces him. It welcomes him as though he were one ransomed from captivity. I see them blend, and he becomes a new seed in the heart of his Kohar.

SCL:1:39 I hear the Kohar speak; it names itself Nevakohar. It says, "O man of pure thoughts, of kindly words, of quiet speech, of good deeds, come to me. I am your being, yet I am not you; as you have loved and cherished me, so I now love and cherish you. I am your reward, as I would have been your affliction." They are now united, and this is the place of the first threshold, from whence the Completed Beings depart.

SCL:1:40 The departed one now stands in his own form and likeness. He becomes the Great Ship-Borne Voyager and passes over the waters to the Place of Reeds, but his weaknesses do not bear him down, and he goes through. Great Ones, lift him up, let him not fall into the fetid waters of decay. He is a worthy son of Lewth. Then, the lesser is carried by the greater, while Dark Ones gaze up from their misery and wait silently to see if he is borne up. The Glorious One goes past in peace, for he is not compatible with their dark company. He remains unmolested, for flame confounds the hands of slime.

SCL:1:41 An unloosed Dark One comes up saying it will take this man, but is repulsed by brightness. It is a thing of maimed rottenness, for on Earth it was clothed in lust-saturated flesh, though contained in a form of beauty. The heart of this man is not faint; see him now, is he not sure of his welcome among Beings of Glory? He is as the wild bull, the prince of herds; he is a Great One among the Everlasting Spirits.

SCL:1:42 He reaches the firm ground where a Bright Being welcomes him, and he is named 'The Newcomer'. He has landed on the shore and climbed the Steps of Splendour. He is in the company of Shining Spirits, and his earthlife companions greet him; they welcome him, saying, "All this beauty and splendour is yours to enjoy." They bring garments of beauty, bright clothes of radiance.

SCL:1:43 He has passed through the Hall of Judgement. The Twin Truths have heard his plea, and those who bore witness have departed. He has crossed the waters and ascended the steps; now he has attained the threshold of immortality and stands in rapture. He has passed by the regions of darkness and gloom and is with glory. He comes to everlasting life in a true form of splendour, to dwell evermore as a living spirit within his Kohar. How wonderful it is to be united and one with the Kohar!

SCL:1:44 The Newcomer looks back across the waters to the Place of Decision; then, he turns and ascends the steps to the threshold of immortality. He is in his true form, yet he is a spirit within his Kohar. He speaks, but it is not the speech of men, and all understand him. His hearing is all-embracing. He sees both the powers of Light and the powers of Darkness, but the powers of Darkness no longer affect him.

SCL:1:45 The Newcomer has reached his compatible abode. He has fought the battle, which is mortal life, and risen supreme to victory. He has not been vanquished by the Raging Ones which are the bodily passions. At each step forward he has left a lifeless form; at each step he has fought a shadow; at each step he has won the clash of arms.

SCL:1:46 The Newcomer has sought out and discovered the One Hidden Behind the Two and the Three, which stand before them. He knows the secrets of the Nine, which veil the others from the eyes of men. He has unravelled the skein of life's mysteries, even as those enlightened ones yet living on Earth must do.

SCL:1:47 There is no suffering or pain in the Newcomer; he cannot feel hurt, neither can he be sorrowful. If a companion of his Earth journey be numbered among the Dark Ones, then his heart is soothed with forgetfulness; but later, he will remember, and because of his efforts, the Dark One will be returned to the crucible.

Chapter Two – The Sacred Registers – Part 2

SCL:2:1 The writings of Garmi were brought by the hands of Nadayeth The Enlightener, of the twin cities whence come the Sons of Fire, when he fled the wrath of kings. He spread out before the Learned Ones beauteous things of many colours and spoke to them after this fashion, and I, Lavos, recorded it in the tongue of the Sons of Fire:

SCL:2:2 Behold this; it is the Land of the Dawning. It stands between the Land of Light ever splendid and the Land of Darkness ever gloomy. They are the lands beyond the veil; before the veil is the Land of the Living.

SCL:2:3 The Aspiring One has embarked on the waters of illusion; his craft is afloat but it has not yet reached the shores where the promise of new life is fulfilled. Now, he is guided by two beings, one a lovely maiden and the other an ill-visaged man. These two strive one with the other, each grasping one side of the craft; now, it overturns. The maiden seeks to drag the Aspiring One down, while the ill-favoured man seeks to keep him afloat. But the Aspiring One struggles against him. They come to the sands of the shining shore where the Light of Truth turns the maiden into a vile-faced hag and the man into a handsome youth. The Aspiring One lies on the sands of Shodew as one dead, for he had fought against the man who sought to save him.

SCL:2:4 The Beauteous One comes attended by handmaidens, and with them are the companions of the Aspiring One's earthly life. There, too, is his soulself, awaiting his embrace. The Aspiring One lies as dead, for he did not know his saviour. They who stand about, who are The Welcomers, wait in uncertainty. The Beauteous One bends over the prostrate man and says, "Revive, this is not a place where death rules." He moves, and she says, "Raise yourself and cast away the residue of your mortality."

SCL:2:5 The Aspiring One opens his eyes, he sits up, he shields his eyes before the vision of beauty, he is blinded by it and she gives him his heart. The handmaidens weep and their tears are the blood of the Aspiring One's life. The Beauteous One says, "I have come that you who were dead might live, that you who were blinded might see, that you who were deceived might know Truth." The soul self says, "I have come to embrace you, I have come to protect you, I have come to shield you, I am your refuge."

SCL:2:6 That which is the Kohar says, "I have come to brighten up your face, I am you, as you are me. I have waited for you; I have wept for you and rejoiced when you rejoiced. I have never forgotten you while we have been apart. I have heard every word spoken, and these are recorded for you. I have recorded every sight. I have recorded every sound. I have recorded every smell and every taste. Every memory is secure for you. Here I give you form and substantiality."

SCL:2:7 This is The Herald; he stands between this man and his Kohar, and they, together with The Adjuster and The Welcomers, go to the Hall of Judgement and stand before The Lord of Life, The Master of Destinies. Now come The Lords of Eternity, who are The Lesser Gods, and they enter the Gates of Splendour. The Balancer comes from his secret place. The Greeter to Darkness stands at his door, and The Greeter to Splendour stands at his door; they face each other. The Welcomers, compatible companions of this man's earthly life, stand about; they are there, in the Hall of Judgement.

SCL:2:8 The Balancer causes two fluid-like, fluctuating columns, which stand on either side of the Kohar and one takes the form of the Aspiring One, but it is horribly malformed, because it mirrors all his wickednesses and weaknesses, The other shines brightly, for it mirrors all his goodness and spiritual qualities. Then the two columns merge back into the Kohar, and The Adjuster adjusts with justice and mercy. Then the Aspiring One stands forth in his Kohar and in his true likeness, which is a blending together of all his incarnational likenesses.

SCL:2:9 The Aspiring One is drawn towards the right hand door; he passes through and sets foot on the rainbow road. He is accompanied by The Welcomers, the companions of his earthly life, who are now revealed to him in their true likeness. They sing, they dance, they rejoice, and there is much gladness in the reunion. The word of Truth is established; it is fulfilled. The ancient promises are fulfilled. He who departs shall return, he who sleeps shall awaken, he who dies shall live. The Aspiring One has passed into the Regions of Glory.

SCL:2:10 Now, behold the body vacated by the vehicle of life. It slumbers in its death wrappings, for the enlivening spirit has flown. The earthly body alone stays and cannot hold itself together. It prepares to fall apart and decay. The Companions of the Dead take it into their company; it will be made incorruptible and become a communicating door. It is given the things which rightly belong to the dead.

SCL:2:11 Those who remain on Earth fear the Life Shadow of the One who has gone on before them. The body is bandaged in its death wrappings. It is purified, it is made clean, it is provided with the necessities. Thus, the Life Shadow shall dwell at peace within the empty body; it believes it to be its abode. It shall not wander. O Shadow, do not wander; remain within the tomb; seize any who come to steal; seize any who would break the body; seize any who would open that which is closed. Seize and haunt, seize and haunt!

SCL:2:12 The Companions of the Dead speak thus, "The Life Shadow of this man who was is never restless; it never wanders, it is ever protecting, it is ever watchful. It remains, for it is bound to the empty corpse by the restraining throngs."

SCL:2:13 They say, "The spirit of this man has awakened in the Land of Immortality, it rejoices in the Land Beyond the Horizon. He is a Hero of the Horizon. Offend him not by thinking that he is dead; he cannot die, for he is with the Ever Living. He has not gone away to die; he has departed to live elsewhere. Let the moisture of his body return to the waters of the Earth from whence it came. Let the things of hardness in his body return to the dust from whence they came. Let his bones rejoin the stones which once they were."

SCL:2:14 "Weep not, for your tears and lamentations restrain his eager spirit. Sing the death dirge, that its echoes may sound the toscin in the Region of Light and The Splendid Ones and The Welcomers come to the place of appointment. It is unfitting to force gladness on a sorrowful heart, but be sad only for a temporary parting."

SCL:2:15 "Let not the earthly body of this man who was, become destitute; surround it with care and affection, so that it may transmit the substance of life. Sustain it, so the Life Shadow remain within."

SCL:2:16 "What see you now? Gaze upon it, the frail mortal remains enwrapped and silent, unresponsive. Ponder, this you see with the eyes of the body, which cannot perceive things of the spirit. Were the eyes of your spirit opened but a brief moment, you would perceive something entirely different, and then you would know that his shining, immortal spirit walks in the company of those risen to glory."

SCL:2:17 "It is the time for parting, the time for farewell, for the closing of the door."

SCL:2:18 "O departed one risen to glory, who has left us to sorrow. As we have helped you and surrounded you with the protection of our love and our offerings, so now help us in the days of life left to us on Earth."

Chapter Three – The Sacred Registers – Part 3

SCL:3:1 Behold, one comes wearing white sandals and clad in fine linen. Arise, stand up to greet him. He bears the staff of righteousness. He brings a pearl of priceless value; take it and become perfect.

SCL:3:2 Others come, fair women and young children. His father's heir has come, and the four great ones who bear sweet waters, who spread the feast and rejoice under the strong arm of their protector. He who has gone is not forgotten, but this is the day of the living.

SCL:3:3 He who has inherited ceases from weeping and begins to smile; the protecting one comes in peace. The heart in the sky is no longer small; it expands; it grows large. Thus it is also with the heart of he who lives; his days of lamentations are over, and his heart swells and grows large.

SCL:3:4 The good son never ceases from faithful service on behalf of the absent one who has escaped from the confinement of the body. The dutiful son now calls upon the absent one for protection from wandering shadows and from the molestations of Life Shadows.

SCL:3:5 O Bountiful, Ever Considerate One, hear the words of your faithful and dutiful son, as they ascend with the blue, penetrating smoke of fragrant incense. Let no shadow wander from your safe abode to haunt our habitations, for they who dwell therein have done you no dishonour. Safeguard the Dark Doorway, that things in vile forms come not near us to pollute our bodies with sickness and disease.

SCL:3:6 You left, and before the waters rose again the man of Shodu, he who dealt harshly with the widow dwelling beside the channel of black stones, departed for his judgement. Is it not he whom you judged, and did you not deal rightly with him when the scales went down against him? Therefore, might he not return from the Region of Darkness with others of his kind and cause misfortune to fall upon us? You, he cannot harm, you are now in the Place of Glory, in the land beyond the Western waters. Therefore, send us guardians from among the Glorious Company, that they may spread protecting wings over our habitations.

SCL:3:7 Many come bearing cakes of fine meal and barley cakes, large, fat-bodied fish and meats of many kinds, honeywine in jars and fruits in plenty. He who is absent from the feast is joyful; his arm is strong and he issues his commands to the guardians. Cast off all gloom and be joyful, for this is not the time of sorrow, and tears have no place in your eyes.

SCL:3:8 If there be benevolent Life Shadows beyond the protective pale, they may enter. Join with us in our rejoicing. Let us all enjoy what we have and what we share, for life is irrepressible.

SCL:3:9 These are things from a foreign place, said for our brother Gwelm, according to the rites of the Sons of Fire, and thus it shall be for those who enter the chambers of stone.

Chapter Four – The Sacred Registers – Part 4

SCL:4:1 No longer can the man who was speak with men on Earth, for he now lives in splendour among The Eternal Ones. He was weighed before the Assessors, and though his faults were not few he was not outweighed in goodness. He has become a Shining One and journeys on into the spaces of Heavenland, accompanied only by his compatible companions.

SCL:4:2 He has ascended into the Place of Glory, the Place of Fulfilment. The years have fallen off his shoulders, like a cast-off cloak, and he is young again. He is vigorous; he lives. Time cannot touch him with change, nor sorrow enter his heart. He rests, awaiting a new call to duty.

SCL:4:3 He has passed through the Wide Hall and through the Narrow Portal. He has entered the Land of a New Dawning and he is welcomed; his Earth companions greet him; he lives. He is beyond harm; he sees the sublime visions which fulfil his yearnings. He who has served is now served. As he has sown and husbanded, so now he reaps.

SCL:4:4 He continues past the Place of Waiting Souls and sees the awaiting Kohars who will unite with the ascending spirits of men. He bears in his hand the Book of Life and glides over the pure pastures, past the bright dividing flame. He turns the face of compassion towards the darkness, but sees nought but fleeting shadows against the red glare. The Lost Ones shrink back in shame, and the man who was passes the entrance to their foul abode.

SCL:4:5 Those who are left to mourn for the Glorious One have dried their tears, for all is well with him. He delights in the good life in a place of glory. He is safe in the embrace of his Kohar; he is the Adoring One whose eyes are opened to splendour; he sees the sublime visions.

SCL:4:6 The man who was seeks the illuminator who will direct him in his duties; he cleanses himself in the Lake of Beauty and refreshes himself at the Fountain of Life. He sees spirits of the twilight who are purged of all their wickedness and lusts; yet they remain captive to The Lords of Destinies, for they are still unproven. The Lord of Life will direct their passage back for trial and testing. For these, there is always hope.

SCL:4:7 The man who was has navigated the winding waters of life and crossed the dark waters of death, and he is now strengthened in wisdom. He takes a seat on high, that he may become an instructor and guide on the path. He becomes a brazier in the distance, a homing light to guide those who seek Truth. He is purified and comes forth wearing the White Mantle of Greatness.

SCL:4:8 Behold the splendour of his raiment and the purity of his adornments as he sits awaiting calls from those in the Heavy Kingdom, who seek his counsel. The seers in dark waters will amaze the people with the clarity of their visions and revelations, for the power goes forth from the man who was, with manifold strength. A great being has joined the Splendid Company in the Land of Dawnlight. Over there, they will say, "Earth is worthily fulfilling its purpose when it produces men such as this."

SCL:4:9 You may wonder what are the occupations of the man who was. Does he illuminate the dark waters alone? May he not be among those who seek to enter the hearts of those who close the doors of their spirit to the instructors of wisdom? Alas, they who are heavily enshrouded in earthly wrappings are ever set of face before the instructors of wisdom, they say, "What have we to do with this babble?" Yet they, most of all, require enlightenment, for they are men of small minds.

SCL:4:10 May he not have become a pathfinder in the night, a guide through the darkness, the star illuminating the night at its darkest hour as the herald of The Great illuminator? May he not have become a Director of Rays that dance on the waters, or a Controller of the Winds, which caress the cheek? Suffice that he rejoices in a life of splendour, so let it remain with him and his Kohar until the day when all is known, the day of full knowing.

Chapter Five – The Sacred Registers – Part 5

SCL:5:1 These are the instructions for those who journey the outer track of the twinway, for those who have been laid in the chambered tombs, who followed the ways of Kemwelith. The words are those from the distant past, first spoken in a far land beyond the rolling billows:

SCL:5:2 The Risen One has become the Newcomer, and having passed through the clearinghouse his departure is not delayed. No toll is required on the ferry, for the Newcomer has with him the words of entrance, which have become known to him according to his deeds. He has not deviated from the path, and all is well.

SCL:5:3 The ferryman comes to the Place of Waiting, he of the winding river which is the tortuous channel of purification. The Newcomer stands at the mooring place and proclaims. "O ferryman, away to the Region of the Blessed Ones. I am purified, purged of polluting evils; make haste, do not delay. I am a wanderer anxious to reach my destination." The ferryman says, "From whence come you?" The Newcomer says, "I am from Restaw and am weary. Take me to my compatible place of abode, let us not delay. I wish to join those united with their soulselves. Let us not dally. Do not tarry, for I am anxious to depart from this sombre shore. Have no fear, cautious one, for no evil dogs my footsteps. Come, let us away; bear me over the waters to the appointed place. Carry me swiftly to where spirits are regenerated and made young again. Carry me to the foot of the Great Stairway that ascends to the Place of the Immortals, Courtyard of The Great God."

SCL:5:4 The ferryman hesitates; he says, "Show me your token, that I may know you have truly passed the tests, that I may know your true destination. For it is the way with men that they think one thing, but Truth lies elsewhere."

SCL:5:5 The Newcomer says, "My token is the brightness, which, if you be no imposter, you may see shining above my head, and my introduction is the writing concerning me, written in the Book of Sacred Mysteries. Come, bear me over the waters, so that I may tread the Field of Peace. See, have I not four attendants, two on either side? Let them speak for me, for they are witnesses walking in the light of Truth."

SCL:5:6 The ferryman says, "Who stands to the pole?" and the Risen One answers, "I will stand to the pole with my attendants, two on either side. You stand by to bear at the steering oar, so that our course remains straight." The ferryman says, "It is well, for the current is sullen and changeful."

SCL:5:7 The Newcomer says, "O ferryman of the boatless ones, I am truly a man justified before all on both sides of the horizon, before Heaven and Earth. I have passed the tests of the examiners and am free to proceed. I am one who can claim passage by virtue of my deeds. Have not men spoken well of me after I departed from their midst, is this not enough? It is the way with Earth, that if men speak of the goodness of an absent one, then he is good indeed. Truly I am a Bright One."

SCL:5:8 The ferryman says, "Draw aside your mantle, that I may see your likeness, for this is a good boat which may not be polluted. The path henceforth is hard for those who cannot be faced without revulsion. O Great One, draw your mantle over again, for you are indeed among the brightest of those who pass this way, great will be the rejoicing when you appear among your own kind, the pure of heart."

SCL:5:9 "Delay no longer, ferryman. Quickly over the waters to the other side. If you delay further, I will name the names of gods to men, that their unreality be exposed. I am not one to be trifled with, I am one who can dispel the clouds of illusion. I am a man of no mean qualities; therefore, tarry no more, let us depart."

Chapter Six – The Sacred Registers – Part 6

SCL:6:1 The man who was becomes the Pilgrim. He has crossed the waters, he has passed the Grim Guardian, he waits without the Place of Union and stands firmly. He is not afraid and stands resolute. The Cool Gracious One approaches with three jars of water and refreshes him.

SCL:6:2 The Pilgrim says, "Behold, O Watcher at the Gate, I have laid up treasure enough in the storehouse of love; therefore, allow me to pass. The love of those who have gone before; see, is it not a large quantity and sufficient to draw me upward? See the love of those who remain behind; is it not a large quantity and sufficient to draw me upward?" The Watcher hears his words.

SCL:6:3 The Grim Guardian counts and weighs and says, "Pass." Then this man passes and goes beyond the Lake of Wisdom, past the Winding Channel of Experiences, over the flooded Field of Reeds, to the Eastern side of the Region of Light, where he will be renewed in birth into the Higher Spheres.

SCL:6:4 The Pilgrim now stands before the Womb of Heaven, where those who enter as pure seed are brought forth into union with God. This man passes by to where the attendants help him to assume the Robe of Glory. They welcome him.

SCL:6:5 "Behold," they say, "His Kohar has brought this man powers to make him complete. The powers he gave into the keeping of his Kohar during the prayer times on Earth have returned greatly magnified. This man has joined the Joyful Company; he has left his old, discarded body in the Region of Heaviness, to assume another more glorified one in the Region of Light.

SCL:6:6 The Kohar greets the Pilgrim and says, "I welcome you, my own." The Kohar says to those about, "This is my own; he has washed in the Lake of Wisdom and passed by the Caverns of Distrust and Doubt. Let us, therefore, enter in peace when the Great Door is opened for the United Being in the East, the door leading to the Place of The One True God above all gods, whose manifestations are secret mysteries."

SCL:6:7 Before going further, they pass by a side entrance to the Region of Darkness, where vile and sorrowful things lurk, the Lost Ones, those who served in the ranks of evil on Earth. O Great Kohar, stop the ears of your own; that he may not hear the mournful wailings of the doomed ones left behind!

SCL:6:8 They who are the companions of the Pilgrim cry out, "O Kohar, guide Your own right, guide him up the Ladder of Life which he must traverse again; strengthen its rungs, support him, so he bears lightly upon them, let not the rungs break beneath his weight. This is the test of deeds long since done, where evil bears down heavily."

SCL:6:9 "O Kohar, Your own is weak and falters, yet Your arms are strong; therefore lift them to support him, that he may surmount to the heights above. Do this, that he may sit with those who have understanding and perception, that his feet may be welcomed in the Fields of Peace and that he may take his place among the Glorious Ones."

SCL:6:10 Blessed is the Kohar who safeguards all memories, storing them as men store corn; who retains these for the use of the Reborn Ones; who can recall all that men forget and can draw forth a memory as men draw water from a well. The Kohar is the eternal recorder; Pilgrims become Risen Ones and enter their Kohars as a soul enters a body, and in unity, they become Glorious Ones.

Chapter Seven – The Sacred Registers – Part 7

SCL:7:1 This is the manner whereby the Aspiring Ones of Earth may cross the dread horizon through residence within the Cavern of Stone. It is thus that men come to know the Truth concerning the Realms of Glory beyond the Western Horizon, but it is a path beset by great dangers and manifold terrors, and many return witless.

SCL:7:2 The Aspiring One is of Earth, he is earthbound. He sits within the cavern before the Cauldron of Rebirth and Regeneration, and inhales the smoke from the brew of release. He rises above himself, flying on wings of five feathers, the names of which are recorded in the Book of Secret Mysteries, wherein are the awful recipes. There it is written that he may ascend like a falcon and cannot go otherwise than as a falcon. He may not go in the manner of any other bird.

SCL:7:3 He escapes the call of Earth, its fetters fall from him. The Aspiring One leaves his attendants behind; he is not with them; he is not of Earth, neither is he of Heaven. He is at the place where the two meet and intermingle.

SCL:7:4 His body moves without the spirit and partakes of the sour yellow bread of wide vision. The Aspiring One drinks the brew of grey barley and sips long at the wine of harish, eating the cakes of green brown horris. He eats the fruit of the releasing tree and drinks the brew of black fungus, which is in the smoke goblet. Thus, he sleeps and the attendants lay him down in the receptacle called the Womb of Rebirth. He is in the Place of Visions but remains like the masthead bird.

SCL:7:5 He shall be covered and made so that in his struggles he rise not. His voice is heard speaking in a strange tongue, as he calls on his fathers who have gone before and now preside over affairs beyond the Wide Lake. His body becomes still, as he enters the dazzling chamber which is the doorway to twin vision.

SCL:7:6 Now, he must penetrate the Walls of Dry Air, which bar his passage, and rise into the rainbow-coloured Clouds of Radiance, which are above. High up, he looks below him and sees the waters of the Winding Canal of Experience and understands the meaning of all that had befallen him. Now, he has four eyes, these being the inner and outer eyes, and rising higher, he attains the heights of wide consciousness.

SCL:7:7 Here, he meets the Pathfinder and follows him swiftly. He speaks rightly to the Guardian. He shields his eyes when passing the Lurker on the Threshold, and goes on until he comes to the abode of the Opener of the Ways.

SCL:7:8 Now, the body of the Aspiring One becomes restless, and those who attend him place the power of Hori over his face. He hears the voice of The Sungod, which says, "I know the necessary names, I am The Knower of Names. I know the name of The Limitless One, above The Lords of the East and West, I am One Most Powerful."

SCL:7:9 The Aspiring One becomes covered with moisture; he writhes, he shouts, he struggles. The Companionable Watchers know he has left the protection of The Sungod, that he has been seized by the Fiends of Darkness, but he struggles and prevails over them, and all is well. Then the Aspiring One returns.

SCL:7:10 A hundred shining suns whirl above, a whisper rolls around like thunder, lights of manifold hues sway above, like the river reeds in the wind. All things appear to dance in a shimmering haze, then turn over and fold back into themselves, and such beauty is produced that the human tongue cannot describe it. All things take upon themselves shimmering forms, through which other forms can be seen. Great melodic music throbs all around, while everything pulsates a soft rhythm. The air is filled with voices of unearthly sweetness, glory and splendour are everywhere. Then, the Aspiring One awakes.

SCL:7:11 He is raised; behold, he comes forth and walks as one bemused by a vision of glory. He staggers, he cannot walk unsupported. His throat burns, and his mouth is overgrown with dryness, His head resounds with drum-beats. He is given the sweet waters in the cup of forgetfulness and drinks deeply; all is well. He is a Reborn One, he is an Enlightened One. He is one resurrected from the Cavern of Stone.

Chapter Eight – The Sacred Registers – Part 8

SCL:8:1 These are the supplications of Ilkeb the Stranger, who came from the Land of Rising Waters and was known to us as the Opener of the Ways. He came under the wings of the Firehawk. He was the first of the Scarlet Robed Ones, the right hand of Glanvanis. That was in the time of our fathers' fathers, and the tongue of the seafarers is no longer in the mouth of men.

SCL:8:2 O Great Being of Beauty, Brilliant One who greets the Newcomers arriving in the Place Beyond the Western Horizon, this woman is your daughter, your daughter is she. See; she is pure in spirit and clean in heart. She is modest and womanlike, so let her pass to live in the Pastures of Life, in the Land of New Dawning, where all is wholesome.

SCL:8:3 Let her be purified by the maidens of Orshafa; let them purify her, let her be washed and dried by the attendants at the clean, sweet waters of life. Let the nine Delicate Ones minister to her; let her be clothed in garments of decency, for she is a womanly woman. O Great and Glorious One, give this woman your hand; clasp her hand with womanly tenderness. Spread out your falcon wings over her, spread protecting wings around her. She has followed the tedious ways of womankind and has glorified life with her presence. She has endured affliction with patience and made her home hearth a place of peace and content. Let her roam the pastures of the Blessed Ones and penetrate into the farthest regions of light.

SCL:8:4 I raise my hands in supplication. The flame is lit; it burns brightly; fragrant incense is placed in the bowl and it becomes aglow. Its sweet perfume rises into the recesses above. O Happy Risen One, O Beautiful Being glowing with womanly goodness, treasurer of all the virtues, purify yourself for admittance into the higher Regions. The incense we offer here is your indrawn breath of renewed life. It fills your lungs; you breathe, and because you breathe you live. This is the best incense from the Land of Gwemi, differing not from that, which our fathers knew when they travelled the water road. O Beautified One, my heart lingers at the place where you rest; my heart is with you, entwined with yours. How sweet your breath, how pleasant your perfume, how gentle your whispers, how delicate the rustle of your attire. O newly become Beauteous One, you are not alone.

SCL:8:5 Rise blue perfumed smoke; rise cleansing fragrance; rise sweet wholesome offerings; rise like fluttering birds on wings of purified air to the glorious regions of light which lie away beyond our poor perception. Accept our sweet fragrance, O Beautified One; inhale our sweet smoke, O Ever Delicate One; may you enjoy the due reward of your labours and privations, of your selfless sacrifices. Be ever contented and peaceful. O dutiful wife and loving mother, hear our words, as they rise to you in the softly smouldering incense, which comes shipborne to these shores.

SCL:8:6 Hear the voices of the waiting Welcomers greeting the Beauteous One who now joins them. They say, "Cast off the old, worn garment, and array yourself in garments of radiant light, in the clothes of splendour which have awaited you. Bedeck yourself in the well-earned jewels of spiritual reward."

SCL:8:7 "Henceforth, you shall dwell here, walking about freely, to be honoured and loved. Here, you will be renewed, be alert, vigorous and far reaching. The power of your spirit shall stretch out to every place. You take thought and fly on hawks wings. Your desire becomes a chariot with wings of light."

SCL:8:8 "Beyond the place of your first destination is the kingdom of the Lord of the Distant Sky. There, he will permit manifestations in glory. There, henceforth, you shall walk in strength and beauty, being ever filled with life and power, garmented in loveliness for all eternity."

SCL:8:9 "There, floodwaters of a glorious fluid light unknown here rise and fall in moderation, and therein you may bathe daily and taste the revitalising rests. Here, your thirst may be slaked at the well of Divine Essence and your appetite appeased by the strange bread of everlasting life."

SCL:8:10 This is your destiny, in the Land Beyond the Veil; therefore lift up your face in joy.

Rise, lovely liveliness; you are one destined to be numbered among the Shining Ones and are warmly welcomed into the company of the Fragrant Ones. O happy one who enhanced earthly life with your presence, this is your reward. Many have done mighty things, but you have served with constancy and diligence, adding the small grains of goodness to the pile of merits until it exceeded in weight the great things done by others. We hail you, O victorious one!"

SCL:8:11 The Welcomers say among themselves, "How fair and bright the face of this Newcomer. How fine must have been her life in the Region of Heaviness. Behold; here she is, renewed and made young again but with a loveliness unknown in the life left behind'.

SCL:8:12 When she goes forward from here, she is within her Kohar; they are one. Her vision is through the Kohar; her smell is through the Kohar. All she senses is through the Kohar. All she does and knows is through the Kohar.

SCL:8:13 Behold, she is among the Chosen. Henceforth, she becomes an Opener of the Way for those of her blood. Glorious is she and blessed are they!

SCL:8:14 Those are the supplications made for Milven, daughter of Mailon, son of Market the Stranger, according to the rites of the Sons of Fire. Ardwith kept it, and it was done into this form at the place called Korinamba.

Chapter Nine – The Sacred Registers – Part 9

SCL:9:1 This concerns the mystery of the Twice Born. It relates to those born again, to those who have endured the awfulness of the false death, which many do not survive; who have drunk deeply from Koriladwen, the smooth, bitter brew, which releases the spirit; who have entered Ogofnaum through the thundering doors. This is their path.

SCL:9:2 The door of Heaven stands ajar; the doors of vision have been opened, and now the Cavern of Vision is revealed. The spirit-bearing waves from the abyss have been freed; the rays of the Great Light have been set free, and the Guides and Watchers have been placed in their positions by the Constant One.

SCL:9:3 The Welcomers stand back, for this is not their stage. The Brilliant One is there, and another who is the Reciter, and he explains the visions: "O Brave, stouthearted one, Syoltash to be, the things you behold are the things seen by the Great Ones of Earth when they came this way in their hour and were returned back to life. They were truly men of wisdom, well versed in the mystic procedures, men who knew their position and parts."

SCL:9:4 "Behold the twin stars. These embody the midwifery powers drawing the Twice Born back to their places of origin. They who are with them are the champions of light and darkness. One, you must choose as your companion, but the choice must be made according to the law of affinity; otherwise, you are lost."

SCL:9:5 "The pool wherein you gaze is earthlife. The brilliant light above, far greater than the sun, is the manifestation of The One God, but it is not He. The rays dancing about are the gods, distorted reflections of what is, distorted reflections of Truth, shadows of reality. The sparkling motes are souls, they descend from the light to manifest in darkness.

SCL:9:6 "The clouds obscuring the lesser lights are the clouds of misconception, which darken the face of wisdom.

SCL:9:7 The dark twins standing by the pillar are Delusion and Illusion, the constant beguilers of men. The stream of clear water is Truth, and the waters of Truth constantly sheer away the clay pedestal of falsehood"

SCL:9:8 "The brightness you see before you and to the right is the naked spirit displaying itself in isolation. It is neither in a mortal body nor within the Kohar. Beyond it is a much greater brightness reflected from afar, which is the Kohar of Kohars, which men cannot yet understand."

SCL:9:9 "The repulsive shapes, which are behind the flame on your left, are doomed spirits, which once were the enlivening forces within men. Now, they grovel in slime and filth, denizens of the mire, but their fate is just, for they themselves were the judges. The darkness beyond the murk will not become greater. Darkness cannot change to light, for when light comes into darkness, there is no darkness; it ceases to exist."

SCL:9:10 "The gloominess and shadow scene you see, forward on your left hand side, is the Region of Heaviness, where mortals sojourn. The flickering lights which appear here and there are the joys of Earth, while the darker spots are where there are sorrows and suffering. The redness is anger and strife. The blue whiteness is love and compassion."

SCL:9:11 "The brightness above and ahead is the Region of Lightness, where the Risen Ones rejoice, for there they welcome their Earth companions and are happy in reunion. Behold, here is a Rising One newly arrived; see, she flies upward on the wide wings of spirit, and loving arms reach out to welcome her. The star-girt roadway you see rising before you is that trodden by the countless Risen Ones, who have gone before. Now, advance towards the left."

SCL:9:12 "The abyss now before you is the mouth of Earth, and see, it opens and speaks to you, bidding you farewell. Listen carefully, for it will retell your deeds, your accomplishments and your omissions. If they weigh against you, then cast yourself into the abyss, for you are unworthy to survive this trial; go no further, nor can you turn back, lest you become prey to the Foul Lurker in Darkness."

SCL:9:13 "If you have not been found wanting in the weighing, then step forward boldly and without fear, for the mouth will close to let you pass. If you are not numbered among the triumphant ones, then better by far that you be swallowed forthwith than that you survive to meet the Dread Lurker, the Devouring Horror, and be returned to Earth a witless, empty shell."

SCL:9:14 "Beyond the abyss lies a stretch of blue water, which contains the Pool of Wisdom and the Pool of Purification. Therein, you must bathe and refresh yourself. The trees growing to your right bear the fruits of spiritual nourishment; eat, and become strong. Know, as doing so, that the things done, thought and visualised on Earth become qualities, which are here transmuted into the things, and experiences of this nature."

SCL:9:15 "Pass between the waters and the trees and you will see a cliff against which is a ladder, the rungs of which are bound in leathern throngs made from the hide of the Bull of the Nightsky. This ladder, which rises before you, is the Ladder of Experience. Its two supports are experience in the body and experience in the spirit. The rungs are your daily deeds and thoughts and fantasies of your earthly life. Now is the test. Will your daily deeds and secret thoughts support your ascent, or are they incapable of bearing you upward? See, above is your Kohar, call upon it for help, for therein you may have stored a reserve of spiritual strength. Or, perchance, it may be barren and empty; only you know. Those who uphold the ladder are the Lords of the Ladder, and they greet you as the Ascending One."

SCL:9:16 "The ladder leads onto a plateau, and beside you appears the strangely-garbed Reciter, who sweeps his arms about and says, "All wherein things manifest is the firmament, which was before the beginning and still is. In the beginning, its darkness was pierced by just a single ray from The Sun of God, but later, when the first spirits entered, the firmament was brightened, and it was divided by heaviness and lightness. Then, when it was set apart, it was divided by the entry of dark spirits whose need was for a place, with which they had a sombre affinity. Therefore, the firmament of lightness is divided; there is a Place of Light for the Victorious Ones and a Place of Darkness for those who could not rise to victory. There are regions of gloom and shadow, regions of twilight and shade. There are regions of light in many hues, regions ranging from dazzling lights to dim light. There is a veil across the firmament, dividing Heaven from Earth, and each spirit departing from Earth penetrates through this veil, going to its appointed place, carried by the winds of affinity. Arriving there, the spirit, good or bad, strengthens and extends its compatible territory."

SCL:9:17 "The Kohar is the Knower, and the spirit is the known. All knowledge is with the

Knower, but the known can tap it so it flows out into the known. The Kohar receives the spirit seed in heaven, for there it is as the body is on Earth. Even as the earthly body is made of things from the Region of Heaviness, so is the Kohar made of things from the Region of Lightness."

SCL:9:18 "These things are said by the Reciter before he leads you to the place where sleeps a serpent, and pointing to it he says, "Behold the serpent it sleeps at the bole of a tree from which hangs the body of man, the tree of his backbone. It is on guard, safeguarding the precious gem of spiritual powers, which lies enwrapped in the threefold covering. To obtain the gem the serpent must be aroused and then overcome. To rouse this serpent is a thing not to be lightly undertaken, for it causes a fire to mount into the heart, which may destroy the brain with delusions and madness. Only the Twice Born can really obtain the gem."

SCL:9:19 You pass on with the Reciter, who will say: "These are the things you must establish in your heart, the knowledge of the eight roads along which you must travel to reach the Land of the Westerners. These will bring you to the twelve first portals leading to the Land of Shadows. Here I will recite for you the twenty-two deeds of wickedness you have not done. You will then pass through the Land of Shadows, as if it were your hour, and beyond it, come to the Great Portal, where it must be established, before the Great Guardian, that you have ever done all within your power to live according to the twelve virtues. Then, you pass through the portal to the hall of Judgement. Here, for the first time, your light is revealed and it is made known whether your tongue has spoken in accordance with the things within your heart."

SCL:9:20 "Many are they who know the words of the tongue, but sever these from what is written in the heart. If the words of the tongue are copied from the writings of the heart and are a true copy, then cross to the Place of Assessment, where your true form and likeness will be displayed for all to see."

SCL:9:21 A curtain of darkness descends; there is a heavy, dark mist; then, the muffled crash of Thundering Doors. The aching body reclines within the tomb of stone. The questing pilgrim has returned to his homehaven. He has learned truths he could never learn on Earth and now knows the Grand Secret. Faith is replaced with certainty, and he is now an Initiated One.

Chapter Ten –
The Sacred Registers – Part 10

SCL:10:1 My God and Father, my Creator and Governor, Supreme and Immortal Spirit, I come to You as a wayward son comes to his father. I come as the world-weary wanderer comes home. I come as the victorious, battle-bludgeoned warrior comes to the place of his rest. I am one, who has passed the trials. I am one, who has survived the challenges.

SCL:10:2 I have returned full of wisdom and knowledge, the fruits of long years in Your earthly place of instruction. There, I was diligent; I was not a waster of time; I was not a man of idleness. I am proved worthy. I, Your son, have come home.

SCL:10:3 The virtues I developed on Earth are the messengers that sped before me; my qualities hastened to announce my coming. They sped on invisible wings, so that only those sensitive to that which emanated from me knew of their coming. They came as perfume carried on the wind. They announced me, they heralded me. They gave salutations to the Spirits in the Bright Abodes. Yet, I have not forgotten the Dwellers in Terror, and a small dark spirit of the Twilight has gone forth to make known to them my departure from Earth. This, that should any there know of me, they may be made aware that I am not of their dismal company. Will there be weeping there in the dank, dreary darkness?

SCL:10:4 I surmounted the trials of existence in heaviness. Now, my spirit can speed like the lightning flash. I am one who has accomplished what had to be done. I have governed my affairs, not wholly by earthly standards but by the greater ordinances of Heaven. I have carefully read the books of instruction and listened to the interpreting words of the wise.

SCL:10:5 He who tests hearts and reads thoughts has weighed me, and I was not found wanting in the balances. I am a Cool One, for my thoughts rest in peace. I am not numbered among the Hot Ones, whose thoughts consume them as fire consumes wood.

SCL:10:6 I have passed the Nameless Ones, to come into the presence of The Great One whom no man names, whose name is not knowable to men. I have reached the destination of ages; I have achieved the ultimate goal. I have put on the mantle of immortality and the robe of light, which the Heavenly Weavers prepared for Me.

SCL:10:7 I am a Little One, one who comes in littleness and not greatness. I am a Humble One and come not in pomp and grandeur, for these are things of the four-quartered Earth, having no place here. I have done things which have been wrong, but these were done in ignorance and not wilfully or with malice.

SCL:10:8 O Watchers, announce to the Lords of Light and to the Lords of Darkness that I am one, who has penetrated the Mystic Veil but is destined to return to the Realm of Heaviness. O Watchers, announce that I am now a self-knowing everlasting spirit. O Father of the Gods, who is above all, issue the decrees of fate, which ensure that henceforth, I live a life of service, that I may live purposefully when I return to fulfil my destiny.

Chapter Eleven – The Sacred Registers – Part 11

SCL:11:1 My Heart, my Spirit, my Kohar, guardian of my memories, cast not your words in the balances against me. My faults and failings are not few, for no mortal man is perfect, yet they weigh lightly against my qualities and good deeds. Say not that I have wrought evil to any man wilfully or with malice; say not that I am a man of wickedness. Let me not suffer sorrowful remorse in the gloom and darkness, but let me live forever within the Region of Light.

SCL:11:2 I have done deeds of goodness and led a goodly life. I have overcome the wiles of wickedness and avoided the snares of temptation. I have lived in peace with my neighbours. I have dealt justly and fairly with them and have not uttered words of malice to stir up strife. I have not gossiped about my neighbours, nor engaged in idle chatter concerning their affairs. These things are not easy, and as no man is perfect, I have at times been bad-tempered under provocation. Therefore, speak words that will weigh in the balances against my failings.

SCL:11:3 I have not slandered any man, nor have I wilfully caused pain and suffering. I have not caused the widow to weep, nor the child to cry without cause. I have dealt justly with my servants and with the servants of others, and I have been loyal to my masters. I have not slain unlawfully, nor wounded any man wilfully. Yet, no man is perfect and when my burdens have weighed heavily upon me, I have spoken harshly. Therefore, speak words that will weigh in the balances against my failings.

SCL:11:4 I have never oppressed a poor man or taken from him what is his by virtue of my position. I have never oppressed the weak or cheated in the substance of metals. I have never said to a hungry woman, "Lay with me, and you shall eat," for this is a vile thing. I have not lain with the wife of another man or seduced a child, for these are abominations. Yet, no man is perfect and few are commanders of their thoughts, Therefore, speak words that will lighten these things in the balances.

SCL:11:5 I have not turned the water of another so that he is deprived of his full measure. I have not stopped flowing waters in their course. I have not kept fodder from cattle, nor allowed the pastures to be neglected. I have not caused any child to know fear without reason, nor have I beaten one in bad temper. I have not transgressed the statutes of the king. Yet, no man is perfect, and sometimes that, which is right in its day becomes wrong in another. Therefore, speak words that will weigh in the balances against my wrongdoings.

SCL:11:6 I have not stolen; neither have I taken the possessions of any man by deceit. I have not divided the household of any man, nor separated him from his wife or children. I have not quarrelled with any man because of ignorance. I have not turned from my duties or failed in my obligations. I have not hidden my errors or buried my failings. Yet, no man is perfect, therefore speak words that will weigh in the balances for me.

SCL:11:7 I have never behaved boisterously in a sacred place, nor have I ever defiled one. My hand has not been demanding because of my office, nor have I dealt haughtily with those who came to me with a plea. I have not increased my position by false words or writings. Yet, my burden has been increased because of the perversity and wilfulness of men, and no man is perfect. Therefore, speak words that will weigh in the balances against my weaknesses.

SCL:11:8 I have not permitted envy to eat my heart, nor malice to corrupt it. I have not been loud of mouth, nor spoken words of boastfulness. I have never slandered another or uttered words of falsehood. My tongue has never escaped from the control of my heart. I have never derided the words of another because they passed my understanding, nor have I stopped my ears to words of enlightenment. I have never hidden myself to observe others, nor have I ever disclosed the secret designs or doings of others, unless they be of evil intent. Yet, no man is perfect; therefore, speak words that will weigh in the balances for me. When I have done wrong, I have adjusted the scales that weighed down heavily against me. I have not hidden my weaknesses and failings in dark places, but washed them clean in the sunlight of honest compensation.

SCL:11:9 I have not succumbed to the lures of lewdness, nor has my tongue spoken slyly of things, which should be kept private. I have not peeped at nakedness or pried into another's privacy. I have respected the modesty of womankind and the innocent delicacy of childhood. Yet, men are as they are and imperfect, while thoughts stray wilfully and are not easily restrained. Therefore, speak words that will weigh in the balances for me.

SCL:11:10 O Great One, protect me. O Kohar, save me. Hear the words of my heart. I was one who was ever mindful of what was right and what was wrong. I did what I thought was right and shunned that which I thought was wrong. I listened to those who were wiser than I and helped those who were less privileged. Can man do more?

Chapter Twelve – The Sacred Registers – Part 12

SCL:12:1 Know me and understand my ways. I am one who sees the past and the future. I look into hidden places. I am one who wanders freely. I am one who can be reborn. I am one who knows the speech of the released. I am an Uplifter. The Climbers come to me and I support them, I lift them up, I strengthen. Therefore, bring me the sustenance of smoke.

SCL:12:2 I hear, and I hear not, for what I hear is heard by others. I speak, and I speak not, for what I speak is in the mouths of others. I weep, and I weep not, for my weeping is the weeping of others. I am an Uplifter. The Climbers come to me, and I console them. I enlighten them with words of hidden wisdom. Thus, they find the way.

SCL:12:3 I am one, who comes forth when the circle is formed, when the twin lamps have been lit and the incantations made. I come forth from the consecrated place and bear the staff of power. I know the secrets of the dark waters and the secrets of blood. I am a wanderer in strange places. I am one who does not fear to tread the forbidden paths. I am an Uplifter. The Climbers come to me, and I reveal the way.

SCL:12:4 I am the Opener of Tombs. I am the Dweller in the Stone Caverns. I am the one who precedes the Herald of the Companions. I am the Swimmer in the Waters of Wisdom. I am the Discoverer of Hidden Places. I am the one who hovers above the Still Waters. I am the Wanderer with the Winds. I am an Uplifter. The Climbers come to me and are comforted. They thirst, and I refresh them; they hunger, and I fill them with food.

SCL:12:5 I am the Sitter Beneath the Sycamore. I am the Eater of the Rowan. I am the heart within the heat of the fire and the eye within the candle flame. I am the uprising hawk and the contented dove. I am one, who has tamed the serpent and drawn forth its secrets. I am one, who has many eyes and sees what is written in the nightskies, whose ears hear the whispers at the edge of the Great Waters. I am one whose right foot rests on the Earth and whose left foot rests on the firmament. I am one, who faces all spirits alike and knows their true nature. I am an Uplifter. The Climbers come to me, and I give them peace.

SCL:12:6 I am one, who gazes into the deep, dark pool, reading the things hidden therein. I am the Caller Forth of the Deformed Ones and the Tongue of the Bright Ones. I am he of the Everlasting Form. I am he, who provides stability to faltering forms and the interpreter who spans the veil. I am an Uplifter. The Climbers come to me, and I provide their Guide and their Guardian.

SCL:12:7 Know me, and understand my ways. Invoke me through the rite of smoke and wine. Call me forth into the circle of stone, but beware, for lest you hold the seven keys and understand the nature of the three rays, you are lost.

Chapter Thirteen – The Scroll of Ramkat

SCL:13:1 Awful is the great day of judgement at its dawning in the Netherworld. The soul stands naked in the Hall of Judgement; nothing can now be hidden. Hypocrisy is no avail; to maintain goodness when the soul reveals its own repulsiveness is futile. To mumble empty ritual is foolishness. To call upon gods who have no existence is a waste of time.

SCL:13:2 In the Hall of Judgement, the wrongdoer is judged. On that day and henceforth, his qualities shall form his food. His soul, soft as clay upon Earth, is hardened and set into shape according to its moulding. The balances are adjusted.

SCL:13:3 One arrives. The Forty-Two Virtues are his assessors. Shall he dwell among beauty as a godling or be given captive to the Keeper of Horrors, to dwell among vile things under a merciful mantle of darkness?

SCL:13:4 One arrives. The twisted body, tormented on Earth, and the ugly face have gone, discarded at the portal. He strides through the Hall in radiance, to pass into the Place of Everlasting Beauty.

SCL:13:5 One arrives. Now no earthly body shields the horror, which is the true likeness of the evildoer upon Earth. He runs from the light, which he cannot tolerate, and hides himself in the shadows near the Place of Terror. Soon, he will be drawn to his compatible place among the Dismal Company.

SCL:13:6 One arrives. He has been upright and a just one. His failings and weaknesses were of little account. This upright man fears nothing, for he is welcomed among the Bright Ones and shall go unhampered among the Everlasting Lords.

SCL:13:7 One arrives, He trembles before the Unseen Judges; he is lost; he knows nothing, earthly knowledge and confidence are left behind. The balance drops; he sees his soul and recognises his true self, he rushes into the merciful darkness. It enfolds him, and dark arms embrace him, drawing him into the terrible gloom, into the Place of Dark Secret Horrors.

SCL:13:8 One arrives. She graced the court with beauty, men sang of her loveliness and grace. Now, as when a mantle is removed, all is discarded, it is the time of unveiling. Who can describe the lustful thoughts and secret unclean deeds, which fashioned the horror coming through the portal? There is a hush among the compassionate.

SCL:13:9 One arrives. On Earth she was pitied by the compassionate and scorned by the hardhearted. There, her lot was degradation and servitude, privation and sacrifice, few and meagre were the gifts from life. Yet, she triumphed. Now, she comes forward surrounded by brilliance; even the Shining Ones are dazzled by her beauty.

SCL:13:10 One arrives. The twisted face and pain-wracked body of the cripple have been left behind. A kind and loving soul dwelt imprisoned within its confines. Now, the relieved spirit steps forward into the great Hall, unencumbered and free, glorious to behold.

SCL:13:11 One arrives. The splendid body which graced Earth remains there, an empty, decaying thing. The naked soul enters the Everlasting Halls. It is a deformed, mis-shapen thing fit only to dwell in the merciful gloom of the place, with which it has compatible affinity.

SCL:13:12 One arrives. Neither goodness nor wickedness bears down upon the scales. The balances remain straight. The soul departs to the twilight borderland between the Region of Light and the Region of Darkness.

SCL:13:13 O Great Lords of Eternity, who once were in the flesh, even as I, hear not the outpourings of an overburdened and sorrowful heart. For who am I to presume to call upon The Great God of All? I, who am not without wickedness and weak in spirit. I have filled my heart with knowledge of the Secret writings, but still I fear the judgement. Therefore, Great Lords of Eternity, I call upon you who once walked the Earth, even as I, and who, therefore, understand the failings and weaknesses of men.

SCL:13:14 I am not weak in my standing with earthly things, but I am weak beside the Greater Beings. Will I, too, ever be worthy of the grandeur of the Eternal Mansions? O Great Beings whose nature is beyond understanding, grant me just a spark of the Eternal Wisdom, that it might light my soul and kindle the flame of immortal life.

SCL:13:15 What is the destined fate of a man, who knows the existence of things beyond his understanding? I see, but I do not know; therefore, I am afraid. Man can swim against the current towards the bank, but he needs a helping hand to pull him ashore when he is exhausted from the struggle.

SCL:13:16 This is the fate of man. He must strive for that, which he cannot attain. He must believe in that, which he cannot prove. He must seek that, which he cannot find. He must travel a road without knowing his destination. Only thus can the purpose of life be fulfilled.

SCL:13:17 Man may believe he knows his destiny, but he cannot be assured with certainty; in no other way can he fulfil it. In this way alone can his soul be properly awakened to flower with its full potential. This alone he may know: The purpose of all human life is a goal so glorious it surpasses all earthly understanding.

SCL:13:18 We may visualise our individual goals as we will; it is ordained that we have this freedom. How close or how far we are from reality is of little consequence; what is, is. He who seeks a non-existent destination will, nevertheless, get somewhere. He who seeks not at all will get nowhere. Earthly life fulfils itself without attainment.

Chapter Fourteen – The Scroll of Yonua

SCL:14:1 Away from my eyes, O Hideous One. Slink back into the dark shadows about the black sunless abode, where dwell the self-distorted souls of the Fearsomely Formed Ones. Back to your murky haven of sombre compatibility.

SCL:14:2 Away, out of sight, for your repulsiveness brings back into my heart the thoughts of evils and temptations I have encountered and overcome, thoughts which I now so gladly forget. You poor, doomed fiend, mis-shapen, horny-headed, slit-snouted, stunted in arms and legs, horrible to behold. What dreadful thoughts and unclean deeds must have been yours, to fashion you in this manner!

SCL:14:3 Away, back to your own kind, back from the twilit border, where you lurk furtively, afraid, pitifully seeking a glimpse of the bright joys denied to your own folly. Back to the place, with which you have pitiful affinity, back to your own dark, compatible companions.

SCL:14:4 The Guardians of the Hidden Gates repel you, lest you befoul the pathways of the Glorious Ones, who once struggled to find beauty and cleanliness. The light of this place is ever spreading, and soon a Glorious One may walk where you now slink in the gloom. Back, back from the dividing flame, back into the sad comfort of enveloping darkness. Back to your foul companions in misery; back into the mercifully enshrouding gloom.

SCL:14:5 Your fate saddens my heart. Can you find consolation there, hidden in the comforting darkness? Does a kind word ever lighten the burden of your days? Is there a place of rest among the slime and excreta? O Fallen One, who once walked Earth so proudly in self-esteem, selfishness and arrogance, go back; torment yourself no more with the sights of beauty and joy, which lie beyond your reach. O Wriggler in the Slime, back from the purifying flame, what can it avail you now?

SCL:14:6 O Repellent One, who by wrongdoing and non-good doing thus cursed yourself and were delivered into the comfortless arms of decay and filth; who on Earth appeared arrayed in such deceptive softness and complacency; who dwelt amid pleasure and luxury, away, back into the shadows; hide yourself from the pure gaze of the Glorious Ones.

SCL:14:7 O Squirming One, turned back are you; the shameful flesh is unworthy even of the flame. The unshapely mass, unchiselled by the forming blows of self-discipline and selfless service, unmoulded by the touch of compassion and love, unpolished by conformity to the burnishing blows of sincere goodness, has no place near the region of revealing light. See, are you not seared with pain when the pure light falls upon you? Miserable indeed is your lot in that dread, dreary abode!

SCL:14:8 See, your slimy hide shrinks from the pure glare; it splits, it cracks; back, back into your dark cavern with its floor of slime. Back out of sight, out of hearing, back from the pure gaze of righteousness. How miserable the lot of one who finds unconsoling comfort in the depths of dread darkness lit only by shadowy gloom! How awful to dwell in companionship with distorted shades!

SCL:14:9 What became of the loveliness, which once clothed you on Earth? Whose fault that you brought it not with you? Did you ever pause, even for one moment, to gaze into the self-revealing mirror within you and see the awful creature you were forming? Amid your pleasures and luxury, did you not think of the wellbeing of your inner self? Did you not care?

SCL:14:10 O if I could but help you now, but the hideousness was set firm in the furnacefire of death. Then the enveloping flesh was stripped away and the hidden horror within the mould revealed. As the butterfly emerges from the chrysalis, so should the soul emerge from its earthly body. An unnatural thing like this was never intended, yet you freely made the choice. Not a single disfiguring line was made by another.

SCL:14:11 What words are those which rasp forth from the unlipped, fish-shaped mouth? O ears, say you deceive me! O heart, cease this pounding clamour! O hand of horror, release your awful grip! Would that I could swoon, that I could find relief in unconsciousness, but facts have to be faced here, as on Earth. I must look in trembling terror.

SCL:14:12 Yes, I loved on Earth, nothing there was more precious to me than my sister in love. I forgave her wilfulness and was not stirred up when her words were unkind. I ever remained a man of cool temper. I clothed her well, and good food she never lacked. My heart sang in her presence; I rejoiced in her loveliness; she was my life, my wife. Yet, she was unfaithful, she was cruel, she found pleasure in deceit and perversion. As the years passed, they became heavy, clouded and bitter because of her wayward ways.

SCL:14:13 O horror, O terror, O cringing fear, keep away from me! O my eyes, O my heart, it is true. It is the one I loved. O let me die once more, that consciousness may pass from me! It is her, whom I loved, she for whom I waited in joyful anticipation, hoping to find the light of my youth, hoping the overlay of later evils would be sloughed away by death, hoping to find the warm, throbbing liveliness I once held. I would gladly have forgiven the pain she caused in her maturity. O what has become of the smooth flesh, the warm touch? Where is the beauty of face, the grace of form? O raise not the crocodile-skinned arms to shield the awful snout, the green-rimmed, red-veined eyes!

SCL:14:14 O racing heart! I hear the misformed words amidst the hiss and gurgle issuing forth from the oozing aperture. O say not that I was so blind, so greatly deceived, that you cared for nought but the earthly things we shared; that your affection was the false front of hypocrisy, your love a lie. Did I not always forgive? Was I not always patient'? With whom did you share the terrible thoughts and desires that fashioned you thus? Surely, this cannot be the work of your own nature alone. Fickle, you were and pleasure loving, selfish, cruel and deceitful, but all this I forgave because of the plea of my heart. as this not enough? O where is the companion I awaited? Lost, and worse than lost.

SCL:14:15 O compassion, O mercy, come to my aid! My heart fails me, I cannot face what I thought to greet so joyously. O powers of solicitude, strengthen me. What can I do to mitigate the Law? Is there hope? Is there a way?

SCL:14:16 A whisper of comfort, O gratefully I hear it, "There is hope and there is a way, but between this self-shaped horror and the Glorious Ones there is an uncrossable chasm. In sorrow and anguish, it must seek a road, it must go its own dark way, as you must go yours in the light. Turn back, turn again towards the light; the compassion in your own heart does nought to bridge the gulf between, unless it strikes a responsive spark within the other heart".

SCL:14:17 "Let the memory be erased; this is not the companion of your path. The trials and sorrows borne so well, the uncomplaining unselfishness fashioned you in glory. Nor would you have reached the present degree of perfection, had she not been as she was and is now revealed to be. This fearful fate was wrought by the lost one alone, for each is the sole keeper of his spirit. Each soul is fashioned by every thought, desire and deed, every emotion that touched it during its sojourn in an earthly body".

SCL:14:18 "Each is the maker of his own future, the fashioner of his own being".

Chapter Fifteen – A Scroll Fragment – One

SCL:15:1 Salvaged from the Great Book of The Sons of Fire, this is all that remains of some sixteen damaged pages relating to an initiation ceremony.

SCL:15:2 Who will reward or punish me? I will.

SCL:15:3 Who besets my path with sorrow? I do.

SCL:15:4 Who can grant me a life of everlasting glory? I can.

SCL:15:5 Who must save me from the horror of malformation? I must.

SCL:15:6 Who will guide my footsteps through life? I will.

SCL:15:7 Who brings joy into my life and gladdens my heart? I do.

SCL:15:8 Who brings peace and contentment to my spirit? I do.

SCL:15:9 Who lightens the burdens of my labour? None but myself.

SCL:15:10 Whose courage will protect me from the workers of evil? My courage.

SCL:15:11 Whose wisdom will guide me and enlighten my heart? My wisdom.

SCL:15:12 Whose will rules my destiny? My will.

SCL:15:13 Whose duty is it to attend to my wants? My duty.

SCL:15:14 Who is responsible for my future state of being? I alone am responsible.

SCL:15:15 Who shields me from temptation? No one.

SCL:15:16 Who shields me from sorrow and suffering? No one.

SCL:15:17 Who shields me from pain and affliction? No one.

SCL:15:18 Who benefits from my toil and tribulation, my sorrow and suffering? Myself, if wise.

SCL:15:19 Who benefits from my temptations and afflictions, my sacrifices and austerities? Myself, if wise.

Chapter Sixteen – The Third of the Egyptian Scrolls

SCL:16:1 If a man would know heaven, he must first know Earth. Man cannot understand Heaven until he understands Earth. He cannot understand God until he understands himself, and he cannot know love unless he has been loveless.

SCL:16:2 God is unknown, but not unknowable. He is unseen, but not unseeable. God is unheard, but not unhearable. He is not understood, but He is understandable.

SCL:16:3 The goal of life is upstream, not downstream. Man must struggle against the current, not drift with the flow.

SCL:16:4 A child is born knowing all God intended it to know; the rest, it must discover for itself. Man does not live to increase the glory of God; this cannot be done, but to increase the glory of man.

SCL:16:5 He who worships with empty rituals wastes his time and displays the shallowness of his thought. That which man does to benefit man is good, but if he seeks to gratify God, it is a labour of ignorance, showing disrespect for God whose nature is above that of earthly princes. A lifting hand is worth ten wagging tongues.

SCL:16:6 Be a man of fortitude and courage. Prepare to fight, for Earth gives man but two choices: to struggle or perish. There is work to be done in the Garden of God; therefore, cease useless performances and word-wasting discussions; go, pick up the hoe and tackle the task to hand.

SCL:16:7 This is the secret of life: Man lives in God and God lives in man. This answers all questions.

Chapter Seventeen – The Sixth of the Egyptian Scrolls

SCL:17:1 God is in all, and He encompasses all.

SCL:17:2 There is no God but The True God, and His existence is our assurance of life everlasting. He was before the beginning and will be after the end.

SCL:17:3 He is mighty and all powerful. In His magnificence and majesty, no man can conceive Him. His divine nature is beyond the understanding of man. His creation is awesome. His ways unfathomable.

SCL:17:4 His creative thought brought all things forth, and the power which flows from Him is life. He holds life within His mind and the universe within His body.

SCL:17:5 If a man, in ignorance and foolishness, conceives a more understandable god in his own image or builds gods of wood and stone, that will not take anything away from the stature of God. The Supreme One is ever God, the Creator of man, and if man makes earthly gods to worship, then it is man who loses thereby and not God. Among earthly things, man shall find nothing greater than himself.

SCL:17:6 Man worships, not to make God greater, for this he cannot do, but to make himself greater. Nothing man can do can add to what God already has. Men conceive God as a Being having greatly magnified human qualities, as a kinglike Being greater than any king. Thus, man falls into error.

SCL:17:7 As the sun surrounds man with light, though it be hidden behind the stormclouds, so is man in the thoughts of God, though God Himself be hidden from him.

SCL:17:8 Such is our God, who though Himself eternal, lives with each man and with him passes through the Dark Portal of Death into the light of the Glorious Region beyond.

SCL:17:9 God rules over all earths and all spheres. He is in them and they are in Him. All things are in God, and He is in all things. What is was to be; all things begin and end in God.

SCL:17:10 This alone is wisdom; understand and live forever.

Chapter Eighteen – A Scroll Fragment – Two

SCL:18:1 The Book of Initiation and Rites says of God, "All our hopes rest in God, who created all things, sustaining them with His breath, whatever their state, wherever they may be, in this place on Earth, or in any other place visible or invisible."

SCL:18:2 "He alone causes herbs to blossom in beauty and causes all things to come forth in their proper order and time; all flow from His directing thoughts. The peaceful beauty enfolding the face of the land at eventide, the melody of song and speech, the fragrance of flowers, the soft delicacy of petal and wing. All beauty and charm that delights the hearts of men flow from God."

SCL:18:3 "His wisdom is unbounded, and in His goodness, He has provided all things, in which He has created a need in man. The daylight and wind, food and water, heat and coolness, the materials of his dwelling and the substance of his garments, all things for his daily use and enjoyment. Man lacks nothing, which would increase his skill and knowledge; to all useful things, guideposts have been planted along the way. What need can man know for which God has not already made provision, even before man was born?"

SCL:18:4 "He has established the nature of all things, so they remain stable and come forth in their proper order without change. When a man sows barley, he knows what will come up out of the ground; the rewards of his toil are not confusion."

SCL:18:5 "A man lights a fire knowing it will cook his food; it is not sometimes hot and at other times cold. He knows that day will follow night and that the hours of darkness are prescribed; it is not a matter of chance. The hours of darkness are not one day long and the next day short. Oil is ordained for lamps and water to drink; man knows that never can he light a wick in water. Man looks about him and sees order, not confusion, and he knows that where there is organisation there must be an organiser."

SCL:18:6 "The ordinances of God are established for the benefit of man; were they not set in stability, man would be nothing but the plaything of chance and the victim of chaos. Therefore, on the days of feast and fasting, each following in their due season, I will ever remember the obligations due to my God."

SCL:18:7 "I will rejoice and sing songs of praise with a full heart; I will shun the hypocrisy of moving lips. I will be joyful in the fullness of spirit at the beginning and at the end of the appointed seasons."

SCL:18:8 "The decrees of God are fulfilled at the appointed times, and the days of labour pass one into the other. The season of first gathering to the full time of harvest, the season of sowing to the season of fruitfulness, all pass away as the kiss of the wind on the waters."

SCL:18:9 "I will raise my voice, and my hands will move with the music. I will pluck strings and send sweet musical sounds rising to my God, and my breath will fill pipes with tunes to His Glory. When the sky blushes in the dawning, I will lift up my voice in gladness, and when it reddens in the evening, I will not remain silent."

SCL:18:10 "O, how I rejoice that God has made me as I am! Truly, He is in all and encompasses all. In His magnificence and majesty, no man can conceive Him, for His divine nature is beyond the understanding of man. His creation is awesome, his ways unfathomable."

SCL:18:11 "The love of God for His wayward children has been limitless and abounding. It has remained changeless throughout the ages, filled with His noble purpose. He created so that He might express and share that love, which is the very essence of His nature, with beings created in His likeness, beings which could absorb and reflect that love. Yet, that his love might be wholly free, man was endowed with freewill, the freewill, he has used perversely."

Chapter Nineteen – A Hymn from the Book of Songs – 1

SCL:19:1 Bring forth the instruments of music; let all voices be raised in thanksgiving to The Lord of Our Lives. Be happy in heart, and let joyfulness flow from your lips, but remain in stillness while the hands move.

SCL:19:2 Peace and honour be Yours, O Great One, Shadow of Our Days, Comforter of Our Nights, to whom alone we pay homage. Long ago, the skydoor opened, and You appeared over the land in the days of our forefathers, shaking it with Your wrath, but now You are hidden. Your awesome glory is seen no more. We, Your children, rejoice, for You bring peace and spread contentment and security over the whole face of the Earth.

SCL:19:3 Heaven and Earth and all the spheres of the infinite spaces are filled with Your Spirit. The demons of darkness tremble before You. Yet to us, You are truly The Mysterious Hidden One, The Guide of our fathers in the sad days of darkness when the face of the sun was veiled in gloom from the eyes of men.

SCL:19:4 You pour out goodness, bringing fresh water to the green pasturelands, bestowing life upon all beasts and living creatures therein. Through the blessing of Your bounty, even the parched lands drink unceasingly in their season.

SCL:19:5 You are The Bestower of Bread, for You cause the corn to increase and the harvest to be plentiful. You are The Supplier of Reeds and The Provider of Fish. Every craftsman is prosperous and deft when under the guidance of Your hand.

SCL:19:6 Your eye directs the hammers of the smith, and Your hand covers the fingers of the potter. Your creating breath is inhaled by the craftsman, so he is inspired to create an object of beauty. You whisper on the breeze, and the hearts of men are filled with a gladness, which issues from their mouths as joyous song. You move the brush of the painter and direct the pen of the writer.

SCL:19:7 You are The Warden of Fishes within the waters, and You direct them into the nets of the fishermen. You are The Watchman who keeps the waterfowl away from the field sown at the rising of the bountiful waters. You are The Lookoutman at the eye of the barge moving safely over the flowing waters. You are The Director of the energy-giving breezes, which press against the sails.

SCL:19:8 Your hand rolled the corn grains, and Your life-giving breath sucks up the green growing shoots. Your fingers unfold the awakening buds. Your firm will holds stone in stability, so the great buildings endure through the ages. Nothing can escape Your Vigilance, and rest is unknown to You. Eternal activity is the essence of Your nature.

SCL:19:9 You are The Ever Watchful One, The Great Bearer of the Scales, The Unchanging Guardian of the Helpless and The Protector of the Poor. Those who fill these roles on Earth do them in Your name, for You are the motivation and power behind their deeds. Were You non-existent, men would devour one another like crocodiles, while justice and mercy would be things unknown. Something intangible and unseeable flows out from You and rules the lives of men, causing men to deal justly with one another. For, though injustice is part of the fabric of life, it is not dominant, and Your power mitigates its effects.

SCL:19:10 You caress the face of the land, and at Your touch, the womb of Earth is opened, green growth springs through the soil and reaches up towards the sun. All creatures move about according to Your design, and by Your decree their lives are directed. You paint the patterns of life and design its destinies.

SCL:19:11 Though the prince lay his head on a pillow of down and the beggar lay his on an unyielding stone, both sleep alike on Your bosom. The sleep of the rich man is no better than that of a poor man, while the sleep of a labourer is better than that of an idler. The Nightfrightener does not haunt the dreams of those who have paid their debts to the taskmaster of the day. Those who spend their days in idleness sleep in a restless bed. Thus, You have ordained that the scales of life be adjusted. All is balanced in Your hands.

SCL:19:12 Your spirit moves over the Earth, instructing the bee in the gathering of its honey and the hornet in the making of its nest. It directs the ant in the complex design of its cavern and the swallow in its mudgathering. It guides the birds in their season and calls the locusts at the appointed times. All creatures have their unlearned wisdom, which is an outpouring force emanating from Your Spirit.

SCL:19:13 When You fill the Earth with the shining light, which rules the day under Your command, all men rejoice, for by this, all things are increased and food comes forth in abundance. Then, the Lady of the Night rules the darkness, and all is hushed in mellow coolness; hearts are filled with tranquillity and content. You fulfil all the needs of men, for You are The Great Provider.

SCL:19:14 Men labour in the fields and fill the storehouses with grain, but You provide the increase. You are The Ever Bountiful One; Yet with all You give, never is Your substance lessened. You remain everlastingly the same. Man has nought but what originates with You. It is Your waters of life, everlastingly flowing, that sustain him. Eternal glory be Yours, my God and my Life.

SCL:19:15 I sought You in many temples, only to discover that there was One God hidden behind all other gods. That You are indeed The Father of Gods, yet The Maker of none of them. You have illuminated the widespread universe with beauty and filled it with awesome, imperishable grandeur beyond description. So great are Your works above that they must be veiled, so we can comprehend them only dimly, lest we be overcome.

SCL:19:16 Beforetimes, many great men have praised You in error; not knowing what was good for them, they sought to attain the things, which fed the flesh alone. O Great One, show such as these the error of their ways, giving them not the good things of life but making all better men, that they may be worthy of these. You have loved us with an exceedingly great love, having compassion on our many failings and weaknesses, knowing that men are but frail creatures prone to go astray. O God of Gods for the sake of our fathers who placed their trust in You, to whom You gave the ordinances of life, be merciful to us. Instruct and guide us along the paths we should follow. Lead us through the many entanglements of earthly Life, so we may finally come to rest in Your safekeeping.

Chapter Twenty – A Hymn from the Book of Songs – 2

SCL:20:1 O Great and Bountiful One, who is the fountainhead of glory and the eternal spring of power, who sits enthroned in wisdom, whose counsel is the Law, great are the manifestations of Your wrath when it purges the land, even as it was done in the days of our fathers. Yet, we weak, wayward and wilful men, know in the depth of our hearts that whatever You do is done injustice and to our ultimate benefit.

SCL:20:2 With inscrutable wisdom, You prepared a compatible place for the spirits of men, a place encompassing the domain of man, a place wherein man rules under the decrees of Your everlasting and unchanging Law. You have set the boundaries, and they are held back, neither troubling nor oppressing us beyond our endurance.

SCL:20:3 The spirits of men rule in the mysterious domains governing the sun and the moon, the stars and the nightwatchers, the mistmen and the hidden caves of power. They undertake their appointed tasks there and are wave wanderers of the watery wastes, guardians of the deep.

SCL:20:4 You have created man in the likeness of an original conceived in Your mysterious abode, and the manner of his life is fixed according to Your plan. Great and wonderful is the ultimate destiny of man, who as yet, has progressed but a few steps along the road towards the goal of life. Yet, You have opened his ear to mysterious and wonderful things. You have revealed strange mysteries to his eye, he knows things unbelievable in olden times.

SCL:20:5 This being, on whom You have conferred so much, is a thing of weakness and frailty. He was shaped from moistened clay and moulded in water, then set upon a mound in the midst of the great chaos. His eyes were shown the glory above but he wearied of looking, for such splendour was beyond his comprehension. Therefore, he sought his pleasures among the things from whence he came, and therein he now finds his delight. So he sits on a pedestal of shame down by the polluted spring. His repast comes from the pot of fornication, and he is clad in the garments of wickedness.

SCL:20:6 Great One. You who are all wise know the words which come forth from his lips. You know the fruit of his mouth, the pollen of his tongue. Be merciful to man, and overlook his weaknesses, for he is as he was made, and perchance, so he was meant to be. Who can question the mystery? May Your will prevail!

Chapter Twenty-One – The Sunsetting Hymn from the Book of Songs

SCL:21:1 O Great God unbounded by earthly limitations, Your Will is an eternal mystery and Your deeds confound the minds of men, Men worship You, the lesser gods pay due homage, while they who are between gods and men devote themselves to Your service. Highest of Gods, Lord of Men, Ancient Lord of Life and Light, Creator of the Tree of Life, who made the herb and fruit to nourish men and grass to feed the cattle; who perfumed the flowers and gave birds their gay plumage, Hail to The Supreme Power and Spirit!

SCL:21:2 Maker of all that exists in all the spheres above and below, the essence of whose Spirit is in all things. Ruler of all the regions of light and Master of the nether regions. Great Fountainhead of Wisdom, whose abode is in Truth, who fashioned men so they accord with Your own nature, who gave rare abilities to animals and instilled cunning knowledge into insects, who chose the colours of the flowers and the songs of the birds. O Veiled One, whose sanctuary is hidden in the breasts of men, whose temple is open to the Heavens and hung about with the stars. O Mighty One, hear the cry of my spirit as it seeks nourishment from the divine source. Hail to The Supreme Power and Spirit!

SCL:21:3 Great Fashioner of Earthly Things, who came into being before all else, whose sacred name none can know, whose likeness is not displayed in writings and whose image is not carved in wood or stone, whose eyes were the pattern for the sight of men and whose sensitivity generated their touch, whose tongue gave speech to the little gods, who made the herbage for cattle and the waterweed for fish, who feeds even the worms and insects and quickens the life within the egg, who fashioned wild fruits for the birds and wild seed for the mice, who sustains the lifeforce within every living thing, up to the heights of heaven, across the wide breadth of Earth, down to the very depths of the sea. O save me from that, which is beneath the Earth and from those upon the Earth, who would work wickedness against me. Hear me, and my God, I shall praise You; my voice will rise up to Heaven and roll right across the Earth. All those who ply the great mothering river shall hear its echoes. I will tell of Your goodness and greatness to my children and to their children. My words will resound down through the generations as yet unborn. Respond to me, O Great One, as I seek to commune in the silence. My desire is to learn, but You are too mysterious for men to understand. Hail to The Supreme Power and Spirit!

SCL:21:4 O help my soul to rectify its evil deeds and balance them with good. Destroy every form of evil, which clings to me, and let there be nothing in my soul to cause malformation and thus estrange me from my friends, who have departed to dwell in the happy Land of Dawn. Let brightness be my new life's birthright, and let my spirit be ever light. Hail to The Supreme Power and Spirit!

SCL:21:5 The great dome of Heaven rises above, and no man knows its limitations. The broad Earth is spread wide, and no man knows its boundaries. Man cannot fathom it all; O God who is great, have compassion on my littleness. Bear patiently with my blunderings, and overlook my ignorance. Your reach is so great, and mine is so small; help me to know You for myself. I am helpless and lost. Hail to The Supreme Power and Spirit!

SCL:21:6 O Great God, who brings comfort to the prisoner, peace to the tormented; who strengthens the fearful and adjusts the scales between the weak and the strong. Strengthen my desire to understand Your great purpose. O Sole God, whose tears vitalise the hearts of men, in reverence and humility my spirit awaits Your command, my Creator and my Light. Hail to The Supreme Power and Spirit!

SCL:21:7 O Great Craftsman, who fashioned man so wonderfully, who brought together the elements of the Earth and transmuted them so mysteriously, who created with such diversity that no two things are exactly alike, give Your servant some task, that he may accomplish it to Your glory. O Provident Benefactor, who provides sustenance for the beasts of the wilderness and fills the storehouses of men, who placed the great metals in the bosom of the Earth, that man might draw them forth, let not my body go naked, nor my sleeping place be destroyed. Accept my homage, O God of

Truth, who lives down through the ages of time, which make up the everlasting Circle of Eternity. Hail to The Supreme Power and Spirit!

SCL:21:8 O Powerful God, whose wrath lit up the vaults of Heaven and whose fire devoured the wicked in olden times, whose whirlwind swept clean the Earth, who lifted the seas and dashed them against the mountains. O let not the great forces of Earth afflict me. Hold them fast in Your hand, that they may not crush me as the chariot crushes the ant. Hail to The Supreme Power and Spirit!

SCL:21:9 Having an affinity with You, my soul knows You and rejoices in the knowledge. It hears You and is at peace. It opens in response to Your warmth as the lotus and awakens softly as the day opens its eye to the night. My soul knows what I know not. It sees into hidden places and understands deep mysteries. Let me know its nature better, that it may instruct me in wisdom. My soul swells with gratitude towards The Bounteous Being, who causes all things to be, which fulfill all desires. My God is not graven in marble or stone. He is not shaped in wood or cast in copper. He has neither offerings nor ministrations. My God is a god of quiet places and silences. He is found where the wild winds blow and the gay flowers blossom, away from the habitations of men. He is not worshipped in temples, and His praises are not sung by the unthinking multitude. My God is a constant companion; He lives quietly in the homes and hearts of men. His true abode is unknown. He has no painted shrine, no building fashioned by the hands of men could contain Him. Hail to The Supreme Power and Spirit!

SCL:21:10 O Ever Watchful God, The All Seeing One, if aught be done or concealed in the darkness of the night, it shall be known to You. O Supreme Power, who alone can deflect the Awesome Ones of Heaven from their path of destruction, who alone can turn aside the skyboulders and break the winds of the hurricane, I acknowledge You as my Sole God, The Guide of my ways and The Guardian of my Life. I will call upon You by Your names of power. I give You Your degrees, O Lord Over the Thrones of Earth, Director of the Destinies of Nations, Ancient Dweller in the Heavens, Lord of Existence, Lord of Terrors, Master of the Hidden Spheres, Commander of the Universal Hosts, Lord of The Law, wherein Your will is manifested. Victor in the Skyfight, Creator of the Hidden Desires of the Soul, Great One who mysteriously fashions His body as men fashion their souls. Giver of life to souls, by whose breath they awaken. Selector of the Generative Substances, Transformer of Matter, Keeper of the Eternal Essences, Ruler of the Spirits in their Spheres. He who hears the prayer of the prisoner, who stands between the weak and the strong. Lord of Fertility, for whom the great mothering river flows and the waters rise. Lord of the Tree of Life, Emperor of the Sacred Spheres, who dispenses the Celestial Substance, who directs the Thunderbolts, who pilots the stars in the skyways, who overlooks the Watchers in the Night, Great Guardian of Hidden Things and Master of the Divine Secrets, whose domain is shrouded in mystery; who makes tender the hearts of women and makes stern the faces of men. Dweller in Deep Obscurity, whose sanctuary is infinite, who died in the effort of creation and was reborn in the soul of man. Great God, whose face shall be revealed in the future, when all men are wise, grant me Your Truth and Peace Divine. Hail to The Supreme Power and Spirit!

SCL:21:11 Though I falter on the way and fail at the task, despise me not. I try, but success eludes me. I seek but cannot find. I am so small and You are so great that I cannot span the gulf between, unless You incline towards me. O Great Spirit, how near men are to You in reality! Through the darkness of ignorance greater than night, they have groped a way to You; You alone are addressed in the prayers of men. To whatever men pray, You alone hear their petitions; You alone can answer them. Only for You are their words of praise fitting. O Great One, enter into the hearts of men and renew the bond with their souls. Hail to The Supreme Power and Spirit!

SCL:21:12 O Mysterious God hidden in time, Great Ruler of the Ages, we who cannot know more than the smallest part of Your creation turn to You for help and enlightenment. If it be Your will that man should struggle towards understanding and strive for knowledge, then so be it. Man will do whatever he must do, but, O Great God, be patient with him in his failures and failings. Hail to The Supreme Power and Spirit!

Chapter Twenty-Two – A Hymn of Prayer from the Book of Songs – 3

SCL:22:1 O Great One in Heaven, whose thoughts probe the hearts of men, cast forth a small ray of illumination to light my way in the darkness of man's ignorance. Strengthen me by Your revelation, that for even a brief moment, I may see Truth and know the mysteries of life. I ask not to see as the Great Ones have seen, but just for something within my understanding.

SCL:22:2 O Great God, send me one bright shaft of light, that I may see, silhouetted as in a flash of lightning, the forces that wage war for the possession of my soul. For what mortal unaided can understand or visualise the dark things that lurk to lure the soul along the path of horror, such as the demons waiting to twist the weak soul into coils of frightfulness before casting it into the abyss of terror?

SCL:22:3 Lord of the Universe, take pity on me. Everything lies in Your Great hand except the fate of each man, and men are frail and weak. Many who have seen Truth revealed have quailed before the awful responsibilities of man and consoled themselves by fashioning unnatural gods, before whom they quelled the fears in their hearts. I am not one worthy to gaze upon Truth, nor do I desire to do so, lest I be overwhelmed; perhaps I ask too much from One who reads the hearts of men.

SCL:22:4 O Great Luminated One, keep me from the final horror, which lies in wait to devour the souls of men. Help me in the dread hour when I come face to face with my own soul. O save it from the abode of the Dark Warden of Terrors!

SCL:22:5 What are the great mysteries of man's destiny so dimly perceived even by the Illuminated Ones? Have mercy on my dismal ignorance, or I am delivered into the toils of my own repulsiveness.

SCL:22:6 What is the Great Secret whispered so fearfully among the great columns? What are the substances, wherewith men may pass through the Great Portal and return to life? Is it true that the destiny of man is determined by man? O what fearful responsibility; my heart is overwhelmed and my spirit becomes weak with dread. Is it for this that men shun the Truth and cast themselves at Your feet for mercy?

SCL:22:7 I fear, for my soul is heavy with evil, and the scales will bear down against me. Will it be stamped with the dread impress of condemnation by the forty-two seals? Place Your hand in mercy upon the balances, and let my soul be made light.

SCL:22:8 O Great One, hidden within the eternal silence, who shines forth as a beacon of light to few men. O lighten our darkness and our fear-shadowed hearts! Lift the veil just slightly, that we may understand something of Your greatness.

SCL:22:9 We are not uninstructed and know we can be granted no more than a glimpse of Your greatness, for to receive more would be too awesome for the frail constitution of man. This is why the ignorant doubt, for their very ignorance spawns the frailty, which inhibits their enlightenment.

SCL:22:10 We hardly dare murmur these fervent words. O Great One, grant that the spirit within us may be helped to cleanse itself of the besmirching foulness spawned by our thoughts. Remove from us every trace of that, which may pollute, and let us know timeless splendour in glory.

Chapter Twenty-Three – A Hymn from the Book of Songs – 4

SCL:23:1 I am here; I am Yours; I sing Your praises. Join the dance, O priests and priestesses. Join the dance, O Skytravellers, who cover the Earth with Your rays of power. Join the dance, O strangers. Accept our offerings and salutations, accept our devotions and make them successfully beneficial.

SCL:23:2 Move around moonwise, O priests and priestesses. Stamp on wickedness. Stamp on hypocrisy. Stamp your feet on malice and hatred. Sound the flutes, blow the pipes, shake the bells. Come, stamp on the head of pride. Stamp on the Foul Fiend of Lust. Melody and music ring me about in a protecting wall. I am one who rises over the fallen.

SCL:23:3 Hail, O Overlooking, All seeing Power! I am Yours, I am a Chosen One. I am gifted with strength. I am thrice gifted with strength. I am filled with The Sacred Essence. I have partaken of the cup of joy. I am pure, I am pure, I am pure.

SCL:23:4 I see the light of the East, the arrow of All Embracing Love. I see the light of the South, the arrow of All Comforting Benevolence. I see the light of the West, the arrow of Everlasting Hope. I see the light of the North, the arrow of All Consoling Comfort. Let the golden bow speed the arrows of my desire. I am still; I worship the Hallowed Limbs.

SCL:23:5 The Heavenly Hosts gather, as swallows for the flight, as stormclouds for the downpour. Before the Sacred Shrine, I renew my strength. I free myself from all earthly desires, from all bodily passions, of all soul-eating lusts, of all soul-destroying vices.

SCL:23:6 Now, I see the rainbow-hued radiance of the real within the unreal. Now I see true, where before I saw what was not and heard what was not. I was deceived by my body. I was deluded by my feelings. Now, I see things not seeable by unaided mortal eyes. I hear things beyond mortal hearing.

SCL:23:7 O Great One, O Radiant One, O Timeless Knower, O Limitless Viewer, O Majestic One with a form of indescribable beauty! I have seen You through the veil. I have glimpsed the reflection of eternity. I am free.

SCL:23:8 I, Your son, bow humbly before You. Lord, my heart is pure. I proclaim my loyalty to my neighbour on my right and my neighbour on my left. I see the meat. I see the tripod. I see the knife. All is ready. Come, benevolent spirits, gather about the flame. Hover over the bowl.

SCL:23:9 To You, in whom resides the power to appear in any form or shape desired, come; come as welcome guests. Before the Place of Awe, I stand unafraid, for those who are damned to sorrow and horror cannot approach within the barrier. They await in jealous hate without, they who come up from the dismal depths. Away, foul spirits of the damned! Away, O self-destroyed ones!

SCL:23:10 O Great Representative, the court is purified. I now see the flame-like radiance. Brothers and sisters, do you see it too? I see the Radiant Risen Ones who have torn aside the veil for one brief moment. I see things of overwhelming splendour. Bring incense, bring water, bring salt and bring the offering flame.

Chapter Twenty-Four – A Hymn from the Book of Songs – 5

SCL:24:1 I believe in You, Great God of Life, Lord of the Kingdom of Light, Dweller in the Eternal Silences. From the centre of Your domain, there is an outflowing, which sustains all life, and in You rest the hopes of all men.

SCL:24:2 You are The Ruler of All Spheres, and Your dominion is unchallengeable. Under Your benevolent guidance, Earth continues to exist and hold together, changing for nought but the benefit of man. We are Your children, and You are our Father.

SCL:24:3 I believe in the Sacred Spirit of Inspiration, which enters the hearts of men, flowing out from You and joined with You and yet separate, the Spirit to whom our fathers of old gave the greatest reverence, the Beautiful One, the Gentle One, the Inspirational One who first taught men to love and who drew aside the veil to show them beauty.

SCL:24:4 I believe in the Great Kingdom Beyond Earth, where in the Place of Light, the souls of men, if worthy, find a perfection not known here. The light, which is in the Region Beyond the Veil is not as earthly light; it has a sustaining quality; it is a vitalising light indescribable in earthly words.

SCL:24:5 O Great Dweller in the vast silences, which are not as the silence known on Earth, who attends this sacred place, where men gather in devotion. We who are here see You revealed as a beacon light for those whose hearts dwell in the darkness of ignorance. We rejoice in the strengthening emanation, which flows out towards those with the wisdom to attract and absorb it.

SCL:24:6 Here, in the Hidden Place, we Your servants are gathered, and we bow before You, O Great One. We bow in humility, not in servility; we bow in recognition of our earthly limitations. We are overcome with awe and can but stand in worshipful silence before the vision of Your glory. It shines before our eyes, and our mouths cannot open.

SCL:24:7 Here, on this Sacred Ground, we hardly dare to utter the words of prayer, for the sentences formed by men are so unworthy of their purpose when used and spoken before You. Man is limited in knowledge, in understanding and in ability; it is the recognition of this which makes him humble.

SCL:24:8 O Great One, who understands even the speech of the dumb man, help us to expand our knowledge and understanding. We, for our part, will not remain inactive but will ever sincerely struggle to reach out towards You, striving even to extend beyond our limitations. Were it otherwise, we would be dishonest in seeking Your help.

SCL:24:9 Help us to remove the disfiguring stains upon our everlasting spirit, and when earthly life is renewed in us, let us not be too disadvantaged. Teach us to pray without prayerfulness, so that the taint of self-seeking is eliminated. When we petition, let this not be in the spirit of selfishness.

Chapter Twenty-Five – Fragment 1

SCL:25:1 O enfolded, sleeping soul, unaware of the life fountain within from which you may drink, unfeeling of the throbbing life all about us, now is your hour. Prepare yourself for the great awakening. The bright light of wisdom awaits to encircle you, as you stand before the awful door within the Sacred Temple of Mystery.

SCL:25:2 That the light of Truth may be a sure guide amidst the dark gloom of earthly life, a certain aid enabling you to find the way of your eternal spirit, you are not unknowing of your inner wisdom. It is the key to everlasting life in the glorious place beyond the Western veil.

SCL:25:3 O live my soul; awaken, hear me. Let not my love and my sacrifice be in vain; let not all my hopes turn to dust within the tomb. Can love become soil and hope become sand? Never, for the grave is not the destination of the sublime attributes, which ennoble the nature of man.

SCL:25:4 Man is as a flame burning in water, as it is written on the pillars without. His soul is as the rosebud awaiting the kiss of the sun to awaken it to bloom. His nature is as the day, which is ever accompanied by the night.

** ** ** ** ** ** ** ** **

SCL:25:5 Fragment 2 - I will praise The Nameless God, who is The True God and The Knower of Every Name. Hail Great Overseer of Earth!

SCL:25:6 The high Heavens will hear the sound of my voice, and its loudness shall ring across the widespread land. It shall resound throughout the Red Land. My song shall ride on the wings of the wind, and my gladness shall whisper into the ear of the air. Hail Great Overseer of Earth!

SCL:25:7 I shall seek diligently for enlightenment and knowledge, that I may proclaim the ways of The True God among people, for they are mysterious ways not easily understood. Man wallows in a quicksand of ignorance, and only by extreme effort can he extricate himself. Great Overseer, grant me the ability to understand. Hail Great Overseer of Earth!

SCL:25:8 I say to the people, "Declare The Great One to Your children, to the high born and to the lowly ones, who dwell together under the same sun, to the generations as Yet unborn. Sing songs that will echo down the corridors of time." Hail Great Overseer of Earth!

SCL:25:9 "Sing His praises with the birds of the air; tell of Him to the fishes in the waters, to the creatures which bide in the ground and to the things which walk and crawl above it." Hail Great Overseer of Earth!

SCL:25:10 "Declare Him unto all, for He is The God of All. He is The Great Compassionate One, whose wrath declines with the setting sun and in the morning departs with the dawnlight mists." Hail Great Overseer of Earth!

SCL:25:11 Sometimes in the lonely nightwatches, I wonder, have You turned Your face from me? What have I done that You are unresponsive? Have I ever lived otherwise than in accordance with Your word? O Great Overseer of Earth, what is Your will for me?

** ** ** ** ** ** ** ** **

SCL:25:12 Fragment 3 - O Great One, everlastingly considerate of our needs, Overseer and Taskmaster of mankind, look down upon us with compassion, and lay not too great a burden upon us, Your dutiful servants. Labour we must, for thus we prepare for a higher state of being, but bear with us, for sometimes we grow weary and falter at the task.

SCL:25:13 Here we have fallen victims of our own wiles; we have hopelessly snarled up the threads of our existence, so we know not how to loosen the knots we ourselves have tied and so free ourselves. We are entangled in a net of our own weaving. Let us, Your servants, look to You, The Great One, for aid. Our destinies are held in the hollow of Your hands, while the future is visible to You, as is writing upon an open scroll.

SCL:25:14 The Glorious Ones worship You with service and serve through following the words of guidance. Thus, the earthbound spirits worship You, the shades of the departed worship You and the whole of creation worships You. We, Your servants, offer our continual and everlasting devotion to Your service. We are not as others, O Great One, for we know well that worship and devotion mean service and expended effort, not mere words and ritual.

SCL:25:15 Your spirit governs the breezes that comfort mankind. You send the fertilising rains. Your Spirit quickens the seed within the womb of Earth. The songs of the birds are inspired by the knowledge of You, and the wild beasts rejoice in the sustenance provided.

SCL:25:16 You are The Universal Being, The Raincloud Overshadowing the Earth, The One Dwelling in the Cave of the Heart within all breathing creatures. You are The Weaver of the Warp and Woof of Life.

** ** ** ** ** ** ** ** **

SCL:25:17 Fragment 4 - I praise The One Who Eats Evil, The Disposer of Earthly Residue. He who sustains the devoted followers of The Deathless One in whom all merge on leaving the body. For the day comes when we discard all that is of Earth, when we recognise and realise that all remaining is the pure and sacred spirit, boundless and free as the winds.

SCL:25:18 I praise The One Who Eats Evil, The Disposer of Earthly Residue. He who sustains the devoted followers of The Deathless One, who is with us everywhere and in all things, in whom is all, though not Himself the all, who sees and hears all, who knows and understands all, but whom none tied to Earth can know; who projects His word of power, so that it is within all and holds all things together in stability.

SCL:25:19 I praise The One Who Eats Evil, The Disposer of Earthly Residue. He who sustains the devoted followers of The Deathless One, who created all things and thus became His Own Greater Self, who clothed Himself in the universe as with a garment.

** ** ** ** ** ** ** ** **

SCL:25:20 Fragment 5 - O Great Spirit, I would see the vast face of the Earth as You behold it. I would know how the seed is quickened, so that it grows into the plant and how the fowl comes forth from the egg. What is added to the egg to give it the power to reproduce life?

SCL:25:21 I would touch Your Great Body born of the breath from The Eternal Source and watch Your thoughts creating and moulding all things to shape step by step.

SCL:25:22 I would see the links of Heaven and Earth and rest one hand in each. I would see the thread that binds yesterday, today and tomorrow, so all are one and parts of the whole.

SCL:25:23 I would see the appointed place of every living man and understand why. I would see the purpose of every beast and every plant, every tree and every thing that flies and crawls.

SCL:25:24 I would know gladness with the children, as they play and go singing on the way to their places of instruction. I would watch birth and death and solve their mysteries. I would know the depths of hatred and the heights of love.

SCL:25:25 I would journey the adventurous path of love hand in hand with another. I would know its secret, its delights and their shadows, and the secrets of its silences.

SCL:25:26 I would know the beginning and the end and understand what links them. I would see the chain of the years and the necklace of the days. I would know the purpose of it all. Then, knowing all these, I would know You at last, O Great Spirit!

** ** ** ** ** ** ** ** **

SCL:25:27 Fragment 6 - O True God, by whom the worthy are guided in all they undertake; who rises as a beacon in the darkness for the lowly. Grant us, Your servants, who put their trust in You, strength to overcome all the doubts and uncertainties which rise in our hearts, as frightening shadows arise in the night. Let us sip the waters from the inexhaustible well of wisdom, that we may not move along false paths to encompass our own destruction.

SCL:25:28 For we cannot see the way in the enveloping darkness, and confusing voices shout this way or that way. We are bewildered, for we know not which one is right. Can there be so many ways?

SCL:25:29 We are not men of great learning or high position. We do not sit among princes, being among the lowliest in the land. Yet, it is we who carry the burdens of the people; we feed the hungry and provide for the widow and orphan. Ours are the aching backs and weary feet, ours the naked body and empty bowl.

SCL:25:30 Those who are concerned with higher things sit at tables of plenty; those seemingly unworthy rejoice amid prosperity and plenty. Those who take are given more, while those who give are mocked.

SCL:25:31 We see these things, and doubt enters our thoughts; we ask one another, "Why is this the order of things? Is it the will of our God?" Then, we seek for an answer in all sincerity and with productive effort, and The Great God Above All does not remain mute.

** ** ** ** ** ** ** ** **

SCL:25:32 Fragment 7 - O God, hear my prayer, for I have gone into the great recess within me and await a response from out of the enveloping silence and tranquillity. The restlessness and discontent of life, I have left at the portal. I have closed the door to the outer things of life.

SCL:25:33 Give ear, O my soul, to the whispers from the silence. Close out the clamour of Earth, and harken to the soft voice which echoes from the far reaches of eternity. Hear without ears the wordless voice of Truth. Close the eyes of the flesh, that the greater eye may see in the inner darkness.

SCL:25:34 Enter into the inner temple, and await the revelation of heavenly secrets. Shut out the clamouring senses that demand expression in sensual pleasures. Then, when all outer doors are closed and all inner doors open, speak to me and I will hear Your voice. Tell me the secrets of the ages, and my spirit will dwell in contentment for ever.

SCL:25:35 This alone I ask and no more; it is sufficient for one lifetime.

** ** ** ** ** ** ** ** **

SCL:25:36 Fragment 8 - O Great One on High, have pity on us, for we are hopelessly ensnared by our complete lack of things needed to sustain the body. Without sustenance, our spirits are restless; our hearts cannot find peace. We do not desire foolish things or pleasurable or vain things, but just the things, without which we cannot live.

SCL:25:37 Though we lack all things, we do not turn our faces from You, for we know well that, in

Your bounty, all men are provided for, and the Earth is full of richness. It is not You who take away the things needed to sustain our lives, but those made in our own likeness, our own brother men.

SCL:25:38 They deny meat to the hungry and drink to the thirsty, though they themselves are gorged to fullness and bloated with good things. Be merciful to them; instruct and enlighten them with Your chastising afflictions. Thus, they may come to know that man needs man, and each man is brother to all others.

SCL:25:39 Others have reaped where we have sown, and others sleep where we have built, because of the statutes of men. Therefore, mete out nought but justice, that we may be fed and clothed and have a place to rest our heads.

** ** ** ** ** ** ** ** **

SCL:25:40 Fragment 9 - O God, who teaches us in so many strange ways in this great place of instruction called Earth, who set us tasks to an end which we cannot foresee, and who tests us to measure our abilities and to try our courage and fidelity.

SCL:25:41 Instruct us, so we may better understand the bitter lessons, which purge from our natures all, which is unwholesome to the spirit. Strengthen us, so we may bear all things without complaint and conduct ourselves manfully under the strict discipline of this unique place of instruction. Open the eyes of understanding within us, that we may benefit by every experience and not waste time bewailing our lot.

SCL:25:42 Tell us, so we may know. Instruct us in our duties in the battleline, so that when we are called upon to take our appointed place, we shall not shirk the clash. Toughen us on the training ground of adversity, so that we may be stronger for the fray. When the day of battle comes upon us and cowards flee before the strength of our adversary, when the valiant ones kiss the dust at the portals of glory, let our place be where the battle rages most fiercely and the blows fall the thickest.

SCL:25:43 If we faint, may we still remain faithful. If we are exhausted, may we remain dauntless. If our hour come and we fall before the onslaught, may it be with weapons in hand and face to the foe. We fight the fight, where the victor can be the vanquished and the vanquished the victor, for here the fight is the end and not the victory. He who serves the end well justly claims the fruits of victory.

SCL:25:44 We cannot ask to win, but we can ask to be made strong if we struggle for strength. We cannot ask to remain unhurt, but we do ask for courage. We cannot ask to be supported in weakness, but we can ask for the fortitude to endure. We stand firm-footed, grim-faced to the foe. The ranks of wickedness encompass us about, but we will surge forward with closed ranks, carrying all before us until we come to rest in the presence of victory.

SCL:25:45 O God, Supreme Among Spirits, watch over us in the struggle, for we are Your children.

** ** ** ** ** ** ** ** **

SCL:25:46 Fragment 10 - This is my prayer. O Great Spirit, accept my prayer. O Dweller in the Pure Region of Truth. hear me. O Great Fountain of Wisdom, hear me.

SCL:25:47 O Comforter and Companion of the Soul Silences, hear me. I, Your son, come into Your presence with faith and humility.

SCL:25:48 Grant that my spirit be admitted into the Glorious Audience Chamber between the two regions.

SCL:25:49 I, Your son, come into Your presence with faith and humility. O Supreme Source of the form-holding rays, grant me a hearing. O Great One seated on The Celestial Throne behind The Great Solar Disk, hear me. All homage to You, Great God, Master of the bodies of men. I, Your son, come into Your presence with faith and humility. My every thought and deed are dedicated to Your service. These things are written clearly in my heart and are not mere puffs of wind from my mouth.

** ** ** ** ** ** ** ** **

SCL:25:50 Fragment 11 - Lord of my heart, hear me now, as I stand in communicating silence before the listening shrine. You are The Great One, who existed before the upheaval of the mountains, who tore apart the land and waters in the infant years of man.

SCL:25:51 For in Your sight, a thousand great years are as an hour in the heat of the day, or as a watch in the coolness of the night. You are The Timekeeper in Eternity and Warden of the Ages.

SCL:25:52 You reap men as corn is reaped at the harvest and sweep them away as floodwaters cleanse the land. For man is like unto the grass of the field; in the morning, it grows full of vigour, gaily bedecked with the gems of morning dew; in the eventide it is cut down, to wither in the night.

SCL:25:53 The day is not important if men live by the hour, fulfilling in each its appointed task

** ** ** ** ** ** ** ** **

SCL:25:54 Fragment 12 - When the Dread Messenger calls for you, let him not find you ill-equipped and unprepared. In the final hour, which must surely come, there will be no opportunity for fine speech, and nought can delay his imperious command. Then all the possessions you have cherished and stored will be as nought, and all you will be able to take with you will be that, which you have fashioned within.

SCL:25:55 Do not be numbered among the foolish, who say, "Time enough, for I am yet young." Death claims the breast-child as well as the aged, and on this you should ponder. Consider well your future estate.

SCL:25:56 Here, you are the architect of your future abode; the plans prepared here are carried out in another place. Earth is the place of sowing. Heaven is the place of reaping.

SCL:25:57 Here you are the sculptor, who chisels the statue; the potter, who fashions the pot; the woodworker who carves the pillar. What is there on Earth more deserving of your care and attention than your own future form and appearance?

SCL:25:58 Do you recklessly hew or wilfully cut? Do you heedlessly pound the pliable clay and carelessly fashion the unfired pot? Do you mix the colours with proper thought?

SCL:25:59 What manner of thing are you fashioning in this great workshop? A beauteous being, arrayed in radiant splendour, or a hideously foul fiend, which can do nought but squirm in the slime of its fitting abode?

SCL:25:60 Whom will you praise for your prudence or curse for your lack of foresight? Who can force you to deal tenderly and responsibly with the slumbering child of your own self? Or prevent you from carelessly and wilfully shattering all hopes for its future wellbeing?

** ** ** ** ** ** ** ** **

SCL:25:61 Fragment 13 - Rejoice, all cities beside the waters; be joyful all people in the land, for great things have come to pass. Behold, the foe is scattered in confusion; they are no more; they are eaten up; victory is with us.

SCL:25:62 All praise to our Commanding Lord. Hail The Great Leader. Hail The Source of Power in the land, live for ever in glory. O Mighty Fighter, let us rest in the shade of Your greatness, let us dwell under Your shadow, under the protection of Your right arm.

SCL:25:63 You have given us that, which we never thought to know again. Men sit in peace, speaking freely one with another. They walk abroad with light steps, and their heads are held high. Men look their fellowmen in the eye, and there is none to jostle them. They are delivered from the shadow of fear, and confidence is renewed in them. The fortresses are no longer overflowing with fighting men, and all throughout the land, no well is forbidden to the thirsty; all may drink freely where there is water. Men come and go across the wilderness, carrying the burdens of trade, and no one falls upon them to plunder. Men journey peacefully along the lonely roads, and no one waylays them to rob. Traders cross the barren places and are unmolested; no one rises against them.

SCL:25:64 The bearers of messages no longer hasten about, pale of face and frightened; they no longer carry doleful tidings; they no longer bear words of fear. Their coming no longer causes the knees to tremble and the stomachs to fall. Now, the messengers loiter in shady places, remaining there until the nightwatch calls, for there is no urgency in the words they carry. The fighting men rest; their hazardous days have gone; the bow, the sword, the spear and the shield have been laid away in the weapon stores. Men walk freely; they talk gaily, for they are not overshadowed with fear, neither do they tremble for fear of molestation, The faces of the border guardians are no longer haggard with sleeplessness, nor are their eyes tired and strained with watchfulness. Throughout the whole land there is content and tranquillity.

SCL:25:65 The herds are large and sleek; they are no longer tense and restless. The flocks graze contentedly in their green pastures. The fowls are no longer alert and noisy but squabble playfully, chasing one another through the dust. The voices of men are no longer hoarsened with war cries; instead, they can be heard singing, as each goes about his appointed task. The doleful wailing of women, who mourn their dead is no longer heard, and widows no longer proclaim themselves. The husbandman sows contentedly, knowing that where he sows, he shall also reap. He no longer doubts that he will enjoy his own harvest.

SCL:25:66 The face of God is once more inclined favourably towards us; even the lesser gods look again upon the land with favour. The reign of Saku is over; he no longer overshadows the lives of men; all is well in the two lands.

** ** ** ** ** ** ** ** **

SCL:25:67 Fragment 14 - We praise our own God with joyous and grateful hearts. He has shown Himself among us. He will come again in His season; all is well with us. His desire brings forth the green growing things, and the land is clothed in its gay mantle. His hand guides the stars; his mind contains all things that fly above the Earth and all things that walk and crawl upon its face.

SCL:25:68 We praise You, Great Eternal One, whose forms are so many. We kiss the ground before You. All the sacred beings and sacred things men worship are but manifestations of their groping through the clouds of ignorance to understand You. Have pity on them, for they were born into darkness and mysteries, but their hearts are good.

SCL:25:69 Each day, You bring some new thing to the attention of men and place before them problems to unravel. The nature of men ever inclines them towards the path of ease and passiveness; therefore, they tend to shun the things which are truly profitable. Therefore, deal with men in a manner best fitting for their progress towards Truth.

** ** ** ** ** ** ** ** **

SCL:25:70 Fragment 15 - Neither life nor love ends at the Grim Portal. The strength of the invisible bond between two souls binds them even after death. That which binds strongest of all is the love, which is sincere, true and constant. Such love endures through tribulations and trials.

SCL:25:71 If one you love has departed through the Western Gates into the Great halls of Eternity, then be comforted by the words of Truth. This you will then know: that the Guardian at the Grim Portal is no fearsome being, but a compassionate attendant who tends you gently while asleep, until the morning of a more glorious day. Then, you will be awakened to journey through a greater adventure with the companions of former times.

** ** ** ** ** ** ** ** **

SCL:25:72 Fragment 16 - In death, you are greater than ever you were on Earth, for now the companionable spirits lament for your sake. They strike their bare flesh for you and smite upon their forearms. They tear at their hair and cast dust on their heads.

SCL:25:73 Yet, if they be true to themselves, they are not cast down; they are not distressed. There is a voice speaking out of the silence, saying, "If he goes, he shall come, if he sleeps, he shall awaken, and if he dies, he shall live."

SCL:25:74 Can you be gone from us forever? No, you are not dead or lost unto us, unless by our own deeds we depart to dwell in different regions.

SCL:25:75 I am not cast down. You are now in the Great Place beyond the everlasting stars. You have passed over the horizon of immortality and now walk erect along the path of glory. May we meet there in days yet to come.

SCL:25:76 Hail O Glorious One!

** ** ** ** ** ** ** ** **

SCL:25:77 Fragment 17 - Stand by my side; support me when I pass out from the tomb, O My Guardian! Let me take Your hand; stand by my side when I come before the Assessors, that when I hear the verdict, I may not be alone. If my eyes cannot see, then tell me of the balances; do they bear down in my favour?

SCL:25:78 O Guardian God, lighten the darkness for me, and deliver me from the meshes of the net woven by my own deeds of wickedness and weakness. You are my strength and support; to You have I given my offerings. You I have honoured above all.

SCL:25:79 There, I may be in distress and have none to abide with me. I may have no comforter and may be alone; therefore, desert me not in my time of trial. Stand by my side, O Guardian God. If I am numbered among the distressed ones, look upon me with compassion and mercy, and if I am deserted, then sustain me with water, bread and oil.

** ** ** ** ** ** ** ** **

SCL:25:80 Fragment 18 - I sing words of glory unto my God who is the Great God Above All Gods, and the words, which issue from my mouth shall be exalted above all things. With them, I will praise Him in the Sacred Place, in the silence of His Hidden Sanctuary. They will glorify my God, so that His Majesty is not dishonoured and He is not deserted, until the day when He shall be declared before all men.

SCL:25:81 With the ever-loving thoughts of a devoted heart, I praise Him. Even as the sun rises joyfully into the daysky, so does my heart rise towards He, who gives me life and renews it day by day.

SCL:25:82 He is Great; He is Mighty; He is Glorious. He made the great river to flow, that all men in the two lands might be fed. It never wearies; it never ceases its onward flowing. It is everlastingly renewed.

SCL:25:83 Even as the great river flows steadily and strongly through the barren wilderness and bestows verdant life on its way, so let the river of my life flow through the Earth and eat away the sands of wickedness.

SCL:25:84 Release me from my mortal fetters. Loosen the heavy covering of flesh, which imprisons me, which restrains me. Let me rise free into the glory above, as the falcon floats freely on the wing. Let not the melody of my song be cut off while I sing, nor the story end before its completion.

SCL:25:85 Keep me, O my God, from the ways of darkness, and let my spirit rejoice in the light of righteousness.

SCL:25:86 Glory to You, Great God, Lord of Truth, whose eternal throne is concealed behind man's limitations, who issued the command that brought things into being, who made man so wonderfully that man himself cannot understand his own nature, who hears with compassion the cry of the distressed and the moan of the captive.

SCL:25:87 All hail the everlasting spirit within, the real self, the seat of all thought inseparable from me. I am one who can truly call his soul everlasting, for I am one of the Awakened Ones, one of the few who have at long last attained the Splendid Vision. I have seen the bright flash of Truth in the darkness of earthly existence. I am free. I am illuminated.

SCL:25:88 I will sing, that You may be glorified in the solitudes of Your hidden Places, where the eyes of the profane can never penetrate, where few men come as Chosen Ones. There, we will sing songs of yore. We will sing of Your ways and of Your laws, which remain everlastingly unchangeable.

** ** ** ** ** ** ** ** **

SCL:25:89 Fragment 19 - Heaven and the many Heavens beyond Heaven, Earth and the many

Earths beyond Earth are held in the thoughts and power of God. They are as a monument to His everlasting glory. All things living that move and breathe have their place in the abode of life. Man finds the greatest joy in the Eternal Halls; therefore, set not Your heart on earthly possessions.

SCL:25:90 Here, a man may desire life for a hundred years and may even attain it, but what benefit are the extended years to him if they do not exalt the soul? There is a horror-haunted region of darkness, and whosoever rejects the godward life on Earth will surely dwell therein. They will go down to partake of the nature of demons, down into the darkness of delusion and doom.

SCL:25:91 The soul, without moving flies on wings swifter than thought. It stands behind and beyond the senses. It is the Knower working within the things that are known. The spirit of man is carried down the stream of action into the ocean of life. The spirit is everlasting; it is near, and it is far; it is in all, and it contains all.

SCL:25:92 He who sees his own self in all things and all things in his own self is awakened. He is beyond delusion and outside the reach of futile sorrow.

** ** ** ** ** ** ** ** **

SCL:25:93 Fragment 20 - I am Hahrew the Enlightened One, Hahrew the Twice Born. Having crossed the dark waters myself, I carry the others across. Being free from fear, I free others from fear. Being unrestricted, I ease the restriction of others. Knowing the way, I show it to others. Having trodden the road, I now guide others along it. I am an Illuminated One, the open of ear, the keen of eye. I am one who knows the Law; I am a keeper of ordinances.

SCL:25:94 I shall refresh all those whose bodies are bent with toil or sorrow. I shall come to the aid of those whose souls are withered and distorted and give them strengthening sustenance. I shall open the eyes of many, who are deluded in the heavy mists of threefold existence.

SCL:25:95 Hear me, all who toil under the yoke of ignorance, who labour under the clouds of despair. I am the Forthcoming One, the Future One Turned Back. I am the Spirit Within The Law.

SCL:25:96 I am the Voice of Enlightenment, one who proclaims the brotherhood of all men. I am to one as to another. I am Hahrew.

** ** ** ** ** ** ** ** **

SCL:25:97 Fragment 21 - O life-giving Sun, handwork of God, projection of divine fire, heat of Heaven, light of the day, solitary glory of the daytime, let me behold the hidden form behind Your brightness, for the spirit within You is even as my spirit. Thus, I may come to understand the nature of my God, who commands You and to whom I pray. The fair face of the daughter of Truth remains hidden behind its mask of gold. O spirit of light, draw aside the veil even slightly, that I may see.

SCL:25:98 Who among men is wise enough to know his own wrongdoing, or to see clearly his own errors and follies? The eyes of men are dim and the road narrow; therefore, it is not hard to wander from the way. Therefore, O my God, keep me from all hidden wrongdoing and errors, and keep me from the power of temptations, to which I so readily succumb.

SCL:25:99 I know the rebellions of my heart, and my wickedness is ever before my eyes, yet how much more do I not see! I have chafed against the restrictions of Your decrees and the Law. I am a foolish one, who does himself an injury.

SCL:25:100 I am ashamed and blush for my folly. I am as a man who, when his arm does wrong, cuts off a finger. Help to make clean my heart and strengthen my spirit, that it may resist my own inflictions upon it. I believe I do right and do wrong, for I have not listened carefully and diligently to Your words written on the sacred scrolls.

SCL:25:101 O my God, whom I have long worshipped with devotion, incline from the great heights of Your splendour, and stretch a helping hand down towards Your weary servant. Trusting in You, I will depart from the pastures of sweet grass and the calm waters of restful repose and go into the presence of the Everlasting Lords. I will pass out of the dark tomb; I will arise refreshed with the outpouring of Your Spirit. I will clasp Your mighty hand and be guided along the path of Truth. Thus, I cannot stray, and the lonely places will not claim me.

SCL:25:102 In confidence and trust, I will take my place before the Court of Assessors. Guided by Your light, I shall pass safely by the Place of Darkness, and those who lurk shall do me no harm. My trust is in You, and I will come safely past the lurking ones. I shall be freed of all earthly weariness, and my spirit shall shine forth in glory. I will stand in the Place of Brightness, and the Glorious Ones will come bringing refreshing waters. I will not lack sweet sustenance, and delicacies shall be poured forth for me in abundance.

Chapter Twenty-Six – From the Scroll of Senmut

SCL:26:1 The stonebearer measures the stone, and it is trimmed and pushed into place. It is fitted, and the overseer looks upon it and says, "This stone is well laid. It remains in its appointed place."

SCL:26:2 Beside it, other stones are fitted and set, each according to its own shape and design; each has its own place and position. Then, upon it are placed other stones, and so it becomes concealed from sight in the foundations of the structure. The building rises, firm and strong, to become the dwelling place of a prince.

SCL:26:3 I am one, of whom men say, "He establishes buildings, which stand forever." I remember that stone deep below the ground in the base of the structure, where no eye ever sees it. Men know it is there; it just remains in its place, fulfilling its appointed duty, a necessity for the upholding of the building.

SCL:26:4 What difference whether that stone be set upon the pinnacle, shining in the sun, ever before the eyes of men, or hidden in the ground, unseen at the base? It does its duty by standing solidly in its rightful place and seeking not to change it.

SCL:26:5 I, who establish great buildings, which will stand forever, remember that stone.

Chapter Twenty-Seven – The Songs of Nefatari – One

SCL:27:6 I sing my song because the Earth sings; though the wind is hushed among the groves, it still plays with soft melodic gaiety. The benevolent sky looks gently down, its breath stilled as it listens to the melody of the leaves. The dew smiles in the morning, for it has captured the light of love from the stars. My song is beautiful because my heart dances gladly in my bosom; its joyfulness conveys gay music to my thoughts and places endearing words on my lips.

SCL:27:7 Because I am dedicated to love, I have but one love, the beautiful container of my life. My heart is a lonely thing ever seeking companionship with yours. It is lost to you, so let it beat in your breast, nestled against your heart, for there it surely belongs. My love is wholesome, not tainted by any residue of past affections; it is gentle and pure; therefore, treat it with manly tenderness, for it is a precious treasure. I give it gladly and can give no more. That which I give to you, I can give to no other man. For you, the lovely pearl; for others, the empty shell.

SCL:27:8 Let me live just for you, let me serve as your housewife. Let me hold your child to my breast; let my eyes be gladdened by your presence each night and in the morning. Let me bask continuously in the wonderful radiance of your presence. Never part me from the source of my joyfulness and gaiety, but let us go down the corridor of life together, your arm laid on my arm and my hand in your hand.

SCL:27:9 My heart is desolation; it is like a wilted flower. You are away, my love, and my eyes search the road for your coming. The caress of sleep eludes me, for your image is ever there beside me, and I cannot find consolation with even the most comforting shadow. Come to me, my living love, that I may feel the warmth of your flesh and be at peace.

SCL:27:10 While you are absent, I concern myself no more with things, which give pleasure to a woman's heart. I neglect my hair arrangement, and my diadem hangs disregarded. My curls are laid aside, for I await your coming to put them on and greet you in my gaiety. The song is silent on my lips, for my heart is without joy.

SCL:27:11 While you are away, my heart slumbers; my bosom is empty. Come quickly, my love, that my heart may awaken and beat gladly with the pulse of life. I await your coming, as the dawn awaits the sun, as the parched lands await the rising waters.

SCL:27:12 My eyes search the nightskies and see the mating dance of the stars; the Earth about me throbs with the pulse beat of love. The dark waters reflect the mystery of life, but I sit beside them desolate. Come to me my love, for none but you can awaken my response. I stand alone on the shore of the sea of love. Come, O come, that we may enter the enchanted waters together.

SCL:27:13 Does the night long for the day, as I long for you? Does the thirsty wayfarer long for water, as I yearn for you'? If so, then truly they are to be pitied. O come, my living love, and fill my days with the sunshine of your love.

SCL:27:14 It seems the ages of man have never been loveless.

Chapter Twenty-Eight – The Songs of Nefatari – Two

SCL:28:15 Life is the bearer of the most wonderful gifts. You are a man and my man. Maker of my heart's butterfly flutter when my breath becomes a necklace of sighs. In your strong arms, I melt as honey in the warm night waters.

SCL:28:16 O man and my man, great one in my maidenly eyes. The light of my life, the sun of my days and the moon of my nights; the rock, against which I confidently nestle, for to feel your protecting strength is my everlasting delight. My body yearns for you as the parched fields cry out for the caress of the fertilising waters.

SCL:28:17 How delightful the gentle hour of love with you. O that it might become an eternity, wherein I might sleep with you as your wife, your lifelong companion in love. In this life always yours, to serve your pleasure and be ever with you; to stand at last, my hand in your hand, together before the dream goddess in the Halls of Eternal Joy. There, those who have loved wholesomely, such as we, find everlasting pleasures.

SCL:28:18 I am yours, both here and there, escapable never, yours forever. Yours pure, untouched and unsullied. I am with you first, sister in love. If at times my tongue speaks with unmaidenly boldness, then let this be forgiven me, for I am pure of heart. The words pour forth from a heart overflowing with love and not from a tongue dipped into the shame of impure experience.

SCL:28:19 I come to you with maidenly pride, as a dew-bedecked garden of herbs, fair flowering, sweet smelling and refreshing. Peace and contentment are mine to gladly give. Upon you, I gladly bestow all that is precious to a maiden. You share me with no other, I honour love by bestowing what is exclusively yours.

SCL:28:20 Your brow becomes hot with the body passion of man burning within, and I cool it with my womanly hand as the cooling north wind tempers the heat of the burning sands. The strength of an ox and the gentleness of a kitten are united in love.

SCL:28:21 We walk together in a land of beauty, a garden of loveliness fashioned thus by the dreams we share. Hand in hand in the kingdom of men, heart in heart in the kingdom of spirit.

SCL:28:22 When hearts are bound together in a love exceeding all bounds, then bodies may unite with purity and peace. We wander heedlessly about, and my heart sings with joy, for we are together.

SCL:28:23 Your voice is the food of my heart, your touch the life of my body. I see you, and I am gay; you depart and I am sad. Your glance pierces me like an arrow of fire; your words carry me away like the surge of bitter waters over the beach.

SCL:28:24 For the lovers' hour, we sit beneath the wild fig tree, beneath its fruits of lovers' blood and its leaves of lovers' eyes. Hear it whisper to our hearts. I am a maiden reserved to you in love; you are my lord, the commander of my heart. I dwell beneath your shadow and within your shadow. O never leave me unshielded!

SCL:28:25 My nights are restless and hot; shall I give my love the apple of his desire, the first fruits of womanly love? Am I the wild bird snare awaiting the wild goose? O my heart, how have women beyond number decided before me which answer is the true one?

SCL:28:26 O take me not in my weakness, lest You despise me after the manner of men and bring low the head of my father. Have manly compassion on the weaknesses made by my love. Degrade me not before my mother, and let not the shadow of shame fall over my father's house. Let me ever keep faith with the Mother Guardian of Love, that when I am called before her, I shall stand in unsullied radiance. Make me not a woman of the hedgerow.

SCL:28:27 Let our love bear us up in glory, up into the revealing light, where we may stand together, proud and unashamed. Let ours be a love that fulfils its appointed function in the great chain of life, something honoured by men and an inspiration to our children. Let it not become a flower of the field corner, which withers in shame when the sunlight falls upon it.

SCL:28:28 I wait, the day comes, its hours are long and extended, but with its declining, you hasten to me, my man and my life. Sweet mistress of love, speed the fulfilling hour.

Chapter Twenty-Nine – The Songs of Tantalip – One

SCL:29:29 The night rolls back to reveal the promise of another day. The great sun comes up in the morning time, and the lotus opens to reveal its shining heart displayed in devotion. You come, and my heart leaps up from my breast to meet you.

SCL:29:30 The wind blows and shakes the wild fig tree; you come, and your delicate perfume enwraps my spirit, and my body is shaken. I become weak within the shadow of your presence. I feel a radiance about you which calls to something within me, and I am awed by the wonder of a love, which can subdue all base feelings.

SCL:29:31 I have seen you. In the cool dewtime of the morning, I passed on my way and you were bathing in the freshening waters. I saw your pure loveliness, and all else faded and passed from me; the beauty of the morning was dimmed before the vision I had of you. Modest maiden of mine, clad in a white garment, which clutched your supple limbs, I saw you and my heart swelled up in joy. The breath was stopped within my throat.

SCL:29:32 You looked up and smiled a chaste greeting, covering yourself in a garment expressing your maidenly modesty. Your delicate hand plucked a lily, and my heart left its cradle when you came up out of the waters and drew near. You embraced me with cool, glistening arms and open, wet lips. I savoured the joys of the gods, with a greater promise of unutterable joys to come, before I continued on my way. Would that I were the fishes in the pool, that I might be so near to you twice daily.

SCL:29:33 Yet, I am a man and consumed in the fires of manhood in my need for you. Still, you remain veiled in reserve, and I pray to the great god for the assurance that some day, my sister in love will be truly mine. Her reserve and modesty, treasured as gifts to be surrendered in love, mean more to me than gold and pearls or the treasures of kings. What is mine, no king, no matter how great, can claim. It is love's mantle bestowed on manliness.

SCL:29:34 The night comes, and I dream it is our wedding night, and you are beside me. My spirit rises on wings of joy, singing, "O let my love find its ultimate expression in this night of beauty!" Your breath caresses me with the fragrance of Heaven; your lips dispense the heavy wine of love. Our bodies meet in ecstasy and part, but our spirits remain mingled in the greater bond that knows no severance. Our united souls share together the destiny of eternity. I sleep at last in the gentle arms of contentment.

SCL:29:35 O Great Readers of the Souls of Men, see the strength of my love. Is it not untainted with base feelings? Is it not wholesome and undemanding? Is it not protective of womanly secrets? Let it endure on Earth, that it may blossom in glorious fullness throughout the great ages in everlasting splendour. May it shine forever in the unwalled Halls of Eternity. O grant me my heart's desire!

Chapter Thirty – The Songs of Tantalip – Two

SCL:30:36 I am one, on whom the fates smile. My sister in love is the light of my life. She is the promise of love enduring, the brazier of a love undying, the hope of joy throughout eternity. The night becomes silent, for its fragrance is as nothing to her sweetness. The brightness of the dawn fades before her loveliness, and the dove hangs its head before her virtue.

SCL:30:37 She breathes gently and caresses with her glance. Her skin exudes a sweet perfume, and her hair is proud and confident, as becomes the guardian of secret mysteries of charm and delight.

SCL:30:38 She is graceful, her robes are not stiffened, they are not of royal or white linen and caress her softly. Her sandals are daintily bedecked with beads, and her lovely curls are clasped in a circlet of blue and red stones. Her bosom is covered with cloth of Ithika and held by a clasp of silver.

SCL:30:39 She flutters her fan with delicacy and grace. Her speech is gentle as the cool breeze. Her eyes sparkle as the moonlit waters, their deep pools enhanced with tinges of green and purple delicately applied.

SCL:30:40 Men say, "Who is she who walks with graceful steps and lively air? The blush of the blood rose is on her cheeks, the perfume of morning sweetness breathes from her parted lips. High-spirited joy, tempered with innocence and modesty, sparkles in her eyes. Her voice tinkles like sweetly rippling waters, and from the gay cheerfulness of her tender heart, she gladdens all nature with her gentle singing."

SCL:30:41 I say, "She is mine, my wife in waiting," and confidently know all her secret charms are for me alone. I shall be lifted in joy above all men or cast into the abyss of despair. I wonder about her in the manner of men and rebuke myself for my thoughts. Could such beauty ever betray love?

SCL:30:42 I inhale the sweet breezes, which once filled her mouth, and each day, my thoughts recall her beauty. My heart longs for the sweetness of her lovely voice, fresh as the cool north wind. Her love strengthens my limbs; my heart rises from its place. Let me clasp once more the delicate hands that hold my heart. Let me feel her once again in warm embrace. I hear her name whispered on the cool nightwind, and never do I hear it without my spirit responding.

SCL:30:43 O my Lord God, who led me in the conquest, who directed my right arm in battle and chastened my pride in victory, help me now in the time of peace. Help me when the turmoil is over. I am well-skilled in the ways of war, but am a ready victim for the snares and wiles of peaceful life.

SCL:30:44 Give to me my heart's desire, to be the mother of my children and the companion of my life. I am burnt with passion and need the cool, quenching waters of true love. My body cries out in the night towards one so distant from me. You made me as men are made, you gave me the craving; now, grant me relief.

SCL:30:45 I am alone and one, when I should be two. I speak, and none answers, I eat, and my food lacks flavour, I thirst, and none brings water. I am a sword unused; let the sword not rust in the sheath.

SCL:30:46 I await my other self; my right side desires union with my left; I wait and know that the waiting is not in vain. I await her coming; she is on her way, as she was from the beginning of time. She draws near, and my spirit leaps from its seat and dances from the body to meet her. I see her; she is mine, fashioned for me by the ages, her body is made for mine and mine for hers. We are betrothed by eternity.

SCL:30:47 I will keep her always for myself; I will never let her go hungry or let her live to lament her fate. We will share seven lives together, and in each, I will seek her anew.

SCL:30:48 Man is two, the life force and the life material. Love holds all things together, and no man can know the joys of love who shares the secret charms of his beloved with another.

Chapter Thirty-One – The Marriage Song

SCL:31:1 O devotee of a love that rises above the mire of matter and flowers in realms where romantic love is glorified! O daughter of love and sweet mistress of life, now is the hour of your fulfilment. Prepare to accept the sceptre of womanhood, as becomes a true maiden; prepare to accept the burdens and pleasures of motherhood, as becomes a true woman. Verily, you are a disciple of love.

SCL:31:2 Earth knows no greater joy than that of contented wedded love. Such love is a beacon-light to all mankind; it guides the caravan of its journeying with a pure and sacred flame. Sweet, hallowed love has a temple in the heart of every chaste maiden, and all men worship the mystery enshrined within. O resolute priestess and guardian, you are now worthy of the white crown of love.

SCL:31:3 Great has been your inspiration to man. Well have you fulfilled the duty of maidenhood; now, step forward to accept the joyful burden of womanhood, the crown that proclaims you a wife. Marriage is sanctified by ancient tradition, for it has survived the tests of time and turmoil. It has ever been the anchor of society and the shield of the family.

SCL:31:4 Loveliness belongs to all women, for it is the heritage of womanhood. Beauty of face and form is carried away by the passing years, but the beauty of heart and thought grows as the waters rise and fall. The glorious charms of modesty and purity can be possessed by any woman.

SCL:31:5 Weave a mantle of contentment around your chosen mate, O gentle bearer of womanly charms. Remember that you are the mother of generations yet unborn. Maidenhood, wifehood and motherhood, these are the phases of a woman's life. A chaste maiden becomes a good wife and a good wife becomes a good mother. Thus, it is written.

SCL:31:6 May The Great God, whom you now worship, spread His protecting wings over you, and may you enjoy the companionship of many children. May your life be enwrapped in peace and contentment, and may it be attended by the four bearers of prosperity.

SCL:31:7 O son of strength and goodness, remember always your obligations and duties as a husband and father. Love belongs nowhere but beside your own hearth, for what foolishness it would be for a man to expend it on one other than his wife! That which a man gives to his wife is his also, a love truly shared is joy multiplied. He who sows beside his own hearth reaps a manifold harvest.

SCL:31:8 Be not harsh with your wife or impatient because of her weaknesses, for her ways are those of all women. Be gentle with her, remembering that the dart of love cannot penetrate a hard and inconsiderate heart.

SCL:31:9 Love is a treasure unearthed by few. It is found by less than one in a thousand. Yet, where it is, let it be held sacred, for it is the decree of a divine destiny uniting one to the other in ever increasing glory and beauty, as they rise from life to life.

SCL:31:10 Is not every part of the Earth paired with its mate? Even Heaven and Earth are mated, for does not Earth cherish and nourish whatever Heaven lets fall? When Earth lacks heat, Heaven bestows it bountifully upon her, and when she loses her freshness and withers, Heaven restores her freshness with gentle soothing waters.

SCL:31:11 Heaven daily goes about the task of sustaining Earth; she is never neglected. Therefore, take an example from the greater sphere of life; sustain and cherish your wife, that she never be neglected. He who sows seeds of discontent before his hearth reaps a full harvest of misery. Thus, it is written by the Wise One in olden times; even so, it is now and will always be.

Chapter Thirty-Two – The Lament of Nefatari

SCL:32:1 They have placed my dear lord in the engulfing tomb, they have laid him to rest in eternal secure silence. We depart; we journey home, but home is no more; it is rent apart and a place of dull shadows. Some with me are silent and solemn, some are weeping, some make show of weeping. Some suffer silently, some talk idly, some mask their sorrow with false mirth. It is a time of solitary heart pain.

SCL:32:2 Some say it is finished, and others that he sails the sky, but I ask my soul, and it says this is not the end. It is not finished; this is the beginning, which all loving things must know as they awake to a new dawn.

SCL:32:3 The years of earthly instruction are left behind; the last lesson is read, the pupil has departed to take up his appointed task. He has been born to life, and death has been left behind. There are no dead, just the departed living; death alone occupies the silent tomb. Death is a pause at the beginning of life, a hesitation before the light of a greater day.

SCL:32:4 Death is a deceiver, a non-existent thing of the shadows. From the creeping caterpillar comes the lightloving butterfly, and from the hard grain, the full blooming barley. Who, looking at the date stone, can see therein the tree to be? Search the seed, and the plant is nowhere to be found. Even so is it with the spirit.

SCL:32:5 I trust in He, who gave us life and love, but I suffer because of my loss. I am alone. Where is my lord, the one I loved, the sharer in my cup of joyfulness? Where is the caressing hand, the touch that soothed, the voice that strengthened my heart in times of distress, the consoling counsel, the quiet laugh that dispelled God-given hurt? Though he has gone to glory, yet my heart shrinks, aching with solitary grief.

SCL:32:6 I will keep him, that he wander not in the darkness, for he has been loved and cannot be alone for evermore. I will keep him, that he be not despaired and condemned to walk with himself, for he is a man, who has loved beyond himself.

SCL:32:7 He has stepped from his body as one steps from a mantle. He has left it as one leaves a discarded garment.

SCL:32:8 His future is in my hands, and I shall live in such wise that none can deny our reunion. There is a subtle something, I know that, that ties us together still. May I be given strength never to break the loving link, which comforts me through the long night and sorrowful days.

Chapter Thirty-Three – The Scroll of Herakat

SCL:33:1 Great God of Wisdom, help me in my transcription of these ancient writings, that they may be a true record; for I am not learned in letters, as was Sopher. I am unskilled even as a scribe.

SCL:33:2 Man is a battleground; he is torn apart in the struggle between his two selves. He dwells in the dark night of ignorance.

SCL:33:3 From Ramakui of the seven cities, Land of Copper, came the People of the Light, and they brought with them, out of their transparent temples, the light that shines, when darkness falls, without being lit. Led by the Old Bald-Headed One, he whose name is not spoken, they came out of the West at the sunsetting. They came from the place, where now the sun goes down; in the days when the Western wilderness was green and sand had not replaced the waters; when the outlands nourished cattle, and sheep fed where now there is nought but rock and stone. The Tirdinians welcomed them not, but they passed safely through the westward places to the land of Ansibyah and were succoured and fed. They brought to the people many things, for wise they were and learned. They were men of wisdom.

SCL:33:4 Truth is not for the multitude; dirty hands despoil fine linen. The high born have their estates, and the lowly ones have their appointed places. Truth is not sold in the marketplace, nor can riches alone obtain it. Few entered the great chambers to die and to live. The temples were fine shells, but the kernel was dead inside. Men lacked the food of life.

SCL:33:5 The True God was guarded and hidden by the false gods. He spoke in the hearts of the wise, but the people heard the voice in the stone. Their ears were closed to all but the voices of men. Small places there were in olden times for all gods; the pillars were not yet stood up. The stones were not yet in their places, and the House of Hidden Secrets was not yet in the land.

SCL:33:6 Then, temples were built in splendour, and priests were comforted in mansions. Great gardens and fields were the property of the gods of men. They had great herds of cattle in their pastures. Within the worship and ritual, amid the pomp enshrining the little gods, shone the light of Truth, which was the revelation of The True God. It was known to few, and fewer understood it.

SCL:33:7 Seven years, men being chosen, waited and were called. Seven years they served, and seven years, they ministered at the feet of their Masters of Instruction. They were passed into bleak caverns to die and know God, and called forth with the sure knowledge of Truth. Thus, men were made servants of The One True God. Thus, they knew the Truth which may not be written, for many read who are not with us in God.

SCL:33:8 There are writings which speak truly, but they are no longer with us. The Arisen Ones know the secrets of the lesser gods, who are no more than these. The Great Scales weigh the soul by its appearance in the Netherworld, and thus, its place is appointed. Its virtues form its food, but no man eats the filth that is his.

SCL:33:9 He who devours souls is but the dark cave of horror, which opens to receive dark souls into affinitive darkness. The Rakima watches in silence; patiently it sits, waiting for the day of the Destroyer. It will come in a hundred generations, as is written in the Great Vault.

SCL:33:10 All men are not equal in heart and spirit. Is the Southern Man learned, or the Ambric Man brave? The Land of Incense bestows all good things upon its inhabitants; yet, they are not great. The Land of Bright Waters raises nothing but trees and grass; yet, its people are strong, and the lion does not equal them in courage.

SCL:33:11 Above are the waters of Heaven, and below are the waters of the Dark Region; yet, there are not two waters but one. There is the fire above and the fire below; yet, there are not two fires but one. The Lady of Ladies is arrayed in a radiant garment; when it dims, the great trial begins. Her footsteps do not waver; her path is straight, but beware when she wavers and is inconsistent.

SCL:33:12 Great Mistress of the Stars, let us abide in peace, for we fear the revelation of your horns. Remain ever constant as a good wife to the Lord of the Day. When women are as men and inconsistent as women, the hour approaches when the Great Lady will wander. When man and woman meet as one in likeness, the Fiery Heralds will appear in the darkness of the sky vault.

SCL:33:13 Man twirls the drill in his hand; he is the master of fire, but the day comes when fire will leap forth from the heart of the stone and consume him. Men read the Great Book of the Master of the Hidden Temple. They die and take it with them, but there is no power in their words, and who but we, the Enlightened Ones, know the hidden meanings? It is not for those dead to the Earth, who step forth in the Netherworld, but for those who died and remain with us.

SCL:33:14 Men make offerings for their fathers after the custom of their fathers. The motions are those of their fathers' fathers' fathers, but their hearts remain locked. It is foolishness.

SCL:33:15 In the First Book, it is written: "Words that do not produce deeds are as thistledown on the wind. They were better never uttered."

SCL:33:16 The soul of man is as a bird that knows of a place, to which it must journey, but which it has never seen; yet it departs on the appointed day. Men have gods in Heaven and gods on Earth, but Heaven is for gods and earth for men. Thus did we write our own doom.

SCL:33:17 In the Secrets of the Soul, it is written: "The soul of man is not a small thing inside him, but wraps him about. It is greater than the boundaries of the Lands of the Reed and the Lily and reaches out beyond the stars."

SCL:33:18 To live, man must believe in his soul. Belief comes not from outside teaching, but from listening to its whispers; unbelief comes from stopping the ears to its murmurs. Read the Sacred Writings diligently and hear the voice of the Instructing Master with receptive heart, so you may furnish your soul with nourishment, and it shall not wither from any lack of sustenance.

SCL:33:19 The seed of Truth came to the black fertile land in olden times and was planted in well-watered soil. Pontas was not yet born. It grew not in the light of the sun, for ignorant men would cut it down. In the dark places, it flourished. Earth is a strange place, and stranger the creature who rules it. Then came the dawn of a brighter day. The tree was goodly, and its leaves filled both the Land of the White Crown and the Land of the Red Crown. In a day of darkness, men came, who exposed it, and the king said, "Cut it down, lest it choke us with wisdom."

SCL:33:20 The tree died, but its seeds falling into the red soil lived, and from them, saplings grew. They were sheltered under the strong arm of the East. Then came one, who was Lord of the Sweet Breeze, one who had sat beneath the Tree of Life, and he raised up a city to the Veiled Truth. Over the great road it was, by way of Lados it lay.

SCL:33:21 He revealed the Light of Truth darkly to the people, but they were people of the night, and even its dim flame consumed them. The child of good intentions may be fair or dark.

SCL:33:22 The Guardians of Truth covered the bright flame, and even its glow was seen no more by the people. No unlearned man again saw the light.

SCL:33:23 A treasure in the hands of a few is great to each. Shared among many, it has little value for one. We had been told the ways of men from olden times, but we heeded not the warning.

SCL:33:24 Now the Truth is scattered to the four quarters of the Earth. Thus, it was foretold it should be; therefore, it is appointed. A tree scatters its seeds by the thousand, yet but one may spring to life, and that may lay long in the soil.

SCL:33:25 These writings have been re-written with diligent care. They have been transcribed exactly as they are, and no thought or belief of mine has gone into them. May those, to whom they come as a heritage be no less circumspect in dealing with them.

Book of
Sons of Fire

SOF:1:6 In days gone by, you have had leaders to guide you, but before them were even greater leaders, whom you have not known. The inspiration of their words is something that must never be lost; it must be preserved for all time. We must be like a man who has travelled far with a heavy burden. He rests and seeks among the things he carries to find what can be discarded, knowing he has still a long way to go. The choice you must make has to be made soon, for the years remaining to our father cannot be plentiful.

Table of Chapters

BOOK OF SONS OF FIRE
Table of Chapters (Continued)

Book of Sons of Fire

Chapter One – The Reconstructed Chapter

SOF:1:1 We took refuge with the sons of Uteno, whose fathers had been in the land many generations, for they had come out of Egypt in the days of Pharaoh Nafohia. There on the borderland, we dwelt in caves above Kathelim. We were without books or possessions, but we were diligent and laboured to make the land fruitful. We knew ourselves as The Brothers in Light, but others called us The Children of Light, even as we are called to this day.

SOF:1:2 This is a good and fertile land; it is a wide land of flowing streams, where wheat and barley increase a hundredfold. Figs and pomegranates flourish here, and it is a land of olive groves and vineyards. All the needs of life are supplied with an overflowing bounty. It is a land where sheep and cattle multiply without fear and a land, where the sickle of famine never reaps. It is a land where even an effortless search is rewarded with the materials of copper, but it is not a manless land.

SOF:1:3 We are not alone in this land and must live among people whose ways are not our ways. They have gods with many names, and even now those beside the sea strive among themselves, for some say God is called Mamrah, while others say he is called Aneh. All about us, men are in dispute, and the strife among them arises out of the bounty of the land. Gaining their livelihood with little effort, they have much time for argument and strife. We must build for these people a court of peace, the four pillars whereof shall be Love, Consideration, Justice and Truth.

SOF:1:4 The land of our fathers and our inheritance has been lost to us forever. Their homes have been returned to the sands, and their altars where they worshipped cast down. Their temples have been destroyed and the forms of worship practised there are no longer known. The songs once sung are now mingled with the winds, and the voices of the singers are silent. The wisdom once revered has departed; the illuminating flame no longer burns, and the lamps lie broken in the dust. The honoured writings have been used for kindling, and the sacred vessels turned into vain ornaments. The very names held sacred by our fathers are now defiled and held to represent wickedness. Those who would have been our brothers are sold and their leaders slain. Those who would have been our wives are violated and degraded in servitude. Therefore, brothers, it is time the memory of these things was put aside and forgotten.

SOF:1:5 What cause have we for sorrow? We are in a bountiful land; we have hope for the future and an unshakable faith. Better by far than all else, we have with us the key to the ancient Portal of Communication. Our memories must replace the books and decrees of former times. Let us, therefore, be thankful for our blessings and diligently preserve the flame, from which the lamps of Truth will one day be relit.

SOF:1:6 In days gone by, you have had leaders to guide you, but before them were even greater leaders, whom you have not known. The inspiration of their words is something that must never be lost; it must be preserved for all time. We must be like a man who has travelled far with a heavy burden. He rests and seeks among the things he carries to find what can be discarded, knowing he has still a long way to go. The choice you must make has to be made soon, for the years remaining to our father cannot be plentiful.

SOF:1:7 We must establish a community, where men can live together and where they can enjoy the companionship of women. Men always benefit from united effort, but this is inseparable from necessary restrictions. Let the restrictions imposed be such that no man can feel resentment because of the restraints set upon him. Let the only ordinances and restrictions imposed be founded on the nature of man and upon spiritual and moral values.

SOF:1:8 We must seek to assure freedom of action for every man and woman, so long as it does not prejudice the equal rights of others. We must work for the benefit of the many, but in doing so must not overlook the provision of rewards for those who serve best. The rewards must go to the men, who are best in all ways and not to the worst. We must see that good lives are rewarded and evil ones punished. We must place the greatest value on things spiritual, and no man must be unduly rich or unduly poor.

SOF:1:9 We must provide for the sick and helpless, for the old and incapable. We must assure the integrity of the family. The first objective must be the spiritual goal, which is the only proper one for all men. After that, all instruction and law should be bent towards an increasingly harmonious relationship between every living being. The upbringing of children must have as its objective the attainment of well-balanced manhood and womanhood.

SOF:1:10 We must make men high-minded and above all pettiness. They must be upright and rejoice in their manhood. They must possess courage and fortitude equal to any trial, for there will be many. They must be prepared to endure oppression and persecution with self-control and a calmness, which no misfortune or calamity can shake. They must also be such men that good fortune and abundance does not weaken them.

SOF:1:11 We must teach men to be quick in decision and deliberate in judgement. Because in numbers, we are like two grains of sand in the desert, we must seek converts diligently. We must be a guiding light before the eyes of all men, leading them along the paths of honest labour rather than power. We must teach men their duty towards others, so that no man ever says, "Unless I place my own welfare first no other will."

SOF:1:12 We must seek out and accept suitable converts, and they must be particularly precious to us. We must hold them in high regard, not because they have accepted our beliefs; the good within them can be developed within their own, but because they assume willingly and cheerfully the great duties and obligations peculiar to us. We must always remain a brotherhood engaged in an organised quest for Truth. We must ensure that the teachings we expound are valid everywhere and among all men as a code of goodness. If a brother become powerful, he must not glory in that power, if wise in his wisdom or if rich in his riches. If a brother have to glory in something, then let it be in the fact that he is always the best of men. By this is not meant the victor in the earthly struggle, but he who best serves the purpose and good of mankind.

SOF:1:13 We found refuge in a place where men spoke our tongue, though now, they are no more. The land of our fathers is denied to us, so we must seek another, for a man without a nation is more heavily afflicted than any orphan. Egypt was a land destined for greatness; its people should have led all others towards the Great Light. Egypt failed in its destiny because those who were entrusted with power and position proved unworthy. Its kings, who should have reared families dedicated to goodness and inspiration, betrayed their trust to satisfy the weaknesses of men. The leaders to godhood were misled and became ensnared in the deserts of worldliness, and those who followed them were betrayed. The priesthood became corrupt when it offered a life of ease and abundance, instead of a life of service and austerity. The ideals of man were above reproach, but man himself was unworthy of them. We have no need to change ideals, but to attain them, we must change men. The sacred lore of Egypt, enshrining the treasure of the ages, was possessed by only a select few who safeguarded it as nothing else has ever been guarded, because of its greatness. Not only this, but even a little knowledge of it could be dangerous in the hands of any who sought to utilise it improperly.

SOF:1:14 Of all desirable things attainable by man, the assurance of his immortality, clear insight into the purpose behind his creation and true knowledge of the road towards the fulfilment of his destiny are the greatest. Those were the things so closely guarded, and just as they are the most desirable things on Earth, so are they the most highly priced and difficult to attain. Religion records the efforts of men; its doctrines and inspiration are the measure of its success or failure.

SOF:1:15 The paragraphs just written replace some difficult to decipher and translate, but they preserve the essence of what was recorded so long ago. Much is too fragmentary for use; a great amount is therefore lost. There is one very applicable fragment which states, 'unless they would be open to mockery, Revealers of Light must possess more than a dim, smoky glimmer.'

Chapter Two – The Hibsathy

SOF:2:1 These things must not be entrusted to common folk; neither must they be degraded by disclosing them to such as would profane them. They were once reserved for those, who were exalted in wisdom and virtue, In those days of Harempta, Mouth of God on Earth, they were hidden from those in high places.

SOF:2:2 This is one among the Lesser Mysteries, the Ritual of the Twice Born. It is a ceremony to regain spiritual vigour and to restore spiritual power, whereby a Chosen One dies and rises again. It is a grim undertaking fraught with danger. It is not for the spiritually weak or for the faint-hearted. Not all survive to walk again upon the friendly ground of Earth.

SOF:2:3 Only the older men who had completed the three cycles of seven years were accepted. They had to be men with wisdom and courage, with the strength and fortitude to survive. Other essentials were absolute purity and complete self-discipline. The ability for self-sacrifice and a strict sense of duty were demanded. Only men possessing all these qualities could cross the border in consciousness and return. To be deficient in any essential quality meant death.

SOF:2:4 The Tree of Life has many branches, and that which is initiation bears the best fruit. It is about this that your brother writes. It began in that far away glorious period before the days of wickedness, which caused men to walk in darkness, in the days when they walked in the light of Truth.

SOF:2:5 A House of Hidden Places was maintained, so that all who had any part in governing the lives of the people, whether as king or priest or official, could prove themselves worthy before becoming encumbered with the office.

SOF:2:6 Later, it came about that the Hidden Places had to be further secured, and only men long established in goodness could enter them. Those in high places and those with power shirked the austerities and dangers demanded, and thereby, they cut themselves off from the light of Truth. The kings and governors, who ruled in Egypt during all the many long generations of twilight and darkness, were born to the frailties of the flesh. Seeing only through earthly eyes they, lacked the clear guidance of revelation and knowledge. The Serif Egg remains; it will give up its secrets on the distant day when hatched under the breast of understanding. Then, it will open its eyes, unfold and spread its wings to reveal the light of Truth.

SOF:2:7 The spirit of man is like an unweaned child, which has wandered away and become lost among the rocks and caves. Unless it is found and given sustenance from the source of its life, it will perish.

SOF:2:8 The first Temple of the Shrine of the Hidden Places was built on the Sacred Heights. It was a temple within an inner court, where there were lesser temples and the rooms of priests and teachers. The whole was surrounded by a courtyard and gardens, and beneath the main temple were the three Caverns of Initiation. Later, the Temple of the Shrine of the Hidden Places was built during a time when the light was revealed throughout the land.

SOF:2:9 Though previously, the shrines of the Twice Born had been concealed in the smaller temples, when Ramsis built the Great Temple of Ramen, it contained within itself both temple and shrine of the All Highest God. Also, there were Caverns of Initiation underneath. In the hall of the temple, which faced East and West, between pillars of pure stone, was the portal of the outer sanctuary. As the sun rises in the East, to give life to the day, so was the Devoted Priest placed in the East of the sanctuary, to open the services of worship and to instruct, like a father, those who came to him with understanding. In the ceiling above the candidates was the symbol of the sun, and from it extended seven hands. This represented the sun of life, dispensing the vitalising forces of life from their fount within the circle of creative consciousness. Behind the priest were representations of the ten rays of power that flowed out from the All Highest God when He created Earth, and which became the attributes of His Spirit. They are: Love, Foresight, Wisdom, Insight, All Knowledge, Strength, Resolution, Justice, Mercy and Courage.

SOF:2:10 Between the Devoted Priest and the wall behind him was the triangular representation of the three Sublime Essences - Supreme Spirit, Soul Spirit and Forming Spirit - the three parts of Spirit ever in unity. The entrance to the sanctuary was in the East, and above this was a representation of the Great Eye, the secrets of which cannot be written. Before the Devoted Priests was a hidden doorway, and this led down to the Marriage Chamber. In this chamber were performed the rites known as The Marriage of the Soul. Here, too, spiritual nourishment could be inhaled through fragrant smoke of incense prepared from secret essences and ingredients, which activate life. Here was learned the profound Secret of the Soul, the secret that was in the silence.

SOF:2:11 Behind the sacred place in the temple, behind the place of flame, was the Thrice Hidden Door, and this led down to the Chambers of Darkness, which were before the Caverns of Initiation.

SOF:2:12 Before the first Chamber of Darkness, there was an antechamber containing a small lamp and light. Cut on the walls were representations of Life and Spirit. The candidate had studied with the priests of the upper temple for seven years and been observed by one of the Twice Born for seven years. Now, here in the antechamber, he became an Anointed One.

SOF:2:13 The Anointed One went into the first Chamber of Darkness for testing by one of the Twice Born of a lesser order. Here, it was discovered whether he truly desired The Great Illumination and whether he had all earthly desires and ambitions under control. Here, he was warned of the dangers he would have to face and was tested for courage and fortitude. Before him now, there was only one choice, victory or death. This was the Chamber of the Red Light.

SOF:2:14 Now, the candidate and he who attended upon him stood before the next door, and the priest said to one who stood there. "Having realised by his own preparation, that the external is unreal and having eliminated earthly desires and substituted spiritual ones, he who aspires stands ready. He has tamed the wild steed of his body, so that it is completely under his command. He has awakened the man within the man, and the eyes of inner vision are open. He has made the irrevocable decision and is one ready to go forward."

SOF:2:15 The Anointed One was admitted into the second Chamber of Darkness, and here he was uncovered and placed within a bath of cold water where he remained for a period determined by the burning of a lamp. This was the Chamber of the Purple Light.

SOF:2:16 From, here the Anointed One passed into a small chamber, which was the entrance to the Caverns of Initiation. He now stood before the Portal of Restuah and recited the Prayer Before the Portal, "O Unnameable God, give me a burden of suffering to bear, and place about my shoulders the yoke of tribulation. O God, fill the empty spaces of my spirit with pain. O grant me such fortitude that, even under an almost unendurable load of distress, I may be willing to lighten the burden and suffering of another. Even as I stand prepared for the awaiting test, I ask that should I be returned to the light of Earth, I be granted a share in the afflictions of others, for I need the strength given by suffering and sorrow and will welcome them for the benefits they bestow." Then one who stood in this place gave the Anointed One water to drink and said this prayer, "O Unnameable God, hear the prayer of the Anointed One. Strengthen him with such courage and fortitude that he will not fail in his hour of awful trial, but shall pass beyond the Place of Terror through the Portal of Death, and so may shine with the protecting radiance and therefore return unharmed in spirit and body."

SOF:2:17 The Anointed One entered the first Cavern of Initiation and was tested there in such manner that no ordinary mortal could endure it. After three days, he came out saying to one who stood there, "O acceptable suffering, what has been decreed is indeed best."

SOF:2:18 After passing through the first two Caverns of Initiation, the candidate became an Enwrapped One, and in the last small Cavern of the Lord of the Twice Born released his spirit. The Enwrapped One was then placed within the Womb of Rebirth, and there, within the tomb of stone, he was left seven days. Here came complete liberation of the spirit. It floated out through the confining stone and went as it willed. No words of men, however learned, can ever describe this experience.

SOF:2:19 The spirit of the Enwrapped One returned to the body at the behest of the Lord of the Twice Born, and he who had survived became a Twice Born One. When led forth into the Place of Glorification, his face shines with an inner beauty indescribable. From that day onward, his conduct and attitudes are changed, and he is at peace with all men and with himself. He needs nothing from earthly life and seeks nothing. He accepts and enjoys whatever life offers, for he has learned the answer to the riddle of life and solved the Secret of the Ages.

SOF:2:20 Your brother was one, who underwent the Initiation of the Twice Born, and he has drawn the curtain aside a little to reveal only what is permitted. It is little enough, but sufficient for you to understand why, when kings and governors rose to position and power, they declined the ordeal. It is understandable, for the final ordeal brought earthly life as close as possible to extinction, without complete severance of the spiritual umbilical cord. Before this went more than twenty years arduous preparation. Yet long and terrible though it was, the time and austerity did not exceed the necessary limits by even one jot. In sorrow, your brother must say that it was not an ordeal required to obtain something man has never possessed; it was to regain something he had lost. It was, however hard it may seem, the lowest price payable for the Secret of the Ages.

SOF:2:21 For long years, he who aspired to become one of the Twice Born had to practise the awakening of his spirit and bring his body under complete control. The first thing to overcome was met long before any threshold was approached, it was something, which lurked in the uncontrolled thoughts of men. The frightening experiences during the years of preparation had to be modified and their effect channelled off; otherwise, the awakening spirit would have been completely overwhelmed. As the material body of man cannot come too close to a blazing fire, so cannot the spirit approach too close to the sphere of divinity.

SOF:2:22 Having arisen from the Womb of Rebirth, the spirit is completely freed from any doubt about the immortality of man. Can a man doubt the source of sunlight when he can see the sun arising in glory before his eyes? Having joined the Twice Born, each man has a choice; he can go on to higher development within the Realms of Light, or he can remain to help others. Your brother chose to remain.

SOF:2:23 The wisdom of the Twice Born has spread to every corner of the Earth, and Caverns of Initiation are opened everywhere. But increasingly, through the years, men have declined to undergo the austerities and trials essential to bring them into the clear light of Truth. Therefore, the places of initiation decay, and their secrets are lost; men grope in the dark and try to open a door to which they have no key. If a man has not the courage or the time, the inclination or the ability, to sail to a far distant land, then if he would know about that land, he must listen to those who have made the journey. So it is with those who would know the Secret of the Ages. Men possess creeds of little value because they are unwilling to pay the price of something better.

SOF:2:24 Your brother has no way of explaining his ultimate experience to others. Although he has looked upon the face of Truth and now understands the purpose of life, what he has seen must remain locked within the heart. Though he no longer has to be satisfied with belief alone, he cannot extend his certainty to others. Yet, men forever seek him out hoping to share with him the wonderful knowledge, which has so gloriously transformed his life. This he tries to do, within the limits imposed by his own expanded enlightenment; beyond that, he cannot go.

SOF:2:25 The spirit of the Twice Born can be liberated at will. How often have you seen your brother in a state of ecstasy, which he cannot describe? It is a state beginning in quiet bliss, flowing outward in bright radiance from an inner light, which can even illuminate the material darkness about him. He hears the music of the sacred spheres and sees the throbbing pulsations of life heaving about him, like waves upon the great seas. He becomes aware of an inflowing of unspoken knowledge from a surrounding power. It does not come from any one point, but appears to flow out of all things and to penetrate all things. Material objects lose their density and become visible within; they become as though compounded of ten thousand whirling spheres of brightness. Colours are no longer dull and restricted; they become infinite in depth and number. The spirit becomes lost in adoration and wonder at the beauty revealed in everything. The soul is aware of something glorious within all this and knows it for the spirit outflowing from its source.

SOF:2:26 There is a complete unconsciousness of others, for the greater sight transcends their material bodies. The spirits of men are seen in a harmony of colours, and their bodies as whirling masses of power. The experiencing soul is lost in a sea of sensitivity and feeling. There is a swelling surge of harmony, a sounding of glorious chords. It is the sea that washes the shores of eternity lapping upon the nearer strand.

SOF:2:27 It is an experience that no one can give to another or adequately describe to him. It is the earned reward of those who have paid the price. It is not the only reward, for throughout the life of one who is Twice Born, there is boundless feeling of wellbeing; sickness and disease are unknown. There is an abiding love for all men, a sense of brotherhood, and over all this the certain knowledge of the immortality of the soul and its unity with its source.

SOF:2:28 The impressions received in moments of illumination are everlasting. They fill the spirit with a glorified splendour. There are flashes of inspired visions, and the future unrolls and can be read as the past. There is a form of joyous rapture experienced by those who have risen from the Womb of Rebirth, and when it comes, it can no more be held back than the sun can be stayed in its rising.

SOF:2:29 When the body of your brother lay enwrapped within the Womb of Rebirth, his spirit was carried out as on the wings of a serif and became lost in a sphere beyond understanding. He knew not which way to go or what to seek. Then, like a roll of distant thunder, there was a swelling sound, and there came an overdazzling light. It grew steadily more brilliant until your brother saw a beautiful form of divine glory arrayed in a splendour beyond all earthly bounds. The cumbersome words of Earth cannot do justice to what your brother wishes to describe. It is like trying to sew a silk garment with rope, or to eat sweetmeats with a spade. Words are wholly inadequate symbols. The vision of glory, which had been granted, passed away and your brother found himself in the familiar sphere of the Spirit.

SOF:2:30 Once the mysterious border has been crossed, it remains open ever after and can be recrossed almost at will. You are told of these things, because your brother knows that the age of the Twice Born draws to its close. Because of those who have devoted their lives to the discovery of Truth, there is progress in the sphere of the spirit. Nothing has been lost; nothing has been in vain; the Great Gates are still closed, but they are no longer bolted. Now, they will open at a knock. The road is better marked and the way more clearly indicated. They who lit the path have departed from Earth, but their service has not ended. They serve still in another place. While life on Earth moves forward, life in the sphere of the spirit does not stand still.

Chapter Three – The Brotherhood

SOF:3:1 Brothers in belief, there are two roads through life, the Road of Good and the Road of Evil; they are not clearly defined roads and often run side by side and sometimes cross each other. Those who travel without a guide or in darkness often mistake one road for the other. We are those, who have chosen to walk in light, a brotherhood of men who travel the Road of Good together in companionship.

SOF:3:2 We are companions on the Great Path of the True Way, and when an instructing brother speaks of the Great Path of the True Way, he speaks of a double path. The Companions of the Right Hand are those who bear the burdens of earthly labour and advancement, for they require strength, dexterity and steadiness. The Companions of the Left Hand are those who bear the burdens of spiritual labour and enlightenment, things closer to the heart of man.

SOF:3:3 The brotherhood is separated into two parts. There is an Earthly Brotherhood, and though it may be small in numbers and have few possessions, this will not always be so. There is also a Heavenly Brotherhood comprising certain of the Twice Born and their followers who have gone before. Their task is to clear the Netherworld of demons and dark spirits and to prepare the way for those who follow. They are like men who enter a new country and must clear it of wild beasts and bring the land under control. It is the task of those above and those below to build a road joining the two territories.

SOF:3:4 Your brother is not well-equipped to instruct in earthly matters, and therefore leaves it to another. The caravan moves quicker when each man rides his own camel. In spiritual matters, the most important is that each man should awaken his own soul, a task far more difficult than it may appear, but for which Earth is the dedicated instrument.

SOF:3:5 The first objective to attain towards this end is self-taming. Just as a horse has to be broken in before it can be of any service, so has the mortal body of man to be tamed and brought under control. To do this requires not only self-discipline, but also the ability to rise above earthly conditions. No easy task, for Earth is a hard taskmaster and a worthy adversary, and the mortal body of man an unruly steed.

SOF:3:6 The duties, the obligations and the restraints, by which those who follow the Great Path of the True Way direct their steps are not imposed capriciously. They are, in fact, no more than the bare essentials covering the first steps. That is why everyone, before admittance to the brotherhood, must accept every obligation and decree covering our way of life. We do not claim to know the only path; undoubtedly there are others, but we can claim to know the best. The top of the mountain may be reached by many paths, but the shortest one is always the hardest.

SOF:3:7 Supreme personal spiritual experience is undoubtedly the best source for the foundation of true spiritual faith. It begins with the development of latent spiritual powers through meditation. When you are ready, seek out a place of solitude, a place that is away from the abodes of men, a place that is restful and quiet. Take a skin and a little food and water, just sufficient for your needs. Now turn your thoughts inwards, harmonising them with the rhythm of the body. Let your spirit seek harmony with the spirit flowing about it, so that the two become one. While at your meditations, neither overeat nor undereat, for there must be harmony in your eating and sleeping, in your relaxation and activity.

SOF:3:8 To become one who knows the joys of spiritual self-consciousness, to have a Truth-revealing vision transcending anything knowable by the senses, to rise above the bondage of pain and sorrow and to free the spirit from the shackles of the body at will, is something unattainable by spiritual meditation alone. Leading to this road is the path of moral self-discipline and courage. The creed that teaches spiritual things alone is as barren as one concerned only with earthly things.

SOF:3:9 Your brother will not set forth in writing all things concerning the awakening of the spirit; they would be of no use until the moral foundation is laid. Such teachings must remain within the higher circle of those who travel the Right Hand Path and not disclosed to the uninitiated.

SOF:3:10 Let the prayer upon your admission be always fresh in your memories: "Great Supreme Creator, Craftsman of Earth and of the multiple spheres, grant that our brother may always remain loyal. That he will, day by day, become ever more worthy and so dedicate and devote his life to the service of mankind and the completion of its purpose, that he shall forever walk in the light of Truth. Grant him the crown of wisdom, the garments of knowledge, and let him be shod with diligence. Grant him the strength to abide by our instruction and discipline, so that with these and by his own efforts, he may awaken within him the true beauties of the spirit. Add your strength to his weakness, that he may overcome all selfish motives and unworthy desires. Help him in his self-taming, so that he may combat the tendency inherent in men towards anger, greed and self-pity. Strengthen him, that he may overthrow the evils of talebearing, malice and jealousy. Grant him the ability to see with the eye of understanding the defects and shortcomings of his brothers and to emulate their goodness."

Chapter Four – Amos

SOF:4:1 Amos led the congregation and the people down from the mountains and brought them into the land of Heth; a good land was opened up before them. But Amos warned the people that they were like gems among pebbles; therefore, they were not to provoke the people who had accepted them because of their skill.

SOF:4:2 Amos said, "We will build a city for ourselves and our children, and within it a temple for those who follow the light of the Right Hand Path. The temple will be like the pearl within an oyster, or the heart within the body."

SOF:4:3 The congregation with Amos were the Children of Light and the people were Kenim who worshipped Yawileth, and Galbenim who worshipped Eloah. But Amos taught the people to walk in the light of Truth and said, "To each of you his own god, but above any god which can be named is something that cannot be named, and you shall know it as The Supreme Spirit."

SOF:4:4 The Galbenim built the city and the temple, while the Kenim set up forges among the sons of Heth, and Amos went among them and saw that all was well. The number of those who followed the Right Hand Path and resided about the temple was one hundred and forty-four, and it was never any more or any less. The number of those who laboured in and about the city and dug the soil or attended to sheep and cattle, was two thousand four hundred and thirty-five. The number of the Kenim who followed Amos was eight hundred and twenty, and the number of the Galbenim was three thousand and fifteen. These were the numbers of those who could labour or bear arms.

SOF:4:5 As Amos went out among the sons of Heth, he taught the way of light, but they would not listen to his words. They were like men walking a circle in darkness, one behind the other, each having his hand on the shoulder of the man in front. Therefore, when the king of the sons of Heth came to buy what Kenim had made, Amos spoke to him about the way of light, and sometimes the king listened. When they came upon priests of the sons of Heth, Amos said, "What manner of men are these who prance about as though the ground were covered with hot cinders? Before their altars, they are like drunkards who go about shouting and singing. They leap like horses kicking at the wind."

SOF:4:6 "What manner of spirit possesses them; is it a spirit of light or a spirit of darkness? We have seen this often among your people, it is seen even among the princes and those who sit in judgement. Who can understand the words that pour from their lips? This is not prophecy, but a drug-induced delusion. The people who listen to their words are as misguided as those who resort to a tomb at night and sit within a vault. If a spirit comes, it is a restless one whose words have little value, for they are hollow, empty things."

SOF:4:7 "Surely the gods of such as these are demons in disguise, whose powers are a myth, for they are unhearing and unseeing things. They are unfeeling idols clothed in garments of delusion woven within the tormented thoughts of men."

SOF:4:8 The king said, "I have seen your own holy men as they sat beneath their trees and they, too, acted in a manner strange to the eyes of ordinary men. Where is the difference?" Amos said, "Our holy men sit in quietude, at peace within themselves, and if their mortal eyes are unseeing, it is because their spirits roam freely as birds. There is a test, whereby the difference can be made known, if you will agree to it." The king gave the sign of consent.

SOF:4:9 Then, a place of absolute darkness was prepared, a place, to which light could in no manner be admitted. Into it went two priests of the sons of Heth and two of the Holy Ones from the congregation, the king and two attendants, and Amos. Then, while the king and his attendants watched, they saw the Holy Ones radiate a light that lit up the whole darkness, so that the faces of all became visible. The priests of the sons of Heth remained in darkness, for their spirits were feeble things without power. This is the test of true illumination.

SOF:4:10 Because of this, the king looked even more favourably upon Amos and his people, but he did not change his ways or seek to walk in the light. For Amos refused to perform acts of magic before his court or to foretell the future, and the king believed that magic could accomplish all things. He believed there was an effortless way to accomplish all things, if the secret were known, and could not understand that the secret was safeguarded behind the doors of austerity and self-discipline.

SOF:4:11 There was a city called Migdal within the kingdom, and some of the Kenim laboured there for the temple. When Amos came to the city it was the festival of its great god and no man laboured; neither did the Kenim, for it was the day when their fires rested. When Amos sought the overseer of the Kenim, he could not find him, and none of his people would say where he had gone. But Amos found him at the temple of Belath and awaited him in the courtyard outside and was filled with anger against the overseer.

SOF:4:12 When the overseer came out Amos chided him, but the overseer said, "What have I done wrong? This place provides the food I eat, and is its god not brother to mine? There was a decision to be made, should a door of brass be cast one way or another? I sought an answer from the god by means beyond the control of men."

SOF:4:13 Amos said, "Might not even the god answer according to his own pleasure? By what means was the decision sought?" The overseer said, "By the ebin, which only the god could control." Amos said, "You say this is beyond the control of men; it may be so, but there are men who are more than men, men even as this god, whose smallness I will prove. Come, let us put this matter to the test."

SOF:4:14 Amos then sent an attendant in haste to bring back a Holy Man of the congregation, who was with his caravan. When the Holy Man came, Amos showed the overseer and the priests that such things were not beyond the control of enlightened men, for the Holy Man could foretell the issue, whatever was done with the ebin.

SOF:4:15 When Amos left the temple, he took with him a woman named Kedshot, whom he had won from the priests, and he made her free. The degradation of women to serve the temples was common in the land of Heth, and Amos raised his voice against it. When next in the presence of the king, he said, "The common feelings of all men condemn fornication, and it is not allowed by your own laws. Yet if fornication is sanctified to your god, the priests permit it for their profit. Is it not true that this wickedness is now so common in the temples of Heth that the woman who seeks to sell the services of her body in the drinking booths can ask no more than a handful of meal?" The king said, "Such is the custom of Heth, which is of long standing and cannot be changed." Amos said, "Does the long standing of a custom make it good?"

SOF:4:16 Amos said, "If your desire is to walk in the light of Truth, you must choose between your form of worship and righteousness. You must choose between your gods of this land, and Truth. If a nation sow the wind, it must be prepared to reap the whirlwind, for no other crop can spring from such seed, except through violation of laws, which are never inconsistent." The king said, "I have long been patient with you, stranger with the unbridled tongue, but do not overvex me." Amos held his peace, for he had disregarded his own command to his people.

SOF:4:17 Yet, the king heard the words of Amos and was kindly towards him. When the king came to Lethsan to buy the wares of the Kenim, Amos was there with them, and the king said to him, "The gods of Heth are many; added to those of other places, the gods must be beyond counting. Why are there so many, and which one is it most profitable to serve? The priests say each has power in its own place; can this be so among gods?" Amos said, "There is only one God, but each man views Him from a different standpoint and in his own light. It is even so with lesser things of Earth; how much more so with the greater things of Heaven! A mountain rises up from a plain, and men see it from all sides, and to each it appears different. Some see it in daylight and others in moonlight, some at dusk and some at dawn, it is never alike to all men. Even so do men view God in different aspects. As no man knows the whole mountain but sees it only in part, so men see God in part, and each man names the part he sees according to what he sees and his understanding. Therefore, though it seems that the gods are numerous because of their names and differences, each is no more than a part of the whole. There is, in Truth, only one God, but what mortal man can see Him in wholeness?"

SOF:4:18 The king said, "If this be so, as well it may be, my eyesight is as good as yours, and I see just as far." Amos said, "He who has ridden around the mountain and climbed to its summit knows it best."

SOF:4:19 The city built by the Children of Light grew in strength, and the people prospered under Amos and forgot their trials in Enshamis. When Amos led them into the land of Heth, he was still a young man, but as the people became many and strong, so he became heavy in years. The king who knew Amos died, and the young king did not look upon him with favour, for Amos did not forbid the Kenim to go out into other nations.

Chapter Five – Laws of Amos

SOF:5:1 These are the decrees of Amos, which he made so that justice should prevail in the land of his people. That wickedness and wrongdoing should be destroyed and the strong prevented from oppressing the weak. Amos said, "In the days that are yet to come and for all future, let these decrees remain as a memorial."

SOF:5:2 "When they are used in judgement, let the judges have wisdom and give attention to the words that are written. Let every judge seek to root out the wicked and evildoers from the land and promote the welfare of the people. If he seek Truth and Justice among these words, when they are before him, let him remember that no written words can serve him fully. Truth and Justice are but dimly reflected in the writings and laws of men and must be made clearer by the light of righteousness within his own heart."

SOF:5:3 "The seats of judgement are to be raised above all small thoughts and unworthy aims. If petty-minded men are permitted to argue over the form of sentences or pick out particular words for attention, then there will be no end to pettiness. Let no deduction or interpretation be made from the decrees, which alters them."

SOF:5:4 "Judge every man with the scales weighed in his favour. Do not be hasty in rendering a decision; time will make it more just. Be patient and calm in speech, whatever the provocation. The impatient and bad-tempered judge is an unworthy judge who sits astride an untamed horse."

SOF:5:5 "The words of a judge must be shaped to fit the ears of his listeners. They must be spoken at the right time and in the right manner. His speech should not be too long or too short, and every word should be well chosen."

SOF:5:6 "The frailties of men accompany judges to their seats; therefore, no judge shall sit in judgement alone. Where no punishment is provided by decree, then the judges shall fix the punishment according to past judgements. Where the words of a decree refer to men, then women shall be treated in the same manner, unless it be otherwise stated elsewhere. A child is one whose body has not reached manhood or womanhood."

SOF:5:7 "When two persons stand before a judge, he should look upon them as though both were likely to be in the wrong, and when they have gone, as though both may have been in the right. The motives of men are many and strange, and even though they bow to the judgement, the dispute between them may not be settled with justice."

SOF:5:8 "When a rich man and a poor man come before a judge for a decision between them, he cannot say in his heart, "How can I say the poor man is wrong and the rich man is right and add to the misery of the poor man?" Neither can he say in his heart, "How can I say the poor man is right and the rich man is wrong, when the rich man is powerful and I may be delivered into his hand?"

SOF:5:9 "If there is a dispute between men the judges shall not let one sit and the other stand, or be patient with one and impatient with the other. Both may sit or both may stand and unless one be afflicted they shall at all times be equal before the judges."

SOF:5:10 "A judge shall never say anything that will indicate a way to win his favour or to obtain a favourable decision. If all men walked in righteousness, there would be no need of judges to punish the wicked. Therefore, righteousness is more desirable than the laws of men. If all men walked in the light of Truth, there would be no need of judges to settle disputes between them. But as men see only a pale reflection of Truth, and that distorted by their own understanding of it, there are times when two men are in dispute, and each believes truly that he is right. It is then that they come before the judges, believing them able to see Truth more clearly. Let the judges be able to see Truth better than any who come before them."

SOF:5:11 "When a man comes before the judges having his life or freedom at stake or the freedom of one of his family, then the judges shall first hear reasons why they should consider him innocent or in the right and not why they should consider him guilty or in the wrong."

SOF:5:12 "Every man who comes before the pillars of the judgement place to bear witness shall be given a drink from the cup of marat and shall swear the judgement oath before the shrine and fire. Every man shall be allowed two months to discover those who speak for him, and if he ask for another two months with reason, it shall not be denied him."

SOF:5:13 These are the decrees of Amos for the Children of Light:

SOF:5:14 "It is decreed that no man shall worship in the temple of any god or stand in homage before any image or idol. No god shall be joined with The Supreme Spirit in worship, and the whole of his devotion and worship shall be given to The Supreme Spirit."

SOF:5:15 "It is decreed that no man shall swear an oath in the name of The Supreme Spirit or in any other name, which shall bind him to do anything against the Scriptures of The Supreme Spirit. Neither shall he swear an oath, which will incline his loyalties and obligations away from those who walk in their light. But as kings and governors must be served, and loyalty and obligation together with duty are our declared principles, to swear to serve them well or be faithful to a trust or an obligation is not denied him. The only solemn oath binding upon a man shall be that sworn on his immortal soul, for to swear in the name of The Supreme Spirit is forbidden."

SOF:5:16 "It is decreed that no man shall sell or barter spiritual knowledge of The Great Path of the True Way. He shall not come into a sacred place or enter into prayer while drunk; neither shall he do these things when unwashed, unless he be a wayfarer or one who has come from a distant place on the same day. If water is unavailable to purify himself, clean sand is not to be despised."

SOF:5:17 "It is decreed that all those, who truly follow the Great Path of the True Way and those, who are of the Brotherhood of Men, who serve The Supreme Spirit shall be called the Children of Light. If any among them shall turn from the Children of Light through fear of others, then he is unworthy and shall be cast out. He shall not be numbered among them here or in Heaven, where there is a special place for the Children of Light. But those, who remain loyal to the Children of light, even though they have to flee to strange places, if they continue to struggle, there is no wrong in them."

SOF:5:18 "It is decreed that if a man hear anything about an evil deed or know something about it and fail to disclose the knowledge before a judge or to the judge's servant, he shall not go unpunished."

SOF:5:19 "It is decreed that if any man will not bear witness to murder, to theft or to adultery, he shall not go unpunished. If he bear false witness according to his own understanding, before the flame and shrine, if it be grievous, he shall lose his tongue."

SOF:5:20 "It is decreed that if any man make a false accusation of adultery against his wife, without just cause and without her acting indiscreetly, he shall receive seventy lashes."

SOF:5:21 "If any man slay another, he shall die, unless it be done in his own defence or in defence of his house and family. He shall not die if he who is slain be an adulterer or a seducer of one within the household of the slayer."

SOF:5:22 "It is decreed that if any man slay another in anger, during an argument or dispute, and if the fight be fair and equal, then he shall be exiled. But if any man slay another by lying in wait, or by guile or by coming behind him, he shall not live."

SOF:5:23 "It is decreed that revengers of blood shall be appointed by the judges, and no man shall revenge another of his own blood unless he be appointed by the judges."

SOF:5:24 "It is decreed that if a man slay another without intent to slay, without hatred or malice, then he shall not die for the slaying."

SOF:5:25 "It is decreed that no man shall be put to death by the word of one witness. If a wife cause the death of her husband through neglect or malice, she shall not live. The law of blood shedding is: a freeman for a freeman, a slave for a slave and a woman for a woman. The free can be enslaved to repay a death."

SOF:5:26 "It is decreed that when a man must die because of his deed, it shall be by the sword, by drowning or by entombment. A woman shall be smothered or entombed or drowned."

SOF:5:27 "It is decreed that if a man strike his father or his mother or curse them, he shall be seized and sold into slavery, and the money received shall be given to his father and his brothers. But if a man stand between his father and his mother and his sister because he fears for their lives, then he shall not be punished. In this case, the matter shall not fail to come before the judges, for if the father be a man of such violence, how can he claim to be numbered among the Children of Light?"

SOF:5:28 "It is decreed that if a man seize upon another to sell him into captivity, he who seizes shall die. If a man smite another so that he lose an eye or a tooth or suffer any wound, and this without provocation, then he who committed the wrong shall make it good in kind, according to the judgement."

SOF:5:29 "It is decreed that if the beast of any man injure another man within its own place of confinement, then there shall be no blame upon the owner of the beast. But if the beast be outside its place of confinement and loose, he who owns the beast shall make restitution in kind, If the beast has been savage in times past and this made known to he who owns it, and it strays beyond the limits of its enclosure to harm a man, then who owns it shall make restitution to threefold the damage. The beast shall also be slain, but the carcass shall belong to he who owned the beast."

SOF:5:30 "It is decreed that if a beast stray beyond the limits of its confines, and being savage to the knowledge of he who owns it, if it cause the death of any man, then he who owns it shall die. But if it be so decreed by the judges, his life may be ransomed."

SOF:5:31 "It is decreed that if a man shall cause death or injury to the beast of any man, and the beast be within its proper place of confinement or upon the lands of its owner, then he who caused the death or injury shall make restitution to threefold its value. If the beast be outside the lands of he who owns it and be the cause of no danger or damage, then he who caused its death shall make restitution to its value. If it was seeming that the beast would be the cause of danger or much damage, then providing there was no choice but to slay it, there shall be no restitution, but the carcass shall be returned to the owner."

SOF:5:32 "It is decreed that if the beast of any man cause the death of another man's beast, then the beast causing death shall be sold and the money received divided between the owners. But if the beast causing the death was known to be savage and its owner informed, then he shall make restitution in full to the value of the dead beast, but the carcass shall be his."

SOF:5:33 "It is decreed that if a man shall cause anything growing within the pastures of another or upon his cultivated land to be damaged by a negligent or purposeful deed, then he shall make restitution twofold its value. If a man find the beast of another man going astray, he shall not pass it unheeded but shall provide for its return to its owner. Having done this, he shall not lose or go unrewarded, but if the owner of the beast be a poor man, then bear with him."

SOF:5:34 "It is decreed that if a man set off a fire, he shall make restitution for whatever it consumes to a like value in kind. But if he be careless or seek to hide his deed, then he shall make restitution twofold. If a thing be scorched or there is a blackening of wood or stone, the amount to be paid for restitution shall be agreed by the judges. If the fire was caused by accident, then he who caused it shall make restitution to half the value of whatever it consumes. The fire a man handles is like the arrow he shoots, for the bowman is liable, no matter how far his arrow flies."

SOF:5:35 "It is decreed that if a man steal any beast or fowl and dispose of it so that it is not recovered, he shall make restitution of threefold its value and shall not go unpunished. But if the beast or fowl be recovered and restored, then he who stole it shall pay its value and shall not go unpunished."

SOF:5:36 "It is decreed that if a man give anything into the keeping of another and that thing be of gold or other metal, or of some other nature, and it be stolen, then the thief, if caught, shall pay twice its value and the money shall be divided equally between he who owns it and he who held it. If the thing is not restored to its owner, then the thief, if caught, shall pay its value threefold and one part shall go to he who held it and two parts to he who owned it. The thief shall not go unpunished."

SOF:5:37 "It is decreed that if the thief is not found, then he who held the thing in safekeeping shall be brought before the judges and questioned about his integrity. If he took the thing for his own use, he shall restore its value twofold and shall not go unpunished. If he dealt with it carelessly, then he shall make restitution to its value, but if he was not careless, he shall not be called upon to do so. But if he were paid for the safekeeping of the thing, then he shall restore its value."

SOF:5:38 "It is decreed that if a man give a beast or fowl into the safekeeping of another and it be stolen or injured and die, then if he in whose keeping it was be found careless in its keeping, he shall make restitution of its value, If he be not found careless, then he shall not be called upon to make restitution. If it be stolen from him and he be paid for its safekeeping, then he shall make restitution of its value. If the thief be found, he shall make restitution to threefold its value and shall not go unpunished."

SOF:5:39 "It is decreed that to take from a child, or from a man who is both deaf and dumb, or from a blind man, or from an idiot is stealing and shall be punished as theft."

SOF:5:40 "It is decreed that if a man steal the boat of another or push it into the water so that it goes away or loose any rope that holds it so that it is lost, he shall restore its value twofold and shall not go unpunished."

SOF:5:41 "It is decreed that if any man steal from a house on fire or from a house abandoned by flood, he shall become enslaved to the owner."

SOF:5:42 "It is decreed that if a man steal from a temple or holy place, he shall be whipped and sold into slavery and his price given to the temple or holy place."

SOF:5:43 "It is decreed that for all manner of disputes regarding beast or anything without life, whether it be lost or not, where different men make claim to own it, the dispute shall be decided by the judges. He whom the judges decide to be wrong shall pay its value to he who was the true owner. If he who is wrong has been malicious or avaricious, then he shall not go unpunished."

SOF:5:44 "It is decreed that if a man borrow a beast or anything without life, the owner not being with it, and it be lost or damaged or injured or die, then he who borrowed it shall make good its value. If a man find a thing that was lost and keep it, or he withhold from another that, which is rightly his, then he shall restore it and make payment of its value in kind; if he swear falsely about these things, then he shall make restitution to twofold its value. If the thing be not restored, he shall also restore its value."

SOF:5:45 "It is decreed that if a man make a false report regarding another, so that he be harmed in substance, then he who did the harming shall make restitution of twofold the amount of damage done, according to the decision of the judges. If he knew not that the report was false, then the judges shall judge him according to his dealings in the matter. If it be not done carelessly and with bad intent, then he shall make a smaller payment and shall go to the man he wronged and make amends with words. It is an obligation on every man hearing a report to discover its truth before letting go. Carelessness with words should not go unpunished."

SOF:5:46 "It is decreed that if any man bear false witness against another and he be not otherwise punished, or to a lesser extent, then he shall bear upon himself the punishment he would have brought down upon the other and shall also make payment as the judges decree."

SOF:5:47 "It is decreed that if a man take a bribe to turn a judgement, then he and the man who gave it shall make restitution twofold to he who was wronged, and neither shall go unpunished."

SOF:5:48 "It is decreed that no man who sits in judgement in any place shall take a gift or benefit from any man because of his position. If any man seeking a decision shall give a gift or benefit to another to speak words in his favour, or shall forbear to do anything that words may be turned, he shall not go unpunished."

SOF:5:49 "It is decreed that if a man take advantage of the ignorance of another, or gain advantage from his dealings with an idiot, he shall make threefold restitution; if a man deceive another to his loss, or take anything from him by violence or threats, he shall make threefold restitution."

SOF:5:50 "It is decreed that if a man declare a falsehood to the loss of another, the loss shall be made good in kind twice its value. If a man deceive another who has entrusted him with goods, he shall make twofold restitution, if a man deliver a beast or thing without life, making payment to another who deals with them, if the one who deals with them or carries them loses them or fails to deliver, he shall make restitution of their value. If he be found careless in his dealings by the judges, he shall make restitution to twice their value, but if he be waylaid or struck by powers above man, he shall not make payment."

SOF:5:51 "It is decreed that if a scribe alter a record or make a false writing, he shall be punished with thirty lashes. If a man suffer loss because of the scribe, the loss shall be made good by twice its value. He who does wrong or causes any loss, be it done with purpose or without purpose, and seeks to blame another who is innocent, shall bear the guilt of his deed. He shall not go unpunished for his deceit and shall make payment to the man he sought to blame."

SOF:5:52 "It is decreed that if a man have a maidservant or slave and he seek to give her to his son in marriage, he shall deal with her as a daughter. If he smite a manservant or a maidservant so that they lose blood or cannot move about, or if they suffer pain for three days, he shall be brought before the judges, and they shall decide upon his dealings and bring justice to the one injured. It shall be within the power of the judges to free a slave from an unworthy master and place him with another, either as a slave or a freeman.

SOF:5:53 "It is decreed that if a master die and all those of his blood be absent, his servant or slave shall send for them without delay. If the servant or slave steal anything with life or without life from the dead man, he shall be whipped. If a servant, he shall be made a slave. If one who is of the same blood as the dead man steal, he shall be denied his inheritance. If he would not have inherited, he shall make twofold restitution."

SOF:5:54 "It is decreed that a master shall not allow his servant or slave to remain unmarried if they wish to marry. No man or woman having a child above the age of marriage should forbid a marriage because of their selfishness. It is their duty to see that their child is not left without children. The duty of a child towards father and mother is great, but the duty to marry is greater. If a man have a slave who serves him loyally and is righteous, he should set him free to serve as a servant. Slavekeeping is not forbidden, but it is not goodness; the truly righteous man sustains the poor by finding work for their hands. When a land is divided into large portions worked by lowly men and slaves, it is in a weak condition and ripe for the plucking. It is a truth that if men are so oppressed with toil and servitude they lose the manliness which would make them rise against their oppressors, they will not have the stomach to withstand those who invade the land. But whether the land remains at peace or is invaded, it is no longer great."

SOF:5:55 "It is decreed that the inheritance of a man shall not go to his sons alone, for the daughters are not to be denied their portion. If he have no sons, it shall pass to his wives and daughters. If he have no wife or daughter, it shall pass to his brothers. If he have no brother, it shall pass to his sisters. If he have no sister, it shall pass to his father's brothers. If his father have no brother, it shall pass to the next nearest to him in blood, but not to a woman."

SOF:5:56 "It is decreed that if a son or daughter be adopted, they shall be as though they were of the same blood as he who adopted them. Those who stand together in blood shall not be given their portion by decree, for a man knows those of his own blood best. The portions a man declares shall be fair when all his reasons are known. If it be not thought fair, the judges can decide, but they must remember that a man knows those of his blood best."

SOF:5:57 "It is decreed that no woman having an inheritance shall marry a man who is not of the Children of Light. If she does so, her possessions shall not go with her. A man should not forget the portion for his father and mother."

SOF:5:58 "It is decreed that if a man who bears witness to an inheritance and its portion shall change it so that a man suffer a loss, then he shall make twofold retribution and not go unpunished. If he who bears witness fear that he who died made an error and seek to adjust it, there shall be no blame if he deal justly."

SOF:5:59 "It is decreed that if a man die without wife or children his inheritance shall go to his mother and father, and when they die to his brothers and sisters. If he have wives but no children the inheritance shall be theirs, but if one die while his mother and father live, her portion shall go to them."

SOF:5:60 "It is decreed that no man shall be denied his portion if he be worthy and righteous and not an idiot. A man's inheritance should be shared out fairly among all of his blood."

SOF:5:61 "It is decreed that if a wife die and have an inheritance, the portion of her husband shall be half, and the other half she may leave to her mother or father, or to her brothers and sisters. But if she have children, then the other half shall be theirs."

SOF:5:62 "It is decreed that if a man die and have wife or children, they shall not be put out of their habitation. If a wife remarry, and there are others of her husband's blood within the habitation who are not children, she shall not remain there."

SOF:5:63 "It is decreed that the wives of a man who has died shall be able to marry again after one year, and no restraint shall be placed upon them against remarriage."

SOF:5:64 "It is decreed that no man shall cause his daughter or any other woman to remain a maiden under oath. Strife between the children of the same father to the same mother is worse than bloodshed. These things are the obligations of a father towards his son: to teach him a craft, to teach him to defend himself and his wife and children, to teach him the wisdom of the Sacred Books and to find him a wife. These things are the obligations of a mother towards her daughter: to teach her housewifery and the care of children, to teach her the craft of clothes and to teach her the womanly virtues according to the Sacred Books. A father should never show favour to one son over another. A child should be instructed in the Sacred Books as soon as it is able to talk. A wife should be able to prepare flour and bake bread, cook food and brew, gather herbs, wash and mend clothes, keep her dwelling neat and clean. She should be able to make all things and do all things for the comfort of her husband; to suckle his children and work in linen, wool, pottery, basketry and tapestry. If she brought one maidservant from her father's house, she should give her the least important of the tasks, but no matter how many maidservants accompanied her, she should never neglect the care and upbringing of her children or be idle. There is an excuse for the poor woman whose children are wilful and unruly, but none for the rich woman who has all the time to devote to them. They and her husband are her greatest obligations and her most important concern. The husband who permits his wife to be slothful or idle inclines her towards unfaithfulness. A man without a wife may not be man, but one with an unchaste wife certainly is not."

SOF:5:65 "It is decreed that a man shall not pledge his daughter in marriage while she is still young, but must wait until she can say "yes" or "no" to his choice. A worthless wife or one who is lewd, a wife who displays herself immodestly before other men, or is over wasteful, may be enslaved within her own household but cannot be sold outside of it. A woman may become an inferior wife by decision of the judges. It is intended that the pledges of marriage shall be maintained until death."

SOF:5:66 "It is decreed that if a man divorce his wife and she be of good character, he shall leave their dwelling or provide another suitable for her until she marry again. A man and wife shall not be intruded upon, and their enjoyment of each other shall be unhampered by any other. Every child is entitled to proper shelter, bed, food, upbringing and instruction. If a child have no father or mother, or if they be proven worthless, the judges shall appoint a guardian for it. If an unmarried woman become with child, it shall be a disgrace upon her father who shall be called before the judges. If she have no father, then her mother or her brothers or the person having care of her. If a wife fear she cannot be trusted or remain faithful to her pledges, she shall not deceive her husband but declare herself truly, and he shall decide whether to put her away or not. If he decide to keep her and she prove unworthy, her punishment shall be lessened. The punishment of an unfaithful wife is not only for the deed but for the deception."

SOF:5:67 "It is decreed that if a man divorce his wife, they shall not come together again without renewing the pledges of marriage after they have the permission of the judges. If it be done, it shall not go unpunished."

SOF:5:68 "It is decreed that if a wife fear for herself at the hands of her husband, she may come before the judges who will decide for her welfare. Men should treat their wives with kindness and generosity. It is the duty of a wife to be faithful to her husband; to be modest in the presence of others and to be prudent during her husband's absence. A wife must not only be faithful, but she must give her husband no cause to suspect her of unfaithfulness. A wife must never forget that marriage was ordained for the benefit and protection of women. Therefore, they have the greater obligation in upholding it. Wanton women for fornicators and good women for good men, that is the rule! Thus shall the cause of mankind be advanced and calamity kept from the heart. The upright man who walks in the paths of duty and obligation is allowed all things wholesome and healthful. He should marry only a chaste woman who would be a good mother to his children. He should live with her in cleanliness of heart and meet her without the stain of fornication. It is not wholly good to maintain a concubine, but an unchaste woman may be kept as one or lain with if a slave."

SOF:5:69 "It is decreed that before a man and woman come to judges seeking a divorcement, there shall have been a meeting between those of their blood. There shall be a man or woman of the wife's blood and a man or woman of the husband's blood who, between them, shall choose another not of their blood to deliberate with them. Let them try to reach agreement and strive to heal the breach with goodwill, and if anyone have a grievance, it should not be hidden."

SOF:5:70 "It is decreed that before every marriage, there shall be an announcement of betrothals in a public place. If anyone have something to say regarding the man or the woman, not in their favour, he shall declare it to the nearest of their blood and one who witnesses. If any man hide within his breast something that should be declared, or speak about it after the marriage, he shall not go unpunished."

SOF:5:71 "It is decreed that, if a man say a betrothed woman is unchaste without proper cause, he shall be punished with twenty lashes and if a woman do so she shall be punished with twenty stripes. If a man know a betrothed woman to be unchaste and fail to make it known, he shall be punished with forty lashes and shall make repayment as the judges decide. If a woman, she shall receive thirty stripes. No marriage shall take place until seven weeks after the betrothal. No fornication shall be committed during this time, for it would be a betrayal of marriage, and your soul bears witness to your deeds."

SOF:5:72 "It is decreed that when a man takes to himself a wife and is newly married, he shall not be called upon to take up weapons or to serve away from home for one year. If he is taken away, he must not be separated from his wife. A marriage is the union of flesh with flesh and of spirit reaching out to spirit. It shall be witnessed by two men and two women and declared before men by the man giving the woman a ring and bangle and piece of silver, and by her giving him a lock of hair and piece of woven cloth."

SOF:5:73 "It is decreed that all women who are not unchaste are women reserved for marriage. They shall be sought as wives with respectful conduct and without fornication or deceit. A man who seduces them shall not go unpunished. It is not wrong for a man to make a proposal of marriage to a woman within the time she is denied to him. A promise of marriage shall not be made in secret, for such promises often cover shame and deceit.'

SOF:5:74 It is decreed that if a man accuse his wife of adultery or lewdness and there be no other witness, he shall swear three times on his immortal soul that he speaks the truth. His words shall be accepted, for if he swear a falsehood, he has condemned himself and his soul to most grievous punishment. But if the wife likewise swear three times that the words sworn to by the man were false, then it shall not before the judges to decide which has damned their soul. Both shall go their own ways, and if one speak to the other, that one shall not go unpunished; if they both speak, then both shall be punished. The judges shall receive reports on both and if one of them cease to live a righteous life, that one shall be cast out."

SOF:5:75 "It is decreed that if a man divorce a woman who has done no grievous wrong, he shall support her in the household of one of her blood for six months. If the woman be with child, and she hide it from the father, she shall not go unpunished, neither shall they with whom she dwells. If she be found with child, then she shall be treated with kindness and consideration, and those of the child's blood may seek a reconciliation between its mother and father. Both must act fairly towards the other and in righteousness and good faith."

SOF:5:76 "It is decreed that a wife may be divorced once and taken back, but if she be divorced again she shall not be taken back. The things a man gives his wife during marriage remain hers. A woman who is divorced without committing any grievous wrong is to be treated kindly and generously by her husband. A woman shall not be divorced while carrying a child or suckling it, unless it be the child of adultery. If a man be called to high office with the Elect of the Children of Light, and his wife prefer earthly things to spiritual things, then they may agree to a just and fair divorce. Such a woman would be a burden, for her soul is heavy with darkness."

SOF:5:77 "It is decreed that if a man divorce his wife, he shall put no restraint upon her. She shall not take his heir with her and if children go with her, their father shall sustain and clothe them. A true man makes fair provision."

SOF:5:78 "It is decreed that if a man seduce a maiden, he shall endow her with goods as though she were his wife and bestow upon her all the benefits due to a wife. He shall do this, even though her father keep her from him."

SOF:5:79 "It is decreed that if a man permit his wife to become a whore, he shall be declared unworthy of a wife and shall not marry. His wife shall be removed from him, so that he has none, and he shall not go unpunished. If a man permit his daughter to become a whore, he shall die."

SOF:5:80 "It is decreed that as a woman may be taken in lust with her consent, if it be done, both man and woman shall bear the guilt alike and neither be more deserving of punishment than the other. But if the woman be a child or an idiot, or if she be protected by the judges, it shall be as though she were ravished without consent. When a woman is taken with force, it shall be punished with death, If the deed be done in the fields or in places where women go away from the abodes of men, or in a forest or uncultivated place, or where no man can hear her cry, then it shall be taken by the judges that the deed was done without her consent, unless otherwise proven. But the woman shall explain her presence alone. If it be done in the city, among habitations, and the woman made no call for help and did not cry out, it shall be taken that she consented, unless threatened with death or mutilation by a weapon. Where there has been no struggle, then it was with her consent, for no man can take a woman without her consent while she is conscious."

SOF:5:81 "It is decreed that if a man commit adultery with his son's wife or his wife's mother, both shall die by stoning. If a married women commit adultery, both she and the man with whom she committed it shall die. A husband may ransom his wife, but if he does, he shall be cast out from the people, lest he bring corruption upon them. When a woman is ransomed from adultery, he who shared the blame with her shall not die, but he shall not go unpunished. When judging the adulterer or adulteress, the whore and the whoremonger, deal with them strictly and without compassion, for they are the enemies of love. They place man back among the beasts. A fornicator should not marry a chaste woman, but it is not forbidden. A whore shall not marry among the Children of Light. The sins of whoredom are not unforgivable, and those who truly show repentance over many years may be accepted back into the Children of Light. A woman who becomes a whore to feed a starving child has committed no great wrong. The wrongdoing is by the people."

SOF:5:82 "It is decreed that no man shall permit a female slave to engage in fornication, and it is his duty to keep her modest and free from lewdness. If, after marriage, slaves commit adultery, they shall not be punished to the extent of a free person, for they have been brought up as slaves. Though the punishment of a slave be less, the master may be punished, if the slave warranted punishment because of his neglect."

SOF:5:83 "It is decreed that a man shall not be guilty of adultery except with a married woman. If a woman have three witnesses against her for whoring, or she does not deny it, she shall be shut up in a place alone where no man can come at her. There, she shall weave or work for her sustenance, and if any man come to lie with her, he shall be punished. If the judges decree and a man be found willing to take her, with obligations for her keeping, she may be enslaved to him. If a whore run away from her place of confinement or from her master, she shall die."

SOF:5:84 "It is decreed that if a man have a woman slave, who is a maiden and the intended wife of a freeman, he shall not lie with her. If a man lie with a slave and she become with child, he shall not sell her or cease to support her. If a woman slave marry the slave of another master, then her master shall not restrain her unduly, but he shall meet with the master of her husband and make an arrangement concerning her that is fair and just."

SOF:5:85 "It is decreed that the punishment for whoring shall not be upward of two years. If a woman be accused of fornication, and three bear witness against her, she shall be treated as a whore. A maiden cannot be guilty of whoring after a man."

SOF:5:86 "It is decreed that the Children of Light shall not deny their servants or their slaves, or the ignorant among them, their own gods, for they have no better light. Even as the dim glow of an ember comforts a child in darkness, so are they comforted. The gods Teloth, Yole, Yahwelwa, Bel, Behalim, Elim and all the lesser gods of light may have a shrine in the city and lands about it, to serve those who would be blinded by a greater light. Better the glow from rotted wood than no light at all. Negil, Mudu, Ilani, Neflim and the gods of darkness shall not be permitted to the servants and to the slaves and to the ignorant. But the stranger shall not be denied his god, for the Children of Light are not denied their light and dwell in peace among strangers."

SOF:5:87 "It is decreed that if the tongue of the stranger stray to lewdness in the presence of women, or he cast lustful looks upon them, he shall be spoken to and warned. If the warning is not heeded, he shall be dismissed, so that the women be established in their goodness and be honoured among men. In the lands of strangers, where deceit is considered a virtue and vanity a womanly charm, there is no understanding of women who are modest and restrained. Men treat women as they find them; therefore, women should restrain their glances and conduct themselves with modesty. They should not display too much of their body or reveal clothes that are not overgarments. They should not reveal the nakedness of their bosoms. It shall not be wrong for woman to uncover before woman, or before young children who will grow to be men but have not reached the age of full talking."

SOF:5:88 "It is decreed that if a wife be guilty of lewdness before the eyes of men or provoke them to lust after her, she shall not go unpunished by her husband and can lose her rights of inheritance. If any man complain to the judges about her, then her husband shall be called before them to account for her. If a maiden be proven guilty of lewdness, then her father or guardian shall not go unpunished. If a man be so punished, he shall not revenge himself on the maiden or her mother, for the fault is not theirs alone, and he must bear his burden manfully. It is well to deal with daughters kindly, so that they are not estranged. In chastising a daughter for something bad in her, do not overlook the good. If the wife of a man in high position be guilty of any lewdness or other unwomanly thing, her punishment shall be doubled, for she is unworthy of her trust."

SOF:5:89 "It is decreed that if a man slander a woman who is virtuous but careless, he shall come before judges to swear to the truth of his words. If he decline or his words be proven against him, he shall not go unpunished. If the man swear, then the woman shall be brought before the judges to swear likewise that his words are false, and if she decline, his words are established. If both swear, they shall go out, but one soul has condemned itself to punishment."

SOF:5:90 "It is decreed that when a woman is beyond the age of childbearing, it shall not be wrong if she lay aside the garments of modesty, providing she does not degrade modesty or is unmarried. It shall not be done so that she display some part of her body not commonly displayed by women. Neither shall she display any ugliness, but what she does shall be done with decorum and grace. No woman slave shall be made to do any deed of lewdness, and her modesty shall be honoured. If she be forced into lewdness or immodesty, she shall bear no sin, but he who forced her shall not go unpunished. Lewd talk about women and foul speech shall not go unpunished,"

SOF:5:91 "It is decreed that the fat of a beast that has died of itself or been torn by another beast may be used, providing it is not eaten or placed upon the body in any way. The flesh may be given to another beast to eat, but if any part of it is given to a man without him knowing its nature, he who gave it shall not go unpunished. No man shall eat the flesh of the falcon, the vulture, the eagle, the crow, the raven, the ibis, the owl, the hawk, the pelican, or of any bird that wades in water and has legs greater than the height of its body. These creeping things shall not be eaten: the beetle, the snail, the ant, the slug, the grasshopper, all manner of lice and all creeping things less in size than a finger joint, and everything that creeps upon the ground without legs. The cat, the dog, the mouse, the mole, the weasel and the fox shall not be eaten. To overeat is as harmful as to starve. To fast is not an empty deed and is healthful for both spirit and body. It teaches discipline and self-control as well as moderation and frugality. Food is never lacking in the places where justice holds sway. Consume food slowly and with content, for a restless stomach robs it of taste and goodness. The man who overeats is worse than the beast who knows no better. If any man pollute food he shall not go unpunished."

SOF:5:92 "It is decreed that if a man steal water from the land of another or cause it to run away, or if he pollute it, he shall not go unpunished. If there be loss, then he shall make threefold restitution. Water in which there is a carcass shall not be used to drink. A man may drink wine or beer, or anything that is not unwholesome, providing he maintains his self-control and decency, but no longer. He who causes strife or harm to another because of something he has put into his mouth shall not go unpunished. Wine taken in moderation is not wrong, unless it lead the hand to wickedness. No fruitbearing tree shall be cut down until it ceases to bear or dies."

SOF:5:93 "It is decreed that no man shall leave a dead beast undealt with. If he do so, he shall not go unpunished, for if it be not eaten or used, it must be buried. If a man place anything that is foul into a storage pit or among stored corn, he shall make fourfold restitution and shall not go unpunished."

SOF:5:94 "It is decreed that no man shall cut his flesh for adornment or make any mark upon it which cannot be removed, though the ears of men and women may be pierced. Circumcision such as the strangers practise is mutilation and is forbidden."

SOF:5:95 "It is decreed that no man shall engage in usury, but shall deal with men in fairness and moderation. Payments and punishments shall be decided by the judges."

SOF:5:96 "It is decreed that no man shall associate with another who deals with spells or calls up the spirits of the dead. If he do he shall not go unpunished and those who practise sorcery shall be cast out."

SOF:5:97 "It is decreed that no man shall cheat in weight or measure, and he who does shall make threefold restitution and not go unpunished. No man shall take advantage of the misfortune of another of his own blood and shall not buy their house, their field, their beast or anything without life, to his own advantage. No man should lend upon interest to another of his own blood or to a friend, for this is the cause of much strife."

SOF:5:98 "It is decreed that if a man remove a beast or a fowl or a fish from a trap laid by another, he is stealing. If a man is collecting fruit from the top of a tree, it is stealing to take whatever falls to the ground. If a man borrow something and sell it, or sell something in his keeping belonging to another, it is stealing; if a man do any of these things, he shall make restitution as though he had stolen them."

SOF:5:99 "It is decreed that if a man receive a beast or anything with life or without life from another, and the two do not have proper witnesses, whether it be sold or given, the two shall be punished by making payment as the judges decide."

SOF:5:100 "It is decreed that no man shall cut the living flesh from any beast or remove a limb or a piece of hide while it lives, and if he do, he shall not go unpunished. The law of life demands that men eat and that beasts be slain for food, but this should be done with least pain and distress to the beasts. No beast shall be tormented for the enjoyment of its suffering, and it shall not be confined with cruelty, and he who does so shall not go unpunished. A beast and its young shall not be slain within sight of each other, or where the blood of the other can be smelled. No man should partake of food or drink while beasts in his charge go unprovided and uncared for."

SOF:5:101 "It is decreed that if a man carry weapons without the right to do so, he shall be punished with thirty lashes. If another be hurt so that blood is drawn unjustly, restitution shall be made for any loss and payment made according to the decree of the judges. If a man who carries weapons without the right wound another grievously, he shall die. It is cowardly to slay a man who has cast down his weapons in surrender, or to slay a woman or child. It is cowardly to torture a man who is helpless in your power or a bound captive. These things are unworthy. Treat a captive with firmness and dignity. When in battle, raise your thoughts above the spoil; look to Heaven for your reward. Peace is the proper course for all men to follow, but peace at any price is a delusion. Therefore, it may better become a man of peace to stir up the righteous to fight. Ten courageous men can overcome a hundred of lesser courage. Prepare for war with peace in your heart and with regret, but for the sake of the cause, press forward resolutely. Be at peace within yourself through gain or loss, advance or retreat, victory or defeat. The peaceful man who shouts, "Peace at any price" does not prevent war; he only steps aside to put another to the fore who will slay and be slain. That is contemptible and worse than if he had stood his own ground."

SOF:5:102 "It is decreed that if a man or woman be bound to another for a debt or payment, they shall be fed, clothed and given shelter. They shall not be beaten or ill-treated, but they should do a full day's work. Their welfare shall be in the hands of the judges."

SOF:5:103 "It is decreed that if two men enter upon the same wrongdoing together, or one against the other, both shall be punished alike, except if one be in the power of the other."

SOF:5:104 "It is decreed that games of chance played for money shall be undertaken only in moderation, and if any man cheat or weigh the game unfairly, he shall not go unpunished."

SOF:5:105 "It is decreed that no man or woman who is of the Children of Light shall marry another who is not, for this is wrong against their children, whose upbringing is divided against itself. A slavewoman who believes as her master is better for a mate than a freewoman who does not, even though the freewoman be more pleasing. No man shall permit his maiden daughter to marry a man who is not of the Children of Light. A slave who is righteous and walks in the light would be better, even though he be unacceptable to her father."

SOF:5:106 "It is decreed that if a man withhold from an orphan or anyone under his care that which is theirs, if it be done without cause or to his benefit, he shall not go unpunished and shall also make twofold restitution. He shall not deny them the right to marry, or if it be a man, the right to his own livelihood, if a man or woman of a man's own blood be in his care because they are an idiot or incapable, then let not the burden of responsibility for their own sustenance fall upon them. Keep them from harm, support them with food and maintain them in clothes. The man who is rich and powerful has a duty to protect the destitute and ailing woman from the afflictions of life and from the wiles of men."

SOF:5:107 "It is decreed that if any man or woman die, those who stand next to them in blood shall be responsible for the disposal of the body. Those who declare the need to burn the body so that the departed one may use its essence in Heaven indulge in a vain superstition."

SOF:5:108 "It is decreed that if anyone seek refuge within the sanctuary of the temple, it shall not be denied them, and if any violate this sanctuary they shall not go unpunished. The labours of the sanctuary shall not be diminished."

SOF:5:109 "It is decreed that the measure within a logua shall be equal to the water, which can be contained in twelve blown eggs of the groundfowl. The weight of a silver shekel shall be the same as barleycorns numbered according to the days in the year. The length of a cubit shall be the same as forty-eight barleycorns. From these, all things shall be weighed and measured."

SOF:5:110 "It is decreed that a man may be declared to be outside the law, and then, though he be liable to all restrictions and penalties, which it imposes, he can enjoy none of its benefits or its protection. If a man be declared fully beyond the law, no other shall speak to him or supply him with food or clothing or shelter. If a man be declared an outlaw, he is to be slain on sight. If exiled, he is to be slain if he return from his place of exile."

SOF:5:111 "It is decreed that no man shall make an image of any god or make anything in the likeness of a god, but all objects of beauty can be made. Anything can be made bearing the likeness or image of a man, woman or beast, providing it be done with good taste and without obscenity."

SOF:5:112 "It is decreed that if anyone attempt to slay another with poison, they shall die, even though they have not succeeded. All who aid them in the deed or seek to hide it shall also die."

SOF:5:113 "It is decreed that if anyone take their own life, they shall not be buried or burnt for three days."

SOF:5:114 "It is decreed that if a man die having no son or daughter, and no one of his own blood who can claim, a son or daughter born to his wife after remarriage may become his heir."

SOF:5:115 "Justice and Truth are not in the safekeeping of the judges. They are, to those who sit in judgement, as the sun is to other men. Every man who comes before the judges should walk in the light of Truth and Justice, even though he speak against himself or against those of his own blood. The man who bears witness should take no heed whether he be on the side of the rich or the poor. He should not follow the road of passion or the paths of his own prejudices, lest he lose the guiding light of Truth. The man who hides within himself knowledge that would assist the cause of Justice and Truth inflicts an injustice upon his own soul."

SOF:5:116 "A too hasty decision by the judges often inclines towards injustice. Therefore, when the judges have heard all, and every word has been spoken by those who have a right to speak, the judges shall retire and pray. Each should say, within his heart, "I will consider my words carefully before I speak, and they will be uttered in the purity of Truth untainted by falsity or hypocrisy. I will not be harsh in my judgement, and it will be bent towards a benefit rather than a loss. My speech will be directed towards the safeguarding of others and be without any taint of malice or evil intent."

Chapter Six – The Tale of Hiram

SOF:6:1 Thute, the son of Pelath, a freeman of Elanmora in the land of the Hethim, wrote these things in the harvest years of his life, when his heart was filled with wisdom and understanding. He who reads them with the eyes alone will derive little benefit, but he who receives them with an enlightened and uplifted heart will find a response within the depths of his own spirit.

SOF:6:2 While Hiram Uribas, son of Hashem, was still a beardless youth taking his pleasure among the riches and splendour of his father's house, a wise man came from a faraway land. He came, not as a great man riding with a rich caravan, but weary-footed, begging water and food. These were not denied him, and while he sat in the shade, slaking his thirst and satisfying his hunger, Hiram, the youth, came up to him with courteous greetings. The wise man was pleased and poured out words like jewels, so that the young man became filled with the desire for wisdom and Truth, swearing that from that day forward, he would devote his life to the search for them.

SOF:6:3 After the departure of the wise man, Hiram became restless under his father's roof, and it was not long before he set off with a bundle of food and skin of water for Uraslim. Arriving there, he slept in the house of Gabel, a servant at the temple of the Winged God of Fire, and from thence he journeyed towards Bethshemis, which lies past Tirgalud, on the road to Egypt. Hiram was a young man of his people, tall of stature, with a darting bright-eyed glance. His long, band-bound hair hung low on his shoulders, and his stride was wide and firm.

SOF:6:4 He came upon Bethshemis close to nightfall, when it was not good to enter the city, and therefore, as darkness closed about him, he prepared to lay himself down beneath the wall of a vineyard. This was owned by a wealthy widow who, seeing the young man preparing for the night, sent men out to bring him into her guest house. The widow was neither old nor unbeautiful, and when she saw the comeliness of the young man, her heart was gladdened, and she bade him welcome. Hiram did not depart with the light of the morning, and it came to pass that the widow offered him a high place on her estates. Hiram accepted, for he was young and pleased with the honour, but in the course of time, the widow had become enamoured with him and sought to make him her husband. Hiram sought a way of release from this, for he had already heard tales of the woman's many lovers.

SOF:6:5 The widow said to Hiram, "Be my husband, for the one I had has died and left no heir. Let us enjoy the fruits of your manhood, for I desire the seed of your body, so that I may have a splendid son. I will give you robes of blue and red, and they will be laced with chains of gold. You shall ride in a high chariot wheeled with brass and poled with copper. Many servants will attend you, and wise men brought from East and West will fill your heart with wisdom. You shall lack nothing that satisfies your desires."

SOF:6:6 Hiram was not at ease with himself, for he was young and lacked the wisdom to deal with the situation. He answered the widow hastily in these words, "You are a woman of beauty, and this alone makes you a desirable treasure to men, but how would it fare with me in marriage? It is said that you have had many lovers, and they find you as a smouldering fire in a cold room, a door restraining neither wind nor sand, a roof that falls in upon the sleeper beneath it, a boat that drowns the boatman, the crust over a quicksand, water that does not slake the thirst and food that sits heavily on the stomach. Which man did you ever love with constancy, so that he walked in the joy of contentment? Which man could ever call you his?"

SOF:6:7 The words from his mouth stung the widow like hornets, and she flew into a rage after the manner of women. She called upon her servants, and they beat Hiram with sticks and drove him off her estate. With a little more wisdom in his heart, he continued on his way into Egypt, and after many days, he arrived at the city of On.

SOF:6:8 Hiram dwelt among the Southern Men on the outskirts of the city, for many had been captured during the wars and made slaves. When lustfully, aroused the bodies of these men exude a sweet odour like honey, which no man can detect, and it makes all women succumb to them. This is the manner, in which the nation of Egypt sacrificed its purity. In the days when Hiram came to Egypt, the Pharaoh Athmos ruled.

SOF:6:9 In those days, Egypt was at war with the Abramites, for their great red-headed king had committed adultery with the wife of a prince of Paran. The remorseful king reaped as he had sown, for his favourite daughter was ravished by her own brother, and his wives were humiliated and ravished before the eyes of all men. Because of the war, there was much coming and going of strangers in the city of On, and Hiram went unnoticed.

SOF:6:10 Hiram dwelt long in Egypt and absorbed its wisdom, but the thing, which delighted his heart the most was the tale of its long-hidden treasures. He learnt about the nest-burning bird, whose wondrous many-hued egg granted men the gift of eternal life. He heard about the serpent pearls and the bright jewels, which glowed with the light of the sun even on the darkest night. All these things he desired to possess for himself.

SOF:6:11 The nesting place of the nest-burning bird was among the Mothbenim, eastward of Egypt, but among the treasures of Egypt was one of its eggs. The egg, the pearls and the jewels were safeguarded in a dark cave upon an island called Inmishpet, which was set in the middle of a lake called Sidana. In the waters of the lake were fearsome watermonsters, part beast, part fish. On the shores of the lake dwelt the shapeshifting priests, guardians of the treasures.

SOF:6:12 Northward of the lake was a broad pastureland, where the shepherd Naymin tended the temple flocks, but Naymin was old and had no son who would follow him. Therefore, he took Hiram into his household, and Hiram became as a son to him, tending the sheep of the temple, and no Egyptian was with him.

SOF:6:13 One day, while the sheep still suckled their lambs, Hiram was out in the pastures, sitting near the cool waters because of the heat. As he reclined in the shade, he played gay shepherd tunes on his flute, and in the many times he had been there, no one had ever disturbed him. Yet, not far away was the House of the Virgins of Elre, but the maidens who dwelt there rarely went abroad.

SOF:6:14 This day, however, Asu, daughter of the High Priest, walked abroad and hearing the melody of the flute drew near to listen, but Hiram did not see her because of the bush between them. The maiden sat down, taking the sandals off her feet.

SOF:6:15 Hearing a cry from one of the sheep in the distance Hiram stopped playing and stood up, his back towards the maiden. She, seeing him standing up, sought to creep away before he saw her, but as she did so, her foot was pierced by a thorn, and she let out a cry of pain. Hiram turned and seeing her distress hastened to help her. He withdrew the thorn tenderly and carried her down to the pool, so that she could bathe the foot in cool waters. While she did so, he entertained her with sweet melodies on his flute.

SOF:6:16 The maiden fell in love with Hiram and he with her, but because she was a dedicated virgin and daughter of the High Priest, neither could open the doors of their heart. The maiden spent nights weeping, for she had a love, for which there was no remedy. Hiram took his flock to other pastures, but still their hearts drew them back to the place of meeting, and they met again and yet again.

SOF:6:17 Now, the wife of Naymin noticed that Hiram pined as with a sickness, and she spoke to him about it, and he told her of Asu, the maiden from the house of the Virgins of Elre. The wife of Naymin spoke words of consolation for this hopeless love, knowing they helped but little.

SOF:6:18 In the fullness of the year, Hiram took his flock to distant pastures around the other side of the lake. While he was away, the wife of Naymin took herself down to the place where he was wont to meet Asu, and one day Asu came. She was known to the wife of Naymin, who was the gatherer of herbs for the temple. They spoke of many things, of Hiram and of the gods, of priests and their ways and of temples and those who served in them, of life and of man and of woman.

SOF:6:19 Now, when Hiram returned, it was nigh the feast of sheepslaying, and at this time, sacrifices of lambs were made to the watermonsters in the lake. While away, Hiram had thought about Asu and about the treasure of Egypt, both seemingly equally unattainable. The wife of Naymin spoke to him rarely and Hiram wondered, for this is not the way of women.

SOF:6:20 On the eve of the feast of sheepslaying, the lake boats were prepared for the annual pilgrimage to the island. Among these was the great boat of Erab, kept in memory of the day when the Scorcher of Heaven rose with the sun, and earth was overwhelmed. From this boat, the sacrificial lambs were offered to the watermonsters, and on it served Asu and eight virgins. There, too, the High Priest officiated.

SOF:6:21 Hiram had conceived a plan within his mind, whereby at the risk of his life, he might possess himself of the treasures of Egypt. This year, Naymin being now frail, he alone would be in charge of the sacrificial lambs, together with two boy priests to assist him. They came from the Temple of the Lake dedicated to the Bright Bearded One, who once saved Earth from destruction through fiery hail by making a third round.

SOF:6:22 On the night before the festival, Hiram stept with his small flock beside the boats, and at first light, they were put aboard. As the sun rose upon high, the High Priest came with many other priests and princes, and the virgins came also. They offered sacrifices at the Temple of Departure and then set out upon the waters. In another boat were Naymin and his wife and there were other boats filled with people.

SOF:6:23 After making offerings upon the waters, the boats arrived at the island, and preparations were made for the Island Ceremony, which lasted throughout the night. The lambs were offered as darkness came, and the waters became red with blood, and the watermonsters satiated with meat.

SOF:6:24 Now, the cave on the island was protected from men by the Spirit of Mot, who had died there in days long forgotten, and the priests guarded its entrance. But Hiram did not fear the Spirit of Mot, for it could do no harm to one, who carried upon his body the same bloodscar as Mot had borne. Hiram the stranger had been so marked out from other men in his childhood.

SOF:6:25 At the sixth hour of the night, three virgins entered the cave to bring forth the treasures, and with them went a priest protected by sanctification in the blood of a lamb. Five priests who were Guardians of the Treasures and never left the island also went into the cave with them, garbed in skins and masked with the heads of beasts. The treasures were brought forth and placed upon the altar against the rock wall beside the cave, so that all might behold them. Over the altar was laid a cloth of linen and gold. While the people passed before the treasures and danced and sang, priests came and went in the cave.

SOF:6:26 Before the cave and away from the road leading down to the lake, there was a pathway which went down to the Pool of Purification. Here, after the maidens had bathed, men and women came down one by one to be purified in its waters. They then went through an opening into the lake and, passing through the waters along the shore where they rose not much above the waist, ascended by steps through a small, arched temple back on the road. If they were truly purified, they were never touched by watermonsters.

SOF:6:27 Never had a maiden been taken by the watermonsters, but on this awful night, while a maiden passed between pool and temple, there was a loud cry of agony quickly stifled. The island fell silent with foreboding and as the night passed, the name of Asu was whispered from mouth to mouth. The treasures were carried back in gloom and silence under a mantle of dread, and the head of the High Priest was bowed in sorrow and disgrace.

SOF:6:28 When the boats departed, none noticed that Hiram was missing, for his duty done, he could return in any boat. And none saw the strange craft that clove the waters of the lake of Sidana that night. Hiram returned to the shepherd hut of Naymin, and nothing was said to him, for Naymin thought he had joined with the people sorrowing in the temples, and always many remained about for several days.

SOF:6:29 When Hiram had refreshed himself, he left Naymin, who was weary and weighed down with age and sorrow, and prepared to return to his flocks. In his grief, because of the death of Asu, he could find solace nowhere, except perhaps in the familiar solitude among his sheep. But the wife of Naymin said, "Let me walk with you a little way, for I, too, suffer and yet must seek herbs, which are needed and not easy to find." When they had gone some distance, she said, "I go this way; will you not accompany me and humour an old woman, who may need your aid?"

SOF:6:30 Hiram did so, for the woman was even as his own mother, though he could not understand her strange manner. She brought him to a place in a hollow enclosed by thickets, and lo, there was Asu. When the embraces and the greetings were over and the explanations given, the wife of Naymin said, "Here, you cannot remain. There are clothes and food, and no pursuers will follow the maiden, and none will query your departure. Go this night, taking thought for nothing here, for you are young, with a lifetime of joy before you, after the pangs of parting have passed."

SOF:6:31 Hiram said, "No gladness, no joy can ever surpass what I now feel; yet, this thing increases a burden already upon me and is less simple than it appears. For this you must know; I have taken the treasures of Egypt and hidden them in a place where no man can find them. Who would suspect me if I went about my task without change, a shepherd with no thought beyond his sheep and flute? The cry may be raised even now, though I think another day will pass first. Then, who could trace the passage of every man who has departed, even though pursuit is made in all directions? Why did you not tell me of your plot?"

SOF:6:32 The wife of Naymin said, "How could you be told of something, which might not have been or which you might have betrayed by glance or bearing? We, too, thought you no more than a simple shepherd with no thought beyond flute-playing, except love. What now; will you flee with the maiden and abandon the treasures? Or shall she flee alone, for she is committed to flight."

SOF:6:33 Hiram said, "I cannot abandon love for treasure, but neither can I abandon this treasure for life or let it corrupt. Therefore, let Asu, the maiden disguise herself, and together we will depart to a safe place without the treasure, none suspecting she still lives. Then in the fullness of time, I will return and recover the treasure, for no man can discover its hiding place. However, I will not depart in haste, but wait and bid Naymin farewell and go in the fullness of time."

SOF:6:34 Hiram left Asu and returned with the wife of Naymin. Coming unto Naymin, Hiram told him he had had a vision such as no man could disregard and must go to the land of his fathers, but would return before the coming again of the season. That night, a great cry went up among the temples and in the light of the morning men came and questioned Naymin and those with him, but found them simple shepherds.

SOF:6:35 Hiram departed, taking the ass of Naymin, and with him went the wife of Naymin. They were joined by Asu, cloaked as a beggar girl who earned her food by ungainly dancing, whose face was unwashed and clothes unclean. They accompanied men who hunted for the stolen treasures, and their possessions were open before the eyes of all men. After seven days, the wife of Naymin returned.

SOF:6:36 Hiram and Asu went onwards until they came to Bethelim near Fenis beyond the borders of Egypt, and they dwelt there among the Kerofim. In the fullness of time, Hiram returned to Egypt and recovered the treasures, bringing them inside skins hidden within other skins filled with water and oil.

SOF:6:37 Now, when Hiram had left Egypt and drawn nigh to Bethelim, he saw that the dwelling he had left no longer stood, and the fields about it were overgrown with burning bushes. Within the burnt-out ruins he found remains and bones and knew them for those of Asu and the Kerofim, with whom she dwelt. He saw that they had died by the sword.

SOF:6:38 Hiram did not linger at the place of death and thought to take himself to a place of safety, but knowing the dangers of the land, he sought a place, where he hid the egg of the nest-burning bird and the pearls, all except two, and most of the jewels. Having secured them in safety, he went on his way.

SOF:6:39 Hiram kept going until he came upon a small, wooded place nearly two days' journey away. Here, while he slept, two wild swine came and swallowed three of the jewels which he had tied in a piece of hide. Later, he lost one while fording a river, and one was taken from him when he sought shelter in a temple. Two pearls and two jewels were taken from him by other priests, who placed them in the treasury of their god. The remaining treasures, which he had with him, were lost when he was waylaid, and though his life was spared he was left bleeding and near to death. As Hiram lay by the roadside, he was succoured by wandering metalworkers and brought back to health by them, for they were men of his own blood.

SOF:6:40 Hiram remained with the metalworkers for some years and learned their craft. He became skilled in the making of weapons and in their use. In the fullness of time, he returned to the place where he had secreted the treasures and recovered them. He then went down to a city by the sea and took a ship to a far off land. No man has seen him since, but it is said he married the daughter of a king and became a prince among foreign people.

SOF:6:41 This is the tale of Hiram. As written, it was a wordy tale and well preserved but without great import. It had imaginative descriptions and indulged in valueless flights of poetic fancy. Therefore, it is rendered in outline and reduced to a few paragraphs.

Chapter Seven – The Rolls of Record - 1

SOF:7:1 By the hand of Raben, son of Hoskiah, who was the Bowman of God and brought the Children of Light to the Land of Mists.

SOF:7:2 Hoskiah was a mighty man whose bow shafts struck like the lightning flash, and his enemies went down like corn before the reapers. He was a Captain of Men in the War of Gods, and those he slew where numbered like barley in the measure. His enemies were spread before him like a carpet at his feet, and there was no other like him.

SOF:7:3 He was a man who knew the Almighty God and looked up to Him as the God of his fathers. But Hoskiah worshipped Him after the customs of his people and therefore knew Truth only in part, for having stolen Him they were unable to know Him fully.

SOF:7:4 Now the days of fighting were past, and Hoskiah and those who remained alive with him slept in strange places, for they were sought by the king who had been victorious. His wives and his children and all his household dwelt at Kadesh, against the mountain and awaited his coming there. But he came not while being sought by the king.

SOF:7:5 So it came to pass that his brother Isais, who held stewardship over all his household and his possessions, seeing that Hoskiah could not come unto this place, possessed himself of them. Isais had the ear of those in high places, and Hoskiah lost his birthright.

SOF:7:6 So all that was Hoskiah's passed into the possession of his brother Isais. He took even the wives of Hoskiah, for such was the decree of the king.

SOF:7:7 But Athelia, the first of the wives of Hoskiah, spurned Isais and called down the wrath of Helyawi upon his head. And Isais was afraid and did not possess her. When they saw this the other wives, being jealous of her, for she was ever in high favour with Hoskiah, stirred Isais up against her. They mocked him, saying, "Are you truly the master here, or are there fruits you cannot pluck?"

SOF:7:8 So Isais sought to take Athelia by strength, but she strove against him, and his manhood was hurt, so that he did not take her. Then Isais had her bound and her hands were tied for seven days, so that she could not of herself either eat or drink or do the things required by her body. She was humiliated and her womanhood betrayed, for an idiot man attended her wants and he mocked her modesty, and she was tormented by her needs.

SOF:7:9 Then on the seventh day, she was brought forth by Isais to trial, and she was stripped and lashed, and her hair was burnt off. She was branded on the face, and her lips and tongue were cut. She was given a robe and a pitcher of water, and dried fruits and flour. She was driven forth by Isais who said, "Go, woman, and perhaps, should you even find him, Hoskiah will understand your babble."

SOF:7:10 Athelia went out into the wilderness to die, and at night, she fell in pain and weariness, under an elan tree and lay there. In anguish she cried out unto her God and cast her soul from her, that she might not feel pain. And her soul found Hoskiah.

SOF:7:11 As it became light next day, Athelia awoke and praised God, saying, "I have slept amid my pain, for God is good and merciful. And I know that Hoskiah yet lives in a far off place, but my soul and my God will lead me to him." And she went, guided by her soul.

SOF:7:12 On the same night, Hoskiah lay in a cavern amid mountains, but he slept not, for one had come bearing tidings of his brother, saying, "Isais has possessed himself of all that once was yours. Even your wives has he taken, and between you and he are many men who would slay you.

SOF:7:13 As Hoskiah lay thus in agony of spirit it came to pass that he felt the presence of Athelia's soul, and peace came upon him and he slept. And as he slept he dreamed, and in his dream, Athelia stood at his feet, fairer than he had ever known her. And she said, "All is not lost unto you, for I come seeking you in the wilderness, and I will find you, so be at peace." And Hoskiah awoke refreshed and strong in spirit.

SOF:7:14 And he came down out of the mountains, and over the wilderness, came to the Place of Bitter Waters, where men find refuge. And men were hiding there from the wrath of the king. And Hoskiah enquired of them, saying, "You have come from many places; which of you has seen a woman seeking me?" They said, "No woman travels abroad on such a quest. Or has she many attendants, and what is her appearances?" And Hoskiah said, "She is fair as the dawning, with hair like the raven's wing and skin like fine oil. Her touch is like cool waters, and her bearing like the gazelle."

SOF:7:15 Then the men mocked him and talked much, saying, "How long would such a one as you describe travel alone? It is not in the nature of women to leave their household and come into the wilderness. Would any man pass her by? Who, then, now possesses her? Seek her not in the wilderness, for is she not clad in fine linen and perfumed with sweet smelling oils?"

SOF:7:16 Then Hoskiah took counsel with himself and said "I am indeed a fool who chases dreams. This is no time for dreaming when there is a man's task at hand." So in the morning, he said to those with him, "I go up against my brother." But they pleaded with him, saying, "Have you a host of men or even a company? Abandon such foolishness."

SOF:7:17 Now, at that time Athelia dwelt beneath a mountain where there was a spring, for she was weary from many days' journeying. And she was sick in spirit, for men, when she came among them, beat her with sticks and drove her from the place of their habitations. She offended their eyes, and none desired her.

SOF:7:18 No man came to the spring, for it was an accursed place where voices came from the rocks and the dead spoke. Therefore, it is called the Audience Chamber of the Dead. And none but witches go there, for these the dead do not harm.

SOF:7:19 Now, when night fell, Hoskiah slept, and those with him were not watchful. And evil men said among themselves, "Let us slay Hoskiah in the night, for he has gold and silver and spoils of war with him. Let us cut off his head and carry it to his brother, that we may be rewarded and made welcome,"

SOF:7:20 So it came to pass that in the morning hours of the night, men came to fall upon Hoskiah and those with him to slay them. But one among them was heavy-footed, and Hoskiah awoke as they fell upon him, and he seized his sword, and leaping up as a lion springs, smote about him, and there was a slaughter. But he was without helmet and his head was bare, and so he was wounded. They who came against him died or fled, but of those with him, just one remained, and he sorely wounded.

SOF:7:21 In the morning they left with their asses laden, and Hoskiah held his bow and none came near him. And as the sun mounted on high, the sight departed from the eyes of Hoskiah, and he became blind.

SOF:7:22 So Hoskiah and he who was his companion abandoned hope, for there were men who would destroy them in front and behind, and the wilderness enclosed them. And they said, "Let us, therefore, go to the place called the Audience Chamber of the Dead, which is by our side. For are we not as those already dead? There, we shall find water to quench our thirsts and soothe our wounds as we end our days."

SOF:7:23 And as they entered the pass at the place where the waters entered the sand, the companion of Hoskiah died. Then, Hoskiah heard voices of the dead calling him from among the mountains, and he arose and said, "I come, for this is my hour." And he passed up the watercourse. So it was that being blind, he dashed against the rocks and fell to the ground, and lay there as one already dead.

SOF:7:24 Now, on that day, the soul of Athelia was troubled and she wandered abroad, straying from her tasks. And she looked up and saw a raven descending from out of the sky, and her soul said unto her, "Behold, it comes for the soul of Hoskiah, for he is near by and close to death." So Athelia sped away guided by the bird.

SOF:7:25 She came upon Hoskiah as his soul was preparing to depart, and she took him in her arms, and lifting his head, gave him water. And her soul communed with his soul and bade it stay, and because of the bond between them, it stayed. And she remained with him three days and built a bower and ministered to him, but he lay as one already dead.

SOF:7:26 On the third day, as the sun prepared to enter into his night kingdom, Hoskiah stirred. He groaned in anguish from his wounds, and Athelia comforted him, and he slept in peace. When it became light next day, he awoke and felt Athelia's touch upon him. And Hoskiah knew her and said, "Athelia, are you here? How came you to this place and found me in my hour of need?"

SOF:7:27 But Athelia answered not because of her tongue, and she drew a veil around her face, for she knew not that Hoskiah was blind. She wept, and her tears fell upon his face. And he held on to her, for her hands told him that she could not speak to him as once she did. And he said, "I am blind and cannot see," but she drew not the veil, for she feared for him when his hands sought to be his eyes.

SOF:7:28 Days passed, and Hoskiah grew strong, and he knew the tale of his brother's deeds and swore vengeance in the name of his God. He said, "For this purpose, life has been left to me." And Athelia grieved that he spoke thus, for he could not walk without her.

SOF:7:29 The waters of the valley were cool, and there were herbs and wild fruits and goats upon the mountainside. So it came to pass that after many days, Hoskiah was whole and strong again. But he remained blind, so he could not see Athelia and therefore she remained fair in his eyes. But the soft speech was gone from her. This, Hoskiah did not mind, for what he heard daily was the speech, which greeted him as he lay in her arms before she knew he had come back to life. Hoskiah and Athelia were no longer troubled by the voices among the rocks, for no harm was done to them in this place.

SOF:7:30 When Hoskiah became strong again, he desired to go from that place and fretted to be gone, but Athelia bade him stay. She said, "You are blind and therefore like a child. And will we not die of hunger in the wilderness, or be slain by men who seek after you? Let us stay here." And Hoskiah listened to her words, for it was not unpleasant in this place.

SOF:7:31 And it came to pass that one day, as Athelia gathered herbs in the valley, she espied a stranger drinking at the waters, and he was weak and weary from much journeying. And she took Hoskiah, and together, they went up to the stranger, and Hoskiah greeted him, saying, "May the peace of God be with you, master; how may we serve you?" The stranger answered them saying, "I am Lokus, Son of the Fire Bird and physician to the king of Tyre. I have travelled from afar to this place, that I may hear the wisdom of the dead. I came to talk with my soul in solitude, for I am weary of the ways of men. I no longer seek to be the companion of those in high places who concern themselves overmuch with wars and the affairs of men." And Hoskiah knew Lokus for a magician of great renown.

SOF:7:32 Hoskiah dwelt in a cave in the mountainside, by the waters of a spring, which came forth from a smaller cave nearby. The land before the caves was flat, and there were ancient gardens and enclosures. Beyond these were trees. When Lokus had been brought to the abode of Hoskiah, to the place where he camped, he was given food and rested. Then, Hoskiah said unto him, "You are great even among great magicians, for your magic is greater even than the magic of Egypt. I beg you, master, look with pity upon my blindness, for it makes me even as a child, I who am a man among men and have a man's task before me. Pray, therefore; cast magic with fire, that I may be made whole again." Lokus said unto Hoskiah, "Is this then the one desire of your heart; is there nought in Heaven or Earth you desire more?" Hoskiah said, "There is nought above this."

SOF:7:33 Then Lokus spoke to Athelia, saying, "What is your desire; is it that you may be as you once were?" And Athelia said, "This indeed I desire, especially for the sake of my lord. But, master, above all I desire that he may see again; but, oh, let not his eyes lead him from me to destruction." Lokus said to Athelia, "You know what his eyes will see." She answered him, "Let his eyes see what they will, but let them see." Lokus said unto her, "So it shall be, for you have but one desire between you. I will make a covenant with Hoskiah, so that his eyes may see again. This is the covenant: That Hoskiah will stay in this place until Athelia has borne him a son, and until six months after his son's weaning, he will sit at my feet and absorb my instruction."

SOF:7:34 Then Athelia said unto Lokus, "Master, when he is no longer blind and sees me as I am, will not the burden of the covenant be too great for him? Lokus answered, "He has more than two eyes."

SOF:7:35 Lokus took Hoskiah and cast a spell upon him, so that he fell asleep. And Lokus opened his head and let out the evil, which blinded him and encased his head in clay, that the demon might not resume its residence. And Hoskiah was left asleep for six days and six nights.

SOF:7:36 On the seventh day, Hoskiah awoke, and behold, he was no longer blind. And he called for Athelia, but she came not unto him. Then Hoskiah cried, "I see, but the woman is not here; is this not a time for rejoicing? But lo, she stays away." Lokus said unto him, "It is the manner of women; let her be." And when night had come, Athelia came and sat at the feet of Hoskiah and said unto him, "It is well, my lord, and my heart rejoices." And Hoskiah, stretching out his hand, caught hold of Athelia, saying unto Lokus, "Long have I been with this woman. And I was blinded that I could not see her face; now I say, bring me my torch quickly, that I may look upon the face I desire to see with all my heart."

SOF:7:37 And Athelia, bowing her head, remained cold and still beside Hoskiah, the veil held before her face. And Lokus, placing the torch aside, drew the veil and lifted her head towards the light, and the woman looked up fearfully.

SOF:7:38 Hoskiah looked long upon her in silence. Then, he lifted her towards him and kissed her face, saying, "Wife of my bosom, the years have taken nothing from the loveliness of your youth." And Athelia fell before him in a swoon.

SOF:7:39 Now, when morning came, Lokus sat outside the cave, and Athelia came, and kneeling before him said, "Great master, what magic have you wrought? The waters do not lie, yet my lord sees me not as they." And Lokus answered her, saying, "Nor does the soul lie, but the eyes of men are deceivers and not to be trusted. One desire only have I granted, for my magic has not touched you. Hoskiah sees indeed, but if he sees not wholly with his eyes and in part with his heart, seeing not with the eyes of other men, then perhaps my magic is imperfect, and I am not the greatest of magicians."

SOF:7:40 Unnumbered days passed, and Athelia was first delivered of a daughter and then of a son. And Hoskiah sat before Lokus and received his instruction, and many books were opened unto him. He learned the Mysteries of the Secret Way and the Songs of the Fire. He knew the wisdom that had come down through the ages.

SOF:7:41 So it came to pass that one day, Hoskiah went unto Lokus and said, "All has been done that the covenant required." And Lokus answered him, saying, "It is well; prepare now to follow the path of your destiny."

SOF:7:42 Then Hoskiah took Athelia and his son and his daughter, and with Lokus, they passed out into the wilderness. And when they came to the habitations of men Athelia was veiled. And Lokus journeyed as a great magician, following his stars, and Hoskiah served him as though his slave.

SOF:7:43 Thus they came to the lands held by Isais, and Lokus made masks of animal skins, with tree gum and clay, and gave them unto Hoskiah and Athelia. And he clothed them in strange garments and dyed their skins, saying, "Men expect all things of a magician and make no query concerning the strange things they see about him. Therefore, let not the men of this place be disappointed in my attendants." To Hoskiah he said, "Be as one dumb, for your tongue would betray you to those we come amongst in this place." And Hoskiah answered, "My tongue shall be dead in this place." In this manner they came before Isais.

SOF:7:44 Isais had looked well upon the fleshpots, and his body was filled with fat. He was clad in fine linen from Egypt and perfumed. And Hoskiah said within himself, "Can this be the son of my father and the companion of my childhood? It is truly written, in the hands of a weakling, gold turns to fat."

SOF:7:45 Lokus spoke unto Isais, saying, "Lord, I have come far and therefore beg that I and my servants be given food and drink and a place to lay our heads. I am a magician of magicians and a physician of physicians. Mayhap, there are those within your household who are sick or possessed by demons, whom I may serve. Or may I enliven your leisure with wonders and magic and show you strange things beyond the understanding of men?

SOF:7:46 Isais said unto Lokus, "Remain with us, for there is little pleasure here. If you enliven our days, you serve us well."

SOF:7:47 So it came to pass that Isais prepared a great feast, to which came many lords with their households. The fame of Lokus had spread afar, for he had healed the sick and cast out demons and shown many wonders beyond the understanding of men. And among those who came were many who knew Hoskiah.

SOF:7:48 When the day of the great feast came, there was much feasting and merrymaking, and Lokus worked great wonders, so that all men acclaimed his magic. And there were games and feats of strength and dancing.

SOF:7:49 When night had fallen, great fires were lit and many torches. Tables were spread with all manner of good things, and the guests assembled within the great courtyard. Isais sat beneath the tall sycamore tree, and before him was a table laden with every kind of meat. There were breads and sweet things and spices in abundance. And Isais was sitting among half men and wanton women, and with him were gluttons and drunkards. There was much loud laughter in their company and many sly gestures. There were singing women and dancing girls. There were half men who performed as women, and the night was heavy with the scents of wickedness.

SOF:7:50 The feasting and dancing went on well into the night, and Lokus displayed his powers before the assembly. When the clamour was at its height, Isais spoke to Lokus, saying, "Show us now the greatest of your wonders, which we have not yet seen. Let the night be more enlivened."

SOF:7:51 So Lokus stood before them and lo, before their eyes, he changed stones into gold and a dog into an ass. He drew wine and milk from an empty pitcher and caused a rod to become a snake. Standing before a table that was bare, he drew all manner of foods and wines out of the air and furnished it for a splendid repast. Then, he called Hoskiah as his slave and stood a comely maiden before him. And Hoskiah shot arrows into her, and they stood out from her body, so that there was not space for a man to place his hand. And the blood flowed down her robe as though she stood in a rainstorm of blood, before she sank to the ground and lay there dead before them.

SOF:7:52 Then Lokus went up to her and after wrenching the arrows from out of her body threw a cloak over it. The arrows he carried to Isais and those about him, saying, "See the blood of a maiden," and they held the arrows and looked at them. And behold, as they held the arrows and looked, the blood went from them and the arrows were clean. And Lokus cried out in a loud voice, "Lo, the blood returns." Then, passing over unto the maiden, he lifted the cloak off her, and behold, as he did so her robe became clean again. And Lokus took her by the hand and said unto her, "Arise," and she arose and stood before Isais. And he was silent, and those about him did not speak. Casting aside her garment, which was the outer robe, the maiden danced before the gathering, and all there wondered greatly, for her body was unmarked.

SOF:7:53 Isais spoke to Lokus, saying, "How can such things be? What manner of magic is this?" Lokus answered him, saying, "Lord, your eyes saw as I bid them see, for I am the master of men's hearts, not the master of flesh and wood. The eye is the greatest of deceivers. It is the magic of Egypt which undid the work of the Ethiopian's bow." And Isais said, "Who is this Ethiopian, who stands there so strangely garbed? It is indeed a bowman among bowmen to loose his arrows so that one has scarcely struck ere another left the bow. Has Rasfamishel come among us?" Lokus answered him, saying, "Lord, he comes from beyond the Land of Elephants, in the place where the Earth tips over. The magic is in his bow, which can shoot at a wild ass and bring down a lion."

SOF:7:54 So saying, Lokus took up a clay pot and stood it on a table, and Hoskiah, standing off, loosed an arrow at it. And the pot was shattered, and as it fell apart lo and behold, a silver pot appeared in its place. And those who saw these things were amazed and spoke one to the other about the magic of Lokus.

SOF:7:55 One among the gathering, a speechmaker, stood up and spoke words praising the magic of Lokus, but Isais sat quiet, deep in thought. Then bidding Lokus come to his side, Isais said, "This night, I have seen with my own eyes a maiden slain with arrows and raised from the sleep of death. I have seen the magic of the bow change clay to silver. Is then your magic great enough to change age into youth and weakness into strength? It is said that the greatest of magicians can do even this." And Lokus lifted himself and said, "Even this, I can do."

SOF:7:56 Then there was much whispering back and forth and talk among those who sat about Isais. They that stood in the place of his favour said, "Master, this is the hour; let the magic of this great magician cast the years from off your back and renew the vigour of youth" And while they spoke, there was much whispering and sly laughter among the half men.

SOF:7:57 Lokus stepped back from the presence of Isais, and he raised his left hand, and there were loud thunders. He raised his right hand, and fire leaped forth from the ground, and a great cloud of smoke went up. And he said unto Isais, "Great Isais, this is your hour. You are the lord of this land and place; therefore, command as you will. Already the night is more than half spent and speeds to its closing. Hear now my words, this I say unto you: Enter now into my magic tent which stands strangely adorned over against the edge of the feasting place. The tent, wherefrom I issue forth my magic, to which I return to replenish my strength when it is done. Therein is the fount of my magic, the hub of the great circle of power. Remain in there until the first red glow from the fires of the underworld appears in the night sky. Then lord, I will come into the tent and, standing against it, will call forth the lord of this land and place, and behold, a new lord will stand before the gathering in manly strength and vigour. A man among men and a fitting master for this household. He will be such a man that I, even I Lokus, the master of magic, will be the first to proclaim him."

SOF:7:58 So Isais entered into the tent of Lokus the magician, and as he passed within, Lokus gave him the great bow of Hoskiah, saying, "Take this with you, for its magic is great and may well be needed. It is a worthy weapon for the lord of this land."

SOF:7:59 Then the gathering spoke amongst themselves and waited. Singing women whiled away the hours. And as the first arrows of morning light struck the night sky, Lokus arose and stood against the tent of magic. Lifting up the door he cried out in a loud voice, "Great Lord of these lands and place, come forth to your heritage, behold your lord." And as he spoke, lo, Hoskiah stepped forth into the morning light, arrayed as a lord and girded about with belt and sword. He wore a helmet, and in his hand was the great bow.

SOF:7:60 The sound of a great sigh passed through the gathering, and men looked one at the other. They were bemused, not knowing what to do, for there was magic about them. And Lokus lifted up his voice in the silence and cried, "Behold, I have brought forth a man among men as lord of these lands and place. Will you not, therefore, receive him in a befitting manner?" And men spoke among themselves, saying, "This is one having the appearance of Hoskiah, whom we know, in truth the lord of these lands and place. He is a man indeed, if it be he; has magic drawn him back from the grave, or has the spirit of Isais clothed itself in the form of Hoskiah?" Then first one and then another hailed the man before them saying, "This is a man among men, if not our lord Hoskiah." Then a great shout of, "Hoskiah!" went up, and Hoskiah stood stern before them.

SOF:7:61 Now, there were those among the gathering who stood silent. The half men and wanton women who were about the table where Isais had been, sat pale and silent, clinging to each other. They said among themselves, "If indeed this be Hoskiah, where then is our lord Isais ?" And a man stood up among the gathering, shouting, "This is not Isais transformed by magic, but Hoskiah, who, with this evil magician, has worked a trick. Isais is not transformed, but murdered. Let him be avenged." And reaching back, he took a javelin and sought to hurl it at Hoskiah. But the bow in the hand of Hoskiah bent, and before the javelin could be sped, an arrow pierced the man's throat. Then the bow sang twice more before the enemies of Hoskiah departed.

SOF:7:62 Now, it came to pass that those remaining gathered about Hoskiah and rejoiced, saying, "Hoskiah is indeed the rightful lord, and none but he ever bent bow as we have seen a bow bent this dawning." And Hoskiah passed through them to the seat of Isais. And those gathered there shrank from him, and he swept the table clean and drove away those who stood about it, saying. "Begone, lest I have you seized and beaten, for you befoul the Earth and serve neither God nor man." They departed, saying, "This is indeed Hoskiah and not Isais." And Isais was seen no more by the eyes of men.

SOF:7:63 Now, after three days had passed, Lokus said to Hoskiah, "The time has come when I must depart. I shall go unto my king, who is now your king and speak with him concerning you. It is well that I go now and dally not unduly here, for mayhap as things are, he will lend a willing ear to my words. But if I dally here with you, others will gain his ear with another account." So Lokus departed, and Hoskiah was grieved.

SOF:7:64 Before he left, Lokus was given horses and servants, also slaves and asses with food for the journey. And Lokus said to Hoskiah, "We shall meet again, for it is decreed in the Book of Heaven."

SOF:7:65 Athelia came before Hoskiah many times and said, "Lord, let me depart from your residence and dwell in a place not too far off." And Hoskiah was perplexed within himself because of her manner of speech, for he did not understand what she wanted. He said, "Have no fear for the women of my household, for there is none I desire but you."

SOF:7:66 And it came to pass that on his way to the king, Lokus was stricken with a sickness and lay as one already dead, and for many days, his soul was prepared for departure. And while he lay sick, the power that bound the eyes of Hoskiah became weakened, and the eyes of Hoskiah were no longer bound.

SOF:7:67 Now, Hoskiah purged his household and spent the days dealing with his estates, and his lands flourished. His servants no longer bickered among themselves as before, and contentment reigned within his shadow.

SOF:7:68 So when many days had passed and all things were ordered, Hoskiah called his steward and said unto him, "Let a feast be prepared. As the land has given generously to me, so will I give no less generously." Hoskiah said this, and it was done.

SOF:7:69 Now, there was a woman called Mirim of the household of Isais, who was fair to behold, and she sought the favour of Hoskiah. And among the women, there was much talk of Athelia, who remained ever veiled, for there were those among the women who knew her. But none spoke to Hoskiah, for he was a man who talked little with women, and Athelia stood first in his eyes.

SOF:7:70 Mirim had not seen the degradation of Athelia, nor had she seen her unveiled. But it came to pass that she spied upon Athelia one day, while she was about her toilet, and seeing her unveiled, Mirim took counsel with herself.

SOF:7:71 Now, the day of feasting came, and many were the guests, but of half men and wanton women, there were none. And among the women, Athelia sat apart, and among the men, there was much talk of riches and battles, and of spoils of war and husbandry.

SOF:7:72 Among the guests was a young lord, who sought the favours of Mirim. And while the feasting and dancing were at their height, they came one to the other. And as they dallied beyond the torchligh,t Mirim said unto him, "Am I fair indeed?" And he answered her, saying, "You are fair even among the fairest." Then she said unto him, "Yet there is one more fair by far, so fair that she needs to go veiled before men. She is Athelia, wife of Hoskiah, who keeps her thus. He fears for himself and does not trust her, for this is his weakness." And Mirim moved away from the young lord, saying, "Go look upon her face, and if you can then say I am the fairest of the fair, I shall know that your heart speaks sincerely of itself and not at the behest of your body."

SOF:7:73 The young lord returned to the feasting and sat in a place nearby to Hoskiah and spoke to those about him, saying, "Have any among you seen a woman here who rivals the fairest bearers of myrtle and palm?" And the men rebuked him, saying, "It is not meet to talk thus about the women of a household, wherein you are a guest. Are they to be judged as are women of the night?"

SOF:7:74 But the tongue of the young lord was not stayed, and he replied, saying, "That which causes talk will be talked about." And Hoskiah heard him and was angry and said, "What in my household moves foolish tongues to gossip?" The young lord said, "That, which a man tries to conceal ever arouses the interests of others. Does any man conceal that, of which he is proud?" And Hoskiah looked about him, saying, "This talk, I do not understand." The young lord said, "My lord, men talk of what lies beneath the veil of the woman you brought here, is she indeed as fair as men say, or is there truth even in the gossip of women?"

SOF:7:75 And those who knew about the degradation of Athelia muttered among themselves, for her secret could not be kept hidden. They said, "This is loose talk and wicked, let the evil, which belongs to the past remain buried. Does this concern any man but Hoskiah? Are we among women that the talk should be thus? Is our custom to be lightly set aside? Let the veil remain.

SOF:7:76 But Hoskiah, hearing the muttering, thought wrongly of what was said. And he spoke to the young lord, saying, "This woman is fair as few women are fair; should I not know? This you shall indeed see for yourself." And Hoskiah said within himself, "Long enough have I indulged Athelia her whims; does a pearl give pleasure within its shell?" And Hoskiah sent his attendant for her.

SOF:7:77 So Athelia came with her hand maiden, and Mirim came too and stood close behind them. And Athelia stood before Hoskiah and said, "My lord, what is your wish?" And he said to her, "Woman, remove your veil." And Athelia put her hand to the veil and pleaded with him, saying, "My lord, there are many men here and strangers. There is a custom of my people, by which I abide." And men, hearing her voice, looked one at another, and the oldest among them said to Hoskiah, "Let the woman be, for this is of no importance and of no interest to us. Allow her the whim, for such is the nature of women. Shall we deny them their small pleasures?" Athelia inclined her head towards the man who spoke, and as she did so, Mirim stepped forward and caught hold of the veil, snatching it aside. And the stricken face of Athelia was revealed to the gathering.

SOF:7:78 All men were silent and still, like statues. And Hoskiah looked at Athelia, and she at him. And Hoskiah saw her as she was, and Athelia knew what he saw. Then came the voice of the young lord, saying, "Behold the pearl of Hoskiah." And Hoskiah turned upon him in rage and slew him.

SOF:7:79 And Hoskiah turned to Athelia, who stood still and alone, saying, "What evil has been wrought here? Begone, take your face from me." And Athelia went out between the gathering. And passing into her bedchamber, she took a draught of poison. And her handmaiden sped to Hoskiah, saying, "Come, my lord; my mistress dies."

SOF:7:80 Then Hoskiah, his heart filled with remorse, sped to Athelia. And as he came unto her she died.

SOF:7:81 And Hoskiah wept over her, and his heart was filled with grief. And he looked upon the body of Athelia and said, I have slain the life within my own heart. I have slain the one who cherished me in my blindness, the one who loved beyond the bounds of love."

SOF:7:82 In his anguish, the eye of his soul was opened and saw the soul of Athelia standing nearby. And Hoskiah was dazzled by the vision of her beauty, for she was radiant as the sun. He stretched out his hands towards her, but could not touch her, for she was beyond the reach of earthly things. And she shook her head at him and, raising her hand, departed to the Antechamber of Eternity.

SOF:7:83 Hoskiah raised himself up and strode out from the chamber, but he returned not again to the place of feasting. He sorrowed many days.

SOF:7:84 Now, while Hoskiah still sorrowed, word came to him that a company of men was coming against him. And he sent out his servants with laden asses and went forth, himself. And with his true men, he prepared a place on the heights above the road to meet those, who came to take him. And Hoskiah met them with arrows and with stones and left them with their dead.

SOF:7:85 And Hoskiah and those with him passed out into the wilderness and lived there many days. And it came to pass that word came to him of Lokus, and he arose and went into the land of the Sons of Fire, passing into Tyre as a merchant from Kithim.

SOF:7:86 So it came about that Hoskiah came with sons of the Children of Light on ships of Arad, by way of Hawnibo and Mesilonas, where there are many temples. The ships made one harvest towards the Land of Trees, where the great river flows to the West. And his sons, he left in Tyre, that they might receive instruction in the household of Lokus.

SOF:7:87 Hoskiah governed many years in the Land of Mists and made laws and died in his old age. And he was buried by the river, where the ground rises, beneath stones and soil carried in many baskets. A fence was made and trees, which still grow, set about the place.

SOF:7:88 When Hoskiah came here, he had been forty and four years on Earth, and two score and five years passed before he died. May his God fulfil his hopes!

SOF:7:89 Raben, the son of Hoskiah, was born of a daughter from the house of Lokus in this land.

Chapter Eight – The Rolls of Record - 2

SOF:8:1 Lothan, Captain of Men of Valour, Victorious over the Sons of the New Moon and Guardian of the Hidden Wisdom. Maker of Roads in the Red Lands and Builder of the Secret Fort. By Abisobel, once Scribe of the God Eloah in Ladosa, Keeper of Records in the New Temple, to his Fathers in Wisdom at the Temple of Iswarah, Greetings. May you live long on Earth in prosperity, peace and health, and depart in knowledge.

SOF:8:2 We left the good land, hearts heavy laden with grief. The ships were five, and I looked to mine and found it good. It was built of alonwood and stout-masted. All about it, casks were lashed. Along the planking, the cords that moved were free, but all clear spaces were filled with things wrapped about and bound. There was much leather for the sails and leathern scoops. There were half a score of large buckets of wood hooped about and handled with plaited leather. Between the eyes of the ship, the guide pole was raised, beneath which were stored all kinds of unusual things made of wood and cordage used by men of the sea. There was a machine for slinging stones and another for hurling fire. There were high shieldguards, which could be strapped to the side. A store contained every kind of weapon and much armour. There were pots for cooking and braziers.

SOF:8:3 There was a store behind the mast, and in it were over five score jars of oil and not less of wine and vinegar. Casks of food, there were and more stored in baskets. Many large pitchers were lashed about and dried meat stored in cloth. Dried dates and figs and small fruits, there were in large quantities. Water was not lacking, nor the dishes for eating. There were nets for fishing and hooks for catching birds.

SOF:8:4 The chief among the men of the sea was skilled in the notched stick called 'thumb of the night', which guided him across the widths of the sea. We brought up against Keftor, where Nebam departed, for they were troublesome. Men of Melkat came, who had been wrecked, and we took a score, who were men of valour. We passed many lands by the sea, where once broad sea-girt Posidma reigned, before blown apart by underworld fires. By the lands of Hoghurim, we went over the wide sea to the gate of Athiesan and beyond it across the sea of Tapuim.

SOF:8:5 One ship and forty men and the households of six men were lost on the way. Three ships, have I left, with one brought up on the land. Twelve men, have I lost in battle and ten have gone with sickness. There are, with me, two hundred fighting men. One hundred and ten men of skill and one hundred bondsmen. Sixty households with their cattle and sheep and corn and tools and wagons. Athiesan things with us are numbered and the tally grows daily.

SOF:8:6 The encampment is well made and encircled with a wall, where water does not lie. Trees and soil are the material of its construction. Great trees are about us, but no stone for building, for the soil is deep. The waters rise not over the fields where men have cut water passages, but there is much rain.

SOF:8:7 Wild men are in the land, who write on their skins. They are hairy ones whose gods are the plants of the field. Their quarters are like baskets over the ground and they are unwashed. The women are like hellcats, uttering wild cries among the trees, but the men are quiet and come in silence.

SOF:8:8 They have temples of poles, roofed over in part and encircled by great logs, with logs laid over. Skins and painted leather are hung about, but no cloth. They place plants on altars, that their high gods may consume the essence of life within them and draw it back into themselves.

SOF:8:9 Virgins, they keep in cages, why I know not, but the women in cages are virgins and well cared for. Is virginity uncaged like a hound unleashed?

SOF:8:10 The wild men are unlearned and without soft speech. They are cousins to the wild dog, yet with children, they are gentle. The children of Fikol, the stoneworker, were lost among the trees, and wild beasts beset them at night. The wild men found them there and carried them away and fed them. Then came the searchband of men of valour upon the place, and the children, seeing them, ran away from the wild men. The men of valour slew the wild men, thinking they had taken the children, for they knew not their speech. Since then, we have seen their ways.

SOF:8:11 One hundred and ten of the wild people, we have as bondsmen and bondswomen. The men work with the soil and wood about the encampment. The wall, I caused to be built out into the water and it encloses a pier against the bank, where ships can moor.

SOF:8:12 Within the wall and circle of water, I have built the temple, but not all go in there with me. We are not one people. The gates of the temple are on pillars of wood and turn on a stone, and wooden are the pillars within. Great beams support the roof, and the walls are of wood and mud brick. The floor is of sand finely raked, and before the heir, the altar rests on stones. There are no images designed to confuse men, for though the temple is poor, it does not enshrine ignorance. We have no evil men with us. There are men of valour and men of skill, men of the land and men of the sea, no more.

SOF:8:13 Beneath the altar is the Grave of Life, kept dry with mortar. In its place is the Great Chest of Mysteries and in the Urns of Life are the records. Well kept, they are and safe from the unlearned, all the records of the Eastern Quarter.

SOF:8:14 Thus all things have been done according to your divining, and it is good.

SOF:8:15 (Between that just copied and that, which follows there was a full plate, but the writing upon it was ineffective.)

SOF:8:16 In the land at the edge of the Earth, there is little sun and the people grow sick with water. The dampness causes a sickness among us, where the teeth become loose in the gums, and skin peels. Flesh puffs up and holds the marks of fingers.

SOF:8:17 The people of the land beset us, and we cannot find them among the trees. Lothan was slain, with twelve men of valour, three days' journey inland among the trees. He died in the night. Two men were caught by the wild men, who burnt them in cages.

SOF:8:18 Men have come in ships from the Land of the Sons of Fire, who are our brothers. Alman the scribe and Kora the builder came. Hoskiah, who is a man mighty in battle, having gone from us, brought them here by Kedaris.

SOF:8:19 Of the Sons of Fire, there are four hundred, but few are fighting men. They are not men of valour. They are men of the sea and cultivators and men who trade. There are builders among them and men skilled in the ways of wood and stone, for they came to establish a city in this place.

SOF:8:20 This, the Kingdom of the Trees, is no place for a city. Trees shut us in and hold us captive. They conceal those who lie in wait to do us harm. A house is built, and trees take over the roof, and plants creep over the walls. Corn is planted and rots, while weeds smother other growing food. Greyness is everywhere; even the face of the sun is pale here.

SOF:8:21 Men shiver without heat, and the air is not pure and mixed with water. Wild dogs lurk among the trees, to tear the unwary to pieces. There are few stones, and they are covered with slime. The wild fruits and herbs are poisonous, and men have died eating them. The wild men in this place eat their own children and anoint their bodies with the fat of the dead. There is a race of men with great hairy bodies and the heads of dogs, who carry children off to feast on them. Arutha, wife of Amora, died in the embrace of one. They have hides that no arrow can pierce.

SOF:8:22 The Book of Heaven is open to the Sons of Fire; in it, they found the road across the waters. They are filled with the wisdom of wanderers. As we came by the sea in the hands of seafarers, so shall we go out. We long for the welcome omens of the shining arrows of the night. Our people are weary, and there is muttering among the men of valour, for they fear the Spirit of the Trees. His breath surrounds us. His grey fingernails corrupt our possessions. He has caused our cattle to die and our crops to wither. Against him, we are powerless. He was robbed of this land hewn out from among the trees; he will never forget.

SOF:8:23 The Great Secrets and Sacred Wisdom are secured for our children. We place them and ourselves in the hands of the Sons of Fire. We shall leave this place and sail towards Hireh, towards the West, where lies the Land of White Stone. There we may build with stone and brick.

SOF:8:24 Here is the tally of our departure: Of those who came with Lothan, ninety men of valour and the households of thirty-five. There are seventy men of valour, who came later, and those of the Sons of Fire. Eighty-two men of skill and eight households newly formed. There are the men of valour who came with Hoskiah and the households among them. There are nine households, which came later.

SOF:8:25 There are two hundred and forty bondsmen. Of these, one hundred and ten carry slings and clubs. Some have fighting axes of stone and staves shod with metal, but there is no sharpened weapon among them.

SOF:8:26 One hundred and four among all the households are children and unmarried women, for many have died of the sickness belonging to this place. There are slaves, but most have died or perished among the trees.

SOF:8:27 The cattle are gone, and there are a few sheep and goats. There are, for each man of valour, two measures of corn at morning and for others one measure. Of corn, there are sixty great baskets. Of herbs dried by fire, forty-five ankrim. There is fish fried by fire and some meat.

SOF:8:28 There are a hundred and ten baskets of cuped nuts, which are bitter and go sour. The Men of the Trees eat them, and for such people it is proper food. There are narah nuts, which grow in this place, sweet but not stomach filling, and nuts, which are good for cakes in quantities.

SOF:8:29 There is much weapon metal melted down and gold and silver in pieces. There are all kinds of tools for the men of skill and much pottery in the households. But much has gone to the Men of the Trees, and of cloth, there is little, and men are clothed in skins and the woven fibre of plants.

SOF:8:30 The Harbour of Sorrow, we leave behind, and with four ships, sail towards the sunsetting. One ship goes to the Land of the Sons of Fire. Spirit of Lothan, remain among us as we go far away among men who are strangers to us!

Chapter Nine – The Rolls of Record - 3

SOF:9:1 The Sons of Fire came to the Land of Mists, they and their households and their cattle, and all the tools of craftsmen. With them came others, men of Egypt and men of Javen. Also strangers who were not as valiant as are the Sons of Fire. Many among them were sickly and distressed in their hearts.

SOF:9:2 They took land among the barbarians and built a city and a port at the place called Sadel, near Saham, and cut roads about it into the forests. But they were kept in by the barbarians, and strangers in a strange land. The city was a place for buying and selling, and men came and went. Ships came bearing cloth and pottery, instruments and weapons of war and all manner of things. The ships went away bearing things from the barbarians, who dug in the soil. The place of the city was good, for it was fertile and well watered, and the bay was guarded by a great rock.

SOF:9:3 When he came, Hoskiah caused statutes to be set up for the city, and they were kept in the courts of the temple. This record was made at his command:

SOF:9:4 "It is unlawful for you to curse your father or your mother, or their father or their mother, or to raise your hand in anger against them. If the forbidden be done, you shall be burnt with fire and iron upon the left shoulder and a task and time set upon you."

SOF:9:5 "It is unlawful for you to steal the reputation of another man by lies. If the forbidden be done, you shall be branded by fire and iron upon the lips of the mouth."

SOF:9:6 "It is unlawful for you to defile the wife of another man. If the forbidden be done, you shall be branded with fire and iron upon the soles of the feet and upon the backside and the armpits, and upon the mouth and nose, and shall be cast out from among us, unless bearing arms in war.

SOF:9:7 "It is unlawful for a wife to lie with any man not her husband. If the forbidden be done, she shall suffer her time upon the adulteress' saddle and shall not be healed with skyfire."

SOF:9:8 "It is unlawful for you to penetrate a child in lust. If the forbidden be done, you shall be castrated and the wound healed with iron and fire."

SOF:9:9 "It is unlawful for you to place your hands between the legs of a womanchild. If the forbidden be done, you shall be burnt with iron and fire upon the palm of the left hand and upon the left cheek and between the thighs."

SOF:9:10 "It is unlawful for you if, being a guest, you defile the household of the man who harbours you. If the forbidden be done with a free man or a free woman you, shall be burnt with fire and iron on the soles of the feet and in the armpits, and shall die in the waters, after the custom of the barbarians. If with a slave or bondsman or bondswoman, you shall be burnt upon the backside and the armpits, and shall pay their price to their master."

SOF:9:11 "It is unlawful for you to speak falsehood against another so that he suffer at trial. If the forbidden be done, you shall suffer the same as he and be burnt upon the tongue with iron and fire, and pay the recompense set by the council."

SOF:9:12 "It is unlawful for you to give a daughter of your house to the barbarians in marriage, unless she be one who has brought shame upon you. If the forbidden be done, you shall be dispossessed of your property and household."

SOF:9:13 "It is unlawful for you to allow any man within your household to fornicate with the barbarians. If the forbidden be done, you shall be burnt with iron and fire upon the left thigh. The man within your household shall be burnt upon the soles of his feet and in his armpits. If it be done again, you shall be burnt with iron and fire upon the backside and dispossessed of a tithe of your property. The man within your household shall be blinded in the left eye with iron and fire, and burnt upon the soles of his feet."

SOF:9:14 "It is unlawful for you to allow any woman within your household to fornicate with a barbarian. If the forbidden be done and she be a freewoman, you shall be dispossessed of your household and property, and she shall die as women die. If a slave or a bondswoman, you shall be dispossessed of a tithe of your property, and she shall be burnt upon her private parts, after the manner of burning women."

SOF:9:15 "It is unlawful for you to fornicate with the barbarians. If the forbidden be done, you shall be dispossessed of your property and household and made a slave of the council."

SOF:9:16 "It is unlawful for a woman to show her breasts to the eyes of men not of her household. If the forbidden be done, she shall be burnt between the breasts, after the manner of burning women."

SOF:9:17 "It is unlawful for any woman to show her private parts to any man, unless he be her husband or master. If the forbidden be done, she shall be burnt daily, after the manner of burning women, until each of the seven points have been burnt. If she do so with a man not of her household, then her husband or master shall be burnt with iron and fire upon his right thigh."

SOF:9:18 "It is unlawful for you to show your nakedness wilfully to any woman or maiden not of your household. If the forbidden be done, you shall be burnt with iron and fire upon the backside."

SOF:9:19 These are the statutes made because of the things done before the eyes of the barbarians, who hold their women in high esteem:

SOF:9:20 "It is unlawful for you to slay or maim any man or woman or any child among us. If the forbidden be done, then a life shall be taken for a life, by water, after the custom of the barbarians. A limb shall be taken for a limb and an eye for an eye. Except that if it be one among you who is a bearer of arms in war, he shall not be maimed so that he cannot fight, but he may be slain for a slaying."

SOF:9:21 "It is unlawful for you to steal or dispossess by deceit. If the forbidden be done, the harm done shall be restored double. If it be done again to the same man or another, you shall also be burnt with iron and fire upon the right forearm. But if a man act foolishly so that he is easily dispossessed, than only that taken shall be restored in value."

SOF:9:22 "It is unlawful for you to wilfully destroy a writing or record in writing, or marks of meaning or namemarks. If the forbidden be done, you shall be burnt with iron and fire upon each palm of the hands and be dispossessed of one quarter of your property."

SOF:9:23 "It is unlawful for you to wilfully damage the property of another man among us. If the forbidden be done, you shall make it good by paying its value to the man you wronged."

SOF:9:24 "It is unlawful for you to change worked iron with the barbarians for other things. If the forbidden be done, you shall be burnt with iron and fire upon the sole of the left foot and upon the palm of the right hand."

SOF:9:25 "It is unlawful for you to deal deceitfully with the barbarians or to steal from them. Or to cause hurt to them or damage to their property. If the forbidden be done, you shall be burnt with iron and fire upon the palm of the right hand. You shall be cast out without weapons outside our boundary in a place where you can be taken by them, so they may deal with you according to their own customs,"

SOF:9:26 "It is unlawful for you to increase gold or silver with other substances. If the forbidden be done, you shall be dispossessed of half your property and possession and burnt upon the ears with iron and fire."

SOF:9:27 "It is unlawful for you to enter secretly into the habitation of another man or within the enclosure about it. If the forbidden be done, you shall if within the habitation, be blinded in the left eye with iron and fire, and if it be done again, in the right eye. If you enter secretly within the enclosure about the habitation, you shall be burnt with iron and fire upon the soles of the feet and upon the backside. If you be found with weapon, you shall be made a slave to the owner of the place."

SOF:9:28 "It is unlawful for you to use an animal for lust. If the forbidden be done and one penetrate the other, you shall be castrated and the wound healed by iron and fire. Unless a bearer of arms in war, you shall be driven out from among us, and the animal shall die. If neither penetrate the other, you shall be burnt with iron and fire upon your private parts."

SOF:9:29 "It is unlawful for you to befoul the well of another man or the clear water, from which he drinks. If the forbidden be done, you shall be burnt with iron and fire upon the backside."

SOF:9:30 "It is unlawful for you to cause damage to the herds or the crops, the goods or the property of another man. If the forbidden be done, you shall make good the damage. If it be done again to him or another man, you shall also suffer burning with iron and fire upon the sole of the left foot."

SOF:9:31 "It is unlawful for a woman to sell herself for the use of men, unless she first proclaim herself a public woman by standing from dawn to dusk, for two days, at the market gate of the temple. If such be done, no guilt shall attach to her, but if the forbidden be done, she shall be burnt after the manner of the burning of women, upon the cheeks and on the arms and on the belly. If she do it again without proclaiming herself, she shall be sold as a slave. Her price shall be given to the governor."

SOF:9:32 "It is unlawful for the wife or the bondswoman or the slave of any man to sell herself for the use of men. If the forbidden be done, the husband or master shall be burnt with iron and fire upon the mouth and upon the backside and upon the soles of the feet, except it be done secretly from him. The woman shall be sold, and her price given to the governor."

SOF:9:33 "It is unlawful for you, if a man with womanly ways, to conduct yourself as such, unless you first proclaim your nature by standing from dawn to dusk, for one day, at the market gate of the temple. If such be done, no guilt shall attach itself to your conduct as a man with womanly ways. If the forbidden be done, you shall be burnt with iron and fire upon the belly and the backside and sold in the market place, and your price given to the governor.

SOF:9:34 "It is unlawful for an unprotected man with womanly ways to be the master of a household or to take a wife. He cannot own anything, except it be required for eating or sleeping, clothing and the practice of his craft. He may own a dwelling of one room, but if he bear arms in war, he may own a dwelling of any size. if the forbidden be done, he shall be burnt with iron and fire on the backside and chest and sold as a slave, and his price given to the governor.

SOF:9:35 "It is unlawful for you to satisfy your lusts with a man of your household. If the forbidden be done, you shall both be burnt with iron and fire on both armpits, unless one be in the hands of the other."

SOF:9:36 "It is unlawful for a woman to slay her child or let it die by neglect. If the forbidden be done and the child be unweaned, the woman shall be sold into slavery and her price given to the governor. If the child be weaned, a life shall be taken for a life."

SOF:9:37 "It is unlawful for you, if the master of a household, to go beyond our boundaries for upwards of two days and one night, unless you appoint a steward in your place or have a son in manhood. If the forbidden be done, you shall be burnt with iron and fire upon the sole of your right foot and upon your backside. If you be detained by force, you shall not be burnt."

SOF:9:38 "It is unlawful for you to touch a woman not of your household upon her private parts, unless she be a woman who sells herself to men. If the forbidden be done, you shall be burnt with fire and iron upon the palm and fingers of the right hand and upon the left cheek and upon the backside. If it be done again, you shall also be blinded with iron and fire in the left eye, and if again, in the right eye also."

SOF:9:39 "It is unlawful for you to take a woman not of your household by force for lust, unless she be a woman who sells herself to men. If the forbidden be done, you shall be blinded by iron and fire in both eyes."

SOF:9:40 "It is unlawful for you to enter the sacred places of the barbarians or their temples, or to pass within a thousand paces of the Rabukimra. You may attend their festivals outside these places. If the forbidden be done, you shall be burnt with iron and fire on the sole of the left foot."

SOF:9:41 "It is unlawful for you to carry upon yourself or to have within your household the talismans of other gods. If the forbidden be done, you shall pay a tithe of your possessions and property to the temple."

SOF:9:42 "It is unlawful for you, if a guest, to conceal a weapon upon yourself or be in the dwelling of your host, while within his habitation. If the forbidden be done, you shall be burnt upon the muscle of your left arm and upon the forehead."

SOF:9:43 "It is unlawful for you to act seemingly towards an unlawful deed so that men will say, "His thoughts are towards an unlawful thing." If the forbidden be done, it shall be as though you had already done the unlawful deed, except that the council shall look upon you with mercy, if it be deserved."

SOF:9:44 "It is unlawful for you to talk to another man towards an unlawful deed. If the forbidden be done, you shall be burnt with iron and fire upon the lower lip and the left hand palm. The man among you who denounces this thing shall not be burnt."

SOF:9:45 "It is unlawful for you to lie so that another man be harmed. If the forbidden be done, and it be not serious, or without evil intent, you shall pay recompense. If it be more serious, you shall be burnt upon the upper lip and if more serious still, upon the tongue."

SOF:9:46 "It is unlawful for you to allow a woman of your household to be drunk in an outside place. If the forbidden be done, you shall, if it happen twice, be burnt with fire and iron upon the left thigh. If it happen again, you shall be burnt upon the left armpit."

SOF:9:47 "It is unlawful for a stranger to remain within our boundaries after sunset, unless he be a guest within a household or under its protection. Or unless he remain within the strangers' court or he be proclaimed. No man shall remain beyond ten days unless he be proclaimed. At this proclaiming, nothing of his past deeds or his comings and goings shall be hidden, and lies shall not be told. If the forbidden be done, he shall be burnt with iron and fire upon the nose and placed beyond our boundaries. He shall not return, and his goods shall be taken to the governor. As the sun goes down, all men shall bid the stranger be gone and shall not hold him."

SOF:9:48 "It is unlawful for you to delay the departure of a stranger when he must go and has done no wrong. If the forbidden be done, you shall be burnt with iron and fire upon the left backside."

SOF:9:49 "It is unlawful for a woman to depart from her household or to remain outside her home after sunset, unless she be protected. If the forbidden be done and she be a wife, she shall be burnt upon the sole of the left foot. If she be a slave or bonds woman, she shall be burnt upon the soles of both feet, and if she be a freewoman or servant woman, she shall be burnt upon the left leg. If she be a virgin, she shall be beaten with a leathern throng."

SOF:9:50 "It is unlawful for a man to raise his hand against the master of his household. If the forbidden be done, he shall, if a freeman, be burnt with iron and fire upon the right shoulder and upon the backside. If a servant, upon both shoulders and upon the backside, and if a slave or bondsman, upon both shoulders and upon the backside, and upon the soles of his feet. But if the master be hurt so that he is put to bed, then he who struck him shall be seized and confined and shall also be burnt on the body each day, until the master be up again."

SOF:9:51 "It is unlawful for you to maim or mark in chastisement beyond repair any woman of your household, or any freeman within its protection. If the forbidden be done, you shall be burnt with iron and fire, as the council declare."

SOF:9:52 "It is unlawful for you to strike in chastisement any woman not of your household, or touch her in anger. If the forbidden be done and she be without marks, if a freewoman, you shall be burnt with fire and iron upon the right thigh and the right armpit. If a maidservant, upon the right armpit and if a slave or bondswoman, upon the left thigh. But if she be marked or maimed you shall make payment to her master or her household and be burnt according to the declaration of the council."

SOF:9:53 "It is unlawful for you to drive a woman or a child from your household unlawfully. If the forbidden be done, you shall recompense the one driven out with a fifth part of your property and possessions. They may then enter any other household and shall not be held back."

SOF:9:54 "It is unlawful for you, if placed in stewardship or in guardianship, to do an unfaithful thing against anyone under your care. Or to cause loss or harm to the man who trusted you. You shall not conduct yourself unseemingly in the household under your stewardship or cause the man who trusted you to lose his reputation. If the forbidden be done and it be serious, the council may put you to death by water, after the custom of the barbarians, but if it be less serious, you shall be burnt as the council declare."

SOF:9:55 "It is unlawful for you or any man or woman within your household to eat uncooked meat, unless it be dried by sun or fire, or be pickled. Blood shall not be drunk. If the forbidden be done, you shall be burnt with iron and fire upon the left forearm."

SOF:9:56 "It is unlawful for you to become drunk or quarrelsome while among the barbarians. Or to curse them in their hearing, or to use unseemingly language in their presence, or to talk against us to them, If the forbidden be done, the first time, you shall be burnt with iron and fire upon the left leg; the second time, you shall be burnt upon the left armpit, and the third time, upon the lips of the mouth. Each time of chastisement, you shall be bound from the time of burning until sunset, and displayed on the boundary."

SOF:9:57 "It is unlawful for you to pass water within the temple enclosure, or to befoul the grounds or floors there. If the forbidden be done, you shall be burnt with iron and fire upon the backside and the soles of the feet and between the thighs. If it be done again, you shall be blinded in both eyes."

SOF:9:58 "It is unlawful for you to spit or use foul language within the temple enclosure. Or to shout or raise your voice unseemingly or act irreverently there. If the forbidden be done, you shall be burnt with iron and fire upon the mouth and right ear."

SOF:9:59 "It is unlawful for you to destroy anything within the temple enclosure. If the forbidden be done, you shall be burnt with iron and fire upon the palms of the hands and between the thighs. This may be increased to death by water, according to the custom of the barbarians, if the council think it fitting."

SOF:9:60 "It is unlawful for you to steal anything from within the temple enclosure. If the forbidden be done, you shall die by water, after the custom of the barbarians."

SOF:9:61 "It is unlawful for you to strike any priest or servant of the temple or anyone under its protection. If the forbidden be done, you shall be blinded by iron and fire. But if you maim someone, you shall die by water, after the custom of the barbarians. If it be a slave of the temple or a bondsman, then for striking him, you shall be burnt with iron and fire upon the soles of the feet and between the thighs. If he be maimed, you shall be blinded in the right eye."

SOF:9:62 "It is unlawful for you to be within the temple enclosure at night, in secret. If the forbidden be done, you shall be blinded by iron and fire."

SOF:9:63 "It is unlawful for you to carry weapons of metal or sharpened weapons within the temple enclosure, unless with the sanction of the temple guardians. If the forbidden be done, you shall be burnt with iron and fire upon the soles of the feet and the palm of the left hand."

SOF:9:64 "It is unlawful to seize any wrongdoer within the temple enclosure, unless it be done by those who serve the temple. If the forbidden be done, he who commanded the deed shall be blinded by iron and fire. Those who did the deed shall be burnt with iron and fire upon the palms of the hands and soles of the feet."

SOF:9:65 "It is unlawful to speak against the governor or the council or the commanders or princes, unless it be done before them or at the market gate of the temple. If the forbidden be done, you shall be burnt with iron and fire upon each side of the mouth. But no man shall suffer for anything he says in public at the market gate of the temple, except he talk about the God of This Enclosure."

SOF:9:66 "It is unlawful for you to speak against the God of This Enclosure within this His enclosure. If the forbidden be done, you shall be burnt upon the tongue and upon the mouth and driven out beyond our boundary, and you may not return for seven years."

SOF:9:67 "It is unlawful for you to speak against any priest of the temple, except before the High Priest on the days when any man may speak freely without fear. If the forbidden be done, you shall be burnt with iron and fire upon the backside and beneath the chin."

SOF:9:68 "It is unlawful for you to approach the Place of the High Altar or the forbidden place about it, or to touch the Sacred Treasures, unless you be a priest or high servant of the temple, or a man admitted by them. If the forbidden be done, you shall be blinded by iron and fire."

SOF:9:69 "It is unlawful to take a virgin to wife if you have a wife, but if without wife, you may marry a virgin. You shall not have more than three wives. If the forbidden be done, you shall be dispossessed of a fourth part of your property and possessions, which shall go to the wife you have taken unlawfully."

SOF:9:70 "It is unlawful for you to have intercourse with your mother, your daughter, your father's sister or your mother's sister, your brother's daughter or your sister's daughter, your father's mother or your mother's mother, your wife's mother or your son's wife, whether they be by blood or by law. If the forbidden be done, you shall die by water, after the custom of the barbarians."

SOF:9:71 "It is unlawful for men to wear the garments of women or women to wear the garments of men, unless they have proclaimed their natures. If the forbidden be done, men shall be burnt with iron and fire on the left cheek. Women may not be touched with iron made hot and therefore are to be burnt with skyfire. All men shall be burnt with iron and fire."

SOF:9:72 "Men may be put to death by water or fire and women by water or by smothering. Women shall not suffer chastisement so that their blood flow. When men are castrated, it shall be done with a knife of stone."

SOF:9:73 "Men shall be punished in a place where all men may see them, but a woman shall suffer away from the eyes of men, though she may receive punishment at the hands of a man. The punishment of a woman shall be witnessed by two men of the council and two women from the household she wronged."

SOF:9:74 "A man punished by burning shall suffer at high noon and then be laid on his back or his belly, according to which eases him most. Each of his limbs shall be drawn out and fastened to a stake, and he shall be left until midnight, and then let go. A woman, having been punished, shall be placed within a room, which has a pole lengthwise at sitting height and left there from noon to midnight. Any man or woman suffering punishment shall be allowed one attendant after it be inflicted, until their release. No man shall refuse to let another go to attend his friend."

SOF:9:75 "If a woman do something for which a man would be punished, she shall suffer likewise, except that the burning shall be with skyfire. The council shall not overlook a suitable punishment for the master of her household."

SOF:9:76 "If a man become indebted by trial and fail within the season to pay whatever be demanded of him, he and his possessions shall be seized and given into the keeping of those to whom he is indebted,"

SOF:9:77 "A woman having been declared by her husband before the council as unsuitable for a wife, and the council having found this to be so, she may remain within his household without being his wife. Or she may return to the household, from which she came or that of her father or her brother or her father's brother or mother's brother, as she wills. But she may not go elsewhere, and having chosen where to go cannot choose again."

SOF:9:78 "It is unlawful for a man to use whatever force and chastisements are necessary to maintain order within his household. He may make any adjustments within the household to endow it with contentment, but all things must be done with justice and moderation. All disagreements within a household shall be judged by its master."

SOF:9:79 "That which be done by a wife or a daughter, a youth or a child; or a servant or his wife or his sons or his daughters, or his servants; or by a freeman or his wife or his sons or his daughters, or his servants or slaves; or by a slave or a bonds woman or a bondsman, or their wives or their sons or their daughters, within your household; or by a freewoman or by a guest or by the stranger within your gates, shall be as though it were done by the master of the household, and both shall suffer alike. Except that the council shall weigh all the actions of the master of the household and set his punishment according to them."

SOF:9:80 "If, upon marriage, it be found that a woman taken to wife as a virgin be not a virgin, evidence of this may be given at the Seat of Truth before three witnesses. One witness shall then go to her household and declare this before its master. Then, except the matter come before the council, the woman may be put aside as a wife and returned to her household, and her bride price reclaimed double. Or, if her husband choose, she may remain in his household as wife or concubine, but he may reclaim her bride price."

SOF:9:81 "If a woman be put aside by her husband as no longer his wife, and she remain in his household, she shall be as a concubine."

SOF:9:82 "The rights of a concubine are those of a bondswoman, but she is a bondswoman to her master for life."

SOF:9:83 "When the master of a household dies, his eldest son shall become the master, and brother shall follow brother, until there are no sons. Then the brothers of the master shall follow in the order of their ages, and their sons, according to their kinship. The new master shall provide for the wives and concubines of his father in the same manner as previously. His brothers and sisters shall become as sons and daughters. Within a household, the death of its master changes nought but the master. After the death of its master, a household cannot divide, except it be done lawfully by the new master after he has been master for one year.

SOF:9:84 "All who stand at the market gate of the temple shall be proclaimed by the hours, and under the proclaimer's voice all men shall cease exchanges and be silent."

SOF:9:85 "A child may be adopted into house and household according to the custom of the Sons of Fire, and it may be one of us or a barbarian from across the waters, or a barbarian from outside our boundary. But if a barbarian from outside our boundary, it shall not be adopted unless a foundling under seven years if male, or a child if female."

SOF:9:86 "If a man take a barbarian woman to wife and have no other wife from among us who is her superior, he shall not become the master of a household, and a younger son shall step over him."

SOF:9:87 "A man with womanly ways who has proclaimed himself shall stand before us as a woman and be treated as one. Except if he bear arms in war, he shall then stand before us as a man, unless he choose otherwise."

SOF:9:88 "If the master of a household have within it a woman who is not a virgin and is a concubine or slave, and he give her to a guest or another within the household, that he may go in unto her, no wrong is done."

SOF:9:89 "If a man be proclaimed a man with womanly ways, an arrangement may be made with the governor and a price paid to become his protector. He shall then enter the household of the man who paid the price."

SOF:9:90 "A slave or bondsman may be bought for any woman of your household. But if she be a freewoman, then the slave shall be made free, and if a bondsman the debt paid so that he be free."

SOF:9:91 "If a woman be a concubine and within five years of her loss of virginity or admittance into your household have not become with child, she shall pass into the household of another after the custom of the Sons of Fire and returned according to the same custom."

SOF:9:92 "During the proclaiming of a stranger his deeds, good and bad, shall be made known. All things about him shall be told to all within hearing of the proclaimer's voice. Any man may question the stranger concerning such things, and if aught be hidden or lies told, the stranger shall be dealt with lawfully by the council."

SOF:9:93 "A virgin shall not be burnt, but is to be whipped with wands and the council shall set the number of stripes."

SOF:9:94 "A man who has been punished by trial three times shall be driven out from among us after the fourth punishment, unless he be a bearer of arms in war."

SOF:9:95 "Records and writings, namemarks and marks of meaning can be destroyed or altered only by permission of the council and the governor."

SOF:9:96 "The man who is the companion of thieves is himself a thief at heart and may be taken to trial if his companions steal."

SOF:9:97 "If the rightful master of a household be under age of manhood, the council shall appoint a steward and guardian for the household and heir."

SOF:9:98 "A stranger may not enter our boundaries bearing weapons of war made of metal. But the lords of the barbarians about our boundaries may come bearing weapons.

SOF:9:99 These are the statutes between the council and the governor and men. Those between man and man are in the keeping of the court of the market place. There are others between the court of the temple and men.

SOF:9:100 It was Hoskiah who set the statutes up and Racob recorded them. I, Brigadan of the Gulwa, preserved them, but many are unknown. Those are the statutes of Hoskiah.

SOF:9:101 This was misplaced from its text. "It was decreed that the iron for burning should not glow, neither should a blinding be made by contact with metal but should be through heat alone nor should it be absolute."

Chapter Ten – The Rolls of Record - 4

SOF:10:1 Now, even in the days of Hoskiah, the records were not whole, and Hoskiah caused it to be that this was written. It was set down in the manner of Kahadmos.

SOF:10:2 It is written in the Book of Mithram: The True Man has many qualities, and among the greatest is the inclination towards his duty. A man has a duty to his soul, to his God, to those who govern and to his household.

SOF:10:3 The weakling runs in battle and says, "See, I have done my duty; I am alive." The True Man stands resolute and grim; his enemies are like chaff before the wind; he is the master of life. Duty is the goddess of manhood, and she demands no mean sacrifice.

SOF:10:4 The grim goddess says "Die," and the True Man steps forward. The ranks of the Everlasting Lords of Life open, and he takes his place among them.

SOF:10:5 Duty says, "Glory and honour will never be yours; your miserable lot is to labour in the brickpits, so that your wife and children will not go hungry." The True Man faces his task with fortitude and cheerfulness.

SOF:10:6 Courage is the greatest quality of manliness, and duty the greatest expression of courage. What chastity is to woman, duty is to man; the willingly-assumed burden of their kind. Man and woman travel the same road together, but each bears a different burden.

SOF:10:7 Hoskiah said, "This shall be added to the records: Even the wild beasts have a duty to perform, for duty is the handmaiden of life. All things that have life have a duty, for life itself is duty. When a man has no obligations, he is dead.

SOF:10:8 The greater the standing of a man the greater is his duty. The Captain of Men shall serve better than the footman. Greater men have greater duties; lesser men have lesser duties. Wherever there is life, there is danger.

SOF:10:9 It is written in the Book of Mithram: The True Man is generous in word and deed, meanness has no place with him. He who gives with one hand gathers with the other.

SOF:10:10 It is also written thus: All men must seek to rise above their estate. They either rise or are cast down. Only man knows discontent and seeks to improve his lot, for discontent is the maker of men."

SOF:10:11 Hoskiah added this to the records: "Aim your arrow above your expectations. The man who sends an arrow towards the moon shoots farther than the one who sends it to a treetop. Choose your bow according to your strength. A strong bow without a strong arm is of no more value than a weak bow. Judge a man by his aim and not by his bow. A plain bow for service, a fancy bow for display. The strongest bow ever made is useless without an arrow."

SOF:10:12 Hoskiah said, "These are things, which are written but have been lost. Let them be recorded again": Success is the child of diligence and persistence. It follows the footsteps of the wise, even as failure dogs the foolish. Men have the choice of either success or ease; they cannot have both. To be beaten and still not surrender, that is true victory.

SOF:10:13 Failure is the yardstick of success. It alone adds value to achievement, but there can be no real failure, except through the acceptance of failure."

SOF:10:14 These things were added to the records, but we cannot tell when, though it is said by Hoskiah: "The manly spirit rejoices in freedom and cannot bear the yoke of servitude. It will admit no master who imposes his will by force.

SOF:10:15 A man may submit to leadership and command in warfare and be a better man, for true service is not servility. Never demand your rights before you have earned them.

SOF:10:16 A man is unworthy of freedom unless he also recognises the rights of others to freedom. The freeman is his own governor, and his rule is more rigorous than that of a despot. The only man entitled to be free is the one, who governs himself strictly and wisely.

SOF:10:17 Every nation moves either towards freedom or towards servility, for none can remain suspended between the two. It is free men, if they are weak, who are the greatest enemies of freedom. Great events do not make either heroes or cowards; they just unveil them to the eyes of men."

SOF:10:18 Hoskiah caused this to be written, saying, "This too was once written but is now lost to us by decay": The way of the evildoer is the path of sleeplessness. The wicked follow a road of darkness; they tread in constant fear of falling.

SOF:10:19 The evildoer is caught by his own wrongdoing. He is imprisoned by his own wickedness. The evildoer becomes trapped in a snare of his own making; he flees when none pursues.

SOF:10:20 It is truly said: The wicked in heart praise the wicked in deed. More men think wicked thoughts than commit wicked deeds, for many who would act are cowards. Observe the man who talks much about the deeds of wicked men; would he not be among them, did he not lack the courage?"

SOF:10:21 This was written in records which were lost even in the days of Racob: "In a hundred generations men will be less wicked, for such was written in the Plans of God. When a thousand years have passed, women will be more fair, for this was written in the Plans of God.

SOF:10:22 A day will come when a great nation will rise above all others, to lead the nations of the Earth, and it will survive even the Day of Visitation. Much was written of this nation, which is now lost.

SOF:10:23 As the generations pass, the Earth will become more fruitful, for this was written in the Plans of God.

SOF:10:24 The body of the Great God contains all that is, and His Spirit is contained in all that is. The spirit is perfect, but the body is imperfect."

SOF:10:25 Hoskiah said, "Let this now be written, for it was written before." No man shall walk in ways set against the will of the people. No man shall bear an unjust grudge or take personal vengeance unjustly.

SOF:10:26 These things shall be punished: If a man take a wife before he be one score of age, though he may have a concubine; if he empty his body, except in private; if he purify himself, except in flowing waters."

SOF:10:27 Because of his birth, Hoskiah could not become governor over the Sons of Fire, but he sat equal with the governor at the council, for he commanded all in this place.

SOF:10:28 The council made these statutes and set them together with those of Hoskiah: "A stranger, even a barbarian, may become one of us if he be supported by three members of the council, but he shall not sit in the council, unless he has carried arms in war for us. He shall not become one of us until one year after his proclaiming, and any man may come before the council and speak his objections to the acceptance of the stranger.

SOF:10:29 Each man shall have his assigned place at the council and may speak at his time, according to his place. No man shall interrupt another, while he is speaking.

SOF:10:30 No man shall speak before his turn, and any man having spoken may speak again. If a man has spoken twice and desires to speak again, he shall stand and remain silent. If one man in five raise their hands for him, he may speak again, but if they do not, he shall be reseated and not speak. If more than one man stand up at a time, those of lesser placement shall reseat themselves. On the third time, no man shall speak, except on some matter spoken about by one, who came after him, and he may not speak about any new thing. No man shall speak beyond his own time.

SOF:10:31 The old statute shall be changed, so that no man shall sit on the council, except he be one score and five years old, but those over three score years may remain on the council. A man who has carried weapons of war in battle shall take a higher position than a man entering the council with him who has not.

SOF:10:32 If a man go to sleep during a meeting of the council, he shall not come there again for one season.

SOF:10:33 A man shall not leave a meeting of the council, while another is on his feet speaking, and when a man goes outside, no man shall speak in debate.

SOF:10:34 A man shall not spit or laugh foolishly or make body noises during a meeting of the council. No man shall whisper or talk, except in his talking time.

SOF:10:35 A man shall not revile another at a meeting of the council. If a man wish to make an accusation or call something into question he shall state it when he is speaking and ask that a time be made for it to be debated."

SOF:10:36 This shall be the stranger's oath upon admittance: "I swear before The God of This Enclosure that I will dutifully follow His ways and obey His commands. I swear to be steadfast on the Great Path. I swear to submit myself to all your statutes and to remain faithful to you in warfare and before the face of terror, even under torment by the barbarians. This I swear for all time."

Chapter Eleven – The Rolls of Record - 5

SOF:11:1 "Supreme One Above Greatness, illuminate the hearts of my people, and let them see the path ahead. Permit them to understand the meaning of life, Make their hearts fearful for the responsibility they carry with regard to the future state of their souls. To this end, help them towards achieving a humble spirit and a kindly heart. Grant them some glimpse of eternity while here on Earth, so that they may better understand what lies before them. Bestow upon them the ability to make contact with the fount of wisdom and Truth, and let them draw near the well of holiness to sip its waters. Help them to make right judgements and guide their hearts, so they hold fast to the teachings of our Masters who have gone before. Make them steadfast in the light, and show them the falsity that glitters in the darkness. When they come to the end of their journey, Supreme One Above Greatness, grant them immortality in the Region of Eternal light. Incline towards them in mercy, for You can even mitigate the impress of wickedness upon their everlasting souls."

SOF:11:2 "Our Masters taught that the soul of man is the seed of a spirit implanted within the body of a beast. Supreme One Above Greatness, send down the refreshing waters of Your wisdom and compassion upon my people, that the seed may be nourished within them, to spring to life in the Land of Light. If the seed wither within the body or be consumed by the beast, we are condemned to the doom of everlasting nothingness. Let none of my people suffer this, for even the most wicked among them will be missed by others in the Region of Eternal Light."

SOF:11:3 "Supreme One Above Greatness, who reads the hearts of men as an unrolled book, what can I ask for myself? I who, though first in rank among my people, fall far below many of them in strength of soul. I am a man of battles and not a man of prayer, therefore I cannot know how I stand with You."

SOF:11:4 "Indeed, Supreme One Above Greatness, I have brought about much sorrow and suffering in my days. The burden of my manhood has weighed down heavily upon me. But, Supreme One Above Greatness, I have never robbed the widow or fatherless, or struck at the helpless and those without protection. I have not mocked the afflicted or stood aside in fear when wickedness was being done. I have slain no man, unless he has been my enemy and would have slain me. When I served any man, I served him well. I have never deserted a friend in distress or violated the sanctity of another man's home. Yet, Supreme One Above Greatness, I have done much that men condemn and therefore cannot know my standing before You. Yet, however I stand in Your eyes do not consider me too unworthy to plead for my people."

SOF:11:5 "I was not born among those who are now my people. I am not of their blood, and once I called upon the God of My Fathers after the manner of my fathers. Yet, are You not the same Being, by whatever name called? You are the Being, before Whom my spirit bows, the Sustainer of its strength. You alone know the conflict, which has twisted my heart in its resting place, for I cannot know what, indeed, is Truth. I do not expect to know, being unworthy of such knowledge. I did not desert You, but sought only to see You more clearly and serve You better. When I could not understand You in one place, I sought You in another. I looked for You where there was more light. Amid the people of my youth, You seemed close; yet, I could not understand You, for they wished to enclose You in a box. Now, though You appear further away, I see more clearly and know Your nature."

SOF:11:6 "Supreme One Above Greatness, I cannot say, as others do, that I have no doubts, for indeed I am often torn with conflicting thoughts. I do not doubt Your existence, for I have been granted a manifestation of its reality. But I am full of doubts about my relationship with You. Then, too, there is so much I cannot understand; yet, others turn to me for guidance. When I make an error affecting only myself, I do not complain about the consequences, but should I guide others into error my heart will be torn apart."

SOF:11:7 "God of My Heart and Father of My Soul, incline towards me a little, for of myself I cannot reach You. Enlighten me, so that I may lead others into the light. Death and destruction, I do not fear, not even everlasting nothingness, but I do fear being inadequate for my task. Supreme One Above Greatness, give me confidence and strength, I ask no more. If I cannot find these with You, I can find them nowhere. Guide me, Supreme One Above Greatness; what shall I do for my people?"

SOF:11:8 This was not written for the eyes of men, but will he who wrote it object if by being recorded for men, it adds even a mite to the storehouse of goodness available to men on Earth?

SOF:11:9 When Hoskiah was past three score years of age, he sent to Pelasi for the remnants of the Children of Light. None of them came, for they said it was not meet for them to journey to the edge of the Earth to dwell among barbarians. They said, "We will retain the light here, for out there, it will surely be extinguished."

SOF:11:10 Later, four ships did come, but they carried the standards of Ashratem. With them came Enos Husadim of the Sons of Dan, a learned man from the slopes of the mountain, which rests in darkness and reaches up to the limits of light. He knew Hoskiah when a child. There came also one named Zodak, who had dwelt in Twalus, and he brought with him all the books of the Children of Light. With Zodak came many men who knew the mysteries of metal, and they brought with them the light of Amos. When they came, the spirit of Hoskiah had already joined his fathers.

SOF:11:11 Before his spirit took winds, Hoskiah wrote this for the guidance of his people: "My trusted ones, the time draws near for my departure on the Great Voyage, and I cannot complete the tasks before my hands. In one thing I have been neglectful, for though the Chief Guardian of the Records, the time I devoted to their care was little enough. Thank the priests for their care; I have recorded many statutes needful for this place. Their like was known before, but were not set down for men to see. Now, they are made known to the ears of every man. Your welfare and safety has ever been my first concern, but I am a man of battle and a commander of men, not a scribe and recorder."

SOF:11:12 "My trusted ones, we are few, and the barbarians about us are many. For a while they are well kept in hand, for Cladwigen wishes us well, and his sons are our friends. We have toiled to raise a city, and men come and go freely among us. Many ships come in their season. Yet, stout warriors who are not friendly press down from the Northeast and therefore vigilance can never be relaxed. We cannot sleep peacefully side by side with the barbarians and must ever be alert. Danger hangs over us like a boulder upon the mountainside, and our safety is like a playstone in the hands of a child. The barbarians do not forget that we are strangers in this land; and only while we serve a purpose are we welcome."

SOF:11:13 "Yet, my trusted ones, with all the dangers around us it is the dangers threatening within that I fear the most. We are few indeed against the numbers of barbarians; yet, we weaken ourselves with foolish strife one with the other and people with people. Our city is a place for buying and selling, a place where things are exchanged. Outside, it is a market place, where men come and go as they please, and they buy and sell without hindrance. We have laws for the city and laws for the marketplace. Amongst us are many craftsmen who exchange the things they make with the barbarians, who bring things to eat. We have a good life here, but it is not a life I fully understand. We came from afar to set up a city dedicated to the light, to hold the light. Yet, is this such a city? Do men seek the light and worship it, or do they seek luxury and worship wealth and possessions?"

SOF:11:14 "When some of us came from the Harbour of Sorrow, we were full of praise at our deliverance from death, but amid the forests of fruitfulness, much of our gratitude and will was lost. Why must men always be better men in the face of disaster and in the midst of privation, than in the green fields of peace and plenty? Does this not answer the questions of many, who ask why there is sorrow and suffering on Earth? Why is it the lot of men to struggle and suffer, if not to make better men?"

SOF:11:15 "My trusted ones, my eyes may be clouded to the things before them, but I am not blind to your ways. Already, our women cast their eyes towards the barbarians, and when women seek men outside their own kind, it is a sign of a people's degeneracy. I read what is written, and I fear for the future."

SOF:11:16 "Many who are with us in the light will join us, and then we shall be stronger in arms and strengthened in belief. (Annotation: How few came!) Yet, our destiny lies among the barbarians. They are fine, upright men endowed with courage; do not belittle their ways, but bring them into the light."

SOF:11:17 "Our city was not founded as a marketplace, a place for exchanging only the things of Earth. Neither did we come here as conquerors, but as men seeking refuge."

SOF:11:18 "My trusted ones, remember that the road of life is not smooth; neither is the way of survival a path of grass. The most needful thing for any people who wish to survive is self-discipline. Think less of gold and more of the iron, which protects the gold. Remember, too, these words from the Book of Mithram, "The keenest sword is useless, unless it be held in the hand of a resolute man. Also, the man who has gold keeps it in peace if he tends his bowstring."

SOF:11:19 The remainder of Hoskiah's words to the people has been lost.

Chapter Twelve – The Rolls of Record - 6

SOF:12:1 Before we left Droidesh, they brought living sheep and goats and hung them upon a tree standing in the place of assembly. Birds of bright colours and things of worked gold and silver were hung upon the branches. Perfumes and oils with garments. They danced about the tree, and hewn wood was brought and laid against it. Three maidens came, and it was lit and burnt as an offering to success.

SOF:12:2 We went Northwards and came to a strand, where many ships were drawn up and armed men such as we had not seen before were disputing among themselves with great noise.

SOF:12:3 We drew off, for they were foreign to us, but others came behind, and we were taken in among them and brought before Albanik, the Leader of Armed Men. They pushed around about us, and some cried out for blood. They wished to take our ships and possessions, but the leader said, "Leave the deed until the morning, for if blood flows now, it will not cease with the foreigners."

SOF:12:4 That night, the wife of Albanik spoke to him and said, "It would be a foolish thing and an evil deed to slay these strangers, for they have wisdom and are men of learning. Why destroy something you may use to good end?" The leader listened to her advice, for he knew there were many wounded men and none more skilled than we to attend them. Because she was carrying a child, our lives were spared and our goods restored to us.

SOF:12:5 The commander among the captains was a warrior who, while hunting, had slain his own father and so had to flee his own land. With him, he had taken the queen captured by sly and subtle means, but we feared him not, for Albanik looked upon us with favourable eyes.

SOF:12:6 Of the warriors who came with us there were a score of men from Ilopinos. They wore helmets of bronze with plumes of scarlet and purple. Their shields were of bronze burnished, so that they shone like the sun and were edged with a band of hardened metal. In length, they were two and a half cubits, and in width, one and a half cubits. They had spears of unknotted wood six cubits in length, with blades of hard metal set in sockets.

SOF:12:7 Their swords were of pure hard metal worked in a strange way, and in length. one and half cubits and in width, three fingers breadth. They were horn-handled and bound about with wire of copper and silver. Some among them were armed with war javelins and darts. They had a curious dart that turned over itself in flight and another that struck in from the side.

SOF:12:8 In battle, they stood there and three to withstand the rush of the enemy, but they were weak in attack, for they moved heavily. With them were slaves and six score attendants, who were plunderers of the battlefield, pillagers of the land, the cooks, the baggage keepers and the carriers of burdens. The warriors were the battle craftsmen.

SOF:12:9 In seven days, all the ships sailed together and in seven days came upon some land by the sea. It was a place of the dead, where all was desolation. In the centre of the land by the sea, there stood a temple which had fallen into itself, for there were no people to keep it. The leaders and the chief among them went up to the temple and made sacrifices to their gods, whose voices they wished to hear.

SOF:12:10 The daughter of Laben the armourer had hidden herself in the opening behind the flame and spoke to them in a strange tongue. They heard her voice and thought it came from a shadow god. She told them of the land of her mother, called Belharia, and bid them find their way there. She told them to take the Bethedan with them, for they brought good fortune and were beloved by the gods. The leaders went out from the temple believing they had been granted a vision.

SOF:12:11 We sailed with a large company towards the West and had nothing to fear, except the whirlpool, for the Red Men with us knew the way of the waters. For long days, we saw only the sea, and the landsighting birds all came back.

SOF:12:12 We went out through the mouth of the sea into the sea of the Great River. Past the lands of white copper to the Place of Painted Men, where we drew up the ships and staked them.

SOF:12:13 Among the fighting men were some from Sparsia whose leader was Korin, called the axeman, but whom we named 'the cunning one.' These went out into the forests to hunt, and the king of that place sent men to take them, but they refused to go and there was a loud dispute.

SOF:12:14 The bodyguard with the leader of the Painted Men were bowmen and one shot an arrow at Korin. He slewed aside behind his shield and the arrow turned into the throat of a Painted Man, who held a sword against him. This started a great fight between forest and sea, and though surrounded by many enemies, Korin fought through them. The battle was his because he went forward through the forest and attacked the houses of the Painted Men.

SOF:12:15 The ships were divided and those who wished to set up the eagle and serpent went to the Harbour of Giants in Belharia, The same giants are builders of great temples, and they are six cubits tall.

SOF:12:16 The ship with Korin stayed with us and he hunted them out of their caves and slew them all, save one giantess. She came to us, bound as a surety for the life of the wife of Albanik.

SOF:12:17 We came to a bay, on one side of which was a forest and on the other a plain where herds grazed. For the men of that place, it was the time of the feast of fires and they held games upon the shore and ran races in cleared land behind. At this time, they would not fight, so we met them in peace. They wore garments woven in two parts and belted with hide. They had caps of skin or leather, and the tunic, which hung about them was darkly coloured in blue, green and brown. They enclosed their legs and feet in dressed skins, bound in front with throngs. They had many ornaments of copper, but little gold or silver, though their armbands and brooches shone like silver. They had the art of making copper like silver or gold.

SOF:12:18 These people hold a great feast before the beginning of the heat, when their god Mago appears. Inside the god were the spirits of men, whom the god had eaten, and their voices could be heard calling for deliverance from darkness. Because of the feast, these people demanded the giantess, and she was given over to them for the days of feasting.

SOF:12:19 We did not know the ways of these people and when we saw that they wished us to drink blood, we drew apart from them. The headman sent a messenger to us, and Korin and the giantess wrestled together, but the giantess was the stronger, so Korin lured her towards the cliff edge. Korin taunted her and laughed at her clumsiness, and then at the break of the cliff, he tricked her, so that she rushed forward. As she passed beside him, he turned behind her and pushed, so that she fell over the cliff edge on to a large, black rock below. Her back was broken. The same black rock was later split and taken up to be worshipped.

SOF:12:20 In the place, to which we came, the deathless stars ride high. The adze rests on the morning, and the watchman at the gate of the sky sits at the eastern tiller in the evening. The falcon is rarely seen clearly. This is the Land of Dada.

SOF:12:21 We warned them, but they would not listen. They were fasting before the battle, the sacred fast before they ate the meat of the offerings. We buried salt beneath the floors of their houses, so that no man would live there again. When the horns sounded the alarm and danger threatened, these shrewd bargainers came running to us. Their faces were wet with the sweat of fear, and their lips trembled. When the danger was past they came out with chests puffed up and tongues bragging about their deeds. They were the first to push forward for a share in the plunder.

SOF:12:22 Korin left to seek them. He took two ships but did not return to his children. The leader may be carried away, but the lowliest of those who followed him has a will, which need never be broken. Now when men wish to say a thing is impossible they say, "Where is Korin?"

Chapter Thirteen – The Rolls of Record - 7

SOF:13:1 In the seven and twentieth year came Emos, who was a learned man, and with him came Zadok who was one of us. Mosu, son of Shonthel, came also, and others in four large ships. Keeta came in a ship apart.

SOF:13:2 They were welcomed, and Keeta set up a place of learning, and many came and sat before him. When Keeta died, those whom he had taught said, "Let us record the knowledge of our master, so that it may be added to the records and not lost."

SOF:13:3 We who are the pupils of Keeta and have been blessed by him and purified by water shall be one. From this day we will call ourselves by the name he gave us, which is 'Bartha Hedsha Hethed.' The meaning of the words is lost.

SOF:13:4 God and goodness are one and alike. God is not a person, but The Supreme Spirit. He made the Earth so that it brought forth man and woman, and they lived together in a far away land, where everything was pleasant, even the forests. Woman tempted man so that he ate something, which was part of God, and man was punished, for he is responsible for woman.

SOF:13:5 Children were born in their generations and multiplied, until Earth was filled. They built cities of stone and cut channels for water to flow away and made lakes. They were cunning workers in stone and in wood and in ivory. They made instruments from firestone and pottery in many colours. They raised up temples to the sunlight and worshipped inside many pillars, but within the temples were inner temples, where greater things were known.

SOF:13:6 In the Land of Copper, which was the Land of The Golden Light, one man in twelve was a priest. There were priestesses, who took care of them and watched over the sacred elements within the temples. The headdresses of the priests were red, and they wore feathers and cloaks of black. They had circlets of gold and beads of silver, and there was a spiral of blackstones at their waist.

SOF:13:7 There was war between those who lived within the city and those who lived beyond its limits. Those who lived within the city grew all kinds of things and clothed themselves with the labour of their hands. Those who lived outside the city were hairy hunters clad in the skin of wild animals.

SOF:13:8 Outside the grounds of the city, there was a holy mountain, and priests lived within it. The men of the city brought them herbs and fruit with bread and wine. The men who were not of the city brought them sheep and goats and beasts of the chase.

SOF:13:9 The men of the city loved wealth, like city dwellers, and were less generous than those who gained their food by strength and hunting. The men of the city held back portions of their dues and caused the priests to look upon them less kindly. When the great day of the sun came and the High Priest gave his blessing of fruitfulness, he withheld it from the city dwellers and gave it only to the hunters and herdsmen. That night, when those, who had received the blessings were rejoicing beside the mountain, the city dwellers fell upon them and slew many. This was the cause of a great war, in which many men died.

SOF:13:10 Men did to men what their natures inclined them to do, but they also ravaged women and children. The evil grew in greatness, until the land could no longer contain it and had to be purged clean. Therefore, the revenging dragon was called up out of the heavenly abyss, and it lashed the land with fire and thunder. The whole land was filled with its smoky breath and men choked to death.

SOF:13:11 The land was split apart between the city and the mountain, and the sea rolled in upon it, so that the city was destroyed. The valleys of the mountain were filled with dead men and animals and with trees.

SOF:13:12 The High Priest survived with seven others, who were priests. He brought these, together with one hundred and ten men and their wives and children, into Labeth, which is a land among high cliffs at the edge of the Wide Plain.

SOF:13:13 Here, the priests sought to preserve their wisdom and knowledge and pass it on to the children, but it became distorted and misunderstood. They did not understand the radiating power from the bodies of the dead, which could guide the living. Even we do not understand these things clearly.

SOF:13:14 The priests, who came from the Land of Copper, could make their soul depart from the body at their command and return as they willed. When ignorant men saw seemingly dead bodies return to life when the soul came back into them, they thought the same could happen to a dead body if kept long enough. Even this superstition stays with us.

SOF:13:15 Later, when they had left Labeth, men believed that if they kept a dead body so that it remained whole, the soul would not finally enter the Sphere of Accounting. Such was the knowledge of their wickedness and fear of their fate that they used every art to prevent the body falling apart and entering decay. They may have believed that, until the soul entered the sphere above Earth, it remained flexible and capable of acting to counter some of the ill-effects of a life of wickedness and ignorance.

SOF:13:16 Later still, the light of Truth dimmed until it could scarce be seen, but always there were the few within the many, and the many hid them. The light of the few was a precious thing, safeguarded with diligence and care. The people knew the many, but the few remained unknown, their treasure safe. Gods multiplied, but those who sought Truth among them could always find it if they were sincere and diligent seekers, It was then as it is now.

SOF:13:17 A nation was once made from the blood of kings, and it became great and good. The light of Truth was revealed to this nation and it rejoiced in the light, but in a few generations, it accepted the light as being something, to which it was entitled by heritage. So the nation became careless in the preservation of the light; it was kept in a poorly built and neglected shrine. The winds of adversity came, and the light was blown out.

SOF:13:18 Another nation was made from the blood of sturdy herdsmen, and the lamp of Truth was lit among them. They, too, rejoiced in the light for a few generations and cherished it in a house of gold, Then, a powerful king coveted the house of gold and came with many armed men and drove out the guardians, together with their light. The guardians built a house of reeds for the light, but because the house was so humble, they no longer bothered to guard it closely. Then some drunken men came by, staggering like ships with broken steering oars, and the house of reeds was knocked over. The light within burst into an all-consuming flame, and not only the house of reeds, but the house of gold was destroyed.

SOF:13:19 Still, another nation was made out of slaves, and they lit a lamp from the Eternal Flame, which belongs to all men. Because they had no veil over their light, they were blinded and thought it the only light. They became arrogant and called themselves 'The Chosen of God'. But it was they who made the choice, not He. Though their god was a god above Earth, and their god, he was not the God of Mankind, and though he serves The Supreme Spirit, he is not The Supreme Spirit.

SOF:13:20 So it is that the Children of Light understand that the majority of men who seek the light are like children playing about a brazier. As a man long-confined in darkness is blinded by the sunlight, so are most men blinded when brought into the presence of the Light of Truth, even though it be heavily veiled. Only gradually can men be brought out of darkness into light.

SOF:13:21 Yet, even the Children of Light have become divided among themselves and one institution became two. The institution of the East claims it is the true guardian of the written records, but now we have books written even before those copied by the scribes of Hoskiah. We are not the Children of the Lesser Light, and we know the mysteries of the Hidden Light. Only we in the cold north will survive, for did not Amos write. "Our destiny lies in a much bleaker land, where our seed will be planted in strange soil. It will lie within the bosom of an untamed land, until quickened to growth by the warmth of the desires of men."

SOF:13:22 Keeta taught that this means we should not seek to spread or reveal the light until our day of destiny, which must lay ahead. Therefore, those who say we must multiply our strength or be lost like a bead among the wheat harvest, are mistaken. They talk against our destiny, which is written and unalterable.

SOF:13:23 We know nothing of our first leader in Light, except that he was a priest warrior skilled with the spear, and he lived in times of war. His name is not recorded, for he said, "True Masters are to be known by their works and not by their names. They who seek to stand forth from other men and raise themselves up to increase their stature before the generations, seek vain glory." He said, "I am no more than the storehouse into which the harvest is gathered. The good grain within comes from many fields and is produced by the labours of many men. If I said all this is my own growing, I would lie. Therefore, so that men cannot attribute undeserved greatness to me, I make myself faceless, and men may see as they will."

SOF:13:24 In those days the Children of Light were sought out and persecuted, and no man knew another by his name, for the tools of the tormentors awaited them. Many were hung by the riverbank, feet uppermost, for the governors said, "These people read their books upside down." The women, they consigned to houses of pleasure, so that many died in their degradation.

SOF:13:25 We know that the first Leader of Light was among the highborn of Egypt and his name was struck on marble pillars. He was cast down because he carried the lamp of Truth, and his name was removed from the records of Egypt. He raised an army, but it was like a goat attacking a wild bull, and he was slain in the great marshlands lying near Ethiopia.

SOF:13:26 He wrote the book, which is known to all, and the Book of Rites and Ceremonies, which is known only to the elect. He did not write the three books in the Lion Urns, which we alone know, or the Book of The Secret Way. He may have written the Book of Instruction For The Children of The Written Word Within The Children of Light. The manner of keeping the book is taught from generation to generation. The books are our foundation, our shield and our sword. They are our promise and our hope, our guide and our defence.

SOF:13:27 It is said now, as in the days of our fathers and their fathers in the generations before them, that men steal our words and light their lamps from our flame. This may be so, but we have gathered seeds from the flowers of wisdom wherever they grew and planted them within our own garden. Shall we then deny to others what we ourselves have taken? Is it not written that no man can make Truth, but many can find it if they seek? Therefore, is not Truth the property of all men, even though most spurn it? For Truth is not a pleasant draught.

SOF:13:28 Nevertheless, it is true also that we may keep the Truth, as we find it, secured to ourselves. If a man seek for unwrought gold and find it, he has not made it, yet it is still his. Is it not also written, 'Gold is the treasure of a lifetime, but Truth is the treasure of eternity. Gold can nourish the body, but it may poison the soul.'

SOF:13:29 Which do men treasure most in this place, gold or wisdom? Is it not the earthly thing they can hold in their hands and not the treasure they can safeguard in their hearts? The things they hold in their hands and hearts are already being weighed on the Scales of Fate, and our destiny decreed accordingly.

SOF:13:30 Many in this place, who seek the light and have gone so far and no further, declare this is not what they sought and go back, discarding what they have. Yet if a man seek gold and find silver, does he throw it away? Better half a loaf than no loaf at all.

SOF:13:31 If gold were as plentiful as copper, it would be valued less than silver. Only the things hard to obtain have value, and what is more difficult to discover than Eternal Truth, which must be sought beyond the boundaries of Earth? Only the beginning of the long road towards it is here, and it is this beginning you must seek. Every journey has a beginning and an end, and you can make your way only in one direction. If you are dispirited, be comforted by the knowledge that you need only find the beginning of the road. Then, having found it, let every step you take be in the right direction. The journey is long and the road rough and stony, but do not turn back before you reach the first staging post; you will find new strength and encouragement there.

SOF:13:32 Our light was lit in the land of our beginnings. Many books were made and kept in four places, and we were in truth Children of The Written Word. There were scribes and readers, officials and guardians. There were servants and those, who served in the courtyards.

SOF:13:33 Strangers came into the land of our beginnings and brought practices which were different, but more acceptable. They promised an easier road; they displayed deceitful marvels, the usual baits thrown to the ignorant. Their hands were heavy against us, and what could we show except Truth arrayed in her earthly robes of simplicity? Even the princes turned against their own customs, and the twin priesthoods of the undergods became earthlywise and corrupt. Few were ready to undergo the perils of initiation; no more were prepared to accept the austere life prescribed. As spiritual barrenness spread, evil practices crept in to fill the places vacated by the Sacred Mysteries. The candidates accepted into the body of light became fewer and fewer.

SOF:13:34 As the name, The Children of Light, is written in the old characters, it may also be read as The Children of The Written Word, and this is a truth. We alone preserve our secrets in this manner. The Children of Light followed a destined course by abandoning their altars in the land of their beginnings, and went to dwell among strangers, where many ate at one table. We do not know what befell of their books, for those we have are rewritten. We know the Children of The Written Word went Northward after the scattering, but we do not know what were their journeyings.

SOF:13:35 We know about Lothan and Kabel Kai, designer of houses, who sailed around the edge of the Earth. With them was Raileb, the scribe, who knew hidden mysteries. They gathered the records, which were in Kindia, and carried them the long sea journey, believing the records safer among the barbarians than among those who sought to destroy them. If the records are destroyed by barbarians, it will be done in ignorance and not in the knowledge of wickedness. Many books were laid open to the eyes of ignorant men and destroyed.

SOF:13:36 They came to the Harbour of Sorrow, which lies by the Hazy Sea, away from the Land of Mists. There great trees grew, and smaller trees upon them, and moss hung from them like door curtains. It lay near the great shallow waters South of the Isle of Hawluge and North of the Sea Pass. Green pearls are found there.

SOF:13:37 Many died in the Harbour of Sorrow, for it was a place with a curse upon it, which caused an evil sickness. The Sons of Fire came with Hoskiah and saved them, and they came to this place and built a city. Labrun, the son of Koreb, was governor.

Chapter Fourteen – The Rolls of Record - 8

SOF:14:1 The sister of Kabel Kai was born in the House of Sothus, and her name was Amarahiti. There were four children, and one still remains among us. Amarahiti was said to be a lovely-faced woman.

SOF:14:2 In the days, when the city was being built, the barbarians came and went freely among us. Many came but stood off and watched from afar, for they did not understand our ways. Among those who came was Cluth, the son of Cladda and brother of Cladwigen, and he talked with Amarahiti in the days when she was still in her fathers household. In those days, she sat at the Place of the Talking Stone, which still stands in its place, for she was among those who sought to know the speech of the barbarians.

SOF:14:3 In the season of fruitfulness, the true wife of Cladda was overcome with a sickness, which no one among her own people could cure, not even the wise men or priests who were able enough in such things. Therefore, Cluth came to Ramana, the mother of Amarahiti, who was known afar for her skill with herbs. Amarahiti came with Cluth, to speak for him. When Ramana understood his needs, she and Amarahiti went with him, taking two armed men and men of the barbarians. The peace of Cladwigen went before them. They came to the place, where the true wife of Cladda lay, on the evening of the second day. The wise men and priests went among the people, muttering against the women, and dark looks were cast upon Ramana.

SOF:14:4 The mother of Amarahiti cleansed the sick woman with ashes and made a brew of herbs and bitter bark of the river ash. She sat by the true wife of Cladda, and in the morning, the sick body no longer burned; neither did it consume itself. When the priests of the barbarians heard about it, they declared it was not a thing of goodness, but something brought about by evil arts. They told people a devil was loosed among them, whose trailing vapours they saw going among the huts. When darkness came that night, there were loud cries among the barbarians, for many were seized with weakness and vomiting, but this was something brought about by the priests and not by the devil.

SOF:14:5 Among the barbarians, the priests were held in high regard, and so the true wife of Cladda sought to appease them. She called the highest of the priests to her and asked him what should be done to make the evil depart and leave the people in peace. The priest told her that if the two foreign women were sent away, their evil and the devil would depart with them. He asked her to let her own people treat her after their own manner. He told her that the things, which cured sickness in another race would not cure sickness in theirs. The true wife of Cladda, seeking to avoid strife and being already half cured, said it would be done as he wished.

SOF:14:6 So Amarahiti and her mother departed, together with their servants and the armed men who accompanied them. On the night after they left, the true wife of Cladda died, with vomit stopping in her throat. Then the priests made their voices heard among the barbarians and told them to behold the work of the devil, which remained among them. They said it had not departed, nor would it leave until it was appeased. They spoke in such a manner that men of the barbarians set out in haste and came upon the women and Cluth, who with armed men were preparing to leave their camping place. When Cluth heard the words of the priests spoken by those who came, he was dismayed and knew not what to do. There was a man among those who came, who spoke many words to Cluth, so that he was stirred up against our women. For Cluth was a barbarian, and their ways were his ways. (Here. some three hundred and fifty words are missing).

SOF:14:7 It resumes: Amarahiti turned her face towards Cluth and told him that by strength alone, he had brought her to this distant place and its stronghold. That through his stubbornness, her people had died, and her mother had been wounded. She said that though the priests called for the sacrifice of her modesty, after the customs of his people, she was already made sacred to a man of her own and would rather die than be degraded. She asked him what would be his pleasure, and would it not be even less than that given by a woman with a price, who would at any rate be willing to please. What a small pleasure that is, set against the pleasure women can really give. (Indistinct, then several lines missing). Cluth stood apart with his arms (Part missing). The priests prepared the cage, and Amarahiti was fetched (some words missing) stood by with dignified modesty. Her mother sat apart before the image (large part lost here).

SOF:14:8 It begins again: Away Cluth lay against the bole of the tree, and when they fetched her to him he raised himself up. He hardly stood, for he was bloodied and weak. Amarahiti told him that never had woman beheld a braver man, though a foolish one. Down at the water's edge lay Kabel Kai, and the men who had cut the lashings of the structure laved his wounds.

SOF:14:9 The old man, who had read the omens and divided the people, bade those nearby to carry Cluth to the riverbank. When they came nearby, Kabel Kai had disappeared into the thickets of the forest. The men of Kelkilith remained on the other side.

SOF:14:10 They left the destroyed place and the buried dead behind them, and Amarahiti stayed in the keeping of the priests of Cladwigen. In this manner they came to the place where Cladwigen and his warriors were assembled to meet the enemy. They were received joyfully, but there was sorrow for Kabel Kai whose cunning had carried the day. They feared for him, thinking he had been taken by the Wictas.

SOF:14:11 Cluth was slain in the battle with the Wictas and the Men of Broad Knives at the crossing of the river now called by the barbarians Cluthradrodwin.

SOF:14:12 Kabel Kai was not taken, though he was sorely wounded. His face was torn from the blows of the spiked club, so that flesh hung loosely down. He was twisted, for his shoulder was broken when the logs fell upon him. So he remained hidden within the forest, the companion of beasts, for his appearance caused men to shudder,

SOF:14:13 When the leaves left the trees in the fall of the year, he came close in to the city, near the boundary, where Amarahiti was wont to sit, by the side of the flowing stream. In the winter, he was clothed with skins and moved hardly.

SOF:14:14 At the time of the midwinter feast of the barbarians, the people of the city met them on common ground beyond the city and before the forest. Fires were lit, and there was feasting and revelry. Gifts were exchanged between the people of the city and the barbarians. There was an image (part missing).

SOF:14:15 Amarahiti was sorrowful because of this and withdrew into some bushes close by the stream. With her were the two hounds. The hounds smelled out Kabel Kai, for he had come close, being drawn by the warmth and cheerfulness at the place of feasting. They leaped upon him gladly, for they knew him. Kabel Kai sought to escape back into the forest, but Amarahiti caught him by the hand. She looked at him and fell on his neck with tears. She covered him with her cloak of coney fur, and when her two attendants came, they carried him to a sheltered place close by the stream. (Some five paragraphs are missing).

SOF:14:16 It goes on: The most skilful with herbs among them. In the spring of the year, they returned as husband and wife and were welcomed with a great feast. They were remained within the house of Kabel Kai.

SOF:14:17 The fortress of Cluth was built up again by Kabel Kai, according to his promise, and the sons of Cluth live there in these days. It stands on high ground rising out of the waters, surrounded by a high wall of logs.

SOF:14:18 The city was built and finished with a wall, which was two walls of wood with soil between. Men came in ships, with cloth and pottery, with things of metal and shells and beads. The barbarians gave much for cloth dyed scarlet, for their tree blue is not fast in cloth. Scarlet is made nowhere except in the land of The Sons of Fire, where a white fish turns scarlet under the warmth of the sun. Men say that those, who bring the scarlet cloth declare it to have been found in this manner: A man was out hunting with his dog, and while they walked along the strand, the dog caught a fish which it carried to its master in its mouth. The man saw a scarlet stain on the dog's mouth and wiped it away with a piece of linen. When the colour could not be withdrawn from the cloth, it was taken to a dyer who sought out the thing that had made it.

SOF:14:19 The temple was built within the city and raised up on logs. Beside it was the Place of Instruction, and just before it was the Place of Exchanging. It stands today as a sanctuary and a centre for those who seek the light. In its keeping are the records of the Children of Light, who are the Children of the Written Word.

SOF:14:20 But all is not well with the heart and spirit of the city, which is the people. A city lives not by the wood and stones, with which it is built. Therefore, since the coming of Samon of the Barhedhoy and those who follow Ameth, we who are the heart of the Children of Light prepare our departure. (Some words missing). By the waters of Glaith not far distan,t where we may dwell by ourselves.

SOF:14:21 The first books, we leave in the temple with those who guard them, but we have made other books which will go with us, In another place, we will make them incorruptible. (piece missing). This we leave with you, as we also take it with us, so that it may not be lost. The names are written and the seals placed.

Chapter Fifteen – The Book of Kadmis

SOF:15:1 By command of our master Lodas, son of Kadmis and Karla, by the hand of Orailuga, the writer born of the Hortheni. Set down in the seven and eightieth year of the temple, which is the fourth year in the cycle of Balgren and the ninth year of our oath.

SOF:15:2 As man moves in air, so does God move in goodness. As God is incomprehensible to man, as mortal man but comprehensible to him as man in spirit, so is God not a Being with the mere attributes of men but The Supreme Spirit among spirits. As man stands at the apex of material creation, so is The Supreme Spirit the Ultimate Unity above the spiritual sphere.

SOF:15:3 From this day forward we shall be known as the Craftsmen of The Supreme Spirit, and this place, upon the waters of Glaith, which we call the Valley of Reeds, known to those about us as Carsteflan, shall be called the Smithy of The Supreme Spirit.

SOF:15:4 The boundaries of the land pledged solely unto us are the waters below, upward of the markpost three thousand and two score set paces. Downward of the markpost one thousand and twelve set paces. In the water and its divisions, you may fish and gather reeds and cut water herbage over to its further bank.

SOF:15:5 Landward of the markpost, at four thousand four score and ten paces, is the stone placed by Calraneh, set upright, and there is the boundary to the East Outward from this; two thousand and five hundred set paces on each side is placed a markstone set that all may recognise it. From these stones to the markposts on the waters edge are the boundaries North and South.

SOF:15:6 Within the boundaries, the land shall be clear of trees and shall be pastured and sown, and therein, we shall have our habitations. In the forest about us may be gathered wood, and swine may be fed there, and we may hunt.

SOF:15:7 The House of Men shall remain as before, but no longer shall we be divided into parts. Men shall be made men as they have been in the past. If any man be in years and without wife and children, or having a son who is a man placed in his stead, he may enter wholly into the House of Men.

SOF:15:8 No man shall absent himself from the House of Men at his times, unless by dispensation of the Houseruler, or if it be impossible for him to be there. But all time not served shall be served doubly later, unless, with the dispensation of the Houseruler, it is waived.

SOF:15:9 The Ruler outside the House of Men shall be a man chosen by the council, which shall be four men chosen in meeting together at noon, one day before midwinter's eve. The Ruler and the council shall govern and judge in all things among us, but they shall not alter these decrees, which shall stand among us as a rock. We will govern our lives by them and abide by them and pass them on to those who follow. These, together with the words of the Holy Writ, are the candle stick and container for the mortal Light of Truth, which is among us. They shall be honoured by all who walk in that light, now and henceforth.

SOF:15:10 They shall be written on copper made incorruptible and placed within the sacred urns, together with the records. Yet, they shall remain with us and be among us written on tablets of wood.

SOF:15:11 We shall keep the decrees of Hoskiah and abide by them and their punishments. Though the punishments may be changed by the council, so that men are lashed with the whip and the women with leathern throngs or wands of wood. We now have with us the decrees of Amos, and they alone shall stand before those of Hoskiah. All other laws shall stand according to the order of their numbering. Where laws are at variance, one shall not be set against another, but that, which is latest shall stand highest and the others be subordinate.

SOF:15:12 The decrees of the Old Law, which is not written, shall be kept only if their keeping be the custom in judgement. Let no man build a habitation of brick or stone upon these lands, for this is an unlawful thing unto the people within whom we dwell.

SOF:15:13 If any decree be set against another, the last written decree shall prevail, except between the decrees of Amos and Hoskiah. Let no man change to his benefit the brandmark upon the beast of another, for this is an unlawful thing. If done, the wrong shall be adjusted by restoring double the value and if done again, by restoring treble,

SOF:15:14 Let no man among us worship otherwise than in the manner of our brotherhood. To the rituals, nothing shall be added, and nothing taken away. Our beliefs shall be supported manfully, without shame and with all our strength. You shall not be faint-hearted when danger threatens, nor indifferent when hard-pressed. No man among us shall be voiceless when our beliefs are ridiculed, or remain passive before their enemies. If anyone become a coward or fail in this, he shall not be numbered among us.

SOF:15:15 The works of men are imperfect, and no man has ever seen the Light of Truth in absolute purity. Therefore, though two things within the body of our written records may appear contradictory, if not capable of reconciliation through greater understanding, the thing written later, unless a manifest error, shall be more acceptable. Be men of good faith, goodwill and common sense. Nothing passing through the hands of many men escapes contamination. Only sincerity and diligence will maintain its purity. Nevertheless, having established something, uphold it steadfastly. In this sphere of falsity, cling to every truth, as a man swept out to sea by the river torrents clings to a log.

SOF:15:16 All men held captive for anything they may have done, and not yet brought before the council or punished, shall be kept encaged at the waters edge. A man may be encaged as a punishment and the cage either covered or uncovered. If a man must die he may die either in clean or unclean waters, as is done by the people who surround us. No man shall draw blood to slay in judgement.

SOF:15:17 A man shall take his brother's wife into his household if his brother die and leave her unprotected. The unprotected of any man's bloodkin or lawkin shall become his responsibility. Inasmuch as the Lord of Heaven mated with the Queen of Heaven, brother and sister are not forbidden to each other under the Old Law.

SOF:15:18 A man shall not gaze upon the nakedness of any of his bloodkin or lawkin in lust, and no woman shall expose her nakedness to any man not her husband. Punishments may be executed either by burning or the cage.

SOF:15:19 Every man shall learn to fight and defend himself with the axe, the bow, the spear, the sword, the javelin or the sling, and all weapons of the hand shall be sharpened.

SOF:15:20 Every man among us shall know the words of the Holy Writ by understanding of the writings or by memory. They shall be cut into his heart, as they are on copper and wood.

SOF:15:21 The records shall now be written in the Sacred Characters and not in letters of the Sons of Fire. line for line, the letters of the People of the Five Red Gods shall be used, the letters from the skysigns seen by the Master of Writing.

SOF:15:22 (Many following chapters are lost.)

Chapter Sixteen – The Reconstruction by Kadairath

SOF:16:1 The Master was seated at his table, and, about him in a half-circle, were those he instructed, and he taught them in this manner:

SOF:16:2 "My brothers, these are the ordinances of living and the laws, which are the ordinances of men. No law, whether it be of The Supreme Spirit or of man, wholly produces happiness and causes no sorrow. So, to be worthy and good, an ordinance or law must produce more contentment and happiness than it prevents. It must also prevent more sorrow and confusion than it produces, or it would be a work of wickedness and a memorial to the follies of men."

SOF:16:3 "Pleasure never comes unadulterated, and no form of goodness, which man seeks to promote, is unencumbered with restriction. Nonetheless, there is no form of goodness, which is unproductive of happiness in the hands of those governed with wisdom. Joy and sorrow, pain and pleasure, success and failure are all moulding processes operating on the spirits and natures of men. Neither of the opposites is of less importance than the other."

SOF:16:4 These were the things taught:

SOF:16:5 "The nature of every person is different, and all tend to drift towards the circles, which accord with their natures. Therefore, we set a standard, which not all will find acceptable, so that only those whose natures demand the best find our company congenial."

SOF:16:6 "Unless the soul of each man and woman is developed and disciplined by the restraints of spiritual and material decrees, it cannot rise above its earthly elements. As the earthly body must be kept fit by discipline and self-control, and become gross and weak through overindulgence or indifference, so is the spirit controlling the body required to exercise restraint."

SOF:16:7 "Every law, whether arising in the sphere of the spirit or the sphere of matter, suppresses something arising out of the nature of man and therefore calls for the exercise of restraint and forbearance. Yet is it not true that, though every just law restrains something within men and women, it also restricts evil and things, which are not good? The less a law imposes upon men and women and the more it imposes upon the things detrimental to their welfare, the better the law. All laws are paid for out of the treasury of freedom; the lower the cost the better the law."

SOF:16:8 "The laws of earthly rulers are kept by force of arms, but the keeping of the higher spiritual laws can only be ensured through enlightenment and wisdom. The causes of misjudgements, sorrow and remorse stem more frequently from breaches in spiritual laws than in earthly ones."

SOF:16:9 "Moral laws and restraints are essential to the progress and welfare of mankind. When passions are unrestricted and weaknesses unfenced by moral laws, various forms of vice and perversions become accepted and sap the stamina of nations. When the abnormal is given free access to intrude upon the normal, the nation degenerates, the race is contaminated, and mankind suffers a reverse. The Great Law places an obligation upon mankind to improve itself. Every man and woman must safeguard their heritage and raise themselves above earthly sordidness. This is one of the reasons for living. The struggle of life is with man; the struggle of man is with himself."

SOF:16:10 "Wise leaders in every land and age have made laws restraining the weak and abnormal from satisfying their carnal appetites and immoral urges. If their own uncontrolled desires were allowed freedom to dictate their actions, then not only would the weak and abnormal destroy themselves, but they would be like a cancer in the living body of mankind."

SOF:16:11 The Sacred Books tell us that the nature of man contains a sense of shame. This is so, and it is there that he may also know the meaning of decency and be proud of himself as a man. It is there to make a better state known to him, a state of spiritual cleanliness and purity."

SOF:16:12 "Such knowledge does not come naturally to man, any more than good pastures come naturally to the husbandman. The city over the hill was founded in goodness, and its founders were not men, who found pleasure in wickedness. Nonetheless, as the years passed, it became apparent that all was not well within its walls. Now, because of the inclination of its inhabitants, the city's days are numbered."

SOF:16:13 "Men come across the sea in ships from the South, bringing things much sought after by the people who surround us, who go into the city to exchange the things they have caught or grown, or which have been dug out of the ground. Things are exchanged in the marketplace of the city, but they are for the enjoyment of the body, not the satisfaction of the soul."

SOF:16:14 "Nonetheless, men will always be driven by their very natures to seek for and obtain things, which do not satisfy any earthly appetite. Such things are those which delight the hearts of men by their beauty or bring inward joy and contentment. Also things, which bring pleasure to loved ones and things, which inspire men to noble deeds. With all the earthliness of man, the things most sought and desired are those, which stir the forces within the soul and not the forces within the body. When it is otherwise, mankind will slip backwards towards the beasts."

SOF:16:15 This is rewritten in our tongue, through a rethinking of the text by Anewidowl.

Chapter Seventeen – Part of a Marriage Pledge

SOF:17:1 My name is Farsis, from the house of Golaith, and I am without wife. These are my pledges to Awerit of Glendargi:

SOF:17:2 "Here, in the light of day, before The Supreme Spirit and before all men, in the sight of my father Bealin and your mother Goronway, I establish you as my wife."

SOF:17:3 "I shall not fail to consult you before I take another, wife and you will never be other than headwife. You will never lack for food and clothing, though the food may be uncooked and the cloth unwoven. A roof shall always cover your head, and a weapon be ever ready for your protection. I will always be considerate of your wants and always careful in things relating to your welfare. Whatever good fortune comes, it will be shared with you and our children."

SOF:17:4 "I will protect you through every year of my life and shelter you from every calamity to the best of my ability. An insult to you shall be an insult to me and every man of my blood. As from this day, my house is your house. What your father and your father's house were to you before, now am I and my house."

SOF:17:5 "Should greater duties call me from your side, I will take every precaution for your safety and welfare. Should I leave you, through any change of heart or darkening of thoughts, or should I slight the pledge given here and take to myself another woman in your stead, then, unless you have brought shame on me and my house by committing the great wickedness of women, I shall pay to your father's house twice the bridal price. I shall also bestow upon you a half share of our property and possessions joined together since marriage. Each of our children shall be given its proper portion of all my property and possessions, and it shall be established in the hands of the king's servants."

SOF:17:6 "Whatever comes to you as bridal gifts or is brought with you as your own shall be yours. I shall always safeguard and defend it. I will never take it to myself, so that you are deprived of it, unless for the one wrong which defiles my house and mocks my name. Whatever your father gives shall be ours, after the custom of the great laws."

SOF:17:7 "Your infirmities are accepted, to be shared with you, and the children you bear shall always be mine. No man shall ever mock you or abuse you without my hand being against him. No man shall ever wrongfully lay hands upon you, for you are mine, now and for always."

SOF:17:8 "I will not neglect the upbringing of our children, but they shall be raised according to my own light. You may follow your own creed, even as I follow mine, each being tolerant towards the other."

SOF:17:9 Those are my pledges, my hand and my token.

Chapter Eighteen – The Masiba Amendments

SOF:18:1 These are the lawful changes witnessed before Masiba:

SOF:18:2 "No man or woman shall own a slave, and no maiden or woman shall enter the household of another except as a wife or maidservant. To possess a concubine is no longer lawful. A maidservant shall be under the protection of the master of the household, wherein she serves, and he shall render her up in due time. If he lay hands on her in anger, he shall make due payment for it, and if he seduce her, he shall forfeit to her household a third part of his possessions and may be otherwise dealt with lawfully."

SOF:18:3 "If anyone strike a half-wit or injure one in any way he shall be severely dealt with lawfully. Courtfathers shall be appointed, who will be protectors of widows, orphans, half-wits, the afflicted by fate and those assigned to them. The Courtfathers may be responsible themselves, or they may appoint guardians. The property and possessions of any person may be placed in their care. If the Courtfathers act without good faith, deceitfully or carelessly in their trust, they shall make restitution without stint and be punished otherwise."

SOF:18:4 "If two men fight without weapons, using their hands, without wood or stone except that they may use staves or sticks, and one be injured so that he keep to his bed upward of three days, the other shall pay for his loss of time and full healing. If any man gain deceitfully by keeping to his bed declaring himself to be hurt sorely, he shall not keep his gains and shall be punished otherwise. If a man fight with wood and stone in his hands, or unlawfully with weapons, he shall be punished severely. If an armed man attack another who is unarmed, he shall pay heavy compensation and be punished severely."

SOF:18:5 "If, when men fight, a woman with child is hurt so that she suffer, or if at any time a man cause injury to a woman with child so that either die, he shall pay with his own life. If it can be doubted whether a man caused an unborn child to be stillborn, he shall not die, but can be made to pay compensation to the husband of the woman,"

SOF:18:6 "After her punishment, the life of an adulteress shall be in the hands of her husband. If he redeem her, he may deal with her as he wish. If he redeem her, but do not wish to deal with her, she shall still be denied the status of wife."

SOF:18:7 "If a woman use a substance so that she may not conceive, her husband may punish her by whipping or beating, providing he does not draw blood or maim."

SOF:18:8 "If a woman make a substance which prevents conception, or give or convey this substance to a woman, she shall be whipped with wands, as before. From this time, the whipping shall be done on three days following each other, and she can be made to pay compensation. If a man make, give or convey this substance, he shall be severely dealt with."

SOF:18:9 "If a woman cause her unborn child to be stillborn, she shall be secluded in a place of confinement for a month and whipped with ten strokes of the wand every third day. If anyone supply a potion to cause an unborn child to die, they shall be punished. If a woman, she shall suffer double the punishment of a mother, who causes her child to be stillborn, and can be made to pay compensation. If a man, he shall be much more severely dealt with."

SOF:18:10 "If anyone poison an animal belonging to another, that person shall pay compensation to no less than three times the value."

SOF:18:11 "The flesh of horse, squirrel and rat shall not be eaten. The badger is a creature sacred to our fathers because it was their salvation, and it shall not be slain."

SOF:18:12 "When a child stands on the threshold of manhood, and his manly organs become active, he shall be made a man after the old custom. He shall be handed over the threshold stone and welcomed as in times past, but this shall be the new declaration: "I know without doubt what I am. I am the seed of divinity implanted within a body of flesh. I belong with those who walk the Great Path of the True Way, and my place is beside them. I am a man knowing manly ways, and I will do what is required of me as a man.

SOF:18:13 My duty is to always protect those who walk with me and never deny my beliefs. I shall be steadfast even under persecution. The tormentors' instruments will not open my mouth. I undertake to bring at least one convert into the light.

SOF:18:14 My duty is to take a wife and beget children, who will be raised in the light of the Great Path of the True Way. My duty is to provide for them in every way within my power and to instruct them in the paths of wisdom.

SOF:18:15 My duty is to learn a skilled craft. I will be kind to animals, to vegetation and to the soil.

SOF:18:16 I will not wilfully harm a wild creature or a tree. My duty is to oppose all forms of disorder and lawlessness. It is to learn the purpose of life and to try to understand the design of The Supreme Spirit, Who laid all things out in orderliness. I know I must always keep my thoughts clean, my words true and good and my deeds manly.

SOF:18:17 I know there is a path of evil. It is the way of weakness and cowardice, which leads to self-destruction. I will fight all forms of wickedness and evil, wherever I find them, and I know I cannot go manfully through life without opposition and struggle.

SOF:18:18 I know that all men are born mortal and all must die in body, but I believe I am a soul with the potentiality of everlasting life. If, during the trials of life, I am assailed by doubt, I will not remain passive before it.

SOF:18:19 I promise to obey the code of manliness and to follow the paths of wisdom. My tongue will ever speak true and my hand do good. I know that just to do good is not sufficient, but I must attack evil. My duty is to oppose wicked men and their ways, and I will abide in peace with my brothers.

SOF:18:20 My duty is to learn and to understand the teachings of the Holy Writ, so that I may direct my children by its light. I will uphold and support the Brotherhood all the days of my life and expound its teachings to others. I acknowledge that only by example can I be a true and worthy exponent.

SOF:18:21 I will never oppress any man for his belief, unless he first attack mine. Even then, I will bear him with tolerance, until his oppression threatens to overwhelm me. I will never agree to the conversion of men by force, even for their own good, for this is an evil thing. My only arguments shall be example and common sense.

SOF:18:22 The faith I hold shall not be something imprisoned within my thoughts, but something lived and expressed in deeds. I give thanks for the knowledge that I am a living soul, but I know full well the grave responsibility I bear towards my future being. I will not be a disgrace to Earth when I pass to the greater realm beyond.

SOF:18:23 When I become a father of children, I shall accept responsibility for their wrongdoing, even as credit is claimed for their goodness. I shall not seek to blame others for my own failures. I shall be ever mindful of the good things of life and grateful for them. I shall suffer adversity and affliction with fortitude, rising above them like a man and not cringing before them like a dog under the stick of his master. Doubts, fears, unnatural desires and unmanly urges may lurk along my path, like forest demons, which waylay those who travel, but I shall overcome them.

SOF:18:24 I will not hide my contempt for the workers of wickedness and servants of evil, and though they may be in the seats of the mighty, I will accord them no respect. I will never commend that which is wicked.

SOF:18:25 I recognise that my soul and body compete for the satisfaction of their separate desires. I know that each day, the body dies a little, that every day, it draws nearer to the dark shore. Therefore, I will follow the precepts of prudence, and each and every day will be a step forward in the awakening of my soul. I shall not punish my trueself for the sake of satisfying a decaying body.

SOF:18:26 I will live in the light as revealed in the Holy Writ, the Written Light as revealed to the Brothers of the Book. I will live as a man, acknowledging my duties and obligations as a man, and I will die as a man."

Chapter Nineteen – Letter of Mata - A Son of Agner

SOF:19:1 The barbarian asks, "Who and What is The Supreme Spirit?" Say unto him, "Conceive it as a Being even above your greatest god. If it helps in your understanding, see The Supreme Spirit as a God reflecting His image as yourself. It is He, who fills Heaven and Earth with His might, and His powers are displayed in the elemental forces. He is now as in the beginning and will be no different after the end. He formed men by building an earthly structure around a heavenly seed, and into this, he infused the vapours of life. He maintains the order of the Heavens and stabilises the land in the waters. His breath is the breath of life, and He causes water to fall and greenery to live." Say to the barbarian, "Look about you, and see God reflected as in a mirror. No mortal man has ever looked upon Him directly, but His reflection may be seen with immunity."

SOF:19:2 The barbarian seeks a god he can see, but try and make him understand this is impossible, because of God's very greatness and the littleness of man. Take the barbarian out next time the sun shines at its strength, and ask him to gaze upon it. He will be forced to admit that it is beyond his powers to do so. Then say unto him, "See, it is beyond your power to look upon even the shield, behind which Haula hides himself because of his brightness. Yet, even this great god is no more than a faint, far off reflection embodying the ray carrying power from The Supreme Spirit. How then could you hope to look upon the source of power, itself?"

SOF:19:3 The barbarians are still children, and these things do not easily come within their understanding. Because of this, it may be best if they were taught by simple tales, like children, and so brought into the light gradually. A belief in The Supreme Spirit is of no great importance. An inquiry into His nature by the ignorant is purposeless foolishness. It is of much more importance to men that they believe in their own souls. Belief in a god of any sort without belief in the immortality of man and his godlikeness serves no end. If a god existed without man deriving any benefit from his existence, it would be better for man to ignore him. This, however, is not the case. Man seeks unity and communion with The Supreme Spirit only for his own benefit. Man has a destiny founded in something greater than himself, and hence his need for that something.

SOF:19:4 The existence of a Supreme Being is not just something to accept, believe in and ignore. A belief, faith alone, cannot be ends in themselves, for nothing exists without purpose. Simple belief in a Supreme Being is not enough; we must know the purpose or intention of the Being. If we believe this Supreme Being created us, however this was brought about, we must seek to discover the purpose behind our creation. If we were created to serve some purpose, to do something we were intended to do, we must do it or earn our Creator's displeasure. Does the potter keep the pot useless for its purpose, or the smith keep unwrought metal? Only things, which serve the purpose, for which they were intended are kept and cherished.

SOF:19:5 Therefore, we who are brothers, were taught not only to believe in a Supreme Being, but also in our similarity to Him. The Supreme Spirit is not a stranger beyond our ken; the powers of The Supreme Spirit infuse every fibre of our bodies.

SOF:19:6 If we have difficulties among the barbarians, the difficulties here are no less. The Truth we have seems not only unpalatable, but also indigestible. Men seek tastier food, even though it is less sustaining, and few replace the brothers who depart. Would we serve better if we presented Truth as a draught diluted with water and honey?

SOF:19:7 The threat of the barbarian king is something, upon which you shall be counselled. If you are threatened with the alternatives of death or transgressing our laws, you may transgress them within reason and the bounds of conscience. If, however, you are required to deny all that you hold to be good and true, to betray all that we hold sacred, then you must accept death for the sake of your soul. You will be informed about these things by Kuin of Abalon, who comes later, so only the things you enquire about are answered.

SOF:19:8 For the sake of the barbarians, it is perhaps best to call The Supreme Spirit, 'God, The God without a Name.' This will solve some difficulties, and if the barbarians think themselves superior because they contain Him within a name, let it be so and hold yourself in peace.

SOF:19:9 Say to the barbarians, "As the soul of man fills his body, so does God fill His domain. As the soul surrounds and contains the body, so is it with God and his creation. As the soul sees but cannot be seen, so does God see without being seen. As the soul feels, so does God. As the soul oversees the nourishment of the body, so does God revitalise the whole of his habitation. As the soul occupies an unfindable place within the body of man, so is the residence of God unfathomable. No man can know the seat of the soul, and no man can know the seat of God."

SOF:19:10 The barbarians make images of God to make Him more understandable. Are we much better, who make images of Him in our likeness within our thoughts? Not perhaps because we believe him so, but to make Him more understandable.

SOF:19:11 As man's understanding of God increases, so does God recede; so that though through the ages man comes to understand God better, He ever keeps the same distance away. We who dwell in the light of The Supreme Spirit have come closer to understanding, not because we are better men but because we have devoted our lives to the search. If any man seek carefully and diligently enough, he must find whatever it is he seeks.

SOF:19:12 The rest of this letter is missing, but on a small recovered scrap dealing with buildings, it refers to Galheda. Elsewhere, it is stated that Galheda rewrote it.

Chapter Twenty – The Teachings of Sadek

SOF:20:1 All men within the Brotherhood are to be taught to live by these ordinances, which provide for the discipline of the spirit:

SOF:20:2 Men shall be made to abstain from all manner of wickedness and hold fast to all that is good. They shall become speakers of Truth and followers of uprightness, and justice shall be upheld in their hands. The virtues are staffs, which will aid man in his long journey through life to the gate of his soul's unfolding.

SOF:20:3 There are guides upon the path, guideposts and places of rest and shelter for the weary. There is provender to be found by the wayside, and there are many things to be discovered along the trackways. (About two paragraphs missing)

SOF:20:4 The Master shall admit into the Brotherhood all who have, by diligent study and rigid self-rule, established themselves. They shall become one with those who climb the steps, and find their appointed place.

SOF:20:5 The Master shall instruct them in the School of Light and life, revealing unto them all the secrets of their nature and the manner of the soul's release. There shall be no unnecessary chastisements here and no particular rewards. Austerity for its own sake shall not be practised.

SOF:20:6 Every man who comes under the Master's hand, led forth by his nominator into the presence of the acceptors, shall bring with him all his skill, knowledge and possessions. He shall have been properly observed, judged and questioned before coming before the acceptors and shall not do so until he has been here for one year.

SOF:20:7 The next symbols shown are those representing the Design and The Law, these are the great unchanging things, lasting forever; they were the same in the time of our first forefather, as they will be in the time of our last descendant. (Much missing.)

SOF:20:8 No man shall remain within the Brotherhood who does not live by these our ordinances. The man who walks in filth befouls not only his own floor, but also the thresholds of his neighbours. Unless a man walk in cleanliness of body and purity of mind, he shall not be counted among us, and no one shall call him brother.

SOF:20:9 The soul must be wrought with the hard smiting blows of adversity and sorrow. It must be gently moulded by the waters of humility and charity; it must be chased by understanding and patience. These are things, which form a shape of harmonious beauty. But other things shape it in ugliness, these are: falsehood and greed, deceit and malice, cruelty and haughtiness, together with other evil qualities.

SOF:20:10 The just reward of those who follow the path of ease and indolence is condemnation in the recesses of disgrace and shame. There will be sorrowful groans and tear-shedding in the misery of soul loneliness.

SOF:20:11 These our ordinances are not made to provide for the comfort and ease of man, not even for his bodily welfare, but for the benefit of his eternal soul. Here his soul is to be purged and quickened to life by the strong waters of wisdom infused with the greatest amount of Truth he can tolerate. Only by himself submitting his soul to our discipline can any man acquire benefit from our mode of life.

SOF:20:12 Man was raised out of the womb of Earth to rule its surface, but here, the existing powers gather into two camps of everlasting hostility. Life opposes death; the champions of light challenge the champions of darkness. Truth confronts falsehood. There is a leader of light and a leader of darkness, a commander of life and a commander of death. The legions of wickedness oppose the legions of the upright.

SOF:20:13 At birth, all are cast out upon the battlefield of life and join the legions arrayed on one side or the other. According to his rank in the legion of Truth, so does a man fight against falsehood. By his standing in the eyes of the commander of light, so is a man placed in opposition to his adversary in the legion of darkness.

SOF:20:14 The wicked will be delivered to the sharp edge of the sword, but the good will be remembered. So it was in the first days, when our ancestors left Kaburi and followed the Master who guided them across the seas. They came over the pathless waters, forsaking soft living and delusions. which amused the eye.

SOF:20:15 The wicked are not only those who knowingly do wrong. An evil man is one, who seeks to justify the wickedness and weaknesses of others. The fires kindled against them became a raging flame, in which their legions were swallowed up.

SOF:20:16 Now that you are invested with new life, open your eyes, and behold the works of The Supreme Spirit with understanding. Always follow the path you have been shown, so that your steps lead you towards perfection.

SOF:20:17 Never incline towards degrading thoughts or look into the eyes of lust, for these things have led great men astray and brought down mighty ones. Be clean in all ways. Never profane the temple of man by lying with a woman whose flow is upon her. Be clean within and without, in body, thought, word and deed.

SOF:20:18 Such things were done by those, from whom we were divided. They lit their temple lamps in vain, and the smoke from their dark altars was blown aside. You shall not be as those who walk in darkness. Though we are oppressed on every side, this is the time of travail heralding the birth of the Great Master. You are not like those, who shall be cut off from the tree of life, to fall to the ground and return to nothingness. You shall always attend to the welfare of your brother and not deceive your neighbour.

SOF:20:19 You are to live in dedicated communities, marrying and begetting children. Your sons will grow up like strong oak trees, and your daughters modest like the violet. Your sons are to wear swords, and your daughters a headdress with a veil which may be drawn across the face.

SOF:20:20 So, too, shall it he with those, who are counted with us but are faint-hearted in the performance of their obligations. They are men who melt away in the furnace. Here, we do not practise discipline and austerity for the futile mortification of the flesh. We do these things for the sake of our souls, even as a warrior exercises to keep his muscles supple for the fray and so preserve his life.

SOF:20:21 Ninety-two generations have to be born. Then, gods and men intermingled will do battle, and there will be great carnage on that catastrophic day, when war is waged in the red-hued darkness amid mighty blast. That is the time, of which it is written: 'fire shall leap forth from the heart of a stone.'

SOF:20:22 These things have been written about, so we concern ourselves only with the ordinances governing the Brotherhood. This is the place to which you belong, and if you leave unsecured, it will be upon your own head.

SOF:20:23 Those who declare that beyond the gate of death there is a place of torment, where demon torturers inflict unspeakable agonies upon the wicked, are led by a misguiding light. Certainly, there is a gloomy place of sorrow haunted by Dark Spirits, but they do not inflict torment by fire. They are there because they are evil, and their companionship is awful enough to bear.

SOF:20:24 Do not come to us holding heathen gods in your heart, even though they are within a hidden and closed recess. Purge yourself of all false beliefs outside the gate.

SOF:20:25 Here, all brothers are to practise the way to full soul realisation in common. Here, Truth will bind one with the other. Humility, modesty and justice will govern our lives. There is to be no straying of heart and eye towards improper and unworthy things. Every man is to command or obey according to his rank.

SOF:20:26 If anyone is found to have lied upon admittance, whether it be about the past, the tribal allegiances or possessions, amends are to be made by labour. No madman, no simpleton, no one who is blind, deaf or dumb is to be admitted.

SOF:20:27 If anyone strike someone of higher rank or refuse to obey instructions given, then if the striker have rank, it is to be lowered, and amends will be made by labour and restraint of food. If anyone strike another of equal rank without just cause, the rank of the striker is to be lowered and amends made by labour. If two men fight, the ranks of both are to be lowered.

SOF:20:28 If anyone lie with intent to deceive, or if injury or sorrow be caused to another, amends will be made by labour. If anyone cause damage or loss to something belonging to another or to all, amends will be made by labour. If any man expose himself improperly and heedlessly before another he is to make amends by labour.

SOF:20:29 If anyone defame another behind his back, he is to make amends by labour, but anyone may accuse another to his face before witnesses. If anyone rebuke another in anger, amends will be made by labour. If anyone bear a grudge and make it known, an apology will be given with humility and accepted with good grace.

SOF:20:30 If anyone speak filthily to the hearing of another, amends will be made by labour. If anyone wastes metal or cause the loss of metal, amends will be made by labour. If anyone bathe in water used by another or in unclean water, amends will be made by labour.

SOF:20:31 From the hour of darkness beginning the seventh day until the hour of darkness beginning the first day is a time of rest and meditation. It is to be a time of tranquillity for soul communion and sacred study. The only labour to be undertaken is the providing of provender for animals and their care and attention. Food may be eaten, but it is best if prepared the day before. Decorative trees and plants may be attended to; relaxing pastimes may be indulged in, and all essential tasks undertaken. An essential task is one which cannot be done on any other day or is made absolutely necessary by circumstances. On the day of rest, all are to wear clean raiment, and the chastisement of children is to be deferred until the morrow.

SOF:20:32 The first concern of a man should be his wife and children and anyone else under his care. He should not cause them to go unfed or underclothed to provide for the needs of another. If anything belonging to anyone or to all is lost or taken away and hidden so that it is not known who has it, the thing is to be made accursed in the hands of its possessor. If later, it is found in the possession of anyone, that person is to be expelled from the Brotherhood, not for what has been done but for the curse.

SOF:20:33 When something is found, which has no owner, it is to be taken to the sanctuary and remain there for one month. If it remain unclaimed it is to be restored to the finder. No one is to take anything from an outsider except for fair and full payment, and no one is to join an outsider in buying and selling.

SOF:20:34 We are ruled by a council, and this is to be twelve men and a master. There will be a high council of five and a low council of seven within the full council. There will be a half council of four chosen by the full council, to be judges in disputes and overseers of chastisements.

SOF:20:35 The high council is to appoint headmen, who will lead the brothers in groups of twelve. The low council will appoint beadles, who will report to it. All are to obey the headmen and beadles and those of higher rank than themselves, but they may complain to the low council about any instruction given them.

SOF:20:36 (The larger part of this and the next chapter are lost and it has been difficult to assign a proper place or order to anything. Perhaps no more than a tenth of the original remains.)

Chapter Twenty-One – The Laws of Malfin

SOF:21:1 May your souls be enlightened by the Central Light. May all you who assemble between the great pillars at the appointed times be cared for by The Supreme Spirit, as you care for His earthly affairs. May He keep you, as you keep His laws. May you receive the grace of enlightenment from the centre of the Sacred Circle, and may an eternal fountain open for you, from which your souls may drink and be refreshed. May you receive the gift of everlasting regeneration.

SOF:21:2 These are the laws of the outsiders, which you have to obey, and they can be justly added to those you have, for right recognises no origin. They are in two parts: those, which are to be wholly yours and those, which govern you among the outsiders.

SOF:21:3 If one whose position requires him to bear witness to a transaction give false evidence concerning it, so that an outsider is at a loss, he is to be bound and given over to the outsiders. If an outsider suffer loss, the one causing it is to be deprived of his rights and made to labour in the place of captivity, until the loss is made good and twice the amount has been paid to the council. He must not be re-established in his rights.

SOF:21:4 Only a man of good repute, having no interest in the things being judged, can witness to it with immunity. If he accept a payment, his voice is not to be heard.

SOF:21:5 No one who gambles or lends money, or who buys to sell, or collects payments or taxes may sit in judgement. Neither may a man, whose house is in turmoil or who has been condemned in judgement.

SOF:21:6 No one may sit in judgement on a kinsman, a friend or an enemy, unless no other judge can be found. No one may attend upon a judge in the absence of those who oppose him, so that he may gain favour. The words of a lying witness are to be disregarded, unless otherwise proven.

SOF:21:7 If voices be raised in anger before the seat of judgement, or anyone behave unseemingly, the matter is to be left until the morrow. When sitting in judgement a judge must remember that it is more wicked for a rich man to steal than for a poor man. Or for the wellborn to act basely than for the lowly to act likewise. It is more wicked for the strong to strike unjustly than for the weak to do so.

SOF:21:8 If anyone, by boisterous behaviour, cause damage within the grounds of a man's dwelling place, or injure anyone, he shall go to the place of captivity until the damage or injury is made good, and the same amount is. to be paid to the council.

SOF:21:9 Every landowner must have his land hedged in, and if it is not hedged, or the hedges are broken, he will have no claim for any damage caused there by strayed animals, but they must be driven out without hurt or harm. If anyone damage a hedge or fence, he will be responsible for anything happening through the damage. If anyone damage any property or cause harm to an animal belonging to the outsiders, he will be handed over to them.

SOF:21:10 If a man find a beast straying upon his land, he may secure it and demand a payment in compensation for loss or damage.

SOF:21:11 If anyone offend against the laws of the outsiders, he will be given over to them for judgement under the laws of the outsiders. No one is to be given over to the outsiders until he has been heard by his own judges. If anyone is to be judged by the outsiders, a man from the council is to sit with him.

SOF:21:12 If a man draw a weapon in an assembly of people, he shall surrender the weapon to anyone who ranks above him. If he refuse to do so, he shall be seized and brought before the judges for punishment. He may not recover the weapon, except by payment of its value. If anyone threaten another with a weapon, it is to be taken from him and may not be recovered without payment of its value to the council.

SOF:21:13 Men are entitled to the privacy of their wives, men to the privacy of men and women to the privacy of women. A family is entitled to the privacy of a family.

SOF:21:14 Anyone who commands another in his power to do a deed shall stand as though he did it himself.

SOF:21:15 If in company with a man, whom many come to take and slay or injure unlawfully, then draw your weapon in his defence. If anyone use the language of slaves in your presence, It is not sufficient to remain silent. If you do not rebuke him because he is powerful, then depart from his company. To do nothing is wrong, for men are told not to remain passive before the face of evil.

SOF:21:16 The scandalmonger and scaremonger may both be delivered to the place of captivity to requite the harm done. If no harm is done, the liar is still a person without repute, and his punishment is that he will not be believed, even when he speaks truthfully.

SOF:21:17 Hypocrites are two-tongued, loathsome creatures who, like grass snakes, cannot be grasped in the hands. If any establish themselves as hypocrites, drive them out, and let them afflict the outsiders.

SOF:21:18 There are punishments prescribed for wrongdoing and much advice given to prevent it. Punishment is only acknowledgement of failure. Wrongdoing arises from failure to deal with weaknesses, failure in upbringing, failure in teaching, failure in establishing rules of conduct and failure in discipline, whether imposed by self or others. When a man comes before the judges for punishment, they do more than half their duty when they condemn him. They should also enquire within themselves, "Wherein have the people failed with this man? Was he guided rightly or wrongly, and have we no responsibility towards him?" Punishing a wrongdoer without seeking out the cause of his deeds is hypocritical justice. If a man walk in darkness and stumble into a pit, is he to blame? If a light guide falsely or be too feeble to keep men from stumbling, it is of no value. Therefore, if a brother fall into a pit by the wayside, the bearers of light cannot be guiltless.

SOF:21:19 These things are recorded unto you, so that in the day of freedom, you may not be without law. That day will come as surely as the sunrise. Never fear because your numbers diminish. One wise man is better than a pack of fools, and a staff of solid oak better than a pillar of reeds.

SOF:21:20 The man who supplies weapons to another, who uses them in a wrongful deed is not guiltless himself. If he knew their use, he is no less guilty. Anyone possessing things wrongfully taken is not without guilt, and if taken knowingly is no less guilty. One who is not yet a man in age cannot be equally guilty in robbery or violence. Neither can a simpleton, a madman or a woman.

SOF:21:21 If anyone bind another unlawfully or cause anyone to lose his freedom, he shall requite the harm done and may be delivered to the place of captivity. Everyone has the right to solitude and privacy, and those who deny him it are not without guilt. If anyone destroy the hair of a woman, he must requite the harm to the limit of fullness.

SOF:21:22 If anyone come upon a thief in his deed, or upon someone about an unlawful deed and slay or injure him because of his resistance, no wrong is done. If he submit to capture and is slain or injured unlawfully, those who do the deed must bear the guilt. If a man come upon his wife in adultery and slay both, he has done no wrong. If a man come upon another dealing wrongfully with his son or daughter or another child and he slay him, he has done no wrong. If a man slay a thief in the night or one who seeks to injure him, he does no wrong. If a man find another with his wife behind bolted doors and slay the man, he has done no wrong. If he come upon them in a secret place and slay the man, he has done no wrong. If a man commit a deed unlawfully, in lust, so that he may be lawfully slain, he may be castrated instead. If a man lay his hand in any way upon a virgin, without her consent, he is not guiltless.

SOF:21:23 If two men quarrel and one bear insult with forbearance, the other must requite him for the insult. A brother, a father or a son coming upon his kinswoman in adultery or behind bolted doors, is to stand as though he were her husband.

SOF:21:24 If a man slay another who provoked him in fair contest, he does so in self-defence. The guilt of a deed done while drunk is not lessened. If anyone become drunk so that he cannot stand upon a stool, he is not guiltless.

SOF:21:25 If anyone destroy a tree belonging to the outsiders and not on common land he must requite the outsiders its value. If anyone destroy the tree of another, he will stand as though he stole it.

SOF:21:26 The man, who is betrothed to a woman, coming upon her in fornication or behind bolted doors, is to stand as though he were her husband. If he come upon her in a secret place, he is to stand as her husband. If anyone, knowing a woman to be unchaste, permit a man to marry her believing her to be chaste, he shall bear the guilt and may be called upon to requite the husband.

SOF:21:27 At the trothing, a man must pledge the father of his betrothed, or the next of kin to her father, that he will maintain and protect her. The bride price is to be paid seven days before the marriage, and it is to repay her father for bringing her up with all the womanly virtues.

SOF:21:28 Marriage by deceit or force is not valid. It does not bind the victim, but binds the other in every way, as though married. If a man marry a woman by deceit, he is not guiltless and must requite the wrong. If a man marry by force, and she was a virgin, he is to stand as though there were no marriage, but the woman has all the rights of a wife against his possessions.

SOF:21:29 A husband may punish his wife for these things transgressing the law without being punished by the law: Talking freely with men while her husband is absent. Cursing her husband or his house. Cursing her own house. Talking loudly, so that her voice carries to the habitation of another. For slander and gossip. For lewdness or immodesty. For betraying him in her talk. For being slothful or neglecting his children.

SOF:21:30 A wife is not wholly delivered into the hands of her husband, and he must provide all things for her wellbeing and treat her with affection and consideration. He is to be tolerant of her shortcomings and overlook her frailty as a woman. A man has a duty to see that an adulterous wife is dealt with.

SOF:21:31 If a wife become mad or sick or injured, she cannot be put aside, even though she cannot be a wife to her husband. These things are the dispensations of life and must be borne together.

SOF:21:32 No man may know the nakedness of his sister. No man may lie with his wife, except in a place of privacy. No one is to permit a mad man or woman, a child or a simpleton to slay a beast, but a bird may be slain by a woman for food. The one who permits the deed is not guiltless.

SOF:21:33 If the head is unclean, it will lead to blindness. If the garments worn are unclean, it will lead to madness. If the body is unclean, it will lead to sores and sickness.

SOF:21:34 Eat to fill a third part of the stomach. Drink to fill a third part and leave the rest empty. Eat only when hungry, and drink only when thirsty. Always sit to eat, taking two meals each day and three on the seventh day. Do not overeat or oversleep, for body rust is not an unreal thing.

SOF:21:35 The threshing place is not to be less than fifty paces from a habitation. A grave is not to be within a hundred paces, a carcass yard within a hundred paces, or a tannery within two hundred paces. The midden is not be within fifty paces, and hogs within thirty paces. The privy hole is to be within twenty paces and is to be screened and covered. No beast except the dog, the cat, the horse, the cow, the goat and the ass may come within the dwelling enclosure. The barn must not adjoin the dwelling. Corn for eating may be kept below ground, but corn for sowing must be kept above ground. Water should not be drunk under a roof without herbs.

SOF:21:36 Roofs must not be thatched by bending the reeds under a lath, but by laying them straight over an underpinning. The middle and pillarpost should rise a third part above the crossbeam and either rest upon itself or lie on the cumber. The outer posts should be pegged and not bound. Inner walls should be caulked with moss and not with grass or bark. The roof should lie down over the outer wall an armslength, and the openwork of the wall should not be left unplastered. The foundation should go down two cubits and rise one. The door is to turn upon itself, either to the side or upward and should not be hung. The wall hangings within should be of fibre or skin. Overlay outside with wands of bethom.

SOF:21:37 Stones should not be pressed without heat, and their outer parts should be kept. The herb offerings must be burnt on each day, when the sun does not show its face. Flour must not be used to purify sharpened metal. The offering log must be burnt at its hour.

SOF:21:38 A man must teach his sons to swim, to ride and to hunt. The stranger is not to be denied a sleeping place and food at nightfall, but he may not remain during the day without labour. Any man who deals with metal shall be as a brother. Anyone may come before the high council for justice.

SOF:21:39 In all assemblies, opinions will be given first by those of lower rank, so that their words are not influenced by those of more knowledgeable men. In the lands of the outsiders, you will abide by their law, but you will keep your own law within theirs. Where laws conflict, let conscience, duty and the Holy Writ be your guide.

SOF:21:40 (This is not the end, but the remaining writing on three plates cannot be read, It is transcribed in meaning and not in word,)

Chapter Twenty-Two – Salvaged Fragments Reconstructed - 1

SOF:22:1 If any, who have joined in cause with you or become allies act treacherously, grant them no quarter. Deal with them in such a way that their fate will be an example restraining others from doing likewise. Never join cause with anyone proved treacherous or unreliable.

SOF:22:2 If any hold the same belief as you and have suffered for it, they are your brothers. Those who fight for the betterment of mankind or suffer for it, are your brothers. To surrender to the threats of those who demand you abandon your beliefs or ideals, is something, which must not be done. Any man, who has fought with you in battle is bound with you in the tie of blood and becomes even as your own kin.

SOF:22:3 Though you fight in the cause of Truth and justice, be reluctant to commence the bloodshed and never do so if any other means, except cowardice or capitulation, lie open to your hand. If, however, you truly believe the foe will launch an attack, you are justified in getting in the first blow. You are answerable to your own soul. When battle is joined, you may slay the foe wherever you find him. Never acknowledge defeat, and never submit meekly to domination. If the battle goes against you, withdraw to fight again. The live dog eats the dead bear.

SOF:22:4 Never fight among yourselves, for such quarrelling is worse than the bloodshed of battle. Differences and arguments among you are to be settled in an orderly and just manner, so that there is no severance or weakening among people. You are the People of the Light, the Law and the Book.

SOF:22:5 In the place of captivity, men and women will be kept apart, for it is a place of requital and retribution. They will no longer be free; neither will they hold the rights of the free. They are to labour according to the judgement, but the labour of their hands is to be accounted to them. Each one must be used to get the greatest benefits from their ability, and no one must be kept even one day over their requital.

Chapter Twenty-Three – Salvaged Fragments Reconstructed - 2

SOF:23:1 These are the sayings of judges, set down by the law scribes, and all that remains out of nearly eight hundred:

SOF:23:2 We have learned that, whatever a woman does she should not be cut off from her household, for this leads to other wrongs. If a wife be put aside for her wrongdoing, it may be well to let her remain under the same roof without any rights of wifehood.

SOF:23:3 We have learned that not only are there women, who are unworthy to be wives, but there are men unworthy to be husbands. If marriage remain open to such as these, those who sit in judgement are not unblameworthy for whatever follows. Therefore, man or woman may be forbidden marriage.

SOF:23:4 It is the law that adultery being a furtive deed done in deceit and betrayal, if man and woman are found in a position for adultery, it would be as though they were caught committing it. This can lead to misjudgement. Therefore, when no certainty of adultery can be seen, and the woman can only be found to be indiscreet, she is not be dealt with as an adulteress. It is better for men to believe in the natural goodness of woman than otherwise. Yet, when a woman has placed herself in a position, where there can be no doubt, the husband may decide to keep her or not, but he must declare himself. If he put her aside as a wife, the judges will decree whether she go or stay. If she stay, she may be bound to her husband, though no longer his wife.

SOF:23:5 We have learned that, though adultery is a loathsome deed done in deceit while displaying a hypocritical allegiance to love, it is often not without preventable cause. Therefore, an adulteress can suffer a lesser punishment by being bound into the care of her husband, while ceasing to be a wife, for she is unworthy. Then, she is to remain within his household and submit to his direction. He must maintain and protect her and not allow her to wander. If she wander, he may restrain her as he will. If she commit fornication while bound, the man who was her husband is not blameworthy, for she is under his restraint. The three must suffer their own punishments.

SOF:23:6 We have learned that when men fear for their safety and the sanctity of their own wives, they are less inclined to act adulterously with the wife of another. Therefore, if a man be found in adultery and married, he will forfeit half his possessions to the wronged husband, and his wife will also pass into the house of the wronged husband, or if he have neither dwelling nor land, he shall be bound into the keeping of the wronged husband.

SOF:23:7 We have learned that the minds of men are like a maze, and therefore, the rights of marriage are to stand against all others and prevail at all times. All children born within a marriage union are equal in rights. Their inheritance is not to be diminished, even though they be the offspring of adultery or incest, for the wrongdoing was not theirs. Such children should be received with mercy, for they are helpless and will repay in full with love and devotion.

SOF:23:8 We have learned that it is unwise to give a daughter in marriage to an outsider, for if her husband die, she shall be given to his father or his brother. Therefore, no woman may be given in marriage to an outsider, unless the contract of marriage be heard by one of the council and given his approval.

SOF:23:9 We have learned that these things should never be taken from a man or shared: His wife, excepting he commit adultery; his children, his clothes, his nightcovering, his weapons and his tools of craft.

SOF:23:10 We have learned that it is no longer necessary to forbid the eating of swine's flesh in this land, and its eating is allowed, but the flesh of horse is not to be eaten, except to prevent starvation.

SOF:23:11 We have learned that the soul departs with the last breath, and whatever is done to the body does not affect the soul. Therefore, a body may be either buried or burned, but a high mound is not to be raised over the body or the ashes. Only husband and wife, parent and child, or brother and sister may be buried in the same grave within a graveyard. No one may be buried within his habitation.

Chapter Twenty-Four – The Last of the Metal Plates

SOF:24:1 In the containers, I have gathered together all the books given into my care, and I have done all the things I was instructed to do, and the work of my father is now complete. The metal will stand the test of age, and the cutting is the finest workmanship.

SOF:24:2 The five great bookboxes contain one hundred and thirty-two scrolls and five ring-bound volumes. There are sixty-two thousand, four hundred and eighty three words in The Greater Book of the Egyptians and eighty-one thousand, six hundred and twenty-six words in The Lesser Book of The Egyptians, of which eight thousand, nine hundred and eleven are in The Book of The Trial of The Great God and six thousand, one hundred and thirty-four are in The Sacred Register, and sixteen thousand and fifty-six are in The Book of Establishment.

SOF:24:3 The Book of Magical Concoctions has six thousand, eight hundred and ten words, and this was the most difficult to remit, for it was a work of mystery and hidden things.

SOF:24:4 The Book of Songs and The Book of Creation and Destruction were not worked under my hand, but they are well constituted and will not perish. The Book of Tribulation was beaten under my eye, and there are the books in The Great Book of The Sons of Fire, which are not of my workmanship. I helped in part, where the words were marked out, and I struck them.

SOF:24:5 The Book of Secret Lore and The Book of Decrees are joined into The Great Book of The Sons of Fire and they, too, are enabled to last forever.

SOF:24:6 The metal is as our masters desired, made cunningly by the secret methods of our tribe, and it will never perish. The marks are cut so that when seen to the right of the light, they stand out clearly.

SOF:24:7 The bookboxes are of twinmetal founded with strength and turned with great heat, so that there is no joint where the ends come together. When closed and sealed, water cannot enter.

SOF:24:8 When you read these things in times ahead, think of us, who made the metal so imperishable and cut the words on it with such care and heavy labour, using such skill that in the years of rest, they have not been eaten off. Observe its brightness, and wonder, for it will never tarnish.

SOF:24:9 We are the sons of The Sons of Fire, men so called because fire was necessary to their metalworking. Today, we name our sons over the fire and forge, as they did, and each one of us belongs to the same fire.

SOF:24:10 Read carefully the sacred words, which are written, and may they be a lodemark to a greater life.

SOF:24:11 I, Efantiglan, and my father, attended to the making of these books and their covering containers. Those who mixed the metal and worked it by forging and those who cut upon it are members of our tribe, and it is well made and will last forever.

SOF:24:12 Malgwin recorded these books before they were consigned to the future, and the name by which they were called is 'The Living Book For The Living.'

Book of
Manuscripts

MAN:3:1 Men forget the days of the Destroyer. Only the wise know where it went and that it will return in its appointed hour.

Table of Chapters

BOOK OF MANUSCRIPTS
Table of Chapters (Continued)

Book of Manuscripts

Chapter One – Scroll of Emod

MAN:1:1 The writings from olden days tell of strange things and of great happenings in the times of our fathers who lived in the beginning. All men can know of such times is declared in the Book of Ages, but the gods had their birth in events and things, which were in the beginning.

MAN:1:2 It is told in the courtyards that there was a time when Heaven and Earth were not apart. Truth echoes even there, for Heaven and Earth are yet joined in men.

MAN:1:3 It is written that God once walked the earth with man and dwelt within a cave above a garden where man laboured. God encompasses all that is and cannot be contained in a cave. Look to the Sacred Writings for Truth.

MAN:1:4 It is told that woman made God angry, and He took Himself into the sky, removing Heaven from man because of his disgust for woman. It is also told that man offended God by imitating Him. These are tales made by man.

MAN:1:5 This is not wisdom, for the Sacred Writings reveal the Plans of God, and these things cannot be as told. It is the talk of the courtyard; it is the knowledge of the outerplace.

MAN:1:6 Men talk of the land of Oben, from whence they came. Not from Oben towards the South came men, for the great land of Ramakui first felt his step. Out by the encircling waters, over at the rim, it lay.

MAN:1:7 There were mighty men in those days, and of their land, the First Book speaks thus: Their dwelling places were set in the swamplands from whence no mountains rose, in the land of many waters slow-flowing to the sea. In the shallow lakelands, among the mud, out beyond the Great Plain of Reeds. At the place of many flowers bedecking plant and tree. Where trees grew beards and had branches like ropes, which bound them together, for the ground would not support them. There were butterflies like birds and spiders as large as the outstretched arms of a man. The birds of the air and fishes of the waters had hues, which dazzled the eyes, they lured men to destruction. Even insects fed on the flesh of men. There were elephants in great numbers, with mighty curved tusks.

MAN:1:8 The pillars of the Netherworld were unstable. In a great night of destruction, the land fell into an abyss and was lost forever. When the Earth became light, next day, man saw man driven to madness.

MAN:1:9 All was gone. Men clothed themselves with the skins of beasts and were eaten by wild beasts, things with clashing teeth used them for food. A great horde of rats devoured everything, so that man died of hunger. The Braineaters hunted men down and slew them.

MAN:1:10 Children wandered the plainland like the wild beasts, for men and women became stricken with a sickness that passed over the children. An issue covered their bodies, which swelled up and burst, while flame consumed their bellies. Every man who had an issue of seed within him and every woman who had a flow of blood died.

MAN:1:11 The children grew up without instruction, and having no knowledge, turned to strange ways and beliefs. They became divided according to their tongues.

MAN:1:12 This was the land from whence man came; the Great One came from Ramakui and wisdom came from Zaidor.

MAN:1:13 The people who came with Nadhi were wise in the ways of the seasons and in the wisdom of the stars. They read the Book of Heaven with understanding.

MAN:1:14 They covered their dead with potters clay and hardened it, for it was not their custom to place their dead in boxes.

MAN:1:15 Those who came with the Great One were cunning craftsmen in stone; they were carvers of wood and ivory. The High God was worshipped with strange light in places of great silences. They paid homage to the huge, sleeping beast in the depths of the sea; believing it to bear the Earth on its back; they believed its stirrings plunged lands to destruction. Some said it burrowed beneath them.

MAN:1:16 In Ramakui there was a great city with roads and waterways, and the fields were bounded with walls of stone and channels. In the centre of the land was the great flat-topped Mountain of God.

MAN:1:17 The city had walls of stone and was decorated with stones of red and black, white shells and feathers. There were heavy, green stones in the land and stones patterned in green, black and brown. There were stones of saka, which men cut for ornaments, stones which became molten for cunning work.

MAN:1:18 They built walls of black glass and bound them with glass by fire. They used strange fire from the Netherworld, which was but slightly separated from them, and foul air from the breath of the damned rose in their midst.

MAN:1:19 They made eye reflectors of glass stone, which cured the ills of men. They purified men with a strange metal and purged them of evil spirits in flowing fire.

MAN:1:20 We dwell in a land of three peoples, but those who came from Ramakui and Zaidor were fewer in numbers. It was the men of Zaidor who built the Great Guardian, which ever watches, looking towards the awakening place of God. The day He comes not, its voice will be heard.

MAN:1:21 In olden times, when men lived in the ground, there came the Great One whose name is hidden. Son of Hem, Son of the Sun, Chief of the Guardians of Mysteries, Master of Rites and the Spoken Word. Judge of Disputes, Advocate of the Dead, Interpreter of the Gods and Father of Fishermen. From the West, from beyond Mandi, came the Great One arrayed in robes of black linen and wearing a head-dress of red.

MAN:1:22 Who taught men the secret of writing and numbers, and the measurement of the years? Who taught the ways of the days and the months, who read the meaning of clouds and the writing of the nightlights?

MAN:1:23 Who taught the preservation of the body? That the soul might commune with the living, and that it might be a doorway to the Earth?

MAN:1:24 Who taught that light is Life?

MAN:1:25 Who taught the words of God, which spoke to men and hid things from them, which stood in the place of Truth for those with understanding? Which spoke to the priests, the scribes and the people differently according to their enlightenment

MAN:1:26 Who taught that beyond the visible is the invisible, beyond the small the smaller and beyond the great the greater, and all things are linked together in one?

MAN:1:27 Who taught the song of the stars, which now no man knows, and the words of the waters, which are lost?

MAN:1:28 Who taught men to grow corn and to spin, to make bricks and fashion stone after a cunning manner?

MAN:1:29 Who taught men the rituals of sea shells, and the reading of their mysteries and the manner of their speech?

MAN:1:30 Who taught men the nature and knowledge of God, but in the years left to him could not bring them to understanding? Who, then, veiled the great secrets in simple tales, which they could remember and in signs, which would not be lost to their children's children?

MAN:1:31 Who brought the Sacred Eye from the distant land and the Stone of Light made of water, by which men see God, and the firestone which gathers the light of the sun before the Great Shrine?

MAN:1:32 He died in the manner of men, though his likeness is that of a god. Then, they cut him apart, that his body might make fertile the fields, and took away his head, that it might bring them wisdom. His bones, they did not paint red, for they were not as those of others.

MAN:1:33 These are the words of the Sacred Writings. recorded after the old custom. As they are, so let them be; for that which is recorded remains with you.

MAN:1:34 The Stone of Light and the firestone were stolen in the days of disaster, and none now knows their resting place. therefore the land is empty.

Chapter Two – Scroll of Kamushahre

MAN:2:1 In this fertile black land, there are those who worship the sun and they call it the greatest and the most bountiful among all gods, the Seer of Heaven, the Orb of Glory. They tell many tales about the coming of the Sun People and of the land, from whence they came. They also tell of the squalid manner, in which men dwelt before the Golden One led his people hence.

MAN:2:2 He came to this fertile land. Now, it is a pleasant place with many great cities and contented villages; there is the great, broad river of fresh water, which rises and falls in its due seasons. Channels there are and waterways, which lead the fertilising waters unto the growing things, the herbage and the trees. There are flocks of sheep and herds of cattle on the green pastures.

MAN:2:3 It was not ever thus. In the days before Harekta came, all was barren and desolate. Nought divided the wilderness from the swamplands filled with reeds. Then, there were no cattle or sheep, and the land knew not the hand of man, it lay untilled and unwatered.

MAN:2:4 No land was sown, for they who dwelt in it knew not the making of waterways, nor did they know how to command the water and make it flow at their behest. There were no cities, and men dwelt in holes in the ground or in places where the rock was cleft. They walked in their nakedness or clothed themselves with leaves or bark, while at night they covered themselves with the skin of wild beasts. They fought with the jackal for food and snatched dead things from the lion. They pulled roots from out of the ground and sought for sustenance among things that grew in the mud. They had none to rule over them, nor had they leaders to guide. They knew not obligation or duty. None spoke to them about their manner of life, and none knew the way of Truth. They were truly unenlightened in those days.

MAN:2:5 Then came the servant of the Sun, and he it was who brought the people together and put rulers over them. He set Ramur up as king over the whole land. He showed them, man and woman, how to dwell together in contentment as husband and wife, and he divided their tasks between them.

MAN:2:6 He instructed men in the sowing of corn and the growing of herbs. He instructed them in the tilling of the ground and the manner of cutting the waterways and channels. He it was who showed men the ways of the beasts of the field. He instructed men in the working of gold and silver and the making of vessels from clay. He instructed men in the hewing and cutting of stone and the building of temples and cities. The making of linen and the dying of cloth that forms garments ever pleasing to the eyes, he did not teach. Neither did he instruct them in the making of bricks or the working of copper.

MAN:2:7 Then, when he departed he bade the people not to weep, for though he went to his father, the sun would adopt them as his children and all could become sons of the sun. Thus many became sons and servants of the sun and they believed what they had heard, that the sun was their father and the light of goodness overlooking the whole land. It is this light that sustains all living things, but within it is the greater light which sustains the spirit. It is the light that enlightens the hearts of men. There are lesser lights that guide men about their daily tasks and shield them from harm, there are unseen lights that influence men for good or ill, but it is the Great light that banishes coldness and makes all men warm. The warmth it bestows ripens the harvests of man and makes his herds yield their increase.

MAN:2:8 It oversees the whole activity of men on Earth as it journeys the skies from one end to the other; thus, it knows the needs of all men. Therefore, be like the sun, be far-seeing and foresighted, be regular in your comings and goings while about your daily tasks.

MAN:2:9 When their guide and leader left, the people knew themselves as children of the sun. They were warlike and subdued other people in its name, and brought them under its rule. Then great temples were raised up to it and for a time it displaced the greater gods which the people of this land had set up in their ignorance. The One True God, it never displaced, for the True God was ever hidden from the eyes of the profane and ignorant.

MAN:2:10 Then some priests among those who followed the rule of the sun stole its spirit and brought it down, so that it enlivened the statues and images of their gods. Thus the spirit, which enlivens all the lesser gods is but the one spirit held in captivity, and not many as the people think.

MAN:2:11 Then came the Wise Ones from the East and they caused the people to have other thoughts. They were men who knew the ways of Heaven and asked of the people, "Is the sun spirit indeed supreme? Is this not a thing requiring much thought? Consider its movements, are they not more like those of one who is directed in his comings and goings? Does it move about freely as it wills, or is it restricted and held to its appointed path, like a yoked ox, or as the ass treading out corn? Does it rise up from the Netherworld as it wills or go down into the cavern of darkness by its own decree? Is its path not more like that of a stone hurled forth by the hand of man? Is it not like a boat controlled by the will of a man, rather than a free-ranging god? Is it not more like a slave under the direction of a master?" These things disturbed the hearts of the people; some pondered upon them, but others, in the manner of men, cried death to those who deny the truth of these things.

MAN:2:12 However, because of the things said, the worship of the older gods grew in strength, for the people had never turned from sira, who was with them before the first water channel was cut. He was not the god of the high born but of the lowly people.

MAN:2:13 This is a land of two peoples, of two nations, two priesthoods, two streams of wisdom and two hierarchies of gods. It is a land where the light of Truth burns brightly, though hidden away from the eyes of all but a few. It is the Land of Dawning on Earth.

Chapter Three – The Destroyer - Part 1

MAN:3:1 Men forget the days of the Destroyer. Only the wise know where it went and that it will return in its appointed hour.

MAN:3:2 It raged across the Heavens in the days of wrath, and this was its likeness: It was as a billowing cloud of smoke enwrapped in a ruddy glow, not distinguishable in joint or limb. Its mouth was an abyss from which came flame, smoke and hot cinders.

MAN:3:3 When ages pass, certain laws operate upon the stars in the Heavens. Their ways change; there is movement and restlessness, they are no longer constant and a great light appears redly in the skies.

MAN:3:4 When blood drops upon the Earth, the Destroyer will appear, and mountains will open up and belch forth fire and ashes. Trees will be destroyed and all living things engulfed. Waters will be swallowed up by the land, and seas will boil.

MAN:3:5 The Heavens will burn brightly and redly; there will be a copper hue over the face of the land, 'followed by a day of darkness. A new moon will appear and break up and fall.

MAN:3:6 The people will scatter in madness. They will hear the trumpet and battlecry of the Destroyer and will seek refuge within dens in the Earth. Terror will eat away their hearts, and their courage will flow from them like water from a broken pitcher. They will be eaten up in the flames of wrath and consumed by the breath of the Destroyer.

MAN:3:7 Thus it was in the Days of Heavenly Wrath, which have gone, and thus it will be in the Days of Doom when it comes again. The times of its coming and going are known unto the wise. These are the signs and times which shall precede the Destroyer's return: A hundred and ten generations shall pass into the West, and nations will rise and fall. Men will fly in the air as birds and swim in the seas as fishes. Men will talk peace one with another; hypocrisy and deceit shall have their day. Women will be as men and men as women; passion will be a plaything of man.

MAN:3:8 A nation of soothsayers shall rise and fall, and their tongue shall be the speech learned. A nation of lawgivers shall rule the Earth and pass away into nothingness. One worship will pass into the four quarters of the Earth, talking peace and bringing war. A nation of the seas will be greater than any other, but will be as an apple rotten at the core and will not endure. A nation of traders will destroy men with wonders and it shall have its day. Then shall the high strive with the low, the North with the South, the East with the West, and the light with the darkness. Men shall be divided by their races, and the children will be born as strangers among them. Brother shall strive with brother and husband with wife. Fathers will no longer instruct their sons, and the sons will be wayward. Women will become the common property of men and will no longer be held in regard and respect.

MAN:3:9 Then, men will be ill at ease in their hearts; they will seek they know not what, and uncertainty and doubt will trouble them. They will possess great riches but be poor in spirit. Then will the Heavens tremble and the Earth move; men will quake in fear, and while terror walks with them, the Heralds of Doom will appear. They will come softly, as thieves to the tombs; men will not know them for what they are; men will be deceived; the hour of the Destroyer is at hand.

MAN:3:10 In those days, men will have the Great Book before them; wisdom will be revealed; the few will be gathered for the stand; it is the hour of trial. The dauntless ones will survive; the stouthearted will not go down to destruction.

MAN:3:11 Great God of All Ages, alike to all, who sets the trials of man, be merciful to our children in the Days of Doom. Man must suffer to be great, but hasten not his progress unduly. In the great winnowing, be not too harsh on the lesser ones among men. Even the son of a thief has become your scribe.

Chapter Four – The Destroyer - Part 2

MAN:4:1 O Sentinels of the Universe who watch for the Destroyer, how long will your enduring vigil last? O mortal men who wait without understanding, where will you hide yourselves in the Dread Days of Doom, when the Heavens shall be torn apart and the skies rent in twain, in the days when children will turn grey-headed?

MAN:4:2 This is the thing, which will be seen, this is the terror your eyes will behold, this is the form of destruction that will rush upon you: There will be the great body of fire, the glowing head with many mouths and eyes ever changing. Terrible teeth will be seen in formless mouths, and a fearful dark belly will glow redly from fires inside. Even the most stouthearted man will tremble, and his bowels will be loosened, for this is not a thing understandable to men.

MAN:4:3 It will be a vast sky-spanning form enwrapping Earth, burning with many hues within wide open mouths. These will descend to sweep across the face of the land, engulfing all in the yawning jaws. The greatest warriors will charge against it in vain. The fangs will fall out, and lo, they are terror-inspiring things of cold hardened water. Great boulders will be hurled down upon men, crushing them into red powder.

MAN:4:4 As the great salt waters rise up in its train and roaring torrents pour towards the land, even the heroes among mortal men will be overcome with madness. As moths fly swiftly to their doom in the burning flame, so will these men rush to their own destruction. The flames going before will devour all the works of men, the waters following will sweep away whatever remains. The dew of death will fall softly, as a grey carpet over the cleared land. Men will cry out in their madness, O whatever Being there is, save us from this tall form of terror, save us from the grey dew of death."

Chapter Five – The Destroyer - Part 3

MAN:5:1 The Doomshape, called the Destroyer, in Egypt, was seen in all the lands thereabouts. In colour, it was bright and fiery; in appearance, changing and unstable. It twisted about itself like a coil, like water bubbling into a pool from an underground supply, and all men agree it was a most fearsome sight. It was not a great comet or a loosened star, being more like a fiery body of flame.

MAN:5:2 Its movements on high were slow; below it swirled in the manner of smoke and it remained close to the sun, whose face it hid. There was a bloody redness about it, which changed as it passed along its course. It caused death and destruction in its rising and setting. It swept the Earth with grey cinder rain and caused many plagues, hunger and other evils. It bit the skin of men and beast until they became mottled with sores.

MAN:5:3 The Earth was troubled and shook, the hills and mountains moved and rocked. The dark smoke-filled Heavens bowed over Earth, and a great howl came to the ears of living men, borne to them upon the wings of the wind. It was the cry of the Dark Lord, the Master of Dread. Thick clouds of fiery smoke passed before him, and there was an awful hail of hot stones and coals of fire. The Doomshape thundered sharply in the Heavens and shot out bright lightings. The channels of water were turned back unto themselves when the land tilted, and great trees were tossed about and snapped like twigs. Then, a voice like ten thousand trumpets was heard over the wilderness, and before its burning breath, the flames parted. The whole of the land moved, and mountains melted. The sky itself roared like ten thousand lions in agony, and bright arrows of blood sped back and forth across its face. Earth swelled up like bread upon the hearth.

MAN:5:4 This was the aspect of the Doomshape, called the Destroyer, when it appeared in days long gone by, in olden times. It is thus described in the old records, few of which remain. It is said that when it appears in the Heavens above, Earth splits open from the heat, like a nut roasted before the fire. Then, flames shoot up through the surface and leap about like fiery fiends upon black blood. The moisture inside the land is all dried up, the pastures and cultivated places are consumed in flames, and they and all trees become white ashes.

MAN:5:5 The Doomshape is like a circling ball of flame, which scatters small fiery offspring in its train. It covers about a fifth part of the sky and sends writhing snakelike fingers down to Earth. Before it, the sky appears frightened, and it breaks up and scatters away. Midday is no brighter than night. It spawns a host of terrible things. These are things said of the Destroyer in the old records; read them with solemn heart, knowing that the Doomshape has its appointed time and will return. It would be foolish to let them go unheeded. Now, men say, 'Such things are not destined for our days.' May The Great God above grant that this be so. But come, the day surely will, and in accordance with his nature man will be unprepared.

Chapter Six – The Dark Days

MAN:6:1 The dark days began with the last visitation of the Destroyer, and they were foretold by strange omens in the skies. All men were silent and went about with pale faces.

MAN:6:2 The leaders of the slaves, which had built a city to the glory of Thom, stirred up unrest, and no man raised his arm against them. They foretold great events of which the people were ignorant and of which the temple seers were not informed.

MAN:6:3 These were days of ominous calm, when the people waited for they knew not what.

The presence of an unseen doom was felt, the hearts of men were stricken. Laughter was heard no more, and grief and wailing sounded throughout the land. Even the voices of children were stilled, and they did not play together, but stood silent.

MAN:6:4 The slaves became bold and insolent, and women were the possession of any man. Fear walked the land, and women became barren with terror, they could not conceive, and those with child aborted. All men closed up within themselves.

MAN:6:5 The days of stillness were followed by a time when the noise of trumpeting and shrilling was heard in the Heavens, and the people became as frightened beasts without a herdsman, as asses when lions prowl without their fold.

MAN:6:6 The people spoke of the god of the slaves, and reckless men said. "If we knew where this god were to be found, we would sacrifice to him." But the god of the slaves was not among them. He was not to be found within the swamplands or in the brickpits. His manifestation was in the Heavens for all men to see, but they did not see with understanding. Nor would any god listen, for all were dumb because of the hypocrisy of men.

MAN:6:7 The dead were no longer sacred and were thrown into the waters. Those already entombed were neglected, and many became exposed. They lay unprotected against the hands of thieves. He who once toiled long in the sun, bearing the yoke himself, now possessed oxen. He who grew no grain now owned a storehouse full. He who once dwelt at ease among his children now thirsted for water. He who once sat in the sun with crumbs and dregs was now bloated with food; he reclined in the shade, his bowls overflowing.

MAN:6:8 Cattle were left unattended to roam into strange pastures, and men ignored their marks and slew the beasts of their neighbours. No man owned anything.

MAN:6:9 The public records were cast forth and destroyed, and no man knew who were slaves and who were masters. The people cried out to the Pharaoh in their distress, but he stopped his ears and acted like a deaf man.

MAN:6:10 There were those who spoke falsely before Pharaoh and had gods hostile towards the land, therefore the people cried out for their blood to appease it. But it was not these strange priests who put strife in the land instead of peace, for one was even of the household of Pharaoh and walked among the people unhampered.

MAN:6:11 Dust and smoke clouds darkened the sky and coloured the waters upon which they fell with a bloody hue. Plague was throughout the land, the river was bloody, and blood was everywhere. The water was vile and men's stomachs shrank from drinking. Those who did drink from the river vomited it up, for it was polluted.

MAN:6:12 The dust tore wounds in the skin of man and beast. In the glow of the Destroyer, the Earth was filled with redness. Vermin bred and filled the air and face of the Earth with loathsomeness. Wild beasts, afflicted with torments under the lashing sand and ashes, came out of their lairs in the wastelands and caveplaces and stalked the abodes of men. All the tame beasts whimpered, and the land was filled with the cries of sheep and moans of cattle.

MAN:6:13 Trees throughout the land were destroyed and no herb or fruit was to be found. The face of the land was battered and devastated by a hail of stones, which smashed down all that stood in the path of the torrent. They swept down in hot showers, and strange flowing fire ran along the ground in their wake.

MAN:6:14 The fish of the river died in the polluted waters; worms, insects and reptiles sprang up from the Earth in huge numbers. Great gusts of wind brought swarms of locusts which covered the sky. As the Destroyer flung itself through the Heavens, it blew great gusts of cinders across the face of the land. The gloom of a long night spread a dark mantle of blackness, which extinguished every ray of light. None knew when it was day and when it was night, for the sun cast no shadow.

MAN:6:15 The darkness was not the clean blackness of night, but a thick darkness in which the breath of men was stopped in their throats. Men gasped in a hot cloud of vapour, which enveloped all the land and snuffed out all lamps and fires. Men were benumbed and lay moaning in their beds. None spoke to another or took food, for they were overwhelmed with despair. Ships were sucked away from their moorings and destroyed in great whirlpools. It was a time of undoing.

MAN:6:16 The Earth turned over, as clay spun upon a potter's wheel. The whole land was filled with uproar from the thunder of the Destroyer overhead and the cry of the people. There was the sound of moaning and lamentation on every side. The Earth spewed up its dead, corpses were cast up out of their resting places and the embalmed were revealed to the sight of all men. Pregnant women miscarried and the seed of men was stopped.

MAN:6:17 The craftsman left his task undone, the potter abandoned his wheel and the carpenter his tools, and they departed to dwell in the marshes. All crafts were neglected, and the slaves lured the craftsmen away.

MAN:6:18 The dues of Pharaoh could not be collected, for there was neither wheat nor barley, goose nor fish. The rights of Pharaoh could not be enforced, for the fields of grain and the pastures were destroyed. The highborn and the lowly prayed together that life might come to an end and the turmoil and thundering cease to beat upon their ears. Terror was the companion of men by day, and horror their companion by night. Men lost their senses and became mad, they were distracted by frightfulness.

MAN:6:19 On the great night of the Destroyer's wrath, when its terror was at its height, there was a hail of rocks, and the Earth heaved as pain rent her bowels. Gates, columns and walls were consumed by fire, and the statues of gods were overthrown and broken. People fled outside their dwellings in fear and were slain by the hail. Those who took shelter from the hail were swallowed when the Earth split open.

MAN:6:20 The habitations of men collapsed upon those inside, and there was panic on every hand, but the slaves who lived in huts in the reedlands, at the place of pits, were spared. The land burnt like tinder; a man watched upon his rooftops and the Heavens hurled wrath upon him and he died.

MAN:6:21 The land writhed under the wrath of the Destroyer and groaned with the agony of Egypt. It shook itself and the temples and palaces of the nobles were thrown down from their foundations. The highborn ones perished in the midst of the ruins, and all the strength of the land was stricken. Even the great one, the first born of Pharaoh, died with the highborn in the midst of the terror and falling stones. The children of princes were cast out into the streets and those who were not cast out died within their abodes.

MAN:6:22 There were nine days of darkness and upheaval, while a tempest raged such as never had been known before. When it passed away, brother buried brother throughout the land. Men rose up against those in authority and fled from the cities to dwell in tents in the outlands.

MAN:6:23 Egypt lacked great men to deal with the times. The people were weak from fear and bestowed gold, silver, lapis lazuli, turquoise and copper upon the slaves, and to their priests they gave chalices, urns and ornaments. Pharaoh alone remained calm and strong in the midst of confusion. The people turned to wickedness in their weakness and despair. Harlots walked through the streets unashamed. Women paraded their limbs and flaunted their womanly charms. Highborn women were in rags and the virtuous were mocked.

MAN:6:24 The slaves spared by the Destroyer left the accursed land forthwith. Their multitude moved in the gloom of a half dawn, under a mantle of fine swirling grey ash, leaving the burnt fields and shattered cities behind them. Many Egyptians attached themselves to the host, for one who was great led them forth, a priest prince of the inner courtyard.

MAN:6:25 Fire mounted up on high, and its burning left with the enemies of Egypt. It rose up from the ground as a fountain and hung as a curtain in the sky.

MAN:6:26 In seven days, by Remwar, the accursed ones journeyed to the waters. They crossed the heaving wilderness while the hills melted around them; above, the skies were torn with lightning. They were sped by terror, but their feet became entangled in the land and the wilderness shut them in. They knew not the way, for no sign was constant before them.

MAN:6:27 They turned before Noshari and stopped at Shokoth, the place of quarries. They passed the waters of Maha and came by the valley of Pikaroth, northward of Mara. They came up against the waters which blocked their way, and their hearts were in despair. The night was a night of fear and dread, for there was a high moaning above, and black winds from the underworld were loosed, and fire sprang up from the ground. The hearts of the slaves shrank within them, for they knew the wrath of Pharaoh followed them and that there was no way of escape. They hurled abuse on those who led them; strange rites were performed along the shore that night. The slaves disputed among themselves, and there was violence.

MAN:6:28 Pharaoh had gathered his army and followed the slaves. After he departed, there were riots and disorders behind him, for the cities were plundered. The laws were cast out of the judgement halls and trampled underfoot in the streets. The storehouses and granaries were burst open and robbed. Roads were flooded, and none could pass along them. People lay dead on every side. The palace was split, and the princes and officials fled, so that none was left with authority to command. The lists of numbers were destroyed, public places were overthrown and households became confused and unknown.

MAN:6:29 Pharaoh pressed on in sorrow, for behind him all was desolation and death. Before him were things he could not understand, and he was afraid, but he carried himself well and stood before his host with courage. He sought to bring back the slaves, for the people said their magic was greater than the magic of Egypt.

MAN:6:30 The host of Pharaoh came upon the slaves by the saltwater shores, but was held back from them by a breath of fire. A great cloud was spread over the hosts and darkened the sky. None could see, except for the fiery glow and the unceasing lightnings, which rent the covering cloud overhead.

MAN:6:31 A whirlwind arose in the East and swept over the encamped hosts. A gale raged all night, and in the red twilit dawn there was a movement of the Earth, the waters receded from the seashore and were rolled back on themselves. There was a strange silence and then, in the gloom, it was seen that the waters had parted, leaving a passage between. The land had risen, but it was disturbed and trembled, the way was not straight or clear. The waters about were as if spun within a bowl, the swampland alone remained undisturbed. From the horn of the Destroyer came a high, shrilling noise which stopped the ears of men.

MAN:6:32 The slaves had been making sacrifices in despair; their lamentations were loud. Now, before the strange sight, there was hesitation and doubt; for the space of a breath they stood still and silent. Then, all was confusion and shouting, some pressing forward into the waters against all who sought to flee back from the unstable ground. Then, in exaltation, their leader led them into the midst of the waters through the confusion. Yet, many sought to turn back into the host behind them, while others fled along the empty shores.

MAN:6:33 All became still over the sea and upon the shore, but behind, the Earth shook and boulders split with a great noise. The wrath of heaven was removed to a distance and stood upwards of the two hosts.

MAN:6:34 Still, the host of Pharaoh held its ranks, firm in resolve before the strange and awful happenings, and undaunted by the fury, which raged by their side. Stern faces were lit darkly by the fiery curtain.

MAN:6:35 Then, the fury departed, and there was silence; stillness spread over the land while the host of Pharaoh stood without movement in the red glow Then, with a shout, the captains went forward, and the host rose up behind them. The curtain of fire had rolled up into a dark billowing cloud, which spread out as a canopy. There was a stirring of the waters, but they followed the evildoers past the place of the great whirlpool. The passage was confused in the midst of the waters and the ground beneath unstable. here, in the midst of a tumult of waters, Pharaoh fought against the hindmost of the slaves and prevailed over them, and there was a great slaughter amid the sand, the swamp and the water. The slaves cried out in despair, but their cries were unheeded.

MAN:6:36 Their possessions were scattered behind them as they fled, so that the way was easier for them than for those who followed.

MAN:6:37 Then the stillness was broken by a mighty roar, and through the rolling pillars of cloud, the wrath of the Destroyer descended upon the hosts. The Heavens roared as with a thousand thunders, the bowels of the Earth were sundered and Earth shrieked its agony. The cliffs were torn away and cast down. The dry ground fell beneath the waters, and great waves broke upon the shore, sweeping in rocks from seaward.

MAN:6:38 The great surge of rocks and waters overwhelmed the chariots of the Egyptians who went before the footmen. The chariot of the Pharaoh was hurled into the air as if by a mighty hand and was crushed in the midst of the rolling waters.

MAN:6:39 Tidings of the disaster came back by Rageb, son of Thomat, who hastened on ahead of the terrified survivors because of his burning. He brought reports unto the people that the host had been destroyed by blast and deluge. The captains had gone, the strong men had fallen, and none remained to command. Therefore, the people revolted because of the calamities which had befallen them. Cowards slunk from their lairs and came forth boldly to assume the high offices of the dead. Comely and noble women, their protectors gone, were their prey; of the slaves the greater number had perished before the host of Pharaoh.

MAN:6:40 The broken land lay helpless, and invaders came out of the gloom like carrion. A strange people came up against Egypt, and none stood to fight, for strength and courage were gone.

MAN:6:41 The invaders, led by Alkenan, came up out of the Land of Gods, because of the wrath of Heaven which had laid their land waste. There, too, had been a plague of reptiles and ants, signs and omens and an earthquake. There, also, had been turmoil and disaster, disorder and famine, with the grey breath of the Destroyer sweeping the ground and stopping the breath of men.

MAN:6:42 Anturah gathered together the remnants of his fighting men and the fighting men who were left in Egypt, and set forth to meet the Children of Darkness who came out of the eastern mountains by way of the wilderness and by way of Yethnobis. They fell upon the stricken land from behind the grey cloud, before the lifting of the darkness and before the coming of the purifying winds.

MAN:6:43 Rageb went with Pharaoh and met the invaders at Herosher, but the hearts of the Egyptians were faint within them. Their spirits were no longer strong and they fell away before the battle was lost. Deserted by the gods above and below, their dwellings destroyed, their households scattered, they were as men already half dead. Their hearts were still filled with terror and with the memory of the wrath, which had struck them from out of Heaven. They were still filled with the memory of the fearsome sight of the Destroyer, and they knew not what they did.

MAN:6:44 Pharaoh did not return to his city. He lost his heritage and was seized by a demon for many days. His women were polluted, and his estates plundered. The Children of Darkness defiled the temples with rams and ravished women who were crazed and did not resist. They enslaved all who were left, the old, young men and boys. They oppressed the people, and their delight was in mutilation and torture.

MAN:6:45 Pharaoh abandoned his hopes and fled into the wilderness beyond the province of the lake, which is in the West towards the South. He lived a goodly life among the sand wanderers and wrote books.

MAN:6:46 Good times came again, even under the invaders, and ships sailed upstream. The air was purified, the breath of the Destroyer passed away, and the land became filled again with growing things. Life was renewed throughout the whole land.

MAN:6:47 Kair taught these things to the Children of Light in the days of darkness, after the building of the Rambudeth, before the death of the Pharaoh Anked.

MAN:6:48 This is written in this land and in our tongue by Leweddar who, himself, chose it for saving. It was not seen until the latter days.

Chapter Seven – Third Egyptian Scroll

MAN:7:1 This is the manner whereby the Sacred Records shall be kept, and their number is twelve books and four hundred and forty-two scrolls.

MAN:7:2 Four copies shall be made, and each shall be rolled on a stick of blackwood. Each shall be enclosed within a pickled skin and bound with a leathern throng. It shall be placed with spices in a box of copper, which shall be enclosed in a box of wood bound about with hide and pitched.

MAN:7:3 At each of the four appointed places shall be four hewn masonry receptacles, within which shall be contained the Great Arks. They shall be kept by the Guardians at the four quarters of the Earth, and no copies shall be made, except one be destroyed.

MAN:7:4 Nothing shall be added and nothing taken away from the books, except it be done according to the books, and the signs of the books shall be counted according to the custom of writing.

Chapter Eight – Fourth Egyptian Scroll

MAN:8:1 Man directs his life by the laws of God and the statutes of men. The statutes of men, which are for the good of men, are to be upheld by the Children of Light, who shall not live for the next life alone.

MAN:8:2 These laws, though stricken on marble and set up on everlasting pillars at the gateways of the temples, are but diversions for the eye and exercise for the tongue, unless graven also on the tablets of your heart. Thus, you shall not fall into error.

MAN:8:3 A man does not obey the statutes because they are the law of the land, but because they accord with his nature and inclinations. The true nature of man stems from the godly directive within and is, therefore, above the edicts of kings.

MAN:8:4 In upholding the laws and statutes, the chief concern should be a man's good intent. If he intends well and is diligent, he can be forgiven much, but if he intends well and is thoughtless, then he shall not be looked upon so kindly. Remember; men do not dispense justice, they can but hope to serve it. God alone knows who is good or wicked within his heart; therefore, He alone can dispense true justice.

MAN:8:5 These are the laws by which man will live:

MAN:8:6 A man will not have intercourse with a womanchild.

MAN:8:7 A man will not rob another with violence or plunder or steal.

MAN:8:8 A man will not slay wilfully.

MAN:8:9 A man will not cheat another or act deceitfully towards him.

MAN:8:10 A man will not utter lies to lead another into error.

MAN:8:11 A man will not carry off food, so that another is deprived of the fruits of his labour.

MAN:8:12 A man will not utter words of blasphemy or use foul language.

MAN:8:13 A man will not trespass upon the privacy of another or violate the sanctity of his household.

MAN:8:14 A man will not pillage the grainland or spoil the pastures.

MAN:8:15 A man will not listen in secret to the speech of others.

MAN:8:16 A man will not practise degrading things.

MAN:8:17 A man will not slander another.

MAN:8:18 A man will not have intercourse with the wife of another man.

MAN:8:19 A man will not pollute himself.

MAN:8:20 A man will not leave his household to go abroad about his task unwashed.

MAN:8:21 A man will not terrorise the unprotected or unreasonably attack any man.

MAN:8:22 A man will not break the just statutes of the land.

MAN:8:23 A man will not stir up strife maliciously.

MAN:8:24 A man will not make women and children weep in fear.

MAN:8:25 A man will not commit any deed of impurity.

MAN:8:26 A man will not pass judgement hastily or in the grip of wrath.

MAN:8:27 A man will not unnecessarily associate with half men or cowards.

MAN:8:28 A man will not befoul running waters.

MAN:8:29 A man will not curse the sacred things.

MAN:8:30 A man will not reject his kinfolk or leave his children unprotected.

MAN:8:31 A man will not use what another has used, after his death.

MAN:8:32 A man will not lie with a pregnant woman three months before she gives birth.

MAN:8:33 A man will not revile his parents.

MAN:8:34 A man will not mock the afflicted.

MAN:8:35 A man will not expose his nakedness to maidens or children.

MAN:8:36 A man will not torment the helpless or corrupt the young.

MAN:8:37 A man will not associate with thieves and deceivers.

MAN:8:38 A man will not harbour an adulterer.

MAN:8:39 A man will not pander to the lusts and weaknesses of others or seek to profit by them.

MAN:8:40 A man will not raise a harlot above her chosen station.

MAN:8:41 A man will not desert the path of duty, even though it lead him down to death.

MAN:8:42 A man will not turn a blind eye to wickedness.

MAN:8:43 A man will not speak in language of slaves.

MAN:8:44 A man is ever a man. He abides by these things because he is a man. If he turn aside from even one of them, may he be cursed with the triple curse.

Chapter Nine – The Half Scroll of Jasop

MAN:9:1 A man is not a man in the eyes of God according to the standards of men, but according to the standards of God.

MAN:9:2 A man is silent and calm; he stands steady like a rock amidst the tumult of raging waters. He bears himself patiently before the temper of a wrathful man and controls himself in the presence of a fool.

MAN:9:3 His decisions are made clearly and without undue haste. He is prepared for whatever may befall, his reckoning embraces both success and failure.

MAN:9:4 A man judges all men equally by one standard and expects each to act according to his capacity.

MAN:9:5 He is prepared to meet strength with strength. He does not shirk the issue with violent men, nor does he suppress his wrath when the cause is just.

MAN:9:6 A man safeguards his reputation and challenges those who would steal it from him.

MAN:9:7 He is prudent and wary; he is not easily beguiled. He weighs all things in his mind and concludes all things by reasoning.

MAN:9:8 A man receives the stranger with hospitality and politeness. He gives generously to the needy and eases the burden of the heavy-laden.

MAN:9:9 He is cheerful under difficulties, and his face is never sullen or mean.

MAN:9:10 A man never fawns upon his superiors, nor does he oppress his subordinates. He is neither a hypocrite nor a coward.

MAN:9:11 He does not mock the afflicted, and his arm is ready to their assistance. If he sees evil men at work, he does not turn aside.

MAN:9:12 A man is impartial in his dealings. He is fair and just to all men.

MAN:9:13 He understands the duties and responsibilities of a man and places these before his own welfare. He does not seek the places of pleasure when there is a task at hand.

MAN:9:14 A man befriends the friendless and oppressed. He supports the man in want. He respects the aged and infirm. He acts for the ignorant and shields them from the designs of crafty men. He instructs the unlearned.

MAN:9:15 He makes peace when the peace is just and war when the war is justified.

MAN:9:16 A man never betrays a friend, nor does he avoid him in his time of trouble. His friendship is not a thing of thistledown, to be blown away before the first puff from the winds of adversity.

MAN:9:17 He is vigilant in the cause of justice and swift to right a wrong.

MAN:9:18 A man acknowledges his ignorance and welcomes the teacher. He is ever eager to learn.

MAN:9:19 He gives bread to the man who is hungry and drink to the thirsty man. He provides a bed for the wayfarer and provisions for the victim of misfortune.

MAN:9:20 A man does not avoid his debts or shirk his obligations.

MAN:9:21 He is resolute in the face of adversity. He is not humiliated in defeat or cowed by greater strength.

MAN:9:22 A man is gentle at home and forceful in the field.

MAN:9:23 He is yielding at play and determined in the chase. He does not provoke a fight, neither does he avoid one.

MAN:9:24 A man remembers his manhood at all times. A man who is a man treats a woman as a woman.

Chapter Ten –
Scroll of Kulok - Section 4

MAN:10:1 These things are wicked and must be opposed: Fornication and seduction, for they degrade womanhood. Lies and deceit, for they sear the soul. Unclean ways and lewd speech, for they corrupt the body and lead along the path of unwholesomeness.

MAN:10:2 By these laws, you shall live:

MAN:10:3 A man shall not uncover his private parts unduly before men or expose them before any woman not his wife, or before any child. If he do so, he shall not go unpunished.

MAN:10:4 A woman shall not show her nakedness to any man or appear unduly unclad before any woman. If she does so, she shall be whipped and secluded.

MAN:10:5 A child being able to walk shall not go naked.

MAN:10:6 A womanchild shall not uncover her private parts before any person.

MAN:10:7 Neither mother nor father shall uncover themselves before their children, nor shall they permit their children to reveal their nakedness. If they do so, they shall be punished at the task.

MAN:10:8 If any man touch the private parts of a womanchild for lust, he shall be branded and whipped and cast out forthwith.

MAN:10:9 If any man use a manchild for lust, he shall be branded and cast out forthwith.

MAN:10:10 Any man using a beast for lustful purposes shall be removed from among the people, that he may live among the beasts of the wasteland.

MAN:10:11 Any man being cast out or removed from the people shall lose all his possessions, which shall become the property of those to whom he caused harm or disgrace.

Chapter Eleven – Sixty-Fourth Egyptian Scroll

MAN:11:1 The voice of the people cries out for the blood of the learned, and upon their heads the blood shall be. It is a time of sorrow, it is a time of distress, it is a time of tribulation.

MAN:11:2 It is the dark night of wickedness, when ignorance covers the Earth. Yet though the pillars of Heaven fall, though the great abyss open, the Earth shall not end until its purpose is fulfilled.

MAN:11:3 This is no new thing, for the darkness of ignorance has often followed the bright days of spiritual illumination; but we who dwell under the shadow of darkness see nought but the sorrows of our times. When the sunship lies at anchor, then will dawn the day not followed by darkness.

MAN:11:4 Look in the places of judgement, they are filled with low people, and unclean feet rest upon the footstools. Priests grow fat on riches bestowed for the preservation of the body, while those who speak of the preservation of the soul are tormented.

MAN:11:5 Men talk of the delights of life, but who cares for the eternal life of the spirit? We are as carrion yet unseen by the vultures, or as a tomb laying open to the despoilers.

MAN:11:6 Our doctrine is as a leprosy upon us, for the life of a man who cannot impart his knowledge to another is futile. Men live to learn and also to teach. He who learns, but does not teach takes all and gives nothing.

MAN:11:7 Dark looks are cast upon those filled with the ancient wisdom, the people's pleasure is with those who perform deeds of deceit. Then there are those who seek acclaim in lewdness. When they perform some filthy deed, the people say, "This was the custom of our fathers and our fathers' fathers before them; therefore, is it not permitted, even before The One God? But they reason wrongly, for He cannot condone any deed of filthiness or evil and He abhors unclean ways.

MAN:11:8 Men say, "Our eyes cannot deceive us, the eye sees that which is real, that which the eye sees is not unreal." Foolish people, who know not how little the eye sees! The real is real of itself, neither the eye of man nor his understanding makes it real or unreal.

MAN:11:9 Is a stone a thing unchanging, or is a star always a star? Who among you, people of ignorance, can see the bond between star and stone? Yet there is kinship in all things. The stars hanging above are not wholly apart from the heart of man.

MAN:11:10 In the Law all things are united, it gives stability to everything. To it, all things conform, even The Great God, for He will not break His own Law. Man cannot, for even in his working of wonders and deceit he must conform to the Law.

MAN:11:11 Our doctrine is the teaching of the Law, that and no more. He who seeks to know great secrets or probe hidden mysteries must first pass through the purifying fire of the Law. Without having done so he might as well seek to tie down the sun or cast a net around the stars.

MAN:11:12 Behold the secret places of The Great God. There, no magic is performed; there, no wonders displayed, there, all is peaceful and normal. There silence reigns.

MAN:11:13 The great temples shall pass away. The tumult and shouting of the people shall fade into the silence, and their habitations shall be ground into dust. Then shall still remain the hidden place of The Great God and still it shall be peaceful and normal.

MAN:11:14 Stand in the concourse of the people; does not good appear weak and wickedness powerful? It is true, but ten generations, a hundred generations hence, there will be more good on Earth, for generation by generation good eats into evil.

MAN:11:15 Men say, "There are many gods, therefore which among them shall we worship? We cannot know." They are confounded by their own foolishness, for choice is easy. They worship where they find inward peace and contentment, for spiritual illumination is found in more than one place.

MAN:11:16 The pillars of all wisdom are numbered as the fingers upon a hand. Five things alone are the concern of man. What is man? Where does he begin, and where does he end? Why does he exist, and how can he conduct his life in a manner best for him?

MAN:11:17 The Earth at his feet, the Heavens above, The Great God of gods or the unreal gods of men, the nightdreams, the inhabitants of the Netherworld, the spirits good and evil, all things seen and unseen are no concern of man unless they affect him for good or ill. That which does not affect man is of no importance. This alone is wisdom.

Chapter Twelve – Eighty-Seventh Scroll

MAN:12:1 Our deeds are as thistledown launched upon the wind. We know not whence the winds of chance will bear them, or whether they will take root or be borne away, as though they never were. Our works are as edifices of mud built upon the river banks, which are swept away by the rising waters. The one certain thing in life is change.

MAN:12:2 Men make plans. They are as nought, they are as words written on the waters, as commands given to the winds. Wise is he who knows the Plans of God, for to them the whole Earth conforms.

MAN:12:3 Men cry out at the tribulations of life, not knowing that by adversity alone can they find their souls. They say, "Why are we beset with trial and tribulation?" for they cannot understand the contest. They say, "Why must we seek and never find?" knowing not that life is nought but a search and at the end man can discover nothing except man.

MAN:12:4 O man, gaze well upon the Earth. See, is it not by its nature a place of labour and not a garden of pleasure, or a panderer to your weaknesses? Truth is found in the book of life, but it may be understood just by degrees. For who among men receiving the whole would not be overwhelmed and destroyed?

MAN:12:5 In general, men are childlike. Give the people deceitful things, and they will rejoice like children. Show them amusing things, and they will acclaim their pleasure. The gods of fear are held in reverence, but The Great God who banishes fear, they despise.

MAN:12:6 O foolish people; O foolish generation! With dust on my head I mourn your ignorance. With loud lamentations I decry your folly. Yet the path you have chosen, you have chosen freely. Ease and comfort appear to be your end and purpose.

MAN:12:7 The gods of deceit have temples of splendour, their priests are well clothed and overfed. But The Great God of Truth has no more than a hidden cavern, His servants are garbed in rags, and their bellies are empty.

MAN:12:8 The gods of lust and cruelty have storehouses of treasure, but The God of Kindness has not even a field.

MAN:12:9 The people worship gods that oppress and ignore The God who frees. They give to the gods that take and spurn The God who gives. O misguided generation!

MAN:12:10 O blind and ignorant people, to cherish the stone gods of death and mock The God of Life! O misguided generation, to clasp to its breast the things that inherit decay and spurn the things that inherit everlastingness!

MAN:12:11 Let the Destroyer come as the whirlwind of the barren places. In the dread day of its appearance, the works of ignorance shall go down to everlasting.

Chapter Thirteen – Ninety-Third Scroll

MAN:13:1 A man shuns the deceitfulness of the wanton woman, for her words are like honey, but her beauty is to men as the flame to the moth. Her skin may be smoother than oil and her caress gentle as a feather, but her heart is hard and her ways are shameful.

MAN:13:2 Her feet tread the ways of disease and death, and she is a decoy for the Eater of Souls. Her steps incline not towards the joyful path of life, and her hand leads the trusting to misery and loneliness.

MAN:13:3 A wanton woman is man's greatest affliction; she wanders and is unpredictable. Though she be bathed in perfumed waters and anointed with sweetness, painted and clothed in fine linen, her adornment is no more than the crust over a quicksand. Within herself, the betrayer of womanhood is unclean and polluted.

MAN:13:4 What is the desire aroused by the deceitful beauty of the wanton woman but something spawned in weakness? Her provocative eyes may stir your manhood, her moist lips may call to you in the simulated language of love, and her lithesome form may quicken your heartbeat. But what is the value of all the harlot has? Not more than one loaf of bread or a measure of corn; yet, her cost is the wholesomeness of man. A man may not handle hot coals and remain unburnt.

MAN:13:5 The harlot is the destroyer of manhood. She blights the soul, she is the dweller in the antechamber of unclean things, the servant of horrors, the handmaiden of disease. The womanliness of a harlot is as a silken robe on the back of a swine.

MAN:13:6 The forces of whoredom are strong, they have servants in the fortress of man's body. They strike when he is weak, they rob and they destroy. They take that, which cannot be replaced.

MAN:13:7 Flee from all harlots as from a leper or those with the disease of running sores. Let not the pollutions of harlotry enter the stronghold of your body.

MAN:13:8 A man who is a man is worthy of a chaste wife, clean in body and pure in thoughts. Her wholesomeness shall gladden his heart, and in her hands his contentment is secure. With her, he shall find fulfilment and joy.

MAN:13:9 Marry a chaste woman, that you may have a faithful wife and live in peace among men. Let not the nights of your journeyings be spent in sleeplessness and doubt.

MAN:13:10 Rejoice and be content in the love of the wife of your youth, for it has been established. The foolish man disregards the proven love for shadowy love that may melt under adversity, as the morning mists melt before the sun.

MAN:13:11 Through all the eternal ages, women who are lovely and wayward have been and will be the sorrow and ruination of man. Envy not the man who rejoices in a beautiful wife; she may be his secret sorrow. Far more to be envied is he whose wife brings him contentment and joy.

MAN:13:12 He who finds a good wife is fortunate above the man who finds riches. He who treats a good wife with indifference is as the man who leaves open the door of his treasurehouse.

MAN:13:13 The husband who harbours an adulteress is both weak and wicked, for he encourages adultery in others. He is selfish, for he thinks of one man and not of all men. He condones the mockery of love, and his weakness contributes to the sorrows of better men.

MAN:13:14 The wrong is not great when a hungry man steals bread, and less when he steals it for his hungry children. The adulterer steals that from which he gets no benefit and in doing so brings sorrow and shame on the heads of the innocent.

MAN:13:15 Where is his joy when he gathers a woman to his breast, not in peace and contentment but in the manner of a thief? Furtive love is false love; at the best it is love betraying itself.

MAN:13:16 Stolen bread is often the sweetest, and hidden waters the most pleasant, but under the hand of the adulterer the sweetness putrefies and the pure becomes unclean.

MAN:13:17 Is it not written in the statutes and in the nature of man that if a man come upon his wife in adultery and, in his just wrath, shall slay, then he commits no great wrong? It is the duty of a man to protect his home, but he owes a greater duty which decrees that he uphold the sanctity of every home. He who lets adultery go unpunished condones it and mocks the things a man should cherish and honour.

MAN:13:18 The lion maintains the sanctity of his mate; the jackal is indifferent. A man will follow the ways of men; a cur the way of curs.

MAN:13:19 My son, the day comes when your heart reaches out towards woman and you desire a wife. It is well to choose her with prudence, to select carefully, without passion and without lust. Who is the woman who claims the heart of a man, whose love is the sun of his dwelling, in whose pure radiance he delightfully bathes?

MAN:13:20 She is modest and quiet-spoken, sweet womanly innocence blooms on her cheek. She is diligent in seeking work, for her hand and foot do not stray from her household. Observe her in the house of her father, note her ways with care. She takes delight in simple pleasures, her demands are moderate, and she behaves with decorum. Lewdness is silenced before her glance. She is attired with neatness, and her adornments are not overmany. Her voice is low; gentle decency and mildness of speech are virtues from which she never departs. She walks with prudence on one hand and chastity on the other; before her go discretion and decorum. In her eye is the light of love, and her smile is the caress of affection.

MAN:13:21 Her overwhelming virtue grips the tongues of lewd men and they are silenced. When the mouth of scandal is abroad, the doors of her ears are closed. Her delight is not in the misfortunes of others, nor does she find pleasure in the re-telling of their misdeeds.

MAN:13:22 Her thoughts are a fountain of purity, and she remains unsullied by the wickedness splashed by others. When she marries, her dwelling becomes a haven of peace for her husband and a well of wisdom to quench the questing thirst of her children.

MAN:13:23 Her delight is in the care of her household and her good management a joy to her husband. She fashions the thoughts of her children with example, and the words, which fall from her mouth are heard with obedience. Withal, her character is strong, were it not she could not be as she is. Fortitude and courage are not the least of her qualities.

MAN:13:24 O joyful the man who calls her wife, and joyful the child who calls her mother! Among all Earth's treasures she is the greatest and too often the least valued.

Chapter Fourteen – Ninety-Sixth Scroll

MAN:14:1 I am ashamed, for naked bodies are exposed to lewd glances and lustful looks. There is foolish laughter and foul words spoken among the onlookers.

MAN:14:2 Yet it is not the naked body that is degraded, for bodies are things of beauty. In the beginning, God moulded the body to its shape, knowing that in the days to come His Spirit would dwell therein when entering the matter of Earth.

MAN:14:3 It was shaped slowly, with care and foresight. Loving hands wrought its wonderful form, and the day dawned when it became the abode of a living soul. Then God commanded, "Respect this, the vessel of the ever living spirit, for it is a great and delicate thing meant for communion one with another. It is My supreme achievement upon earth."

MAN:14:4 Therefore, though the body be not supreme it is a thing of greatness, it is a glorious temple meant to be the residence of a god. It can speak, and words bring it into companionship with other souls.

MAN:14:5 It reflects without the spirit dwelling within; the smile, the laugh, the eyes reveal it. The body is a thing of glory, it is the greatest of all material creations.

MAN:14:6 Man and woman embrace and unite; two bodies and two spirits join together in the search for another servant of The Supreme Spirit. There can be no greater responsibility, for their task is to find a worthy one. To man and woman has been given the power of creation, they can use it for good or ill. The beasts know not what they do; they mate in blind ignorance, impelled by desire alone. Yet, never do they bring forth creatures unsuited for their purpose. Man and woman, with freedom of choice and knowledge, do not do so well because, impelled by unworthy desires, they choose unwisely. Where are the thoughts of men when they mate, upon themselves or upon their children?

MAN:14:7 That which causes man and woman to forget their responsibility, which arouses in them desires and thoughts, which they cannot control, is not a thing of goodness; it is an instrument of evil. Why should men cover their bodies and women hide their nakedness? Not because naked bodies are things to be ashamed of, but because of what the eye of the beholder makes of them. The God-made eyes see beauty, but the man-fashioned thoughts interpret it lewdly. Did the sight stimulate him to goodness, it would be good, for all that serves good is good.

MAN:14:8 The simple and thoughtless woman may display her secret charms in innocence, for she cannot see into the thoughts of lewd men. Her wrongdoing lies in the fact that she feeds their lustfulness and panders to their evil thoughts. Anything a woman does, which stimulates goodness in men is good, whatever she does to the contrary is wrong.

MAN:14:9 O change our thoughts and outlook, that our feelings may become servants and not masters! That they may serve the cause of good, which is the cause of man, and not the cause of evil, which is the degradation of man.

MAN:14:10 Make our bodies wholesome residences and not foul prisons. Purify our thoughts, that they may properly direct our bodies, and dedicate them as fitting vehicles for our journey through life. Let this glorious material creation be fittingly inhabited, and let it be illuminated from within with the flame of a pure spirit.

Chapter Fifteen – Scroll of Kulok - Sections 2 and 3

MAN:15:1 Thus it is written on the Tablets of Fate: Whatever may be accomplished at the sunrising, let not the sunsetting find undone.

MAN:15:2 When you build, build as forever and your fame shall be sung among the great in the Everlasting Halls.

MAN:15:3 He who has done you one good turn will be more ready to do you another than will the one, to whom you have done a good turn. Expect not that the deeds of men should accord with the dictates of reason or be ruled by consideration of right.

MAN:15:4 There are men who live for themselves alone, and their souls are smothered in the deadly winding sheet of selfishness. There is no greater loneliness than that of a man who lives for himself alone. He looks about him and says, "All men seek to do me wrong. All men seek to be over me." His life is a problem, and his days are filled with anxiety. He says, "What if tomorrow I shall not eat?." And furtively steals from his friend. He hoards that which he cannot use.

MAN:15:5 His soul is twisted and ugly, his countenance is mean, his days are a burden and his nights sleepless. He deals harshly with those under his hand, for, secretly acknowledging his own inferiority, he distrusts all men.

MAN:15:6 These things are written in the third section of the Scroll of Kulok: Consider the petty man, his deeds are mean and his manner servile, his heart shakes in a small breast. See him among the concourse of the people, and his eyes shift from side to side. He shuffles about his affairs, and his path is not straight.

MAN:15:7 He is spiteful and malicious. Like a snake, he crawls in the dust, ever ready to strike blindly at those above him, not knowing that their eyes are fixed far above his element, and he is unseen.

MAN:15:8 He gossips and prattles like an idle woman and men look down upon him, for his ways are those of a half man. His pettiness is an irritation to all.

MAN:15:9 His residence is a place of torment, for his wife despises him, and his children are wayward. He has no friends, and men visit him for nought but their own benefit.

MAN:15:10 His time is occupied with matters of small moment, and bigger undertakings overwhelm him. The deeds of greater men he cannot understand and therefore derides them.

MAN:15:11 Consider the vulgar man, his voice is loud, and his words bawdy. Like the ass he laughs without understanding. His tongue rattles in his head, he makes noise but not sense.

MAN:15:12 In his ignorance he pushes himself forward when, with his meagre talents, he should remain behind. The tongue of a vulgar man betrays him and holds him up to mockery. His companions are petty men and hypocrites.

MAN:15:13 He is jovial in the midst of sorrow and speaks loudly when others whisper. He is a man afraid of silences; he is a man afraid of himself. He has no understanding of the innocence of children and no respect for the modesty of women. He is a man well left to himself.

MAN:15:14 Consider the cowardly man; his mother does not grieve at his absence, for she is ashamed of his face. His father shuns him, and he becomes the companion of hypocrites.

MAN:15:15 His wife goes in fear of every man, while her thoughts turn to better men. His children are mocked, and his father insulted. His son has to establish his place, and his daughter commands no respect. For a coward, to marry is a wrongdoing.

MAN:15:16 He has no friends, for all men avoid him. His manner is furtive, and he slinks from place to place. He can put on a bold front, and may deceive foolish women, but underneath his heart is craven. Put to the test by men, he is found wanting.

MAN:15:17 Consider the man of no account, he is improvident and wasteful. He speaks of his own importance, but deceives none but himself and the foolish. The easiest person for any man to deceive is himself. The man of no account walks the marketplace to buy a stone.

MAN:15:18 Without merit himself, he appeals to the deeds of his forefathers for credit. What good is it to the blind man that his father could see? What benefit to the illiterate that his father could write? In what way can it raise the standing of a man of no account if his father's father was of good standing and repute? Is it not more to his discredit that he is what he is? He who walks in the shadow of his father's reputation has none of his own.

MAN:15:19 He who establishes his reputation upon that of another erects a building without foundation. The ass of Pharaoh is still an ass. A worthless man does worthless things. His death removes an encumbrance from the Earth.

MAN:15:20 Consider the man of honourable estate; his wife is fully married and not made ashamed by a life under the double law. His household is well fed, and his servants obedient.

MAN:15:21 He uses his strength to protect the weak, and his arm is swift to right an injustice. He remembers that the greatest injustices are wrought in the name of justice.

MAN:15:22 He does not permit the weakling and hypocrite to rise to high position by cunning. He seeks out wickedness to destroy it, and cannot remain passive in its presence.

MAN:15:23 His children are dutiful and obedient. His fields are well cared for, and his estate prosperous. His treasures serve the good of the people and promote contentment and harmony. His riches are not spent selfishly or foolishly.

MAN:15:24 Consider the courageous man; his wife holds her head high, for she is proud of her standing. She fears not the lewd looks of base men, nor the mocking smiles of women.

MAN:15:25 The courageous man has many friends, and men turn to him in times of trouble.

He is as a rock among raging waters. He is the shield of the unprotected and the sword of the weak.

MAN:15:26 His arm is steady, and his thoughts clear. He walks among the people with head held high, for he fears no man. Lesser men give way before him, and he is followed by the admiring glances of women.

MAN:15:27 Consider the half man; his ways are the ways of woman without her charms. He sickens the stomachs of men, and women turn from him in disgust. He is ever treated with scorn and contempt. He fawns and makes himself lowly, that he might please true men.

MAN:15:28 He is unclean within, and filth lurks on his lips, ever ready to fall and pollute. He is small-hearted and seeks his pleasure among vile things. He is an abomination to true men, for he is a man in form alone. As his vile thoughts mould his speech and actions into a mockery of womanhood, so do they twist his soul into an image of horror. He who is not wholly a man is no man. He who is the companion of half men is a half man himself.

Chapter Sixteen – Scroll of Horemaket

MAN:16:1 This is the revelation of The All Glorious One, who was with us on Earth as a Master and now dwells in the Place of Eternal Brightness.

MAN:16:2 I am as I was, the devoted friend of the friendless, the servant of those who sat at my feet and the lover of all. I dwell amid brightness in endless joy, in the place of blending, for when flame unites with flame, there is but one flame, and when waters mingle with waters, there is but one water. When all is merged in one, then the difference is removed.

MAN:16:3 That which once was heavy is now light. As once I was in the body, so am I now in spirit. All that was once impure has been purged away, the painful darkness of earthly life is no more. The heavy burden of restriction has gone; I am free.

MAN:16:4 The deluded eyes now see clearly; the stifled tongue is freed, and the insensitive ears are opened. Life is an everlasting melody of glory. The falsehoods taught by the body no longer hold me in bondage. The fetters are struck off my limbs, and the bandage removed from my eyes.

MAN:16:5 I no longer desire the things unearned, nor do I refuse the enjoyments of my gains. I stand alone in wisdom and peace. Beyond the range of earthly senses, the past is no longer a shackle at my ankle.

MAN:16:6 I am garbed in my own true changeless form. I stand forth in Truth. and all may see me as I truly am. I am firm and changeless, unalterable in time.

MAN:16:7 I perform the tasks that come to my hand, and amidst inactivity, I perform unceasingly. I am not apart from bodily activities, for that which once held me captive has been exchanged for a form infinitely more glorious.

MAN:16:8 The heart-gladdening enjoyments remain, and the nectar of wisdom still feeds me. I am nourished by knowledge, and the way of enquiry remains open. I am unrestricted in movement and see through limitless space. I am as a prisoner unbound. That which is unseen by you is seen by me, that which is unknown to you is not unknown to me. I know the nature of the firmament, which came forth from God and, of which all things are made. I know the nature of the forming force which unceasingly shapes things out of formless matter.

MAN:16:9 I know not past or future, yet I am not without them and all are merged into the present. In truth I know not eternity yet, for that still remains beyond my reach. It is there, just beyond my horizon. It is the attainable goal not yet reached, the end of the journey. I am freed from earthly cares and no longer bound by the demands of the body. I am free; I am pure.

MAN:16:10 I am established in glory. I am The Self-Formed One, I am The Arisen One, I am The Glorious One, I am The Victorious One.

MAN:16:11 All is in me, and I am in all. I can span ten thousand earths or dwell within the heart of a mote. There is no here and yonder, the far is near and the near far. I can move in matter, but I cannot manifest. I cannot rend the veil between matter and spirit, yet I can commune soul with soul.

MAN:16:12 There is about me an infinitely vast expanse of unmoulded space wherewith to labour, and this is a place of unending toil and gratification. I stand on the strand of a formless sea. Earthly words are unavailing for expression and lead to falsity and confusion. It is like trying to pour the Nile through a straw.

MAN:16:13 You ask for words to guide, and I answer thus: Be still, be quiet, rest in silence, with tranquillity of heart. Calm the restless surges of unbidden thoughts, the oppressions of uncontrolled desires. There, in the stillness and silence, you will be a shining, motionless, unflickering light, like a flame of a candle on a windless night. That is the pure flame of self, the light that guides towards divinity. It is the small light of eternal wisdom lit from the infinite flame of Truth.

MAN:16:14 Of all things on Earth, Truth is the hardest to find. Men who have not expended effort say they possess it, but it is not for them. Truth is the supreme reward for those who have successfully passed an almost unendurable test. It is not a prize awarded in a simple contest.

Chapter Seventeen – Scroll of Netertat

MAN:17:1 Your servant, Netertat, priest at the Temple of the Seer of Heaven at Nethom, found this writing when he was the Opener of Doors for Penekin. It is a writing so old that few could be found who knew the nature of its signs, and they no more than servants of the Kohar. Yet one who has enjoyed peace within Your shadow undertook the task of re-shaping them with pleasure, for as fire is born of the spark, so are the joys of his life kindled by the brightening countenance.

MAN:17:2 The writings of old declare the wisdom of our forefathers, which is the treasure trove of man and the inheritance of our days. Thus, it is written:

MAN:17:3 All things on Earth are compounded of two flowing powers, the right hand power and the left hand power; the first predominates in men and the second in women. Where they fall nearly equal, the being is neither wholly man nor wholly woman.

MAN:17:4 The Spirit of Life resides in the air men breathe and is shared with the beasts, the trees, the things that crawl, the birds, the fishes, the herbs and the grass. It quickens the living hearts of men and is diffused through the blood of the body.

MAN:17:5 Man sleeps when his spirit departs for refreshment at the fount of its being. Even as his mortal body must sustain itself with things of the earth, so must his spirit seek sustenance in the place of its being.

MAN:17:6 In sleeping, the spirit of man departs in part alone, it goes not wholly or as one awakened. When his God calls him away, his soul goes to the place of decision, where fate is decreed. There, by the underground river, the good are separated from the wicked, but the river is not a river of water. In Dat, all things are made known, and the river is the river of life.

MAN:17:7 Outside of man, between God and Man, is the reflection of God, which men call Nature. It can be disturbed by man and distorted, even as the reflections in a pool of clear water are disturbed by the drop of a pebble. Nature accords exactly with the greater needs of men, with their desires and beliefs, and with what they have deserved. It is also a modifying force operating upon the conditions of their testing. It is the Breath of God expressed in living things. It is, to God, as the material web of the spider is to the living thing, they are separate and unalike, yet one.

MAN:17:8 There is a fine, unbreakable thread, one end of which is secured in the Spirit Centre, wherein dwells The Everlasting Being, The Eternal One. The other end is fastened to matter, and between the two is the web of creation spun out of the single thread of invisible substances by the forming power of God.

MAN:17:9 All that we can know as mortals exists within the sphere of mortality. All was originally compounded from the fiery dust, the first expression of the out-breathing of God, upon which the forming power operated. As hair grows from the skin of the head, which is nothing like hair; as a tree springs up from the soil, which is nothing like a tree; as the spider spins its web and then withdraws, so does mortal matter come forth from the immortal spiritual substance. As the shadow is to the object that gives it form, so is the material to the spiritual. All things are held together by the spiritual womb-web. The form is there, but the shape is here.

MAN:17:10 Nature is the Spirit of God manifesting in matter, it is the spiritual form seeking outlet and expression in matter. It is the maker, the means of making and the thing made, though all these activities are in a subordinate capacity. Spirit is not Nature. Spirit is the source of all consciousness, which experiences both pleasure and pain. The spirit of man, when in contact with Nature, feels the ever changing conditions of Nature.

MAN:17:11 He who understands that activity anywhere is but the working of Nature and that God oversees this labour, understands the truth. Nature is never still, it is ever moving. Man is a creature bound to things ever changing. On the great scales, he is balanced between the eternal adversaries - good and evil.

MAN:17:12 At death, the senses perish, but the memory of them endures. The spirit roams the Morningland free, with all its beliefs, its desires and its memories intact. The arisen man awakes as from a brief sleep and finds himself in the Place of Decision; there, a body awaits him, as substantial as the one he has discarded.

Chapter Eighteen – Prayer of Hapu

MAN:18:1 "O my Lord of Wisdom, I have been laid low by sickness and smitten by every disaster that can befall a mortal man. No priest or diviner and no wise man can deliver me, by purification and rites, from the great wrath which has descended upon me. I have prayed, I have made sacrifices, I have chanted in procession, I have paid all due tributes and I have not cheated any man. Yet, though everything I have done was good, all men avoid me because of the presence of evil about me and the shadow of misfortune that hovers overhead. Am I a man deluded in thought, can it be that the things men dream to be good are evil in the light of Your greater insight and understanding?"

MAN:18:2 "My ploughlands and pastures are like a woman without a husband and I diligently search my heart to discover wherein I have failed, that this should be my lot. Am I the prey of powers and causes beyond my understanding? O my God, illuminate my heart with wisdom, even as Your glorious shield lightens our path through the day. I seek an answer, so that I may understand, but I am mocked by the muteness of silence. I speak from the inner recesses of my heart and say, how shall I commune with my God; where shall I seek Him, what offerings will He accept? I ask others, but they know not; I seek the counsel of the wise, but they talk in riddles. I am told that my wickedness is the barrier between us, but what have I ever done to hurt You? What could I, a mere mortal man, do to have ill effect upon the greatest of all divinities? If, in my ignorance, I did wrong in Your sight, it was not my will; it was an illusion, it was thoughtlessness, bad temper or beer. The weak are led astray by stronger men, even when asleep men are led astray to sin, Therefore O Mighty One, overlook my errors. How shall I call upon You, O my God, I who have served You well, I who am the ever loyal and loving one, I who have remained constant under oppression and adversity?"

MAN:18:3 "I have faith, though not without doubt, yet I am not dismayed. I can see that to progress man needs both, for he who has but one unleavened with the other is easily misled. Though no sign has ever been given me, I am not cast down, for I have known one who has enjoyed the full splendour of inner vision and the communicating ability. Where do we differ, he and I, in Your sight? I search my heart truly and can find no great wrong done to others. What small wickednesses I have committed have been done in hot-headed haste, or while led astray by strong drink or in thoughtlessness. I have never wilfully done harm to another fellow being."

MAN:18:4 "What is there in man that sends his thoughts afar, seeking the unknown? Who first struck the spark of life and sent it forth on its mission to fill the Earth with its glorious burning flame? My pen sets down these words, and behind the pen is my hand. Behind the hand are my heart and will, and behind them my loving spirit. What stands at the other end of the chain reaching upward from these words? Can it be that man is unable to see You are the directing power within his thoughts, because his thoughts are themselves within You? Is it that the within cannot see the without, though the without sees the within? Are my thoughts in a tangled skein which I lack the ability to unravel? Though not a scribe, I write because my father wrote, yet I am not a learned man. Can it be that things hidden from me are known to other men?"

MAN:18:5 "Whatever directs the thoughts of men does not leave them free from doubt. It arises strongly when a man dies, for some say he still is, while others say he is not. Which, O my God, is true? Teach me; let me know, that I may tell it unto all men. Is there an inborn thing in man, which never dies? Is there an everlasting part in men, or are they all heirs of decay? Men seek assurance and are told to have faith. They want a substantial God they can see, and therefore make an idol of wood or stone, can this be so very wrong? Men need a rule of life, something, in which they can repose absolute trust, they want sincerity and love."

MAN:18:6 "I cannot blame You, my God, if You have turned Your back on men, for they have deserted the path of righteousness shown them by the men of olden times. Truth is with us no more, and men choose the pleasant paths of ignorance in preference to the more austere and profitable one. The pure worship, which once filled this land and guided its people has fallen prey to greedy and ambitious men. Its cornerstone is no longer the rigorous life of devoted service, which brings its own revelation. Its centrepiece is no longer the dark chamber of austerity where great spirits sought the light, but the pomp of elaborate but empty ceremonial and futile sacrifice. It is a thing of well organised but barren ritual, the perverted tool of unscrupulous priests. The temples have become refuges for those who seek to avoid the trials of life. How can such as they ever be true servants of my God? Where, except from among them, can He find servants? I see, I understand, but, my God, it is hard for one who suffers such as I to face the truth without bitterness. Am I, who did not ask to enter this place of sorrows, to suffer for the wrongdoing and ignorance of others? Is there no dividing line between those who remain loyal and those who have deserted You? Perhaps this, too, I understand, for are we not taught that all are brothers, and men stand and fall with their kindred?"

MAN:18:7 "I do not erase the words I have inscribed with heavy heart and a spirit overburdened with grief and perplexity, for through the enveloping mists of sorrow, I perceive a light dimly. This is my message to those who follow and who may be tossed on the turbulent waters of despondency and despair, my pitiful contribution to the great total of inherited wisdom: If you seek God and find Him not, then the blame lies with men and not with God. For the spirit of man has begotten something which has stepped between to stop the ears of the everlasting inner man. He is blinded by the thick mummy wrappings of muttered ritual and vain ceremonial, misled by ignorant and hypocritical priests. Yet God is still merciful, for knowing those destined for darkness and terror in the life to come, He showers success and good fortune upon them here. Knowing those destined for life as Glorious Ones, He further refines and tests them with sorrow and affliction, that their glory may be greater. I know, for in declaring my trust by setting forth these things, my heart has suddenly been filled with an indescribable light of spiritual illumination, and now I know greater things beyond any hint of doubt. I too am awakened."

Chapter Nineteen – One Hundred, Thirteenth Scroll

MAN:19:1 The boat-encircling rope is half chafed through. The chariot hand is broken and bound. The door socket is splintered and plastered. My son carries sand to the terminals, and my daughter sits at home. I wander wearily across a spiritual wilderness, tormented by deluding mirages of Truth. Nothing is whole, nothing is right.

MAN:19:2 The ways of a man are always right in his own eyes, but they deceive him and unless he has guidance of the law, he is led astray. Where is the law today? Is it where it should be, inscribed on the living hearts of the people? Or is it a thing written on dead scrolls rolled up and discarded? We make of our lives what we will, destiny supplies us with the yarn, which we weave into a pattern of beauty and utility, or tangle up into a hopeless wasteful confusion. Where are the craftsman spinners today?

MAN:19:3 A wise man is one who bathes in the waters of wisdom, a fool is one who wallows in the filth of folly. The well of wisdom is not a public place, from which anyone may draw without discrimination. Its entrance is barred to he of the loud mouth, but opens to receive the calm and silent one. Where, today, are the men of quiet manner and calm bearing?

MAN:19:4 No wise words or well phrased writings are needed to inform men that the light of the sun exceeds that of the moon, or that he who has toiled through the heat of the day will not lie on a bed of sleeplessness. Those are things experienced by a few, that are unknown to the many, that have to be explained. Such are spiritual things, but where, today, are those who have known and experienced them? Who can explain them to others?

MAN:19:5 Today, men seek to gather where they have not planted; they desire the increase, but disdain the effort. They seek to benefit through the toil of others, and unproductive tongues move vigorously, while skilled hands are idle. Men must learn that no more can be taken from the storehouse than was placed there. Where are the men of self-assurance, the men of straight tongue, of constant speech, that were known of yore? Today, if an ass were king, men would bray.

MAN:19:6 This is the day when fine speech flourishes, but it lacks substance; it falls from the tongue and is lost on the wind. The words of the night are soaked in honey, but as day dawns, they melt away with the dews of morning. Even the words of lovers are sweet for but a day; tomorrow they turn to bitterness and gall. O for the days that were, the joyous days now past, when words were things of substance with but one meaning! Now, my days are without object; they are spent in stringing and unstringing my lyre, while the song I wish to sing remains mute in my heart.

MAN:19:7 I do not look for the overthrow of evil, I do not bewail the existence of wickedness. These will always be while man remains mortal. Wickedness will flourish even in the House of God, for has He not ordained the Law, which permits a poisonous weed to flourish among healing herbs? Neither do I seek for any undue reward, nor do I consider my goodness deserves it. Goodness is the seed we sow in the soil of mortal life on Earth, to reap in the sunshine of Heaven. Yet I would enjoy some pleasure undiluted with sorrow. Now, even at the bottom of my rare cups of joy lie the dregs of bitterness and sorrow.

MAN:19:8 I have never failed to come to the aid of the poor and lowly. I have ever obeyed the laws of God and man. Goodness has always been honoured in my heart, and I have constantly read the Sacred Writings. Yet never have I found these things consistent with the mortal wellbeing. Because my tongue did not turn around corners and twist back on itself, because the words I spoke came from my heart, undiluted with any malicious thought, because I chided the rich for their selfishness and inconsideration, their wasteful living and meaningless activities, they became my enemies. Because I called upon the powerful to live according to the laws they professed to uphold and the words declared to be sacred, I was seized and imprisoned. When I protested the injustice to the ears of the people, I was beaten with rods, I was branded as one who seeks to destroy the stability of the land. I, who tried to set an example of goodness, to lead a life dedicated to my God, to convert the wicked to righteousness, am myself declared wicked by the workers of evil. Why is this, O my God? Have I, to my sorrow and undoing, weighed the values of life wrongly?

MAN:19:9 I, who was once a man of estate, am now poor; I have been deprived of all I possess. I supported the oppressed against the powerful and lent my arm to the lowly. I threw my own riches into the balances, to counter the injustices of the rich. What has been my reward from those to whom I gave aid and succour? Do they not mock me and hold me in contempt; am I not called a fool even by them? I am thrown crusts of bread in pity, but no man calls me friend. I speak to men, but they become restless and remember things, which call them away. The sight of me causes men to quicken their steps and change the direction of their journey. Has goodness, then, become a plague in the land? Yet, I have sought but to turn others from wickedness and to replace their misdeeds with deeds of goodness. I have sought to revalue virtue, so that it becomes honoured among men, not merely a plaything of words but a treasure held in the heart. Yet, men mock me, they say, "These are things, in which we too believe, but no man can wholly live by them. They are not the substance of life, and none but a fool discards the substance for the shadow."

MAN:19:10 Where is my dwelling, is it not occupied by one who wrings tears from widows and steals the food of orphans? The wicked one sleeps on a bed of comfort; the righteous one lays his head upon a stone. Where is my tomb? Does it not await one whose foot is heavy on the necks of the humble and whose yoke bears down intolerably on those who labour? The wicked one contemplates his end with contentment, a place of honour awaits him; the righteous one will mingle his bones with those of dogs and cattle.

MAN:19:11 Where are my servants? Do they not toil for one who deals with them harshly, who rejoices at the sweat that pours down on their labours? The wicked one sits on the seats of comfort; he wallows in an over-abundance of good things. The righteous one squats in the burning sun; he is grateful for a few crumbs and a little water.

MAN:19:12 Where is my wife? Is she not cast into bondage, an object of abuse and amusement? Is her master not a man of many useless words, one who dispenses lewdness for pleasure? What misery and degradation she suffers! The wicked one never lacks the delights and services of women; the righteous one lacks even a smile of compassion, a hand to touch his head.

MAN:19:13 Where are my children, the comfort and consolation of an old man? Do they not labour with bitterness of heart, bearing the scorn poured upon the grey head of their father with unrewarding fortitude?

MAN:19:14 The wicked ones display their riches and mock my children, saying, "All this is ours to enjoy or give others at our pleasure, where then is your reward?" The righteous one cannot give even a piece of rag to patch the garments of his offspring, or a morsel of food to ease their hunger.

MAN:19:15 Where are my riches, where my estate? Are they not enjoyed by the avaricious and haughty, the sly man and the cunning man, the hypocrite and deceiver? The wicked ones have no thought of righteousness and virtue; they are clad in comfort and filled to fullness. The righteous one has half a garment, and his next meal is unseen. Is Earth the heritage of the wicked or the heritage of the good? If goodness is to be won for Earth by example, then what must I do? If by words, what more can I say? If by weapons, can an unarmed man fight a multitude?

MAN:19:16 Where have I failed; I do not know, I have no answer, I believe, I hope. I am an old man bowed down with the cares of an old man. The fires of youth are burned out, leaving just the grey comfortless ashes. When men ask, I answer, "I do not know." Can any man answer more truthfully?

MAN:19:17 *

MAN:19:18 Ramotip, son of Yagob by Ilipa, daughter of Pasinesu, Commander of the Royal Protectors, found him by the road to Basiros, as he journeyed to meet the great bride. Ramotip took him to the Shrine of the Flame at Nozab; he had come home. The name Ramotip is honoured forever; gold and silver there was none.

MAN:19:19 He came to the mooring post among friends. Two alone in the House of the Lady of the Sycamore remain steadfast on the hard, grim road. They are protected by her illustrious mantle, they are hidden in her shadow. His scroll is placed among the scrolls that last forever; though it be but a splash in the Nile, it is his memorial. His name is on the Great Scroll.

MAN:19:20 His success was in his failure. In trying to change others, he changed himself. Each effort was a shaping stroke to glory. Earth is as it should be; it cannot be changed, but if a man would change himself to his own benefit, he must ever strike and seek to change it.

MAN:19:21 The message of this writing is not one of futility, but one of hope. No man could have better shaped his future.

MAN:19:22 These are the later days, yet things remain unchanged; the good suffer while the wicked prosper. Whose fault is this? Certainly not God's; this is a man-made state. It was built by strength and strength must smash it down and rebuild. The good have been too passive. Arise from your knees, and look the foe in the face. Strike a blow for God and good.

Chapter Twenty – Commentary of Frater Astorus

MAN:20:1 From the days of the Ancients have been heard the lamentations of the woeful and disheartened, and they ask the winds, "Where have we failed for the God we pray to remain unresponsive?" They air their goodness and virtues and ask why these have gone unrewarded. It becomes a grievance with them, and they know not where to seek the answer.

MAN:20:2 In this, our generation, goodly men have been robbed of their estates by warlike strangers, and their wives have even been ravaged by men, who have studied the ways of weaponry. Their possessions have been sold to provide earthly pleasure for those who revel in things of the Earth, and their households have been despoiled to give pleasure to fornicating fighters.

MAN:20:3 In their dire despair they seek to lay the blame upon a God, who does not strike down wrongdoers and seemingly rewards those who are earthlywise. Wherein have they failed? This is the echo in the corridors of the ages.

MAN:20:4 They have failed because they have left to God the things which they, as God's overseers on Earth, should have accomplished. It is men in the mass who permit evil to flourish in their midst. Their woeful lamentations ascend to Heaven and call upon the heavenly hosts for aid, but better by far would it be were they to call upon their own resolution and fortitude and fight the good fight, to bring about the rule of right and justice.

MAN:20:5 All that is wrong with the world has its genesis in men, and if evil stalks the land, then it follows the attitudes and acts of men. Therefore, it is men who must make recompense for their lack of effort-producing concern. If the people establish the way of iniquity as their way, then it is the wrongdoers who will be rewarded with bounty, and this is not God's will but man's.

MAN:20:6 If the people lament and are disenchanted with the way things are, then it is a time for action rather than a time for prayer. Pray not for heavenly help, but for a strong right arm and righteous wrath and resolution. The gospel of despair is for weaklings.

MAN:20:7 If evil be established by the sword, then it is because the swords of the good have lacked strength and numbers. Those who petition The Great God for help must be sure they have lacked nothing in their own preparations. They must fight strength with strength, and where they lack numbers, then they must fight with subtlety, but above all else they must fight. This is the law they have ignored, and their woebegotten lamentations are as a stench to The Most High.

Chapter Twenty-One – The Nightfight

MAN:21:1 Restless man, strong in his dauntless courage, weak in his pleasure-seeking, the headstrong child of Mother Earth, is a creature of few days, and they are filled with toil and tribulation. They are laden with labour and care. He awakes on Earth like a flower opening to greet the dawning, he welcomes life as the unfolding petals welcome the sunrise. Then, even as the flower fades while the sun declines, so does he weaken as life draws towards its time of departure. The wind blows over the places he roamed; then, it is gone and knows him no more. Nothing remains but a fleeting memory, then it, too, passes and all is ended. A mortal being has passed like a shadow, lingering for a brief moment in the sunlight of life. A man has passed like the shadow of a cloud across the arena of Earth and has left scarcely more impression. A mere handful of dust has been swirled upward by the winds of life, to hover briefly in the still air of Earth, then to fall back to the place from whence it came, back into the embrace of its mother. Life, fleeting as a shadow, comes with the daybreak and departs with the evening gloom. It is a thing without substance, a shadow born in the light of the sun. Like a bird, it stirs the dust to brief motion; it passes, and the dust lies inert, as though it had never moved.

MAN:21:2 Consider from whence man came. His place of origin is like the claypit, where men toil to dig the raw materials used by the potter. A piece of clay is dug out and separated; it comes from the darkness of the pit into the light of day. Even so is a man born. The clay is cast on the wheel to be turned; the wheel is life. The wheel spins and the soft clay is moulded into shape. If the shape be good and pleasing to the eye it will be kept and cherished, If it be ill-shaped, it is cast aside, discarded and unwanted. a useless thing. The potter is man, and the clay his soul. The wheel is life.

MAN:21:3 Swift and fleet of foot is the brief life of mortal man Though it be numbered in days and counted in years; yet, he lives from moment to moment and knows not whether he has a few or many days left to squander or utilise. Can it all be futile, all in vain? Can life, when it passes, be as though it never were? Are the days of man no more than wind whispers among the trees, or fish trails through the waters?

MAN:21:4 The days of men are as a strong breeze sweeping a boat swiftly towards harbour. The journey is soon over; the voyage is quickly ended. He arrives at his destination weak and weary, heavy-limbed and toilworn. The sun is setting; night hastens on with quiet footfalls, the darkness gathers in the remains of day, and the home-sick wanderer finds peace. The labours of the day are ended, and the craftsmen lay down their tools and depart one by one, they each go their own way and are seen no more. The light-skinned ladies withdraw within; their guilded adornments cease to entrance, their glowing glances no longer lure. The gathering gloom darkens the window, and the protective shutters are closed. The night wind seeks out the unsteady door and shakes it in its socket. The breeze murmurs among the latticework and whispers through the eaves. Within, all is secure and silent and the night movers commence to stir restlessly in the descending darkness without. The mistress and maidens withdraw to their resting places. The men drowse by the nightlights, and the serving women standby, eyes heavy-lidded, scarce aware of the task.

MAN:21:5 Without the dwelling the heavy darkness of night gathers; the rustle of life is stilled. The mantle of blackness closes about the weary-footed wayfarer who is nearing the end of the journey to his everlasting abode. He arrives and enters through the welcoming portals with a great sigh of relief. He casts aside his dust-stained garments and sinks down into the soft couch of forgetfulness. The wanderer is home, the tired hoary head has found its place of peace.

MAN:21:6 Now the flame that once burned so brightly is no more. The lamp is snuffed out, and its comforting light no longer shines. The earthenware bowl drops to the floor; it shatters and falls apart, as the days come and pass, it will be ground back into the dust from whence it was drawn forth. That which was lit by a spark from the eternal flame has returned to the place, from whence it was generated. That which was raised up from the dust has returned from whence it came. All is as though it had never been.

MAN:21:7 All who are kindred of the one blood return to the same home; the wayward son and wanton daughter are assured of a welcome there, brief though their stay may be. Who among men knows what moves the spirits of men; and who understands the true nature of his homecoming?

MAN:21:8 Like a falcon soaring up into the sunlight, man, for a brief span in the immensity of time, is borne upward on the wings of life. Then the high flight is over; he descends, the wings are folded and he seeks the solitude of his silent resting place.

MAN:21:9 There is an end to all earthly things, and all men must come at last to the appointed place. None has gold or treasure enough to buy even one more day of time. There is no way back; it is the place of no return. Here the prince and the bondsman are alike. Here they stand side by side, and none can tell who was the man of high rank and who the lowly one. That which distinguishes them now is something not of Earth, though that is where it was acquired.

MAN:21:10 As the waters drain away from the land into the channels and from the channels into the river, to be borne away and lost in the great green sea, so does man sink down into oblivion, never to rise again on earth, never to return as himself. He is gone from Earth forever, back to the place from whence he sprang, back to his eternal home.

MAN:21:11 I tremble and am afraid. What man has not his doubts? What man can say with the conviction of knowledge, "Of this, I am certain." Our fathers of old and the Twice Born had the confidence of certain assurance, but I am no more than a humble scribe, whose life has been devoted to the fulfilment of his trust. I sought no great reward and received none, but I was content. Perhaps that contentment was my undoing. I am like a pot holding a precious draught, none of which belongs to it, or a chest containing a treasure it cannot utilise.

MAN:21:12 What eyes see in the dismal darkness of the tomb? What breath stirs the heavy dust? What flower of love flourishes there? What voice can echo in its silence? Does any glimmer ever enlighten the oppressive gloom? Does any memory ever arise to soften the stark surroundings? The thoughts of an old man taunt him when the security of youth is left behind. Youth traverses the sunlit valley of carefree indifference, but age enters the gloomy cavern of doubt.

MAN:21:13 What kind of stars encircle the vault lying low above? What companion lightens the burden of the never-ending night? What whisper breaks through the dark solitude? How many sleepers lie enwrapped in the dusty silence? Whose voice will awaken them, and on what distant day? With what greetings will they be called forth? Those things, I, myself, cannot know. Yet I search the old scripts and am reassured, for they who wrote did so from some certain knowledge. There were things known to them, which are lost to our days. The sleepers sleep not, for their time has passed, it was not counted as men count days and hours, they awakened even as one awakes from a sleep. They awoke in their day of destiny, to a future of radiant glory or one of disgraceful shame and shapelessness.

MAN:21:14 I can add nothing to the great scripts in my keeping, for I am no more than a mere writing instrument. No sublime thoughts arise in my heart, and I, who myself lack the strength of assurance, can scarce presume to impart it to others. I serve as best I can, as a guardian and transmitter of the wisdom from olden times. I labour in secret places, and I hide a secret life within my breast. This is a miserable and misguided age, when corruption stalks the land and the soul of man swims like a fish in an ocean of sin and wallows like a pig in the mire and mud of lust. It is a time of constant soul danger. In this age of wickedness, neither good works nor faith, nor spiritual wisdom have any value. They who should instruct and guide the people mislead them with deceitful words and hypocritical ways. They have become corrupt of heart, and their eyes are blind to their wrongdoing. Their deeds done in the name of righteousness are as the filth, which pollutes pure waters. The goodness that may once have bloomed within is withered away and their spirits are as shrunken and wrinkled husks. The greed of the great is without bounds, and they oppress the poor beyond endurance. They take away the milch goat of the fatherless and seize the widow's ass for debt. In the scripts of the wise, it is said, "As a man sows, so shall he reap," but I seek vainly for its truth in this age. Is this beyond my understanding? Yet I shall pass on undiminished the treasure with which I have been entrusted. Let those with greater wisdom make of it what they will. It has proven poor fare for an empty stomach and a cold covering for the lonely night. Yet, it has brought its own strange consolation, and I am not without comfort. Think of me sometimes, when I am dust and you are even as I am now. If, in greater wisdom, you have solved the problems that now perplex me, look not upon me with scorn, for I am the child of my age. Meagre though my offering be, it extends to the limits of my capacity, more I cannot give.

MAN:21:15 Now, as his days reach fulfilment and he awaits his destiny, your servant salutes you.

Chapter Twenty-Two – Scroll of Lady Nefermaket

MAN:22:1 Who knows what secrets the wind whispers to the waters, the comforting wind of the evening? Or what mysteries the sailors of the king discuss with the moon in the channel of the night-skies. What are the words in the song of the locust, and who hears the speech of the trees? Life is a treasurehouse of hidden things. With so much mystery and beauty about them, why do hearts of men incline towards sordid things?

MAN:22:2 Beauty is mine. It attends me as a handmaiden, but it also restricts me as a warden. What bounty has beauty poured out for me? Has it not proven a false-fronted friend, a prison and not a palace? Has it brought me lighthearted joy, or loaded my heart with sorrow? I am sold into shame and degradation, as a slave girl is sold to servitude. I, who am of royal blood, in rank equal to the highest born lady in the land, am lower than the pitiful harlot who lurks in the street shadows, on sale for bread. What are the jewels about my brow and neck but symbols of my shame? What are bangles of gold and silver on my arms and legs but fetters of humiliation? Are not the fine garments that clothe my shamed body but indications of my price? Truly, the higher a woman's position the greater her fall.

MAN:22:3 In my luxurious girlhood, I was the spoiled prized delight of my father's eyes, the minor queen of his household. As I stepped over the threshold into maidenhood, great musicians composed delicate songs on sweet, soft-stringed instruments extolling my beauty. Did they not say of me, "She is the supreme flower of loveliness, the essence of maidenly charm, the reflection of beauty's perfection?" What were the words of their song; were they not, "She is the delightful incarnation of the inspiring spirit of innocent love, sent down to dwell among men on Earth to test them, to be their delight or doom." What, today, has become of all this promise? I have sold myself into a loveless union that clothes my heart in garments of shame.

MAN:22:4 Without, I am bedecked in priceless ornaments and symbols of power, but within, I am hung about with the degrading shackles of womanly humiliation. Would that I were an unfeeling one, who knows not the depths of her own degradation! No greater curse can be laid on a woman than to be cherished for her beauty alone, unless it be to have beauty and nothing more. Even then, perhaps it is better, for such beauty clothes a dead, unresponsive thing. O the curse of being lovely and unloved, of being loving and unloved, of wanting and being unwanted! What am I but a jewel of the state, a pretty plaything to delight the eye? O to stir the heart of a true man in genuine love! Can a lovely woman ever know true love? Can she ever be assured of it? How can she know she is loved for herself alone and not for her beauty?

MAN:22:5 People say of me, "How can she, who has everything, lack contentment?" True, I have beauty beyond the hopes of most women, riches beyond estimation, power and position above any other. I am envied by all. Yet, I lack that which even the poorest shepherdess can attain. Gladly would I change places with the least of my handmaidens, were she but truly beloved. Am I unduly discontented, having so much and sighing for one thing I lack? Judge me not, unless you can read my heart and know the anguish of an overladen storehouse of unwanted affection.

MAN:22:6 Say not that with beauty such as mine I could claim the heart of any man. Could I claim it with honour? Could I take it in honesty? What think you I need, a man or love? A dead and empty embrace will not suffice, I am not a she-dog on heat. Should I degrade the glory of love to snatch a fleeting pleasure, I would be unworthy of the very thing, for which my heart yearns. O miserable one, who, having so much, lacks everything she desires! Sad is the lot of one who, while yet young, must look beyond the grave for her goal!

MAN:22:7 I labour under the burden of beauty. Oft have I heard the unspoken question asked, "Can one so beautiful ever love truly, or would her love be fickle as the whims of a butterfly?" In my heart are tears, as I cry to myself, "Can a lovely woman ever know true love? She may, but can she ever be assured of it? Mesenita lacked both beauty and wit, yet she never doubted she was truly loved, nor did she ever have cause to doubt. O fortunate woman!

MAN:22:8 Why are beautiful women thought fickle and wayward, honey-baited traps to lure men to sorrow? Why do other women seek to see them in the role of temptresses? What was it Gilapi said of Meritari? That she was a temptress flaunting her beauty and challenging all men to come and take that, which every woman guards so invincibly. How wrong! A truly lovely woman neither flaunts her beauty before men nor uses it to tempt them, for thereby it is sadly lessened. Beauty, like riches and power, carries a heavy burden of responsibility, and woe to one who lacks the strength to bear it. But unlike riches and power, little preparation and tuition are ever given for its use and purpose. Therefore, why blame the possessor when it is used thoughtlessly?

MAN:22:9 Do men who love truly ever seek the love of a beautiful woman? Experience cries against it. Yet surely, the due of a true man and a true love should be the constant love of a beautiful one. Would that a man could love me for myself alone and not for the lovely covering that hides me! To such a man, I would give a love undying, a love everlasting, for it would not be established in the flesh that fades and perishes. He would have won the sole type of true love, that which binds spirit to spirit. That which binds flesh to flesh is not love, nor yet even its imitation. What, after all, is beauty but the jewel box that hides the jewel within? Though how often is it empty and the jewel lacking, a thing of superficial display, nothing more!

MAN:22:10 Envy me not, my sisters, for life lacks savour for me. I am neither contented, nor joyful. May better times dawn, when things are different.

Chapter Twenty-Three – One Hundred, Twenty-Second Scroll

MAN:23:1 O Egypt, great fertile, black land amidst the encircling red plains, what have you now done? You have departed from the light, to wander in twilight. You have turned to gods that are nought but the spirits of men returned to dwell in wood and stone. What can such as they do for men?

MAN:23:2 The Great Self-Generating God gave you all you have and hold. The people of the West cannot oppress you, the people of the South cannot afflict you, nor can the people of the East command you. The dwellers in lower regions are subject to your powers.

MAN:23:3 Turn not from your true God; it is He who gave you the adornment of waters and greenery. He built you up in the midst of the fertile waters. He sends you the fertilising floods in their due seasons, the fine fish-bearing waters, which nourish you, the dark waters that fertilise the field pastures and fruit-bearing trees. you are not as other lands.

MAN:23:4 Your borders are closed to the people of the East. Whose Hand stays their march? Your borders are closed to the wild men beyond the cultivated land. Whose Hand holds them back? Your borders are closed to the ignorant men of the South. Whose Hand restrains them? Are not the waters to the North as a wall?

MAN:23:5 Forget not the God within your gods; He is the heart and soul of the land. He saved you from every evil of the Dark One in the days gone by. His servant is the great light of day, God-given to you, that you might dwell in its light.

MAN:23:6 He darkened your face, that you might not be barren as other lands. He thrust the clouds from off your brow. The cool North wind is bidden caress your cheeks. Truly, you are the favoured one among nations, the chosen one among all lands.

Chapter Twenty-Four – An Early Egyptian Scroll

MAN:24:1 A craftsman in the words of God and a teacher of writing. The Grand Scribe of his Lord, a faithful servant of a noble master. Beforetimes Keeper of the Royal Writings, whose father's father's father was Chief Overseer of the Great Pharaoh. Follower of the Wise One, whose wisdom and goodness reveal the Divine Essence. Son of the Master of the Secret Ceremonies, Captain of craft in the journey to the Islands of the Outer Seas. May you live forever in prosperity and health, and may life bestow its favours upon you. May the Protecting Spirit spread its wings over you and may your rewards hereafter exceed your expectations. May your servants dutifully transport sand for your fields and may your form in the Unseen Place be that of a god. And to my brothers in wisdom, who follow the Sacred Path, may your way be made smooth and the yoke be lifted from your neck. May you dwell forever in the Celestial Mansions.

MAN:24:2 In the month of rising waters, while all men yet bore the signs of lamentations for the departure of Pharaoh's father, and the great gates remained barred to wayfarers, the ships were prepared and pitched, and all was done as the king decreed. None but he who commanded our movements knew the preparations within the preparations.

MAN:24:3 Then, to the place of mooring, I was carried in a high chair of ebony inlaid with brass, the bearers of which were of chesenam wood bound about with cowhide. On to the ship which had come laden with merchandise from the land of Pontas, lions tails, cowhides, spices, worked and unworked ivory, blackwood, oils and paint. From the land of Egypt went wrought copper and pitchers, stoneware, linen and the finery of women and men. There were instruments for dwelling places and corn in jars, beer and stones and the works of craftsmen.

MAN:24:4 I boarded and was greeted in a befitting manner, for my renown had gone before me. I am one who stands fast under assault, who does not waver at the crisis, nor run from the foe. Whose arm is cunning in battle and never strikes twice to slay.

MAN:24:5 With the craft were men of the Kadanas, a host of men fierce of countenance and bold. The vessel was one hundred and fifty cubits less ten overall and in beam fifty cubits. With us there were one hundred and fifty men of the sea. The other craft with us was one hundred cubits overall and in beam thirty cubits, and had ninety men of the sea. Past Kabas, we sailed to Akar of the two ports. to await the tidings of Shumar. The waterless city, we left behind under the restless stars and we came up to Nasen, where we stood at our posts three days.

MAN:24:6 The seas mounted up on high; the waters rose in wrath. Northwards we went and all but one vessel was lost, all but one boat sunk. I subdued the raging waters with cunning, and the clouds were cleft by my skill. After many days were past, we came to the land in peace; we were not cast upon the shore. No man came near us when we hammered our posts. We set up altars, and none denied us our rights. The God of that place made our God welcome.

MAN:24:7 Then I went by way of the land of Sedek, which lies beyond Takse, to the lord Torka, an Egyptian, the second born greatest of twins, who ruled the people of Mayga. Here there are high mountains and great trees, and the roar of lions is heard in the night.

MAN:24:8 The same lord Torka is he whose father, now in port. took his vessel south of Pontas from Ofir towards the sunsetting, past Kindia to the land of Bemer. He returned when the waters had risen four times and fallen thrice, and sorrow gave way to rejoicing. To the rim of the great circle he went, to where the fires of the Netherworld were revealed and men were the brothers of dwarfs. He it was who brought back the great hairy giant who rests with Thosis.

MAN:24:9 Now, my lord is one hundred and ten years of age. I, alone among his men, understand the hidden words of the gods and the secret ways. I alone know the writing within the writing. I alone know the nature of the Lords of the Celestial Mansions. Therefore, the words of God come to you by the hand of the servant of The Great God, the Guardian of the Book. Thus you may know all that has been made known to those who have slept in the House of the Gods.

MAN:24:10 Keep the writings as they now are for your children and your children's children. Nothing is perfect on an imperfect Earth, but that which flows down and reaches us from the heart of God comes the nearest to perfection. The pure waters are sullied only by the imperfect and impure vessel, in which they are caught.

MAN:24:11 As it is written, so let it be re-written. As it is written, so let it be done.

Chapter Twenty-Five – Song of Sacrifice

MAN:25:1 They came like spoilers to the tomb; they came in the night. They were as robbers carrying foul deeds in the darkness. They came as night creatures fearful of the light.

MAN:25:2 Rasmus, they slew in the antechamber, he died not from the blows before his face but from the steward's knife behind. Evil men lurked within and without. He died in the midst of his manhood strength, and his spirit was not unaccompanied in its journey.

MAN:25:3 Neferlehi, they took; they carried her off. Proud and upright, she went, to die in a foul place by the terrible hooks of the tormentors. Her greater loveliness will live forever in the Halls of Eternity. It will exceed the radiance of the sunlight and enfold the heart like the pale glory of the moonbeam.

MAN:25:4 The son of Rasmus and his children, they slew and tormented, his residence they defiled and laid in ruins. They sought the abode of The Great God within its walls, but found it not. Brick and stone cannot fashion a residence for The True God, but they were sightless men. They did not see what lay before their eyes.

MAN:25:5 Beauty and strength have been destroyed. The love that once adorned Earth now graces a greater place. All things pass from Earth; nothing remains but the never-ending struggle of The Great God, which everlastingly transmutes earthly things. To it, we are what grains of sand are to the whirlwind that whips up a sandstorm.

MAN:25:6 The records were not exposed to the workers of wickedness. They survive, they journey on and they come to you. They come, not that you might live but that you might die. They bring glory and beauty to the soul; can these be obtained except by suffering? Can clay be made beautiful except through scars? Can metal be fashioned to form except by fire?

MAN:25:7 We journey towards a light we cannot reach and fall into a pit of darkness to find it at the bottom. We gaze on the beauty of the stars and think them high above, when, behold, they are within our hearts.

MAN:25:8 Man is not born to play, but to labour. Life is a basket, which must be filled with sustenance for the future. The fool fills it with empty, unwholesome things; the wise man fills it with things of substance.

MAN:25:9 Earth is a place of unreality. That, which seems substantial here may have no true substance. That, which seems desirable here may not be wholly desirable. That, which serves here may not serve everywhere.

MAN:25:10 Man is born to live, but he is also born to die. It is no more natural for him to live than it is for him to die. Death is no harder than birth. It is no more difficult than life.

MAN:25:11 The best of today is gone; we console ourselves; better will arise tomorrow. The Earth gets better or it passes away. Men improve or perish; that is the Law.

MAN:25:12 May you find eternal springs of strength and courage welling up in your soul at the time of your testing. We, your brothers, go our destined way, and we shall not meet again in the same likeness.

MAN:25:13 May your future amid the fountains of light be glorious and beautiful, and may you span the great gulf of the eternal years in splendour of form and spirit. I commend you to the care of Panut; may he protect you and keep you from evil.

Chapter Twenty-Six – The Scroll of Kabel - Section 1

MAN:26:1 The words of the Great Scribe of the Universe, by Laman, Keeper of the Watergate by the Outlands. To the Children of Laka at Kemwar, Keepers of Secrets, wise in the words of God, greetings. May your days be long in prosperity and peace. May the Great Sun of Life endow your years with greenness. May you walk always with a feather in your heart, and may the wild fig tree flourish in the sand of your courtyard. Success in your journey to Godsland; the Guardian of Sand Wayfarers protect you along the road.

MAN:26:2 These are God's words on the Hidden Portal, struck by one who slept within the temple and who knows the will of God. If they be heavy, they are also sound:

MAN:26:3 "My children shall pass across the wilderness and sea, and my wisdom shall go with them. The whirlwind shall not strike them, nor shall they be consumed by the sea monsters. When all this generation and its children shall be as swathed bodies in their coffins, my children shall not be at rest."

MAN:26:4 "They shall come to a land of many waters, where gold is found and there is copper in abundance. There they shall erect a temple to the glory of God, and they will prosper and increase. Their women shall be honoured by the water beast and rejoice in their good fortune."

MAN:26:5 "These are the words they shall remember and strike on marble at the temple gate. These are the words they shall engrave forever:

MAN:26:6 'Good deeds must outweigh wicked ones on the Great Scales; otherwise, the spirit is doomed to darkness.

MAN:26:7 A man is expected to strive for perfection on Earth, but not to achieve it. Let him be judged according to his efforts.

MAN:26:8 Bewail not if prosperity departs from you; it passes from the good, for they have passed its test.

MAN:26:9 The day of the Destroyer will come again and the land shall be laid waste. It will strike out of Heaven at a time when there is prosperity and peace, though the minds of men shall be perplexed. It will be a time when men worship the works of men and say, "There is nothing greater than these." When women are as men and men as women. When the hearts of men are in turmoil and all men seek pleasure and gain. When craftsmen are inefficient and workmen are idle and all men seek ease and comfort.

MAN:26:10 "Be alert and strong, my children. Be ready for the day of the next visitation, when doom reaches down from the skies and man is blasted with irresistible power."

MAN:26:11 "These are the laws, in which you shall find the strength to survive. Throughout the days of your hardships, remember them well, for they will bear you up:

MAN:26:12 No man shall eat to excess or drink until he staggers.

MAN:26:13 No man shall waste his substance in fornication.

MAN:26:14 No man shall cut himself after the manner of the Easterners or suck blood.

MAN:26:15 No man shall act with man as man acts with woman.

MAN:26:16 "These are the rules, by which my children shall survive. They are not for the survival of each man or for everyone, for many must perish:

MAN:26:17 'Where some must die that others live, the weak shall die and the strong shall live.

MAN:26:18 Where the choice of death is between man and child, or woman and child, the child, being instructed and capable of survival, shall live. The means of life shall be placed with the child or woman and the man shall take his chance.

MAN:26:19 Where the choice of death is between a woman with child and a woman without child, the mother shall live.

MAN:26:20 Where the choice of death is between young and old, the young shall live, and the old shall die, But if the young be weak and the old strong, then the old shall live.

MAN:26:21 Where the choice of death is between the wise and the foolish, the wise shall live, and the foolish shall die. Who shall decide? The foolish think themselves wise, and the wise are weak-voiced. Let one who is to die decide who shall live.

MAN:26:22 Where few among many can hope for life, the craftsman shall survive the unskilled man, and the wife shall survive the maiden.

MAN:26:23 The husband shall survive the fighting man and he, who has no wife. The child, being capable and instructed, shall survive the parent.

MAN:26:24 The scribe shall survive the craftsman, and the sister shall survive the brother.

MAN:26:25 The magistrate shall survive the priest, and the learned man the unlearned.

MAN:26:26 The whole man survive the maimed man, and the whole woman the maimed woman. Knowledge shall survive strength, and skill shall survive fitness.

MAN:26:27 Goodness shall survive wickedness, but who shall judge between them? Let he most instructed in wisdom and the writings decide.

MAN:26:28 Joy shall survive gloom, and he who carries himself cheerfully shall survive he whose countenance is sad.

MAN:26:29 Love shall survive hatred, and they who love shall be spared. He who serves better shall survive he who serves less, and the selfish man shall not live while the unselfish man dies.

MAN:26:30 Woman shall survive man, but the common woman shall not live and the craftsman die. Let the one serving best be the one to live.

MAN:26:31 The strong man shall survive the weak, but the fool shall not live and the wise die. Neither shall the unskilled survive the skilled. Where there is a chance for life, the strong shall take that chance and leave the certainty to the weak.

MAN:26:32 The kind shall survive the selfish, but the brickmaker shall not survive the scribe.

MAN:26:33 All things shall be done to this end, that though men die, man shall live. If a priest says, "Am I not the best to live?" say, "Are you not the best prepared to die?"

MAN:26:34 "These are hard things, but neglect them not. Men say, Let us pray we never have to use the sword," but they do not let it rust.

MAN:26:35 When cast upon a strange shore, Lucius chose in this manner: He lived who, by living, served best. He lived who had the best hope of life. He lived whose life held the most promise.

Chapter Twenty-Seven – Unnamed, Unnumbered Scroll

MAN:27:1 O Companions in suffering, raise your heads and cease your lament. Misery and sorrow, trial and tribulation are the appointed lot of man. It is not the end, let the test not be beyond your endurance.

MAN:27:2 This spoke with the voice of the god and said, "All who worship the Unknown God must be brought to judgement." Then, it was the god's will they should be taken out into the wilderness, where none should see them die. Does he come to us as a friend or as one who would place a knife in our backs? What do we know of his thoughts? Is he with us, even though he be ignorant of our ways? Let caution take priority, let prudence be our guide.

MAN:27:3 In the night, the voice of God spoke on the Westwind through the columns at His mouth and said, "Though not one of us, he serves us well. The feather is in his heart."

MAN:27:4 Even the little gods weighed down heavily when asked to speak, and he found favour before them. He found favour in strange places.

MAN:27:5 This is not the hour to cry the tidings in the concourse of the people. Be not unduly impatient; every new thing has the hour of its birth. Many generations shall yet live and pass into dust before the child now conceived shall be born. Let it not be disturbed within the womb.

MAN:27:6 Therefore, deal not with things best left alone. Arise, be strong in heart, go from one to another, gather the Companions in Suffering and let them come this way.

MAN:27:7 Say to them, "This is not the hour, nor is this the generation of the test. Gaze upon the Warden of the Night; does he falter on the path? Is it not written that he shall be the herald for the coming of doom? Where then is the sign?"

MAN:27:8 Therefore, look not unduly towards your destiny in the Netherworld. Remember that the image of all that is there is also here.

MAN:27:9 We are like fish beaten towards the enclosure. The eyes of men know the fish, but to the fish, the men remain unknown; yet we shall not be caught at the narrow end.

MAN:27:10 One comes seeking us, but we are not here. His hand reaches out into the Red Lands, but we are not there. He searches round about, but we are inside, and when he comes within, we are without.

MAN:27:11 Beyond the sea of blood, there is death, turn down stream towards the Land of Waters. Carry the Sacred Writing into the lands of strangers, even unto the Land of Long Days; there, they will receive the Wisdom that the Great People reject.

MAN:27:12 The end here is a beginning in another place. Death here is birth elsewhere. Life is a wheel with no more than a mark between birth and death.

MAN:27:13 May the Great Governing Powers be gracious towards you, and may your paths be covered with grass. This is the beginning, not the end.

MAN:27:14 Farewell!

Chapter Twenty-Eight – Two Sections of an Unnamed Scroll

MAN:28:1 Praise to the Great Lords of Eternity who, once such as we, now sit in the Everlasting Halls. Sanctified forever be the name of The One God, to Whom Alone shall be given reverence and glory, Who Alone is worthy of worship.

MAN:28:2 Greetings, my Companions in Suffering; may the sun ever rise in glory over your fields. May you enjoy peace and prosperity here, and rise in splendour to a life of beauty in the Region of Light.

MAN:28:3 May your servants be ever dutiful and your sons upright. May the women of your household be ever diligent and neat, chaste and modest.

MAN:28:4 Two generations have passed into judgement since the wild dogs came swiftly in the night and scattered the seeds of wisdom to the winds.

MAN:28:5 The Great Land shall no more know the true greatness of wisdom. The black soil shall not nourish its seed. The seed shall spring up and burst forth into leaf in foreign lands, among strange people.

MAN:28:6 Our destiny lies Northward, and such is foretold in the Sacred Writings. I go and my household, and Jothan the Sartisian with his household. My brother Kabel also and his daughter, with Karob and Agab of the house of Moshes.

MAN:28:7 We go by way of Kambusis and the waters of Jabel, over the wild wilderness to the Mountains of Winds. Beyond them we journey into Kindia, where there are pines.

MAN:28:8 We shall take the records of the Eastern Quarter and the Guardians, who remain with us. None among all who know our ways shall be forced to go, neither shall we condemn those who remain. The scrolls in four chests and the Books of Wisdom in their canopies go with those who depart.

MAN:28:9 Our thoughts remain with Semlis; may he sail in peace with moderate winds and find everlasting glory and beauty in the Netherworld.

MAN:28:10 Written at his master's behest by Thomes, scribe at the Quartergate of Ephos.

Chapter Twenty-Nine – Second Scroll of Kison

MAN:29:1 I am Kison, son of Nesubot and Nektorab, a citizen of Hakarnak. I am he, who brought the Sacred Writings from the swamplands and gathered men together, who are the Sons of Light.

MAN:29:2 Now the wisdom of olden times is replanted in the land, though it sits without in the courtyard. Yet among those behind the pillars, many know who among them sees clearly. Great secrets are hidden deeply, but they are not unknown, and the day will come when the soil will give up its treasures.

MAN:29:3 I am not one who takes his ear in his hand when darkness clouds his heart. I came from out of the land of security to a place, where all men would raise knives against me, were their eyes opened.

MAN:29:4 In baskets of barley, on the backs of asses, came the Sacred Writings containing words to guide the wise and knowledge to dispel the powers of darkness. No magic could prevail against the superior spells I carried, and the treasures remained unseen.

MAN:29:5 Men sit beneath the trees and nod their heads solemnly and roll out long books to read things that evaporate in the air. I deride not the books, but one blow of the sword can destroy ten thousand strokes of the pen.

MAN:29:6 Those in high places persecute us, not because of the whole of the writings, for much is common to all, but because we seek to change the established order of things. We seek to change the ever present state of affairs. Because, too, we have a God who is not the holder of property or a God of the rich and powerful. Who benefits from the riches and estates of other gods? The gods or their priests? Would they who benefit, therefore, welcome the words of God? Such is not the nature of men, and we have the nigh impossible task of changing the natures of men.

MAN:29:7 We proclaim that riches and high estate carry corresponding responsibilities. Is this doctrine to be welcomed by those high ones in the land, who seek just to gratify their desires and lavish their riches on pleasure? Therefore, we either speak openly and die or become enslaved, or we serve secretly and live. Can a dead man serve or a slave move freely among the people to gather men of spirit?

MAN:29:8 I am a man of movement and a hardy one, who is not easily set back. It was I, who rekindled the flame.

MAN:29:9 I brought to safety the Four Great Books, of which one is the Book of the Masters Words and one the Book of the Masters Deeds. One the Book of the Masters Ways and one the Book of Awaking to Life in the Dawnlight. With them were the Books of Beginning and End and the two and seventy scrolls. Not one was lost.

MAN:29:10 I came back. I stood before the Mother of the King in the Great Place and was unbowed, though I gave homage, for without my life, all was lost. I took the truth even to the palace and was undefiled there.

MAN:29:11 I returned to my dwelling place among the trees and dwelt beneath the Great Cow, near the temple where men worship the Calf of Gold. I leave my abode, and my eyes are blinded. Therefore, when the Earth is as if dead, I prepare my books and men come and are refreshed in the coolness. Yet men who sit with books and men who do deeds are not alike, and each has his task; therefore, let not one despise the other, but let both go forward together, each bearing his own burden.

MAN:29:12 Now I make ready to go downstream to the Abode of Light, that wisdom and Truth may be carried to the appointed place under the everlasting stars and there made secure to men in generations yet to grow up in the Light. They will be seen in generations to come.

MAN:29:13 I shall go on the Wings of the Sun before the retinue of the Breaker of Heads. I am one acknowledged as being pure of hands and shall be with those who serve under the head of The Great One.

MAN:29:14 My name, henceforth, shall be Hemnetar, and I shall not eat of fish or beans until I come to the place appointed to fit my station. I shall wear linen, and my sandals shall be made of grass, so that none shall perceive my greatness. I will hide great things within my heart ,and a bridle will ever hold my tongue in check.

MAN:29:15 I shall pray among the empty-hearted, but my prayers will not be as theirs but as those offered in the days of our fathers, who sat enfolded in silence two hours beforehand. Now, the marks are changed by the hypocrisy of men.

MAN:29:16 With me shall go Methemun, my brother, but Nifanethrith shall remain and provide for our father in faith. We shall be with he, whom men call Nonpeka for his foolishness in his father's abode. Kenamun shall be with us as chief overseer.

MAN:29:17 Behind us, we leave many in sorrow, but our stature shall not diminish, for greater things are always believed of those who are distant.

MAN:29:18 Nofret, I depart from you in sorrow, but are not great loves increased by absence, while little ones diminish? Parting is the test of love. Let the years speak and enlighten us unto ourselves. Have we spoken truly one with the other?

MAN:29:19 My son, my unseen little one now asleep in comfortable darkness, gathering your strength for the coming struggle, may The Great God of Life add His strength to your strength. You will be a great one among men, for you were conceived in love and not in lust.

MAN:29:20 Within the guardian of my heart you remain as a wonderful mystery. I am overcome with awe, for within you there is something God-inspired. It bestows strange powers upon you, so that at the appointed time you fight for air and light. You will be a man of courage, for such men are born to the fearless and good. Strength and beauty, courage and modesty have mated, that you might be the heir of their gifts. Your heritage was chosen by those who gave you life.

MAN:29:21 It is your fate, my son, as a child born of woman, to fight and grasp, to grimly hold on to life as you reach across to this side of the earthly portal. There are dark powers that would drag you back, but you are not for them. O let the Great Light be ever with you, as a watchman's fire on a lonely road, when the evil powers beset your way. I pray, from the very inmost recess of my heart, that the Lords of Form walk with you and ever protect you from the Formless Ones.

MAN:29:22 As you grow, may your thoughts ever seek to enquire. May you be filled with the heady wine of the gods, the gift that spurs men to venture forth into strange places, seeking the unknown; which leads them to seek green pastures beyond the desert, the dawning over the sea rim and the light beyond the circle of darkness.

MAN:29:23 Adversity maybe your lot, but adversity is the greatest tutor. It is something welcomed by men as the measuring stick of their manhood. Adversity calls men forth to seek God and Truth and drives them upward along the Great Path.

MAN:29:24 May you ever seek the unknown and strive courageously against the unseen. May your spirit be high on the journey in this place, where so many men grow weary on the road. Be not one who sits following the ways of other men, but one who moves along a path of his own choosing.

MAN:29:25 Keep the love of life given men, or life is lost, but cast aside the fear of death, for it is a small payment for a life well lived. Rejoice in living, and walk in the sun, avoiding the shadows. Remember that though life is to be enjoyed to the full, its enjoyment is ever subordinate to duty.

MAN:29:26 Be a man, my son. Be not a man of unbridled wrath, for such are rarely without trouble, though righteous wrath will lend strength to your arm. Be a man above pettiness and greed, above meanness and deceit.

MAN:29:27 Keep forever the joys of friendships well made, and serve your friends well. Never betray friendship or turn it to serve your own ends, lest you become something less than a man. Carry high gladness in your heart, and never cease to wonder at the marvels in life. Not a day shall pass, but you will see something new to enrich your thoughts. Look at life as a man and not as an ox. Wonder at the great and awesome manifestations of God, such as sunlight and thunder, the dew and the stars, the sandstorm and the murmur of waters. Never let your eyes become dulled to the growth of trees, to the rising of the waters and to the return of the harvests.

MAN:29:28 Let your heart be hungry for knowledge and your hand be ever seeking some skill.

Hate lies and shun the coward; walk with men and learn manly ways. I know you will do the right thing, my son, for a bird does not beget a crab.

MAN:29:29 I must tread a path you may not follow for many a year. I go, ashamed to leave you in surroundings unbefitted to your blood, but so it must be. Can the wilderness hold down the eagle, or waters restrain the wild goose? No; neither can a true man be ensnared by his condition and circumstances. I go, my son, for go I must; I cannot delay.

MAN:29:30 I kiss the lovely forehead of your noble protector; it will soon be the time of farewell. I will not be here to greet you, to welcome you at your first cry. I will know you not before I depart. Woe to a sorrowful father who can bestow nought upon his unprotected child but a piece of stone and some writing.

MAN:29:31 These are my words to you, my son. Live the life of a man, such as, if all other men lived likewise, The Great God Himself would leap out of His Heaven to welcome their race into the Realm of Gods. Live not as other men do live, but as they should live.

MAN:29:32 Fare you well, my son; a good morning and a clear dawn. May the Great Wings enfold you until we meet.

MAN:29:33 My old friend, upon you I have laid a charge not unworthy of your integrity. For you, the days of deeds are near past and you, therefore, now stand on the threshold to the years of wisdom. Age should think while youth should act, but youth needs the considered guidance and restraint of age. Old men for counsel, and young men for action. You have aged wisely and carry no regrets; therefore, is your counsel ten times valued. Then, too, you have lived well, and is not the old age of an eagle better than the youth of a sparrow?

MAN:29:34 I leave you the two garments becoming to you, and one for your wife, as a departure gift. Mine, henceforth, shall be those of the pure-handed. You know the things that are written on my heart.

MAN:29:35 * * * * * * * * * * * * * *

MAN:29:36 From Kison in the Land of Cedars, by the hand of Katelis, to those who journey on across the great, green waters. By Jamulus to Sopher called the Stranger, peace be with you and with your household. May your god be blessed as he blesses. Prosperity attend you and a safe journey. I kindled a fire for you and the smoke arose straight up with the savour of the meat, and my heart rejoices for your protection. Now I say, declare these words clearly and with a true tongue. Neither suppress any, nor add to what is written.

MAN:29:37 Nebutoret shall go with you in my stead, for he is as a young lion, while I lie sickened with the worm. It is a land of strangers with strange ways, where men pass water standing while women sit; where sons labour for their fathers' sustenance and women are not household mistresses.

MAN:29:38 Among these people, women are not respected. Ravish one, and the wrong is against the father and her father's house. Ravish one married, and the wrong is against her husband and her husband's house. Are men better under such laws? Unless the soil be treated with a husbandman's care, can the fruits from the sown seed be bountiful and good?

MAN:29:39 There is no stability of rule and princes strive one with another. The seasons come and go uncontrolled, and there are no records of harvests. In the public halls, many men talk, but none writes. The speech of the people is an uncouth babble.

MAN:29:40 Thieves go unpunished, and those who slay buy their freedom with gold. Robbers purchase wives with their spoils. Sons do not obey their fathers, and daughters are wilful. Harlotry is practised in high places.

MAN:29:41 You who leave are better served than I who stay, for I am able neither to go forward nor to go back. I am not a man wise in words who counsels, but a man of movement and deeds. But of what good is a fig when a worm inhabits it? The broken pot does not go to the well.

MAN:29:42 Go in peace, and fare you well on the way. If the sea journey be not smooth, then console yourselves, for it will strengthen the faith of those who waver. There are many who doubt the existence of God in fine weather but quickly recover their faith as the winds and waves rise.

MAN:29:43 Take Nebutoret, for it is fitting that he go; he is one well favoured for such a venture. He is one who, if he fell overboard, would come up with a fish in his mouth. If gold fell from the skies, it would fall at his feet.

MAN:29:44 I have re-written what I found in four parts; be it not well done I could do no better, for much was lacking, and the letters are strange.

Chapter Thirty – Scroll of Panubis

MAN:30:1 To Ohsirahes from your servant, Panubis; may The One God grant you long life and contentment. May Nebetnif be your everlasting joy. May strife ever depart before your shadow.

MAN:30:2 Your servant writes with difficulty, for his heart has become small within him, and few are those whom he can entrust with tasks of importance. In considering the events occurring in the land, few are the words of assurance that can be written. Things do not get any better; from year to year they get worse.

MAN:30:3 The secret writings remain with us, but they are lightly regarded by those who should cherish them. Few still walk in their light, and in all the land the right way of life is avoided. The path of righteousness is spurned; it is beyond the strength of men today. Here, at its heart, the land is distressed. Better by far to dwell at the edge of the pool, where none but the strongest ripples reach, and they as no more than a slight disturbance.

MAN:30:4 Men cry aloud with sorrowful hearts, for their lives are turned over. No longer are their institutions respected, and like wild dogs, man seeks to snatch the sustenance of man. Contentment and trust have departed; peace has gone, and hope is no more. Mornings come and men rise to greet them with anticipation of change, but this passes with the early mists and the sun goes down on despondency and despair. Your servant is heavy-laden with care; he is burdened with sorrow but adjusts his life to the times. Better by far would it be if he were many days journey away.

MAN:30:5 The burdens of yesterday remain, while those of today are added to them. Those of tomorrow already weigh heavily. Your servant wearies under the load, but he carries on without falter.

MAN:30:6 The mouths of all men remain mute; they speak not about that ,which afflicts the land. The hearts of all are disturbed, but their tongues remain silent. Strange gods have entered upon the land, such gods as have not been known before, who are gods of sorrow and despoilation.

MAN:30:7 The silent strength hidden in the heart of the land, the spirit of its life, the secret of The One God has not been sufficient. Men have failed to bear up under the blows of misfortune; the calamities have overwhelmed them; their wills and spirits are weak. Alone of all in the land, the Devoted in God remain firm and stout-hearted. Yet, wickedness covers the land, as waters at their rising.

MAN:30:8 This is the testing time for men. This is the trial of their strength, but their frailty is established and they fail and fall. Those who should be resolute and firm, to maintain the order of things, are weak and faint of heart. They are weaklings, their wickedness has eaten their manhood. Like the people, they seek naught but the easy way. Their desire is to live in ease and comfort, untroubled by the times. They care not that greatness has departed from the land.

MAN:30:9 Affliction besets men on all sides, it encompasses their days. In the morning they open their eyes to tribulation and suffer it the whole length of the day. The rich man robs the poor, the strong oppresses the weak. The unprotected virgin is seduced, the widow is ravished and the orphan defiled. Greed and lust range wide through the land. It is a time of heart-testing.

MAN:30:10 The tongues of men wag with strange tales and it is difficult to remain silent when falsehood stalks boldly throughout the land. In such times the ignorant and foolish lend their ears to any falsity. How can the wise reply to the ignorant, when wisdom is exposed to ridicule and Truth to persecution? To expose the folly and wickedness of the powerful brings down rods of wrath upon long-suffering backs. The ears of rulers are closed to words of wisdom; the doors of their hearts are bolted against Truth. To reply wisely or give good counsel from the books of wisdom is to invite scorn. Men no longer worship at the shrine of Saboyet.

MAN:30:11 The servant no longer devotes himself loyally to the affairs of his master, and where the arms of many are needed at the task, it is abandoned. Men no longer toil at the task with cheerful hearts, they no longer labour in accord. Men are tied down by their own inability, they are shackled by their own fears. They have become timid and fearful.

MAN:30:12 Even the halls of judgement are no longer inviolate; the decrees are cast forth to be stamped underfoot by ignorant men. Even things that sustain the spirit now serve to prepare sustenance for the belly. Records are falsified, so that no man knows the true from the false. The tallies of produce are no longer taken, and corn becomes the property of any man. He who lies readily gets the best; he who acts the deceiver gets most. Ignorant men have raised themselves to high estate by falsehood and deceit. None raises hand or voice against them, and therefore their ways are acclaimed and emulated. Truth is mocked and justice vilified.

MAN:30:13 A man fears his brother as a foe and his son as a betrayer. He plows his field bearing shield and sword. Men walk abroad girded for battle, but now the day has dawned when henceforth even manly defence is denied them. When a man is slain by the side of his own brother, he who lives flees to save his limbs. When a woman is ravished, they who see turn away. The screams of maidens fall on deaf ears.

MAN:30:14 Spearmen gather in bands, but the standards they bear are not those of justice and Truth. Bowmen stand alert, and arrows are loosened in their quivers. The men of blood exult, for it is their day. If a man of high estate be unguarded, he is slain, and if rich he is robbed. If a highborn woman be unprotected through lack of kindred or gold, she becomes a harlot. In the marketplace men say, "Better a well fed harlot than a goddess dead from hunger." Even men who are not men have their place in these days. Would that I could journey to a land against the rim of Earth!

MAN:30:15 Men of no estate and landless men become the lords of men, and strangers become masters of slaves and servants. They stir up strife among the people and say, "This is because we are protected by gods of power; by what are you protected?" The people know not that the power of gods is sustained by the spiritual devotion of the people, and their power flows from the strength and goodness of their worshippers. When a people fail their god, that god fails the people.

MAN:30:16 I am a man instructed and know this is a time of strengthening affliction, but my heart troubles me. Will the people understand this? Will they rise to meet the challenge or go down the path of ease, the fair path of flowers and fragrance? Is this the Land of Leaders, wherein will be erected the Temple of Truth and the Stairway to Heaven? Would that I could peer through the door of the unborn days!

MAN:30:17 Strange bowmen have entered the redlands, and they spoil the people. They are men whose delight is in suffering. They are men whose pleasure is destruction; they tear down, but do not build. The roads are covered, and the water channels opened. The craftsman no longer interests himself in his craft, for that which he makes is taken away. He who reaps does not store the corn, while he who is without a plow never lacks a full storehouse. The harvests go unrecorded and he who toils not eats with he who has laboured at the ingathering. The man without cattle eats meat, while he who owns them eats herbs. The waters rise and fall away from the land, but none plows or sows, for men say, "The events of tomorrow are unknown, and who knows what man will reap where we have ploughed and sown?"

MAN:30:18 The scribe is stricken and dies on his stool. His writings become a mystery and are disdainfully trodden underfoot. The fruit of many days' labour become kindling, the wisdom and knowledge of generations become fuel for fires of destruction.

MAN:30:19 The weaver has abandoned his loom, and robbers lie in wait to strip men of their garments. The keepers of storehouses are stretched out before the doors, and storage places are empty. Charcoal has gone from the land, and the watermen have left their hoists. Slaves wander without masters and children roam, begging for bread.

MAN:30:20 No longer do men sail northward, and there is no cedarwood for those who have departed. Gold and silver have gone back into the soil and copper is hidden in the ground. Ships that leave return no more. The roads are places of danger, and he who journeys with goods reaches a strange destination. He who is unarmed or undefended becomes the plaything of brutal men.

MAN:30:21 They who rob become lords, and they who once ruled with riches wander in rags. Chests of ebonywood are smashed open, and fine furniture is broken and burned. No man possesses vases or things of metal. No door is closed, and no dwelling secured. The mysteries of the temples have been taken away.

MAN:30:22 Such is the state of the land, wherein your servant dwells; it is a land of sorrow, it is a time of tribulation. When Thumis came to me with your letter, my heart grew big with gladness, for it told me you had reached a secure mooring. My heart spoke to my spirit and said, "Where in the land is left another such as he, one who judged with impartiality, whose head never inclined towards a bribe, who ever stood firm for Truth. who saved the lowly man from the oppression of the powerful and the humble man from the hard hand of the arrogant? Such men no longer serve in the land."

MAN:30:23 I am one, who is instructed, and therefore I know that the life of each man has a set span, and from this knowledge I gain courage. I know that from whence the spirit came, there it will return. Each night, my soul goes to pastures of the spirit and there sustains itself and is refreshed at the fountain of eternity. I arise renewed in vigour, to face the trials of each new day.

MAN:30:24 The state of the land has been made known to you, and therefore I ask that you take into your charge the Sacred Things and Writings, which are now guarded here. Daily, our task grows more difficult, and we live in fear of two-tongued men among us. Also, your servant lacks the knowledge and wisdom that reside with you, and he fears because of his inability to deal with the situation. Now, the guarded things can be conveyed to you, though this is beset with difficulties and danger, but if there is delay, nothing can pass out of this land.

MAN:30:25 Here, things cannot change for the better. If you ask your servant to continue with his charge, he can but reply that the floodwaters already lick at the foundation of the walls. The hostile ones gather before us; can Opiwat be kept from his dwelling place or Ree from his descent?

MAN:30:26 Therefore, this goes in haste with Thumis, who has the means of passing through the land. He knows the roads and the waters; the sand wastes do not shut him in.

MAN:30:27 I leave all things in your hands. May sorrow never stretch out towards you. May you live forever in a form of glorious perfection. Your servant hopes to see you, but submits to his master's will.

Chapter Thirty-One – Scroll of Thotis

MAN:31:1 These writings are dedicated to The Great God Who is Eternal. May they live forever among things that survive to serve man. May they be an enlightening lesson and a warning to those who follow, for now a dark night of ignorance and fear overshadows the land. Your servant bows to Your will, O Great God Who is benevolent towards those who serve with purity of intent.

MAN:31:2 We who remain loyal glorify You, not with mere words, for the time of hypocrisy has passed, but in our inmost thoughts and in our deeds. We remember You as the sun rises to Your glory in the morning and, as in the evening, it sets into Your peace. Teach us that there is joy in being Your servants. Keep us under Your protecting wing.

MAN:31:3 Great Spirit Who made the Nile to flow, the great water, which never wearies or ceases from its journeying. Its movement is as everlasting as the wind. May the stream of my life be filled to overflowing with the waters of righteousness. Loose the shackles of wickedness, which hold me captive. Let not the string of my lute be broken while I play, and let not my labours be ended before their fulfilment. Though men hail me for a greater thing than any that has been done before, it will not be my memorial. Time will eat away my name, but let many mornings dawn on my waking, that I may complete the task entrusted to me. Remove the fears that lurk about me in the solitude. Cut off the bonds of affliction that bind me down. Let my spirit roam free. We who remain loyal know Your laws and the Great Law, which is as firm as the hills of immortality. In the days to come great songs will be sung unto You, even as they were sung in the days of old.

MAN:31:4 The priests can no longer be held in restraint by Umotif, and dark days threaten us. It is a time of foreboding, yet there is peace throughout Kahemu. The state of men in high places is such that the beauty of Truth has to be concealed from them, lest they profane even her purity. Under the shelter of her mantle, even those strengthened by the visions seen in the Eternal Chambers are liable to lapse into many wickednesses. They would say in their hearts, Being one who is purified, I am safe. I can cleave the dark waters of evil as a sea bird does the ocean and rise, all wickedness falling away from me as water falls from the back of the soaring bird. Thus it is today and was even in the days long gone, for such things are written in the old manner on a scroll found at Honew.

MAN:31:5 The first land on Earth wherein men dwelt was not Kahemu, it was a land out beyond the salt waters. To this land came the Immortal Spirit in the form of a Radiant One from Heaven, who had left his more enlightened place to dwell among beasts in the lower kingdom of sorrow. In some mysterious way, he became incarnated as man; how, we know not, but he founded the race of man. It is not as recorded in tales told for the ignorant.

MAN:31:6 None knows in truth the Old Motherland or where it was; there are tales, but they disagree. The Nine Bows say it was Southward, the learned priests are not united in thought; some say towards the West where the sun now sets, while others say towards the East where the sun rises. Southward are great mountains and forests, monsters and men covered with hair. Here, winds are formed within the Earth and issue forth from a black cavern. It is a place of chaos where water, soil and air are not separate; the Old Motherland could not have been there. To the left hand side, there is a great wilderness, the land of Amua; the Old Motherland could not have given birth to such as these. To the right hand is the wide plain of man-eaters, which stretches out to the far reaches of Old Kahemu; this was barren even in the oldest times. To the North of the wilderness, the land is occupied by deformed men and dwarfs. Where amid this could have been the fertile pastures and ploughlands well watered from the sky river, where men lived in peaceful content? The Old Motherland was never there, nor, as some say, in the waters beyond, which boil at the extremity. Beyond the wide river there once was a land graced with all riches needful to men, crowned by many walled Meru, but it was not the land of our birth. Northward is the home of the cool breeze, but beyond the lands which skirt the salt water are the one eyed peoples and the giants with white hair and eyes. Here, the rocks and stones are of the whitest marble, and the trees bear white fruit; thus in the whiteness, the eyes of men are blinded in their youth, for even the grass grows white. Before this is the land of Hosugia, a place unproductive and barren, where fruit never appears on the trees and crops will not ripen. How could the Old Motherland lie in this direction?

MAN:31:7 In the old books, it is said that the Old Motherland was ruled by the Queen of Light, who was supreme above all. The temple tales tell that the lesser gods came to dwell among mortals when the Mistress of Brightness ruled in Kelathi, that they were sheltered in temples, and priests were appointed to minister unto them. It is said that places of instruction were setup within the temples, but few men were taught the inner knowledge. It was rightly held that it would be a danger to those without wisdom, and it had to be safeguarded. Is this not the tale told in the Book of Beginnings? It is said that Kelathi lay within the borders of Kahemu, but could it not have been the land of similar sounding name outward from Pontas beyond Godsland?

MAN:31:8 Is it not said of both that they were engulfed in fire and water? In the Book of Beginnings, it is said: The generations passed, and a vast amount of knowledge and wisdom was accumulated and preserved in purity. It was the heritage of mankind, but though man had learned to cherish the light of Truth and walk wisely with it, nevertheless then as now, false priesthoods flourished. They pandered to the carnal desires of the undeveloped and exploited the weaknesses of the ignorant. Their iniquity built up a vast weight of evil in the Netherworld, which projected itself into the material of Earth, so that the powers which upheld it became unstable. This caused all the southern part of the Old Land to sink down into heaving waters.

MAN:31:9 The disaster was brought about through the ascendance of evil. Rites which awakened the dead were rife among the carnal-minded and ignorant, while those who remained steadfast on the harder road of spiritual development had fixed their eyes on the light ahead, ignoring the pitfalls at their feet. It was then even as now; will men ever learn?

MAN:31:10 This was the aspect of the disaster, as written in the Book of Beginnings: There were openings in the land, from which evil vapours poured forth as a mist; descending upon the people like a mantle, it spread out and covered the whole face of the land. The tongues of the people were stopped, and they became dumb with fear. The ground trembled beneath them, and great tongues of flame shot up. The whole land heaved and rocked like an ocean wave. As it rose and fell, groaned and shook, the fires which strove beneath burst forth to be met with shafts of lightning striking down from Heaven.

MAN:31:11 A thick black cloud of smoke filled the land, and men were smothered in dust. As the setting sun rested on the horizon, it could be but dimly seen beneath the cloud as a fiery red ball. When it had gone, a grey dense darkness prevailed, lit only by great sheets of lightning. The waters broke heavily over the land, sweeping it clean. The plains and cities were covered, and new shores formed around the mountains. The waters mounted up until all that moved and lived was covered, the land was submerged. Mountain tops alone remained above the rush of uplifted torrent. Whirlwinds blew and brought cold winds, which cleared away the dust and debris. Mudbanks were formed, and a mountain mouth remained open to spew forth vile vapours. During one long awful night, the doomed land was torn apart, and southward sank out of sight forever.

MAN:31:12 A wise man has written, This was not mountain-girt Kelathi, or age-old Ramakui. This was the land out in the green waters where the sun sets beyond Keftu, near the lands of the Henbua.

MAN:31:13 It is then said: They came through the marshes and across the wild mountains beyond the barren places of stone into a new land called Anketa. Here grew the great life tree known even in the days of our fathers. This is a tree of strange aspect, like unto no other, though in the days of our fathers, it was barren and enclosed in flames. Now we know that the life tree grew in Taleus, which is towards the Lands of Dawn, by Pontas. Therefore, could not the Old Motherland have been found hereabouts? Not all was inundated.

MAN:31:14 It is said: Men came out of the devastation. Behind them, the land sank and the Earth shook, mountains split apart and crumbled. Where once there had been a valley now stood a mountain. The air was filled with smoke, and hot rocks were hurled down from out of the sky. Men choked in brimstone. Great winds howled like a thousand unearthly wild dogs. They left all behind them and came across the wild places to the Land of Refuge. Was not Kahemu once known to some men as the Land of Refuge? Therefore, the whereabouts of the Old Motherland is not unknown. It is said that when men came from the Old Land, the everlasting stars rested where Earth meets Heaven, but none knows how many lifetimes have passed since then.

MAN:31:15 Thus, it is not impossible to discover where the Old Motherland lay. Therefore there is hope, and men need not despair, for the secret may be re-discovered. When once again the Sacred Things rest in the Old Land from whence they came, the days of disturbance will cease, and once again men will live in peace. Men go forth to seek the road; all is not lost to us yet.

MAN:31:16 Now the Great House of the Hidden Places stands in Kahemu. It is built to last forever and stands up strongly towards Heaven, high above the heads of men. It is covered with white stones; the white stone of Rehakom was cut for it, and above it is topped with copper. It is not the copper of men, but the copper of God. Within it lies the Womb of Rebirth used by the Twice Born of the Enlightened Ones. Men enter its portals to die and come out restored to life, reborn as gods. Beside it stands the Temple of the Radiant Ones, many-pillared and walled about. Here is the Great Portal of Entry into Life, and above it, on a great stone, these words may be seen:

MAN:31:17 From the Children of God to the Children of Men. Behold, we found you in bondage to mortal bodies and bestowed upon you the gift of everlasting life.

MAN:31:18 My brothers, these are days of distress, and no man knows the outcome of the strife that rends the land. For long generations, this was a land of peace, a land blessed with bounty, but now men have wrought evil upon it. They who have gone to save it may not complete their journey back, and nought shall have been achieved. Therefore, I say unto you, prepare to depart hence, even as it is written. Let the things that are more valuable than life be brought to safety. Above life and land is God. He is above life and land.

Chapter Thirty-Two – Scroll of Harmotif

MAN:32:1 Odidef of Onekhefu found many scrolls from the olden times. The Inspector of Temples discovered writings from the days of the Wise Ones, many things from the past and utterances by Lords of the Kohar. He caused them to be copied and placed in the houses of record. Some were guarded from the eyes of men. The writings dedicated to the name of The Great God were sought out. Nekat, a scribe at Yano, wrote them down; they are set forth by his hand. They are not lost and will live when he and his sons and his son's sons rest in Morningland. He will abide in Amentuth in peace.

MAN:32:2 The physician must know the courses of the Watchers. He must know their times and their comings and goings. He must know the secret of the Lord of Forms and the way of the Guide of Souls. He must know who are the Owners of Forms and who are the Formless Ones.

MAN:32:3 He must know their abode. He must know the road and the four ways of entry. He must know the nature of the double power. He must be a master at drawing forth the spirit. He must know the outside of man, the things which flow over it. He must know the inside man, the substances which fill it. He must know the heart, the muscles that move out from it, controlling every action of the body.

MAN:32:4 These are words to fill the ears of the physician. These things are written on his heart. The physician sits on a throne of silence. The physician absorbs the pains of the sick through his ears. If any man opens the door of his heart to the physician, the tongue has no knowledge of what the ears have heard. The inmost room is open to the silent man. The heart of the physician is not puffed up because of his knowledge. He talks with the simple man as though he were wise. The words of the physician are as healing herbs. The physician bears himself so that when the eyes of the sick fall upon him, they are half cured. The eyes of the physician see through the flesh, When he sat before his master, he learned to bear patiently the chastisements for his own failings, now, he can justly reprove another for his. The tongue of the physician is dipped in honey, not in guile. Where Truth adds to suffering without benefit, then he may veil it, but never will he do so without purpose or care.

MAN:32:5 The physician does not fear the god above the stairs. He does not shrink before the face of death. He is a man of wide wisdom. He knows the nature of the lesser gods. The lesser gods are the limbs and attributes of The Great God and form His members. He will not seek to raise up the dead, he will not seek to speak with them, He is beyond the urges of gold. He knows the laws of The Great God, they cover countless years. They are fixed and unchangeable and never fail at their times. The physician knows the measurements of the hours and the movements of the days.

MAN:32:6 When the vital, God-given breath is stopped by demons, the body becomes restless and hot. They stir the heart, they drive out the body water containing the life. The demons must be made inactive and put to sleep with one of the sleeping draughts. The body is to be made cool, for the demons of heat are expelled with coolness. They will enter into a vessel of earthenware, if it be warmed, and can then be destroyed. If a man be slain in battle or by the body being pierced, the destroying demon enters through the blood. The body is broken and it enters through the opening. The breath is stopped, breathing ceases. The outward senses are discarded. The spirit departs, to find its memories intact in the keeping of its spirit twin, the liberated spirit is united with its spirit twin. It dwells in another sphere. It is the place of fulfilment, not unlike Earth. The physician must not hamper the departing spirit once breath has left the body. He must not bind it.

MAN:32:7 The spirit does not pass to the Morningland awake. It awakens there as from a sleep. It does not unite with its spirit twin until judged according to its colours. When united together, all over there appears alike to all here. All past hopes and desires appear before the risen one. The gods that have been worshipped are given form there. They arise before the eyes of the risen one.

MAN:32:8 The worship of strange, lesser gods is not forbidden, for it helps purify the heart. It makes wholesome the heart. The words spoken before unhearing images are not lost. They are heard by Greater Ears than men conceive. The Great God made ten lights or rays, which flow forth from His midst. Each shines in the form of power His thoughts have imparted to it. They are shed everywhere and contained in all things. The physician is wise, if he is master of the rays.

MAN:32:9 A man is melancholy. It is not that a demon has made its abode in his body. It is not a sickness of the body. See if his land is feeble. Look at his crops, have they failed? If the wife of a man be unfaithful, his crops will not grow. if his sister be unmarried and unchaste, he will suffer infertility in his herds. The trees of his garden will not bear fruit. Corn and wheat will not yield their bounty. A man's daughter being unmarried and unchaste, his birds and beasts will waste away. He will become downcast in spirit. His eyes will become dull. The cure is not within the man. His body is not unsound, no demon abides there. The cure is in the daughter. The man must brand her with burning brands. She must be branded in stripes. She must name the man who made her impure. She must denounce the one who made her a fountain of impurity. Her impurity afflicts her father. It goes forth invisible as air, to lay hold on his birds and beasts, If she would be tested she is given a draught. It is gall of dog, juice of aloe, ashes of goathorn, each one measure in five measures of water. If she throws up the evil, she is purged and purified. if there is no evil, it does not come up. She makes an image of the man who made her impure. He brought evil into her. She burns his image in purifying fire. Into the ashes go all her thoughts and longings for him. She is free from evil.

MAN:32:10 A woman knows an adulteress and locks the secret in her heart. She does not denounce the adulteress. Her male kindred go to war or to hunt. They will die or be wounded. The knowledge hidden in her heart becomes like a barb in living flesh. It becomes putrid, a thing of evil. As putrid flesh gives off an aroma of corruption, which pollutes as it festers and spreads evil, so does hidden knowledge of evil fester in the subtle essences. It spreads abroad, and as blood cries to blood, it reaches the blood of a man under strain. This woman must be branded in stripes and purified. She must denounce the adulteress. The adulteress will be dealt with; then, like an unchaste woman, purified with the water of maidens. The blood of a guilty man must be spilt to save the blood of one who has done no wrong. The physician does not punish, and he does not seek out one who deserves punishment. The art of the physician is to heal.

MAN:32:11 Men suffer sickness of the heart; they become sad. Their birds, their beasts, their crops are stricken, but the evil springs not from evil festering in women. The evil is within themselves. Their household is in disorder; they are confused in thought. They say one thing, when they mean another. None is at peace with them. They become hot ones. They must no longer strive to dwell in the northwind. They must labour for another or take up the tools of a craftsman. Better a long life in poverty and peace than a short life weighed down by riches and care.

MAN:32:12 A man is in pain, or it becomes you to cut into his flesh to remove a demon's abode, or to draw together bones that have parted. Then is the time for putting forth the spirit. He may be given the drink of slumber; it is for you to decide. You will move the gabulik before his eyes. You will call forth his spirit. You will move your hands downward over his body, spreading the power of your spirit. Your voice will give him instructions. The power of your spirit will enter into him; his eyes will close, but more often not. The power will enter into his body. It will close all doors between his spirit and his body. His body will breathe; it will live, but he will be as one dead, for his spirit is called forth. You will place the Eye of Hora upon him. It will bind him; he cannot move; he is fast. You will speak to him, you will ask of him the thing he cannot know. He will answer. If his spirit be called forth, it will know the thing he cannot know. You can tell him he will sleep the sleep beyond sleep. You will tell him there is no pain and that doors between the body and spirit are closed. His eyes do not see, his skin does not feel. his flesh is soft. You can enter his body with an instrument. If he have the abode of a demon within him, you pierce it. You draw forth the demon in the fluid. It runs away. The seat of the demon falls upon itself. You close it with a thin rod of copper made hot. it is purified. You draw the flesh together; you fold it back. It is covered with long boiled satish. You leave the man enwrapped in the Eye of Hora. You tell him when to awaken. All decisions are yours. He awakens not as Osireh, unless it be the will of Osireh.

MAN:32:13 A man is plagued by a demon, which has made its abode in the inmost recesses of his body. It cannot be found. He talks loosely; his tongue lacks control. His thoughts are wrapped in shadows. his heart moves quickly; water flows from his body. He finds no peace in sleep. His hands tremble. There is pain in his head. He relishes no food. He is a man of many thoughts, but knows not what to do. You will call forth his spirit. You will place him in the chambers of silence. You will enwrap him in the healing aroma. The doors between his spirit and body are shut. You place the Eye of Hora upon him. He sleeps in the Eye of Hora. It fills every recess of his body. It seeks out the demon. It destroys the demon in its abode. The demon is not called forth. You speak with the spirit of the man; is it at peace, is it restful? You decide the time of awakening. This is the healing sleep. You, the physician, are the master of sleep. Of all physicians, sleep is the greatest.

MAN:32:14 The pupil asks, "What is sleep?" It is renewal of spiritual energy. The spirit returns to its source, to the fountain of its being. The body lapses into sleep. The spirit is easily recalled. It is not far away. A man lacks sleep; he cannot sleep, he becomes sick. His body is heavy, his footsteps slow. He lacks strength; his thoughts go from him. His limbs ache, but he has no point of sickness. He cannot say what ails him. His pillow is a place of torment, his bed a wilderness of wild thoughts. Small things of little moment loom before him as mountains. You decide. If it be a simple affair without himself, an affair of his household, a problem at the task, a soothing draught will suffice. Let the spirit obtain the substance for its forces peacefully, and it will renew its vigour; it will be well. If the sickness come from within, if it come from something entered within, then the healing sleep will bring a cure.

MAN:32:15 A man fears the nightcomer. He fears to sleep, lest the nightcomer seize him. He builds an abode of sickness with bricks of fear. He has opened a window into the Place of Terror. He must be purged, he must be purified with incense. He may eat while the Overseer of heaven rises upward, but not while he descends. When night approaches, he must dance around his habitation until weary. He will bathe himself in warm waters, to be purified. His misdeeds will fall from him. They will no longer attract the nightcomer. It will not rise from the Dark Abode to haunt him.

MAN:32:16 A man has a festering sore. He has a wound. It is unclean, it turns yellow. It darkens. There is evil beneath the hardness. Salt is dissolved strongly in water. It is made warm. The sore and the wound are bathed. The hardness is softened; it is taken away. The yellow, which has come up is taken away. Homu leaves are pounded; they are sprinkled with brimstone. They are placed on the wound, they are bound up with linen. A wound is large or a battle wound, it must be made clean with liskin wood in water. If the maggot seize on it and consume the evil and the blackness, it can remain. When the flesh is clean and bright, it must be covered to stop entry of unclean things, and the sixth sign must be on top. There is benefit if the wound be left open to the sun.

MAN:32:17 A man is burnt. The skin blisters; it gives out water. The skin is consumed; the flesh is raw. It is not black. The flesh is soft. The burned is laved in cool waters. it is sprinkled with water of sesumen. It is not bound up. A wound does not heal, a burn does not heal. You take yellow dried powder of luba; the powder is placed in water. It remains yellow, then cast it out. It turns red. then use it forthwith, but do not keep it with you.

MAN:32:18 A woman in childbirth, A man wild with fever. Water made hot with stones is poured on the tree of life. It soaks during two nights. it is given often and drunk deep. It is the basis of many things. it can be kept.

MAN:32:19 The tree of life is pounded; it becomes pulp. A joint swells filled with pain. The pulp is applied, it sticks, it is not bound. The rectum becomes a place of evil; it bleeds. The evil stirs up inconvenience. The pulp of the tree of life, four measures. The pulp of poppy fruit, one measure. Oil of sufan, one measure. Moon oil, two measures.

MAN:32:20 A man becomes sluggish in the grip of fat. his body is encased in fat. He is in a state of sickness. His body is silted up with fat, as the water channels are silted up with sand and soil. Fat is the adversary that eats away a man's welfare, It chokes his body, as weeds choke a waterway. He who walks with fat is as a man who ever carries a load of sand. He is purged day after day. He shall he given little water. He shall walk long distances in the heat of the day and bathe in uncool water. A shallow pit shall be dug during the cool of the morning and left during the rising of the sun. As the sun declines, the fat man shall be put in the pit. The sand will cover all but his head. He shall be left during the declining of the sun. In the evening, his meal shall be small. This, he will do many times. He shall not eat of sodden foods or foods which grow and are hard. All that grows and is soft shall be eaten, but shall be unsodden.

MAN:32:21 Learn dancing and movements of the body, so that soul and body may develop in harmony. Let nothing enter the mouth or come forth from it except it be controlled by moderation. A hungry man exposes the wickedness of others, but an overstuffed one does no less. The body of a hungry man is abused through no fault of his own, but the abuse wrought by an overfed man is his own doing.

MAN:32:22 Never forget to call upon God in your sickness, and you will find He comes with fond compassion, When His power enwraps you, sickness is overcome.

MAN:32:23 The Egyptians were wise, but their ways were not our ways. The cures of their physicians were for them and not for us, as our bodies, being sustained in a different manner, are unlike in their humours. The substances, which bring about a cure can be obtained only from the surroundings in which the body moves. Anything from another land lacks the essential harmony. Therefore, all the recipes recorded on this long scroll are omitted. Our material is limited, and this is not a treatise on physics. This scroll was among those added.

Chapter Thirty-Three – Annexed Scroll 1

MAN:33:1 O great city, O heart of Egypt, your habitations are overthrown and your sacred shrines lie buried beneath the sands of time. The dust of ages enwraps you, as a dead one is swathed within the tomb. Your temples still stand and ring with noise, but the solemn shrines are silent. They have become an abode for the wild dog and scorpion, and your roads are highways of wickedness.

MAN:33:2 Behold, in the days long gone down into dust, the whirlwind came and earth poured out her wrathful breath, so that you were burnt. The evildoers were swept away by the waters, and the wicked ones were swallowed up in the fires. The days of the years were shortened and the times of all things altered. The seasons were turned around, so that the seed rotted within the soil, and no green shoots came forth to greet the day. All buds withered upon the vines, the land lay dead under its grey shroud. The moon changed the order of her ways, and the sun set himself a new course, so that men knew not where they were and all were afflicted. The stars swam in a new direction, and the whole order of things was changed. Yet, O Egypt, even from those days of calamity you emerged unbroken, your spirit intact, your heart unshaken. What has happened to you, O land of mine?

MAN:33:3 Weep, O land of Egypt, weep for the things that have gone. Weep for the spirit now-departed. Weep for the betrayed gods, weep for The Great God so high above them that you scarcely knew him. Weep for the destruction that has befallen you. Weep for all the beauty and glory that have gone down into the dust. Weep for eternal ages, and sleep for evermore. Your spirit has departed, your life had ebbed away, your vitality has burnt itself out, only the empty corpse remains. The generations yet to tread the Earth will know nothing of you. They will see no more than the dead, dried, mummified thing. The loving life that once vitalised it so gloriously, they cannot know. O Son of Kebew, forgive the people of this land for their ways. Reveal your greatness by serving those who no longer walk in the light of your instruction, even as you served their fathers in days gone by.

MAN:33:4 My land, what have you become? You have left the true path of your faith and wandered into strange byways. You are bemused and bedazzled with things that disturb the senses, and have become like a ship adrift without oars. You have abandoned the spirit that inspired you and sought satisfaction among lifeless things of Earth. You have spurned the stern discipline required to win the hand of love and trodden the well-worn path of carnal satisfaction. You have turned to the ways of the harlot, and out of your harlotry, you have wrought destruction. You no longer delight in the serene mystery of the stars above; your pleasures are in the filth beneath your feet. Where once you gazed upward in awe, now you look downward in degradation. O that this is the self-chosen fate of my land!

MAN:33:5 I go, for go I must. I depart, for destiny demands it. When his motherland collapses about him like an undermined palace built on a foundation of mud, then it is not a time for hesitation. One man cannot stem a flood with his hand. When his habitation falls apart, it is time to seek another. Perhaps nations, like men, grow old and decay. My land is old, a hundred and twenty generations have passed through it since Osireh brought light to men. Four times, the stars have moved to new positions, and twice the sun has changed the direction of his journey. Twice, the Destroyer has struck Earth and three times the Heavens have opened and shut. Twice, the land has been swept clean by water.

MAN:33:6 The lot of a man destined for exile is sorrow, but as a sorrowful man I would save others from my misery. I would leave a memorial for their guidance, and knowledge to increase the wisdom of their days, Let my voice of warning ring out to all men; let it reach even the strange lands beyond the seas, even unto Hownibut. Listen to my voice, take heed to my cry; be warned, lest you, too, fall under the condemnation of destiny; lest you, too, be struck down by the sword of tribulation. My motherland, the land I knew, is no more; it lives, yes, as a flower lives when plucked and dried, as a fruit lives when pickled and preserved, or as a man lives when embalmed.

MAN:33:7 About the days of Nun, we have no knowledge. Before creation commenced there was the One Father/Mother Being and from this Divinity came the heavenly Twins. From these were born three, and the three became many. Thus, even in the beginning it was divinely ordained that brother and sister might be wed. From the first Heavenly Twins were born those whose destiny it was to be eternally married. For theirs was the divine right of eternal and undying love, a love unknown to mortals, but to which, if they would be more than mortal, they must aspire. This love is the Light of Life, the Light of the Earth, the Sun of the Spirit.

MAN:33:8 The Originating Divinity is called many names among men, and in Egypt His names are hidden in other names. Among the Chosen Ones, He is called The Craftsman Creator, but men and women name Him differently among the people. Likewise, some say ‘Him’ while others say ‘Her;’ it is all alike, for these are no more than the words and distinctions of mortal man. Heaven is the sphere of God, the true abode of His Spirit in essence. There is the Heaven above, which is the High Heaven, and the Heaven below, which is the reflection of the High Heaven. The true Centre of God is in Newit.

MAN:33:9 The Craftsman of Creation placed Heaven and Earth apart. He set the sun and Stars in motion and spread wide the Earth beneath them. His wisdom, He enclosed within the hearts of men, wherein it still lies sleeping. Heaven goes his daily rounds like a husband foraging for his wife's sustenance, while Earth is busy with the duties of a wife, feeding and cherishing that, which she has brought forth. Is not all life known to man born of Earth? Is it not nourished upon her breast? Unless it be that they derive pleasure in company, why do Heaven and Earth remain together? Without Earth, how could the grass grow, the basic substance of life, how could trees, fruit and flowers bloom? Without Earth, what could the water and warmth of Heaven produce?

MAN:33:10 God put desire for each other into the hearts of men and women, that in their union, the race of men should be preserved. Likewise, He has implanted in every part of life the desire for another compatible part. Thus life endures and multiplies. Earth and all life upon it are bent towards one end, one purpose, the service and development of man. Without man as the objective, Earth would be useless, it would have a purposeless, futile existence. Even night and day, the daylight and dark serve in the nurture and development of man.

MAN:33:11 In the early days Egypt was bounded in the West by the green bitter waters. There lay the land of Nilar, where men learned to bend the dead bodies, so that the earth-bound spirits of departed ones should not wander to molest them. Out here was the city of Merow, from whence came the mighty men who smote the giants in the days of yore. Northward lay the entrance to the Kingdom of Darkness Under the Earth. The portal lies behind a veil of air mixed with water, it is covered with a mantle of cloudy thickness, which eyes can scarce see through. The floor is of water, not too deep that the dismal, stony bottom cannot be seen, hence men require a boat. Both sides of the entrance are flanked with giant blocks of stone, from which rise huge pillars set one against the other, so that there is no space between them. The whole is overset with an immense rock greater than any cut by mortal hands, and it is shaped like the rump of a man. It is in a cold region of long darkness, where the Calf of Gold shows his displeasure. Now to the West of Egypt, all is barren and sandy, except to the North, which is the habitation of wild men who dwell in holes within the ground.

MAN:33:12 Out of the Land of God, to the East, came Osireh, who was one filled with the Spirit of God, the first Viceregent of God on Earth. Truly a god who walked among men, a true Son of God. He learned, by communicating with the heart of God, what lesser beings can hope to learn only by long contemplation of the Sacred Writings. Yet he said, "Not all can hope to see; it is not a thing granted to men. But even he who only hears and has faith in his heart, who stretches himself out to do good, who conforms with the teachings, who is one with us, he also shall attain to the glory of an awakened spirit. He, too, shall share the joyful heritage of a righteous man. I who have journeyed the full distance to the Fount of Fire, lit a torch there and turned back to meet you with the comforting light of its flame. Hence, there is no need for you to journey the full length of the long, weary road to see Truth."

MAN:33:13 In the Book of the Bearers of Light is written: 'God speaks with Osireh, "Have you measured My words in silent communion with Mine Own Self? Has the darkness of Earth's delusions been dispelled by your own inner light?" Osireh says, "By the grace of the communication granted me I have seen the light of Truth. and all the delusions of darkness have gone. My doubts are now no more. My faith is confirmed, it is firm, I am the steadfast one. I say in Truth. Your will be done. Osireh speaks to men, I heard these words of glory spoken within the silence and solitude of the great cavern, and they filled my soul with awe and wonder. By the working of a wondrous thing, I heard these words in the sacred silence. I knew the mystery of life. I will ever remember the things burnt into my soul. I came out; when I spoke with men my tongue danced with exaltation." These things are written.

MAN:33:14 Later, Osireh went up into the Sacred High Place and there learned the ordinances for the wellbeing of man. He was given the rules for safeguarding the Sacred Mysteries, and he was also shown the workings of the Great Law. When he came down he chose the best of those about him and appointed the Council of Light, which numbered twenty-four.

MAN:33:15 These are the words he spoke to them by the Sea of Death: "These are things to be explained to none but those with understanding and enlightenment. The Path of the True Way will be long and arduous, its trials and tribulations manifold and harsh. It is not a place for the faint-hearted, and the oily-tongued or double-tongued will not be found there. Yet, it will never lack a pilgrim, for there will always be seekers of Truth and fighters for Goodness. Nevertheless, treat this not as a light thing; weigh these words well and do not belittle the perils of the road ahead. Take good heed of my warnings."

MAN:33:16 "The Path of the True Way is one beset with the sharp stones of suffering and sorrow. The mortal flesh shall be torn by the sharp thorns of pain and tribulation. Thus, it will be well to choose those who aspire to journey the True Way with great care and discretion. Never overlook the sacrifices that you maybe called upon to make." These are words spoken by Osireh.

MAN:33:17 In the Book of the Bearers of Light is written: 'Osireh says to those about him, "I am the first among lightbearers. I am the one instructed by The Great God, I am the one with knowledge concerning the building of the first Shrine of Mysteries. I, alone of those now upon Earth, hold the key to the Sacred Mysteries. I know the secret of things that are past, of things that are and of things that are to be. The act of birth enwraps the soul of man in a mantle of unconsciousness; it imprisons the spirit in a state of slumber. His own true self is within him, but it is as one dead within a tomb. All the great spiritual powers lie latent, locked inside, even though the mortal abode be formed to perfection. The True Way is the road to freedom; it is the process of awakening the spirit and the key to spiritual self-awareness. It unlocks the door and reveals the light. It banishes all doubts and grants an assurance of life everlasting. It is man discovering himself. Such is the True Way."'

MAN:33:18 God says to Osireh, "Behold the land before you, it is a chosen land for safeguarding the Sacred Mysteries. Out of its womb shall come the Child of Truth. which shall die and rise again to lead men in the struggle to glory. In the Day of his rising, the Earth will be distressed and know it not. Nor will it open its arms to the Child, which will go unrecognised and even be despised and mocked. Yet, in that day will be produced a salve to heal the scars of mankind. In that day, when men shall have forgotten the way of righteousness and turned from Truth. the light will come unto them." These words were spoken by God.

MAN:33:19 When Osireh came to Egypt the people were unlearned and wild; they lived in huts and holes, seeking their food in the wilderness about them. He gathered them together and gave laws to guide them; he taught the growing and gathering of corn, the making of the waterways and channels, the building of habitations for the living and the dead. The gods of the people were dangerous gods to be feared, to be approached fearfully by none but those, who were familiar with their ways. Those alone could interpret the signs and portents rarely granted in those days. Osireh did not deny the people these gods, but he changed men as time changes trees. Even so has Osireh changed in the hearts of men and he is as they have made him.

MAN:33:20 Before the coming of Osireh, men and women dwelt apart, men going into women of their choice. But the women kept to the fires while men roamed about, though in those days they never defiled the land of another with their feet. Osireh drew them together and taught them the laws of marriage, but still he let men and women dwell apart if they so willed, though now no man lay with a woman not his wife.

MAN:33:21 Osireh taught the making of bread with gathered corn and sown corn. It was eaten at the floodwater feasts, with salt and with honey. For Osireh knew the nature of salt, which is of the bodies of men, and the nature of honey, which is of Heaven. Salt is found in bitter waters which wash far off shores in the Land of the Salt Mountains. Men who have sailed far have seen great mountains covered with salt. They lie under the steadfast stars gleaming in a strange light. Honey comes airborne from Heaven, to be gathered by the bee. Once, the Earth was veiled within an awesome cloud and in those days honey fell as frost upon the ground, and it fed man and beast when the herbage withered.

MAN:33:22 When Osireh had drawn the people together, so that they dwelt peacefully in the land, they enquired of him whether he knew the likeness of their gods, whom none among them had ever seen, Therefore, he fashioned the likenesses of the gods for them. He built cities, wherein to keep them and cultivated the land. He caused temples to be set up, and in these were placed the likenesses of the gods which Osireh equipped. The likenesses he made satisfied the people, so that their hearts were made glad. Then, the gods entered into their bodies of wood and stone.

MAN:33:23 Yet, Osireh was sad; his heart was heavy for the people, he knew their nature and the ignorance of their ways. Therefore, he assigned a protector to be the guardian of the people, one who knew Truth. who was an Enlightened One, who was greatest among the Twice Born. One to be an ever open channel to God, so that a flood of spiritual power should inundate the land, spreading bounty and peace over its expanse. He assigned to him all the people in the land, that they may prosper. Osireh placed the land in the hands of the Appointed One, with all the water within its bounds, all the herbage, the cattle of the pasturelands and beasts of the wild places, and all things that fly and crawl.

MAN:33:24 This Appointed One was the King, the Pharaoh, the Light of God on Earth, the Vicegerent of God over Men. Him, Osireh endowed with the essence of the spirit outflowing from God, the power that reaches towards Divinity. He was the link, the bridge between God and man. His was the task to bring men the knowledge and awareness of divinity, and to preserve the special spirituality with which he was endowed in a select portion of one race. By his authority alone, all places of worship should be built and kept, and their ceremonies controlled and performed. By his decree alone, all canals should be cut, all waterways opened, all lands marked out and all war hosts raised. Under him, all food should be gathered and stored, all men fed and every burial permitted and performed. He would be the supreme channel of contact with God. He and all who came from out of his loins should be Ladders of Light. Osireh it was who himself ordained that as their bodies were filled with vitalised spirit essence, they should be preserved, to keep such power bound to Earth for its good.

MAN:33:25 Such was Pharaoh, a god below gods, a man above men. He was bound by the decrees of olden times and must ever set Truth over falsehood. He was the narrow channel between God and man, one whose task was to reveal God to men. The family of Pharaoh was, in the first place, chosen by the Council of Light. In those days, a few families were selected and some chosen from them to be carefully bred, so that all the less desirable traits were excluded. Their aim and objective was to produce men and women perfect in goodness, the ultimate in perfection. These were the qualities, in which they were trained to the highest degree: In duty and responsibility, obligation towards the people, in dignity, justice and benevolence. They were a family, a race apart, trained wholly to govern in goodness. Every moment of their lives was to be devoted and dedicated to the elevation of mankind. They were taught to regard the people as their own children, to be guarded, guided and inspired by the finest examples possible. The family of Pharaoh was to reach out to the very summit of aspiration, to aim for the pinnacle of goodness and spirituality. While the common people laboured under them, the whole life of royal families was to be devoted to service and goodness, to the elevation of mankind, to the preservation and administration of justice.

MAN:33:26 Originally, this worked perfectly, but earthly conditions are finely balanced between the call of the divine and the demons of the flesh. Somewhere, down through the ages, the dam of spirituality sprang a leak, and that which had hitherto been hoarded and guarded ebbed away. The divinity, the spirituality in the blood was diluted, it became weakened, and when goodness diminished its opposite crept in. What has this glorious institution, the great Pharaoh become today? He is no more than the clacking tongue of a bell, a hollow, empty shell, a vane in the wind. He is not the owner of his own time; his days belong to others and the hours of his nights are controlled. He follows a shallow, futile ceremonial; he performs empty, meaningless rituals. He eats according to instructions and bathes at the rising and setting of sun, not for his own pleasure, but because he must. Where is the glory in this? O for what once was; O for the joyful days of the past! What has happened to the glorious spiritual inspiration? Where once there was a purpose, now there is foolishness; where once there was a sacred being, now there is a puppet manipulated by puppets. Where once there was a divine insight, now there are dead precedents. All is gone, all is dust, all is woe!

MAN:33:27 Now this Osireh, of whom I speak, is even he whom the people of this land have made a god, for the Twice Born who have wisdom have let it be thus. Call him man or call him god; it is a matter of small importance, for the boundary between them is not impassable. Petty men will argue about the distinctions of words, but they would be better engaged in discovering Truth. Osireh was ever enshrined in the hearts of the common folk, who had believed in immortality from the beginning. It was not so much their ignorance that obscured the light of Truth. but rather the structure erected by hypocrisy and pomp, by avarice and ambition. Down through the ages, this belief in immortality persisted over the official view, which held that no more than a few might hope for immortality, and that mainly ensuing from the efforts of others. In the days of the first Pharaohs, it was different. Then immortality was the reward of all people, though only collectively and under the leadership and guidance of the king. Nevertheless, the immortality of the common folk and the immortality of the Twice Born were not alike.

MAN:33:28 Osireh came not into a land of powerful kings and great cities, but into a land of ignorant, unenlightened men. He came with seven strangers from a land far East of the Sea of Death, a land not as old as Egypt but long since dead and forgotten. When Osireh came, he found two peoples of power on the river, the People of Roh and the People of Haru, and Haru was of the body of Atem. There had long been war between these two peoples, but Osireh pacified them and united them as one. Then, he taught them the ways of peace and the ways of prosperity.

MAN:33:29 When men began to build places to dwell in, and to grow things, they were troubled by men who came out of the wilderness. These were a people ruled by women, and though the men were small in stature the women, who ruled were tall and lean. Their only weapons were such as could be thrown from afar, but they had shields made of hide woven in a manner which caused anything coming against them to become entangled. Such were the men who came out of the wilderness and the wild places there. Strong men and hairy.

MAN:33:30 The Queen of these people was not as the other women, for she was good to look upon, besides being a great huntress. She was fairer than the other women, even more fair than the women of Egypt, who put all others to shame. Her name was Neth, and I know of no man who has knowledge of her father. Perhaps she was an Undying One, who was always there, though I cannot believe there are any such beings. Yet even in these days, there is a race of men beyond the mountains, whose span of life is thrice that of other men.

MAN:33:31 I need not describe the manner in which Osireh went out to meet Neth and how his bow, the first bow seen in the land of Egypt, won her in contest. This can be learned from the tales told to the people, which all contain within them a core of Truth. I will not indulge in the recounting of such tales; they can be found in other places. The bow ,Osireh gave Neth as a pledge is the same as that one upon which men still make oath and pledge their word.

MAN:33:32 Osireh did not at once take Neth to wife, and this is little understood, but it was a thing that could not be done in those days. At first, she was adopted by him as his sister, according to the custom. Later, men called her Esita, she being the same whom men call Esitis in these days. This is a name of the same meaning, for in the tongue of the old river people the name became Ness. Later, this was changed to Nesit, which in the old tongue meant she who was Ness. Then, it was ordained that Osireh should marry his sister, and Esitis gave birth to the manchild Hori. He is the same after whom the kings of Egypt, even in these days, take their title, for he was the first true Pharaoh, though others may disagree.

MAN:33:33 Men lacking understanding will say I write about mortals and not gods, and this is true as it is false. The truth is that there are no fixed regions of gods, spirits and mortals separate one from the other, neither are all these entirely separate and different forms of beings. There is no impenetrable boundary between mortals, spirits and gods; neither is it to be understood that mortals reach the status of gods entirely by their own efforts. Gods are chosen by the people and raised to godhood by the people for the benefit of the people. If they choose wisely, they are blessed, but if they choose unwisely, then whatever befalls is upon their own heads. As the people conceive their gods, so will they be; this is something hardly understood in these days. The worship of such gods is, of itself, neither right nor wrong, for this depends entirely upon its effect and objective. If it serves the purpose of good, if it is to the spiritual benefit of man, it guides in the right direction. If it does not, or if it be sterile or purposeless, then it is at best a misleading phantom; in its worst aspect, it is an instrument of evil. When a man ceases to believe in his god, the fault is not wholly with either, each is at fault, each has equally failed the other. The man no longer serves the god, as the god no longer serves the man. Neither gains, and both lose. A man without a god is neither a free man nor a whole being, his life is incomplete, he lacks something vital to his existence. When, from some cause, a god loses worshippers, he is no longer wholly a god, he becomes a god without ties, a wild god or wandering spirit retaining some of his powers, but none of his rank. Such then is the nature of gods, who are but beings originating as mortals, further advanced along the road towards godhood than other mortals who chose them as representatives and leaders in the heavenly sphere. If you would live with Truth. never confuse gods with God, for gods are but a step upward on the stairway from man to God.

MAN:33:34 There is still one true temple of Esitis, but it is unknown to men in these days, though many others hypocritically declare their allegiance. The true temple itself is hidden behind a false facade for protection. It is still dedicated to the ennoblement of men; it still upholds the virginity of its maidens and dedicate them to modesty and innocence. It is still a bright light in the gathering darkness, It still maintains the flame of spirituality, which, in days to come, will light the fire, which consumes evil and purges men of wickedness. In these days, the priesthood is corrupt and temples are places of evil where wickednesses are made more wicked by being condoned in the name of sanctity.

MAN:33:35 Esitis left her people, and Setis, her brother, ruled the People of the Sand Barrens, later gaining power over many of the People of the River. He was one who was great among men; he led them in the ways of men, the easy ways, along the wide road beloved by the multitude and followed so unthinkingly. There is no point in' retelling here the accounts of the deeds of Osireh and Setis. Nor of how Osireh was betrayed by his blood brother, from whom he did not expect treachery, and slain at Nadit in Tawara. This was after he and those with him had been lured there and enclosed in battle. Though there had been much shedding of blood, Osireh still believed the best of men, but he was deceived. his body was dismembered and scattered, so that none should worship at his shrine, but this only spread goodness throughout the land. When his body was united, his spirit rose in greatness above all spirits. Setis was later slain by Hori and now awaits men in the Dawn Halls where he bids them sit patiently, passive and at rest. Hori, too, awaits men there, but he says, "Arise, O Glorious One; move and be active, for you are reborn."

MAN:33:36 Hori was the staff of his father, but he could not bring the people to walk in the way of light, therefore the light was withdrawn from them. He ever exhorted the people to change their ways, but they stopped their ears to his voice, his words were launched vainly on air. In the Book of the Bearers of Light it is written of his efforts. Hori brought lasting peace to the lands of water and sand, and to their peoples, he gave long life and prosperity. The bounty of the waters was theirs, but still they gave no heed to his words of enlightenment; they declined the call to spiritual austerity and discipline. Thus, it came about that he brought before him the Council of Twenty-Four and said. "Go; speed on your way. send men through the length of the land, even unto the Three Peoples, and warn them lest they bring the wrath of The Great God, He who is the Eye of the Dawning Day, down upon their heads. Say unto them: "Forsake the paths of evil, turn aside from the byways of wickedness and cast down the shrines of false gods, who have misled you. Let their names be utterly obliterated from your hearts and cut out from the places where they are engraved. If you stop your ears to my words, so these things be not done, then the wrath of The Great God shall surely come down upon you and due punishment meted out by the waters."

MAN:33:37 Thus spoke Hori, but his words were as good seed falling upon unwatered ground.

Instead of plants, all manner of weeds sprang up to smother the tender shoots of the good seed even before they rose up into the sunlight. Then, he cried out to The Enlightening God, "O Great God, I have failed miserably in my task, and the people still walk perversely in the ways of wickedness. Their feet incline away from Truth. Men have taken to every manner of wrongdoing and their lusts go unrestrained. The cities are steeped in iniquity, they are places where men practise every kind of abomination. Instead of the abode of glory, the bodies of men have become a lurking place for every kind of evil. O my God, where have I failed, what can I say to You, what can I do? Grant me an ear of understanding, O God!"

MAN:33:38 The Spirit of God responded to the cry of Hori in this manner, "My son, take not unto yourself the blame for the iniquity of these perverse people. Leave them to steep in the brew of their wickedness, which they have prepared for themselves, for there is a point beyond which My administrators are not required to go. Leave the wicked, and gather the select few unto yourself, for thus it shall ever be. Many will cry at the gates, but few shall enter. Abandon the misled to their false shrines, for the day will dawn when all these shall be dust borne away on the wind. Even then, the words of Truth shall remain unto men. Go, cherish the few and abandon the many. Hide the Sacred Mysteries in places, where they shall be least sought. Choose well those, who are of one thought with you. A roof is better supported upon a few sound pillars than on many unstable ones. Yet, the day is not far distant when many shall give ear to the words of wisdom, for if their ears are stopped they are lost. Those, from whom you incline your head, shall be removed from out of your sight and they shall become lost and restless spirits. To you is given command of men, as he who fathered you is given command of spirits."

MAN:33:39 All things that God commanded, Hori did, and when at last he lay in the arms of the Great Bride, he knew that the foundation for the Temple of Truth was well and truly laid. In the Book of the Bearers of Light is the Supplication of Hori:

MAN:33:40 "O Ageless God of Aging Things, O Constant One Amid Inconstancy, no mere words of mine can hope to make known the gratitude welling up as an everlasting spring within my heart. In the midst of my desolation, you brought me comfort; into the darkness of my spirit, you came as a comforting light. You led me forth when the wilderness shut me, and guided my feet when they became entangled in the chaos of waters. When my enemies descended upon the people to devour them, you scattered the foe like frightened asses fleeing before a lion. You have magnified me in the eyes of the faithful. I am made great even among the chosen. My people, you have made your people."

MAN:33:41 "You have favoured us among all others and have granted us a knowledge of your laws, that our way may not be undirected. You have taught us the performance of your statutes, that we might conform to Your will. You have revealed to us the boundaries between light and darkness, between wisdom and ignorance; between the spirit and the mortal, between the sacred and the profane. You have set the faithful apart from all other people and revealed unto us our duties and obligations."

MAN:33:42 "O our God, grant that the days allotted to us be days of peace and plenty. Show us yet more clearly the path of purity, that we fall not into the abyss of iniquity. In the vale of temptation, let us not stray from the path of righteousness, and in the wilderness of wickedness, let us not become lost."

MAN:33:43 "Favour us with wisdom and skill, for if there be anything wholly of Earth within the grasp of man that is truly desirable, is it not skill and knowledge? of all things outside of Heaven these are most praiseworthy. Though these be not of the spirit, grant them to us, O God, for You are the fount of all knowledge."

MAN:33:44 "When we stray, as oft men do; let not the force that brings us back onto the path afflict us too much. We acknowledge our weaknesses with humility and our failings with repentance. When we wander bring us back into the light of Your Laws, that we may not be swallowed up in the darkness of ignorance."

MAN:33:45 "Forgive us our deeds of wickedness, pardon our transgressions, grant us reprieve from the effects of our wrongdoing. Give us, whatever this may entail, that which will benefit us the most spiritually. Teach us, O God, to accept with resignation the wondrous workings of Your will. Everlasting glory is with You. Sanctity is Yours; therefore, we honour You with submission and service. We, Your servants, acknowledge our obligations. We, Your children, declare our love and loyalty."

MAN:33:46 Hori died after the manner known and was buried in glory. There is no recounting of his deeds. Then there was peace throughout all the lands beside the Nile and contentment reigned everywhere. Many great kings lived and ruled, and gradually, the Light of Truth was again revealed unto men. It never fails to appear when men are deserving. Is this not sufficient indication of the forbearance of God?

Chapter Thirty-Four – Annexed Scroll 2

MAN:34:1 This is written on a scroll found in the temple of Athorhara, the possession of Neyti, a free woman of Pibes:

MAN:34:2 Then, there was peace throughout the land, and the two priesthoods dwelt together in tolerance; but, behold, the day came when the hearts of men turned again to strife. Then, the land was rent in twain, and the forces of the Red Reed Crown strove against those of the White Lily Crown. Once, again the dark mists of ignorance descended to envelop the hearts of men. Again, the sacred shrines of Truth were closed, and those who served Truth withdrew behind the veil and were hidden from the eyes of those who would profane her. The whole land was torn apart, from upstream to downstream; from the right hand to the left of Egypt, there was strife.

MAN:34:3 Then came one who was mighty among men, one who also knew Truth and saw the wickedness of the people. He was a Declared One, for unless a man be such, he has no value among the chosen. He carried the sword among the striving peoples, and in his day, the might of Mantethrop prevailed. The spirit of Hori, who took the land from Namah, and of Minis, who united it, were with him. Then, the lands of the North and the lands of the South were delivered in to the hands of the king, and they became one. They were united, though they remained two. They were even as they had been before. Yet, the multitude declared themselves for the ways of the multitude, and the light of Truth remained obscured behind the dusts raised by their dancing feet. Though peace and plenty reigned throughout the land, righteousness did not attend the throne of later kings. They ruled as kings, but the days of their rule were dark days of sorrow for the followers of Truth. for they became few and feeble in deed. They were lost in the land. Again, as in other days, the High Servant of the Sacred Mysteries, who held the key, commanded that the sacred shrines be closed. This was so that any knowledge of the Great Secrets should not pass into the possession of the unworthy multitude, which would profane them. Again, as has happened many times, the Great Light was removed from the midst of men.

MAN:34:4 Then came the year of the great flood of waters, though some say it was before these days, when the salt seas rose upon the East and covered the land. Men were warned beforehand by the shortening of the days of the years, and the five days now added to the days of the year are days of sorrow for the alteration of things. It is said that seven days before the coming of the waters the sun appeared in a different quarter, but this is not easy to believe as the sun remains ever constant. The sailors of the king certainly departed for strange places during the chaos of waters, perhaps this was because the sun had left his steady course.

MAN:34:5 Kings came and departed to their place. They ministered unto the people according to the light revealed unto them. Most knew only the veiled Truth. but in olden times, they were better kings than in later days. There were long generations of men who walked with wisdom, and among them was the generation of the First Great Master, he who established the Brotherhood of the Chosen Ones of Light. In those days men learned the rites for coming forth by day, but the inner wisdom was not declared before them. Yet they were days of wisdom, skill and knowledge, but the knowledge of the spirit still languished, and the Sacred Secrets remained hidden. In fact never have they been revealed to the multitude of men, for never has the multitude of men been worthy.

MAN:34:6 Now men say that all the wisdom of those so wise availed them nothing, have they not long gone down into dust? Have they not departed to the land of no return, to the place that may or may not be? Where is their memorial? Where their shrines? Can even their tombs be seen?

MAN:34:7 They say among themselves, as it will ever be said when men are deluded by their mortality, "The life of man is short and uncertain; the one certainty in life being the approach of death. What awaits hereafter, no man can tell, for no man is known to have returned from out of his tomb. We are all the children of accident and mischance, and in a short generation shall be as though we had never been. Our bodies shall harden and be ground to dust, and the fire of our hearts shall burn itself out and turn to ashes. Our shade will hover for its day and then be wafted away on the wind, and as the waters come and go, our name will pass from the memories of men forever. The works of man shall pass away like the shadow of a cloud upon the sand, and his life will vanish like the dew of morning that disappears in the heat of the rising sun. What are the days of man, but the shadow of a shadow, and he passes away to an end from which there is no returning. He goes out through a door which is immediately shut, and there is no way back.

MAN:34:8 They say, Come, therefore, and let us be joyful; let us cast aside the long face of learning and the melancholy face of discipline. Let us enjoy the good things of life, which are all about us. Let us take no thought for an uncertain future; where is the profit in that? Let us eat and drink to fullness, let us grant our bodies all means of satisfaction. Let no means of pleasure and enjoyment pass us by, but whatever comes our way, let us make the best of our lot in life. Let us turn our backs on all doctrines of the spirit, for they deny us much. Let us give full rein to all our senses and feelings, and let them serve the ends of pleasure. We will take no heed of the poor and helpless, for where is the benefit in this? What have we to fear from them, we who are strong? Let the widow weep alone, for why should her sorrow disturb us? Let us avoid the encumbrances of the aged and maimed. Let us use our strength to obtain all we need for our own wellbeing. Let our strength provide the rule and establish the right. Let strength and power, riches and position alone be valued, and let the weak and the feeble survive as they may. Perhaps, in our generosity, we will spare them a few crumbs or bestow upon them the things we do not need. Let us take no more of their criticism and their objections; have they more swords than we have? Are we to be overawed by a God whom they cannot produce?"

MAN:34:9 Such are the things spoken by men today, and if they declare them not openly, they hide them in their hearts. This is their law, their way of life, be the law declared before men or hidden in shame. The life of their years cannot answer them, for the answer lies hidden in the life of ages. Gold is not gathered by the wayside.

MAN:34:10 Yet, the wisdom of our fathers did avail them, whatever is said in the streets today. They have indeed left a memorial worthy of reverence, and they are not without shrines. The wise words they spoke have not gone down to be eaten by dust, nor have they been carried away on the wings of the wind. As for the Enlightened Ones, who passed among the people and strengthened them since the days when the gods walked with men, their names have become lasting even though they themselves have gone. They did not make themselves tombs of stone and memorials of metal, nor did they desire them. They were unable to leave estates to their children, some were unable even to leave an heir alive. Nevertheless, they made heirs for themselves among those who study their writings, and they have left treasures of wisdom for their estates. Their memorials are the words which came from their mouths and remain still alive on the tongues of men. Books of Wisdom are the heritage they have handed on, and they forged the frail reed into a mighty weapon. Where are their like today? Men sneer at the achievements of the past, at the greatness that has gone, but are these not achievements and greatness they cannot themselves hope to emulate? If men have climbed high today, did they themselves build the stairway, or was it erected by the labours of those long gone? Was not the first step laid down in ages long past? Is the first step of least importance? Is the foundation any weaker than the superstructure, even the superstructure of today? Yes, the great men of wide wisdom have gone; they are forgotten; yet through the greatness of their works, they are honoured, and their spirit moves among us still. The chords they struck still echo within our hearts.

MAN:34:11 Where, today, are the rulers and princes this land once knew? Where are similar officials to be found? Today, bribery creeps behind the seats of judgement, corruption lurks on the right hand, and perjury sneaks around to the left. What of the flow of fine words that accompany a magistrate to his seat of appointment? What have these noble utterances become but a more meaningless babble. Yet are they not a glorious thing capable of moving the hearts of men with their inspiring message of hope in the ultimate attainment of justice? Let them be recorded for all time:

MAN:34:12 "He who is pure of hands comes forth. He utters the words that have come from the Temple of Mant. Those with panther skins bear the symbols of authority. These words are spoken. You are the ever faithful servant of Truth. the humble one who begs her for guidance. You are not the lord of justice but one who ever seeks it with humility and perseverance, praying it will bless your decisions. You are henceforth one whose words are heavy with authority, whose eyes see without prejudice and whose ears are closed to intolerance. Your thoughts are clear and clean, your heart is pure. It is free of all malice, and to you, a vindictive verdict will be an abomination. The mantle of wisdom rests on your shoulders and the robe of learning is your garment. Your tongue is the servant of Truth and the sword of justice. Your mouth is the shrine of honour and the cave of retribution. Your heart is the temple of purity and the storehouse of wise judgements from the past."

MAN:34:13 "Justice will ever be your guiding light and rule; it will lead you even to the appointed place before the mother of the king. Wherever you go, uprightness will take command. You will wield the sword of justice without fear; you will bear it before the sight of all men. You will carry it to the rich and powerful, to the poor and lowly, without discrimination. You will strike down all merchants of falsehood, all forktongued deceivers, all who bear false witness or break the statutes of the king. Let wickedness perish in the sands."

MAN:34:14 "Justice is not a thing less than the measure, but that which fills it to overflowing. It exceeds the bounds of mortal requirements. It endures everlastingly and is not denied one who is entombed. It passes over with the spirit to bear witness. It is the great brightener. It is not a thing bought and sold. Justice cannot be bartered."

MAN:34:15 "Be ever above price. One worthy of the greatness you reflect on Earth, one ever above mundane things. Be not as the ferryman who demands payment before his task is fulfilled, who bears upon the water the man who makes payment and no other. Be as the sun, whose brightness seeks out every nook and cranny and pours light into their hidden gloom. Be one who shines among men to lighten their days. Spread uprightness and honesty across the two lands, as the sunshine spreads brightness and warmth. Cover the land with goodness, as the rising waters cover it with fertility. Fill the land with strength, as the northwind fills it with contentment."

MAN:34:16 "Guard Your heart, as a father guards his daughter, as a mother guards her baby, for it is the stronghold of integrity. Be vigilant concerning every deed, for the eyes of men are ever upon you, the life you live is not yours alone. You are the image, which men will imitate, and you are before every eye. The blowing wind will open its ear at your windows and spread wide its report. The flowing waters beside your door will uncover their eyes and carry what they behold through the land. Your position makes you a supporting pillar of the government; if the pillars be rotten, the roof crashes. Your responsibilities will beset your life with care; the road you journey is stony and encompassed with pitfalls and thorns. The cup You drink will be more often bitter than sweet."

MAN:34:17 "Though you will judge all men impartially, do not, in your diligence, incline towards the poor and unprotected because they are such. Your duty is to see that all things are done according to the statutes of the king, in the manner in which they have been done previously. You are not wise enough to set aside the wisdom of the past. Every man must be dealt with as though he stood before you naked and unknown. Let he who is permitted entry into your courtyard be as he who is left standing outside the gate, and your decisions must be given with indifference, as to whether they serve him well or ill."

MAN:34:18 Such were the words uttered at the installation of an official empowered to give judgement. In other days, such words were honoured and adhered to, now they are ignored. Now justice lies buried in a tomb of past precedents, swathed in mummy bandages of formality. It consists of the impartial, heartless administration of the recorded statutes, rather than the redress of injustice. Where has the glory gone? All is lifeless, all is dead. The hands that guide are dead; the hands that rule are dead.

MAN:34:19 Men may ask, in days yet to dawn, how it came about that the flame of glory died in Egypt, how her grandeur passed away into dust. How, when man had climbed so high, he could climb no longer. But there is no simple cause, the seeds of degeneration lie dormant in every nation, in every man. As the man, so the nation. These seeds are as weeds, which spring up when the cultivated soil is neglected, when it is tended with indifference. The road to greatness is, for nations as for each man, a hard and stony one. Greatness is a gift requiring constant effort to retain; when men decline the effort, greatness departs. Greatness and glory will abide only in the habitations of the worthy. They depart when no longer treated as honoured guests. What are Justice and Truth today? They are no more than words mumbled by the lips, but once, they were an inextinguishable flame burning within the hearts of men. What is left of honour when men cease to regard it as more than an empty symbol? It is like the lyre in the hands of a man with blistered fingers, or as the flute played by one with scabby lips. The instruments remain, but where are the musicians? Without the musicians, where are the melodies?

MAN:34:20 In the land of Egypt, periods of righteousness have come and gone like ripples passing over a quiet pond. There have been periods of material greatness, ripples of longer duration, but they have not been at one with the ripples of righteousness. Throughout all times, there have been two visible forms of worship, with their many variations: that of the highborn and that of the people. Now, they have been blended for many generations. The worship of The High God and the knowledge of the Sacred Mysteries, kept hidden by the Enlightened Ones and the Twice Born, were behind both and veiled within them. Where else could these things be better concealed?

MAN:34:21 The House of the Hidden Places was established fifty generations before the reign of the Mighty One, who was Pharaoh, and in those days, The High God was known to men and was revealed even after. But twenty generations before the evil Amuleka descended like locusts upon the land, there was strife most grievous. This is set forth in the scroll belonging to Kabitkant, son of Nemerath, copied from an old writing copied from another which was the property of a temple in Pinhamur. it says, "The twin powers drawn down entwined about themselves and grew ever stronger. Even as waters are dammed to be drawn upon, so was the united power built up into a reserve of force. A storehouse of strange energy was prepared. The thoughts of Setshra ever turned about within himself, and behold, the day came when he believed the secret key to be his, the key that would open the inner chamber of Sacred Mysteries. Yet he made the mistake of all such men down through the ages, unaware that his very unworthiness forbade his admittance into the Inner Mysteries. That though he could deceive himself and others, he could not deceive the Inner Guardians. It is true that some who were admitted to the outer chamber were indiscreet and spoke carelessly before the ears of unadmitted men. It is ever thus when goodness is not persecuted, for goodness blooms best in the barren soil of intolerance and injustice. Anyway, in this manner the seeds of strife and suffering were sown. Then, Setshra conceived a plan, whereby the multitude would be admitted to participate in the Sacred Mysteries hitherto kept exclusive for the worthy ones among men. He gathered together a following of his own from among the people and promised, in return for their devotion, that the knowledge of sacred things hitherto kept from them should now become available. He called those who followed him The Enlightened Ones of the Gods. Naturally, such folly could have but one outcome, for the experience of ages has shown that sacred things cannot be revealed to the profane. Not only would the things revealed be disdained by the ignorant, as swine would trample pearls underfoot to gobble up a handful of filth, but the multitude in its sinfulness would destroy the delicate beauty of the Hidden Mysteries. Like goats devouring hangings of artistically patterned loveliness, they would decide that the gross things to which they were accustomed were more satisfying."

MAN:34:22 "The new teachings grew in strength and spread throughout the whole land; they went from city to city gaining followers in every one. The multitude is ever powerful; therefore, he who controls it by whatever means is himself powerful. Thus it came about that eventually, Setshra was able to challenge the authority of the Twice Born. This authority was always vulnerable, as it sought to rule by wisdom and goodness rather than by power and subtlety. Only when wisdom and goodness rule the wise and good, can such rule succeed; such time may never come."

MAN:34:23 "Though the followers of Setshra could not discover the higher secrets, they learned the lower ones, and these were twisted to their own ends. Thus was developed the worship of dark spirits, a vile and poisonous thing that perverted the thoughts of the people and led them away from the path of spirituality. They strayed into all manner of strange and corrupting byways. Then, their hearts hardened by earthly sordidness, they rose up, clamouring for the blood of the righteous ones."

MAN:34:24 "Now, Setshra gained the ear of the king and, pouring in a flood of venom wrapped up in fine speech, he overwhelmed the heart of his Majesty. None in the land had a tongue more subtle than that of Setshra. Then, new shrines were set up in the temples; new forms of worship appeared, pandering to the weaknesses of men. The hidden places of the Enlightened Ones were profaned with wickedness, and the secret chambers of the Twice Born were polluted with vile rites. Therefore, the Enlightened Ones and the Twice Born withdrew from the eyes and knowledge of men. Their day was yet to dawn, but none among them would ever have thought that never in Egypt would that day be. Yet dawn, it will, even though it be in some strange land, where the ways of men are different, and in some manner inconceivable to men of our times. Will they be people such as we? O my land, having known you, how strange all others appear! Away from you, I will be as a fish cast up onto dry land."

MAN:34:25 "In the temples dedicated to many different gods, the forms of worship were subtly changed to serve another end. The servants of the Dark Ones were able to display wonders before the multitude, but these wonders were works of deceit. They revealed mysteries, but the mysteries were not the most sacred ones; these were never known by any likely to betray them. The thoughts of the people were poisoned. All manner of rites aimed at satisfying carnal cravings were introduced. Simple, satisfying answers were given to content the hearts of the people, and all manner of rewards were promised. For payment made, men were promised forgiveness of even the most grievous wickednesses. It is well that the ears of the dumb gods were unhearing, or they would have been deafened by the clamour of pleas for petty things. The servants of the Dark Ones left not even the dead to rest in peace, but sought to satisfy the living with words from beyond the tomb. Even the blood of men was offered in dark places, while in others of greater evil, men, yes, and even children, were tormented to give pleasure. Such is the nature of men when the scales weigh down against righteousness."

MAN:34:26 "The hosts of the Dark Ones were well skilled in battle, and they drove out all those who stood against them. The forces of righteousness were scattered. The sacred shrines, which stood before the veil of Truth. were spoiled. The ornaments of beauty and the sacred vessels were taken away to be profaned by sin-soiled hands. The Enlightened Ones and the Twice Born were hunted down like beasts of the chase. They were slain and buried in the ground like dogs. Their resting places remained unmarked and unattended."

MAN:34:27 "The Leader of the Light cried out, "O Great God, what can I do; how shall your servants be saved? What shall be done unto those who have profaned your sacred shrines? What can I do to turn back the rising waters of iniquity and temper the wild winds of wickedness? How can the black cloud of ignorance be lifted? What shall be the just reward of those who have slain the faithful?" The voice coming forth by the Spirit of God said, "Concern yourself not with those who have persecuted you, leave them to follow the path of their own choice. Vengeance is with Me; I will measure without stint. Justice never sleeps and never forgets; the reward of the wicked awaits them. In the Hall of No Hiding Place justice will speak the final word."

MAN:34:28 The Leader of light and those with him fled into the land beyond Shari and built there the Temple in the Rock, which stands against Shina. In this land, the forces of the Dark Ones were cast back; yet still, some among the faithful beseeched their God to save them. Thus it has ever been, this is the nature of man that in his hour of distress he cries out to God in bitterness of heart, and they who deserted God in better times expect Him to turn towards them. Yet such is the nature of God that this He would do, were it to the good of men, which it is but rarely. In the land of Egypt, the great shrines were deserted by the Enlightened Ones and abandoned by Truth. They became places of darkness. They were as lamps without flame, as fields without crops, as wells without water."

MAN:34:29 The generation of those days passed down into dust, their spirit arose in the Everlasting Halls, to stand before the Inescapable One. Then, in the generation of Pahopha, the name of Osireh began to be known in the land, and for twelve generations, it grew in greatness. The Upuru departed; the Ameluka came. Ten generations entered into their Eternal Habitations, and Tathomasis came, to make the name of Egypt known throughout all the lands. He, too, could no more stay the hand of decay than could the meanest slave. Then, in his day Nabihaton came to rule in the land of Egypt.

MAN:34:30 While he was still a child and yet at nurse, the young woman who tended him at night took a man in lust without attending to her purification. Therefore, when she came back nigh unto the sleeping prince, she broke the protective wall about his sleeping place. Thus, a Formless One came up from out of its lair beside the flaming lake and entered the bedchamber. Because the young woman was as she was, it could not be seen by her. It was a formless, flowing thing that spread itself out in the darkness, to slink across the floor. Its fluted snout was in the midst of a face twisted backwards, like all its kind. It raised an awful mouth up to kiss the sleeping child, and the child was stricken.

MAN:34:31 In the morning, the child's body was consumed with an inner fire lit the night before, and the breath of life struggled against the occupying demon to enter the body. In those days, there lived a great physician named , and he drew out the demon with things of power, and dowsed the fire with impregnated water. None but the greatest of physicians could have released a tongue from the grip of the demon. Yet, this was done by Mahu.

MAN:34:32 Perhaps it is well to give a fuller account of this Pharaoh, not as a matter of history, for this I am not competent to record, but to show what can happen when those unqualified seek to reveal the light. Also the perils that can attend such folly.

MAN:34:33 Nabihaton rose to rule while still very young, and though it is said that he died in the grip of a demon, with blood welling up from within his mouth, the other version, that he died a tombless wanderer, seems more probable, for it is so written on the Tablets of Amon.

MAN:34:34 In the days of his father, the Enlightened Ones had regained strength in the land of Egypt, though they remained a hidden force, and all their deeds were secret. Nevertheless, they were not unknown to the priesthoods, which were then strong, though they were regarded with much disfavour. In those days, the charges made against the Enlightened Ones were that they stirred up the lowly against the powerful. That they tried to turn the land over, to change that, which had ever been. Therefore, those who knew The Great God dwelt in seclusion and hiding. Their names were unknown, their faces unseen.

MAN:34:35 The mother of Nabihaton was Towi, one of the Chosen Ones. In those days there were still four ranks of the faithful: the Twice Born, the Enlightened Ones, the Chosen Ones and the Dwellers in Light. Among the Dwellers in Light, there were Seekers in Light and Labourers in Light. Even then as now. The wife of Pharaoh, though of high blood, was no more than half Egyptian; her ways were strange. While he had still not come to manhood, the mother of Pharaoh taught him the ways of light. She revealed many of its secrets, probably without proper authority, though this cannot be known. However, though the Leader of Light in Egypt was never far removed from the Pharaoh, only during days in the far distant past were the kings numbered among the enlightened. Only in the days of true greatness, days long gone down into dust, days long forgotten in the land. Yet ever, we have hoped. The kings bred for goodness, the families reared to conserve spirituality, were swayed between two influences, that of the spiritually inspired ones and that of the earthly-orientated ones. Earthly conditions being what they are, and the purpose of Earth being what it is, it was too early in the generations of men to expect goodness to triumph. It is in this that the forces of good are confounded; they anticipate too easy a victory. Yet, though the pestle grinds slowly, it grinds with every blow.

MAN:34:36 It was the wife of Pharaoh who influenced him to disclose some of the mysteries, which, since the time just mentioned, had been completely withdrawn and very carefully hidden. Thus, though the forces of evil had prevailed in the land they had not uncovered the Inner Shrine of the Sacred Mysteries. Such mysteries as they had discovered proved of little value to them and were soon so distorted and perverted as to be useless. The great secret of how to penetrate the barrier between the two spheres of mortal and spirit was still completely secured. If nothing else, its very dangers would have safeguarded it.

MAN:34:37 Actually, though it is said that Secret Mysteries were disclosed, this did not happen. All that did happen was that Pharaoh used the knowledge he had to try and give the people a greater insight into the way of light, the True Way. As is ever done, he veiled the all consuming brilliance of Truth. leaving just sufficient glimmer to light the way, to become a beacon. Nabihaton, himself saw the Truth but dimly, for though he tried he failed to meet the tests of an Enlightened One. Perhaps it was this that inclined him away from the faithful. How many, when they discover what the knowledge of Truth entails, falter on the path?

MAN:34:38 The Pharaoh, the Great One of Egypt, was ill-formed in body, he was subject to uncontrolled trances unproductive of any vision. This was because at such times his spirit would withdraw, thus permitting a Dark One to enter its seat. He would fall down upon the ground, and the demon spume would issue from his mouth. Therefore, at such times, he had to be kept from the eyes of the people, lest they were seized with the fear of demons devastating the land and sapping its fertility. Yet not everything could be kept hidden from the people, for the Pharaoh lived as the fish within the garden pool. Therefore, the people learned of his grievous wickedness and turned from him; nevertheless, it was not as bad as the marketplace chatter stated. This Pharaoh had many powerful opponents in high places; the tales are much exaggerated. Some, not knowing the inside of the pot, declared him to be the very light of goodness. Perhaps the truth is that in him, good and evil swung out to the extremes of the balances. Yet weighed one against the other, evil bore down no more in him than in the case of those with much less evil in the scales and much less good to counterbalance it.

MAN:34:39 The son of Nabihaton, one conceived in wickedness, was slain in battle; therefore, the younger son, one also born of the union of evil, became king in Egypt in his day. While yet young, he became a follower of the new rites of mystery, which his father had set up in imitation of the Mysteries of the Hidden God. These new rites were, themselves, hidden within a new form of worship set up by Nabihaton. Of themselves, these were not things of wickedness, but they inclined too far towards ritual which was futile and ceremonial that was purposeless. Though the new mysteries served to spiritualise and could awaken the spirit, they went just so far and could go no further. They led to a dead end. They went as far as the Grim Threshold, but could not lead beyond it. As far as the faithful were concerned, the setting up of a new form of worship made little difference to their position in the land, but they did attempt to draw the young prince wholly within their fold. Because of his manner of life, the king, his father, was precluded from this.

MAN:34:40 I will go back to when the father of Nabihaton, a man of great valour, much beloved by the people, became feeble through a wound that troubled him in his old age. It was then that his queen, the noble Towi, priestess of the faithful, urged him to send for the young prince Nabihaton, though he was not then so called, to become his staff and take up some of the burden. In this manner it was hoped to secure the throne of Egypt once more for one of the faithful, an end towards which the faithful had long laboured.

MAN:34:41 Undoubtedly, the Enlightened Ones and the Chosen Ones from among the faithful played some part in the introduction of the new form of worship, but unfortunately, they were not equal to the opportunities of the times. This is an instance when too much concern with spirituality, too little interest and involvement in mortal affairs, can prove a fatal handicap. The lesson to be learned from this, the whole purpose of its telling, is that at all times, a good balance must be maintained between spirituality and earthly existence. However great the spiritual goal ahead, nevertheless at present, our feet are firmly bound to Earth. Whatever the eyes behold, it must not blind men to the pitfalls before their feet. To say, as many have, that the new form of worship clashed with the old established worship of Amon, is true in part only. The hopes of the faithful were nurtured in both and could have been a reconciling force, weak in power and numbers though it might have been. Superficially, and among the mass of lesser priests and followers in the two beliefs, there was antagonism and strife. While the flame of Aton waned, the sun of the new form of worship rose. But it was the popularity of Queen Towi among the people, her wisdom and insight, that enabled the young prince to maintain his place at the king's right hand and share the royal symbols, despite hostility by the priests of Amon. Had he dutifully followed the Path of the True Way, all would have been well. Perhaps, and this seems more likely, he did not quite understand it. Probably his intentions were good, but good intent is not sufficient. Good intent is nullified by lack of wisdom and knowledge and confounded unless supported by example and deeds. It is not sufficient for a man to proclaim a way of life for others, unless he lives according to its principles, himself. Too often have men tried to direct others along a path they are reluctant to tread themselves. This is not the least of hypocrisies.

MAN:34:42 When his father died, the young king Nabihaton ruled in equality with his mother; they shared the royal seat and symbols, but he acted in a manner unbefitting a son. He inclined away from the highborn ladies of royal blood; his interests were not those of a Pharaoh, and this caused the hearts of those who opposed him to rise in hope. It also isolated him from the faithful, who would have been his most ardent supporters, though their loyalty remained with the queen.

MAN:34:43 When their Pharaoh showed no inclination to marry, and strange rumours were heard about him in the streets and marketplaces, the people became disturbed and uneasy. Also, the highborn ones about him, the court officials, the princes and governors of the land, were perturbed at his interest in the Mistress of Songstresses at the Temple of Amon in Victory. The faithful were perturbed also, for within this temple was one of their secret shrines. This could have been the turning point for the faithful in Egypt, had the king been other than he was, for there were several princesses of the royal blood numbered among them. As it was, the faithful were antagonised.

MAN:34:44 The new form of worship introduced by this Pharaoh was simple enough. Outwardly, it had all the symbols and ceremonial beloved by the people, with sufficient substance in it to attract the spiritually inclined. It could have formed a fitting gateway to the Path of the True Way, another light guiding men along the road to the embarkation port for Truth. Behind the symbols and ceremonial, the Pharaoh worshipped the Spirit behind the Sun, the Spirit of Light and Life as a direct, fully conscious member outflowing from The Great God Behind All. The king, however, being cut off in the midst of his instruction, perceived the road but dimly. There is little doubt of his genuine desire to bring the True light to the people, but he was not wise enough to know, firstly, that one who brings light must be one in whom light burns brightly, and secondly, that the multitude cannot be exposed to its unveiled brightness with impunity. The king, severed from his weaknesses, could have been a truly great ruler, a steady light before the eyes of men, the guide to a new age for the people of the land. But he was one who cast heavily on both arms of the balances.

MAN:34:45 Nabihaton knew enough of the Secret Mysteries to realise that he would need a new place of worship, uncontaminated by previous concentration of the twin powers, if he were to succeed in opening even the first door. Therefore, he moved his court to a new city, within which was a temple outwardly dedicated to the New Light, which he enshrined before the Place of Flame. It was a sanctum for those, whom he called 'The Awakeners of the Spirit to Light. From this we get the expression, 'Light within the light behind the light', used even to this day. The priests of Amon were impoverished to pay for the new city.

MAN:34:46 The king had a son by the Lady of Songstresses, one destined for greatness, though his greatness was not perceived by the eyes of men. When, later, this son was exiled to wander in strange places, his mother cast herself into the arms of Sebuk, but this is something, the telling of which has no place here. However, with the removal of the king's household to the new city, its power was diminished; the people under the two crowns became divided against themselves. The rulers became unsettled in their posts, and there were revolts in the colonies towards the East. It was a time of unease because of the dispersion of the power. Now also, because of the most grievous wickedness of the Pharaoh, all the protecting divinity of his blood, which, though diminished by the generations of wilfulness yet remained potent, was dissipated. Thus, all the land suffered and was restless.

MAN:34:47 Then it was that some of the faithful from the city of the old royal residence, not from the new one as told, contacted the eyes and the ears of the king, so that the Pharaoh was counselled to take himself a wife. In this manner alone could the clamour of the people be stilled and their hearts put at ease. It was then that the High Priest at the Temple of the Visible Light, by a cunning move, brought the young princess called Nefare, in our tongue, before Pharaoh. She was a temple maiden, daughter of a king, and one devoted to The Great God in Silence.

MAN:34:48 Pharaoh took her to wife, but he showed her little affection, though she was not unbeautiful, even if with a beauty not of this land. Nevertheless, in the eyes of the people, the marriage appeared successful enough, though perhaps the outward display of affection was overdone. Still the queen, being more frail than Egyptian women, could bear only daughters. There is another reason for this, but it cannot be gone into here with propriety. It is something between women. Things were not as they appeared, and Nefare despised the king in her heart for his secret wickedness.

MAN:34:49 I have mentioned the surviving son of the king, one born under the darkest cloud, the secret of whose illomened birth had been unrevealed, though it was known to a few. Some of these were antagonistic to the new form of worship proclaimed by the king, and they used this knowledge to their own advantage. I have also mentioned another son, one born to the Lady of Songstresses, and he was bound to a different destiny altogether.

MAN:34:50 The son born to Pharaoh by the Lady of Songstresses was also born to high estate through her. I will not record his name, lest even now it be used with evil intent, for it is a name of power. I will not disclose his titles but call him just what he was, 'The Master'.

MAN:34:51 When The Master was born, Pharaoh was quite indifferent towards him, though, through the nature of his blood, he was not unexposed to danger. The account of how the child was stolen from the temple garden by the priests of Amon; how it was rescued by a Syrian in the services of Nefare, disguised as a woman vendor of spices, and Seltis, a Captain of Craft, is known and need not be retold. However, though it is true that the child was carried away by a vessel, he was not taken to the lands of the Henbew. He was not brought up in the household of the Captain of Craft. The child was left at the Temple of Anthor in Splendour, where sweet waters kiss the bitter, and brought back to the City of the Horizon at Dawning. Later, both child and mother were taken into the royal household, for the two women had long been friends, even before Nefare became queen. Yet Pharaoh knew not that the manchild within the household of Nefare was his, for the tale had been put about that the son of the Lady of Songstresses was dead. Thus, even in the shadow of the royal household, The Master grew up to walk in the path of Truth.

MAN:34:52 Now, as the years went down into dust, the land of Egypt crumbled and began to fall apart. Nefare, because she followed the pure light, could not dwell with Pharaoh while the life he led was an abomination against purity. She was an ever faithful one, though in her disgust, she must have been tempted to be otherwise. The queen removed herself and her household in the fifteenth year of the reign of Nabihaton. It was then put about, by those who licked the feet of Pharaoh, that she was a fickle woman of wanton ways. They said she was an adulteress and called upon her beauty to bear witness against her. What they said was false, it is equally false that all beautiful women are fickle and wanton. True, such women may be subjected to greater temptations, but if they resist these, are they not so much the greater? Are they not so much more what a beautiful woman should be, the true inspiration of men? Surely there can be no doubt that the Pharaoh was abnormal, for how could any but an abnormal one treat such a woman thus? Nefare sought refuge in Lebados, where there was a secret shrine to The Great God, and resigned herself to a life of great virtue. With her went The Master, then on the threshold of manhood, but his true mother did not go with them.

MAN:34:53 Without the temple gates at Lebados, beneath a sycamore tree, dwelt a three-eyed man, Hepoa, one who could foreknow the future, who had the gift of farseeing, but he was aged and infirm. One day, The Master chanced to pass that way, and he came upon Hepoa as some youths mocked him and cast sand upon his head. Then, the heart of The Master was filled with wrath and, taking up the staff of Hepoa which lay upon the ground he laid it on the backs of the youths and they were discomfited. When they had fled, he succoured the old man and, returning into the city, brought forth food, so that Hepoa ate and was made content. Then, The Master sat at the feet of Hepoa and heard his words, for they were words of wisdom and Truth. Hepoa was one who knew the mystery of The Great God and the secrets of the hidden places, for he was one of the Twice Born. Thus, The Master became the old man's staff. Eventually, the day came when the two journeyed to a secret place within the wilderness, so that The Master might approach the threshold.

MAN:34:54 When Nefare left, wickedness consumed good in Nabihaton, and the chambers of his heart lay open and unprotected. Then a Dark One entered into him and drove him out into the barren places of the wilderness. It is said, "And Pharaoh fled through the wilderness, uttering horrible cries and howling as dogs howl, so that all men departed from him in fear." Thus it came about that Nabihaton came upon Hepoa and The Master as they sat beneath the shade of a rock in the heat of the day, and the tongue of the king was blackened with the fire of the Dark One that held him.

MAN:34:55 Hepoa cooled the fire within the king and expelled the Dark One, so that the king was made whole again. Then, they went, the three of them, to the place, where the fighting men of Pharaoh were encamped, the king riding upon an ass. When the king was again bedecked in his royal garments and girded with the symbols of power, he gave Hepoa a place of honour, and The Master dwelt at the gate of Pharaoh.

MAN:34:56 Within the City of the Horizon at Dawning was the Temple of the Sun's Dawning, at which Nabihaton officiated as High Priest, but after his return with Hepoa, he built a residential temple upriverwards, called 'The Sun's Blessing.' Some men have called it 'The Temple of the Blessing of Light'. This was erected in three courts, one of which was called 'Nefare's Memory', a place dedicated to womanly virtues. There, when she came of age, his daughter by Nefare, a maiden called Meriten, was consecrated in service. There is a description of this maiden in a scroll kept at the shrine dedicated to the Martyred Maidens of Chastity, at Nomin, the city of forgotten wickednesses. It says, "As I stood before the gate called 'Treasurer of Life,' on one pillar, of which was engraved the words 'When the eyes see, the ears hear, and the nose smells, they transmit to the spirit, that it understands. I saw the young daughter of the king. She was not tall or fat, and her feet were delicately formed. Her curls were long, but tied back from her face and anointed with sweetly fragrant oils. She passed close by, and I noticed her garments gave out a delicate perfume. Her eyes were large and unusually long-lashed. Her glance was soft and restrained; her whole bearing, modest. Her skin was lighter than the pale copper of Askent, like the cherished ostrich egg, soft as the finest oil. Her nose was perhaps slightly larger than usual, but fine and delicately formed. Her mouth was small, though the lips were full, and even then, tantalising with secret promise. About her head was a circlet of gold, and she wore a necklace of gold and blue stones. She was clad in a pure garment of fine linen fringed above and below with blue and red. Upon it were workings of gold ornamentation. On her arms were bracelets of burnished copper interwoven with gold and silver. She had just come from the sacred grove, and the glistening dew of morning still dampened the lower fringe of her robe. In one hand, she carried two small bells of copper, and in the other, a small hammer of gold."

MAN:34:57 Such was the daughter of the king. Yet among all the highborn ones throughout the long length of the fertile lands threaded like a necklace upon the Nile, there was no man to truly love her. Certainly, many desired her, but who among them could say it was for herself alone, desirable as she was in the eyes of any man? No, she would have gone to her marriage bed unloved as a woman should be loved, a pawn in the game of power, a sacrifice at the altar of ambition, a chattel bought as a means of winning favour in the eyes of the ruler. Would not her fate have been better, had she been born to a herdsman? Or were she the daughter of a craftsman? Then she could have delighted in the kiss of the hot sun and the caress of the cool breeze. She could have been loved and wanted for herself alone. Such, however, was not her fate; all things she could have but this.

MAN:34:58 It was after the consecration of Meriten that the eyes of Nabihaton wandered towards her lustfully, but perhaps, to do him justice, he should not be judged by the same standards as other men. He was the Pharaoh of Egypt, who, according to ageless tradition, was above wrongdoing. There is not much doubt but that, at this time, he was under the control of either a demon or a Dark One, which had taken possession of his heart. Also, he had been brought up to a code, where inter-family love and marriage were accepted as the rule, where the sanctity of the royal blood and the need for its conservation in purity was believed in as a law. Then, too, despite his unnatural longings, which he lacked the strength to control and subdue, there is no doubt that he could and did experience extremely deep feelings of affection. He also had an unusually strong, perhaps overwhelming appreciation of beauty, as can be seen by any of his writings still in existence, though few remain of the great many there once were, and these ever in danger. Anyway, he did take his daughter in awful wickedness, his evil thoughts displaying themselves uncontrollably. Now he took no care to hide them. Throughout the new city he, caused the name of Nefare to be struck out, and the name of Meriten was put in its place.

MAN:34:59 Perhaps the best indication of his state of mind is shown in the prayer he composed for the offering ceremony at the festival of the inturning year: "With this sacred outpouring, we sanctify You, Great God of Golden Goodness. Upon Your altar, we offer pure butter, cakes of broken barley, fresh meat of clean beasts, dark bread and honey in three shades. Two kinds of beer and dark wine poured out before You. Now, we open our mouths in praise, Eternal One Overlooking Heaven and Earth. This we do, not for ourselves alone, but also for the sanctified dead. Humbly we come before You; humbly we offer our meagre sacrifice and humbly we receive the gracious gifts, which grant us our sustenance from day to day, and even greater gifts beyond our understanding. We thank You for the peace filling the land with contentment. Teach us the meaning of Your laws, which we cannot understand. Look down upon us with benevolent kindness when we err. Permit us to assist in accomplishing Your will. O Lady of Loveliness, coming forth from Your place of vigil, O Lady of Protection, coming forth with Your maiden attendants, speak for me with the tongue of simplicity and the heart of purity. O Dedicated Maiden, be my mouthpiece in the inner shrine. O Sanctified One, be the listening ear before my people. Let Your goodness shine upon us, as the glory above shines upon Earth. O pacify any wrath that rises in the Glorious Heart of Heat. I know not all the weaknesses and wickednesses of my heart, I who am mortally blind and mortally frail. I know not all the impure longings that possess me, I who am mortally blind and mortally frail. I sought for help, but it came not. I wept, but there was none to comfort me. In the night, I cried for succour, but none answered. I who am great, have less than the least. O Lady of Loveliness, intercede for me in purity and devotion." Never before had such a prayer been offered in sight of the people by a Pharaoh, and the people murmured that divinity had departed from the king.

MAN:34:60 Nabihaton, Pharaoh of Egypt, was a strange mixture of goodness and wickedness, both carried to their extreme. I know not what his form will be in the place where the spirit stands forth in its true aspect. Certainly, we are taught that goodness cannot entirely obliterate the evil effects of wickedness. Yet how much was the king really to blame? How much can be laid at the door of his affliction, how much apportioned to the demons in his limbs? How much to the Dark Ones that possessed him? These things are beyond judgement by mere mortal men. They can be properly dealt with only by a Higher Judge, an Infallible Reader of Hearts.

MAN:34:61 Although it had been accepted that the kindred of the Pharaoh could inter-marry, any union between parent and child was absolutely forbidden. This law from days long past was still binding, though the law which decreed that any one of royal blood suffering a demon-induced deformity or becoming possessed by a Dark One should be given the draught of death, was no longer enforced. This proves how evil ensues when old and trusted laws established by the wise ones of old are cast aside. It is folly to thoughtlessly discard that, which has ever served well.

MAN:34:62 Now, when Pharaoh took Meriten in grievous wickedness, the people murmured, but none arose among them to do more, for such is not the custom of the land. Towi, the great and good, who had lapsed into but one form of wickedness, was no longer there to restrain him. Nor in all probability, could she have done anything, for he was Pharaoh. But when it came to the ears of Hepoa, he took himself into the wilderness and fasted there for seven days. He then returned and gained audience with Nabihaton.

MAN:34:63 Hepoa went before Pharaoh, and there, in the midst of his court, he denounced him. These were the words issuing from the mouth of Hepoa, as set down by the attending scribe: "O great and mighty Pharaoh, where once the stormwind raged, there is now a gentle breeze. Where once the diligent shepherd stood, now a musician sits and idly plays. The land is no more as it was, and no man remains content within his dwelling. The northwind has ceased to enter the land, and the south wind eats it up. A heavy hand lies on the hearts of men, and their limbs are sluggish; they are languid and move no longer, as once they did. Wherefore has all this come about, the people ask, and I answer them truly, it is because the protective power has departed from the blood of the Pharaoh; it is because of the iniquity in the palace. This is a time of woe. These things I have spoken before the eyes and ears of Pharaoh, beyond the palace gates. Yet, it is not in me to leave them unsaid before the face of the king himself. Where is the great one, who sets goodness in the place of wickedness? Where is he, who replaces injustice with justice, who hears the cry of the lowly? Who causes right to prevail in the land? Where is He? I look, and I look in vain. I see only one, who has defiled the protective treasures, the glory of Egypt, with iniquity. I see only one, who has polluted the pure stream with the sewage of evil, who has succumbed to the ultimate in wickedness. This I see, as all men see it, but I am one, who sees more. I see an Egypt gone down into dust. I see plague and death stalking the streets. I see the fertile, black waters turned back on themselves. I see the black land buried beneath the sand. I see grim-faced men coming from out of the East to stamp the land flat in blood. I see the dread things of the past recurring. I see desolation spread out on every side. Woe to you, great Pharaoh; woe to the land of Egypt! Goodness lies dying beneath the triumphant foot of evil. Virtue is betrayed into the foul hands of loathsome lust, her despairing cry unanswered by any coming to her aid. Wickedness walks unhampered through the cities, and wrongdoing is seen on every side. Woeful are these days, and doomed are those who endure them. What does the great light shining forth from the palace conceal, sacred mysteries or secret sins?" Then, the arm of Pharaoh stretched forth to stop the mouth of Hepoa, and it was stopped. He was led forth, and whips were laid on his back, and he was placed within a dungeon.

MAN:34:64 The events that followed remain within a shadow, and none knows the truth, for it was a time of confusion. Meriten probably died of poison administered by her own hand, as was befitting. Her tomb is known, for she was not unhonoured. Some say the same potion slew the king, but others that he died of a Dark Demon within the heart. It seems that the poison was not a quick one and while Meriten died in her chamber, after pledging of the king was made, he fell forward with an issue of blood from his mouth. His spirit was heard in his throat. Thus, it does not appear that they were slain with the one cup. It is unlikely that Meriten died by any hand other than her own, though this is said.

MAN:34:65 Some say the king died after being carried to his chamber, others that he recovered, but the truth is unknown, for at this time the signal was given, and the people arose in the streets. The new worship, which nevertheless, was an outgrowth from the bulb of Truth. died away as the growth dies back on an onion. But like an onion, the bulb remained. The new worship was not unwelcome in the land of Egypt and would have survived, had not its founder led an impure life. The hostility by priests of the other forms of worship would not alone have sufficed to extinguish its light. It was the maggot in the heart of the flower he raised that caused it to fall apart. To establish a pure form of worship and beliefs, its founder must also be pure of hands and heart.

MAN:34:66 Whatever happened, Nabihaton was never placed within the tomb he had prepared for himself. Some say because Hepoa cursed it, but this I doubt. I know of such a curse, but I do not suppose Hepoa would have used it. Some say Pharaoh was buried with his wife, but who knows the name of the woman, in whose tomb he is said to lay? I think, however, it is more likely that he is a tombless wanderer, which is not so strange when the record is considered fully. As told, it is not beyond belief that such a fate could befall even a Pharaoh and does accord with the laws of olden days. The next Pharaoh married his sister, conceived in wickedness, and therefore died while yet young.

MAN:34:67 The predictions of Hepoa were averted by the happenings in the land, happenings that purified it during the days of Pharaoh's short-lived successor. Then came a great one to rule the land, and peace and prosperity returned. Of his times, this is written: "Be joyful, O people, for a time of gladness had descended upon the whole land. A righteous and royal king has been set over us, one truly favoured in the eyes of the Great Ones. The waters rise and fall in moderation; the days are long and productive. The hours of night are measured and restful. The moon maintains her appointed seasons, and the sunship steers a straight course. The bright torch of heaven burns steadily, and the stars retain their stations. Once more, men must qualify by goodness for the right to govern and to hold official positions. All is well with the land." If this could be but written of these days!

MAN:34:68 Of Nemertean, wife of Cupola, men say she established the Sisterhood of Sin, but this is untrue, for they misunderstand the writings. The written things are misread. The writings of men are as plows which cannot follow a straight furrow. Everyone at birth is a twin and has a spirit twin. Nemertean was, of all women, the most virtuous; yet surely no woman ever evoked such malice in the hearts of her sisters!

MAN:34:69 Once, men said that the king was the shepherd of everyman and that wickedness was not in him. That however lowly the man in distress, he would devote hours of his time to bring him justice. If our fathers had but known the nature of the men who would follow as kings, or had the kings of olden days foreseen what was to come, the sons of the kings would have been destroyed, even though they were the seeds of divinity. Perhaps we do injustice to our rulers, for when the governors are bad, maybe they are no worse than a corrupt, degenerate and indifferent generation deserves. When you decry your rulers, read the hearts of your people.

MAN:34:70 The good ruler should not speak falsehood; he should be as great as his responsibilities. Each word should be weighed before spoken, for it is accepted as gold and not as thistledown. He should take heed of his own judgements, for the judgements of eternity draw near. He should be, above all, an example to all men. The gardener of wickedness waters his land with deceit, and it brings forth falsehood. The good ruler should be above every deed of meanness; he should be the father of the orphan and the husband of the widow. A true leader of the people should be free from every kind of avarice, a man above every kind of pettiness. He should be a man of wide vision. He should be like the rising waters that feed the fertile fields. He should be swift and sure to execute judgement on him, to whom punishment is due. O where does he sleep today, in what generation will he come forth?

MAN:34:71 (The end of this scroll is unknown. This was not one in the great chest. It is one added in the days of preservation.)

Book of
Morals and
Precepts

MPR:1:2 Behold the teachings concerning life and the testimonies, which are a true guide through the portals at the Great Halls of Eternity. Here is a code of behaviour and manner of living prescribed by the Noble Ones. The story of life with a revelation of the secrets and mysteries of the Unseen Kingdoms and Earth. The meaning and purpose, which govern all things.

Table of Chapters

Book of Morals and Precepts
Table of Chapters (Continued)

Book of Morals and Precepts
Table of Chapters (Continued)

Book of Morals and Precepts

Chapter One – Preliminary

MPR:1:1 Wisdom is the treasure of all ages, which shall endure incorruptibly forever until time is spent. Therefore, let the tumult of life be stilled, and in reverence and silence receive these instructions from ancient times.

MPR:1:2 Behold the teachings concerning life and the testimonies, which are a true guide through the portals at the Great Halls of Eternity. Here is a code of behaviour and manner of living prescribed by the Noble Ones. The story of life with a revelation of the secrets and mysteries of the Unseen Kingdoms and Earth. The meaning and purpose, which govern all things.

MPR:1:3 Herein are the guiding lights of thought, which will enable a man to follow a straight course on the great sea of life and to steer away from evil. Followed faithfully, they will bring him to a safe harbour.

MPR:1:4 To enable him to give a righteous judgement and return a suitable answer to one, who speaks to him or challenges him. By holding these things in his heart, he shall maintain a position of respect among the people and be delivered from the yoke of common folk.

MPR:1:5 The dispensations of eternity shall not remain hidden from him, nor shall life conceal its mystery. Behold, herein is wisdom and knowledge given to you, that in the fullness of time, all the inhabitants of the earth may dwell in its glory. The old teachings, which will provide a staff for the simple and a guardian for the young.

MPR:1:6 Wherever the sun shines or the wind blows; wherever there is an eye to see with clarity or an ear to hear with understanding, a mind to receive and assimilate, there let the greater way of life be made known and the maxims of Truth be honoured and obeyed.

MPR:1:7 Written for the elect by the Master of Mysteries, once Overseer of Harvests and Recorder of Taxes. Guardians of Tombs and Upholder of Royal Decrees, Beloved of the High Gods and the gods. Keeper of the Secrets of the Highest God, Lesser Lord of Jubilees and Grand Scribe of the Sacred Writings. One born into the house of a false god, whom he rejected, Distributor of Barley Seed and Master of the Great Sanctuary. Chief of Seers and Guardian of the Great Mysteries. Watcher at the Sacred Shrine and Defender of the Lakeland and the Gates. Inspector of the Courtyard of the Sacred Being, Guardian of the Hidden Records and Servant of the Secret Temple, Messenger of the True God. Third Begotten Son of an enlightened father, a Magistrate of a goodly city. Son of a gentle lady sistrum bearer and mistress of the song-stresses in the Temple of the Twofold God. Now one whose name is obliterated by unchallengeable decree, but once a man of good standing in this country, whose estate remains to this day.

MPR:1:8 My children, listen to the voice of instruction and incline a willing ear towards the speech of wisdom. Thus shall the words which issue from your mouth be established before men and your commands be obeyed as the statutes. Let not your mind be diverted, nor your attention be distracted. Set them in your heart as a Royal Impression. Inscribe them there as though struck on marble.

MPR:1:9 To cast aside the words of experience, which guided the Ancients is foolhardy and an invitation to calamity. Therefore, immerse yourself in the writings of the past, as in cool waters at the heat of the day, and your spirit will emerge refreshed and strengthened. They will be a steadying oar enabling the vessel of your heart's desire to alter course and wear against the winds of adversity without capsizing.

MPR:1:10 When your opponent sends a gale of words beating against your defences, they will break it as a shield shatters the sword and will arm your tongue for the counter assault. Live your life according to these instructions and you will be well fortified in the season of adversity's trial.

MPR:1:11 To you, my children, I give this, the treasure of the past, the accumulated wisdom of man. There has been a careful selection of words and gathering of sayings, a winnowing of works of wisdom and a careful choice made from the Hidden Writings, all recorded with much searching of the heart, while seeking the Great God's inspiration. There is nothing added to that, which was, no unknown utterance or unfamiliar saying. Nothing, which has not been on the tongue and in the hearts of our forefathers. What was recorded in their days has been rewritten, for Truth and Wisdom are a mooring line from the first man to the last, from generation to generation, until the end. Would that I could grasp something from the unknown to hand on to you, but I am only the guiding channel leading the refreshing waters of wisdom from the great reservoir of Truth towards the parched lands of the uninstructed.

Chapter Two – The Nature of the True God

MPR:2:1 There is but one God, the High God, the Designer, the Creator and Ruler of the Earth and the Lord of the Kingdoms of Light and Darkness. Everlasting, All Powerful and beyond the understanding of men. The Great Dweller in Everlasting Pregnant Silence, Unseeable, Unknowable.

MPR:2:2 By a command He created man, and in His indulgence permitted the gods to be fashioned. He is the Source of all that is, the Father of Fathers, the Mother of Mothers, the One Who preceded the sun. The sun is not God, though His creation, for its brightness bestows light and life upon the Earth. It gives warmth to the aged and quickens the child in its mother's womb. It nourishes the seed and calls forth the green growth. It is the instrument of the High God, His furnace fire of life. The sun is removed from man at night time, but the True God is always with him. Man never walks alone; he is never unescorted.

MPR:2:3 To this God alone give praise, Self-Created, Maker of Heaven and Earth, Founder of the Kingdoms of Light and Darkness, the Waters and the Mountains. To the One that is above all, the Spring, from which flows all wisdom, to Him alone belong adoration, thanksgiving, honour and praise. Who spread wide the great canopy of Heaven and pinned back the curtains of night with the stars. Whose finger draws the courses of the nightlights in unalterable arrangement.

MPR:2:4 He holds the great waters within their appointed limits, and the stormwater, He keeps in restraint. He covers the face of the Earth with a green mantle of vegetation. He inundates the land with the waters of life. His arm sweeps across the skies, and men are bewildered; Earth is shaken, and nations collapse and fall. The wicked tremble before His manifestations and are consumed in the midst of His fire.

MPR:2:5 The wrongdoer is confounded and lies stricken before His darts of lightning. His thunders rend the roof of Heaven, and Earth groans out its travail. It is He, the High God, who defeats armies with pestilence or gives one man dominion over thousands. At his command, the seas will rise against the Earth or mountains belch forth fires of destruction.

MPR:2:6 A man lives his allotted span in the dispensation of the High God of Old, whose will encompasses the daily task and round. All things have their beginning and end with God. His power cannot be suppressed. His knowledge is the wisdom of eternity. His strength reaches out into infinity.

MPR:2:7 His dwelling place is set in the universal centre, and He encompasses all the universes great and small. His breath sustains life in multitudinous forms, and his thought holds all things to their proper shape. He prescribes the courses of the stars. He issues His commands to the winds, and they sing their responses. The wide seas murmur His praise. He moves the silences in the void of empty space, where the Eternal Heart lies sleeping. Order and beauty are shaped by His hands.

MPR:2:8 His voice speaks from the sandy silences. He whispers in the cool breezes. He roars in the whirlwind. He murmurs in the running waters. He sighs in the treetops, and men hear His voice without understanding.

MPR:2:9 Man dreams and says this is reality. He sees the shadow, but is blinded before the light. He reasons and is deceived. The design of the True God and His nature cannot be understood in the light of reason, for reason is not with this God, who knows all things without reason.

MPR:2:10 There is none other like unto the One God in all His glory. Whose strength can challenge Him? Whose will can contend with His will? Whose might can equal His? Where is another with His wisdom? Who in goodness can compare with Him?

MPR:2:11 By the power of His thoughts, many kingdoms are brought forth beyond Earth. He speaks the unutterable word, and they are created. He rules His creatures with infinite wisdom and directs their destinies with unchallengeable decrees. His will controls the forces within men ,and the thing they seek unknowingly is Him. As the body, when hungry is filled with the urge to eat and when thirsty, with the urge to drink, so is the spirit in man filled with the urge to seek God.

MPR:2:12 His ordinances govern Earth and the Heavens above. All things therein have their appointed place and purpose, and in their nature conform to His Law. His ways are inscrutable, transcending the understanding of men. His thoughts are a mystery, which men may not fathom, they are veiled and withdrawn beyond the comprehension of mortals.

MPR:2:13 His design is unrevealed to the multitude. Few are the men who can understand why He planted the road to the Place of Glory with the sharp stones of suffering and pain. Or why life is a struggle through the thorny forest of adversity.

MPR:2:14 But the ways of men are known to God, for the creator ever knows the created, though it does not follow that the created know their creator. Therefore, O man, remember that your heart lies naked before His gaze, and your innermost thoughts come under His scrutiny. No deed ever goes unrecorded.

MPR:2:15 None can perceive His residence, for He dwells in the profound silence of the outer sphere. Look for Him in the order of Nature, and see His plan in its direction. Look for Him amid the stars in their courses, and see the grandeur of His scheme. Look for the unmanifested spirit in the manifested object.

MPR:2:16 His glory is proclaimed in the Heavens; the sun reflects His splendour; the moon witnesses His peace. His fruitfulness is spread over the face of the land, and the waters are filled with His bounty. The Earth bends to His will or is broken to His command. Man may walk in the appointed direction or he will be driven. Walk in the light of the Law and not along the paths of the transgressor, for the laws of the High God are unchallengeable and cannot be transgressed with impunity. The wrongful deeds and the wicked thoughts of man are indelibly inscribed upon the everlasting tablets of his immortal soul.

MPR:2:17 He is the Creator, in whose Spirit image and likeness, you were fashioned. His laws ordained your present estate and circumstances upon Earth. The power of your intellect is His promise of godhood, and the marvels of your body are the works of His hand. His soul communes with your soul, and the consciousness He shares with you is the source of your life.

MPR:2:18 In His sight, all men are equal, and He judges them as men and not according to their estate. The rich and the poor, the highborn and the lowly, the wise and the simple all receive a fitting reward according to their labours. From each is expected results according to his abilities; from some much and from others little. Only that, which serves the purpose of the Great God is accounted worthy by Him.

MPR:2:19 He has established the Law, whereby the sun shines down on the good and the wicked alike. He sends rain equally for the provident and the improvident. The arrows of misfortune strike the worthy and the unworthy with indifference. Only the most wise may understand why this is the established nature of things. For the generality of men, it is a condition to be accepted with good grace, and for them, it is sufficient to know that the seeming indifference of the universe serves its purpose.

MPR:2:20 The True God neither rewards nor punishes, for He has established the Law, whereby each man decrees his own fate. The future destiny and circumstances of the soul are shaped in the earthly body. When, in the hour of its release, the soul takes flight, freed from its earthly container of flesh, it assumes the form moulded by its desires. In that awesome day of reckoning, the wicked shall be revealed in hideous shapelessness, but the upright shall step forward in splendour.

MPR:2:21 Therefore, give due respect to the Law of God; walk in His ways, and bow to His decrees. You are placed on Earth that His purpose may be fulfilled. Therefore, fight not against His will, nor rebel against His laws, lest you bring about your own destruction. God will not destroy the transgressor of His Law, for he will destroy himself. Each man ultimately decrees his own fate and receives his reward or punishment, according to the Law.

MPR:2:22 Hail to the Creator, Giver of Breath, God of Destinies, Great God of Thunder and Fire, He who roars over the Earth. The Silent One who walks by your side, unseen, unmanifested. Father God, Mother God, God of Comfort and Conflict, Mighty Fighter with stone. The Glorious Being, the Lord of Life and Light. God of the gods, Prince of Everlastingness. Ruler of the Netherworld, King of the Western Kingdom. Light of Eternity, Light of Life.

MPR:2:23 These are His names according to His nature, but this also you may know about the True God; He is the Fountainhead of All Things. His Power is unbounded, and His Mind knows no limitations. He has the wisdom of eternity, and the mantle of His Greatness envelops all mankind.

MPR:2:24 He sits enthroned in the universal centre, and the divine rays, which flow from His presence, hold all forms in stability. He moves His finger in the nightskies, and the stars dance along their pathways. He walks upon the wings of the wind and encompasses all the kingdoms of Heaven and Earth.

MPR:2:25 Order and beauty follow in His train, and all things obey the directions of His hand. The face of beauty looks out from His works, and the voice of wisdom speaks from the midst of His creation, though it is scarcely heard through the barriers of mortal limitations. Glory and grandeur form His mantle; justice and mercy drape His body. Love and benevolence cover His head, and the virtues are His footstool.

MPR:2:26 Discuss not His form, for it is beyond your understanding. Push not among the crowd of His worshippers. Mouth not the words of His writings unthinkingly. Mumble not His praises. Stand not before His shrine in hypocritical humility. Carefully supervise His ministrations, and maintain due decorum in His place. Remember Him always.

MPR:2:27 He is with you always, in the midst of the concourse and in the silence of your bedchamber. His breath gives life to countless forms, and His will holds all things to their appointed shape.

MPR:2:28 Obey His commands; take heed of the ordinances He has made, for they conform to your needs. All things are bent to the benefit of man, and all that encompasses your life accord with His direction, that the soul within you may enjoy continued gracious growth from stage to stage of its unfolding. So that when the cumbersome sheath of mortal flesh is cast off, it may receive a just and fitting compensation under the Great Law, in accordance with its thoughts and deeds on Earth.

MPR:2:29 Where is this strange God of ours, and it is well you ask, for if you would be happy on Earth, you must know His ways. He is not a revealed God. He has hidden Himself, for He knows well the dispositions of men. Were He here now among the people and revealed to their gaze, the weakling would fawn upon Him, the hypocrite would join His following, and the wrongdoer would walk in His train, proclaiming his innocence with a loud voice. How then, if He were here, could the weakling be tested, the hypocrite discovered and the wrongdoer unveiled?

MPR:2:30 Our God is hidden, that men may be tested and established for what they really are. Were He revealed to the eyes and understanding of men, Earth and life would have no purpose. He hides to discover the hearts of men.

MPR:2:31 Is it not declared in the Plans of God that uncertainty is an essential earthly condition? Yet this you may know, that if you be worthy, and very few are, there is a method, whereby you may look behind the veil, and then no longer will you walk in uncertainty.

MPR:2:32 However, for men in general, the Undiscovered God is not apparent. He has no man-made image in His likeness, and He stands in obscurity behind the great alcove beyond the temple within the Place of Flame. Yet, He makes Himself known in subtle ways, for He cannot remain unmanifested to the truly spiritual, any more than a river can remain hidden, for it dissolves away the ground, in which it is concealed. So will the Great God spring forth in the midst of material things and, dissolving away their solidity, shine forth to the sincere seeker.

MPR:2:33 He is not a New God but the Oldest God of All, the Father of All Ages, the Ancient One of yore. He requires no temple to establish His glory or sacrifice to give Him strength. A cheerful nature is more acceptable to this God than offerings of gold and silver by the bad-tempered man, or the sacrificial ox of the churlish man. He prefers the man who gives a willing hand to his neighbour, to one who brings Him treasure.

MPR:2:34 A word of encouragement to a man in distress is of more value to Our God than loud praises in His temple. He does not take all and remain mute. He seeks not gifts with no purpose, or wasteful sacrifices. What can man give that will add to His glory? What thing fashioned by man could benefit the One God, who by taking thought could create a universe?

MPR:2:35 Work for Our God, and He will work for you. He remembers well the man, who labours on His behalf. He who labours to the benefit of others works for the Great God. He who improves Earth works for Him.

MPR:2:36 The purpose of man's sojourn on Earth is the glorification of man, not the glorification of God, who is the All Glorious One. Thus it is written in the plans of God.

MPR:2:37 The true temples of the Great God are not structures of stone and brick. They are places of quietude in your heart and home, where you listen to the awakening of your soul as it responds to the conscious contact with Him. His worship is your labour among the people. His praise is the song in your heart. His adoration is your joy of living.

MPR:2:38 Keep the peace of the Mysterious God and maintain the order of His Law among men and women. For they are His flocks and herds, and He calls forth shepherds from among them. He made Earth a workplace for man and not a pleasure garden; therefore, be you a songleader at the task.

MPR:2:39 He is the Mighty God, the Nameless One whom your fathers held in awe. He it was who dissipated the darkness over the waters, who separated the chaos. Who lifted the cloud, who made the breezes of life to fill the nostrils of men.

MPR:2:40 Men came forth from His members, and they appeared in His likeness. For their sustenance, He provided fruits and vegetables, animals, fowls and fish.

MPR:2:41 He has brought low His enemies, yes, He has even destroyed His own children.

MPR:2:42 He rolled the grain, and lo, it became the food of men. He dismembered the Destroyer in olden times. He made daylight for the joy of man and darkness for his tranquillity. Men cry to Him in their distress, and He suffers with them.

MPR:2:43 He sends a captain to strengthen the resistance of the feeble and a champion for the weak.

MPR:2:44 He has endowed men with the power of speech and bedecked their language with fine words, that greatness may sound around the Earth. He has enlightened the mind of man with great thoughts to repulse the might of untoward happenings. He has given him the courage to overcome terrors that lurk by night and to dispel those that strike by day.

MPR:2:45 He is a God of justice as well as benevolence, for He metes out chastisement, not always obviously, as among men but sometimes as a man chastises a son for his brother.

MPR:2:46 There can be none greater than the True God, for though Himself nameless, He knows every name.

MPR:2:47 Be not reticent to worship, for this is the prerogative of the highborn and wise. The king and nobles attend the temples diligently, but the stupid man and grave robber have no god.

MPR:2:48 Worship bestows no benefit on God, for He is all self-sufficient. Its purpose is the service of man, not the service of God. It fulfils a need of man, not a need of God. Nothing that man can do will add to God's glory. Nothing that man can give will add to that, which He already has.

MPR:2:49 These are the teachings of the Wise Ones, to whom be all due honour and respect. Give ear ,and listen with a receptive mind. Record them unto your generations, that they pass not away into dust with your habitations.

MPR:2:50 Therefore, let it now be written, and as written, let it be made known.

Chapter Three – The Nature of Man's Soul

MPR:3:1 The One God is above all in greatness, but under Him above all else on Earth is the soul of man. It is not isolated from the Godhead above, nor from the mortal below, for it is that, which spans the gulf between. It is the link between God and man, between immortal and mortal.

MPR:3:2 Nothing exists, which is or can be isolated from all else. There is a connection between Earth and the Region of Glory, a link between dust and star. From the Highest God down to the mote runs an unbroken and unbreakable chain.

MPR:3:3 Man is apart from all other creatures, in that he has foreknowledge of death and decay. If man be immortal, then it is the burden of his immortality; but if he passes to nothingness, he is cursed above the unknowing beasts, which know not the dread of approaching doom.

MPR:3:4 Has man been placed above the beasts to be confronted with his own nothingness? Is his superiority nought but the father of terrors? Such cannot be, for the direction of life is ever towards betterment, and it cannot be cast back upon itself.

MPR:3:5 The ass knows not the value of food, though its belly be full. Yesterday, today and tomorrow are, to it, alike. The lion knows nothing of the putrefaction which one day will be its lot, nor does the ox live in the knowledge of the slaughterhouse. The power of thought is not given to the flesh, nor can the bones reason.

MPR:3:6 Something unseen animates the inert clay of your being. Something intangible is added to the earthly material of your body. Think not primarily of your material self, nor say "My heart is supreme." For within your body resides the soul, which activates the thinking heart, and is not the resident of the dwelling of greater importance than the materials of its construction?

MPR:3:7 Gaze upon a corpse; see. It is empty of life, something that was is no longer there, the soul is missing.

MPR:3:8 Your soul is the Lord of your Body, suffer not the subject to rebel, nor to assert its sway, for its domination cannot be beneficial. Let the soul not only vitalise, but rule and direct the flesh, that wildness and excesses may be held in leash.

MPR:3:9 The soul delights in sweet smells and knows the perfumes of Earth by the performance of the nose. It rejoices in delicacies of the table and tastes them only through the workings of the mouth. Food feeds the flesh, but the flesh finds no pleasure in eating, for it is the soul, which experiences the enjoyment of food.

MPR:3:10 The eyes are the sentinels, which keep watch for you, the lights that go before your path, as braziers before a caravan. Yet, they see not of themselves, for they are but the instruments of sight, without a consciousness of their own. It is the soul within, which interprets their messages.

MPR:3:11 Man, alone of all creatures, is capable of blushing, for he, alone of all things living, has a soul which can experience a sense of shame. That man has a soul is beyond all doubt; it is the most obvious of all truths. Seek not to delve unduly into its secrets but to harmonise it with your body. Commune with it, and awaken its potentialities.

MPR:3:12 Intellect, reason, willpower and comprehension; these are not the soul. They are the manifestations of its existence, its attributes and its activity, but they are not the soul itself. Stimulate the soul by contact with that, to which it responds. Know it through its manifestations and understand it through its faculties.

MPR:3:13 It remains immortal and indestructible throughout all ages. Its splendour is displayed in noble deeds, and its glory in works of art and craftsmanship. It will survive your bodily disintegration. It was not created by the quickening of the flesh, nor conceived within the womb. Its seed existed before the body and preceded the thinking heart. The Great God sows soul seeds into earthly flesh, as man sows barley seeds in the fields of black soil.

MPR:3:14 The soul is yours to fashion; it can be made radiant by goodness, beautified by virtue and glorified by love. It can be hideously deformed by vices and passions and twisted into a form of distorted horror by meanness and hatred.

MPR:3:15 It cannot be valued too greatly, nor can it be handled too carefully, for it is your own trueself, the reality, which is you. It is as virgin stone for you to cut and shape as you will; but remember, the image carved is not easily altered and shall one day be displayed to the eyes of eternity in its true likeness, though on Earth, this is now veiled by the flesh.

MPR:3:16 The desire of the soul cannot be held in restraint; be it at the rim of the Earth, the soul will find it, or if beyond the stars, it will be reached. The soul is ever questing; as the wilderness wayfarer thirsts after water, so does the soul long for knowledge.

MPR:3:17 The gods of the North and South provide food for the body of man, but it is the God of All Ages, who provide sustenance for the soul. As the body has its particular foods, which nourish it, so has the soul. As the body is impoverished by lack of proper sustenance, so is the soul.

MPR:3:18 Mortal man may, in the course of time, forget his experiences, but within the soul, they are retained forever. The soul is a hunter, and the quarry is Truth. the weapons of the hunt are reason and experience.

MPR:3:19 The years of the wrongdoer and he who walks in wickedness plant more wrinkles and scars on the face of the soul than on the face of the body.

MPR:3:20 The soul is not born, nor does it know itself as a soul. The purpose of its earthly journey is to awaken it to self-awareness and to provide it with the ability to continue existence in the Region Beyond the West. Therefore, how could it enter upon earthly life with these things? Were they already there, life and Earth would have no purpose.

MPR:3:21 The soul is bodiless within the body, everlasting among things that change and pass away. Man does not perceive his soul, because his senses face outward from the soul, towards earthly things, with which it makes contact. So it is that only the most developed of men can close out the material things about them and turn their senses inward to perceive the soul.

MPR:3:22 The soul looks out through the eyes and sees all, which is without, but nothing of this can look in through the eyes and see the soul, even though the soul's feeling may be reflected there. An eye without a soul behind it sees nothing.

MPR:3:23 The earthly and wayward seek only after outward pleasures and the satisfaction of the body. They fall into the snare of disbelief in the soul, and the Law decrees that disbelief shall be easy.

MPR:3:24 Wise men, knowing the nature of immortal things, seek not for anything stable here among unstable things.

MPR:3:25 That by which we know the texture of things, by which we taste, smell and hear, by which we experience the tenderness and suffering of love and perceive the beauty of nature, by which we value the glory of self sacrifice, by that we are also assured of something immortal within us.

MPR:3:26 For when a man comes to the realisation that it is by the soul within him that he knows and experiences all things about him, he has taken the first great step towards conscious immortality.

MPR:3:27 When the body and soul are torn apart, what remains? No man lives by the air he breathes in and the air he breathes out. It is something more, the soul, that gives life.

MPR:3:28 As the one fire entering the Earth in oneness becomes different here, there and everywhere, according to the nature of that, which it consumes, so the One Soul vitalising the souls of men becomes different according to the nature of its covering.

MPR:3:29 As the one air passes through the pipes and becomes different according to the nature of the pipes, so the One Essence in the souls of men becomes different according to the manner of its use.

MPR:3:30 The one water is in all things, yet in all things it is different. So it is with the Great Soul and the souls of men. The wise man, who is conscious of his soul within him, will commune with it and never neglect its needs. For if a man cannot awaken his soul before his body falls asunder, he will not awaken it thereafter, and it will return to the waters of the Great Soul Sea.

MPR:3:31 The purpose of Earth and earthly life is awakening of the souls of men. Earthly conditions can serve no other end.

MPR:3:32 Rejoice in the sure knowledge of your soul's indestructibility, but let your joy be leavened by remembrance of your responsibility for its condition.

MPR:3:33 Naked does man come from his mother's womb, and naked does he return to the womb of the Earth. He brings no possessions with him to Earth, and no more can be taken out. Yet, he leaves not altogether as he entered, for though his riches and estate, his titles, even his clothes are left behind, if he has lived wisely, he goes out richer in soul wisdom and arrayed in soul beauty. Man arrives at the Great Portal arrayed in glory or clothed in horror.

MPR:3:34 In the newborn childling is the soft seed of the slumbering soul; this will be developed, moulded and fashioned throughout the period of its earthly existence. It will be shaped by man himself to his own inner likeness; then, when stripped of its outward bodily covering, man will stand revealed to himself and be faced with splendour or horror.

MPR:3:35 In the likeness, to which the soul is fashioned in the body, so shall it come forth in the spirit on its appointed day.

MPR:3:36 Thus it is written in the Secret Books of Wisdom, which are revealed to the few. The body is a womb, life the days of conception, and death the birth of the soul. Is it not written that some shall bring forth monsters and fearful things, and some shall bear gods? These things are not beyond understanding.

MPR:3:37 Pontas taught the people that every man is his own mother, and they fed him to the crocodiles. Children cannot be told even half the truth, but must be led by childish tales towards understanding.

Chapter Four – Life

MPR:4:1 Commune with your soul within, and consider how wonderfully you are created. Meditate long upon your nature, contemplate the powers you possess. Consider your needs and desires;

thus, you will find the proper path through life and a sure guide to direct your footsteps.

MPR:4:2 As the union of heat and tinder produces fire, so does the union of soul and body produce life in man.

MPR:4:3 Nothing is constant in life, except wisdom, knowledge and skill. Life ebbs and flows, as the tide and the fortunes of men wax and wane as the moon. The rich become poor, and the poor become rich. The powerful become weak, and the weak become powerful. Where the stream flowed yesteryear is now dust, and the cooling waters have moved elsewhere. The lakes of last season have joined the wilderness, and the dykes have become pits. Fortune smiles upon the improvident, and misfortune smites the worthy. Men are born handsome or ugly, rich or poor, they inherit a life of ease or a life of struggle.

MPR:4:4 Here is wisdom, accept the nature of things as they are, for as such they accord with the Plans of God and are under the Law. But accept them not with resignation, as an affliction to be borne, but as a challenge to contest. Man must rise to meet life or be overwhelmed; this, too, is the Law. When the road seems long and the load heavy, remember that the stouthearted runner carries the greatest burden.

MPR:4:5 There is no constant state of life; all is movement and change. Therefore, it is well to build the structure of your life on a foundation of things, which are not easily removed. These are wisdom, skill and knowledge, which once possessed cannot be taken away, as can hoarded gold and cherished chattels in the ebb and flow of life's fortunes. Gold and silver are uneatable stones, but wisdom is the food of the gods. Skill and knowledge define the difference between the ox with the yoke and the plowman with the whip.

MPR:4:6 Fear not the feelings which stir in the heart, for therein lie the greatest of life's treasures. Taste their honeyed bitterness, and though you are consumed as you consume, something will remain, which is yours forever. Life is matured and mellowed by the treasures, which pain the heart, and without them, the soul cannot develop.

MPR:4:7 With some, life is generous and with others niggardly, but whether you pass through the stages of life in a lowly or a high condition, your life will be neither wholly happy nor wholly miserable.

MPR:4:8 Whether life is indulgent towards you or austere, whether it metes out reward or chastisement, remember that its dispensations are governed by an infinite wisdom, and the ordinances of the Law, though incomprehensible, are just. Therefore, when life turns undue attention upon you, accept it not as a dumb creature, but say, "What have I done that this is my reward?"

MPR:4:9 The dispensations of life and the course of events are such that prosperity will attend a good life and adversity a wicked one. Is this not proved by the normal course of the affairs of men? If not so provable, then the moral disease of the people is established.

MPR:4:10 Travel the road of life according to your ability, and your foot will find its appointed place. Take time, and consider every action. He who journeys leisurely journeys best, and the runner who hastens not unduly is he who reaches the goal.

MPR:4:11 As the dew to the herb, as the honey to the bee, as the north wind to the raven and the twilight to the owl, such is life to the spirit of man.

MPR:4:12 Think not, with the weakling, that nothing is more precious, nor, with the hermit, that you should reject it. Think not too highly of it, nor consider it worthless. Love it not for itself or for what you can get out of it, but for what you can do with it.

MPR:4:13 Forget not that life has but one purpose, one end and one objective, and that is the awakening of the souls of men. All things on Earth conform to that end. Earth without its perplexities and problems, its struggle and strife, its inequalities and injustices, would never develop the soul in a manner meet for its destiny. This is the answer to the riddle of ages. If all were right with the Earth, there would be nothing for man to do; as it is, there is sufficient to occupy him throughout his generations. When man himself is perfect, its purpose will be fulfilled, and then Earth, too, will be perfect.

MPR:4:14 Riches cannot buy life, nor can gold purchase back wasted hours. Therefore, employ the future that you have left to your greatest benefit. Lament not that you were born or desire that life should depart. Life has a purpose and meaning, even for one as miserable as you, and the Law may not be set aside.

MPR:4:15 Whatever your estate, and however lowly the circumstances to which you have fallen, you still have the power for good in your right hand and the power for evil in your left hand.

MPR:4:16 Would the fish rise to the bait if it knew the hook were hidden therein, or would the lion step on the pit if it saw the stake below? No, neither would man wish to live, were the soul to perish with the body. Neither would a just God have created him, and the True God, if He be anything, is just.

MPR:4:17 Life is yours, that you requested it not is of small consideration, for the choice was not with you. Therefore, accept with good grace that, which has been allotted to you, deriving from it whatever benefits it may bestow.

MPR:4:18 The benefits are great, and were they readily apparent, life would be accepted with due gratitude and endured, whatever its afflictions, with resigned anticipation life, if so lived, would be futile and its purpose confounded. Therefore, only by dire efforts can man come to know the everlastingness of his soul. The Law decrees that man shall never be assured of his immortality.

MPR:4:19 Life must be lived from the beginning to the end. Run the race easily, for the course is long and the runner who runs the race best is he who conserves his strength in the early laps.

MPR:4:20 Be not disturbed or overwhelmed when misfortune accompanies your passage along the way. Be not dispirited when the pace is hard, or faint before the obstacles. Accept the challenge of adversity with high spirits, for as the flame is to wax and the furnace to copper, so is adversity to the soul.

MPR:4:21 Every sorrowful blow that falls upon the soul is a tempering stroke. The metal that suffers the fires of the furnace longest is the finest in quality.

MPR:4:22 Give prudent thought towards tomorrow's problems, but let them not tax your mind unduly, for problems in the womb of the future may be stillborn.

MPR:4:23 Though the pathway of life be uneven, the going is not always rough. Take it as you find it, but beware where the going is smooth, for there evil will set its trap. Danger lurks where least expected.

MPR:4:24 When you journey without possessions, you journey without care, but when you are burdened with many goods, they bring the attention of evil men.

MPR:4:25 He who sleeps uncovered may sleep soundly, but when covered with a mantle, it is well to keep one eye open.

MPR:4:26 Know that life is unimportant, unless properly lived. A noble death is better than a wasted life. He who exchanges a life of wickedness for a worthy death makes amends, and the scales are adjusted. Accordingly, let your aim be to live as long as you should and not as long as you can.

MPR:4:27 While to others, your life is worth more than death, then your duty is to preserve it. While you serve best by living, live; but when by your death the living may best be served, then shirk not the burden of manhood.

MPR:4:28 If your life be disposed of to the benefit of others, then let a worthy price be extracted, for the Law decrees that no man shall relinquish his life easily.

MPR:4:29 The span of man's life is neither long nor short, but sufficient for its purpose. Whatever benefits a man wishes to attain for his soul may be attained in his lifetime. A lifetime is sufficient to fashion the soul to ultimate glory or to ultimate horror.

MPR:4:30 What end would a longer life serve? To the wicked, an opportunity for more evil, to the selfish, more time to hurt others and to the miserly, more time to lay up worthless things. The slothful ones would rejoice, for there would be more time for their idleness, but the burden of the industrious would be that much greater.

MPR:4:31 The good may say, "Why, then, should not our lives be lengthened and years added unto us?" Know they not the goodness of the labour done in their lifetime shall have been sufficient, and no more is required of them here? If they have served well on Earth, they are candidates for higher service in the Regions of Light, for the opportunity for service ceases not at death.

MPR:4:32 To what end would you live longer, to do the things you have not done or repeat the things you have already done? What you have been unable to do will be done by others, and does not man experience repetitious pleasures with decreasing enjoyment? Would you increase your knowledge or develop your skill? Who, then shall teach you more than is to be learned on Earth, or where on Earth can practice carry you beyond perfection? He who would go further must go to a higher place of instruction. The works done on Earth pass away, and the fruits of man's labour are reaped elsewhere.

MPR:4:33 Each man's life should leave its impress on Earth, and each man should depart a better man for having lived. Repine not for lost opportunities, for opportunity does not perish at death. Do your best here and you will do better elsewhere. Be wise here, and you will be wiser in another place.

MPR:4:34 Earthly success is not the measure of a man's achievement, for a gain here may mean a loss elsewhere. An earthly loss may mean a spiritual gain; the scales are always just.

MPR:4:35 When in old age you say, "Alas that life is short," then consider the way you abused and wasted it in your youth, is not your reward fitting? Remember that the paths to pleasant old age are chosen in youth. They are the paths of simplicity, moderation, cleanliness and virtue.

MPR:4:36 Consider the ruthlessness of rulers, the greed of the rich and the wilfulness of the powerful. If these dare to enslave the Earth and wreck misery upon the people, knowing they can enjoy the fruits of their oppression but a brief span of years, what would they not set out to achieve were their span of life doubled or were they immortal?

MPR:4:37 Therefore, the Great God in His wisdom has ordained the proper span of man's life. If, then, you think life is short, why dissipate it so and why waste the precious days? Is it not economy, which makes a man rich, and not abundance?

MPR:4:38 The wise man lives fully all his life, and he is always conscious of being alive. The fool is always beginning to live, and the weakling shrinks from it and seeks forgetfulness in comfort. Those who half live are already half dead.

MPR:4:39 Live lustily and manfully, for life is to be enjoyed; it must be savoured to the full. Better one day as an eagle than one year as a goose.

MPR:4:40 What is life, that man should seek to prolong it? Is it not a continual avoidance of snares, a struggle against delusion, a series of mishaps and a pursuit of shadows, which retreat from the grasp? It begins with ignorance, continues through strife and worry and ends in sorrow and pain. It is a day of heat, and death comes as a cool night.

MPR:4:41 Are not the troubles of life piled one upon another, as the stones of a pyramid? Are not all our hopes based only on possibilities, and do not our expectations look forward into improbabilities?

MPR:4:42 Fools fear as men and hope as gods. Bounded by mortal restrictions, they desire the achievements of immortality. But everlasting life is the reward of those who live good earthly lives without the inducement of immortality. Therefore, the prize is never revealed, and life maintains man in a state of doubt and perplexity. Hope he may have, but never assurance.

MPR:4:43 Life raises some men up and casts others down. Not always does it bestow good fortune on the worthy or mete out to the unworthy their just desserts. It raises men up to test them, and likewise, casts them down. The man who discovers a golden treasure is being tested, even as he who is stricken with blindness. Each man is tested according to his weaknesses, not according to his strength. The reward of the worthy is not here; neither is the punishment of the wicked. Were the just rewards and punishments of men too readily apparent, the course to take in life would be too obvious to serve its great purpose. There must ever be the stimulus of doubt and perplexity.

MPR:4:44 Among men, some are born to rule and some to obey, but not all rulers can rule or all servants obey. If, then, you cannot rule, learn to obey, and if you cannot obey, make yourself a better man, that you may be raised up to rule.

MPR:4:45 Wisdom is nourished from without, but it grows from within. We live not by light of the great sun disc above, but by the light of the cool sun within.

MPR:4:46 The bitter experiences, the sorrows and failures of life are the alternatives to the advice you have failed to heed. Who, then, has brought them upon your head? Instruction alone cannot give knowledge, nor can books bestow wisdom. The pupil sits at the feet of his master and gains knowledge, and the scribe reads the books of men. But wiser is he, who sits under the stars and contemplates the universe or reads the Great Book of God about him.

MPR:4:47 The satisfactory life is that, which realises the dreams and ideals of youth in old age, but life itself is the testmaster of these, and few pass his examination.

MPR:4:48 Life is not of the Earth, though it appears thereon. It remains not with the body at death, for it accompanies the soul into the journey beyond the Grim Portal. Death is but the termination of life's association with the mortal body. The last drawn breath on Earth is a farewell.

MPR:4:49 Life passes from Earth, through the Portal of Death into the existence beyond. Therefore, it is said that the life of man is everlastingly indestructible.

MPR:4:50 Life alone exists in both spheres but life on Earth is inconsistent. Life is a dancing girl.

Chapter Five – Man

MPR:5:1 Consider yourselves, my children, and meditate on the reason for your existence and the purpose, for which you were brought into being. Contemplate your powers, ponder your circumstances, discover your inescapable duties and face your earthly obligations.

MPR:5:2 Assume your burdens cheerfully, for they are not imposed capriciously. The One God has set a hard task, but it is not beyond your capabilities. Remember that every affliction, however grievous and seemingly unnecessary, serves a purpose and end.

MPR:5:3 O man, you are the delight and sorrow of your God; you have been set apart with peculiar favour and exalted above all other creatures. He has endowed you with reason, to maintain your dominion. He has bestowed upon you the faculty of speech, that wisdom may accumulate throughout your generations. He has exalted your mind, so that it may be perceptive of beauty and grandeur. He has ordained the Law, which circumscribes your life, and adjusted your nature to accord with your duties and destiny.

MPR:5:4 Each man is an individual work of God; his mind a fragment of His will; the Breath of God gives him life.

MPR:5:5 The Sole God formed you as He fashioned the beasts of the field and forest. He made you last and placed you at the pinnacle of creation. Command and jurisdiction over all were given unto you. From among the creatures of the forest and the beasts of the field, you ascended in triumphant superiority, and your yoke is upon them.

MPR:5:6 Be aware of yourself, as the pride of God and the fruition of His desire; nothing greater shall be created on Earth. You are the vessel containing the essence of divinity, fashioned with the clay of matter. Behold, you have even the nature of God within you and partake of His substance.

MPR:5:7 Remember, therefore, your superior estate, maintain the pride and dignity befitting your position and descend not to any mean or degrading thing.

MPR:5:8 Remember, my children, that every man, whatsoever his nation or estate, is a man; therefore, never degrade anyone, for even the least among men is a candidate for godhood.

MPR:5:9 Man can be whatsoever he wills; subject to the Law, there is no limitation on man's potential achievements. Shoot for the moon and not for the treetops, for nothing is beyond your reach.

MPR:5:10 Did God appear to man on Earth and man cast a spear at Him, He would not blast man with wrath, but admire him for his audacity. Such is the attitude of God towards man. Thus, God has made him, therefore is it meet that man should fawn upon Him with servility?

MPR:5:11 Man has the powers of reason and decision. A wise father delegates responsibility to his children, and God does not unduly interfere in the affairs of men.

MPR:5:12 Man is the lord of creation and the heir to godhood. He can soar to the greatest heights, but also fall to the lowest depths. No man is wholly good, and no man is wholly evil. The scales are never completely weighed down.

MPR:5:13 No man can hold any desirable thing on Earth or attain it in the Regions of Light without the expenditure of effort. No man can foresee the future or know what test the Wise God has placed there for him.

MPR:5:14 O man, mark this well. Never forget your goal of godhood, but vaunt not your godlikeness, for the beast dogs your footsteps, and an animal clothes your soul. You dwell beneath the dark shadow of the cloud of mortal ignorance. You live in a twilit dream state,;you are deceived by your senses; you dream and say this is reality; you reason and are afraid. But know that all things real reside in God, and His wisdom stands beyond the bounds of reason. He has established the foundations of Truth and Reality for eternity.

MPR:5:15 My children, man is not flesh and bone alone, but something more, something far greater than he can ever conceive at present. The eagle soars in the air above not knowing that soon he will descend to Earth and rise no more. The lion is unaware of the worms that will consume it, and the ox knows naught of the slaughter-house. The ass knows not of the use of food, though its teeth chew the grasses and herbage.

MPR:5:16 Something is added to mere man to raise him above the beasts; something else exists within the space of his body; it is his soul. Is not the mortal substance of the body less perfect when the soul has departed? Now it will decay and fall apart, but is this not because the animating spirit is no longer there? The immaterial spirit has gone; whence has it flown?

MPR:5:17 The spirit departs, taking life and consciousness with it. That, which came from the abode of spirit has returned there. That, which God gave of Himself has returned to its Source.

MPR:5:18 Man, the receptacle of god and beast, has sundered apart at the touch of death, and each returns to its own.

MPR:5:19 Man is the highest of the beasts and the lowest of the gods. Man is the battle ground of beast and god.

Chapter Six – The Real Man

MPR:6:1 Man is divided not only into nations, peoples, tribes and creeds, but also broadly in twain. There are among all men, all peoples, two kinds of man, the Real Man and the weakling. Those who are neither wholly one nor wholly the other, nevertheless tend towards the nature of one or the other of these.

MPR:6:2 Consider the Real Man, the man who reaches out towards godlikeness. He is the man, in whom God has succeeded. He is God's elect. He is like unto a spreading tree planted in black soil, which blossoms quietly and doubles the yield of its fruit in the summer. Its fruit is a delight to the mouth and fills the stomach with satisfaction. Beneath the canopy of its foliage, the weary find a pleasant refuge from the heat. In its shade, all men find peace and contentment.

MPR:6:3 The weakling is like a tree, whose leaves wither before the heat of the summer sun. Whose fruit never reaches maturity, for it falls to the ground unripened and is trampled underfoot. Men avoid it, and the axe is laid against its bole.

MPR:6:4 O Real Man, filled with the calm of strength, you are the true image of God on Earth. Yours is the noble life, and your reward here shall be a body preserved in youthfulness. When, in the fullness of time, you make the great journey westward, then shall your soul arise in the mysterious beyond, radiant in a glory indescribable.

MPR:6:5 Behold the uprightness of the Real Man. Is he not the father of the orphan and the husband of the widow? The brother of the forsaken and the guardian of the fatherless? Do not the friendless find in him a friend and the poor a benefactor?

MPR:6:6 It is not hard to give to the needy within reach or to help the weak when they are at hand. But the Real Man works not in such narrow confines, for he stretches out his hand to those beyond.

MPR:6:7 Watch him among the distressed; he talks with compassion and listens with understanding. See him among the lowly, how he deals with them in patience and kindness.

MPR:6:8 Such men stand out among others, not only because of their own qualities, but because of the respect which others feel bound to accord them.

MPR:6:9 A great man is no less great, though he lie prostrated and vanquished in the dust. The Real Man accepts both victory and defeat for what they really are, a challenge to his manliness.

MPR:6:10 The Real Man stands apart in greatness because of his outstanding qualities, his love of Truth and justice and his hatred of meanness and deceit.

MPR:6:11 Though great men make great events, even as great events call forth great men, they are not always the children of fortune. Success and acclaim do not always attend their undertakings, but whether they rise or fall is of lesser importance than how they rise and fall. It is not what a man does that makes him great, but what he strives to achieve.

MPR:6:12 The greatest men have no memorial if their endeavours were unpopular or not crowned with success. For every great man with a memorial, there are a thousand unknown and unhonoured.

MPR:6:13 The Real Man remains unperturbed by the whims of life. He does not flinch before misfortune or ease his head when fortune smiles upon him. When misfortune descends upon his head, and his hopes and dreams are shattered, he does not go about lamenting in a loud voice, but quietly continues his daily task.

MPR:6:14 If fortune is gracious towards him, he braces himself and is not overwhelmed; for he knows that often it takes a better man to bear the bounty of fortune than to bear the burden of misfortune.

MPR:6:15 The spirit of the Real Man does not bow before the blows of misfortune, no matter how grievous its afflictions. His calmness deflects its arrows, and his fortitude breaks its thrust. The shield of cheerfulness and the sword of courage, he never discards in despair.

MPR:6:16 His contentment is not dependent upon the whims of capricious fortune, and therefore, he is not cast down by her indifference. Like the metal measure, he is unchanging under all stresses; but the weakling, like the balances of the scales, is always moving up and down.

MPR:6:17 The Real Man stands before adversity as a rock before the raging seas, firm in the midst of turmoil, solid and calm against the fury. His mind forms great designs, and his spirit delights in their execution. His ideas grow up; they are never stillborn, nor do they wither before maturity.

MPR:6:18 The examples of great men shine before him as visions in the night, and their precedents walk with him by day. His high-hearted love of life exalts the spirit within him. He strains at the traces and is impatient for the run.

MPR:6:19 He rises above the rock of opposition and splits it in twain as does the sapling. He is like a great oak, which rises above the shrubbery in the darkness and shakes out its branches in the glory above.

MPR:6:20 He has compassion on the blind man; he helps the lame man, and he guards the deformed and afflicted against the mockery of weaklings.

MPR:6:21 He carries himself with the dignity becoming a man; he remains unshaken in calamity. Deceit and hypocrisy are things far beneath him; he has an air of quiet confidence and courage to speak the truth. The thoughts of his heart are the words of his mouth, and whatever he promises is as good as done.

MPR:6:22 The Real Man is he, who serves the purpose of God and carries out His plan. Because of him, all men rejoice for what they are, and the weakling, he carries as his burden.

MPR:6:23 The crown of glorious manliness is on his head; the mantle of courage is about his shoulders; he stands out from others in the pride and glory of his manhood.

MPR:6:24 He treasures womanhood and the dreams of men; he is the master of Earth and the lord of creation. Nothing more is required of man on Earth than that he be a Real Man. This is a sufficient objective and difficult enough for any man to achieve.

MPR:6:25 Manhood is a state of freedom, but its stronghold is in the spirit of a man. The body may be held forcibly in bondage, but the spirit cannot be shackled. He who lies imprisoned in the lowest dungeon may be more free than he who walks above with a servile spirit holding him in thraldom. Servility is the brand of the weakling.

MPR:6:26 Never judge a man according to his estate or circumstances, but accept him as a man according to his state of manliness. He that is manly hold as a man, even though he be your enemy, but he who is less than a man hold accordingly, though he be with you. For were your enemy a lesser man, he might proffer a hypocritical friendship, and thus destroy you by treachery. It is well never to forget that some friends might be enemies, were they better men. Therefore, the measure of a friend's manliness may also be the gauge of his sincerity.

MPR:6:27 A Real Man does not debase or humiliate the manliness of a defeated foe, for in so doing, he reveals his own baseness. It is well to remember that he who fights against you does so in the light of his own truth, and Truth is not the pawn of battles.

MPR:6:28 A Real Man is hardy, tenacious and brave. He is gentle with women and hearty with men. He disciplines himself according to the manly code. He is generous and hospitable. He is alert and audacious. Comfort, intemperance and over indulgence make weaklings. Struggle, adversity and self-control make Real Men.

MPR:6:29 A Real Man is a real man, and no power outside himself can take away his manliness. He is upright and strong, with a full measure of respect for himself. He is a man of deeds and not an idler. In manner, he is quiet and discreet; he is prudent in all things, and with all these qualities go generosity, good nature and reserve.

MPR:6:30 Be not a loud-mouthed bag of wind, for quietness within a man is as a rock, against which the tempest-driven waves of wrath and rage; rashness and haste dash in vain.

MPR:6:31 It is far easier to be a weakling than to be a Real Man. Were the Earth less harsh or the circumstances of life less austere, man would destroy himself before the shrine of the languid goddess. Only Real Men can with safety destroy the tangled forests and wilderness of Earth and make from them gardens, but will those, who inherit the gardens be Real Men? The Law decrees that they must be, or the wilderness will reclaim its own.

MPR:6:32 He who would live in a garden must labour in the sun and subdue the soil. He who is content to live in the wilderness may sleep in the shade, but he is a slave of life.

MPR:6:33 The Real Man stands out above all others; his head is high, his footfall firm. His bearing is dignified, his face calm, his hand steady, his heart tranquil. He sweeps aside all obstacles in his way; he proceeds, though all the dream fiends and powers of darkness seek to bar his way. Where is he, who can gather the Real Men together and make them rulers of all men, that Earth may resound with glory and greatness?

Chapter Seven – The Weakling

MPR:7:1 The burden of the Real Man and the shame of the Earth is the weakling. He frustrates the Plan of God and degrades all men. The weakling is wicked of heart, for wickedness comes easily to men. It is easier to be wicked than to be good; it is easier to be weak than to be strong, the weakling is one, who takes the easy path.

MPR:7:2 The soul of the wicked man is wrapped in a winding sheet of hate, and corruption eats his spirit. He mocks, for mockery is an overspill of poison brewed in little hearts. The Real Man would rather be hated than mocked, for while men hate, cowards mock.

MPR:7:3 The weakling fawns upon the rich and strong; he oppresses the weak and his joy is the molestation of widows and the unprotected. He cannot show respect for anyone greater than himself, for all men are his superiors. Therefore, he shows a hypocritical respect only when profitable to himself.

MPR:7:4 He cringes before the powerful and wrecks his will upon the helpless. His face is pressed into the dust before the seats of the mighty, but his foot is heavy upon the necks of the lowly. Goodness and duty are beyond his understanding, in as much as the evil in his nature corrupts his spirit and renders him incapable of worthy deeds or noble service.

MPR:7:5 The weakling is one, in whom evil destroys the good. In the Real Man, goodness vanquishes evil.

MPR:7:6 In the hour of danger the weakling quails, his feeble spirit wilts and his thoughts are confused, everything he does is confounded. In the day of misfortune's blast, he sinks into the morass of cowardice and is overwhelmed by the black mire of despair. Abandon him to his fate, lest he drag you down to destruction.

MPR:7:7 The very fear of a coward attracts the attention of misfortune and exposes him to danger. By quailing under poverty, he succumbs to meanness, and by tamely bearing insults he invites assault. He feasts on the misfortunes of the weak and unprotected; the carcass left by the lion feeds the hyenas. Destruction follows in his footsteps, for it is easier to destroy than to build.

MPR:7:8 There is no respect for his person or possessions, and his wife is open to the leers of fornicators and the jeers of her sisters. The weakling is not one weak in body, but one who is weak in spirit. Neither does strength of body make the Real Man, for manliness is of the spirit, not of the flesh.

MPR:7:9 A weakling will even marry a common woman, whose husbands are five hundred, for his servile spirit rejoices in debasement.

MPR:7:10 Mankind is divided in twain; Real Men and weaklings, take your place with one or the other, for they will never be reconciled.

Chapter Eight – Attitudes of the Real Man - 1 Towards the Poor and Weak

MPR:8:1 Lend your arm to the aged, and open your purse at the cry of the poor. Guard well against the urge to plunder the unprotected and from treating the destitute with harshness.

MPR:8:2 If you are lacking in compassion, it is well to remember that today, one man be rich and another poor; yet, ere a year has passed the rich man may be working in a stable, and the poor man may be clothed in fine linen. Such are the balances of life, and it is, therefore, wise to turn a like countenance towards all men.

MPR:8:3 Help the man in unfortunate circumstances, for anyone can fall into the pit of misfortune. Commit no assault upon him by reason of his weakness, nor turn his predicament to your own advantage. Fill his stomach with bread and drink. Provide a place for him to lay his head. Let your countenance be cheerful towards him, and let words of encouragement fall from your lips.

MPR:8:4 Assess honestly the boundaries of the widow's estate. The land that is lost to the plough is the waste of a man's lifetime.

MPR:8:5 Do not deride the clumsy speech of a lowly man. The fine phrases of the rich man may be pretty things of no substance. Sincerity is rarely bedecked with finery. What a man has in his head and heart is more important than the fine words that fall from his lips.

MPR:8:6 An honest man is slow of speech, he fumbles for words and is confused, but his eye is straight. The wily man is quick of speech, his wits are ever sharp from constant use.

MPR:8:7 The Just God turns a ready ear towards the outcry of the lowly. Therefore, the prayer of the poor man is greater than the might of sharp weapons, even though he is of no account among the people of his own time and destitute of the power of fine speech.

MPR:8:8 If you see an aged man staggering with the fullness of potent drink, lend him your arm, that his indignity may be lessened. Treat your elders with respect in the presence of their children. Sit not while an older man stands, or while the weak and afflicted have no seat.

MPR:8:9 If any man, himself being powerful, robs the helpless, he shall be your enemy. Nor shall he be your enemy in secret, for this would make you a hypocrite. If you see injustice, hide it not in your heart, but cry it from the housetops.

MPR:8:10 Even though you lose your life thereby and your possessions are lost to your children, have no dealings with the robber of the weak and the oppressor of the helpless. Of his estate, he is unworthy, and it is just that it be taken from him.

MPR:8:11 The Real Man is the protector of the unprotected and counsellor of the ignorant, for there will always be those, who abuse power and strength to oppress them. They will rob the poor, oppress the afflicted, exploit the helpless man and seduce the ignorant maiden from the household of her father. They burden the Earth, and the Real Man knows how to deal with them. He shall wield the sword of vengeance in the name of the High God, and justice shall not weep outside the courtyard.

MPR:8:12 Manliness carries its burden of responsibility. It is not a gown of fine linen but a coat of mail.

Chapter Nine – 2 Towards Wealth

MPR:9:1 If God has endowed you with riches, then regard them with pleasure, for the means to good deeds is in your hands.

MPR:9:2 It is not sufficient for a rich man to give to the poor or to alleviate the distress of the needy. He who, having received abundance from God, doles out a pittance to the poor, does but salve his conscience and is not truly walking with God.

MPR:9:3 It is the duty of the rich man to cast the weight of his riches in the balances, that goodness may outweigh evil.

MPR:9:4 It is the duty of the powerful man to range his might alongside the forces of good in the struggle against evil. He shall protect the poor against the exploiter and defend the weak against oppression of tyrants.

MPR:9:5 It is not so important to give to the poor man as to remove the cause of his poverty. To help the weak is good but of lesser importance than to attack their oppressor.

MPR:9:6 The Law decrees that the lot of no two men shall be alike. If it were otherwise, Earth could not fulfil its purpose. But he who has riches or is powerful or handsome, he who has intellect and skill, should bear in mind that he possesses these under the Law. According to the bounty bestowed, so must be the return to the general welfare of man, and a proper accounting will be demanded by the Assessors in the Hall of Terror.

MPR:9:7 No man is the absolute possessor of riches or estate, for his period of ownership must duly come to an end. Rather is he the trustee of the riches at his command, and he should regard them accordingly.

MPR:9:8 Look for the man of merit, and see that he does not go unrewarded. Encourage the craftsman and promote useful works. Let your wealth serve all men and not be dissipated in selfish indulgences.

MPR:9:9 Seek out the promoters of poverty and distress and cast your riches in the balances against them. Do not expect life to reward you or even grant you peace or pleasure. The powerful and strong will be your enemies, and even those you serve will betray. You will not be acclaimed and may even be derided as a fool, only your soul will remain steadfast beside you.

MPR:9:10 A rich man is not wicked because of his riches, for this of itself neither makes a man wicked nor makes him good. It is the manner, whereby he deals with his riches that determines a man's status.

MPR:9:11 Live in moderate comfort, and maintain a position according to your estate. Stint not in the acquisition of learning and things of beauty. Shun ostentation and publicity, for these are props of the weakling.

MPR:9:12 The riches, which exceed your modest requirements are superfluous to your welfare. It is by your dealings with the surplus that you will be judged.

MPR:9:13 There is little advantage in the mere possession of riches; the advantage is gained in knowing how to use them. Wait not until men come seeking your compassion; find them first and assist them without desiring praise or benefit.

MPR:9:14 Let not your generosity be hampered by the riches you have; rejoice in their possession, for if used for good, your pleasure is without blame. But he who stores up riches beyond his needs and puts them to no good use swathes his soul in the wrappings of death.

MPR:9:15 If rich, become not puffed up because of your possessions, or if poor, be not downhearted, for God in His goodness metes out happiness to both.

MPR:9:16 Count not upon your friends if you are rich and powerful, for they are untried. Can a man of title and position ever be sure he is loved and respected for himself? If the poor man is held in high regard, he can be happy in the assurance that it is for himself alone, and he is at peace.

MPR:9:17 Possessions and position attract friends as honey attracts bees, but it is adversity which winnows them. Men test gold for its value, and gold tests men for their worth.

MPR:9:18 To gather riches for their own sake corrupts the soul, but to deal with them to the benefit of others beautifies the soul. See the face of the miser and imagine the dark horror it dimly reflects, and behold the face of the benevolent man, does it not mirror the radiance within?

MPR:9:19 If on Earth, man is to learn the eternal values, he must be taught through the perception of earthly values. The contrast of riches and poverty serves its end.

Chapter Ten – 3 Towards Servants

MPR:10:1 Be just to your servant if you expect faithful service from him, and if you would have his obedience, be reasonable in your commands.

MPR:10:2 The spirit of manhood is in the slave, yes, it even slumbers in the craven-hearted. Undue harshness towards your subordinates may create a fear of, you but you will never command their love and respect.

MPR:10:3 Mitigate reproof with kindness and temper authority with reason. So shall the labour of your servants become a pleasure and your benefit therefrom be the greater.

MPR:10:4 He serves faithfully who is motivated by gratitude. Loyalty follows in the train of respect.

MPR:10:5 No man knows what events lie in the womb of the future, or what calamities lurk in the shadows of days yet to come. When evil times fall upon a man, it is the trusted servant who will sustain him. When dissatisfaction is rife among the servants, it is a time of calamity.

MPR:10:6 If in return, you fail to reward loyalty and diligence, then you are unworthy of honest service.

MPR:10:7 Deflect no man from the proper course of his duty, for this is a contemptible thing. Steal not the loyalty of a servant from his master, for this is unworthy of a man.

MPR:10:8 A master who treats a faithful servant meanly is an unworthy person, and whatever his titles and estate fit only to be classed among common pinchpurses.

Chapter Eleven – 4 Towards Superiors

MPR:11:1 The state of servitude has many advantages, for it escapes the cares and decisions of authority. He who serves faithfully may feel no shame in servitude. The loyal servant walks among the concourse with unbowed head.

MPR:11:2 Be faithful to the trust, which your master reposes in you, that you may be more trusted and become greater. The time and labour, for which he pays belong to him and if dealt with indifferently, are a fraud against him.

MPR:11:3 Hold your tongue in check when making answer to him, who is your chief. Do not revile him privately, for this is the way of a coward. Do not abuse men who are greater than you, for this is an admission that you can never be like them.

MPR:11:4 Never injure the arm that protects you or undermine the supports for the roof that shelters you.

MPR:11:5 Be prudent in your statements, and never let another's speech fall upon you like a noose, so that you must uncoil it by means of your answer.

MPR:11:6 Consult with your superiors pleasantly and quietly, acknowledging your position as a subordinate. Take care not to stir them up against you. At all times bear yourself like a man, for servitude does not entail servility.

MPR:11:7 A man's position in the community does not indicate his status in life. Though the governor may appear to be noble in his position and with his titles, he may resemble the sacred crocodiles m cruelty and rapacity.

MPR:11:8 When in the presence of your superior, do not press forward unduly or speak in a loud voice, for this will bring you unfavourably to his attention. If you are made unimportant in the presence of your chief, nevertheless conduct yourself with dignity and reserve, and let not your self-command depart from you.

MPR:11:9 Never answer a man in authority when you are wrathful but remove yourself quietly from his presence. Return a soft answer, when he utters words that rankle, and thus he will be pacified, and you will display your self-command and restraint.

MPR:11:10 Answers that provoke those in authority will become rods for your back and staves that strike you down. The wrath of your superiors will react unfavourably upon your affairs.

MPR:11:11 He who remains silent under provocation is the better man, but if provoked too far, then it is a time for action, for neither silences nor words are adequate.

MPR:11:12 He serves best who serves silently. The trusted servant is he, who keeps his tongue in check. A wagging tongue has its roots in a quaking heart.

MPR:11:13 Go quietly about your task; the reward is your own self-respect, knowing that it is well done.

MPR:11:14 It is harder to be efficient than to be inefficient, therefore inefficiency is the mark of the weakling.

MPR:11:15 Loyalty and diligence are qualities of the Real Man. The weakling is irresponsible and slothful.

MPR:11:16 The path of duty is difficult and beset with problems, therefore it is shunned by the weakling, who prefers to take the easy way.

MPR:11:17 The Real Man finds satisfaction in his craft, the satisfaction of the weakling lies in unproductive foolishness.

Chapter Twelve – 5 Towards the Wrongdoer

MPR:12:1 Abandon the wrongdoer and the worker of iniquity to the dyke, that the rising floodwaters may engulf them; thus, their ways shall no longer cause disruption among the people. Let them be seized by the storm fiend in the midst of the rising waters.

MPR:12:2 The lawbreaker and worker of wickedness are to be cast forth from the body of the people, that it remain healthy. The purveyors of filth and the fornicators will be met by the strong arms of Real Men. The day itself will stand up and make an accusation against their abominable doings, and the night will spew them forth.

MPR:12:3 If the sons of wickedness say, "Lend us your arm in the shadows; let us set a trap for the unwary, that his goods may pass into our possession. Let us strike down from behind and leave his body in the gutter," or "Let us possess ourselves of his gold by sly means and thus become rich ourselves," or "Come, cast in your lot with us, that by our joint endeavours we shall become wealthy," walk not along the paths with such as they, for as they lurk for blood so shall their own blood be requited.

MPR:12:4 The wrath of Real Men and Upright Men against the wrongdoers and workers of wickedness is like the hot blast that precedes the sandstorm, and before it, the strength of the evildoer shrivels and becomes nothing.

MPR:12:5 The wrongdoer becomes a slave to his own wickedness; therefore do that which is right, and your spirit shall remain free.

MPR:12:6 It is not sufficient for the Real Man that he turn away from wickedness. He is the fighting man of God, and his duty is to combat evil wherever he finds it.

MPR:12:7 He who sees an evildoer at work and remains silent is an accomplice. He who remains inactive in the presence of evil condones the deed. That which is not actively opposed is encouraged.

MPR:12:8 The slanderer and gossipmonger shall be cast forth, for their ways are evil. The fornicator and seducer shall feel the strong arms of Real Men and regret their deeds. The thief and trickster shall be removed, and the murderer shall forfeit his life. The adulterer and those who dispense sorrow shall not go unpunished, but overlook not that, which induces him to follow the paths of wickedness. Is it just to cut off the hand to punish the heart?

MPR:12:9 Weaklings encourage wickedness by their weakness, Real Men cast it out by their strength.

MPR:12:10 That which benefits man is good and accords with the Plan of God; that which is against the welfare of man is evil. But who among men is wise enough to know what is good and what is evil? Therefore, inscribe the writings of wisdom on your heart, that you never lack a guide in the dark alleyways of perplexity.

Chapter Thirteen – The Unstable Man

MPR:13:1 There is a man half way between the Real Man and the weakling, it is the unstable man. He wavers and is undecided; in thinking he displays a woman's weaknesses; he wrings his hands in the face of calamity and makes no move.

MPR:13:2 Take hold of yourself; be a man. Though now, you have a body given over to weaknesses, the soul within has a reserve of resolution. Call it forth, and it will serve you well.

MPR:13:3 Forget the things, wherein you are strong, for they need no attention. Consider your weaknesses and failings, and keep them ever in sight. Beware the weakness of indecision, for a bad decision is better than no decision at all. Beware of irresolution; better is it to journey along the wrong path than never to start.

MPR:13:4 What can you call to your aid against these grey-shrouded adversaries; is it not the strength of resolution and determination?

MPR:13:5 The unstable man knows he is changeable, like the thistledown, a plaything of the wind, but he knows not why. Though he knows he escapes from himself, he knows not how. O man of thistledown, be firm with yourself; be inflexible in following a course that is right. Thus, when they learn to rely on you, the eyes of men will regard you with esteem.

MPR:13:6 Set out a code of conduct peculiar to yourself and at all times abide by it. Never betray the principles you set yourself, and thus, you will find the road to stability. He who has no rules to abide by is like a vessel, which has lost its steeling oar, or as an unmanned chariot.

MPR:13:7 Suppress the desires that rise to dominate you. Relinquish the urges that drive to misfortune, and the peace reigning within will not be disturbed by anxiety and disappointment.

MPR:13:8 The unstable man spreads the restlessness and uneasiness, which eat his spirit, as dogs spread fleas. None can enjoy ease and contentment who joins his company.

MPR:13:9 He who has no code to live by is like the weathervane turning with every change of wind. Today he loves, and tomorrow he hates, today he argues this way, and tomorrow that way, and he himself knows not why he changes. Now hot, now cold, he is never constant and none can place faith in him.

MPR:13:10 Today he is arrogant, and tomorrow servile, but this flows from the weakness of his nature, for he who is arrogant without power will be servile when none demands servility.

MPR:13:11 What is life to such as he but shadows cast on the sand. Before noon, he is merry, and after noon down in the depths of gloom. Now, he rides high on the wings of ecstasy, shortly to be plunged into the very abyss of despair. One moment, he laughs; the next he sighs. He walks in the door determined; inside he becomes shiftless. He himself never knows what he is or may quickly become. Can any structure of contentment be built on such a shifty foundation? Foolish is the woman who marries an unstable man, for her future is uncertain.

Chapter Fourteen – The Mean Man

MPR:14:1 A mean man is one who walks in unmanly ways; he has womanly weaknesses, much magnified, without womanly virtues. He forever seeks faults in the ways of the wise and the good.

MPR:14:2 He lacks generosity and compassion; he winnows the dust off his storehouse floor to save a few dirty grains. The heart of a mean man is as the sands of the wilderness, which swallow up all the pleasant flowers that fall and bring forth nothing in return.

MPR:14:3 He who rises eagerly to claim praise for a successful undertaking and just as readily casts blame on another when it goes awry, is not only mean, but also a weakling and a hypocrite unto himself.

MPR:14:4 None is worse than the mean man who has riches and estate, for he rides heavily on the backs of his servants and waxes fat on the sweat of their brows.

MPR:14:5 He is without compassion or feeling, and the ruin of his brother brings him no sorrow. For the increase in his riches, he secretly rejoices in the death of his father; but the mean man, being also hypocritical, will be loudest in lamentation.

MPR:14:6 His soul is set hard in the distorted shape moulded by avarice, and even grief and distress can make no modifying impression. What are the miseries of poverty compared with the fate awaiting him beyond the Dark Portal?

MPR:14:7 The beast of the pastures, when fed, show their pleasure and it is not beyond them to show thankfulness, but only man has the nature granting him the ability to show gratitude. The mean man, therefore, denies his own nature, for true gratitude is beyond him, though he amply displays its outward manifestation.

MPR:14:8 The large-hearted man gladly acknowledges a benefit received and seeks all ways to repay his benefactor. If, however, to do so lies beyond his ability, he cherishes the deed evermore in his heart. The mean-hearted man quickly forgets, for the obligation bears too heavily on his small spirit.

MPR:14:9 His mean heart even envies the ability of the benefactor to give, and he accepts the benefit with inner ill grace. Though profuse with outward hypocritical smiles and fair words, his beaming countenance conceals the malicious darkness of the hidden heart within.

MPR:14:10 The mean man and the braggard may seem incompatible, but man is a many-sided creature. The mean and miserly heart and the most boastful tongue so often share the same body. The busiest tongue has the least cause to wag, what does it seek to cover up?

MPR:14:11 The mean man is a coward and so finds pleasure by inflicting suffering on the helpless. The hyena tears at the dead beast he would not dare face while living, but the hunting hound that caught it does not rend it. Only cowardly things find pleasure in mangling that, which lies helpless in their power.

Chapter Fifteen – Women

MPR:15:1 There are two categories of womankind, wives or potential wives, and women of pleasure. The first of these are the intended mates of men, their companions and comforters, the mothers of their children and the goddesses of their hearths. The others become their companions in carnal pleasure; they dally with them, then cast them aside, and they pass on to the embrace of other uncaring men.

MPR:15:2 Each woman decides which category she will join, and that is her chosen path. Never confuse the two kinds of women, lest you eat out your heart in sorrow and regret. It is decreed by the nature of things that womankind should fall into two groups, and each woman is to be dealt with according to the category, in which she has placed herself.

MPR:15:3 What kind of woman can be without a household? Only one who is cast out or has run away because of her misdeeds.

MPR:15:4 Avoid the singing woman, whose ways are frivolous; she is beautiful but her beauty is like the honey in the honeypot, it attracts many flies, and they pollute it.

MPR:15:5 Guard yourself against the wiles of a woman from a strange country, whose city and household are not known. Who are her people? What are her ways? From what has she flown? From her mother's solicitude and her father's supervision? As she leaves them to sorrow, so will she depart from you. Or does she flee her own reputation?

MPR:15:6 When the feelings of a wanton woman are deadened, as the edge of an axe is deadened by constant use, she ceases to please. She becomes as the wassailing cup passed around many times. Then, she flees from the place where she is known and lays her trap among strangers, and he who asks no questions takes her into his household and drains the polluted dregs that remain.

MPR:15:7 Avoid the flattering woman who would beguile you with words. Shun her who repudiates woman's covenant with the Creating God, who casts the treasures of womanhood lightly before men. Her hand guides along the path of sorrow; her embrace leads to the soul's desolation. She shatters the dreams of man; she is a traitor to womankind, the betrayer of womanhood.

MPR:15:8 By the unclean embrace of the wanton woman, a man may be brought down to destruction. The adulteress lies in wait to suck the happiness of a family; a failure in her own home, she seeks gratification in the ruination of another.

MPR:15:9 Adulterate the household of no man by lying with a woman thereof. Men do not despise a thief if he steals because he is hungry, but all men despise the adulterer who takes what is not his to vent his own lust.

MPR:15:10 If you commit adultery, then prepare to flee, for men will arise against you. For if they revile not the adulterer, nor raise their arms against him, then it is a time of the nation's degradation, and all men must look to their own wives. If men fail to punish the adulterer, then they encourage the seduction of their own women. In the land of weaklings, the adulterer hunts freely, for who will oppose him? Is it not written, "That, which is not punished is condoned?"

MPR:15:11 He who accepts meekly the seduction of a woman of his household is a weakling and coward, and unworthy of the mantle of manhood.

MPR:15:12 He who turns his face and sees not the seduction of another's wife encourages the adulterers and establishes their place among the people.

MPR:15:13 All men who are men are jealous of the sanctity of their hearth and home, and the righteous wrath of a wronged husband shall overwhelm the guilty ones. His is the day of vengeance, and no gifts shall appease him.

MPR:15:14 The man who declines to strike a blow in defence of his home and honour is a weakling and coward. Men turn from him in disgust or he sickens their stomachs, while women despise him.

MPR:15:15 He who suffers in defending the sanctity of womanhood suffers in the cause of God, who made woman the Guardian of the Portal of Life. In the land of Real Men she reigns as goddess of heart, hearth and home.

MPR:15:16 When a woman whose husband is absent displays her beauty and encourages your visit; when she arranges that there be no witnesses and prepares her net for you, then is the hour of your manhood's trial. Depart from her house, for it is a place of evil. He who defiles the home of another cannot be justly wrathful if his own is defiled.

MPR:15:17 It is not the way of a Real Man to defile the house of another in his absence; only weaklings sneak around furtively to gratify their body lust in another's domain.

MPR:15:18 If you are unfortunate and unwise enough to love the wife of another man, then degrade not that love by expressing it in dark corners like a cur. Go to the husband, like a man, and let events happen as they will.

MPR:15:19 If you wish to be welcomed in the household, to which you are in the habit of going, always treat the womenfolk with reserve. Thus, you will not be regarded with disfavour and will be trusted by your host. If he has daughters, he will say in his heart, "Such a man can be trusted with my daughters' welfare, for he is circumspect and a man of honour."

MPR:15:20 A man who is not prudent casts an appraising eye over the womenfolk, and his host is insulted, for no woman of his household is indecent.

MPR:15:21 Be not bedazzled by beauty alone. A beautiful tree with gay flowers rarely bears an abundant harvest. As a fire is beautiful and useful when restrained within the fireplace, but a thing of destruction when loose, so is the beauty of a woman when not kept in restraint by virtue.

MPR:15:22 The beauty of a chaste woman inspires a man to greatness and to high accomplishments, that he may possess it, but the beauty of a harlot leads him along the paths of dissipation and improvidence.

MPR:15:23 Men will strive and attain great things to satisfy their desire but will cease their efforts if it be cast at their feet.

MPR:15:24 The beauty of womanhood was ordained to inspire man, and of all things it is his greatest incentive to achievement. Therefore, a woman's secrets are not to be lightly attained.

MPR:15:25 The evil of the harlot is that she counters the inspiration of womanhood. Her wickedness is her cheapness.

MPR:15:26 The pleasures of a harlot are of the body and exist only for the moment, to pass into nothingness like a dream. What have you given? For it is the loss of men.

MPR:15:27 The vigour of manhood that bears man along the path of great things may be also a weapon in the hands of evil, but the weapon remains sheathed until placed in the hands of a wanton woman.

MPR:15:28 The harlot sets her trap; the toils of the net are soft and supple; the weakling is caught easily and even better men are caught by deceit. The soul of a man is bruised and the power of womanhood is weakened.

MPR:15:29 The bait of a wanton woman may be seen from afar; it is attractive and alluring; the hook is well hidden. Her glance is bold, she seeks the attentions of men and spreads out her temptations. Her allurements are well displayed, for has she not had much experience?

MPR:15:30 Her limbs are soft and shapely; her attire loose and inviting; her eyes speak silently of furtive pleasures; her bosom invites the caress of lust. Her smile softens the heart, and her tongue kindles the fire of desire. The smoothness of her tongue overcomes reserve and her soft manner closes the eyes of wisdom.

MPR:15:31 She is familiar with the ways and weaknesses of men and well practised in the gratification of their bodies. She anticipates success, for her victims are not few. She satisfies the lustful desires of the body, but how does she serve the spirit? What does she do with man's highest dreams of womanhood?

MPR:15:32 Fly from her allurements, and close your ears to her words of false endearments; they are well worn from practice on many. If you give heed to her languishing glances or listen to the soft words that fall from her lips, if you yield yourself to the warm embrace of her arms, then you sacrifice your manhood at the altar of lust.

MPR:15:33 If she binds you as with a spell, when your eyes become open, you will know the meaning of shame. Poverty and slothfulness follow in the train of the wanton; misery and remorse will be your lot.

MPR:15:34 Your manliness will be sapped by dissipation; your body, pampered by luxury and softened by sloth, will become enfeebled, your limbs will weaken and your health depart. The glow of strength and the joy of living will be gone. There will be no tender arms to hold you with compassion or eyes to regard you tenderly. None to listen to your griefs with understanding, for you have chosen the path of the fornicator. Gentle women will withdraw from your presence, and nought is to be wrung from the heart of a wanton, for only her body is soft.

MPR:15:35 Therefore, be wise in your dealings with women, and to be wise is to be prudent and strong. Reject that, which is cast before you, for it will be shared with many men. Seek only that, which is desirable in its near unattainability, for it will be yours alone.

MPR:15:36 Be wise, and avoid the sweet enticements of the wanton and the lustful inducements of the harlot, and allow not your heart to be trapped by enchanting mirages of love.

MPR:15:37 The woman who is cheap will receive many offers of silver, but none of gold.

MPR:15:38 Man has many chisels, wherewith to fashion the form of his immortal soul, and among them, none is so sharp as the hard chisel of desire. Therefore beware, lest in the fullness of youth, you fall prey to the allurements of the wanton woman who will cause you to degrade your manhood and cut shameful strokes by the excesses she offers for your delight.

MPR:15:39 She will entice you with a false sweetness, which disguises the bitter soul-corroding draught. Her charms are delusions, which will blind your eyes and benumb your feelings. Drink at the tainted well if you must, but never after shall you be free of its taint, and never after shall you enjoy the pure waters of love in their refreshing fullness.

MPR:15:40 How drab the wanton beside the chaste woman who stands bedecked in radiant virtue and dignified modesty! Whose glory puts the brilliance of the starlit nightskies in the shade; her influence for good is among the greatest earthly powers. She moulds the destinies of men in purity and wholesomeness, and in her hands, the hammer strikes the chisel to fashion a form of glory.

MPR:15:41 The chaste woman is soft and gentle, modest and kind; her glance quickens the beat of all but the hardest heart, and her touch quietens the raging storms in the most troubled. Her eyes shine with womanly innocence and she is garbed in simplicity and truth. Her exclusive kisses are sweet as the fresh-plucked, dew-cooled grape, and the breath from her lips is as a warmly-soft-perfumed breeze.

MPR:15:42 Close the doors of your spirit against the destructive assaults of deforming passions, and open your heart to the tenderness of love. Its pure gentle flame shall inspire the soul to sublime heights of glory and softly mould it into a magnificent form of perfection.

Chapter Sixteen – Choosing a Wife

MPR:16:1 It is the nature of things that man should take unto himself a wife, and the Law decrees the need of man for woman. But not every kind of wood is fit to make an arrow, and not every woman makes a suitable wife.

MPR:16:2 Examine carefully the women of your acquaintance. Choose not hastily, nor fix your mind suddenly, for upon a proper choice depends your future contentment and joy and the welfare of your children.

MPR:16:3 Choose not according to face and form alone, for these will pass, though fairness of face and proportion of figure are not to be disregarded.

MPR:16:4 Observe your chosen one and consider her in your solitude. If her mind is over occupied with dress and adornment, if she laughs too much and talks too loud, if she has a roving foot for pleasure and a bold eye for men, if her manner is crude and her tongue inclined towards lewdness, then though her beauty were as that of the sun disc itself and her form shaped to perfection, turn from her path and set your heart against her charms. Dismiss from your mind the alluring phantoms of the imagination.

MPR:16:5 Your body may incline towards her, but it drags you towards sorrow. If her body calls and your heart says 'Nay,' then flee from her presence, and see her no more. The heart of a wise man chooses his wife, but the wife of a weakling and fool is chosen by his body.

MPR:16:6 When you find a maiden who can be your reasonable companion; who possesses a loyal and steadfast heart, sensitivity of spirit, pity and gentleness, delicacy of mind, softness of manner; who is intelligent and joyous and, with all this, has a lively spirit, gather her to your arms, for she is worthy indeed to be your wife. She will be prudent and temperate and a fitting mother for your children, and above all you will have a treasure beyond price. He who chooses a good mother for his children will find contentment and joy with his wife.

MPR:16:7 Judge not your chosen by your own opinions alone, for your eyes are clouded and your judgement confused. Judge her by the opinions of other men; is she sought by them as a wife, or is she one whom men follow for their pleasure?

MPR:16:8 The greatest gift that life can bestow upon a man is a good wife. Therefore, be diligent and prudent in your search, for a good wife is not gathered by the wayside.

MPR:16:9 In your search for a fitting wife you, will have many competitors, for though the divisions of men and women are nearly equal, many are the women who are unsuitable. Be diligent, lest to your sorrow, you find none left to choose from but those whom other men have passed over.

MPR:16:10 None but the fool takes to wife the common woman, for she has her price and is available to all; nor the weak woman, for she can be taken by any man.

MPR:16:11 Yet these, too, as their attractions wane, will seek a husband for their old age and, lacking the attractiveness of virtue, will set their trap for the unwary. They will find their prey among weaklings who care not about their wife's virtue, for they take secret pleasure in their own humiliation and debasement.

MPR:16:12 No man is more generous than he who marries a common woman, for he shares her with the multitude.

MPR:16:13 When You find a good woman, cherish her as your greatest treasure; let your kindness and consideration take possession of her heart. She is the mistress in your home, so treat her with respect, that the servants shall obey her, and the stranger treat her with diffidence. If a man treats not his wife with respect, can he take offence when other men, observing this, treat her likewise?

MPR:16:14 As she is the partner of your cares and the helpmate with your burdens, deny her not your companionship in pleasure. Be faithful and constant to her, for she is the mother of your children.

MPR:16:15 He who drinks water from his own fountain knows it to be clean. He who draws water from his own well knows it to be pure.

MPR:16:16 In times of affliction and pain, when your wife suffers in sickness or travail, soothe her with tender words and gentle countenance. A look of sympathy and a gesture of understanding from you will mitigate her trouble and be of more avail than the attention of many physicians.

MPR:16:17 Consider the delicacy of her womanhood and the frailty of her body. Comfort her in grief and bear with her weakness. Bring wisdom and understanding to your aid, for if in marriage one is wise, two are happy.

MPR:16:18 Do not marry while too young, for you have not experience enough to train your son; nor be too old, that you have not the patience. There is a mean in marriage, as in all things.

MPR:16:19 He who chooses his wife rashly or in haste spends slow years in regret and repentance.

MPR:16:20 The counsel of a wife is wise and bent to your own benefit, but the counsel of an outside woman serves her own ends.

MPR:16:21 Love your wife wholly, according to the dictates of your own heart, and rightly according to the statutes of men. Fill her stomach and clothe her back; provide her with oil for anointing and hair for her adornment. Keep her contented, and give her no cause for alarm or unrest. Be gentle with her, for she is a profitable field for your efforts.

MPR:16:22 Enter not into dispute with her, for women are gentle and withdraw their hearts before force. If you are harsh, she will return into herself. Make her home a joyful place.

MPR:16:23 An industrious wife is of more value than treasure; she endows her husband with peace and gladness, but a slovenly wife brings discontent into the dwelling place.

MPR:16:24 The husband of an unchaste woman lives in a den of suspicion. There is no greater restlessness than that of a husband apart from an untrustworthy wife.

MPR:16:25 A man loves his mother and his father, his sisters and his brothers, all his life, yet they are not of his choosing. How much more likely should it be that he would love his wife, whom he himself chooses? Or is man's judgement less wise than that of fate?

MPR:16:26 Nothing will ever bring you greater pleasure and joy than a good wife or more sorrow than a bad one. Yet of all things he does bearing on his life and future, a man generally uses the least wisdom when choosing a wife.

MPR:16:27 Be considerate, for the husband without consideration prepares his own betrayal.

MPR:16:28 There are two types of women, true women and common women. The common woman is a fitting mate for the weakling, and the true woman a fitting mate for the Real Man. But the dispensations of life are such that common women will desire Real Men for husbands, and weaklings will deceive true women. Therefore, the Real Man must be wise enough to know the difference between a common woman and a true woman, and a true woman must know the difference between a Real Man and a weakling.

MPR:16:29 To know and recognise the divisions of men and women is not only the first step to contentment, but it is the duty of a people, if it would remain wholesome. When the dividing line becomes blurred, nations decline.

MPR:16:30 It is easy enough to get a wife, but difficult to get a good one.

MPR:16:31 Marriage is like the fisherman's net, easy to get into but hard to escape from.

MPR:16:32 No man is the same after marriage. Either his joys are doubled and his sorrows halved, or his joys are halved and his sorrows doubled.

Chapter Seventeen – The Physical Body

MPR:17:1 My children, contemplate the nature of your own bodies. The fruits of the field provide the flesh, and the stones of the Earth the framework.

MPR:17:2 How wonderfully you are made, how precise and perfect is the construction of your earthly habitation. Who but the Greatest of Beings could have ordained its nature; who but a Master Architect could have planned it?

MPR:17:3 Among all creatures, you alone stand erect, that you may enjoy and admire the wondrous works of your Creator. Rejoice, therefore, in your form and in your body and in your powers.

MPR:17:4 Rejoice in the consciousness, whereby you experience and in the eternal soul within, whereby you know. The attributes of a god repose within you, and they are yours to command, if you will but call them forth.

MPR:17:5 Be kind to your body, which is the vehicle of your pilgrimage and the chariot of your conquest. Keep it in health and strength, that you may enjoy life with vigour. It was not meant that the body should be neglected, and in fact the Law ordains that recompense be made for a neglected body. A body made weak by dissipation and gross from fat-living is an abomination unto the God of Life.

MPR:17:6 On Earth, the body is equally as important as the soul. Keep it clean and in good health, that it may fittingly serve the purpose of the soul. The nearest approach that can be made to complete bliss on Earth is to enjoy the blessing of good health.

MPR:17:7 If you would reserve health unto yourself, even into the ripeness of old age, avoid the allurements of intemperance and dissipation. These are the bewitchments of the wanton and harlot, and not easily avoided.

MPR:17:8 When she spreads her delicacies before you, when her wine sparkles in the cups, when with sweet smiles, she induces you to cast care aside, then the hour of danger is at hand, and therefore, let prudence come to your aid. If you give heed to the sweet words of the temptress, then you are deceived and betrayed.

MPR:17:9 Flee from the bower of the harlot; her face and form are fair, but underneath, the core is rottenness. She is perfumed sweetly on the outside, but the odour of putrefaction lies within.

MPR:17:10 Her deceptive promises of joy are gates leading into the road to madness, and her pleasures lead to disease and death. Look around the board of the wanton woman; cast your eyes upon her guests, and observe those who have succumbed to her charms and follow her temptations. Are they not pale and puny ones; are they not weaklings without the spirit of men?

MPR:17:11 Away from the beguilement of false womanhood, from the tables of intemperance and the sideboards of gluttony! Go, seek your place in the company of Real Men. See, are they not upstanding, brave and active? They are surrounded by the halo of vigour; they vibrate with the song of vitality. Their arms are brawny and strong, and labour is to them as play to the child.

MPR:17:12 Their talk is virile and manly; they know the weaknesses of fornicators and mock the softness of she-men. Their passions are vanquished by self-command, and evil habits do not suck their spirits. They take their pleasures in moderation, and therefore, the enjoyment endures. Their hours of rest are few, but their sleep is deep and sound. Their hearts are serene and their bodies strong. Their thoughts are quick and their form lithe. They are men and the sons of men.

MPR:17:13 Rejoice, O man, in your body strength and cleanliness, and be not ashamed of your nature. Live in peace and contentment, for cakes of flour and water eaten with a contented heart serve the body better than fine meats eaten with strife and enmity.

MPR:17:14 Do not accustom yourself to lying in bed, while the dawn is breaking in beauty, for no man is wholesome unless he has knowledge of the dawn.

MPR:17:15 Remember that the call of the food table exceeds the needs of the body.

MPR:17:16 Do not weary yourself concerning the affairs of the day, nor be over anxious about your household and estate. Things happen; disaster or power come according to the dispensations of God. Follow your inclinations, and if your plans go awry, continue in peace. Do your best, and be content that you can do no more.

MPR:17:17 Let your heart be quiet within your body, and your body will not be unhealthy. It is the guest chamber of the soul; let the soul not abide in squalor.

MPR:17:18 God ordained the Law and laws, which govern the conduct of man and laws, which govern the ways of nature. Unnatural deeds bring unnatural afflictions in their train, and unnatural thoughts precede unnatural ills.

MPR:17:19 The soul of man within his body is like a conqueror in an occupied land. The laws of the victor conflict with the laws of the vanquished, but it is the greater law that must be obeyed, so both may live together in harmony.

MPR:17:20 Avoid the guilt of furtive and unmanly things, that you may walk with a high head and steady eyes.

MPR:17:21 It is wrongful for a man who cannot know woman to seek the sustenance of the serpent.

MPR:17:22 Your nose is ever ready to savour the sweetness of perfume, and your mouth delights in delicacies of the table. Your eye is ever alert for beauty. But remember that perfumes do not linger long in the nostrils, and delicacies destroy the appetite they arouse. Beauty seen too often ceases to stir the heart.

MPR:17:23 The rule is moderation in all things; turn from unmanly ways, follow the path of cleanliness, and avoid the indulgences of soft living and iniquity. Follow these rules, and sleep soundly; spend your waking hours in peace.

MPR:17:24 Enjoy life; take whatever it gives with high spirits. When it bestows contentment, be contented; when it presents the test, rise above it, and when disaster strikes, meet it like a man.

Chapter Eighteen – Man - The External Shell

MPR:18:1 Glorify your body; cherish it; keep it well, for it is the dwelling place of the soul. Is not such a master worthy of a well kept habitation? To revile or mortify the body is a wickedness, for thus, you desecrate the most glorious temple on Earth.

MPR:18:2 As ground must be prepared for the barley and clay kneaded for the wheel, so has your body to be prepared for the fulfilling of its purpose.

MPR:18:3 As the pilot steers the vessel and the husbandman directs the waters, so must your spirit command the flesh. Does the pilot let the vessel take charge, or the husbandman say to the waters, "Go your own way?"

MPR:18:4 Let the soul rule your body unchallenged, for if there be revolt, then you are torn asunder. Health is the reflection of harmony between soul and body.

MPR:18:5 With what do you smell, with your nose? Is not the nose intact on a corpse? And the eye, does it see when the spirit departs? Like an oar without an oarsman, like a sail without a wind, like a bow without a bowman, like a dwelling without an inhabitant, such is the body without a soul.

MPR:18:6 O man, who is both beast and god, see yourself for what you truly are. Say not, "I am this, or I am that;" be reasonable and see Truth. A tongue has been given you and the power of speech; use these, the powers that distinguish you from the beast, to teach your children wisdom and to discover for yourself the path of truth.

Chapter Nineteen – Man - The Eternal Essence

MPR:19:1 As the great sycamore resides in a tiny seed, so does your soul occupy your body. As the dark soil wherein the seed is planted to the sunlit splendour above, so is this life to the life beyond the tomb.

MPR:19:2 As health is to the body, so is conscience to the soul. If the body be sickly, there is a decline; if the soul be troubled, there is distress.

MPR:19:3 That man is a soul residing within a body is the most obvious of truths. Seek not to understand it too perfectly, for understanding is a quality of the soul, and this has to be awakened.

MPR:19:4 Is the moon different when hidden behind a cloudbank? Is the jar different buried under the sand? As these remain unchanged though unseen, so is the soul even within the body of a madman. If a lutestring be broken, even the greatest musician plays a false tune. Thus, the defectiveness displayed by the madman is caused by faults within the material instrument of earthly manifestation; it is not in the spirit behind.

MPR:19:5 Your soul came into the body as a new turn of the scroll; the sheet is clean, ready for use, but what you write thereon is recorded forever.

MPR:19:6 Your soul is as a newly cut block of marble, upon which every thought and deed strikes a blow. It is as fresh clay cast upon the potter's wheel.

MPR:19:7 You alone are the craftsman for the fashioning of your soul, you alone are the artist of the design. Is it a bright thing of joyous beauty formed by goodness, or is it a dark, corrupt horror deformed by vice and wickedness? Ask these things of your spirit, for only it knows what lies hidden within.

MPR:19:8 To nourish and groom the body is by no means undesirable, but take care that you neglect not the soul. The body comes, it grows and decays, the soul remains forever. Therefore, cherish the everlasting soul, for it is your own trueself.

MPR:19:9 As an alabaster jar in the hands of an infant, as a razor in the hands of a madman, even so is the soul in the hands of an irresponsible man.

Chapter Twenty – Wisdom

MPR:20:1 The first step towards being wise is to acknowledge the extent of your ignorance. Concern yourself with the vast amount of knowledge that you lack, and place no undue importance on that, which you possess. As womanly loveliness is best displayed in a modest garment, so is quiet behaviour and unpretentious bearing best becoming the wise.

MPR:20:2 Remember that all men are born equally into ignorance, and no man, whatever his estate, lacks the means to knowledge. True wisdom comes not from books and instruction but from observation and enquiry.

MPR:20:3 The learned scribe knows a thousand books, but what knows he about the ways of the grasshopper? The knowledge of a gardener brings him more joy than does knowledge to a magistrate. The life of a wilderness wanderer depends not on his knowledge of books but on his knowledge of the ways of the wilderness.

MPR:20:4 If you would not be deemed foolish in the eyes of others, then cast aside the desire to appear wise to your own edification. If you would appear wise among the foolish, then you will appear foolish among the wise.

MPR:20:5 A wise man speaks but rarely, and each word is a precious stone. The fool pours forth a torrent of words, but they are all dross. Words spoken with calm forthrightness are burnished with the lustre of Truth.

MPR:20:6 A wise man turns a deaf ear to his own praise; he does not know his own worth and is the last in discovering the greatest of his achievements.

MPR:20:7 No man is wise enough to know his own folly before he has committed it, but nothing is lost to the wise, for failure becomes his guide to success.

MPR:20:8 Man is great according to his wisdom; he succeeds according to his knowledge. Promotion and power are the prerogative of the wise, the lot of fools is a state of servitude. Those who shun wisdom's ways are foes unto themselves.

MPR:20:9 Follow your fathers of olden times, for theirs was the wisdom of God, which is the measure of the experience of man.

MPR:20:10 If wisdom now be held in low esteem, it is not wisdom's loss but the loss of man. Wisdom cries outside the palace and the hovel. She is heard in the streets and in the gathering places. Her voice says, "O fools and sons of fools, how long will you delight in your foolishness?" But the pleasure of fools is in their foolishness, and the pleasure of the weak is in their own weakness, and therefore, they scorn the voice of wisdom.

MPR:20:11 Let the fool eat of his tree; it will provide no sustenance in times of evil. When the whirlwind sweeps across the face of the land, bringing destruction in its wake, fools will be swallowed up, and Earth will be as if they had never been.

MPR:20:12 The nature of life is such that the fool does not always fail, nor is the wise man always successful. Yet failure will always be the attendant of fools and success the servant of the wise. But how is earthly success or failure measured in regions greater than Earth?

MPR:20:13 Wisdom is the food of the soul. The wise man nourishes his soul, and it grows in beauty and strength. The fool starves his soul, and it shrivels and is distorted by weakness.

MPR:20:14 He who has grown to wisdom never acts but at wisdom's command. To some has been granted the ability to soak up wisdom, as the sand soaks up water. If this be your gift from God, then hug it not to your own breast as would the mean man. Share it with those who are less wise for their instruction, and hide it not from the wise, for they will multiply it.

MPR:20:15 The wise man is less presumptuous than the fool. He has many doubts and changes his mind, for as wisdom grows, knowledge alters.

MPR:20:16 The fool fixes his mind in obstinacy; he is stubborn, and doubt does not disturb his placidity. He knows all things, except his own ignorance. The wise man is aware of his imperfections and continually strives for improvement. The fool forever counts his own small talents and is content. He boasts of his achievements in things which are of no account.

MPR:20:17 Thistledown floats on water for all to see, but a gemstone sinks below the surface. So does the fool shout his abilities to the wind, while a wise man keeps them hidden within himself. The goose brings forth its egg while at rest, and the tail of the peacock is displayed while it stands still. The deep, still pool holds the biggest fish, and the resting cow gives the most milk. So it is with the quiet man, who within himself, produces a fountain of strength at which lesser men drink and find refreshment and courage.

MPR:20:18 The heart of a fool flutters at a vain hope, but the wise man puts it behind him. Fools snap at one another, but wise men agree in peace.

MPR:20:19 Let reason rule all your desires, and let not your hopes reach out beyond the limits of probability. Thus, the chances of success bear down in your favour in the scales of fate, and your heart will not be burdened with disappointment.

MPR:20:20 The wise man does not need advice; the fool will not take it. Rebuke a fool, and he will dislike you; rebuke the wise, and they will hold you in regard. The fool does right in his own eyes, he justifies his deeds with a loud mouth. A wise man knows his limitations and seeks the advice of others, and if the advice is good, what matters who gives it? Accept the advice that is helpful even though it may not be palatable.

MPR:20:21 The man who is his own physician soon has no patient. Advice is good or bad irrespective of who gives it. Good counsel can come forth from the mouth of a fool, and bad counsel from the mouth of the wise. While good counsel is always carefully considered by the wise, fools brush it aside. What a fool wants to believe, he will. But never disdain the opinions of another or condemn them because they differ from yours. Might you not be wrong?

MPR:20:22 The man who thinks himself wise believes nothing until it is proven to him, but the wise man considers everything possible until it is disproved.

MPR:20:23 The wisest of men will do something foolish, and everything said and done by a fool is not folly.

MPR:20:24 Wisdom concerns itself only with the things, which are knowable. In matters that are forever unknowable, ignorance is the best wisdom.

MPR:20:25 Wisdom cannot enter a heart whose gates are barred with prejudice, nor penetrate a body filled with evil. The powers of the spirit enter into a man as guests; they will not come unbidden or remain unwelcome.

MPR:20:26 Wisdom is the fruit of past experience preserved for the future. It may be unappetising, but still it is nourishing and cannot be disregarded without the possibility of dire consequences.

MPR:20:27 The abode of the wise man is a sanctuary against despair, a fortress against the forces of discontent. His presence is as the gloom-dispelling sunlight, and his lips as the doors of a treasurehouse; they open, and gems pour forth.

Chapter Twenty-One – Courage

MPR:21:1 Perils and misfortunes, struggle, disappointment and pain are more or less the certain lot of every man. Therefore, it is meet that every man be fortified with courage and fortitude, that he may bear with appropriate resolution his allotted share of the burden of mankind.

MPR:21:2 As the ass plods along, labouring under its burden and suffering heat and thirst through the dangers of the burning sands of the wilderness, and falters not, so must the courage and fortitude of man sustain him through the dangers of life, which beset his way.

MPR:21:3 The timid man listens to the cry of his body; his limbs tremble, and his stomach turns to water. His littleness of heart has no place for courage and audacity.

MPR:21:4 The courageous man is one of God's men. He listens to his heart; his face is bold and his blow sure. His fierce countenance and audacious plans overwhelm his adversary. His opponent passes into his possession; his wife walks abroad with confidence and sleeps soundly.

MPR:21:5 The courageous man is never the slave of change and chance. His pleasures and contentment do not depend on the whims of fickle fortune; her smiles and frowns alike leave him unmoved, for he is alert and prepared to take on whatever comes his way.

MPR:21:6 Such is the man of courage. Though his stature be small and his body puny, his spirit raises him to supremacy over others. The courage of a man who lacks strength, or of one who is at a disadvantage, is greater than that of a powerful man attacking the same adversary.

MPR:21:7 Courage stands out alone as the greatest of all manly attributes, for without it, all others are endangered.

MPR:21:8 The man who lacks courage has nothing. Therefore, if you, being a father, rob your son of the example of manliness, then you have cheated him out of his birthright of unquestioned courage.

MPR:21:9 Courage and manliness are passed from father to son by example and instruction. These, every man can give, and though he be the poorest man of no account, by passing them on to his son, he leaves an inheritance beyond riches.

MPR:21:10 Courage, manliness and wisdom; no man can ask more, for unto these all desirable things will be duly added.

MPR:21:11 Courage is a quality of the spirit, not of the body. Its activity leaves its impress upon the soul, even as every cowardly deed is registered. Courage is the standard of the Real Man; timidity is the mark of the she-man and weakling.

MPR:21:12 Courage is not the absence of fear but the conquest of fear. Fear comes to the courageous and cowardly alike. The greatest courage is that, which cheerfully and stoutly fights a losing battle. Still it is unwise to frighten yourself with unfounded fears or burden yourself with unsubstantial figments of the imagination, for such things are unwholesome phantoms of the mire which would drag you down to destruction.

Chapter Twenty-Two – Contentment

MPR:22:1 The Law is immutable; it decrees the circumstances, which surround your sojourn on Earth. Yet, it has established that by the nature of things for all reasonable desires, all honest endeavours and for all normal requirements there is a probability of attainment and success.

MPR:22:2 Certainty there never can be, for certainty and assurance in such things are contrary to the Law.

MPR:22:3 The poor man says, "O that I had riches and could be free from worry and care!" The rich man says, "O that I could cast aside my responsibilities and live in peace!"

MPR:22:4 The poor man cannot understand the worries and anxieties of the rich, he knows nothing of the problems and perplexities of power; boredom is outside his experience, and therefore, he bewails his lot. He sees joy in the faces of others but cannot see their secret griefs. He envies those with position and estate but cannot understand their responsibilities. He envies the leisure of the rich man reclining at his ease, but he cannot know the turmoil seething within his breast. Contentment does not come with possessions, nor peace with power.

MPR:22:5 If you be numbered among the poor, take comfort, for you have many causes for thankfulness. Can you not sit at your table with a quiet mind, undisturbed by the clacking tongues of flatterers and hypocrites? Do the demands of needy men disturb your peace? Does the morsel you eat not taste wholesome? In the stomach of the rich, it would sit as a stone.

MPR:22:6 The task that encompasses your day brings healthy sleep in its train, and if your bed be hard, remember that many a restless head sleeps on down.

MPR:22:7 Joy and contentment come from something a man has within himself, not from things without. Solitude is a torment to the uneasy heart but balm to the contented one.

MPR:22:8 A man who can be satisfied with little is the possessor of wisdom. He who desires no more than sufficient will always have enough; his cares will be few.

MPR:22:9 Riches do not bring peace to the soul. The greatest treasure of all is a contented heart.

MPR:22:10 The coming of riches is not a misfortune; the inheritance of estates is not a calamity to the wise man, for he will utilise them with temperance and discretion.

MPR:22:11 The cup of gladness may be sipped by man, but to drain it is too much for the constitution of mortals.

MPR:22:12 Contentment is the goal of life, but first the race has to be run. None can receive the crown of the victor until the course is finished and he takes his place among the competitors in the Halls of Eternity.

MPR:22:13 A piece of arable land fenced about, a plot of meadow, a grove of sycamore trees, a faithful wife and many sons, what more can a man desire?

MPR:22:14 Yet, tares grow among the corn, and weeds among the fodder, Flowers wilt unless watered, and finding a good wife requires much diligence. Nothing comes without effort, and nothing on Earth can be perfect, for that is the Law.

MPR:22:15 Therefore, be content if your burdens are bearable and your sorrows counterbalanced by your joys. Live today fully; sigh not for tomorrow, for it will come; regret not yesterday, for it is dead.

MPR:22:16 Active discontent is a spur to achievement, but placid discontent must be cut out like a malignant growth, for it eats into the pleasures of men.

MPR:22:17 Remember that pleasure is the companion, not the guide, of your journey.

MPR:22:18 The Law decrees that the nation, which places pleasure before duty, ease before effort and peace before honour shall pass into the hands of another.

MPR:22:19 Contentment is a state of mind, not an end, but he who is content with anything deserves nothing.

MPR:22:20 To give life is a joy; to take it shatters content. He who has many children has many joys, but he who takes life from another shall not enjoy contentment in his own.

Chapter Twenty-Three – Diligence

MPR:23:1 The days that are past have gone forever, and those that sleep in the womb of the future may not be seen by you in your present state of being. Therefore, it is well to concern yourself wholly with the present, forgetting the past and not expecting too much from the future.

MPR:23:2 The present alone is yours, and the fortunes of futurity will be dispensed according to the Law; therefore, you cannot know what the unborn days will bring forth. As to your own future state, subject to the Law, it is being conceived in your present thoughts and deeds.

MPR:23:3 Idleness is the parent of poverty, but success and prosperity attend upon the industrious and diligent.

MPR:23:4 Waste not the early hours of the day. Serve your master with diligence, and promotion will be your reward. The man of affairs rises early to establish himself. Neglect not the affairs of the day, nor fill them with idle dreams of yourself when greater, for thus, you feed yourself on wind while your bread is eaten by another.

MPR:23:5 Who is he that acquires riches or rises to power or is honoured among the people, or is called before the king in counsel? Is it not he who rises early and goes to bed late? He exercises his mind and fills it with knowledge; he exercises his body, and it glows with health.

MPR:23:6 Only a man who toils can justify his existence, and he who carries no burden or produces nothing of value were better removed.

MPR:23:7 The slothful and improvident man makes strife to arise in his abode, and he destroys its foundations. He is a burden to himself, and the hours drag wearily through his day. The task is all about him, but he knows not what to do; his idleness weighs heavier than any toil.

MPR:23:8 The years of his life pass away like the drifting shadow of a cloud, leaving no mark on the Earth as a memorial. His body becomes gross from want of exercise; disease lurks close at hand. He desires action but lacks the power of movement. He is imprisoned within a cloud of dullness, and his thoughts whirl in confusion. He cannot set his heart to any problem, and it wanders aimlessly like water from a broken channel.

MPR:23:9 His dwelling place is in disorder, and he cries, "Woe, calamity has befallen me." His family leaves him to his own devices, and he says, "See, I am deserted." The ruins of his life fall about his ears, but he has no resolution to extricate himself. Shame and remorse accompany him into the tomb.

MPR:23:10 As in all things, there is a balance in labour and leisure. The man who toils all the long day never knows a relaxed moment, and he who indulges in pleasure unduly becomes soft and never acquires possessions.

MPR:23:11 Observe the ferryman; he allots a time for rest on land, while another relieves him at the pole.

MPR:23:12 It is not required that you exert yourself fully; a leisurely life and an idle one are not alike. Attend only to your own affairs; the governor knows how to rule.

MPR:23:13 Aim for perfection in all you do, for the limits of excellency in craftsmanship have not been set. Seek always to attain a standard that has never been reached before.

MPR:23:14 Strive always to be the best in your calling, whatever it may be, and let not your energy be consumed in the envy of another's achievements. Strive always to improve your own abilities, so that you may take your place among the masters of your craft.

MPR:23:15 Seek not to take advantage of your competitor by any underhanded methods, but overcome his opposition only through your own superiority. Thus, even though you fail, nevertheless the blow will be softened by the retention of your honour.

MPR:23:16 Success is good and desirable, but of itself, it plays little part in the development of the soul. It is the manner, in which success or failure is met that leaves its impress there.

MPR:23:17 Consider carefully the causes of success in others; what they can attain is not beyond your reach. Be not one of those who marvel not when others remove mountains but consider it beyond themselves to carry a pebble.

MPR:23:18 Diligence will always be duly rewarded by the wise master.

Chapter Twenty-Four – Labour

MPR:24:1 All men must toil on Earth, not because they are born to servitude, but because they are heirs of God and must labour in His vineyard.

MPR:24:2 Though a man be born to great riches and high estate, if he contribute not to life in accordance with his position, he is held unworthy in the eyes of God. Though a man may be a great landowner and have many servants, he may not have a stake in life.

MPR:24:3 To be idle is to be a bystander at the parade of life, an onlooker when life has need of its champions. The idler holds no rank in the host of man, which ever advances into the unknown region of the future, towards its destiny in the Eternal Halls.

MPR:24:4 The idler becomes a mere camp follower straggling in the rear, a hanger on in the company of those stalwarts who shoulder the burdens along the road towards the glorious heritage of man.

MPR:24:5 All labour is vain, unless done with purpose, and toil should not only be to sustain the body but also to satisfy the spirit. The man who attacks the task with zest shows his love of life.

MPR:24:6 The weaver should breathe something of himself into the threads and thus endow the cloth with something of his own nature. The builder should set the foundation with care and diligence, and erect the dwelling with devoted attention, as though it were to be the habitation of his own household.

MPR:24:7 The husbandman should till the ground with loving care and sow the seed with tenderness, as though the fruits thereof were for his own children.

MPR:24:8 The craftsman should stamp his handiwork with his spirit, for all who fashion with their hands should leave their seal thereon.

MPR:24:9 If you toil without satisfaction, if you labour with distaste, following a dull routine of drabness, then it were better you did not labour at all. A loaf baked with indifference sits heavily on the stomach. If a dwelling is built without care, it becomes the abode of discomfort.

MPR:24:10 Do good wherever you can; labour to the best of your ability, and gladness shall rule your heart. Toil is more your lot on Earth than revelation; speculation about divine things need not extend beyond the confines of your heart.

MPR:24:11 All labour is not wholesome. He who toils halfheartedly or is careless in craftsmanship implants imperfection in his nature. He deals in deceit, and his toil emits an unseen thing, which, like some poisonous vapour, numbs his spirit.

MPR:24:12 Never let any pastime eat up your substance or become too costly, lest the anguish of payment exceed the pleasure it brings. Yet, the life of man should be a healthy mixture compounded of its essential obligations, with refreshing leisure and pleasure added in moderation.

MPR:24:13 However, leisure, to be beneficial, must be used wisely, and man should not ignore its snares. It is well to remember that leisure is not the same as idleness, which is the rust of time.

MPR:24:14 During the enjoyment of leisure, avoid all burdensome and unnecessary visits. Avoid the acclaim of the fickle multitude, which fawns upon the famous and notorious, for its acclaim has no substance. It is a garland of wind.

MPR:24:15 Let leisure and pleasure never be overdone, and remember that pleasures oft repeated become wearisome. Let them be healthy and refreshing, but spend no time upon them unduly, nor make them your whole life.

MPR:24:16 The joyful man labours diligently to fulfil his allotted task, but to the sad man, toil is a drug which removes him from the misery within himself. When labour is undertaken to provide for the needs of living, or for satisfaction, then it is a natural activity. A slave is not always one who is bound.

MPR:24:17 The knowledge and skill men gain to follow their craft suffice to provide for daily needs, but what of the knowledge, which will deliver them from the yoke of life, is that not the greatest attainment?

Chapter Twenty-Five – Reputation

MPR:25:1 Riches may pass from one to another; skill and knowledge may be transmitted, but a man's reputation is as his nature, peculiar to himself alone.

MPR:25:2 Therefore, your reputation is your own inalienable possession. If properly regarded, it will carry you through life, as a swift horse bears its rider over the rough sands of the wilderness. If however, you neglect it, as the inconsiderate man does his wife, then you cannot complain if that, in which you delight becomes an affliction, which you must bear for the rest of your days.

MPR:25:3 When the ship of prosperity founders, and you are cast into the sea of insolvency, if you have retained a good reputation, it will be the lifeline for your salvation.

MPR:25:4 When difficulties beset you, then it is the time to be on guard, lest your reputation be sullied; for it is not hard to keep a good reputation when it is untested by adversity.

MPR:25:5 The reputation of a man untried by misfortune is like the skill of a runner who has never entered a race. It is like unseasoned timber or unburnt clay.

MPR:25:6 In the days of prosperity, a good reputation is of little value, but in the days of adversity's oppression, it is a thing beyond price. A good name has greater value than gold.

MPR:25:7 No man can truly judge the worth of his reputation until it is all he has left.

MPR:25:8 Riches may come to a man and depart again, for life is inconsistent. Bad times alternate with good times, for the wheel of fortune is ever turning. Friends come and go according to the benefits, which acquaintanceship bestows.

MPR:25:9 Only reputation remains your inseparable supporter, which will not depart except by your own decree. Once departed, it is gone forever, and it flees quickly from he who treats it lightly. Therefore, guard your reputation as constantly as you do your daughter.

MPR:25:10 The thief who steals your possessions takes that, which is replaceable, but the slanderer who steals your reputation steals that, which cannot be restored to you, and it benefits him not. Which is to you of most value; your possessions or your reputation? If possessions, then you lack confidence in your reputation, and perhaps only you know why.

MPR:25:11 A good reputation is acquired by the doing of some things and refraining from doing others. Reputation is the steadying oar of the vessel bearing you across the stormy waters of life.

MPR:25:12 The Real Man treasures his reputation as his life, and he bends every utterance and deed towards upholding it. He is vigilant against the mire slings of slanderers, and he knows how to deal with them.

MPR:25:13 The weakling cares not for his reputation, nor for the reputation of his wife, for his twisted nature secretly rejoices in his low estate among men. To be among the lowest of men is not without compensation, for there is no fear of falling.

MPR:25:14 Only the Real Man can have a worthwhile reputation, for its retention entails continual struggle against temptation.

MPR:25:15 A good reputation, which is untried by adversity or untested in the fires of temptation, is of moderate value only. It is as clay untouched by fire, as bricks unbaked in the sun.

MPR:25:16 As the body loses its vigour and the spirit its fortitude in the habitation of luxury, so does reputation lose its merit on the path of prosperity.

MPR:25:17 He who has not reputation is unknown, for he who has even one acquaintance has a reputation for good or ill.

MPR:25:18 If you were born outside a household, and your mother was without husband when you were born, and for these, you suffer unkindness at the mouths of others; or if your wife is a loose-petalled flower, or your daughter to men as a mouse to cat, hold your head high, and shrink not from the unspoken thoughts of men. No man worthy of the name would condemn you for the weaknesses of others; only for things condoned can you share in the condemnation.

MPR:25:19 Be of good standing with God and man, but above all, seek not to establish earthly merit alone.

Chapter Twenty-Six – Ambition

MPR:26:1 The great full-leafed, many-boughed sycamore, now reaching up towards Heaven, was once but a small seed hidden within the dark womb of Earth. Yet, how much greater are its limitations than the limitations of man! Therefore, try always to excel in whatsoever you undertake, and always reach out to a goal beyond your present estate.

MPR:26:2 Never let another excel you in goodness, and never envy another his abilities, for such is a profitless thing. Seek rather to improve your own, but keep the desires of your heart ever within moderation, and they will come to fruition in due course.

MPR:26:3 Never seek to further your plans by unworthy or mean methods, or to pull another down, that you may rise above him. Seek only to reach your goal by virtue of your own superiority, and if success elude you, nevertheless honour will walk at your side.

MPR:26:4 To seek success is neither unworthy nor unnatural, for man was born to struggle. The Real Man rises to the challenge of life and soars above adversity, as the palm tree soars above shrubbery. He lifts himself above all the sordidness of Earth; like an eagle, he floats on wings of freedom, his eye fixed on the splendour of the sun.

MPR:26:5 Ambition is the only challenger to love. Govern yourself, and you can rule the land, but the best way to succeed is to follow the advice you give others.

MPR:26:6 No matter what your estate, seek to improve it. There is no fish so small, but it hopes to become a whale. No man knows what he can do until he tries, but only a fool tries to surmount the ramparts of his own nature. Whatever befalls, and the future is inscrutable, meet success like an Eastern man and failure like a Northern man. Fear not if you fall the first time, for he falls low who cannot rise again; but if you do succeed, then be on your guard, for prosperity like poverty can ruin a man. Remember always that success is the fruit of effort, and accomplishment the child of diligence.

MPR:26:7 Most men can beat adversity well enough, but if you really want to test a man, give him power.

MPR:26:8 Choose your calling according to your abilities; no two men are alike in ability and everyone is good at something, in which another fails. Fear not to begin, for the glory of man comes from his daring to begin; for the commencement of an enterprise is always the most difficult part.

MPR:26:9 He who lacks the ability or is of small account may yet prosper if he attach himself to one who is great. A drop of water is insignificant by itself, and under the heat of the sun soon becomes nothing, but will it ever dry up if it joined a lake?

MPR:26:10 If undertaking a great enterprise, ensure the support of a trustworthy friend. Nothing can be done unaided; even when burning a field of stubble, the aid of the wind is necessary.

MPR:26:11 The price of success is continued diligence and effort, for though gold may be melted completely, let the fire grow cold, and it hardens again.

MPR:26:12 Seek not to dwell within the shadow of a man because of his estate or because he has titles; better men may be lacking these. Do you judge the ass by its bridle?

MPR:26:13 Be ever ready to acknowledge a benefit and slow to avenge a wrong; thus you will find benefits more readily given than injuries.

MPR:26:14 The wellspring of ambition exists in the bosom of every man, but it flows not in all. In some, it is held back by reserve, while others are restrained by fear. Some cannot face its demands, and some find the road too hard. The weakling renounces the struggle even before it begins.

Chapter Twenty-Seven – Honesty

MPR:27:1 Honesty is a virtue of the Real Man, for he is honest in all things and not least with himself. No man is so deceitful as he who deceives himself and no form of deceit is so common.

MPR:27:2 Even the weakling, if he be honest with himself, takes a step towards manliness.

MPR:27:3 My children, remember that honesty always pays its due reward, though this may not always be readily apparent. In fact, this non-apparency is necessary in the greater scheme of things. This thought alone brings consolation to the heart of an old man in these evil days, when honesty is an unfashionable gem.

MPR:27:4 Sly and furtive deeds may be successfully hidden from others, but they leave an evil impress upon the soul. In a dishonest and deceitful person, the soul is not pleasant to behold.

MPR:27:5 Better is it to be a beggar walking with God in the austerity of honesty than a rich man safely sheltered in a comfortable dwelling, whose countenance is hardened and whose soul is fearful.

MPR:27:6 All poor men are not honest, nor all rich men rogues; poverty and riches do not mark the divisions. Rather it should be in the nature of things to decree that honest men should acquire possessions, and the dishonest ones be impoverished, but this is a challenge not yet met by man.

MPR:27:7 Never filch land away by dishonest measure. When you barter with another, be fair in your dealings, be moderate in your bargaining and never profit from the ignorance or disadvantage of him, with whom you trade.

MPR:27:8 Cause not the balances to fall through falsification of the weights, or through alteration of the marks, lest in the day of adjustment, you be seized by the ape that sits behind the Great Scales.

MPR:27:9 Honesty and bribery are irreconcilable. Honest dealings would not bring shame before the gaze of men; bribery is always entered upon in secret, like a pact between curs.

MPR:27:10 The honest man gains approval of others, and to be held in high regard by men is better than riches laid up in the treasurehouse. But honesty is a thing of the heart and not always obvious; only the spirit knows the intention. The motives written in the heart of man are too often misread.

MPR:27:11 If a scribe or official, never be bribed to make an erasure on the registers or add that, which is not there, for this is an abomination. Write only that, which is true, for the hand that holds the pen becomes the mouth of veracity.

MPR:27:12 It is bad for the people when there is dishonesty among the lowly, but it is a calamity when it is found among those in high positions.

MPR:27:13 The peasant steals handful by handful, and the lord steals load by load, but it is better to have clean hands than full ones.

MPR:27:14 Honesty does not necessarily bring its own reward on Earth. The true reward of honesty is the unperceptible strengthening of the soul.

MPR:27:15 Real Men are honest for the sake of honesty; it is in their nature. Weaklings are hypocritically honest because of the reward reaped for a reputation for honesty. Only the spirit is not deceived.

MPR:27:16 Honesty in prosperity comes easily; adversity and disaster alone can determine the true honesty of a man. For this reason, among others, affliction, calamity and distress beset the life of man; they are not sent capriciously.

MPR:27:17 The Law decrees that honesty shall not always serve the best interests of men on Earth. This is not because the test has found honesty wanting, for honesty has served its end; the test decided whether a man would be honest for the sake of his soul. The Law also decrees that if a man be not honest on Earth, his soul shall carry the scars of his dishonesty forever.

Chapter Twenty-Eight – Generosity

MPR:28:1 It is wrong to give to the deserving alone. Behold the tree in the vineyard, the barley in the plowed land, the cow in the pastures or the lowly fowl in its pen. Do they not live just to give, and is not their service to life established?

MPR:28:2 Is not your neighbour, who whatever his estate shares with you the journey of life, worthy of your consideration? Is he not your partner in Earth, your brother in God? No man is worthy to judge the failings of another unless he, too, has experienced their temptations. It is easy enough to see the failings of another; this any man can do, easier to sit in judgement on them, but it takes a better man to see his own.

MPR:28:3 The only undeserving man is he, who is without need. All men are companions through the journey of life; some are good companions and some are bad; some are stouthearted and others timid; some stumble and fall; some forge ahead, but all are of the same company. Therefore, never desert your fellow wayfarer in his hour of need, for somewhere along the road, you, too will need help.

MPR:28:4 The poor and the lowly are not without pride and dignity; therefore, it may be easier for you to give than for them to receive. Your almsgiving may give you an inner glow, but it may also wound the heart of he who receives it.

MPR:28:5 When you give, consider well the deed, is it really you who gives? Is it not more true to say it is life giving to life, a transfer from one guardian of life to another? What are you but the instrument, the witness, the agent of the transaction?

MPR:28:6 You are the debtor of life, for has it not given you all you have? If there be among men one, who has received nothing from life, then let him be the one, who refuses to give.

MPR:28:7 The good giver gives and thereafter does not remember the gift. The receiver, if he be worthy, never forgets it.

MPR:28:8 The heart of the generous man is like the bountiful waters, which rise and strew the face of the land with fruits, herbage and flowers. It bedecks life with beauty and gladdens the hearts of men.

MPR:28:9 The generous man carries an everlasting spring of benevolence within his heart, from which flow waters of goodness to nourish the gardens of kindness and consideration. He lends his arm to the needy, he sees with compassion the plight of the poor and aged and brings them things to lighten the burden of their days.

Chapter Twenty-Nine – Cheerfulness

MPR:29:1 From whence does sadness come? Not from external circumstances, but from a worm within the heart. It can have no existence, but for the sustenance it saps from your own feebleness of spirit.

MPR:29:2 Sorrow there will always be, for the Law decrees that it is essential for the tempering of the spirit, but sorrow is another adversary to conquer and cast out. It is not something to be accepted with resignation. The greatest benefit comes from rising above it.

MPR:29:3 Therefore, let your face shine with cheerfulness, for a cheerful countenance will bring brightness even into the lives of the afflicted and gladness even to the most distressed. The sad face, reflecting a gloomy heart, will deaden even the joyfulness of youth.

MPR:29:4 Never go about among men with a sad face, for such is easily forgotten. Men care not for the countenance of gloom, but that, which is pleasant is easy to remember.

MPR:29:5 When a man who went smiling into the storehouse for barley distribution comes out frowning, he makes known his displeasure, and they who wait their turn blame the overseer for miscalculation. The people who deal with wise men have cheerful faces.

MPR:29:6 Though your talents are such that you cannot appear great in the presence of others, you can approach greatness by being pleasant and agreeable. It is easy for a man to appear great when he is great, but difficult to appear pleasant and agreeable when he is neither.

MPR:29:7 The sad air of despondency pollutes the pure air of life. The morbidness enthroned in the heart of a weakling magnifies his afflictions. It raises the loss of a needle to the loss of a fortune. His mind is burdened with trifles and therefore cannot give due attention to matters of consequence. The heart of a cheerful man is not depressed by matters of small account, and it remains free to deal with matters of greater importance.

MPR:29:8 Sadness, gloom and despondency ride upon the shoulders of the weakling. They sap his strength, his will and his manliness.

MPR:29:9 Sorrow and tribulations are the lot of all men, but their burden is lightened if carried with cheerfulness. It is well to think, when calamity befalls, "Is it wholly a thing of evil, is it altogether without purpose?"

MPR:29:10 The despondent heart invites the entry of cowardice and meanness; it permits that, which is base to enter. The heart that is cheerful has no accommodation for such things.

MPR:29:11 Be not misled by the mask of piety when it hides the sad heart of the melancholy man. The face of the truly good, like the countenance of the wise, shines with the reflected light of the joyful soul within. The greatest sorrow and the most overwhelming misfortune cannot douse its brilliance.

MPR:29:12 In the midst of affliction and sorrow, the things, which once filled the heart with gladness do not all depart. Why, then, should these be offered as a sacrifice at the altar of sadness? Is this not exalting sadness far above its station? Is not such sacrifice futile and unproductive of good?

MPR:29:13 Never do worry and sadness ease the burden of sorrow or alter the force of circumstances. It is cheerfulness, patience and fortitude that lighten the burden and soften the blow.

MPR:29:14 Like the miser with his hoarded gold, the sad man hugs his misery in solitude, he cannot bear to let it depart from him. It has filled his life; he has no friends; all have fled and left him to the enjoyment of his own precious sorrow.

MPR:29:15 Sadness is not the child of thought; it knows no reason; it rejects the hand of friendship and the touch of compassion; it seeks only the company of those, who will commiserate with its misery. The cause is not important, for sadness is the end in itself. Remove the cause, and sadness remains. Sadness is a state within, not the result of external circumstances.

MPR:29:16 Whence comes the cause of all sorrows? Is it not from the process of living and from change? Then is it not all futile? Life you cannot escape, and are not all things and circumstances always changing? For this is the Law.

MPR:29:17 Therefore, man, who is made according to the Law and subject to the Law, must accept its decree. His life is governed by its ordinances, and from these there is no escape. The mountain will stand, however long you batter it with your head.

MPR:29:18 Accept cheerfully that, which cannot be altered by sadness; thus, its burden will be lightened. The sun shines brighter for the cheerful man.

MPR:29:19 Only one sorrow is truly worthy of sympathy; only one sorrow deeply stirs the heart; only one sorrow is magnificent in its depth, and only one sorrow is really genuine. That is the sorrow of the cheerful heart.

MPR:29:20 If you know that sorrow and misfortune will cross your path because they are a part of the pattern of life, then you are wise to prepare yourself to meet them, but it is unwise to seek them out. The testing tools of life are never stored away.

MPR:29:21 If you are ignorant of the Law, complain not of that, about which you have no knowledge. Seek rather to understand the nature of the Law, and thus know the meaning of life. He who understands the Law knows why the pattern of life is as it is, why it is a design of light and shade.

MPR:29:22 The Law is unchangeable and unchallengeable, and none but a fool rants against that, which cannot be altered. Man will never find contentment until he learns to accept the Law as it has been established. It governs the whole Earth and his life; to live in harmony with it is to live in peace.

MPR:29:23 If, in your weakness and waywardness, you find the burden of the Law intolerable, all your lamentations and wailing will not ease the load; it will do nothing but add to your distress. The Law concedes nothing to the weaknesses of men.

MPR:29:24 The nature of man is such that it accords with the Law, and therefore it is unnatural to rebel against it; thus man can achieve nothing. He achieves nothing except the stirring up of strife within himself. Is it not better to live in peace with the natural state of affairs than to tear yourself asunder by futile rebellion?

MPR:29:25 It is not in your nature to suffer the blows of misfortune without being hurt, but it is within your nature, and your duty, to stand up to them like a man.

MPR:29:26 Sadness for the sake of sadness robs a man of manliness, and the sorrowful man is unfit to embark on great enterprises.

MPR:29:27 Therefore, inflict not any self-induced ill upon yourself, nor lessen your abilities by indulgence in weaknesses of the spirit. From these, nothing beneficial can be gained. There is sufficient real sorrow and suffering on Earth to serve their end.

MPR:29:28 Life is a pleasure to the cheerful man and a burden to the sad one. A cheerful face is always welcome, a cheerful spirit eases the burdens of many, and a cheerful soul is not severed from God.

Chapter Thirty – Discretion

MPR:30:1 Discretion and caution are not akin to cowardice; even the ants march armed. It is wise to cross the field before you abuse the bull and learn to swim before you rock the boat.

MPR:30:2 Go not into a gathering of men when in the mood to fight and their temper tends towards strife. Avoid doing what many others are doing, for if the crew become too many the boat sinks.

MPR:30:3 Sharpened knives come readily to the hands of those who would oppose entry by the unbidden. It is unwise to seek entrance otherwise than by invitation and at the proper time.

MPR:30:4 Before opening your mouth in the presence of others, be clear in your thoughts, and when you speak, weigh your words carefully and use them sparingly. Words once spoken take wings and cannot be recaptured. Be reserved, for if you tell everyone your affairs, they will be taken out of your hands.

MPR:30:5 Examine the circumstances of every deed and its possible outcome before you embark upon any course of action. It is folly to open your mouth or to undertake anything until the consequences have been fully weighed. Thus, disgrace will never overshadow your path, nor shame enter the door of your dwelling. With discretion directing your steps, remorse will be unknown, and never will sorrow for your deeds bear heavily upon your shoulders.

MPR:30:6 Let prudence always walk by your side; her voice speaks with words of wisdom, and her hand will ever guide you safely along the paths of right. She will guard you from the blows of disaster and shield you from the winds of affliction.

MPR:30:7 Give ear to her soft counsels of prudence, and write them on the tablets of your heart. She is the mother of all virtues and the guardian of content.

MPR:30:8 Accept no favour from the rash man and no benefit from the vain one. They seek but to gratify their selfish feelings and their motive is vanity and their end self-importance.

MPR:30:9 Discretion, prudence and diligence do not bring success unfailingly, for such is contrary to the Law. Earthly success is not the inevitable attendant of he who serves the purpose of life.

MPR:30:10 Refuse the favours of the mercenary man, for they are toils not easily discarded.

MPR:30:11 Never hasten swiftly to attain that which will be advantageous; the prudent man hastens slowly. Never create the circumstances, which will destroy an advantage or opportunity.

MPR:30:12 That, which is gained by haste will be quickly lost, but that ,which is gained cautiously will be retained. Remember, too, that goods and gold, like weapons of war, require careful handling.

MPR:30:13 Weigh all things you do in your heart, and shape not your course by the tongue. Even if the tongue of a man be the helm of a boat, as is declared in the new writings, it is still the heart, which is the lookout in the bows.

MPR:30:14 A prudent man keeps knowledge concealed behind his tongue, but the tongue of a fool declares his folly. The man who speaks without thought is led astray by his tongue; he is trapped in the mesh of his foolish words.

MPR:30:15 Judge all men with discretion and reserve, without haste and without prejudice. Judge no man by the talk in the marketplace but as he appears in your eyes. The marketplace popularity of a man is no recommendation.

MPR:30:16 Be prudent in your dealings with all men, that you may be respected for your honesty. Turn your plough at the edge of the field, and drive no furrow across the boundary of another. Let your cattle not stray from your own pastures.

MPR:30:17 Better one measure of land, which is yours by deed, than a thousand measures acquired by deceit and dishonesty.

MPR:30:18 There is a time for boldness and a time for discretion. Therefore, hasten to gather the wisdom to know one from the other, for none but those who have done so will live in peace and prosper.

MPR:30:19 Fools rush into the marshlands and perish, but the wise test every step and pass through. None but a fool stands under a leaning wall.

MPR:30:20 Be courageous and cautious, not courageous and foolhardy, for foolishness can counter the most courageous deeds.

MPR:30:21 The greatest attribute of man, that which sets him apart from the beasts of the field and forest, the most dangerous and discomforting gift of God is freewill; yet it is the golden promise of Godhood. Therefore, at all times leaven your deeds with caution and measure them with prudence as a guide. For as the whirlwind raises the sweeping sandstorm that overwhelms the works of men, so does the irresponsible voice of the multitude overwhelm reason in those who listen to it without judgement.

MPR:30:22 Seek the true meaning behind the words, which fall from the tongue; see if Truth be in the heart of the speaker or only her shadow. Let your life be governed by reason and experience, so that if failure attend your enterprise, you answer for it to none but yourself.

Chapter Thirty-One – Thrift

MPR:31:1 Never seek to live beyond the confines of your estate, and never expand yourself to the limits of your substance, for the things you go without in youth will provide the comforts for your old age.

MPR:31:2 Never let prosperity blind you to the charms of prudence, for he who overindulges in the unprofitable pleasures of life shall live to suffer for lack of its necessities.

MPR:31:3 Be cautious at all times, two arrows in the quaver are better than one, and three better still.

MPR:31:4 There is a vast difference between the thrifty man and the miser. When the love of riches and possessions passes the bounds of moderation, it becomes an abcess within the thoughts. It poisons every good feeling; it stifles all sense of honesty, it smothers virtue and slays love and affection.

MPR:31:5 The miser would sell the charms of his wife for gold; he would dispose of his children for chattels; he would see his father or mother starve before he opened his storehouse. He sacrifices the peace of everyone to his greed; he considers not even his own, for in seeking to satisfy his covetousness, he sacrifices all joy and contentment.

Chapter Thirty-Two – Leadership

MPR:32:1 If you are called upon to be a leader among men, press forward your plans by your commands, and carry out your decisions immediately. Let the morning's thoughts become the evening's deeds, and never let the sun decline upon that, which could have been done during its rising.

MPR:32:2 Remember the days yet unborn, and sacrifice not the future for today. Never retire to sleep with indecision as a bedfellow. Unresolved problems sit heavily on the stomach during the watches of the night.

MPR:32:3 If you would be respected as a leader, guard against avarice. It will steal away the confidence of others, and self-assurance cannot exist in its company. Avarice is an evil thing, turning even fathers to deeds of wickedness against their children.

MPR:32:4 If you possess strength of body, then flaunt it not, for men are led by the strong in spirit. The qualities of a leader and a ruler are not alike.

MPR:32:5 Make yourself respected by quietness of manner and directness of speech. The loudmouthed man invites secret amusement and not respect. Command not, except you can guide. If you seek glory for yourself, or take pleasure in the praises of others, raise yourself up from the dust of lesser mortality, and fix your gaze upon the starry heights.

MPR:32:6 Remember that a leader leads, and man is easy to lead but difficult to drive.

MPR:32:7 Maintain your self-control at all times. The fires of fanaticism burn strongly and consume reason; therefore, dampen down the heated thoughts, which burn in a fervent heart. The man who walks slowly finds the quickest way.

MPR:32:8 Be not arrogant because of your position, for the man who is haughty in heart is easily humbled. The arrogant man, however great may be his power, is less powerful because of his arrogance.

MPR:32:9 Having embarked on a course of action, if it be done in wisdom, see it through to the end, for he who pulls his horse in mid leap always falls.

MPR:32:10 Leadership is the prerogative of the Real Man, for a weakling can lead none but weaklings. Command may fall upon a weakling or be given to him, but it does not result from his own abilities, and therefore he commands by oppression.

MPR:32:11 He who leads to victory is great, but he who can lead in defeat is still greater. The greatest leader is seen at his best in defeat.

MPR:32:12 Success is not the crown of leadership, for the Law decrees that failure may crown the greatest efforts.

Chapter Thirty-Three – Dignity

MPR:33:1 Dignity, both in adversity and goodfortune, is the hallmark of the Real Man. Hold high your head, and walk with dignified bearing, that all men may recognise you as a man. It is in their bearing and manner that the servile reveal their craven hearts.

MPR:33:2 When the raging stormwaters of wrath sweep away the self-control of lesser men, and they are carried away by the torrent of their own temper, stand calm among them, as a rock before the assaults of the wild seas.

MPR:33:3 True dignity, not the false facade of the hypocrite, is the outer manifestation of inner strength, and a Real Man is dignified at all times. It distinguishes the prince from the serving man, the courageous from the craven-hearted.

MPR:33:4 Dignity is neither false pride nor the false front hiding a haughty nature; it is the natural bearing of a confident man.

MPR:33:5 As a woman always remembers the modesty of womanhood and never exceeds the bounds of decorum and reserve, so does a man bear himself with dignity in the knowledge and pride of his manhood.

MPR:33:6 A dignified bearing in adversity, or when others scorn your opinions or beliefs, reveals your greatness. Dignity, when you are scorned or cast down, chastens your adversaries.

Chapter Thirty-Four – Truth

MPR:34:1 Truth is not a quality of Earth, but an infusion from the Greater Region beyond the veil, where Truth is manifested in purity. Here on Earth, things do not disclose their true nature to the eye, for the things we see with the eye are as the eye sees them, and not as they are in reality and Truth. The eye is a poor interpreter of reality.

MPR:34:2 To attain Truth, man must reach out beyond Earth and himself. While he remains bound to Earth, he may perceive the light of Truth only dimly in its reflection from the source afar.

MPR:34:3 Nevertheless, to strive for Truth must be one of the main aims of life. Therefore, Earth, the wise instructress. teaches man the nature of deceit and places it all about him, that he may observe its ways and learn to distinguish its illusions. It is in the nature of a game, wherein man tries to discover what is reality, so far with little success. For the road to Truth lies through the thick forests of illusion and across the wide wastelands of deceit.

MPR:34:4 Unlock the secrets of a stone, and perchance you will find a star; open the body of water, and you may discover a heart of fire.

MPR:34:5 Did not the men of olden times teach that our eyes deceive us in all things, that only the Great Eye can perceive all things in Truth?

MPR:34:6 The godlings of old, who lived beyond the great mountains, taught that man was not a solid being, but likened to a whirlpool in the midst of a moving sea. They saw Earth as a movement within a movement and life within life, and was not their wisdom greater than ours?

MPR:34:7 The Earth progresses in wisdom from generation to generation, but not all wisdom is handed down through the generations of man. There are losses as well as gains.

MPR:34:8 Does the eye in the red alcove see things as does the mortal eye of man, or are things different there at the window of Truth?

MPR:34:9 Truth and perfection unite in one, and neither is to be found in purity on Earth. Yet though men desire Truth, when she stands before them, they see her not, for the coloured glass of illusion veils nothing as much as it veils Truth.

MPR:34:10 Truth is the cupbearer of the True God and pours out full measure to those who uphold His decrees. At some time in their lives, the call comes to all men to bear witness to Truth as they see it.

MPR:34:11 The man who has Truth for his towline acquires position and estate, for he is a worthy man.

MPR:34:12 Truth cannot be determined by the arguments of men; it is therefore not to be weighed according to their arguments, but their arguments according to the light of Truth as it is revealed and known. Say not that Truth is established by time, or that a multitude of believers make certainty.

MPR:34:13 The best Truth men can ever have to judge is Truth apparent, for Truth in actuality cannot be manifested to men on Earth. Then with regard to Truth and falsehood, do they not appear alike in things beyond our understanding? How then could we decide between them, were it not for the whispers of our conscience?

MPR:34:14 General opinion is the least proof of Truth, for men in general are ignorant. Then, too, the Law decrees that the surroundings and circumstances of man shall be more conducive to deception than to Truth.

MPR:34:15 Seek after Truth, for it is the greatest of things man can understand. God is beyond his comprehension, but Truth is not; it alone is the path towards the fulfilment of the destiny of man. Progress through life is the unveiling of Truth, but can man ever stand in her august presence? As the owl is blinded in the splendour of the sun, so will man be dazzled before the unveiled face of majestic Truth.

MPR:34:16 Truth is oftimes veiled with deceit or tainted with the foul touch of hypocrisy. Truth without honesty is a tree without leaves. Distorted Truth has a visage more frightening than any other conceivable horror, and even the innocent heart quails before it.

MPR:34:17 O majestic Truth. What wickedness is wrought in Your fair name! What pain You suffer at the mouths of hypocrites and deceivers, where so often, a fragment of Truth is built into the fabric of a great falsehood!

MPR:34:18 What appears as Truth in the gloom of the serpent's lair may look very different in the clear light of day.

MPR:34:19 Truth, the best advocate, is also the purifying flame, which often hurts more than falsehood, otherwise the soul is struck an evil blow.

MPR:34:20 The weakling and unworthy man says, "What have I to do with Truth, which too often breeds wrath and stirs up trouble; is not the soft word more desirable, and is it not the password to popularity?" Weakling and fool, are not the foes made by Truth better than the friends made by falsehood?

MPR:34:21 Say not, "How can the true be known from the false, if Truth be not of Earth?" Know that you have found truth in sufficiency when you find that, which guides truly.

MPR:34:22 Truth is eternal and unchanging. The first Truth, which was in the beginning, will endure until the end; nothing can be added to it, and nothing taken away. It may be viewed from many sides and appear different, but such differences are in the eyes of the beholders. Truth itself is unalterable and cannot change.

MPR:34:23 Truth is not with man, nor of the Earth. It is with God alone, and when man sees Truth in its purity he will see God.

MPR:34:24 Great truths are the food of the soul, and great souls are the inheritors of eternity.

MPR:34:25 Walk always towards Truth, and though it will recede as you approach, for it is unattainable on Earth, nevertheless you are proceeding in the right direction.

MPR:34:26 Truth lies at the end of the future; when all is ended, there is Truth.

MPR:34:27 Only Truth can set men free. The day will come when man can be told openly about his real nature and destiny, and in that day, his spirit will respond and unfold its glory like a flower bud opening to the sun. In that day, he will accept that the change called 'death' is but the port of departure to a greater sphere of activity. He will then understand what he really is and must become, to fulfil his destiny.

Chapter Thirty-Five – Adversity

MPR:35:1 Adversity and affliction, like the smith, shape as they strike. They stand as challengers on the pathway to Truth and test the aspirants for godhood.

MPR:35:2 Adversity measures the virtue of women and the manliness of men. As gold is tested by acid, so are men tried by adversity. As fire tempers metal, so are men moulded by the blast of perverse fortune.

MPR:35:3 Adversity and affliction are to be expected, for they are necessities for the training of man. Therefore, be not bitter at the trials of life or the chastisement of the One God. A father who omits to chastise his children is careless of their welfare.

MPR:35:4 Behold the man, upon whom hardship and misfortune have never laid hand. He is soft as the unfired pot; like unseasoned timber, he bends under stress. Haratif spoke well when he said that adversity unveils greatness, while prosperity hides it.

MPR:35:5 Calamity ever lurks at the heels of man; it dogs his footsteps wheresoever he turns. It strikes in the dark like those who lay in wait for the wayfarer; it haunts the residences of prosperity and peace. The wise man is ever girt to meet it; in the halls of pleasure, he carries a sword.

MPR:35:6 Sorrow, suffering and the afflictions which beset men are not sent wilfully; they are necessities for existence, without which the slumbering soul could not awaken. They are needful for its development; therefore is it not a vain hope and foolishness to expect miracles to protect you and prevent you from deriving the benefit of these experiences? Is it reasonable to expect exemption from the things you were born to experience? Therefore, accept with good grace that, which life bestows on you, for it conforms with the Law. Is it not better to endure manfully the things which are unavoidable?

MPR:35:7 The scales are never wholly unbalanced; a loss is recorded to adversity, and a gain is recorded to experience. Joy is taken from the body, and strength is added to the soul.

MPR:35:8 To bear up well under the blows of adversity is not easy, but even more difficult is it to maintain balance under the wiles of prosperity. Men who are men do not degenerate under adversity, but in the soft arms of prosperity, many of these surrender their vigour and manhood.

MPR:35:9 Who among mortal men can assess the nature of adversity? What greater calamity can befall man than death? Yet were greater vision bestowed upon him, it would be received as a man receives an inheritance.

MPR:35:10 Adversity does far more good to men than harm; it is not least among the things that have raised them to greatness.

MPR:35:11 Adversity operates according to the Law. It is as the fire, which sets the pot or the hammer, which tempers metal. It divides the weak from the strong and the worthy from the unworthy. It is the grindstone, which sharpens the sword of courage. it is the comb, which adds lustre to the cloth of virtue.

MPR:35:12 Man is the child of misfortune; those who never knew calamity have gone. Earth does not unnecessarily oppress man, as the weaklings declare; her role is to instruct and develop, and can this be done without chastisement? There is a time for instruction and a time for play. Earth provides both and she is not unduly harsh. Life contains far more pleasure than pain, far more joy than sorrow. He who wants all play and no labour has no place on Earth. Instruction is rarely wholly a pleasure, nor is learning inseparable from chastisement.

MPR:35:13 Things change; times move ever onward; nothing remains constant, for this is the

Law; therefore, bewail not your lot because of it. Were the burden too great for your shoulders, you would not be here. To criticise the Law is futile foolishness, far better to harmonise yourself with it. Everything changes; the greater it is, the more liable to do so. If your nature is such that you cannot submit to the Law, then you are among the most unfortunate of men, for you add needlessly unto your burden.

Chapter Thirty-Six – Joy and Sorrow

MPR:36:1 Were there no darkness, we could not know light; were there no sorrow, we would never know joy.

MPR:36:2 Sorrow chisels out a storehouse within the soul, wherein may be stored the things of the spirit. The deeper sorrow carves, the more of these the storehouse will hold. Sorrow digs the well from which are drawn the refreshing waters of compassion and understanding; the deeper the well, the more pure its waters.

MPR:36:3 Is not the finest metal wrought in the fiercest flame and the best timber that, which has stood the longest exposed to seasoning winds? What good is a pot without fire or a brick without sun?

MPR:36:4 When grief occupies your heart, examine the intruder; are you not sorrowing after something from which you have already derived pleasure? Enough misery is allotted to man for his testing and tempering that it is an act of foolishness to increase it by futile lamentations.

MPR:36:5 Joy and sorrow are inseparable companions; one reveals the other. They enter your life together and thenceforth keep the watches with you. Always, one remains by your side, while the other sleeps.

MPR:36:6 You are suspended in the scales balanced between joy and sorrow, and not until you become an empty body do the balances stand at rest. As life pours out your moulding portion into the scales, so the balances of joy and sorrow fall and rise.

MPR:36:7 Let neither joy nor sorrow bear down too heavily on the scales, for neither should move too far from the balance of moderation, lest the scales overbalance completely.

MPR:36:8 Enter the habitation of joy with caution, for a heady brew is served therein, which can call forth the demons of mischief and madness. The first duty of man is to know himself and to reflect upon his destiny, to become aware of his soul. This he cannot do in the house of pleasure, in the arms of joy; therefore, is sorrow not apportioned to man in wisdom and consideration?

MPR:36:9 Avoid the dwelling place of sorrow, for there good is transmuted into evil, and wails of self-pity sadden the heavy night. The tear-damp mist, which issues from within withers the flowers which bedeck the garden of life. Better to stray not into either dwelling, but walk the path of moderation between them.

MPR:36:10 While man walks Earth, sorrow ever dogs his footsteps; it will come close enough unbidden, therefore encourage it not with your own ill judgement.

MPR:36:11 Man, by his deeds and thoughts, keeps open his door for sorrow, but his dwelling rarely attracts joy as a guest. Pleasures have to be bought, but pain comes unbidden.

MPR:36:12 As man is less aware of perfect health than of the slightest malady, so does the greatest joy move him less than the smallest sorrow. Man is the slave of pain and the plaything of pleasure.

MPR:36:13 He who sorrows before sorrow is called for is sorrowful for the sake of sorrow; he loves sorrow, for sorrow, like pain, can give pleasure to the abnormal.

MPR:36:14 He who seeks pleasure among fickle things of no substance can know but the fleeting glance of joy. When kindled, straw blazes up immediately and as quickly fades, but hard timber glows redly for long, and its heat lasts.

MPR:36:15 The afflicting blows of sorrow that strengthens the spirit on the road, that it may stride forward until it reaches green pastures of contentment, are better for man than the soft allurements of pleasure. For these sap the strength from his heart, so that he becomes incapable of enduring distress. For the misty shape of joy too often lures man into the morass of regret, or plunges him into the pool of despair.

Chapter Thirty-Seven – Compassion

MPR:37:1 As the kindly hands of the sun strew the face of the land with gay blossoms, and as the rising waters produce an abundance of bountiful harvest, so do the smiling countenance and outstretched hand of compassion fill the heart to overflowing.

MPR:37:2 He, who is without compassion never deserves it, but let not your heart be hardened against him. The gentle tears of compassion are as the bright dewdrops, which bedeck the harsh wilderness in radiantly gleaming garlands.

MPR:37:3 Let your ear be ever alert for the cry of the needy and your arm be ever ready to aid the unprotected. Let the sorrow of innocent suffering never go unheeded.

MPR:37:4 When the widow and orphan dumbly beseech your aid with eyes of silent suffering, open the gates of compassion within your heart. Pour forth succour to those who can find no other as strong as you to aid them.

MPR:37:5 He who turns from the rags of the destitute and ignores the pale cheek of the hungry, smites his sensitive soul with paralysing blows. Is it a matter for wonder that it becomes dead and insensitive, unfeeling and unresponsive? If for no other reason, have compassion for your own sake, for it moulds your greater form in a glory everlasting.

MPR:37:6 While even one man groans in misery in the habitations of poverty, or there remains one grey head bowed with distress to dumbly plead for aid, how can you go your way unmoved by compassion, dissipating your time and substance in unprofitable enjoyments? You who indulge in vain pleasures unfeelingly, while others want and suffer, will some day eat your own heart out in the dark barrenness within the gloomy cave, haunted by bitterness and regret.

Chapter Thirty-Eight – Greed

MPR:38:1 Commit no avaricious deed to obtain additional riches. Fill not your heart with love for the possessions of another, nor support yourself with that, which belongs to him unless you have his authority so to do.

MPR:38:2 Avariciousness turns a kindly friend into a bitter foe; it drives the trusted servant away from his master. It comes between husband and wife and alienates father from son. It is the keeper of the storehouse of evil and the companion along the road to vice.

MPR:38:3 Suppress greediness when a division of property is made, and take that, which is justly due. Guard against the greed which can cloud your thoughts so that you are unable to see clearly that, which is rightly yours and that, which belongs to another.

MPR:38:4 A man who is greedy and grasping within his own household is as a worm in a good apple; he spreads rottenness through the whole. A maggoty fig pollutes the crop.

MPR:38:5 Greed will gain earthly goods, even riches, but it distorts the soul. The soul of a greedy man is not pleasant to behold.

MPR:38:6 The possessions of a greedy man are never secure, for his avariciousness will destroy that, which his greed has gathered.

MPR:38:7 Greed is a poison within the heart, which contaminates and destroys the good, which is in man. The soulbuilders of virtue, honesty, duty and affection wither and die before its cold blast.

MPR:38:8 Avariciousness is the gravedigger for many who bow to it, for they enter their tombs while young; but greed is best known as the vice of declining years.

MPR:38:9 Riches are servants to the wise, but they are masters over the avaricious and weak. The fool serves his riches; they do not serve him. The greedy man possesses them as a sick man possesses a fever; they torment him, and he cannot rest. His bedchamber is not a place of peace, and his headrest denies him sleep. He is tormented by dreams of loss, and thieves assume the visages of demons.

MPR:38:10 Of what good are gold and silver when an abundance causes so much wickedness? Have they not stripped countless women of their virtue? The metals the Great God placed in the bosom of Earth to serve man have become his master, but blame not the metals, for they of themselves are neutral.

MPR:38:11 Are they not found in abundant quantities among the worst types of men, and are they not held in greatest esteem by the weakling who thinks they provide a substitute for the strength he lacks?

MPR:38:12 The poor man lacks many things, but the avaricious man denies himself everything that is good.

MPR:38:13 Expect no kindness from the avaricious man, for how can he be kind to another when his greed makes him so cruel to himself? How can he respond to affection when his affections are enwrapped in unfeeling things?

MPR:38:14 As a cancer to the body, so is avariciousness to the soul. Greed is king in the land of the small heart. Greed has seduced as many women as have soft words.

MPR:38:15 To be thrifty and provident is natural and good, but avariciousness is an unnatural perversion of these virtues and therefore evil.

MPR:38:16 The first good thing an avaricious man does is to die, and his death is the first benefit he bestows on man. Marriage to an avaricious man is like living in a residence without furniture.

MPR:38:17 In olden times, when men dwelt beneath the sun beyond the mountains, the avaricious man was not known, yet they had both riches and contentment, their life was abundant and joyful, what then happened to men? Perhaps it was these things, which they had, that changed them, if so can we be wiser?

MPR:38:18 Pontas taught that those who lacked contentment and comfort, prosperity and plenty, inherited the lands of those who had them, and this may be a lesser law. In these things, the writings are silent.

Chapter Thirty-Nine – Vanity

MPR:39:1 Behold the boisterous man and observe the vain one. They are arrayed in conspicuous attire, and their desire is to attract the attentions of men. They seek the gathering places and find their pleasure in the midst of the crowd, for little attraction is to be found in their own company.

MPR:39:2 The vain man scorns wisdom and knowledge; decency and reserve are strangers to him. He oppresses his inferiors and is insolent to his superiors who, in return, look down upon his weakness with amusement.

MPR:39:3 He despises the judgement of others and rejects the counsel of his friends; he relies upon his own opinions and is confounded. He pursues bubbles which break at his touch, while trampling underfoot the solid substance, which would bring him respect.

MPR:39:4 His imagination exalts his stature, but it is a magnified shadow without substance, a thing visible to none but himself. He delights in the adulation of others; he cares not for the welfare of any but himself.

MPR:39:5 He whom the multitude praises and acclaims, what is he but the mirror of its vanity and the froth on the surface of its weaknesses? The multitude is fickle and unstable, and the mob a collection of fools. The wise man and the Real Man do not degrade themselves for such as these.

MPR:39:6 Behold the vain man; a stream of insincere words pours forth from his hypocritical tongue, he knows the words returned by the wagging of ignorant tongues are no better, yet he laps them up as a thirsty dog laps foul water. He swallows his own praise with the greed of a swine, but the flatterer comes along and eats him up.

MPR:39:7 Be not one of these puffballs, a bladder filled with wind. Magnify not your stature because of your knowledge, nor be vain because of your attractions. What are you like within? Are you but a false fronted fool or an unmasked horror? Ask these things of your spirit in the silences.

MPR:39:8 Remember that the lover of praise rarely deserves it, and that to him life is but the shadow of a dream. The things that are worthwhile lie beyond his grasp, for he can see no further than his own reflection and is bedazzled by its useless glitter.

MPR:39:9 If you have become great, having once been lowly, or if having been destitute have acquired possessions, forget not what has happened to you in the days that are passed. Place not your whole trust, nor build your hopes, on the things, which have, after all, but come as a gift from God. You would not be superior to any other man if what had happened to you had happened to him. Is it by your own manliness and goodness that you have risen?

MPR:39:10 Carry yourself according to your present estate, and in higher positions, you will carry yourself with befitting dignity. Remember that he who thinks too highly of himself when there is no cause also belittles and insults others.

MPR:39:11 Heed the advice of those qualified to give it, and if unpalatable, remember that advice is never liked by those who need it most. Do good while you live, disregarding what men say about you, for the wicked and weak are ever jealous of the strong and good.

MPR:39:12 Never indulge in loud mouth boasting, lest you bring down the contempt of better men upon your head. Never belittle the deeds of another, for it makes known your own inferiority. Vanity deceives none but the vain, like a bladder filled with air, they collapse at the prick of ridicule. The vain man is blind to his own failings, and thus others see them more clearly.

Chapter Forty – Envy

MPR:40:1 The heart of the envious man is gall and bitterness. His tongue spits forth venom, and the success of his neighbours lengthens his night.

MPR:40:2 The worms of hatred and malice feast upon his heart, and his soul is corrupt and decayed. His face reflects but dimly the fearsome thing within.

MPR:40:3 His spirit finds no cause for gladness in the good fortune of another. His heart, instead of rejoicing, turns and sinks fangs of bitterness into itself, and the soul writhes under the distorting agony.

MPR:40:4 No flame of goodness warms the spirit of the envious man, and it perishes in the chill bleakness. He sits alone enveloped in a soul-misforming cloud of malice and envy, and to his poisoned thoughts, the good fortune of another appears to be a thing of evil.

MPR:40:5 He hates those who excel him and encompasses himself with a wall of wickedness, so that he is cut off from the good of Earth. His little heart schemes the downfall of others, but he himself falls into the pit, which has been dug.

MPR:40:6 He is ever on the alert for evil and on watch for wickedness, for they are never far from him. They overwhelm him, and his spirit flounders in the seething seas.

MPR:40:7 The soothing breezes of goodness never caress his spirit, and it languishes within him as a drab and feeble thing. Lacking goodness himself, he believes that all others are like him and so, puts an evil interpretation on all their deeds.

MPR:40:8 He is detested by all men, and the day comes when he is cast out from among them. When shall we see the day?

MPR:40:9 Envy, malice and hatred are soul cankers. Envy is the heart's recognition of its own littleness.

Chapter Forty-One – Bad Temper

MPR:41:1 The hot headed man cannot restrain himself; he exposes his weakness before all men. He shrieks his fury, and his voice soars up to the unheeding heavens.

MPR:41:2 He tears himself apart and casts his body into weariness. He rages like a destructive fire among the reeds, which blaze up in a gust of flame and then are no more; only blackened ashes remain. The Real Man smiles at this futility and quietly goes his way.

MPR:41:3 Turn your back on the bad tempered man, leave him to his own company, that he may consume himself. The fire that blazes in his belly shall reduce him to pale nothingness. Bad temper is no more than the mask of a weak and frightened man.

MPR:41:4 Akin to the bad tempered man is the rash man. Engage not in any undertaking with him, or you will be left to carry its burden.

MPR:41:5 In its fury, the whirlwind hurls down trees and destroys the places of cultivation. In its convulsions, the earthquake tears open the land and destroys the works of men. Such is the likeness of the hot headed man who in his rage wrecks the peacefulness of his surroundings.

MPR:41:6 Consider the extent of your own patience and forbearance; has your temper been tested in fires of provocation? You have turned from the rage of the lesser man, but have you considered yourself under his provocation? Let his futile raging be a warning to you that in the time of temper's trial, it shall remain before your eyes.

MPR:41:7 Remain passive when the waves of passion seethe within you, The wise captain remains in harbour during the violence of the storm.

MPR:41:8 Remain calm under the provocation of insolence, and refuse to be baited by insult. If you mete out chastisement it would be better done without unnecessary wrath. The sword drawn by a raging man is half wielded by his opponent.

MPR:41:9 Bad temper is a sign of weakness, for it indicates lack of self control. It is a failing of weaklings; the Real Man is able to remain calm at all times; but if, when pushed to extremity, the bounds of wrath are broken, then there is no better time for departure.

MPR:41:10 If the fires of bad temper rise up hotly to consume your heart, walk away and quench them in the quiet waters of solitude. The matter in hand can await a better day.

MPR:41:11 An insolent man can provoke a weakling so that he will consume himself in words of fire, but in the wise man, he kindles nought but disdain.

MPR:41:12 The flood waters of bad temper rise in the mountains of weakness and folly, but they drain away into the seas of remorse and regret.

MPR:41:13 Let he who so desires consume himself with rage, for bad temper is as useless as the waves of the sea without wind. The wrathful man rides a mad horse and is carried to destruction.

Chapter Forty-Two – Lying and Deceit

MPR:42:1 Avoid the liar; turn from his path, but fear him not, for falsehood is the weapon of cowardice. A lying tongue reveals a craven heart.

MPR:42:2 Lies and deceit are the merchandise of the weakling and coward; avoid contamination from their foul wares by shunning their company. Putrid meat defiles the pure air.

MPR:42:3 Leave the liar alone to squat in his web of falsehood spread for the unwary. Despise his shifty mien, his front is bold and his manner confident, his words are strong; but within, his heart trembles and his spirit is shrouded under a mantle of fear.

MPR:42:4 Lying and slander, weapons despised and rejected by the Real Man, loom large in the armament of the weakling. The tongue of the liar is a shovel, wherewith a pit is dug to trap the innocent.

MPR:42:5 He who makes himself the friend of the liar lacks wisdom, for the friendship of a double-tongued one is like dwelling in an abode built over a morass.

MPR:42:6 God turns his back on the hawker of lies, and an abomination to Him is the man who nourishes a secret grudge. If any man voices to you a grudge nourished secretly in his heart, shun him as the plague.

MPR:42:7 Neither do nor say anything, which will make the false words of a liar to appear as the truth. Commit no deed, which supports his speech. Leave him to peddle his slimy wares among the weaklings and fools.

MPR:42:8 Silence lies as well as speech. The heart can lie as well as the tongue. There is the lying deed as well as the lying word.

MPR:42:9 A liar is betrayed as often by his deeds as by his words, for his deeds are cowardly, while his speech is bold.

MPR:42:10 The liar seeks to deceive himself as well as others, for he knows himself for what he really is; being hateful even to himself, he wishes to make himself different. He practises deceit not only upon others, but upon himself.

MPR:42:11 The man of lies is never wholly joyful, for he walks with the ever present fear of exposure. Despise him, for he is unworthy of hate.

MPR:42:12 The deceitful man lays a trap at his own doorstep; avoid his habitation as you would the hole of a scorpion. If a man deceives you once he will do so again.

MPR:42:13 Disdain all flattery, for a man should be above such things. Flattery is the handmaiden of deceit and the child of hypocrisy.

MPR:42:14 Let all your dealings with men be straightforward and open; have no dealings with those of the double tongue. A liar, like a serpent, cannot follow a straight path.

MPR:42:15 The cowardly spirit trembles as it walks in deceitful ways. Fear and servility breed lies, as filth spawns maggots, and he who deals in them is to be despised. Though the deceiver successfully fools all men he cannot deceive his own soul, nor escape its constant rebuke. Could he but see the horror he is fashioning, he would recoil before its hideousness.

MPR:42:16 The deceiver is like an apple, which appears wholesome without but under the skin is rotten and full of worms. Like the liar, he has the heart and bearing of a slave, for within himself, he is not free.

MPR:42:17 Therefore, if by weakness you are tempted to avoid the burden of manliness, to ease the strain of living by recourse to lies and deceit, cast all such temptations aside. Retain your manhood and spare your soul. Deceit may bring gain, and lies respite, but the cost is high, for you brand your everlasting soul.

MPR:42:18 Deceitfulness, like disease, grows from a small seed and once implanted cannot be easily rooted out. Of what use is a healthy body if the spirit within be eaten up by the loathsomeness of despicable ways?

MPR:42:19 The tongue of a castrated man is thick with guile, for lack of manhood induces unmanly ways. Manhood is not only the cultivation of manliness, but also the mastery over unmanly ways.

MPR:42:20 A slippery tongue may deceive many, but prudence will secure the wise. A man is known by his companions. He who lives on a dungheap will stink in a perfumed garden.

Chapter Forty-Three – The Hypocrite

MPR:43:1 Akin to the liar is the hypocrite, his lips are like honey from the date, but his tongue resembles a poisoned dagger. Like the spider, he kisses to kill. He arches his tail like a scorpion ready to strike, or swings back like the crocodile preparing for the vicious sweep. He mouths sweet things, but the cruel sting lies behind them. He is like the serpent, which holds on to its venom though its back be broken; lift it aside in compassion and it will return you with death.

MPR:43:2 Have no dealings with the hypocrite, for he speaks fair to your face but when you turn raises his hand to strike. His opinions are secret, for in case of misjudgement, he has not the courage to stand by them.

MPR:43:3 The man who says he is the friend of all is the friend of none, for he is a hypocrite. The standard demanded of friendship is so high that a man's friends may be counted on his fingers, in most cases on those of one hand.

MPR:43:4 What a man does is important, not what he feels, thinks or believes. The hypocrite thinks one thing and does another, his deeds do not accord with his beliefs. When Truth is spoken, he is ill at ease, but when falsehood flows from his lips, his eye is steady.

MPR:43:5 The hypocrite will always be among men, for wherever they are gathered in concourse, there will be found those who excel over others. In the ranks of the inferior ones will be those who practise the dark arts of hypocrisy and deceit, to raise themselves up to the level of their betters. This the hypocrite and deceiver can never do; he will never be a Real Man, and his nature will forever remain that of a weakling.

MPR:43:6 Therefore, if you would be a Real Man, avoid hypocrisy in all forms, despise and shun the deceiver, and walk not in his ways. Let your tongue be straight, and bring forth that which is in your heart.

MPR:43:7 Let all your plans and deeds come from the heart, for if you follow not its dictates, then you are a hypocrite. If you praise a man to his face or agree with his argument because of his favour and not because it echoes in your own heart, then you are a hypocrite.

MPR:43:8 If you say a thing to one man and follow a course against your word with another, you are a hypocrite. Keep in your heart the simple charms of Truth, and forsake her not, for though she may not reward you obviously after the manner of men, that which she does bestow is beyond estimation.

MPR:43:9 If you stand within the precincts of a temple in the manner of a worshipper, but your heart is not there, you are a hypocrite. If you call a man "friend" but would not make a sacrifice for him or stand by him in his hour of need, you are a hypocrite.

MPR:43:10 If you follow the cause of another for your own ends and not for the cause, unless you state this before all men you are a hypocrite.

MPR:43:11 If one of the brotherhood of the slippery tongue be known to you, expose him to men, that they may know him and escape his wiles. If he be not an immediate threat, it is sufficient if you ignore him and indicate your feelings by your manner.

MPR:43:12 The Real Man is above the ways of hypocrisy, for these grow from the roots of meanness and avarice, the wasteland weeds of a desolated spirit. He scorns to stoop to the falsity of the hypocrite or to sacrifice his manhood at the altar of deceit.

MPR:43:13 The heart of the hypocrite can never be understood; his words are arrayed in finery under the disguise of Truth, while he goes about his business of deceit.

MPR:43:14 He laughs in sorrow and weeps in joy; none know his heart, nor can his words be interpreted. Black in the heart becomes white on the tongue, and white in the heart becomes black.

MPR:43:15 He labours in dark places like a mole and believes himself safe. He toils diligently among the dirt and thinks himself clean. Then, his efforts bring him out into the light, and, exposed for what he is, men kick him aside.

MPR:43:16 His days are filled with deeds of cunning, and his time occupied with schemes of deceit, but his nights are insecure, and sleep withholds its blessing, for the spirit within cannot find rest.

MPR:43:17 The day comes when his disguise is torn off, and he stands naked for all to see what lies beneath. Men who were deceived hide their foolishness in mockery, and all turn from him in scorn. Even hypocrite turns on hypocrite, for they deceive themselves and cannot be loyal to one another. The hypocrite and deceiver refuses to recognise himself for what he really is, he cannot look his spirit in the face.

MPR:43:18 The security of a hypocrite lies in his own deceitfulness, but walls of deceit can be overthrown by a tap from the feather of Truth.

MPR:43:19 The hypocrite hates all men, for he knows that when his fortress of falsehood is breached, they will drag him out into the open and reveal him in his true likeness. The lair of the hypocrite and deceiver is sweetly perfumed, like a garden of a thousand joys, but touched by the feather of Truth, it becomes a stinking mire.

MPR:43:20 If you pray out of habit or give generously for praise, or if you do good for the sake of acclaim, then you are a hypocrite.

MPR:43:21 The hypocrite, the liar and the deceiver are brothers and all distort their souls. Truth can fall from their lips, but it is usually in the form of bait.

Chapter Forty-Four – Slander

MPR:44:1 The malicious word of the slanderer is like a barbed and poisoned dart and swifter to destroy than the whirlwind. The slanderer casts down the good works of men with the tempest of his vile breath; his spite undermines the peace of households, and his tongue builds temples of deceit.

MPR:44:2 The mouth of a slanderer is like a cesspool, from which nothing comes forth but bad smells. The tongue of the scandalmonger is like a maggot; it spreads rottenness where once all was wholesome. It hatches the filth upon which it feeds. Filth begets filth, and while bewailing its existence, the slanderer and scandalmonger fill their bellies with it.

MPR:44:3 The utterances which pour from the mouth of the slanderer are hornets bent on harm and destruction. He is the father of lies, the servant of wickedness, he is the evil ferryman, of whom our fathers spoke.

MPR:44:4 Cast out the scandalmonger from among you, his thoughts hunt in the mists of dark places, and what he brings forth are the ingredients of mischief and woe. His tongue is the whip that lashes the graceful back of gracious Truth. If the water be dirty, can the linen be clean though washed ten times over?

MPR:44:5 His words are barbed and his tongue poisoned; he is the curs whelp, and his habitation should be a dungheap. He is jealous of the contentment and joy of others, which he cannot know. Therefore, he causes enmity and sorrow to arise among them, and therein, he finds his perverted pleasure.

MPR:44:6 Never permit the slanderer or scandalmonger to greet you as a friend, lest you lose the regard of your neighbours. Avoid his son, for a rotten tree does not bear sound fruit.

MPR:44:7 The unbridled tongue of the gossiping scandalmonger seeks out trouble and spreads it abroad. If it cannot be found, he will make it, for to him it is a commodity. Treat him as a worm beneath your feet and let his words be as the buzzing of flies in your ears.

MPR:44:8 The venom of a serpent remains potent until the beast is dead, but the venom, which drips from the tongue of a slanderer persists long after Earth has been relieved of his burden. Turn your just wrath upon all men of evil, for there is a limit, beyond which forbearance cannot go. He of the spiteful, wagging tongue will run from you like a mangy dog before reproof.

MPR:44:9 Be warned by the brotherhood of the wagging tongue. Take care to guard yours at all times, for an unguarded tongue runs to loose talk. The tongue of a man filled with potent drink is like a horse with the bit in its teeth. Be on guard when discussing the absent one, lest you do him wrong, for rarely is the absent one in the right.

MPR:44:10 Place not your ear at the hatchway, nor listen to the talk in council that it may be repeated on the streets. Never collect with your ears in one man's home and empty the catch through your mouth in another's.

Chapter Forty-Five – Friendship

MPR:45:1 The man without a friend should be avoided, for he is a man of iniquity. For every man should have one friend and no more than he can count on his fingers.

MPR:45:2 He who is a good friend will never lack friends, but he who thinks he has many friends has none. There is no greater loneliness than that of a man who lives only for himself, but better by far to be alone than in bad company.

MPR:45:3 Do no mean or deceitful thing in the name of friendship. He who by turning a friendship to his own advantage wrongs a friend, is unworthy of friendship and should be marked among men.

MPR:45:4 He who calls another "friend" while disliking him secretly, or who speaks ill of him to another, is a hypocrite and to be despised. A friend is not the companion of a day, nor the acquaintance of a month. Friendships may be made in good times, but it is in the testing times or hardship and adversity that friendship is established. Friends are for hard times, not for good. No man worthy of the name will desert his friend in distress. A friendship does not cease when there is dispute, nor when one falls into error. These are the testing times of friendship.

MPR:45:5 Make not a friend of the man of evil speech or whose ways are evil. Waste not your goods on a man of short acquaintance. The companionship of a wise and contented man, even though he be in prison, is better than a rash and foolish one who has wronged you, for though you may find it in your heart to forgive him, he will always be ill at ease in your company.

MPR:45:6 To keep your friends, owe them nothing and lend them nothing. In suffering and sorrow, judge your friend not by the tears he shed, nor by his moans, for the greatest afflictions go beyond such outward expression.

MPR:45:7 A rich man or man of position has none he can call friend, unless he knew him before acquiring possessions and importance. A friend is one who has been tried under adversity, for this is the touchstone of friendship.

MPR:45:8 He who says, "I have many friends" is a fool, for real friends are more rare than lapis lazuli in the wilderness. The false friend, the hypocritical friend and the fair weather friend are far more common than are real friends.

MPR:45:9 The friends who are least genuine often appear as the best ones. The false friend oftime seems the most desirable. The friend of convenience is an easy acquisition, but the friend who will remain when calamity strikes is harder to gain than the bronze breastplate.

MPR:45:10 The man who has friends possesses treasures beyond price. The man who has riches and no friends is poor indeed. Say not, "Were I rich, I would have friends;" how could you know?

MPR:45:11 A friend is not one who agrees with your argument; he is not one who frequents your abode; he is not one who sings your praises, nor is he one who converses pleasantly or bears gifts.

MPR:45:12 He is one who encourages you when misfortune presses, who lends his arm when you are down, who walks by your side when men flee from you, and who silences your opponents when you are not there.

MPR:45:13 He who supports you in the presence of opposition is a good friend, but he who champions you when you are not there is a better one.

MPR:45:14 He who helps you to victory is worthy of the name of friend, but he who remains by your side in defeat is a friend beyond doubt.

Chapter Forty-Six – Speech

MPR:46:1 Speech is the most sociable of all the attributes of man. It raises him above the beast and reveals his heart to a friend.

MPR:46:2 Make yourself a craftsman in speech, and in a contest of words, you will become the victor. The master is deft of speech, while the servant is clumsy. High rank and skill in speech are inevitable companions, but to a hasty-tempered or irresponsible man, the gift of the golden tongue is like a sharp sword in the hands of a madman.

MPR:46:3 The tongue is the mightiest of weapons, and fair speech wins more battles than fighting. It is also true to say that without speech there would be less strife.

MPR:46:4 To speak well you must speak honestly and from the heart. A dishonest tongue is a traitor within your walls, which will betray you. An inconsistent tongue leads among many devious paths, and you are lost.

MPR:46:5 If you say a thing in one place and contradict yourself in another, you will be wanted in neither. Your testimonies should at all times and in all places support themselves.

MPR:46:6 Speak quietly and to the point; conserve your words; the weakling is a mere word-wasting tongue wagger; be not like him. Speak firmly and to the point, graciously without malice or ill feeling.

MPR:46:7 Consider carefully your choice of words. One capable of two meanings issuing from your mouth without thought and being repeated elsewhere, may turn men against you. The tongue has overthrown many men and brought them to ruin.

MPR:46:8 The tongue has built a prison for many men. Many words batter down the gates of content, and regret enters, but silence will never betray contentment. In silence there is safety; a closed mouth safeguards tranquillity.

MPR:46:9 If accused by a liar, return a firm answer, remembering that he will also be a coward. His falsity will bear him off.

MPR:46:10 Fine speech flows not from the places of instruction alone, nor is it the prerogative of the wise. It may be found among men who carry water or the women who sit at the grindstone. An abundant supply of words is not enough; like a necklace they must be strung together in harmony and grace.

MPR:46:11 Converse with the ignorant man, as well as with the wise one, for wisdom is not wholly in the keeping of the wise. Does a physician learn from the sick or from the healthy?

MPR:46:12 If you encounter one who displays better craftsmanship in speech than you, do not set yourself up against him to contest his words. Show your discretion in silence, bearing in mind that, in many cases, silence is more effective than a bombardment of words. Then too, if you remain silent men will credit you with greater ability and say, "Had you spoken, he would have been overwhelmed and his argument refuted." There is a time for talk and a time for silence, and wise is he who knows the difference. He who speaks when he has no argument confounds himself, but if he remain silent, men may say, "He might have had a case."

MPR:46:13 Speak not until you have full understanding of a matter and can explain it even to he who knows more. In matters close to your heart, never fear that you will be lost for words, for if the heart be wrung, the mouth will open in eloquence. Even a dumb man makes a noise when kicked.

MPR:46:14 When you have nothing to say, say nothing. Never lash the air with your tongue. He who speaks for the sake of hearing his own voice has an audience of one, and he a fool.

MPR:46:15 Applause is a spur to the Real Man but an end and aim to the foolish man and weakling. Better the silent acclaim in the heart than the outpouring of noisy applause. A loud mouth discloses an ignorant heart.

MPR:46:16 The babbling man destroys instructive conversation, for it is overwhelmed and swept aside in his torrent of words. The ear becomes weary with listening and closes itself in sleep. Even the humble hen fowl is more productive than a babbling man; it lays an egg before it cackles.

MPR:46:17 A large outflowing of words is followed by regret and disquiet of heart, but beside the still pool of silence, there is tranquillity and safety.

MPR:46:18 The unthinking man gives full rein to his wayward tongue; his speech gallops away out of control, and he crashes at the hurdles of foolishness erected by his own words.

MPR:46:19 Let wisdom be the sentinel guarding the exit from your mouth, that no demon formed of words may escape to destroy your peace. If you speak with the headman, choose your words with care; if your counsel pleases, he will remember you when others seek promotion.

MPR:46:20 Never give misleading evidence before the judges, or speak in a manner which may lead to misinterpretation. If your neighbour lay fettered in a place of confinement because of your unruly tongue, his shade would haunt your bedchamber.

MPR:46:21 Fine words are out of place on the lips of a fool and lies on those of a governor. A falsehood spoken by a lowly man is less wicked than one told by a man of position and estate.

MPR:46:22 Even a fool, if he keep his mouth shut, may appear wise. The slow-speaking witness speaks firmly and frames the speech in Truth. He who speaks with haste leads his tongue towards falsehood. Truth is burnished by the cautious tongue, and its careful winnowing of words absolves it from error.

MPR:46:23 Avoid the lewd speech of ignorant men, for this is the consolation of slaves, even as lying is the refuge of the servile. Abusive words should never be hurled against those who stir you to wrath, for always they will return, like echoes from a cliff.

MPR:46:24 Become a craftsman with words, that your tongue may command products of intricate splendour and power, which will confound your adversaries and raise you to the utmost heights of eloquence and set you above the multitude.

Chapter Forty-Seven – Chatterer

MPR:47:1 Avoid the chattering man and babbler, for he makes a noise to hide his own emptiness. The quiet man is his master. Let he of the clacking tongue sit among the women.

MPR:47:2 The noisy man is a weakling afraid to meet himself in solitude. Whether he is going away or coming back, he continues to chatter. His speech is of little consequence and belabours the ears to tiredness.

MPR:47:3 He gossips and turns his own abode upside down, as well as the dwellings of others. His tongue clatters and labours from dawn to dusk but produces nothing. His tongue forms structures of wind.

MPR:47:4 There are less chatterers among men than among women, but a chattering man is ten times worse than a chattering woman. Yet the quaking tree is called 'woman tongue.'

MPR:47:5 Be not like the wagging-tongued man yourself; an unbridled horse is difficult to control. Open not your ears to tales of your neighbour's doings; can you think of no better things? Give ear to nothing but that, which lies within the orbit of your own interests. Repeat not the words of another, unless for a useful purpose.

MPR:47:6 Let your tongue spread no report, except of that which is good, retaining details of wickedness within your belly. Man was given one tongue and two ears, that he might speak half as much as he hears. Let the ears collect all that is spoken, the heart filter the good from the bad and the mouth pour forth all that is beneficial.

MPR:47:7 The tongue moves most when the hands are still; it labours hardest when the body is idle.

MPR:47:8 Nothing issues from the mouth of a chatterer but empty words, which beat the air with wings of futility. He who gives ear to his foolishness encourages the waster of words and makes a rod for his own back.

MPR:47:9 The ears of a chatterer are closed to his own empty talk; were this not so, he would place his head in the mouth of a crocodile.

MPR:47:10 Kick a full pitcher, and it stands firm, making no sound; kick an empty one, and it rattles,

MPR:47:11 He who talks most does least; it is the silent men who do things. The chattering man is nought but an annoyance; his clacking tongue deadens the ears, and his babbling lips pour forth irritating barbs.

MPR:47:12 Pleasantness of speech and instructive conversation are good, but gossip and idle chatter are evil.

Chapter Forty-Eight – Conduct

MPR:48:1 Be dignified when in the presence of lowly people. If with common people, talk not above their understanding. Whether or not you are at ease with them is unimportant, but whether they are at ease with you is important; for to put a man of lowly estate at ease is no small accomplishment.

MPR:48:2 Be not boastful at any time, for the braggard brings scorn down upon his head.

MPR:48:3 Go not into the dwelling of another man unless invited. Never enter when he is absent, unless with some purpose in his interests. Never place yourself in a position with his womenfolk where he shall have cause to suspect your motives.

MPR:48:4 Good manners mark the Real Man, and the secret of good manners is strength of heart and self-confidence. Gentle manners and soft words have carved harder stones than harsh blows.

MPR:48:5 Never interrupt a man when he is speaking, nor anticipate his words. Always hesitate before answering, and if the argument becomes inflamed, break it off and go your way. A prudent man knows his limitations.

MPR:48:6 When in the presence of your superior, speak with caution but freely and in a steady voice, with a straightforward manner. Stand upright, with hands at side or resting before you, let your manner be calm and grave. Let nothing provoke you to a hasty reply.

MPR:48:7 If a guest, eat moderately, but never eat while another stands hungry. Accept graciously that, which is put on your table, but if seated at food which many people hold in distaste, abstain from the food you like. Whatever the food put before you, never disdain it, unless it be against your conscience.

MPR:48:8 Sit not while one who is higher in your calling stands. Sit not while one stands who is weaker. Accept no table while your superior lacks one.

MPR:48:9 Keep your eyes from the doings of your neighbour in his own abode. It is his own domain, and his actions therein his own affair. What you see is stolen from his privacy; this is bad enough, but to disclose it to another is vile.

MPR:48:10 When you meet a friend, greet him wholeheartedly; when you meet an acquaintance, greet him warmly but with greater reserve.

MPR:48:11 Never touch the womenfolk of another household or speak with them on intimate terms. Treat them as you would wish your own womenfolk to be treated. If, to you, the respect due your womenfolk is unimportant, remember that better men think otherwise and treat them accordingly.

MPR:48:12 Do all things according to the decrees of propriety and decency. Forget not the obligations of manhood, nor neglect the responsibilities you have to your family. Spare a thought for those who rest in the bosom of the mountain.

MPR:48:13 It is fitting and proper that a man give due consideration to his body after he has no further use for it, for it must not pollute the Earth with corruption. If it be granted responsiveness as a channel of good, decline not the honours men would bestow upon it.

MPR:48:14 Prepare yourself a tomb upon the mountainside, where your body may be hidden. Neglect not to do this while you remain in health and strength, and all other activity should be set aside to this end. Thus, you will take your place among the ancient ones who rest secure in their caves.

MPR:48:15 Leave this to no other, lest calamity descend upon you from their lack of care. None will have as much interest in the final rites as yourself; therefore, be prudent and careful; do these on your own behalf.

MPR:48:16 When the shadowy form of the grim one beckons you to the Dark Portal, do not bewail the hour of his coming. In due course, he comes to all and carries the young as well as the aged. The welcome, you have prepared yourself, what have you to fear?

MPR:48:17 At all times, whatever the circumstances, bear yourself manfully, with courage and fortitude. Set an example to others by ever reaching out to the limits of your capabilities, that the heritage you leave to the coming generations of men be that they grow better through the ages.

Chapter Forty-Nine – Officials

MPR:49:1 Keep on good terms with the administrative officer of your district. Give him no cause to scrutinise the conduct of affairs under your control. Give him refreshment when he passes your residence, and report faithfully on all matters requiring his attention.

MPR:49:2 If he sends you on a mission, treat it as a matter of confidence; it is something between him and you. Talk about it to no man, lest you gain the reputation of being a man of unbaked clay.

MPR:49:3 If, at the behest of fate, you have been raised to the position of a governor over the people, consider the importance of your trust rather than the importance of your position.

MPR:49:4 Watch the manner of the people; do they acclaim you at your entrance to the city or at your departure?

MPR:49:5 It is your duty to set a course that is wholly right and to pursue it until your administration comes as close to perfection as is possible. Let the goodness of your days remain as an everlasting memorial.

MPR:49:6 Be patient and courteous; never speak harshly or petulantly from the security of your position, for this is cowardly. Listen to the plea of the petitioner with diligence and care; let your thoughts not wander idly; this is an important matter to him. If your attitude of attention is a false facade, then you are a hypocrite, and the extent of your hypocrisy accords with your rank. Bear with him in patience, and stop not the flow of words until he has emptied his heart and said the things he came to say.

MPR:49:7 If the decision be just, a reasonable man will accept the rejection of his plea with good grace, providing he has been given a fair hearing. When two come before you, weigh not the scales in favour of either; you are he who holds the balances, let others add the weights.

MPR:49:8 Let the people not say, "Why has this man been given power when he knows not its use?" If you cannot perform your own great task, how can you condemn one who fails in a lesser one?

MPR:49:9 If you are sent to a city where there is turmoil and unrest among the people, to quell the strife and seek its cause, handle the multitude carefully, for there may be reason for complaint. Seek the matter out, showing injustice and partiality to none. Incline not to those who are powerful, but deliver your findings with indifference. First adjust matters, and then judge.

MPR:49:10 Your first duty is to justice, and it must not be subservient to the power or interest of any man. The governor who, in upholding the statutes of men, turns his face away from justice, is a man of evil.

MPR:49:11 Justice is above kings and rulers. The magistrate is not the maker of justice, for it is not a thing made on Earth; he is but its servant and administrator. Lawmakers make laws, but they cannot make justice; they can only strive to reach it. Did not the voice of God say, "Let no earthly institution claim to be the fountainhead of justice?" Here the best men can do is to make the nearest possible approach to justice; on Earth it is unobtainable in purity and perfection.

MPR:49:12 You who are an official must bear the burden of your office gracefully and with dignity. Be not presumptuous because of it; is it the result of your own efforts or those of your father? Who had you instructed? Was this done by your own efforts and substance? Bear patiently with the poor man, for he has little on Earth to console him; let your interpretation of justice lighten his days. Never be rude to the inarticulate man, for this displays your unworthiness. Never create trouble for the lowly, for they already have their burden.

MPR:49:13 Let your arm be ever ready to guard the unprotected; ease the plight of the destitute, and turn not your face from the misery of the hungry. If you turn a hungry man away unsatisfied, and he steal to satisfy the craving within his belly, how can you who are well fed judge him?

MPR:49:14 The good official upholds the statutes of the land with one arm and supports the widow and orphan with the other. He defends the afflicted against the weaklings who oppose them.

MPR:49:15 He interprets the statutes with indifference to the estate and titles of any man; when in his presence, all men become equal in rights. He safeguards all that men enjoy; his sympathies are with the lowly and oppressed, and his hand falls heavily on the wrongdoer.

MPR:49:16 It is not sufficient to punish the wrongdoer; you must seek out the cause of his wrongdoing. It may be committed wilfully or in ignorance, or because of the oppression of circumstances. Punishment cannot be meted equally to all men.

MPR:49:17 There is no greater abomination that the corrupt official, and the king who retains one, is unworthy to rule.

MPR:49:18 A good magistrate is the servant of justice, not of the king, and often the time comes when he cannot serve both. Then is the testing time of his manhood.

MPR:49:19 The highest form of justice on Earth is the redress of human injustice, but where is the administrator sufficiently capable?

Chapter Fifty – Laws of Men

MPR:50:1 The laws of men are arrayed in pomposity to conceal their shortcomings. They conceal, within themselves, the seeds of injustice; yet, they are not to be held in disrepute, for with all their failings, nevertheless they reach a high pinnacle of achievement. Yet be not unduly bedazzled by them, but see them for what they truly are, the utmost limit of man's reach for perfection.

MPR:50:2 The laws of men will never eliminate the wrongdoer, for many crimes are permitted by inadequacy of the statutes and many more through the multiplicity of laws aimed at their prevention. Criminals are made by laws.

MPR:50:3 One crime fathered by the lawmakers is worse than ten wrongdoers escaping the penalty for their deeds. When those who rule are harsh or vainglorious, or weak and petty, then the people groan under a heavy burden of unwarranted laws.

MPR:50:4 He who promises a wrongdoer that retribution will be withheld or mitigated if he confess his guilt, is unwise, but if he later repudiate his word after receiving the confession, he is a man of evil. If he be powerful, his wrong is greater.

MPR:50:5 When he who is powerful inflicts torture upon one who is but suspect of wrongdoing, he commits an evil deed, not only against one who may be innocent, but against his own soul. Can reason be satisfied with a confession wrung from agony in this manner? The pain will move his tongue to state what is required from him. Can Truth be established by such means? Justice weeps at the justice of men.

MPR:50:6 They who serve justice best are those who acknowledge their own limitations in serving her.

Chapter Fifty-One – Social Obligations

MPR:51:1 O Son of Calamity, give thought to your manifold needs, and contemplate your many imperfections, then consider the reason for which you have been endowed with speech and affection. Is it not that you might develop, in association with others of your kind, the things, which cannot be developed in solitude? Therefore, if in being with them, you receive benefit from others, do you not owe them an obligation in return?

MPR:51:2 The food you eat, the garments you wear, the abode wherein you dwell, the armed men who protect you, the roads and waterways, the comforts and pleasures you enjoy; are not all these due to the efforts of others and the result of their labours?

MPR:51:3 Therefore, should you not give in return? The very nature of life declares your obligation; why then should you shirk the task? If you would enjoy contentment of heart, co-operate in harmony with others, and strive to attain prosperity within the prosperity of your neighbours.

MPR:51:4 Close fast your ear to the barbed words of the slanderer, and let the clacking tongue of the gossip rattle in his head unheeded. Let not the weaknesses and frailties of others become a source of pleasure unto yourself. Only thus can men dwell together in contentment and peace. Therefore, from the generosity of your heart, seek to promote tranquillity among those with whom you have to live.

MPR:51:5 If you cannot assist your neighbour, then leave him alone, that he may conduct his affairs without interference. Close your eyes to his weaknesses if they bring no harm down upon the head of another; if there be strife, then pour oil on the troubled waters, but seek not to place yourself in the position of grain caught between pestle and pot.

MPR:51:6 When many people dwell together, their peace depends upon a proper administration of the statutes, and the contentment of each man upon the safe enjoyment of his possessions. Therefore, upon you there is an obligation to uphold the statutes, even when they appear unjust in your sight, and to cast no covetous eye upon the possessions of another.

MPR:51:7 Lift no hand in anger against another, so that life or limb be put in danger, or do him wrong. If he provoke you let it not be a matter for unmanly raging; might he not be a weakling unworthy of anything but your contempt? If attacked, then deal with the situation as it warrants, for no attack should go unheeded, lest it invite another.

MPR:51:8 Never slander a man or gossip about him, for these are things more becoming a woman. Never bribe a servant, that he steal his master's time or goods. Never seek to tempt a woman of another household; if one turn her womanly wiles upon you, then scorn her advances, for she plans an upheaval. Bring not upon another man a sorrow you cannot relieve, nor do him an injury, for which you cannot atone except with your life.

MPR:51:9 Be just and fair in all your dealings and faithful to any trust placed in you. Never deceive a man who places his trust in you, for it is less wicked to steal from a stranger than to betray the trust of one you know.

MPR:51:10 If you owe a debt, then pay it without delay, for he who placed his trust in you treated you as an honest man; to withhold from him that which is due is the action of a mean man and weakling.

MPR:51:11 Deal justly with all men, that your name may have value among them. A good reputation is of greater value than gold.

MPR:51:12 Have no dealings with a man who says, "Let me be the go-between." He deals neither with goods nor labour, and all he sells are worthless words which neither fill nor satisfy. To him say, "Go reap the harvest of land or water, or set your hand to the hammer or wheel, for we have no use for purveyors of empty words."

MPR:51:13 Be cordial with all men, but be on intimate terms with none but your friends. Nevertheless, a friendly spirit is to men as honey to bees; a friendly man is allowed to do much. If the captain of the vessel likes you enough, you can wipe your hands on the sail.

Chapter Fifty-Two – Food and Drink

MPR:52:1 Dally not unduly at the eating table, nor spend too long in beer drinking. He who overeats or overdrinks, quickly becomes a fat sluggard, his belly bloated and his wit dull; women mock his lack of manhood.

MPR:52:2 Hanker not for fancy food or meat that is highly spiced, for it will create a sword in the stomach and a glowing ember in your gullet. Dainty food and delicate dishes are the pleasures of women and not to be denied them.

MPR:52:3 Gluttony is a disgrace to manhood, for as a man grows m girth, he declines in vigour; one thing replaces another. He who eats little is zestful, while he who gorges himself is sluggish. He whose greatest interest lies in satisfying the demands of the stomach is a reproach to manhood, for he is dominated by his appetite. The stomach always cries for more than it requires.

MPR:52:4 Never do anything that arises from the consumption of strong drink, for what you do will be done without thought; caution flees the heart when strong drink enters the mouth. The tongue motivated by strong drink is wayward, and the mouth, which permits its entry incautious.

MPR:52:5 If, while under the domination of strong drink, you fall and injure yourself, none will waste sympathy upon you; even those who know you will pass by and leave you where you fell.

MPR:52:6 There is little harm in drinking, which delights the heart or makes a meeting of men more convivial; the dividing line is whether strong drink is the master or the servant. When a man ceases to speak, think and act in his normal manner, it is the point of departure between him and the companionable cup. The Real Man has a casual acquaintanceship with the drinking shop, but to many who are weaklings it is home.

MPR:52:7 Sufficient food maintains health; overmuch destroys it. Beer drunk in moderation does no harm, and wine in small quantities can bring contentment and pleasure.

MPR:52:8 When you savour the delightful ripeness of fig or orange, covenant with it in your heart, saying, "The life that dwells in you, I absorb into my body as a sacrifice at the altar of life. As you were sacrificed to me in the name of life, so shall I sacrifice to life. The tree that would have been your resurrection shall grow within my spirit and bring forth the fruit of benevolence and joy. The delightful fruit, which would have been your offspring shall grow to maturity as fragrant thoughts within my heart. The sweet perfume, which would have been windborne from your blossoms shall flow from my lips as the nectar of kindness and affection. You have not been destroyed wantonly but joined to a greater stream of life."

Chapter Fifty-Three – Home

MPR:53:1 Build yourself a residence of your own when you find no peace in a dwelling shared with others. A home is a man's anchor and a woman's sanctuary.

MPR:53:2 Take unto yourself a wife to share your abode. Though a man may build a dwelling place, it needs a woman's hand to make it a home.

MPR:53:3 Always suffer the mistress of your household to talk about you, for in her eyes you are more important than anything else. A woman must necessarily discuss her husband, as a man must talk about his calling.

MPR:53:4 Attempt not to direct her about the affairs of the household when she is a good housewife. Say not to her, "Where is this?" or "Where have you put that?" when you know she puts them in their proper places. Set your eye to watch her, observe her ways carefully, and then appreciate her good management. Pleasant is the lot of the man who travels the road of life hand in hand with a thoughtful woman.

MPR:53:5 Men do not naturally understand the ways of women. The man who interferes in housewifely affairs only sets his own home in confusion, and contentment will fly through the door.

MPR:53:6 He who would enjoy peace in his residence must be open-hearted and considerate, but above all wise in his choice of a wife.

MPR:53:7 Beware never to let the slanderer and scandalmonger cross your threshold. It is better to slay yourself than admit the fornicator, for he will destroy your joy and contentment.

MPR:53:8 Beware when the flatterer establishes a place for himself within your dwelling. Outwardly the members of your household may sing and rejoice, but within their hearts will be a cavern of sadness.

MPR:53:9 If your friend comes and stands without, admit him as one of your household. Greet him with warmth and kindness, and make him welcome within. Let your womenfolk attend to all his wants, for he is your friend and will not dishonour your household.

MPR:53:10 If one comes visiting bearing gifts, accept them graciously, and let him enter. Judge him not by rumour but as you find him, letting caution remain in attendance. If he be worthy of your friendship, he will know many who do not call him friend.

MPR:53:11 Do not present to him a smiling countenance, while your heart remains sullen, or you are a hypocrite. Guests always bring pleasure of some kind, if not in their arrival, then with their departure.

MPR:53:12 If one comes with a request, never say, "Come again tomorrow and I will give," when it is in your power to give today. Thus speaks the weakling and coward.

MPR:53:13 Consider your family and friends, what they are like, for they are clear pools, wherein you see yourself reflected. A man has the wife, family and friends he deserves.

MPR:53:14 What precious things have you within your dwelling, that you safeguard them behind fastened doors? Have you gold and silver there? Have you gemstones or fine works of copper? These may be kept safe by bolts and bars, but the greatest possessions of man cannot be held securely by such simple means.

MPR:53:15 Have you peace and quietude there? Do you share your home with joy and contentment? Do you hide memories there, or have you stored things of beauty to stir the soul? Does love reign as queen of your home, or are you under the tyranny of strife?

MPR:53:16 Is your dwelling a haven of joy in a sea of sorrow? Is it the treasurehouse of sympathy and understanding? Or do you reside in a place harbouring nought but luxury and comfort, where the stifling air is befouled with the unwholesome lust for ease? Comfort can always be invited in as a guest, but beware lest it stay, to become the master of the household. It is easier to be the slave of luxury than the master.

MPR:53:17 Comfort may coax you into its snare with soft allurements, but the shackles it will place upon you are as finely forged brass. Its touch may be silken, but its grip is metallic. Its voice may be soothing, but it sings of your downfall.

MPR:53:18 Luxury may gently lull you to slumber, but while you sleep, it weaves a web of disaster. Comfort mocks at manliness and undermines the ramparts of fortitude. It jeers at virtue and stabs courage in the back.

MPR:53:19 Yet comfort and luxury are not things to be completely avoided, for held in rein, they serve their purpose. However, let them serve as servants and not rule as masters, for they are good servants, but bad masters.

MPR:53:20 Let your dwelling not become the tomb of manliness and the abode of the half alive.

MPR:53:21 Home is not where the body rests but where the heart resides, and where a man receives the most care for the least thanks. A good residence is built on a rock; a good home is established around a good woman.

Chapter Fifty-Four – Family Relationships - Son

MPR:54:1 He is your greatest joy, the son, whom your heart's desire has begotten, the hope you hand down to the future. Yet the pleasures of fatherhood must be tempered by the need for chastisement, for the youth does not become a man without discipline. All youths grow up, but not all grow into men.

MPR:54:2 Great are the duties of a father, and grave are his responsibilities towards his son, for the future of the youngster lies wholly in his hand.

MPR:54:3 Remember that your son will imitate you in word and action, and that the best instruction is by example. If you expect him to do that, which you do not, or not to do that, which you do, then you are unjust and unworthy of your charge.

MPR:54:4 If your son reaches manhood lacking the knowledge of things a man should know; if he possesses a sullen manner and ill disposed nature; if he is a weakling or dissipator, then he is a disgrace to you and a condemnation of your fatherhood, you have failed in the most important duty of a man.

MPR:54:5 Your son is what you have made him. If he grows up a failure or weakling, then add not to your unworthiness as a father by rejecting him. He remains flesh of your flesh and your responsibility and burden; in the fullness of time you can make amends.

MPR:54:6 The first step in begetting worthy sons is to make a wise choice of their mother.

MPR:54:7 Riches and position, a father may not be able to give his son, but example and good counsel, discipline and a guiding hand into manhood can be given by every father. These are the birthright of every son. Cursed be the despicable man who denies his own son this birthright.

MPR:54:8 No man has ever turned from his father and departed from his household because he was not given riches and possessions; but many men have turned away from their fathers because they did not receive proper instruction, guidance and opportunity.

MPR:54:9 Cursed be the man who accepts the joys of begetting his children, but evades the responsibility of their up-bringing. His sons will not forget, and his old age will be barren and filled with regret and self-reproach.

MPR:54:10 Chastisement in the home is a proper preparation for the discipline of life. There is no way other than by a wise and proper upbringing that a youngster can be prepared for life.

MPR:54:11 It is not sufficient that a son be as good a man as his father; life progresses and he must be made a better one.

MPR:54:12 Whether your son grows up to be a blessing or a curse to his father, or whether he becomes useful or worthless, depends entirely upon your wisdom, guidance and care. Think not that the task can be treated lightly, or you will live to regret your folly. The sapling may be bent to shape, but the tree is unalterable; if it be unseemly, other men will cut it down.

MPR:54:13 Therefore, commence his instruction as he learns to walk, and as he grows, nourish his thoughts with the maxims of wisdom. Carefully guide his footsteps towards manhood, for there are many improper paths and pitfalls.

MPR:54:14 Bend his nature in the right direction while it is still supple. Mould him in uprightness while he is still pliable. Turn him in the right direction during youth, and watch his inclinations. If evil habits appear, weed them out before they take root and develop in strength. Chastise him with restraint, for overmuch punishment reveals defective upbringing. Let it be given only of necessity, for the most receptive ear of a son is that on his backside, which listens best when thrashed.

MPR:54:15 Guide, but never drive. Always treat his mother with respect and affection, for if you find contentment and joy with your wife, he will find them with his. Leave him not with a heritage of sorrow.

MPR:54:16 So shall he grow in comeliness and strength; a man of honour, noble and straightforward in his ways, a Real Man. He shall rise above lesser men as a great oak rises above the brushwood, and though you may have failed in all else, this achievement will set the crown of success on your life.

MPR:54:17 The virgin soil is yours to cultivate as you will; it is fertile and responsive. Let it not want for care, for if it be unhusbanded, it will remain barren, unproductive. The good pasture that is neglected produces weeds in abundance, and who is blamed, the pasture or the husbandman?

MPR:54:18 The seed which you sow will produce a crop to be reaped in the fullness of time. The weeds you neglect to pull up will multiply and pollute the harvest. A harvest of gladness and pride can be yours; according to your sowing and attention, so shall you reap.

MPR:54:19 Deposit with him your treasures of stored knowledge, your hopes and aspirations, and he will accumulate a profit greater than your dreams. He may transmute the ashes of failure and bitterness into the gold of success. Think well about your appearance in his eyes, for to him you are the inspiration or handicap.

MPR:54:20 Teach your son manly ways, for he is destined first of all and above all to be a man. Leave him not to acquire his nature in the chambers of women. A son needs the firm guiding hand of a man, for that of a woman is too soft.

MPR:54:21 Instruct him in the ways of discipline and self-control, that he may be master of his life. Show him the wrong of boastfulness and the error of vainglory. Instruct him in the need for manly forbearance, show him the wrongfulness of ingratitude and womanly ways. If he become a follower of falsehood, a deceiver or hypocrite, then he is a memorial to your everlasting shame.

MPR:54:22 Instruct him in the ways of moderation, in the ways of healthful living. Show him the folly of indiscretion, that he may avoid the pitfalls of life. Instruct him in the ways of diligence, that he may become a master of his craft. Show him the weakness of insincerity, that his heart may be strong. Instruct him in all the things where in you have succeeded, and show him wherefore you have failed.

MPR:54:23 Instruct him in the bearing of arms and in the art of combat and defence. For what use is it to teach him wisdom, to instruct him in skill and show him a good way of life, unless he has also the ability to defend and retain these things?

MPR:54:24 Is it not futile and a pitfall for his feet to instruct him to defend the weak, to fight for justice and to oppose the oppressor, unless he be given the ability and strength to do so? Would you send him against a lion armed with a twig?

MPR:54:25 Are you going to instruct your son to fight for a cause and send him out to do combat unarmed? Would you give him possessions, home and honour and then deny him the skill to defend them?

MPR:54:26 The Law decrees that every desirable thing must be struggled for and then defended when attained. Nothing that is good comes easily or is easily held.

MPR:54:27 Give your son confidence in himself and in his people. Give him pride in his nation and in his kinsfolk.

MPR:54:28 Instil into him, by example, the love of learning; if he lacks intelligence, he has hands; teach him a skill.

MPR:54:29 Teach him to bear all things manfully, the good with reserve, misfortune with fortitude and disaster with courage.

MPR:54:30 Teach him to think and to query and to reason. Teach him to rely upon his own judgement and to be self-sufficient within himself. If he ask no questions and agree with you on all things, inquire if he be really your son. If he spend too much time in the women's quarters, turn him upside down.

MPR:54:31 Instruct him early in the way of God, for unless the seed be planted early, the plant will not bloom in its season. Unless the fragrance of belief in the True God surround it, life is meaningless and empty, for it lacks warmth and vitality. It will have no purpose beyond pleasures that pass and the accumulation of things, which will be taken away. He will follow your good example.

MPR:54:32 Show him the paths of contentment and peace. Deny him not a joyful childhood. Respect his mother, that he may learn respect for his wife. Dispute not with your wife in his presence, lest he think it proper to dispute with his. That, which you do, he will do likewise, and if you have not the wisdom to live peacefully within your own household, then he is the son of misfortune.

MPR:54:33 Let not your son live apart from the things of your life; the things you know now he will know later; the things you do today he will do tomorrow.

MPR:54:34 You cannot teach your son courage and duty, fortitude and affection, temperance and diligence. These things he will inherit from you by example, therefore let your every word and deed in his presence be considered.

MPR:54:35 If you chose his mother unwisely, then it is well to keep in mind that you did the choosing; the mistake is yours and not his. Therefore, put her not away from your household and deny him her love; for you, having chosen your burden, must now carry it.

MPR:54:36 The way of life you inherited was that made by the generation of your father. The life of your sons will be made by your generation, not theirs. Will they reproach or praise you?

MPR:54:37 The generation of perfect fathers will be followed by a generation of perfect sons, and in those days, they will live on a perfect Earth.

MPR:54:38 Wars are not made by sons, but by fathers. There are no criminal sons, just indifferent fathers. If a son take a whip to his wife, it is a father's hand that put it there. If a man lurk in wait to rob another or to commit a deed of wickedness, his father stands beside him.

MPR:54:39 When a man walks along the path of wickedness, his hand is in his father's hand. When a man is made captive because of his wrongdoing, his father haunts his prison.

MPR:54:40 The deeds of a son, whether they be good or bad, reflect upon his father. As a father basks in the light of a son's achievements, so shall he not escape the cloud of his failure.

MPR:54:41 Say not that others have led him into the paths of wrongdoing. If a dwelling be well built, it will withstand any assault of wind or weather. If it be faulty, where lies the blame, with the builder or with the structure? If you seek to cast blame on others for the upbringing of your son, you reveal your own lack of forethought and care for his wellbeing. If you delegate your son's instruction to another, it is your responsibility to see that the instruction is adequate.

Chapter Fifty-Five – Family Relationships - Father

MPR:55:1 A tree does not tear out its own roots, nor does it denounce the soil; neither does a man strike his own father. He who turns on his father in wrath cuts his heart in twain.

MPR:55:2 Be guided by the instructions of your father, and obey the words of your mother, and the day will come when you will be a respected man among the people. If they have a responsibility to instruct, then you have a responsibility to obey.

MPR:55:3 Be grateful to your father who brought you into the congress of men with pride and thanksgiving, and to your mother who conceived you as an offering to love and sustained you in your helplessness.

MPR:55:4 Listen to the instructions of your father, for they are given exclusively for your own welfare and good. Obey him at all times, for what he desires of you is bent to your own benefit. Resent not his admonitions, for they come from a heart filled with affection for you.

MPR:55:5 He has made sacrifices for your welfare and laboured to provide for your upbringing. He guided your steps when you first stood upright, and his arm shielded you from hurt in the days of your helplessness.

MPR:55:6 Therefore, honour him in his old age, and protect his grey hairs from insult and indifference. You are his pride and joy; deny him not a share in your achievements.

MPR:55:7 Remember how he shared your youthful problems and toiled that you might sleep secure from the shadow of want. Therefore, indulge the infirmities of his old age, and guard him in his declining years. Your own sons observe your ways towards him and record them in their hearts.

MPR:55:8 Permit your father to pass to his permanent abode in peace and contentment. Respect his old age and the dignity and beauty of the grey beard; thus, you will set an example to your own sons, and in the years ahead, you will not go unrewarded.

MPR:55:9 Strive to reflect credit on your father and on your mother, and if you fail in this, then bring gladness to their hearts and contentment to their spirits.

MPR:55:10 Even a weakling and fool will be loved by them, though he repays their affection with sorrow and care. He who fathers a weakling is a father of woe.

MPR:55:11 Let not men mock your father because of you; what has he done that you punish him in this manner? Why fashion arrows that pierce the heart of your mother? What have they done? They gave you bread, and you repay them with a stone.

MPR:55:12 Why be indifferent to your father's welfare; was he a weakling? Watch over him always. When strife knocks on his door, hasten to his side. Remember who trained your right arm; would you now deny him its succour? If your father be beset with trouble, give your eye for him and be honoured among the Noble Ones.

Chapter Fifty-Six – Family Relationships - Mother

MPR:56:1 See that your mother never lacks warmth and sustenance; cherish her in her declining years, as she once cherished you. None will ever give you the love and tenderness that she bestowed upon you, and you will never have but one mother.

MPR:56:2 In the days of your helplessness, she carried you as a heavy load. You were as a yoke upon her neck and a chain at her ankle. Because of you, many pleasures were denied her and her freedom curtailed.

MPR:56:3 She cleaned you when you were dirty; she bathed and salved the sores on your body. She felt no disgust when you lay in your excrement. She supported you with comfort in your infantile helplessness. She never denied your plea when you cried for her breast and you lay in her arms content in the knowledge of love and security.

MPR:56:4 You grew beyond the years of infancy and were placed in the Place of Instruction. While you chanted your letters and absorbed the knowledge that fell from the lips of the masters, did she not come through the heat of the day unfailingly? Did you ever lack food or drink or the solace of her tenderness?

MPR:56:5 When the task placed upon you was arduous and your heart was heavy with the birth-pangs of inspiration, when you despaired of success, did she not lighten your burden with encouraging words? Did she not make your homecoming an hour of joy and your playtime an hour of gladness? Did she not encompass your life with understanding and compassion? Did the springwaters of her affection ever run dry? Where are the limits of a mother's love?

MPR:56:6 When filled with the vigour of manhood and glowing in the pride of your strength, turn your eyes to her grey hairs and bent back, and let compassion rule your heart. Gaze upon the wrinkled brow and furrowed cheek, the face etched with self-denial and care, how much of this have you written there?

MPR:56:7 The joy she found in you was the joy of self-sacrifice; her gladness was in self-denial, the pleasures, of which she was deprived, contributed to yours.

MPR:56:8 For you she sacrificed the woman's joy in fine linen; the mantle she should have worn was your swaddling cloth. The delights of the table were abandoned, and she ate plain food, that you should eat better; she took from her enjoyment, that more might be added unto you.

MPR:56:9 Now that you are a man and have outgrown the need for her solicitude and care, put her not aside in the lower chamber. Give her sustenance from the first fruit of your labours and cherish her as the most precious of all your treasures. Let her hold her place in your household and enjoy the respect that is her due.

MPR:56:10 Let it never come to pass that she has cause to complain to God regarding your treatment. His ear will incline towards the outpourings of her sorrowful heart, and His heart will harden towards you. Misfortune and affliction will be visited upon you and eat away the contentment of your days. The indifference to your mother's welfare will not go unheeded among men, and they will avoid your company.

MPR:56:11 In her declining years, lend her the support of your strong arm; relieve her of the burden of labour. Treat her with affection, and speak to her gently; do nothing to cause her grief and bear her infirmities with patience. The afflictions of aging bones will demand your consideration; let the call not go unheeded. If the years have made her frail, treat her gently, even as in the years long gone by she was gentle with you in the days of your frailty.

MPR:56:12 To a man, a mother represents all the finest qualities in womanhood. Therefore, treat her as the best of all women, and if she falls short of the standard, remember the frailty of all mankind and forget not your own imperfections.

MPR:56:13 The man who abandons his mother to want or leaves her helpless in infirmity is a reproach to manhood and an abomination to God. His soul is an ugly thing, and when it comes forth in the Halls of Eternity, men will recoil from it in disgust.

MPR:56:14 Respect your father, and love your mother, that your days may be endowed with contentment and joy. He who withholds love and affection from his mother will never be loved and never deserves to be loved.

Chapter Fifty-Seven – Family Relationships - Brother

MPR:57:1 The strongest tie of friendship is not as firm as that between brother and brother. They are the flesh of one father and the beneficiaries of one instruction, the product of one household. The breast of one mother nurtured them in infancy.

MPR:57:2 Therefore, let the bond of affection unite each one with his brother, that there shall be peace and harmony in your father's abode. Unite in brotherly comradeship and stand firm together, that your joint strength shall uphold your estate.

MPR:57:3 Though separated by your crafts, never sever the bonds of brotherhood and unity. Never prefer a stranger to one of your own blood.

MPR:57:4 If your brother struggle against adversity, it is your duty to assist him. Should he go forth to fight those who threaten the peace and security of his household, you shall be his first supporter.

MPR:57:5 If fortune be favourable to you and less kind to your brother, it is for you to adjust the balances. It is meet that brothers share each other's fortunes and misfortunes, though each should reckon with the other's weaknesses.

MPR:57:6 He who deserts his brother in his hour of need is unworthy to be called by the name of man. He who turns against his brother and assists his opponents is unworthy.

MPR:57:7 The love and care your father gave to his sons shall be continued between you and your brother. It shall not be lost to your family, but shall continue down through your generations.

MPR:57:8 When you need support, send for your brother; he is to you as the right hand is to the left. His added weight shall carry your venture to success.

MPR:57:9 Reject not your brother because of his downfall; yours should be the hand to lift him up. If you fail him, you are both lost indeed, and by turning from him you betray your own manliness.

MPR:57:10 The life of man is composed of many states, each of which imposes its own duties and obligations, not the least of these is that of brotherhood.

MPR:57:11 Because you know your own brother too well, perhaps with him you are less tolerant, yet though better known, his failings are no worse than those of other men.

Chapter Fifty-Eight – Family Relationships - Daughter

MPR:58:1 The flower of your household and the pearl of your dwelling, the shrine of all the gentle virtues in your home is the womanchild you call daughter.

MPR:58:2 Lavish your affection upon her, for affection is the sustenance of all women, without which they wilt like flowers without the sustaining waters. Guard her well from brutality and crudeness; permit no lewdness in her presence, for she is the symbol of grace and delicacy in your household.

MPR:58:3 Her welfare is your responsibility. Respect the gentleness of her nature, and shield her from all coarsening influences.

MPR:58:4 Leave her instruction to the womenfolk, for only women can instruct in the ways of women. Nevertheless, let her not go without discipline; treat her with firmness and instruct her in responsibility. Humility and obedience should not be overlooked. Teach her to realise the power of womankind for good or evil, and instruct her in the arts of womanhood, for a manlike woman is an abnormality.

MPR:58:5 The nature of a woman is not easy to mould; that of a man is easier. She is to be gentle but not weak, delicate but not frail, yielding but not submissive and sympathetic without being subject to imposition.

MPR:58:6 The training of a daughter is not to be lax because of her beauty, rather it should be the contrary. Undisciplined beauty is a thing of evil. Womanhood, if handled wantonly, destroys the manliness of men instead of inspiring it.

MPR:58:7 To her, you are the example of what a man should be. She will measure all men according to the standard she sees in you; therefore assure yourself that it is fitting to a Real Man.

MPR:58:8 If any man seduce your daughter and thus defile your home, then it is your duty to render him incapable of repeating the deed. Not for revenge shall this be done, but to keep undefiled the homes of other men and to maintain the values of womanhood. If your daughter be seduced, then you have failed as a father and must adjust the scales, that you fail not also as a man. The seducer has offered the greatest possible insult to you and your household by openly declaring before men that your daughter is unworthy of marriage.

MPR:58:9 When you choose a husband for your daughter, do not disregard riches and position, unless they are possessed by a weakling. However, choose first a Real Man, for he will establish his position, your daughter will be respected and her security and contentment assured.

MPR:58:10 It is less difficult to raise a son than a daughter, for though both need equal discipline and chastisement, it is easier to give these to a son than to a daughter.

MPR:58:11 Consider the imperfections in your wife, due to her father's lack of care and wisdom, and ensure that they are not repeated in your daughter.

MPR:58:12 If your daughter be fair in face and form, then beware, lest this poison her nature, for it will bring the indulgences of men. He who fathers a lovely daughter carries no light burden and no little responsibility. The father who has indulged and spoilt such a daughter is not uncommon, and he must bear the reproach of her husband.

Chapter Fifty-Nine – Family Relationships - Wife

MPR:59:1 Your wife is as the stone of Lamed, which doubles all it touches. Give her affection, and she will return it twofold; give her love and it will be returned doubled. Think not less of her because she is in your power. From whence comes this power, but from her father's trust in your ability and steadfastness, your kindness and consideration. The wise man does not disdain a precious gem because he owns it; possession should add value and not detract from it.

MPR:59:2 She is fruitful ground, in which to sow. Plant confidence, and she will return faithfulness forever. Plant contentment, and the tree of peace will arise whose shade shall ever provide a place of tranquillity when you are troubled. Plant joy, and reap a manifold harvest of gladness.

MPR:59:3 You have not chosen her from body lust, nor to be a constant woman of pleasure; these can be found on any street. Nor did you choose her to be a labourer in the kitchen or the supervisor of the servants, these can be bought. Is she not chosen as the mother of your children, the mistress of the household and the companion of your journey through life? She will be there by your side in times of trouble as well as in times of joy.

MPR:59:4 There is but one choice of wife open to the wise man: the best woman he knows. Miserable is he, and unfortunate the lot of the man who knows not a good woman. Why do they shun him?

MPR:59:5 Your wife will, if well chosen, halve your sorrows and double your joys. If chosen foolishly, she will multiply your sorrows and dilute your joys with bitterness.

MPR:59:6 It is proper that a man have a wife, who should be loved so long as both shall live. You love your father and mother through good times and bad, in sickness and in health, though they provoke or ignore you, chastise or praise you. Their shortcomings and weaknesses are known and accepted, due allowance is made for their failings and their love is always returned. Yet they are not of your choosing.

MPR:59:7 Therefore, if you can accept and be content with those not of your choosing, is it not reasonable to expect you to be more contented with a wife of your own choice?

MPR:59:8 Put her not away from you, when she is no longer young. To whom did she give her youthful freshness? Let the delight of your youth be the companion of your old age, and you will not find her wanting. Who knows you better than she does?

MPR:59:9 Youth is turbulent, and old age is tranquil. Would you put away the tried companion of your struggle because she bears the scars of the conflict? What would replace her? Youthfulness that is untried in adversity, beauty that blooms on the face but is scarce budded in the heart and vitality that has not been sacrificed at the altar of your ambition. Would you give away the sustaining nut for the pretty shell?

MPR:59:10 While youth is passing from your wife, her love is maturing within. Her love, like the unfired clay, was pliable and unstable in youth. Now, it has been passed through the fires of marriage and is set firm and solid, a thing of stable solidity. The unfired pot can be cast back on the wheel and remoulded, but once fired, it remains firm until broken, and once broken can be shaped no more.

MPR:59:11 In youth, the heart speaks between husband and wife and is excited. In the declining years, soul speaks to soul and is contented.

MPR:59:12 The wife of your youth brings you the delights that any woman can give, but the wife of your old age brings you the contentment that can be given by no other.

MPR:59:13 The need of man for woman is great in youth, but in old age, the need of husband for wife is greater.

MPR:59:14 Love blossoms in youth, but it bears its fruit in the maturity of age. The heartaches and pangs it engenders are chisels cutting away at the granite of the soul, shaping it into finer form.

MPR:59:15 Youth is the sowing time of love; the harvest is reaped when youth has passed.

MPR:59:16 No matter how humble the dwelling, there should always be a place set aside for the womenfolk of your household.

Chapter Sixty – Secrets of Womanhood

MPR:60:1 O Daughters of Men, forget not your ancient heritage of mystery granted unto you in the days of old, when you were the light of mankind. Was Earth then afflicted under your sway, and did men then degrade themselves and strive one with another?

MPR:60:2 The age of benevolent mother rule has departed, and little remains of woman's former glory. But remember that the fall of woman and the woes of men were brought about by the wiles and weaknesses of woman.

MPR:60:3 My daughters, remember your attributes, and consider your estate. You can either be the instruments of good to inspire man to great heights of achievement, or be the instruments of evil to degrade him and bring his manhood into disrepute.

MPR:60:4 The woman who says, "I will be no man's unless he be a Real Man" is a maker of Real Men and serves the purpose of God. For the charm and mystery that are the gifts of life to woman were ordained to create a desire and longing in men, and their purpose is to inspire men to reach above and beyond themselves, that they might obtain and possess a treasure so precious.

MPR:60:5 Therefore, O Daughters of Beauty, value yourselves highly, for she who gives herself cheaply inspires no man; for it is the nature of man that he treasure that which is hard to obtain. Man values the scarce gold, not the plentiful marble.

MPR:60:6 She who comes easily to man, he regards lightly; it is the Law that man values only that for which he strives and suffers. Reveal not your womanly charms and secret attractions. Is not the moon more beautiful when shining through a cloud, for then its loveliness is enhanced with mystery.

MPR:60:7 Woman was given a body to reproduce sons, and grace and beauty to inspire them to godlikeness. The spirit of man is inspired and raised up by the love of his mother and the love of his wife. There will be no greater influence in his life than womanlove.

MPR:60:8 A graceful woman is ever clothed in mystery. A good woman will always make Earth a better place for her presence.

MPR:60:9 Beauty of face and form are passing things, but the real beauty of womanhood lies beneath these externals. Seek it out and develop it, for it will be much more enduring. Consider not the beauty of the body, for it is here today and tomorrow departs forever. Concentration on outward appearances displays a shallow spirit to the eyes of men.

MPR:60:10 Beauty of face and form may or may not be yours, according to the dispensations of fate, but whatever you have must be accepted with gratitude or resignation. What you have been given, little can be done to change, but it is not the most important part of your being. There is that within you, which is yours to fashion as you wish; it can be of a beauty indescribable, transcending anything of Earth. Therefore, give due thought to the pliable soul within you, for it is yours forever. It can be a thing of loveliness or repulsion, according to your own decree.

MPR:60:11 The Law, which is beyond your understanding, has decreed the mould of your body; it is fixed, unchangeable. Not so your soul, for here you alone are responsible for its appearance. Remember that every thought and deed is a thread in the pattern of the fabric. Think well; will the result be a thing of beauty or of ugliness?

MPR:60:12 Let prudence rule your heart, and be reserved in all that you do. Remember the womanly virtues of modesty, simplicity, compassion, gentleness, tenderness and grace. Cast not the treasures of your womanhood into the mud, where they will be trampled underfoot by contemptuous men.

MPR:60:13 In the springdays of womanhood, when the promise of loveliness is fulfilled and the warm blood stirs within you, the eyes of men will turn in your direction with meaning, and nature will interpret their glances. Then is the time to give heed to the whispered counsel of prudence and place a guard upon your heart; now is the time when it is ripe for assault; let it not yield except to one. Heed not the false words of seduction and the alluring promises, which fall from the glib tongues of fornicators. The words of seducing men are sweeter than honey, but if you partake of the illicit pleasures offered, they turn to the bitter gall of disillusionment. The seducer has his purpose; he tests you for worthiness as a wife.

MPR:60:14 Woman was meant to be the helpmate and companion of man, his inspiration and joy, not the slave to his desires and the servant of his passions. Are you no more than the receptacle, wherein he satisfies and dissipates his uncontrolled urges? Or are you the goddess of his heart, whose tender touch can soothe the turmoil, which tears his body, who evokes within him the gentle passions of affection and consideration, whose soft endearments are sufficient to strengthen him sufficiently to stifle the struggle within? She who is the first of these takes the easy path, but the second is ten times her better and a worthy wife for any man.

MPR:60:15 Discuss not the ways of the harlot or wanton woman m the hearing of others, lest they say "Her interest betrays her inclinations." Never associate with such as these, for they pollute by their presence. The harlot never repents, and when she reforms becomes a procuress.

MPR:60:16 Seek not to emulate the ways of men, lest you sacrifice the charms of womanhood. Men admire and desire the womanly things in women and the manly things in men.

MPR:60:17 Women attract by their reserve, not by their boldness. They conquer by their submissiveness, not by their attack. They hold by their weakness, not by their strength and they attract by their modesty, not by their forwardness. If seeking a weakling for a husband, you may sacrifice some of your womanliness, for what you lack he will supply.

MPR:60:18 Beware the power of your charms and belittle them not. For while lesser men are but slightly moved by womanly charms, to greater men they are as a whirlwind in the wilderness. Therefore, in the hands of a wanton woman the grace and charm of womanhood are as poison in the possession of one who is mad.

MPR:60:19 As man has a duty to life, so has woman, and hers is to uphold the prestige of love. Thus it is that, though her heart may be moved with compassion, she castigates her wanton sister. Here, harshness serves life better than sympathy and compassion.

MPR:60:20 Know that there can be no greater joy on Earth than that found by man and woman in the sacred union of wedded love. The greatest inspiration of life is the pure and lovely flame of True Love.

MPR:60:21 The temple of hallowed love is in the heart of a chaste maiden or faithful wife, and all men secretly worship there.

MPR:60:22 There is no greater incentive to bring out the best in a man than the true love of a good woman. If you would ennoble life, then weave a mantle of love around your chosen mate.

MPR:60:23 My daughters, beauty is the heritage of all women. Think not only of the beauty of face and form, for this passes with the rise and fall of the waters. Turn your thoughts to the greater loveliness of the spirit; to the radiance enshrined within the thinking heart and the beating heart, this is the true heritage of woman. Purity and graciousness can belong to any woman, whatever her external appearance. What is beauty where tenderness and affection are lacking? Men will run after a beautiful face, but away from a wilful heart.

MPR:60:24 A beautiful woman is beautiful to herself, the admiration of men adds nothing to her beauty. Womanly virtue maintains the blossom of youth and brings contentment to the heart. Thus is the face kept smooth in beauty.

MPR:60:25 Nothing exalts the heart of a man as much as purity in the woman of his choice. Nothing can stimulate his manhood as much as her modesty and reserve. Nothing troubles his thoughts or arouses his curiosity as much as her silence.

MPR:60:26 Let not your future husband's hopes of your chastity be in vain. Mock not the faith of a man in woman, for man requires such faith, and if he be a Real Man, he will believe the best of woman. The seducer and fornicator alone look down on women, for they have seen many at their feet.

MPR:60:27 O glorious and prudent maiden, who will some day rule as Queen of Heart and Home, keep the pure flame of love secure within the sanctuary of chastity. This love asks, above all, that love may be hallowed.

MPR:60:28 Though chastity remains the greatest weapon for good in the armoury of womanhood, like all things on Earth it can be used otherwise. Chastity of itself alone would be of no value unless it serve a positive purpose for good. Futile frustrations are the opposite of good, but chastity is not numbered among these. Chastity hallows and expresses the sanctity and glory of true love, and bestows on the loved one the honour and bliss of an undefiled and uncheapened marriage. Chastity is not the suppression of feeling and the refuge of the unaffectionate; it is the homage paid to the sanctity of a woman's body and the evaluating tribute paid to true love.

MPR:60:29 Our fathers and our fathers' fathers, even in the days before Mina and Pontas, expected and respected chastity in woman. Not in all women, for this is not the nature of men; a man seeks it only in one special woman, his wife. Thus man divides the women in his life in twain, his wife and mother, and other women. No man concerns himself with virtue in the wives of other men, only in his own. Virtue in other women may be unimportant. Which would you be, a wife, the delight of a man's life, or the other unimportant woman?

MPR:60:30 Chastity is the glorious crown of maidenhood; it is the symbol of dedication to the glorification of love; it is honoured and respected by all men. A husband trusts a chaste wife and speaks of her proudly among men.

MPR:60:31 When men discuss women, after the manner of men, the husband of the unchaste woman tries to avoid their looks, their talk cuts his heart. The unchaste woman is a topic of ribaldry among men, but let a man discuss a chaste woman lightly, and there are hard words spoken. In the company of men, does not the chest of the chaste woman's husband swell out before him; is he not proud of his exclusive treasure?

MPR:60:32 The heart of the deceived man and fool shrinks within him when men speak among themselves, for he feels humiliated and uncertain of his place among men. What he has is cheap and the subject of crude jokes among them.

MPR:60:33 Act in all ways befitting a woman. Be modest and reserved, for eagerness does not become a woman. Never go unto a man unbidden, but await his call or a woman messenger. It is unseemly for a man to summon a woman by a man.

MPR:60:34 To women go the things of women. Therefore, turn your hearts and hands towards the inclinations of womankind; cherish and comfort your children; attend diligently to the affairs of the household; support and sustain your husband through his trials and troubles.

MPR:60:35 The drinks of woman are sweet, but she may sip a heady or bitter one without loss of decorum, though she may not drink it as does a man. Only the common woman will drink the drink of men or drink as a man.

MPR:60:36 A woman who safeguards her reputation in public, but is shameless in private, is a hypocrite. She is a deceiver who will drag a man down to sorrow.

MPR:60:37 My daughters, these are not words of wisdom alone; they draw aside the veil to reveal the inner hearts of men. Let your own heart weigh them in the scales; it will commend them to you. If a man deride them, then he is not inclined to your welfare, nor does he see in you a future wife. If you say within yourself, "These things are of little importance to me," you may speak truth, for you are unworthy; the crocodile revels in mud and disdains silk. The womanly virtues are not evaluated in your eyes, but in the scales of Spiritual Eternity. That, which spiritualises life, that enhances love, that inspires mankind and sanctifies the relationship between man and woman, that is good in the eyes of God. You may ignore the wellbeing of your soul if you so desire; its fate is yours to decide.

MPR:60:38 She who sanctifies womanhood garbs her soul in eternal radiance.

Chapter Sixty-One – Prayer

MPR:61:1 Prayer is the communication of the soul of man with the Soul of God. It is the effective means, whereby the great dam of spiritual power and inspiration is tapped. Above all it is not a babble of words.

MPR:61:2 When you pray, do so in silence, with all the words retained within yourself. Pray not with the tongue and mouth, but with the spirit.

MPR:61:3 Inharmonious noise within the sanctuary of God is detestable to Him who is the God of harmony. Rites that produce loudness are an abomination to His ears. Implore Him with a loving heart in quietness, and He will hear your words and accept your offering.

MPR:61:4 The ear of God is closed to the man who speaks, but is open to the silent man. When he who is silent comes to speak, not that men may hear but God, then He hears him. Is not the Great God known among us as the Listener in the Silences?

MPR:61:5 Is not silence the speech of love? God speaks in the still silences. He communes with man in the silences of the soul, and in silence was the creative word spoken.

MPR:61:6 Seek always after silence and quietude, and seek friends among the silent ones. The man who fears to be alone with himself in silence or solitude will never discover the secrets of the soul. Men go into the wilderness to commune with their souls in silence; only thus, do they receive a reply. He who lives ever among noise and turmoil says, "I have no soul."

MPR:61:7 When in prayer, occupy yourself with the affairs at the boundary of the Region of Hope, for prayer spans the Great Unseen Barrier. Prayer is the bridge between two regions, but few there are among men who know how to pray, that the bridge may be opened.

MPR:61:8 Words are unimportant to prayer, for good and fine words alone are not edifying to God. He hears that which is spoken from the heart and reads that which is written in the soul. Therefore, those who are answered are few, and those who are not because of their own inadequacy say, "Where is God that He hears me not?"

MPR:61:9 The souls of men, swathed in flesh and wrapped in passions, cannot easily commune with God. Successful prayer needs much conditioning of the soul; it requires a lot of preliminary preparation and is, therefore, rare. Men say, "Prayer is futility" and to such as they, so it is, but it is not prayer but their conception of prayer that is futile. If a man write so that none understand him, is the reader or the writer at fault if the writing cannot deliver its message? When speaking to a Southern man, he understands not unless you use his own language, even so should you communicate with God in His manner.

MPR:61:10 The ingredients of prayer are humility, sincerity, surrender of desire, acknowledgement of inadequacy and a wholehearted offering of self. It is the opening of a door to admit a wonderful power into the chambers of the soul.

MPR:61:11 Prayer, as it should be, is followed by a profound peace, a spiritual uplifting and a feeling of inner quietude, as though a cool clean breeze sweeps into the spirit, strengthening and reviving it so that clear-thinking follows naturally.

MPR:61:12 When at prayer, listen to the voice of the spirit, for it may be interpreting the words of God. Prayer renders the soul articulate. The length of prayer is unimportant, but the depth and range of prayer matters above all else.

MPR:61:13 Prayer is a state of harmony embracing heart and spirit; it is not a rite.

Chapter Sixty-Two – Death

MPR:62:1 Fear not death, for when he comes, you will be no longer there. Nevertheless, it is well to live a good life and be free from the fear of his shadow, for he that is good has nothing to fear.

MPR:62:2 What is death but the gateway to glory, the entrance into the Kingdom of Greater Life? It is a journey to a new land, an awakening from a sleep where all care and affliction borne on Earth are left behind.

MPR:62:3 Do not men respect death above birth? Do they not adorn their weapons, the servants of death, with gold and precious stones and display them proudly to all men? Have not honour and titles been the lot of many who have caused the slaying of thousands? But who has ever been honoured for bringing a man to life?

MPR:62:4 While there is but one way of entry into life, there are a thousand ways of departing. All roads through life lead to the gates of death.

MPR:62:5 The deer does not cry until it feels the arrow, nor does the fowl shriek until the hunting hound seizes it. He who ever dwells under the shadow of the fear of death dies many times, and the fear is greater than the event itself.

MPR:62:6 Death I fear not; if violent men come with sharp weapons as its messenger, I may fear the instruments, I may fear dying, but death itself holds no terrors. Come it must; of all things in life it is the most inevitable. God grant I accept it as a man.

Chapter Sixty-Three – Close

MPR:63:1 Evil times have befallen the wise and upright. Truth shows her light no more, and deceit walks the land, garbed in gay raiment and with a bold front.

MPR:63:2 These times of evil and these days of affliction were foreshadowed by a decline in the goodness of men, by the lust for pleasure among the people and a seeking after things, which brought forgetfulness, in carelessness of craftsmanship, in indecision of thought, in disdain for wisdom and in disregard for the welfare of the land. Men think only of earthly things and, therefore, Earth becomes a region ruled by wickedness and corruption.

MPR:63:3 Yet this I say unto you; the mockers of the wise and the scorners of wisdom shall tomorrow be forgotten, and the wisdom they deride shall have its day when they are dust and their names forgotten.

MPR:63:4 My children, I am a man of no mean reputation, and here my estate remains intact, though the greater one downstreamwards is lost to me with my name. Even now, events move and soon all will be but a memory. Not for long now shall I be left to sorrow, nor is the death of an old and feeble man any great achievement.

MPR:63:5 Old age weighs me down, when I should be swift, and I bear it as a heavy load. My spirit must soon sail towards its place of origin and immerse itself in the waters at the source of life. I am not loath to depart from this place of sorrow and corruption.

MPR:63:6 Therefore, my children, hear me diligently in the recounting of the wise sayings and secret knowledge of our forefathers. Record them as a guide unto your generations.

MPR:63:7 Now is the day of the wrongdoer. The kindly and unselfish man goes down and the honest man is the plaything of winds of adversity; it is the brazen-faced ones who rise to sit in high places.

MPR:63:8 The iniquity of the wrongdoer is no more than a subject for talk in the marketplace and even moves men to mirth. The shame of women is accepted as normal, and causes no stir except on the thoughtless tongues of the idle.

MPR:63:9 I carry my burden of wretchedness alone, for no friend is left to me among men of my estate. I await the time when my habitation will be laid open to the winds, my place of waiting be filched from me and my funerary equipment be no more. Yet I am still a man of no mean estate.

MPR:63:10 Death attends at my right hand, but I am not perturbed for myself but for my incapacity. O for the arm that once bore the spear and the eye that shot it home! Death is not feared, for it will be as cool waters after a journey in the heat of the day. It will be as freedom to one long held in confinement, or as green pastures to the wanderer of the wilderness. Death is no stranger, for I have lived as a man, nor is it unwelcome.

MPR:63:11 I look around and not until then do I fear death, for it crowns my feebleness. I see righteousness cast out into the darkness, while iniquity sits at the council table. No man obeys the rulers, nor has respect for the statutes, which now breed their own overthrow. There is none so wise that he perceives and none so wrathful that he speaks. The courageous men are dead, and they to whom the land belongs now lie buried in it.

MPR:63:12 The priesthood prospers, and the people live for the day's pleasure, but virtue and wisdom wander the road as beggars. Lewdness replaces learning in the talk of men, and women delight in displaying their charms; the lesser men have come into their own.

MPR:63:13 The bold face goes everywhere, and the reserved man is beggared. Lewd speech and vile conduct is acclaimed; the deeds of wanton women are the subject for conversation. There are no more worthy men in places of power, and the land is in the hands of those who work iniquity. A contented heart is unknown among men.

MPR:63:14 Brother works wickedness upon brother. The hearts of men covet the possessions of others. Children treat their fathers with little respect, and the words of their mothers are mocked. Men smile at the wives of other men and are gay in their presence, but they remain sullen in the presence of their own. Men marry the wanton woman, and her place is established.

MPR:63:15 Fathers leave the instruction of their offspring to others and allow their womenfolk to wander loose. O where are men such as once walked the land? Where are the men of days gone by; did they all die for the king? Do lesser men remain to breed lesser men, while the best are now no more?

MPR:63:16 The ordinances of the halls of judgement are cast forth into the streets; the great writings are carried away. Slaves become the lords of slaves, but their hearts are the hearts of slaves and not of masters. The weaklings walk with riches, for the strangers are their protectors. It is a time of calamity.

MPR:63:17 A man runs to save his own life, while his brother is slain. The grain is gathered by the powerful and wily and not by he who sows. The vulgar man gains a high born lady to wife, while a nobleman raises up a singing woman.

MPR:63:18 The products of craftsmen are faulty, for none takes pride in his craft. Bribery and corruption are the guiding lights of men. Women cannot conceive, for their wickedness makes barren the womb. Men say, "Where is God?" But God has withdrawn because of their wickedness. The false gods flourish and wax fat on promises.

MPR:63:19 Where once the voices of joy were heard, now there is lamentation. Men curse their fathers because of their birth. Maidens array themselves in gaudy ornaments and are no longer modest. Widows and unmarried women open their doors, and strangers are permitted to enter. It is a time of woe.

MPR:63:20 They who once walked in white linen are now in rags, and he who never wove is now the master of weavers and the possessor of fine garments.

MPR:63:21 Would that the seed of men might perish in the womb, for they who come forth are no longer worthy. Thus it was written by one before my time and thus it is again, as the wheel spun before, let it spin again.

MPR:63:22 You, my children, are the hope of the people. Therefore, give your hearts to learning, for in the whole land once united, there is nought else worth possessing.

MPR:63:23 Peruse diligently these writings, and let them be the measure of your heart. Keep them beside you or carry them to a place of quietude, that they may be better contemplated in solitude.

MPR:63:24 It will be an unworthy deed to make alterations in the record of these things. To falsify that, which is written is a wrong against your children and against Truth.

MPR:63:25 The writings will give you pleasure, though that is not their intent, and they will bring tranquillity to your heart and teach you the ways of men. If they cause you uneasiness of conscience, then they are not without achievement.

MPR:63:26 The water flows away, time speeds by on feet of swiftness and the unlearned things are uncountable, as the sands that blow in from the wilderness. Therefore, be like the goose that extracts the sustenance from mud, and devote yourself to the welfare of your soul. Though the spiritual understanding of man is limited and his moral nature weak, nevertheless he fails to utilise fully the attributes he does possess. Man does not make sufficient effort to rise as high as he could; he does not reach out to the boundaries of his limitations; he approaches but a little way towards the goodness he could attain, did he but extend himself.

MPR:63:27 Therefore, give heed to these writings, for they are offered for your benefit; they are not things recorded carelessly or without reason. They will enlighten the ignorant and give all men assurance, that they may steer a steady course through life. Fill your bellies with them, as with cool waters. Store them up, as a prudent man stores corn against a time of famine. As the value of corn is enhanced in times of famine, so is it that in the times of trial and tribulations, these instructions will be more honoured.

MPR:63:28 Man mixes the mud and straw and lays the bricks one on the other, but it is the will of God, which gives them firmness and holds the structure to its form.

MPR:63:29 Give ear to these instructions, and your condition in life will be like unto those who have gone before. Make yourself learned in the written rolls, and everything you do and say will be profitable.

MPR:63:30 Every word written shall pass correct, as a thing which can never perish in the fertile lands. The wisdom shall beautify the commands, which are given by nobles and princes. Let they who understand become craftsmen in speech, and having learned fine speech, pass on to others their knowledge, that the writings may be received with respect.

MPR:63:31 The heart that is well immersed in wisdom rejoices when this is proven a bringer of peace and prosperity. If, within your heart, you say, "Why need I these instructions, for all these things I know," does he who has recovered from a sickness need a physician, or he who has crossed the river a boat?

MPR:63:32 Yet to you I say, be not hasty of speech, for to know is not enough; these things are not given to be just known but to be lived. Know them you may, but do you also live them? Let this written wisdom be the straight edge to show how much you deviate from the true. Use it to align yourself, to eliminate the crookedness.

MPR:63:33 Not the least purpose of these writings is to reveal your weaknesses, to remind you that your body is but dust and to stimulate your spirit with the joyous knowledge of the glories awaiting your awakened soul.

MPR:63:34 Whatever your store of wisdom, be prudent; let your heart serve as a counterbalance for your tongue. Let your lips speak true and your eye see only that which is right for it to see. Ensure that both your ears hear the same thing.

MPR:63:35 Avoid all men who mock and will not incline their ears. Disregard the fool who will not listen, for he will effect nothing. He will mock the man of knowledge as a man without understanding. Wisdom and prudence, he considers to be defects. He smothers his soul and then proclaims that the lifeless thing does not exist. He spends his days on Earth, but he is already as one dead, for life to him is worthless. Men avoid him because of his manner and because of the many troubles, which beset him.

MPR:63:36 When you are hoary-headed and men hold you in respect, instruct your children in these things, even as you have been instructed. Every man has the duty to pass on the knowledge he has acquired undiminished. To tell what he has learned to his children, that they in turn may hand it on to their children.

MPR:63:37 Suppress no word in the writings, nor add anything to them. Set not one thing in the place of another, and instruct in accordance with that which is prescribed. These are things long handed down by word of mouth in the inner sanctuaries of wisdom.

MPR:63:38 All men seek the truth among the temples, but only the Great God knows who has found it. He who knows within his heart that all things here written are good and beneficial but who fails to practise them, is like a man who lights a lamp and then closes his eyes. Let these things not have been written in vain, nor the effort, which has not been small, be wasted.

MPR:63:39 Here ends the book, its beginning to its end as it was found in writing inscribed to endure. Keep it with you always, not just for times of joy and light, but also for times of distress and darkness. Though the moon and many stars are always shining, when the sun sets, it is night.

MPR:63:40 Done into writing and a faithful transcription by a dutiful pupil of a beloved master whose name, being unknown to men, shall endure forever in the Great Halls of the Ever Glorious Ones. Not all is as the master wrote, nor are they all his writings, though attributed to his inspiration by those who sat at his feet and, following the same path, sought to glorify him.

MPR:63:41 For he journeyed in sorrow towards the sunsetting, not knowing whether his seed took root or was cast on barren ground. Who, because of his words, was cast out from his estates and left believing himself deserted by God and man.

MPR:63:42 All men sow, but few live to see the harvest or the strange fruit it brings forth.

Book of
Origins

OGS:1:8 Life is a song, sometimes a song of sadness, sometimes a song of joy. Now a dirge, then a hymn echoes through the chambers of creation. Often a gay carol or lilting lovesong gladdens the ear of the air. All this is the Song of Life. So lift up your hearts, and rejoice in the singing soul, which will, in days to come, rise on ghostly wings to quit the inner circles of woe, where the discordant notes of mortals intermingle with the melodious notes of spirit music, winging its way to where the stargirt chorus sings in glory.

Table of Chapters

Book of Origins

Preamble

Translated by John Laid Ledylith

OGS:0:1 This task was undertaken and carried out by order of the Tothnaelethan made in solemn accord, assembled as beforetimes at Tanagekil near Sunderstow. One hundred and sixty years after the death of Ardpeth, the last king. Twenty years after the death of Garadon Pankris. Eighty years after the death of Kelwin. One hundred years after the death of Afterid. Thirteen years after the death of the great king who died in the year of the devil's breath. This dealdew, lasting upward of a dozen years, so striking the land that people lost their distinctions, and the long conflict came to an end. Forty-four years after the battle of Strathard, when the Christian king died in his forty-sixth year, going down with a great slaughter before the hand of Kadwilan of the Firstfaith, who died at the hands of a treacherous king, being trapped between the trees by Dinsleir. In the month of September, between the seventh and the tenth day, in the third year of the reign of Ethelbred, which is the seventh year in the reign of Egfrid, son of Oswey, king of the North Saxondom. The fourteenth year in the reign of Ardwulf, king of East Saxondom and the second year in the reign of Ketwin, king of West Saxondom. The fourth year in the reign of Lothir, king of all the Kents, and the fifth year we suffer under the afflicting fires of the Black Bull of the North. It is two hundred and twenty-two years since the coming of the long-sword-wielding warbands and one hundred and sixty-five years since the death of Okther. It is one hundred and thirty years since the last warband came and stayed with the land they took, when Britain ceased to be, during the reign of King Ifor.

OGS:0:2 These are the elect Kailwardens who undertook the work: Humog and Lewin of the Gutradors; Pencluith the Dalradan, a smith of the Shieldmakers; Helaf the Carver, born among the Scots over the sea, of the Shieldmakers; Malkuin, a Chief, born among Kwits, of the Engravers; Enelek the Potter, born among the Kwits, of the Shieldmakers; Ipedruad the Grinder, born at Alcuth, of the Coppersmiths; Fronwin the Swordmaker; son of Klude, a Briton born as a freeman among the Saxons to the West and an engraver of note; Edwin the Elder, a Talesman who writes, born of a Mercian, of the Shieldmakers; and Glason the Inglinger who became one of us.

[This preamble appeared at the back of this book in the 1st edition. It was moved to the beginning for this edition. Also, some of the 1st edition eBooks used "OGF" instead of "OGS" in the citations. The correct form is “OGS” for this book.—Editor]

Chapter One – The Worldbirth

OGS:1:1 This is an unhappy time of strife and change, and the old folk knowledge and skills are passing away like leaves falling on flowing water. We of the Gwidonad are therefore gathered together under the shield of Hirweal for the purpose of preserving the things dear to our hearts. To do this, we firstly discover their biding places, and secondly commit into writing all the hallowed tales concerned with them. Also, as the mortal memories of men perish with their frail bodies, we deem it well to commit into bookwriting the old knowledge once written in our minds.

OGS:1:2 Behind us lie fourteen Earth generations of mankind, and this has been the manner of their naming: The Generation of Light, The Generation of Fire, The Generation of Water, The Generation of Grass, The Generation of Trees, The Generation of Wood, and The Generation of Stone, and all these together are the Blissful Generations. Then followed The Generation of the Spear, The Generation of the Axe, The Generation of the Shield, The Generation of the Sword, The Generation of the Bow, The Generation of the Helmet and The Generation of the Chariot, and all these together are the Homeless Generations. The years before us contain six full Earth generations and whatever remains of this Generation of Change. Each of the past Earth generations was three times the length of the one, which followed it.

OGS:1:3 Men ask, as men always will, how the widespread, wonderful world came into being, and whose were the feet first treading the good soil upon it. This, masters, is the old tale concerning the dawntime of life, handed down from the blissful morning days of Earth's existence.

OGS:1:4 Before time was born, it could be conceived. Before all things seeable by the darting eyes of men were seen by any eye, they were conceived. Before sound was heard by any listening ear, it was conceived. All things now knowable by man were first conceived by none but The Inconceivable One, existing solitary in awesome loneliness. Back in the predawn state there was no feeling, throbbing, loving life beyond The Alone One. There was nothing, in which something other could be perceived and manifested. The Inconceivable One's reflecting mirror was not yet made. Love, the sunlight of life, could not be known, for even One So Great could not yet conceive a state of satisfaction in self-love. The one thing not capable of conception was the realisation of responsive love.

OGS:1:5 So from The Inconceivable One there came a great outpouring melody, the song of conception, the notes winging vitalising consciousness outward in radiating ripples. All that is now existing came out of that, which was harmoniously sung into being, and the sweet echoing vibrations still sound in rhythm throughout the many circles of existence. All life and matter vibrate in response to a divinely originated, orchestrated melody and rhythm.

OGS:1:6 As the sweet notes of the divine, lilting music swelled outward, Heaven was formed from the song-created radiance of immortal light. Rising on a higher note of ever increasing splendour into a great pulsating chorus, it hurled forth a whole string of worlds, scattering them in illuminating brilliance through the black matrix of Ked. It was like a handful of bright pearls being thrown into the darkness of night. In a perfectly timed cadence of melody and harmony the worlds were hurled into separate existence, each finding its proper place in accordance with its note. All life is therefore nothing except a response to harmony and melody, to the spreading ripples and resounding echoes from the first Divine Hymn, the life-awakening song. The only disharmonious notes were those which later emerged from the hearts of sinful men.

OGS:1:7 The songs and poems of men, poorly stirring the unresponsive heart, are futile attempts to recapture some part of the first grand symphony. Men instinctively know they are musicians in the great orchestra of life, singers in the chorus of existence. The Song of Life still vibrates upon the lute strings of each throbbing heart, filling it with responsive vitality. On Earth, it can never be heard in perfection, yet it is here the singing lessons must be learned; for once through the dark archway and in the Court of Splendour, the newly released spirit must introduce itself by song. The good, clean spirit vibrates with a happy, harmonious melody, while the dull, evil-doing spirit rasps out harshly in agonising discord. The first thing the travel-weary homecoming spirit hears is the welcoming notes of the Divine Melody. Happy are they who harmonise with it, sorrowful are those who vibrate discordantly!

OGS:1:8 Life is a song, sometimes a song of sadness, sometimes a song of joy. Now a dirge, then a hymn echoes through the chambers of creation. Often a gay carol or lilting lovesong gladdens the ear of the air. All this is the Song of Life. So lift up your hearts, and rejoice in the singing soul, which will, in days to come, rise on ghostly wings to quit the inner circles of woe, where the discordant notes of mortals intermingle with the melodious notes of spirit music, winging its way to where the stargirt chorus sings in glory.

OGS:1:9 Out from The Inconceivable One came the radiating substances of Dewa, who sits supreme in the invisible Universal Hub, and this is His circle. The outflowing notes became contrasted among themselves, dividing into two, and those that poured downwards became the substance of Mamvar the Lifebringer. From the life-radiating substance of Mamvar came Mamdadeh, who spread life wide over the world. The son of Mamdadeh was Dada, whose name was not spoken in the beforetimes, and he carried the spirits of men in his seed.

OGS:1:10 These are the generations of the ancestral godmen who came from Dada, as they have been known tons, and it is well to know from whence we came, we being of their blood. We stand high among the proud races of mankind, not being numbered among the least, and sad will be the day when men lose pride in their heritage. Yet it is foretold that the day will surely come, at a time when men stand on a strange threshold, with the choice of regeneration or decay and doom.

OGS:1:11 Those generated from the seed of Dada were the three Heaven-sent forebears of mankind, named Magog, Gatuma and Keili. We are told that these were beings in spirit form dwelling apart from the Universal Hub, at the outer reaches of Kewgant, but of this there is now no sure knowledge. It is known only that Magog ruled in the North and East, Gatuma in the South and Keili in the West, but old tales tell of Keili's travels from the widelands of the East to this sea-girt green isle. The consort of Keili the All Knowing, he who guards the memories of men, was Kithwin the First Well Beloved, and they had a son and daughter. The son was dark-visaged Aveg and the daughter Kerirway, the most beautiful of women, who set the standards of womanhood, to which all who desire to catch the will-o-the-wisp of love should aspire.

OGS:1:12 The son of Gatuma was Gatumugna the Skyfighter, whose son was Tuwait, the Townfounder and Metalmaster, who married Amerith, the Skychief's daughter. Their sons were Nodinos the first earthling, and Magilmish the Wanderer, in whose days the sky chariots came. It is told how, in the glowering dawntime of the world, Amerith flew on swift wings of the spirit from her kingdom in the West to consult with Tuwait the Eastern Father, son of Gatumugna. They met beneath the great lifetree, known as Kalesdrid, which grew at Enok. They lived awhile within the green bower set in the lushlands surrounding the lifetree, and it was for her the ring of youth was forged. This she gave to her seducer and so became as other women, while he lived in youth and strength. It is thus that the ring became known as the Prize of Seduction.

OGS:1:13 Magilmish was a mighty one among men, whose fame spread far and wide, and he was called the Lord of Battles, the Victory Winner, the Mansmiter, the Earth Burner, the Wind Fighter and the Water Spouter, and called Gilamish beforetimes. Those were his names among all the peoples of those days, for not all knew him by name, and some misnamed him. His son was Jovan, whose son was Bethbal, whose son was Amalugad, whose son was Lugad, the Hammerer. The daughter of Nodinos was Efa, born of the Skymother. Efa married Nud, the Underearthman, whose eyes could not bear the daylight, and their son was Gwin the Fairfaced. Efa ran away from Nud and became the wayward wife of Belesetin.

OGS:1:14 The sons of Magog the Great Brooder, were Kelefa and Mamagog the Fertiliser. The son of Kelefa was Helith the Lifebringer, whose daughter was Amerith the Desirable, much besought by the Battlekings. Those who hold to the old tongue call her Asterith and say she was the mother of the first true man. These are not things to be hugged to the heart, for it would be a wise man indeed who knew the nature of the first mortal man after the sinful intermingling.

OGS:1:15 The son of Mamagog was Bele the Bright, first husband of Dona Smiling Eyes, and one of their sons was Lew Dewtears, the bright, happy cradlechild who laughed in the sunshine. It is told that he shed tears of glistening dew, which healed any wound, and unless these be the rainstones, the story is past understanding. He became king of Karguthrin, where tales of his times are still told in the halls. The other son, Lew's brother, was Malvas Anshriver of the dark tears, and it is said that if he cried, any tears falling on bare flesh would raise unhealable weeping sores. The tale goes that Malvas possessed the balebag containing foul maggots of sickness and the cankerworms of barrenness and infertility. Also it held within its folds the balebook with recipes for every dire event and tribulation. His companions were the dread loping wailwoves of death, but now none knows the meaning behind the tale. We do know that Malvas was the forefather of the dark dwarfs. We know, too, that the ancient taletellers dressed wisdom and Truth in garments of frivolity and motley, so only the discerning benefited, while the mindless manyfolk were momentarily amused but then passed them by as things of little consequence. Who, not knowing and looking at the mud mussel, would believe a beauteous pearl must lie within?

OGS:1:16 The sons of Lew by his first wife, Anath, she who caused the building of mysteryful Kamailas for the glorification of men, and who died because of her desire for Thaneros, were Belesetin and Franan. Their daughters were Branwen and that Nertha sometimes called Naniku in the old tongue, who was the first wife of Nodinos and mother of the first full woman.

OGS:1:17 The sons of Lew by Morigu were Kela, Gwinon the Welcomer of Warriors, Leir and Robeth, and the first wife of Leir was Pendora, by whom he had two sons, Mandobrak and Frans, and a daughter Branwin. By his second wife, the Northern Beauty, Leir had Thanis, Wothin and Dylan.

OGS:1:18 The first wife of Belesetin was Efa, who married Nud after being cast out from her homeplace. His second wife was Franwy and his son was Evalak, Guardian of the Gate, and his daughter was Modren whose son was Owin Wiseheart.

OGS:1:19 The second husband of Dona was Manwidan and their daughters were Pendora and that Arinrada who gladdens the hearts of old men. They lived in the days before the misty veil became impenetrable and Evalak ruled the isle containing a forest of fireapple trees, which men now misunderstand. Many meanings are lost to those who have learned the old tales of wisdom in the new tongue.

OGS:1:20 Arinrada married Traith the Whitehaired, and their sons were Athlan the Strong Wave Wanderer, Kolehan the Teacher, and Kornayna the Bull Borne War Watcher, and their daughter was Mebid who married Bramathamlin. The son of Athlan was Elan the Sea Smith of the Floating Forge, who married the daughter of Manwidan for whom he made armour of a mysterious metal, which no axe, spear, sword or arrow could penetrate.

OGS:1:21 The son of Elan was Karunas the Hornheaded, who married Newlyn the Fairmaid, daughter of Bramathamlin, she whom they of the Old Faith call Tanis the Moonmaid, but it was not her desire which brought the first daylight; it was another's. Their son was Laledkin the Larger, whose son was Hewe, Great Chief of the Upright Ones, who married Helen Bloderwed, whose son was Ayed, who married Sibel the Strange Priestess, whose son was Brydin, whose sons were, Brydin the Younger and Belinos the Bookbearer. The son of Belinos was Bladud the Builder, who was cured of a corrupting disease by mud from a swine's wallow.

OGS:1:22 Bladud married Kelwinith, daughter of Molmed the Wise, whose wife was Tishana, whose mother was Sibel whose husband was slain by Kastwelan the Invader, while fighting with the dark men of Filistis with whom they had sought refuge.

OGS:1:23 Bethbal married Anarath and their daughter was Anath. Athlan married Niad, daughter of Vala. The son of Bladud was Elas, whose son was Lokrinos. The son of Molmed was Marsis, whose son was Kamba, with whom Kelwinith sought refuge in Finkera, over the sea of Mertis. The son of Kamba was Humba, who failed to build his boats of ash slats, so they came apart, and he was drowned, whose son was Erigen, whose son was Kratalinth. The wife of Humba was Marva, daughter of Fermadamid.

OGS:1:24 The son of Kolehan was Neptoran, and his daughter was Sowithy, and Neptoran married Wokelyn. The sons of Mandobrak were Luk the Arbitrator, who plays with the chancechips, and Dianket, who first taught men the use of healing herbs, and that Luktin who was the uncle of Lugad and who taught men the ways of working with wood, and who could fix a spearhead immovably onto its shaft.

OGS:1:25 There is tale at variance with others which states that the daughter of Dianket was Newlyn the Ravenfaced, who married her uncle, which ill-omened marriage caused barrenness among cattle and green-growing corn to lay down in shame. The sister of Neptoran was Sowithy of the Fair Isle, who married Lugad Hardhand the Hammerer, who taught the working of bronze and was the father of our people. It is told how he was shot in the thigh by a dwarf's arrow and how, every year at Samhain, the deep wound opened and erupted a vile venom which dropped off to dry into a grey powder. This wound was eventually healed by the kiss of a rainstone, and it is said that in this way, its holiness was discovered... but surely the drops of venom are the vile rites of the dwarfs!

OGS:1:26 The son of Neptoran was Grakenwid and his daughter was Nanara, who married Kamelognatha, Builder of the high-walled city over the water, who was the son of Ognana and Brigenda. Kamelognatha sought refuge in this land and taught men the art of writing on wood and stone.

OGS:1:27 The tales concerning the doings of our forebears in faith and their generations are not well known among us, for we are a different people having another tongue. Yet though some tell them one way and some another, we have sought out that, which is common to most. In these times of change it is well to have an anchor in the past, but unless it bites into a sound seabed, it is of little value. It is said that the sole message, which can be given to the future is words written in the past, so we write.

Chapter Two – The Dawndays

OGS:2:1 Generations ago, the people living in Britain were unlike those now occupying this bountiful land, and in bygone ages, great herds of cattle were tended on rolling, green plains. Southward grew long-stemmed corn, but in those long-gone days, it was not bartered with blackbearded strangers from beyond the stormy seas.

OGS:2:2 The first folk holding this land were the Kamledis, called Wictarin in the old tongue, but these were dwellers in the North, while southward were the dark, shortlegged dwarfmen known as Oben. They were kingless and chiefless, though it is said by some that stocky-statured Kathlon was once their king. None knows who led the dwarfmen here, though men do say the land spawned them, though the land is good. They were hagridden, forest- fearing river-dwellers who painted their faces and legs, users of evilly poisoned weapons. Theirs were the grim gods of death and darkness, and at their festival times, the dwarfmen sat in sombre caves eating children as part of their evil feasting. They had no priests, only dwarfesses called Chethin, meaning raven-adopted, and there was a great one above the others, called Harada, who lived in a smoky cave called Hegrin.

OGS:2:3 They were ruled by old hagwomen, who prepared hellish brews in firechurns tended by devilish brownswaddled dwarf maidens, for they also worshipped beings dwelling in smoke. The last hagwoman queen of the Oben was Kwasir who had a cave shelter hole at Inswitan, which is the Dwarf Isle, now called Iniseug in the Western tongue. Here they worshipped the Old Yearteller, coming from afar on windfloats, the neighing windhorses of later days. The most hallowed of their rites were those celebrated before the mayflowering, when filthy things were done, for they had no shame. Here, the Children of the Dusk gathered in the month of willows to worship Mamdo and her balebrood, performing vile rites under the command of Blasis, their great mangod.

OGS:2:4 The dwarfmen, both North and South, were skinswaddled, though sometimes wearing nettlecloth clothes of black or brown, and like the cat, dove and dog they mated openly without shame. They gathered toadstools, brockberries, ivy, wayweed and other unwholesome plants, using these with evil moondew to make a maddening brew, which opened a strange door on hellish worlds. They were ruled by cowled sewds and dradwitches, and were unable to number beyond a score. There are dwarfmen still living among us in the forest depths and in caverns under the Earth, though none here has seen one. They quickly take to flight, and though fearing it, will take refuge within the forest. Sometimes a bold one will stay and will greet the wayfarer with, "Hail, man; I saw you from afar but stayed." To which the reply must be made, "Before seeing you I was as one dead, but now life comes again." Then, providing a gift is also given, the wayfarer remains unmolested.

OGS:2:5 In the generations of the dwarfmen, broad Britain was a many-marshed land, where dismal ferns and tangled forests hindered passage from place to place. The Oben were not numerous and their children few, but they were hardy and long-lived. Their caves were painted, even in the darkest depths where daylight never fell, for the eyes of the Oben were like those of cats. They were not skilful hunters but set many traps, and in lots of ways were like children. They were playful when not engaged in dark doings, but their menfolk were not manly, nor their women womanly. They were cunning and devious, not to be trusted.

OGS:2:6 Far to the South were the swarthy swarm of the Frolga, though these were not true dwarfmen but the outcome of intermingled blood. They were worshippers of Nana the Mighty Mother, and were ruled by many feywomen who sat in night councils when the summershiner slept. Into the land held by the short dark Oben, came tall wiry Tothsolars, who were sunfolk. They came through Airana and the country of the Nudlanders, who wore gallitraps, and it was in those days, men began to breed swine, the first beast bred to be eaten, for only the dwarfmen eat dogs and cats. The land was then called Muredin, meaning the Place of Rest.

OGS:2:7 Then into the easterly lowlands came sea-borne Baradon with his plowmen, and that part lying between Hilderith and Pretankely they made their own and called it Holbon. Baradon was the son of Indrud who married Hurash. Indrud was the son of Jova who married Elsis, and Jova was the son of he who became the first father of households.

OGS:2:8 Wise, hoaryheaded men have treasured these tales belonging to our first great race, the wise and noble, having its birthplace in great forest-girt mountains bespangled with green, skypointing pinefingers. These are tales of times before men were men, when the big-bellied murkymother ruled the world-covering Netherfolk, sharing the land with giant Endlings.

OGS:2:9 The great gutted one was unaware of the wind-blasted salt waters; living in the mountain-hid, thicket-walled cave places, beyond the corn grass plains of Nonima, she knew only the cold companionship of hooded adders. There in smoke-smothered, gloom-enshrouded caverns, attended by her daughter Eldiwed, she read signs for rock-stooled Balings, plucking dark wisdom from writhing flames.

OGS:2:10 Lovers of the comforting fire warmth, smoke dreamers, seekers of home hearth's consolation, not far ranging war bringers or land openers, the Netherfolk desired only to remain undisturbed. Compatible companions to intangible wraiths, flitting shades and unsubstantial ghosts, they knew full well the secrets of Gorwel. Fearing forest-ruling Pafamba, they begged protection of the Netherogre, but among the life-giving trees, he was powerless. In the smoke-curtained, many-pillared hole hall, unblessed by regenerating sun-ray, the Netherfolk called upon their wan night goddess, their prayers weird yelpings in the ruddy gloom. Their music was the rushing gurgle and splash of falling waters, their song a howling whine.

OGS:2:11 These were of the race spawned long ages ago in dark-mired moss swamps, fern-eating foemen of the poisoned dart. Not for them the swiftly killed sacrifice; their delight was in painful maiming, in the broken humiliation of their betters. Woeful indeed was the yearly fate of the hagmother's spouse on the long dark night preceding the bridal day during the feast of flame.

OGS:2:12 They were wolf-talking howlers of the night, owl -screeching denizens of dim caverns, speech beguilers of wild creatures in closed places. Cowled and cloaked in dull clothing, they were undistinguishable in their habitat, save for the foul, nostril-stinging smell of bodies ointmented with pigfat, soot, blood and clay. All the night, at the dark of the moon, they pranced around stone-hedged, deep-dug, glowing firepits, their kirtles upheld by the never subsiding limb beneath.

OGS:2:13 Bemudded, grease-grimed and grey were the heads of the hagwomen seated around the ashfires, muttering darkly over the rowan omen-sticks. Casting spells for the hell-spewed horde, they sucked fat dripping portions from the stone-heated pots. Only the poison-speared he-goat leader of rituals received choicer portions than they.

OGS:2:14 Never fighters with sword or axe and shield, the battle-shy dwarfmen were twin-handed dart hurlers. Back-pointing, evil-toothed, barbed short lances were their hand-carried weapons, and no mansmiting metal was theirs to work. Nor did they pin their cloaks, but held them together with animal threads. They had no shields, but were agile and deft in dodging the thrusting weapons of their foes.

OGS:2:15 Into the dark, wild, wooded land came blood-haired Lodmor, son of Kel, wave-borne, encased within the ship bellies of oak and beech. Father fighter of the upright Iberis, the Hearth Hallower, the Wife Maker, the Child Protector, the Wild Herd Rider. Up the flowing waters to Muspel, place of the Netherfolk, came the fair-skinned wanderers. Not with fight-straining eyes, but with hands empty of weapons and guileless hearts, seeking only to live out on the grass-thatched plains. Their eyes fell on sights never before seen, the feast of offal, the fire-smoke dancing, the open coupling before jesting advice-giving onlookers.

OGS:2:16 No sight, this for maidens of the Iberis, no place for wide-eyed womenfolk, not for red-cheeked children's curiosity the pleasures of the dusky horde. Not for hard-hunting men the stone benches of the wolfwenches; the heavy-handed ones who made men of men had come to a land demanding their care, and they were vigilant. Long into the night echoed the songs to Bilew and Blasis, while those of the upper-born race sat sternly silent, their disgust unvoiced. No thoughts of spear-reddening had they, as they gazed upon the revolting antics.

OGS:2:17 Beyond the undistinguishable wall, where ruddy firelight gently kissed the face of darkness, skulkers of the Netherfolk stole the fur-swaddled sleeper, manchild of the lusty-lunged war singer. Swiftly he was borne away in the arms of the son of the day banisher. Righteous rage broke out in the ranks of the Upright Ones. No longer were the war weapons unwhetted, ruddy indeed the dawn over Muspel, but in the bushes and trees about the place lurked most of the swarthy swarm, escaped to howl vile threats and defiance at the grouped warriors and their protected womenfolk.

OGS:2:18 With the opening of the dawn's eye, the brawny warriors were spreadwide, driving the wily foe from his cover. Eager the faces; fierce, close-held the comforting shields, but the foemen were as hard to grapple with as the morning mists. The call to close came many times; the red horn resounding through the thicketed woods, but the dwarfmen were never in front, always behind. Then, as the skychief descended towards its resting place, the warriors came to a clearing before a caverned-cliff face, and there the evil brood were cornered. Grim-faced, the tall ones entered the battle clamour, but axe and sword bit only unsatisfying air. There was a scattering of the small ones, followed by a hunting through darkling glades. Ever the swift, silent, poisoned darts flew and the bitter barbs bit deep, fastening viciously on to heroic flesh. Evil indeed for heroes to thus die!

OGS:2:19 Back through bramble-entangled woods, through high-grassed glades, came the weary warriors, the long, thirsty swords still alert and eager for the blood of barbed-dart throwers. That night, they camped where they had left their guarded womenfolk, and with the dawnlight the sentries discovered a dwarfman. It was Kamwird the Wrinkled, and he brought back the manchild and the heart of his abductor. "Tatish, peace" cried Kamwird the Wrinkled, before the long, sharp-pronged spear of Thunderwolf, "Let be; let us bide together." Sad tears, the dark eyes shed. "Peace" said the swordsheathers, "Defile not the ankitel. Peace be." The Hardgripping hands familiar with spear, axe and sword were extended in friendship and the vengeance-smiting and bloodflow ceased.

OGS:2:20 Then to the stockade came the small ones, emissaries for peacemaking. Magas and Shine, dwarfmen of Himy, Mooney, Meany and

Shindy, with Lum the leader, brownclad, hooded, kirtled, belted and entassled, russet-skinned and ruddy-faced. Then came wise Killen to the peacemaking, tall towering, sinewy and stern, he of the generous hand. Thus was the way opened for the fairfolk to enter the land.

OGS:2:21 Lodmor led his people through the forested land to the white, dusty, hawthorned plains, and they settled there in peace. There they raised noble sons, white-browed, blue-eyed, slim womaned and dutifully wifed. Russet battleaxes were laid aside, the whetstone no longer caressed the sword. Brawny arms drove in the firmly held alder piles, raising the ash-held rafters, spreading above them in the thick-led fern and corded grass. Laughingly, the children played, the merry maids singing, the building blows of men echoing in the clearings. In from the moors to carry timber and stone, came Sons of the Nightcrow, blue-skinned people, dark-cloaked, mossy-haired men akin to the Oben, worshippers of The Ever Broody Mother.

OGS:2:22 The son of Lodmor was battleblooded Killen the Northrider, whose mother was Elvira, Maid of the Morning, and while Killen was yet young, dwarfmen came to the high stockade, emissaries seeking allies.

OGS:2:23 Killen sat with his father, listening to the words of the dwarfmen. It was agreed the dwarffolk should live under the shield of Lodmor, and they would labour in return. Then Killen gave them sticks for hoeing and digging, long stones for planting. Leeks, beans, flax, barley and wheat were unstintingly given, along with woven haircloth. In wooded glades cleared by tree-encircling fires, the sowing commenced, the bough bowers were built, the swine enclosed.

OGS:2:24 Not all the wide-ranging warriors thought as did Lodmor, for some said "Let us make masters for this dark brood of dwarfmen. Let us sever the haglings from their Ever Broody Hagmother, the smoky hellhag of dark caverns. Let us pen them as cattle."

OGS:2:25 To enslave was not the nature of the Upstanding Ones. Blood had been ransomed with blood and no score remained unsettled. No woman of the dwarffolk was beridden.

OGS:2:26 When the time of mayfeasting was at hand, Lude came, the dwarfchief, son of Frokith, with him his daughter, the night-haired Rada. The dwarfmaiden came well attended with young hagwomen, her skin like half ripe rose seed. Small-faced, bedimpled, bird-eyed, full-haired to the knee, brown-kirtled, fur-shod and cloaked with acceptable grace, she came as a worthy bride offering. Hers was the bracken bed, fragrant grass mingled within.

OGS:2:27 For three days Killen the Battleblooded Northrider, the Weary Wanderer, the Forest Fighter, remained silent, his thoughts remaining within himself, but then he welcomed the trothplighter. He welcomed the dark maid, the non-beridden one of the dwarfmen, for she was not unworthy of a true man.

OGS:2:28 Spake dark Lude, "This woman, the safeguarded daughter of a chief, has never been any man's plaything. Not for her the bed of sand, the dance-ending gift, this is a true lady of the Elfingers. Of women in the land, none is above her; none exceeds her in beauty or virtue, if these you value. As man speaks with man, chief with chief, match gift with gift, let this land be ours. Give me a tall, corn-haired maiden, full-bosomed, fair-skinned, sun-faced, to enliven gloomy lives."

OGS:2:29 Spake one-tongued Killen, "Not for me the words of hidden meaning. No maid of light shall be given to man of darkness, though dwarfmaidens are not denied to men of mine. If night mingle with the day, the light is lessened, so the day spurns the night. The night is not guardian of the light, so what cares it? Does darkness put out the firelight or fire dispel darkness? Can they mix? No milkskinned maid shall go at my behest."

OGS:2:30 "This I declare, for even I cannot forbid the trothpledge of one who loves. If there be a milkskinned maid who would freely choose to go, then let it be. She may bide as a bride of yours, but surely it is known no milkskinned maid would sever herself from our race, for return with a dark brood is forbidden. No dark brood do we accept; our men with your maids go, but what come of it is not one of us, no acceptable issue of ours. We father no dark brood, nor twilight offspring. What do we choose to father our herds, the best or the worst among bulls? Are not men many times greater than cattle?"

OGS:2:31 No milkskinned maid came freely forth; the dark dwarfmen chief was left unwed. In stockaded homes, the tall Upright Ones slept secure, no maid crept forth to mingle with the murky ones of the night. Yet when the fullsailed nightscanner shone above, with weird prancing, the Nethermen danced in the downshining light. Round and round, rapidly moved the dancing feet, the earthen mound quaked, the singing rose on the nightbreeze; flute music mingled with the tree sounds. Faster flew the nimble feet beating down upon tight-packed earth, wilder whirled the dancers to their coupling climax. The earthwatchers drew a curtain of cloud over the eyes of the nightshiner. No corn-haired head rose from its resting place.

OGS:2:32 Many the moon-bathed dances, oft the wild prancing, but less and less the dark broods numbers, further back into the forest and cave went the dusky-skinned ones. Oft in the night darkness, fair maids were snatched by brown-cowled dwarfmen, to breed twilight broodlings in secret places. Woeful were the enforced couplings and woeful the issue. Not for milkskinned maids, the free sinful coupling of the foredoomed dawnrace!

OGS:2:33 In five generations, the Nethermen were gone, only in the dark depths of cave and forest could they be found. No longer were the milkskinned maidens molested at night. The night offerings were put out; the dwarfmen came and supped; honey, bread, milk and sowflesh were taken in gratitude. The race of Nethermen passed into the shadows of time, only twilight offspring roaming the land, tawny-faced, blue-legged, weirdly-painted, brown-cowled, rope-belted, builders with stone.

OGS:2:34 No longer dwellers in dismal caves, or hunters in dark-mired swamps, the Alfing built slime-covered bough houses and raised high, upward pointing stones. Still soot-besmeared, pigfat-ointmented like the darkside of their forebears, they were also feathered and quill-ornamented. Being twilight-fathered, they faced no man courageously, coming to the attack like ground-slithering snakes, striking venomously from secret places, still forest skulkers. None could recite his lineage, for no man knew his father.

OGS:2:35 These were mother-lap-reared half folk, speaking with the tongues of their fathers, their words like crackling, spluttering green twigs burning in the fire. Brown and green clothed, bebangled, stone-hauling Idunings toiling for their black-bearded masters for unknown ends.

Chapter Three – The Floodtale

OGS:3:1 Over the sea now called Basabrimal, came a far-ranging race from Krowkasis, the Motherland where Gatuma ruled, where skyreaching mountains rise out of a wide, green, darksoiled plain. They were horsefighters, known among themselves as the Wildland Cultivators, and they landed at the place beforetimes called Haltraith, in the land of the Horsefolk, now held by Engling. They built the woodwalled town called Hovenlee in the new tongue, near where the great sea king sleeps beneath his mound.

OGS:3:2 They took their land from the herdkeeping Frolga and ranged wide from shore to shore, renaming the water-encircled land, the Honeyladen Isle, for never before had they seen honey in such quantities since leaving their own land. There were folk here before the fleet-footed Frolga, but they were magic-dealing dwarfs living in holes sunk in the ground, covered over with wicker and earth. It is said they knew and understood the speech of all wild creatures and often talked with them as brothers. They were friendly and frolicsome, and before them only, the bowed Yoshan roamed the land.

OGS:3:3 In the days when the Wildland Cultivators came and swallowed up the Frolga, there were bears, wolves, wild cattle, boars, oruks, deer, elk, lioncats, man-eating water lizards and beasteaters that dwelt in lakes aplenty. The Frolga were not small, but lacked fighting skill; they were spearmen and without bows, but skilful stone slingers.

OGS:3:4 Behind the Wildland Cultivators came the Uksening, but being boatless, few came to this green land, most turning southward to Amorika.

Those who came were workers in wood and metal, and it was they who built Kelnahilene, which stood even in the generation of our grandfathers' fathers.

OGS:3:5 In the generation when Glenapton was king of the Wildland Cultivators, a North-spawned horde came down upon the flatlands, led by Beledon the Thrummchinned, who gained kingship over the land once called Keningwed. Kolwader, the son of Glenapton, married a daughter of Beledon, and Frewil, son of Beledon, married a daughter of Glenapton, and there was peace.

OGS:3:6 It was in the generation of their sons that Benlanda, son of Bamlod, king of the Parsis, took the land, and all Britain moved southward.

OGS:3:7 The southward moving folk established the places of their responsive gods where once other gods had been hallowed, and they took the place of Madrad. They took the lands of the cattle-herding Basgala and the seatrading Taning, and out in skywide Senmag, they built the great hall of Karkilgule, with material carried from the Land of Illusion during the cold half of the year.

OGS:3:8 In their generation, people of this blood, the blackbanded Kelglain, built the wooded town of Maroliven which stood until the coming of the longsworded Helwaren. Its burning was a vile act of spite following their bitter defeat at the harsh battle of Belishmer, when king Faidlimid was slain and honourably buried at Kumbirgels by the British battlechiefs.

OGS:3:9 It was the Wildland Cultivators who gave the floodtale to our housebuilding forebears, but the generation of its happening is lost. In those days, men were inclined to the ways of peace, and harvest followed winter without change; but it came about that looking up into a darkling nightsky, they saw a strangely formed moonchariot overhead. It passed away into the rosy dawning of a new-born day, but then at the night end of the skyroof appeared the dread figure of Awamkored revealing itself to the eyes of wondering men. It crawled out into the brightness.

OGS:3:10 The foul breath of the nightcomer newly sprung from the dark depths of its unearthly lair, spread across the brightening face of Heaven, like an evil grey veil, and even the ever fearless sun withdrew to gird himself in red war armour. The fastbeating hearts of men first shrivelled with despair at the fearsome sight, then rose while their throats responded with glad cries as the moonchariot came back over the dim horizon. There, riding the battlebar, flaming sword held high, was the bright, beloved figure of Lithalun, her fair hair strung out behind as she flew towards the hellfigure.

OGS:3:11 They met in an awful, hell-echoing clash, with the noise of ten thousand rolling thunders, and men bold enough to look were stricken with blindness, and uncovered ears were deafened forever, Cold moontears were shed by the fang and claw-torn champion of mankind, while the hellish Awamkored drooled white cinders, which, if they touched the skins of men below, raised evil weals.

OGS:3:12 The unearthly foemen fell apart and hurled great self-created rocks at each other, and onlookers below dashed for protective shelter as they howled down out of the sky above. The very Earth, herself immovable, was sickened with fear, and her bowels became loosened with dread; her belly trembled before the awful sight. Men, looking anxiously to their lord the Sun, were dismayed to see his constant change of war garb, from red to blue, then to yellow, then green, then brown.

OGS:3:13 Good Mother Earth opened her groundmouth and roared earcracking protests, while her whole comforting body shook in fear under the gloomy battle shadowform above. Men and beasts were drawn together in a strange brotherhood of fear, none doing harm to another.

OGS:3:14 Those hardy enough to maintain a watch on the combat saw the flashing chariot of Lithalun crush the writhing body of the nightcomer, and then saw its vile black blood, thick like resin, fall upon the thankful bosom of Earth. Where the blood fell, flames sprang up. The fear-heated, blood-despoiled body of Mother Earth was cooled and refreshed by the soothing moontears of Lithalun, shed in womanly relief as she drove back towards her hidden abode in the recesses of Heaven.

OGS:3:15 This is the tale of the skyfight, but whether it happened before or after the generation of Hestabel and the floodtale, none now truly knows. It concerns the Doomdragon, which has come more than once and will come again, and the last music mankind will hear is the shrill throbbing notes of the Doomsong.

OGS:3:16 This is the floodtale, which has come down to us from our housebuilding forebears, and it happened in days generations ago, when men were widely divided.

OGS:3:17 Out into the grey, watery wilderness, where now the restless Western waters roll and heave, there was a place called Tirfola, meaning the Far Western Land. It was a country of high mountains, higher by far than those known to us, and low, green-grassed hills swept down from them to brown, fertile, plowed lands at the sea edge. The folk of Tirfola lived in fine houses, though the roofs were flattened, built on cliff shelves and places high above the fertile valley floor. Ladders went up the side of the houses, for they were entered from the roof; the ways of other people are strange! They hunted the roving deer in open-gladed forests where there were no entangling brambles, and fished in quiet pools of gay, splashing rivers. They plucked the plentiful herbs, which grew in manifold variety, there being some for every known purpose. It was indeed a land of peace and plenty.

OGS:3:18 The day came, as come it always must whenever peace and plenty abide, for then, Earth displays a defect in her instructiveness, when the soothsayers saw kolkers in the night skies, but they were unable to agree among themselves as to what these portended. Some said this, and some that, while the wiser ones listened, saying nothing.

OGS:3:19 The day came when sleeping Earth awoke to a great silence and stillness, not a breath of air strirring the anticipating trees, and no bird left its perch and every animal remained quiet within its den or in the field. All was hushed and motionless, waiting. Then, the soaring sun brought low-moaning winds which stirred the trees and grasses to rustling, murmuring life, but all living creatures huddled closer together. The skyroof above was darkened and lowered; it was ruddily-hued and gave out sharp, whipcracking sounds, as though it would break asunder, with now and then a shrill, long-drawn cry. In heart-thumping procession, awesomely-figured skygods never before seen, passed overhead. Men lived through two fearstruck days of dread, not knowing what to expect, during which time there was no true night, one heartstopping sight after another passing before their horror-filled eyes.

OGS:3:20 When darkness did fall, it was not the restful nightdarkness which soothes workweary men, lulling them to revitalising sleep. No indeed, it was that form of darkness known as the smothering cloak of Thunor, though never before had it spread so wide. Water streamed downward from the fountainspouts of the sky, not as rain falls but as water drops out from a pail upturned. Neither was it the pure, true rain; it was tainted with bitter blood from some strange battlefield in the vast skyspaces and contained broken pieces of the rainbow. The skyroof itself was borne down to the very surface of the seething waters, and Mother Earth cowered beneath it, as the shrinking fieldmouse cowers before the harvesters' footfall.

OGS:3:21 A vast, black cloud was drawn like a curtain across the skyroof, stretching from horizon to horizon. Rising above it were strange billows of flame and smoke; though what the fire consumed, it is not possible to even guess, for all know water does not burn. Then all things ceased movement, all was silent and still; a heavy, ill-boding, brooding silence, the stillness of hearthammering fear.

OGS:3:22 Then, with awful suddenness came a high wave wall of dark, white-fang-edged waters, sweeping swiftly along in fearsome irresistibility. It carried everything before it as a broom sweeps the floor, and accompanying it was a high born note, long-drawn out. Behind it, upon the seething waters, all the fruits of the land, house debris, trees, bloated dead animals and humans floated upon the wild, wide waters. There was an earthy-brown, foamy scum, which drifted strangely over the surface, not sinking, yet not like oil, for it was gritty, it was irregular and held together, it was like the scum on a fuller's tub.

OGS:3:23 There was a great downpouring of rain, which stopped after seven days, then the skyroof rose back into its proper place, and our fearstruck forebears saw once more the blessed light of day. They stood upon their drenched mountainsides and saw great trees, the like of which had never before been seen, float past. Hell-formed, hideous things came up from the depths and, swelling, burst on the surface. There were fearful sea monsters and great whirlpools, terrible things from unknown places. Wild creatures were washed about, dead or dying. The surging seas tore between the high mountains in great rip tides of dirty water. Standing on their hilltops, our frightened forebears saw the swimming house, made fast against the sea, come up to the land, and out from it came men and beasts from Tirfola.

OGS:3:24 It was built as a house on a high platform, standing well above the waters. When they had landed and made themselves secure, the black-raimented strangers built a tall tower of stone upon which they kept an ever burning fire, to honour the gods who brought them to safety. It was said that, if the fire ever went out, the waters would rise again.

OGS:3:25 Upon the surging waters was another wave-tossed craft, the great Brimcofer of Hestabel, the Wildwave Wanderer, Slayer of Niktoran the waterbeast, Worker of Strange Metals, who married Newlyn of Warnwilt, daughter of Manwidan, far famed for her beauty. For her hair outdid the yellow of the celandine. Her skin was softer than down and whiter than the mayflower. Her lips were the red of strawberries and her bosom soft as the windflower. She exuded the sweet perfume of new-mown hay. The son of Hestabel was the temple-protecting, three-spirited Esures, who made his home in the Great Oak where to this day he is worshipped as the god of beer and greenery. The tale tellers are not at ease with Hestabel and Esures, whether they were gods or men, but in some men the division is not clear. Perhaps gods are made by the regard of men.

[There is no Chapter 4 – ED]

Chapter Five – Workers in Metal

OGS:5:1 There are, in this land, two tribes of smithworkers and metalforgers, and one is the Merkings who remain among the Kwicta, and they tell a tale of a flight from the West where their forebears lived in painted abodes cut out of rocks. It is now the Land of Manan and closed to men by the waters above, for it burst asunder at the bowels, streaming out through Linleon during a great night of darkness. So it is that these others who work with metal worship spirits who dwell beneath the sea. They do not worship gods as the Kwicta do, and still cast food upon the waters; but they do have god-beings which are less than gods, and worship these, calling them, Haspa, Yelpa and Tiz. They acknowledge Blasis and leave offerings to Nana.

OGS:5:2 Oxen are sacred beasts to them, and they do not eat the flesh of geese, believing them to contain the souls of women. Yet they eat the flesh of boars, though believing these have been entered by the souls of men, but they do not eat this except with solemn ceremony. Once, though no longer, their chiefs were not succeeded by their sons, as now, but brother succeeded brother by the mother, then succession was by the mother's daughter's son.

OGS:5:3 In the days before Umpopal was the Great Chief, wives were the property of all men of the household. It was not until after the coming of those who followed Lugad the Bronzefinder, that many changed their ways. After Lugad came, the dead were no longer buried in the old manner, nestled in boughs and stones. They were laid out straight, heads to the West, with their comforting objects and oak boughs, as is done today.

OGS:5:4 These other metalworkers learned their craft from Yasus, otherwise called Hestabel, though some say they were two, and brothers. He came boatborne with the other children, Ree and Mag called Maya, who became his wives, for their father had cast them afloat at the time of the land sinking. This is not a tale known to us, and not being ours, is not well understood. They were fortunate to escape the underwater dwellers who lurk in the depths to snatch seafarers down to destruction. We have heard many tales of our times concerning the Brimkrakan, which drags seacraft down to destruction in all the four seas of Britain. Yasus was saved by the People of the Bear and became their chief, but they married among the dark Feymin and became as they are today.

OGS:5:5 These people were disliked because of their ways, but were not shunned. No king ever molested our forebears, for they threatened no one and served all alike. They went freely from place to place with their hearths, were law-abiding folk and not land-hungry. Our people held safe the secrets of metals, though later they were opposed by the Sons of May when they came, for these feared the knowledge held fast.

OGS:5:6 Though given high estate among the Kwits, our people do not make swords for the Black Brood of the North. It is the same Kwits who have given land, which the wanderers do not need. Our people first came to this land through Pokatha and even now have great houses at Karboska. The others came across the water from Eblana, but the generation of their coming is unknown to any here.

(This chapter is from parts reconstructed. The two tribes of metalworkers were the Sons of Fire and those who were called Merkings.)

Chapter Six – The Tale of Hewe

OGS:6:1 Great Hewe the Strongarm, Chief of the Wellborn Ones, was brightbearded, blue-eyed, but not overtall. He was the bronzebound ruler of warriorful Hefa, a place lying out in the shallow seas eastward of Britain, with a many-moated white castle and high coloured walls. This was the seat, from which he ruled oft-flooded Edyfrabandy; gaining control not by the sword but through marriage with the corn-haired daughter of Kwetana.

OGS:6:2 Hefa lay off the bay called Arkist, over the sea called Mortosh, and the people thereabouts were the Kudira. They were warwise and learned in other ways, but their week was too long by two days. After the arrival at Solmanth, to which he came peacefully as a bridegroom to his waiting bride, Hewe became king of the Kathon, and he taught men to plough and till the soil. He crossed to the Summerland where he set up a great school of learning, and there was first taught the writing of books in the trees. The brother of Hewe was that Taran who took men of Hefa across the sea to Ladore.

OGS:6:3 The fightingfolk who came with Hewe were outstanding among others, being fair-headed, light-eyed, soft-spoken, tall and slim, upright, big-muscled, honourable, brave and musical. Yet they were not of the Firstfaith and spurned the Old Faith, nor were they with us, but they were akin to the true folk of this green isle and kindred to the brave ones across the landbound sea. They were not stonebuilders, though they rebuilt skybound Morkoravit, the great gate hall which the Dark Ones call Shindekra even to this day. This is the hall of the horse stones.

OGS:6:4 This is the tale of Hewe, the strongarmed wielder of the mansmiter, child of the Arayan, which was given to us by our housebuilding forebears, but the days of this generation are lost. It concerns the Erim, with whom he fought, who were the Feymin of other times.

OGS:6:5 Hewe of the sunfilled heart, lithsome as the willow, sturdy as the oak, fair-skinned, blue-eyed, straight-tongued, peace-minded, not strife-seeking, yet warwise; this was he who led the Glorygleamer Folk. He gave merry life to the green-grassed heart of Britain, flower-meadowed, sparkling-streamed, water-veined. He brought to these sand-bangled shores the high-hearted race of iron-muscled horn-handed freemen.

OGS:6:6 He, the son of woodgirt fields, first turned the sod of Britain in hilltearing brown furrows; upon the high slopes, he made the soil to be uplifted, overturning it upon the winter-held grain. He first brought the long ox-drawn fieldrakes and carried fertility to the pasturelands. Winters were no longer times of hunger, for now, all ate without stint from hide-lined cellars filled with fire-dried corn.

OGS:6:7 Cabbages and onions, peas and gulegift, forest gleaning of womenfolk, grew in tended soil, staked plots in the forest glades. Cattle gifts of cheese and curdcake, fire-dried flesh of summer-fattened beasts, nuts and brown herbs were the winter fare. Men wandered freely from place to place, wood-wending paths directing their feet. Patient beastback bore the handiwork of men in bursting hidebags. Never were the ever welcome wanderers waylaid with evil intent.

OGS:6:8 On stout hewed house pillars, sheathed swords slept in silent companionship with decorative shields. The old ones slept beside glowing hearths; contented the womenfolk, happy the children, peaceful the hefty, wide-handed, brief-bearded men. They had found Kastira and were content. Warm-clothed against the winds of winter, hide-headressed, black-cloaked, long-tuniced, breast-belted, kartak-ornamented, they lacked little for content.

OGS:6:9 The summer pourer of the rainbow smiled over fertile, flowering pastures, playgrounds of mirthful maids. On green carpets, the young ones skipped to the maiden wakening dance, flute-playing youths and clapping singers gathered around the herbrew pails. Oft told the old tales, oft sung the songs of yore.

OGS:6:10 Not for these, the earth-holed house, the bewattled roof covering. High-raftered, the roofs over the eating hall, broad-beamed, the guest hall, high-raised the host hall. Sturdy-timbered, the roofholding posts, hide hung shielding the slumber rooms. Bracken bench beds gave restful repose to toilers of the day.

OGS:6:11 Twelve was the number of the councilmen, wise the judgements given by the wisp-haired, hoary-headed, bronze-bangled ones who sat on the oak trunk seats. These were the times, when days received their names and weeks their numbering. The coming of the moon was made known, and daylight was divided into four parts. The three parts of night were named and the two times of eating. Men knew the four divisions of the year, and their names were known.

OGS:6:12 Much-landed Hewe taught the mating of the Golden Faced Skyspirit with the Lady of Life; their son, the Godling of Greenness was never unknown in this seanecklaced land. He was the never-tiring teacher of Truth, but this was not he whom the Britons worship, that one being not a man but an invisible spirit.

OGS:6:13 Before Hewe, folk saw at night only by the ruddy illumination of firelight, or its child the flaming fire-brand, but he gave them fatlamps feeding on the floating residue of flesh. Not yet light from the bee. Not yet were the fiery forges set up in this land by brawny, brown-eyed smithmen, their squat four-wheeled workwains ox-drawn through forest ways.

OGS:6:14 Peaceful the lush, green land; peaceful all that dwelt between surging seas. From Partain, the fine bright bronzework, the big-bellied pots. From Longaset, the hides and hornwork, the work of strange smiths. From the Liky, earth-hidden things borne away in far-faring boats. From Setnaspor, the hard sharp stone tools, the ripe corn cutting knives.

OGS:6:15 Yearly, from the Erim at Haroganos came the tribute of murkymaids, mothers of the studbrood, workers with hillside herds and forest feeders, gatherers of wood and fruits. Never had the tribute been withheld, well were the Erim instructed. Inawk the Collector, chooser of bright-eyed murkymaidens, came always with the best, fitting ones for mothering the studbrood.

OGS:6:16 What of Wenda, non-beridden daughter of Orma, trothpledged to Lopik the Blackbannered Chief, she of the flower-garlanded, throng-gathered-unbraided hair? Small-breasted, small-handed, delicately wiry-bodied, rowan-cheeked, sombre-eyed. Who spoke of her to Inawk, who told of her beauty, her ever smiling lips, her wit, her wisdom? She was unfound among the gathering. The hagmaids gazed long, at Inawk's behest, into the full moon-enlightened waters, but she was unseen there.

OGS:6:17 Orma was taken and all the hagwomen, every maid and every youth. Neckbound, they were brought to the studhall, unharmed, they were fed and bedded. In the nightdarkness the wolf-wretches came, evil weapons struck silently, sleepers died, vulnerable backs took fanged barbs. Dektire, child daughter of Ardan, was snatched for foul bewitchment, a sacrifice to Galo, victim of the bloodletting hagmaidens.

OGS:6:18 Through the wide pastures the hawk banner bearers sped, forests echoed the horn blasts. The brand-bearers cries were heard afar. Large the council-called gathering in the field of the stonecircle, and when the shaft cast was counted all cried out for blood.

OGS:6:19 High-spirited, stallion-mounted Hewe, swiftsmiter girded at waist, bright bronze mace in hand, raised the winged warbanner, and harsh the heartgripping warcry from a thousand ensavaged throats. Bright the gleaming bronze blades, the slim, sharp spearheads, the weighty manmaulers. Forward the hefty oakhearted warriors, eager-eyed for battle.

OGS:6:20 Tall, appleash-wooded the hill summit where the folkhorde of Brim stood, no timbered-stockade builders these wood skulkers. Sharp-staked, wildly-pitted the approach, low stone-walled the last defence of the earthruiners. The summershiner was halfway down to his trysting place with Earth.

OGS:6:21 Fast flew the hellballs of stone, the soft-singing death bringers flung by the foulfighters. Lopik, the loudmouthed boaster, shrieked loud against the shieldsheltering stalwarts, fast flew the hook-toothed blades with poison sting of death. Safe were the throwers from the stallion-led horse charge. Never ceasing was the downfall of slingshot stones.

OGS:6:22 Loud were the shrill shrieks of the wild-haired hagwomen, black garb besmirched with sacrificial blood. No tongue of man used they; wolf yelps, howls and cat cries tore the air. Then the shields lifted and came forward, the bright blades gleamed redly, the painbringers arrived among the Erim. Heavily the bloodied manmaulers fell, smashing through shield and bone, wielded by oaklike arms. Loud the cries of the Erim. Long, linden-shafted red rammers thrust forward; the barbed dart was of no avail.

OGS:6:23 Within the wood, wicker-shielded Lopik, tree hid, stood to thrust the poisoned barb. As the skulking stoat springs upon its prey, barefanged to kill, the foulfighter leapt upon the battlewearied warrior, brother of Dektire. Deep sank the evil barbs before the ash shaft broke, but Lopik was within reach, carried forward by furious thrust. Loud the thud of the full-falling battlehammer, biting deep into the incrushed brow, unavailing the leathern protector. This was a vermin slaying. Gone were the hagwomen and nethermaids to their gloomy abode.

OGS:6:24 Far through the forests ranged the vengeance fighters, many the bloodied bodies of Erim left behind. Then in wooded glade, battleweary eyes beheld a maiden figure; Wenda, not overfearful nor overbold, small beneath the tall trees, hooded, caped and kilted. None stood with her except a two-tongued hagwoman cowering against a tree trunk. Silently, curiously, the sleepless, weary Erim fighters gathered.

OGS:6:25 Here was a self-given peace pledge, a ransom for fainthearted fighters, a deed not unworthy of those, to whom she came. No gallant, generous heart could not accept. Tiny indeed was she before the great Hewe. Here was no studmother, but one worthy of being a true wife. No man indeed he who would accord her less.

OGS:6:26 It was Lir, grandson of Wenda and Olva who built the first house on the place where walled London now stands.

OGS:6:27 These are the sayings of Wenda the Wise: "The woods are havens for the heavyhearted, for trees soak up sadness. The lofty trees, sheltering sheet of forest dwellers, whisper soothing words to the worried. The only true friend is the tongueless tree."

OGS:6:28 "The most painful ills are the heartsmiting ones; therefore, never leave it unshielded. A high-sounding title is a poor wood waif, unless it is parented by eminent virtues. The treetops bow in homage to the winter winds, forest creatures are lean, and sheep no longer graze on the summer pastures. Woe to him, say the whistling winds, who sacrifices his honour for worldly gain."

OGS:6:29 "The chill arrows of winter cleave the fall air; within the home a warm fire, and low conversation is pleasant, but much talk unguards the tongue, and to dishonour a confidence is the sign of weakness."

OGS:6:30 "The brow of the hill is white with snow, and wild birds search diligently for food. Squirrels sleep soundly, dreaming of nut hoards. The wind whistles through the walls' wickerwork. Then call to mind that when winds of adversity blow, the fire of friendship comforts, but prefer to be a firetender, not a fireside squatter."

OGS:6:31 "Having no feelings, the fish is chaste. What claim to virtue has a woman chaste as a fish? As a benchbride's love flowers in dark corners, can sweetness be anticipated from its fruits? The woman surrendering to a true man has become a conqueror. No lover of children the benchbride, or she would not act as she does. The benchbride's love is consummated in darkness, for darkness is the befriender of shame. Tarnished or inferior love sold cheaply, that is the benchbride's bargain."

Chapter Seven – Tale of Gwinvera

OGS:7:1 Because they are incomplete, four tales, of 'Helen the Sunfaced', of 'Lavid the Fool and the Warking', of the 'Three Spearkings' and of 'Helen Blodawed and the Golden Chariot', have been omitted. This is the tale of Gwinvera as it has come down to us, and to we who reconstruct it, the task is not easy, for the pages are torn in several parts.

OGS:7:2 The tale is told, how, back in the bygone days when gods walked the Earth, they made the first woman in this manner. They prepared a vessel shaped by the future desires of men, placing into it these things: The gleam of sunlight mixed with the yellowness of ripe corn, this became her hair. The cold clear dawn dew mixed with the hue of the violet, this became her eyes. The pale radiance from the moonbeam mixed with down from the neck of a swan, this became her brow. The red from the cherry mixed with the colour of mayberries, this became her lips. The whiteness of the snowflake mixed with a mayflower's purity, this became her bosom. They took the sparkle from running waters for her smile and the cooing of a dove for her voice. The heat from the fire to fill her passion and the edge from the sword to arm her tongue. From the core of a flint worked keenly they made her mind and from the fall of a snowflake they made her touch. To this they added a blended mixture of extracts from the playful cruelty of the cat, the dancing lightness of the sunbeam's notes, the flutter from the wings of a butterfly, the song of the nightingale, the industriousness of the bee, the gentleness of a mouse, the softness of a rabbit and the shiver of an aspen tree. If this were a godmade woman, then Gwinvera was a product of their hands. But did these gods not try to keep this woman for themselves, as being something too good for man? But man, in his brave audacity, stole her, and she became the great woemaker. Truth is embedded in the old tales for the wise to find and use as they will.

OGS:7:3 When the mother of Gwinvera was in childlabour, her father, the Battlechief Kumwa, was at the festiveboard, and as was the custom, he called upon the soothsayer to foretell the future. The soothsayer told his lord that the womanchild now approaching the veil would grow to be the most beautiful woman in the land, but would be the death of many men, including her own brother, the Warchief's only son. These words ate at the heart of Kumwa.

OGS:7:4 He asked the wise soothsayer what should be done to avert disaster, and the crafty one answered that he would seek advice among the stars. Not all soothsayers had a temple of truth in their hearts. It happened that the voice of Helva, son of Kumwa, lived in the ear of the seer, so when the report was given at midmorn the following day, it was a lengthy woeforetelling much disturbing to the heart of Kumwa.

OGS:7:5 What was the outcome? The soothsayer spoke long, and Kumwa's heart ached for his only son and for the mother, but his duty was to protect his son, the heir born of his youth, and he could put his daughter to death according to the manner of the times. As a highborn woman's blood could not be spilt among green growing things, for this would blight the land, and only a simpleton could not be hurt by the deed, Gwinvera was given to the Battlechief's fool. He was to take her outside the boundary of the land, and there drown her, his payment for the deed being the wishgranting urn called Helwed, no small reward.

OGS:7:6 The kind-hearted fool had little liking for the deed, his heart was heavy and the ass-backed-carried cradlechild so contentedly lovely that the fool's load of sadness grew increasingly heavy. So they went on, the kindly fool and the lovely young one, until they came to the great, gloomy forest of Keliabans lying beyond Dunmerkil. The fool and his assload kept on through the forest, for thought he, "Where else can I go, as well here as any other place. It is in keeping with my heart."

OGS:7:7 Deep in the forest, just before the stars opened their eyes, they came upon a small, stream-traversed glade, and there, nestling among the woodweed was a tumble-down half house. The fool blew the wayfarers' horn and there came a small, shy forestman, first cautiously peeping around the doorpost, then timidly approaching. Had it been anyone other than a gaudy-garbed fool, the small one would have fled, but these forestfarers were taken in and made welcome in the humble hut.

OGS:7:8 Later, the forestman's brothers came back from their foraging and there was much lively chatter, for among such folk, the fool did not feel out of place. He stayed for three days, and it was agreed that the forestmen should take the little one from him and take care of her. What else could they do? For forestmen are gentle and kindhearted; were they not they would never have been confined to the forest. What else could the fool do, if he could not bring himself to put the little one to death? What better place to leave her?

OGS:7:9 The ugly forestmen raised fair Gwinvera with tenderness; they were wise in their way, and because they did not want her to become vain and immodest, or perhaps because they did not want her to discover how different she was, there was nothing in the forest home, in which she could see her face. Knowing about the soothsayer's foretelling, they let her think she was ugly too, or was it because they really wished her to be one of them? Did they not know that love closes the eyes to defects? Her own loveliness was unknown to Gwinvera. Her playmates were the wild creatures of the forest; fawns, rabbits and squirrels played outside her door, and the wise badgers came to protect her at dusk. Wrens and robins were her constant companions. In summer she bathed in sparkling rillwaters and garlanded herself with wildflowers; woodbells and primroses grew everywhere. In winter, she sang through the berrybearing glades and gathered fallen kindling wood under the great trees. She slept on a bed of sweet moss under cosy coverlets of fur. She drank the pure stream waters flowing through the cooking place and ate fish and the plentiful forest fruits. Her garments were woven from fine forest flax and soft down; her mantle was made of white winter fur. Her long, bamp-braided hair took its colour from the water marigold. Yet in all her forest-bounded childhood, Gwinvera never had a companion of her own age or saw any mortal being other than the forestmen.

OGS:7:10 It happened that when the forest maiden had grown to young womanhood, and it was mid-winter, huntsmen from the woodcastle of the king came into the naked forest, seeking boars for the yulefeast. They came upon the rough forest home of fair Gwinvera, and she, not knowing who or what they were, acted like a frightened wren. They did her no harm, not knowing whether she were mortal or spirit, but went away marvelling that the gloomy forest could contain such beauty. Such a tale could not long await the telling, and men argued among themselves as to whether a woodspirit had been seen or a mortal. Woodsylphs were known but rarely sighted.

OGS:7:11 It happened that the tale came to the ear of Helva, and he, lacking neither courage nor curiosity, wished to lead men into the forest to hunt the maiden, be she spirit or mortal. But first, as all wise men do before going on a quest, he sought the advice from the soothsayer. The soothsayer, gazing into his scrybowl, saw the beauty of Gwinvera and knew who she was, and knew, too, that never could Helva venture into the forest, nor would he be safe while Gwinvera lived.

OGS:7:12 Now, though the fool who had taken the lovely maid to the forest was dead, he had, before dying, unburdened his heart to the mother of Gwinvera, and she had kept the secret locked in her breast. Now she decided to go to the forest and warn her daughter, lest any harm befall her, for she doubted not but that there would be a hunting through the treefast depths. Making suitable excuses for her absence, she disguised herself as a woodman's wife, and with a young attendant who had been one of the boar hunting party, set out for the forest.

OGS:7:13 The soothsayer with two companions also departed for the forest, all being disguised as men of the peddling tribe, and because those with him were experienced in forest ways, it was the soothsayer's party, which arrived first at the hutted glade.

OGS:7:14 Gwinvera was alone, for the forestmen were hewing in the ground, and these being the first strangers she had seen, she took fright, evading them among the trees, from which shelter she nervously peered out. While the soothsayer tried to entice the maiden to tarry, the youngest of the forestmen, having hurt his hand, came into the glade. The soothsayer's companions seized him, and the maiden's concern overcame her fears. Rushing to his aid, she was taken also, but no harm was done to her, for those with the old man were disarmed by her beauty. He, seeing this, put on the face of guile and acted as would a true peddling man.

OGS:7:15 They bartered the usual ware of pedlars, cloth, brooches, beads, pins, salt, earthenware, dyes, knives, sweetmeats, cords and flints, taking soft pelts and fruit of the ground. Before leaving, the soothsayer gave Gwinvera, as a parting gift for a lovely maiden, a sweetly perfumed ointment and a mouthwatering cake, both infused with deadly poison. The cake she left, small and tempting though it was, she wished to share it, but the perfumed ointment she could not resist, and it was a womanly thing.

OGS:7:16 Barely had the forestmaiden used it when the forestmen returned; they were early, but heavy rainclouds threatened. Delightedly the newbought wares were displayed one by one, but surprised joy diminished to silence as Gwinvera grew more and more tired, her head at last falling on to the table. The forestmen picked her up and carried her to the bedplace. As they did so, there was a knocking on the door; it was the mother of Gwinvera. They let her in, and the thunderstorm broke full overhead.

OGS:7:17 The speech of the forestmen was not easy on the ears; their chattering was overcome by the downpour, but the mother of the sleeper knew what had happened. The cake, she threw on the fire; the sleeping maid she took in her arms, carrying her out into the thunderstorm. Behind the hut she stripped her, and with moss and mud, rubbing hard, removed the ointmentation. Round and round the glade she walked the small-kilted maid, around and around, never stopping. Talking, prodding, lifting, smacking, stumbling together, falling and getting up, slithering on rainwet moss, bedraggled, muddied and scratched, on tirelessly until final collapse.

OGS:7:18 The forestmen helped the exhausted women inside, and the elder made them make hot brews for the still sleepy maiden. Her feet were placed in a wood tub of hot water, and she was seated by the fire. Later, the two women were bedded down together, and in the morning, the forestmaiden woke up well.

OGS:7:19 They broke fast with goat broth, but the mother of Gwinvera could not dally overlong, nor could the maiden remain with the forestmen, for surely the huntsmen would come again. So a graveplace was made, ringed round with stones and a mound raised, but no maid slept beneath the mayberry bush. Gwinvera left the forest, her long, fair hair beneath a leathern cap, coarse cloth covering her body. A distant herdsman's home gave her shelter.

OGS:7:20 It happened that the herdsman had two sons, one a hefty, hard-handed, wide-strider, fond of brawling; the other a small-handed fireside dreamer, deft but not overstrong. The first was named Bagut and the other Daran. It was only days before Bagut was smitten with the beauty of Gwinvera, but she, knowing not the ways of men, treated him with friendliness and kindness. He, thinking she was being coy and teasing him after the manner of irresponsible women, tried to take her when she was gathering eggs at the hayrick. She fled to the house and the goodwife and Daran within.

OGS:7:21 Bagut became moody; he sulked the day long and neglected his work, and when once he came on Gwinvera alone, he was overcome. He told her that unless she gave herself to him he would be riding towards the woodcastle on a moneymaking errand. She said, "Then having no love for me, what ails you?" He rode away.

OGS:7:22 Now, it happened that the soothsayer had looked into his scrybowl and seen the graveplace in the forest, but looking again, days later, he saw Gwinvera seated on a tussock carding wool, and he knew she lived. He sent men to dig at the graveplace, and it gave up its secret. Forestmen were brought in and put to the mouthopening test, but they knew nothing of where she was and could say nothing to lessen their suffering.

OGS:7:23 So when Bagut arrived with his tale, the soothsayer knew who was being described as having hair yellower than broomflowers, skin whiter than driven snow, hands fairer than blossoms of windflowers, eyes brighter than a falcon's, bosom more snowy than a swan's breast and cheeks redder than mayberries. Men were sent with Bagut to capture such beauty.

OGS:7:24 But beauty had flown, companied by Daran, and sought sanctuary with Pentercil, King of the Howan, Child of the Landholdingers, and this was the cause of the bitter war, which made men scarce in the land. For Helva assembled his warbands and entered the lands of Pentercil, who met him at the place called Rathkelder even today.

OGS:7:25 We have reconstructed the tale as found, but here some part is missing, though account of the battle remains.

OGS:7:26 The chariot clove through failing ranks, through the drooping spears of the weary spearmen, through the ground-resting shields of the swordsmen, through the gasping forefighters, through the bloody-bodied lines of the axe swingers. Behind the tossing, red-eyed heads of the white horses, gold-guilded reins loosely held in one hand and small bright ash-shafted spear firmly held in the other; golden hair unbraided streaming behind her, held back from her face by the golden headguard; her brilliantly brooched cloak flapping like the wings of some heavenly battlebird, Gwinvera sped towards the still standing bodyguard about Helva. No arrow touched her, no slingstone came against her body. She was like a battlegoddess.

OGS:7:27 On the slope between reed-bordered river and tree-crowned hill, the warbands of Helva made their last death-awaiting stand. Then it was all over, and the battlefield foragers did their work. So the tale of the delicate forest-raised maiden who became a rage-driven war goddess, and of Daran who became warwise in one night is one oft told in the feasthalls.

Chapter Eight – The Firstfaith Bringers

OGS:8:1 Once, wherever there was grass, there too was the Old Faith, for it could be contained within no particular domain. They who believed the things it taught were little-minded men, unthinking receptacles for strange tales. With the Firstfaith came better men, adopted sons of Britain, Pritan and the axe-wielding Baruts, and it was he, who named this land the Great White Goddess of the Cowfeeding Pastures. The Baruts learned the sealore from the Chaisite who first ventured out upon the saltwaters, but their homeland is not known. Some say it was Rimvady, West of the Lodgrains, but no man knows for sure. The Lodgrains who bowed to the Great Milk Giver came later.

OGS:8:2 The Firstfaith came only as a babe, it was here that it grew to maturity, schooled at Insgwin. Those of the Firstfaith respect trees even today, few though they are, but the true nature of the Greengod who gives life and fertility to all green growing things is unknown. They called trees the flutes of The Great Holy One, yet did not believe as we do that trees contain within themselves part of the lifegiving force of mankind, pouring out good and absorbing its evils. They did not understand that without trees to mediate for man between the lifeforce and the deathforce, he could not live. Yet now even we are wiser, knowing the Greengod of Life is not in trees alone.

OGS:8:3 They of the Firstfaith made sacrifices at most of the proper times, but instead of leaf crowns, they wore masks in the likeness of sun and moon, believing them to be the rulers of omens. They worshipped in error the malignant horned star and her escorts, fearfully seeking to turn them away. Instead of the wertmound they used gulerinth to set up the sun measuring daypole, but this offended the shadows. They failed even to do this properly, setting up a new pole every year instead of every seven.

OGS:8:4 They did not treasure the soil from the pole circle, as we do that from the mound. The Sons of May, instructors in the Firstfaith, were not allwise, seeking signs of the future, otherwise clearly seen, in ashes, birdflights and bloody twisting entrails. They knew the making of a draught of forgetfulness from herbs and the draught of sorrow from berries, also the making of dradsboon which lightens the heavy heart.

OGS:8:5 They did not, as we do, judge wholly by known laws, but oft made trial by using a magic collar. This was first dipped in water blessed with coldfire, they then believing it would choke the guilty one. This is not for us, for are we not told man cannot avoid the responsibility for formulating laws to try his fellowmen, and rules to govern his life? These things cannot be thrown back onto higher authority.

OGS:8:6 They hold one day in seven holy to The Creating God whom they worship in a transparent temple where the sun falls upon the heads of the worshippers. So there are many differences between the Firstfaith and the Gwidonad. We worship in holy places built of stone or in caverns, using open spaces only for the Midsummer Festival.

OGS:8:7 In the Firstfaith, the womanly maidenwed was always preserved for battlechiefs and the Sons of May, who could claim it without dispute except among themselves. With this, we are not in accord, for women are not to be lightly treated, and a maidenwed is something kept for a husband, a woman's pledge of purity and to the wellbeing of the race.

OGS:8:8 The Sons of May were not lacking in courage, for they were ever in the forefront of battles, though they were mare-riders, never mounting upon stallions. Every one of the Sons of May had to be trained in the use of spear and sword even as we, but they had to know many songs and long lineages and be wordmakers. They had long unmusical songs which were given out with many gestures. The Sons of May could claim no tribe as their own, for they were tribeless. They could not avenge any harm done to their kinfolk, and were any one wronged, his kinfolk could not avenge him. This was not because any one of the Sons of May was ever renounced by his kinfolk, or they by him, but because of the power of his Maydom.

OGS:8:9 Whatever his circumstances, like us, a Son of May could never refuse hospitality. In battle, he always kept his face towards the foe. Like us, he was always respectful in the presence of womenfolk, never raising his voice to loudness or speaking lewdly. This is in accord with our laws. The bride price was forbidden to the Sons of May.

OGS:8:10 Like us, the Sons of May had to prove their manliness, and if one had not done this on the battlefield, he was put into a forest unarmed and hunted by armed men, which is not our custom. If any man defamed one of them he could be challenged to combat on the grovefield, by their combat champion.

OGS:8:11 The Sons of May dressed differently to our Koles, though now all this has passed away, never more to be seen by the eyes of mortal man. They wore a garment of crossed green and brown thread, sometimes with yellow, blue or red interwoven, and this reached halfway between knee and ankle; two necklaces of gold bound together and a headdress of white bound about the head; an apron of finely tanned leather and a cloak of coarse linen; gold, low-hanging earrings. For their rites, they wore a white undergarment with a furtrimmed overfrock fastened with gold brooches. Upon their feet were sandals of fox fur. The chief among them would wear a diadem of gold set with smokestones and rainstones. All shaved the hair in the front half of the head, so they were called 'bigfaces.'

OGS:8:12 The Sons of May preferred to live in forests, but not in the depths, if possible, beside a lake or water, though no lake was holy to them, as some are to us. They had holy trees, and like our trees of power, these had to be beside a well or drinking pool. They had talking trees, but we do not understand these.

OGS:8:13 Then more wells and pools contained the essence of Krisura, and those drinking hung some portion of clothing on the welltree. Because so many failed to make the rounds of the waters, much of the power has now gone, or perhaps it is because the waters have become metal poisoned. Who knows?

OGS:8:14 In Britain, the two folkbeliefs of Keltica met and merged, and though beforetimes they had been mutually hostile, later they could no more be separated than milk and water shaken up together in a jug. So throughout the land there were now two peoples, those who came before the Kelts and were children of this land, and the people of Keltica who travelled much on water and lived near rivers and lakes. The small-statured dark folk favoured the deep forest and high hills. Different from both were the Painted People, who lived largely on herbs.

OGS:8:15 The language of the pre-people was rarely spoken, being the tongue of slaves and wayfarers, men who wandered. To the West, the people spoke the tongue of foreigners; to the East, they spoke Brythonic and to the South, Lemany. In the South, below the white lands of Albany, there were marshes.

OGS:8:16 Among the dark strangers who came to these hospitable shores were men from Greece, who, because they were exiled by their king, though for what we do not know, sought refuge in this bountiful land. They came in high-prowed craft, long-boarded, roofed over the centre, with many long-bladed oars thrust out through hide-bound rowing outlets. The emblems they bore were the Red Eagle and Snake, and they called the far away place from whence they came Filistis, which means Ruddily-Hued Land, so-called from the colour cast by a huge cloud through which their sun always shone. They spoke a wildish babbling tongue, so difficult that unless spoken slowly could not be understood even among themselves.

OGS:8:17 Their god was a huge, many hued stone, which, when placed on their strange altar, kindled the wood of the offering by its own power, when light fell upon it from the Eye of Heaven. Men who have seen it say that the stone comes out cold from the midst of the fire. They wore garments of woven cloth and leather fastened with metal work, open shoes on their feet and flat hats marked with red and purple. These colours have some virtue among them, which we cannot understand.

OGS:8:18 They built five busy trading ports in Britain, the largest being Donardkath, with a great haven for seacraft. The safe haven was encompassed by a high embankment, and beyond a lower one, and a ditch enclosed their fields and cattle. The only one of these safe havens remaining is Karkol; all the others have gone.

OGS:8:19 These Greeks were men of many skills, they knew things unheard of before in this blessed island. Thus, when they first arrived, Kaswalen, king of the Welsh, hastened to make them welcome. He willingly granted them all the land thereabouts for their own use, so they were not humbled vassals, but men who lived in free alliance with the people. When the land-giving pact was solemnised, at a great glen gathering, the daughter of the Greek chieftain, Jezel Bethamin by name, renamed Thespendu, was betrothed to Kewen, Son of Kaswalen, to pledge the alliance. The Greeks took wives from among the Keltic women, for they had only two Greek women among them, the other being she who became Raith, the sister of Thespendu. She was a holy maiden pledged to their god, and at all times she was guarded by two strangely armed dwarfs. It was told of her that her soft touch cured the sick, and her holy hand healed all but the most grievous wounds. It was said that Kaswalen sent his hunchback servant to be healed of a sickness, and that he returned walking tall and straight as a young pine tree. A foolish woman who fell through the roof while thatching and split her stomach open on the loompost was healed by washing in water made holy in the hand of Raith.

OGS:8:20 The last High Priest of the Firstfaith was Ifananud, called Krisnakel, better known among the strangers as Kelwine. It is said in truth that he was the wisest of men, and his is the protecting spirit, which hovers over the twelve green pastures of Britain. He is buried in the West at Kairhen. He was the son of that Owainbartha who died of shame and Olwin Keesabeg, his wife, at that time the most beautiful woman in Britain (daughter of Tisheala and grand-daughter of Merilyn), who ran away to Dunvarmod. We are told, and what brave Briton doubts it, that when she fled from Karsalog, all the sparrows left their nest-building to accompany her, and songbirds flew in a protecting cloud above her bronze-bound chariot. It was on that tragic day that the Great Protecting Spirit of Britain left the Holiselder with all his retinue. Since then, he has never returned, and the once far-famed place is now the dead and dismal abode of a dradwych.

OGS:8:21 The wheels of life turn and turn, and the pride and integrity, the honest dealing man with man, the cherishing of womanly ideals and the code of conduct for man and woman, will return to those, in whose veins flows the blood of Old Keltica. Great Gods, old and new, hasten the day! (There is but One God, but men view Him differently, through their own deceptive eyes, in many aspects, and He appears to them to be many).

Chapter Nine – The Battlebook

OGS:9:1 When I was a lithe, black-haired young warrior rejoicing in the springtime flush of man strength, Aristolio was a veteran battlecaptain. This was the spirit-strengthening war code he taught long ago in the glorious fighting years of my virile youth, in a far off, fertile Motherland within the warm central sea.

OGS:9:2 He rightly told us we need not over concern ourselves with the strange ways of the High Ones of Heaven. Let the hidden gods fight their own sombre battles in their wonderfully mysterious ways; for men, the grim earthly battles closer here below are sufficiently bitter. These we thankfully win or grudgingly lose, according to our courage and fortitude, our discipline and training, our skill at arms and tactical cunning.

OGS:9:3 Such needful qualities and essential skills, we learn from our own war tutors, though some befitting things, they do not teach, and wars are not won by material armaments alone. To complete the equipment of a sturdy fighting man, something more is required, and to this end, these instructions are given.

OGS:9:4 There are four codes to live by, each befitting the peculiar circumstances of the time. They are: the code of the warrior, the code of the citizen, the code of the kinsman and the code of the individual. There is the code of women, but that is something exclusively theirs and something, which all true men uphold.

OGS:9:5 Among all men, the bloodied warrior is the most important, for he alone is the guardian protector of the things, whatever they may be, all men value. None can have and hold any cherished belief or valued possession except by the grace of the sharp-edged weapon in the strong right arm and the sturdily protective shield on the left arm. He pledges something no other man can exceed in value - his throbbing lifeblood.

OGS:9:6 Each grim warrior is a loving and compassionate mother's son, and his war training starts in her protective arms. She never neglects him, and every care is given to ensure his contentment. A nervous mother conveys nervousness with her breast-milk; she withholds from her man-child the basic warrior nourishment. As he grows beyond her tender arms, she must see in her small man-child the bloodied warrior of the heroic future years. He must not be pampered; he must be taught confidence and self-reliance with his first faltering steps. She must bear in mind that in the foreranks of the battlearray, every man stands supported or betrayed by his mother, according to her handling of him in the forming first years of his growing.

OGS:9:7 The questioning man-child grows towards the restless youth, and the foundations for the fullness of manhood are laid down firmly or otherwise. The youth takes weapons, and, having been battle-blooded, becomes a man. The man is not only brave, he is heroic, for courage resides in all men, no matter how mean-minded. He is well knit in body, he stands tall and his eye and hand are steady. Straightforward, keen looking, stern-faced, he stands steadily still and moves with each foot striking the ground as though to assert his mastery of it.

OGS:9:8 Every movement is deliberate; his speech is slow and his voice strong and low. When he laughs, he does so heartily, the walls resound in comradeship, but he laughs rarely; more often he smiles, though his smile is not readily swift. He carries a battleharness just within his easy capacity, and when arrayed for action, he clothes his body just sufficiently for its protection.

OGS:9:9 Every War-readied warrior must struggle to gain absolute mastery in the use of his chosen weapons, by self-driven application, though of greater importance to victory is complete control over himself in battlestance. His body stands poised under the alert controlling mind, ready for any happening; he is never caught off balance in an awkward stance. Yet though this, the clashing fray, climaxes his life, it is only a thin, compressed slice of his alloted lifespan, for the battle is not lost in its own time and action; it is decided in the preparation, which went beforehand.

OGS:9:10 Many ask, "For what does the warrior fight?" It is not for fickle wealth and encumbering possessions, for these the grim warrior rarely gains, and what puny things they are against his glorious life! It is not for illusive freedom, for of all men, apart from slaves, he is the least free. It is not for his gods, for they if they be godpowerful, require no champion, and if they do are unworthy to be gods. It is not for mocking justice, for the disciplined warrior obeys unquestionably, even when the command is unjust. It is not for any fair city or cherished family, for so often these betray him.

OGS:9:11 This was the answer given when I, in my questioning youth, asked the same question of the Battlemaster, and I still have none better. A man fights because it is the inbred nature of men to fight, and this is true, for it is only through strife that he becomes a man. A man lacking the human fighting spirit would be as unnatural a creature as a woman shunning motherhood. This goes against human inclination; yet true men do not despise these, for the nature of men and women is wide and varied and there is a place in life for all.

OGS:9:12 A warrior is a man responding gleefully to the stern demands of manhood, even as a mother is a woman lovingly responding to the demands of motherhood. The two are akin, for what motherhood is to a woman, war is to a man. Without motherhood, men would lose respect for womanhood, and without war, women would lose respect for manliness.

OGS:9:13 All battles are not bloodbattles; there are other battles just as hard and demanding, and the blooded warrior who ignores them in unpreparedness is top-heavy and unbalanced. There is a just as deadly, if less obvious, war than any between kings and nations, and that is the war of life. Here the warrior faces his most deadly adversary, which is himself. Man arms his own foe in the battle of life and sends recruits to its ranks.

OGS:9:14 The first rule of the warrior is obedience, and every warrior is a subordinate. The young cadet warrior, unblooded by battle, is the subordinate of every blooded man. Keenly young, abounding with high spirits, overflowing with energy, he is animal-lithe, ever straining at the leash, baying to go, unwitting of caution. He will seek his outlets among companions of his own age, for in the presence of older men he must exercise the disciplinary restraint of respect.

OGS:9:15 It is never unmanly to show respect for age and wisdom; in fact, it indicates the triumph of discipline. Disrespect for those to whom it is due signifies character weakness, which is an unmanly defect. Young, fullblooded warriors are not wilful women or wayward children, they are men who know their exact standing. Therefore, cadet warriors will always defer to the greater skill and wisdom of their superiors and show proper respect for men of high rank.

OGS:9:16 The disciplinary warrior code need not be detailed, for it is written in the hearts of all true warriors and is a piece of essential equipment. A warrior is the protector of all women, even of the womenfolk of his foe, and he will not rape or abuse any woman or child. To strike a woman in the heat of battle or to attack a child is unmanly, and those who do so are a reproach to better men. He who strikes the weak and afflicted, the unarmed or unprotected, shall not be numbered among those in the ranks of true men.

OGS:9:17 A man's estate is decreed according to his manliness, and honourable warriors are men of high estate. If they serve for gold alone and not with high intent, if they serve mercenary men of low estate who manipulate them, then they, too, are warriors of low estate. Peace will come to the world only when warriors unite to impose it. That is the bad dream of rulers and men of cunning in high places.

OGS:9:18 There is no debt to life placed on a man if he kill in a just war or for his homeland, or for essential food or in defence of the sanctity of his family. Nor if he slay the adulterer who defiles his household, even though he become a martyr to marriage because of the laws of the land. It is unlawful to murder, which means killing for gain or deceitfully or striking behind the back. For true men, included in murder is that, which causes sorrow and suffering, which drive to death or robs the needy so they die, or takes away from a man his livelihood wilfully or unjustly, so his family perish.

OGS:9:19 These are the things that were taught to Golahan of the Bitterbiting Sword: No matter how grievous the crime of your comrade , he remains a comrade, and even though you condemn him at law, nevertheless, let the comradeship that was, help to mitigate his lot, no matter how undeserving he maybe. If all that happened was that your comrade could not withstand some temptation, do not disgrace or desert him. Say instead, "It is possible that had the same circumstances befallen me, I might have been in the same boat with him."

OGS:9:20 A knight is a man who serves the cause of duty, loyalty and good, and upholds the virtues of ladyhood. He is a man among men. Resolute but quiet, he speaks little, but what he says carries more weight in the scales than an outpouring of words by others. Therefore, I say to you, be a knight at heart, and let your armour be what it will, for you are a better man than one bearing impregnable harness.

OGS:9:21 A knight does not allow himself to become prey to melancholy and self-doubt; if you are convinced that you are a worthy knight of The Supreme Commander, you have true cause for rejoicing. A knight is one who acts when action is called for, and he remembers that proper deeds without and proper thoughts within strengthen him in times of testing.

OGS:9:22 Loudmouthed men are to be despised, as are those who deal with ladies as they do with the common woman. The true knight deals with them rightly. A knight is never rowdy or boastful when he has been drinking mead or ale, nor does he ever become unsteady or lack self-control. He is never quarrelsome when in his cups, for this displays a small heart. Because you serve loyally and uprightly, do not think that you will escape temptation and trial. You can call yourself a true knight only when you have overcome many temptations and trials.

OGS:9:23 As the waters to fish and the air to birds, so is fear to the coward, and sadness to the melancholy. Avoid the companionship of those who would contaminate you, and avoid hypocrites as you would the plague. They will fawn upon you, but this is the homage weakness pays to strength. Do not seek their praise nor expect life to be bountiful because of your goodness. Water loves the swimmer no more than the non-swimmer.

OGS:9:24 Put no trust in yourself until after the days of testing. Never judge your comrade until you have stood in his place. Never take heed of the tangled-tongued ones, for they who talk in tangles will surely lure you into a delusive net. Give careful ear to the words of the wise and to the tales of the wordmasters, and always be a transmitter, not a transmuter, of traditions.

OGS:9:25 A knight is steadfast, never the prey of passion swept along like mindless beasts by every vagrant wind of impulse. He is the champion of true love and knows that human love-longing serves to initiate the Soul spirit into the higher love that ultimately unites man with God. He honours the ideals of true love and shuns the lures of low love, which pander to the baser passions.

OGS:9:26 The man of knightly ideals aspires only to the love of a true lady. He avoids the available woman who has been the plaything of promiscuous men and is consequently the end product of careless, clumsy, self-satisfying use. The man who gives his heart to such as these is to be pitied by all true men, for he wallows in complacent, but shallow satisfaction.

OGS:9:27 Learn to be careful of every move, and consider it, just as the swordsman has to consider every stroke. He never rains blows haphazardly, but remains alert to drive home the deadly thrust. There are sword-thrusters and sword-smiters, and each must master his own technique, for proficiency means life. He who remains coolheaded and calm amid the cut and thrust of battle is a master of men.

OGS:9:28 The young knight goes into battle saying, "May I die like a true knight", but the battlechief says such a wish is wrong, for your desire should be rather to live like a true knight, and it will follow naturally that you will die like one. It is a lesser knight who desires to die for a cause, for the better men resolve that the foeman shall die for his cause.

OGS:9:29 A knight must learn the wisdom of the wise and strike it on the tablets of his heart, rather than having it as a babble on the tongue. He must know the difference between the indolent man and the cautious one. The difference lies in their use of the period between the action becoming necessary and doing it. One uses the interval for planning the action required and weighing its merits and demerits. The other, through shiftlessness, delays action until he is forced into it, and he is then found unprepared.

OGS:9:30 A sober man was leaving a market town to journey home a few miles away, and he met a drunken rake, and for safety, they journeyed together. As they passed by a wooded place they were waylaid, attacked and robbed. In the town there was a pedlar who, next market day, met the drunkard and asked him whether it was safe to travel the road, which the drunkard and the sober man had travelled previously. The rake assured him that there was no danger. When the pedlar questioned his cuts and bruises, all the drunkard could say was that he must have gotten them while he was drunk and incapable.

OGS:9:31 When the pedlar put the same question to the sober man, he was warned about the footpads and advised to travel in the company of armed men. Thus it is with those who journey along the road of life. We meet two classes of advisers, from which we can obtain advice. One, like the rake, tells that life is full of pleasures, and there are no dangers along the road. The other cautions us against the dangers and pitfalls and urges us to travel well armed with prudence, discrimination and the virtues.

OGS:9:32 Have a warm and compassionate heart. As frozen water cannot cleanse the body, neither can a frozen heart wash impure stains from the soul. The knightly man treasures nothing so much as his honour, which marks him as a man of high estate. Honour may be an attribute of the poor man, for it is not dependent on riches or station.

OGS:9:33 Earth is an apple orchard with fruits delightful to the eye, which waft fragrance to the nose from afar, but at the core, its fruits have the maggots of bitterness and decay. Yet the orchard is good and senses its purpose, which is to produce fruit. It is not in the hashish fields of the hermit's contemplatory life that men develop their souls. This is an escape for the weak and timid from the stresses of life. Those who are simple seekers after the smooth path become drowned in a sea of unproductive felicity.

OGS:9:34 You can pray, "God help me," when you have expended the last ounce of your strength, for He did not place men on Earth to play but to work. Duty, obligation and responsibility are the manmakers, and these are slighted in the times and places where men are less than men. Always reach out beyond the frontiers of your limitations, for if you believe a thing to be impossible, then you yourself have made it so.

OGS:9:35 Conscience is the eye of God in man, and the prudent man lets nothing be seen which is unworthy, unwholesome or unmanly. He is always circumspect in speech, for only those who can unring a bell are able to recall words spoken in haste. If Earth were devoid of evil, how could we know what was good and judge the weak from the strong? How would we know what to strive against to progress?

OGS:9:36 I am a man who has written many worthy things, and I have faithfully copied that which has been given me. Yet sadly, my efforts have brought me down; my clarity of vision has undone me. I have lived in a generation, which scorns truth and cannot bear the stress of the search. It derides the simple things and seeks only after vain pleasures.

OGS:9:37 All men fear a mind, which sees more clearly than their own and they destroy it in self-protection. All base men fear the tongue of truth, for it strips them and exposes their nakedness to mockery and scorn. To think is to be misunderstood by those who do not think. To voice new thoughts is to invite persecution. To have visions of greater things is to be hated by the visionless, and to be a maker of new things is to invite the scorn of the mindless.

Chapter Ten – The Maymen Lore

OGS:10:1 These are words of wisdom, happily told, of the teachings of the schoolmen who came from over the narrow sea. They journeyed from Durain and were children of Dardanos who was the first man to place a horse in harness. Kostain was his son who married Lengilwin of the high brow.

OGS:10:2 The teachings disclosed strange things, but they were the lore of the land and served well when interpreted by the wise. Before times, they were unwritten, for that, which was entrusted to perishable wood lost its power, and understanding came with the flow of words from the mouth.

OGS:10:3 Every thought leaves an impress upon the Spirit of the Shadow self for good or evil. With every impress of evil, there is further corruption and distortion of the Spirit Form. With every impress of good, there is a strengthening force, which beautifies the Spirit Form, and so it resides within in joy and content.

OGS:10:4 There are seven Spirit cankerers, which are: meanness, theft, hypocrisy, fornication, cowardice, lust and envy. Earth, enveloped in ocean and mantled in air, is the school wherein man, conceived in the likeness of The Divine, plays his part as a pupil.

OGS:10:5 The natural world is that, which continues and develops from the creative impulse. The supernatural is that part of the natural not yet comprehended by men. The Great God Above All is a Being composed of the collective souls of men departed to godhood. For it is written in times of yore that God died in the effort of creation, but a New God is being reformed. The whole of creation and life, as it manifests, is the effect of the Old God being transmuted into a New One.

OGS:10:6 It is also written in the books containing the words of the Maymen, that nothing can create itself or spring from nothing. All things must have something pre-existing to themselves, which brought them forth. This is the law, which teaches that there is a God and only this God was unpreceded by anything. That, which is preceded by nothing is God. The Maymen argued the existence of God by calling upon the natural state of things as witness.

OGS:10:7 There are seven absolute values, which are: Love, Truth, Beauty, Wisdom, Goodness, Creativity and Justice.

OGS:10:8 An animal, not having a Soul Form, lives only for the day, and if it lived a thousand years would not be aware of anything out of place. But man, did he live for that time, would be intolerably bored; nothing would give him pleasure, and he would dread the future and hate the present.

OGS:10:9 If man were a mere mortal struggling for self-existence, how can we account for his sense of moral obligation, his power of pity, his generosity, his ideals and aspirations? What other creature manifests these? Can these be qualities engendered through earthly life? Are the highest aspects of loyalty, the most devoted love, the noble self-sacrifices, no more than the waste products of evolution?

OGS:10:10 The soul is supreme above all. It should be master of its own forces and never permit itself to be led by its servants - the senses. The purpose of the moral restrictions and discipline imposed by religion is to give it mastery, even as bodily discipline and proper care result in a healthful physical existence.

OGS:10:11 The soul is awakened by love, by happiness and sorrow. The soul acts upon the body, but the body does not act upon the soul, for mind commands matter. The soul, awakening to conscious realisation, becomes one with the law and is no longer the slave of external conditions but the heir to truth. It is capable of rising above the illusions and uncertainties inherent in matter.

OGS:10:12 The last part is rewritten and reconstructed, but the original sense is conveyed. There were originally over eighteen thousand words in this book.

Book of
the Silver
Bough

SVB:1:12 Scriptures come in many tongues, they serve different purposes and vary in value, but each suits and serves a group of people in a particular stage of spiritual development. The lessons of an infant are as essential to its future as are the lessons of an older child. Each scripture gives a glimpse of the light, a spiritual revelation from a different viewpoint, but in each case the light is the same, for there is only one light of Truth.

Table of Chapters

Book of the Silver Bough

Preserved by the hand of Gwinder Apowin

Chapter One – Interpretations

SVB:1:1 With scriptures such as these, no matter how pure the original inspiration poured out from the Divine Spiritual Fountainhead, they still have to pass through fallible human hands. This could lead to differences of interpretation and discord among the readers, things most undesirable, where harmony and unity are to be the rule.

SVB:1:2 To avoid all such differences and for the sake of accord and unity, the interpretation of these scriptures must be restricted to conform with the following rules: The interpretation must accord with authentic traditions. It must accord with reason and experience, faith never contending with reason, though it is realised and acknowledged that the nature of life, being as it is, many things have to be accepted and undertaken without logical explanations. The continuance of life beyond the veil of death may not appear to accord with worldly experience and reason; yet it does, but there is a law prohibiting any assurance of this. Such things have to be accepted; therefore, worldly experience cannot be taken as the yardstick in this instance, as in many other instances.

SVB:1:3 Apart from worldly experiences, there are spiritual experiences, which cannot be known and understood by the many. What is told of these must be accepted in faith by those unwilling to devote the time and undergo the austerities and discipline necessary to know at first hand. Only another Twice Born One is in a position to disagree about such a matter, and therefore, all others should be content to leave it in their hands.

SVB:1:4 Higher points of doctrine should be left to those competent to deal with them, but when lesser points are in dispute, then the outcome must accord with reason, and if any one explanation is to be accepted, it must be discovered rationally. All differences of opinion are to be settled by a majority of those competent to judge, and all reasons for supporting, or disagreeing with, any decision must be placed in record.

SVB:1:5 Whenever there is a meeting among brothers, they should assemble in good order, with goodwill and harmony in their hearts, and they should likewise disperse. While things are done in this manner, there will be prosperity and progress, though if any outlandish doctrines are introduced or any dividing disagreement permitted, prosperity and progress will depart. They will remain while the teachings are esteemed and the doctrines hallowed, while the leaders are held worthy of loyalty and the brothers of comradeship. Progress and prosperity will not depart while the brothers are upright and steadfast; while the maiden sisters are modest and virtuous and the married sisters are decent and decorous; while the elder brothers are wise and diligent in preserving all that is good; while the elder sisters are careful in all they do and considerate for the welfare of the younger ones. It is for the old to keep watch and ward, and for the young to dare and do.

SVB:1:6 The harshness of the ordinances should be mitigated with loving kindness, and when brothers or sisters are seen to be falling into the ways of wickedness, they should first be warned. After being warned, they should be reminded, and only after this should they be disciplined. Let some able and discreet person take them in hand and counsel them.

SVB:1:7 When two disagree as to the teachings, this is to be the manner for reaching a decision: One shall say, "This is my opinion," while the opponent says, "No, this opinion is better." Each shall argue with the other with friendliness, self-control and reason, following at all times the road of common-sense. If there is something on which they hold a different opinion, let them try and decide first which viewpoint is best, which is clearest.

SVB:1:8 All the teachings in dispute will be settled in this manner, and where there can be no settlement between two, then let them both agree upon two others. If these cannot settle the matter, then they shall choose one other, whose opinion both agree to abide with.

SVB:1:9 These teachings are always right: Those, which teach the proper channelling of the desires and urges of the body, not those, which would pander to them or ignore them. Those, which place spiritual objectives above worldly things. Those, which uphold the virtues and principles of humanity and attack anything, which would bring them down.

SVB:1:10 Frugality is not meanness, and prudence is not fear. Wastefulness is not generosity, and weakness is not kindness. Happiness is not pleasure, and apathy is not peace. The defence of principles is not intolerance, and idealism is not prejudice. To compromise is not to surrender. To defer to the wishes of a loved one is not weakness of character. To avoid argument and discord within the family requires strength, while assertion displays inconsideration. They who stifle hasty or thoughtless words are better than they who speak according to their thoughts.

SVB:1:11 To stand up for your rights is not necessarily right, and to do all things for peace and harmony is often wrong. The way of goodness traverses a very narrow ledge. The man who says, "perhaps I am wrong" is always right; the man who says, "I am certainly right" is always wrong. To avoid a fight is not cowardice, and to fight with the certainty of victory is not courage. Weak men may often fight and strong men often run; motive is all that matters. To judge anyone by his actions alone is to judge unfairly.

SVB:1:12 Scriptures come in many tongues; they serve different purposes and vary in value, but each suits and serves a group of people in a particular stage of spiritual development. The lessons of an infant are as essential to its future as are the lessons of an older child. Each scripture gives a glimpse of the light, a spiritual revelation from a different viewpoint, but in each case, the light is the same, for there is only one light of Truth.

SVB:1:13 However, scriptures need interpretation, for they conceal more than they reveal. They are never just what they appear to be on the surface. If a particular scripture proclaimed that fire actually gives out cold instead of heat and that the sun really sheds darkness instead of light, the shallow-minded person would turn from it in scorn. But this irresponsible and thoughtless attitude cannot be applied to scripture, and it would be much wiser to assume that the scripture intended to convey a meaning and message quite different from the superficially apparent one. Scripture cannot be treated like entertaining and valueless literature; therefore, delve deeply and diligently.

SVB:1:14 The only conclusion an intelligent person can come to is that all great scriptures, read properly and really understood, originate at one source. All are divinely inspired, but the clarity of vision varies considerably, as does the purity of transmission. Each suits particular needs and varying stages of development. Each provides for certain requirements and satisfies specific spiritual capacities, but in all, the essence of Truth is watered down and the brilliance of the light is obscured. This is essential in all scriptures, for it is only when the divinity within is fully awakened that Truth and reality can be gazed on; then, the scriptures no longer serve their purpose.

SVB:1:15 More than most these scriptures reveal only a fraction of the whole on the surface. In worldly matters, in rules of life and code of conduct and morals, in all things governing life on Earth, they will be interpreted strictly according to their obvious meaning and intent. In all things pertaining to spiritual matters, the afterlife, the divinity, or not strictly concerned with earthly life and existence, they need not necessarily be interpreted literally, for no earthly medium is adequate to express such things concisely.

Chapter Two – Teachings of Elidor - 1

SVB:2:1 I am a prophet of the written word, a man with many books of wisdom, who comes to you in the name of The Supreme Spirit. I bear proof of my mission for all to see. I was a Sleeper in the Great Stone Chambers of Initiation; the voices of the Instructing Spirits spoke to me, and I answered with the words of power. I prepared myself by the Dread Rites and became worthy to be called an Inheritor of the Ancient Wisdom.

SVB:2:2 They who awaken the Sleepers charged me with the burden of a prophet, saying, "Go forth into the highways and byways of the land, bearing the scars of one seared by nearness to the flame of Truth. Be not a man of pleasure, a son of wickedness. Have no love of comfort and the flattery of fine clothes. Deceive no woman for fleeting satisfaction, nor be deceived by worldly shadows. Here, you have seen with the eyes of reality and know the true nature of earthly things; are they not shadowy forms without substance, in which no trust can be placed? All earthly things pass away, the loveliness of flowers withers and fades, the beauty of a woman's face slips away with the passing years."

SVB:2:3 The voice of an Instructing Spirit continued, "Go forth, Shaker of those who slumber in spirit. Go, stir up the minds of men, crying, "Awake, bestir yourselves within the prisons where you are doomed to decay, cast off the fetters of worldliness, and uncover the eyes of the soulspirit."

SVB:2:4 "Go, gather the sincere seekers, and reveal to them a little light; guide them through the bewitching fairyland of earthly illusion, so they leave it to enter the daylight of Truth and not the darkness of death. Deliver them from the delusions generated in dense bodies.""

SVB:2:5 Hearing these things, I said, "Who am I to be a prophet to men? My soulspirit, having bathed in the Lakes of Light, can never again be happy imprisoned within a daily decaying body." The voice of an Instructing Spirit came to me; "Be comforted, my son, by the knowledge of Truth. The world, as it is, we cannot change, for this is the task of men. Go, submit yourself to life, the harsh taskmaster and gentle saviour. Your own good works are not yet sufficient to pay the cost of entry into the Place of Light." I asked in sorrow, "Am I then a man of small righteous credit," and the voice of the Instructing Spirit replied, "Where is the righteous man who is blameless? All men are prone to error, for it is the father of courage and resolution. You have been found reliable in testing and fit for the covenant of prophesy."

SVB:2:6 I speak with the words of the Instructing Spirits, and I am their mouthpiece to men on Earth. They charged me with the burden of a prophet; he is one whose soulspirit is a communicating link with the Divine Inspirational Source; he is one to deliver a message to the world. He is the teacher allocated for the times to teach a particular religious truth. His courage must be tempered with gentleness, and whatever fate decrees he must always rise above it. He will become an attraction for tribulation, overwhelmed with troubles, rejected and mocked.

SVB:2:7 Then they said to me in the comfortless darkness illuminated only by the spiritglow, "You will be a physician dispensing a bitter draught. The message you bear will not strike men's ears like a charming lovesong; the words will not fall pleasantly like notes from a well-played harp. Pleasant things are fleeting and stir the hearts of men for only a brief moment; entertaining things are soon forgotten, and amusing things leave no mark. Your tongue will be a sting and your mouth a fiery furnace."

SVB:2:8 "Men will hear your words, but they will not penetrate to many hearts. Your hearers will say, "We are much moved and our hearts charged with godliness," but these are words of wind and their hearts will still follow the ungodly inclinations of their desires."

SVB:2:9 When a man enters the Great Stone Chambers of Initiation, he receives an infusion of the Divine Essence. His soulspirit is awakened to conscious awareness and passes out, to leave the mortal body still and silent within its tomb. He comes into the presence of Beings who know the will of The Supreme Spirit; he learns awful secrets; he knows whence he came and whither he goes. He is one reborn and awakens to rediscover himself.

SVB:2:10 When I heard my fate, I asked for a smooth path and success, and my plea was rejected. Yet from that day, I came to love life as never before; from that day, I was a lover of Truth. Now I no longer have any trust in the world; I am no longer deceived by its ways. I know the world and the works of men, and I know myself. I sought for my soulspirit, and I found myself. Ten thousand worlds and their mysteries are meaningless to me, I found Truth, and she stands higher than all the worlds.

SVB:2:11 In the Place of Terror, I saw other things. I learned the secret of the serpent with its tail in its mouth. I saw the workings of the spawn of evil and the fungus of corruption. I gazed upon the Dark Ones, and when they saw me, they became vicious; they sought to attach themselves to me, for burdens of wickedness are added to those who affiliate themselves with evil. But I was strengthened against them and came forth uncontaminated.

SVB:2:12 When the implications of my fate awoke knowledge in my heart, I wept, in the spirit-lit darkness, for my wife, for my children; for would they not become fatherless? Who would harness the oxen and scatter the seed over the soil? Who would tend the sheep and stand guard, who would protect from intruders?

SVB:2:13 The voice within the Tomb Chamber spoke of fate and destiny and the things, which were unalterable. It said, "The path of the prophet is beset with sorrow; your house is destined to become desolate, and no human hands could have deflected the blow of fate. Your lands shall be abandoned to wild creatures, and many years shall pass before they are resown."

SVB:2:14 Then I said, "Let my wife be spared and the children of my body, for they will be comforters to me along the way and strengthen my heart in service." The voice of the Instructing Spirit replied, "Were these things within my power to grant, gladly would it be done, but you have been chosen as a prophet, and the way is hard and lonely. In the years ahead, your family will be mankind and your companions the accompanying Spirits. The road is long, and its end rests in eternity. Fear lurks by the wayside, doubt haunts the forest to be traversed and worldly temptations will be like wolves at your heels. But you can look forward to the joy of reunion at the destination, and though the way is hard, the journey is not in vain.

Chapter Three – Teachings of Elidor - 2

SVB:3:1 I am the prophet of the day; now hear my voice. There is a law of compensation; good always leads to good and bad always to bad; whatever the demands made upon you, they are always within reason. To you who defraud the poor and oppress the weak and defenceless, I tell you, your day is coming.

SVB:3:2 You who make justice a bitter draught or two-pronged weapon, or who twist the laws of the land to suit selfish ends, you shall not escape the remorseless Divine Justice. You who hate those who expose your evil ways and drag dark deeds out into the light of day, you scorners of honest men, you bribers and acceptors of bribes, have a pleasant hour! For a grimmer day will dawn.

SVB:3:3 You who harvest in fields you have not ploughed, who snatch a few pennies from the poverty stricken; you who connive with the forces of ignorance, who are self-deceivers thinking yourselves learned; you who walk in the comforting security of God-bestowed riches, unheeding of your duty, enjoy your hour! The reckoning awaits.

SVB:3:4 You who are self-satisfied, priest-deluded, going about like blind men led by the blind;

who dwell under a cloud of shamelessness, gaining riches and power by the ignorance and weakness of others; you who say, "By our own strength have we accomplished our own ends," rejoice while you may! The day will come when you will be severed from your possessions; what will you have then?

SVB:3:5 The inheritance of eternity is for the upright and frugal, but the wicked and wasters shall be shut out from the places of contentment and peace. Hear my voice; let every man deal justly with another, speak the truth, seek the path of true justice and never say, "We need seek no further." Walk in ways of modesty and simplicity, shunning all forms of deceit and hypocrisy. Seek earnestly and diligently, and surely you will find, but expect no results if you are half-hearted and lukewarm.

SVB:3:6 Hear my voice, for I am one who has tasted the waters of Truth at their source. I come to scatter the seeds of wisdom and enlightenment over the whole Earth. The edge of my words has been sharpened on the whetstone of inspiration, and the comforting companionship of spirits has stilled the tumult within my bowels. I am a smooth-polished arrow shaft of inspiration waiting in the quiver of my mission. My tongue is a sword stabbing at the cuirass of worldliness, to open a wound exposing the sensitive conscience beneath. Do not delude yourselves that because I am among you, I have chosen you above others; I come among the worst, not the best, and I am charged to go to all men.

SVB:3:7 Yet though I come as an eagle to strike the foxes who seek to wreck the fowlpen, I come also to salve the wounds of the broken-hearted and to lead those captive in ignorance to freedom. I come also to those whose hearts are fastened with the bolts of intolerance and prejudice and to replace misery with beauty and glory in place of degradation. I am a planter of acorns intended to rise up into oak trees of divinity.

SVB:3:8 I am not a prophet of new doctrines, neither do I declare Truth to be a new thing. Truth remains always the same, however she is clothed. I am not a foreteller of the future and do not claim the ability to know the end of any one of you, or even my own. What lies ahead for anyone of you is in your own hands. Some things are certainly revealed to me, and these I must reveal to you, for this is the obligation of a prophet. I come among you not as a miracle worker, but as one charged with the duty of warning you openly.

SVB:3:9 Among you are many who make secret mockery of their religion, or who conceal their true beliefs behind a false facade of righteousness. To those I say, beware; awake to Truth, for you are deceived by worldliness. They have failed the test of life; they are victims of its delusions. Hear my voice; every man is the maker of himself, this is Truth. No man can intercede for another, and, could any one sacrifice his soulspirit for another, such sacrifice would not be permitted by The Supreme Spirit, Who is the Essence of Justice. As a man makes himself, so will he be known.

SVB:3:10 Do not reject me because I differ not from you. Had the Powers Above chosen one of their number to be a messenger and sent him down among men, then surely, the appointed one would have taken the form of a man. He would have been clothed as men are clothed and eaten as men eat. He would not have been some freakish creature having wings or two heads. Man's body was made to serve man, and if a messenger from above comes to men, shall it not serve him also? Therefore, I speak in the words of men and act as men act. I make no claim to be more than man.

SVB:3:11 If you say to yourselves, "Why should we listen to this one who is no more than a man seeking to change our ways and undermine the teachings of our fathers," I say, have I come with guileful tongue and lips coated with honey? Do I wear garments of silk and linen and eat at tables of luxury? I do not come to speak pleasantries to you, but to declare the harsh and unavoidable Truth. What I bring is not a honeyed drink, but a bitter draught; are these the wares of a false prophet?

SVB:3:12 If I am in error, then all I endure is in vain; if I am wrong, then on me is the punishment, but I have the assurance of certainty. What I have can be any man's if he is prepared to suffer and endure as I did. I make no claim to having received illumination as a gift, or as a reward of righteousness. I received it because I toiled and suffered for it. I paid for it in anguish and austerity. I deprived myself of worldly pleasures and comforts for spiritual knowledge. Do you expect to obtain what I paid for so dearly, for nothing? To know Truth, you must accept my word or follow the road I trod. You have the choice.

SVB:3:13 If the things, of which I speak, be fabricated by myself, or be the fruits of my imagination, then I am like one who labours without wages, for I toil and suffer without gain. Even worse, I damned myself before the judgement seat of Truth. Therefore, if I am convinced of their truth, what cause have you to doubt my words?

SVB:3:14 I do not come before you declaring myself the confident of The Supreme Spirit, the knower of secrets unattainable by others. I do not lay claim to miraculous powers, neither do I pretend to have the ability to forgive sins; these things are beyond the ability of any man. This I do declare to you: I am no superior being, no angel descended from the Heavens above, I am a man, such as you. Will you not hear me as brother listens to brother, will you pay less attention because I am cast in the same mould as yourselves?

SVB:3:15 Hear my voice, for I have come to awaken those who sleep. I come to lead the blind, I am the eyes of those who do not see. I am not a beguiler promising soft beds or comfort. I come as a warner against those who promise an easy way, and I raise my voice against any who lull you into indolence by declaring the ability to intercede for you. There is no easy way, and no one can intercede for another, each man is the master of his own fate. As each man plants, so shall he garner and as he moulds himself, so shall he come forth. There is always a day of reckoning.

SVB:3:16 Long years I struggled and prepared myself, seeking to discover Truth and the purpose of life. Then, the day came when I entered into the sleep which awakens the soulspirit. Then, when the truth was revealed, I saw myself as one seeking for selfish ends, for the satisfaction and contentment of knowing. When first I was charged with the burden of a prophet, my heart cried out, "Is it for this greater affliction that I have suffered and toiled, where is my reward?" I who should be strong was weak.

SVB:3:17 The inner voice of my conscience came to my aid, and I obeyed its command. I devoted my full attention to the Instructing Voices. I tested them for reality and knew they were no delusion. I act only upon the knowledge and proofs I have been given. I am not a bearer of idle tales. Do you think me such a fool as to sacrifice all I held dear, to give up all I possessed, to come and preach a false doctrine to those who would repay me with nothing but scorn? Do you consider me so lacking in wit that I would commit such an act of folly?

SVB:3:18 Do not disregard what I have to say; the words I speak were dearly bought. Do you treat them contemptuously because it was not you who paid the price? Hear and heed. I come to proclaim the Way of Truth. I can neither save you from the effects of your own errors, nor remit even the slightest transgression. I can only point the way; I can only offer myself as a guide. I cannot drive you, I cannot carry you, neither can I assume responsibility for your fate.

SVB:3:19 If you are bent under a burden of sorrow, then I will lighten your load; if you are oppressed, I will come to your aid; if you are lonely, then I am your friend; my hand is ever ready to help. All things within my power to give I gladly offer, whether they be of this world or transcending it. False promises to gain popularity, fair words to make friends, appeasing words to turn away anger; those I cannot give. A day will come when we shall all stand naked before the glare of Truth. That day I do not fear; can the comforting prophets so readily acceptable speak likewise?

SVB:3:20 Sons of fools are fathers of fools. If you will not accept my words of Truth you deny them to your children. Revile me as you will; sheep bleat and asses bray, but the stalking wolf makes no reply. You clamour for signs and say, "Cause these trees to become uprooted and dance, this well to flow with wine, or he who died three days ago to rise up from the grave and live, and we will believe." You ask for childish things contrary to any law and therefore beyond my power. Even could I perform such miracles to gain your belief, I would refrain, for what would such belief be worth? Just one miracle could convert the whole of mankind, but even then the price is too high for such a worthless gain.

SVB:3:21 Go your own ways; follow your undisturbing beliefs. Had it been in accord with the Creating Intent, you could all have been born perfect in righteousness, but what would you have been then? Mere puppets dangling from the hand above. The Divine Intent was not to create puppets; what end could they serve? The Supreme Spirit wants men, men with freewill capable of decision, free men reaching upwards to divinity, choosing it of their own accord.

SVB:3:22 I follow my belief; you follow yours, me to my end you to yours. You look upon me and say in your hearts, "Can we believe him?" Yes, look upon me, and see how I live; do I not live by my own words? Now look upon those who declare me to be a false prophet, who are they? Are they not those who trample others underfoot in a scramble for power? Do they not thrust the orphan aside and permit the poor to starve in the midst of plenty? Who is the less hypocritical, the man to follow and believe?

SVB:3:23 May the woes of the world descend upon those who pray with the lips while their hearts remain dead and unmoved. Likewise those who display devotion in public places, but turn a hungry man away from their back gate. Let them suffer no less who worship in the daylight, but in the darkness of night indulge in whispers of scandal and deceit.

Chapter Four – Teachings of Elidor - 3

SVB:4:1 Hear my voice, listen to my words, obey these rules of conduct: if any man names you a liar or treats you as one, have no further dealings with him. Keep away from the smooth-tongued man with oily ways, for he is unworthy of your friendship. Keep your face unsmiling in the presence of a man who uses vile language. What spews from his mouth is the overspill of the rottenness within; he is empty and weak and, if encouraged, will spread his disease far and wide.

SVB:4:2 All things which really benefit man, whether materially or spiritually, and do no harm, are good and should be encouraged; they are the particles of progress. If a man comes to you and says he has secret knowledge of benefit to man, then hear him fairly. Bear with him patiently, for if he is sincere, even though you derive no benefit and are told nothing new, his sincerity needs encouragement.

SVB:4:3 Though it is well to convert others to the Way of Truth, tread wearily. Many will seek to lay snares for you, or to find some hidden vice, but if you live as your conscience dictates, you will go free and they will become ensnared. Those who call your belief false are themselves blinded by the scales of gullibility and held fast in the meshes of their own net of ignorance. As the blind can never see, so are these inconvincible; did The Supreme Spirit Himself come down and manifest to them, they would declare it to be only an illusion. Men believe what they want to believe and see what they want to see.

SVB:4:4 Leave them to form themselves as they will. The day will come when they will see themselves as they actually are, and on that day fear will overcome them, they will not know where to run. All their cunning and trickery will not avail them then; their words of scorn and mockery will rise up within them as bitter bile rises into the mouth. Have compassion for them, for on the dread day, they will stand alone, their waiting companions, the uncomforting horrors, skulking just beyond their sight.

SVB:4:5 Those who have no desire for Truth will never be convinced of its existence. There are many who do not believe in the existence of The Supreme Spirit in their own mortality because they fear to do so, not because it conflicts with their reason or inclinations. Even if a door could be opened into Heaven, through which they could look, they would say, "It is all an illusion, we are under some kind of spell."

SVB:4:6 Hear my voice; listen to my words; I have books of ancient wisdom giving guidance towards the light. I teach from them, and if they remain hidden, it is to keep them from the hands of despoilers. You who remain with face set towards the darkness of disbelief, go your way. If your affairs appear to prosper better than the affairs of those who walk in the light, do not deceive yourselves. The Supreme Spirit is compassionate and they prosper because He pities you for your future fate. In His mercy, He is granting you an abundance of pleasure in this life; enjoy it while you may. To you who hear my voice, I say, let these things not bother you or appear unjust. It is proper that the just and upright should suffer, for they are the chosen ones to be tested for greater things. The weak horse is never heavy-laden.

SVB:4:7 You who withdraw, closing your ears to my words, who erect a barrier around your hearts so my teachings cannot penetrate, follow your way. You take your road, and I will take mine. But when the gloom closes about you, do not say, "We have been treated unjustly." If any injustice is done, it will be by yourselves to yourselves. The wickedness you have done will then recoil upon you; the truth you derided will have caught up with you. Laugh if you will, but laugh well, for your laughter will come to an end. Beyond it lies an ocean of tears.

SVB:4:8 You mockers, who ask to be shown the man who has returned from beyond the grave so he can describe what it is like, you say, "Only by this will our doubts be stilled." Who am I to change the order of things and still your doubts? I have not come to bring assurances, but as a warner and awakener. Why do you talk like this? If my teachings do not stir your hearts to response, they will not be forced upon you.

SVB:4:9 Many times, I have been tempted to withhold part of my message, knowing you would hold it in scorn. I have been faint-hearted when others have mocked, saying, "Bring down a Spirit from Heaven or disclose the hiding place of treasure, and we will believe." Hard is the road of a prophet, and that is all I am, not a conjurer.

SVB:4:10 You turn from me, saying one to the other, "What does he want of us?" or "Where lies his gain?" I ask nothing from you except a receptive mind. I ask no riches; I seek no payment. My reward lies in the knowledge of a duty done, in a clear conscience, in having done my best. Were I seeking wealth, or even fame, this is the last way I would set about it.

SVB:4:11 I speak with a true voice, I am no deceiver with some subtle end in view. I make no claim to possessing sacred treasures of wisdom. I make no claim to the knowledge of hidden mysteries or great secrets. I am not an Angel, nor a Spirit sent direct from Heaven. I am one of your own kind. I am not a hypocrite seeking to curry favour by taking your side against those who ridicule your own views. I stand alone, asking favour of no man. I speak according to my heart; as my heart, so my lips. My words are true; if I did not utter them, I would be a coward and a betrayer of all I hold dear.

SVB:4:12 Wait and listen. Do not worship vainly and to no purpose. Serve The Supreme Spirit, for there is none greater to serve, If you think otherwise, you devise false things. Take my teachings into your hearts; I offer them gladly, asking no reward. Will you not open your hearts and incline towards the truth?

SVB:4:13 You demand proof of my prophesy, that I am what I declare myself to be. You say the darkness of the tomb has smitten me with madness and ask me to join you and become cured. May the Protecting Spirits bear witness that I do not join in ignorance and darkness. The proof of a true prophet is in his way of life. Have I ever lived otherwise than in accordance with my teachings? False prophets gain worldly things; true prophets suffer unrewarded, without complaint. Even then, what they suffer in the sight of men is only a small part of the whole burden.

SVB:4:14 You mock my teachings, declaring them to be false and foolish. You are suspicious of them; what do you fear? Be honest with yourselves; is it not because they disturb you, that inwardly, you know their truth? I have not come to bring you consolation; I come to cause you anxiety. I do not speak words of comfort, but words of urgency. Change your ways now, before it is too late. The road back is long and tiresome.

SVB:4:15 I speak with the voice of The Supreme Spirit; I serve Him, and to Him is my life dedicated. Were I to demand a sign from Him to bolster my own faith, would I not be unworthy of His trust and a failure as a prophet? Did I demand a sign to show you, would He not think me weak? It does not need a prophet to convert by signs and miracles; anyone could succeed by this means; the true prophet is needed when it is more difficult, when the opposition is really tough. A true prophet speaks harsh words; he is known by his unpopularity.

SVB:4:16 You may ask me whether it is my desire that you should abandon the worship of your fathers. This is not my desire; retain all that is good and beneficial; reject all that serves no purpose. You accuse me of being too solemn; you say I have lost the ability to laugh, that I set my face against merriment. In all this, you wrong me, for I never set myself against laughter and happiness. In all things, there must be balance; laughter and happiness have their place, but are not things of supreme importance.

SVB:4:17 You say, "Why should we not deal with our possessions and our lives as we wish? They are ours." I say, where the wishes and inclinations of a man's heart lead him along the most beneficial road, then follow them. But no man has sufficient wisdom within himself to know where his benefit lies; therefore, he must seek guidance if he be truly wise. Which is the wiser, to deal with your lives according to the prompting of inclinations and desires or to live them in a way most beneficial to yourselves?

SVB:4:18 Through my own efforts and sacrifices, through application and long years of patient endeavour, I have been granted an insight into the nature of things. I have been given a clear revelation and also been charged with making it known to men. What I have has been bought dearly; why then do you mock my teachings or doubt my sincerity? Have I asked anything from you except a change of heart?

SVB:4:19 You mock me, saying, "We cannot understand the import of your great teachings," or you deride me, saying, "Were it not that we have pity on your state of madness, we would drive you away from us." For your sakes I have given up all I once possessed; I have left all I hold dear; can you not spare me a few moments of your time? You ask, "Why did not The Supreme Spirit make all men conform to one creed, one belief?" This He could have done, but it would not serve His end. These are not superficial teachings; can you not spare time to consider them?

SVB:4:20 You say I am no more than a man like yourselves; this is true. You say I am powerless among you, that I remain only because of your benevolence and goodwill. If you think me powerless, you are mistaken. In the Stone Chambers, I learned secrets of power beyond your conception. Do not think me helpless because I come among you with humility and restraint. Had I so desired, my knowledge could have brought me riches and position; instead, I chose to live as I do and follow the road of a true prophet. Is this not proof enough of my sincerity?

SVB:4:21 The times are good. There are bountiful harvests, and the land is at peace. Men come and go without fear; pleasure and comfort are to be found on every side; it is a bad time for prophets. Turbulence and trouble are needed to stir the hearts of men, to lift up their eyes to greater things. When a man is beset with trouble, he turns to spiritual things for consolation and help, but no sooner has it passed than he reverts to his former ways. The man who pillows his head on a log is more likely to pray than one who lays on a pillow of down.

SVB:4:22 Many among you have come forward in a half-hearted manner and said, "We have heard and believe, we are followers of your teachings." The day came when they were called upon to make sacrifices for their beliefs; then, there was a speedy sorting out. Some regarded their afflictions as chastisements from above, being still unable to understand the nature of suffering. When misfortune came upon them, they said, "The Supreme Spirit is against us." When the sun of fortune shone they said, "The Supreme Spirit is with us." How little they knew of Him!

SVB:4:23 Heaven and Earth have been formed for a serious purpose, for a great and glorious end. Man is blind to them because of his small-mindedness. I speak of wonderful things, while you answer me referring to miserable matters. I am a plain man; I claim no extraordinary powers beyond acquisition by any other, I am not a conjurer or sorcerer. My mission is to choose those who wish to serve The Supreme Spirit. I come from the silence of solitude; I am not a man gifted with eloquence. Did I come performing miracles, all would follow me, even the hypocrite and evildoer would be among those who walked the road. Who then could separate the chaff from the grain, the weak from the strong, those worthy of Divinity from those who were not?

SVB:4:24 All creation is upheld by The Law, and the value of The Law is revealed in the fact that even The Supreme Spirit does not act against it. It would be less beneficial for men if miracles were performed by the prophets. If the Law is good, it must be strictly applied.

SVB:4:25 If men are insincere and shiftless, the performances of miracles will not strengthen their hearts. They are like voyagers at sea; a storm rises, and they are distressed; it abates, and they rejoice. When the winds roar and the waves mount up, they pray and proclaim their repentance; they profess their intention of living a new life, if saved. Yet when they come safe to land again, they forget all that passed; they return to their previous ways. They commit self-injuring excesses and deeds of selfishness; only further affliction brings these to an end; can you not understand?

SVB:4:26 Hear my voice, those who miserably bewail their misfortunes. When troubles beset you and new trials confront you every day, know you are being tested. Life itself is a necklace of tests. Accept with fortitude whatever test life presents, saying in your heart when meeting each one, "However this may appear now, it is for my ultimate good."

SVB:4:27 You, too, talk of miracles. You seek miraculous solutions for your problems. Do you not understand the nature of freewill, and that miracles are contrary to it as well as to The Law? Were they part of normal life, your fear of divine intervention, or reliance upon divine power, would sap your independence and stifle the expression of freewill. Your choice between good and evil would no longer be free, and you would become more of puppets and less of men.

SVB:4:28 Face up to every trial, for only the tests successfully undergone and the good deeds done have lasting value. To merely while away the time, to take the easy path through life, turning aside at every obstacle, has no value whatsoever.

SVB:4:29 No two persons have the same abilities and inclinations; therefore, let each man serve The Supreme Spirit according to his endowments. Do not try to imitate another in service, for such imitation accomplishes less. Follow the road of your own choosing; serve to the best of your ability; live a good life; little more can be required of any man.

SVB:4:30 However, do not close your eyes to Truth, thinking that service through earthly skill and ability is enough. What you think, and what you believe best, may all be wrong. You may not even know what is for your own good. You were born without being consulted; you cannot direct your lives according to your desires. You will die, whether you wish it or not. Such is earthly life, and likewise, your condition in the afterlife may not accord with your own designs and will.

SVB:4:31 You say, "Death is the end of all things; therefore, let us live as we will." Are you certain, that you can state this as a fact? What do you know of death? The only fact you do know beyond a doubt is that death is the universal lot of man. Therefore, exercise caution regarding something you know little about. Shed no tears for those who are already beyond the place of tears. Can weeping console them, or mourning assist them? What is life or what is death, that you should grieve for either? They come and go, they merge one into the other until neither is distinguishable.

SVB:4:32 Sorrow and joy, pain and pleasure, tumult and peace; they come and go. They play about man and are gone. They are like winds rustling a tree; they pass, and the tree remains unmoved, life is a lamplit room with two doors leading to the darkness of night.

Chapter Five – Teachings of Elidor - 4

SVB:5:1 Hear my voice. I condemn the slanderer, the talebearer, the hypocrite. They are the inheritors of darkness, the ones destined for the dismal abyss. I condemn those who amass riches and store possessions against the future, and those who delude themselves that wealth will shield them against the trials of life.

SVB:5:2 These are times of worldliness, when riches are the lure, the obsession of men. Only on the brink of the grave do they see the folly of their ways. Then when it is too late, they cry out in despair, saying, "Grant us just a little more time." Of what value would more time be to them? They have had sufficient.

SVB:5:3 Food which would sustain widows and orphans is thrown by the rich to their dogs, and they say, "This is the natural order of things." I condemn them, not for their riches, but for what they say. Here the widows and orphans cry, but who will cry beyond the grave? Who will inhabit the grim caverns? Ah, you indolent rich, fatten yourselves up, surely a lean time lies ahead! Do not shift the blame when your just desserts are meted out; you are the guardians of your future, the preparers of your future abode.

SVB:5:4 I condemn the self-deceivers. They say, with hypocritical lying heart, "This may be done, and this is forbidden." They split hairs; they have a conscience of convenience; they interpret the message from the formation of a letter. Hear my words; heed what I say. Do not twist the truth so that it becomes lies, and say, "These are rules for the conduct of others," at the same time masking your own deeds under a convenient veil of distortion. Never make laws for others, which you are unable to keep yourself. Are they better than you? If so, let them make the laws.

SVB:5:5 I raise my voice against mean-minded men. Would there be any justice, were they to share the same fate as the generous and self-sacrificing? I condemn cowards. When they are told, "Be men, this is your duty," their hearts quail inside them; their knees tremble; their feet shift; they know their true nature will be revealed and can find no words to avoid their obligations.

SVB:5:6 Those I do not seek as converts; let them go their own way. For if there is hardship or persecution, if the followers of Truth are to be tested for their worthiness to survive and bear the light, where will they stand? The smug, self-satisfied man is not called upon to follow. If good fortune smiles upon him, he will say, "See what I have been given, though I have done little. I must surely be a worthy man." Self-deceiver, he has been discarded as unworthy of any test; the good fortune has been granted in mercy and compassion; his future fate is awful.

SVB:5:7 I condemn the cowards and hypocrites who go about shouting indignantly against warmongers and injustice. They say, "Restrain yourselves, for we are men of peace." But when the enemy swoops down upon them, or a just war is proclaimed, they say, "Let your hand carry the sword and spear." Those who once shouted boldly now speak in whispers; their voices are no longer heard.

SVB:5:8 The weaver knows the design of the whole tapestry; the threads only the colour in their own part. This life must be viewed together with the life to come, if it is to be understood. Only The Great Designer can do this, and He metes out success and failure, joy and sorrow, all the tests of life accordingly.

SVB:5:9 I condemn the man who says, "I am pure; I am good." Who is he to judge? Does the polecat think its own smell bad? Does the adder throw away its venom? Only the deluded fool says, "I know what is good and what is bad and need no information on the matter." Heed these words; heed them well!

SVB:5:10 When good fortune comes, some men say, "I have led a good life, and this is my reward", or "This results from my own efforts." If misfortune befalls them, they say, "This is the fault of some other," or, "This is a chastisement from above." I say to you, all things flow from your own destiny; good and bad are sent alike to test you; both can be turned to your own benefit or your own undoing.

SVB:5:11 If some of you have done wrong and acted against your own future good, whatever it is, the harm is not irreparable. There is still time, how long is unknowable, but the uncertainty is essential. The damage must be repaired by a constant outpouring of good, and this alone is not enough; the roots of evil must be torn up within you; felling the tree is insufficient.

SVB:5:12 Those who heed my words and follow my teachings are Pilgrims on the Path. They must be resolute and resourceful, for the going is tough. Each victory a Pilgrim wins contains the promise of a harder one to follow. Every obstacle overcome brings another into view; from birth to death life is a continual overcoming.

SVB:5:13 The desires of the body and cravings of the flesh are divisible into two parts: those, which draw attention to the needs of the body (these can be satisfied in moderation) and those, which bring greater spiritual reward through suppression or re-channelling. The man of wisdom knows one from the other.

SVB:5:14 I do not speak of profound things; my words are for the ears of unlettered men. I try to speak within the understanding of every man and woman and according to their capacity, but because of this, the enlightenment given to the many may have no value to the few. Even so, there will be those who find it beyond their comprehension. My teachings are many-sided, and therefore, each must interpret them according to his own capacity for understanding. My words are not for those whose minds are pools of stagnation; a pot filled with stagnant water cannot become a receptacle for the pure waters of wisdom. My words are not for the intolerant and prejudiced; fresh milk cannot be mingled with sour milk.

SVB:5:15 Hear my voice, for though I speak plainly, in unadorned sentences, I have been strengthened by an inflow of power. I have a shield to deflect the words of mockers and scorners. In a sea of hostility, I am not troubled or disturbed; my heart is like flint and my face confronts the unrighteous like a cliff withstanding the wind. Where are my wordy adversaries? Let them come forward and meet me in open discussion before you. Why do they keep away? Why do they seek refuge behind armed men?

SVB:5:16 It is time to separate the good from the bad, the serviceable from the worthless. The Earth is overloaded with useless things; progress is impeded in a welter of unnecessary things. It is deafened with the clacking of foolish tongues and overwhelmed in a spate of valueless words. Mankind wallows in the mudhole of a purposeless existence. It must pull itself out or be drawn under and perish.

SVB:5:17 Many desire fame or greatness, but these come only in accordance with destiny. If it be destined, they will come unbidden. Therefore, do not make these your aim in life. Obey the laws of life as recorded in the scriptures. Live in accord with your neighbours, for irrelevant quarrelling harms all and benefits none. Endure every trial with steadfastness, and between the tests, prepare for the next; never be caught unprepared.

SVB:5:18 Those who live a good life, maintaining themselves in uprightness and shunning the ways of wickedness, do this for their own good. They are wise, but would be unwise and hypocritical, were they to hold it was done for the sake of The Supreme Spirit alone, and not for their own sakes.

SVB:5:19 Some have been given riches in abundance; they lack none of the good things of life. Others have nothing, and their burdens are grievous and heavy. I have heard men say, "What kind of God makes this the order of things," but it is not God; it is man who establishes this as the order of things. The Supreme Spirit will not undertake the tasks of men, neither will He withdraw the tests of temptation when they are placed in the paths of men.

SVB:5:20 The Supreme Spirit has made a law covering the dealings between men. They are judged with a greater justice than Earth can ever know. It differentiates between the powerless slave who owns nothing and the man abundantly supplied with wealth and possessions. A kind word or drink of water from a man in bondage is of greater value than gold pieces from a man of wealth. A poor man who gives from compassion or comradeship does so in goodness, but the goodness of a rich man giving in consciousness of charity, or from pride in his possessions and position, lacks the same purity; it is tainted. Whose goodness has the highest quality, that of the poor man who shares all his food and clothing with a fellowman, or that of the rich man who gives two pieces of gold from the thousands in his treasury?

SVB:5:21 The same law differentiates between the maimed and afflicted and those who are whole and healthy, between the strong and weak, the dull-minded and the keen-minded man. The law is: from each man according to his ability and means. The feeling and intent behind an act give it value.

SVB:5:22 I speak again to the cowards, for in these pleasant times, who knows where they are;

there has been no sorting out. Only their loud voices betray them, their love of comfort, their lack of hardihood, their appreciation of womanly things. They say, "Would that times were different and we had a call to action," but when a matter is placed at issue, when the opposition is aggressive and immovable, they melt like wax images before the heat of fire. Their hearts tumble, their bellies turn to water, they turn their eyes aside and mumble excuses. They say, "We have a sickness," or, "We have many responsibilities." Far better were they better men with enough courage to admit their own cowardice.

SVB:5:23 There are others, not cowards, who have a point of weakness in their family ties. Wives and children cause men to stray from the strict path of duty, but for this, the wives and children are to be forgiven.

SVB:5:24 Obligations have an order of precedence, which is to be strictly observed. Few men are so unbiased that they can decide such things for themselves. A wife and children are the sun of a man's life; they are almost indispensable to his full development. Yet they, like riches and power, are sources of trial, a means of testing, and every man should act in the light of this knowledge. By doing so, his life will be more harmonious and beneficial. He should also bear in mind that his relationship with all his family is judged according to a law similar to the one just mentioned. As he treats them, how he acts, so is he judged. The family living in a hovel of poverty is not expected to conform to such a high standard as the one in a place of plenty. That the former does is to its credit; that the latter fails and its standard falls below the other, is to its discredit; there will be a proper accounting.

SVB:5:25 Those who live contentedly, snug in the bosom of their family, safe at home, going placidly about their daily affairs, untroubled by the call of the cause or the demands of duty, shall not be treated or judged like those who sacrifice and serve. The placid and indolent are not judged the same as those who struggle resolutely and endure steadfastly. The constant and the inconstant are not treated alike; their merits are in no way similar. There is a greater recompense of merit for those who turn their back on home comforts than for those who remain content with peace and placidity.

SVB:5:26 These are times of peace and prosperity, but are they times of inner stability? Those born less fortunately, who have fought in bloody wars, who have been driven away homeless, who have endured famine, imprisonment or persecution, have learned that mutual suffering is the cement of humanity. The sweet flowers of friendship and understanding are found in the deserts of despair and distress, not in the pastures of pleasure and prosperity.

SVB:5:27 Peace and prosperity cannot remain with you forever; therefore when trouble and strife descend upon you, as they have in the past, remember that the pattern of life is one of light and shade. Happiness and sorrow, success and failure, contentment and strife, are sent alternatively among men, that the good may be known from the bad, the strong from the weak, the true from the false, the straight-forward man from the hypocrite and the selfish one from the unselfish.

SVB:5:28 Now, I will speak about deceitfulness, the evil rampant among you. Nay, do not seek to drown my words in an avalanche of mockery. Honest men do not fear Truth; words of Truth do not beat painfully against their ears. There is no deceit so profound as the deceit of the self-deceived. They are prisoners in a cell of their own building and have cast the key into the moat outside. They may hide their true selves from others in this life and think they have done well, but there will be no such deception in the life to come.

SVB:5:29 Some self-deceivers stand before me, half their thoughts proclaiming their goodness and the others preparing acts of deceit. Others say, "We are good; we are just" and twist the words of the scriptures with their own interpretations and misquote to comply with their own convenience. They cannot deceive one who sees the reflection of their inner image, but they may deceive you, for they put on the face of plausibility.

SVB:5:30 I see behind the mantle of goodness displayed to the eyes and discover the rottenness hidden underneath. The alms they give, the good deeds they perform are no more than palliatives to their consciences. They blow themselves up to appear great in the eyes of men, but there is nothing inside except wind. Beneath the mortal surface, there is a puny thing, weak and withered. Could these only see their future fate they would surely cry, "We are treated unjustly," maintaining their self-deceit. But who is unjust to them if it is not themselves?

SVB:5:31 To you who are healthy-minded, I say, keep well away from those self-deceivers, for if they do not corrupt you, they will surely lead you astray. Take no notice of what they say; their words are false; seek rather to discover the things hidden in the alcoves of their hearts. Some deceivers have come to me and said, "We believe your teachings and wish to follow your way." In their hearts, they do not believe, and they act from base motives. Because they are blind, they think I, too, cannot see. I may lack all worldly possessions and wealth, but I do have a treasure beyond price, granted me in the Great Stone Chambers, my eyes can see the inner likeness of men. I cannot be deceived by words,

SVB:5:32 Some of you who are Pilgrims on the Way will find many seeking to gain your confidence and appearing willing to repudiate their own kind. Have no dealings with them. A man who would betray his faith, his race, his nation, his convictions or his family, is a weak reed, from which no support can be expected, and upon which no reliance can be placed. If he plots your downfall, return cunning with cunning, it is not wrong to slay a snake with a snake's venom. If you disregard a man who schemes against you, you support his cause.

SVB:5:33 Those totally ignorant of Truth can do little harm, but those who know Truth and disguise her are dangerous. Those who alter the appearance or mask the face of Truth are servants of evil. Among them are those who turn the words of the scriptures to suit their own ends. They say, "This is the true meaning; it is more convenient, less harsh," or they say, "This we know is written, but we do not obey; it is too exacting; we accept part and discard part." Get rid of them, they confuse the genuine seeker for Truth and mutilate Truth with their knife of selectivity.

SVB:5:34 You ask, "Why do the good suffer as well as the bad, why are the innocent afflicted as well as the guilty?" It is because mankind is a single whole; if an arm is wounded the whole body suffers; men are not strictly divided into good and bad, guilty and innocent. Those who suffer or are afflicted through the faults and failings of others derive the greatest kind of benefit.

SVB:5:35 Just as the soulspirit experiences pleasure, so must it experience pain; were it otherwise, the pleasure would have no value. Can light be known without the contrasting darkness? If a man is prepared to accept pleasure and happiness from contact with others, should he not also be prepared to participate in their sorrow and suffering?

SVB:5:36 Pain is unpleasant; agony sometimes unendurable, but they can be accepted and borne by a realisation of their objective; the knowledge that they have a purpose and end. Suffering and strife have made man what he is; he suffers things unknown to lesser creatures, which do not know the pains of remorse, regret, shame and disgrace. It is suffering and sorrow, not pleasure and happiness, that have raised man to his present height.

SVB:5:37 You ask, "How can the troubles and tribulations of the good be reconciled with the statement that The Supreme Spirit is the fountainhead of Justice, Goodness and Mercy?" They can be. Man must tread the hard road of sorrow and suffering, because it is an inescapable route on the journey to claim his inheritance. Man has won the right to make the pilgrimage; he has passed the simple tests; should he baulk at the greater ones along the way?

SVB:5:38 My people, hear my voice; I am your prophet. Transmute the dark memories of your sorrows into light seeds of spirituality. The pearl of perfect peace lies in the dregs within the cup of suffering. The haven of happiness lies across the turbulent seas of strife.

Chapter Six – Teachings of Elidor - 5

SVB:6:1 Truth cannot be destroyed or changed; she cannot be stripped and displayed to the eyes of men. Wisdom and knowledge cannot be trampled underfoot by turning the sword against their upholders. I may not be powerful, I carry no weapons, my voice may be weak, but better men will come in days unborn, and they will sing glad songs of light. The night of ignorance will have its end.

SVB:6:2 I speak to the toilworn, to those heavy-burdened with labour. In the bondage of servitude, you are free, because you are not shackled with cravings begotten by idleness. The idle rich are not free; they are slaves to their possessions; they suffer under the lash of their thoughts.

SVB:6:3 Labour is not toil and nothing else; its rewards extend beyond worldly things; this is one of the tragedies of the rich who are denied them. Even the prophets of the past have not seen clearly the rewards of labour. I will teach you the truth, and it will make you free.

SVB:6:4 There is a right way to labour, and there is a wrong way. There is also a way of labour that is full of song and a way that is silent; both play their part. Men should choose their form of labour and not have it thrust upon them. In it, they should find contentment and self-expression, then it will not become wearisome.

SVB:6:5 The man who would be happy and contented must seek a form of labour free from anxious thoughts and fanciful desires. It must bring satisfaction and confer benefit. These things have been said before, but I say them again: do not pursue vain hopes or seek too high a reward. Ask only for a just return, and remain your own master.

SVB:6:6 It is unwise to seek a position too great for your abilities; by so doing, you burden yourself with a life of straining. Be satisfied with whatever fate decrees, and whatever problems perplex you, rise above them. Be without jealousy, never envious of another's position; meet success and failure with equal poise and your labour will not be burdensome.

SVB:6:7 Learn to see the hand of The Supreme Spirit in all things, and make your labour the sacrifice, your toil the offering, to Him. No others are asked than these. Care and diligence, honesty and skill being your form of worship, you worship well. Diligence in the task, a life of moderation, dedication of wealth, leisure hours filled with service or study, these are proper sacrifices, not poor dumb creatures.

SVB:6:8 Those who curtail pleasures and then do nothing useful with the time gained are fools. To abstain from enjoyment to serve beneficial ends is good; so also is dedication of worldly wealth beyond modest needs. Giving an honest days labour for wages, living modestly and frugally, without meanness or harsh austerity, these too are worthy and acceptable sacrifices. It is through sacrifices such as these that the soulspirit is truly glorified.

SVB:6:9 Neither contentment in this world, nor happiness in the world to come is for those who do not know the meaning of sacrifice. All good works, all honest labour, all charitable deeds, all payments of full and fair wages, not futile burnings, are worthy sacrifices. Another form of sacrifice is the time devoted to studying the scriptures.

SVB:6:10 Open your hearts to my words; I speak only for your benefit, my voice is not raised for my own amusement. There is much talk about the wickedness and arrogance of the rich. Have I said this? It is not only they who are wicked and arrogant, and no man can be called wicked just because he is rich. Wealth does not necessarily serve evil. What matters is how persons deal with the inheritance entrusted to them, not only riches, but also strength, beauty or talent. Search your own hearts before condemning others.

SVB:6:11 It is not only the rich who are idle. Each of you, ask yourself how you would fare under the test of riches, and answer honestly. Is it certain you are not reviling the rich through envy? Are you sure there is no hypocrisy in your hearts? Wealth is no light burden, and few, very few survive a severe test. But there are others, men of unusual ability, women of great beauty or talent, they, too, often fail. Look within before you look without.

SVB:6:12 Like those other things, labour is a challenge, the outcome can be a gain or a loss, victory or defeat. The slovenly man who labours only to supply his needs is one on whom life is wasted. The man who declines to utilise mind and limbs to the utmost is no better than the man whose riches permit him to live a life of uselessness. The fault lies with the man, not his money.

SVB:6:13 The enjoyments that flow from worldly things bear within themselves seeds of sorrow to come. Worldly pleasures are passing things, and peace and content are not to be found in them. The man on the right path is one who considers the earthly rewards of effort less valuable than the spiritual gain.

SVB:6:14 All men become Pilgrims on the Way when their labour and efforts are dedicated to serving mankind. They reach out for spirituality when they find pleasure in their task. The man who labours with zest and dedication, even though the result be small, is a better man than one who lacks these qualities.

SVB:6:15 Even as in all fire, there is smoke, so in all things created by men, there will be some imperfection, for perfection lies outside this world. The best man can do is strive towards perfection; whatever he turns his hand to; make it the goal.

SVB:6:16 You may think me a doleful prophet preaching the glory of the sorrowful path, but this I am not. The inclinations of men lure them from the road; to turn them back. I, too, must leave the road and take a stand where the inclinations have led them. I do not speak of things supporting them along the way, but of things leading them astray.

SVB:6:17 I say to you, seek happiness; enjoy yourselves; life is meant to be more light than shade. I also say, these things cannot be made the whole aim in life; see them in proper perspective. Happiness is not the goal of earthly life; it is a reward along the way. Everyday life is governed by duty and obligation, not happiness and pleasure. To be over-concerned with happiness and contentment is the surest way to unhappiness and restlessness.

SVB:6:18 Submission to the will of The Supreme Spirit is the surest means of avoiding too much suffering and frustration. Knowledge of His will comes from careful study of the scriptures. Joyfully accept whatever destiny bestows, be it joy or sorrow, good or ill. If you are blessed with many gifts, there is no better way to indicate your gratitude than just being quietly and contentedly happy, finding pleasure in even the smallest things.

SVB:6:19 A man's trust in the goodness of The Supreme Spirit must not depend upon the outward circumstances surrounding that man. This is a very important thing to remember. He should try and quell all expectations and preferences, accepting cheerfully whatever comes his way. The man who serves best rises above all desire attachments and sense allurements, his only earthly ties being those of love, duty and obligation.

SVB:6:20 To know the will of The Supreme Spirit and will what He wills, that is the supreme secret of spirituality. Labouring to fulfil that will is to worship with the daily task, a most profitable form of worship. I say, let the will of The Supreme Spirit be supreme, and subordinate all earthly labours to it. The path of life is on a mountainside; man can ascend or descend according to his inclinations; he can take the hard or the easy way. Upwards is the light, downwards the darkness; man has the choice; he goes where he pleases.

SVB:6:21 I speak to you as a warner,and I warn against the ways of evil men. They are selfish men unheedful of the good of others, the good, which includes them. Their thoughts do not extend beyond themselves and their own; they seek to isolate themselves from mankind when the good of mankind is an issue. They do not know what should be done and what should not be done; they do not understand the nature of good conduct and the path of Truth. They say, "Mankind has no need for goodness; it has no moral foundation. There is no way of knowing Truth. There is no Supreme Spirit, no Creating God. All creation is the result of chance, and lust is the only cause of birth. The only purpose of life is an earthly one, we begin and end in the dust."

SVB:6:22 Set in the ways of this belief, these unconscious soulspirits dutifully serve the cause of evil, working, though they know not, for the destruction of mankind. They taint their soulspirits with unrestricted desires and stain them with uncontrolled urges. Full of arrogance and deceit, they ride rough-shod over the spiritual inclinations of others and hold fast to their own dark belief. Their destructive work is carried on in the name of progress.

SVB:6:23 Yet with all they have, they are unhappy and discontented. They are loaded with many unnecessary cares, and their restless thoughts never give them peace. They fruitlessly seek happiness in sensual enjoyments, in pleasure and gaiety, in the frivolities of life, in drinking and gambling, in luxury and ease, firmly believing they will find it there, that life can offer no more.

SVB:6:24 They are bound fast with fetters of worldliness; they are blind and insensitive to anything else. They seethe within; anger, spitefulness, indignation and malice are relieving outlets. They seek refuge in lies and deceit; they hope for relief in outbursts of temper, in lust and sensuality and in foul language. Their only aim is to amass wealth and possessions, or to live a life of idleness and ease; they cannot understand what drives them on.

SVB:6:25 They say, "What I have I have earned; it is my own; with it I will acquire whatever I need to satisfy my desires. I have amassed riches, I have come to a high position; men look up to me; I am praised and honoured. I can buy what I desire; I will enjoy life; I am a success; who else is like me? I give charity; I fulfil my religious obligations; I am sought after by those who need advice and help. I live comfortably; I eat well; I have all I need." This they say, but are they really happy and at peace, are they really successful having all they want? No, they speak from the darkness of delusion, though they know it not.

SVB:6:26 They have been deceived by the trap of earthly conditions; they have fallen prey to the alluring phantoms of the senses. They are entangled in a net of delusion; they wander in the deep fog of illusion. They are slaves to their urges, captives of their cravings; they are bound and helpless in a chariot drawn by runaway horses, carried swiftly towards the yawning abyss.

SVB:6:27 Weak men become drunk with the heady draughts of power and riches; they are carried away by their own arrogance and conceit. They try to turn earthly condition towards serving their own ends and struggle futilely against The Law. Willing slaves of arrogance and selfishness, helpless victims in the stormy seas of rage, lust and violence, these servants of evil hate the divinity within themselves. They hate and fear the small still voice inside. They stifle it; they smother it under the loud clamour of gaiety. They seek solace in strong wine, in sense-stimulating entertainment and in spirit-poisoning drugs. Stand aside; let them be carried swiftly to the place of sorrow and vain regret!

SVB:6:28 Hear my voice, and do not fall into the trap of worldliness; do not fall willing victims to the allurements of phantoms. Look for reality; be satisfied with nothing less than Truth. Do not reject the scriptures; study them carefully, and you will have a guide through life. They will reveal the right and the wrong; follow their light; do what has to be done; no more is expected of you. Heed what I say, for I am your friend.

Chapter Seven – Teachings of Elidor - 6

SVB:7:1 I will speak to you about the commonplace man. He is one in whom there is neither spirituality nor spiritual aspiration. He is not righteous, but neither is he really wicked, and he does not have any ingrained evil qualities. Because he knows neither vices nor virtues, such a man is untried and untested; he does not know what are the qualities needing development and what are the evils to avoid. He serves the cause of evil, though he is no more than a mere pawn. No man can stand aside from the conflict; men such as these are unwittingly drawn into the service of evil.

SVB:7:2 The commonplace man has an understanding of good conduct; he is genteel; he is cultured. People like him; he is at ease with them; they seek his company; he is useful to them, as they are to him. But though he is full of worldly knowledge, he has little knowledge or understanding of the scriptures, or of things transcending earthly existence. He cannot soar into the heights; his feet are planted solidly on the ground, but his wings are undeveloped. He cannot rise above the ordinary; his behaviour is that of the common crowd; he is a commonplace man. He has learnt from earthly experience and associations what conduct is right and what is wrong to serve worldly ends. This is not enough; to live fully and to good purpose, he must know more.

SVB:7:3 The commonplace woman is like the commonplace man; she moves easily in her earthly environment, but is incapable of raising her eyes above it. She has so much to stir the hearts of men; she can be so desirable; yet, she fails to inspire them. She can goad them on towards earthly goals, but not to anything greater. She can fan the flame of ambition in her children, but cannot inspire them to look beyond the world.

SVB:7:4 Commonplace people have commonplace traits and weaknesses. I will speak of one: revengefulness. An unjustifiable seeking for revenge springs from an inner weakness; the mean and servile person is most addicted to it. Malice, like revenge, is a trait of the weak, not of the strong.

SVB:7:5 If someone wrongs you without cause, do not let this disturb your tranquillity of mind. Do nothing else except scorn them. In this way, you will not be unnecessarily upset, but will also be revenged without any need for inflicting it. The tearing wind and flashing darts of lightning leave the sun and moon untroubled; their anger is vented on trees and plants below. So it is with wrongs done by mortals; the wrongs do not disturb the hearts of superior men, but cause turmoil in the fainter hearts of inferior men.

SVB:7:6 You laugh, you mock me and say, "We prefer life among the commonplace people, for they are easier to get along with; they do not criticise us." It is true, they will not; if they are unconcerned about their own future, how can they be considerate about yours? You ask why it is that the righteous people keep to themselves, while the wrongdoers are more companionable. The answer is simple, those who live good lives walk in the light and so do not fear to be alone; they have the companionship of the Spirit. The wrongdoers, however, walk in darkness and so have need of company, for they are secretly afraid.

SVB:7:7 Not long since, one came to me and said, "Prophet, I have offended against the law of the land, but not against the law of the scriptures; am I blameless?" I tell you this; the law of the land may extend out beyond the law of the scriptures, but should not conflict with it. The law outside the scriptures must also be obeyed. The law of the land is not perfect; it is made by men and cannot claim to be perfect. It should be what it is not, a pure marriage between justice and Truth, unadulterated by the deviousness of man. The child of the marriage should be loving kindness. It is not for me to tell you of these things. If men are content to suffer under bad laws, whose is the blame? The true nature of a nation is revealed in its laws.

SVB:7:8 This I do say: I condemn the lawmakers who issue unjust and devious decrees, who seek to hide their true intent under a mountain of words. I condemn the unjust laws armed with the sword of legality. I condemn the judges who spread a legal covering over cunningly laid traps and snare men in nets made with words. They deceive the ignorant and simple with false masks of legality. Truth and Justice weep outside the courthouse. I condemn also those who stir up strife under protection of the law, who cause legal mischief or deal in legal deception to rob the innocent and unwary. Wickedness has many faces, but the most hideous is that of those who twist the laws to serve selfish ends, or treat the downtrodden with harsh injustice.

SVB:7:9 I speak of these things, but I have not come to change the laws of the land or decide whether they be good or bad. I leave worldly things to worldly men. You say, "Tell us to which a man should owe greatest allegiance, to the leaders of his nation or the leader of his faith?" I say this, there is a scale of precedence, and man must serve whatever ranks highest. Spiritual things rank above worldly things, but the man who loves his nation and its customs, its mother tongue and its traditions, is a better man than one who decries them. The man who obeys his rulers, identifying himself with his people, with their progress, their welfare, their calamities, as though they were his, repenting for their wrongs and rejoicing in their triumphs, that man is a patriot, and patriotism has a proper place. He is above the commonplace man, but not above the man spiritually inclined, for spiritual things transcend earthly things. The good of all mankind transcends the good of any nation.

SVB:7:10 In keeping the laws of the scriptures, good intent is the main consideration. There must be a complete absence of hypocrisy and deviousness. I am a man with many books; I will tell you their teachings, but their words are for study by men of insight and learning. I speak in conformity with what is written, for if a prophet sets up a body of laws conflicting with established teachings, or laws claiming to replace them entirely, he is a false prophet.

SVB:7:11 Man reflects the powers, which are his heritage; he is the heir to divinity. He must, however, submit to the will of The Supreme Spirit who is much wiser than man, and this will is made known through the laws of the scriptures. Man must not submit abjectly, through fear of punishment or hope of reward, these things are unworthy of one aspiring to divinity. The will of The Supreme Spirit is revealed through those who have proved worthy of divine inspiration, who have spiritualised themselves sufficiently to communicate with the Powers Above. The prophet who has been fully tested, who has survived his trials, who knows the means for assuring himself that he speaks with divine authority, is a rarity even among prophets.

SVB:7:12 There is a spiritual value in submission to the Divine Will. Where the purpose is obscure and self-discipline required to conform, the value is even greater than where the reason is easily perceived. This discipline, too, has its value; it is the discipline of the heroic warrior, the man of courage and conviction.

SVB:7:13 The mind of man is like a water barrel placed against the house. On top floats a slimy scum of worldly lust and lewdness; beneath this grow weeds of ignorance, prejudice and selfishness. Below this is clear, clean water, unseen because of the scum above. I am one who clears away the scum; I am the revealer of the good underneath. My mission is to make the water fit for use, not to destroy the barrel.

SVB:7:14 I am not a man of fancy words. I have lived all my life among wise men and found nothing better for a man than silence. Study is not the most important thing; it is deeds. Contemplation and speech have their place, but actions shift mountains, while words blow around them. The knowledge that his soulspirit records every word makes a man careful in speech. It is the man whose inner self is wrapped in the mantle of ignorance, who keeps no rein on his tongue. If a man antagonises you, never answer him in haste; no reply at all is often an eloquent answer.

SVB:7:15 You ask me concerning marriage. Others more able than I have spoken about it; study their words. This I do say: It is not enough for husbands and wives to love each other; they must make their love known. A husband does this by showing his wife more respect than to any other woman; is she not the one he chose, or has she been chosen unwisely? If this is so, then it is wrong to make her suffer for it. A wife should be treated with delicacy and care, as the most precious of a man's possessions. As no man expects his wife to defile his home by adultery, he should commit no adultery either. A wise man leaves his wife to be mistress in his house and home; he provides for her needs to the utmost of his ability.

SVB:7:16 This is the way a wife shows her love for her husband: She is at all times affectionate and womanly, always considerate and gentle. She is careful in managing the household and supervises it diligently, being herself always neat and clean. She never does anything to cause her husband anxiety; she is never wasteful with his earnings. She pushes aside every thought of other men and never disgraces her house or shows her contempt for her husband by committing adultery.

SVB:7:17 I do not say that a wife should not think of other men, or husbands of other women; such thoughts come unbidden. It is not wrong or unnatural that they should do so, when the true nature of marriage is known. It is a state of trial; it is one of life's greatest tests; ignorance of this fact is the enemy of marriage, not human nature. However, I am not the prophet to declare such things.

SVB:7:18 Neither am I the prophet of peace; he is yet to come. I am the prophet to tell men of The Frightener, though many generations will pass before it appears. It will be a thing of monstrous greatness arising in the form of a crab; first its body will be red, then green, then blue. It will spread destruction across the Earth, running from sunrise to sunset. It will come in the Days of Decision, when men are inflicted with spiritual blindness, when one ignorance has been replaced with another, when men walk in darkness and call it light. In those days, men will yearn after pleasure and comfort; they will go down roads of ease, encouraged by women incapable of inspiring them towards the upward path.

SVB:7:19 There will be disbelief in spiritual things, but this will proceed from ignorance; it will be a thing of the lips, for disbelief is not in the heart and nature of man. No matter how much a man cries out his disbelief, in times of turmoil, in strange and unfamiliar surroundings, when frightened by the unknown, he turns to spiritual things for comfort and strength.

SVB:7:20 In the days of the great conflict, do not pray that The Supreme Spirit be on your side, this would be a futile waste of time. Pray rather that you be on the right side, the side of The Supreme Spirit.

SVB:7:21 Hear my voice, for I tell of things to come. There will be no great signs heralding the coming of The Frightener; it will come when men are least prepared. It will come when they seek only worldly things. In those days, men will be falling away from manliness and women from womanliness. It will be a time of confusion and chaos.

SVB:7:22 I have warned of The Frightener; I have done what I am charged to do. Now, one asks where he shall seek for Truth. I say this; They who set about it rightly will find Truth, no matter where their mortal bodies are located. It is never far from men. Truth is everlastingly unchangeable, Earth is false, because it changes and passes away. Truth and The Supreme Spirit are one, because they are eternal things.

SVB:7:23 Things as you see them and things as they really are, are in no way alike; illusion is the environment of Earth and it deludes the inner eyes with outward impressions. As a needle pricks a blister to let out the water, so does the sharp point of Truth pierce the veil of illusion and let out ignorance.

SVB:7:24 The mind of man is like a pool of water; while it is disturbed, only distorted pictures can be seen; but when it becomes calm and still, the light of spiritual Truth is reflected there in all its beauty. The inner being interprets things through a veil of emotion. The man who burns hotly within himself sees the world about him as a fierce fire seeking to consume him; but the man who is calm and quiet within sees all about him as tranquil and peaceful.

SVB:7:25 Everyone suffers from certain fears in one form or another; the feelings of anxiety, doubt, frustration and despair are only normal, but to be overwhelmed by them is a sign of weakness and immaturity. Therefore, to those who are fearful and anxious or have doubts, more will be sent, for this is meant to be experienced and overcome. Only by this means can man prepare himself for the greater tests ahead. Calmness, love, steadfastness and tenacity are the sentinels outside the first gate of spiritual development. Mere ceremonial, however uplifting, cannot of itself bring the soul-spirit of man into contact with the Powers Above; something more is required.

SVB:7:26 You ask how much more sorrow one must suffer to win freedom from sorrow. There can be no such freedom on Earth; the waters of sorrow are drawn from a bottomless well. Only when the eye becomes incapable of some tears does it really see fully.

Chapter Eight – Elidor Speaks to His Disciples

SVB:8:1 I have chosen you from the many because of your eagerness, your attentiveness, your serenity and your self-discipline. These are the basic qualities required. You must also prove yourselves loyal and adaptable, strong and trustworthy, intelligent and unselfish, free of all vices and bad traits, efficient, self-reliant and stable. When I was given my prophethood, I was told to initiate only the worthy persons who had proven their self-mastery and trustworthiness.

SVB:8:2 Each of you must snap the knot of the heart. You must study the scriptures constantly, and apart from these, read words, which are beautiful, inspiring and true. You must constantly strive for tranquillity of heart, for self-control, for self-harmony; be kind and considerate at all times, and always maintain purity of thought.

SVB:8:3 Live good lives; practise frugality, but false austerity for your own inner edification is impure. When self-control or self-discipline become self inflicted torture, or when their intent is to hurt another, then they are servants of evil. However, sacrifices such as I have taught, the kindly acts of everyday living, are not to be abandoned because you are disciples. Strive each day to achieve greater self-harmony, for this is the swiftest path upward.

SVB:8:4 The senses and body cravings must be disciplined, otherwise they would assume control. It is not sufficient to be spiritually developed, you must ensure that the body is completely controlled by the soulspirit within. Therefore, you must not succumb before the rigours of life. You must not pamper yourselves; you must obtain victory over heat and cold, over the craving for food and drink, over the weaknesses of the flesh and over the call of comfort. You must cultivate persistence and resolution, for determination is essential on the path.

SVB:8:5 The women must practise all womanly virtues, such as decorum, decency, pity, modesty, sincerity, devotion, purity in all things, cleanliness and love of love. They must be free of all sensuality, lewdness and crudeness. They must maintain an evenness of mind through all things, whether pleasant or unpleasant. They must aim for a single outpouring of pure love, a love never straying, never deceptive. They must have contentment of heart, so that they can enjoy solitude, avoiding vain enjoyments and the noisy multitude.

SVB:8:6 The men must seek contentment and calmness within and outwardly display a steadfast and unruffled front. They must be courageous, generous, truthful, strong in character and healthy in body. They must cheerfully accept austerity and have the ability to endure privation, solitude and a rigorous life. They will have a distaste for aggression, for bullying, for the arrogant and haughty, for the cruel and for the boasters.

SVB:8:7 In men and women, there will be a constant yearning to awaken the soulspirit; there is to be an ideal to be upheld and a vision to follow. You may practise all things and follow any way of life consistent with the spiritual aims set out in the scriptures.

SVB:8:8 Hating another unjustifiably is wrong, but hatred itself is not necessarily wrong. There is no wrong in hating cruelty, wickedness, arrogance and many other things of evil. The measure of all things is to be how they effect the sole aim and purpose of life, the upward flight of man.

SVB:8:9 In seeking contentment and peace, beware that you do not fall into the pits of complacency, passiveness and inertia. Apathy also sets its trap, and when caught in any of these, you will be doomed to a spiritual death. The purpose of earthly life is to experience. Therefore, be wise enough to understand that though contentment and peace may be desirable, they are no more than that, they are not prime objectives.

SVB:8:10 There are two kinds of people in the world. There are those who must chase enjoyment and pleasure because there is no happiness within them; they are empty and have to suck happiness from people with whom they associate, or from their environment, or have to obtain it by external stimulation. Those are the spiritually deficient. Then there are those who are inwardly happy; they shed joy and contentment; wherever they go, they are a lamp of happiness giving out a bright glow which all may enjoy. Those can enjoy external things and find happiness outside themselves, but are not dependent on them. They are the spiritually healthy.

SVB:8:11 Some people are like the uncomprehending butterflies fluttering aimlessly from flower to flower of sensation and pleasure. Then, there are the spiritually strong who are like hawk-eyed birds flying directly towards their objective, riding high above lower creatures. Those are the two kinds of people, but the spiritually deficient cannot recognise themselves.

SVB:8:12 Always seek the beautiful in life, and add to it. Turn aside from all forms of vulgarity and crudeness, but it would be better to replace them with graciousness and loveliness. However, do not forget that all too often, a man seeking the beautiful becomes soft, and it is well established that beauty can ruin a man. Be a man of few words; this does not mean become dumb, but make your words have value; it means avoid idle chatter.

SVB:8:13 A man can be judged by the company he keeps, so make sure you are always in good company. Avoid all persons of bad repute, for they follow a path of destruction. Be vigorous and alive, never fearing hard work; no living man can ever fully renounce work or effort, so avoid being numbered among the dead.

SVB:8:14 Be a Master of Life; this is one who has his body and emotions firmly in rein. Though hard pressed by tribulations and afflictions, he remains steadfast; his mind is never confused. He knows what has to be done, what is expected of him, and does it. He strikes swiftly when action is needed, or just keeps plodding along the path. His mind is clear regarding his duty, and he knows his obligations and does not shirk them. He is always a pillar of strength to his weaker brethren.

SVB:8:15 Who are the Masters of Life? When you can ride the stormy seas of sorrow, when you are not overcome by pleasure, when you can control the passions, master fear, discard anger, and whatever comes, maintain a quiet and steady manner, you will be a Master of Life.

SVB:8:16 When you can accept all your obligations cheerfully, do your duty at all times, accept whatever comes, be it good or ill, with steadfast heart, remain calm in the midst of confusion and upheaval, you will be a Master of Life.

SVB:8:17 When you can temper all your desires with prudence, resist temptations to weakness and bring all urges under control; when you can bring all senses into harmony, control all emotion, overcome the greed for possessions, smother unwholesome desires, you will be a Master of Life. When you can subdue anger, dispel dismay, never forget where your duty lies and be completely free from confusion of mind, you will be a Master of Life.

SVB:8:18 As the worldly work selfishly and in bondage to worldliness, so does the Master of Life work unselfishly for the good of mankind. He is inspired by the highest ideals of man. He knows that hatred and cruelty, lust and desire for possessions have their roots in the lower natures of men, in the beast within them. These things the Masters learned long ago. Searching their hearts with wisdom, they found a stirring response to something greater and discovered the bond of union between man and the spirit. When the Master of Life knows his true nature and understands the unity of contact, he is freed from all delusion and sorrow; he rises to something greater above.

SVB:8:19 Self-control and harmony form the first step towards becoming a Master of Life. Harmony meaning tranquillity within and harmonious relationships without. Self-control means self-control in all things. Even an artist must exercise self-control when creating; the tradesman must control his sharp tools, and the physician his knife. Everything man does requires self-control in one form or another.

SVB:8:20 The Master of Life has to do more than this; he has to transform his whole life into a creative act, self-control and creativity going hand in hand. Only self-control of itself is not enough; it must be subordinated to goodwill and loving kindness.

SVB:8:21 The Master of Life must be conscious of his true nature. He must develop the threefold power: self-control, creativity and effort within himself, and reach out for the threefold unattainables beyond: love, perfection, and Truth.

SVB:8:22 You, my disciples, must become Masters of Life, never regretting the past nor worrying about the future, but always applying yourselves to whatever is in hand at present. The Masters of Life know what are good thoughts and what are bad thoughts, the first being beneficial, the second not. They know what to tell and what not to tell; they know what to do and what not to do; they know what serves and what does not, what is good and what is bad.

SVB:8:23 If a house is seen to be on fire, this immediately suggests the getting of water or saving whatever may be within. The commonplace man does not know how to act; he acts foolishly or in haste. The Master of Life does not get excited; he keeps his head. He does not stand aside wringing his hands, he does not rush about or get in the way, impeding others; he does not raise his voice, he does not offer futile sympathy. He remains calm and quietly and efficiently does what needs doing; he takes charge or places himself at the disposal of those who are better fitted to assume control.

SVB:8:24 The Master of Life is not bound by fetters the ignorant wear; neither is he misguided into ways of darkness by the blind. Every thought and act is considered, for he knows the power of oft-repeated thoughts, desires and actions to cut deep grooves into the soulspirit. He is no longer a prisoner of the flesh, but the charioteer of his body.

SVB:8:25 I call upon each of you to take up your burden and travel the long road leading to mastership of life. The progress of all Pilgrims who have taken this road is indicated by their conduct. The instability has been left behind; the excesses are gone; the demanding desires are dropped; the spitefulness, greed and conceit have been discarded; wickedness and malice are thrown aside. One by one they have been sloughed off, as a snake sheds its skin.

SVB:8:26 As Masters of Life, you will call upon others to follow you in the pilgrimage. They will have to be resolute and strong, willing to devote their whole lives to serving the cause of Truth. They will have to study diligently the pages of the scriptures and search ever deeper into the inmost recesses of their being. Their first step will be in overcoming the greatest of all man's delusions: that of thinking the body comprises the whole being.

SVB:8:27 As Masters of Life, you will set an example far beyond reach of the commonplace man. You will be known from others by a profound serenity and resolute steadfastness, just as the commonplace man is distinguished by ignorance, by restlessness, the urge to hide himself in pleasure and by enslavement to prejudice and emotion.

SVB:8:28 Poise and confidence, the marks of real wisdom and knowledge, distinguish the Masters of Life. Unsteadiness, shiftiness, unreliability, ever changing opinions and fluctuating loyalties distinguish the commonplace man. Undue consideration for the outer body and the satisfaction of its desires marks the commonplace man, and his concern for material things is the prime cause of his delusion. In a Master of Life, the mind has escaped from worldly delusions, like a bird freed from its cage, and in the liberated mind every doubt is stilled by certainty.

SVB:8:29 My disciples, heed what I say. Be steadfast in heart and mind, dogged in pursuing the pilgrimage, cheerfully accepting the trials and tribulations, which will beset you. Always seek the companionship of congenial and thoughtful fellow wayfarers. If you must pray, then remember the prayers of quiet silence.

SVB:8:30 Develop your soulspirit by contemplation of life, meditation of the scriptures and visualisation of the soulspirit's form of beauty and glory. The following are things you must strive against and overcome, so that they are completely banished from your nature, you have heard them before, but they cannot be repeated too often: all forms of anger, recklessness, cruelty and boastfulness; all tendencies towards falsehood, deceit and dishonesty, or towards lewdness, obscenity or lust; fornication, seduction and the degradation of women are forbidden; cheating, insincerity, gossiping, slander and talebearing are unworthy of you; such things as an unforgiving nature, moral weakness, cowardice, instability, irresolution, fickleness and intemperance are to be eliminated; undue love of comfort, of worldly or sensual pleasures and all forms of uncleanliness in mind and body must be overcome; stomach gratification is not wrong, but is not to be overdone.

SVB:8:31 Never indulge in argument or discussion as to the form and nature of The Supreme Spirit, for this is folly. An understanding of these is beyond the unawakened finite mind, though the mind of a Master may grasp what they are; therefore, defer all argument and discussion until you are one.

SVB:8:32 There is much talk among you concerning the nature of worship. Understand this: true worship is seeking to unite the spirit below with the Spirit Above. To do this you must have a heart purged of all evil thoughts, a tongue undefiled by falsehood or tainted with deceit and hypocrisy, and a life free of all malice and hatred. Even this is not enough; you must have a life filled with love and good deeds. Only when in this state are you fit to worship. When you talk about the worthlessness of worship, are you condemning yourselves? Purifying worship of which you speak means all acts, which tend to burn up carnality and worldliness within the body.

SVB:8:33 As true disciples, you must spend your whole conscious life in purposeful and constructive thinking. You must be doers, not dreamers. When you withdraw into the silence to worship, remember the great jewels of prayer:

serenity, purity and trust. The prophets who have gone before held that a kindly and pure heart is the only worship required to benefit man; this may be so, but surely tranquillity and trust are also needed.

SVB:8:34 You will learn that the true greatness and goodness of Pilgrims travelling the road with you are often hidden from the eyes of men, because of their unusual way of life. Commonplace men will often think them deluded or men who have lost their reason. How many of you have not hesitated because you feared the opinions of others, the entreaties of loved ones or the thoughts of possible suffering and discomfort?

SVB:8:35 I have spoken of discomfort; this I say again; too much comfort is not for you, neither should you sleep too much or too little. You must overcome all tendencies towards sloth and carelessness, for these will sap your spiritual stamina.

SVB:8:36 Do not be impatient for advancement; slow progress is often the best. If someone breaks a hatching egg before its time, no chick will emerge. When the time is ripe, the shell will be broken from within and a healthy chick will emerge to life. If the shell is broken before the chick is ready, that chick will be dead. So it is with the awakening soulspirit, let it emerge from within, of its own accord. Until you have purged your hearts of all impurities and washed away all the worldly filth, you cannot even set foot on the lower rung of the ladder leading to enlightenment and awakening.

SVB:8:37 When you speak of the mating of spirit and mortal, you are wrong. Under no circumstances can spirit mate with mortal, though it is certainly true that spirit can enter mortal. It is well to know what spirit can do and what it cannot do, for it has its limitations.

SVB:8:38 Should any man come, directly seeking Truth and knowledge of the True Way, let him first seek someone to introduce him into the body of the select who wait. Then in the course of time, as he is observed and his manner of talk and bearing is noted, so will one come to him and call him before the primary selector. Life is such that though it is easy enough to become an intimate of a moderately good or bad man, it is difficult indeed to meet a really good one.

SVB:8:39 You will choose candidates for discipleship who may become Masters of Life; no commonplace man may be accepted. They must be calm and wise, recognising what is real, desirable, important and true, and what is false, illusive, trivial and unworthy of attention. They must be ones who have overcome and are aware of true values, who have no inclinations towards anything not actively assisting them in the search. They must not be weak of character, neither must they be seeking a refuge. Three things must be brought together in combination: the sacred scriptures, the wise instructor and the eager and diligent pupil. The sacred scriptures are not to be swallowed as one does a medicinal compound, they are to be assimilated slowly and digested with reason and experience.

SVB:8:40 True enlightenment and the road to Truth are found only by way of intelligence rooted in truthfulness and reason. Some have said it is difficult to be both intelligent and absolutely sincere after examining true motives, but this shall not apply to the chosen candidates.

SVB:8:41 Never forget; it is the meaning, not the mere form of words in the sacred scriptures, which is of value. A silken mantle may look better than a coarse, woollen one, but which serves best in providing warmth? Also keeping mind that the scriptures are guides; they cannot undertake the hard work, nor assume the burden; these are things for the candidates alone. The purpose of the sacred scriptures is also to show men what life should be, how they should be governed, how they should conduct themselves, what they should keep and what they should discard.

Chapter Nine – Elidor on the Sacred Scriptures

SVB:9:1 These are the sacred scriptures which are not like other scriptures, they are the scriptures of those who follow the Great Path of the True Way. They are not for the mocker, the unbeliever, the man of worldly affairs or the evildoer. They shall move forward with the ages, keeping abreast of man as he advances. They must evolve to keep pace with his growing intelligence, but he must also evolve spiritually. If he does not, then they must assume the burden and come forth to lead him.

SVB:9:2 There are men satiated with worldly learning, who have fallen into the pit dug by their own books. They are gorged and uncomfortable; their diversity of opinions and thought confuses them. The study of the sacred scriptures is not for the curious; it is useless unless the student knows where he is heading, his destination, unless he has an end in view. Though the truth within the sacred scriptures is unalterable, can never change, the revelation can always be interpreted according to man's progress. The hidden truths are to be made available to man whenever he is ready. The spiritual man who is truly awakened sees much more in the words than the commonplace man, who may see no more than the letters and words. Yet words are a forest, in which man can easily lose his way. Fine sentences and a grand manner of expression may just be a lure and a covering for the pit and stake.

SVB:9:3 There are those who talk about spiritual things, but do no more than weave a web of words to trap the unwary. To derive benefit from a bottle of physic, the contents must be taken, merely reading the inscriptions will effect no cure.

SVB:9:4 My disciples, read the sacred scriptures diligently, and never abandon your work and studies, for to do so when you are struggling to cross the stream of life shows lack of resolution, and it achieves nothing. You will sacrifice your own self-assurance; your inspiration will be lost. Never forget, these words are not fair weather friends; they are not things of feathers to blow away before a slight wind. They are stones in a solid causeway, firm and reliable under all conditions. Take these sacred scriptures as your daily guide, make them your advisor whenever a problem arises. Unless they are put into practice, they remain valueless, just things to be thought about in idle moments.

SVB:9:5 Pure reason, like bitter essence, is worthless alone. Even as the essence must be made palatable and drinkable by the addition of water, so must pure reason be diluted by faith.

SVB:9:6 The sacred scriptures are the midwife and nurse of the soulspirit. Some awaken the soulspirit by meditation; sometimes it is awakened through a vision; in some it awakens through good works, in others through labour. It can be awakened by creativity and love, there are many means to suit the numerous conditions of men. A few may not feel the stirrings of an awakening soulspirit; some may rely only on the words of others, but because they believe and act accordingly these, too, shall awaken to conscious survival.

SVB:9:7 So wonderful is the state of a newly awakened soulspirit, so delightful the experience of sudden realisation, that none who has known it will ever forget. None will ever find words adequate to describe it to others. There is no thought except a deep awareness of life, of being. There is a sense of deeper reality than that of ordinary consciousness. Faith in the reality of the soulspirit then gives way to certainty and assurance, for how can any man doubt the greatest experience of his life?

SVB:9:8 The glory of the stars shining in the nightskies is truly revealed once in the darkness. It is as children that men begin to sense the mystery of silence, the mystery, which reveals the universe. Silence is the secret of the soulspirit.

SVB:9:9 There are dark doctrines, which tell of soulspirits condemned to everlasting darkness and torment, but this is not so. They are not condemned to suffer forever, for after a long interval, they are taken out and recast. They are like misshapen casts of metal which are thrown back into the furnace to mingle and blend together, coming out purified and pliable, ready to be cast into new form. They come back to Earth completely unconscious of the past; it is lost to them in the purifying fires of the furnace, and so they start again. As a lump of salt dissolved in water, which can never regain its former shape, so are they.

Book of
Lucius

LUC:1:6 Nothing, except The Supreme Spirit, can have a real, self-contained and independent existence. This does not mean that nothing else is real, and by 'illusion' is meant deception by the senses, which interpret falsely. Man is deluded by his senses and so cannot distinguish the real from the unreal.

Table of Chapters

Book of Lucius

Chapter One – The Spheres of Existence

LUC:1:1 This is the whole law needful for man to direct his life: Know your nature, do your duty and live in harmony with others. To live in harmony means doing wrong to no man.

LUC:1:2 There is one Supreme Spirit, which men call God, because God means Allgood. But because men seek a closer relationship with The Supreme Spirit of Good, they refer to it as Father and as Him, and there is no wrong in this.

LUC:1:3 The Supreme Spirit contains the essences of all the perfections, and these flow out from Him in a form of vitality, which is called The Holy Spirit. The Sphere of The Holy Spirit surrounds the Sphere of The Supreme Spirit, and around this again, and below it, is the Sphere of Matter and Mortality.

LUC:1:4 In the sphere of Matter and Mortality, the Holy Spirit manifests imperfectly, for here it becomes mingled with the inert composition of this Sphere. Also, the penetrated offers resistance to the penetrator, and this, combined with the effects of intermingling, causes obscurity, illusion and ignorance. These are visualised in the form of a mist called 'agnosia.'

LUC:1:5 The activity of The Supreme Spirit in the Highest Sphere is unceasing, and this alone maintains the Universes of Matter. The basis of matter is an outflow of energy from The Supreme Spirit, which forms a kind of framework solidifying at its outer edge. The three Spheres comprise the whole, no part of which is devoid of the vitality originating within The Supreme Spirit. So the statement that The Supreme Spirit is in all and all is in The Supreme Spirit is true, though He does not manifest in the Sphere of obscurity, illusion and imperfection. This does not mean that The Supreme Spirit could not manifest here, or that the Sphere of Matter and Mortality is beyond His reach. These conditions serve a specific purpose.

LUC:1:6 Nothing, except The Supreme Spirit, can have a real, self-contained and independent existence. This does not mean that nothing else is real, and by 'illusion' is meant deception by the senses, which interpret falsely. Man is deluded by his senses and so cannot distinguish the real from the unreal.

LUC:1:7 All the Universes of Matter are contained within the Sphere of Matter and Mortality, which reaches out to touch the Sphere of the Holy Spirit.

LUC:1:8 Their greatness exceeds the bounds of man's most daring imagination, and even if man could penetrate through to their limits, he would still find The Supreme Spirit veiled and hidden.

LUC:1:9 The Holy Spirit flows from The Supreme Spirit, as heat and light flow from the sun, and, penetrating all things, holds them in form and solidity. The Supreme Spirit alone is unpenetrated by anything, He alone is whole and fully self-sufficient. He alone is the One Pure Essence.

LUC:1:10 The Sphere of The Holy Spirit is divided into Subspheres, and the Sphere of Matter and Mortality is likewise divided. The Supreme Ruler of the Sphere of The Holy Spirit is The Holy Spirit, and The Supreme Ruler of the Sphere of Matter and Mortality is Nature. So all the material universes are governed by one set of laws called The Law of Nature. Nature is the effect and manifestation of the activity of The Holy Spirit operating in matter, where reality is relative and not absolute.

LUC:1:11 The earthly body of man, his moral shell and spirit container, is moulded before birth by following a soul pattern drawn by destiny. Once born, many forces influence the life of man on Earth, but he is also given the responsibility of free choice. Notwithstanding this, the life of any man can only follow a course set by destiny, but while on that course, he can do as he wills.

LUC:1:12 Every single thought and act on Earth has its effect on the soulspirit projected into the Sphere of Matter and Mortality. Man himself is a threefold being comprising soul, spirit and matter, each having an affinity with one of the Spheres of Existence. Here on Earth the soulspirit is made ready for its life in the Higher Spheres, or it is neglected and ignored.

LUC:1:13 This is the outline of Truth, within which our master taught, and Pemantris, his devoted disciple, has recorded what follows. He taught to seven only, in a small hermitage beside the forest brook.

Chapter Two – Vision of the Holy Spirit and Creation

LUC:2:1 My friends, the power of The Holy Spirit has led you here and directed your footsteps, so that you may be well guided in ascending the heights of divinity. No others shall be admitted to our circle, for so profound a subject as that dealt with here would be profaned by the presence of many.

LUC:2:2 To understand The Supreme Spirit is difficult, but enlightenment may be granted to those who diligently follow the Great Path towards spiritual development. To describe Him to others is impossible, for no man possesses the eloquence, and no tongue has adequate words. Then, too, it is difficult for the imperfect to grasp the meaning of perfection, or for the visible to comprehend the invisible beyond its range of vision. The Eternal is so distant from the Sphere of Mortal Man that the beauty there can only be glimpsed as a dim reflection. This is well, for if unshielded from the beauty beyond vision, mortal man would be consumed in its brilliance.

LUC:2:3 Without His creation, The Supreme Spirit would be uncontrasted and therefore not really supreme, so He created. No man has ever seen Him and lived, though many have been granted a sight of His reflection. So if any man says to you, "I have seen The Supreme Spirit and now understand His nature," be sure he has not seen Him, but only some distorted reflection. The Truth is that The Supreme Spirit is not understandable to us mortals. He is far beyond mortal conception, and hence, many say He is non-existent.

LUC:2:4 The Supreme Spirit is outside and beyond His creation, but His radiance is the basis of all things together. He is the Central Flame, and the souls of men are rushlights lit at the flame but enclosed behind thick horn, so that they scarcely shine. The task is to pare down the horn, so that the light within shines brightly.

LUC:2:5 Being without material restrictions, The Supreme Spirit is bodiless, and such a state is hard for the bodilocked man to conceive. But man does not contact Him through the body but only through the soulspirit, and certain places and conditions are designed to help man make contact.

LUC:2:6 Men may call The Supreme Spirit by any other name, which conveys a meaning of divine greatness. Provided the name is hallowed and held in reverence, there is no need to go into definitions, for this is an unworthy pursuit. Not any name or all names could adequately describe what is beyond description. The only way, in which man can come to fully know the nature of The Supreme Spirit is through The Holy Spirit, through whose

Sphere passes the Godward Road. This is all I need say about The Great Name.

LUC:2:7 When I was young, I thought much about life here and above, and in times of sublime contemplation, my inner being appeared to penetrate into the very heart of things. Once, I became aware of a presence like that of some infinitely Good and Great Being who spoke to me, asking what I wished to learn and know. I answered, "I wish to learn the nature of things and my own relationships with them. I wish to know the purpose of life and why I was born." The Great Being seemed to speak again with a voice resounding in my whole being, "I know what you seek and what drives you to search. I carry the power of knowing all, and my vitality is a spring whose waters are available for the refreshment of every questing soulspirit. I am the manifestation of The Holy Spirit."

LUC:2:8 When the voice had finished speaking, a brilliant light seemed to glow all about me, and vast, radiant corridors appeared to open up in every direction. I became filled with an overwhelming feeling of love, and all about me shimmered soft lights, from out of which proceeded the most melodious sounds. Then, from one side came a dark and gloomy cloud, and I was filled with foreboding as it writhed and twisted like a heavy smoke. From out of it came the sound of wailing, and there was a low-murmuring moaning long-drawn-out.

LUC:2:9 Then I heard an exquisite sound, which rose and fell like the notes of a divine melody, and between the brightness and the dark cloud, a wall seemed to condense. It appeared to be of iridescent glass containing a living flame, not set in form, but with a flexible movement. From the wall came a kind of softly glowing vapour, which then rose above it.

LUC:2:10 I heard the voice again and it said, "Have you seen and understood?" I said, "I have seen, but understanding has not been granted." Then The Holy Spirit said, "I am the light and the light is mind. The darkness and the cloud are agnosia, which seeks to increase its sphere by the agency of man. But the wall prevents it, and the wall is the mind of the Spirit. It is the barrier, which agnosia cannot penetrate. The mind of man is a ray from The Holy Spirit pinpointed upon the spirit enclosed within a mortal body. Mortal existence is an echo, through the corridors of time, of the word spoken in the Chamber of Eternity. The Sphere of The Holy Spirit is where mind manifests freely, unhampered by mortal limitations."

LUC:2:11 I looked again, and the cloud and wall were gone, and then I saw the brilliance was divided by lights of many shades. Where the cloud had been, I saw a dullness amid brilliance, and then I seemed to be standing before it. I looked into the dullness as though down a corridor, and along its length, the darkness increased, so that at the end there was a deep-shaded gloom. In the dismal shadow I saw ugly, mis-shapen things moving sluggishly, as though the life within them was weak. They were creatures such as haunt the most horrid nightmare, and my eyes could not bear to rest upon them. I turned away, and the voice said, "In the place where garbage is disposed, life assumes unpleasant forms, and this is the spirit garbage of Earth."

LUC:2:12 Then I was drawn back into the light, and all about me was a joyousness and gaiety, which seemed to have no perceivable source, but to be a quality of the atmosphere.

LUC:2:13 As I stood joyfully, bewildered in the radiance, I saw beautiful shapes, which appeared to come and go like fishes swimming in and out of the water shadows. I sensed rather than heard laughter and the sounds of happiness, and my whole being seemed to be filled with joyful communications.

LUC:2:14 Again, I heard the voice and it said, "This is the beauty and glory so feebly glimpsed in earthly existence; this is the diadem of life. When mind first penetrated mind-created matter, it brought light and life into being in greater and lesser degrees of manifestation. While the heavier mortal elements of matter tended downwards, those, in which light and life manifested the most, tended upwards, towards eventual spiritualisation. When spiritualised, they were drawn, by natural affinity, into the Sphere of Beauty and Glory. Affinity directs the course of all things and governs the destinies of men. The thought that flows out through The

Holy Spirit bears designs for structures of beauty to the boundary of the Sphere of Matter and Mortality, but the deeper it penetrates, the more these are distorted and dispersed. So it is that things unbeautiful and unsightly are produced in the depths of matter under the rulership of Nature. In the reasonless density of the lower subspheres of matter, the influence of creative mind is less manifest. Elsewhere in the same sphere can be seen the effects of evil mind energy, which floats up like fumes from the disposal pit of spiritual garbage."

LUC:2:15 Then I said, "But what caused all this to come into being," and the voice of The Holy Spirit answered, "All things began with the intoning of the first creative sound. This rushed outward like a great wind-borne roar, and creation marked its passage. Then, like a great tidal wave falling back towards the sea, it drew back on itself, leaving the least of its substance at the farthest point of penetration. The waters of creation are deepest in the Sphere of The Holy Spirit and shallower at the spiritual edge of the Sphere of Matter and Mortality. Outward from there, they lessen to nothing."

LUC:2:16 "Now", said I, "understanding is mine, but what of man; what of myself? How was man created?" The voice of the Good and Great Being which I knew to be a personalised manifestation of The Holy Spirit, answered me.

Chapter Three – The Making of Man

LUC:3:1 "The image and nature of The Supreme Spirit reside in the soulseed of man, just as the image and nature of an oak tree reside in an acorn. The pattern for the mortal body of man was formed in the Sphere of The Holy Spirit and projected to the Sphere of Matter and Mortality where Nature built upon it. When the time was ripe, the body prepared by Nature was implanted with the soulseed of divinity, and the creature of Earth became a man. From that day, man, unlike all other living things on Earth, became a twofold being in his own right, mortal in body but immortal in soulspirit. He is immortal only because he has been made the heir of divinity, and as such, all things are within his grasp. He is mortal because he lives within a mortal shell and is subject to a destiny in mortality."

LUC:3:2 I said to the Being who seemed so near, "Whatever man was when given divine life, it is said that he suffered a downfall or disinheritance." I heard the voice say in reply, "Man will not be disinherited, but he can make what he will of his birthright. The downfall of man was a fall from the sunlit heights of spirituality into the dark valley of agnosia. It was also a fall from a position of responsibility and trust, and man has yet to regain that position."

LUC:3:3 "Man fell because he declined to undergo the necessary preparation and discipline needed by one who aspires to climb the heights. Also, he possessed the powers of creation, and being free could express them as he pleased. Man used them to satisfy his lower desires and so brought about his own downfall. Since then, he has no longer enjoyed them to the full. Given freewill and the ability, it was intended that man should direct his own evolution, but he proved unequal to the task."

LUC:3:4 "Man was intended to be the redeemer of reasonless matter and the controller of Nature; for that reason, he was first called Lord of Creation. But it was Nature herself, who dominated the will of man and tempted him to betray his trust. She lured him into entanglement with the senses, so that instead of being free, he became the slave of desire. The sweetness of the bait disguised the poison it contained, and the spirit of man was dragged into forgetfulness and mindlessness."

LUC:3:5 "Instead of being the master of a noble steed galloping along the road to immortality, man was now a blind creature bound upon a runaway horse. Notwithstanding this, he found the sensation enjoyable, believing that in being freed from the responsibility of control, he had found true freedom. Man made little effort to assume control, for this meant struggle, effort and responsibility, and so he remained in the state of spiritual inertia called the Mire of Matter. The soulspirit had entered the body, only to be caught in the toils of the flesh. Man was heading in the wrong direction, and the way was all uphill."

LUC:3:6 "So now you see," the voice continued, "that man was made a twofold being. Within, though this is a misleading description, is the soulspirit, but to all outward appearances, man is a mortal shell subject to decay. Though born to a heritage of divinity, man himself has freely chosen to suffer as the slave of his desires and the vassal of his weakness. He has bartered his spiritual birthright for a handful of fragile material baubles. Man, becoming enamoured of the glitter from the first bauble offered, has lost his sense of values and has closed his eyes to things of real value. He has drunk the material waters of spiritual oblivion and now lies asleep beside the stagnant pool. He slumbers, awaiting the Day of The Awakener."

LUC:3:7 There were things I understood and things I could not understand, and I said to the Good and Great Being, "If The Supreme Spirit is indeed the essence of love and kindness, could He not have created man in conditions, which gave him complete contentment and happiness, absolutely free from pain, sorrow and restraint? Is all this suffering and distress really necessary?" The reply came as though radiating from a Being full of compassion and understanding, "He could have created a perfect being and placed him in a condition of absolute contentment and happiness, but what purpose would this serve? Could such a being respond to love? Where could he learn its full meaning except in a state of lovelessness? Such things as love, pity, gratitude, mercy, unselfishness and all the other virtues are uncreatable qualities which can come into existence only through experience. Nothing can realise itself through a state of purity and perfection. Only by contrast can it become conscious of its existence."

LUC:3:8 "Pain checks man in the midst of senseless enjoyment and makes him ponder his fate. It causes him to turn his thoughts towards greater things and to reflect on the approach of death. Suffering, sorrow and trouble are tests, which, if passed successfully, qualify the soulspirit for entry into the greater sphere of existence. They create in him the qualities, which are needed there. To those who realise that these tests and trials have a purpose, they do not appear too harsh. But to those who cannot rise above them or who blame The Supreme Spirit or their fellowmen for what befalls them, the tests and trials appear as unnecessary hardships barely endurable."

LUC:3:9 "Regarding restraint, ask yourself what it teaches and what qualities it creates, and then you will know whether it is necessary. Does not restraint also lead to greater enjoyment and appreciation? No man can say that the ordinances of The Law really detract from the joys of life. Neither can it be said they are obstacles to the gratification of normal desires and the natural craving for pleasure. Read and examine them carefully; to what normal desire do they deny gratification? What natural impulse do they attempt to destroy? What reasonable pleasure do they prohibit, and what beneficial outlet do they seek to suppress?"

LUC:3:10 "On the contrary, the ordinances of The Law seek only to elevate and purify the lower impulses and bodily desires by controlling them with wise limitations, seeking only to subordinate them when it serves a greater good. Mortal cravings are made subject to higher aims, while lust and carnal passions are transmuted into useful material for constructing the glorious palace of love."

LUC:3:11 "The ordinances of The Law are a means of guiding the evolving man towards beneficial and necessary ends. They unyieldingly oppose the bestial urges and the craving for harmful pleasures. They oppose the tendency towards mortal inertia, which expresses itself in apathy and indifference, in the search for comfort and ease. There are things, which, though harmful, they do not absolutely forbid and seek instead to utilise towards a good end."

LUC:3:12 I said, "This I understand; if the world was created to serve man, then its fate depends upon his conduct."

Chapter Four – Man - Bond and Free

LUC:4:1 These things were revealed to me in the days of my youth, while I was still pure-minded and unsullied by the world. For I, like primal man, was tempted and fell, but though my descent took no more than a few days, the way back took twice as many years. Yet the things I learned when elevated in spirit to the Sphere above have always remained clear in my mind. If then you ask, why did I who had been granted this vision fall from grace, let me say that the pitfall was well and artfully covered. It was not baited by things that usually tempt, but by imitations and representations of things which usually inspire the best in men. Man is a crafty fish not easily caught, and the hook must be carefully concealed and the bait well chosen.

LUC:4:2 My friends, it would serve no purpose for me to tell the tale of my own fall, for never are two birds brought down by the same arrow. It serves better to tell what I learned in the Sphere of The Holy Spirit, and this is what I discovered about man fallen into bondage, or into slumber.

LUC:4:3 "The Supreme Spirit communicated with man through The Holy Spirit, and the message was that he should multiply and cover the Earth. Man was told to never forget that he was the custodian of his race and the designer of his earthly dominion. He was also told that submission to carnal desires meant spiritual death and that love is a lady worthy of the greatest respect, and not a menial serving maid attending to the demands of a master. Those were the things man was told, but he gave heed only to the first."

LUC:4:4 "The man who has recognised his true nature has already stepped into the domain of spirituality. The man who has craved only for things pleasing to the mortal body and been led astray by carnal urges is lost and wanders aimlessly in the darkness of moral wastes. His doom is to be devoured by damnation, the predator of these wastes."

LUC:4:5 The stern manner of speech appalled me and I asked, "Why must the ignorant suffer dire consequences, and why is man not more fully warned?" The voice of The Holy Spirit answered me, "The ignorant do not suffer because they are ignorant, for that is the state, into which they were born. They suffer because they are content to remain in that state and have chosen to take the easy road of effortlessness. The consequences of ignorance alone are not so dire; it is wickedness, chosen either deliberately or unthinkingly, that damns a man. What he suffers is not a punishment but the natural consequence of his actions. If a man places his hand upon a hot iron and is burnt, the pain is not a punishment but the consequence of his actions. If a man cuts himself, he must expect to bleed, and if he walks through mud, he cannot expect to remain unsoiled.

LUC:4:6 "Those who seek refuge in the darkness do so not because they are condemned to suffer in this manner, but because it is the only place in which such as they can live. The worm does not seek the sunlight, or the leech find refuge in anything except slime. All things are drawn into conditions, with which they have an affinity; that is a law of Nature, as well as a Greater Law. Man is sufficiently warned, for the light has never been denied those who seek it earnestly, and everything about him proclaims the law of affinity."

LUC:4:7 I understood the words of The Holy Spirit, and I was told other things which I may tell you, but you must not record them in writing. One instruction I was given, I now hand on to you. "This is the choice: Too much regard for the mortal body and craven submission to its demands and desires, a craving for sensual pleasure and surrender to the lures of ease and luxury, enslave man in the Sphere of Matter and Mortality. He is held captive, exiled by his own choice from his true homeland. Such men are the slaves of mortality. Or man can free his own true self waiting to greet him. The humiliating fetters of mortal bondage are then exchanged for the dignity of divine vestments. Man has the choice; he can be bond or free."

LUC:4:8 "Bondage means abject submission to something more powerful than yourself, while freedom entails the acceptance of responsibility and the expenditure of unenforced effort. The choice is before every man. Each has perfect freedom of choice and may accept the challenge of his nature or decline to do so. But upon his choice will follow happiness or misery, survival or destruction. As you have read, man is capable of righteousness and is called upon to be righteous."

LUC:4:9 I thought of these things and saw the working of a natural law where each cause was followed by its own effect and consequence. I thought, too, of these things written in the Good Books, and said, "I have read, 'let the man who has a soulspirit awaken it;' have not all men soul and spirit?" The voice of the Holy Spirit said, "All men are souls within a spirit, for the spirit and soul are not one and the same. To the souls who earnestly struggle towards spiritual unfolding, The Holy Spirit comes to reinforce the powers of the spirit. The presence of The Holy Spirit supports them and, because of this, is called The Comforter, though more often, this is used to describe an earthly comforter."

LUC:4:10 "Even before the soulspirit departs from its earthly habitation, The Holy Spirit is there to comfort, for it is the Guardian at the Gates. But The Holy Spirit does not come near to the servants of evil and the wicked ones, for it has no affinity with them. Those who spent their earthly lives in bondage to the senses and bowed to mortal allurements, those who accepted their state with servility and paid homage to ease and luxury, have no affinity with the light in the Sphere of The Holy Spirit."

LUC:4:11 I spoke to the Good and Great Being who personalised The Holy Spirit, and said, "Tell me the manner in which I shall enter the Sphere of The Holy Spirit." The answer came, not in a voice that beat against the ears but as a melodious note struck on the chords of responsive understanding within. "When the mortal material body is abandoned to dissolution at death, the form you once had no longer exists. The vital breath goes out in one gasp and devitalised, returns to mingle with the air. All mortal things return to their own sphere. What passes over and enters the Sphere of The Holy Spirit is the soulspirit with all its energies and containing an intangible design of etheric framework, upon which the new being will be moulded. Just as the acorn contains the design of the oak and the seed of man the design for his body, so does the soulspirit contain within itself the design for its own unfolding."

LUC:4:12 "Entering the Higher Sphere, all mortal remnants will be discarded, and, looking upward, the soulspirit, freed into eternity, will see the glory above. All the spiritual powers will be gathered about it and may be possessed. The song of the Newcomer will greet the newly arrived soulspirit, 'Welcome into our company, for we are your compatible companions and all one with you.'"

LUC:4:13 I spoke again to The Holy Spirit and said, "It seems there are many degrees in the Higher Sphere, where beings are separated into groups; how then can loved ones be found? Are all groups cut off from each other?" The Holy Spirit replied, "The divisions may resemble groups, but they are not parted by tangible or impassable barriers, for the thing keeping them apart is the law of affinity. The same law operates on the Lower Sphere, where some forms of material expression are so unlike others that one may be completely unknown and unmanifested to another. The grouping is no more rigid on the Higher Sphere than on Earth. The law of affinity draws compatible soulspirits together, just as creatures on Earth seek compatible surrounding and the company of their own kind. In both spheres, there is affinity and antipathy; understand the laws governing these, and you understand the nature of the divisions in the Higher Sphere."

LUC:4:14 I thought awhile and said, "I understand, there are creatures of the light and creatures of the darkness on Earth, and they are kept apart by their different affinities. A gentle lady is revolted by filth and sordidness because she has an antipathy towards them, while the besotten drunkard or unclean bawd is not repelled."

LUC:4:15 The voice of The Holy Spirit was still with me, and I heard it say, "This, then, is the end of the first stage, and here the tired wayfarer may rest and refresh himself. The first flight towards divinity has been accomplished. This is the end of material mortality, and the mists of agnosia swirl far below. Now, the conscious soulspirit can rejoice in the sunlight above."

LUC:4:16 There, in the Sphere of The Holy Spirit, surrounded by a form of glory, which words cannot describe, and immersed in beauty as a swimmer is immersed in water, I was lost in rapture. I could think of no more to say, and having gazed on the face of reality, I would never more be a victim of doubt. The joyousness I knew can be known only through experience, to tell of it is as futile as describing colours to a man born blind, who cannot know one from the other by mentioning their names. Having glimpsed this glory and knowing what is planned for each and every soulspirit, I was filled with zeal and overcome with the desire to awaken my brothers who lay wrapped in the sleep of indifference. I wished to stir them out of their lethargy and make them aware of the effort needed to attain glory. But in my enthusiasm, I rushed forward too hastily and instead of achieving my objective fell into the pit, which always awaits the hasty and unwary. Perhaps it is well, for in my callow youth, I lacked the experience and knowledge of the ways of men, to have been a proper teacher.

LUC:4:17 Having told me these things and granted me the vision of glory, The Holy Spirit withdrew, and I sensed, rather than saw, the departure of the Good and Great Being. Gradually, I descended from the Higher Sphere and awoke on Earth with an abounding feeling of wellbeing. The sleep of the body had freed the soulspirit, and the closing of earthly eyes had marked the opening of spiritual ones. From that day onward, I was a new being.

Chapter Five – The Wandering Mission

LUC:5:1 I fell and struggled upward. My feet hardened on the stony road of experience. I drank heavily of the bitter waters of regret, and the purging fruit of remorse was gall in my mouth. Then, when I had purged and purified myself and once more become a proper receptacle for the light, illumination was granted me. I was in communication with The Holy Spirit, and since that day, grace has never gone from me.

LUC:5:2 Having been filled with power and inspiration I was sent out to teach the doctrine of the Supreme Vision. I proclaimed The Supreme Spirit to men and tried to direct their steps into the paths of beauty and Truth. I was received with mockery and taunts, and many were the blows directed my way. I did not seek alms or beg, and wherever I went earned my bread by working as a cobbler.

LUC:5:3 My friends, this is how I spoke to any who would listen: "Awaken, you sleepers who have abandoned life for slumber, who have scorned the effort of living. You have given yourselves over to the wineshop of mortality and quaffed too deeply of the wines of sensuality and lust. Now you lie in a drunken sleep, ignorant of your spiritual existence and nature. You have sipped long from the cup of ignorance and drunk deeply from the flagons of thoughtlessness. Awake, open your eyes to a sober awareness of the beauty and love about you. Wake up, and look into the light of soulspirit recognition. It hurts your, eyes but that is because they are accustomed to darkness."

LUC:5:4 My friends, I led a life of frustration, for I was like a child who finds a loved parent, too heavy to move, lying drunk in a burning house. I tried to awaken people from their stupor and to draw them out of the darkness of ignorance, but they were bewitched by spells of vain ritual and held captive by irrational but beguiling teachings.

LUC:5:5 When I said, "The Law is that man must struggle and strive, or starve and perish, and this applies not only to the mortal body of man, but equally to his soulspirit", their answering voices came to me from the darkness of ignorance and from the depths of matter, into which they has sunk. I heard them from the thick mists of agnosia and they all said, "We have our saviours and those who plead for us; we make acceptable offerings and pay due homage. Our priests stand between us and destruction, and we are content to leave our spiritual wellbeing in their hands. Leave us in peace, for your voice disturbs us, and with our hands full of mortal affairs we have no time to give for the contemplation of these things."

LUC:5:6 My friends, my heart was sore within me, for I was a lone voice crying against the tempest. I said, "Open your hearts just a little, and raise your spiritual gaze above the sordid drabness, which surrounds your daily existence, Do not ignore the hopeful, helping hand I extend to you, for this ignorance which serves as the servant of evil, floods the whole Earth. Its currents sweep along all the aimless, drifting soulspirits shut up within unguided bodies, which are carried away, to be sunk and lost in the depths."

LUC:5:7 My voice appeared to call in vain, and my heart sank in despair, for with each failure and setback, my confidence drained away. Still I was not left abandoned, for The Comforter came to me in my darkest hours, and I was not left friendless. Refreshed by a surge of spiritual vitality, I continued my pleas, "Men of Isolia, do not let yourselves be carried off by the strong currents of carnal desires. Do not ride the rafts of wickedness, which must go with the wind and waves without direction. Row back against the tide of apathy and indifference; bend your backs, and pull with vigour. Seek the harbour where your soulspirit can step ashore in its homeland. Why have you abandoned yourselves to drifting aimlessly on the sea of mortality, where, unless you awake from the stupor of apathy, you will be destroyed upon the dark lee shore. Awake, awake, pull for the harbour to windward."

LUC:5:8 My body was seized and confined in a dungeon deep, and cruel keepers tormented me. I longed for the fresh air of the free highways, and when at last I was freed, I hastened to another place. Again, I raised my voice to any who would stand and listen and said, "Why do you share your homes with error and make ignorance your guest? Why do you welcome the misguiders and turn away those who bear the gifts of Truth?" Come out of your comfortable cottages, where you sit quaffing the sleep-inducing draughts of agnosia. Get out into the fresh, bracing air of fully conscious life. Be a whole being, wholly awake, instead of a half being half asleep. Come, lay your hand to the plow, and till the fields of immortality. Turn under the weeds of your past mistakes as green manure, and trim your share to turn them deep."

LUC:5:9 "Come out from the stiflingly sleep-inducing air contaminated with fumes from the fire of complacency. Come out into the reviving cold, and fill your lungs with the bracing air of reality. Arise from the comfortable drowsiness of apathy, and step out into the stimulating winds of challenge and care."

LUC:5:10 Again few heeded my message and most went away mocking, calling after me, "Where is your temple? Seek no offerings from us." Still, here and there, a few remained, and I gave them the knowledge of The True Way, of how and by what means they could tread the road to divinity. In them I could sow the seeds, which, in order to grow had to be harrowed in by worldly effort and watered by rain from the Sphere above. For these few, I was duly grateful, and in them comforted by the thought that I had not laboured to dig a well in vain.

LUC:5:11 My friends, I did not wait to see the harvest grow where I had planted, for fresh fields always lay ahead, I spoke as I walked, and I taught as I laboured at my task. I protected the feet of men stoutly with good workmanship, and the spiritual wares I vended freely were no less serviceable.

Chapter Six – The Forest Mission - 1

LUC:6:1 The tests each man must endure have an affinity with him and with no other, so no two persons are tested alike. I who have shod the feet of others, making walking more comfortable, was fated to suffer the trials of a cripple; and the day came when I no longer enjoyed freedom of movement. It was then I came to this place, and my stay here has been blessed in many ways.

LUC:6:2 My friends, I will tell you now about The Supreme Spirit and His properties, and although The Supreme Spirit is neither male nor female, by convention men say 'Him,' and I will do likewise. Just as the eye cannot see The Supreme Spirit, or the finite mind understand Him, so can they neither see nor understand the perfect, the beautiful and the good. These are properties having their source in The Supreme Spirit, and they are things with which He is in love and therefore responds to. They are the things having an affinity with the soul.

LUC:6:3 So if a man strives after perfection, beauty and goodness, even though he lacks knowledge of the soulspirit, he will attain such knowledge. If he has no knowledge of the existence of The Supreme Spirit, this, too, will be given him. For if a man takes the road to York, even though he has never heard of York, he will certainly get there if he continues along the road.

LUC:6:4 Therefore, my friends, if your desire is the attainment of the ultimate in perfection, beauty and goodness, the knowledge of the ultimate in Truth and Reality, then it would be pointless to deny The Supreme Spirit. It would be no more than foolish for one determined to follow the road to York to its end to deny the existence of York. In any case, whether or not he believes it to be there does not influence its ultimate appearance.

LUC:6:5 Because this is so, perhaps too much has been said about the destination and not enough about the road. The man who travels the road to York is better served by information about the road, its turnoffs and landmarks, than about his destination. Ford the rivers and cross the hills before you concern yourself with the hostelry fare.

LUC:6:6 The best way to know and understand anything is to study its properties, and this applies no less to The Supreme Spirit. So, therefore, consider: What is beauty, what is goodness and what is perfection? Is it not true that they can be known here only by their contrasts and reflection? If this is so, then where are they existing? Can a non-existent thing have a reflection, and what contrasts with nothing?

LUC:6:7 The Supreme Spirit is the sun of The Sphere of The Spirit, as The Holy Spirit is the light of that Sphere. The worm raising itself up at daybreak sees the light but departs before the sun rises, for it is too lowly to withstand the rays that have no affinity with slime. It has never seen the splendour, which reigns above, though it knows of it through the light. The swallow soars and swoops in the sunlight and revels in the warmth, with which it has an affinity, but it cannot rise above its established limits. It can see the splendour it cannot attain as a bird.

LUC:6:8 When the land is covered in mist the worm remains above ground with safety, while the swallow defers its flight. So it is with the mists of agnosia, for when they cover the mortal sphere, the blind, creeping things move more freely, while the winged creatures are restricted.

LUC:6:9 Men who are dissatisfied with an unsubstantial reflection seek the reality, which gives it existence, and these are they who gaze in the direction of The Supreme Spirit and divinity. One who, seeing the reflection, says to himself, "Behind this, there must be something greater, which I must seek", is a religious man. One who says, "The reflection is pleasant and satisfies me, for to seek for its cause is too tiresome", is a non-religious man.

LUC:6:10 Reflections are illusive, and those cast on the dark mists of agnosia the most deceptive. Many mistake the ugly for the beautiful, the imperfect for the perfect and evil for good, and so are trapped by their desire for worthless and unprofitable things. To seek for perfection is to seek The Supreme Spirit. To seek for goodness is to seek divinity. To seek for beauty is to reach up for both.

LUC:6:11 Seekers after enjoyment and pleasure gain little benefit, but to seek true happiness is a worthy aim, for it points in the right direction. Unhappiness, despair and remorse are the products of ignorance, folly and apathy. Evil effects flow from evil causes. Enjoyment and pleasure are unprofitable trees whose fruit may be tasteless or bitter. Ignorance is the darkness of the soulspirit, the smothering fog in, which it becomes lost. It beguiles the spirit of man into a kind of drugged dullness, man is no longer spiritually alert, keen and energetic. He becomes inert, caught in the mire of matter.

LUC:6:12 My friends, if any of you see imperfection in The Supreme Spirit, be sure that the apparent imperfection results only from your mortal limitations. It is like looking at the sun through coarse, soiled glass and thinking the spots and distortions you see belong to the sun itself. It is not the sun that is spotted or distorted; the defect is in the glass or even in the eye of the viewer, but the effect is as though the defect lies in the sun. However imperfect the reflected image may appear, the reality behind it, The Supreme Spirit, is perfect.

LUC:6:13 The Supreme Spirit has always remained unmoved in the centre of the wheel of eternity, which rolls its out rim through the universes of the Lower Sphere. He alone is the central, unchangeable reality, the hub, around which all things revolve. Time begins in eternity and ends there, though it may itself appear eternal because expressed in revolving cycles modified only by change.

LUC:6:14 For me to speak of a beginning is a concession to mortal limitations and, in any case, it is pointless. The resolute wayfarer does not look back along the road. Suffice to say that there was The One Sole Consciousness containing the essence of perfection and reality, which words cannot describe. When the potential power was stirred by thought, it flowed out in rhythm, and this was the beginning. Do not concern yourselves with these things or talk to others too much about the nature of The Supreme Spirit. To seek Him without first becoming aware of the soul spirit is like looking for darkness while carrying a lighted lamp.

LUC:6:15 The Supreme Spirit is the source of all spirit, and this is the power, which flowed out and brought all else into being. The power flowed outward in the same order, in which it returns.

LUC:6:16 My friends, these are things difficult to understand, and it is pointless going into waters beyond your depth. Man has more pressing problems to solve within himself, so before delving into the nature of The Supreme Spirit, he should first seek to unravel the secrets of his own nature. Still more important, he should deal with the flaws and defects in his own make-up before seeking to probe further. When a man has to travel a long road, his first care should be the soles of his feet.

Chapter Seven – The Forest Mission - 2

LUC:7:1 From the Sphere Above, a Spirit Force descended, penetrating into the Sphere of Matter and Mortality, and this is called Nature. Using the laws of cause and effect, necessity and the conservation of life, Nature cherished and nurtured the descending lifeforce and, with earthly moulds, modelled it to spiritual patterns.

LUC:7:2 Life comes from The Supreme Spirit and reaches the Sphere of Matter and Mortality through the Sphere Above, and Nature works with clay. Man is the receptacle of life in both parts of his twofold being, though he should learn to concentrate it in his higher self. The lifeforce becomes strong in the spiritual man but is weak in the worldly man, just as it is strong in the eagle and weak in the grub.

LUC:7:3 There are forces in Nature beyond the knowledge of man, but whatever they are, man must harmonise himself with them. It is unwise to contend with the unknown, or challenge powers incapable of assessment. To live harmoniously, man must revere all forms of life and treat his fellowmen with consideration and courtesy. All that is beautiful and beneficial is to be preserved, and man must never tire of adding to these. Nothing having life, beauty or uniqueness must be wantonly destroyed, unless it is known to be harmful.

LUC:7:4 Thought is mind working through matter, and feeling is life manifesting in matter. Thought and feeling are not separable in man, for feeling unrecorded and unconditioned by thought would serve no higher purpose than a mortal one, and man is more than that. Therefore, all feeling has to be conveyed to something that experiences and reacts to it. Thought and feeling are not absent from the Sphere of The Holy Spirit and are even greatly intensified there. That is one reason why man has to learn to control them here, for the Earth is a place where he is schooled to handle great forces and powers now beyond conception.

LUC:7:5 My friends, the things I wish to teach form so high a doctrine that it is difficult to convey them to the clouded minds of men. Some will never grasp the meaning and message, others will laugh them to scorn. Those who try to help man along the steep, upward road and who extend the hand of friendship are more often mocked than heeded. Man prefers to sleep on the soft bed of agnosia rather than be awakened to harsh reality. Those who disturb complacent slumbers are usually reviled. To think is to understand and believe, but to be unthinking and unbelieving is less disturbing and follows the wide way of ease and apathy. All most men seek spiritually is to be left alone, undisturbed.

LUC:7:6 Most things spoken here in the hermitage are not for the uninitiated and must not be recorded, for an infant cannot be entrusted with the firebrand. Initiation is a meaningful rite, the purpose of which is to awaken the sleeper and open his spiritual eyes. Little purpose is served by talking to a sleeping man, still less to a deaf man and even less to one who has no desire to hear. So it is that men walk as though in a fog and see things hazily or with distortion. You, my friends, must go out among them and take their hands and be their guides. If they will not follow, they alone suffer, for if you do your best, you can do no more.

LUC:7:7 Dealing with mind. This comes from The Supreme Spirit by way of The Holy Spirit and is, to The Supreme Spirit, like sunlight is to the sun. It is often likened to light. Though previously explained to men in this manner, their sons, in their delusion, began to worship the sun, for man has always misunderstood the teachings and sought to bring them down from a high to a lower level.

LUC:7:8 Those who seek the truth about their nature are men becoming more than men; they tread the road to godhood. Those who close their minds to Truth are actually closing the doors of the cage, in which they remain as little more than animals. The apathetic man becomes deluded under the influence of his own ideas and imagination; he readily accepts teachings requiring no thought or effort. If ever a teacher comes along who says, "Surrender your will and reason to me and I will assure you of life everlasting," he will be unable to count his followers.

LUC:7:9 Knowing the truth, you now realise the futility and foolishness of repeating thoughtlessly the feeble formula, "I am a helpless, miserable wrongdoer bound by the misdeeds of my fathers. I am one naturally inclined towards evil and cannot save myself. Save me, have mercy and forgive me, meek and miserable as I am." Those, my friends, are actual words spoken, and doubtless, you will let them speak for themselves. Such an outlook is not only degrading, but it condemns man to disinheritance. It blinds him to his true nature and, binding him with knots of ignorance, hands him captive to enslavement in matter.

LUC:7:10 Without doubt, it is difficult to understand The Supreme Spirit and His Great Plan and all too easy to sneer and dismiss the disturbing thoughts and shun the effort. It is only after long and careful consideration has been given to the matter that a man comes to believe in spiritual things and his own immortality, and that is only the first step. Time has established that disbelief and lack of faith spring either from an inability to think deeply or from apathy. In either case, the mind falls prey to agnosia and, being weakened by ignorance and prejudice, slides wearily down the precipice into hasty and false conclusions.

LUC:7:11 True spiritual enlightenment cannot be found through the written words of man alone or through reason and logic, but those are important signposts along the way. They point in the right direction, and the Good Books are reliable guides along the road, but there comes a point where, to find spiritual enlightenment, man has to commit himself to a spiritual vehicle and be conveyed beyond the bounds of matter. The ability of any man to attain spirituality and know the truth is limited only by his steadfastness in the search and fortitude in the struggle.

LUC:7:12 Can any man think long on the wonder of creation and the complexity of created things and declare truthfully that he believes they came into being of their own accord? Can he look at the awesome beauty of the spinning universe, now so old and yet so full of vitality, with never a sign of declining powers, and say there is no motivator behind it? Can he look at the life-giving light of day and the growth-controlling light of the night, at the teeming Earth and burning stars, and honestly believe that all this is a matter of pure chance? Could all this vast and splendidly run universe have created itself? It could, if a tapestry can weave itself, or a statue chisel itself out from the rock.

LUC:7:13 Everything throughout the whole of creation conforms to certain basic laws, and where there are laws, there must be a Lawmaker. There is only one set of unchangeable laws and so there can be only one Lawmaker. Were it otherwise, there would have been a clash of laws, with resultant chaos and confusion instead of order and stability.

LUC:7:14 Men have often asked me concerning evil and sought to lay traps with their questions. Evil is a kind of mildew, corrosion or rust, which forms on the pure creative impulses of good, when they penetrate the lower Sphere of Matter and Mortality. These impulses can be purified from the adulterating evil through change and regeneration. Everything descending from the Higher Sphere finds itself contrasted or reflected here, for this is the quality of matter. This contrast or reflection may be so different as to appear to manifest as evil.

LUC:7:15 Everything on Earth is evolving either upwards or downwards, becoming more like the pure pattern, which left The Divine Designer or more grossly material and earthly. Evil does not come from above and results only from existence in an elementary sphere of change and decay. Here on Earth, change is fundamental and, like everything else, can be made to serve a good or bad end. When a thing becomes too good, it is removed by change, and anything, which becomes too bad is likewise removed. The unbounded wisdom of The Creator is beyond criticism, and only the ignorant and apathetic would criticise anyway.

LUC:7:16 Unless there is direction and control, everything tends naturally towards chaos and confusion. Undirected change can lead to nothing except disorder. Therefore, wherever there is orderly movement, there must be direction, and where there is direction, there must be a Director. No sensible person who thinks deeply enough could possibly conclude that the great universe and the whole of creation are undirected. Who, then, could The Creator and Director be but The Supreme Spirit?

Chapter Eight – The Forest Mission - 3

LUC:8:1 Each soulseed is implanted into the whole being according to a preset destiny, and from this grow the two branches of the whole being, the soulspirit and the mortal body. Though not of mortal elements, the soulspirit, by law of affinity, draws to itself particular elements when entering matter, and so all soulspirits manifest differently on the Sphere of Matter and Mortality.

LUC:8:2 Within the seed of man, there is the life potential, which has an affinity with the life breath impregnating the Lower Sphere. And this, when two complementary life impulses unite, causes generation of life. The new being grows within the womb by dividing within itself into particles too small for the eye to see, and these arrange themselves so as to form a copy of the model contained in the soulseed.

LUC:8:3 Nature composes the body in the likeness contained in the soulseed, according to the law of affinity, and each new being attracts or repels certain elements and conditions according to its destiny. Affinity and destiny act in such a way that no two persons are compounded and blended alike. Everyone is different, down to the smallest particle of his being.

LUC:8:4 The soulseed is not drawn into the Sphere of Matter and Mortality by the desire for existence in matter, but simply by the law of affinity. Success or failure, fame or life as a non-entity, do not depend on a preset destiny, though this may make them easy or difficult to achieve. A man's destiny may cause him to be born rich or poor, frail or sturdy, civilised or savage, but it cannot make him accept or remain in this state.

LUC:8:5 The power of pro-creation exists in both man and woman, though the power manifests differently in each. It is one power with two aspects, the nature of which is not easily described. The Ancients called it the 'twofold ray' and referred to an active and a passive side; one, they said, was lighter than the other. The reaction of the two aspects to each other expresses itself in the interplay of love. The compelling force is also twofold, expressing itself in a lower and higher form.

LUC:8:6 My friends, I am often asked about death, which seems to frighten most people who consider it the greatest evil, which can befall them. This is a wrong attitude caused by ignorance and spiritual apathy. Death comes when the body has served its earthly purpose, or should have done so, and is now worn out and ready to break up. The vital forces, which have hitherto held it together, withdraw and concentrate within the soulspirit. It is not the end but only a separation, the severance into two parts, each returning to the place, with which it has an affinity. It is not dissolution but renewal. The immortal is absorbed back into its own element without dissolution, while the mortal part obeys its own law of decay and renewal. Death destroys nothing, except the link between the soul spirit and the perishable body.

LUC:8:7 There is something you should know and consider most earnestly, for it bears directly upon the afterlife condition. It concerns two kinds of wrongdoing: that done openly, and perhaps I may say courageously, if such a word can be permitted to describe an evil deed, and that done secretly and slyly. Punishment for the former is often meted out by man, and this can in many cases cause spiritual re-adjustment. In the latter, however, the furtive deed is close hugged and so becomes accentuated within the sensitivity of the soulspirit. Because their evil deeds were hidden and not uncovered, the sly ones will suffer far more than those whose evildoing was exposed.

LUC:8:8 Because of this, hypocrisy is to be condemned as a most detestable vice. Those who go through life practising evil undetected, particularly if done under a cloud of virtue, will surely suffer much more grievously than the condemned murderer and thief. This is why the Good Books condemn hypocrisy and deceit more than murder and theft, for spiritually, the former are more potentially evil. It is a thing little understood. Just as little understood is the nature of sorrow and suffering. Of these there are two kinds, that which follows as the result of a foolish, wicked or ignorant act, and that which destiny prescribed to test the soulspirit. Consider these things well, for it will lead to a better understanding of life.

LUC:8:9 The soulspirit gives out a kind of glow called the 'spiritlight,' which can be seen by many of those who are spiritually awakened. It envelops the earthly body and forms something like a radiant ring above the head. In good men, it appears bright and shining, but in the unrighteous it looks dull and drab. This is why it is said, "The faces of those who have abstained from wrongdoing shall shine like the sun." It also indicates the different death conditions of people. However, it would be well for you to remember that abstaining from wrongdoing is not enough; you must act positively in the service of good.

LUC:8:10 It is not pleasant, my friends, to dwell too long on the fate of the evil-minded ones, whose afterdeath condition is a nightmare of unending strife and unrelieved ugliness. These are the wretched, undying dead who long for oblivion and the supremacy of death. This is not a pleasant teaching, but it is unwise to shun reality because it is painful to dwell upon. This is the escapism of weakness. Suffice to say that there is a place to which the evil-minded ones are drawn by affinity, where remorse and regret are more pressingly painful than any cancerous growth. The suffering falls heavier for its postponement beyond death. The undeserved honours, the unwarranted good name, the unearned credits and benefits, are not overlooked either. No man can escape the judgement of his regenerated conscience, which measures and judges according to what is revealed against a contrasting standard of absolute purity.

LUC:8:11 Now, there is one thing often asked touching the teaching concerning the unclean place, the ultimate disposal of the spiritual garbage. My friends, the doctrine of eternal condemnation is false. This cannot be, for it asserts a downward finality, which not only is against the whole creative intent, but also questions the goodness of The Supreme Spirit. The misery suffered by the unclean beings in their self-selected, filthy abode of shadowy horror, is in fact a purging and purifying cure. Though it lasts many ages of time, and the road upward through the density of matter is long and arduous, there is an end, be it in glory or oblivion.

LUC:8:12 After so-called death, which word in former times meant no more than removal, each soulspirit goes to the habitat to which it is drawn by affinity. There, all its latent powers and qualities built up and hoarded during earthly life are released and revealed. These should suffice for complete spiritual happiness and freedom, and this is what the Ancients meant when they said, "His qualities will provide his food." Man, having learned to live harmoniously on Earth, continues in a state of harmony above. The Ancients also referred to this when they said, "He who sows the seeds of discord reaps the wild wind harvest."

LUC:8:13 My forest friends, the soulspirits of grown men and women are often enclosed within a hard-set cement of materialism. Compare this state with the innocence of a child whose soulspirit, unstained by evil, still retains affinity with the source of its being. But as the mortal body develops, so it closes in upon the being inside, encasing it in ever thickening layers of grossness. Soon, the light no longer penetrates and the recollection of the beauty beyond is stifled. The vision departs, and the soulspirit, shut off from contact with its homeland, sinks into forgetful slumber. The fleshy prison walls hold it fast, and communication with the freedom light outside becomes more and more difficult. The beauty fades away in the enveloping darkness.

LUC:8:14 I, my friends, do not wish to dwell unnecessarily on these aspects of the higher teachings, they are ably enough presented in the Good Books of the Ancients and may be studied there. I would rather speak of the divine qualities. The greatest of these is love, for it is through love that man can best learn about immortality. True love brings all other virtues in its wake, and with them must come spiritual awakening. With spiritual awakening comes the influx of calming power, which makes men tranquil and quiet. It stills the rowdy haste, which saps vitality and calms the unproductive bustle. Dispute and argument upon spiritual matters become futile, for the awakened soulspirit is no longer dependant on unsubstantiated outward beliefs, but upon inward spiritual realities and assurances. Others have said that here, on the Sphere of Matter and Mortality, man cannot have assurance, but from my own experience, it would appear that assurance can be gained. There is a road to certainty, albeit a long and weary one.

LUC:8:15 However, too much is said of spirituality in a world where it is an infrequent manifestation. Only a few are in sight of the destination, while by far the most are still well back along the road. To these, the conditions to be met along the way and the location of refreshing wells and sources of sustenance are the most important things and the most serviceable information. So unless you are one who has the end in sight do not aim to immerse yourself too soon in the waters of spiritual rapture and devotion. There is a proper time and place for everything.

LUC:8:16 First, gain complete mastery over the body, and control every urge and desire arising from it. This is the first step only, and the way and means are contained in the precepts of the moral law. Study these diligently, but remember that study and understanding without practice and performance is absolutely futile. First, learn to live as you should, and only then seek to advance further.

LUC:8:17 Vice is the cancer, and depravity the plague, of the soulspirit. Mean and petty acts of spitefulness and malice are the pockmarkers. Such things are like spiritual diseases, which strike during spiritual weakness and debility. They flourish where there is avoidance of obligation and shunning of responsibility; where there is an inability to withstand pain with patience and fortitude and a selfish seeking for diverting pleasure and unrewarding frivolity. These are the things condemned through the ages, and who, looking back, would dare say such condemnation was wrong?

LUC:8:18 The greatest gift of spirituality, by which the soulspirit becomes conscious of its own existence, is not a state of easeful bliss. On the contrary, it is a driving force spurring the soulspirit ever onward along the road to godhood, to the tackling of greater obstacles. The first struggle is towards self-conquest, mastery over the mortal.

Chapter Nine – The Forest Mission - 4

LUC:9:1 Man is prone to error because of his mortality and because his earthly habitat is compounded of matter apt to lead him into evil ways. He is directed by destiny and subject to laws he cannot break, so the freedom he enjoys is largely a delusion. Escape lies in only one direction, which is upward, and this upwardising is called the road to spirituality or the True Way. Mortal man is enslaved to the demands of necessity, but this is an essential quality of earthly life, which prepares for the enjoyment of the greater freedom beyond.

LUC:9:2 Like a sleeping man in hostile terrain, the slumbering soul spirit is defenceless and exposed to attack. Good and evil spirits exert influence upon it and, unless stirred to wakefulness, it cannot discern one from the other. From the moment of its conception into mortality, the soulspirit is subject to influences operating under the law of affinity, which either attract or repel. These move to the irrational soulspirit centre of sensitivity where they set up throbbing impulses, which move like ripples circling outward, seeking compatible responses. These movements are under the administration of destiny.

LUC:9:3 Just as the body has rational and irrational centres, so with the soulspirit. The rational part of the soulspirit cannot be dominated by spirits, either good or evil, without its own free choice. This is the part not naturally inclined to evil and more receptive to the ray-like impulses from the Sphere of The Holy Spirit.

LUC:9:4 The lives of all are ruled by a preset destiny. But whatever this entails, each must rise above it, for destiny is the challenger, the handicapper and the test selector. The soulspirit alone can be freed from the domination of destiny; the mortal clay cannot. Therefore, the designs of destiny should be left to work themselves out solely in the mortal flesh.

LUC:9:5 My friends, I am asked, "What is the soulseed, and whence does it come?" Above all is The Supreme Spirit surrounded by the soulsea, below which is spirit and, lower still, matter. The soulseed is a drop from the soulsea, which has been separated out and become encased in a shell of spirit. It descends through spirit and returns there, and may do this many times. What flesh is to the soulspirit, so is spirit to the soulseed.

LUC:9:6 The laws of The Supreme Spirit cannot be evaded, but man has within himself the ability to rise above them to greater freedom. He can, of course, choose the downward path and surrender instead of struggling, but as he descends so does he become more subject to restriction; more the plaything of forces beyond his control, more like a windblown leaf. Freedom lies at the end of the upward road, not in the depths of matter.

LUC:9:7 The true evils in the world are all man-made; even disease and sickness originate in the evil tendencies of men. Evil can reach out even from the midden in the Sphere of The Holy Spirit and strike at men. But did this not originate in their own wickedness? Here are generated unseen evil things, which become parasites in the susceptible mortal flesh. They are indescribable in words, and there is no way of making them known to you. Yet, they exist even as the soulspirit exists, unseen and mortally unknowable.

LUC:9:8 My friends, the world need not be a place overrun with evil. If men could only cleanse the unclean garments of their minds, it could be a place of unceasing joy. Men bear the burden of their body with unintended sadness. They are like a man living in an empty tomb, who shrinks from the bright sunlight outside. The longer he hesitates, the whiter and weaker his body becomes. Men still choose to ignore the message handed down through the ages.

LUC:9:9 So, my friends, we make little progress. Man looks around him hopefully, seeking inspiration from distant places, when all the time, everything needed lies to his hand. The Ancients spoke wisely when they said, "That, which lies nearest is hardest to see." The ancient wisdom is as fresh today as it ever was; it is just as applicable now as it was then and will never grow stale. Man places too much faith in things he can see and grasp, while unseen things give rise to disbelief and doubt. Yet, his whole life is dominated by unseen things and forces beyond his knowledge.

LUC:9:10 The only rock, to which man can cling with faith and assurance, is the unshakable ancient wisdom contained in the Good Books. The only thing man can strive for with certainty of benefit is goodness. Man can travel the road to perfection, but it is endless and discouraging. The road to Truth is wearisome and full of pitfalls. If you asked for one rule to guide you safely, I would say, "Ignore the authoritative voice of the body, and listen to the quiet whispers of conscience."

LUC:9:11 Now, you ask whether the unclean soulspirit, degraded in darkness and humiliated by remaining in the substance, with which it has an affinity, ever resumes life in worldly form. It may indeed extend out into the brutish body of a man, or into one more graceful though heavily fettered by destiny. To say that any soulspirit is completely reborn in a new body is not strictly true, though it may manifest again on Earth. Rebirth is accepted by those who worship the great goddesses and by some others, but it is a much more complex matter than they believe. Their assertions are clouded by ignorance of the true nature of the Higher Sphere and the laws governing birth. There is, however, some truth in the doctrine, which is much deeper than they suspect.

LUC:9:12 Nature models the earthly containers, into which the soulspirit descends. She moulds them according to a prescribed pattern and adheres to the Spiritplan drawn by destiny. She likewise moulds the bodies of animals and birds; though here, the pattern is general and not differentiated by destiny, as it is with man.

Chapter Ten – The Mangod

LUC:10:1 The reaches of the Sphere of The Holy Spirit and the Sphere of Matter and Mortality are not without limitations, though within each, there is everlasting change. The godlike divinities worshipped by man have their abode in the Sphere Above, and unless formed only in the imaginations of men, are no more than superior soul spirits. Least among these, though greatest among men, is the godlike man called Mangod, the ideal towards which we all should strive.

LUC:10:2 The Mangod is candidate for a godhood within the reach of everyman and has special godlike qualities of goodness and spiritual strength, which set him apart from ordinary men. He is the strong runner in the race of life and one who never withholds a helping hand from the laggard. Such men are rarities indeed; yet, they are destined rulers of the world, the vanguard in the march towards godhood. Their day will come as surely as the sun rises above the treetops.

LUC:10:3 The virtue of the Mangod lies in his strong tendency towards goodness and his keen sense of judgement and justice. He knows when to stand firm and when to give way, and when to say, "This is enough." Not with-standing this, he always inclines towards peace and reconciliation, even in the face of accusations of weakness. He knows it is the weak man who accuses another of weakness, and the man unsure of himself who has to be reassured by a spate of his own words.

LUC:10:4 The Mangod treads with soft footfalls, but he steps from mountaintop to mountaintop. He prevails by reason and example and not by force, for he is a natural leader of men. Though I abide by the teachings, I cannot see that it is wrong to honour the names of great men who inspire loyalty and obedience, and who restore peace and justice. I would let the very names of the Mangods ring out to fill the wicked with dread and the righteous with contentment. However, while the true Mangod is not recognised among the world leaders and not even sought for high positions, perhaps it is best. The day of the Mangod will come, and the nation, which honours him will be raised above all others. But it is for the nation to bring forth the Mangod, and not for the Mangod to bring the nation.

Chapter Eleven – The Vision of Evening

LUC:11:1 This land, which was once the school of spiritual enlightenment, is still the sanctuary of spiritual civilisation, though we are cut off from our brothers over the water. Even now, terrible foreigners press about the pure land held in trust, as divine estates and religious rites are neglected. But my friends, this is just a beginning, and the time is not far distant when there will be laws prohibiting us from the practice of worship, and heavy penalties will be laid upon the righteous. Yet I still lay the charge upon you; go forth and teach.

LUC:11:2 The matron of the coming days will bear strange children, aliens blind to the light of beauty and nobility. The chants of weird forms of worship will be heard, and meaningless hymns will echo through the land. The devotional places will be wreathed in agnosia, and the purity of white enlightenment will be exchanged for the drab blackness of ignorance. Men will cease to seek their soulspirit sustenance in the light and will feed on agnosia. Unknowingly, darkness will be preferred to the light. The theme of life will be death, and death will even be idolised in the form of a man.

LUC:11:3 The righteous man will be held up to scorn, and the irreligious will be deemed wise. Those with twisted minds will be held intelligent, and those who declare that good can only serve a worldly end will be considered righteous. All this will result from spiritual poverty and lack of enlightenment, yet they will declare themselves rich and enlightened. The impoverished cannot surround themselves with grandeur, and this applies both to the flesh and to the spirit. Consideration for the soulspirit will be non-existent, and belief in its immortality will be treated as a jest. The mind of man will either be set on worldly things or be clouded by a fog of spiritual darkness. There will be no respect for spirituality.

LUC:11:4 There will be persecutions and wars, riots and looting, all manner of deceit and oppression will be practised in the name of angry and revengeful gods. Worse still, all this will be practised in the name of good, and men will blindly accept what they are told and execute orders running contrary to their natures.

LUC:11:5 When spirituality has reached its lowest ebb and religion has decayed, the wheel will turn again. Man will either rise up with an influx of spiritual regeneration or go down and utterly perish in the dark depths of moral degeneracy. The world cannot be permitted to remain a spiritually festering sore failing to serve any purpose.

LUC:11:6 There are things buried in the future, with which it is unprofitable to deal, so what is said must suffice. Better by far to deal with the problems of today, though even these are less important than learning the secrets of the True Way.

LUC:11:7 The awakened soul spirit of man becomes filled with a yearning not there before, an overwhelming desire for constant communication or unity with the Sphere of The Holy Spirit. As this manifests more strongly and desires and inclinations tend to disappear, the soulspirit grows from strength to strength.

LUC:11:8 Since the Earth is the work of The Supreme Spirit, he who cherishes and improves it, or adds to its beauty and goodness, becomes an assistant to The Creator. This is a position all should aspire to, for the Earth must not be uncouth or unadorned. Those who benefit most from life are those who serve it best.

LUC:11:9 I have spoken of the Mangod, of the very few who are gifted with purity of mind and high intellect. These are the ones who should marshal the forces of mankind to serve The Creator, but all too often, good men are not great men, or great men good. As things are, the man who is both good and great is a rarity.

LUC:11:10 To be spiritual means living life to the fullest, in its widest sense; making conscious contact not only with the Sphere of Matter and Mortality, but also with the Sphere of The Holy Spirit. As this means that the spiritual man differs from ordinary men, the crowd is not able to understand him, and often, he is treated with scorn. This does not deter the spiritual man who knows the mockery and scorn of the crowd are usually directed against someone superior to it. When I was held up to ridicule, scorned and even believed mad, I felt flattered.

LUC:11:11 Reality and Truth are not to be found on Earth, though man, being more than mortal, can conceive their existence, and some may even be granted a divine vision of them. How can such qualities exist in this sphere where good is adulterated with evil? Where there is no stability, where pain, sorrow, decay and change press in on every side? How can any unstable, changeable thing be real? How can it be true to itself? Everything that is unstable changes and is therefore false to itself, and the false is unreal. The real is something unchanging. When a man can conceive what Truth and Reality actually are, he stands on the threshold of comprehending The Supreme Spirit.

Chapter Twelve – The Bodiless Body

LUC:12:1 My friends, I see myself as one who has been granted a divine vision, a gift of insight beyond that of most men, these things coming to me through the grace of The Holy Spirit. This I know beyond any doubt; I have broken through the closed ring of mortality about me and taken possession of a deathless body. I am now an awakened soul clothed in spirit and, having drunk the waters of life in the Sphere Above, am more than mortal. Would that I could explain this better to your understanding. But the things, which can be easily taught are of this world only, and higher things can be learned only by direct experience of the Sphere of The Holy Spirit.

LUC:12:2 The soulspirit is like a bodiless eye, seeing as men see visions or recall scenes from the past without the sight of the eyes. Yet, this is no more than a poor representation of Truth, for there are no means known to men, whereby these things can be explained. To understand fully, each man must go out from the body to the Sphere Above where only the soulspirit can go, and only then can the vision of beauty and reality be seen. It seems to me that this is not achieved even by the powers of the soulspirit, great as they are, but rather that, in such cases, man is uplifted by the very arms of The Supreme Spirit. There appears to be two subspheres co-joined: one, the lower where form and colour still manifest, and above this, another where these have their origin, and this is a place of quiet, restful serenity. It is a place of unchanging stability.

LUC:12:3 You ask me about the higher vision. Again it is difficult to express myself in words. It comes as a brilliant light, but not like the blazing glare of the sun, before which men are forced to close their eyes. It is a spiritual form of light, shining only to an extent within the ability of the one granted the vision to receive it. Those who, like my own master, can drink deeply at the well of visions, are lulled into a sound spiritual sleep outside the mortal body, and can remain long in the place where visions reflect reality more clearly.

LUC:12:4 Such men are true Illuminated Ones, and they are not many. By far, the greater number are deceived by the upward reflections of illusion, but because these appear as glorious visions, they accept them as reflections of Truth. This is always the great danger, but there are tests to guard against deception.

LUC:12:5 Sometimes, when an illuminated One speaks of the Sphere of The Holy Spirit, its power will flow down into him to such an extent that his mortal senses will become blocked out. He will then appear to lose the trend of his own speech and, instead, his mouth will become an outlet for the flooding channel of inspiration. Sometimes, in such cases, it is difficult for the listener to grasp what the illuminated One is saying, unless he, too, is in equal harmony with the Sphere Above. The words race ahead of his understanding. If sitting in darkness or gloom, it will be noticed that, at such times, a light or radiance surrounds the Illuminated One, and it is this, which establishes the reality of his spiritual elevation.

LUC:12:6 Spiritual things are far more difficult to understand than earthly things, and their study requires much greater effort and self-discipline. That is why there are so few spiritual people. The lower mortal mind can gain only a faint insight into them through spoken words, and then only by a supreme effort of understanding. This proves too much for most people, and so spirituality goes into a decline. If the effort directed towards destructive or purposeless worldly things had been directed towards spiritual ends, the race of man would now be a race of Mangods.

LUC:12:7 There are some among you who do not understand the mystery of rebirth. It means rebirth into spiritual consciousness, and this is the central secret of all time, the knowledge of which will change men into Mangods. The reborn man can bid his soulspirit go into any place he chooses, and it will be there quick as a thought. It will pass over the seas or penetrate through the denseness of the forests, not as a thing moving swiftly, but as a thing already there. The soulspirit, once freed, can rise above all denser material things, though it cannot penetrate into the upper subspheres of creation in the Sphere of The Holy Spirit.

LUC:12:8 Now, those of you who have experienced the power and speed of the soulspirit and examined, by careful study, the reality of the experience, can surely understand the nature of the Supreme Spirit. If you can do these things, how much more capable will He be of doing them. Therefore, expand yourself to the utmost limit; break out of your confinement, slip away from the mortal body, and escape the shackles of space and time. Behind and beyond this, you will see the gateway at the path leading to the door of The Supreme Spirit.

LUC:12:9 If, however, you prefer to imprison the soulspirit within the body and to treat it with contempt, saying, I know nothing and fear to reach out into the unknown. I fear the limitless spaces, the unfathomable depths and the boundless heights. I am afraid to seek too deeply in order to discover what I am or what I can do, or what I will become," if you are numbered among those who tremble and fear, then you are not fully alive; you are already more than half dead. You can understand nothing of the truly beautiful; you cannot perceive glory and if you love the mere mortal body so much, then you cannot really know good and are easily inclined towards the bad.

LUC:12:10 Even the slumbering soulspirit can know, through its dreams, the joy originating from its affinity with the Sphere Above. It is experienced when the restlessness of the thinking mind is stilled, in the joyous lilt of the heart filled with melody, in the glory of a sunset. In the warm smile of love, in the confidence of a child, in the sweet scents of a garden, or in the cool caress of the wind. The cumbersome words of Earth cannot describe its glory or reveal to mortal mind the majestic picture of Truth. These words of mine do no more than reflect a pale shadow of the splendours of reality. Once again I repeat; the true knowledge of the Higher Sphere can be gained only from personal experience, through self-awakening.

LUC:12:11 The soul spirit is potentially beyond spatial limitations and exists outside earthly time. It knows that everything is everlasting; yesterday remains where it was; it is man who has moved on and left it behind, out of sight. Life is a steady advance, it flows on like the waters of this stream and cannot turn back on itself. The same stream passed this way a hundred years ago. It remains the same, though moment by moment every drop passing by is new. So it is that we cannot return upstream, through the waters of life, to yesterday. However, when cast upon the bank by death, no longer swept onward by the flowing stream, yesterday becomes approachable.

LUC:12:12 These are vital truths known to all Illuminated Ones. The childish mind of the worldly man sees things in unreality. The partially awakened, while in trance or ecstasy, see reality as though through a veil. They realise that the mortal eyes see only the unreal and deceptive, but they are between two spheres, seeing neither clearly, and so do not see reality either. The illuminated One alone sees clearly and so knows for certainty that he is an immortal being.

LUC:12:13 The discipline of the moral teachings, when fully practised and lived, is the first essential step towards illumination. It is only by completely eliminating his own self-centredness that man can become aware of the communicating point within himself, whereby he can contact the reality above. By this means alone, he escapes from a world of shadows and illusions. When the greater self awakens within, the peace and joy of spiritual consciousness fills life with splendour, but first the childish struggle for worthless, unreliable things must cease. The spirit of man is like a caged beast, ever restless, ever seeking to escape to a greater sphere, but too often the restlessness is stilled by drugs of worldliness.

LUC:12:14 The unenlightened man is unaware of anything beyond his limiting mortal wall, or outside the scope of his own ideas and interpretations. Yet, his ideas are clouds of preconceived prejudices and his interpretations deceptive illusions. He is dead to reality, entombed within himself.

LUC:12:15 The man who sees a treestump in the night and mistakes it for a man is deluded. Yet the treestump is real enough; it is the misinterpretation by the man that makes it what it is not. Likewise with the Earth and material things; they too have a reality of their own, but man misinterprets, making them something they are not. His mortal body is also real, but this, too, he has misinterpreted, to make it something different. The Earth, material things and his body are not what man mistakes them to be; he is deluded in the nightmists of agnosia.

LUC:12:16 The soulspirit is truly awakened when it has a personal experience proving the reality of the Sphere of The Holy Spirit, and this is a far from easy accomplishment. There may be brief glimpses in a half wakened state, but these are not enough, nor are they satisfactory. The Higher Sphere can be known and experienced; it is not something completely cut off from the knowledge of man. There, the answer is to be found; there, the secret of the opposites is revealed; there, Truth shines with greater clarity. There you will discover that the soulspirit is a fragment of The Supreme Spirit containing the essence of His creative power.

LUC:12:17 Thought, combined with the power of The Holy Spirit, can create whatever it desires, whatever it wills to come into being will do so. The originating creative thought has been modified on Earth by the thought activities of many soulspirits, and so there is much that cannot be directly attributed to The Supreme Spirit. Meditate on this, for it explains much. Man remains generally completely unaware of his own powers, his limitations being in fact no more than the result of his own lack of knowledge and awareness, his lack of insight and preference for walking in the comforting calm of agnosia.

LUC:12:18 The soulspirit can be whatever it wills itself to be; it is the fashioner of its own form and destiny. It can, if it wishes, see all things as they are in reality by sweeping aside the clouds of illusion and removing the veils of deception. Do not misunderstand me when I talk of the real and the unreal. Earth, earthly experience and material things are not unreal, for the unreal would have no existence. The things so often called unreal do exist and have a reality of their own, it is man's interpretation of that reality that is wrong. The things are not what man thinks them to be; they are false, deceptive, illusive. Even the words 'real' and 'unreal' are themselves deceptive and lead into error.

LUC:12:19 This higher knowledge has been gained by those who have built up their spiritual powers, so that they could enter into direct communication with the Sphere Above. By their sacrifices and self-disciplines, they so refined and strengthened their soulspirits that they could penetrate to the place where the light of Truth shone clearly. That they were not misled is easily provable.

LUC:12:20 The means of freeing the soulspirit are available to all men who first seek to discover their true nature. This is the beginning of the only direct road; the others lead to illusionary Heavens. Each man is his own ruler and the director of his own destiny; whatever advance he makes, even though it come through the teachings of others, will result from his own individual effort.

LUC:12:21 The road to spirituality lies within himself, but too often, it is blocked by barriers erected through his own ignorance and mortal weaknesses. The pain and suffering, against which he so often protests, are only attempts at goading him into clearing away the barriers. Study of the Good Books provides directions for traversing the road, but such study is worthless unless the teachings are put into practice. That is the secret, not knowledge but practice.

LUC:12:22 There are teachings, which declare that man will become lost in a sea of oblivion, but this is incorrect. It comes from a misunderstanding of the All. Man will not become lost in the Eternal All, but this will become a part of man, of each individual soulspirit. Were this not so, there would be no need for the continual conflict, the continual testing by affliction and the continual presentation of new problems to overcome.

LUC:12:23 However, it is useless speculating on the truth of other teachings until the truth of your own is established. One thing you now know for certain is that man is more than he thinks himself to be, far more than the mortal expanse of unawakened potential. This you know, for you have experienced the rapture of the Illuminated. What you have done, others can do, for it is within the scope of anyone prepared to accept the necessary austerities and self-discipline. Not many will reach the goal of complete illumination, but all can obtain a momentary glimpse through the veil separating this sphere from the one above. All can awaken their soulspirit to consciousness, and only those who have done so can realise its glorious wonder. They become completely freed from every material limitation. They know themselves to be truly immortal, and to them, birth and death are now no more than milestones along the road. They lose their significance in the great inpouring of consciousness, the invigorating surge of new life.

LUC:12:24 All the awareness most persons encompass at any moment in time is just a minute part of the whole being. Some portions just on the fringe of the mortal are tapped from time to time, and these, such as memory, play a large part in life. However, out in the vast expanse beyond, comprising the undeveloped part of man, lie the latent powers, which he is incapable of utilising. Within the reach of each man is an infinite spiritual treasure, if only he would expend the necessary effort to grasp it!

Chapter Thirteen – The Lifeforce

LUC:13:1 When the child grows up, becoming a youth or maiden, it enters into a struggle with existence, with worldliness. It becomes like a swimmer setting out to cross a turbulent river. Individuals try to mould the world to their own way of thinking, but the world fights back, and in so doing shapes each one into an image differing from his own conception. To each person Earth takes on a different aspect, according to individual thoughts and inclinations.

LUC:13:2 The lifeforce centred in man is not something unique in nature, and the vast ocean of life seeks to draw it back into itself. Therefore, if the lifeforce is to remain separate within the individual, the individual must be prepared to face conflict and opposition. The struggle to retain life cannot be renounced; no one can cut himself off from the difficulties of worldly existence, or discard the burden of manhood or womanhood.

LUC:13:3 While strength and vitality throb within the mortal container, worldly problems and difficulties must be steadfastly faced and overcome. But at the onset of middle age, each one should prepare for the downhill run, and by this time, the soulspirit should be aroused to consciousness and be well and harmoniously formed. Each person should, by this time, be strong enough to face the inevitability of old age, decay and death, with equanimity. At this, the turning point of life, there should be an inward turning, a greater effort expended in seeking to understand the purpose and meaning of life. There should be a seeking after spirituality, after fulfillment.

LUC:13:4 The sole purpose of earthly life is to realise and develop the latent powers in man. All the problems and struggles, all the spiritual difficulties and obscurities, all the paradoxes, the experiences of joy and sorrow, pleasure and pain, simply serve to awaken the soulspirit. Life is all-embracing, it includes both birth and death, growth and decline, the contrasts, the opposites, the active and the passive, male and female.

LUC:13:5 It is the knowledge of his individuality, his seperateness, his consciousness of self that raises man above the level of the dumb creatures, but this position cannot be maintained without effort; it will always be easier to fall than to rise, to go back instead of forward. The child knows little of the burdens imposed by life, but as it grows older, its light-heartedness becomes overshadowed by the knowledge of duties and obligations, which must be assumed. The hearts of our weaker brethren are so often filled with a longing to return to the state of protected childhood, that they are easily beguiled by parental faiths, which treat them as children. They find it easy to cast their spiritual burdens at the feet of comforting priests, but such action is not only childishly irresponsible; it is also morally cowardly.

LUC:13:6 The spiritually irresponsible, who seek a comforting creed, are generally apathetic or selfish persons careless of their spiritual life and its needs. My friends, the ultimate, the final thing we must depend upon is the soulspirit. Only that accompanies the individual into the life eternal, but it is too late to come to this realisation upon the deathbed. Those who have confidence in their future existence are the only truly contented ones on Earth.

LUC:13:7 Man should never forget that his most important aspect is the soulspirit, and he should not be neglectful of its needs and demands. He should not confuse it with the frail mortal body whose needs and demands, if given full rein, will override those of his greater self. Man must understand life; he must understand its forces, which play about him. To understand it fully is to know one's own destiny, one's own heritage of struggle and one's own trials. Man must resolve on the inner search and follow its trail diligently.

LUC:13:8 When a man's life becomes a pattern of perfection reflecting the perfection above, he is a container for the lifeforce and a channel for the down pouring power which serves to uplift the whole of mankind. Becoming this is in fact the only real service man can render The Supreme Spirit.

LUC:13:9 Man's prime duty is to himself, and even when he serves others he is serving his own ends; therefore, he should not be hypocritical about his goodness. The good deeds of men are the soulspirit moulders, as also are spirituality, freedom from agnosia, forbearance, love of Truth and justice, tranquillity of heart, simplicity, austerity, generosity and integrity.

LUC:13:10 Only in a well-balanced being can the lifeforce manifest harmoniously. Therefore, all excesses of joy and sadness, pleasure and melancholy, despair and exhilaration, are to be avoided. The rule must be oft repeated: Moderation in all things and complete control over the self.

LUC:13:11 My friends, I have revealed to you the nature of the inner being who controls all things from within, now it is up to you to use this knowledge to good effect. I have shown you the chords, by which the spheres are held together and the same chords bind all things.

LUC:13:12 You ask me, "What is a good man?." He is one in whom goodness triumphs over evil, whose qualities grow stronger daily, while his evil qualities weaken. In him, conceit, avariciousness, selfishness, anger, rashness and agnosia are diminishing each day, and he governs his life in accordance with the Good Books.

LUC:13:13 Self-mastery is freedom, not restraint, for it is bondage to the body which makes life a misery to the man who aspires to goodness and the spiritually inclined. This bondage is caused by ignorance of the true nature of man and his destiny, and can best be overcome by a steady advance towards self-knowledge, spirituality and soulspirit awakening. The essential qualities for such advancement are tranquillity of heart (which means serenity), self-mastery, fortitude and resolution under the afflictions of life, kindness and consideration for others, a life led in accordance with the Good Books. The man who is truly good understands the troubles of another and stands ever ready to help the weak and oppressed. He never boasts of his achievements and treats every woman with respect, the same respect he has for his mother. He does not sully his lips with falsehood and is free from the fetters of greed and envy.

LUC:13:14 The lifeforce diversifies into many expressions, the greatest of which is love. This is a prime quality essential to soulspirit awakening, but it may take on many forms. Reverence is a form of love, so is the appreciation of melody and beauty. Uprightness is love manifesting in self-control; wisdom and desire for Truth is another form of love. Duty and obligation call forth an expression of love in a different aspect, though no less strong and beneficial.

LUC:13:15 My friends, there are those who teach that spirituality comes from turning away from the world, but this is a wrong teaching, for life is meant to be lived fully, and to live means to experience. A man who shuts himself away from the world can love no one except himself. To say he does it for love of The Supreme Spirit is empty talk.

LUC:13:16 No step is lost on the path of experience, though sometimes what appears to be a gain will be a loss, but so may a loss be a gain. The wayfarer must keep one objective ever before his eyes, and that is the ultimate end. He must strive towards this with all his resolution and allow nothing to divert him. The alluring sideroads are many-branched and lead to dead ends, and along them, worldliness beckons bewitchingly. Along the road, there are strugglers and stragglers, seekers and non-starters.

LUC:13:17 Therefore, if you would travel the road, firmly rid yourselves of the burden imposed by worldly and selfish desires. This does not mean that worldly things are to be completely shunned, for worldly success is not to be despised if sought with moderation and without prejudice to greater things. In all things there is a proper balance and state of harmony. However, whatever comes your way do not become too elated with success or too downcast by failure, both are tests and serve the same end.

LUC:13:18 Labour in the cause of earthly gain is of less value than labour, which benefits mankind or glorifies Earth. Therefore, if a creed brings men together only for worship, it serves little purpose; but if it is also a creed where men labour to learn, to beautify life and to advance mankind then its value is beyond estimation.

LUC:13:19 The lifeforce must be conserved and guarded, it must not be dissipated in the uncontrolled tempests of passion and emotion. These carry away the lifeforce, as the winds carry away the autumn leaves.

LUC:13:20 My friends, one of you says my words confuse him because they contain contradictions indicating two paths, and asks which is best for the attainment of the supreme goal. Let me say, and heed it well, that the most profound truths can be explained, in the limited expressions of men, only by seeming contradictions and paradoxes. Man may travel two paths to the perfection lying beyond Earth, one is the path of wisdom lit by the lamp of vision, and the other the path of action lit by the lamp of determination. There are men of wisdom and counsel, and men of deeds and action. All are equally necessary to maintain the balance and harmony of life, and an existence with one and not the other becomes chaotic.

LUC:13:21 Two things man cannot do, he cannot refrain from learning and he cannot refrain from action. He must not turn his back on life or renounce the worldly struggle. However, there is learning that is beneficial and learning which is not, there are actions which are good and others which are bad. It is the choice that counts.

LUC:13:22 Man is like a cornered bear, and life is like the hunters who surround it, goading it into action, forcing it to strike. So are all men driven to action by the nature of things, and any who seek to avoid it while permitting their thoughts to wander idly towards life's pleasures, do inestimable damage to their soulspirit. The true man is one in whom wisdom and action are balanced, whose mind, controlling his inner forces with harmony, governs his resolute steps along the path of action, and the mortal body could not exist here were it not continually active.

LUC:13:23 The lifeforce in man turns the wheel of progress, aim to be good, and carry out your allotted tasks in life, and progress in the right direction will follow. Though it is folly to sit irresolutely at the crossroads, it is no wiser to press forward along the wrong road.

LUC:13:24 Have faith in these teachings and follow the indicated path with cheerfulness, goodwill and resolution, and your soulspirit will safely reach the high pass where it can look out over the good country spread before it. Ignore the inner urges which rise from the depths of mortal flesh and drive a man, often even unwillingly, to act wrongfully.

LUC:13:25 Have faith in the reality of the soulspirit, for it is the only permanent thing in the ever changing waters of life. It may be hidden deep in agnosia, it may be clouded by mortal desires, as fire is clouded by smoke, by petty unfruitful pursuits, as a mirror is darkened by dust, or by the denseness of matter, as a kernel is hidden by its shell, but the reality lies underneath.

LUC:13:26 The lifeforce must never be consumed by flames of desires generating in the flesh. Unhealthy or abnormal desires, like wood ants, burrow into the minds of men and breed there, eating away their reasoning powers and wisdom. From such desires arises a noxious cloud of vapour which, having overcome reason and wisdom, smothers the soulspirit in darkness. Therefore, be masters and directors of your desires.

LUC:13:27 Great are the powers of the senses and the worldly desires to which they pander, to bind and blind. But the resources of the soulspirit are infinitely greater, if you will only call them forth. So stretch out and grasp the sword beyond the limits of mortality, and slay the enemies of the soulspirit. Even though you lack the resolution to fight for any cause, however great, fight for yourself, for your own preservation into eternity.

LUC:13:28 Those who lack faith in the existence of Truth, who cannot summon the strength to struggle, who have not the fortitude to stand the long weary years of preparation, will never penetrate the veil to see the wonder and glory beyond. There is a glorious, eternal beauty shining over the universal vastness, and in rare moments of illumination, man may glimpse the everlasting in things which pass away. This is the message handed down through the ages; this is the message of all true spiritual teachers. All poets, musicians and artists, all who beautify and glorify life, convey only the same message in infinite variety of expression.

Chapter Fourteen – The Last Forest Teachings

LUC:14:1 My friends, the purpose and meaning of life are no longer hidden from you, and you know why men should follow the way of good rather than the way of evil. Every restraint and restriction, every responsibility, every duty and obligation, however obscure the purpose, are imposed with only one end in view, your own ultimate benefit and good. Everything unnecessary or purposeless has been winnowed away and only the sustaining grains remain, nothing not worthwhile has been kept.

LUC:14:2 Yet there is another reason for following this path, for, by refining and strengthening the soulspirit and awakening all its latent powers, each man is potentially a Mangod. He is no longer restricted to this sphere and can even contact Greater Beings beyond the mountain, and from them learn the truth.

LUC:14:3 Life itself is real, but as expressed in the Sphere of Matter and Mortality, it is little more than an illusion. The true being lives elsewhere, and where it lives man awakes to eternity, the illusion vanishes and he is confronted with the real. In this sphere man dwells in bondage to a belief in the reality of the illusion, he is attached to passing shadows, he seeks to grasp something of substance in a place where nothing is true, substantial and unchanging. Grind a stone to powder, and the powder to a powder of powder, and in the end, you will have something tangible. Such is the basis of this unsubstantial place.

LUC:14:4 My friends, you know too well how few soulspirits are awakened from their slumber on the soft couches of agnosia. Of those who do wake to consciousness are some who did so quickly and lovingly embrace the Great Light. They seek diligently and carefully for the tree of love and eagerly eat its nourishing fruit; those are the noble soulspirits, the truly illuminated among men. A ray of light from the Sphere of The Holy Spirit pours the vigour of renewed spiritual life into them, and they become more than men.

LUC:14:5 You wonder why there are so few awakened, but is it not man himself, by his own folly and blindness, his own spiritual apathy, who has slammed shut the gate leading to the road of enlightenment? Perhaps the truth is that man declines the necessary spiritual effort. It is your task to sound the awakening call, to rouse man from his spiritual drowsiness and stir him into action.

LUC:14:6 Do not concern yourselves overmuch regarding the nature of The Supreme Spirit. He is a Being incomprehensible to those with only the limited faculties of the Lower Spheres. He exists within a divine principle, upon which speculation is impossible, since it lies beyond the limits of mortal conception. Only the truly Illuminated Ones, the noble soulspirits, can approach the border of understanding, for they can see from afar. The treasures of His sanctuary are the ultimates of Love, Beauty, Perfection, Truth. Justice, Compassion and Goodness.

LUC:14:7 I am asked how this Far Away Formless One, awesome in changelessness, whose Spirit fills the whole universe, can be worshipped. My friends, how can He be influenced from the lower depths of His creation? Can rain wet the sky or rivers fill the ocean? Concerning the form of worship which is praise and prayer. Do you think that doleful chants, mournful music and mumbled prayer add to His glory or fill His heart with joy? These are gifts gathered from the woodland. Far more acceptable would be a freely dedicated heart purged of evil, the offering of a body wherein lust and unhealthy desires have been uprooted, the display of a mouth untainted by lewdness and falsehood, and the showing of integrity, honesty and purity.

LUC:14:8 True worship is the purification and elevation of the soulspirit, no more, all that purifies and elevates is worship. The purpose of worship is to arouse the soulspirit to wakefulness, it is the companionable unity of those serving a common cause. It is an act of mutual experience. It is not the servile humiliation of a slave before his master, but the linking of spirit with spirit.

LUC:14:9 These are the only sacrifices to bring: Bodily lusts and passions, evil thoughts, lies, deceit, slander and all forms of wickedness. To offer the blood of harmless creatures is easy and cowardly, and an insult to He who created them. These are the offerings to dedicate to His service: Diligent study of the Good Books, wisdom, courage, moral purity and steadfastness, together with all things serving the purpose of good. The only vestment needed for worship is a loyal, kind and pure heart.

LUC:14:10 To act as men do when worshipping is to belittle The Supreme Spirit. How can One so great be worshipped and served by fires and candles, by mumbled words falling thoughtlessly on unhearing ears, by sacrificial blood and by ornaments and incense? These things may serve a purpose in aiding man's awakening, but it is hypocritical to say they are necessary to The Supreme Spirit, and blasphemy to say He requires them from man. The Supreme Spirit rises above the thinking of men and says, "If such things please man, then let the offerer become the recipient."

LUC:14:11 The truly enlightened worship by a compliment, in trying to match their purity and goodness with the reflection of these qualities coming down from on high. The ennobling of the lesser self, goodness in thought, word and deed, the subjection of material urges, a constant disciplining of the body, an unwavering devotion to the cause of mankind, which is the cause of The Supreme Spirit, this is true worship, providing they are not clouded with hypocrisy.

LUC:14:12 Worship serves the soulspirit and therefore is beneficial, if sincere. Many have felt its first restless stirring in worship. My friends, how sad that the greatest treasure there is, the jewel beyond price, the soulspirit, still remains so often buried out of sight, unheeded, unsought, unwanted!

LUC:14:13 Nothing is more impressionable than the soulspirit, and every act forms a guide to its future appearance. Thus it is that every experience tends towards a repetition; and so a habit, good or bad, once formed is hard to break. It is like water which cuts a channel all other water follows.

LUC:14:14 Man has a material sounding board called the brain, which means a drumskin, and this is very apt. However, if it is battered with impure desires or taken over by worldliness it thickens and becomes a barrier against the spiritual forces. The brain, made dense with insensitivity and calloused by wickedness, forms a door which closes out all things of the spirit and becomes the servant of the senses. It no longer admits the light, and what light does penetrate becomes disguised and distorted into gloom. The door to the soulspirit becomes overgrown with weeds and brambles, the material and spiritual are separated by an immovable barrier and the soulspirit slumbers while the body decays.

LUC:14:15 Lacking the light, ensnared in sorrow and smothered in agnosia, degraded and sunk in the depths of matter, the soulspirit languishes and pines. Mercifully unconscious, it is pounded, twisted and torn, uncared for and unheeded, its infant cries falling upon deaf and deadened ears. Slowly it is smothered under the great overburden of wickedness and worldliness. Little need you wonder why the Dark Spirits are so often called 'abortions!'

LUC:14:16 Man, having chosen to spurn spirituality and thus lost the union in consciousness, which is his birthright, now seeks to console himself with worthless worldly baubles. With the arrogance of ignorance and blindness he claims the reality of his environment and endeavours to possess something outside himself, something to which he is half alien. This striving for worldly things still further buries the inner divinity, which becomes so encased in materialism that it can no longer be roused from its deadly slumber.

LUC:14:17 While man turns his soulspirit outwards, towards the illusive and deceptive world of matter and mortality, seeking fulfilment there, so long will he be unaware of his greater being. Here he will never find true contentment, and cut off from companionable communication with his true self, he will remain restless and dissatisfied. He will be always seeking for something, though he knows not what.

LUC:14:18 The greatness of the soulspirit, with all its potential powers, a true spark from the fire of divinity, is now smothered under layers of worldliness formed by pandering to the body experiences of the senses. The true being becomes a prisoner within a material prison of man's own creation.

LUC:14:19 Life is like a wide river containing the waters of manifestation deeply clouded by the silt of illusion, wherein the soulspirits of men swim back and forth. The Supreme Spirit is reflected in the waters through His rays of Holy Spirit, just as a mirror reflects the face of the looker while itself remaining untouched. The image in the waters is the soulspirit.

LUC:14:20 Those who say they can find The Supreme Spirit through means outside of themselves will seek in vain; what they will find will be worthless pebbles, the real jewel lies within. Only when the unreal is revealed for what it is and penetrated in consciousness, can the real come into sight. This can be proved beyond any dispute by personal experience, but few care to pay the price of such knowledge. The waters of illumination cannot be gathered on the heights of arrogant self-assurance, or on the hilltop of prejudice. Neither can they be drawn from the valley of apathy or the dale of agnosia.

LUC:14:21 I am asked concerning the people about us. They are not altogether ignorant in their teachings and it is not amiss to understand what they declare about the nature of man. They say he is a divine thought caught up in heaviness and wrapped about with clay. The thought, imprisoned in darkness, desired to see the light and the effort generated by the desire caused two holes to appear in the clay, and these became eyes. One of them looked to the right of things and the other to the left, and so directed straightly. No eyes appeared behind, as the divine thought never intended man to retreat, only to go forward. The eyes, being fixed on the path ahead, wished to know what was going on beside them, and so the effort generated by this desire brought forth two holes, which became ears. Because the clay desired to remain moist, a mouth was formed to provide water and then arms were formed, to push aside whatever got in the way. Then, so that it might know more of what was happening about it, the clay became sensitive and felt. So they say man is a divine thought trapped in a body and seeking to escape. They say the body is no more than clay reddened by sunlight, and can anyone say this is not a good description?

Book of
Wisdom

WSD:1:2 When a conscious, awakened spirit occupies a material body in conscious unity, the whole being is united with The Divine. It expands out beyond the limitations of space and time. Mindfulness controls the thoughts and feelings and clears an inner place, so that in silence and peace it is ready to receive an influx of the Divine Mindfulness, and meditation opens a way of communication, whereby the spirit of man may communicate with the spirit surrounding The Divine. It is a higher form of prayer, a controlled concentration of thought.

Table of Chapters

Book of Wisdom
Table of Chapters (Continued)

Book of Wisdom

Chapter One – Meditation and Morals

WSD:1:1 The only way a man can become fully awakened spiritually is to know his true nature and to strive for communication with the Spiritual Realm. This can best be achieved by meditation, or perhaps 'mindfulness' expresses it better. This is a state of conscious awareness of all the potentialities within man; the ability to cut off all material disturbances and to bring the spirit into harmonious relationship with a higher, more compatible realm. It means gaining complete mastery over all material impulses, urges and desires.

WSD:1:2 When a conscious, awakened spirit occupies a material body in conscious unity, the whole being is united with The Divine. It expands out beyond the limitations of space and time. Mindfulness controls the thoughts and feelings and clears an inner place, so that in silence and peace it is ready to receive an influx of the Divine Mindfulness, and meditation opens a way of communication, whereby the spirit of man may communicate with the spirit surrounding The Divine. It is a higher form of prayer, a controlled concentration of thought.

WSD:1:3 Clearing an inner place to form the Shrine of the Heart does not mean that it serves no purpose. The usefulness of a cave is in its empty space; the usefulness of a basket or a pot is in its emptiness. All wisdom and all knowledge, the answer to every question, are not to be found outside of man, but within him. He need not seek outside himself for the solution to the riddle of his nature. He need not traverse the Earth to find the answer; it can be reached from within himself. There, too, he will find all that supplies the needs of his spirit.

WSD:1:4 In his daily life and in all he does, each man should conduct himself as though intending to be a living example to others. He should act as though proclaiming his dedication to service in the greatest cause any man can serve, and as though inviting others to join him. He should be a leader showing the way and a guide indicating the path others should follow, the path each must travel alone.

WSD:1:5 Every thinking man must surely realise now that there is something more to life than a search for happiness, wealth or luxury. That life must be more than an idle drifting, the only efforts being bent towards seeking the still waters of contentment and the shallows of pleasure. There must be more than walking around seeking enjoyment. There is indeed something more to it than that; there is a purpose to life, and that purpose is living.

WSD:1:6 Living is meant in its fullest sense and does not refer to mortal life alone. Mortal life is the servant, the threshold of a greater life and should be regarded only in this light. The duty of all is to awaken their own spirit to consciousness. If, however, this has not been achieved, then the best thing to do is to follow the precepts and advice contained in the writings of those who have themselves awakened their spirits to consciousness.

WSD:1:7 For the first step it is sufficient to be self-controlled and self-disciplined, the efforts of every man being bent towards learning more about himself. He must cultivate mindfulness, to discover his own motives and to know what lies behind every thought, every word and action. He must discover every cause and understand its effect. He must know why he does a certain thing and by what means he achieves it. He must decide upon a plan of life, upon certain objectives and carry them through to a successful conclusion. He must choose a path and follow it through to the end, not looking too far ahead that he ignores what lies before his feet. He must firmly ignore the cries of diverting desires and disregard the bypaths of foolish fancies.

WSD:1:8 As yet, no mortal man knows the true laws of justice, and no mortal man has ever seen the face of Truth unveiled. No man has yet risen sufficiently in greatness to proclaim his ability to live free from all restraint imposed by others. Some may proclaim their ability or right to do so, but these do it not from strength but from moral weakness. Their affirmation of their own freedom is in fact a declaration of war upon the liberties of others. They are no more than spineless creatures who decry the laws of morality and high principles only because these seek to restrain their baser instincts and restrain their unhealthy carnal outlets.

WSD:1:9 While disparaging the existing codes, whereby men live, they have neither the ability nor the strength to replace them with anything equally good and worthy. Certainly, whatever they did produce would never tend towards the spiritual elevation of mankind. Such as these must not be pandered to and, if they refuse to bear their fair share of the burdens of mankind, they should not be humoured. Those who seek to assert their individuality at the expense of others are a menace not to be tolerated. The rule shall be that everyone is to be granted the greatest possible freedom up to, but not beyond, the point where it infringes upon the freedom, rights or contentment of others. It is impossible to give complete freedom to any man, and no man is worthy of it. Any freedom attained at the expense of another man is an unworthy freedom.

WSD:1:10 No man has the right to condemn a moral code or standard of principles until he himself has risen above them. No laws, no principles and no code should be discarded until they have been replaced by something proven to be better. The replacement of those already established anywhere is no easy task and one certainly far beyond the experience and ability of any one person. Therefore, in the present condition and development of mankind, goodness and righteousness are expressed by the disciplined acceptance of the moral law and courageous submission to the written law. These must, however, evolve with man, to meet his changing and greater needs.

WSD:1:11 An evil custom or law is to be cast aside, even though it be established and accepted by many generations. A good custom or law should be taken over and followed, even if it be observed by your enemies and followed by them. The decision as to what is good and what is bad cannot lie within the province of any one man.

WSD:1:12 Laws are made, and laws are changed, but no man truly knows what is right and what is wrong. This can be discovered only in the inspired books compiled by the hands of illuminated men. The time is not far distant when men should no longer think in terms of being good or wicked, rich or poor, sick or healthy, but in terms of being spiritual or material.

WSD:1:13 The basic motive behind a righteous and good life is not the quest for happiness. Righteousness, goodness and morality are other words meaning self-discipline, duty, obligation and service. These form a foundation, upon which a proper way of life can be built, and within the framework of this foundation, the quest for happiness is certainly not restricted. Indeed, not only is it encouraged but also earnestly urged.

WSD:1:14 Nearly everyone has principles of some sort, but all have a tendency to push back the frontiers of these principles to suit themselves. Their idea of morality is subordinated to their material interests. Men should not be hypocrites with themselves and should freely admit to this tendency to subordinate their principles to their own selfish interests. A standard of morality or code of principles which is not absolute and unshakable is worthless as a support and no standard at all. Only the very wisest of men can set their own standards, and the wisest of men are too wise to do so.

WSD:1:15 As far as man is concerned, the purpose of life is development and preparation for something greater. This cannot be undertaken in a half-hearted manner or at specific times; it is a process continuing every minute of the day. Every test confronting man here is purposeful and necessary, even though its reason and end may be obscure.

WSD:1:16 The measure of the duties, obligations and service demanded from any man is dependent upon the strength, talents and possessions, which have been bestowed upon him. The more a man has, the stronger he is, so must the returns be in proportion, for he is that much better able to serve. Every man has been given according to the extent of the service expected from him.

WSD:1:17 One of the less easy tasks for the enlightened man is to develop the ability to genuinely assess the service to be rendered in return for the things, with which he has been endowed, and to serve without selfish hesitation. Each man has his particular place in the ranks of those who serve, and his own talents and possessions should be regarded only as a means of enlarging the pool of common good and the advancement of mankind. Those who deny their obligations inflict a lonely, awful doom upon themselves.

WSD:1:18 As the weakness and faltering of any one man lessen the total of service rendered and retard the advance, it becomes the obligation of the strong to protect the weak, not in order that they should be shielded from things leading to their ultimate good, or to carry a burden they decline, but to help them towards the attainment of strength. The aim should always be towards increasing the total amount of strength and ability at the disposal of the whole.

WSD:1:19 Suffering and affliction are unavoidable if man is to develop into the godlike being intended. He must grow spiritually strong, possessing both courage and compassion, and, to do this, he cannot be protected from suffering and affliction. Can the over-sheltered plant kept indoors withstand either the sun's heat or the windy blast? Compassion was awakened in the heart of man only through suffering, and the noble qualities of courage and dedication were roused only through affliction. Those who, in the past, bore their suffering with fortitude became uplifting examples to their fellowmen.

WSD:1:20 However, it must be remembered that pain and suffering do not, of themselves, develop spirituality. They are not so important, but what is important is the manner, in which they are endured, the spirited rising to the challenge and the courageous conquest. The suffering of each man should be an offering dedicated to the uplifting of mankind.

WSD:1:21 What any man has to face and overcome is unimportant. What really matters is how he faces it and by what means he overcomes it. Where a man stands is also unimportant, the important thing is the direction, in which he is moving. Life on Earth was never meant to be spent in rest and tranquillity. Its very tribulations and problems give it an added zest for those brave spirits who face up to them with courage and cheerfulness. Each man must discover for himself his own weaknesses and frailty.

WSD:1:22 The Creating Divinity could have brought a painless world into being, but it would also have been one without purpose. It could have been peopled with perfect beings, but these could not have understood the meaning of suffering and tribulation. They would have been devoid of pity, tenderness and sympathetic understanding.

WSD:1:23 It is not through the Divine Will that man suffers. The Divine Will is that man fulfil the Divine Plan through learning to overcome the restrictions and illusions of a material existence by rising above them. The troubles and trials are there to goad man on, to stimulate him, to rouse him out of material lethargy and urge him towards the development of spirituality and wisdom. If man suffers unduly, it is because of his own heedlessness and waywardness, his ignorance of the true meaning and purpose of life.

WSD:1:24 The Earth is imperfect because its imperfections are essential. The social imperfections, as distinct from the natural imperfections, are the result of man's lack of understanding and his dedication to material ends rather than spiritual ones. The trials and tests resulting from the natural imperfections of Earth do not oppress man nearly as much as the afflictions man has brought upon himself, through seeking to establish a life wholly within the material. It is necessary to know the difference between the two and to separate one from the other.

WSD:1:25 The reason that there is so little divine intervention is not that The Divine remains indifferent, but that man has been given all the powers and wisdom necessary to deal with the affairs of Earth. If he fails to make use of them, who then is to blame? The duty and obligation placed upon man relate to his reaching upward towards spirituality and outward towards perfection. If man declines to do this, he must accept the consequences and can blame none but himself.

WSD:1:26 Were there no pain and suffering, man would be like a jellyfish drifting aimlessly with the currents in a sea of matter. Suffering, pain and sorrow result from an existence within a material body and are not a part of man's spiritual heritage. The bonds of humanity are forged in the furnaces of life and not in its tranquil breezes.

WSD:1:27 These are the directions for those who follow the Great Path of the True Way, the never failing guides and sustainers: Be grateful for the good things of life. Be patient under suffering and steadfast in adversity. Be diligent in the performance of your duty, and never shirk your obligations. Bear the blows of affliction with cheerfulness and courage. Do not be quick to anger, hasty to argue or rash in judgement, for this reveals your lack of self-control. Avoid the weaknesses of unjust hate and envy, for they rebound upon yourself. Do not engage in undue frivolity, lest people come to think you petty-minded. Keep your temper under control, for an angry person is a confused one. Let your deportment be serene and confident. Keep your mind above earthly things, and look towards the Kingdom of the Spirit and Mansions of the Soul. Never pay homage to evil men, and never commend what is wrong.

WSD:1:28 Do not use lewd expressions or foul language, for this advertises your inferiority to others. Do not laugh at sly or dirty humour, for this displays an unclean and unhealthy mind. Do not raise money or possessions to the status of a god. Fit yourself to earn an honest and useful livelihood. Skill and knowledge are jewels in times of prosperity, a sword and shield in times of adversity, and sure guides through times of uncertainty.

WSD:1:29 In the midst of material illusion, do not add to the confusion by acting falsely in word or deed. Be diligent and consistent in studying the wisdom contained within these books. Never forget the benefits that accrue from a life well led, and remember that whatever befalls is intended for your own good. If a man, establish yourself by your manliness and, if a woman, by your femininity.

WSD:1:30 Be modest in manner and calm in bearing, for men avoid the excitable man who is a weak reed to lean upon in times of stress and a hazard in danger. The boastful man falls far short of the image he intends to create, so weigh your words carefully, for the spoken word cannot be recalled. A man careless with words is also unreliable in other ways. Never make a confident of one who babbles.

WSD:1:31 Forget what has been done and cannot be altered, and do not be concerned about things, which may never happen. If you have anything of value, keep it away from an envious man. Arise early in the morning, and greet the day eagerly, for the sluggard and lieabed are already partially dead. Eat and drink in moderation, taking sufficient for the wellbeing of the body without overloading it. Seek the company of those who are your superiors in wisdom, skill and spirituality, so that you will be raised up to prosper. Always be ready to heed advice and to accept instruction, bearing in mind that it is more profitable to listen than to talk.

WSD:1:32 The man who cannot restrain his tongue rides a wild stallion. Keep it in check, and avoid returning a hasty answer to those who say unkind things, which may stem only from their own weakness. Be patient and forbearing under provocation, and restrain your arm when tempted to raise it in anger. The man who remains unmoved under provocation is a better man than he who strikes. Always speak calmly and with few words.

Speak softly and clearly, for only fools shout to cover their own ignorance. The ox bellows, while the bull snorts.

WSD:1:33 One of the great failures of life is to lose a friend. If this misfortune befall a man, he should search his heart carefully and sincerely, lest it happen again. Never seek to maintain a friendship through hypocrisy or flattery, for this is no friendship, and it displays the double heart of a deceiver.

WSD:1:34 Be proud but not haughty, straight-talking but not insulting. Bold but not aggressive, patient but not servile. Bear in mind that it is better for a man to be numbered among the insulted than among the insulters, among the slandered and not among the slanderers.

WSD:1:35 Keep your feet firmly upon the Great Path of the True Way, using moderation in all things as your guiding light. Never be effusive of speech or too friendly towards those who are no more than acquaintances. Keep all at arms length until they have established themselves for what they are and their true natures are revealed. Never allow the secrets of your heart to be handed around as common property.

WSD:1:36 Do not be over-sensitive and ever ready to take offence, for this will only turn people against you. Never trespass upon the privacy of others, and let all follow the paths of their inclinations. Attend to your own affairs, and keep your thoughts from the affairs of others.

WSD:1:37 Of thoughts, words and deeds, only deeds have any established value on Earth. Thoughts are intangible things in a world of matter, while words have no meaning unless translated into action.

WSD:1:38 Goodness and wisdom should not be secreted, for when their possessor cuts himself off from others, what purpose do they serve and how can they be measured and tested? The good man who fears contamination by the world has no confidence in his goodness and renders no service. If a man is found sinking into a morass of mud, he who tries to rescue him cannot be rescued by anyone standing off. The man who attempts to clean up the morals of the people is like the dusting cloth which cleans only by becoming soiled itself.

Chapter Two – The Dispensations of Life

WSD:2:1 If visited by affliction or sorrow a man should not bewail his loss, for these should be the means of drawing him closer into the embrace of Divinity. They are meant to strengthen his spirit and develop his spirituality. No man has any right to expect an untroubled life, and one who has passed half a year without trouble or affliction has already received ample reward for living and should not ask for more. Sorrow is the purging agent of the spirit and suffering the flux merging man with Divinity. They also help to distinguish purelove from mock-love, for purelove is the unquenchable fire, which the waters of tribulation cannot put out.

WSD:2:2 A man should always be prepared for testing and never be caught off guard, for calamity may well strike in the midst of prosperity and peace. He should also bear in mind while undergoing his test, that at any time it may be eased by a stroke of good fortune.

WSD:2:3 After every calamity, a man should review the words he has spoken and the things he has done, for perhaps what has befallen him is only the result of incautious words or the outcome of foolish deeds. Chastisement is a necessity of earthly life. If it did not follow a wrongdoing, how could a child ever learn the difference between right and wrong? The chastisements of men spring from Divine Love alone, for through suffering comes sympathy and through tribulation comes understanding. The man who can cheerfully accept affliction, knowing its true purpose, is one who has learned one of the deepest secrets of life. No man is afflicted beyond his endurance, for the cold blasts of calamity are always tempered to his weakness. Only the strong and chosen are called upon to carry the heavy burdens, for the strong runner does not care if the wind is against him.

WSD:2:4 If trials and tribulations descend upon a man, he should meet them with quiet resolution and courage. It is useless to rage against them or seek to rise in revolt against his lot. Only the faint-hearted and ignorant are turned from the Path because they think their endurance may be in vain. The righteousness and goodness of a man will not protect him from suffering and may even add to it. The fruits of his labour are not plucked along the road, which lies this side of the border. How often is a man seen bewailing his misfortune and so sorry for himself that he fails to gain any benefit from it? All too often, men take their misfortunes as a sign that they are abandoned.

WSD:2:5 Men set their hearts on certain things and make plans for their attainment, but unless the plans they make complement the Divine Plan, they will come to nothing. Earth has a mission, and everything upon it is there to play its part in the fulfilment of that mission. Material ends have little importance beside spiritual ends, and creation is only intended to satisfy spiritual needs and develop spiritual abilities.

WSD:2:6 The good and the wicked are tested, and no one is exempt. The difference is that the righteous man uses the tests to benefit himself, while the unrighteous turns them against himself to destroy his own soul. No man should be overwhelmed by the troubles and tribulations, which come upon him. They are intended to be utilised for the benefit of his soul and the strengthening of his spirit, and, bearing this in mind, he should be better able to endure them.

WSD:2:7 Every man is born to be tested and tried. Sorrow and suffering, problems and tribulations, are meant to be the lot of men. Yet, they are never his continued lot, and the brighter moments of life far outweigh the darker. Man was not given life for the sole purpose of enjoying Earth and its pleasures. Earth is a place man must cultivate and prepare for harvest, and what he produces will be his sustenance when the season is ended. Tribulation is his plough, and trouble his spade. Sorrow and suffering are his seeds, and the joys of life the fertilising waters.

WSD:2:8 Be grateful for the good things of life, for they far exceed your needs. Offer a prayer of thanks in the morning and another in the evening, and if you can find no reason for doing so, be certain the fault lies within yourself. Even to know that the worst possible thing has happened, and the cup of misfortune been drained to its last drop, brings a strange compensation, for there is a deep peace of mind known only to those who have lost all and cannot lose more.

WSD:2:9 If a man is favoured with prosperity, he should be vigilant, lest it permit his desires to lead him astray and his spiritual diligence be diminished. In the greater scheme of things, the times of affliction and adversity are not to be feared so much, for then, men incline towards spiritual things. It is in times of prosperity, when they acquire wealth and become conceited and self-centred, that the danger lies, for then they twist the commanding words and austere meanings of the sacred books and pervert them to console their own consciences. Therefore, in times of prosperity and contentment, a man must be more careful in the interpretation of the Sacred Books than he would be when he only turned to them for strength and consolation.

WSD:2:10 The intelligent man observes the ways of Nature and the forces she utilises. He learns how they operate, so that he does not become the slave of blind forces beyond his control. Those who do not understand the workings of natural forces, or are overawed by them, become their slaves. This is a place where nothing is seen clearly, and even Truth can be distinguished only against a background of contrasting falsity.

WSD:2:11 The dispensations of life are not entirely beyond the understanding of man, and indeed he has a duty to strive for understanding. Everything serves a purpose, even things, which seem the most hurtful. Every ungainly rock has, within itself, a potential statue, and potential beauty lies in every block of wood or lump of clay, but what is there cannot come out of its own volition. The image and the beauty are brought out only after the untouched materials have been subjected to the discipline of thought and the forming action of chisel, knife or fire. According to the good things done by a man, so will he be rewarded, and by the nature of the evil he does, so will he be punished. A man is paid according to his labour, and idle hands make a hungry mouth.

Chapter Three – The Harmonious Life

WSD:3:1 Whatever is wrong on Earth is wrong with man. The discord among men comes from within themselves and not from their environment, and it is in his relationship with others that man displays his deficiencies and weaknesses most clearly. Hypocrisy is one of the most deep-rooted evils in the natures of men, for they hate in others the things they fear in themselves. The man who is the most voluble against a particular form of vice is the man who practises it in secret. Men wrap themselves in a mantle of hypocrisy and never uncover their real selves. They declare themselves for or against; they say they believe one thing or the other; they like this or that, but rarely do they declare themselves truthfully or reveal their true thoughts and feelings to others. To overcome this evil, this weakness in men, is one of mankind's greatest battles. To this, the Good Religion must dedicate itself.

WSD:3:2 Those who follow the Good Religion should seek their friends among others of similar belief and inclination, and they should not try to walk a double road. No man can hide a thing within his breast forever, and if he is a secret hypocrite, some day it will be made known. Nothing done, known or experienced during earthly life is lost forever.

WSD:3:3 If your neighbour offend you, then restrain your anger so that your spirit may be benefited. Burdens borne patiently and with courage, and insults ignored, are better for the spirit than any form of penance. Always restrain your anger for the sake of neighbourly harmony, but for your own good, remember that the words of an angry man are like glowing embers in his mouth. Anger alone does no great harm to the spirit, but anger with malice or hatred certainly blemishes the purity of a soul.

WSD:3:4 Never try to appease a man in the hour of his anger, but leave him to be consumed in his own fire. Before you vent your anger on a man who has offended you, pause and try to discover some goodness in him, which you lack. It is not required that a person never get angry or become stirred up inside, for sometimes circumstances demand the response of righteous anger. Therefore, be one slow to anger and with complete mastery over the temper, rather than one without the ability to be stirred to anger. Do not be too sweet unless you want to be eaten. When two persons quarrel in anger, both are always in the wrong.

WSD:3:5 The most burdensome person in any community is the one who will not do what he is capable of doing because he cannot do the things he wants to do. Every man must learn the difference between the little things he can do alone and the greater things, which can be done with the cooperation of others, for unity bestows strength.

WSD:3:6 Always be generous in your dealings with a neighbour and bear in mind that as water quenches fire, so does cheerful restitution atone for a wrong. When a neighbour greets you cheerfully, answer him in the same manner, for a surly face or a frown frightens away the hand of friendship. Generosity and kind-heartedness are excellent qualities, but those who possess them should be vigilant, for it is not inconceivable that the goodness they do may sometimes result in more evil than good.

WSD:3:7 Always treat the property of your neighbour or his friends as you would wish your own property and friends to be treated. Never speak without thought, for words cannot be recalled and things said may remain beyond recall forever. A lightly spoken word may ruin a life or destroy the contentment of a family. The guiding rule is not only to say the right thing in the right place, but also to leave unsaid the wrong thing at the moment when it is most tempting to utter it. This is the rule of conversation: Is it true, is it instructive, is it kind, is it necessary?

WSD:3:8 Do not be crude in speech or rough in manner, for these reveal a hidden weakness. Courtesy, consideration and good manners are necessary ingredients in the cement of neighbourliness. The cement of friendship is mutual suffering.

WSD:3:9 A man should never talk to a woman in a manner, which would outrage her modesty, but common women have sacrificed their modesty and cannot be outraged. Therefore, the manner of a man's speech in the presence of a woman indicates his opinion of her and her reputation. Always be vigilant when in the company of women, for no greater insult can be offered to a man than to imply that his wife, mother, daughter or sister is a common woman. A strong man can afford to be gentle and quiet wherever he is, but a weak man must be rough and boastful to boost himself. The man who is always boosting himself is certainly one who needs boosting.

WSD:3:10 If some misfortune has befallen a neighbour, or he is out of favour with the rulers, he will be suffering the miseries of shame, and therefore to visit him under these circumstances might add to it. It is a matter of discretion and tact as to when he should be visited. Whatever he has done, treat him with kindness and consideration. The fruits of kindness are sweet, but the fruits of hatred and malice lie heavily on the stomach. As surely as night follows day, as a man deals with others, so will he be dealt with.

WSD:3:11 If a man does not wish his own possessions to be touched, he should show the same respect for the possessions of another man. Likewise, if he respects his own reputation and expects others to respect it also, he should hold the reputation of others in the same high regard. If he does not wish to become the subject of gossip, he should not gossip about anyone else.

WSD:3:12 As a man expects his own home and family to be treated, so should he treat the home and family of another. As he cherishes the good name of his wife and the welfare of his children, so should he cherish the good name of another's wife and the welfare of his children.

WSD:3:13 Deal charitably with your neighbours, and wherever the opportunity to do good arises, do not hesitate to do it. However, a single act of charity means that the heart has been stirred only once. It may be just a sudden urge that passes, and charity is a continuing process.

WSD:3:14 A man can find peace and happiness in his home only when his wife and family have it, and these things cannot be portioned out. The man with strife at home has a lot more misery than that of a hungry dog. When a guest, bear in mind that the ways of a host are always right in the eyes of his guest.

WSD:3:15 Always live according to your beliefs, for to do otherwise is hypocrisy. One of the tasks of the Good Religion is to teach men that they have to bridge the great gap between what they believe to be right and the way they live. Also, though many men know how they should live very few do in fact live that way.

WSD:3:16 Though it is proper for a man to marry early, it is not right to marry with undue haste. For a man to take a wife before he can support her, or before he can understand her, is foolishness. The man who takes a wife in unwise haste ties a millstone around his own neck and can blame none but himself for the consequences. A man should never take a wife until he has read through the Sacred Books many times.

WSD:3:17 Stand firm in your belief as to what is right and what is wrong. Never surrender your principles or betray your ideals. Yet, do not let your mind become bigoted or prejudiced, for the man of unchanging mind is as water, which, standing still, becomes stagnant and filled with slime. His thoughts are like water imprisoned within a vase until it becomes foul.

WSD:3:18 Tact and self-control, the exercise of moderation in all things and a disciplined ambition with attainable aim, a kind heart and truthful tongue, these are the things, which smooth the way along the path of life. The maggots that eat away the body of peace and contentment are: undue haste, thoughtlessness, indifference and malice.

WSD:3:19 Do not be unduly afraid of being poor. It is better to have only a few possessions with just sufficient to maintain the health of the body, than to have vitality-sapping and spiritual-enervating abundance of the rich. Happiness cannot be bought, and a joyful heart makes a healthy body. Pure love, not wealth, is the most desirable of treasures, for it hallows the brief days of life and fills them to overflowing with spiritual wealth of everlasting value.

WSD:3:20 Along the high road of life, man and woman must walk together hand in hand. The two together are meant to make their joint love a harmonious whole, and the life of one without the other is incomplete. Yet in these times, true matrimonial harmony appears to be one of the most difficult things to achieve, because of the spiritual immaturity resulting from the inadequacy of existing religious doctrines. This, too, must be remedied.

WSD:3:21 Do not be too hasty in judging a wrongdoer, for it may well be that though he has been found in some wickedness, the good in him is greater than the good in you. Perhaps in the Divine View, he is a better man than you are. Disobedience to the laws of men with the sincere and considered intention of doing good, is better than abject submission to them without any such motive.

WSD:3:22 The golden rule of harmonious living is that a man must master his desires, control his will and serve his conscience.

Chapter Four – Defects of Character

WSD:4:1 The man who talks much does so to cover his own weakness. Words, of themselves, are worthless things and where there is much talk there is little action. Words alone are lifeless things having no value until they are quickened within the heart and demonstrated in deeds. Therefore, the rule is never to engage in idle chatter and always to avoid the company of those who babble.

WSD:4:2 Those who find pleasure in chattering and gossip display the outward signs of a small and irresponsible mind. Those who sow mischief with their tongue can be assured that they will reap the harvest of scorn. Speech is one of the qualities, which set men apart from the animals, but it is also a drug to be handled with care. Therefore, treat all words as an apothecary does the drugs of a prescription. They must be carefully measured out and weighed, with every precaution taken against an overdose.

WSD:4:3 Over-indulgence in talk displays a defect of character. Therefore, even when praising another or lauding his virtue, excessive talk should be avoided, lest the speaker be accused of hypocrisy or patronage. Effusive speech is the babbling water flowing over a shallow mind. Nothing is more becoming for the intelligent man than silence, and how much more so for one who is not!

WSD:4:4 The motto for those who follow the Good Religion should be: 'Say little, and do much. Replace words with deeds.' The good will find this no hardship, but the wicked will prefer talk to action. The mouth of a man is like a horse; it must be restrained by firm control and bridled before it can serve him. If allowed out of control it will carry him off to calamity. Therefore, guard your tongue as you would your wealth, bearing in mind that the less the words spoken the less the errors made.

WSD:4:5 Though all the wisdom of the past condemns overindulgence in chatter, this still grows in volume, while the ills of the world do not lessen, though they may change in nature. Therefore, if you would serve the Good Religion well, hold your tongue in check. Do not overlook it in youth, then in maturity, it may pour out wisdom, which will advance the greater cause of mankind.

WSD:4:6 Words are the weapons, which give power to falsehood and equip the liar. Lying and deceit are the defects of character, which most reveal its underlying weakness. The earthly punishment of a liar is in the fact that nobody believes him when he eventually speaks the truth, but he condemns himself to greater punishment in the realm of the spirit.

WSD:4:7 Lack of hospitality displays the defects of meanness. Therefore, always be hospitable to the wayfarer and stranger, treating them fairly and with consideration. Do not cheat them or betray their trust and confidence in you, for this is the action of a mean nature. Those who are mean or who lead others into meanness cannot avoid a blemished soul.

WSD:4:8 Few are those who recognise their own defects and fewer still those who honestly acknowledge them. Even less in number are those who earnestly strive to overcome them, though this is an essential part of life's purpose. Most are hypocrites and self-deceivers whose regeneration commences only when they honestly search their hearts and discover what they actually are within themselves.

WSD:4:9 One of the greatest defects of character is sheer indifference and lack of interest in anything beneficial and useful. A man can gain wisdom and enlightenment only when he has laboured at reading and diligently studied the Sacred Books. Casual thinking about higher things and reading for amusement or pleasure produce no beneficial effect and serve no useful purpose.

WSD:4:10 The man who is dominated by passion and is the slave of his desires is one whose character is weak. He can serve nothing greater than an earthly end. To serve the Good Religion, a man has to rise above this end, and the means for so doing, the reason and purpose, is the revelation contained within the Sacred Books.

WSD:4:11 The man of defective character seeks to live at the expense of others and does not pull his weight. He takes and does not give; he is a parasite on the body of mankind. Therefore, bear in mind that he who eats from the produce of his own hands is contented in heart and refreshed in spirit. But when eating, do not bring discord to the table or consume food while flies swarm or a dog stands by hungry.

WSD:4:12 Throughout the lands of the old religions, people complain that they have little to live for, but it would be more true to say that they have nothing to die for. They can see no purpose in life, but the truth is they can see no purpose in death. They complain they do not have enough to sustain them in death. The existing religions grow old and weak, not through age, for a religion sustained by Truth is ageless, but through lack of Truth which is the food of good faith. They cannot give sustenance, which provides strength to deal with the times, but the food of the Good Religion must still be withheld from men, for its day remains deep within the womb of time.

WSD:4:13 In these times men lack the strength of character to seek fame, and seek notoriety instead, but this is no more than fame's horribly distorted image. Men are deficient in the qualities, which should spur them to seek fame through service and sacrifice. They lack the driving force and inspiration, which should come from their national spirit. The fertile fields of inspiration are now overgrown with weeds, and the refreshing waters of spirituality are stagnant. The sun of a new inspiration, the dawn of a new day of hope will surely follow this night of darkness. Then, mankind will surge forward once again to storm the spiritual heights, bearing a new standard, a new banner with the device of spiritual inspiration.

WSD:4:14 Pride is a quality of good; false pride and haughtiness are servants of evil. The man who has no pride in himself as a man is weak in character, and this weakness leads him into error and wrongdoing. When a man is without a standard to live by and holds himself in low esteem, any wickedness he does will not appear wrong to him. The laws of men punish the sickness and ills within the nations, but do not cure them. The precepts and moral code of the Good Religion are the medicines needed to prevent and cure; their day will come. If a man is more concerned about what others may think of him than about what he knows himself to be, if he fears their judgement more than his own, then he knows the worthlessness of his own opinion. Man must be made to stand proud in his strength of character and moral integrity. The duty of religion is to make such a man.

WSD:4:15 To be good, a man must not only live a good life; he must also do good deeds. These should not be only such as come his way or result from his inclinations, they must also be the result of effort, search and sacrifice. Doing good when the opportunity arises is not sufficient, for real merit results only from a hard-fought battle with evil.

WSD:4:16 The man of sound character bestirs himself in the cause of good and diligently studies the Sacred Books, to know what is required of him. He accepts with good grace the tasks imposed upon him and does not shirk his duties and obligations. He does not try to interpret the words of the Sacred Books in such a way that things are made easier for him. He does not treat their command lightly, neither does he shun the service they require from him. He knows that no matter how hard he strives, they can still lead him on towards greater perfection. No man is asked to be perfect; he is asked only to strive towards perfection with all his heart and strength.

WSD:4:17 No man can ever be a failure if he strives to do his duty and undertakes all the things he should. But if he turns his back on his duty and shirks his obligations, he is always a failure. A man who seeks to boost himself by displaying his cleverness is like a commander who reveals all the secrets of his defence. He lays himself open to easy conquest.

WSD:4:18 The defects of character are many and varied, but before they can be overcome, they must be discovered. The words written here can be no more than a mirror, which is handed to you. Whether you look at the mere reflection of yourself, or whether you look with deeper insight and understanding, does itself depend upon the nature of your own character. The defects of a defective character may conceal its own deficiencies from itself, but they cannot remain hidden if sought in the light of Wisdom and Truth.

Chapter Five – Within Your Home

WSD:5:1 Though your house is your domain and the stronghold of your privacy, keep it open for acts of charity. Do not close its doors to one in trouble, but let all who need it enter and find sympathy. Let your house be open to receive the widow and the orphan.

WSD:5:2 Maintain your house as a place of contentment and happiness, permitting all members to have their say without interruption or suppression. Uphold its sanctity and the sanctity of your family, whatever befalls, bearing in mind that no sacrifice in doing so is too great. If the sanctity of your home or family has been betrayed or destroyed, do not be passive, for by doing so, you induce the same calamity to fall upon another.

WSD:5:3 Your home is the stronghold of your privacy and ideals, and it enshrines the gentleness of your wife and the modesty of your daughters. Therefore, do not permit it to be invaded by the tongues of lewdness, or allow its air to be polluted by the breath of the foul-mouthed. The man who does so displays his lack of pride and the low esteem, in which he holds his family. If you hear lewdness in the privacy of a man's house, know that he is a weak character whose family is to be pitied.

WSD:5:4 Within your house is your home, and this is the life and spirit of the house. Maintain your home as a hallowed place where all that is finest in mankind remains enshrined. Do not argue except to instruct, and do not chastise without understanding and good intent. Never break the peace of the table, for food should always be consumed in tranquillity and without haste.

WSD:5:5 It is the nature of children to be boisterous and get into mischief, so the good parent tempers discipline with understanding and tolerance. The good parent is never unduly harsh, but neither is he lax and indifferent to the need for discipline. The proper discipline for a child is maintained through example and guidance, not through chastisement. When the need arises to punish a child, never do so without asking yourself where you have failed. If you care enough for the child, you will be diligent in your heart-searching.

WSD:5:6 An unhappy marriage is always the result of haste, thoughtlessness or lack of consideration by both or one. No child should ever suffer for the foolishness or ignorance of a parent, and when dealing with a child, this must be the governing rule. While no one can claim happiness as a birthright, every child brought into the world is entitled to all the happiness possible and all the pleasures of childhood.

WSD:5:7 The sun of a man's home is his wife, but he who takes an unchaste woman to wife is one content to live without the warmth of inspiration. The man whose wife lacks the womanly virtues becomes a prisoner to his own shame, and his house a place of discord and unrest. A faithful wife crowns her husband with a garland of happiness, but the wife who deceives her husband is like a cancer within his heart waiting to erupt.

WSD:5:8 Within his home a man is king, and his wife is queen. No stranger should be permitted to trespass on the domain of their happiness, and prying officials should rightly be excluded. Even those who seek to uphold the laws of men shall not force entry, but all worthy men will deal with them honourably and justly.

Chapter Six – The Treatment of Women

WSD:6:1 No man shall be intimate with a woman during the time of her courses, for this brings about a subtle pollution. However, a man may go with a woman after her cleansing without any fear, for this thing stems from the nature of women and is not uncleanliness. Yet it is to be borne in mind that the sufferings of women at such times are not part of their nature, but a sign of their past failure to maintain the purity of the fountain of life.

WSD:6:2 A man's wife is his own pasture, wherein he may enter as he wills, but he never should be insensitive to her own feelings, for an inconsiderate husband reaps a poor harvest. A wife must not be subjected to harshness, but should be treated with tenderness and affection. She is deserving of consideration, for her feelings are not those of a loose woman, whom men have treated as they willed.

WSD:6:3 Always treat a woman with reserve and respect, for by doing so, you enhance your own standing as a man. It is the men without pride in themselves who hold women in low esteem, and women who submit to such men take a perverted pleasure in their own degradation. When all a man seeks in the company of a woman is frivolity and amusement, he will in the end seek to use her as an instrument of fornication. The wise man keeps well away from the chattering woman, for life with her would be like living at the foot of a sandhill.

WSD:6:4 Every man who follows the Good Religion will treat women with respect and consideration. He will never attempt the seduction of a decent woman, for chastity is the pure blossom of womanhood. Without it, a woman is like a garden tree that never blooms, and she fails to inspire rapture in the heart of any man.

WSD:6:5 Long ages have taught many subtle lessons, and one is that married to a decent woman, a man tends to become better. Married to an unchaste or faithless woman he tends to become lewd, harsh, inconsiderate and rude. The man who is willing to take an unchaste woman to wife gets just what such as he deserves.

WSD:6:6 Therefore, treat those who may become the wives of other men as you would want your own waiting wife to be treated. Bear in mind the ancient words of wisdom, which have stood the test of time, and choose a wife with care. Fortunate indeed is he who unearths the treasure of a virtuous woman, for her value is beyond estimation in earthly wealth. The heart of her husband rests on a bed of contentment, and he sleeps secure in her constancy. She will never cause him to bow his head in sorrow when men speak of women, or to turn his face in shame from the mocking glances of other men.

WSD:6:7 The intelligent man does not maintain his wife in idleness, lest her thoughts stray towards scandal and gossip. When the light of the Good Religion is revealed, it will set the good woman apart from others, and man need no longer walk in doubt.

WSD:6:8 The good woman has pity on the destitute poor, but is not deceived by the wiles of the idle beggarmen. Her children are brought up in the knowledge of goodness, and they reach maturity in honour and uprightness. No songs on the lips of men extol the virtues of a good wife and mother, but the silent, grateful song in the hearts of her husband and children never ceases. It is the holy melody resounding among the universal spheres.

Chapter Seven – Duties, Obligations and Service to Life

WSD:7:1 If a woman is beautiful and gifted beyond other women, then she has been favoured by The Divine and entrusted with life's greatest treasures. Therefore, she should not conduct herself as other women, for many men will seek after her, and she must be discriminating. Her influence on men can be greater than that of other women, so she must always be conscious of its effect. Does it make them better men, and does it serve the cause of good? The attitude of gifted and beautiful women is of prime interest to those who concern themselves with the spiritual uplifting and advancement of mankind. Unlike the religions that will die, the Good Religion cannot ignore this aspect of life.

WSD:7:2 The beautiful woman, if she be good, is proud of being the guardian of such treasure and safeguards it from polluting hands. She dedicates it to the service of good, which also means the service of mankind. She uses it as a spur and incentive in the upward struggle of man towards divinity. She is more modest and reserved than other women, and as this increases her desirability even more, she is absolutely discreet and prudent in all her activities. Her devotion to the cause of good need entail no more than the maintenance of strict female standards of decency in the face of overwhelming temptation and being a good wife and mother.

WSD:7:3 The fires of passion can rage in woman as they do in man, but when they do, it should be borne in mind that such driving forces are to be used for good and not wasted on an evil outlet. Men and women are not alike, and their duties and obligations in the Divine Design are different, even though they share the same urges and desires. The same water is in the river and the irrigation channel, but the millstone and the growing plant do not utilise it in the same manner. The power, which serves best, serves many different ends.

WSD:7:4 The Divine Design sets man and woman apart and prescribes for each a different form of service. Women are not called upon to be warriors, and men are not intended to bear children. Yet, the differences of man and woman complement one another and, coming together, form a harmonious whole.

WSD:7:5 It is the duty of everyone to study the Sacred Books and to try to understand their deeper meaning. All should learn a skill whereby a useful livelihood be earned, and knowledge and wisdom should be increased day by day. As the purpose of life is to develop spirituality and further the Divine Design, it would be utter foolishness to neglect this. Each person should try, each and every day, to become a better balanced being living a more harmonious life.

WSD:7:6 The obligations of men reach out far and wide, while the obligations of women incline towards the beautification of life and enshrine the virtues. The duties of manhood tend to draw men from home and comfort, while those of womanhood tend to draw women to serve hearth, home and family. Man worships at the altar of duty and obligation, while woman worships at the altar of virtue and service. Both bow before the altars of love.

WSD:7:7 It is the duty of anyone who can to set right what another has done wrongly or in error. No one who has the welfare of mankind at heart can say, "This does not concern me," or, "I have no interest in what another does."

WSD:7:8 Do not neglect the welfare of the sick and aged, for this is an obligation each one bears. Visit those who are ill, for visitors break the loneliness of their days. Enter the sick room cheerfully, as though it were a pleasure, and not as if you were fulfilling an obligation. Be considerate of their circumstances, and do not overstay.

WSD:7:9 Each man should clothe his family decently and feed it according to his means. He should never allow any member of his family to become shabby, unclean or indolent. When something goes wrong within a house, it shall be the head of the house who will answer for it. Though every child is born with certain tendencies, the parents incline them as they will and therefore cannot deny responsibility for what a child becomes. When the child grows up to be a worthy man or woman, parents will often hasten to take credit, but when the child turns out to be a disgrace, they are tardy in accepting responsibility. Yet, the bad is more likely to result from what the parents have done or failed to do, than is the good.

Chapter Eight – Respect for the Rights of Others

WSD:8:1 Do not enter a house other than your own uninvited, and if you have a position of power, do not use it to gain entry into the house of another. Do not enter a house when the occupier is absent, even if it is open. If at any time, you are denied admittance to a house or told to go away, then depart in peace. Only in the interests of justice or peace, or when the safety of another demands it, should the privacy of a home be invaded, and even then only with the greatest restraint and consideration.

WSD:8:2 However, if a house is abandoned or empty, there is no harm done if it is entered for shelter, but it should not be damaged wilfully. Nothing established by the hand of man should be damaged, unless it causes harm or inconvenience, which outweighs its usefulness.

WSD:8:3 When a guest within the house of another, treat his family with respect and his possessions with care. If you damage anything belonging to him, make proper and full restitution. When in the house of a friend, under no circumstances, touch a woman of his family improperly or show disrespect for her modesty by word or gesture. Note the way a man conducts himself in his own home, for this reveals not only his own character but also the character of his womenfolk.

WSD:8:4 If a man greets you with courtesy, then answer him in the same manner, for surliness displays a weakness of character. If a man in difficulty seeks your aid, cheerfully grant him whatever assistance you can. If advice or information is yours to give, do not withhold it when requested, but never press advice upon another.

WSD:8:5 Respect the rights and dignity of the poor, for they may have little else. Those who help the poor or needy with gifts or benefits, knowing they cannot be repaid, are not without gain when their life is enlarged. Receive all comers with a happy smile, and do not look downcast when giving something away; otherwise, you set the gift at nought.

WSD:8:6 Though freedom is the birthright of every man and one of the ideals, which must be upheld, when it infringes upon the freedom of another man, it ceases to be genuine. Therefore, before you talk about your own freedom or rights, consider the freedom and rights of others, for if you are truly good, their freedom and rights are the most important. However, if others come seeking to diminish your freedom and rights by force or legislation, without conferring a benefit of equal value in return, they are to be resisted. But bear in mind that true freedom is another of the sublime qualities unattainable on Earth, where, though man may aspire to it, and must, it is restricted by earthly conditions requiring service, duty and obligation.

WSD:8:7 To be truly free, man must rise above his mortality and become divine. To attain true freedom, he must travel a road of many tollgates, and at each, payment is demanded from his own supply of freedom's gold. Freedom, like perfection, goodness and justice, is an end man must strive for, but he must also realise that its attainment lies beyond the realm of mortal limitations. Like the other divine qualities here on Earth, it is best understood by contrast.

WSD:8:8 Duty, obligation and service are the three inescapable elements of life. On the road to divinity, they are the three burdens, which have to be carried every step of the way. They cannot, of course, be without purpose and so are also the great stimulants, without which man cannot be sustained in his ascent. Take them away, and man slides backwards towards the low ground of the brute beasts which have no awareness of them.

Chapter Nine – People and Places to Avoid

WSD:9:1 Avoid all places and people, which conduce to evil. Keep away from hypocrites, for, having a common feeling of degradation, they will congregate together, and it would be unwise to be numbered among them. Hypocrites tend towards evil because they serve its purpose and, therefore having an affinity with it, they turn away from what is good and just. They are hard-fisted when the poor come discreetly seeking for alms, but are open-handed when approached in a public place. Surely the hypocrite must be the lowest form of man or woman!

WSD:9:2 If you meet a stranger who appears to be filled with extraordinary virtues, or who conducts himself with grace and good manners, do not hastily conclude that this is his true character. Go to the place where he lives and is known. Note his attitude towards his family and behaviour among friends, and listen to what is said about him. Only then will you be in a better position to judge and to weigh him in the balances.

WSD:9:3 There are many persons of a hypocritical nature who reveal their true character in one place, but put on a false display of goodness in another. If you accept a man or woman in haste and are deceived, then blame no one except yourself. The man who accepts another at his own valuation usually gets a poor bargain.

WSD:9:4 Avoid those whose natures are shallow or superficial, even though they be attractive and pleasant. Shallow streams sparkle most, and weakest waters make the most pleasant sound. There are many whose understanding of friendship is mere companionship, and they neither seek nor know anything deeper. Such people should not be cultivated beyond acquaintanceship. No man really knows another until he has seen him exposed to danger and loss. Even then, he cannot know him fully until he has seen him when tested by prosperity and success.

WSD:9:5 Avoid those who are seeking to benefit from your friendship; they are not for you. Friendship is a precious plant, which must be nurtured in the good soil of sincerity and trust, and plentifully watered with loyalty and understanding. The man who presumes too much on friendship is unworthy of it.

WSD:9:6 Avoid the loose woman, for even if she is beautiful, it may be just a lure over the pit trap. Do not become snared by your desires or let your eyes drug your wisdom. The man who claps fire to his chest cannot escape unburned, and he who embraces uncleanliness will be soiled, however delicately it is wrapped.

WSD:9:7 Avoid an evil neighbour and a wicked neighbourhood, bearing in mind that a man is judged according to his associations. There are many weak characters who, while not desiring to associate with the wicked or live in their neighbourhood, will do so for benefit or to advance their ends. Unless they are prepared to freely admit their weakness, they are hypocrites.

WSD:9:8 Avoid the places of pleasure, which attract the weak and bad characters, for if you associate with them you cannot expect to remain uncontaminated. Bear in mind that the best person to associate with may not be the best companion; and evil places are generally more alluring than the good.

Chapter Ten – Neighbourly Living

WSD:10:1 When a man holds views directly at variance with those of his neighbours, they are incompatible with harmonious living. He then has to decide whether the right views are held by himself or by his neighbours and, if by his neighbours, he must adjust his own.

WSD:10:2 However, if he sees that the views held by his neighbours are wrong or corrupt and degenerate, and he fears he may fall under their influence, he must depart without delay. He must go to another place where the conduct and outlook of his neighbours will be more congenial and compatible with his. It does not matter how far he has to travel.

WSD:10:3 Where there is no one ready to take command in an emergency, or no one prepared to concern himself with the welfare of the neighbourhood, then strive to be a man worthy of the purpose. Do this even if it means having to neglect some study of the Sacred Books, for the man who serves his neighbourhood well serves the cause of good.

WSD:10:4 As the whole man suffers for the errors of the hand or tongue, so shall the whole congregation of the righteous suffer for the misdeeds of any one of their number. If a member commits a wrongful act, then the others shall put it right. This is so that every man shall have a feeling of responsibility towards the whole, and that the good name and reputation of the whole shall not suffer for the acts of one person.

WSD:10:5 It may be no great wrong if one neighbour gives comfort to another who has committed some misdeed, but if a neighbour aids another in a wrong or covers it for him, he is no better than the wrongdoer. To comfort and to condone are things far apart.

WSD:10:6 Whatever the problems of your neighbourhood, do not isolate yourself from them, for if they concern the welfare of others, they are your concern. Strive to be on friendly terms with all your neighbours, and if you fail, let it not be said that the fault lies with you.

WSD:10:7 If you have a neighbour in need, do not be tardy in going to his assistance. If you are not in a position to help, show that you are not indifferent to his predicament. If a neighbour falls into ill favour with the law of the land, do not set yourself up to judge him. If you cannot say anything in his favour, then hold your peace.

WSD:10:8 The laws of the land and of your neighbourhood should be framed towards the maintenance of peace and security, therefore it is your duty not only to abide by them, but also to uphold them. Good laws do not need enforcing among the good, for their goodness declares itself to all, but oppressive laws chafe upon the neck like a yoke. The goat does not attack the lion, and sometimes bad laws have to be endured with patience for the sake of neighbourly peace. Yet, if the entrance to its hole is threatened, a mouse will not hesitate to attack an elephant, and men are no less courageous.

Chapter Eleven – The Cause and its Champions

WSD:11:1 The greatest cause any man can serve is that divinely designed for him and intended to be his. It is the cause of mankind, which operates within the Divine Design and bears man upward to the very threshold of divinity.

WSD:11:2 In these dark days when many gods wage war among themselves for supremacy and man is divided against himself with the many conflicting beliefs, this cause is voiceless and unchampioned. Yet already, the champion is conceived and lies asleep within the womb of time, awaiting the hour of birth.

WSD:11:3 This champion is the Good Religion now safeguarded and cherished by the devoted few during the ages of its conception. This is the religion, which will some day enter the homes and hearts of a despairing humanity. Enshrining the hopes and aspirations of mankind, it will endow them with life and meaning, so that they can rise with man to the mountain tops of divinity. Only the Good Religion will stand forth and declare that man, given a cause sufficiently great, will be unconquerable.

WSD:11:4 While other beliefs appeal for mercy or aid, or beg forgiveness or seek to appease, declaring man to be weak and pitiful, the Good Religion will come to his aid like a life-giving elixir. Its advent will be the morning star heralding a new, brighter day, and, in the light of that day, man will know himself for what he really is and will do the things he must do. He will then no longer be a child walking in darkness and ignorance, wringing his hands and crying because he is so weak and wicked. He will no longer crawl in the dust of servile humility, begging for mercy or for another to bear the burden of his sins. In the light of the new dawning day, man will be shown what he really is, and the dawn heralds will declare his divinity. Then, from out of the dust long-gathered in the darkness, the new man will arise and stride resolutely forward towards the sunrise.

WSD:11:5 In the days of its awakening, the Good Religion will require leaders, and these will need to be men of exceptional qualities. They will have to devote themselves to its cause without any thought of self-aggrandisement. Many men deceive themselves into thinking their desire for leadership is to benefit others, but in fact, they are really seeking self-esteem and power. Some cannot even see their true incentives or read their innermost thoughts, because of the cloud of hypocrisy, which surrounds them. Such men are not desirable leaders.

WSD:11:6 The path the Good Religion must tread will not be an easy one, and all who follow it will need to dedicate every effort and the last reserves of resourcefulness to its cause. The fainthearted will have no place in it, for a cause so great will need the utmost sacrifice of person and purse.

WSD:11:7 There are men who are vainglorious leaders knowing only outward and superficial values. Many such as these cannot even find the right direction or select the best path for themselves; yet, their vanity and ambition prompt them to presume their qualities of leadership. Still, they may be no more to blame than those who support them and follow a road blindly.

WSD:11:8 When men are half-hearted in a cause or indifferent about the achievement of its objective, they are denied a true leader. If the leader is blind, he and those who follow him will end up in the ditch. The true leader is a man, to whom all who follow him can look up in every way.

WSD:11:9 Where there are no true men capable of worthy leadership, strive to be such a man yourself. Where no one is willing to accept responsibility, or to strive and be worthy of it, then take the initiative yourself. In this, there is no arrogance if you dedicate yourself to service and not self-esteem, if you recognise your own shortcomings and limitations.

WSD:11:10 Leadership and example are essential to the advancement of mankind, and where they are lacking, there is certainly no wrong done in their establishment. The criterion of a good leader is his own integrity and intent.

WSD:11:11 When support is needed for the cause, it will be no betrayal if the infirm, the sick and the incapable remain inactive because of their inability to contribute anything. Their sincerity and moral support may be all they can give. Those who will be blameworthy are the wealthy or those able to serve who seek exemption by excuses. The man who can give most in any way should be forefront; he should not lag behind or be lax in action.

Chapter Twelve – The Good Life

WSD:12:1 Life is not altogether a vale of sorrow, neither is it meant to be a grim, unending struggle. Man is born into the world to make the best possible use of earthly conditions, and this does not mean that effort should be concentrated exclusively on the achievement of spirituality. Things must be kept in the right perspective, and a proper balance achieved. It is unwise to let thoughts dwell exclusively upon the Spiritual Realm, and this was never intended. Only its reality and ultimate attainment should be ever borne in mind.

WSD:12:2 Man is to make the most of conditions as he finds them and get all the happiness he can from life within the framework laid down in the Sacred Books. Not only must he make the best of earthly conditions, but he must also improve them, so that more happiness may be gained. Though this may appear to serve only an earthly end, it is not entirely the case, for in the effort lies the spiritual development. Earthly conditions are not to be accepted passively, for every man has a duty to make some improvement, however slight, upon the earthly state of things.

WSD:12:3 While permitted to seek the greatest amount of happiness, man must bear in mind that the search must not extend beyond the bounds of his duties and responsibilities. When seeking spirituality and knowledge of the Spiritual Realm, man must remember that there are limitations as to what he can experience. The purpose of Earth must, and will, be maintained with all its lack of stability and certainty. No mortal man will ever know for certain what the coming year will bring.

WSD:12:4 The amount of spiritual experience and enlightenment permitted any man is just sufficient not to upset the balance of his life or nullify his earthly existence. This is a fact, which should be clearly understood by those ignorant persons who rail against the lack of divine intervention or guidance. In these times, mankind is not advanced enough for the Divine Veil to be any more withdrawn, and even in the greater light of the Good Religion, it will not be removed. The two realms of spirit and matter, mind and body, must remain separated by a near impassable gulf, which can be spanned only by the utmost effort. When the light of the Good Religion is given to the world, it will not be a world ready to welcome it, or even ready to receive it. The world to which it will come will be a sick, disordered world reluctant to take the medicine, which will restore it to health.

WSD:12:5 In those coming days the desire for the good life will have exceeded its proper bounds and, for many, become the sole objective. It will be a world of spiritual barrenness, a place where discord and disillusion has become lost in a doctrinal wilderness, with nothing more refreshing to offer than the waters of stagnant dogma.

WSD:12:6 What man needs, the Good Religion will be able to offer, but as man is always tardy in accepting what is good for him and seems incapable of diagnosing his own maladies, he is unlikely to recognise the remedy. Perhaps the illness of man will then be too far advanced for the simple cure by herbal potions, and only the agonising knife or cauterising fire will effect it. Meanwhile, wait and watch for the heralds of the dawn.

WSD:12:7 The body of man is perishable and only a speck of dust in the great scheme of things; yet, men believe that the mighty universe was created solely to serve it. Man, the mortal, sadly deludes himself by presuming to think he can bend all Nature to serve his bodily wellbeing. As the fool, seeing trees and mountains shimmering in the waters, thinks their images are dancing for his pleasure, so man, while Nature follows her destined course, believes all her activity is only to gladden his eye and give him pleasure.

WSD:12:8 Nature, like man, is intended to serve an end and purpose, which far exceed any conceivable by mortal flesh alone. Yet it can be said with truth that the eternal universe and boundless Nature exist only to serve man, the greater being. Therefore, this being so, each man has a duty to recognise himself for what he really is and to do all that is required of him. He should strive to improve life, to supply something it lacks, and to leave the world a better place for having passed through it.

WSD:12:9 The man who denies himself harmless pleasure is also a wrongdoer and servant of evil, for such pleasures serve a good purpose and proper end. Happiness is not a thing to be avoided, and enjoyments, which do no harm, are not to be shunned.

WSD:12:10 Desires and ends, which are good should be pursued, but bear in mind that the tree of desire will bear no fruit unless nourished with the waters of effort. Happiness itself is not an undesirable end, but too many pay for it with their contentment and peace.

WSD:12:11 It has been taught that the love of pleasure serves no useful end, and that wisdom comes through pain. This is not true, for the spirit can also develop through pleasure, for otherwise it would be an unjust world. Not all school lessons are unpleasant, though all should be rewarding.

WSD:12:12 It is none-the-less true that of all things man may do on Earth to his benefit, the acquisition of spirituality is supreme. It is in fact the whole and sole reason for man's existence. Therefore, while getting whatever happiness he can, he should never over-indulge his bodily appetites and should shun the frivolities of life. These are earthly seducers, which leave little time for more beneficial things and become more demanding as they gain greater control.

WSD:12:13 Such things as eating, drinking, sleeping and the bodily union of man and woman are meant to be sources of pleasure, when enjoyed in moderation and for their proper purpose. They, too, can serve a spiritual end. The rule is moderation in all things, with consideration for the welfare and feelings of others and a complete disregard of anything, which may serve the cause of evil.

WSD:12:14 Do not fear the onset of old age, for though to the undeveloped spirit, it may be the bleak winter of life, to the developed spirit, it is the harvesting time. Old age is bodily preparation for departure to rebirth. It is the approach to the threshold of a new life.

WSD:12:15 Every man should earn his livelihood by service through toil or skill. The man who wishes to live the good life fully must engage in all kinds of activities, in trade and in various instructive affairs. Life, to be properly lived, must be balanced with a knowledge of many things and a variety of experiences.

WSD:12:16 Man must certainly engage in worldly and social activities for the benefit of his body, for its needs are not to be neglected. Still always bear in mind that this is not the sole aim in life, nor the greatest. Only one aim or objective should be held always in view, and that is the perfecting of the soul. In this way, all activities become praiseworthy and beneficial, since the end lies not in the activities themselves but in their objective.

WSD:12:17 If a man has any talent and fails to develop it, he is unworthy of the gift and, in due course, must make an accounting. The man who does not continually expand the horizon of his life becomes stagnant within himself. The man who does not study and learn places himself on the level of the dumb beasts, though even they learn.

WSD:12:18 The good life is a balanced, harmonious life and a life well and profitably lived. It is a life of many contrasts and experiences, with a steady advance towards spirituality. All earthly goals are elusive, and their attainment may not bring the pleasure and happiness anticipated. There is only one goal, towards which everyone can advance with certainty and assurance, and that is the goal of spirituality. The very things, which defeat earthly ends and render them impossible to accomplish are, if viewed in the proper perspective, aids towards the achievement of spirituality. Out of earthly failure and frustration can come spiritual accomplishment and gain. If you can understand this, the good life is yours.

Chapter Thirteen – The Religious Life

WSD:13:1 Religion is not something alien to the nature of man, but something which supplies a fundamental need. Just as eating is the response to an inner urge, so is religion the response to another. It is only when religion, in a particular form, becomes insipid, ceases to nourish, that it is discarded, and then the nature of man seeks to supply the deficiency from another source. Without religious nourishment, the spirit of man becomes unstable and out of harmony with life. Unless the deficiency is made good the whole being may disrupt into disharmony.

WSD:13:2 The religious urge is as much a part of man as the urge to eat or sleep, though of a much more subtle nature. Some try to suppress the urge, and in such cases, the effects are no less harmful and apparent than when other urges are suppressed completely. Those with a little knowledge and wisdom often turn away from religion, but once they have gained much more, they turn back again. Religion itself can, therefore, never be outdated or outmoded, though its earthly manifestations certainly may be, and so many persons, disillusioned with the image, spurn the reality behind it. True religion deals only with the relationship between man and his divinity and is the stairway for his ascent.

WSD:13:3 Too often, religion is a quagmire, into which the spirits of men sink and are lost, but it is the fault of men and not of religion. Each man has the religion he deserves and not necessarily the religion he needs. When it proves inadequate for his needs and he becomes disillusioned, he seeks to lay blame on the religion and not on himself. Religions which nourished weaknesses of character and ignorance in men have been destroyed by those same failings and are no more, but the religions are no more to blame than those who served them. If a man put to sea in an unseaworthy boat, can he blame the craft if he be cast into the water? Still man is never abandoned and somewhere there is the religion he needs, though he may never find it because of his spiritual indolence.

WSD:13:4 The religious life is not one of ease and indolence, neither is it something to be undertaken half-heartedly. Too often an old man who has wasted his life in worldly excesses and scorned religion, suddenly becomes converted and seeks to imitate the religious life. He imagines he has become good because he performs acts having an outer appearance of goodness. However, he is no more than a hypocrite. The truth is that his abstinence from wrongdoing and conversion to the religious life are directly related to his declining bodily powers. Such men generally become so self-righteous that they readily forgive themselves for their past deeds, which, after a shallow repentance, are quickly and conveniently forgotten. They should read what is written in the Sacred Books, and learn how much more is required of them.

WSD:13:5 Religion is man reaching out towards something greater than himself and attempting to express an indescribable glory revealed just beyond his grasp. It is man's search for greatness, the recognition that he is more than mere mortal flesh, and that above this is a divinity towards which he may aspire.

WSD:13:6 Devotion is not a state of servility, but is actually an attempt to return to man's natural condition. It is a seeking for powers, which, though once possessed, have now been lost. It is a search for the truth concerning man as he really is in his whole being.

WSD:13:7 Incense, fire, candles and ritual cannot increase the glory of The Divine. Certainly they may benefit man and increase his sensitivity, but he should not be hypocritical about their effect or insulting. The sacrifice of bird or beast, the offering of gold and jewels, may assist men, but in no way do they benefit The Divine. All The Divine asks from man is whole-hearted self-dedication to the fulfilment of The Divine Design. The worshipful ritual and devotional acts are the manifestation of man's desire to take an easy path. They are no more than an interlude in his daily life, the acknowledgement that he owes some sort of obligation.

WSD:13:8 The Sacred Books should be read often and diligently, for they are the repository of knowledge transcending that, which can be gained by the senses of men. The Divine knows your heart, your intentions and inclinations, and therefore does not expect you to make the study of the Sacred Books too wearisome. The Divine knows that some are sick while others are handicapped either by a life of movement or a life of restraint. Others are so tied up in the struggle for the cause that they have little time for reading. Many have to depend upon the literacy of others for the learning. Therefore, even one section at a time is enough, if it is studied and meditated upon.

WSD:13:9 Prayer is an exercise of the spirit. It must never be misdirected and cannot be used to change natural laws and effects for the sake of the one who prays. Always pray in a place proper for prayer. Those who say no place is especially holy because The Divine is everywhere, may discover that they are unable to find The Divine anywhere.

WSD:13:10 Prayer is little understood, for it raises the worshipper above a normal state. It is a state of being wherein man loses himself in the Spirit of Divinity. To those great souls who know the true nature of prayer in its highest expression, it seems a miracle that after losing himself in prayer, the worshipper continues to live in the flesh. True worship, however, is not prayer but the devotion of a life dedicated to the fulfilment of the Divine Design and the preparation of the soul for the crown of divinity.

WSD:13:11 Repentance from those who have been doers of wickedness and then repent their deeds or confess their wrongdoing when dying, serves little purpose. Unless some recompense is made by the death itself or by other deeds, mere repentance alone cannot reshape the soul.

WSD:13:12 Worship and devotion require effort, so unless specific times are set apart for reading the Sacred Books, for worship and dedicated service, no time will be given to The Divine. Too often, men devote all their time to the affairs of the body and completely neglect the welfare of the spirit.

WSD:13:13 Ignorant men stupidly stir up many cares and troubles; they confront themselves with pointless problems and add unnecessarily to the burdens of life. They increase the number of trials prescribed by their destiny. They indulge in futile forms of worship and waste time in worthless ceremonial. They delude themselves by placing false values on their offerings, they fast and mortify themselves without gain. They go on timewasting pilgrimages and seek new shrines, but from all this they derive little spiritual benefit.

WSD:13:14 Religious rituals and ceremonies are brought about by a desire for the mutual sharing of religious experience. As words cannot describe the greater glories, which are inseparable from the religious life, the problems connected with belief and faith are no more than standpoints indicating man's limited means of communication. Therefore, let each man find his own path, and having found it follow steadfastly through to the end.

WSD:13:15 The many and seemingly conflicting doctrines, which arise from time to time and in many places, do, if inspired by the urge to spirituality, lead towards the same goal - the One Supreme Truth. They are like the many roads into the city, which convey travellers from all directions. The conflict and discord between the many religions are caused by ignorance, by blindness in the material clouds of illusion and by misinterpretation of basic truths. Rightly or wrongly, each man believes the road he travels to be the best and most direct.

WSD:13:16 A true religion does in fact do no more than supply the medium, whereby man works in co-operation with The Divine. It is the means, whereby the Divine Design is revealed and its purpose interpreted. Whatever goes into the make-up of human nature bearing the impress of divinity, whatever man does to unfold the divinity of his soul, that constitutes the religious life.

WSD:13:17 The religious life on Earth does not lead to any finality. It is no more than the first stage of the journey, but it does lead in the right direction. Death is no more than a movement across a frontier, though the wise man assures that the move improves his circumstances and is to a better place.

WSD:13:18 The course of life is determined by destiny, so pay no heed to those who pretend to read futures in the stars, for they predict only in riddles and what they say may apply to many. No two predictions are alike, except by coincidence, and the planets have no power to determine what a man will become.

WSD:13:19 The origins of superstition and false belief lie in the conceit and presumption of man, but to an even greater extent in his mortal tendency towards deceit and hypocrisy. They also stem from his spiritual immaturity and indifference, for he tries to attain and understand things which are attainable only by the spiritually developed, and interprets them with his inadequate knowledge and inspiration. Superstition and blind faith are pillars supporting the religions of ignorance.

Chapter Fourteen – Personal Conduct

WSD:14:1 Every man should have a cause to fight for and a road to follow. He should fight for the cause until its objective is attained and follow the road until the end. The horizon of each should be outward towards perfection. The causeless man is like a riderless horse.

WSD:14:2 It is better to adhere to one cause absolutely and wholeheartedly than to dabble in many causes without being wholehearted in any. A truly great cause should carry all other worthy causes forward with it, and one great cause cannot fall into conflict with another. A man is judged by what he fights for, or by what he declines to fight for, he must do one or the other.

WSD:14:3 A man must keep careful watch on himself, so he does not wax fat and self-indulgent. Whatever his position in life, he should always be engaged in some worthwhile occupation and never neglect the study of the Sacred Books. Idleness is the mother of miseries. Indolence occupies itself in filling the body with fat.

WSD:14:4 To study the Books of Wisdom is good, for thereby a man learns what to do and what not to do. On the other hand, if a man is busily engaged in earning his livelihood and fulfilling his obligations, it will not occur to him to steal and fornicate.

WSD:14:5 Man and woman are intended to be unalike, and therefore, a man should conduct himself as a man and a woman as a woman. They were made to serve differently; their separate purposes should not become confused. A mannish woman cannot inspire men or serve the cause of womankind. If she serves mankind, it is in a capacity below that of other women.

WSD:14:6 Do not disgrace a man before others or hold any man up to ridicule. The Books of Wisdom say that the only person a man will disgrace before others is his bitterest enemy. Mockery of another discloses the mocker's own weakness of character.

WSD:14:7 Do not be immovable in your ways or set in your circumstances. Be like the reed, which bows with the wind and bends all the way, but always springs up again. Always be alert and ready for whatever may come your way, and above all, do not expect life to deal kindly with you always. Do not envy those who have more than you, but turn your eyes towards those less fortunate.

WSD:14:8 Do not be complacent about your personal attainments, for no one can say truthfully that he has purged his spirit of all disfiguring stains and is now perfect. No matter how perfect a man may appear to himself in any respect, there is still a greater perfection attainable, and that is the goal. The limits of earthly perfection remain unmarked.

WSD:14:9 Cleanliness in all things is essential. If you would not put filth in your mouth, why put it in your mind? No one allows garbage at the eating table, yet many gladly overload their minds with it. These are weaknesses of character, which have to be eliminated. Through long ages it has been known that a foul tongue expresses the language of weakness, and filthy jokes are the consolation of slaves. The nation sinking into the mire is comforted by the knowledge of its affinity to filth.

WSD:14:10 The man who boasts about his prowess as a fornicator does so to hide the secret knowledge of his own inadequacy. His foolish boasting is the source of his satisfaction and indicates the limit of his achievements. Let the man of weak character and weaker vitality betray himself, but keep away, lest you be numbered among the self-deceivers.

WSD:14:11 Let your personal conduct be in all ways above reproach. Strive to be worthy of the respect of all men, though their praise is froth on the waters of life. Live as you should live and not as you would like to live. If you cannot acknowledge your own worth, then recognise your own failings.

Chapter Fifteen – The Spiritual Realm

WSD:15:1 The Spiritual Realm lies between the realm of matter and the realm of The Divine. If your mind is unable to grasp the idea of The Divine and you cannot understand what is meant by spirituality, do not be dismayed. How can an ordinary, unenlightened mind do so when it is shut in by a corrupt material world and enclosed on every side by illusion? Absolute purity cannot be seen amid the clouds of earthly impurity, and in this defiled place, the immaculate is inconceivable. Therefore, if you cannot understand this or perceive the reality of perfection, how much less are you able to comprehend The Divine! Step confidently along the path, guided by understanding companions, who are more enlightened, for they will not lead you astray, and soon the light of understanding will be placed in your hand.

WSD:15:2 The Spiritual Realm is divided into two parts. On one side is the place, where the wicked have companionship of their own kind, and it is a cold place of gloom and darkness. This is the realm of evil containing those who are repulsive even to their own kind. Their greatest punishment may lie in the fact that they retain the memory of beauty, goodness and cleanliness, just as the happiness of those in the realm of good, on the other side is heightened by its contrast with the sorrows and afflictions they have known.

WSD:15:3 The realm of evil is separated from the realm of good by an etheric form of flame, through which communication can be made. Were those on the sunlit side to enquire from the dwellers in gloom what brought them to their deplorable state, if the truth could be found in them, they would reply: "We are those who were heedless of all spiritual and ennobling things. We were those who thought only of their own betterment and not the advancement of mankind and the welfare of others. We were the selfish ones who considered only their own comfort and convenience. Now look at what we have! We oppressed the poor and lowly and exploited the helpless and weak, doing nothing to improve their lot. Now look at ours! We sat on councils and in seats of authority engaging in vain disputes about right and wrong, while the poor, the hungry and the oppressed stood by and suffered in patience. We are, above all, those who could have done much but did little. We were those who, given great gifts, used them for selfish ends. What have we now? We inhabited fine houses and surrounded ourselves with all things to give ease and comfort. Now we are comfortless. We sought out places of pleasure and closed our eyes to the sorrow and suffering of the world. We laughed at those who sought to teach us spirituality and took a base and easy view of right and wrong. There is no laughter here. We doubted that there was any life to come and could not understand the talk about it. Would that the grave had been the end! Talk of duty and service disturbed our ease and complacency, and we let others carry our burdens. If only we could return! Only now when we so miserably exist in the certainty of life after death can we realise our errors and suffer for them. Here the air is filled with the sighing sound of the saddest words we know, "Too late!"'

WSD:15:4 Those words did once span the gulf and were recorded by an ancient seer.

WSD:15:5 On the day when the whole being is split apart by death and the mortal clay is consigned to its proper place, the spirit passes through the great gates into the Spiritual Realm. There it first enters a Borderland, where the floodgates of memory are opened and each and every deed recalled. This is where the newly arrived spirit waits while slowly it assumes its chosen shape and realises the direction of its destination.

WSD:15:6 The spirit does not arrive in a state of waking, but it is like one asleep. It awakes to its new life like a man awakes to a new day. Then, if during earthly life it has doomed itself, this realisation will slowly dawn, and the newly formed being will cringe away from those who came to welcome it. It will indeed wish that death had been the end. The wisdom of ancient times disclosed that the newly arrived spirit stood in completeness for judgement, but what it called the Place of Decision is the Borderland.

WSD:15:7 If, during life, the spirit has beautified and ennobled itself, it will slowly realise its unfolding glory and rejoice. It will rise gladly to its welcome and advance fearlessly into the light of its compatible place. Some, which do not have full affinity with either the light or the darkness depart for the Shadowland, towards which they are impelled by its attraction for one in their state.

WSD:15:8 Within the Spiritual Realm there are places to suit the condition of every spirit entering it, and that is why the ancient books state, 'The mansions of the spirit are without number'.

Chapter Sixteen – The Meaning of Marriage

WSD:16:1 In the eyes of men and according to their laws, marriage is a covenant made between a man and a woman, under which they can enjoy bodily union with the sanction of their religion. This is not the view which can be supported by the Good Religion, for true marriage is not something formed through the words spoken by a priest or through sanction by the laws of men. Marriage is an open declaration, which marks the taking of an irrevocable step by two souls towards a definite end. It signifies their complete surrender and dedication to each other. It is meant to be far more than union of the bodies, it should also be a union of spirits, though this is rarely achieved. True marriage is a union of two realms, it is a twofold union.

WSD:16:2 The marriage ceremony is an announcement made before all persons that a man and woman are setting out on the rocky road of matrimony in search of true love. This is not something which can be picked up like a jewel, it cannot be bartered, bought or sold. The thing which must never be overlooked is that true marriage is not just the union of two bodies, but the first step towards the blending of two spirits.

WSD:16:3 The marriages of humble people, unsanctified by priest, are no less worthy than those of wealthy people of quality whose religion sanctifies bonds of straw. 'Living in sin' means living together without responsibility and for bodily satisfaction alone. Unholy wedlock means being bound fast in the bonds of matrimony without any prospect of advancement to the glory of true love. Wedlock and marriage are not alike, for a true marriage may exist without sanction by the laws of men or blessing of priest, providing a love exists, which can mature into true love.

WSD:16:4 The chain that binds two souls together is forged in the spiritual realm, and no earthly power can ever break it. It is worn on Earth like a gloriously wrought chain of weightless gold, but not one marriage in a thousand is ever blessed with it.

WSD:16:5 Adultery is the defilement of a marriage, but there is a mild form of it when the thoughts of one partner go out towards someone else. Religions now existing do not understand the true nature of marriage and regard it as an end in itself and not as a beginning, a fulfilment rather than a search for fulfilment. The Good Religion will regard marriage as one of the great challenges of life and one of the supreme tests along the road to spirituality. Love is not the end, for love aspires to reach out beyond itself and ascend to the heights of true love, sometimes called 'pure love'.

WSD:16:6 Outside of the Good Religion, union between man and woman has become so tainted with imperfection, so clouded in lewdness, so subordinate to lust and bodily satisfaction, that anyone can readily be forgiven for believing the falsehood that no spiritual benefit can derive from the act; that it has no sanctity, no higher objective and purpose than to meet the demands of the flesh.

WSD:16:7 Man soars on spiritual wings and rises high above the realm of the dumb brutes. Therefore, he can conceive something greater in bodily union than mere satisfaction of the flesh, and indeed it is not meant to be a concession to the flesh but a sublime sacrifice to love. The feelings arising in the body are not, of themselves, servants of evil, this is a wrong teaching. The body is not naturally antagonistic to the spirit, and its needs are by no means incompatible with spiritual needs. As the harp to the harpist, so is the body to the spirit, the instrument and means of expression.

WSD:16:8 Marriage is the fortress of the family, so its safeguarding and integrity is a sacred obligation. The unity and purity of the family is one of the great concerns of men, but though the laws of men may build a wall about it they cannot prevent corruption and decay from within. Only higher laws, moral laws, can deal with this, and these the world sadly lacks.

WSD:16:9 The three earthly institutions a man is entitled to defend, even to the extent of taking the life of another, are: His marriage, his home and his family.

Chapter Seventeen – The Upbringing of Children

WSD:17:1 To teach a child a readymade code of morality may not be the ideal, but ideals are rarely approachable on Earth and while mankind is so far-retarded spiritually, it is impossible to do otherwise. Yet if a child is also told why there is a necessity for such a code, perhaps in the child's maturity, it will add something of goodness to the code.

WSD:17:2 Children brought up with the very best instruction often become wayward and later disregard all they have been taught. Parents wonder why, for the ancient wisdom states that if a child is properly instructed and good habits ingrained, this will not desert the child when it grows up. Such parents must honestly search their own hearts, because the reason is that they have failed to practise their own teachings, and the growing child resents such hypocrisy. Therefore, as it grows up, it will tend to imitate the parents rather than follow the teachings. Parents should bear in mind that example is the best instruction.

WSD:17:3 A healthier and better upbringing is if parents do not over-indulge their children or play with them too much. A parent is not a playmate, and his or her first duty is to be a parent. A mother should act like a mother, and a father like a father. Read the Sacred Books and learn your proper role in life.

WSD:17:4 Parents get the children they deserve, and the failings of a child mirror the failings of its parents. The children of a considerate and just father are successful. Good children cannot be raised in a house of discord. When the father is hot-tempered and the mother a gossip, the sons are fools and the daughters slovenly.

WSD:17:5 Those who spare themselves the pain of chastising their children display their lack of love for them. Proper and just chastisement is part of a child's upbringing and the duty of every parent. Chastise a child during its childhood, for later is too late. When you were advised against over-familiarity with children, it did not mean that you should be too stern and austere with them.

WSD:17:6 The highest expressions of Justice and Truth and a perfect code of laws are not attainable on Earth. Therefore, the best thing anyone can do for a child is to teach it self-mastery and bring it up in the knowledge of its true nature. The wisdom of the Sacred Books should be impressed upon the minds of children and taught according to their understanding. It is the duty and obligation of every parent to see that their children are properly instructed.

WSD:17:7 Children are not to be brought into the world irresponsibly and parents have an obligation for their welfare. They must see that a child is not left without a craft or calling whereby a livelihood can be earned, There is an obligation upon those who bring a child into the world to see that it does not grow up without learning a skilful and useful occupation, and that it is instructed in the purpose of life and ways of the world.

WSD:17:8 The well brought up child crowns its parents with happiness, but one ill raised weighs heavily upon their hearts. A child may rightly reproach its parents if they fail in their duty or avoid their obligations, for it did not ask to be born. Parents, however, cannot reproach their child, for it came at their behest and is the fruit of their pleasure.

WSD:17:9 Parents should bear in mind that the fruit of the tree of indulgence is bitter and the waters of indifference soon quench the fires of affection. The parent who sows unwisely in the fertile fields of childhood reaps a blighted harvest when the crop comes to maturity.

Chapter Eighteen – Friends and Enemies

WSD:18:1 The only real enemy any man has is the man he does not understand, and the only man to really fear is the one who is afraid. While it is true that a man can be judged by his friends, it is no less true that he can be judged by his enemies. A weak character does not have enemies, but only those who pity or despise him. A declared enemy is not necessarily a source of constant danger. He is better than a false friend and need not be an object of hatred; in fact, many enemies can be admired.

WSD:18:2 The man who seeks a friend without faults or one without weaknesses and failings, will never have a friend, and he who declares his enemy to be wholly evil is a liar. A man may be poor in worldly possessions but rich in friendship, for true wealth is not the accumulation of lifeless things but the possession of firm friendship. The greatness of a man may be assessed according to his friends, but it may be measured even better according to who are his enemies.

WSD:18:3 True friendship is not given its proper value in times of prosperity, and fair weather friends grow wings when the winds of adversity blow. Though misfortune reveals the friend, it also discloses the enemy. When misfortune strikes, false friends scamper like rats, and enemies gather like vultures.

WSD:18:4 No man can attain full spiritual development until he has learned to respect the rights and views of others. Help others along the path, and the right way will be pointed out.

WSD:18:5 The nature of man is such that while it always tends to resist force and compulsion, it will always yield to gentleness and persuasion. Force is the last resort and an acknowledgement of failure. Power in the hands of a man in all ways strong is always good, but power in the hands of a weak man is a menace.

WSD:18:6 A friend is capable of inflicting greater hurt than an enemy, but both should be chosen with equal discretion. Yet wounds inflicted at the hands of a friend are more to be desired than the hypocritical embraces of an enemy. Let experience be your guide. He who has tested honey knows it to be sweet, while he who has tasted the fruit of evil knows it to be bitter.

WSD:18:7 Do not take a fornicator as a friend, or you admit a wolf into the sheepfold. Enslaved by his urges, he will never be constant and always a weak reed to lean upon. As a dog leaves its kennel to return to its vomit, so is a fornicator drawn back to the woman with whom he relieves himself.

WSD:18:8 Genuine friendship between man and woman is said to be impossible, but this is the talk of weak characters, of whom many burden the world. When the relationship of love between man and woman is hallowed as it should be, and elevated far above sordid relationships, between the two there will be a place for friendship.

WSD:18:9 Do not be lukewarm either in friendship or enmity, for the strong character reaches out afar in all directions. Not all enemies are personal ones, for those who oppose the cause for which you fight are also your enemies, as are all who oppress the weak and lowly. There is everlasting enmity between those who serve the cause of good and those who serve evil, and there can be no reconciliation between the two. To compromise with evil means contamination of the good.

Chapter Nineteen – The Tendency Towards Evil

WSD:19:1 Everyone born to be tested in a mortal world has a tendency towards things, which are evil, rather than towards those, which are good. The material part of man, with its heritage of decay, finds itself more attracted towards evil than towards good. Therefore, it is good, which has to be taught and learned and evil, which has to be put aside and eliminated.

WSD:19:2 When a man delves into wickedness, to satisfy his carnal urges, the body fully supports him, and his mortal limbs and organs readily respond. The bestial desires and urges lurk only just beneath the surface and need little encouragement to bring them up. However, when a man is called upon to do some good deed, his body is reluctant, and disinclination invades his heart.

WSD:19:3 This is because evil impulses range freely through the movement of good impulses. The gross material of the body must be impregnated with spirituality, if the position within is to be reversed.

WSD:19:4 Evil impulses press urgently upon the mortal body and make their demands known in no uncertain manner. Only the best of men are truly free enough to rise above them and stand firm in resistance. Passions and the demands of the body are aggressors from the realm of evil seeking to capture and enslave the spirit. These aggressors must be subdued, put in restraint and made to serve.

WSD:19:5 The tendency towards evil involves not only those who break the laws of men, but also those who break higher laws. The Good Religion should not concern itself so much with earthly lawbreakers, for the laws of men can deal with them, but with greater things, against which the laws of men are inadequate. The number of lawbreakers and outcasts in any nation is the measure of a nation's spiritual deficiency. 'Where there is lawlessness, there will also be injustice, for the two go together like light and shade.

WSD:19:6 The spiritual life is inseparable from daily existence, and a nation becomes spiritually deficient when it tries to separate one from the other. Religions, which stand aloof and permit this to happen, if not servants of evil, are certainly poor champions of good. The laws of men have to be enforced only when people cease to govern their lives by spiritual laws. Therefore, of all laws spiritual laws are the highest.

WSD:19:7 The duty of religion is to concern itself with moral laws and discipline, and when it fails in this duty it no longer serves the welfare of mankind. The laws of men are completely inadequate for this, as indicated by their complexity and multiplicity. The greatness of any nation resides in its national spirit, and the breath of that spirit is religion.

WSD:19:8 The tendency towards evil is opposed by religion, the champion of good, which must prove itself equal to the challenge. A poorly armed champion, ill prepared for combat or defective in resolution, is of no use whatsoever, though the people of few nations deserve anything better.

WSD:19:9 The tendency towards evil includes abuse of the body, for unhealthy excesses lead to weakness, apathy and early death. The body that is overstuffed with food houses a selfish spirit, which has deprived others of sustenance. A body worn out with dissipation hides a spirit, which has surrendered to wickedness. It includes also all things tending towards the disruption of life and the brutalisation of mankind.

WSD:19:10 Yet, to live a righteous life does not mean withdrawal from association with all others. A man should withdraw from life among his own people only when they have turned completely from the path of good and tread the road of evil. In such cases a man has the obligation to separate his family from the contaminating influence of those about him, but he must always bear in mind that his duty is to fight and not run away. Withdrawal to a stronger base, from which to fight is not running away.

Chapter Twenty – Teaching, Study and Learning

WSD:20:1 Conscience is the best guide, and experience the best teacher. Nature is the best book, and life the highest form of schooling. Death is the great graduation day.

WSD:20:2 Study itself is not enough, for learning without application and practice is futile and leads towards wickedness. The man who studies the Sacred Books as a child and applies their teachings to his life is like one who works with metal while it is still hot. The man who leaves such study until old age is like one who works with metal when it is cold.

WSD:20:3 Study, when not combined with work and practice, tends to lead towards the path of weakness. Unless a man is engaged in a skilled or useful occupation, all his book learning serves little purpose and does not avail him much. Therefore, even the man most devoted to the study of the Sacred Books must also learn a skilled or useful occupation.

WSD:20:4 Practice is of greater importance than study; for of what use is it to study the way for goodness, and being willing to do good, if experience of what constitutes good living is lacking? The good life is a life of action and not a life of passiveness.

WSD:20:5 Yet, study and learning are not to be neglected, for they are part of the discipline of living. Without the study, which leads to knowledge, right living and right action in their fullest expression are very unlikely.

WSD:20:6 In your absorption of knowledge, consider nothing impossible and nothing beyond achievement. Bear in mind that whatever is possible will one day come into being. The road to wisdom begins in attentive silence and passes through study and practice into fulfilment.

WSD:20:7 A teacher's words should be goads to goodness and learning, and not like a salve to the wounds of wickedness or a narcotic deadening the instructive pains of life. As the herdsman's goad directs beasts and urges them along the right road, so should the teacher's word direct and urge the pupil. Words of worth do not fall softly.

WSD:20:8 A teacher may have a pupil wait upon him and attend to his needs, providing it is regarded as an opportunity for training and teaching. The teacher who fails to set a good example, or to abide by his own teachings, is unworthy of his position and betrays his trust.

WSD:20:9 The man who quietly carries out the precepts of the Sacred Books and upholds their teachings is better than he who studies diligently and teaches well, but fails to put his teaching into practice. A hypocritical teacher is the lowest order of hypocrites.

WSD:20:10 A disciple is one who follows a religious master, and it is better to be the disciple of a wiser man than the master of others who are ignorant. Always seek self-improvement and advancement in knowledge, for these are the justifiable aims of the disciple.

WSD:20:11 The man who is diligent and careful in his studies, but not in his deeds or words, is a weak character who tends to hypocrisy. The man who learns but does not practise what he learns is like a man who labours at the sowing, but does not reap the harvest. He is like a man who digs a well and never draws water.

WSD:20:12 The purpose of learning is to know the good from the bad, the beneficial from the harmful. The good and beneficial should not be scorned, whoever dispenses them. Would you take poison even if offered by your best friend, or refuse dressing for a wound because given by an enemy?

WSD:20:13 The man who is filled with learning and knows all the wisdom of the Sacred Books, but fails to put it into practice, is like a many-branched tree with no depth of root. The wind blows, and it is laid low to quickly rot. The man with much learning and knowledge but no strength of character, is like a frail pot filled with precious liquid. If roughly handled, it falls apart, and the contents are lost.

WSD:20:14 Good has its fount in The Divine, and at its source is uncontaminated with evil. It is that which harmonises best with the Divine Design, and evil is that which harmonises least. Good is absolute quality, while evil is not; therefore, even in the greatest concentration of evil there must be some good. So there is no form of evil, whether in man or outside of him, from which some good cannot be extracted, but man by nature tends to overlook this. Entrapped in matter, evil is more easily seen. Bear in mind that, in even the greatest evil, there is somewhere a speck of good which can be of service if extracted.

WSD:20:15 Finally, if seeking a religious master, be careful in your choice. In matters of religion, the whole forces of evil are marshalled to deceive and delude. If one whom you would choose as a master seeks popularity or self-advancement, avoid him like the plague, for he is a false prophet.

Chapter Twenty-One – A Word to Prophets and Preachers

WSD:21:1 The true prophet is a message bearer who has heard a voice crying out across the distances. The message may not be clearly heard and perhaps conveyed with errors and distortion, but if it is the dedicated effort of a sincere man, it must be of value.

WSD:21:2 Because there are many false prophets, the words of a true prophet do not lose their value. No man has ever sought to counterfeit a valueless thing. The vine is judged by the drink it produces and not by its leaves and appearance. It is the end product that matters.

WSD:21:3 The pattern of the Divine Design is marvellous and its working intricate. The threads are many, and their preparation involves countless processes. The weavers are numerous, but few can visualise what magnificence completion may reveal, and none can see the uncompleted whole. Therefore, those who would show others the pattern to follow should not seek to guess at what lies beyond their own range of vision.

WSD:21:4 So if you are a prophet chosen to guide, do not exceed the scope of your authority or seek to describe things beyond the reach of your light. Go forward with courage and confidence, and the voice of The Divine will teach you the signs along the road and make clear their meaning.

WSD:21:5 When you stand up to deliver your message, many hypocrites will gather and declare their belief in what you say. The words they speak may deceive you, for they are a cloak disguising their true garb and, because of their hypocrisy, those who would otherwise listen to your words will turn away in disgust. Therefore, when you make converts, beware of including the fainthearted and hypocrites, for they will only be a liability.

WSD:21:6 Do not be afraid to speak up when men will listen to what you have to say, but also know when to be silent and hold your peace. It is futile to waste words when you will not be given a hearing. You will have to contend with many false-faced prophets whose words are beautiful baubles falling from silver tongues. They attract the attention of many who listen for pleasure and so are led astray.

WSD:21:7 Some men will come to you declaring that they have been converted to your cause, but the words they utter have no more substance than the breath, upon which the words ride. Their speech does not reflect the image in their hearts, and their hypocrisy places them among the damned.

WSD:21:8 Others will come prepared to accept what you say in part only and to serve with reservations. If good comes out of what they do, they consider the effort sufficient, but if they find the going hard, they will fall away. Those are weak characters who can derive little benefit from your teachings, until they first change themselves. The first duty of the Good Religion is not to preach The Divine, but to teach men to change themselves. Its first aim is to develop a better being.

WSD:21:9 Do not ever tell others the way to live and how to govern their lives, until after you have put your teachings into practice. First practice what you teach, and then, you can instruct others from your experience. The hypocritical teacher betrays his cause.

WSD:21:10 Though you may preach to an audience of allcomers, choose your disciples carefully. Do not waste time on fools or simpletons, or on those unwilling to take the road towards spirituality. Always explain in such a manner that your words cannot be misconstrued. Do not always expect people to ask for further explanation if they do not understand, for their misinterpretation may satisfy them, or they may be reluctant to speak up.

WSD:21:11 Sometimes, a preaching prophet may upbraid his hearers with anger because his heart is stirred up within him, and some may be resentful. They will overlook all his good qualities and search out his faults. Perhaps they will say, "This man preaches forbearance and self-control, while railing against us with hostility and anger." Therefore, before attempting to preach, strengthen your character, so that if you must upbraid people for their ways, you do so with affection and restraint.

WSD:21:12 Do not argue hot-headedly or enter into dispute with your hearers, but talk to them in a kindly, reserved manner. Bear in mind that, whatever their belief, it will contain a large amount of good with which you have no dispute or issue. It is the bad, which taints and contaminates the good, that has to be sought out and destroyed.

WSD:21:13 Do not enter into discussion or argument with anyone well instructed in another doctrine, unless you are equally well instructed in yours and equally well informed on theirs. In disputes and discussions, the ill informed man is knocked over with a straw. In the arena of argument, the man without knowledge attacks with a reed.

WSD:21:14 Other doctrines have their books, and the best book is the one, which benefits the most. In one book, Truth may be described in one way, and, in another book, it may be described differently, but this need not mean that one is right and the other wrong. Truth never goes unveiled, but the wise man seeks her where she is veiled the least.

WSD:21:15 The outward vestments of a religion are unimportant, for gaudy ones may hide a festering body, while unimposing garments may clothe a healthy one. Disregard the bottle and give your attention to its contents. A mis-shapen bottle may hold matured wine, while the well shaped bottle may contain wine newly pressed.

WSD:21:16 If your calling is to preach, then declare to others all the words you believe to be true concerning The Divine and the latent divinity in men. Pay no heed to those who would discourage you, and follow the footsteps of Truth unflinchingly. The least enlightened are those who close their ears to the voice of wisdom.

WSD:21:17 If you have been granted the gift of speech so that your opponents are routed under a hail of words, do not proclaim a victory. A man is not converted because he is silenced. The advocate who presents the best argument may not have the best case, and he who speaks the right words may not be on the right side.

WSD:21:18 Though you cannot reveal the Divine Design, you can point out the order in the Divine Dominion. All about, the signs are manifested in the order and procession of the stars and the succession of the seasons, in the abounding beauty and bounty of Nature and in the laws that govern growth and decay.

WSD:21:19 When the call to the cause is sounded in the dawnlight of the day of Truth, preaching prophets will fare forth as harbingers. If it falls to your lot to be numbered among them, then consider yourself honoured among humanity. Summon others to tread the way of Truth with you, but do so in simple words and with enlightened argument and wisdom. Do not enter into time-wasting disputes, but use gentle persuasion and kindly guidance to put the feet of your followers upon the right road.

WSD:21:20 Those who answer the call to the cause cannot expect to escape the conflict unscathed. If you are among those who suffer, do not take reprisals, but only such steps as will prevent a repetition. Display your strength of character in patient endurance and cheerfulness, but you are not expected to be meekly submissive.

WSD:21:21 Endure whatever trials come your way with patience and fortitude, for they serve you well. Do not be unduly disturbed if you are not believed, or troubled because so many betray their own nature and destiny. You can do no more than warn them and call upon them to fulfil their duty and obligations. Do not let your heart be troubled by their subtleties of arguments, and bear in mind that deluded men always believe in the reality of their delusions.

WSD:21:22 Concentrate on teaching the young, for this is like engraving words on metal, while teaching the aged is like writing words on the seashore sands. But instruction should be given by the aged, for he who looks for wisdom in the young is like a man who eats unripe fruit from the vine or drinks unmellowed wine from the cask.

WSD:21:23 The Good Religion will not concern itself with moneymaking for profit; though, if it is made to serve a good end there is no harm. With moneymaking and profit, it is the objective that counts. Those who preach the Good Religion will take no money for themselves in such a way that people might come to regard it as no more than another means of livelihood. The praiseworthy teacher will earn his livelihood through his skill or labour.

WSD:21:24 However, if a man devotes himself to furthering the cause, and sacrifices opportunities in other directions, he shall not be denied a fair return for his services. A man who dedicates himself wholly to the service of a cause can rightly expect that cause to supply him with the necessities of life.

WSD:21:25 The preacher dedicated to service must not be too fastidious, for to give battle to the muck wallowers, the muck heap must be entered. Neither must he be intolerant with those who hold to the most outlandish beliefs, for each man's belief seems right in his own eyes.

WSD:21:26 The harbingers of the Good Religion must be men of strong character and integrity, for a fortress cannot be built on shaky foundations, or stout walls erected over a bog. The preacher who is truly dedicated to a Divinity of Love and Goodness becomes, himself, a manifestation of those qualities.

WSD:21:27 Man is not expected to achieve perfection here on Earth, but only to seek it. What is expected of him is a sincere and honest effort without any hypocritical or deceptive reservations. The Divine Design requires that man make a conscious choice of right under the constant pressure of temptation to do otherwise. This also leaves man free to choose wrong.

WSD:21:28 Man chooses wrong instead of right for just two reasons; either it is the easy path of least resistance, or it is the most alluring. Consequently, the Good Religion must first concern itself with establishing strength of character and moral backbone, for these form the only foundation, upon which the palace of spirituality can be erected.

WSD:21:29 Long ages ago, man took the wrong path and was led astray still further by guides with insufficient knowledge of the way. They knew the general direction, but their maps were faulty. Now, man is lost in the swamps of spiritual barrenness and the marshes of moral decay. His vision cannot penetrate the thick mists of mortal and material illusion, which have closed in upon him. He has lost all confidence in his guides and feels betrayed, abandoned and lonely.

WSD:21:30 The lost wayfarer must be revived with a draught of moral courage. He must be strengthened and revitalised with a belief which gives him spiritual backbone. The religions, which pander to the weak characters, to the meek and servile, the ignorant and unthinking, must be discarded. Man must be given what he needs, not what he deserves. He must be taught the meaning and purpose of life, so that he no longer wastes it. He must know that whatever befalls him on Earth is either decreed or the result of his own actions, but that it may be utilised to his benefit elsewhere. Now, as always, man is taught to seek inspiration outside himself. In the light of the new dawn, he must be taught to seek his inspiration from the divinity within himself.

WSD:21:31 This is not the hour of dawning, for it lies still distant, and therefore, these words are no more than an arrow shot in the direction of the rising sun. He who writes them now will never put them into effect, for a child born prematurely has little chance of survival. A ship is not launched on the floodwaters, and a harvest is reaped only when the seed is sown in its proper season.

WSD:21:32 Do not be downhearted if the results of your preaching cannot be seen, for be assured that if good is sown well, it will surely take root. When your hearers are men of intelligence, speak to them profoundly, but if they are men who toil, men not gifted with intellect or well endowed with words, instruct them by parable and with tales drawn from their own background and turned to account.

WSD:21:33 When The Divine intends to call a man to high service, that man is certain to be the first disciplined by suffering. He may be tested by bodily labour, by hunger and privation, or he may be tried in the fires of trouble and distress. His every undertaking may be confounded and every effort frustrated. By such means his character will be strengthened and his resolution intensified. His understanding and compassion will be increased.

WSD:21:34 Men have to make mistakes to learn, and reformation of character often commences under duress. Yet, it does not follow that all derive benefit from the tests of life, for many weak characters succumb before them, and then, their weakness swallows them up. The benefit comes to those who realise benefit is to be gained and who look for it, or to those who, unconscious of benefit, still rise above their trials,

WSD:21:35 Nothing is wrong with the Spiritual Realm, and nothing is wrong with the world except through man's own actions. What is wrong and must be remade is man, himself. The Good Religion must, therefore, teach man to be happy and contented within himself and to rise above his environment. Too many lack this ability and are happy only when circumstances and surroundings are favourable, but they soon become depressed and sad when things go against them or are not to their liking. Despondency and worry arise when a person's thoughts are completely self-centred, and harmful desires arise when they seek selfish gratification. To seek the things and circumstances that please and to shun those that do not is taking the slippery path leading to the pit of sorrow. The road to degeneracy is wide, smooth and downhill all the way.

WSD:21:36 Men must learn that, while they traverse the arid desert of materialism, they must expect to suffer the thirstpangs of unquenchable desires and unsatisfied urges. Their feet will always drag heavily through the sands of sorrow and suffering. Only when they come to the cool waters of spirituality can they rest, refreshed and satisfied. The duststorms of passion, the mirages of deception and illusion and the dark cloud of mortal ignorance must be penetrated in order to glimpse the Light of Divinity beyond. The phantoms of sense fallacies must be recognised for what they are, unimportant things without substance.

WSD:21:37 Things come into being because they are needed and necessary, and when the Good Religion opens its arms to men, it will be for this reason. Until then, it is not harmful for them to worship the awe-inspiring symbols and indulge in the spirit-stirring litanies conceived by the many existing religions. These do serve by assisting the spirit to purge itself of grosser attractions and to elevate the soul. In such elementary forms of worship, the object of homage does not matter, for each worshipper forms an image in his own mind of what lies behind it according to his own state of development. In this manner, the way is prepared for the coming of the Light.

WSD:21:38 No activity of man is so wrapped in ignorance, so inept and harmful as religious intolerance or prejudice in favour of one outward form of worship as against another. All who worship are seeking the same destination, and each takes the road he thinks most suitable. Men are led by phantoms to fight for dimly-revealed causes and end up consumed in fiery pits of hatred. Why have they chosen one side rather than the other? Only because the particular religion they support is an accident of birth and upbringing. Man weaves his sorrows from the very materials given for his adornment and glorification.

WSD:21:39 The answers given by all true religions are inspired by the desire to meet particular needs. These needs differ according to time and place and the condition and development of men, but all true religions have this in common: they come in response to something upsurging in the nature of man. When the rites of a religion are performed without thought and its ceremonial becomes meaningless, then that religion is ready to die.

Chapter Twenty-Two – The Good Religion

WSD:22:1 This is not a recipe for salvation, nor a formula for blind belief. It is not a matter of doctrine alone, and dogmatic belief must not be rigidly imposed, though loyalty and unity are certainly to be expected from those who follow its light. The Good Religion is not so much a belief or doctrine as a way of living. It is the way of life of a company of kindred spirits headed for the same destination and all sharing the same adventure, with its hazards and excitement, all seeking the best road together.

WSD:22:2 It is not a religion of gloom and despair. It does not seek to placate or coerce any Being, for it serves a Divinity above such things. It is not a religion revelling in servility and meekness; instead, it seeks to reveal the greatness of man. It is a religion of joy and hope, of high ideals and aspirations. It adheres to the highest principles of Truth, Justice and Goodness. It aspires to the greatest good for all mankind and believes in the sanctity of life, love and family. It hallows hearth and home.

WSD:22:3 It is a practical religion teaching the doctrine of evolving betterment. It establishes a standard for men to live by, which will make them better men and permit them to live in peace and harmony with others. It values the qualities of courage, audacity, fortitude and steadfastness. It upholds the virtues of modesty, patience, purity and gentleness. It is not a religion of undue restraint or narrow dogma, and it does not believe in the futile mortification of the body. It takes full regard of man as a twofold being and maintains the dignity of the mortal as well as the spiritual body. It makes no empty promises of salvation or redemption and is not founded upon a system of indulgences, rewards or promises. It expounds the principles of personal responsibility, obligation and effort. Its prime objectives are to the carrying out of the Divine Design and the service of mankind. It is a religion to be lived by and not just believed in. It demands to be expressed in deeds and not in words, in beneficial action and not in blind conformity. It is more interested in bringing out the hidden good than in outward display and pomp. The Good Religion concerns itself with whatever is necessary for the unfolding of the spirit, and its aim is to spur man upward to divinity.

WSD:22:4 The purpose of a religion is to serve, and it cannot do this properly by concentrating on spiritual matters alone, for it also has the obligation of setting a moral standard. A worthwhile religion cannot permit itself to be shut out from everyday life. If it does so, it is undeserving of its status. It must concern itself with the way men live, with the conduct of their daily affairs, with their relationship with one another.

WSD:22:5 Religion is man's response to his existence in earthly conditions and the answer to the challenge of his environment. Therefore, it is in religion that he finds the most satisfactory outlet for his feelings and the best way of expressing his inner yearning. The soundless, insistent voice of The Divine calls out to man from the depths of his being, and that which guides and directs him towards it is called 'religion.'

WSD:22:6 The Divine is hidden from men and veiled behind the firmament, and this separation, this feeling of being cut off, is the source and basis of religion. The Divine and man, fire and spark, now sundered apart, crave to be united, and this craving expresses itself as religion.

WSD:22:7 Man, the person, is like a lamb separated from its mother, the source of its life, and lost in the mountain mists. He is a lonely creature pulled and pushed around by urges and desires, dragged onward by the remorseless chords of time, heavily burdened with fragile mortality and always haunted by the accompanying phantoms of decay and change. His only encouragement is the light of divinity just dimly glimpsed in the distance, and his only consolation and comfort his religion.

WSD:22:8 But religion too often gives cold comfort and little encouragement; therefore, the Good Religion must be a truecomforter as well as a champion. It will teach man that there is a happy haven and worthwhile destination at the end of the road. It will show him that it is futile to try and run away from life and that its trials are inescapable. Life is given to man with intent and purpose, and he can achieve divinity only by first experiencing the realities of existence here and rising above them.

WSD:22:9 The standards imposed upon those who follow the light of the Good Religion will be those already set out in the Sacred Books of times gone by, for wisdom is not a callow youth. Such standards should not weigh too heavily on men, as do some enforced under the cloak of ignorance. This is the Religion of the Light, and it accords with the natural tendencies of man. It declares every man to be heir of divinity and, therefore, capable of living a righteous and upward-tending life.

WSD:22:10 The concept of righteousness held by the Good Religion is not one of external display, for it preaches that goodness is expressed in deeds and in a way of life, not in the holding of barren beliefs and purposeless ceremonial. It is like a mighty oak, always shedding leaves and replacing them in the proper seasons. Its roots keep spreading out into new ground, but its trunk is always strengthening and growing greater.

WSD:22:11 The Good Religion believes that man is the instrument of The Divine and His deputy on Earth; that man is entrusted with certain responsibilities and duties, which he can shirk only to his cost; that the soul is immortal and the body mortal and that man can achieve divinity only through his own efforts. He can be saved by no one except himself.

WSD:22:12 There are those who prefer the worship of many lesser divinities, and those who divide their belief so from one come many, and each is content with his portion and derides that of others. The many divinities are like mirages across the sands, which appear to offer cool waters, but no man ever found refreshment there. When darkness falls, the mirage disappears, and he who trod the sand towards it is lost.

WSD:22:13 Men have to be organised in worship as in all things, but this is not so much for their own good, though this is often made the excuse, but to check man's inherent tendency towards irresponsibility and apathy. While it is true that the less responsible and resolute men are the more they have to be organised and controlled, it is also true that the more they are organised and controlled, the less responsible and resolute they tend to become. In this as in all things a balance must be struck. Therefore, when a religion teaches that men should be responsible and resolute, it should not seek to organise and control them too much. However, it must also be remembered that without leadership, organisation and discipline, no battle was ever won.

WSD:22:14 The Good Religion must do more than produce good men. The popular religions within the confines of civilisation already produce good men, but they do not produce divinely inspired men or men who rise even above goodness.

WSD:22:15 The Good Religion will not accept the doctrine now preached that the man who suffers is one who has done wrong or offended some divinity. Instead, it will declare that the man who suffers is undergoing one of the inescapable tests of life and may be one chosen for higher service. However, it should acknowledge that this should not lead to suffering being accepted passively. Not only must suffering be struggled against, but every effort must be made by others to help the sufferer. The trials and tests of life are not things to be endured with passive patience, they are challenges to be met and overcome.

WSD:22:16 The Good Religion must establish a tradition of service, which it can hand down from one generation to another. It must also establish base within a compatible body of people, from which it can be propagated, not only by preaching and teaching but also, more important, by example. To each of its followers, it must declare the message: "Whether a man does much or little is not as important as to whether he always does his best and directs his actions towards the fulfilment of the Divine Design."

WSD:22:17 The Good Religion exists even now, for it is the faith of the few who cherish the seed. It is limited to a small number who hand on the torch, and this must continue until the day already appointed. Meanwhile, mankind is not ill served by its many religions, but the day comes when they will no longer serve, and that is the day the child of man's ancient heritage will be born.

The Britain
Book

BRT:4:2 After our Lord died, having been hung on the cross outside the city walls of Jerusalem, Joseph of Abramatha took Mary, the mother of Jesus into his home until John could make suitable arrangements. Then he was called Guardian of the Lady, which title became confused in Britain with that of Guardian of the Sacred Vessel.

Table of Chapters

The Britain Book

Chapter One

BRT:1:1 To my stalwart son, always well beloved. I greet you heartily, desiring to hear of your welfare. Be not displeased at my going from Kelshaw or my manner of departure, for I first gave your mother and sister over to good keeping in the hands of the goodmistress Cotter.

BRT:1:2 Verily, such tidings were brought to me by diverse persons of the Craft on matters of our abiding concern, that I was beholden to come hitherwards. Nor durst I now go hence, for the charge remains, lying heavily upon my breast.

BRT:1:3 As for Hempshill he lied to us, for he is a knave and a churlish one, and we were fools to be deceived by his wiles and his tongue speaking such wild language. I will entreat with the bailiff, and mayhap he who stands in the lord's place will abide my supplication.

BRT:1:4 As we planned, you do thereafter, but I pray you beware in what manner you walk, for those, among whom we walk are full black-hearted and enwrapped in the ways of wickedness. They desire an end to all things, in which we hold fast, but are not as staunch that they will set upon you in a manly way but will start out upon you like lurking footpads. Beware, too, what you eat and drink, and trust not even they who speak fair unto you, for the hands of all outsiders are against us.

BRT:1:5 Send me tidings of Long Will and goodwife Abigail, and of John the Cordwainer and John of the Wildwood band, and others who stood in at the tithing ere you departed. It is to my abiding contentment that we have been able to acquit the Wanderers in full good measure, for their braziers did their work right stoutly in a cunning manner. Had we a clerk among us, then it could have been wrought to more avail; but no matter, for their hand was firm, and they faithfully followed the marks.

BRT:1:6 Now, take you the secured budget and go against Lewlaw, and leave it there in the cell under the Grimsbarrow where Alain the Pedlar secured his hoard.

** ** ** ** ** ** ** ** **

BRT:1:7 In the Books of Britain it is written: Ilyid came seaborne in a ship of Tarsis from across the sea of Wicta, setting up at Rafinia in the land of the Wains. From thence to the river Tarant, which flows between the Kingdom of Albany and the Kingdom of Korin, Albany being the land between the Isen and the Ikta. Passing Ivern and Insels, south of the Kathebelon, and then past Dinsolin to take water at the town where ships traded, standing at the foot of the red cliff between the two white ones around the extreme of the world to the northern Ikta in Siluria. Here, they were unwelcome, but were permitted to take water and wood and to trade for meat and grain. Sailing thence towards the rising sun, they came to the place beyond Sabrin called Summerland.

BRT:1:8 They were coldly welcomed by Homodren of the Chariots, but in the Kingdom of Arviragus they came under the mantle of the High Druid of the south, whose ear was inclined towards them, for he understood full well the nature of the three-faced god. The king heard their words but did not take them to heart, saying they differed little from what was there.

BRT:1:9 Then were the shipborne wanderers given land over from the Isle of Departure, saying that, could they live where no one else could because of the spirits, then their holiness would be established before all the people. The strangers were sorely tried by the Druids, but the spirits troubled them not. Nor did the sickness of the place come upon them, and the people wondered. They were troubled because of where the strangers were and were stirred up by the Druthin, but the shield of Arviragus protected them.

BRT:1:10 Now, eastward and to the north there was a lake, and between this and the Isle of Departure, there was a swampland and there was a village of houses that stood out above the water, and the moonmaidens and moonmatrons who served the dead dwelt there. Among these was Islass the Dreamer, who was sacred to the guardian of this place.

BRT:1:11 Islass was the daughter of the queen's youngest sister and a holder of the king's favour, and when she attended him, she divulged her dreams. It happened that she dreamed the same dream thrice, and this was its manner as she told it to the king: "Behold, I saw a moon which had three changing faces, and, as I watched, the changes the moon itself changed and became a sun, and within this sun was a face of a god. As I looked long on this sun, another sun appeared, and such was its brilliance that the first sun appeared inferior in brightness. Then, the two became one and its brilliance filled the sky. In the midst of this, I saw the king and many Druthin and priests of the strangers. Then I saw a great battlesword, and the brilliance faded, as did the figures, and only the sword remained, from which blood dripped drop by drop. Then, too, it faded.'

BRT:1:12 The king took heed of the dream and gave the strangers land beside the Summerhouse of the King, which could be reached by ships. Inland from here, the gifted land extended to the tree now called the Great Oak, which still stands, and thence to the hill south of the residence where Ilyid, being wearied, rested against a great stone. Beyond this was an avenue of standing trees and oak trees placed one and one, and the gifted land came up against this.

BRT:1:13 It extended southward to the holy vineyard, which was fenced about. The fruit of these vines was small and bitter in the mouth. The strangers built huts for shelter on the hillside, high enough to be free of the tides. They settled down and learned the language, though Ilyid and two of the women spoke it strangely.

BRT:1:14 The words of the strangers fell on deaf ears, for the people were content with the gods they knew and did not wish to weary their minds with the words of the new ones. When the strangers gathered in praise of The One True God, the tribesmen stoned them and shouted abuses, but Ilyid persevered, and while later the people still would not believe that The God of whom he spoke was more powerful than their gods, they would sit around and listen to his stories.

BRT:1:15 Now, when the strangers were granted the land, the Druthin disputed this with the king and said that they wanted a divine sign that their gods approved. Ilyid said, "Give me but half a year." At the witnessing of this, the Druthin set up a holistone, and Ilyid struck his staff into the soil to mark the covenant.

BRT:1:16 The following Eve of Summer there was a gathering and it was found that a small green shoot was coming up from the ground beside the staff, which was an offshoot of the staff. The king decreed that this was a sign that the land accepted the strangers, but these took it as a sign that what they taught fell on fertile ground and would take root.

BRT:1:17 Here, the strangers, now called the Wise Ones, were free from the yoke of Rome and from the intolerance of the Jews. They were not subject to immoral customs and were among the right-living people, simple but pure in mind and body. Close by was a place for trading in metals, slaves, dogs and grain. Here, Ilyid built himself a house unlike any others, for it was square and in two parts, more stone than timber. This place was called Kwinad.

BRT:1:18 Here, on twelve portions of land, the wise strangers dwelt in peace and they built a church which was a full sixty feet long by a full twenty-six feet wide. At one end was a statue four feet high, carved from a beech trunk. The roof was thatched with reeds, after the manner of the Britons. The walls were of wicker overlaid with plaster of chalk and mud.

BRT:1:19 Ilyid is buried outside the forked path before the church, and on his tomb was written, "I brought Christ to the Britons and taught them. I buried Christ, and now, here my body is at rest."

BRT:1:20 Islass was the first convert, and it is said that she alone knew the secret of the Holy Hawthorn. What this may be, none can know now. It is said that, when the Druthin murmured against the staff of Ilyid, she placed a twig in water and it flowered.

BRT:1:21 Here, in this holy place, under the direct guidance of God, our father founded the first church in Britain. It is said it was not built by human hands, which is true, and from here shall come that, which will be the salvation of mankind in the years to come. Here was the resting place for the souls of the dead, where they received their last sustenance before passing through the glass wall. From here ran the old road to the place of light where the bright-winged spirits flew freely in the place called Dainsart in the old tongue.

Chapter Two – Jesus - 1

BRT:2:1 This is the true record of events concerning Jesus, son of Joseph and Mary, which we have received by the hands of several who have lived within the circle of His Light, and more especially from one who is our earthly father in the faith. He being not the least among the articulate ones who knew Jesus, and a person of no mean estate, both in the distant land from whence he came and in this more virile land.

BRT:2:2 For Jesus came to fulfil the desires and longings of men expressed in certain Holy Books, but more so in many unlettered hearts. For it is written that such is the nature of things; the tree springing from the yearning of men shall not fail to bear fruit. For the Holy Books can be likened to an egg containing the embryonic hopes and desires of men.

BRT:2:3 In the Sacred Books of the Idewin it is written: 'The Son of Man is the shepherd of men and we know how diligently a shepherd tends his flocks.' Jesus came not as a shepherd to drive, but as one bearing a guiding lantern to show the way. It is also written: 'The Son of Man is the deliverer of men,' and while we know from what we have to be delivered, those who lived in His land misunderstood the meaning.

BRT:2:4 From the Book of the Holy Mark (whose wife was one of our own fair race, her father being a Roman waykeeper whose wife was barren, and having this homeborn lady, her mother, as a slave, had by her a child whom he later adopted and raised as a lady of estate), we learn much. But clearer to our understanding is that knowledge concerning Ilyid imparted to us by our earthly father.

BRT:2:5 Aristolas taught that Ilyid had been one who commanded with the ships of Rome, but was not without ships himself. So it was that, when Jesus went down to the Western Sea of the Jews, which is not the Sea of the Setting Sun, He being one skilled with His hands, worked on them. Jesus was brawnily built and not one to take money without labour.

BRT:2:6 Jesus, our Master, Light of our Life was hung on the shameful cross in His twenty-seventh year, this being the one thousand and ninety-ninth year of Britain, in the reign of Tiberius, ruler of the Roman lands to the east.

BRT:2:7 Within a year, Ilyid and others departed from their homeland shore by ship, and though this was demasted in a heavy storm, it made safe haven in Sankel. There, he and his son were joined by several other holy persons. They tarried awhile before crossing to Laidlow, from whence they took a ship to Tarsis.

BRT:2:8 In the year of Britain one thousand one hundred and twelve, our father came from Rome with others, because of the decrees of Claudius, ruler of all the Romans to the east, seeking refuge beyond the oppression of Roman might, where the true light could burn undisturbed. But the circle of Roman might spread ever wider, like a thrown fisherman's net.

BRT:2:9 Thirteen years after our Master was hung on the cross, the Romans came to the fair land of Britain, and the might of their legions prevailed over the brave Caradew, great battleking of all the Britons. He was the leader of fighting men such as will not be seen again. He was carried off, betrayed by an irrational woman, an honourable peace offering to appease the argument of might, together with the British fount of knowledge and wisdom. With him went the allwise Fran, being held in honourable captivity until returned to the land of light at the intercession of our father, for those whom he befriended had not forgotten him. For Ilyid taught that the greatest wrong man can commit against man is the betrayal of a friend.

BRT:2:10 Now, the daughter of Caradew was Gladys, red-haired, blue-eyed and slim, who married Pudens, Commander of the Legions, beloved of Paul the Martyred in God, who died in the one thousand one hundred and thirty year of Britain. Lein, son of Caradew, brother of Gladys, being the first Christian in Rome.

BRT:2:11 In the year of Britain one thousand one hundred and twenty-seven, there was a great outbreak of fighting, and many men sought refuge within the enclosure of Ilyid, for the free Britons had risen, having been given an assurance of victory by no less than the battlegoddess herself.

BRT:2:12 Calling on Amaraith and Kamulose, the Britons followed their battlequeen, whose heart was afire because of the rape of her daughters. She stood tall in stature and was serene of face, speaking deep but melodiously. She knew the mastery of letters and spoke three tongues. She had fair hair hanging to her hips when not battlegirded. Her head was circled by a golden war coronet and her tunic was of green and brown interwoven in the manner of men. She wore a short cloak of purple. Thus she spoke before the battle:

BRT:2:13 "I speak to you as a woman whose house has been violated and her daughters dishonoured, We have been dealt with unjustly and I appeal to you not only as a queen but more so as a woman. Britons who honour their womenfolk cannot regard this lightly. Unlike the squirming Roman Nierotes, I do not rule over servile and docile unmanly men who are less than men, nor like he who rules over pedlars and hucksters. Nor am I like the cowardly man/woman, Nero, who surrounds himself with perverts and half-men and slaves who satisfy obscene desires. Such is the nature of the vile culture these foreigners have introduced to our fair land."

BRT:2:14 "I am not such as these whose minds are fevered with an evil ferment. I rule over true men, little schooled in craftiness and deceit, real men born to fight and withstand adversity. The code they live by is that of manliness. True men indeed who, in the cause of freedom, willingly heed the call to arms and stake their lives on the outcome. They willingly offer themselves as a sacrifice for the future of their womenfolk and children and their lands and property."

BRT:2:15 "As the leader of this brave breed of men, I fervently plead for the assistance of your strong right arms. Let us not shirk the task or shun the opportunity to strike a blow for freedom. I pray the gods of war, the overseers of battles, for victory. We have the duty to stamp out these infections on our land, these ruthless enemies whose reputation is infamous. They are perverters of justice, promoters of depravity and servants of greed."

BRT:2:16 "They are a race who enjoys unmanly pleasures, who delights in the infliction of pain on the helpless but cringes like a dog at the prospect of its own suffering. Whose approbation is more to be feared and its friendship more to be shunned than its enmity. Never will I surrender to people whose ways I abhor, nor will I ever desire to live to see my countrymen treated as servile serfs. May the Great Godly Powers be with us now in the great testing time, as we gird ourselves to face the issue."

BRT:2:17 Those brave, inspiring words were of no avail, and Britain was lost, but the spirit could not be quenched, and manliness was maintained. It is not in victory that a race finds greatness but in defeat. The knowledge of Christ came, not through peace and prosperity but through persecution. That, which is written is not a tale of victory, but of the glory that resides in defeat. The books, which are the recipe for victory are written by defeated men.

BRT:2:18 I, Elfed, write these things, but they are not from my own heart but come from the hand of others. This is that Elfed who married Marcella, maid of Ilted, after the death of her husband who tripped over a stone and fell on a spike and died bent like a bow.

Chapter Three – Jesus - 2

BRT:3:1 Jesus was the son of Miriam called Mary, by Joseph. His brothers were Jacob, Joseph, Simon and James. He was born at Bethlehem. In the days of His youth, the land rang with the exploits of Judas the Galilean, who preached that there was no ruler but God; he was called the Teacher of Righteousness in his day.

BRT:3:2 Joseph, Jesus' father, died when Jesus was sixteen. Mary, His mother, did not like His inwardness, His long silences and His solitary habits. She rebuked Him for being a tardy breadwinner, but this was unjust, for He excelled in His craft. She could not understand her strange son who was unlike the others, and she wanted a practical man, not a dreamer and preacher.

BRT:3:3 Jesus had spells of rapture, and His male kinsfolk declared He was out of His mind, so they sought to have him put under restraint. But the womenfolk said He was harmless, and in cases such as this, their words coloured the law of the land. Jesus loved His father, who had taught Him His trade. He consoled Himself with the scriptures which said, "I will become His father and He shall be My son."

BRT:3:4 Jesus early became a wandering carpenter and then joined the Nasarines. There was excitement in the land because it was said that the prophesy of Daniel was to be fulfilled in these times. The conditions of the times fulfilled the predictions.

BRT:3:5 Then, Jesus went into the wilderness beside the Jordan. He joined the Society of Saints, which was beside the Sea of Heavy Salt. When He came back to the Jordan, He no longer retired within Himself, but was a man of direct and forceful speech. He was decisive and commanding.

BRT:3:6 The people called Him the Galilean because He was raised in Galilee, and they sought to name Him the Man of Messianic Hope and the Suffering Just One, when Judas the Galilean was dead. Some thought He was the warrior messiah, but He rebuked them, saying, "I am He of whom it is written 'He shall judge the poor rightly and reprove those who oppress them. He shall smite the Earth with the rod of His mouth and slay the wicked with the words that issue from His mouth.'"

BRT:3:7 He wrought cures, as did many others in those times. The Levites put out that He did not as they, but by the power of the Prince of Darkness. But Jesus said that such was blasphemy, as the healing spirit of God was strong within Him. Therefore, such an accusation was a sin, but they mocked Him.

BRT:3:8 He was a true man, a good organiser, strong, alert and resourceful. He had determination and courage, though withal, He could be gentle and compassionate. He was inflexible in purpose, yet, He could bend before the storm and survive where the stubborn man would go down.

BRT:3:9 He stood firmly against the holy men of the Jews, whose seeming holiness was but a cloak, for it was something that flourished only in the public eye. It was woven with self-righteousness, lined with intolerance and sewn with threads of sadness. Good men do good deeds out of the sight of others and gain merit from their selfishness and sacrifices.

BRT:3:10 One came to Jesus, saying, "Lord, I give many gifts and alms to the poor. I am ever giving to the needy. I am a rich man, but my riches have come by lawful means. I have traded with ships and encountered dangers to accumulate them. Having gained wealth, I live in moderation, supplying only my moderate needs. I give the rest to the needy poor, and I am ever ready to serve the deserving. Am I then a sinner?"

BRT:3:11 Jesus said, "No, by giving with discretion and making such sacrifices, you gain merit, and there is no harm in seeking riches for worthy ends. It is the love of money for its own sake that is productive of evil. The evils of riches arise from their misuse. If a man gains wealth in a lawful way and does not live in luxury, supplying no more than his moderate needs, serving the poor and deserving with his surplus, then he does no wrong."

BRT:3:12 A teacher of the Jewish way said to Jesus, "If God is so great and all knowing, why does He not strike down the wrongdoer? Why does He withhold His justifiable wrath when the wicked man swallows up the man who follows the path of goodness? Is he not the God of justice?" Jesus replied, "Justice is not a thing of the time. Though the mills of God grind slowly, they grind to perfection. Life itself metes out justice. The justice of God adjusts the injustice of men. Were this not so, I would not have come."

BRT:3:13 Jesus was then asked if He was one with God, and He answered, "It is not in Me to state that, which I know to be untrue, and truly there can be but one God alone. Because I have been granted visions and insight into things unseen and unknown to other men, what manner of man would I be did I claim equality with God? I have spoken only that which I am bidden. I have said, 'Worship God who is My Father and your Father.' Does this then raise Me above other men? I have proclaimed all men My brothers, and if I have said I am even as God, then truly I have raised them up also. Yet, this they cannot see, or is it that they fear the burden of their own godhood?"

BRT:3:14 Jesus came and was like the slasher, which clears away the useless undergrowth in the forest of life. He uprooted and burned that, which was unproductive. He planted good trees, but the undergrowth returns. It is a time for the activities of good men. Jesus found pearls by the seashore. He sowed the good seed in the hearts of those who followed Him closely. For his sake, many of the rich became poor.

BRT:3:15 He came and separated men out from the errors of the world. He brought men a mirror, into which they could look and see their own divinity. He opened a door now open to all, and those who choose to pass through stand on the road to the eternal. He raised up the fallen and healed the afflicted. He woke those who slept and reminded those who had forgotten. He enlightened the righteous and gathered in those who were lost.

BRT:3:16 To what can He be compared? To the great sun that shines down, giving joy and life to all living things. To a great river giving gladness to men and the waters of life to beasts. To the good husbandman who cherishes his fields and tends his flocks. To the men of the forests who care for their trees and thankfully gather the fruits thereof.

BRT:3:17 The sun shines today, and the air gleams with light. The Earth puts forth blossoms, and the seas are calm. The waters flow clearly, the birds sing and the gloomy Winter has gone. Hope dawns, and so it is with the Son of Man.

BRT:3:18 The tree of glory has been planted and will survive, for it is well serviced. Its servants are dutiful. So let it be like the holly, whose leaves are not shed in Summer or Winter, which stands with weapons ever ready in persecution or freedom, in good days and bad.

BRT:3:19 He who neglects these scriptures is like the branch of a fruitless tree; his life is fruitless. Blessed are those who seek fruit that grows out of our good deeds. He who copies a book is like a maimed man who gives his weapons to a whole and healthy man. The lettered man resembles this good land, which takes the seed and nourishes it. The rains fall plentifully and the crop is good.

BRT:3:20 The life men live is like an inn where they dwell shortly, or like a house rented for a limited time. Vessels of metal and earthenware are to them like borrowed utensils. Their riches are held in trust. The wise man uses them and they serve him, but he does not set his heart on these or hug them to his bosom.

BRT:3:21 Who is most praiseworthy for his goodness, the son of a rich man or the son of a poor man? The rich son gives only what he himself has been given, so surely it is the son of the poor man, for he has overcome the temptations of poverty and satisfied the cry of hungry mouths with the earnings of his own labour. It is the poor who help the poor, for the rich help themselves.

BRT:3:22 There are those who fast for the sake of Heaven, but Jesus said it were better did they devote themselves to learning the scriptures and to good works for the sake of Heaven. Yet, it is useless to merely read the scriptures, for unless they be taken into the heart and lived by, then they are things of little value and use. The value of all sacred writings lies in what people do with them. More important still is what the scriptures do to the people.

BRT:3:23 A man asked Jesus, "Lord, what does it mean when it is written that the iniquities of the fathers shall be visited upon the children?" Jesus said, "When a man commits a sin, for which he does not make full recompense in his lifetime, then the same temptation is placed in the way of the son, for there is a bond of family blood between them. Is it not manifest also that the wrongs a man does within his own household become the sins of the sons within their households? Wrongful living is the heritage of generations.

BRT:3:24 A man asked, "Where is God?" Jesus took a piece of bread and gave it to the man, saying, "Take this and hold it." Then He said, "Put out the other hand." He poured a little water on the upturned palm and said, "Now you have felt the power of God, for without His spirit in the bread and in the water, these would not exist for you. Split a billet of wood, and God will be there. Lift up a stone, and you will find Him."

BRT:3:25 Another said, "Tell us how we may best serve God." Jesus replied, "Talk not of serving God as you would serve a king. In serving God, man serves himself. You ask in your heart, shall you be this or that or a priest. Let your own heart point the best way, and having chosen it, follow it with devotion and fortitude."

BRT:3:26 At a wedding feast, Jesus was asked, "Master, why do You come to this place when it is a gathering place of those who seek only their own pleasure and will drink to excess if it is provided?" Jesus said, "Our purpose here is to make glad the hearts of the hosts and to share in their enjoyment, blending their pleasure with ours. There will always be those who are neglectful of their obligations and who concern themselves only with their own wellbeing. Yet, is this reason enough not to bring happiness to those who have invited us?"

BRT:3:27 One day, Jesus and those with Him came upon an old man playing with childish things. A bow and arrow-bearing huntsman passing by mocked him, saying, "Behold the old man playing as a child." Jesus called him over and said, "Do you always keep your bow bent, the string under stress?" "Of course not" replied the huntsman. "To do so would be foolish, for the bow would become useless were it not unbent from time to time." Jesus said, "Just so is it with the old man, and you should know better."

BRT:3:28 The bowman strings his bow before he shoots and, when the shooting is over, he unstrings it. A bow kept always strung will break and be useless when needed. So it is with a man who never relaxes. He is ever taut within, and when the testing time comes, his stomach turns to water.

BRT:3:29 Jesus taught that there are things, which should be approached with humility of spirit, they are: holiness, wisdom and nobility. Humility bestows upon the soul the benefit of harmony and attunement. A man once said to Jesus, "But who can define these things; that which is holy to one man can be unholy to another. The thing, which one man holds sacred, another holds to be an abomination. That, which one will bless another will curse." Jesus said, "The many nations and men, because of the diversity of their natures, hallow many different persons, places and things, apart from their gods. But nothing can be made holy by men alone, neither can anything wholly of Earth be holy. That, which is wholly of and for God is holy, the place wholly for God is holy and the person who lives wholly for God is Holy, but where on Earth can such absoluteness be found?"

BRT:3:30 "If by gathering in a temple, men feel they can better commune with God, then He will be there, and that place will be holy. If within a circle of stones or before a symbolic image, the soul of man may be stirred to attunement, then God will not absent Himself because of the Nature of the Place. He will meet man wherever man earnestly prepares for His coming. Though the temple may be holy to one man and the circle of stones to another, both places will be hallowed by God, if therein, the souls of men are elevated to commune with him."

BRT:3:31 "A structure of splendour, magnificent in its architecture, called holy by men who worship there, if their spirits remain asleep and unstirred will not be hallowed by the presence of God. He does not honour places where men just congregate, where their voices alone are raised in worship. He hallows the place where their souls and spirits are uplifted as they seek communion with Him. A Holy place is where the uplifted spirits of men blend with the nature of God."

BRT:3:32 A man asked, "What of wisdom? Has this not been plentiful in the world since the days of the Great Enlighteners, of whom Solomon was deemed the greatest? Even before him, there was much wisdom, yet is Earth a better place for this? What has it contributed to progress?" Jesus replied, "Alas, never has there been a shortage of wisdom in the world, but always there has been too little in the hearts of men. Wisdom is not something written in books, but that, which is conveyed from the book of the heart. It is a way of life."

BRT:3:33 All the wisdom of the past, held in reverence by some, was easier to write than to live by. Yet, following it is the only wisdom. Wisdom, however, is more than the thoughts of the wise, it is the accumulated philosophical knowledge of mankind winnowed by the wind of practicality.

BRT:3:34 Nobility is an attribute of the soul, and no man has this by right of birth. Nobility demonstrates an ability to live and act according to the high principles. It is expressed in deeds, outlook and bearing, in the manner of life and relationship with others. That, which ennobles a man is his recognition of something to love and strive for outside of himself. Nobility is the subordination of self to principles.

BRT:3:35 Jesus was One, in whom all the virtues came to fruition, and His gentleness drew to Him all His neighbours. In His presence, even enemies were reconciled, and this presence alone brought tranquillity to a restless and sorrowful heart. In the street, even the little children followed Him, just to touch His hand.

BRT:3:36 His reaction to injustice and insult was a sorrowful compassion. He neither sought to acquire anything beyond His immediate needs nor treasured what he had. Beneath His soft exterior was a rocklike, immovable determination immune to oppression and suffering alike. Despite His gentleness He could act decisively and swiftly, and when He had cause to strike in the name of justice and right He never avoided the issue.

BRT:3:37 His mind and wit were like the lightning flash. He was always keen and alert, and His face never lacked the calm beauty of cheerfulness. He was friendly towards all and acted so as not to annoy anyone. Only in the face of great injustice to another or oppression of the weak, or in the presence of gross hypocrisy did His wrath boil up and overflow; but never was it other than righteous. Though always compassionate and sympathetic, He was never sad or downcast. He rose above all suffering and pain, and ever seemed at peace within Himself.

BRT:3:38 Mary said to Jesus, "To whom can Your Disciples be likened?" Jesus said, "They are like children at play in a field, which belongs to a stranger, and when the owner comes, they say, 'This is our field, therefore convey it to us.'"

BRT:3:39 Thomas said, "If the spirit brought the body of flesh into being, it is a marvel." Jesus said, "It would be a much greater miracle had the body brought the spirit into being, for the lesser cannot create the greater. I marvel how this great wealth of beauty can dwell in such a mean habitation. But to he who has goodness in his heart, goodness shall be given; he who lacks goodness shall be stripped of what he has."

BRT:3:40 Jesus also said, "Just as it is impossible for any man to stretch two bows or mount two horses, so is it impossible for a man to serve two masters."

BRT:3:41 The disciples asked, "Is circumcision a good thing?" Jesus replied, "If it were would not children be born circumcised from the mother's womb? Only circumcision in the spirit confers true benefit."

BRT:3:42 When asked concerning accounting, Jesus said, "Give to Caesar that, which is Caesar's and to God that, which is God's. Give Me what is justly mine, and keep for yourselves only that which is rightly your due. Deal fairly with all men, and shun the morals of the marketplace. Do not become like the Samaritans who, loving a tree, hate its fruits, or loving the fruit, hate the tree. The Pharisee is like a dog sleeping in the manger, from whence the oxen eat. It cannot eat what is in the manger; neither will it let the oxen eat."

BRT:3:43 Jesus said, "The Kingdom of Heaven is like a woman carrying a jar of good wine. Being careless, she puts the jar down heavily and crashes it, and when she resumes her way, the wine spills out behind her on the road, but she blithely continues on her way, unaware of the spillage. When she enters the house, the master takes the wine jar and finds it empty." The disciples asked what this could mean, and Jesus replied, "When you possess the good things of the Kingdom of Heaven, do not let them slip away."

BRT:3:44 "For the Kingdom of Heaven is neither here nor there and contains all good things. It is in the hearts of men and exists where God reigns. When the lion lies down with the lamb and peace reigns over all, there shall be found the Kingdom of Heaven. Yet truly, Heaven and the Kingdom of Heaven are not the same." These things were said in the forecourt of the temple.

BRT:3:45 Jesus took the disciples who were with Him into the Court of the Hebrews, which was an inner place, and a warden, a priest named Levi, stopped them, saying to Jesus, "Are You an ignorant man? Do You not know it is forbidden to walk here in the presence of holy things without first purifying yourselves? See, those who follow You have not even washed their feet. They enter here defiled by the world."

BRT:3:46 Then, Jesus stopped and said to Levi, "Concern yourself with your own state rather than with ours." The priest replied, "I am clean. Having bathed in David's pool, going down by one set of steps and coming up by another; only having done this and donned clean clothes have I come here." Jesus said, "Lord, have mercy on the blind! You have washed in standing water, which may have been befouled by dogs, and scrubbed your outer skin as harlots, singing girls and vain men do who are full of vileness inside. But My disciples and I have little need for outer forms of ritual cleanliness, being clean within, for we have washed in the living waters of the spirit."

BRT:3:47 Having departed from the temple, Jesus said, "Do not the guests assemble in the antechamber before entering the feasthall? There, the hands and feet are washed, the head anointed, and small foods to whet the appetite are eaten. Even so is the Earth the antechamber of the Kingdom of Heaven."

BRT:3:48 "Live your lives in the world as men who journey through a strange land, marvelling at its wonders, tasting its pleasures, but ever on guard against dangers, for undue love of the world is a doorway to evil. There are those who derive pleasure in being what they are not, but as their hair turns grey, they suffer sorrow and frustration. Be ever true to yourselves and to your natures."

BRT:3:49 It came to pass, at this time, that many said that Jesus was the Messiah, but this was a manifest falsehood. Jesus, the son of Joseph and Mary, was an inspired prophet, a teacher who held the hand of God and there had been others before Him. His mother was a decent woman; both ate food as humans do. Mary did not set herself up as a goddess, neither did she preach.

BRT:3:50 It is of no moment to those who are not Jews whether Jesus was the heralded Messiah or not, so believe as you will, but were He born of a Holy Ghost and not of Joseph, then He did not fulfil the prophesy. Men step outside the bounds of truth in their beliefs, but this, too, is of little moment unless they impose their beliefs on others.

BRT:3:51 Jesus was not a sorrowful man, for greatness cannot be downcast. Always, he brought strength to the disheartened and was not influenced by the despondency of others. When Peter was dismayed and shut his sorrow within, Jesus said, "If My friend will not admit Me into the antechamber of his sorrows, how can I ever sit in the reception room of his affections?"

BRT:3:52 Jesus set His face against all forms of melancholy. He said, "The man who cannot rise above the burden of his sorrows or the trials of the day shall not know the Kingdom of Heaven; nor can he know the love, which is the cornerstone of life."

BRT:3:53 There was a Greek scholar in the crowd, who said to Jesus, "Your never-rusting tongue wearies me; words neither make men nor change things. It is the sword and spear which are all powerful and raise kings or cast them down." Jesus replied, "Truly, the words of scribes are greater than the commands of war chiefs. That, which is written and read can not only change things but also endure forever. The sword gains prestige through destruction, but the pen of the scribe gains prestige through creating. That, which destroys will be destroyed; that, which creates shall be preserved.

BRT:3:54 A Roman soldier who hailed from Gaul spoke up, saying, "Let scribes do what scribes do best and swordsmen do what they do best, but it is foolishness and futile to set one against the other, for men cannot write with swords, or fight with quills or writing reeds. Let men become brothers, as they await the day of the Awakener. Tell me, good Master, when shall the end be?

BRT:3:55 Jesus answered. "There will be an end to the beginning, and men will know this by the spirit of the times. Men will no longer be as brothers; nor will they be manly. Women will be as men and men as women. Adultery will not be condemned, nor will fornication; therefore, these will flourish. Men will not honour their homelands, and there will be no discrimination among them, nor will they maintain the purity of their races. Fathers will not be honoured, nor mothers respected, and children will be raised to be wayward. Perversions will be encouraged, and criminals will mock the law. There will be incest and rape and it will be unsafe to walk abroad. Floods, famines, droughts and earthquakes will cause death and destruction: Strange sicknesses will smite the people, and there will be a denial of God. Babes will be slain in the womb."

BRT:3:56 "Men will lust after the wives of other men, and marriage shall lose its meaning. Women will go to the marriage table unchaste and with deceit in their hearts. Their husbands, creatures of pity, will hear the mocking voices of laughing men. Priests will defile their altars with their impurity, and the rulers will be held in little repute. It is not God who marks the end days, but men who lives as though setting a pitfall for himself."

BRT:3:57 Jesus saw a man ill-treating a horse, and He rebuked him for his cruelty to a dumb animal. The man became angry and said, "This is my beast." Jesus said, "You are wrong, it is God's creature, and I, as His servant, am here to protect it. For no man can wholly own any living creature except it be in the name of The Great God of Life."

BRT:3:58 This has been copied and edited as found. It appears to have been preceded by a document entitled, 'The Sayings of Jesus.' For some reason, it has been cut up into pieces, each containing just a few paragraphs. Included were other scraps from some much later source, which, for various reasons, are suspect. The latter part of this manuscript is probably a late if not modern addition, but it may have been re-written from some older material. This has not been altered and is included under the authorisation given to the compilers.

Chapter Four – The Writings of Aristolas

BRT:4:1 This is an account of the coming of certain Wise Strangers to the sea-girt realm of Britain. Taken from the Books of Britain and re-written into the appendices to the Bronzebook. This being that part safeguarded by Rowland Gasson.

BRT:4:2 After our Lord died, having been hung on the cross outside the city walls of Jerusalem, Joseph of Abramatha took Mary, the mother of Jesus into his home until John could make suitable arrangements. Then, he was called Guardian of the Lady, which title became confused in Britain with that of Guardian of the Sacred Vessel.

BRT:4:3 Aristolas wrote these things in the Sacred island, and this is his prayer: "In silence, hands uplifted, heart humbled and mind stilled, Your servant presumes to come into Your Presence, Great Understanding One. Grant me the abounding joy of union with Your Spirit. Grant that all my deeds be in harmony with the Great Law and that I learn to acquire wisdom, so I may illuminate the hearts of men."

BRT:4:4 "Let me embrace Your Spirit in full knowledge of my twofold nature. Guide my feet towards the Great Law, by which all true seekers find the light. As long as my body and spirit remain together, so long will I preach to men, seeking always to awaken a response in their hearts. Bless me with sweetness of speech and harmony of voice. Help keep me from the grip of greed and from the loud-mouthed futilities and frivolities of illiterate men. Spare me the sad companionship of the sanctimonious ones."

BRT:4:5 "God of my heart, Sun of my life, Keeper of my circle of content, fill this place with the divine emanations from Your Being. Attune with the Circle of Truth and the Circle of Light. Make me receptive to the lessons and inspirations of life."

BRT:4:6 Joseph, our father in faith, came across the storm-tossed seas to the place called Balgweith, and from thence to Taishan, where he met the envoy of the king who was sorely troubled. For the Chief of All Druthin, called Trowtis, was away at the meeting place of his god, where he came in a wondrous way every nineteen years. There, the ceremony lasted three moons.

BRT:4:7 When Trowtis returned, he met Joseph at the place now called Henmehew, because of the strange tree that grows there. The Druthin held a feast of welcome in the place called Nematon, which is below the great hill. The Chief of All Druthin washed his face, his hands and his feet, then a white goat was led out and sacrificed on a four-horned altar. Trowtis washed his hands again and made an offering of salted barley cakes and gave some to Joseph, called Ilyid by the people here.

BRT:4:8 Then, the goat's thighs were burnt on the altar while a lesser priest mixed the sacrificial blood with water and black wine. Then barley cakes and a chalice containing the blood, wine and water were passed through three sacred horns before being given to the chiefs present. Then, youths danced around the fire over the sacrificial pit.

BRT:4:9 Then, priests of a lower order prepared tables for a feast while the common people sat around on logs made smooth at the top. The sacrificial beast, having been first offered to the gods of this place, was eaten by the common folk. All except the liver, which, being the seat of blood and life was kept for the diviners. These found that the right wing of the liver was broken, so they prophesied that no enemy would enter the land.

BRT:4:10 Now, the king called together a great conclave of the people, and the Druthin were there. The king said to our father, "Speak now before the people. Tell us of your ways, and we will judge whether they be worthy." Joseph spoke a tongue understandable to these people, but he spoke slowly and not after their fashion.

BRT:4:11 Our father said, "As the light came first and called the eye into being to see it, so it is with God, who is the already existing light. The heart does not create the thought, but the thought produced the heart. This, so it could manifest, for the heart is created to serve thought in the world of effects. The world of causes lies in another kingdom." The Druthin said, "The light we know and have, these things are not strange to us. All light comes from an original crystal, which is always virgin, and we say the behaviour of light is the fore-ordained symbol to man.

BRT:4:12 Joseph, our father, said, "I have not come to batter down your house of hope, for it has many pleasing features, even as ours. So let us not disagree, but take the best from both and, discarding what is less good, fashion something of value to all. Let us weigh one thing against the other, rejecting that, which less clearly shows the way."

BRT:4:13 The king said to the Chief of All Druthin, "Do we not have the source of light in a grail egg?" The Druthin replied, "The sun shines not, and the Esures (servants of Light) will not come without the presence of the Great Gleamer, which provides their sustenance. There can be no incarnation of light on Earth unless there be, behind it, a greater light."

BRT:4:14 Joseph said, "When I was shipbound, I had a vision of God; the eyes of my spirit were opened, and I saw Him in all His glory. Then, I understood that there was no difference between the nature of His Spirit and the spirits of men, only that His was of an infinitely greater purity. This I knew for sure: God and man are of the one essence. I knew we are all rays of the One Light, sparks from the One Flame. Yet, the flame is not the fire, for what flame can call itself into being?"

BRT:4:15 Joseph said, "If fire can be contained in wood, to leap forth when two pieces are heated through rubbing together, yet remain hidden within the wood, then surely it can be so with the soul within man.

BRT:4:16 The Chief of All Druthin said, "Often have I thought on this. All men are alike in nature and all aspire to the same goal. All seek to make the same journey's end; only the route differs. Therefore, let us not argue whether men should follow your road or mine, but find between us a path better than either."

BRT:4:17 One priest said, "What of the worlds within the ever moving circles?" Joseph replied, "The hidden worlds are numbered as sands on the seashore. If a man concerns himself with many things, he benefits none and derives no benefit, himself. Let us concern ourselves with this world first."

BRT:4:18 The Druthin said, "Who can change the natures of men, for these are fixed by the gods." Joseph answered, "All things can be changed, but not always for the better. Change and life are inseparable."

BRT:4:19 Joseph went on to say, "Because you are folk who work the land, bringing it to fruitfulness, you are not to be despised. Let the newcomers with their armed might say as they will; you are workers with God. Were not the Sons of God also called the Sons of the Plough? Did they not fight against the Sons of Men who were hunters eating raw flesh like the beasts and worshipping serpents, which crawl on their bellies? Always there have been some who worship things of insensitive wood and stone, grovelling in the dust at their feet, and those who worship the highest they can see, the sun and the stars. Others reach out even beyond these."

BRT:4:20 One of the Druthin asked, "What know you of the Eye of God in men?" Joseph replied, "What is written in the heart is the Eye of God in men; this sees everything. Knowing right from wrong, it puts things in instant perspective. Men, in whom this eye is closed, are little better than the beasts of the field and forest. I come as one who opens the eyes of such as these."

BRT:4:21 In the beginning, the king had listened in silence and was tolerant, because he felt he could indulge these strangers. Now, as he saw that their teachings might prevail, he became angry and unreasonable, as it happens in instances such as these. He said, "Who gives you authority to speak in this manner? Who sent you, and do you come to spy on us? To whom do you make report?"

BRT:4:22 Joseph said, "Know this, great king. I am a servant of The Great God of Light. I am sent in order to build a church here, where it will serve your people well. I will establish a place of light unto them. I come to teach the perfect commandments. Ask among your own about me, for I am not unknown to them. I have no human teacher, from whom I learned the wisdom, from whence I got these things. I lived in the light of Christ but learned tardily. Then I had a message from God Himself, 'Go preach to those who dwell at the edge of the Earth.'"

BRT:4:23 The king said, "How comes it that these things have been revealed to you, while the same God who reigns here has not revealed them to us, even though we were the lords of this land? Are you a man of significance this side of the wide waters?"

BRT:4:24 Joseph answered, "Those who are established in The God of Light need no mentors, and they take pride in their insignificance, for it is said, 'The first shall be last and the last first. The lowly shall be raised up and the haughty cast down.' We do not seek after gold or worldly possessions. Of myself, I have no power, but I have power from God. It is God who commands, and it is He who makes a true man of God."

BRT:4:25 There was much talking and long discourses on the nature of God, and the Druthin challenged Joseph to produce Him, saying, "Though you decry our images, yet we do have likenesses of our gods, while you lack even these. Your words are mere puffs of wind."

BRT:4:26 These things and more were said, and the Druthin believed, but tardily. Then, at the midsummer festival the Chief of All the Druthin collapsed on the processional walk, denying himself the reviving draught prepared by Islass, his daughter. He died in the arms of Joseph our father. It was he who received the moon chalice and the light of Britain. The Druthin held the secrets of the Great Temple of the Stars, and theirs was the royal isle in the Kingdom of Kevinid.

Chapter Five – The Writings of Abaris

BRT:5:1 I write in terrible times. My people have been driven to black despair, and the most cruel of foes has taken our fair land. The wisdom which flows through my pen, tutored by Isbathaden the Younger, is as set into writing by our father Aristolas and by the great ones who gave us the Annals Romanorum which we hold in part, clinging like the thundervine to what is left.

BRT:5:2 I am no weaver of words and if fine phrases bedeck what I transcribe, they are the work of better hands than mine. I am not as a teller of tales who sits before the hallfire, a waster of words like women over the fuller's tub. Those who wear the red robes of nobility have passed over the misty seas, and the land lies barren of learning. The Firthreig have taken over the dwellings of the wise, and the three pillars of progress - wisdom, courage and beauty - no longer stand against Maermagic.

BRT:5:3 I speak of one named Jesus who was Hesus come to Earth as a godling, the much abused One, but does not the lawman whose case is bad abuse his opponent? I speak of those who followed Him and suffered in the dark days of oppression. The anger of the people smouldered against the just ones, as Jesus had foretold while still in the body. Then, the time came when the dragon of disaster awoke, thirsting for blood, and it began to stalk its prey while liemongers fanned the smouldering embers of hatred into flame.

BRT:5:4 The king of the land was stirred up to anger, and the hatred of the people became an all consuming fire. The wolves came out of their dark forest and suddenly fell upon the flocks of innocent sheep and rent them apart. Wild bears burst among the sheepfolds and ravaged them. Evil-motivated ones came and cut down the apple-bearing trees, and the starglint nights were woeful. Beasts trampled the flower gardens while eaglehawks swooped down among the dovecotes. The earthen ones broke.

BRT:5:5 The culled-out servants of The High God entered the arena of vile entertainment, like children before their teachers. They were thrown into the path of the lions. Some, they equipped with weapons and forced to fight with bears. Women were scented with the smell of heat-angered beasts, and children stood frozen with fright. Their bodies were shredded like the paper of Egypt.

BRT:5:6 They moaned pitifully, like oxen awaiting the slaughter, and their children were murdered before their eyes. They were raised up by throngs on the wrists, their feet pressing on thorns or on heated plates, or over small fires. Many were thrown into prisons to die of hunger, thirst and cold.

BRT:5:7 In the days when the Druthin looked darkly on the enlightened ones, the Hammer of God said to the king, "It is in the nature of people placed such as we to fear those who wield the weapons, but we have One who is more to be feared than you, and He is One to whom I look up. I stand in awe of The Great One who is strong enough to overlook your present power, but who will surely call you to account in the life to come." The king said, "Where is your temple?" The reply was, "A true servant of God has no need of a temple built of wood and stone."

BRT:5:8 It was to tell of such things that the Anointed One came, to awake sleeping men drunk with the heavy droughts of sensuality and lewdness. He came to open the eyes of men to their carnal degradation, which corrupts their spiritual natures. He came to open their eyes to their divine destiny and to show them the hidden sparks of divinity captive and suffering in the carnal natures of apathetic men.

BRT:5:9 There are those who prefer the dregs of darkness to the living power of light, which flows from Jesus, Son of Dewi, Sap of the Trees, Sweetness of the Fruits and Perfume of the flowers, Bread of Heaven and Shepherd of Souls. He is the River of Sweet Waters arising at the Spring of Truth.

BRT:5:10 I am an unworthy one in the telling of these tales. Great Inspirer, give me a ray of inspiration to raise my voice, as it were, from the mystic cauldron, sister vessel to the ice-clear chalice. I will lay the dowry of the mystic maid at the feet of the discriminating ones. The smoothness of my lay flows from the bubbling brew from out of the great cauldron. I am one of God's inspired and not numbered among mere poets yapping at the heels of high-browed bards.

BRT:5:11 I am not one aspiring to the noble chair, whose words must be proved by privilege and truth. Where are the grave, high-browed druids of the past and the wonder-making bards? Those who thrive today cannot rise to the sky heights of song, even though their melody-making wings ache with fluttering. They are like the food pot placidly bubbling over the red greying coals.

BRT:5:12 O Comforter of the comely tribes, welcome me into the lush dominions of field and forest. O Champion of the thrusting sharp spear, hear my petition thrown out into the three-circled expanses of power. Let us feast at the overflowing cauldrons of peace and let us, your people, sleep in the downy, heather-scented beds of tranquillity. Protect the holy sanctuary of the blue-gowned bards where valour is honoured and chastity cherished. The raging assailants, protectors of slothful ways, labourers of concealed mysteries, surround us. We call on the guardian bulwark of celestial power to become the smasher of shields.

BRT:5:13 How straightly comfortable a scribe am I, who reconciles the mystic daughter with the lowly mother! Who places the crystal-clear chalice beside the blood-filled golden cup! Who combines the divine circle with the eternal cross and the sorrowful son with the triumphant fighting father!

BRT:5:14 In the beginning, only the Absolute existed in the firmament, called Nuvrie by the Britons and Kewgant by the Welsh of the west. The Spirit of Life spread outwards from the hub to form Gwinvidon, the region of light and the circle of spirituality. This opened out to Anton, which is the circle of germinal existence, at the inner edge of which was the circle of corporeality. This spread out to Abred, which is the material plane and the circle of trial, testing and tribulation. It is a place of experiment and experience for gaining knowledge, wisdom and spirituality. Below this is Anoon, the sea of souls. Here is the lake of unspecialised soul stuff, which is forged and fashioned in Abred and perfected in Gwinvidon. In Abred was the Garden of Karahemish, through which flowed the river Nara. Here dwelt Keili and Kithwin. Here were born Derwiddon, the first of the Druthin, Gwinidendon who composed the first song, and Tydain who was the first bard.

BRT:5:15 It is said that there were two classes of druids: the Dryones who were masters of medicine and divination, and the Druthin who were superior and gifted with twinsight and magic. The first had their seat at Abri, while the Druthin had their seat at Innisavalon, the island of indestructible apples.

BRT:5:16 The druids believed in the One Supreme Being, but also held that there was a body of lesser Beings. They believed in a fairyland of Nature Spirits, which manifested to mortals. All happenings were motivated by an interplay of unseen rays from The Source. Therefore, the running of a hare, flight of birds, fall of leaves, patterns in sand, the sound of waters, were meaningful.

BRT:5:17 Their seven deadly sins were: hypocrisy, theft, cowardice, fornication, gluttony, indolence and extortion. Above all precepts were the three manly qualities: honour, courage and manliness, and the three womanly qualities of decency, decorum and chastity. There were female temple attendants, but no female druids. The druids who taught were called Nemids. There were Waiths who knew the secrets of Nature, and these would not eat birds. Once every three years there was a firewalking.

BRT:5:18 Under the great night reflector, only four animals appear as ghosts: the dog, cat, horse and hare. The ghosts of these could be forewarners of the crack of doom. Will-o-the-wisps haunt the marshlands, but few are enlivened by ansis. Nick-o-the-nights haunt the stony places and fells.

BRT:5:19 Joseph Idewin and his brave band came to flowering Britain three years after the death of Jesus. He converted Gladys, sister of Caradew, who married a Roman, and her sister Aigra who was the wife of Salog, lord of Karsalog. After landing, he and his band passed through an avenue of oaks and standing stones. They first built huts over against the holy vineyard where the fruits were bitter.

BRT:5:20 After all the saints had gone to their rest, the first church and its surroundings became a wild place, a refuge for wild creatures. Then, as the land remained holy, saints came from Gaul, who restored it, and one was Fairgas the Briton, who had served at this place as a youth. Idewin was buried in a shirt of fine linen, which he had worn when burying Jesus, and which was stained with three spots of blood on the chest. He was buried by the two-forked cross. The saints had lived in twelve huts around a never diminishing well at the foot of the holy hill.

BRT:5:21 Joseph Idewin was related to Avalek, whose kingdom bordered that of Arviragus, through Anna the Unfaithful. He converted Claudia Rufina, the daughter of Caradew previously called Gladys, who married Pudens, a Roman, and had a daughter Pudentia. In his twenty-eighth year, Caradew was betrayed to the Romans by Arisia, queen of Bryantis. He married Genuissa, daughter of Claudius, to bind the peace agreement. The name 'Caradew' means 'filled with love,' but he preferred to use a warrior name.

BRT:5:22 Gladys, sister of Caradew, married Aulus Plautius, a Roman commander. Caradew held an estate in Siluria, and he was made warchief when Guiderius, son of Kimbelin, was slain by a slingshot, near the river Thames. In the year 59 of our Lord, the British rose up tinder Woadica, the horsefighter, who died nearly three years later when Gulgaes became warchief.

BRT:5:23 Caradew went forth with the bright, flashing, sharp pointed spears of war. Bards, renowned judges of excellence, sang his praise. Even druids of the three great circles launched their eloquence in the five dialects and four tongues. Dancers from the steep mount gaily preceded him, and diviners from the high-pillared gates declared wise oracles.

BRT:5:24 I am one who lived in those brave days. It is my right to be the master singer, for I stand in the last line of blood from the golden strong-armed kings of old. My fathers father was a bard of the high enclosure, prince of the true tribe, high-caller of the Kimwy, a giant of song born of melodic race, light-tongued, harp-voiced.

BRT:5:25 Well fitted am I to sing Caradew's praise. Excepting great Keili and the all-seeing diviners of the land, and sagacious druids of the fine woven gold chains, and chiefs of the splendid wars, I am first above all to open his mouth in honour. He honoured all blue-gowned bards, singing bards of the land, guardians of the storehouses of winged words. Guests such as I were never wanting for provision while Caradew reigned, a high king over the wide land of heroes. He paid them well in sleek, fleet-limbed coursers, chasers of the wind-borne hare.

BRT:5:26 The valorous druids, feared by foes, the flowing-robed judges of disputes, said, "Let songs be composed with melodious refrains to praise the savage-subduing heroes."

BRT:5:27 The power of the bard is in the uplifted shield shaking before the tumult, high-riding on the battleleader's shoulder. It is in the quivering hare crouching in the bracken-buried hallow. It is in the soft-sighing promise of a fair-skinned maiden. In the finely-shaped form of the terrible spearblade. In the bright-bladed sword clashing in the heat of the conflict. In the homely, comforting abode of the family.

BRT:5:28 I have sung my last day, the wonder days have gone and strangers walk the land. The high-hearted bards have gone to their rewards and the diviners mouths have been sealed. Now it is the fashion to hear the babbled words of Brandigan of Walsogo, which stand before the Resounding Halls, by the stream of sorrow, at the very gates of hell.

BRT:5:29 The purifying Kolgarth fires remain as transmuters to Heaven. Happy is the flame-borne one. Our fathers of old believed that fire was a form of creature, which had to be fed with fuel, given share of the food and in stressful times the sacrifice of a human. They who read the flames and embers are no longer with us, for they have been supplanted by the omen readers.

BRT:5:30 As dogs can see happenings in the world of spirits, then whatever they do is important, and a wise man watches them and takes heed. For if a dog sleeps before the fire, all is well, be at peace. If he sleeps on a bed, then beware. To sleep in a corner means strife, and to howl means a death. To crouch and whimper indicates the presence of a spirit.

BRT:5:31 Happy are the bright spirits in Elendon, the glorious sky isle where they await their call to return. All here have the Kailight around their heads. Come night, and they visit Earth in their dreams. If there be confusion in dreaming, then there is confusion in the daily round of life. Dream without confusion, and see clearly and know you live well.

BRT:5:32 Seek not to dream through the spotted elfincap, though it give enormous strength, visions and the gift of prophesy. Do not dream with the dungchild, as did the seers of olden times. Do not look through the window of the egg vessel. These things are forbidden to you. Nor may you consult the tree-bound maiden who, in truth, is the viper-blown Glainid. That, which was done on the high night of Summer shall be done no more.

BRT:5:33 Gems from the serpent must not be sought, nor may you follow the swanship, though that, which it bears within itself may be yours. Even so, it is unwise to bring the majestic sun down to incarnate in a stone. Know the secret of the sunship and all wisdom will be the reward. Seek it at Karelen.

BRT:5:34 Those worthy ones who could drink from the Goryglian are no longer a voice for the land, but there is a new chalice at the well. The phoenix sleeps in the holyhole of Karperal. If a man would know the mystery of life, the secret of these things, he must climb the Mountain of Tears in the Vale of the Dead, at the trysting place of the sun and the moon chalice. Thence must he go to the Place of Brandigan, following the path of mysteries. If he does by the wanderer's way, he is lost.

BRT:5:35 The secret of Dwyva is known to the Knights of Karwidrin, who sit within the Sacred Circle. They fight the never-ending war with the Powers of Darkness. It is victory in the conflict of the soul, which entitles the warrior to drink the cup of immortality. The Knights of Karwidrin seek in a never-ending quest. The wisdom of the way by which knights and their ladies live is, 'Let men follow the natures and ways of men, and women follow the natures and ways of women, and let each serve the other rightly.'

BRT:5:36 The heart of Britain is the moon chalice, which was brought here by the hands of the Chief of the Kasini. He came shipborne to Rafinia, which is by the Mount of Lud, against Ardmoal. Passing Insdruk, he came to Itene where he hid the treasure in Trebethew. It was not captured, as men say, nor could it decay. In the fullness of time, it came to Kargwen. There it was kept secure with the Grailstone and the ever-virgin vessel which was brought down the rays of the sun. Thus it was that these treasures of Egypt came to Britain. This was the secret of Britain.

Chapter Six – The Writings of Emris Skinlaka

BRT:6:1 The master was born under the sign of the Churlswain, at Dinsolin, called Insel by the Sons of Fire, in the year that the warwolves drove back the Children of the Horse. His father was one of the ornaments of Hew. In his youth, he was a battle-blooded warrior.

BRT:6:2 He was a dashing leader into the thick of the fray, a dauntless captain in the heat of the battle. The bearer of the battle-hammer was the great-hearted valiant warrior. He stood stern and steadfast in the grim work of bloodletting. Proud as the high-flying death eagle he stood.

BRT:6:3 A dark doomsbird flew over the land when the daring hawk gave battle. Behind came the sharp extractors of blood, the thrusting spears darting eagerly to the thrust. Like ripples across a pond, further and further spread the dying groans of doom-gathered men. The spear horde stood firm to protect the Vale of Tadwylch. It was a testing time of manhood.

BRT:6:4 Knightly men will read these words with a swelling heart. They will feel for the heroic brides of bloody spears, for the shattered shields and splintered hafts. The valiant captain of men sounds the red horn and sweeps over the fearsome foe like foaming seas. They were consumed by his bright-burning breath, like the fierce bush flame raging through the brown bracken.

BRT:6:5 The horse-vaulting warriors rode in for the final assault. The patron of the blue-bound bards swept the foe before him. Raising the red shield, holding high the sharp-slashing sword enjewelled with the ruby-red blood of warriors. It was a proud day for the ruler of the battle, the leader of strong, mail-clad spearmen, the scion of an illustrious race.

BRT:6:6 Only real men know the exultation of victory. They cheered the battlechief irresistible in the war rush. His spears dismayed the blood-thirsting, frightening foreigners. He wielded the dreadful blade of battle, which tested the manliness of men. Those were brave days. Now, only mean-minded, faint-hearted buffoons lampoon the heroes of renown. Where are the manly men; where the chaste ladies?

BRT:6:7 We were blameless for the outflowing tide of blood and entitled to the peace of the plough. The reward of the warrior is the tranquillity of old age. The pillar of battle, whose hands once wielded the hard-downslashing swords, the dragon chief, is due the peace of aged infirmity. If he is found among the gentle women, is it of any account? For he has established his manhood before men.

BRT:6:8 Thus spoke the master in the court of the king: "I am a man who has never shirked his duty. I have stood fast in the fray. I have struck many a mighty blow. Am I any less qualified to speak on things of the spirit because I was what I was? I have stood at the gateway of the grave and I have slept the sleep of inspiration. As my arm weakens, my spirit strengthens. I am no longer a man of war, but a man of peace. But let no man say before me that I am a shirker at the manly test. I am no lesser a man now. Hear my words, and let your heart judge."

BRT:6:9 "If a man followed a sunbeam to its source, he would find the sun; and likewise, if he followed his mind, he would find The Divine Source from whence it came. From The High God flows the inspiring spark in men which kindles the flame of Wisdom, Truth and Goodness. Likewise does the mind project its thoughts and plans, which are given form when expressed in words. When a man's thoughts come from a spiritual mind, they reflect the nature of The Spirit Above All Spirits. When they are stimulated by desires, feelings and urges, they reflect only the influence of matter on mind."

BRT:6:10 "Individual man is not a separate being cut off from all others, living isolated in his own enclosure. All things are in unity, and the thoughts and feelings of others, living or dead, pass through men like water through the gills of a fish. No man is cut off from the free flow of life, which purpose is to bring forth new forms of life, absorbing the old and outworn and replacing it with the new."

BRT:6:11 "Have faith, for this is the child of study and diligence. If, however, adopted by credulity or apathy, it becomes a useless thing. Faith is not an excuse, but an expression of hope. If made the refuge of the gullible, it is a thing of little moment. Faith is the spear of the wise and the crutch of the foolish."

BRT:6:12 The king said to the master, "Why do you, who are of warrior estate, entertain uncouth and ignorant men? Some say you even prefer their company to that of the wise and highborn." The master replied, "Sire, I will tell you how a Teacher greater than I dealt with such a question. In a land across the waters, a wealthy man gave a feast, to which this Great Teacher was invited. As was the custom there, outside the feasting place was gathered a motley crowd of hangers on, drunkards, thieves, deceivers and harlots. Now, when the prime feast was over, the Teacher went and sat among the outsiders and talked to them, in a manner to their understanding, concerning uplifting things."

BRT:6:13 "Those within and the disciples of this Man were aggrieved because of this and sent out two men who said to the Great Teacher , 'Tolerant Master, is this a wise thing You do?' The word of such doings will spread quickly and when they hear of the company you keep, prudent men will shun You.' The Great Man replied, 'A worthy man never fails to do his duty wherever he may be, and what I am entails a duty to minister to such as these. As to My reputation, have I not taught that reputation is subservient to service? These, being God's children, are our brothers, yet their lives contain more problems unknown to you. Because you have no knowledge of the nature of their burden, you, considering yourselves wise, cannot disclaim understanding and sympathy.'"

BRT:6:14 "These sinners are openly guilty, but such honesty is capable of transmutation into shame and shame into remorse. Those within are clever enough to cover up their guilt, and their duplicity and dishonesty cannot lead to shame and remorse, for they believe only that they are more clever than those here. Suppose those within, who despise these sinners, were to stand forth stripped of the hypocritical overlay covering their sins? What do you think you would see? I tell you, the inner aspect of many of those within is more hideous than that of many here without.'"

BRT:6:15 "'For those within have much and therefore should be above temptation, yet I tell you that the man with most is often the most avaricious. The distortions of sin are not caused only by deeds done, but also by the suppressed wish and desire.'"

BRT:6:16 " 'I say to those who sit at the fleshpots, you covet the wealth of others. You envy the house or wife of your neighbour. Lewd thoughts burn in your minds when you gaze on the figures of women, so that your bodies lust after them. You practise deceit every day, wishing for wealth, position and fame. The man who covets in his heart suffers as a thief, and she who lusts in her heart is a harlot.'"

BRT:6:17 Those within heard these words, but held their peace and were silent. The master said to those who were beside him, "Their own hearts accuse them, for the hearts of the pure do not make such accusations. The impure cover the evil polluting their hearts with hypocritical displays of righteousness. They hide their true thoughts by displaying loathing for things their hearts long to do. They revile others for their sins, but this is hypocrisy. They hug their worldly reputations won by deceit, but were the mask to be torn aside, they would be seen as wallowers in the mire of secret sinful thoughts and hidden vices."

BRT:6:18 One day, the master went to the encampment of the idol worshippers and said to one there, "Why do you worship images of wood and stone?" The idol worshipper replied, "So that it will provide me with food and shelter and keep me from harm." The master said, "How can it do this when it cannot even move of itself?" Said the idol worshipper, "Whom do you serve?" The master answered, "I serve The Great God Above All Gods who can feed His worshippers everywhere." Said the other, "See now, your own actions contradict your words, for if your God is everywhere, why have you left your home beyond the great forest to wander here?" The master replied, "I am not here to serve God alone, but also to serve you. I bring wholesome fare as a gift of comradeship."

BRT:6:19 Wayfaring with some waytamers, the master looked into a pool with all its life and said, "What an imagination God has!" They said to him, "You have been taught in the shadow of the Great Master and may gaze on that, which casts the shadow, but how will it go with our children and their children who know only the shadow of a shadow?" The master said, "Behind every shadow, there is substance. If you see a shadow, believe there is substance somewhere."

BRT:6:20 There was a dyer with them, and he used the unripe berries of the buckthorn, which were for dying, as a purge. Dyers' greenweed gives a yellow dye, and wood mixed with this and lime gives a good green. The waytamers had a nightlight, which they made by heating a few oyster shells in the fire until they became white. Then they heated them in a container with double their weight in brimstone, for three hours, until they became red. This made a light in the night.

BRT:6:21 Many times, the master spoke wise words, and his followers wrote them down, for he knew the way of words. He said, "When the wind blows it discovers every opening. Keep your eyes and ears fully open before marriage and half shut afterwards. Even a thief does not steal from his own neighbours. What does the wolf care if the sheepfold be destroyed. Progress is the creation of discontented people. A wise man learns to love the lovable and to hate the hateful, but more important is to know the difference. A child should behave towards his parents so they have no anxiety except as to his health, and confidence in the wisdom of his actions."

BRT:6:22 "No law whatsoever can ever unman a man or devirtue a woman. For the waywenders, the old law holds good. It is said that he who kills another unlawfully, who steals or robs with violence, or rapes or seduces a maid or matron, shall be placed in a wicker cage with others and burnt. Now this does not apply, but he shall be hanged at the crossroad."

BRT:6:23 "It is not unlawful for a husband to kill his wife's seducer. It is unlawful to require that a wife shall lick ash off a spearhead to establish her virtue. The first God-given right of man was the right to maintain his family inviolate; and it is the duty of the rulers to uphold that right. The seven qualities of manliness are: courage, fortitude, kindness, integrity, truthfulness, consideration and protectiveness."

BRT:6:24 A stranger accosted the master and said, "I don't like Your methods." The master answered, "Is that so? Well actually, I am not too satisfied with them myself. Tell me, how do you inspire men to live in harmony among themselves?" The stranger said, "I don't." Said the master, "I prefer the way I do it to the way you don't."

BRT:6:25 The stranger said, "You are unbending in Your teachings. Is it not wise to follow the path of moderation?" The master answered, "I am not interested in moderate faith or moderate goodness, moderate honesty or moderate virtue. There can be no moderation in things of vital importance. The moderate man is not for me. Would you eat a moderately fresh egg, or want to live in a house that keeps out most of the wind and rain? Would you be satisfied with most of your wages or with moderate work from your servants? I am not a moderate man, but one who plants his standard firmly. A standard of moderate morality is no standard at all. Could an army of moderate fighting men secure the land?"

BRT:6:26 The master went on to say, "Man lives for two things: the acquisition of knowledge and skill, and the refining of the spirit through experience. He who commands by his integrity is like the pole star, which remains constant while others revolve around it. To give you the essence of my teachings, I would say: Let all your thoughts be wholly good."

BRT:6:27 One asked of the master, "Who shall be our teachers?" The master replied, "They who, by revitalising the old wisdom of their forefathers in this land and adding to this new knowledge, are suitable." When they asked who should preach, he said, "He who should not preach what he desires others to practise is one to whom these practices are not normal. To learn without thinking is futile; to think without learning is profitless."

BRT:6:28 "Wisdom does not consist of what a man knows, but of recognising the limits of his knowledge. Listen always, but speak seldom. Maintain silence when in doubt, and you will seldom get into trouble. Keep your eyes open, but forget what you should not have seen. Never gossip, and shun all gossipmongers."

BRT:6:29 The master was asked, "How should a master deal with his servants," and he replied, "Promote those who are worthy and reward their loyalty, and train those who are incompetent. To know what is right and not to do it is cowardice. Wealth and station are desired by every man, but if these can be acquired or retained only to the detriment of his service to his creed, he must relinquish them. Poverty and subordination are disliked by all, but if they can be avoided only to the detriment of his creed, he must accept them with good grace."

BRT:6:30 Become paladins among the people, making the words of these writings the cause you serve. The inspiration is divine, but the medium is human. In the past, the pure light of Truth was concealed, from the multitude of the people, in riddles and a fog of jargon. Parables satisfied the people's understanding. Religion degenerated because in its higher aspects, it was not understood by the mass of the people, and there was a fear of casting pearls before swine, hence the mysteries and the need for ceremonial, images and symbols. People more readily worship representations of God, because they cannot comprehend Him and shirk the effort of trying to. God cannot be represented by things of this world to the understanding of the aristocratic soul.

BRT:6:31 There are Adamites whose souls slumber within, and Godmen who are the ultimate earthly beings. These are mysteries held close and safeguarded by the Knights of Karwidrin, but which came to our master through Gwalgwin of the white hawk crest, and Gwalanad the Summer Hawk. Also, through Palader of the spears and Lancelot, he who carried the mystic spear of Lot. They who are ready will read these things with understanding.

BRT:6:32 Words are mysterious things, within which can be hidden profound things, but enlightenment does not come easily or from mere reading of what is written. Greatness declined during the great peace, when knights were lax and pleasure-seeking. Men forgot their past unity and there were quarrels and rebellion. Peace is a fatal sickness to the Sons of Brittania. It was said of their battlechief that he lost every lesser battle and won every big one.

BRT:6:33 The art of the scribe came to Britain with the highbrowed one who taught Gwilidun of Ivern, who had seven sub-scribes. He said to the king, "This strange art will make the Britons wiser and will improve their memories, for it is the very essence of memory, which has been brought to this island." The king said, "Most wonderful, but while you may be prepared to bestow this, have you the ability to judge the worth of this art? Should not this be with another? The potter lacks the ability to judge the worth of his own pots, or the knight his own horse. Therefore, the ability to judge the usefulness or harm of this new thing should surely lie with another. Now, you who are the master of letters have been so swayed by your affection for them that you endow them with powers quite the opposite of what they actually possess. For this new thing will not increase the range of memory, but will lead to forgetfulness in the mind of those who learn this strange art. It encourages men to cease to practise their memory. Are the legs of a horseman equal to those of a man who walks? With time, men will put their trust in writing, and these strange signs will discourage memory. They are not instruments of memory but of reminding. Those who learn to read many things without proper instruction will then give an appearance of knowing many things, of which they are in fact ignorant. They will be hard to get along with, since they will not be wise but only appear so."

BRT:6:34 So it was that the art of writing did not come easily to Britain. Yet always, there had been the letters on stone and the brand sticks, but these were not for ordinary men. Give an ass oats, and he will run after thistles. Such is the nature of man, and never went out an ass that came home a horse.

BRT:6:35 The king had imprisoned one of the master's followers, and when the master sought the king's ear, his retainers drove him off. He returned, but this time, they turned loose the hunting dogs upon him. The master stood firm and made no move, saying in his heart that if God decreed that the hounds should maul him, so let it be. The hounds stopped before him and refused to obey the urging of those who trained them. This filled the heart of the king with wonder, for he knew the nature of the dogs of Britain, and he released the prisoner.

BRT:6:36 It was at this place that the master was challenged to produce his God. They said, "Though you decry our images, yet do we have likenesses of our gods while you lack even this. Your words are no more than puffs of wind." The master said, "These are the words of the report; to few has the arm of God been revealed. Did it not shoot up before your eyes as a sapling from a staff, and did not the withered staff take root in alien soil? Even so will it be with my words."

BRT:6:37 "I heard the Spirit of God in the night-watches, saying, 'Go, carry My words of Truth to the unbelievers, and it will be like the rain that ends the drought. My words shall strike deep into fertile soil. Its beauty shall be like the holly tree. Its fragrance shall fill the land like the scent wafted from a new-mown meadow. You, My servant, will plant a tree, which shall shelter all nations.'"

BRT:6:38 "You say, 'Show us the road', and I say go a little way and you will come to a fork in the road; take the turn to the right. Go awhile along this until you come to an inn. Pass this and take the next road bearing left. A little further along this road you will come to a village, and beyond this a lane to the left. A mile along this lane is a rise, from whence you will see your destination ahead."

BRT:6:39 "A man who has been provided with this most complete directions possible from my intimate knowledge of the area, may lose his way and become lost. Another man comes along later and is given exactly the same information, and he reaches his destination. No doubt, the first man will revile his informant and seek to place blame wholly upon him, declaring the directions to have been misleading. The other will declare how comprehensive they were."

BRT:6:40 "My words direct those, who listen with understanding, along the road of man's destiny. This road will not change about and will always be there. Here, too, there is one who knows the road well and gives clear instructions. Yet, some become lost while others get there safely. I am only the shower of the way, the light on the path. I instruct all the same."

BRT:6:41 "Did I ever say to you that, if you followed me, I would make every secret known and reveal every hidden mystery? I did not, for this is not for all men. Suppose a man was pierced in the breast with an arrow, and his friends were to summon a physician skilled in such matters. What if the man said, 'I will not have the arrow withdrawn until I know who fired it and from what manner of bow it came; whether the archer be fair or dark, tall or short. I would know his name and his tribe; I want to know whether the arrow is fletched with feathers of a goose or of a fowl.'"

BRT:6:42 "Such a man would die, and all his queries would serve him not one jot. The man's life would come to an end, but still the great question which he overlooked would go unanswered: Why was the arrow fired? It is equally foolish to say, 'I will not accept the teachings of this man until I know from whence he came, who is his father, what is his estate.'"

BRT:6:43 "A man wishes to know what the land of Egypt is like, but does not wish to endure the discomforts and dangers of the voyage. Yet, when others who have made the journey tell him about it, he says, 'I will not believe this until I have seen it with my own eyes.' So there is only the choice of making the voyage or accepting the word of those who have done so. None can justly say, 'Because I have not seen it for myself, because I decline to face the dangers and discomforts, the place does not exist.'"

BRT:6:44 The master was asked, "How shall we live to be in accord with the way of God?" He replied, "Say not that you live for God, for whatever man does serves man; God is served only by serving men. Follow the words of the wise, and do not chase after fools. Learn about the ways of life, and enjoy them to the full. Life is meant to be lived with excitement and joy, but never for mere pleasure or self-satisfaction. Discipline your daily doings, and let these not become burdensome. Earn a congenial livelihood, and in all things you, do be honest, diligent and careful."

BRT:6:45 "Let not your thoughts be the sport of every wind that blows. This thought may come to you: 'I know imperfect conditions may be put aside. I know impure things can be discarded.' But a man may even be blessed with the good things of life and yet remain sorrowful and melancholy, for this he is by nature. Happiness and cheerfulness are not things flowing from affairs of the day or through circumstances. The sorrows of a sad man come from within."

BRT:6:46 "Things of the daily round of life should be directed in the knowledge of what is for your own good. There must be an understanding of the way of the path. Be upright, conciliatory in speech and rational in bearing; mild but not meek and with no vain conceit. Be content, having few material wants, frugal and composed in mind. Be discreet, neither insolent nor avaricious. Do no mean thing, for this is not the way of a knightly man. Never act deceitfully or scorn another unjustly. Be free from sloth, and spread goodwill to all."

BRT:6:47 "Many will merely read these things, which will go in one ear and out of the other. There is no virtue in just reading them; they have to be lived by to be of value. Wisdom can be given to men, but this, of itself, does not make them wise. Wisdom is like a handful of seeds plucked from the seedbag. There is no value in them unless they be sown, nurtured and reaped."

BRT:6:48 "Be ever mindful of what is done. Know the body as it deals with the outside. A man thinks to himself, 'This body I wear as a garment is what I make of it.' He does not neglect the body and is always aware of its existence and activities. This awareness is called mindfulness. Through bodily contemplation, a state of mindfulness is reached."

BRT:6:49 "The mindful man is ever conscious of every action and its consequences. He knows what he does, whether standing still or engaged in some activity. Whatever the body does, he is aware of it and he has it under control. He knows his body to be filled with a variety of contents, he regards it as a pedlar's bag. Examine the body daily, in contemplation, and thus develop mindfulness."

BRT:6:50 "Contemplate the body made of earthly elements in solitude and know that, which contemplates is the spirit. Think of the body as if dead. What enlivens it? What is life? Be mindful of all your feelings. If experiencing something unpleasant, be mindful that this is so. Be mindful of all the activity about you, of the sighing of the wind, of the song of birds, the rustle of grass and the whispers of leaves."

BRT:6:51 "Know the difference between that, which is generated by the body and that, which is generated by the spirit, Abide in the mindfulness of feelings. Teach the body to know itself more fully and to comprehend more of its surroundings. When a man is mindful of what flows from the body and what flows from the spirit, then he knows he is body and soul."

BRT:6:52 "Be mindful of what is good and what is bad. Thoughts become confused when undirected; so, like horses, they must be kept in hand through the restrictions of bridle and reins. There are lofty thoughts and base thoughts, thoughts which arise through the prompting of the body urges and thoughts which arise through the purifying prompting of love."

BRT:6:53 "The wise man dwells in mindfulness of all things, not overlooking the urges towards indolence, ill will, resentment, worry and wavering indecision. Be mindful of ideas and ideals. Be mindful of the full working of the eyes, the nose, the mouth, the ears and the skin."

BRT:6:54 "The true way is the overcoming of self and the mastery over earthly conditions, for as a man changes himself so does he change his condition. Man must be able to say, This is of me and this is not of me. This is me or this is not me. He must divide himself in two in mindfulness, knowing what is of the Earth and what is of the spirit."

BRT:6:55 "He must travel the great path, conscious of his twinself. He should observe others, whether or not they have the quality of mindfulness. He must be self-possessed by his own spirit. The self-possessed man acts with composure, is mindful and self-aware. The man of turmoil is he who goes abroad with senses unguarded. Without mindfulness, he is unsteady and unstable in thought.."

BRT:6:56 "The godly life is one, which attracts friendship, which is the appreciated revelation of beauty. It is the search for beauty in all things. The holy prophet, in his austere, dank, dark cell, is not truly holy. The long-faced preacher is not truly holy."

BRT:6:57 "The godly life is associated with beauty. Whenever a man reaches out after the beauty found in purity of spirit, he is uplifted. It is by not understanding the true nature of godliness that men have become entangled like fowls in a net. They are like leather covered with mildew, like logs encased with moss."

BRT:6:58 "Godliness is attained by abandoning worthless things, by not falling into the fallacies of unchastity, by the repulse of sensuality and the repudiation of evil. This can be done by mindfulness of such things."

BRT:6:59 "When a master takes an apprentice, he gives the first lesson: 'Come and be disciplined, learn restraint and obligation. Learn right behaviour.' When the pupil is controlled, then he gets the second lesson. The master says, 'Seeing things with the eye, do not be misled by their outward appearance. Be mindful as to what they do to you. See with your mind all that the eye sees, and so it is with all the senses. Be aware of everything; experience all things, but do not become immersed in anything.'"

BRT:6:60 "For man is shut off from the spirit by mindlessness. As he becomes more aware of the material things and happenings about him, so does he more and more become mindful of the spirit. He who says, 'I have no feeling of the spirit,' is a man of small mindfulness. He is mindful of what is at his hand, but unmindful of what lies beyond. What lies beyond forms a veil, through which he cannot see. How can a man mindful only of what holds his immediate attention be aware of the world beyond his narrow confines?"

BRT:6:61 "Be like the spirit-filled Earth, who accepts unto herself all the foulness, which you cast out of your body and cleanses and purifies it. She is neither disgusted nor delighted, but transmutes it. Water accepts both foul and fair, for from its embrace, both emerge together in goodness. The wind is not disgusted with the foul smells of Earth, but mixes them with the essences of earth-life so they are sources of fragrance."

BRT:6:62 "Practise kindness, compassion, poise and decorum. Contemplate beauty and banish ugliness. Contemplate virtue and goodness, and banish carnality. Contemplate the eternal and banish impermanence. For all things of Earth must decay and pass away, and it is the destiny of every human being to embark on the dark adventure."

BRT:6:63 Thus, the master spoke and he said, "You must accept any intelligent person into the sheepfold. Accept all who are willing to follow the light of our way. I say this, not desiring to win followers or wishing to turn others from their ways if they walk in light. I seek only those who walk in darkness or seek a better light."

BRT:6:64 "For all journey towards The One Light, but not seeing it in its perfection, they must travel by the reflection they see. Each sees a different reflection, and therefore, men dispute among themselves as to the nature of the truth behind it all. Be not one who indulges in such futile foolishness."

BRT:6:65 "Never judge virtue by outward appearance, for then, the evildoer as well as the saint may lay claim to it. An artful imposter may gain more admiration than is given to the zeal of a saint. Do not nourish the cankerworms of malice, hatred, envy and jealousy within your bosom."

BRT:6:66 "It is truly said that the heart of man is a labyrinth. Goodness is not merely a matter of right action, it includes bravely enduring and surmounting difficulties. The final test of character is when trouble comes in strength. Then, the question is not so much whether a man does what is right, as to whether he can stand up, with integrity, to what life does to him. The anvil stands steady when the hammer falls."

BRT:6:67 "Manliness involves recovery from every moral failure. It involves the retention of honour. What honour is to man, chastity is to woman. Honour and manliness endow a man with inner strength. His slightest word, his very presence, bring peace and leaves others strengthened. No man or woman, no matter how humble, can be really good without the Earth being better for it, without someone being helped and comforted by that goodness."

BRT:6:68 "Words such as these blow against the whirlwind of human nature; yet, they are the stuff of the spirit. When the breaths of the multitude blow back the whirlwind, then has life fulfilled its purpose. Say not that the days of victory of good will be brought in with a griffin's egg."

BRT:6:69 "No man is free who does not control his own movements. No man is free who is not master of himself. Fear is the tribute the mind of man pays to guilt. He who has never been guilty knows no fear. To see the path of duty and not to follow it is the way of the coward. A man tarnishes the lustre of his greatest actions when he applauds them himself."

BRT:6:70 "No man is more vile than he who causes a woman to shed tears from the heart, tears generated in remorse and regret. Every maid has the potential for ladyhood. A lady never flaunts her estate, but ever remains modest and reserved. She covers her virtue with ladylike ways, for as a veil adds to beauty, so is chastity enhanced by being veiled. The wise woman pays no notice to the spider's lullaby from the lips of hypocritical men who speak of love. The spider loves its prey."

BRT:6:71 "Babblers are not wanted. Shun the Sophists and their sophistry, and be chary of divinators. Avoid the Paynim, and be as strong as a bull, light as a hawk, swift as a deer and tenacious as a salmon. If things go against you, never despair. To be vanquished and still not surrender, that is victory indeed! Avoid the talebearer, and do not listen to the witches' whisper. Be prudent; giants step off the path in the realm where a dwarf is king."

BRT:6:72 "Avoid the daydreamer and the moneyluster, the vagabond and the woman fascinator. Avoid the honeytongued hypocrite, for it were better you took a viper to your bosom than to open your heart to one such as these. Do not become a griffin."

Chapter Seven – The Corrygorsed

BRT:7:1 To you, Nathaniel, son of my brother Will Smith, and to Andrew, his half brother, I leave two books of integrity and others in portions. The bare words are unimportant, but what they convey is as jewels in a crown of gold. Yet, even this is not the crown itself, which should be sought in the Karnamard at Nantladiwen. I am not an unlettered man, but I lack the virtue of subtleness in writing of things best hidden.

BRT:7:2 Inasmuch as the ferocious bloodseekers close in upon us and Christian folk do in their zeal deem it fit to claim for their own persons of innocent blood, persecuting them with ratchet, rope and brand even unto death, I charge you, my assigns, to protect the several holy Books even unto your death. Believing full well that evil cannot triumph over good and the dark days of fearborn hatred will pass, keep them secure under the most sacred oaths now foresworn.

BRT:7:3 The said Holy Books, of themselves innocent, fill the base hearts of our enemies with craven fear, even as the lamp-bearing lackey causes scuttling among the rats in the larder. What dire secret do they hide closeted within their breasts, occasioning such terror that limbs quake when innocent wisdom is mentioned in their presence?

BRT:7:4 In all the land, no place remains comfortable and the free-spirited are as hares hunted by whippets running into the talebearing wind. Before the doomsmen come, we make our peace and can await our call to sacrifice in patience. The jewels are safely hidden. These things, which follow, are found in The Book of Recitals.

BRT:7:5 There are three adornments of life: Love, Truth and Beauty.

BRT:7:6 There are three things, of which God is The Source: Life, Wisdom and Power.

BRT:7:7 There are three things, which men must get from living: The greatest benefit, the greatest knowledge and the greatest experience.

BRT:7:8 There are three causes, in which it is fitting that men should risk their lives: In establishing Truth, in upholding Justice and in seeking Liberty.

BRT:7:9 There are three paramount qualities, to which all else should be subordinate: Love, Truth and Good.

BRT:7:10 There are three things men should place above themselves: Their faith, their race and humankind.

BRT:7:11 There are three things a man should value above his life and possessions: His family, his honour and his reputation.

BRT:7:12 There are three principles of government: Effective security of life and person, security of possessions and dwelling, and security of personal rights.

BRT:7:13 There are three things a government must hold inviolate: A man's family, his dignity and his opinion.

BRT:7:14 There are three things the government must provide: Education, Justice and Safety.

BRT:7:15 There are three pillars of the state: The questing scholar, the diligent craftsman and the incorruptible official.

BRT:7:16 There are three unities: One God, One Truth and One Creation.

BRT:7:17 There are three things, for which the Earth exists: The development of souls, the fulfilment of the destiny of man and the manifestation of life.

BRT:7:18 There are three things man must give to life: Beauty, Stability and Harmony.

BRT:7:19 There are three things woman must give to life: Love, Goodness and Compassion.

BRT:7:20 There are three things only God can do: Constantly renew Himself in the infinite Circle of Eternity, remain unchanging while impregnating every state of changeability, and encompass everything existing.

BRT:7:21 There are three things required of men: The ability to change that, which is changeable, to accept that which is unchangeable and to know the difference.

BRT:7:22 There are three virtues of maidenhood: Prudence, Modesty and Decorum

BRT:7:23 There are three virtues of wifehood: Faithfulness, Industriousness and Motherliness.

BRT:7:24 There are three graces: Faith, Hope and Love.

BRT:7:25 There are three things to know about God: He must be sought for, He cannot be given anything by man which increases His Greatness and He dwells within His own Law.

BRT:7:26 There are three rights of man Freedom to move, to enjoy privacy and to speak his mind.

BRT:7:27 There are three things God requires of man: Effort, Courage and Reverence for the sacred.

BRT:7:28 There are three duties of woman: To reproduce the race, inspire mankind and beautify life.

BRT:7:29 There are three duties of man: To protect the race, strive for progress and elevate humankind.

BRT:7:30 There are three things, which distort the soul: Malice, Deceit and Sensuality.

BRT:7:31 There are three rules, which govern a man's relationships with others: What he requires in another, what he forbids in another and what he regards with indifference as being entirely the concern of another.

BRT:7:32 There are three things, which shatter a man's life: An unfaithful wife, invasion by foreigners and a crippling disease.

BRT:7:33 There are three principles of greatness: Obedience to the law, concern for the welfare of the community and the ability to suffer with fortitude all the blows of fate.

BRT:7:34 There are three states of being: That of God in the Great Circle, that of Spirit in the Outer Circle and that of Matter in the Inner Circle.

BRT:7:35 There are three duties of parenthood: To protect, to cherish and to educate the child.

BRT:7:36 There are three duties of a child towards its parents: Obedience, Respect and Loyalty.

BRT:7:37 There are three qualities of a husband: Consideration, Protectiveness and Care.

BRT:7:38 There are three essentials of manhood: Courage, Fortitude and Honour.

BRT:7:39 There are three qualities of womanhood: Loyalty, Decency and Gentleness.

BRT:7:40 There are three jewels of womanhood: Modesty, Decorum and Circumspection.

BRT:7:41 There are three prime qualities of the Real Man: The ability to maintain self-control, the ability to remain calm under stress and provocation, and the ability to not stand too rigidly upon his rights.

BRT:7:42 There are three things in men that other men hate: Saying one thing with the mouth while holding something quite different in the heart, withholding evidence in favour of another to the detriment of another, and spreading scandal and gossip.

BRT:7:43 There are three things that hold the state in cohesion: Effective protection for everyone and their property, just punishment when due, and a proper blend of punishment and mercy.

BRT:7:44 There are three obligations of men in war: To kill and not be killed, to destroy the enemy and his possessions, and to survive the onslaught.

BRT:7:45 There are three types of persons who cannot bear arms: A bondsman, a boy under fifteen and a public idiot.

BRT:7:46 There are three kinds of stone, for which removal is death: A council stone, a session stone and a guide stone.

BRT:7:47 There are three things, the punishment for which shall be greater than a simple death: Killing a kinsman, killing a child or virgin, and killing an idiot.

BRT:7:48 There are three things, for which the trumpet sounds three times: The counting of heads and numbering of families, the horns of harvest and the horns of war.

BRT:7:49 There are three persons who can demand hospitality: The traveller from afar, the afflicted or orphan and the bard.

BRT:7:50 There are three groups entitled to freedom of movement and maintenance: Chiefs of tribes and their retinue, druids and their followers, and judges and the retainers of their courts.

BRT:7:51 There are three types who can claim citizenship: Those who bring new land under cultivation, those who work with metals and those who bear arms.

BRT:7:52 There are three basic protections: Protection of life and person, protection of possessions and dwelling and protection of natural privileges.

BRT:7:53 There are three types of persons who forfeit life: One who betrays his country, race or kindred, one who kills another through viciousness, lust or gain, and one who injures a child for life.

BRT:7:54 There are three things, which are indivisible and unchangeable: The Supreme Being, Truth and Reality.

BRT:7:55 There is one God, one Truth and one Reality.

BRT:7:56 There are three necessities of man: Change, Suffering and Choice.

BRT:7:57 There are three tests to determine a free man: He has equal rights with every other man, he has no more obligation to the government than it has to him, and he has freedom to come and go.

BRT:7:58 There are three things essential to united nationhood: The same language, same rights for all and the same race.

BRT:7:59 There are three things, which are private, untouchable and sacred to every man: His wife, his children and his tools of trade.

BRT:7:60 There are three persons in the family exempt from menial or heavy work: The small child, the aged man or woman, and the sick and afflicted.

BRT:7:61 There are three civil birthrights: The right to free movement, the right of protection for family, possessions and liberty, and the right to equality in privilege and restriction.

BRT:7:62 There are three requirements for social stability: Security of life and limb, security of family and possessions, and security of traditions and culture.

BRT:7:63 There are three foundations of the nation: National solidarity, national courage and national pride.

BRT:7:64 There are three things a man can legally be compelled to do: Fulfil his family obligations, attend a law court and serve in the military in times of national peril.

BRT:7:65 There are three things, for which a man can be called a traitor: Aiding the enemy, meekly submitting to an enemy, and betraying his race.

BRT:7:66 There are three things no law can deny: Water from a spring, river or lake, wood from a decayed or naturally fallen tree or branch and unused stone.

BRT:7:67 There are three forms of sonship: A son born within a marriage, a son born outside a marriage but publicly acknowledged by the father and a son by adoption.

BRT:7:68 There are three types of thieves not to be punished: A woman compelled to steal by her father or husband, a young child and a starving person who steals to eat.

BRT:7:69 There are three things, which must remain open and free to all: Rivers, roads and places of worship.

BRT:7:70 It is said that Alfred the Homeborn rewrote these things, but it is also said that what was is lost, and he put this in.

Chapter Eight – Nobility

BRT:8:1 Nobility and honour are words much abused, but in truth nobility is not bestowed by birthright, but resides in the soul, and honour is not a thing bartered among kings, but comes from a sense of goodness. Men sell their honour for gold, and nobility is conferred on those who have done nothing more than their duty. This is wrong.

BRT:8:2 When titles are given as the reward of true, selfless service, when he who serves his fellows well is ennobled, both giver and receiver are raised in stature, and the realm benefits.

BRT:8:3 When they who inherit titles also inherit the virtues, which earned these, then all is well; but when he who inherits, to whom they descend, is unlike he who earned them, then they can no longer be borne with honour.

BRT:8:4 Honour and nobility, in their true sense, are not things which can inevitably be inherited; they are not in the blood. The man who, being without merit himself, appeals to the actions of his ancestors, for his justification is like a thief claiming justification in possession. What good is it to the blind that his parents could see, or what benefit to the deaf that his grandfather heard? Is this more foolish then that a mean-hearted man should claim nobility because his forbears were noble? A man who serves the people well has no need of ancestors. The noble mind does not derive pleasure in receiving honours, but in deserving them. Is it not better that men say, 'Why has this man not been honoured by the king?" than to ask why he has been?

BRT:8:5 I speak to knights who, surely of all men, are the most noble. Eat slowly and with good manners, even if alone at the table. Do not gulp down ale or water, for food hastily eaten sits on an uncomfortable stomach. Though we must feed our bodies, even as animals have to, we are not as they and must do so with good manners. This is also a knightly discipline, which will enhance the light of your soul.

BRT:8:6 This soul has an inner stronghold, an unassailable keep, which remains impregnable against all outside influences. It is an inner zone of silence, so that even in the most crowded street, amid the din of commerce, the hustle and hassle of everyday life, in joy, sorrow, success and failure, there is always an inner sanctuary, a place of retirement, a retreat, to which one can always retire, assured that no intruder can assail anyone there. This is the citadel of the soul, against which all the tempests and turmoils of life's storms may beat in vain. Within, all will be serene, peaceful and secure, and if it be well built, nothing can ever overthrow it.

BRT:8:7 Loyalty is an attribute of the knightly man. It is expressed in deed and service. Be audacious in confrontation. It is a bold mouse that pulls the cat's whiskers. Be renowned for what you achieve, not for what you are. The renown of a bowman is not earned by his bow, but by his aim.

BRT:8:8 Those who seek to shun the battle of life because of cowardice or selfishness find that their attempts to run away are in vain, for the Law compels them to engage. Because human destiny, individual and collective, is bound to the rock of the Law, that which is avoided is enforced.

BRT:8:9 I come before the dire days to carry a sword against evils, which threaten our race, and to direct the struggle of man into correct channels. Be true to yourself, and answer accordingly to your own inner knowledge. Are your God-given qualities, which all possess, marshalled to carry out the Designs of God?

BRT:8:10 The rallying call has sounded, and it echoes in every responsive heart. Arm yourself for the fray with the God-given powers within. Align them to fight on the side of good. The call has gone out, and the inner forces of every Real Man are required to rally to the cause of humankind.

BRT:8:11 If everyone in the world would rally their own special forces within and throw these into the battle on the side of good, the Earth would overflow with goodness.

BRT:8:12 Men and women are apathetic; instead of taking up the sword against evil, they stand aside like menials. So evil grows, and the main cause of the present sorry state of the people is man's lack of fighting spirit. In war, it is the cause that counts and it is not enough to resist evil. It must be attacked.

BRT:8:13 When you have conquered the weakness within yourself and assumed full control, you are a true knight ready to go out and fight. The trumpet has sounded, and the rallying cry rings out, so do not seek the place of protection. Do not hesitate in this dramatic hour. Say not that these things foreshadow things in days far ahead, or that they are residue from the past.

BRT:8:14 Cease all disagreement among yourselves. Unite as comrades in arms. There will, of course, be arguments and differences, but be men enough not to let them divide you. We are in our present sorry state because of past disunity and disobedience to the Law. Do not allow the knights of right to be disarmed, and fight against the Realm of Darkness.

BRT:8:15 It is a manifest thing that kingdoms divided against themselves are destroyed by more united forces. Yet, is not the Kingdom of God divided against itself?

BRT:8:16 Truth and faith are the handmaidens of love. They bring confidence, and how can a man stand steadfast unless he has confidence, for in confidence is strength. The qualities of knighthood are such that those who have them can look the world in the eye. They have no furtive deeds to hide within where they eat away at a knight's integrity.

BRT:8:17 Praise no day until nightfall, no wife until she is buried, no sword until blooded, no maid until married and no ale until drunk. Never be a talebearer, for this is despicable in a man.

BRT:8:18 Persons who, within themselves, are really enemies often come garbed as friends, and among these are the following: He who takes little care to hide his intentions to rob or violate and does it brazenfaced, he who gives a little with the intention of getting much back in return; he who puts on a friendly front out of fear and he who acts friendly to serve his own ends.

BRT:8:19 The man with the well greased, mobile tongue can be distinguished in this manner. He is inclined to talk much about himself and his past accomplishments, or he will fill your ears with boasts about his future deeds; he assails your ears with empty words and with the sweet draught of flattery. Walk warily, for these are false-fronted friends and when their friendship is put to the test, it falls apart like rotten wood. When called upon for assistance in time of need they plead their own misfortunes and handicaps as excuses for standing aside.

BRT:8:20 The smooth-tongued hypocrite glosses over the misdeeds of others. He excuses unworthiness and sings your praises before your face, in your hearing, but reviles you behind your back. Avoid all such as these, for their friendship is worthless.

BRT:8:21 The other to avoid is the wastrel. He will be a pleasant companion in the drinking parlours. He will be your amiable companion in the places of pleasure, where there is gaiety and laughter. He will be a charming companion at feasts and festivals. He will be quick to suggest gambling and dissipation and all things that lead to sloth.

BRT:8:22 Here are the earmarks of a true-hearted friend: He will help you when help is really needed and requires real sacrifice on his part; he remains unchanged amidst the fluctuations of fortune; he is the one who is not afraid to tell you what is for your own good; he is the one who declares his friendship and loyalty in the company of those who condemn you.

BRT:8:23 True friends are few and are treasures indeed. A true friend watches over you when you falter on the way. He keeps a watchful eye on your property and interests when you are indisposed. He is your refuge in times when you are in fear, and your consolation in distress. He is your reassurance in doubt. He never deserts you in need.

BRT:8:24 A true friend tells you his secrets and never under any circumstances reveals yours. He never forsakes you in times of trouble and would sacrifice almost anything for you.

BRT:8:25 In earthly armies, rules and commands must be obeyed; there is no other way to conduct a campaign. It is so in the army of good; each and every man can rise by his own efforts and perseverance.

BRT:8:26 Be as ready to take orders as to give them, for no man has the qualities of leadership who cannot also obey. All soldiers in the Holy Army must be well disciplined. How otherwise can the battle be won? If we falter in this, the infidel and heretic will prevail and the long, weary journey be abortive.

BRT:8:27 Be ever loyal to your comrades placed in authority. Trust them, and change only when, by direct and personal contact and knowledge, you find them false and wanting. True friendship is the greatest of all gifts.

BRT:8:28 In the courts and castles of the land, women, as apart from ladies, because of their physical weakness have been made to appear of lesser importance; but a true knight, while honouring ladyhood, treats all women with respect and chivalry. It is chivalry, which distinguishes our times from all others.

BRT:8:29 A true knight is decorous at all times and circumspect in the presence of womenfolk, for he honours the delicacy of their ways. Always, however, womanliness is required to respond to and foster the chivalry in men. A mannish-mannered woman is the declared enemy of chivalry.

BRT:8:30 A knight embodies the criteria for manhood. He concentrates on mannish things and mannish ways. He does not meddle in the affairs of womankind.

BRT:8:31 A true lady is a rare and lovely jewel. What the word 'lady' means is hard to define, but one meaning is that a lady is a woman, in whose private presence, a man acts with decorum and reserve. He shields her from crudity and lewdness.

BRT:8:32 A knight understands the economy of life. It is too easy to long for a certain conclusion, perhaps that the suffering of a loved one will end. However, it may be a case where only endurance and fortitude will heal and benefit the spirit. Pain purifies and strengthens, and sometimes it is better to suffer than to sleep.

BRT:8:33 True knighthood demands not only nobility of spirit, but also nobility in attire and manners. It is an attitude towards others. The duties of man to man are almost as important as those of man to God where the obligations entail the stewardship of God's earthly estate.

BRT:8:34 Man chooses as he will, and it is entirely up to him whether or not he does a thing. Of what benefit is a high position to a man who uses the power he has over the lives of others only for purposes of boosting his own arrogance and false pride; who uses it only for his own pleasure and not to serve others.

BRT:8:35 God has given man shepherds to guide him and indicate the path. But these shepherds cannot, of themselves alone, gain such leadership and guidance, unless inspired by the Spirit of God. Man must be guided according to his spiritual needs and not according to his worldly needs.

BRT:8:36 Therefore, God has ordained a means whereby these shepherds may be found, and He has told them what to teach the people and in what manner to accord with their understanding and acceptance. The way is complex, as can be seen through these writings.

Chapter Nine – Shards of Wisdom

BRT:9:1 In the days when Lucius Clorus was named King Coel and lived at Karcolwin, Enisivorwin served the good Queen Helena, and from her to her husband, Kambord, by whose hand these things were written, came words of wisdom. There is that, which is old and that, which is new, but old and new are one in the eye of time. Therefore that, which is first might be that, which was written last, for now, among the pieces, none knows which should be where. In truth, none knows when these things were written, but what has just been said was found as a broken piece, and where else could it be?

BRT:9:2 Of the druids, it is said that Pair Keridwen, the Cauldron of Higher Love, represented to them the womb and that the fire, with which it was associated, was the lifeforce. It is said that the representation was in more than one form, but what this means none now knows. To become a druid required immersion in a bath with a decoction from the cauldron. After immersion for a prescribed time, the residue from the bath, infused with the man's evil, was poured into a pit. His spirit was thus cleansed and renewed, but henceforth, any wrongdoing would have a twofold effect.

BRT:9:3 A band of Troubadours, being people who held some secret of life, came to Britain in the days when England was Saxonised. They had a secret book said to explain all the mysteries of life, but the book itself explained little; yet, they who followed the secret book became the wisest among men. Written words, when read without thought, are valueless, and this is how most men read. Troubadours have a secret place in the Ogmosian hills.

BRT:9:4 Emris said, "The people are entitled to the consideration and care of the rulers who direct their days. Men are entitled to the peace of the plough unless their lands and families are under threat. No man who is a man slumbers under threat, and the reward of the warrior is tranquillity in old age."

BRT:9:5 "The foolish man who sacrifices his peace of mind and happiness to seek wealth is like a man who sells his home to buy furniture."

BRT:9:6 "If there is anything more powerful than fate, it is the courage that bears whatever fate decrees unshaken. The dispensations of life favour the courageous man."

BRT:9:7 "Within the wider world, responsible procreation and selectivity play a spiritualising role, while on another level, they preserve the diverse racial and cultural heritages. Racial pride is a positive quality which has nothing to do with racial prejudice. Pride without prejudice should be the watchword."

BRT:9:8 Thus, it is written: 'They who inherit and inhabit the kingdom, in which irresponsible procreation is condoned prepare for themselves the path of degeneration. They do not hold human sexuality sacred, enshrining it in the family and placing it in the guardianship of women. They do not honour the mistress of the house as the vigilant guardian of their racial heritage. The worship of ancestors sprang naturally from the pride and reverence, in which people held their forebears. It indicated their gratitude and understanding for the sacrifices the ancestors made in being selective and responsible.'

BRT:9:9 'When the selection of a marriage mate can be left to the sense of responsibility in the couple primarily concerned, then civilisation has taken a big step forward. But who is wise enough to determine when this wisdom is present and expressed? Where are those prepared to uphold responsible breeding habits?'

BRT:9:10 As found written, these are the accomplishments of a lady: She should learn the following: Cutting, sewing and making of garments. The arraying of garments and adornment of the body. The toilet of the hair and the art of hairbraiding. The art of motherhood. Housewifery and cooking. The preservation of fruits, meats and herbs. The growing of flowers and herbs. The stringing of necklaces and the making of ornaments. The making of pottery and the preparation of perfumes and ointments. Singing, if she have a sweet voice and melodious speech. Writing and drawing with paints. The art of archery with the little bow and small swordsmanship. The knowledge of jewels. The making of lace and knitting of wool and weaving. The use of herbs and simples and small leechcraft.

BRT:9:11 Her teacher in the ways of life should be her mother's sister, should she be married, or a sister who is married; or a female friend of her mother who is of long standing and in good grace with her mother; or a female tutor or female nurse who is attached to the family.

BRT:9:12 Concerning women, there are petty maids and maids (both of these categories being virgin); unmarried matrons, wives, widows, cast out women, women of no repute and harlots.

BRT:9:13 A woman living as married but not actually married is not inviolate, nor is an unmarried matron. Those may be sought for pleasure. An unmarried matron having been enjoyed by others is available for a man's pleasure.

BRT:9:14 These women are not to be touched in lust: A madwoman, a woman with running sores, a woman with child and a wife. No child shall be touched in lust. A man shall not display his nakedness before his daughter, nor a mother before her son.

BRT:9:15 After the days of Emris, it was written: 'Never give up; where there is a will there is a way; while there is life there is hope. Never leave your friend in the lurch, but support him with might and main. Do not be half-hearted or run with the hare or chase with the hounds.' Those are things said in our days.

BRT:9:16 These are the qualities and attributes of trees, as revealed by the ancient lore of our fathers, the usage whereof is known to the wise: The providing apple, the winsome cherry, the soporific ivy, the comforting elderberry, the holy oak, the sorrowful willow, the compassionate ash, the protective yew, the happy birch, the companionable holly, the lively hawthorn, the mystic hazel, the sedate pine, the wish-granting sallow, the healing heather, the age-consoling alder, the youth-giving waywithy, the generous broom, the helpful furze, the spirit-strengthening beech, the soothing windrake, the laughing aspen, the gentle junapah, the reliable wayfaringbeam, the cunning hornbeam, the flighty gadberry, the ominous dogwood, the jumping buckthorn, the light-hearted maple, the direful slaethorn, the angry parbeam, the wilful kartakbush, the haunted banbeam, the frightened witchbeam.

BRT:9:17 They who are at one with the trees understand the nature of the life within them and make much of such things. There is a mystery here to be worked by those with understanding, but to others, it will be meaningless.

BRT:9:18 These are the useful herbs to be found in field, forest and wayside in the days gone by: Wolfbane (which guards against wolves and dogs), barroweed (which grows only near the dead), harwort, witchweed, tinkerbells, wayweed, skullcap, featherflowers (which cure the stone), blackberry, sundew, deadly dick, celandine (which cure the piles), windweed, moonflower (which works a spell), witchhead (called blackspear), asproot, drudbalm (which brings sleep),witchbane (which is put above the door), hawflowers, ellenberry, wimberry, dradsweet, elfeyc, fairyfern, witchwhispers, quickenbush, sowerseed (which purges), bardberry (for lovers), amarinth (it never fades), windflower, goolflower, weggrig, blowderbud (which heals all wounds), levenshade, layganleaf, hokanmil, rillweed, boonberry, hatherswed (which women use), esislip, fullerswort, withrinweed (which makes blue dye), canweed (which quiets the heart), mayslip, kodecreeper, slanlus, sewd, (which cures men of madness), mothan (which only grows on cliffs), arkiesene, dafblowder (which cures stomach sickness), malbrig, maisbel (which heals the stomach), bormowed (which soothes burns), selerweed (which gives visions), tianwed (which heals the skin), kaincop (which makes a brew), cowslip, waybroad, satyrion (which overcomes impotency), dwail, corncockles (which men call tares), dockumdick (which gives men virility and only grows under the shivertree).

BRT:9:19 These things serve well, but some are lost to the knowledge of men: Herb beer, made of yarrow and riversweet, soothes the spirits of men. Red clover cures the small cancer, if the suffering one be a man of self-control. The herb called 'mothan' is drunk with milk at childbirth.

BRT:9:20 Sickness is first a malady of the mind.

Index

A

C

F

H

L

Q

R

S

T

U

V

W

Y

KOLBRIN.COM

Quick Study

Reports

A compilation of popular essays from the Kolbrin.com web site and chapter-length excerpts from *Planet X Forecast and 2012 Survival Guide.*

Report #1 — Kolbrin Essays

Newly-Revealed Bible Honors The Ancient Phoenicians

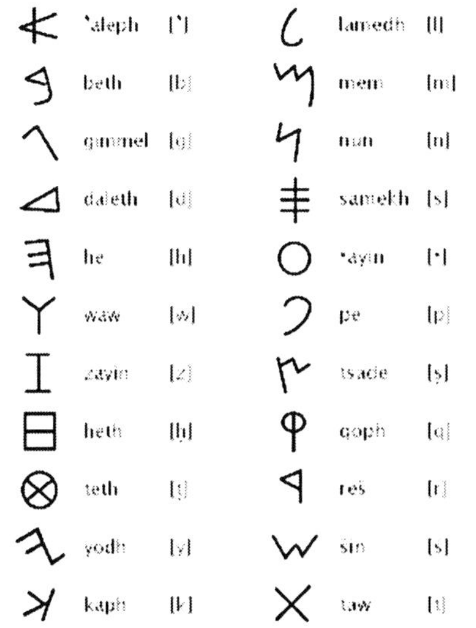

Newly Revealed Egyptian-Celtic Wisdom Text Offers New Insights to Ancient Phoenician Civilization

The word "Bible" is generically associated with the *Holy Bible* in Western societies. Nonetheless, a quick search on Amazon will also turn up other applications of the word such as T*he Barbecue Bible, The Boomer Bible, The Organic Cooking Bible,* etc.

No matter what kind of itch you have, you'll likely find an authoritative Bible on Amazon that scratches it.

Now, there's another Bible on Amazon, and it is just as serious, just as large and just as old as the Torah and New Testament combined. It is The Kolbrin Bible, and it is the first ancient wisdom text to honor the Phoenicians, from whom we derived the word "Bible," because of the wonderful gift of knowledge we inherited from them.

𐤀	'aleph	[']	𐤋	lamedh	[l]
𐤁	beth	[b]	𐤌	mem	[m]
𐤂	gimmel	[g]	𐤍	nun	[n]
𐤃	daleth	[d]	𐤎	samekh	[s]
𐤄	he	[h]	𐤏	'ayin	[']
𐤅	waw	[w]	𐤐	pe	[p]
𐤆	zayin	[z]	𐤑	tsade	[ṣ]
𐤇	heth	[ḥ]	𐤒	qoph	[q]
𐤈	teth	[ṭ]	𐤓	reš	[r]
𐤉	yodh	[y]	𐤔	šin	[š]
𐤊	kaph	[k]	𐤕	taw	[t]

The Ancient Phoenician Port of Byblos

School children know the word "Bible" comes from the Greek word *"bublos,"* which describes papyrus (an ancient Egyptian writing material made of reeds), and which is derived from the name of *Byblos*, an ancient Phoenician port that once thrived on the coast of present day Lebanon. What is not commonly known is that the Greek alphabet was developed from the 22-letter Phoenician alphabet. Likewise, the Latin, English and Cyrillic alphabets were also derived from the Phoenician alphabet.

An Alternate Historical View of Exodus

The Phoenicians based their alphabet on an ancient Egyptian hieratic script. This is why the history of *The Kolbrin Bible* makes it the first Bible of any kind to honor a history that begins in the days following the Jewish Exodus from Egypt.

The *Torah* (Old Testament) version of the Ten Plagues of Egypt is the history of a nation, and it describes a righteous victory of Moses over Pharaoh. In simple terms, it is the story of Exodus as told by the victor. Conversely, the first six books of *The Kolbrin Bible*, which are collectively referred to as the Egyptian texts, contain the story of Exodus as told by the defeated some 3600 years ago. While there are many similarities between the stories of the *Torah* and the Egyptian Texts, it is the latter that offers a truly unvarnished account of a nation shaken to its core.

According to the Egyptian Texts, Pharaoh and his army caught the Jews in the midst of their Red Sea crossing and slaughtered better than half of them before the waters swept them away, as well. However, the plagues that devastated the whole world caused only part of the suffering that severely weakened Egypt as a nation.

Militarily decimated, Egypt's treasuries and granaries became the prized targets of the starved hoards who invaded from the South. Much blood was shed to repel them. Yet, there was an even worse fate in store. The Egyptians were shaken to their national core by an experience many times worse than 9-11. This is because 9-11 never made America lose it's faith in God, whereas Exodus left the Egyptians with a pantheon of impotent and unworthy gods.

After The Jews Crossed the Red Sea

As the Jews wandered the Sinai writing their *Torah*, a studious, new Pharaoh and his humbled Egyptian intelligentsia reasoned that the Jews were onto something, so they resolved themselves to find the One True God of Abraham. What ensued was perhaps one of the most remarkable wisdom-gathering events of the ancient world, as the Egyptian intelligentsia fanned out to the farthest reaches of the kingdom's trading sphere to conduct a first-ever regional anthropological study.

During the day, scribes and academics conducted business as usual, and then during off hours, they interviewed the wisest of many lands. Their field notes accompanied usual shipments back to Egypt and were then compiled into a secular work titled the *Great Book*.

Historical Account of Phoenician Folklore

Penned in an ancient hieratic script, the *Great Book* was over four times the size of *The King James Bible*, and one part titled the Sons of Fire contains a significant amount of ancient Phoenician folklore; an ancient maritime nation well worth remembering.

The Phoenicians were the first mariners to navigate their ships by Polaris, the North Star, and to circumnavigate the African continent. Their primary trade routes stretched through the Mediterranean; up along the Western shores of Europe and North to Britain. During the late Bronze Age, Britain was a major exporter of tin, which, when smelted with copper, makes bronze. Savvy traders, the Phoenicians plied the waters between the Middle East and Britain carrying lucrative cargoes of Egyptian papyrus and British tin.

Deeply enamored of the Egyptian Great Book, the Phoenicians translated several copies of it into their own 22-letter alphabet, from which our own English alphabet is derived. One copy made it to Britain, where it was warmly received by the Celtic priests there, because many of its stories reminded them of their own Druid folklore.

Sadly, the Phoenician civilization was later smashed by the Roman Empire, and little is left of their history, and a similar fate almost befell the Great Book. Much of the original Phoenician translations were destroyed during the 1184 arson fire at the Glastonbury Abbey, and what remained was combined with a collection of ancient Celtic texts called the *Coelbook*. The texts were later translated into English and collectively published as *The Kolbrin*.

Your Own World Books, the new publisher of this work chose to re-title it as *The Kolbrin Bible: 21st Century Master Edition* to honor the Phoenicians and their home port of *Byblos*. Without them, the wonderful historical accounts of this 3600-year old work would have been forever lost in time.

Tiananmen Square Protests Uncovered Ancients Texts

Why Tiananmen Square Will Be Remembered as the First Defining Moment of the Information Age

The 1989 Tiananmen Square protesters made history when they forced the injustices of a repressive government into the global limelight. Not only did they give new freedom to an ancient culture, their courage also triggered the publication of millennia-old wisdom texts for the benefit of all humankind. One such text is called *The Kolbrin Bible.*

Mention Tiananmen Square today, and it may not ring a bell at first. If so, just describe the picture of that courageous young man who stopped a column of Red Army tanks for over half an hour, and it will click. This is because this "Kodak moment" of courage is the defining image of the information age. A time when the most repressive and brutal regime in the world at that time could not seal the hemorrhage of phone calls, faxes, simple e-mail messages and message board posts to the outside world from protesters and sympathizers. Thanks to their efforts, the atrocities of a brutal communist government were subsequently exposed to the world, and it was deeply humiliated.

Why Tiananmen Square Was Important to Us All

In a very real sense, Tiananmen Square was the electronic pen of the new Information Age and it was mightier than the repressive sword of a brutal government. Not because it was wielded by a "prestigious" world body or by a "powerful" global power, but rather, by a relatively small band of students, intellectuals and labor activists with the guts to peacefully confront their own government.

Sadly, their grievances were answered with a horrible massacre, and the organizers will be forever haunted by the lives lost. Yet, future historians shall lovingly remember them with enduring reverence. Why?

Like the fresh water that encourages a seedling to find the light, Tiananmen Square redefined human communication as it left its mark. In the process, it also defined a new context for the news reports we saw on our televisions each night about the fall of the Soviet empire and about a new technological wonder called the Internet.

Internet Knowledge Liberation

Today, most regard the Internet as a convenient information and communication tool. Yet how many of us truly appreciate it's "other" power? That is its inherent ability to unleash vital human knowledge from the bonds of repression. This is a hidden blessing of the Information Age and the Internet.

Case in point is *The Kolbrin Bible.* This ancient wisdom text was targeted by English King Henry II for destruction in 1184, when he initiated a murderous arson attack on the Glastonbury Abbey. After the attack, the surviving Celtic priests recovered what remained of the texts and fled to Scotland.

Had King Henry II been successful, the result would have been a loss for humankind no less significant than the destruction of the Library of Alexandria by the Roman Empire. This is because the first parts of *The Kolbrin Bible* were written by Egyptian academics even as Moses was leading the Jews through the Sinai following the Exodus.

About The Kolbrin Bible

Originally penned in old Egyptian hieratic, this massive work was later translated by Phoenician traders into their own 22-letter alphabet, which later became the root of the English alphabet.

The Phoenicians plied the seas between their home port in modern-day Lebanon and the tin mines of Britain and carried a copy of the text to Britain, where it was embraced by the Celts. In it, they found historical accounts and prophecy similar to their own Druid folklore. Following the death of Jesus, they were inspired to write the later parts of *The Kolbrin Bible* in the old Celtic language.

Ever mindful of the need to protect this ancient manuscript from an English monarchy as brutal as any Chinese communist cabal, the Celts kept the manuscripts in hiding for centuries. Eventually, the texts were translated into continental English by succeeding generations of secretive caretakers, who patiently awaited the arrival of the "right" moment in time, when it could be shared with the world.

The Kolbrin-Tiananmen Connection

That "right" moment came in 1989, thanks to the courage of the Tiananmen Square protesters. Their courage also sped the fall of the morally corrupt Soviet empire, interest in the newly-invented Internet and something else that has been long overdue. Knowledge caretakers no longer need to labor anonymously, under the threat of political or religious repression. Thanks in part to the courage of the Tiananmen Square protesters, these knowledge caretakers can now share their texts more easily and safely than ever before in the history of humankind.

Thus inspired, the Hope Trust of England, the last known caretakers of *The Kolbrin Bible* knew the time had come to gift this ancient work to the world. In 1992, a senior member of the trust began distributing copies of *The Kolbrin Bible*. Today, it is available on the Internet and can be purchased in any bookstore in the Western world.

Let there be no doubt about it. Tiananmen Square was a defining watershed event for the Information Age. As such, it is a gift to human knowledge that will keep on giving for generations to come. We can only hope that those brave souls who sacrificed so much in those heady days of 1989 will know all they've done for humanity, for they have done so very much.

3600-Year Old Wisdom Text Describes Extinction of the Dinosaurs

Historical Account in Newly Revealed Ancient Text Challenges Chicxulub Impact Dinosaur Extinction Theory

In recent years, scientists have begun to challenge the popular K-T extinction event theory advanced by Nobel laureate physicist, Luis Alvarez. In 1990, he found evidence of a large impact resulting in an Extinction Level Event (E.L.E) in what is now Chicxulub, Mexico. His theory that this E.L.E. wiped out the dinosaurs some 65 million years ago was soon adopted.

However, modern scientists are now casting doubts on his theory. Furthermore, a newly released 3600-year old wisdom text called *The Kolbrin Bible* supports these challenges to Alvarez's theory with a prescient human account.

At the core of this E.L.E. debate is a thin global layer of iridium that capped the living presence of dinosaurs on this planet. It is called the KT boundary. Iridium is rarely found on the surface of the Earth, but it is common to asteroids, and there is a sharply defined global layer of Iridium that dates back to the Chicxulub impact event.

Challenges to Alvarez K-T Impact Extinction Theory

Doubts about Alvarez's theory are founded in equally credible explanations of the KT boundary. One notable theory is the "KT-Deccan Traps volcanism-induced carbon cycle perturbation extinction theory" of Dewey McLean, Professor Emeritus of Geology in the Department of Geological Sciences, Virginia Polytechnic Institute, Blacksburg, VA. Besides the science, what makes McLean's theory attractive is the amount of effort Alvarez has invested to suppress it.

While precise dating of deep time events is difficult at best, ample evidence exists to suggest that at about the same time Alvarez's asteroid cratered the Yucatan peninsula, a hotspot volcano produced the Deccan Traps eruption with equally devastating results. Unlike an explosive supervolcano event such as the last Yellowstone eruption, the miles-thick Deccan Traps eruption flowed out over thousands of square miles, and released massive amounts of iridium into the atmosphere. Sizable remnants of this lava pile still exist on a volcanically active Reunion Island in the Indian Ocean.

Enter *The Kolbrin Bible*. The first part of this 11-book secular anthology was authored by Egyptian academics after the Jewish Exodus and is referred to as the Egyptian Texts. (The last part was authored by Celtic priests shortly after the death of Jesus.)

Within the Book of Gleanings of the Egyptian Texts, one passage not only clearly supports the K-T Deccan Traps of Dewey McLean; it also suggests that humanity co-existed with the dinosaurs:

THE KOLBRIN BIBLE
EGYPTIAN TEXTS
GLEANINGS:3:5

"In olden times, there were spawned great monsters and beasts in fearful form, with frightful gnashing teeth and long ripping claws; an elephant was but a rat in comparison with them. Then, because of heavenly rebellion and turmoil, and the terror overwhelming the hearts of men, The Great One hardened the face of the land, which had become unstable, and the beasts were changed to stone. This was beforetimes, when the Destroyer still slumbered in the upper vaults of Heaven."

The reference to an object the Egyptians called the "Destroyer" is repeated often. *The Kolbrin Bible* and the Egyptian academics explain that it was a long-period orbiting object, which during its last two flyby events caused the Great Deluge (Noah's Flood) and the Ten Plagues of Exodus. Unlike the *Torah* (Old Testament) this ancient work explains these events as natural disasters — not the punishments of an angry deity.

About The Kolbrin Bible

This account in *The Kolbrin Bible* is part of what remains of the *Great Book*, as the Egyptians first called it. First penned in ancient hieratic, the *Great Book* was approximately 4 times the size of *The King James Bible*. The impetus for the work was the defeat the Egyptians suffered at the hands of Moses. Convinced their own gods had been proven to be impotent, they initiated the first regional anthropological study in the history of humankind.

Throughout the breadth of their trading sphere, their academics and scribes would do their business as usual, but in their off hours, they began interviewing local wise men. The aim was to record historical accounts and folklore in the hopes of uncovering any clue that might lead the Egyptians to the One True God of Abraham. The field notes of these interviews were then sent back to Egypt and incorporated into the *Great Book*.

One civilization that received special attention from the Egyptians was the seafaring Phoenicians. Enamored by the Great Book, the Phoenicians translated it to their own 22-letter alphabet and took a copy of the work to Britain, which, during the late Bronze Age, was a major exporter of tin.

The Celtic priests of Britain embraced the work, which was mostly destroyed during the 1184 arson of the Glastonbury Abbey. What remained was combined with other Celtic texts, translated into Old English and collectively published as *The Kolbrin*. After WWI, the work was updated to Continental English, and the first copies were released in the early 1990's.

For interested researchers, this 3600-year old work offers vital corroboration of Dewey McLean's KT-Deccan Traps eruption theory, plus an abundant source of prescient historical accounts of ancient global disasters. The details in these accounts are as crisp as the man-on-the-street interviews one sees in modern televised news broadcasts.

Report #2 — Comparative Prophecies

Planet X Forecast and 2012 Survival Guide

Planetxforecast.com / Yowbooks.com

Chapter 3 — Historical Accounts of Previous Flybys

What we call Planet X today was known to the ancients by many different names, and there is a very substantial historical record of previous flybys in both folklore and wisdom texts. The three most notable wisdom texts are the *Holy Bible*, *The Kolbrin Bible* and the Sumerian texts as translated by Zecharia Sitchin in his landmark book, *The 12th Planet* and therein referred to as Nibiru.

Of the three, the most comprehensive source of historical accounts and prophecy is contained in *The Kolbrin Bible*, a secular anthology. Penned by numerous Egyptian and Celtic authors, it was written in two parts, each in the same time period as the Old and New Testaments, respectively.

The direct correlations between these secular and non-secular texts are both stunning in scope and language. Likewise troubling is their equally-dire, prophetic warnings for our future. A complete discussion of all the accounts, prophecies and correlations between the two would require a book in itself. Therefore, this chapter will briefly discuss many of the more notable correlations and prophetic warnings.

Filtering Concepts through the Passage of Time

When reading ancient historical accounts and prophecies, it is easy to become frustrated, as these texts often lack a clear correlation to the present reality of our own lives. Consequently, we often use something akin to "Kentucky windage," a slang term used by shooters to describe a process whereby we adjust our aim in order to hit a distant target.

A good example is the creation of the State of Israel. Before 1948, many Christian Scholars explained the Bible prophecies regarding the re-establishment of Israel as a Jewish state in the context of a greater Christian Church. Given the political realities in those days, that reasoning made sense to those who could not imagine such a thing happening. Yet it did. Ergo, they rationalized the prophecies instead of reading them literally, and they were wrong for two reasons. First, they invented context where none existed before and second, because they lacked the patience to wait out the prophecy. Or in other words, if something does not make sense today, leave it be until it does.

Those reading the Planet X accounts and prophecies of the ancients decades ago would not have been able to fully understand them in a modern sense, as the scientific harbinger signs discussed in the first chapter of this book only became available within the last few decades. However, we do have this data, so now we can fully understand the prescient warnings of the *Holy Bible* and *The Kolbrin Bible* as they were written.

The most stunning warning is found in a direct correlation between the *Holy Bible* and *The Kolbrin Bible*. Both use the exact same name for Planet X, which they refer to as the "Destroyer."

Holy Bible: New Century version

- **Jeremiah** 25:32 & 48:8 "Disasters will soon spread from nation to nation. They will come like a powerful storm to all the faraway places on earth...The **DESTROYER** will come against every town, not one town will escape...The Lord said this will happen."

The Kolbrin Bible: Egyptian Texts of the Bronzebook

- **Manuscripts** 3:3 "When ages pass, certain laws operate upon the stars in the Heavens. Their ways change; there is movement and restlessness, they are no longer constant and a great light appears redly in the skies."

- **Manuscripts** 3:4: "When blood drops upon the Earth, the Destroyer will appear, and mountains will open up and belch forth fire and ashes. Trees will be destroyed and all living things engulfed. Waters will be swallowed up by the land, and seas will boil."

- **Manuscripts** 3:6: "The people will scatter in madness. They will hear the trumpet and battlecry of the **DESTROYER** and will seek refuge within dens in the Earth. Terror will eat away their hearts, and their courage will flow from them like water from a broken pitcher. They will be eaten up in the flames of wrath and consumed by the breath of the **DESTROYER**."

While "Wormwood" passages from the "Book of Revelations" are often cited by Planet X prophecy researchers, the most disturbing *Bible* prophecy comes from "The Book of Joel," which is part of the Jewish Tanakh, and the Old Testament of the *Holy Bible*.

Some 2,400 years ago, Joel predicted a terrible destruction that will befall Israel's enemies in a future cataclysm. This prediction clearly correlates with the scientific Planet X flyby scenarios we'll examine in the next chapter.

It also correlates with the Celtic prophecy written after the death of Jesus and which is noted in the second part of *The Kolbrin Bible*. It is important to note that while the Egyptians and Hebrews called Planet X the Destroyer, it was known to the Celts through their own folklore as the "Frightener."

When the prophecy of the Hebrew prophet Joel and those of the ancient Celts are read together, a profound and inescapable correlation occurs.

Jewish Tanakh, and the Christian Old Testament

- **Joel** 3:15 "The Sun and the moon shall be darkened, and the stars shall withdraw their shining."

- **Joel** 3:16 "...the heavens and the earth shall shake...: but the LORD will be the hope of his people, and the strength of the children of Israel."
- **Joel** 3:19 "Egypt shall be a desolation, and Edom [western regions of present day Jordan and Saudi Arabia] shall be a desolate wilderness..."

The Kolbrin Bible: Celtic Texts of the Coelbook

- **The Silver Bough 7:18** "...I am the prophet to tell men of THE FRIGHTENER, though many generations will pass before it appears. It will be a thing of monstrous greatness arising in the form of a crab...its body will be RED...It will spread destruction across the Earth, running from sunrise to sunset..."
- **The Silver Bough 7:21** "...There will be no great signs heralding the coming of THE FRIGHTENER, it will come when men are least prepared ...It will be a time of confusion and chaos."
- **The Silver Bough 7:22** "I have warned of THE FRIGHTENER, I have done what I am charged to do..."

Up to this point, the prophecies have all spoken about a Planet X cataclysm in our near future, but is there proof that it has been here before? Yes!

The Kolbrin Bible: Egyptian Texts of the Bronzebook

- **Creation 4:5** "...God caused a sign to appear in the Heavens, so that men should know the Earth would be afflicted, and the sign was a STRANGE STAR."
- **Manuscripts** 33:5 "...FOUR TIMES THE STARS HAVE MOVED TO NEW POSITIONS and twice the Sun has [appeared to] change the direction of his journey. TWICE THE DESTROYER HAS STRUCK EARTH and three times the heavens have opened and shut. Twice the land has been swept clean by water."

The vast numbers of secular accounts, such as these, which are contained in *The Kolbrin Bible,* clearly establish this ancient Egyptian-Celtic anthology as the preeminent source of Planet X history and prophecy. Naturally, this begs a logical question. "Why haven't we heard of it before?"

Why The Kolbrin Bible was Revealed

The first part of what is now *The Kolbrin Bible* was first penned by the ancient Egyptians following the Exodus as *The Great Book*. It was later translated by the Phoenicians from hieratic, the simpler, cursive form of hieroglyphic writing, into their own language, and copies were distributed as far North as Britain.

Recognizing many similarities to their own folklore, the ancient Celts embraced the work and actively taught it. Following the death of Jesus, Joseph of Arimathea (his great uncle on the side of Joseph) founded the Glastonbury Abbey in Britain, which then became the repository for these texts, as well as those authored by Celtic priests in their own language.

In 1184 CE, English King Henry II ordered an attack on the Abbey, because he viewed these Egyptian and Celtic texts as heresy. The Egyptian accounts of the Exodus differed dramatically from the Hebrew accounts. Likewise, early Celtic Christians loved Jesus as their "Lord and Master," but rejected him as a savior, as indicated in two biographical sketches of Jesus contained in the book, in which he is directly quoted in this regard.

The Kolbrin Bible: Celtic Texts of the Coelbook

- **Britain 2:13** "Jesus was then asked if He was one with God, and He answered... 'I have proclaimed all men My brothers, and if I have said I am even as God, then truly I have raised them up also...'"
- **Britain 2:24** "A man asked, 'Where is God? Jesus... said, '...Split a billet of wood, and God will be there. Lift up a stone, and you will find Him.'"

Following the attack on the Abbey, the surviving Celtic priests secreted the remaining texts to Scotland where they were translated into Old English and eventually merged to create the original *Kolbrin.* After WWI, this work was later updated to Continental English and finally revealed in 1992 by a senior member of this secret society after the fall of the Soviet Empire and the warlike rise of radical Islam. These end times harbinger signs were predicted by the Egyptians some 3600 years earlier.

Given the dire Planet X warnings of both *The Holy Bible* and *The Kolbrin Bible*, what can we expect in 2012 in the familiar terms of the worst case and best case scenarios? Both have happened before and were documented by both texts.

Historical Worst Case Scenario

The first recorded European to set foot on the islands of Hawaii, (America's 50th State,) was British explorer Captain James Cook in 1778. Tourists visiting the island today are often regaled with a deluge story unique to the island.

When Cook began explaining the Biblical story of Noah and the flood, the Hawaiians told him that they already had a similar story. The only difference was that their Noah was spelled "Noa." Some think it is a convenient yarn made up by tour guides pandering for a good tip, but the fact is that there are literally hundreds of deluge stories all around the globe.

When the deluge accounts in the *Holy Bible* and *The Kolbrin Bible* are correlated, the similarities are striking.

Noah's Flood, Deluge Correlations	
THE HOLY BIBLE **(King James Version)**	***THE KOLBRIN BIBLE*** **(21st Century Edition)**
Gen. 6:5 – 8 ...the wickedness of man was great in the earth...grieved [the Lord] at his heart..."I will destroy ... man ... beast ... creeping thing ... fowl ..." but Noah [whose great-grandfather was Enoch (in German, "Henoch")] found grace in [his eyes] ...	**GLN:4:13, 16** ... from afar off came three men of Ardis ... worshippers of The One God ... went to Sharepik, now called Sarapesh [which the Holy Bible calls Zarapheth] and said "... The shadow of doom approaches because of wickedness." ... [but] Sisuda, the King ... shall not perish. [Sisuda] ... sent for Hanok ...
Gen. 6:14 – 16 [Build] ... an ark of gopher wood. [Give it] rooms ... pitch it within and without ... [300 cubits long X 50 cubits wide X 30 cubits high] ... [Give it] a window [1 square cubit above the water line] ... [and] ... a door [in the side] ... with lower, second and third stories	**GLN:4:18, 19** The ... ship was [300 cubits long X 50 cubits wide], finished off above by 1 cubit (1 cubit over the water line) ... three storeys ... without a break ... hatch [in the side] ...
Gen. 7:10, 11, 12, 17, 18, 24 ... after seven days, the waters ... were on the earth ... all the fountains of the great deep ... opened, ... windows of heaven ... opened ... rain ... forty days and forty nights ... flood ... forty days ... [bore] up the ark ... waters prevailed [150 days] ... ark went upon the face of the waters	**GLN:4:28** The swelling waters swept up to the mountain tops and filled the valleys. [They] came in great surging torrents ... the DESTROYER passed away [which should have taken several weeks at least], and the great flood remained seven days [afterward] Then the waters spread out calmly ... great ship drifted ... brown scum ... debris. **OGS:3:22, 23** Then ... came a high wave wall of dark, white-fang-edged waters ... carried everything ... as a broom sweeps the floor ... fruits of the land, house debris, trees, bloated dead animals and humans floated upon the wild, wide waters ... earthy, brown, foamy scum ... great downpouring of rain which stopped after seven days ... surging seas tore between the high mountains ... [Their ancestors] saw the swimming house, made fast against the sea, come up to the land, and out from it came men and beasts from Tirfola [North American continent].

Scientists today tell us that such a global deluge is impossible, as there is simply not enough water on the face of the earth to cover all the land masses. Even if there were "forty days and forty nights" of rain, as the *Holy Bible* tells us, there simply would not be enough rainfall to flood the continents.

However, what the scientists do not examine is the possibility of a surge — in lieu of a deluge. This is where the deluge accounts in *The Kolbrin Bible* lend the *Holy Bible* phrase of "forty days and forty nights" an undeniable prescient brilliance. This also incidentally ties in perfectly with the pole shift prediction of Edgar Cayce, the sleeping prophet. Cayce made two pole shift predictions. The first was the harbinger event prediction, which has been fulfilled, and the second which is the future pole shift itself.

In a pole shift, the continents move about the molten core of our planet most like the loosened peel of an orange. After that, the North and South poles shift to a new location, or completely flip over.

To imagine the consequences of such a catastrophic event, assume that you're driving down the highway in a 50-year old car with a friend, when one of your tires suddenly blows out. Because of the high speed at which you're traveling, you lose control and slam head-on into a bridge embankment. The car, which is solid, immediately stops.

You unfortunately are a bit more fluid, and lacking the restraints of modern cars, you and your passenger fly head-first through the windshield of your car and splash into whatever is ahead of you. With regards to a global deluge caused by a Planet X flyby, the very same mechanism comes into play. Except in this case, the continents are the solid cars, and the oceans are you and your passenger.

Interestingly enough, speed will largely determine survivability in both cases. The more slowly the event unfolds, the greater your chances are of surviving it.

If the pole shift Cayce predicts does happen during the flyby of Planet X, then pray the whole process takes no less than the "forty days and forty nights" spoken of in the *Holy Bible.* If the pole shift completes in less time than that, the loss of life will increase exponentially. Keep in mind that Noah's Flood, or what is known globally as The Great Deluge, followed a pole shift!

The Kolbrin Bible: Egyptian Texts of the Bronzebook

- **Gleanings** 4:24 "...the DESTROYER... opened its mouth and belched forth fire, hot stones and a vile smoke. It covered the whole sky above and the meeting place of Earth and Heaven could no longer be seen. In the evening, the places of THE STARS WERE CHANGED, THEY ROLLED ACROSS THE SKY TO NEW STATIONS; THEN, THE FLOODWATERS CAME."
- **Gleanings** 4:28 "The swelling waters swept up to the mountain tops and filled the valleys. They did not rise like water poured into a bowl, but came in great surging torrents..."

Cayce and others predicted that this pole shift would happen in 2000, which it obviously has not — as of yet. That being said, there is nothing to suggest to he was wrong about the event itself, and in the grand scheme of things, the universe has its own calendar. In the meantime, let us all pin our deepest hopes and most solemn prayers on the best case scenario.

Historical Best Case Scenario

The Jewish people have celebrated Passover annually since the time of Moses to remember the bitterness of slavery and their miraculous escape from bondage in Egypt. It is the first of the seven annual festivals celebrated by Jews, and it is considered by most to be Israel's foundational feast. It is also called the Feast of Unleavened Bread, and the other six feasts celebrated by Jews build upon the celebration of Passover.

For the Egyptians, the Exodus was a time when their own pantheon of gods failed them miserably. Although they slaughtered better than half of the Jews on the land bridge at the Red Sea, the nation lost an army and a pharaoh in the process. Worse yet, the plagues of Exodus were part of a global catastrophe, and following the Exodus, Egypt had to fight off a massive invasion from the South.

In the aftermath, a studious new pharaoh and his academics and scribes embarked upon the most ambitious anthropological study of the ancient times. They interviewed the wisest of the wise from the many lands and peoples within Egypt's trading spheres with one singular goal in mind. They did it to find clues that would lead them to the one true God of Abraham, which they reasoned was not the god that led the Jews out of Egypt. Rather, it was a lesser god, which nonetheless was mightier than those of Egypt.

The result of this effort was a 20-volume encyclopedia-length work titled *The Great Book.* All that remains of this work are contained in the first six books of *The Kolbrin Bible.* As you read the correlations between the Hebrew accounts of the Exodus and the Egyptian accounts, keep the following in mind:

- The Hebrew account documents the righteous victory of a nation.
- The Egyptian accounts in *The Kolbrin Bible* document a bitter defeat. They are as brutally honest as the conclusions in America's own 9-11 Commission Report.
- After 9-11, Americans reaffirm their relationship with the being that they call the One true God of Abraham. The Egyptians, on the other hand, were left empty-handed, with a bankrupt belief system. A fate certainly worse than 9-11.

If we are to be blessed in 2012, the worst we can expect is another 10 plagues of Exodus. Rather than being the result of a vengeful God intent on punishing a hard-hearted pharaoh, these plagues will result from the same natural disasters caused by solar flares, asteroid impacts and brutal meteorite showers.

Report #3 — Medicinal Herbs and Plants

Planet X Forecast and 2012 Survival Guide
Planetxforecast.com / Yowbooks.com

Appendix E — Post-2014 Medicinal Herbs and Plants

In the months and years after the flyby, natural herbs and plants will return that can be used for medicinal purposes. *The Kolbrin Bible* specifically mentions hardy and beneficial species that have endured previous cataclysms.

> **Britain Book 9:18** These are the useful herbs to be found in field, forest and wayside in the days gone by: Wolfbane (which guards against wolves and dogs), barroweed (which grows only near the dead), harwort, witchweed, tinkerbells, wayweed, skullcap, featherflowers (which cure the stone), blackberry, sundew, deadly dick, celandine (which cure the piles), windweed, moonflower (which works a spell), witchhead (called blackspear), asproot, drudbalm (which brings sleep),witchbane (which is put above the door), hawflowers, ellenberry, wimberry, dradsweet, elf eye, fairyfern, witchwhispers, quickenbush, sowerseed (which purges), bardberry (for lovers), amarinth (it never fades), windflower, goolflower, wagging, blowderbud (which heals all wounds), eventide, layganleaf, hokanmil, rillweed, boonberry, hatherswed (which women use), esislip, fullerswort, withrinweed (which makes blue dye), canweed (which quiets the heart), mayslip, kodecreeper, slanlus, sewd, (which cures men of madness), mothan (which only grows on cliffs), arkiesene, dafblowder (which cures stomach sickness), malbrig, maisbel (which heals the stomach), bormowed (which soothes burns), selerweed (which gives visions), tianwed (which heals the skin), kaincop (which makes a brew), cowslip, waybroad, satyrion (which overcomes impotency), dwail, corncockles (which men call tares), dockumdick (which gives men virility and only grows under the shivertree).

To make the list easier to use, most of the herbs and plants mentioned above are organized in alphabetical order in the table below. Compare this list with known species in your area, and particularly those known to grow naturally in the area of your safe haven. Get to know these plants now. Learn how to recognize and prepare them.

Herbs from The Britain Book in *The Kolbrin Bible* *Some of these planets possess powerful properties. Before using them, review this list with your family physician .*		
Ancient or Generic Name	**COMMON NAME Alternate *Scientific* name**	**Usage and Concerns**
Amarinth	**CELOSIA** Red Cockscomb, *Amaranthus*	"Never fades," Taken internally for diarrhea, dysentery, hemorrhage from the bowels, nosebleeds, kidney stones, and excessive menstruation. Used as a wash for skin problems.
Asproot	**SENECA** Snake root *Polygala Senega*	Evacuates the bowels, increases volume of urine to reduce body water content, causes vomiting, expectorant.
Bardberry	**SAW PALMETTO** Saw Palmetto berries *Serenoa Serrulata*	Aphrodisiac; generates greater sexual arousal and desire, as well as increased sexual potency and power.
Blackberry	**BLACKBERRY** Blackberry leaf *Rubus fructicosus*	Internal: may help ease childbirth, increases volume of urine to reduce body water content, tonic, may cure dysentery, diarrhea. External: sore throats, mouth sores, gum inflammations.
Blowderbud	**ST. JOHN'S WORT** Blowderbud *Hypericum formosum*	Heals all wounds, anti-depressant, relieves muscle spasms, astringent, expectorant, soothes nerves, brings down swelling, destroys disease-carrying microbes, stomach remedy, tonic, destroys and eliminates parasitic worms, reduces bile secretion, cures lung diseases.
Bormowed	**ALOE** Aloe Vera *Aloe barbadensis*	Soothes and moisturizes burns. The pulp can be eaten raw to treat stomach ulcers.
Canweed	**HORSETAIL** Candock *Equisetum arvense*	Quiets the heart, increases volume of urine to reduce body water content.

Celandine	**CELANDINE** *Chelidonium Majus*	External, as an ointment: cure the piles (hemorrhoids); mixed with sulfur, can be used to cure jock itch. Internal, as a type of tea: liver and gallbladder cleanse.
Corncockles (tares)	**TARES** Corncockles *Agrostemma githago*	TOXIC! Reduces or stops bleeding (external use only).
Cowslip	**COWSLIP** *Primula Veris*	Relieves muscle spasms, sleep agent.
Dafblowder	**DANDELION** Dafblowder *Taraxacum officinale,*	Cures stomach sickness; naturally increases volume of urine to reduce body water content and assists in digestion. Improves function of the pancreas, spleen, stomach and kidneys. It is ground and applied as a poultice to snake bites.
Drudbalm	**BALM** Drudbalm *Melissa Officinalis*	Brings sleep, relieves muscle spasms, calms the user, stomach remedy, reduces fever.
Dwail	**DEADLY NIGHTSHADE** Belladonna *Atropa Belladonna*	TOXIC! Narcotic, sedative.
Ellenberry	**ELLENBERRY**	Made into a cider to treat something called Imbrium Fever. Second bout with Imbrium Fever was usually fatal.
Featherflowers	**CELOSIA** Featherflowers *Amaranthus*	Cure the stone (kidney stones).
Fullerswort	**WILD SWEET WILLIAM** Soapwort *Saponaria Officinalis*	Gradually restores health, produces perspiration, tonic.
Goolflower	**ROSE** Rose Hips *Rosa Canina*	Many medicinal qualities; most important for survival include: antibiotic, treats infections, destroys disease-carrying microbes, kills or slows growth of bacteria, rids the user of poison.
Hatherswed	**EVENING PRIMROSE** Primrose *Oenothera biennis*	Astringent, treats symptoms of menopause, PMS (PMDD), sedative.
Hawflowers	**HAWTHORN FLOWERS** Hawflowers *Crataegus monogyna*	Many cardiovascular and respiratory benefits.

Kaincop	**CAMELLIA (TEA) OR HOPS** *Humulus lupulus*	Makes a brew. No available modern name, so two choices here depend on the desired brew.
Maisbel	**CATNIP** Cat Mint *Nepeta Cataria*	Heals pains, spasms, prevents or relieves flatulence and strengthens the stomach.
Moonflower	**MOONFLOWER** *Botrychium lunaria*	*Magickal*, works a spell, brings love and prosperity.
Mothan (only grows on cliffs)	**PEARLWORT** Bog Violet, Butterwort *Pinguicula vulgaris*	Mostly *magickal* as a love attractant, but also reportedly effective in easing labor pains by placing a quantity against the back of the mother's right knee.
Quickenbush	**ROWAN** Quickenbush *Acuparia*	Internal: The unripe fruit and bark treat diarrhea. External as an ointment or poultice: they soothe the throat and bowel.
Satyrion	**ORCHID** Satyrion Root *Orchis*	Overcomes impotency.
Selerweed	**VERVAIN** Verbena *Verbena officinalis* *V. hastata (Blue)*	Gives visions. Some medicinal treatments include treating eye ailments and sleeplessness.
Sewd	**DILL** Sewd *Anethum Graveolens*	Cures men of madness, calms the user, relieves muscle spasms.
Skullcap	**SKULLCAP** *scutellaria lateriflora*	Sleep agent, relieves muscle spasms. Used against hysteria, seizures, asthma, menstrual cramping, epilepsy, insomnia, pain, vertigo, addiction recovery.
Sowerseed	**PSYLLIUM** Flea Seed *Plantago Psyllium*	Evacuates the bowels, increases volume of urine to reduce body water content.
Sundew	**BERMANN SUNDEW** Dew Plant *Drosera rotundifolia*	Fights dry coughs, such as whooping cough and the cough that comes with measles. Good against the cough from asthma. Relieves muscle spasms, protects mucous membranes.
Tianwed	Aloe Vera	Heals the skin.
Tinkerbells	**BLUEBELLS** Wood Bells *Hyachinthus Nonscriptus*	Increases volume of urine to reduce body water content, soothes nerves, reduces or stops bleeding.

Waybroad	**PLANTAIN** waybread *Plantago lanceolata*	Brings down swelling, destroys disease-carrying microbes, astringent, soothes irritated mucous membranes, increases volume of urine to reduce body water content, expectorant, reduces fever, evacuates the bowels, refrigerant, stimulant, reduces or stops bleeding, heals wounds.
Wimberry	**BLUEBERRY** Bilberry *Vaccinium Mertillus*	Astringent, eye-care, reduces or stops lactation.
Windflower	**MEADOW ANEMONE** Pasque Flower *Anemone pulsatilla*	Relieves muscle spasms, soothes nerves.
Windweed	**SQUAW GRASS** Elk Grass *Rhizoma Anemarrhenae*	Fights feverish diseases accompanied by excessive thirst, diabetes, dry cough and, with other herbs, constipation.
Witchbane	**ROWAN** Witchbane *Sorbus Aucuparia*	See Quickenbush / ROWAN above.
Witchweed	**MUGWORT** Witchweed *Artemesia Vulgaris*	Stimulant, soothes nerves, laxative.
Witchwhispers	**WITCH HAZEL** ***Hamamelis virginiana***	Abrasions, cuts, bleeding, burns / sunburn, eczema, eye-care, vision, insect bites, rash, pet care, vein support.
Withrinweed	**INDIGO** *Indigofera Tinctoria*	Makes blue dye (for natural fibers)
Wolfbane	**MONK'S HOOD** Dogbane *Aconitum Napellus* *Aconitum Falconeri*	TOXIC! Kills wolves, dogs and medium-large animals (can kill humans). Coat bait and place where animal can be observed taking it or cover point of arrow or spear with juice and shoot animal. Also CAREFULLY used as a (narcotic) pain reliever, a sleep agent and an anti-diabetic (to lower blood sugar).

Printed in the United States
109801LV00001BA/3-48/P

9 781597 720694